Encyclopedia of Jewish American Popular Culture

Encyclopedia of Jewish American Popular Culture

Edited by

Jack R. Fischel with Susan M. Ortmann

GREENWOOD PRESS
Westport, Connecticut • London

Library of Congress Cataloging-in-Publication Data

Encyclopedia of Jewish American popular culture / edited by Jack R. Fischel with Susan M. Ortmann.
p. cm.
Includes bibliographical references and index.
ISBN: 978–0–313–33989–9 (alk. paper)
1. Jews—United States—Encyclopedias. 2. Jews in popular culture—United States—Encyclopedias. 3. United States—Civilization—Jewish influences—Encyclopedias. 4. United States—Ethnic relations—Encyclopedias. I. Fischel, Jack.
E184.35.E54 2009
305.892'407303—dc22 2008028513

British Library Cataloguing in Publication Data is available.

Library of Congress Catalog Card Number: 2008028513
ISBN: 978–0–313–33989–9

First published in 2009

Greenwood Press, 88 Post Road West, Westport, CT 06881
An imprint of Greenwood Publishing Group, Inc.
www.greenwood.com

Printed in the United States of America

The paper used in this book complies with the Permanent Paper Standard issued by the National Information Standards Organization (Z39.48-1984).

10 9 8 7 6 5 4 3 2 1

To Emily
From Grandpa Jack with Love.
This Is Your Heritage, Always Be Proud of It
And to Ethan and Emma
From Grandma with Love,
Always Remember, This Is Your Heritage Too.
Grandma Debbie Would Be Proud of You and So Am I.

Contents

List of Entries	ix
Guide to Related Topics	xiii
Acknowledgments	xix
Introduction	xxi
The Encyclopedia	1
Bibliography	459
Index	475
About the Editors and Contributors	485

List of Entries

Abzug, Bella
Adler, Mortimer
Albom, Mitch
Allen, Woody
Annenberg, Walter
Apple, Max
Arbus, Diane
Arkin, Alan
Artists
Bacall, Lauren
Bamberger, Louis
Beastie Boys
Bellow, Saul
Benny, Jack
Berger, Isaac (Ike)
Berle, Milton
Berlin, Irving
Bernstein, Leonard
Bikel, Theodore
Black, Jack
Blume, Judy
Boteach, Shmuley
Brice, Fanny
The Brill Building Songwriters
Broncho Billy
Brooks, Albert
Brooks, Mel
Brothers, Joyce
Bruce, Lenny
Buchwald, Art
Burns, George
Buttons, Red
Caesar, Sid
Cahan, Abraham
Cantor, Eddie
Cantors in America
Capp, Al
Carlebach, Shlomo
Carlisle Hart, Kitty
The Catskills
Chabon, Michael
Chayefsky, Paddy
Chess
Children's Literature
Cobb, Lee J.
The Coen Brothers
Colen, Daniel
Comedy
Comic Books
Copland, Aaron
Copperfield, David
Curtis, Tony
Curtiz, Michael
Dance
David, Larry
Davis, Sammy, Jr.
Dershowitz, Alan
Detective Fiction
Diamond, Neil
Doctorow, E. L.
Douglas, Kirk
Dreyfuss, Richard

Dylan, Bob
Einstein, Albert
Eisner, William
Ephron, Nora
Exodus
Falk, Peter
Fashion
Feiffer, Jules
Feldshuh, Tovah
Ferber, Edna
Fiddler on the Roof
Fierstein, Harvey
Film
Film Stars
Finkel, Fyvush
Fisher, Eddie
Foer, Jonathan Safran
Food
Food Industry
Freud, Sigmund
Friedan, Betty
Friedman, Debbie
Friedman, Kinky
Friedman, Thomas
Fuchs, Leo
Gangsters
Garfield, John
Gehry, Frank
Gentleman's Agreement
Gershwin, George
Ginott, Haim G.
Ginsberg, Allen
Gittlesohn, Rabbi Roland B.
Glass, Philip
Goddard, Paulette
Golden, Harry
Goodman, Benny
Goodman, Paul
Grade, Chaim
Green, Gerald
Green, Shawn David
Greenberg, Hank
Hecht, Ben
Heeb Magazine
Heller, Joseph
Heschel, Abraham Joshua
Hoffman, Dustin
Holidays and Rituals
Holliday, Judy
Hollywood Moguls
The Holocaust in American Culture
Holocaust Remembrance Day
Houdini, Harry
Hurok, Sol
Jazz and Blues
The Jazz Singer
Jessel, George
Jewish Daily Forward
Jewish Delicatessens
Jewish Museums
Jewish Women and Popular Culture
Joel, Billy
Johansson, Scarlett
Jolson, Al
Jong, Erica
Journalism
Jungreis, Esther
Katz, Mickey
Kaye, Danny
Kazin, Alfred
King, Alan
King, Larry
Kissinger, Henry
Klezmer Music
Klugman, Jack
Koch, Edward
Koppel, Ted
Koufax, Sandy
Kramer, Stanley
Kubrick, Stanley
Kunitz, Stanley Jasspon
Kushner, Harold S.
Landau, Martin
Latin Music
Lazarus, Emma
Leibovitz, Annie
Leonard, Benny
Lerner, Rabbi Michael
Levin, Ira
Levin, Meyer
Lewis, Jerry
Lewis, Shari
Lewisohn, Ludwig
Lieberman, Joseph
Liebman, Joshua Loth
Linden, Hal
Literature
Lorre, Peter

Lumet, Sidney
Mailer, Norman
Malamud, Bernard
Mamet, David
Manilow, Barry
Manischewitz Family
Marcus, David "Mickey"
The Marx Brothers
Maslow, Sophie
Mason, Jackie
Matisyahu, Hasidic MC
Merrill, Robert
Miller, Arthur
The Minsky Brothers
Mostel, Zero
Myerson, Bess
Newman, Paul
Nimoy, Leonard
Odets, Clifford
Ozick, Cynthia
Paley, William
Patinkin, Mandy
Pekar, Harvey
Perlman, Itzhak
Picon, Molly
Pinsky, Robert
Plain, Belva
Popular Music
Popular Psychology
Portman, Natalie
Potok, Chaim
Radio
Ramone, Joey
Rand, Ayn
Randall, Tony
Rap and Hip Hop Music
Reich, Steven
Reiner, Rob
Reubens, Paul
Rice, Elmer
The Ritz Brothers
Rivera, Geraldo
Rivers, Joan
Robbins, Harold
Robbins, Jerome
Robinson, Edward G.
Rock and Roll
Rose, Billy
Rosenblatt, "Yossele" Josef
Ross, Barney
Rosten, Leo
Roth, David Lee
Roth, Henry
Roth, Philip
Rubin, Rick
Sagan, Carl
Sales, Soupy
Salinger, Jerome
Sandler, Adam
Sarnoff, David
Schary, (Isidore) Dore
Schindler's List
Schulberg, Budd
Schwartz, Maurice
Science Fiction
Seinfeld, Jerry
Sendak, Maurice
Shatner, William
Sheldon, Sidney
Shore, Dinah
Sills, Beverly
Silverman, Sarah
Simmons, Gene
Simon, Neil
Simon, Paul
Singer, Isaac Bashevis
Sitcoms
Skulnik, Menasha
Sondheim, Stephen
Sontag, Susan
Spelling, Aaron
Spiegelman, Art
Spielberg, Steven
Spitz, Mark
Sports
Steinem, Gloria
Stern, Howard
Stewart, Jon
Stiller, Ben
Stone, Irving
Streisand, Barbra
Susann, Jacqueline
Television
Television Stars
Theater
The Three Stooges
Tin Pan Alley
Todd, Mike

Toklas, Alice B.
Toys and Games
Trilling, Lionel
Tuchman, Barbara
Turow, Scott
United States Holocaust Memorial Museum
Uris, Leon
Van Buren, Abigail
Vaudeville
Wallace, Irving
Wallace, Mike
Wallach, Eli
Walters, Barbara
Westheimer, Dr. Ruth
West Side Story
Wiesel, Elie
Wilder, Gene
Winchell, Walter
Winkler, Henry
Winters, Shelley
World of Our Fathers
Wouk, Herman
Yiddish
Yiddish Film
Yiddish Theater
Youngman, Henny

Guide to Related Topics

Arts (See Literature, Music, Theater)
Arbus, Diane
Artists
Colen, Daniel
Dance
Gehry, Frank
Ginsberg, Allen
Kunitz, Stanley Jasspon
Leibovitz, Annie
Maslow, Sophie
Pinsky, Robert

Business, Managers
Bamberger, Louis
Fashion
Food Industry
Hollywood Moguls
Hurok, Sol
Sarnoff, David
Toys and Games

Comedy
Benny, Jack
Berle, Milton
Brooks, Mel
Bruce, Lenny
Burns, George
Caesar, Sid
Comedy
David, Larry
Fuchs, Leo
King, Alan
Lewis, Jerry
The Marx Brothers
Mason, Jackie
The Ritz Brothers
Rivers, Joan
Sales, Soupy
Sandler, Adam
Seinfeld, Jerry
Sitcoms
Stern, Howard
Stewart, Jon
Stiller, Ben
The Three Stooges
Wilder, Gene
Youngman, Henny

Comic Books
Capp, Al
Comic Books
Eisner, William
Feiffer, Jules
Pekar, Harvey
Spiegelman, Art

Entertainment (See Film, Music, Television, Theater)
The Catskills
Copperfield, David
Houdini, Harry

Film, Film Stars, and Industry
Allen, Woody
Arkin, Alan
Bacall, Lauren
Black, Jack
Broncho Billy
Brooks, Albert
Brooks, Mel
Bruce, Lenny
Buttons, Red
Carlisle Hart, Kitty
Chayefsky, Paddy
Cobb, Lee J.
The Coen Brothers
Curtis, Tony
Curtiz, Michael
Davis, Sammy, Jr.
Douglas, Kirk
Dreyfuss, Richard
Ephron, Nora
Exodus
Falk, Peter
Fiddler on the Roof
Film
Film Stars
Garfield, John
Gentleman's Agreement
Goddard, Paulette
Hoffman, Dustin
Holliday, Judy
Hollywood Moguls
The Jazz Singer
Johansson, Scarlett
Kaye, Danny
Klugman, Jack
Kramer, Stanley
Kubrick, Stanley
Landau, Martin
Lewis, Jerry
Lorre, Peter
Lumet, Sidney
Mamet, David
The Marx Brothers
Mostel, Zero
Newman, Paul
Patinkin, Mandy
Portman, Natalie
Randall, Tony
Reiner, Rob
The Ritz Brothers
Robinson, Edward G.
Sandler, Adam
Schary, (Isidore) Dore
Schindler's List
Schulberg, Budd
Shatner, William
Silverman, Sarah
Skulnik, Menasha
Spielberg, Steven
Stiller, Ben
Streisand, Barbra
The Three Stooges
Todd, Mike
Wallach, Eli
Wilder, Gene
Winters, Shelley
Yiddish Film

Food
Food
Food Industry
Jewish Delicatessens
Manischewitz Family

Games
Chess

Literature, Fiction, Nonfiction
Apple, Max
Bellow, Saul
Blume, Judy
Chabon, Michael
Children's Literature
Detective Fiction
Doctorow, E. L.
Exodus
Ferber, Edna
Foer, Jonathan Safran
Friedman, Kinky
Gentleman's Agreement
Ginsberg, Allen
Goodman, Paul
Grade, Chaim
Green, Gerald
Heller, Joseph
Jong, Erica
Kazin, Alfred
Lazarus, Emma

Levin, Ira
Levin, Meyer
Lewisohn, Ludwig
Liebman, Joshua Loth
Literature
Mailer, Norman
Malamud, Bernard
Mamet, David
Miller, Arthur
Odets, Clifford
Ozick, Cynthia
Plain, Belva
Potok, Chaim
Rand, Ayn
Rice, Elmer
Robbins, Harold
Rosten, Leo
Roth, Henry
Roth, Philip
Sagan, Carl
Salinger, Jerome
Science Fiction
Sendak, Maurice
Sheldon, Sidney
Singer, Isaac Bashevis
Sontag, Susan
Stone, Irving
Susann, Jacqueline
Toklas, Alice B.
Trilling, Lionel
Tuchman, Barbara
Turow, Scott
Uris, Leon
Wallace, Irving
Wiesel, Elie
World of Our Fathers
Wouk, Herman

Media and Journalism
Albom, Mitch
Annenberg, Walter
Buchwald, Art
Cahan, Abraham
Friedman, Thomas
Golden, Harry
Hecht, Ben
Heeb Magazine
Jewish Daily Forward
Journalism
King, Larry
Koppel, Ted
Mailer, Norman
Rivera, Geraldo
Sarnoff, David
Trilling, Lionel
Van Buren, Abigail
Wallace, Mike
Walters, Barbara
Winchell, Walter

Military
Gittlesohn, Rabbi Roland B.
Marcus, David "Mickey"

Miscellaneous
Gangsters

Museums
Jewish Museums
United States Holocaust Memorial Museum

Music
Beastie Boys
Berlin, Irving
Bernstein, Leonard
Bikel, Theodore
Black, Jack
Brice, Fanny
The Brill Building Songwriters
Copland, Aaron
Davis, Sammy, Jr.
Diamond, Neil
Dylan, Bob
Fisher, Eddie
Friedman, Debbie
Friedman, Kinky
Gershwin, George
Glass, Philip
Goodman, Benny
Jazz and Blues
Joel, Billy
Jolson, Al
Katz, Mickey
Klezmer Music
Latin Music
Manilow, Barry
Matisyahu, Hasidic MC

Merrill, Robert
Patinkin, Mandy
Perlman, Itzhak
Popular Music
Ramone, Joey
Rap and Hip Hop Music
Reich, Steven
Rock and Roll
Rose, Billy
Rosenblatt, "Yossele" Josef
Roth, David Lee
Rubin, Rick
Shore, Dinah
Sills, Beverly
Simmons, Gene
Simon, Paul
Sondheim, Stephen
Streisand, Barbra
Tin Pan Alley

Politics, Government
Abzug, Bella
Friedman, Kinky
Kissinger, Henry
Koch, Edward
Lieberman, Joseph
Marcus, David "Mickey"

Radio
Benny, Jack
Berle, Milton
Burns, George
Caesar, Sid
Cantor, Eddie
Carlisle Hart, Kitty
Jessel, George
Liebman, Joshua Loth
Radio
Sarnoff, David
Stern, Howard
Winchell, Walter
Youngman, Henny

Religion, Religious Theory
Boteach, Shmuley
Cantors in America
Carlebach, Shlomo
Friedman, Debbie
Gittlesohn, Rabbi Roland B.
Heschel, Abraham Joshua
Holidays and Rituals
Jungreis, Esther
Kushner, Harold S.
Lerner, Rabbi Michael
Rosenblatt, "Yossele" Josef

Science
Einstein, Albert
Freud, Sigmund
Popular Psychology
Sagan, Carl
Science Fiction

Social Sciences, Humanities
Adler, Mortimer
Brothers, Joyce
Dershowitz, Alan
Freud, Sigmund
Ginott, Haim G.
Goodman, Paul
The Holocaust in American Culture
Holocaust Remembrance Day
Jewish Museums
Popular Psychology
Sontag, Susan
Tuchman, Barbara
United States Holocaust Memorial Museum
Westheimer, Dr. Ruth
Wiesel, Elie
Yiddish

Sports
Berger, Isaac (Ike)
Green, Shawn David
Greenberg, Hank
Koufax, Sandy
Leonard, Benny
Ross, Barney
Spitz, Mark
Sports

Television
Benny, Jack
Berle, Milton
Burns, George
Caesar, Sid
Chayefsky, Paddy

David, Larry
Falk, Peter
Jessel, George
King, Larry
Klugman, Jack
Koppel, Ted
Landau, Martin
Lewis, Shari
Linden, Hal
Myerson, Bess
Nimoy, Leonard
Paley, William
Patinkin, Mandy
Randall, Tony
Reiner, Rob
Reubens, Paul
Rivers, Joan
Sales, Soupy
Sarnoff, David
Seinfeld, Jerry
Shatner, William
Shore, Dinah
Sitcoms
Skulnik, Menasha
Spelling, Aaron
Stewart, Jon
Television
Television Stars
The Three Stooges
Wallace, Mike
Walters, Barbara
Winkler, Henry
Youngman, Henny

Theater, Vaudeville, Yiddish Theater

Brice, Fanny
Cantor, Eddie
Feldshuh, Tovah
Fiddler on the Roof
Fierstein, Harvey
Finkel, Fyvush
Fuchs, Leo
Jolson, Al
Linden, Hal
The Marx Brothers
Maslow, Sophie
Mason, Jackie
Miller, Arthur
The Minsky Brothers
Mostel, Zero
Odets, Clifford
Picon, Molly
Rice, Elmer
The Ritz Brothers
Robbins, Jerome
Schary, (Isidore) Dore
Schwartz, Maurice
Simon, Neil
Skulnik, Menasha
Sondheim, Stephen
Theater
Vaudeville
Wallach, Eli
West Side Story
Yiddish Theater

Women's Movement

Abzug, Bella
Ephron, Nora
Friedan, Betty
Jewish Women and Popular Culture
Jong, Erica
Sontag, Susan
Steinem, Gloria
Toklas, Alice B.

Yiddish

Yiddish
Yiddish Film
Yiddish Theater

Acknowledgments

The publication of the *Encyclopedia of Jewish American Popular Culture* would not have been possible without the assistance of many people. The list of names of those who contributed their advice and expertise to the project is a long one, but special recognition should be given to the following, who were instrumental in moving the encyclopedia in the right direction. Stephen Whitfield provided not only his sage advice but also recommended many of the contributors who fill the pages of the encyclopedia; Sy Colen is not only a great friend but someone who used his expertise in the field of popular art to make important suggestions and recommendations as to who to include in the volume; Patricia Erens's expertise, patience, and suggestions in regard to Jews in film contributed enormously to the completion of the project; Rabbi Jack Paskoff, Congregation Shaarai Shomayim, Lancaster, Pennsylvania, was particularly helpful on questions of Jewish religious identity; Jonathan Lauer gave his sage advice in regard to matters pertaining to the encyclopedia; Leroy Hopkins was always available to write a needed essay or entry; and David Zubatsky shared his vast knowledge of popular culture and offered ever-valuable suggestions. We thank Maggie Eichler for her willingness to assist with the project, Nicole Oktela for her assistance in tracking down bibliographical material, and Janet Dotterer and Janet Kacskos, members of the Millersville University staff, who were helpful in identifying and providing photos for the encyclopedia. We also thank the *Forward* for permission to adapt Steve Whitfield's article on the 50th anniversary of *West Side Story* for the encyclopedia.

Susan Ortmann, who teaches history at Millersville University, is singled out for her outstanding contribution to the organization of the encyclopedia. Enough cannot be said in regard to her understanding of what needed to be done to complete the project. For Sue no task was too difficult, especially in dealing with the detail work that is necessary in a project of this kind. The completion of the encyclopedia is a testimony to her organizational ability.

Our spouses, Julie and PJ, are thanked for putting up with the myriad phone calls, meetings, and living with the project for so many years.

Finally, both Sue and I thank Kristi Ward, our editor at Greenwood Press, for her thoughtful suggestions and guidance in steering the project to its conclusion, and Elizabeth Claeys, who proofread the manuscript and offered numerous helpful suggestions that made the *Encyclopedia of Jewish American Popular Culture* the quality reference work we hoped it would be.

Jack Fischel

Introduction

The *Encyclopedia of Jewish American Popular Culture* provides over 250 entries on the Jewish contribution to popular culture in America. The encyclopedia is divided between a series of comprehensive essays on subjects such as artists, film, drama, music in its many different formats, vaudeville, radio, television, and many other areas where Jews have made their contribution to the overall American experience. These essays provide an "overview" of a particular subject, and shorter entries provide a snapshot of a noteworthy personality or event. In choosing the entries, we have attempted to balance the past history of Jewish popular culture in America with noteworthy entries that reflect contemporary Jewish contributions. Admittedly, the choice of entries is subjective, but we have attempted to imagine what the reader would expect to find in perusing the volume and have weighed these expectations with an effort to balance the past with the present. Although the reader will find less about Jewish religious culture than secular, the process of selection recognizes that although a Woody Allen or Lenny Bruce have greater name recognition than that of Shlomo Carlebach, both have made important contributions to overall culture. Balancing religious contributions with secular ones is never an easy task, and it would be remiss not to include places for an Abraham Joshua Heschel or Elie Wiesel, alongside that of more secular popular culture figures such as Bob Dylan and Barbra Streisand. In the case of religious personalities and popular entertainers, we selected entries that struck us as culturally important—likely to remain important for the foreseeable future—and, wherever possible, as reflecting their "Jewishness."

We attempted to include those topics that general readers would expect to find in such a work, but we also tried to include important aspects of Jewish culture that might not be familiar. As we distance ourselves from the generation of immigrant Jews who arrived in the United States in the nineteenth and twentieth centuries, we acknowledge the cultural influences they brought with them, which both entertained and informed them about the new world they were in. We have not forgotten this aspect of the Jewish contribution to American cultural life, so the reader will also find essays on aspects of Yiddish culture in America: film, the stage, and the language itself. Many personalities from the Yiddish-speaking world were either influenced by or graduated from their environment to make important contributions to the general American culture. Indeed, one may argue that the unique contribution of American

Jews to the world of entertainment came not in their influence on "highbrow culture" but from their innovative, vibrant, and profound contributions to the world of popular entertainment. Can we truly imagine an American popular culture without the influence of Irving Berlin, Broadway musicals, Will Eisner, and the Hollywood moguls who shaped the growth of the film industry?

In developing the *Encyclopedia of Jewish American Popular Culture,* we enlisted the best possible people to write the essays and entries. In identifying contributors we utilized the expertise of our distinguished advisory board, some of whom wrote for the encyclopedia and others of whom recommended the names of scholars or shared expertise in a particular area. Some of the writers are themselves expert in the fields for which they contribute essays, such as Cantor Jacob Ben-Zion Mendelson; others are journalists, teachers, and scholars. Wherever possible, we urged our contributors to include the Jewish connection in the subjects that they wrote about. Sometimes, as with people like Isaac Bashevis Singer or Elie Wiesel, the Jewishness of their identities is well known; other times the connection is not so evident, as with the entries on Lenny Bruce or Diane Arbus.

The encyclopedia is intended to be a user-friendly A–Z work, with cross-references, a helpful further reading section at the end of each entry, a general bibliography at the end, and a comprehensive index. The intended audience for the work ranges from the general reader to high school and college students to researchers and academics interested in the subject of the Jewish contribution to American popular culture.

THE JEWS AND AMERICAN POPULAR CULTURE

Although there has been a Jewish presence in the United States since its founding, its population has never exceeded more than three percent of the population. Yet the Jewish contribution to all aspects of American culture has been enormous, especially in regard to popular culture. Indeed, it would be hard to imagine what American culture would be like without the contribution of Jewish talent in such areas of mass culture as film, comedy, comic books, Tin Pan Alley, rock and roll, the stage, television, radio, literature, and so on.

So who were these Jews? Where did they come from, and more important, how much of their Jewish ethnicity factored into the contribution they made to American culture? Another way of asking this question is did their creativity occur because they were Jewish or was that incidental to their work?

The *Encyclopedia of Jewish American Popular Culture* may be construed as a celebration of the contribution of American Jews to overall culture. Yet, it is important to note that in the hundreds of biographical entries ranging from Hank Greenberg and Dustin Hoffman to Leonard Bernstein and Natalie Portman, as well as the many essays dealing with Jewish contribution to subjects such as fashion, food, popular psychology, the stage, vaudeville, the place of the Holocaust in American culture, film, sports, and so on, much of the influence arrived with the cultural baggage that some three million Jews brought with them from Eastern Europe to America in the years between 1880–1914. This subculture has not been forgotten in this encyclopedia, and the reader can expect to find essays and short entries on the Yiddish theater, film, newspapers, cantorial music, language, and the personalities who bridged the world of Yiddish culture and pop culture—for example, Molly Picon, Fyvush Finkel, Sidney Lumet, Leo Fuchs, "Yossele" Josef Rosenblatt, and many others.

In choosing what and who to include, it became apparent that the process of assimilation and intermarriage has made the question of "who is a Jew" a difficult one. For many Jews, the operative definition, as defined by halacha, or Jewish law, is simply that any one born from a Jewish mother is a Jew. In recent years this definition, at least in the United States, has been broadened by Reform Judaism to include as Jews those born with either a Jewish mother or father and who identify as a Jew. There is also the issue of conversion. In Judaism, a convert to the faith must be accepted as an equal on all counts alongside all Jewish people. The three most famous conversions to Judaism in American popular culture were Marilyn Monroe, Elizabeth Taylor, and Sammy Davis Jr. Both Monroe and Taylor were excluded from the volume, but the reader will find an entry on Sammy Davis Jr. This at best is a judgment call. As far as research indicates, there is little evidence that the late Marilyn Monroe, after her divorce from Arthur Miller, or Elizabeth Taylor, after her divorce from crooner Eddie Fisher, ever identified with the Jewish community or Jewish life in general. This is not the case with Sammy Davis Jr., who took his conversion to Judaism seriously. In making the selection of entries, the editor has chosen to use the inclusive definition of who is a Jew—that is, anyone who has converted to Judaism, has a Jewish father or mother, and identifies as a Jew—fully realizing that within the world of celebrity, there are those born to Jewish parents who would define their Jewishness as an accident of birth.

Scholars and specialists from many fields have contributed their research to this project, eager to chronicle the distinctive contribution of Jews to American popular culture. We hope that this reference work will meet the needs of students at all levels but will also be of interest to the general public and those who enjoy reading about the events and intriguing personalities that have shaped so much of American culture.

A

ABZUG, BELLA (1920–1998)

Lawyer, politician, and civil rights advocate Bella Abzug was the first Jewish congresswomen (1971–1977). A New York Democrat, Abzug was committed to the fight for social justice. Among her accomplishments were a number of firsts: Abzug was among the first politicians supporting gay rights, among the first to defend clients prosecuted by the 1950s House Un-American Activities Committee, among the first in Congress to call for President Nixon's impeachment, and the first to introduce a law banning discrimination against women when obtaining credit. Bills she sponsored that became law include the Freedom of Information Act; the Sunshine Act, which insists on government transparency; and the Right to Privacy Act, which grants citizens the right to obtain government records concerning themselves. Abzug also fought for passage of the Equal Rights Amendment. A passionate Zionist, Abzug was a strong supporter of Israel and fought against the United Nations' Zionism is Racism Resolution (1975).

You might call Abzug a founding mother: she played a major role in creating the Women Strike for Peace organization (1961) and moved it to oppose the Vietnam War and atomic testing. She co-founded the National Women's Political Caucus (1971); co-founded the international Women's Environment and Development Organization (1990)—WEDO—and guided WEDO to cosponsor the first World Conference on Breast Cancer (1997).

Abzug was born in 1920 to Esther and Emanuel Savitsky, Russian Jewish immigrants who settled in the Bronx. Her father owned a butcher shop where she often served customers. She attended Hebrew school and observed the Sabbath. As she grew older, she taught in religious school. Subsequently, Abzug attended the Jewish Theological Seminary for advanced religious training. When her father died, in 1933, she defied tradition and said Kaddish (prayer for the dead) for him. Abzug, a member of Hadassah and B'nai B'rith, exercised her speaking talents to raise money for Israel.

Abzug attended Hunter College, a tuition-free college, majoring in political science. At Hunter, she became president of the student council and after graduation was awarded a scholarship to Columbia University Law School. Extremely intelligent, she became editor of the *Columbia Law Review*. In 1945, she married Martin Abzug, a partner in a shirt manufacturing company. The marriage lasted until his death in 1986. The couple produced two children, Eve and Liz. By

1947, Abzug had practiced law for 25 years. She specialized in labor law and civil rights cases. Abzug endangered her life in 1950 when she went to Mississippi to defend an African-American falsely accused of rape. At age 50 she ran and won election to Congress, then held the seat for three terms. Subsequently, she ran a losing campaign against Patrick Moynihan for the Senate in 1976 and afterward was unable to win an election.

From 1980 on Abzug resumed her law practice and participated in various national and international organizations promoting the rights and welfare of women, and in 1984 she wrote *Gender Gap: Bella Abzug's Guide to Political Power.* She remained active in the Democratic Party, serving as a delegate to the Democratic National Convention five times. Abzug was a colorful personality who was recognized by her broad-brimmed hat. She contracted breast cancer in 1998 and subsequently heart disease. She died of complications following heart surgery in 1998. She was 77 years old.

Philip Rosen

Further Reading: Levine, Suzanne Marin and Mary Thon. *Bella Abzug: One Tough Broad from the Bronx.* New York: Farrar, Straus and Giroux, 2007.

ADLER, MORTIMER (1902–2001)

Educator and philosopher Mortimer Jerome Adler was born into a nonobservant Jewish family in New York City on December 28, 1902. In anticipation of becoming a journalist, he dropped out of high school at the age of 14 and became a secretary and copy boy for the *New York Sun*. In order to improve his writing, Adler began to take night classes at Columbia University. It was at Columbia that Adler's love for philosophy emerged. Adler remarked that, whereas John Stuart Mills, who influenced him a great deal, could read Greek and had read Plato by 15, he himself did not even know who Socrates was at 15. After reading some dialogues by Plato lent to him by a friend, Adler decided to enroll at Columbia and study philosophy. He was awarded a scholarship. Adler never finished his undergraduate degree because he did not complete the physical education courses required (Columbia awarded him an honorary BA in 1984). Yet Adler's knowledge of the history of ideas was so impressive that Columbia allowed him to enroll in graduate school and eventually awarded him a PhD in philosophy.

A self-proclaimed "nuisance" to his professors at Columbia, including John Dewey and Irwin Edman, Adler became a teacher in the honors program (today, the core curriculum) during the 1920s, a program that stressed the "great books" of western civilization. Adler subsequently carried his interest in "great books" to a number of other institutions, including the University of Chicago and the University of North Carolina–Chapel Hill. He also helped to found the Institute for Philosophical Research and the Aspen Institute; there he taught business leaders about the great books for over 40 years.

Throughout his career Adler took his bearings from two fundamental commitments, one methodological and the other practical. Adler was an advocate for an interdisciplinary approach to the study of ideas, one which integrated the study of philosophy with science, literature, and religion. Also, his work was always written or developed with the ordinary person in mind, taking seriously the first line of *Metaphysics,* by Aristotle (one of Adler's philosophical heroes), that "all men desire to know by nature." Or, as Adler believed, all individuals have traces of philosophical insight in moments of reflection.

This practical turn manifested itself in a multitude of ways throughout his career. Adler was editorial board chairman of the *Encyclopedia Britannica* and creator of Britannica's 54-volume *Great Books of the Western World*. He founded the Paideia Project, a plan for the reform of public education that revolves around a curriculum based in part on the Socratic method and which was introduced in selected elementary and secondary schools in Oakland, Atlanta, and Chicago. Adler was also chairman and co-founder with

Max Weismann of the Center for the Study of the Great Ideas and editor in chief of its journal *Philosophy is Everybody's Business*. He developed with Bill Moyers a television series entitled *Six Great Ideas* that aired on PBS. Frequently Adler was a guest on television, appearing on *The Dick Cavett Show* and *Firing Line,* and was interviewed a number of times by **Mike Wallace** on ABC on the theme of survival and freedom in contemporary America. Between 1953 and 1954 Adler hosted a half-hour, weekly television series entitled *The Great Ideas*. These programs were produced by the Institute for Philosophical Research and were carried on ABC as a public service. At times, Adler's counsel could be found in the nation's newspapers. For instance, in 1960, *U.S. News & World Report* interviewed Adler on how well the country was educating its children. Adler died on June 28, 2001.

Joshua Fischel

Further Reading: Adler, Mortimer. *How to Read a Book: A Guide to Reading the Great Book.* New York: Touchstone Publishing, 1966. ———. *A Second Look in the Rearview Mirror: Further Autobiographical Reflections of a Philosopher at Large.* New York: St. Martin's Press, 1992. ———. *Six Great Ideas: Truth-Goodness-Beauty-Liberty-Equality- Justice.* New York: Simon and Schuster, 1997.

ALBOM, MITCH (1958–)

Mitch Albom, the acclaimed sportswriter and author of the *New York Times* bestseller *Tuesdays with Morrie,* was born into a Jewish household on May 23, 1958, in Philadelphia, Pennsylvania. He received a bachelor of arts degree in sociology from Brandeis University before completing his master of arts in journalism and business from Columbia University.

Albom's career in sports journalism began with the *Ft. Lauderdale News* (now the *Sun Sentinel*) but his national popularity increased after joining the *Detroit Free Press* in July 1985. Since then he has won the Associated Press Sports Editors national column writing contest 13 times, more than any other sportswriter. Albom appears on television and radio shows, including the *Monday Sports Albom* and *The Mitch Albom Show,* and he is regularly featured on ESPN's *The Sports Reporters,* a nationally televised Sunday morning sports show.

Albom, a prolific writer, wrote *Tuesdays with Morrie* (1997), a memoir of the insightful conversations he had with a beloved and dying professor, which spent four years atop the *New York Times* bestseller list. Oprah Winfrey's television version of Albom's *Tuesdays with Morrie* aired in December 1999 and garnered four Emmy nominations including best television film. Albom's *The Five People You Meet in Heaven* (2003) has sold over eight million copies. Both of these books, as well as several comedies, have been adapted for the stage. A television version of Albom's latest book, *For One More Day,* aired on ABC in December 2007.

Albom is actively involved with his community and is associated with several charitable organizations. In 1989, he helped found The Dream Fund, providing disadvantaged children access to the arts. In 1998, he organized A Time to Help, a volunteer group that assists other charities, such as Habitat for Humanity and Meals on Wheels. He also formed SAY Detroit, an umbrella organization that funds Detroit-area homeless shelters. Albom's all-writers rock band, the Rock Bottom Reminders, raises money for literacy.

Albom and his wife Janine currently reside in Michigan.

Maury I. Wiseman

Further Reading: Albom, Mitch. *The Five People You Meet in Heaven,* New York: Hyperion Books, 2003. ———. *For One More Day,* New York: Hyperion, 2006. ———. *Tuesdays with Morrie,* New York: Doubleday, 1997.

ALLEN, WOODY (1938–)

Comedian, writer, director, and producer of films, Woody Allen was born Allen Stewart Konegisberg and raised in the Flatbush section of Brooklyn, where he attended Midwood High School. His father, Martin, and mother, Nettea Cherry, who were born and raised on the Lower East Side of Manhattan, were not particularly observant Jews, but they sent Allen to Hebrew schools for eight years, where he was Bar Mitzvahed in 1951. During his early years, Allen spoke **Yiddish**, but that appears to be the extent of his Jewish upbringing, and as an adult he claimed no religious affiliation. After high school graduation, Allen entered New York University. Never a good student, Allen even failed a film course and was eventually expelled; he later briefly enrolled in the City College of New York but never obtained a college degree.

Allen began his professional career writing jokes for David O. Alber, an agent who proceeded to sell his gags to newspapers. Subsequently, at age 16, Woody Allen was discovered by comedian Milt Kamen, who was instrumental in getting him his first writing opportunity—composing gags for **Sid Caesar**. By 1957, Allen was writing scripts for *The Ed Sullivan Show, The Tonight Show, Caesar's Hour,* and other **television** shows. From 1961 to 1964, Allen was a stand-up comedian in New York comedy clubs. He also wrote short stories for *The New Yorker* magazine. It was during this period that Allen developed the traits that would identify his subsequent screen character—a sexually obsessed, neurotic, and intellectual persona. Nightclubs, television appearances, and film made him a popular personality in the field of entertainment, to the extent that he appeared on the cover of *Life* magazine in 1969.

Woody Allen's first screenplay was *What's New Pussycat* (1965), and his screen persona as an insecure and sex-obsessed character was fully realized in the James Bond parody *Casino Royale* (1967). Dissatisfied with working for other directors and producers, he began to write, produce, direct, and act in his own films, which included *Love and Death* (1975), *Interiors* (1978), *Zelig* (1983), *Broadway Danny Rose* (1984), *Purple Rose of Cairo* (1985), *Radio Days* (1987), and *Crimes and Misdemeanors* (1989). His movies have won 14 Academy Award nominations, and he has been awarded 3 Oscars. Three films have won film awards: an Oscar for *Anne Hall* (1977), a Cesar for Best Foreign Film for *Manhattan* (1980), and Best Screenplay for *Hannah and Her Sisters* (1986). During the 1990s, Allen directed *Alice* (1990); *Husbands and Wives* (1992), which won two Oscar nominations; *Shadows and Fog* (1992); *Manhattan Murder Mystery* (1993); *Bullets over Broadway* (1994); *Mighty Aphrodite* (1995), a musical; *Everyone Says I Love You* (1996); *Deconstructing Harry* (1997); *Celebrity* (1998); and *Sweet and Lowdown* (1999).

The start of the new century witnessed somewhat of a decline in Allen's work, with *Small Time Crooks* (2000), *The Curse of the Jade Scorpion* (2001), *Hollywood Ending* (2002), *Anything Else* (2003), and *Melinda and Melinda* (2004). But *Match Point* (2005) was one of Allen's most successful films and generally received very positive reviews. It is also a markedly darker picture than Allen's earlier films. In *Match Point* Allen shifts his focus from the intellectual upper class of New York to the moneyed upper class of London. While different from Allen's many critical satires, *Match Point* still has undertones of social critique. This is clearest in the theme of luck, which works on several levels in the film. *Match Point* earned more than $23 million domestically (more than any of his films in nearly 20 years) and earned over $62 million in international box office sales. *Match Point* earned Allen his first Academy Award nomination since 1998 for Best Original Screenplay and also earned directing and writing nominations at the Golden Globes, his first Globe nominations since 1987. *Match Point* was followed by *Cassandra's Dream* (2007) and *Vicky Cristina Barcelona* (2008).

As successful as Woody Allen has been in film, he has also made his mark in theater. In 1960 Allen wrote sketches for the revue *A to Z,* but his most successful work was his writing for *Don't Drink the Water* (1968), a comedy which ran for 598 performances on Broadway and has been revived frequently by road companies throughout the country. The success of his first play was followed by *Play it Again, Sam* (1969), starring his future leading lady Diane Keaton. The show ran for 453 performances, was nominated for three

Tony Awards, and subsequently was made into a film (1972), which was directed by Herbert Ross. In the film, Woody Allen played a neurotic film critic who has trouble with women and is consumed by movies, particularly his favorite film of all time, *Casablanca*. His future costar Diane Keaton reprised her stage role in the film.

Other Allen contributions to the theater include his early 1970s one-act play *God and Death,* which later was made into his film *Shadows and Fog; The Floating Light Bulb* (1981), which was a commercial flop; and the one-act play *Central Park West* (1995).

In addition to articles published in magazines such as *The New Yorker,* Allen has also authored four books: *Getting Even* (1978), *Without Feathers* (1983), *Side Effects* (1986), and *Mere Anarchy* (2007).

Influenced by the films of Ingmar Bergman, Allen's works often are written in a somber and philosophical vein. His films explore the meaning of life and death, guilt and retribution, morality and immorality, anxiety and sexuality, as well as dealing with the characters' obsession with sex. Often his characters are Jews who struggle with identity. He uses Yiddishisms in his dialogue and Hasidic rabbis in parodies. *Annie Hall,* his most honored film, juxtaposes his Jewish background with Annie's (Diane Keaton) WASP heritage, reproducing a central theme of Jewish-American literature—the Jewish male's pursuit of the shiksa (Gentile female). In the film, Allen portrays himself as a neurotic, intellectual, indecisive schlemiel.

Allen has been accused of Jewish self-hatred, because his films portray Judaism (see his ridicule of Yom Kippur in *Annie Hall* and *Radio Days* (1987) and his Jewish characters in a consistently negative manner. But Allen has also used his films to present Jewish fears, desires, and paranoia, as expressed in *Zelig* (1983), a story about the desperate effort of Jews to achieve total assimilation into American mainstream society. Lawrence J. Epstein has written in *The Haunted Smile* that Allen's characters are not Jewish by religion or ethnicity but by their Jewish consciousness and temperament. Elsewhere, Epstein notes that Woody Allen's focus on themes of adultery (see *Crimes and Misdemeanors,* for example) reflected not only his own sexual tensions but that "Jewish audiences could see in such adultery their own unfaithfulness to Jewish tradition" (*Haunted Smile,* 2001). Allen's first two marriages were to Jewish women: Herlene Rosen (1956–1962) and Louise Lasser (1966–1968). He had strong romantic attachments to two Gentile leading ladies, Diane Keaton and Mia Farrow. With Mia he fathered a son, Roman. He eventually married Soon-Yi Previn, the adopted daughter of Mia. Soon is 35 years his junior. The couple adopted two daughters. *See also* **Comedy**; **Film**.

Philip Rosen

Further Reading: Allen, Woody. *Side Effects.* New York: Random House, 1980. ———. *Without Feathers.* New York: Ballantine Books, 1983. Epstein, Lawrence J. *The Haunted Smile.* New York: Public Affairs, 2001. Lax, Eric. *Woody Allen: A Biography.* New York: Vintage, 1992.

ANNENBERG, WALTER (1908–2002)

A publishing and broadcasting mogul, diplomat, art collector, confidant of presidents, and philanthropist, Walter Annenberg was known as one of the world's richest and most generous men. He also had a reputation for vindictiveness and was not reluctant to use his media power against his personal and political enemies In 1885, Annenberg's father, Moses, immigrated to the United States with his German Jewish family. Moses Annenberg started in the newspaper business, working to increase circulation for William Randolph Hearst. Reputed to associate with notorious gangsters such as Meyer Lansky, Annenberg purchased the *Daily Racing Form* in the early 1920s, and, using bribes and strong-arm tactics, he parlayed this asset into a small media empire that ultimately included the *Philadelphia Inquirer.* Moses Annenberg pled guilty to tax evasion charges in 1939, served two years in prison, and died days after his release.

Age 32 at the time of his father's imprisonment, Walter Annenberg took control of the family business, which he renamed Triangle Publications. In the 1940s, he launched *Seventeen Magazine,* a huge success. Annenberg followed in the 1950s with his greatest publishing success, *TV Guide,* which at its height sold 20 million copies per week. One of his Philadelphia television stations developed the hit show *American Bandstand.* His successful media ventures made Annenberg a fantastically wealthy man. In 1988, Annenberg sold his publishing empire to Rupert Murdoch for $3.2 billion.

In 1969, Annenberg was appointed ambassador to Great Britain by President Richard Nixon. He served until 1974. Although his appointment was met in some quarters by derision, Annenberg became a popular ambassador, the only one from the United States to be named a Knight Commander, Order of the British Empire.

A lifelong supporter of conservative political causes and candidates, Annenberg was intimate friends with Presidents Nixon and Reagan. He used his publishing clout to derail campaigns of candidates he opposed. One such attack was made against Milton Shapp, who ran for the Pennsylvania governorship in 1966.

He was also was notorious for ordering his media outlets to ignore celebrities and institutions who earned his ire. After a contract dispute with the Philadelphia Warriors basketball team regarding a lease on an Annenberg-owned arena, his Philadelphia newspapers ignored the team and its games for the rest of the season.

Annenberg's philanthropy encompassed a wide variety of causes and recipients, and the amount of his largess could be staggering. It is estimated that his gifts during his lifetime exceeded $2.5 billion. A non-practicing Jew, he was generous to Jewish organizations, especially the United Jewish Appeal, and to Israel. Education was Annenberg's most significant philanthropic target in dollar terms. He made a $50 million grant to the United Negro College Fund, as well as million-dollar gifts to the U.S. Army, Navy, and Air Force academies. Annenberg's gifts to the Universities of Pennsylvania and Southern California to fund their respective Annenberg Schools for Communication reached the hundreds of millions. And, in 1993, after receiving criticism for giving so much to private education and ignoring the public schools, Annenberg made a $500 million gift intended to help reform public education. Since his death in 2002 at age 94, the Annenberg Foundation continues to give hundreds of millions to support education, youth development, the arts, the environment, and health and human services. *See also* **Journalism**.

Howard C. Ellis

Further Reading: Altschuler, Glenn C., and David I. Grossvogel. *Changing Channels: America in TV Guide.* Urbana, IL: University of Illinois Press, 1992. Cooney, John. *The Annenbergs: The Salvaging of a Tainted Dynasty.* New York: Simon and Schuster, 1982. Ogden, Christopher. *Legacy: A Biography of Moses and Walter Annenberg.* New York: Little, Brown and Company, 1999.

APPLE, MAX (1941–)

Max Isaac Apple is an American short story writer, memoirist, novelist, and screenwriter whose literary works are known for warmth, humor, and use of historical figures as fictional characters. Apple has been favorably compared to writers John Barth, **Philip Roth**, and **Woody Allen**.

Apple was born in Grand Rapids, Michigan in 1941. A self-described "professional grandson," Mottele was raised in a home steeped in the Yiddish humor of his two Lithuanian Jewish grandparents. Growing up in that household, Apple reflected, was like living in two worlds, that of nineteenth-century Lithuania and walking out the door to twentieth-century America. Apple earned both a BA (1963) and PhD (1970) at the University of Michigan, and then embarked on a career as a "nonacademic" professor of literature, first at Reed College in Portland, Oregon, and, since 1972, at Rice University in Houston, Texas. While still an undergraduate, Apple received Michigan's Hopwood Prize for writing. Other

Hopwood recipients include playwright **Arthur Miller** and Apple's daughter, Jessica Apple. He has also been the recipient of a Guggenheim Fellowship, the Jesse Jones Award in 1976 for *The Oranging of America* and in 1985 for *Free Agent,* and the *Hadassah Magazine* Ribalous Award for Best Jewish Fiction in 1985.

Apple's best-known works are memoirs of his grandparents: *I Love Gootie: My Grandmother's Story,* and *Roommates: My Grandfather's Story,* the former work describing what it was like being raised in America by a Yiddish-speaking grandmother. Apple co-wrote the screenplay for the movie version of *Roommates* (1995), which starred **Peter Falk**.

In his short story collection, *The Oranging of America,* Apple used such historic figures as **Norman Mailer** and Howard Johnson as cultural images that served to satirize social norms. Apple's oeuvre includes two novels: *Zip: A Story of the Left and the Right* (1978) and *Free Agents,* published in 1984. Apple also wrote the screenplay for the 1981 film *Smokey Bites the Dust.* His most recent publication is a series of short stories titled *The Jew of Home Depot and Other Stories* (2007). *See also* **Literature**.

Kurt F. Stone

Further Reading: Apple, Max. *I Love Gootie: My Grandmother's Story.* New York: Grand Central Publishing, 1998. ———. *Roommates: My Grandfather's Story.* Grand Central Publishing, 1994.

ARBUS, DIANE (1923–1971)

Noted for her photos of people on the fringe of society, Diane Arbus revolutionized documentary and street photography. With a deadpan shooting style and a fascination with society's fringe, Diane Arbus revolutionized documentary and street photography. Born Diane Nemerov on March 14, 1923, she was the daughter of David and Gertrude, who owned Russek's, a Fifth Avenue department store in New York. As part of her privileged upbringing, she attended the Ethical Culture School in New York. At age 18, she married army photographer Allan Arbus, who helped her develop an interest in photography. Together, they took photographs for Russek's, as well as fashion magazines, including *Harper's Bazaar.* The Arbuses had two daughters, Doon and Amy, before divorcing in 1959.

While studying at Manhattan's New School for Social Research with photographer Lisette Model, Arbus began to move from commercial work toward fine art photography. Recognizing the uniqueness of Arbus's work, Model encouraged her to continue shooting. Fascinated with identity and street photography, Arbus's portraits were of marginalized people or "freaks." She included in her work midgets, giants, twins, triplets, transvestites, and circus people. Arbus's shooting style was disarmingly straightforward and original. As her subjects stared into the lens of the camera, Arbus rendered them as honest, harsh, and—at times—grotesque. Arbus's photographs earned wide critical attention. She was awarded Guggenheim Fellowships in 1963 and 1966, which offered her the freedom to concentrate on her personal work, featured in the New Documents exhibition at the Museum of Modern Art in 1967. Between 1966 and 1971, Arbus taught college photography at the Parson's School of Design in New York and the Rhode Island School of Design.

On July 28, 1971, Diane Arbus committed suicide. She has since become one of the twentieth century's most revered artists. Her photographs continue to influence contemporary photography. In 1972, Aperture Press published *Diane Arbus,* a posthumous monograph of her photographs. The book has remained in print for over three decades. Two new books on Arbus were published in 2003: *Diane Arbus Revelations* and *Diane Arbus: Family Albums.* In 2006, a loosely related fictional feature film was produced—*Fur: An Imaginary Portrait of Diane Arbus. See also* **Film**.

Shauna Frischkorn

Further Reading: Bosworth, Patricia. *Diane Arbus: A Biography.* New York: W.W. Norton and Company, 1976. *Going Where I've Never Been Before: The Photographs of Diane Arbus.* Videocassette. Camera Three Productions, 1989.

ARKIN, ALAN (1934–)

Noted Oscar-winning actor, writer, and director Alan Arkin was born on March 26, 1934 in Brooklyn, New York to David and Beatrice. The Arkins have been described as Jewish intellectuals. He is of German and Russian descent. When Arkin was 12, his family moved from Brooklyn to Los Angeles, where he eventually attended Franklin High School and Los Angeles City College.

Both of his parents opposed the Red Scare of the 1950s. The anticommunist movement cost his father, a writer, teacher, and artist, his job. Arkin's father died before his dismissal was reversed. Ironically, Arkin earned his first Academy Award nomination for his performance in *The Russians Are Coming, the Russians Are Coming* (1966), in which he played a Soviet submariner.

Since his first feature-film appearance in 1957's *Calypso Heat Wave,* Arkin has appeared in almost 90 films and television programs. He is perhaps most recognized for his role as Captain Yossarian in the 1970 film *Catch-22.* During the course of his acting career, he has received critical acclaim and numerous awards and recognitions.

Though best known as an actor, Arkin is an accomplished musician, writer, director, and film producer. In 1956 he wrote "The Banana Boat Song," which became a hit for the calypso singer Henry Belafonte, and in his 1957 feature-film debut, he sang lead with the Tarriers. He also recorded and performed with the Babysitters, a folk-music group, for 10 years beginning in 1958. A prolific writer, Arkin has written numerous movies, children's stories, and science fiction books. Since 1967 he has directed 10 movies, including the 1993 film *Samuel Beckett is Coming Soon,* which he also produced.

Arkin continues to be a commercially viable and highly regarded actor. Since 2000 he has appeared in numerous commercially successful and critically acclaimed films including *Arigo* (2000), which he wrote and directed; *America's Sweethearts* (2001); *And Starring Pancho Villa As Himself* (2003); and *Little Miss Sunshine* (2006), for which he was awarded an Oscar for Best Supporting Actor. He appeared in two films in 2008—a remake of the television series *Get Smart* and *Sunshine Cleaning.* *See also* **Film**.

Danny Rigby

Further Reading: Arkin, Alan. *Halfway through the Door: First Steps on a Path of Enlightenment.* Harper San Francisco, 1984. ———. *The Lemming Condition.* Harper One, 1989.

ARTISTS

At the turn of the twentieth century, Paris was the center of advanced art. Artists from across Europe and America headed for this caldron of creativity. Among the most talented Jewish arrivals were Chaim Soutine, from Belarus; Marc Chagall, a Russian; Jules Pascin, a Bulgarian; an Italian, Amadeo Modigliani; and an American, Max Weber.

Max Weber (1881–1961), born in Bialystock, arrived in Brooklyn with his family when he was 10. He returned to Europe as an art student in 1905 and took full advantage of the opportunities that Paris offered: he befriended the great, naïf painter, Henri Rousseau; studied art with Henri Matisse; and attended gatherings at the salon of Gertrude Stein, on whose walls hung a major collection of modern art. Weber was mesmerized by Cubism.

In 1910, shortly after Weber returned to the United States, he was given a show at the pioneering gallery of Alfred Steiglitz. The general public, however, was still not ready for modern art. Unable to sell his work at that time, Weber became a teacher at the Art Students League in New York City and advocated modernism and Cubism, qualities that are reflected in his own paintings and sculptures. Later in his career, he also portrayed Jewish subjects, like Hasidim in the ecstasy of prayer and dance. In 1934, he painted *The Talmudists,* which was hung at Jewish Theological Seminary.

During World War I the pioneering modernist Marcel Duchamp spent time in the States. His painting *Nude Descending the Stairs,* shown at the groundbreaking Armory Show of 1913 earned him immediate notoriety. When this elegant, reserved, aristocratic European met Emmanuel Radnitzky (1890–1976)—five feet, three and a half inches; ebullient; humorous; and artistically inventive—a lasting friendship was formed. The artistic radicalism of Duchamp, three years his senior, inspired the American to explore art at the very edges of its frontiers. Radnitzky yearned to distance himself from his Jewish identity and his family. His father's job as a sewing machine operator in a sweatshop made him feel ashamed. He changed his name to Man Ray, a perfect avant-garde moniker for a modern artist with a future, but no past.

Man Ray's struggle to distance himself from his past surfaced in a 1920 sculpture consisting of a sewing machine carefully wrapped in a blanket and tied securely by a strong rope. On one side he attached a small sign: "Do not disturb," written in three languages. Fortunately, this desperate need to sever the familial umbilical cord, a theme that haunted him, also inspired Ray to create glorious pieces of radical art.

In July 1921, Man Ray headed for Paris. He was welcomed by Duchamp, who speedily brought him to Café Certa to meet the Dada circle. Even without a grasp of the French language, Man Ray still impressed the group. Later in the year, before the opening of his first show in Paris, Man Ray was absorbed by a simple tailor's iron. He attached 14 nails in a line to its flat side and created an icon of modern art. He had transformed the iron into a spiked weapon.

Kiki of Montparnasse, shapely and volatile, became Man Ray's favorite photographic model and his lover. Kiki is the subject of some of his most revered photographs. In "Blanche et Noir" (1926), her face lies flat on a table and a black African mask stands upright, balanced by Kiki's hand. The image is unforgettable—simple, powerful and poetic. But Kiki was not a passive partner. During a quarrel, Kiki, who knew his vulnerabilities, attacked him as a "filthy Jew." Escape from his past was a Sisyphean challenge.

Man Ray's innovations and achievements in the arts—photography, painting and sculpture—earned him an international reputation and honors. His achievements in photography contributed to its evolution into an art form.

In 1940, as Nazi armies advanced, Man Ray returned to the United States along with a distinguished cohort of European artists. Their presence acted as a stimulus, a challenge, and an inspiration to American artists who were coming to maturation and leading the charge into abstract art. It was the success of the Abstract Expressionists—Jackson Pollock and Willem de Kooning—that led to New York becoming the center of the art world. Three Jewish abstract artists were part of this elite group—Barnett Newman, Adolph Gottlieb, and Mark Rothko. They were considered, along with Clifford Still, the spiritual wing of the movement. All four were determined to express the sublime in their art.

Mark Rothko (1902–1970), was born in Latvia. His father, distanced from traditional Judaism, nevertheless decided that one of his children should learn Torah. Mark was chosen to enter a cheder. Three was the typical age for a male child to begin his formal religious studies. Mark spent seven years in the cheder before the family moved to America. He studied Jewish texts for long hours each day.

It was the normative design of a page of Jewish religious literature that directly influenced the composition of this great painter's mature art. Study a printed page of Torah: the biblical text in one block occupies perhaps a third of the page, and would, considering its primacy, be printed in bold and large lettering. Other texts, those of the classical commentaries on the Bible, appear in other rectangular blocks of space written in smaller letters. Rothko's mature style copies this basic design. However, he replaced the blocks of text with colors, and he tried to make these blocks of color as sublime and numinous as the words of the Torah. Rothko's signature style, achieved in 1949, is as Jewish as Chagall's, even though Chagall portrays *shtetl* scenes, while Rothko offered abstractions.

Sadly, Rothko suffered from depression and as it deepened in the late 1950s, the brilliant colors of his palette—oranges, yellows, reds, blues, and purples—began to darken. By 1964, dark colors dominate, and by 1970, the year he committed suicide, light had vanished from his paintings.

Barnett Newman (1905–1970), a New York native whose parents had immigrated from Lomza, Poland, had the good fortune to have the renowned art critic Thomas Hess praise his mature art and its Jewish iconography. Hess leafed through books in Newman's library until he discovered the key to Newman's inspiration in the book of Genesis and in volumes of mystical Jewish literature. He found underlined passages and handwritten notes that revealed ideas that influenced Newman's "Zip" paintings. The Zip was a line or lines of color that divided a field of color. Newman opined that his first Zip painting, *Onement,* ushered in his mature art phase and was a watershed moment in his life. The title, *Onement,* was an abbreviated version of "(at)onement." Among his other works inspired by Jewish ideas are *Genesis, Primordial Light, Day One,* and *Abraham.* His large painting *Vir Heroicus Sublimis* (1950–1951) and his 25-foot-high sculpture *Broken Obelisk* (1963–1967) are frequently displayed at the Museum of Modern Art in New York City.

Adolph Gottlieb (1903–1974), returning from Europe after studying museum collections and gallery shows, settled into the lifestyle of a professional artist. His level of sophistication and his artistic ambitions impressed his younger friend Barnett Newman and other neophytes. Newman and Gottlieb first met at the Art Students League. In 1931, he introduced Newman to Milton Avery and Mark Rothko. They would meet at Avery's home to study his powerful and original work. That the lessons were not lost becomes clear when one compares the mature work of these three artists with Avery's.

Gottlieb viewed his art as the expression of his subconscious. Throughout the 1940s, Gottlieb's signature style was the pictograph. He divided each canvas into boxes and painted a simple form in each box—the outline of a body feature or a purely decorative element. In the 1950s, a new style emerged. In *Blast II* (1957) a flaming red circle floats in an expanse of white, and below the circle is a black amorphous shape.

Gottlieb is credited with initiating the historic protest by New York artists against the Metropolitan Museum for consistently selecting conservative judges for its modern art competitions. Gottlieb drafted a strong statement of protest that was signed by 28 leading artists. All agreed not to enter the competition. On May 22, 1950, the letter made the front page of the *New York Times. Life* covered the story. Its group photograph of "the Irascibles," as they were dubbed, added to the uproar. The successful protest educated the public, turned the spotlight on the artists of the New York School and put pressure on the Met to change its attitude toward advanced art. Gottlieb had proved his mettle as artist and social activist.

Philip Guston (Goldstein) (1913–1980) became a highly respected member of the Abstract Expressionist cohort. During the 1960s he began to find abstraction too confining, and by 1970 he was ready to assert his personal and artistic freedom. At the time he was 57, not an easy age to begin anew. But Guston came from a family that faced the obstacles and challenges of starting life anew. His family left Odessa and immigrated to Montreal in 1913. In 1920, they pursued their dreams in Los Angeles. Guston's father could not attain a position in his trade and was forced to work as a junkman. His failures led to his suicide. It was 10-year-old Philip, the youngest of seven, who discovered his father's body hanging in a shed.

A closet in the crowded living space, illuminated by a single, bare light bulb, became Guston's sanctuary. There he made comic drawings. His mother recognized his talent and encouraged his art. At Manual Arts High School, Guston met Jackson Pollock and they became friends. One charismatic teacher introduced them to modern European art. Both left school before graduation. Pollock later headed for New

York City and in 1935, at his urging, Guston followed him.

Guston's early work is realistic. Mexican mural painting, with which he had some working experience, inspired him, and social realism was a natural philosophical base. The subjects of several of his paintings in this genre are of Ku Klux Klan members—intimidating, armed, hooded, and violent. Ultimately, the fervor and commitment of the Abstract Expressionists with whom he associated, as well as the excitement of their art, captivated Guston, and in the postwar years he produced abstract work that was elegant and lyrical.

When Guston showed his new work in 1970, the critics and the artists were dumbfounded and angry. Peter Schjedahl, an esteemed critic, hated the work and called it "raucous figuration" (Wilson, 227). His new style of painting was a mix of absurd and comic realism. It was as if a paintbrush instead of a pen had been handed to Samuel Beckett at the point when he was ready to start working on *Waiting for Godot*. Guston filled his paintings with crudely painted objects and people—mostly parts of people. The work was filled with round heads with one eye, ridiculously hooded figures, and legs as thin as pipes; naked light bulbs, piles of shoes, and cigarettes and butts.

The hooded Klan figures no longer intimidate; they are defanged. Guston implied that they represent the artist. In one of his later works, the hooded figure is painting a self-portrait. Did he perceive the KKK as a neutered movement? What about the stacks of shoes or pipelike legs? Do they relate to victims of the **Holocaust**? Do the assorted objects refer to the junk his father collected in the streets of Los Angeles, probably feeling humiliated as he called out, "alte zachen, alte zachen"? Anyone walking the streets of New York City could find in the garbage many of the mundane objects seen in Guston's paintings.

Unlike Guston, the august and proud Louise Nevelson behaved more like Guston's father. She scavenged the piles of detritus, but solely for the wood. Nevelson (1899–1988) was born Louise Berliatsky in Kiev, Ukraine. Her father, who owned a thriving lumber business, brought the family to Rockport, Maine in 1905 and successfully established the same business. Louise always wanted to be an artist. To accomplish this goal she knew she would have to leave Maine. In 1920, she accepted a proposal of marriage. The Nevelsons settled in a suburb of New York City and two years later Louise gave birth to a son, Myron.

Nevelson never adapted to life as a suburban housewife. She took courses, studied art and drama, endured emotional crises, and felt unfulfilled. When her husband's business suffered reverses, the Nevelsons moved to Brooklyn. Finally, Louise realized that to become a serious artist she had to abdicate her roles as wife and mother. In 1931, she left her husband, placed her son in her parents' care, and headed for Munich, Germany. She studied painting with the renowned teacher Hans Hoffman and always remembered that on her way to class each day she passed the home of Adolf Hitler.

Upon her return to the States, Nevelson settled in New York City, established a studio, and began her routine of foraging for wooden remnants: boards of all proportions and qualities; turned wood that had served as the legs of table desks and beds; carved pieces; curved arms of chairs; even toilet seats. She would then build a series of shallow boxes of the same size. In each box she would arrange and rearrange a group of remnants until she was satisfied with the composition. When all the boxes for the sculpture were completed, Nevelson painted them all black. If her plan was to create a sculpture with 18 boxes, she would perceive it as having 3 stacks of 6 boxes each. Many of these works are masterpieces.

Later in her career, Nevelson became more flexible. She might attach wood remnants to a beam six or seven feet long and develop a three-dimensional sculpture that stood upright. She also created assemblages without the box. She created two important pieces that paid *Homage to the Six Million*.

Unlike Nevelson, Mark di Suvero (1933–) yearned to work in steel. Finances forced him to start his career "on the cheap," which meant finding wood for sculptures. He scavenged for beams of considerable girth, the type found at demolition sites, so heavy that he had to drag them through the street. His studio was in the East Village—half way round the world from his birthplace—Shanghai, China, where his father, a Jew from Venice and a former ship captain, represented the government of Italy.

Abstract Expressionist art became di Suvero's primary source of inspiration. In place of the spare, bold, aggressive slashes of black paint that Franz Kline brushed on his canvas, di Suvero used thick beams of wood to build complex sculptures. A work might also have a chair or a tire hanging at the end of a beam. In 1960, di Suvero was crushed in an elevator accident. It was three years before he could walk again. During that period he began welding metal. The time came when he was prepared to use steel construction girders as the primary building block for his sculptures. This meant he could work big. *Yes for Lady Day,* of 1966–1969, measures 54 feet by 40 feet by 35 feet. It is perhaps not surprising that his sculptures evoke a sense of awe and monumentality. It is surprising that these large works of great originality also radiate a sense of elegance, grace, and enchantment. One powerful wood and steel sculpture, 22 feet by 30 feet, is titled *Praise for Elohim Adonai* (Praise for the God of Our Fathers).

Di Suvero led a campaign that resulted in the establishment of Socrates Sculpture Park in Long Island City, on the shores of the East River. It is an outdoor site that invites younger, emerging sculptors to show their work. An extensive collection of his major pieces are located at Storm King Art Center, near Newburgh, New York. To see 10 of his major steel sculptures spread out across acres provides a unique experience.

If one drives south from Storm King Art Center, it is possible to enter the Bronx and pass the neighborhood where George Segal's father had his kosher butcher store. He gave it up to buy a chicken farm near South Brunswick, New Jersey, an area and an occupation which attracted a number of Jewish socialists and Zionists from the greater New York area. Segal grew up on this chicken farm. He began his art career as a painter, but painting left him unfulfilled. His friend Allan Kaprow found himself in a similar quandary. The two aspiring artists discussed alternatives to Abstract Expressionism and struggled to find niches in art that would satisfy them. For Kaprow, the breakthrough came in the form of staged events he called "happenings." Robert Hughes describes it as a variant of performance art. Segal's path led him to sculpture of the human figure. He progressed to placing these figures within specific, familiar settings. The method of sculpture was unusual. Segal would wrap the body of friends or family members in cloth strips soaked in plaster, while that person struck a desired pose. Once the plaster was hard, like a doctor removing a cast, Segal would saw through the plaster and remove it. He would then reattach the pieces. Later in his career he would cast the plaster in bronze, with a patina that had the same color and surface as the original.

Segal's environments capture a familiar scene, a moment in time. Yet they are timeless creations. In 1965, Segal's father died, and six months later the son created *The Butcher Shop,* an installation in which the viewer sees a sign, "KOSHER MEAT," printed in Hebrew. There is a stainless steel bar with a series of hooks. A dead goose hangs from one hook and a hacksaw from another. In the background is the butcher, holding a cleaver in one hand and a chicken in the other. The scene is affecting. The objects are authentic, whereas the butcher and the poultry are white apparitions. One Segal sculpture stands on permanent display in the Port Authority Bus Terminal in New York City. Three travelers form a line by a door through which we assume they will pass to board a bus. Segal has poignantly captured their unease, exhaustion, and resolve.

When looking at photographs of Eva Hesse (1933–1970), one is struck by her eternal youth, as if she were caught in a time warp. Reading her biography removes such illusions. There are no photos of her aging because she died of cancer at age 34. Although her art career was brief and her life tragic, her work is memorable and continues to influence the work of contemporary artists.

Hesse was born in Hamburg, Germany. In 1938, the family fled and settled in New York City. Her sensitive mother, haunted by the upheavals in her life and the horrors of Nazism, took her own life in 1945. Eva received her BA from Yale in 1959. Her early drawings were abstract. A series of ink drawings done in 1964 foreshadowed her use of tubes, wires, and ropes connected or emerging from other forms in her sculptures. By 1965, her major work was in sculpture. There are many sausage-like forms attached to each other with strips of surgical hose, as seen in the work *Ingeminate*. The sculpture *Hangup* (1966) is a challenging and puzzling piece. It consists of two basic forms: an empty picture frame has its four sides wrapped in cloth and cord and is hanging on a wall. A steel rod emerges from the top slat near the right end, sweeps down and away from the frame, and reaches the floor several feet from the wall, at which point it loops and stretches back toward the wall, entering the bottom slat of the frame near the left end.

The artist Richard Serra saw a photo of the piece and was so impressed that he called Hesse, and they met for the first time. Hesse went on to create wondrous works of art with such materials as latex, fiberglass, polyethylene, wire, and plaster. She used repetition of forms—whether circles or squares—with hanging wires and tubes. Like many other sculptors, she needed to employ fabricators to deal with these materials and transform her drawing into sculptures. It is interesting that the Arko Workshop that Hesse used was staffed by men who were all Holocaust survivors, with numbers tattooed on their arms. Though Hesse left no hint that her work is related to the Holocaust, entering a room filled with her sculpture is to enter an eerie, haunted space, permeated by tragic memories.

Standing in front of a sculpture by Hesse's friend Richard Serra (1939–) evokes a sense of awe, a rush of adrenaline, and a thrill. Like di Suvero, Serra loves to work in steel and to work big. Instead of the construction beam, Serra's large creations use sheets of steel—15 feet wide and 2 inches thick. Only massive, highly specialized machinery can shape Serra's creations. They are frequently curved and sometimes circular. There is only one entrance into the center of the circular pieces, which Serra refers to as torqued ellipses. Being in close quarters with Serra's monumental sculptures leads one to feel both security and danger. The thick, high steel walls are fortress-like. They offer protection. They also overwhelm and intimidate. What if they should fall is a question that strikes fear in the viewer. Withal these ambivalent feelings, they are magnificent works of art.

Serra has also created a series of smaller sculptures made with pieces of steel that lean against each other. A delicate balance ensures their stability. Or he wedges a large sheet of steel in the corner of a room. The precarious positions of heavy objects provide marvelous arrangements that induce anxiety and awe.

Who is this man who offers us steel fortresses for protection and for intimidation? Who creates objects in such equipoise that one hopes he never exhibits his work in a region beset by earthquakes? His own words provide us with insights. While struggling to create a piece of sculpture for a synagogue in Germany, Serra recalled that at age five he asked his mother, Gladys Feinberg, " 'What are we? Who are we? Where are we from?' One day she answered me. 'If I tell you, you must promise never to tell anyone, never. We are Jewish.' " Serra comments: "I was raised in fear, in deceit, in embarrassment, in denial. I was told not to admit who I was, not to admit what I was" (van Voolen, 2006, 167).

Serra created the sculpture *Gravity* for the **United States Holocaust Memorial Museum**. A statement he made about it has relevance for the work of all the artists presented in this essay: "We face the fear of unbearable weight . . . the weight of history" (van Voolen, 2006, 167).

Sy Colen

Further Reading: Fineberg, Jonathan. *Art Since 1940.* New York: Harry N. Abrams, Inc., 1995. Hughes, Robert. *American Visions.* New York: Alfred A. Knopf, 1997. Van Voolen, Edward. *Jewish Art and Culture.* Munich: Prestel, 2006. Wilson, Martin, ed. *The Hydrogen Jukebox: The Selected Writings of Peter Schjeldahl, 1978–90.* Berkeley, CA: University of California Press, 1991, 227.

B

BACALL, LAUREN (1924–)

Star of stage and screen Lauren Bacall, originally Betty Joan Perske, was born on September 16, 1924 in New York City to a middle-class family. Her father and mother, William Perske, a salesman, and Natalie Weinstein-Bacall, a secretary, were German Jewish immigrants. They divorced when Bacall was five years old. Although she did not maintain a relationship with her father, she remained attached to her mother throughout her life. Bacall moved her mother to California when she became a Hollywood actress.

Bacall knew at a young age that she wanted to be a performer. After completing high school, she attended the American Academy of Dramatic Arts. She began her career as an off-Broadway actress and had a brief career in modeling. Acclaimed director Howard Hawks spotted her picture on the front page of *Harper's Bazaar* and cast her in the film *To Have and Have Not* (1944). The film was significant for Bacall. It was the first of over 40 films in her career, and there she met her first husband, Humphrey Bogart, who she married in 1945 (her marriage to Jason Robards Jr., following Bogart's death, was a short one).

As her career flourished, she was offered many scripts but turned down those that did not interest her. Although this gave her the reputation of being difficult to work with, her success continued. She was best known for her roles in the popular film noir genre of the 1940s and often costarred with Humphrey Bogart. The two acted in such productions as *The Big Sleep* (1946), *Dark Passage* (1947), and *Key Largo* (1948). Bacall was an accomplished and versatile actress who took on a variety of film roles, ranging from the slapstick comedy of *Designing Women* in 1957 to the tear-jerker *Written on the Wind* (1956), as well as such memorable films as *Young Man with a Horn* (1950), *Bright Leaf* (1950), *The Cobweb* and *Blood Alley* (1955), *Murder on the Orient Express* (1974), *Dogville* (2003), and *Manderlay* (2005).

In 1993, Bacall was selected for Hollywood's Cecil B. DeMille Award, and in 1996 she won the Screen Actors Guild Award for Best Supporting Actress—Motion Picture for her role in *The Mirror Has Two Faces.* A year later Bacall received a Golden Globe Award for the same film role.

In addition to her career in film, Bacall was also an accomplished stage actress. In 1970 she won a Tony Award for Best Leading Actress in a Musical for *Applause,* and a Tony Award in 1981 for *Woman of the Year.*

Bacall moved beyond acting at times to work as a political activist and campaigned for Adlai

Stevenson, the Democratic Party presidential candidate in 1952. Additionally, in 1978 she published her first book, *By Myself.* This was followed by *Now* in 1994 and *By Myself and Then Some* in 2004. In these autobiographical accounts of her life, Bacall addressed her Jewish ethnicity. After receiving her "big-break" in the film *To Have and To Have Not,* she was made aware that director Howard Hawkes was an outspoken anti-Semite. As Bacall informs the reader, "I bit my tongue." With regard to the courtship period which led to her marriage to Humphrey Bogart, Bacall writes: "Fearfully, I told Bogart that I was a Jew . . . I had to ask the question that had been so much on my mind—I had to get it straight. Did it matter to him that I was Jewish? Hell, no—what mattered to him was me, how I thought, how I felt, what kind of person I was, not my religion. He couldn't care less—why did I even ask? He couldn't really understand my anxiety, but he'd never felt it himself—he wasn't Jewish. Being singled out for such a thing was inconceivable to him. It was a big weight off my shoulders—I was relieved to have it in the open, it had been lurking too long in the unfinished--business department of my mind" (Bacall, 2005).

Bacall and Bogart had two children, Steve and Leslie. Steve was sent to Sunday school at All Saints Episopal Church, but although her son enjoyed attending, "he couldn't continue without being a church member. Bogie's feeling was that the main reason for having the children christened was that, with discrimination still rampant in the world, it would give them one less hurdle to jump in life's Olympics . . . I, with my family--ingrained Jewish background, bucked it—it felt too strange to me. True, I didn't go to synagogue, but I felt totally Jewish and always would. I certainly didn't intend to convert to Episcopalianism for the children, or to deny my own heritage. At the same time I knew how important it could be to a child to have a religious identity" (ibid.). Thus Bacall reasoned that according to Halacha (Jewish law), the children were Jewish because they had a Jewish mother.

Bacall writes extensively about her travels to Great Britain, France, India, but curiously not to Israel. About the only time in her book that Bacall's Jewish background was recognized in a public context was at the Jewish funeral for her mother, Natalie Bacall. As noted by Donald Harrison in his review of *By Myself and Then Some,* "unless, Queen Esther-like, Bacall has been working for Jewish causes behind the scenes, one fears that with Natalie's passing, so too did this family's attachment to Jewish peoplehood" (Harrison, *Jewishsightseeing.com,* July 23, 2006). *See also* **Film.**

Gabriela Lupatkin

Further Reading: Bacall, Lauren. *By Myself and Then Some.* New York: Harper-Collins Books, 2005.

BAMBERGER, LOUIS (1855–1944)

Jewish philanthropist and department store magnate Louis Bamberger was born in 1855 to Elkan and Theresa Hutzler Bamberger, German Jewish immigrants. With 23 years of experience working in a family-owned dry goods business in Baltimore, Maryland and New York, Bamberger struck out on his own and in 1892 opened what became New Jersey's largest department store, L. Bamberger and Co., in the city of Newark. In 1911, Newark was the third largest manufacturing center in the nation and home to a significant Jewish population, numbering around 50,000.

As a German Jew, Bamberger joined reform Temple B'nai Jeshurun, Newark's oldest synagogue. He socialized at Mountain Ridge Country Club, the first Jewish country club to welcome Newark's Jews.

As the owner of a successful department store, Bamberger was a "merchant prince" during a period in American history (1890–1929) when department stores provided an unprecedented flow of consumer goods designed to appeal to the rising middle classes. Bamberger was the master of advertising and promotion for the products he sold. Historian Jan Whitaker's *Service and Style* confirms that none, "absolutely none, outsold, out styled, out promoted, out advertised, or did more for their respective cities than Louis Bamberger" (Whitaker, 2006).

By World War I, Bamberger's role as a public benefactor had become legend. His civic initiatives supported the arts, provided music scholarships, built a Jewish hospital, founded a YM-YWHA, spearheaded the movement to create a united federation of Jewish agencies, and established neighborhood houses and orphanages for first-generation Jewish immigrants. His generosity earned him the respect of those who came to solicit his advice and financial support. Much of his philanthropy was done anonymously. Bamberger, a founder of Newark Museum in 1909, donated land and a completed building for the museum, which remains one of America's great small-city museums.

The sale of L. Bamberger and Co. to R. H. Macy in 1929 provided Bamberger with another opportunity to put his wealth to work. Trying to break new ground in the philanthropic world, Bamberger settled on an idea proposed by Rockefeller Foundation's Abraham Flexner. Bamberger, in concert with his sister, Caroline Bamberger Fuld, agreed in 1930 to fund the world-renowned think tank Institute of Advanced Study, located in Princeton, New Jersey. **Albert Einstein** spent the last years of his life at the institute. It is in this New Jersey think tank that Louis Bamberger's quiet philanthropy continues to exert influence in an ever-changing world of great ideas. *See also* **Einstein, Albert**.

Linda Forgosh

Further Reading: Goodwin, George M. "A New Jewish Elite: Curators, Directors, and Benefactors of American Art Museums." *Modern Judaism* 18, no. 1 (1998). Whitaker, Jan. *Service and Style.* New York: St. Martin's Press, 2006.

BEASTIE BOYS

The Beastie Boys are a talented, respected white hip-hop music group from New York City, who also happen to be Jewish. The members are Mike D, MCA, and Ad-Rock. The group plays both rap and rock and have been successful in both genres. Their debut album *Licensed to Ill* (1986) reached number one in the charts.

All three members of the group came from wealthy middle-class Jewish families. Mike D, born Mike Diamond, November 20, 1966; MCA, born Adam Yauch, August 5, 1965; and Ad-Rock, born Adam Horovitz, October 31, 1967, became involved in New York City's punk underground when they were teenagers in the 1980s. Diamond and Yauch formed the Beastie Boys with drummer Kate Schellenbach and guitarist John Berry in 1981. Both Schellenbach and Berry left the band in 1983, and the Beastie Boys added Horovitz, the son of playwright Israel Horovitz, whom they had met a year before. The revamped group's first rap single was "Cookie Puss" (1983), and by 1984 they had abandoned punk for rap.

Under the label of **Rick Rubin** and Russell Simmons' Def Jam, whom they joined with in 1984, the Beasties transformed their underground punk group into an MTV rap phenomenon, producing *License to Ill.* They engaged with Run-DMC, the single most important group in hip hop's colorful history, LL Cool J (thanks to Adam Horowitz) and Public Enemy. In the *License to Ill* album, the Beastie Boys recorded Run-DMC's "Slow and Low" and hired their bodyguard Wendell Fite, aka DJ Hurricane. The two bands jammed together and enjoyed a frank camaraderie. The emblematic hit on *License to Ill* is the goof song "Fight For Your Right," transforming the joke into a short-lived reality in which the Beastie Boys turn into jock favorites. Nevertheless, sexual fantasies and machismo embedded with a warholesque teenage *TV Guide* concept on life are just sideshows to musical creativity and chutzpah. Released in 1986, the album sold nine million copies and became the biggest-selling rap album of the 1980s.

Leaving Def Jam for the Dust Brothers, the Beastie Boys discovered layers of music through instrumentals. They moved to Los Angeles and built their own studio, where they worked with engineer Mario Caldato and keyboard player

Mark Nishita. As Joe Levy wrote in *Rolling Stone Magazine, License to Ill* reveals a **Three Stooges** aggressive comic band, while *Paul's Boutique* (1989) approaches the comic surrealism of the **Marx Brothers**. Societal concerns about AIDS, racism, and the homeless are all part of this formidable musical bouillabaisse.

Check Your Head (1992) has the studio night birds fly from the 1970s on, exploring musical limits, from the hardcore explosion "Time for Livin' " to the psychedelic soothing jam "Something's Got To Give." Blending colors and mall smiles nurtured the album, which took almost three years to record. *Ill Communication* (1994) marked their comeback to New York. The song "Root Down" is a tribute to their formative years, discovering music on subway rides to school and then travelling back home to watch sitcoms.

"Sabotage," a *Starsky & Hutch* spoof, has all the necessary power to carry the album to success. With success comes responsibility, and the band involves itself in many causes, especially Tibetan freedom. Adam Yauch, who met fleeing Tibetans in Nepal, is very involved with Buddhism and attends the Dalai Lama's teachings focusing on patience. The text studied inspires him to rap "Bodhisattva Vow."

The Beastie Boys move from hip-hop icons to independent heralds on the New York scene. The group produces their own and other bands' work under their Grand Royal banner (sold in 2003 via an Internet auction). The album *Hello Nasty* (1998) carries the hard rap, James Bond spoof "Body Movin' " and retro futuristic manga "Intergalactic," as well as instrumental pieces and gentle ballads. September 25, 1999 the Beastie Boys performed with Elvis Costello for *SNL*'s 25th anniversary special. Two months later the anthology *The Sound of Science* came out. *To the 5 Boroughs* was released in 2004. This Beastie Boys' sixth album is dedicated to the city where they grew up, discovered music, and shared their lives with myriads of New Yorkers. In their "Open Letter To NYC" they sing: "Since 911 we're still livin' / And lovin' life we've been given." September 11 is a trauma which the Beastie Boys address with a janus-type attitude. They look forward by promoting New York's rebirth and potential; yet, they look back to remember its history. In 2007, the Beastie Boys came back with *The Mix-Up*. If confusion arises about the Beastie Boys it is only because labeling them is problematic since they reference many genres and produce independent and creative music. *See also* **Rap and Hip Hop Music**.

Steve Krief

Further Reading: Cunningham, Steve. "License to Chill." *New Times* (Broward Palm Beach, FL), March 6 2008.

BELLOW, SAUL (1915–2005)

Saul Bellow, who won the Nobel prize for literature in 1976, has written some of the most important works in contemporary American fiction. The Nobel Laureate includes among his major works such classics as *The Adventures of Augie March, Mr. Sammler's Planet,* and *Herzog.* As well received as his fiction has been in the United States, Bellow's writing has also commanded serious international critical attention for over 50 years. He was a bold neoconservative voice, who began his writing career in the aftermath of World War II. Shaped by the Holocaust and the Cold War, his novels, short stories, and novellas defended the embattled human soul.

He was born in Lachine, Montreal, Canada on June 10, 1915, the fourth child of Abraham and Lescha (Liza) Belo. His parents were originally from St. Petersburg, Russia. In 1918, the family moved to Montreal's St. Dominique street, a poor Jewish neighborhood replete with rats and assorted immigrants, many of whom later appeared in his fiction. In 1918, at the age of three, he watched funeral corteges go his past window with victims of the Spanish influenza epidemic. Five years later he spent six months in a sanatorium fighting tuberculosis. While there he saw many children die and became obsessed with death. Humboldt's Park, Chicago, his next childhood home, was full of multiracial tenements, which also captured his imagination and shaped his early fiction. It was a neighborhood dedicated to the pursuit of art, culture, and ideas. Better still, it was rich in idiomatic immigrant English, Yiddish, Hebrew, and Russian.

By 1933 Bellow, a determined intellectual and socialist, entered the University of Chicago, and he transferred the following year to Northwestern University to study anthropology. He graduated in 1937 with a BA and honors in sociology and went to New York to become a writer. By Christmas he was back in Chicago, married to his first wife, Anita Goshkin, and working on his first book, *Dangling Man.* "Two Morning Monologues" and "The Mexican General" appeared in print in 1942. On June 5, 1942 Bellow was inducted into the Merchant Marine. When Bellow resumed writing he found apocalyptic Romanticism an outdated, imitative literary formula, quite antithetical to his Jewish optimism. The rest of his career was dedicated to denouncing destructive Faustian individualism, unproven existentialism, the then-fashionable alienation ethics, nihilism, and fears of the collapse of Western civilization. Like the American transcendentalists he loved, he believed in a unitary Romantic self and decried imitative "Wastelanders" who, unlike T. S. Eliot's World War I generation, had not earned their pessimism.

In 1944, Bellow's first son, Gregory, was born, and *Dangling Man* was reviewed by nearly every major journal and newspaper in the country. It was praised for its style, brilliance of thought, and its sharp, cutting language. The themes of individual freedom, moral responsibility, and social contract, along with Bellow's choice of a first-person male protagonist, characterized his work for the next 40 years. *The Victim* (1947), his second novella, was written to a Flaubertian standard and explores victimization, the paranoia of the post-Holocaust Jewish American consciousness, and the psychological effects of anti-Semitism in America.

He was awarded a Guggenheim Fellowship (1948), and from 1948–1950 Bellow was in bomb-ravaged Paris or traveling throughout Europe working on languages. He abandoned work on a huge and reportedly gloomy manuscript called "The Crab and the Butterfly" and began work on the ebullient *The Adventures of Augie March*. In 1953 he told interviewer Harvey Breit that: "The great pleasure of the book was that it came easily" (*New York Times*). Despite his anxiety about confronting a WASP worldview, he abandoned former Flaubertian standards and wrote of the Russian immigrant experience in Chicago—its character, language, habits, and their embrace of the American experience. In 1949, he published two more short stories, "Dora" and "Sermon by Dr. Pep," and in 1950, "The Trip to Galena." In 1951 he published "Looking for Mr. Green," "By the Rock Wall," and "Address by Gooley McDowell to the Hasbeen's Club of Chicago." In 1952, he received the National Institute of Arts and Letters Award and was made Creative Writing Fellow at Princeton University. In 1954 "Leaving the Yellow House" appeared, and soon after, Bellow received a Ford Foundation grant.

By 1955 Bellow was lecturing in Poland, West Germany, and other European countries. In 1956, he married Alexandra Tsachacbasov, his second wife, and was divorced in 1960. During this period Bellow was writing of *Henderson the Rain King,* battling house repairs, dealing with lack of money, feeling bored, attending family funerals, and mourning the deaths of childhood friends. Surrounded by death, Bellow escaped to a symbolic Africa of the soul in *Henderson the Rain King* (1959). In this novel he attacks the modernist legacy of late Romantic despair. He decries the notion that twentieth-century life is terminally broken and disordered. He also protests the idea that the novel is dead. He places blame for all these untruths on European nihilists and existentialists, as well as British and American university professors who convinced students that Joyce, Mann, Proust, Eliot, and Lawrence were the last literary prophets or models. This, Bellow argued, caused misguided contemporary novelists to embrace early modern "wasteland" views instead of making their own assessments.

Adam, Bellow's second son, was born in January 1957, but in 1961 Saul Bellow married Susan Alexandra Glassman, his third wife. He received an Honorary Doctor of Letters from Northwestern University in 1962, and he celebrated the arrival of his third son, Daniel. This same year he joined the prestigious Committee on Social Thought at the University of Chicago and worked on a draft of his first play, "The Last Analysis." In the fall of 1963 he received an Honorary Doctor of Letters by Bard College. When *Herzog* (1964) appeared, it was hailed as a great masterwork. Herzog is an unstrung divorcee whose *magnum opus* on Romanticism will never be finished. In a series of letters written to various European philosophers of doom and gloom, he wages war on nihilism. This novel is the comic vehicle for Bellow's description of his own divorce traumas. In 1965, Bellow received the James L. Dow Award and the Fomentor Award, as well as the National Book Award for *Herzog*. When "The Last Analysis," opened on Broadway, it closed after only two weeks. During 1965 Bellow received many honors for *Herzog*, including the International Literary Prize. By 1967 he had published "The Old System," and he also made an important trip to Israel to report on the Six Day War for *Newsday*.

By this time critics were noticing that Bellow had created no fully-imagined women characters. Bellow, never fond of critics, despised feminist critics and resented the presence of women and international faculty members hired at the University of Chicago. He was unapologetic about being primarily interested in men, and in particular, those with poetic sensibility and spiritual hankerings. In 1968, his first short story collection, *Mosby's Memoirs and Other Stories,* appeared, he divorced Susan Glassman, won the French Croix de Chevalier des Arts et Lettres, and received an award from B'nai B'rith.

In 1971 he won the National Book Award for *Mr. Sammler's Planet* (1969). Also in 1971 "The Last Analysis" was performed in an off-Broadway theater, only to close in just five weeks.

Bellow wrote *Humboldt's Gift* (1975) and vigorously registered in essays and in fiction his disapproval of Freud's reductive notions of the human unconscious. He was also seriously studying anthroposophical theories of the transcendent. Bellow enrolled himself in anthroposophy in order to move beyond the textual, or discourse, barriers blocking higher consciousness. In *Humboldt's Gift* Bellow reveals how badly Modernism diminished the inner lives of artists and poets; how sensibility has failed, and how humanism has been bankrupted by a destructive rationalism. He also laments the diminution of the private life in the contemporary age. Yet the novel concludes with an affirmation of the reality of the soul's intuitions and the transcendent.

During the decade of the 1970s Bellow had published "Zetland: By a Character Witness" (1974), "Burdens of a Lone Survivor" (1974), and *Humboldt's Gift* (1975). In 1975 he had married his fourth wife, Romanian mathematician Alexandra Ionescu Tulcea, and in 1976 he was awarded the Nobel Prize for Literature. Sadly, *To Jerusalem and Back: A Personal Account* was poorly received. Soon after, he visited Bucharest with his wife, Alexandra, and began work on *The Dean's December*. In 1978, he published one of his most beloved short stories "A Silver Dish." In 1984, *Him With His Foot in His Mouth* appeared. It is a collection of short fiction and was followed by *More Die of Heartbreak* (1987). In 1989 *A Theft* and *The Bellarosa Connection,* two novellas, appeared as paperbacks. It was an unprecedented event in the publishing world. *A Theft* details the tragicomic failure of modern heterosexual relationships and features Bellow's first attempt at a female protagonist. Bellow's demythologization of romantic love in "Gogmagogsville" again hinges on the ironic portrayal of a male protagonist torn between desire for ultimate union with the female and the simultaneous pursuit of the rational. *The Bellarosa Connection* features an unnamed narrator, an elderly man, trying to recapture a lost relationship with the remarkable and mysterious Sorella Fonstein and her Holocaust-survivor husband, Harry.

It all Adds Up, Bellow's collected essays, appeared in 1994 to mixed reviews. In 1997 *The*

Actual, another novella, appeared in hardback. This novella features an old adolescent love resumed. *Ravelstein* (2000) is a powerful autoethnographic short fiction work written as a memorial to his great friend the late Allan Bloom of the University of Chicago. The book chronicles the very special brotherhood of two famous first-generation male Russian Jewish American intellectuals. It records Bellow's personal recovery of the origins of his own Jewish voice, Jewish humor, Jewish anxiety, and Jewish intellectual life. Thoroughly voiced and performative, *Ravelstein* is a small masterpiece full of jokes, one-liners, and Catskill comedian gags. It captures a distinctly first-generation Russian Jewish American voice, its neuroses, manners, affectations, cultural collisions, and ethical humanism.

When Bellow died in 2005, his reported work-in-progress, "All Marbles Still Accounted For," had still not appeared. His wife and literary executor, Janice Freedman, whom he married in 1989, recently dispatched all of his papers and manuscripts to the Regenstein Library at the University of Chicago.

Bellow's reputation as a major American literary figure is established, as is his preeminence in the post-World War II European literary landscape. Critics now comment on Bellow's gender ideologies, his comedy, his intellectual and social analyses, his protagonists' racial attitudes, his use of first-person male monologues, his social realism, his concentration on Jewish American masculinity, his testy neoconservatism, and his undeniable, if circumscribed, ethical and moral brilliance. Most of all they acknowledge his enormous intellectual command. He is the late twentieth-century writer who established the quintessentially twentieth-century American urban voice of twentieth-century American literature. British writer Martin Amis calls Bellow and Nabokov the two greatest twentieth-century writers. *See also* **Literature**.

Gloria Cronin

Further Reading: Atlas, James. *Bellow: A Biography.* New York: Random House, 2000. Kennedy, Eugene. "Saul Bellow Teaches an 'Object' Lesson." *Chicago Tribune,* May 31, 1987, sec. 14: 3, 5. Kulshrestha, Chirantan. "A Conversation with Saul Bellow." *Chicago Review* 23.4–24.1 (1972): 7–15. *The New York Times Book Review,* September 20, 1953. Roudane, Matthew C. "An Interview with Saul Bellow." *Contemporary Literature* 25.3 (1984): 265–80. "Saul Bellow." *Playboy Review* (May 1995): 59–68, 166–70.

BENNY, JACK (1894–1974)

Jack Benny was a star of vaudeville, Broadway, movies, radio, and television. The son of eastern European Jewish immigrants, Meyer and Emma Kubelsky, he was born Benjamin Kubelsky in Chicago. The circumstances of his birth, early life, and long and successful entertainment career must be seen in the context of ethnicity and the Jewish immigrant experience. Both were formative experiences in his public persona.

His parents shared the immigrant's desire for success and tried to impress it on their son. Emma Kubelsky, a lover of music, even decided to have her son born in Chicago, rather than Waukegan, where the family lived, because she believed that Chicago was a more appropriate birthplace for a great artist. Meyer Kubelsky, a haberdasher by trade, supported his wife's dream by paying for music lessons for young Benjamin.

His parents' dream was thwarted—not by lack of talent, but by Benjamin's aversion to practicing. In his posthumously published autobiography, Benny related in self-deprecating humor that he was a dreamer and uninterested in school, homework, or sports. In fact, he flunked all his academic subjects in public school and only graduated to high school because the principal was glad to be rid of him.

High school was no different. Again flunking all his subjects, Benny recalls how his father hired a tutor for him and he still failed. His father then enrolled him in Waukegan Business College, and he was expelled. In a last final attempt to secure a future for his son, Meyer Kubelsky took him into the family business. Here he soon demonstrated a remarkable lack of aptitude for business, and his father fired him. This series of failures, while daunting, was the impetus to Jack Benny's future success. Determined to make his own way and find a niche for himself, he turned to a comfortable venue: entertainment.

The decision to entertain led to confrontation with the problem of ethnic identity. Benny largely avoided talking about his own religious beliefs in his memoir, but mentioned that his parents were devoutly orthodox and that he met his future wife at a family Seder. In contrast, his daughter relates how Christmas was always celebrated with all the trappings one would expect in a Christian household.

Ethnic identity was central to Benny's comedy, however. The evolution of his stage name is an amusing bit of ethic identity. He was twice threatened with lawsuits because his name sounded too much like those of other performers. As Benjamin Kubelsky, the violinist Jan Kubelik took umbrage to the similarity. As Benny K. Benny, the vaudevillian Ben Bernie threatened suit. Finally, he assumed the first name used by sailors of the day (he served in the navy in World War I)—"Jack"—and applied it to his actual first name: Jack Benny.

Twentieth-century America was a contentious period in which race and ethnicity were a constant struggle. Benny transcended both in an unique manner. In his successful radio and then television programs, he submerged himself in an eclectic ensemble of comedic talents that included the African American Eddie Anderson, the remarkable Jewish mime Mel Blanc, and Benny's wife Mary Livingston (a cousin of the **Marx Brothers**). Benny served as a comic foil whose vanity, parsimony, and egotism were the very same stereotypes used to label Jews. Benny used them for comic effect so that people laughed about him and not his Jewishness.

The quality of his comedy differed greatly from the heavy-handed racial stereotyping of the contemporary Amos and Andy duo, initially created by white performers in vocal blackface. Jack Benny became an American cultural icon whose exaggerated character flaws obscured his real character. Benny died in 1974. *See also* **Comedy**; **Radio**.

Leroy T. Hopkins Jr.

Further Reading: Benny, Jack, and Joan Benny, *Sunday Nights at Seven: The Jack Benny Story.* New York: Warner Books, 1990. Fein, Irving. *Jack Benny: An Intimate Biography.* New York: Putnam, 1976. Josefsberg, Milt. *The Jack Benny Show.* New Rochelle, NY: Arlington House, 1977.

BERG, GERTRUDE

See **Radio**; **Sitcoms**; **Television**

BERGER, ISAAC (IKE) (1936–)

Considered by many to be the greatest living featherweight weight lifter in American history, Isaac Berger was born on November 16, 1936 in Israel, to Rabbi Baruch and Chaya Rivkah Berger. He was one of six children: Miriam, Meir, Samuel, Leon, and Moshe Berger.

Berger grew up in an Orthodox Jewish household and was therefore a yeshiva student. In 1948, during Israel's War of Independence, he was wounded by shrapnel. During the war, it was Isaac's chore to go out daily to obtain food for his family and neighbors. It was about three miles each way and he had to watch out for artillery shell fragments and snipers.

In 1950, only one year after becoming a Bar Mitzvah, at the age of 14, Berger and his family migrated to the United States and settled in Brooklyn, New York. Berger was fascinated by the city's playgrounds and participated in many sports. He could not, however, get over his physical stature and was self-conscious about his size and physique (he was about an even 5 feet and 90 pounds as a teenager), and he decided to do something about his stature. Isaac began lifting weights and soon was pressing 125 pounds. He decided to compete as a weight lifter with the York BB Club, and, in 1955 at the age of 19, he won the national AAU championship. He went on to win the title a total of eight times, from 1955–1961 and again in 1964. Ike Berger was the first featherweight to lift over 800 pounds and press double his own body weight. Berger was a technically flawless lifter; his best lift was the press.

In 1957, Ike Berger competed in the fifth Maccabiah Games, representing the United States and winning the gold medal. He became the first athlete ever to establish a world record in Israel by pressing 258 pounds in the featherweight class. The following year, 1958, he won the world championship in the featherweight class. He went on to win the world title again in 1961 and finished second in 1957, 1959, and 1963. Berger was also the Pan American Games champion in 1959 and 1963. His greatest accomplishment came four days before the 1960 Rome Olympics, when Berger broke four world records: the press (264 pounds), the snatch (255 pounds), the clean-and-jerk (336 pounds), and total weight (853 pounds).

The longest weight lifting competition in Olympic history took place in 1960—it was the featherweight championship battle between Ike Berger, the defending champion, and Yevgeny Minayev of the Soviet Union. It lasted 10 hours, finally ending at 4:00 A.M., when Berger failed to lift 341 pounds in the jerk. Berger injured his muscles during this competition and subsequently placed second at the 1960 Olympics. He had beaten Minayev six times in a row prior to entering the Olympics, but this time he had to settle for second.

Berger always approached weights as a soldier would view the enemy. Because he hated weights, he sought to defeat the "enemy" by lifting them. At the same time, after victory in a weight lifting contest and hearing the applause, the euphoria which attends victory turned his hatred into love and respect for the sport.

Berger won the U.S. featherweight championship seven times, from 1955 through 1961 and in 1964. He was world champion in 1958 and 1961, finishing second in 1957, 1959, and 1963. He set a world record of 722.6 pounds for three lifts when he won the Olympic gold medal in 1956. Berger added the 1964 silver medal to the one he had claimed in 1960, and he was the Pan American Games featherweight champion in 1959 and in 1963. The Dominican Republic issued a postage stamp with his picture on it as a tribute to him.

Isaac Berger retired from his most impressive professional competitive weight lifting career as a 3-time world featherweight weight lifting champion, winner of 3 Olympic medals, owner of 23 world weight lifting records, and 12-time United States national titleholder.

Berger was the first featherweight in history to lift more than 886 pounds and the first to press double his body weight. His 1964 Olympic record of 336 pounds in the jerk made him pound-for-pound the strongest man in the world; he was a modern-day Samson, and his record stood for nine years. He was undefeated in six competitions against the Soviet Union.

Since Berger was born into a rabbinic and cantorial family, his father Baruch was a rabbi-cantor, his brother Leon is a cantor and choral director, and his brothers Meir (Mark) and Moshe are rabbi-cantors. It seemed only natural for Berger to follow his family's example. In 1965, Isaac began a three-year program at the New York College of Music to prepare himself for the cantorate.

Ike Berger is considered by many to be the greatest featherweight weight lifter in American history. In 1980, the International Jewish Sports Hall of Fame inducted Berger into its hall of fame. Our "modern-day Samson" Isaac Berger was also inducted into the USA Weightlifting Hall of Fame in York, Pennsylvania. Isaac presently resides in New York City with his family.

Israel J. Barzak

Further Reading: Taylor, Paul. *Jews and the Olympic Games.* Sussex, UK: Sussex Academic Press, 2004.

BERLE, MILTON (1908–2002)

Mendel "Milton Berle" Berlinger was an Emmy-winning comedian and actor, known As "Mr. Television" and "Uncle Miltie" during television's golden age. Berlinger was born on July 12, 1908 in New York City. When he was five years old he won Charlie Chaplin look-alike contests as well as appearing as a child actor in silent movies, beginning with *The Perils of Pauline* (1914). His mother liked the idea of a show business career, and Berle became a regular on the **vaudeville** circuit and continuing to find work in silent films. He performed in the Palace Theater in New York and became the youngest master of ceremonies on Broadway. Ultimately, he became one of the highest-paid comedians in show business. His show business career would last some 80 years.

Milton Berle was a star of stage, film, radio, and most of all, television. In the course of his career he authored and published some 400 songs. His television show *The Texaco Star Theater* made him a familiar personality to millions of viewers and brought him his greatest success. He was credited with helping to sell millions of television sets to the American people, who were eager to see his comedy and variety show. Sometimes he was called "Mr. Television," sometimes he was the viewers' "Uncle Miltie."

Berle was a slapstick comedian. At times he dressed as a woman, and viewers who did not recognize that it was Uncle Miltie thought he was a sexy middle-aged lady. He said that laughter or making people laugh was the most important part of his life. "A good laugh is better than anything." He appeared as himself in such films as **Woody Allen**'s *Broadway Danny Rose* (1948), *The Perils of Pauline* (1914), and *I Hear Laughter* (1999). He was one of the first to be inducted into the National Comedy Hall of Fame, as well as the California Hall of Fame in 2007. He was married four times, twice to the same woman. Milton Berle died in 2002. *See also* **Comedy**; **Television**.

Herbert M. Druks

Further Reading: Berle, Milton, and Haskel Frankel. *Milton Berle: An Autobiography with Haskel Frankel.* New York: Dell, 1994.

BERLIN, IRVING (1888–1989)

One of the most prolific songwriters in American entertainment history, Irving Berlin was born Israel Isidore Baline. He arrived in America with his parents from Russia in 1893, where the family escaped from the pogroms directed at the country's Jewish population. The family settled in Manhattan's Lower East Side, where his father earned a living as a cantor and worked certifying kosher meat. Although the family was Orthodox, Berlin did not show a propensity to be an observant Jew. Instead, like other immigrant children of the time, Berlin spent more time playing in the streets than as a scholar. When his father died in 1896, young Berlin found himself forced to help support his family, which included seven other siblings. Israel Baline went to work selling newspapers but was soon attracted to the saloons of Chinatown, where he listened to performers sing or play musical instruments. Israel, like his father, had a pleasant voice and soon found employment as an assistant to a popular street singer called Blind Sol. Subsequently, he found employment at Callahan's and Chatham restaurants and eventually worked with composer and publisher Harry von Tilzer, a Jewish composer best known for his classic song "Take Me Out to the Ballgame." Baline was paid five dollars a week to plug von Tilzer's songs at Tony Pastor's Music Hall in Union Square.

It was about this time that Baline began composing songs, although he could not read music. In 1906, Baline got a steady job at the Pelham Café in Chinatown both as a waiter and busboy, but throughout the evening he also sang popular songs. In 1907 Israel published his first song, "Marie From Sunny Italy," and although he did not make much money from the song, he decided that he was not only a singer but a composer, and he changed his name to Irving Berlin. Perhaps Baline thought that changing his name to one that sounded more "American" would help make him more marketable. Berlin's first major hit was his "ragtime" song "Alexander's Ragtime Band" in 1911. Berlin composed three additional ragtime tunes, "Mysterious Rag," "The Ragtime Violin," and "Everybody's Doin' It Now," and within the space of a few months he sold more than one million copies of the sheet music and ushered in the nation's ragtime dance craze.

Subsequently, Berlin wrote songs for the Ziegfeld Follies, and one of his songs, "A Pretty Girl is Like a Melody," became the group's theme song. In 1914 he wrote his first Broadway show, *Watch Your Step,* which featured Vernon and Irene Castle. As Berlin became an established songwriter, young talent sought to work for him; one of them, **George Gershwin**, was encouraged by Berlin to pursue his career in show business. Gershwin would always be grateful to Berlin for recognizing his talent and encouraging him to write his compositions and songs.

Berlin was also devoted to his mother, and despite his indifference to Judaism, he promised his mother that he would say the Kaddish prayer when she passed on. He kept his word when she died in 1922.

When America declared war against Germany in 1917, Berlin sought to enlist in the army, but when doctors discovered that he suffered from nervous indigestion, he was exempted from army combat duty. He proceeded to ask that he be assigned to an entertainment unit, which led to his placement in the army infantry as a private. Ultimately, he was promoted to the rank of sergeant, but not before he produced a show to raise money for an army entertainment center. The show was *Yip Yip Yaphank,* which opened on July 26, 1918 at New York's Century Theater. The show produced two Berlin hit songs, "Oh, How I Hate to Get Up in the Morning," which sold more than a million and a half copies, and "Mandy."

In 1926, Berlin married Ellin Mackay, the daughter of Clarence H. Mackay, the multimillionaire founder of the Comstock Lode Mining Company. A devout Catholic, Clarence McKay was also an anti-Semite, who threatened to disinherit his daughter for marrying a Jew. This was the second marriage for Berlin; his first wife, Dorothy Goetz, also a non-Jew, died of typhoid fever five months after the wedding. The Berlins subsequently had three daughters. A son, Irving Berlin Jr., died as an infant on Christmas Day, and Ellin Berlin's former friends attributed the death as "God's punishment for marrying a Jew." Despite opposition from her father and being ostracized by her circle of friends, the marriage was a happy one. When Irving's father-in-law lost his fortune after the stock market crash in 1929, Berlin offered him his financial assistance.

From the 1920s through the 1950s, Irving Berlin wrote many hit songs which included "Blue Skies," "Always," "Say It Isn't So," "How Deep Is the Ocean," "All Alone," and hundreds of others. Berlin also composed for the movies, as well as for Broadway, which included his most successful shows, *Annie Get Your Gun* (1946) and *Call Me Madam (1950).* It was during this period that he wrote "God Bless America" for the 1943 film *This Is the Army.* The song that many regarded as America's second national anthem was initially composed for *Yip Yip Yaphank,* as a patriotic tribute to the United States Army, but Berlin decided against using it. As the United States fought World War II, however, radio star Kate Smith asked Berlin to compose a new patriotic song. Berlin adhered to the request and wrote the song that expressed his love for America, "God Bless America." It was Kate Smith who convinced him to use the song in the film, and her rendition of the song that has been associated with it ever since. In 1942, Berlin wrote songs for the film *Holiday Inn,* which included "White Christmas,"—one of the most-recorded songs in history, and also one of the most controversial. First sung by Bing Crosby, it sold over 30 million copies when released. The irony of the song, however, was not lost on Berlin's critics, who noted that the son of a cantor, brought up in an Orthodox Jewish home, had composed one of America's most popular Christmas songs. Anticipating the culture wars of the late twentieth century, it was pointed out that Berlin had taken "Christ out of Christmas," thus contributing to the commercialization of a holiday that celebrated the birth of the Messiah.

For the agnostic Berlin, religion, unlike patriotism, was never important. He viewed Christmas as an American holiday as much as was the Fourth of July. Indeed, Berlin's celebration of America is evidenced by his composing songs for each

American holiday: "Easter Parade," "Let's Say It with Firecrackers," for July 4, "Plenty to be Thankful" for Thanksgiving, and "Let's Start the New Year Right," for New Year's.

Irving Berlin composed over 3,000 songs, 17 film scores, and 21 scores for Broadway shows. In 1968, Berlin was awarded the Grammy Lifetime Achievement Award, and one of his last public appearances was his attendance at the centennial celebrations for the Statue of Liberty in 1986. He died of a heart attack in New York City at age of 101 and was buried in a Jewish cemetery as he had requested. *See also* **The Brill Building Songwriters**; **Popular Music**; **Theater**.

Herbert M. Druks

Further Reading: Bergreen, Laurence. *As Thousands Cheer: The Life of Irving Berlin.* New York: Da Capo Press, 1996.

BERNSTEIN, LEONARD (1918–1990)

American composer of classical music and Broadway musicals, Leonard Bernstein was also a pianist, author, television personality, and the first American-born concert conductor to receive international acclaim. Leonard Bernstein was born to an upper-middle class Jewish family in Lawrence, Massachusetts on August 25, 1918. His parents, Samuel Joseph and Jennie Bernstein, were Russian immigrants. He learned to love music, and when he was 10 his aunt gave his family a piano. He began to play by ear and to compose simple songs. Soon his family gave him piano lessons. He attended Boston Latin School and graduated from Harvard in 1939 with a degree in music. He continued his studies of music at the Curtis Institute of Music in Philadelphia, where he studied conducting with Fritz Reiner, piano with Isabella Vengerova, and orchestration with Randall Thompson.

His first work, the Clarinet Sonata, was published as World War II. Bernstein's first classical music compositions were the Piano Trio (1937) and Sonata for Clarinet and Piano (1939). He subsequently produced operas for the Boston Institute of Modern Art, and in September 1942, he received an appointment as assistant conductor to Serge Koussevitsky in Tanglewood, Massachusetts. It was at Tanglewood that he conducted and taught master classes and established a lifelong friendship with **Aaron Copland**. His career moved swiftly thereafter. In 1942–1943 he conducted concerts in New York and was appointed assistant conductor of the New York Philharmonic. On November 13, 1943, he replaced a conductor who took sick at the Philharmonic. He did so well that the *New York Times* gave him an excellent review.

Bernstein was a sensitive man, composer, and conductor. He expressed that sensitivity in such composition as *Candide, Mass, Kaddish,* the *Jeremiah* Symphony and *Age of Anxiety.* He likewise added his talents to popular compositions such as *Fancy Free, Wonderful Town,* ***West Side Story*** and *The Dybbuk.* Some of his other compositions include *Trouble in Tahiti,* a one-act opera; *Touches,* a piano composition; and *A Musical Toast,* in memory of Andre Kostelanetz.

One of Bernstein's many favorite musical activities was his Young People's Concerts, which he conducted at Lincoln Center and broadcast on television. After the death of his wife he resigned as director of the New York Philharmonic, and the Philharmonic honored him with the title of conductor laureate.

He led a liberated style of life and was an innovator in orchestral as well as popular music. He performed Copland's *Piano Variations* so often that he considered it to be his trademark. Bernstein programmed, performed, and recorded Copland's orchestral works, some of them more than once. Among the composers he rendered were: Haydn, Beethoven, Mahler, Brahms, and Sibelius.

Bernstein did not forsake his Jewish identity. He traveled to Israel on a number of occasions. One of the most dramatic moments of his visits to Israel was when in 1967 he came to visit the Western Wall, which had finally been liberated after hundreds of years of occupation. He did not hide his true feelings. He cried openly as if he were a Hasidic rabbi.

In 1943, he completed his Symphony no. 1: *Jeremiah*. Twenty years later he composed his *Kaddish* and dedicated it "To the Beloved Memory of John F. Kennedy," which was performed by the Israel Philharmonic Orchestra. Among his other compositions were *Riffs for Solo Clarinet and Jazz Ensemble* (1949) and *Serenade for Violin, Strings and Percussion* (1954). The operas composed by Bernstein included *Trouble in Tahiti* (1952) and *A Quiet Place* (1983). The ballets he composed with **Jerome Robbins** were-*Facsimile* (1946) and *The Dybbuk* (1975). He wrote the score for *On the Waterfront* (1954) and incidental music for Broadway plays such as*Peter Pan* (1950) and *The Lark* (1955). Bernstein composed for such musicals as *On the Town* (1944) with Betty Comden and Adolph Green; *Wonderful Town* (1953); *Candide* (1956) with Richard Wilbur and Lillian Hellman; *West Side Story* with Jerome Robbins, **Stephen Sondheim**, and Arthur Laurents; and *1900 Pennsylvania Avenue* with Alan Jay Lerner.

In 1978, the Israeli Philharmonic commemorated his dedication and his devotion to Israel. In 1988 the Israel Philharmonic bestowed him the title of laureate conductor. In 1985, he received a Grammy Lifetime Achievement Award. That same year he received an Emmy Award for his music compositions. Among his publications were *The Joy of Music* (1959), *The Infinite Variety of Music* (1966), *The Unanswered Questions* (1976), *Six Lectures at Harvard University* (1972–1973), *Findings* (1982).

In December 1989, he conducted Berlin Celebration Concerts on both sides of the Berlin wall, as it was being dismantled. In 1990, the Praemium Imperiate Japan Arts Association presented Bernstein with an award for his lifetime achievements in the arts. He used the $100,000 prize from that award to inaugurate the Bernstein Education Through the Arts foundation.

He was a musician who pioneered in many fields of music and achieved greatness in all of them. But above all, he was a humanitarian who fought for human rights for all peoples and carried his love and devotion to Israel and the Jewish people in his heart. This giant of music died on October 14, 1990. *See also* **Popular Music**; **Theater**; ***West Side Story***.

Herbert M. Druks

Further Reading: Burton, Humphrey. *Leonard Bernstein*. New York: Doubleday, 1994. Peyser, Joan. *Bernstein, a Biography*. New York: Beach Tree Books, 1987.

BIKEL, THEODORE (1924–)

Theodore Bikel is the very definition of a renaissance man, Jewish and otherwise. His achievements are remarkable for both their quantity and diversity and include successes as an actor and singer in the arenas of the legitimate stage, concert halls, movies, and television; as a translator of lyrics; and as an activist and spokesperson for progressive and Jewish causes. He has himself acknowledged his multifaceted abilities, saying, "professionally, I can count three or four separate existences" (Bikel, 1994).

Theodor Meir Bikel—named for Herzl, on whose birthday he was born, hence the original missing "e"—was born in Vienna on May 2, 1924, to Josef and Miriam Bikel. The household was secular, but traditional; his father was a socialist and Zionist. Bikel left Austria at 13, making aliya with his family to what was then Palestine. Already multilingual then, he speaks seven languages. His ambition was to become a linguistics teacher, but acting proved too strong an inducement, and in 1943 he joined the famed Habimah Theater. His first professional role was a small part in the play *Tevye, the Milkman,* a forerunner of ***Fiddler on the Roof***, in which he has played the lead over 2,000 times since 1967. He became a cofounder the next year of the Cameri Theater of Tel Aviv.

After the war, Bikel enrolled in the Royal Academy of Dramatic Art in London, graduating in 1948. Laurence Olivier cast him in a small part in *A Streetcar Named Desire,* and he eventually played both lead roles. He scored many stage successes in London, where he also began playing guitar and singing folk music. Bikel came to settle in America in 1954;, he became an American citizen in 1961. In 1959, he originated the role of Baron von Trapp in *The Sound of Music* on Broadway, garnering a Tony nomination for Best Featured Actor in a Musical. Other Broadway shows he starred in are *Tonight in Samarkand, The Rope Dancers,* and *The Lark.*

He made the first of his more than 30 screen appearances in *The African Queen* (1951) and appeared in, among other films, *The Defiant Ones* (1958)—his Sheriff Max Muller earned him an Oscar nomination,*My Fair Lady* (1964), *The Russians Are Coming, the Russians Are Coming* (1965), *Benefit of the Doubt* (1992), and *Shadow Conspiracy* (1996).

Opera is also on the versatile entertainer's résumé, including appearances in *La Gazza Ladra* (1989) and *The Abduction from the Seraglio* (1992).

On the small screen, Bikel has played many diverse parts, earning Emmy nominations and receiving one in 1988 for his starring role as a West Coast pioneer in *Harris Newmark,* a PBS special. He has been featured in numerous specials and has guest-starred on such series as *All In the Family, Murder She Wrote, Dynasty, Falcon Crest,* and*Twilight Zone* and has hosted public service programs focusing on music, religion, and education. He portrayed Henry Kissinger in the 1989 television movie *The Final Days* and Russian Sergey Rozhenko in a 1990 episode of *Star Trek: The Next Generation.* He was Mr. Van Daan in a 1967 production of *The Diary of Anne Frank,* a hijacked passenger in *Victory at Entebbe* in 1976, and a troubled Holocaust survivor in a 1992 episode of *L.A. Law.*

Bikel wrote for and was featured on the classic radio and television show *The Eternal Light* and appeared on the daytime dramas *Look Up And Live* and *Directions.* He also had a 90-minute television special, *One Night Stand* and a weekly radio program, *At Home With Theodore Bikel.* A cofounder in 1961 of the Newport Folk Festival, Bikel made his concert debut as a folk singer at Carnegie Hall in 1956, and through the years has appeared in concerts, often accompanied by symphony orchestras, in the United States, Canada, Europe, Israel, New Zealand, and Australia. He has recorded more than 35 albums, including cast recordings of *The Sound of Music* (1960), *The King and I* (1964), and *Bravo Bikel!,* a 1959 live recording from Carnegie Hall.

The author of *Folksongs and Footnotes* (1961), Bikel is a lecturer and frequent contributor to journals and publications. *Theo: The Autobiography of Theodore Bikel* was issued in 1994 and republished in paperback in 2002.

An activist in the civil rights movement and a leader of civic organizations, Bikel served as a delegate to the 1968 Democratic Convention in Chicago. He has held leadership positions with numerous bodies, including Actors' Equity Association, the International Federation of Actors, Amnesty International (USA), the National Council on the Arts, and the Associated Actors and Artistes of America. Although he has characterized himself as "a general practitioner in the world of the arts," Bikel also said, "but, when I toil in the field of Jewish culture, which I frequently do, I am indeed a Jewish artist" (Bikel, 1994).

It was as a Jewish artist that he coauthored and costarred in the theatrical work *Greetings Sholem Aleichem Lives* in 1997. More than half his music recordings tap into Jewish culture, offering Yiddish and Israeli folk songs, holiday selections, and songs of World War II partisans and the Soviet Jewry movement. His audio recordings include *Tevye, the Dairyman,* stories of Sholem Aleichem, and *O Jerusalem,* the 1972 novel on the founding of Israel. Among the orchestral works he has performed are *The Poetry and Prophecy of the Old Testament* by Dov Seltzer, *King David* by Arthur Honegger, and *A Survivor from Warsaw* by Arnold Schoenberg.

Bikel received a doctor of humane letters from Hebrew Union College, served as senior vice president of the American Jewish Congress, and, in 2006, received the Maggid Award from the World Union for Progressive Judaism. In January

2007, he was elected to chair Meretz USA's board of directors.

Bikel provided the narration for two major works in the Milken Archive of American Jewish Music: Ernst Toch's *Cantata of the Bitter Herbs and Ahava-Brotherhood* by David Diamond, celebrating the 350th anniversary of the arrival of the first Jews in America.

Describing himself as a "secular, cultural Jew," Bikel has said that he likes the customs, rituals, and traditions of the religion, as well as synagogues for their communal aspects and "concentration on the Hebrew language." About his signature role, he has said, "Well, Tevye is my own grandfather, a very knowledgeable, traditional Jew, but he was also rebellious in a sense" (Bikel, 1994). Bikel has attributed his efforts to nurture Jewish culture to his deep concern over the threat of the loss of many of its aspects, foremost among them the **Yiddish** language

Bikel had a brief marriage to Ofra Ichilov in the 1950s. He and his second wife, Rita Weinberg Call, whom he wed in 1967, have two children, Robert and Daniel. Bikel lives in California and Connecticut. *See also* **Film**; **Theater**.

Abby Meth Kanter

Further Reading: Bikel, Theodore. *Autobiography of Theodore Bikel.* New York: Harper Collins, 1994. Theodore Bikel Web Site: www.bikel.com.

BLACK, JACK (1969–)

Born Thomas Jack Black, Jack Black is a Jewish American film and television actor as well as a musician. He was born in Hermosa Beach, California, the only son of two satellite engineers, Thomas William Black (who was a convert to Judaism) and Judith Cohen. At age 10, his parents were divorced, and he was raised by his mother in Culver City. Black attended Hebrew school and was Bar Mitzvahed but never went to synagogue again. He developed his desire to act following a Passover Seder. The year was 1979 and Black was invited to play a game of "Freeze" after the Seder. The basically improvisational game unleashed something inside of him that led to his desire to become an actor. Black attended Culver City High School and then transferred to Crossroads School for Arts and Sciences in Santa Monica. After graduation he attended the University of California–Los Angeles, where he came under the tutelage of Tim Robbins, who later cast him in *Bob Roberts,* his first film role (1992). He also had recurring roles on the HBO sketch comedy series *Mr. Snow.* Black's acting career began in television and appeared in such prime time television shows as *The X-Files, Northern Exposure,* and *Picket Fences.* He also appeared in small roles in films such as *Demolition Man* (1993), *Waterworld* (1995), *Mars Attack* (1995), *Dead Man Walking* (1995), *The Cable Guy* (1996), and *Enemy of the State* (1998), among others. His breakthrough role was as John Cusack's coworker in *High Fidelity* (2000), but he became best known in popular culture for starring in the 2003 hit comedy *School of Rock,* in which he played a rocker who finds himself teaching musical theory in a private school. Soon after, he appeared in leading roles in such films as *Saving Silverman* (2001), *Shallow Hal* (2001), *Orange County, Envy* (2002), and *King Kong* (2005). In 2006, Black starred in *Nacho Libre* and *Tenacious D: The Pick of Destiny.* He played Kate Winslet's love interest in *The Holiday* (2006), and in 2007 he starred in *Margot at the Wedding,* with Nicole Kidman and Jennifer Jason Leigh. Black is also the lead singer for the rock comedy band Tenacious D, the subject of his 2006 film. The band owes much of its popularity to Black's unorthodox, humorous lyrics. Black married Tanya Haden, the daughter of jazz double bassist Charlie Haden, in 2006, and they have a son, Samuel Jason. *See also* **Film**.

Jack R. Fischel

Further Reading: Handler, Daniel. "Interview with Jack Black." *Believer,* July/August 2008.

BLUME, JUDY (1939–)

Popular bestselling author of novels for children and young adults, Judy Blume was born Judy

Sussman in Elizabeth, New Jersey on February 12, 1938 to Rudolph and Esther Sussman. She received a BS degree in education in 1961 from New York University. Her first marriage was to John Blume in 1959, which ended in divorce in 1975. The couple bore two children, Randy Lee (1961) and Lawrence Andrew (1963). Judy Blume's second marriage was to Thomas Kitchens, and they divorced in 1978. She subsequently married her present husband, George Cooper, a writer of nonfiction books, with whom she has one stepdaughter, Amanda.

Judy Blume is best known for her authentic depiction of American adolescence. Blume was a pioneer of realism in children's literature. She dared to write about topics like menstruation, divorce, intermarriage, popularity, pimples, fitting in, and training bras. *Are You There God? It's Me, Margaret* (1970), broke new ground by dealing frankly with divorce and getting one's period. *Then Again, Maybe I Won't* (1971) used believable characters and straightforward language to introduce a generation of adolescents to wet dreams and the beginning of sexual desire. Similarly, her young adult novel *Forever* (1975) presented a detailed, no-holds-barred depiction of teenage sex and losing one's virginity.

Blume's books, quickly embraced by her readers, were less popular with librarians and teachers. Readers were hungry for believable characters with whom they could identify, characters who dealt with real-life challenges. The honesty and lack of embarrassment in her approach to difficult subject matter made it possible for adolescents to feel that they were not alone.

Blume is a prolific writer, having published more than 20 picture books, young- and middle-reader chapter books, and young adult fiction, as well as three adult novels. Blume's books for younger children deal sensitively, and humorously, with the issues that plague pre-adolescents, as in the sibling problems of *Tales of a Fourth Grade Nothing* (1972). This beloved book introduced characters who lived on in the Fudge series, including *Superfudge* (1980), *Fudge-a-Mania* (1990), and *Double Fudge* (2002). *Starring Sally J. Freedman as Herself* (1977) is the book that Blume has called her most autobiographical. The book features a Jewish girl living in Miami in 1947, trying to make sense out of becoming an adolescent as the adults around her grapple with life after World War II.

A frequent target of censorship herself, Blume has been active in the fight against the banning of books in schools and libraries. She edited the collection *Places I Never Meant to Be: Original Stories by Censored Writers* (1999) and served on the board of the National Coalition Against Censorship.

Blume has won many awards and accolades for her work, including many readers' choice awards. *Are You There God? It's Me, Margaret* was named an Outstanding Book of the Year by the *New York Times* (1970), as was *Blubber* (1974). *Forever* was named an American Library Association Margaret A. Edwards Award for Outstanding Literature for Young Adults (1974). *Tiger Eyes* (1981), was named Best Book for Young Adults by the *School Library Journal*. Blume was named the Most Admired Author in the Heroes of Young America Poll by *World Almanac* (1989) and was given a Civil Liberties Award by the American Civil Liberties Union (1986). In 1996 Blume was awarded the Margaret A. Edwards Award for Lifetime Achievement from the American Library Association. *See also* **Children's Literature**.

Hara Person

Further Reading: Wilson, Nance. "Judy Blume." In *The Continuum Encyclopedia of Children's Literature,* edited by Bernice E. Cullinan and Diane G. Person. New York: Continuum Publishing, 2001.

BOTEACH, SHMULEY (1966–)

Rabbi Shmuley Boteach, the "rabbi to the stars," was born on November 19, 1966 in Los Angeles, California. A disciple of the late Rebbe Menachem Mendel Schneerson, whom he first met at the age of 13, Boteach received his rabbinical ordination from the Chabad-Lubavitch movement in 1988, after studying for three years at Torat Emet Yeshiva in Jerusalem. Following his ordination, he was sent by the Lubavitcher movement, as part of its outreach program, as a *shliach* (emissary) to Oxford University in England.

During his 11-year residence at Oxford he founded the L'Chaim Society, an organization which encourages young Jewish students to participate in Jewish culture and religious practices. While at Oxford, Boteach served as rabbi to the university's Jewish students. During these years, he hosted and debated some of the world's leading intellectuals, statesmen, and entertainers—a list that included Mikhail Gorbachev, Stephen Hawking, Shimon Peres, Deepak Chopra, Benjamin Netanyahu, **Elie Wiesel**, Christopher Hitchens, Yitzchak Shamir, Richard Dawkins, Javier Perez de Cuellar, Simon Wiesenthal, Michael Jackson, and Colin Blakemore, to name but a few.

Rabbi Boteach is the author of 18 books, including *Kosher Sex* (Doubleday, 1992), which became a bestseller, made him a celebrity, and was excerpted in *Playboy.* Boteach has appeared on radio and television shows such as *Oprah, The Today Show, The View,* and *The O'Reilly Factor.* He hosts his own television series, *Shalom at Home,* which made its debut on The Learning Channel (TLC) in 2006. The show focuses on troubled families and how they can overcome their problems.

Rabbi Boteach retained his connection to L'Chaim Society and moved the group to link with the Heal the Kids foundation which he founded with Michael Jackson (the charity is no longer in operation). When Jackson was accused of child molestation, Boteach initially defended him, but he has since disavowed his relationship with the pop star. In 1994, Boteach invited Prime Minister Yitzhak Rabin to speak at L'Chaim, although the *rebbe* opposed the invitation because of his opposition to the prime minister's land-for-peace proposal. Boteach broke with the Chabad movement over this issue.

While Boteach has been criticized for commercializing Judaism, he has also been praised for projecting a positive image of Judaism into mainstream America. In its March 25, 2007 issue, *Newsweek* listed Rabbi Boteach as one of the Top 50 Rabbis and described him as "the most famous rabbi in America."

Rabbi Boteach is married to his Australian wife Debbie, and they have eight children.

His most recent book is *Shalom in the House* (Meredith Books, 2007), which is based on his television series.

Judith Lupatkin

Further Reading: Boteach, Shmuley, and Uri Geller. *Confessions of a Psychic and a Rabbi.* New York: Element Books, 2000.

BRICE, FANNY (1891–1951)

Popular comedienne and singer who is best remembered for her many stage, radio, and film appearances, as well as for being the creator and star of the top-rated radio comedy series *The Baby Snooks Show,* Fanny Brice was born Fania Borach on Manhattan's Lower East Side. Brice was the third of four children of Rose Stern, a Hungarian immigrant, and Charles Borach, who left Alsace to come to the United States. Brice's father was a bartender in a Bowery, New York tavern, and Stern was a seamstress manufacturing fur coats.

A less than enthusiastic student, Brice ended her formal schooling around her eighth grade year. After winning an amateur night competition in 1906 at the Keeney Theater on Fulton Street in Brooklyn, she explored her dream of becoming a professional entertainer. In 1910, she was asked by Max Spiegel to appear in *The College Girls.* He was also producing a benefit and asked her to perform in it as well. Brice asked Irving Berlin to write songs for her to sing in the benefit, and he composed her signature number, "Sadie Salome, Go Home." The lyrics told of a Jewish dancer who stunned her family by becoming a performer. Infusing the song with her Yiddish accent helped make it a hit. This success prompted Brice to tap into her ethnic background when future opportunities arose to play Jewish characters.

For the next 40 years, Brice entertained audiences in burlesque, vaudeville, film, and musical performances. Brice became one of America's renowned performers, integrating her ability to introduce unconventional humor into her performances. Brice's comic genius moved her into a genre men had long dominated.

She starred in nine Ziegfeld Follies between 1910 and 1936. Brice sang "My Man" in the 1921 Follies, recorded it under the Victor label, and also sang it in the 1930 film titled *My Man*. Along with "Second Hand Rose," "My Man" became associated with Ms. Brice. Her singing career included cuts for the Victor and Columbia labels. She was posthumously recognized for her 1921 recording of "My Man" by the Grammy Hall of Fame.

Her theater credits include *The Whirl of Society* and *Honeymoon Express,* in which she played a flirtatious Yiddish woman, and Jerome Kern's *Nobody Home*.

Awarded a star on the Hollywood Walk of Fame, Brice's film career encompassed almost 20 years, beginning with *My Man* (1928) and ending with *Ziegfeld's Follies* (1946). Included in her film repertoire are *Be Yourself* (1930), *Sweet and Low* (1930), *The Great Ziegfeld* (1936), *Rose of Washington Square* (1938), and *Everybody Sing* (1938). Baby Snooks was created after Brice's role in *Sweet and Low,* where she introduced Babykins, a three-year-old in a high chair. This Brice character remained part of her radio performances for 10 years.

In 1968, a film based on her life was made into the Oscar-nominated *Funny Girl* (Columbia), starring **Barbra Streisand** in the Brice role.

Brice was married three times, but little is known about her first husband. Brice had two children, William and Frances, with her second husband, Nickie Arnstein—the marriage ended in divorce, as did her third marriage, to **Billy Rose**. Fanny Brice died at the age of 59, of a cerebral hemorrhage, in Los Angeles in 1951. *See also* **Theater**.

Robert Ruder

Further Reading: Goldman, Herbert. *Fanny Brice: The Original Funny Girl.* Cambridge: Oxford University Press, 1993.

THE BRILL BUILDING SONGWRITERS

The Brill Building, with its Art Deco and Neo-Gothic façade, stands at 1619 Broadway in Manhattan. Completed in 1931, it was named after the three Brill brothers who owned a clothing store on the ground floor. After buying the entire building they found that, because of the Great Depression, the only people interested in renting offices were music publishers. In 1962, during the time that most concerns us, the Brill Building contained 165 music businesses, ranging from composers to publishers to demo-makers (who recorded a version of the song so the likely recording artist could hear what it might sound like) and record promoters.

Tin Pan Alley is the name given to the area of West 28th Street, just off Broadway, where the American music business was centered from the late nineteenth century to the time of the Great Depression. Many renowned Jewish composers were associated with Tin Pan Alley, including **George Gershwin**, whose opera *Porgy and Bess* premiered in 1935, and **Irving Berlin**, who wrote "White Christmas" in 1940. The composers who worked in the Brill Building represent the most important connection between the older, Tin Pan Alley writers and the composers centered in 1619 Broadway, who worked in the era after the rise of **rock and roll**.

Whereas the composers of Tin Pan Alley targeted adult, middle-class whites as their primary audience, from the mid-1950s forward, the Brill Building composers aimed at a mostly white, teenage audience. The concept of "teenager" was new. The grouping of "teenagers," occupying a time between childhood and adulthood, came into society in the decade after World War II. The rapid expansion of the American economy, coupled with the development of the consumer society, gave young people a disposable income and products to buy. This was very different for young people. At the same time, by 1959, almost 50 percent of women were married before they reached 19. It was in this context that rock and roll found its audience.

In histories of post-World War II **popular music**, the so-called Brill Building sound is rarely given its due. Often, it is referred to as the music that comes between the demise of the first era of rock and roll and rhythm and blues—typified in artists such as Chuck Berry, Little Richard, Bill Haley and the Comets, Gene Vincent, and, most famously, Elvis Presley—and the era characterized as the British Invasion, when American popular music was reinvigorated by the music of groups from the United Kingdom as musically diverse as the Beatles, the Rolling Stones, the Yardbirds, and Herman's Hermits. This dates the high point of the public acceptance of the Brill Building sound to roughly between 1958, when Presley entered the army, and 1964, when the Beatles first toured. However, as we shall see, these dates are by no means definitive.

What, then, was the Brill Building sound? In the first instance, songs associated with the Brill Building sound share a significant amount in common with the Tin Pan Alley tradition. Most importantly this includes the formal structure of the songs, which tended to consist of 32 bars and be organized in terms of AABA; that is, verse, verse, bridge, verse. Similarly, like many Tin Pan Alley songs, the songs of the Brill Building tended to focus on personal relationships, especially on love and the loss of the loved one. In the songs of the Brill Building, however, these were tailored towards the joys and anxieties of teenagers. At the same time, what tended to distinguish the Brill Building sound from other popular music of its time was the tendency to use more complex melodies and harmonies than was usual. In addition, the Brill Building sound made innovative use of instrumentation, such as strings, that had previously been the purview of classical music, and often used Latin rhythms. As importantly, Brill Building music tended to utilize elements of African American music, often making use of vocal stylings characteristic of rhythm and blues—and, indeed, many songs typical of the Brill Building sound were sung by African American artists such as the Drifters and many girl groups such as the Ronettes and the Shirelles. The characteristic Brill Building sound was composed on a piano rather than guitar.

The Jewish composing duo of Burt Bacharach and Hal David demonstrate well the musical connections between the Brill Building establishment and the newer Brill Building sound of the late 1950s and 1960s. Bacharach was born in 1928 in Kansas City, and his parents moved to Queens when he was four. Bacharach studied music at a number of institutions, including McGill University and the Mannes School of Music. During the 1950s he worked as an accompanist and, in the late 1950s and early 1960s, worked with Marlene Dietrich. He started writing with Hal David in 1957 when both worked for the famous Paramount Music Company. Born in 1921, Hal David was following in the footsteps of his brother Mack by choosing a career as a composer. By the time he started working with Bacharach, David had already cowritten songs recorded by Frank Sinatra and Teresa Brewer, among others. Bacharach and David's compositions, many of them sung by Dionne Warwick—whom Bacharach identified as the ideal singer for the often unusual melodies he wrote—included "Make It Easy on Yourself," "Don't Make Me Over," "Anyone Who Had a Heart," "Walk on By," and "I Say a Little Prayer."

Warwick was signed to Scepter Records in 1962, a label started by Florence Greenberg in 1959 with the signing of the Shirelles. The Jewish Greenberg had been a bored New Jersey housewife looking for a way to occupy her time. In 1960, Greenberg moved the Scepter Records office from 1673 Broadway to 1650 Broadway in order to be closer to the songwriters who were beginning to supply the material for her artists. Greenberg finally sold Scepter in 1976. Through the 1960s, in addition to Warwick, Scepter, and its subsidiary Wand, had success with Chuck Jackson, Maxine Brown, and others, including the seminal garage rock version of "Louie, Louie" by the Kingsmen in 1963—in retrospect, an omen of the end of the dominance of the Brill Building sound.

The company which epitomized the Jewish connection with the Brill Building sound was formed by the Jewish Don Kirshner and Al Nevins in 1958. It was called Aldon Music, using the first letters in the founders' forenames. Kirshner was 21. Nevins was twice that age and brought to the company a wealth of experience in the music industry, having been a cofounder of the Three Suns, for whom he had produced and written songs as well as performing as a violinist and guitarist. Kirshner, the son of a tailor, hailed from the Bronx. With a degree in business administration and a fascination with popular music, Kirshner joined up with Nevins to form a publishing company. Almost all Aldon's cohort of 18 writers were Jewish. The company's first signing was the composing pair of Neil Sedaka and Howard Greenfield. Sedaka's mother was Ashkenazic and his father Sephardic. Greenfield's Jewish parents lived in the same block of flats in Brighton Beach as Sedaka's. Sedaka and Greenfield wrote "Stupid Cupid," a hit for Connie Francis, and then numerous hits for Sedaka himself, including "Oh! Carol," "Calender Girl," "Happy Birthday Sweet Sixteen," and "Breaking Up Is Hard to Do." Greenfield also wrote with another Aldon signing, Jack Keller, coming up with hits for Connie Francis with "Everybody's Somebody's Fool" and "My Heart Has a Mind of Its Own." They also worked together on Jimmy Clanton's "Venus in Blue Jeans," among other hits.

Kirshner and Nevins subsequently signed Carole King, born Carole Klein, who wrote many hits with Gerry Goffin. King and Goffin married in 1960, divorcing eight years later. Goffin and King's first major hit was "Will You Love Me Tomorrow?," a song of desire and uncertainty that struck a chord with American teenagers and reached number one on the Billboard singles chart in 1961. It was sung by the Shirelles. Goffin and King continued to write hits through the 1960s, including "Run to Him" and "Take Good Care of My Baby" by Bobby Vee, "When My Little Girl Is Smiling" and "Up On the Roof" by the Drifters, Aretha Franklin's "(You Make Me Feel Like) A Natural Woman," and the Monkees' "Another Pleasant Valley Sunday," among many others. Two other important Aldon composing collaborations were Barry Mann and Cynthia Weil, and Jeff Barry and Ellie Greenwich. All were Jewish, though Greenwich's father was Catholic. Among other hits, Mann and Weil wrote "On Broadway" for the Drifters and "Uptown" for the Crystals.

Barry had already been writing and recording songs before he met Greenwich, whom he married in 1962. Barry and Greenwich often worked with Phil Spector, writing many of the songs that Spector went on to produce with girl groups using his "Wall of Sound" technique. These songs include "Be My Baby" and "Baby I Love You" for the Ronettes and the Crystals' "Da Doo Ron Ron" and "Then He Kissed Me." Barry and Greenwich went on to write a number of hots for the Jewish girl group the Shangri-Las, including "Leader of the Pack" (with George "Shadow" Morton), "Out in the Streets," and "Give Us Your Blessings'

It is important to return to Phil Spector to understand more fully the ramifying influence of Jews in the music business around this time. Spector was not strictly a Brill Building composer but, as an auteur producer, his work, most of it in Los Angeles at the Gold Star recording studio, utilized predominantly songs by Aldon composers. Spector was born into a Jewish household in the Bronx in 1940. After his father's suicide in 1949, Spector's mother took him and his sister to start a new life in Los Angeles. Spector's first hit composition was "To Know Him Is to Love Him," a song inspired by the epitaph on his father's gravestone. Spector recorded the song with a group of Jewish friends who called themselves the Teddy Bears. The song reached number one on the Billboard chart in December 1958.

Spector became a producer working primarily with Barry and Greenwich but also, for example, recording Mann and Weil's "He's Sure the Boy I Love" with the Crystals. In 1964 Spector recorded one of his last, and most remarkable, productions, the Righteous Brothers' "You've Lost That Lovin'

Feeling," written in conjunction with Mann and Weil, and, in 1966, what was to be his crowning achievement, though not recognized as such at the time, Ike and Tina Turner's "River Deep—Mountain High," written again with Barry and Greenwich. Spector evolved a style of recording which fused the sound of the song with a large number of instruments and a great deal of echo so that the listener felt overwhelmed by the sonic assault. He described his productions as "little symphonies for kids" and thought they should be played at high volume.

Central to the evolution of the Brill Building sound were two other pairs of Jewish songwriters—Jerry Leiber and Mike Stoller and Doc Pomus and Mort Schuman. Both Leiber and Stoller were born in 1933. Leiber was born in Baltimore, but his family moved to Los Angeles in 1945 after his father died. Stoller spent the first 16 years of his life in Queens. In 1949 his family also moved to Los Angeles. Leiber and Stoller's early songs were written in the burgeoning rhythm and blues style for African American artists. In 1952 Big Mama Thornton had success with "Hound Dog," remade in 1956 by Elvis Presley. While the writers had a number six hit on the Billboard chart in 1955 with "Black Denim Trousers and Motorcycle Boots" by the white group the Cheers, Leiber and Stoller found continuing success writing for the African American doo-wop group the Robins, who released many singles on Leiber and Stoller's own label, Spark Records. The Robins split up and became the Coasters, and Leiber and Stoller were signed by Atlantic as producers and composers, continuing to write for, and record, the Coasters. Leiber and Stoller went on to even greater success with the Drifters, for whom they produced many songs written by Aldon composers, including Goffin and King, and Pomus and Schuman. In 1964 Leiber and Stoller started the Red Bird label, releasing tracks by the Dixie Cups, the Shangri-Las, and Dee Dee Warwick, among others, many of them written by Barry and Greenwich.

Doc Pomus was born Jerome Felder in 1925 in Brooklyn. He contracted polio when he was six, leaving him to walk using crutches. Pomus started out as a rhythm and blues singer. By 1957 he had shifted his emphasis to composing. He worked for Hill and Range Songs, a music publishing firm started by Australian Jewish immigrants Jean and Julian Aberbach in 1945 and situated in 1650 Broadway. By this time Pomus was working with Mort Schuman, who was much younger than him and had more understanding of what white teenagers wanted in their music. Pomus and Schuman wrote songs recorded by teen heart-throbs such as Fabian and Bobby Rydell. Later, they wrote many songs recorded by the Drifters, including "Save the Last Dance for Me," which reached number one in 1960. Pomus and Schuman also wrote many songs recorded by Elvis Presley, including "Little Sister," "Suspicion," and "Viva Las Vegas." It is worth noting that many other songs recorded by Elvis Presley, such as "Got a Lot o' Livin' to Do," "Wooden Heart," and "Follow That Dream" were written by Ben Weisman, who also worked for Hill and Range.

Another Brill Building songwriter in the same mold as Leiber and Stoller and Pomus was Bert Berns. Born in 1929 to Russian Jewish migrants, Berns worked as a Brill Building writer and then in 1963 replaced Leiber and Stoller as the house producer at Atlantic. Among his many compositions he wrote Solomon Burke's "Cry to Me" and cowrote "Everybody Needs Somebody to Love," and the Isley Brothers' "Twist and Shout," cowritten with Phil Medley. In 1965 he cowrote the McCoys' "Hang On Sloopy" with Wes Farrell and cowrote the Strangeloves' "I Want Candy" with the members of the group. The Strangeloves were three Jewish Brill Building songwriters who had decided that the best way to beat the British Invasion was to join it. Berns also wrote Erma Franklin's "Piece of My Heart" with another Jewish composer known for his rhythm and blues compositions, Jerry Ragovoy. The song was later covered by Janis Joplin. Neil Diamond, who worked in 1650 Broadway for April-Blackwood, recorded his first songs for Berns' Bang Records label.

One of the critical changes brought about by the British Invasion was that artists started to write more of their own songs. However, the shift was by no means immediate or, indeed, ever complete. John Lennon and Paul McCartney famously remarked that Goffin and King were their favorite songwriters and their first album, *Please Please Me,* contained no less than three Brill Building compositions, "Chains" by Goffin and King, "Baby It's You" by Bacharach, David, and Luther Dixon, and "Twist and Shout" by Medley and Berns.

The mostly Jewish composers who produced the music known collectively as the Brill Building sound synthesized sonic elements of African American music, Latin music, and early, white rock and roll, along with the emphasis on melody that had characterized the popular music produced in Tin Pan Alley in the early part of the twentieth century. They also angled the songs they wrote towards the new, teenage record-buying audience. In successfully combining all these sources, these composers produced a music that has a right to be considered a national American music. Certainly, at a time when the United States was still culturally divided by race, the music of the Brill Building composers transcended this divide more successfully than any other music of its time. *See also* **Popular Music**; **Rock and Roll**.

Jon Stratton

Further Reading: Brown, M. *Tearing Down the Wall of Sound: The Rise and Fall of Phil Spector.* London: Bloomsbury, 2007. Emerson, K. *Always Magic in the Air: The Bomp and Brilliance of the Brill Building Era.* New York: Viking, 2005. Inglis, I. "'Some Kind of Wonderful': The Creative Legacy of the Brill Building," *American Music* 21, no. 2 (2003): 214–35.

BRONCHO BILLY (1880–1971)

The son of Esther and Henry Aaronson, Max Aaronson, born in Little Rock, Arkansas, would eventually become the world's first movie star. After failing as a cotton broker, Max Aaronson moved to New York around 1900, where, adopting the name "Gilbert M. Anderson," he failed at becoming a stage actor. At the suggestion of a theatrical agent, Anderson went to the Edison Company, where he began acting in "flickers."

Finding his métier, Anderson played three different roles in Edwin S. Porter's groundbreaking 1903 film *The Great Train Robbery.* Joining Vitagraph, Anderson began writing, directing, and starring in his own films. Teaming with Chicago theatrical producer George K. Spoor, Anderson founded Essanay (from "S and A"—Spoor and Anderson). In 1907, Anderson created the character "Broncho Billy," which he would play in nearly 400 pictures. Often turning out three one-reel pictures a week, Broncho Billy became internationally famous. Tall, portly, and afraid of horses, Broncho Billy set the standard for all future western stars, from Tom Mix to John Wayne.

As producers, Anderson and Spoor also created the popular series "Alibi Ike" and the "Snakeville Comedies." In 1915, Anderson signed Charles Chaplin to a one-year contract for the astronomical sum of $1,250 a week. During his year with Essanay—now having relocated to California—Chaplin experimented with his character, adding the pathos and sublimity which would gain him recognition as a cinematic genius.

In 1916, Anderson sold his interest in Essanay and retired from acting. In the late 'teens and early twenties, he produced a series of comedy shorts starring Stan Laurel. Ruined by the crash of 1929, Anderson returned to California, where he lived the remainder of his life in relative obscurity. In 1957, he was presented an honorary Oscar as a motion picture pioneer. Anderson died at the Motion Picture Country Home, Woodland Hills, California in 1971. He was 91.

Kurt F. Stone

Further Reading: Haist, Paul. "G. M. Anderson, nee Max Aronson: Reel Cowboy." *Jewish Review* 45 (April 2003): 20, 27. Kiehn, David. *Broncho Billy and the Essanay Film Company.* Berkeley, CA: Farwell Books, 2003.

BROOKS, ALBERT (1947–)

Academy Award-nominated actor, writer, comedian, and director Albert Lawrence Einstein (Brooks) was born into a show business family in Beverly Hills, California on July 22, 1947. His father, Harry Einstein, was the radio comedian "Parkyarkarkus"; his mother, the actress Thelma (Goodman) Leeds. Brooks attended Beverly Hills High School along with future stars **Richard Dreyfuss** and **Rob Reiner**. He dropped out of Carnegie Tech after a single year in order to focus on a comedy career. He changed his name to "Brooks" in order to avoid confusion with the iconic physicist. Honing his skills at stand-up comedy, Brooks became a regular on late-night variety and talk shows by the late 1960s. His onstage persona—an egotistic narcissist—greatly influenced other postmodern comics like Steve Martin and Andy Kaufman.

After recording two successful comedy albums, Brooks gave up the comedy circuit in order to become a filmmaker. After directing a half-dozen short films for the first season of *Saturday Night Live,* he appeared in his first film, Martin Scorsese's *Taxi Driver.* In 1979, Brooks directed his first feature film, *Real Life,* a send-up of PBS's *An American Family.* Throughout the 1980s and 1990s, Brooks wrote and directed a string of critically acclaimed comedies, including *Lost in America* (1985), *Defending Your Life* (1991), and *Mother* (1996). In 1987, Brooks was nominated for an Academy Award for Best Supporting Actor for his role as an insecure network television reporter in *Broadcast News.*

In recent years, Brooks has appeared as a guest voice on *The Simpsons* and as the voice of "Marlin" in *Finding Nemo.* In 2005, Brooks wrote, directed, and starred in *Looking for Comedy in the Muslim World.* The film, which stars Brooks as a filmmaker commissioned by the U.S. government to find out what makes Muslim people laugh, received limited distribution.

Before his 1997 marriage to artist Kimberly Shlain, Brooks was romantically linked to singer Linda Ronstadt and actresses Carrie Fisher, Julie Haggerty, and Kathryn Harrold. Albert Brooks's older brother, Bob Einstein, is the comedian "Super Dave Osborne." *See also* **Film.**

Kurt F. Stone

Further Reading: Kaufman, Peter. "The Background on Albert Brooks." *The Buffalo News,* January 22, 2006.

BROOKS, MEL (1926–)

Perhaps one of the most accomplished performers in the history of the entertainment industry, Mel Brooks remains a successful director, comedian, writer, actor, and producer. Brooks has the distinction of having won an Emmy, a Grammy, an Oscar, and a Tony award. The phrase "too Jewish" circulated through the entertainment industry about Mel Brooks's "shtick." Performing a comedy duo with Carl Reiner, he doubted that a record which included "The 2000 Year Old Man in the Year 2000" would sell. In 1960, it took a non-Jew, Steve Allen, to convince Brooks and Reiner of their comedic potential. Allen paid for the recording and invited the duo to play the bit on his show for their first television appearance together. The record was nominated for a Grammy.

Melvin Kaminsky was born in Brooklyn in 1926 to Polish Jewish parents. He changed his name to his mother's maiden name, Brookman, after she was left to raise the family alone when her husband died at the age of 34. Often bullied as a child, Brooks gained confidence working as a drummer and tummler at the **Catskills**, where he was a stand-up comedian. He began his friendship with **Sid Caesar** and again changed his name. This time he chose "Brooks" so as not to be confused with the musician Max Kaminsky. In 1944, he enlisted in the army and served as a combat engineer. After the war, Brooks, promoted to the rank of corporal, remained in Germany and entertained the soldiers. Discharged, Brooks was employed by Caesar, first as a writer for *The Admiral Broadway Revue,* then *Your Show of Shows* and *Caesar's Comedy Hour.* It was during this period that he worked with **Neil Simon**, **Woody Allen**, and Carl Reiner. He invented characters for Caesar throughout the 1950s and worked in improvisational acts in Manhattan comedy clubs with fellow Jewish comedians Carl Reiner and Mel Tolkin.

Brooks married Florence Baum in 1951 and divorced her in 1961. The couple had three children. In 1961, a guest appearance on a Perry Como television special changed his life. He met actress Anne Bancroft, whom he married in 1964, and they remained together until her death in 2005. They had one child.

While writing for the sitcom *Get Smart* with Buck Henry, Brooks began work on perhaps his most successful work, *The Producers.* Originally titled *Springtime for Hitler,* the movie version of *The Producers* (1968), starring **Zero Mostel** and **Gene Wilder**, was awarded an Oscar for Best Original Screenplay. The subsequent Broadway musical, which won a Tony as Best Musical (2001), was a major hit and was later filmed (2005) with the original cast leads of Nathan Lane and Matthew Broderick. Brooks is one of the dozen artists who have won at least one Oscar, Emmys (3), Grammys (3), and Tony Awards (3). A musical version of his film *Young Frankenstein* opened on Broadway in November 2007. The body of Brooks's work reflects the diversity of his talent: comedian, actor, writer, director, producer, and singer. In 1998, Brooks won a Grammy for Best Spoken Comedy Album for *The 2000 Year Old Man in the Year 2000,* with Carl Reiner.

With regard to Brooks's film oeuvre, he has created many cult comedies—*Blazing Saddles* (1974),*Young Frankenstein* (1974), *High Anxiety* (1977)—and unusual firsts, such as *Silent Movie* (1976), where performers, including Marty Feldman, Dom DeLuise, Sid Caesar, and Anne Bancroft, coerce mime Marcel Marceau to utter the movie's only word. Other comedies include*The Twelve Chairs* (1970), *History of the World: Part 1* (1981), *Spaceballs* (1987), and *Robin Hood: Men in Tights* (1993). Although he is best known for his comedies, Brooks has also produced such films as David Lynch's *The Elephant Man* and David Cronenberg's *The Fly.*

Not a practicing Jew, Brooks remains very proud of his Jewish heritage and once, reflecting on his ethnicity, stated: "Look at Jewish history. Unrelieved lamenting would be intolerable. So, for every ten Jews beating their breasts, God designated one to be crazy and amuse the breast beaters. By the time I was five I knew I was that one" (Parish, 2007). *See also* **Comedy**; **Theater**.

Steve Krief

Further Reading: Parish, James Robert.*It's Good to Be the King: The Seriously Funny Life of Mel Brooks.* Hoboken, NJ: Wiley, 2007.

BROTHERS, JOYCE (1928–)

Joyce Brothers, "America's psychologist," was born Joyce Diane Bauer. Her parents, Morris K. Bauer and Estelle Rappaport, were both attorneys. Brothers and her younger sister, Elaine, grew up in a middle-class Jewish household in Queens, New York. She credits her parents for her strong sense of ethics and her belief in God. Brothers graduated from Far Rockaway High School in 1943 and entered Cornell University, where she graduated with a degree in psychology, and went on for her MA at Columbia University. While at Columbia, Brothers met and married a medical student, Milton Brothers, as well receiving her PhD in 1953.

Brothers' daughter, Lisa, was born in 1953 while Milton Brothers was doing his internship. She gave up teaching at both Columbia and Hunter College because she strongly believed that early childhood development is dependent on one parent being at home. When funds became tight on her husband's intern pay, Brothers decided to try out for the television show *The $64,000 Question.* Already sharing an interest in boxing with her husband, Brothers studied *The Boxing Encyclopedia* in preparation for the show. She is the only woman to win the top prize.

In the show's sequel, *The $64,000 Challenge,* she won $134,000 by pitting her boxing

Dr. Joyce Brothers, a child psychologist and television personality whose celebrity status was due to winning the $64,000 prize on boxing knowledge on the popular *The $64,000 Question* television program. She is seen here in a July 22, 1956 photo shortly after winning the prize with a picture of boxer James J. Parker. [AP Photo]

knowledge against experts. Her appearance on these two shows led to her hosting a television interview show called *Sports Showcase.* In 1958 Brothers convinced NBC to try a call-in show in which she gave advice on topics such as love, marriage, and sex. *The Dr. Joyce Brothers Show* had such strong audience response that NBC syndicated it nationwide and then added a late-night version. The later time slot allowed Brothers to tackle subjects such as impotence, menopause, and sexual response.

Brothers' popularity expanded with a call-in radio show, a column that was syndicated in 350 newspapers, and a monthly advice column in *Good Housekeeping* magazine that lasted for 40 years. In the 1970s she spoke out against sexual bias and encouraged textbook publishers to eliminate sexist attitudes. Brothers was named one of America's "most admired women" in Gallup polls six times. She wrote 10 books dealing with the family and psychology, which included discussions of strong self-image, vulnerability, risk, love and trust, failure, manipulation, and the importance of listening.

Her most popular book, *Widowed,* was written in 1989 when she recounted her personal journey out of near-suicidal grief over the loss of her husband, Milton, to cancer after their 39-year marriage. Brothers has appeared in 18 movies, in most cases showing a fine sense of humor in playing herself. Her easygoing manner and playful spirit made her a frequent guest on *The Johnny Carson Show.*

Brothers' popularity as a psychological advisor occurred at the same time that other Jewish women became important for similar purposes. **Abigail Van Buren** and Ann Landers also began their advice columns in the 1950s and remained in vogue, as Brothers did, through the 1990s. Andrew Heinze, in his book *Jews and the American Soul: Human Nature in the Twentieth Century,* contends that the rise of these and other Jewish women to positions of real influence in American society was due in part to the moral sensibility they had learned from the Hebrew Bible.

It is true that much of Brothers' advice is based on the Jewish principla of musar (the term refers to the nineteenth-century moralist movement in Judaism which emphasized ethical study and conduct). In concise, clear language with a commonsense tone, Brothers makes frequent reference to self-discipline, emotional control, moderation, consequences, gradual improvement, and reserved optimism as solutions to personal and relationship problems. *See also* **Popular Psychology.**

Marion Schotz

Further Reading: Brothers, Joyce. *Widowed.* New York: Ballantine Books, 1990. Heinze, A. R. *Jews and the American Soul: Human Nature in the Twentieth Century.* Princeton: Princeton University Press, 2004.

BRUCE, LENNY (1925–1966)

The irreverent social satirist Lenny Bruce was the first comedian to use jokes about religion, drugs, racism, and sex on stage. He was also the first to use his "humor" to show the broken mirror of American society, starting with his own raw life experiences

Leonard Alfred Schneider was born on Long Island, the son of Mickey and Sadie Schneider, who divorced in 1933. At age 17, he enlisted in the navy, and following his discharge in 1946, he changed his name to Lenny Bruce. He proceeded to study acting in Hollywood under the GI Bill. His mother Sadie, a dancer (stage name Sally Marr), was instrumental in getting her son his first experience on stage, when he replaced an ill master of ceremonies at a strip club. When two hecklers at the bar greeted him with, "Bring on the broads!" Bruce replied: "I would, but you'd remain alone at the bar." His first laugh! Bruce struggled as a comic, performing in amateur contests and suburban strip clubs. He built his act on mixing Yiddishisms with the rhythm of jazz. In Baltimore, Bruce was introduced to Honey Harlowe (Harriet Lloyd), a stripper, whom he later married (1951). They had one child, Kitty. The couple divorced in 1957.

In 1947, Bruce made his debut as a comic and impressionist at a Brooklyn nightclub, but his big break came in 1948 when he appeared on the *Arthur Godfrey Talent Scouts Show.* He continued to play in comedy clubs, refining what became his comedy routines. At the same time, Bruce worked on a screenplay that became his first film, *Dance Hall Racket* (1953), which he also appeared in with his wife and mother. During 1954, he cowrote the children's film *The Rocket Man,* as well as *Dream Follies,* a low budget film about burlesque.

His well received appearance in 1958 at *Ann's 440,* a comedy club in San Francisco, led to Bruce's rising celebrity, resulting in a contract with Fantasy Records, where he released four albums, which included comedy routines and satirical interviews on the themes that made him famous —jazz, politics, patriotism, religion, drugs, race, Jewishness, and so on. Subsequently, the albums were compiled and re-released as *The Lenny Bruce Originals.*

Bruce's success caught Hugh Hefner's eye. Hefner was so impressed with Bruce's talent that he arranged for him to perform at Chicago's Cloister Club and later invited him to the premiere of *Playboy's Penthouse* television show. In 1959, Bruce performed on *The Steve Allen Show* and on New York City's public television station, channel thirteen's *The World of Lenny Bruce.*

In 1961, Bruce performed at Carnegie Hall. Due to a blizzard that covered the East Coast, he barely arrived in Manhattan, where, under five feet of snow and a curfew, he found the auditorium jammed. Bruce gave a two-hour stream of consciousness performance, taking the crowd on a roller-coaster ride in which he satirized a meeting between Christ and Moses at St. Patrick's Cathedral, Billy Graham in a Vegas strip show, a member of the Ku Klux Klan lusting after Lena Horne, and a mimic being shot after impersonating JFK at the inauguration speech.

Bruce's act was not appreciated by everyone, and he was labeled a "sick comedian" by *Time* magazine. Columnist **Walter Winchell** referred to him as "America's No. 1 Vomic." In 1961 Bruce was arrested for violating the California Obscenity Code for using the word "cocksucker" in his routine at the Jazz Workshop in San Francisco. Although the jury acquitted him, the trial is considered a landmark in the fight to preserve the freedoms set forth in the first amendment. Bruce was regularly monitored and harassed by law enforcement agencies and forced to defend his comic routines in court. A drug user, after three arrests, his career was all but over. Bruce died of a drug overdose on August 3, 1966.

Summarizing the influence of his Jewish upbringing on his work, Kenneth Von Gunden wrote, "inspired by the funny men he observed in Jewish neighborhoods—nonprofessional comics whose angry in-group situational humor used the language of the Jewish lower classes to skewer the foibles and insanity of everyday life—Bruce incorporated their Jewish 'spritz' into his act and made it his own" (Von Gunden, 1992).

Lenny Bruce's life has inspired works in many different mediums of the entertainment industry, including Bob Fosse's film biography *Lenny* (1974), which starred **Dustin Hoffman**; documentaries by Fred Baker, Robert Weide, and Elan Gale; an autobiography published by Hugh Hefner; a judicial study by Ronald Collins and David Skover; and songs by Nico and Simon and Garfunkel. He appears on the Beatles' *Sergeant Pepper's* cover and has influenced such comedians as Richard Pryor, George Carlin, Eddie Murphy, Bill Hicks, and Sam Kinison. **Bob Dylan** has often begun concerts with a song written in 1981 entitled "Lenny Bruce." The poet recalls the short cab ride they shared and the influence Bruce had on him and generations to come. *See also* **Comedy**.

Steve Krief

Further Reading: Barry, Julian. *Lenny: A Play Based on His Life and Words of Lenny Bruce.* New York: Grove Press, 1971. Goldman, Albert. *Ladies and Gentlemen: LENNY BRUCE!!* New York: Random House, 1974. Von Gunden, Kenneth. "Bruce, Lenny." *Jewish American History and Culture.* New York: Garland Publishing, 1992.

BUCHWALD, ART (1925–2007)

Buchwald, an American humorist, was born October 20, 1925 to a Jewish family in Mount Vernon, New York. He was the youngest of four children and the only son. His father, Joseph Buchwald, immigrated from Austria to avoid military service and started a drapery-making business in the United States. His mother, the former Helen Klineberger, a Hungarian Jew, suffered delusions and was placed in a mental institution shortly after her son's birth. She spent the remaining 35 years of her life there, never known by her son.

When his father's business failed in the Great Depression, five-year-old Buchwald was separated from his other parent, sent to live in the Hebrew Orphan Asylum in New York, and was placed in several foster homes, including a boarding house for sick children run by Seventh-Day Adventists. He, his sisters, and his father were eventually reunited in Hollis, Queens.

Buchwald left high school, lied about his age, and joined the U.S. Marines. He served from 1942–1945, two years of which were spent in the Pacific with the Fourth Marine Air Wing. He was discharged as a sergeant, and under the GI Bill he enrolled at the University of Southern California, where he became managing editor of the university magazine, *Wampus,* and wrote a column for its newspaper, *The Daily Trojan.*

When the university discovered that he did not have a high school diploma, Buchwald was permitted to continue his studies but was deemed ineligible for a degree (although he received an honorary doctorate from the same university 33 years later and established a scholarship for "the most irreverent" journalism student). He left the university in 1948, using a war bonus check to travel to Paris, France. There he was eventually hired by the European edition of the *New York Herald Tribune* to write a column, "Paris After Dark." Its success led to a second column in 1951, "Mostly About People," and the two were soon merged as "Europe's Lighter Side," a piece that quickly became popular on both sides of the Atlantic.

Buchwald met fashion publicist Ann McCarry in Paris, and the couple was married in 1952. She died in 1994. They adopted three children —Joel from Ireland, Connie from Spain, and Jennifer from France. Buchwald is also rumored to have had a brief affair with Marilyn Monroe and to have introduced the star to Judaism.

He returned to the United States in 1962, becoming a fixture in Washington, while spending most summers at a home on Martha's Vineyard. At its peak in 1972, his *Washington Post* column appeared three times a week and was syndicated in 550 newspapers around the world. Buchwald also authored over 30 books, including *Too Soon to Say Goodbye* (2007), which chronicled his five months spent at the Washington Home and Community Hospice, a time when he chose to discontinue dialysis treatment for diabetes mellitus. Though he was expecting to die, his kidneys instead continued working, and he left the hospice to live in the Washington home of his son,

Joel. Buchwald finally did succumb to kidney failure on January 17, 2007. The next day, the *New York Times* web site posted a video obituary recorded by Buchwald himself, in which he posthumously announced: "Hi. I'm Art Buchwald, and I just died."

Buchwald, the most widely read newspaper humorist of his time, was once called a "Will Rogers with chutzpah." In 1982 he was awarded the Pulitzer Prize for Outstanding Commentary. Four years later, Buchwald was elected to the American Academy and Institute of Arts and Letters. *See also* **Journalism**.

Barry Kornhauser

Further Reading: Buchwald, Art. *I'll Always Have Paris.* New York: G.P. Putnam, 1995. ———. *Leaving Home: A Memoir.* New York: G.P. Putnam's, 1994. ———. *Too Soon to Say Goodbye.* New York: Random House, 2007.

BURNS, GEORGE (1896–1996)

A comedian, actor, and writer, Burns's career spanned **vaudeville**, **film**, and **television** both with and without his wife Gracie Allen. At age 79, his career was rejuvenated, and he became one of the entertainment industry's most popular personalities until his death at age 100. Burns was born Nathan Birnbaum in New York City. He began his career in vaudeville as a child, and his career spanned more than 70 years, including appearances in motion pictures, radio, and television. Burns had a taste for show business, and by the time he was seven, he and his friends had formed a singing group called the Pee Wee Quartet. Amateur shows led to small-time vaudeville, where Burns faced rejection time and again, often gaining jobs from people who had fired him earlier by simply changing his professional name.

Usually working as part of a song-and-snappy-patter team, he was in the process of breaking up with his partner, Billy Lorraine, in 1922 when he met a pretty young singer/dancer named Gracie Allen. The new team displayed Gracie as the "straight man" and George the comic, but so ingenuous and lightheaded was Gracie's delivery that the audience laughed at her questions and not George's answers. Burns realized he would have to reverse the roles and become the straight man for the act to succeed, and within a few years "Burns and Allen" was one of the most successful acts in vaudeville, with George writing the material and Gracie garnering the laughs.

George and Gracie married in 1926; thereafter, the team worked on stage, in radio, in movies (first in a series of one-reel comedies, then making their feature debut in 1932's *The Big Broadcast*), and ultimately on television, seldom failing to bring down the house with their basic "dizzy lady, long-suffering man" routine.

By the mid-1930s, the energetic young couple was ready to start a family, so they adopted a baby girl, Sandy, and a baby boy, Ronnie. The family moved into a permanent home in Beverly Hills, where the children grew up and where George resided until his death. *The Burns and Allen Show* remained one of the top radio shows during its nearly 20-year run. By 1950, George felt they were ready for the new medium of television. The show transferred well, and for the next eight years on CBS, Burns and Allen entertained audiences with plots revolving around home life, neighbors, and even vaudeville routines.

Though the public at large believed that Gracie had all the talent, show business insiders knew that the act would have been nothing without George's brilliant comic input; indeed, George was often referred to by his peers as "the Comedian's Comedian." Gracie decided to retire in 1958, after which George went out on his own in television and in nightclubs, to less-than-spectacular success. After Gracie's death in 1964, George concentrated on television production (he had vested interests in several series, among them *Mr. Ed*) and for a few years tried using other comic actresses in the "Gracie" role for club appearances. But it was not the same; George Burns would be first to admit there was only one Gracie Allen.

In 1975, at age 79 and less than a year after having triple bypass surgery, George rekindled another career. Burns enhanced his popularity late in life as a dramatic and comedic actor in films. He garnered an Academy Award (at age 80, the oldest person to have done so) for Best Supporting Actor for his role in *The Sunshine Boys* (1975). It was certainly true, as George quipped at the podium during his acceptance speech, "if you stay in the business long enough and get to be old enough, you get to be new again!" He later starred in such popular films as *Oh, God!* (1977) and *Eighteen Again* (1988). He also published books, including *Dr. Burns' Prescription for Happiness* (1985) and a tribute to his wife, *Gracie, A Love Story* (1988). In 1988, he received a Kennedy Center Award for lifetime achievement.

In 1986 and 1991 Burns appeared in television specials that celebrated his 90th and 95th birthdays, respectively. In January 1996 he celebrated his 100th birthday and then quietly passed into entertainment history on March 9. *See also* **Comedy**; **Television**; **Vaudeville**.

Leslie Rabkin

Further Reading: Burns, George. *Gracie: A Love Story.* New York: Signer, 1991. Fagen, Herb, and George Burns. *George Burns: In His Own Words.* New York: Carroll and Graf, 1996.

BUTTONS, RED (1919–2006)

Comedian and award-winning actor Red Buttons's *The Red Buttons Show* was one of television's most popular programs during the 1950s. Red Buttons was born on February 5, 1919 in New York City, to Michael and Sophie Chwatt. His given name was Aaron Chwatt. Buttons's father was born in Poland and was a millinery worker. Aaron Chwatt grew up in a pretty tough East Side neighborhood in New York.

When his family moved to the Bronx, he was enrolled in Evander Childs High School where he excelled at soccer. After graduating he held a variety of manual labor jobs, and in 1953, he answered an advertisement to work as a bellboy at Ryan's Tavern. The owners of the tavern gave him a uniform with 48 buttons. The buttons and his red hair prompted customers to call him Red Buttons.

Buttons made his show business debut in the **Catskills**. A talent scout who watched him perform was delighted with his ability to do impressions and sing. He got Buttons a job at the Gaeity Theatre in New York.

Jose Ferrer, an established actor, saw Buttons' act and in 1941 helped him get a role in a musical comedy film called *The Admiral Takes a Wife.* The film was never released because its planned opening was set for three days after the Japanese attacked Pearl Harbor. Buttons continued to perform in **vaudeville** until he was drafted into the army in 1943. Moss Hart asked Buttons to perform for his *Winged Victory* play that was presented by the U.S. Army Air Forces. Buttons played the role of "Whitey" for 200 performances, and he later played the same role in the film version for 20th Century Fox.

In 1945 Buttons was sent to Europe and was one of the entertainers in the Big Three (Russia, United States, Britain) Conference in Potsdam in 1945. A year later he won a small part in the James Cagney film *Rue Madeliene* and then performed in the musical *Barefoot Boy with Cheek.* Buttons continued to play theatrical roles. In 1951, he was put in a production about the life of Joe E. Lewis.

Two years later, Buttons was given a weekly **television** show. In that program he developed his theme song and dance—"Ho, ho, ho, strange things are happening." As he sang and danced, he held a cupped hand to his ear. The performance seemed very much like a Hasidic melody and dance.

Buttons's show was a success, but it lasted only two years. When the show ended his career declined. He made occasional appearances on *The Perry Como Show* and had one legitimate stage role. In 1957, he got a break with the part of "Sergeant Kelly" in the Warner Brothers film *Sayonara,* which was based on the Michener novel. His performance was touching and well received. In 1958 he received an Oscar for his role as Kelly.

With his star once again rising, Buttons was back in demand on television. He made several other films, including *Imitation General* and *Hatari.* At five feet six inches tall, and 140 pounds, Buttons said of himself, "I'm a little guy and that is what I play all the time. A little guy and his troubles" (Rothstein, 2006).

Buttons was happily married to Harriet van Horne and died at age 87 in July of 2006. *See also* **Film**; **Film Stars**; **Television**; **Vaudeville**.

Herbert M. Druks

Further Reading: Rothstein, Mervyn. "Comedian Red Buttons Dies at 87." *New York Times,* July 14, 2006.

C

CAESAR, SID (1922–)

Sid Caesar, age 86 (born September 8, 1922 in Yonkers, New York), has had a long and distinguished career in show business. But he will be forever remembered for a single blazing decade of work in three television series—*Admiral Broadway Revue* (1949–1950), *Your Show of Shows* (1950–1954), and *Caesar's Hour* (1954–1957). These live shows set standards for television comedy that have never been equaled. In the early days of television, when the medium was wide open for invention, Caesar and his company of actors and writers stepped in to invent it. Caesar, who had a genius for send-up and satire, pioneered skit comedy for television. He was endlessly inventive and could find comedy anywhere, from modern jazz to foreign films, from urban domesticity to bullfighting, from silent film to Italian opera, from performing seals to Bavarian mechanical clocks. Nothing was safe from his satirical radar, except politics and Jewishness. His shows flourished during the Cold War, and if he was reckless as a parodist, he knew the limits imposed by his time.

Teamed with Imogene Coca on *Your Show of Shows* and Nanette Fabray on *Caesar's Hour,* Caesar created a boisterous, kinetic comedy that showcased his skills at mimicry and satire, at verbal agility and physical exuberance. But above all it was a comedy of character. His shows featured the regular appearances of "the Professor," the bedraggled master of befuddlement who faked his way through the subjects of magic or sleep or mountain climbing—for example, Professor Ludwig von Spacebrain, expert on jet propulsion. He created a dazed jazz musician called Progress Hornsby, whose band included a player on radar, because "whenever we play, we must be warned in case we approach the melody." (Hornsby also allowed Caesar to play saxophone, at which he was quite adept.) With Imogene Coca, he played the Hickenloopers, whose bickering marriage was a comedy of love and pratfalls, and dozens of one-timers: bullfighters, bicycle thieves, mobsters, German generals, U-boat captains, alcoholics, corporate executives, operatic clowns, and "farkokhte" samurai.

The most verbal of comedians, Caesar was the master of doubletalk, a supersonic babble that could sound like German, French, Japanese, or Italian, with just enough **Yiddish** sprinkled in to remind the audience that the comics were Jewish. Caesar has claimed that he learned to imitate languages by hanging out at his parents' 24-hour delicatessen and imitating the customers. But if his comedy tended to burst out in verbal thunder and emotional lightning, Caesar could also mime brilliantly: he pantomimed to the *1812 Overture,* imitated the workings of the great clock of Baverhof, Bavaria, and mimicked a trained seal act so brilliantly that seals could take lessons. He carved up foreign movies like they were cold cuts. Along with Carl Reiner and Imogene Coca, Caesar sliced and diced Vittorio de Sica's *The Bicycle Thief* into a Caesar salad titled "La Bicycletta"; he Caeserized the Japanese film *Ugetsu* into "U-bet-U," a samurai send-up that has Caesar, Reiner, and the impish Howard Morris making sukiyaki out of the Japanese language. Hollywood was also on the fast food menu, as *From Here to Eternity* was fricasseed into "From Here to Obscurity," and *Sunset Boulevard* got half baked into "Aggravation Boulevard."

Supporting Caesar was a dream team of comedy writers that included Larry Gelbart, Neil and Danny Simon, Mel Tolkin, **Mel Brooks**, Lucille Kallen, Carl Reiner (who was also Caesar's onstage straight man), and **Woody Allen**. Neil Simon called it the "Harvard of comedy" and Caesar himself compared it to the nineteenth-century company of French Impressionists. Rarely has so much comic talent and madcap anarchy been let loose in one room and been ordered to write a show in three days, since the show was written on Monday through Wednesday each week. They worked together in a state of pandemonium, creating brilliant routines and leaving behind vapor trails that glowed in the sunset for decades, including the 1982 film *My Favorite Year,* directed by Richard Benjamin, and **Neil Simon**'s play, *Laughter on the 23rd Floor.* Television's *The Dick Van Dyke Show* (1961–1966), produced by Reiner, was based on the life of a television scriptwriter. Brooks and Reiner's "2000-Year-Old Man" routines were first improvised during those writing sessions. Stories could be told about each of them. Larry Gelbart, for example, later creator of *M*A*S*H,* had come over to Caesar from Bob Hope, who called Caesar up and offered him an oil well for Gelbart's return.

This high-water mark of television comedy was also an ending. When tape became the standard of television and live performance ended in 1957, *Caesar's Hour* became even harder to stage —as many as six takes of a scene rather than one—while being more controlled in performance, as actors lost their spontaneity. NBC pulled the plug at the end of that year, and though there were aftershocks in Caesar's career, the mad, wild ride of the early 1950s was over. It took its toll on Caesar, who became an insomniac, an alcoholic, and a drug user during those years, afflictions he now speaks of openly. Some of the show's routines, including a silent film, *A Drunk There Was,* drew substantially on Caesar's experiences. All testimony confirms that rehearsals could break out into emotional storms, as Caesar flew into rages and tore up sets and put his hands through doors. Thirty-nine-week seasons of live television extended Caesar to the limits of his powers, and he wore himself out doing them.

Caesar has called the great American film comics, like Buster Keaton, Charlie Chaplin, and W. C. Fields, his heroes, and the best of his work places him in that heroic company. We are fortunate to have the kinescopes of the great programs that Caesar himself kept (see the New Video Group series, 2004), after NBC had destroyed theirs, as enduring evidence of Sid Caesar's genius and of how much remains fresh and alive and funny after a half century. *See also* **Comedy**.

Mark Shechner

Further Reading: Caesar, Sid, with Bill Davidson. *Where Have I Been: An Autobiography.* New York: Crown Publishers, 1982 Caesar, Sid, and Eddy Friedfeld. *Caesar's Hours: My Life in Comedy, with Love and Laughter.* New York: Public Affairs, 2003. *The Sid Caesar Collection—The Fan Favorites—50th Anniversary Edition.* Starring Sid Caesar, Carl Reiner, Imogene Coca, et al. 3-CDs. New Video Group, 2004.

CAHAN, ABRAHAM (1860–1951)

Abraham Cahan was the founder, and editor, of the Yiddish news daily *Forverts* (***Jewish Daily***

An undated photo of Abraham Cahan, the founder of the *Jewish Daily Forward* in 1897. An ardent socialist, he arrived in New York City from Russia in 1882 and immediately championed the cause of the immigrant Jewish working class in America. Cahan was also the author of the American Jewish classic novel *The Rise of David Levinsky* in 1917. [Forward Association]

Forward), the leading Yiddish newspaper in the world, and a writer in English of realist fiction, some of which has been adapted for the screen. His writing focused on the American popular imagination on Jewish "ghetto life" in the legendary Lower East Side of New York during the great wave of immigration from 1880 to 1920. He was a pivotal figure in the development of a modern secular Jewish culture in America that was based on East European roots but which embraced the new nation's traditions. He also set an activist agenda for Jewish intellectuals, who advocated labor reform, civil rights, and combating anti-Semitism.

Cahan was born in Podberezhye, Lithuania, into a religiously Orthodox family and studied for the rabbinate, following in the footsteps of his grandfather and father who taught Hebrew and Talmud. But Cahan secretly absorbed secular knowledge, sympathized with revolutionary politics, and studied Russian before entering the Teachers Institute of Vilna, which he graduated from in 1881. Later that year he immigrated to the United States to escape the arrest of suspected revolutionaries after the assassination of Russia's Czar Alexander II. He arrived in New York City in 1882. Cahan became involved in socialist labor organizations and published in their Yiddish periodicals. He gained notice with an unsolicited article in English on the coronation of Czar Alexander III in *New York World,* which was followed by essays in literary criticism, as well as short stories in *The Sun, Evening Post,* and *Workmen's Advocate*. His first novel, *Yekl: A Tale of the New York Ghetto,* was published in 1896, and a year later he founded the *Forverts*.

A notable feature of the *Forverts* that entered into popular culture was the "Bintel Brief" ("Bundle of Letters"), an advice column for newly arrived immigrants. Cahan would often answer queries about adjusting to the strange or menacing ways of America with assurances that the new land was hospitable. He encouraged the abandonment of superstitions and ignorance associated with the old country and urged readers to take advantage of educational opportunities and work for social progress in their new country. Literary critics have questioned whether the letters were authentic or were fabricated to advance Cahan's social agenda. Samples from the "Bintel Brief" were translated and edited by Isaac Metzker into a popular book and legal authority. **Alan Dershowitz** used the title for a column in the English weekly *Forward* in 2007.

Cahan followed *Yekl* with *The Imported Bridegroom, and Other Stories* (1898), which, along with his first novel, was made into a film. *Yekl* was turned into *Hester Street* (1975) by director Joan Micklin Silver. The film featured both English and **Yiddish** dialogue with actress Carol Kane in the lead role. Director Pamela Berger kept Cahan's title *The Imported Bridegroom* in her 1990 film about an immigrant who arranges a marriage for his Americanized daughter to a old-country Talmudic scholar. The star of the film was Avi Hoffman, who also appeared in the musical stage production of *The Rise of David Levinsky* in the 1980s and again in the New Vista Theater Company production in 2007.

Famed editor, critic, and novelist William Dean Howells (1837–1920) helped boost Cahan's reputation as he praised *Yekl* and compared Cahan's talent to renowned American writer Stephen Crane. Earlier, Howells consulted Cahan to learn about labor unions for his novel *A Traveler from Altruria* (1892). Howells encouraged Cahan to write in English and Cahan modeled *The Rise of David Levinsky* (1917) on Howell's *The Rise of Silas Lapham* (1885). Both Levinsky and Lapham struggle with their moral sensibilities, but for Levinsky there are also deeper questions of ethnic identity and intellectual aspirations. Cahan described immigrants to the Lower East Side as variations of the human condition rather than as racial types, which Howells tended to do. More ethnically sensitive, Cahan nonetheless also worried about stereotyping, although he harshly depicted Jews who became tools of commercialism. *See also* **Film**; ***Jewish Daily Forward***; **Literature**; **Yiddish**.

Simon J. Bronner

Further Reading: Marovitz, Sanford E. *Abraham Cahan*. New York: Twayne, 1996. Rischin, Moses, ed. *Grandma Never Lived in America: The New Journalism of Abraham Cahan*. Bloomington, IN: Indiana University Press, 1985.

CANTOR, EDDIE (1892–1964)

Cantor was a comedian, singer, film and stage actor, as well as a beloved television personality, who was familiar to millions of fans because of his top-rated radio show which revealed intimate stories and amusing anecdotes about his wife, Ida, and five children. Known by his nickname "Banjo Eyes," Cantor's large eyes became his trademark, often exaggerated in illustrations and leading to his appearance on Broadway in the musical *Banjo Eyes* (1941). Eddie Cantor was born Edward Israel Iskowitz, on January 31, 1892, in the Lower East Side, New York. His parents died by the time he was two years old, and his grandmother took him under her wing. His education was cut short while still in grammar school. Instead of school, Cantor sang songs and did imitations on street corners for pennies.

Thanks to Ida Tobias, his sweetheart, he entered an amateur night contest at the Miners Bowery Theater. He won $5, which was about a week's wages at that time. A few days later, a burlesque establishment hired him to entertain for $15 a week. While performing as a singing waiter in a Coney Island bar, Cantor was accompanied on the piano by Jimmy Durante. Cantor was subsequently hired by the **vaudeville** team of Bedini and Arthur which required him to perform in blackface.

Gus Edwards, a producer, saw Cantor in the vaudeville act and hired him to play a blackface butler in the *Kid Kabaret* revue. Soon thereafter *Charlot's* revue asked him to sing and dance using his blackface costume. Since he was making a regular salary, he asked Ida Tobias for her hand in marriage. They married on June 9, 1914. The couple had five daughters, and in his various shows he began to mention that he would also like to have a son. Somehow, the Cantors never quite managed that. Ultimately, one of his daughters gave birth to a son. He got the news while he was entertaining an audience of 5,000 people. It was, he said, "perfection" to have five daughters and now a boy grandchild.

Producer Florenz Ziegfeld hired Cantor as a comedian. He was on his way to great success and handsome financial rewards. Cantor became a "smashing hit" in *Kid Boots,* which opened in 1923. Five years later Ziegfeld got him a lead in role in *Whoopee.* It was his second greatest success. The stock market crash of 1929 changed Cantor's fortunes, because most, if not all, of his savings of $2 million were tied up in the market.

Crash or no crash, the show went on. In 1931, Cantor made his first radio appearance on *The Rudy Vallee Show.* When Cantor got his own radio show, he introduced the practice of having a live audience preview his forthcoming broadcast. In effect, he rehearsed his show for the audience. This innovation made his show a great success. It was on his radio show that he introduced such talented people as Dianna Durbin and **Dinah Shore**.

Cantor became a highly paid star, but when he spoke out against certain public figures as fascists, his career went into decline. Comedian **Jack Benny** used his influence to get Cantor back on the air after radio executives refused to employ him.

Cantor also made a number of films. While his films were not great, they were entertaining. Among his films were *The Kid from Spain* (1932), *Roman Scandals* (1933), *Strike Me Pink* (1936), *Ali Baba Goes to Town* (1937), and *Little Mothers* (1940). In 1941, he appeared as Erwin in a play called *Banjo Eyes,* a musical comedy based upon *Three Men on a Horse*. Among the songs that he made famous were "If You Knew Susie," "Dinah," "Making Whoopee," and "Ma He's Making Eyes at Me."

His NBC radio show *Time to Smile* was broadcast from 1940–1946, but then he turned to the relatively new medium of television in 1950 on the NBC *Colgate Comedy Hour*. He appeared on the show once a month and rotated with such stars as Dean Martin, **Jerry Lewis**, and Jimmy Durante, among others

Two years later he suffered a heart attack. He returned to the *Colgate Comedy Hour,* and a film biography called *The Eddie Cantor Story* was made to memorialize his life.

Cantor believed that charity and service were the "rent we pay for our room on earth." He was involved in various works for institutions and organizations such as New York University; Temple University; American War Veterans; Surprise Lake Camp, a YMHA camp near Cold Springs, New York; the March of Dimes; and State of Israel Bonds.

Eddie Cantor died on October 10, 1964 at the age of 72 years. *See also* **Film**; **Radio**; **Shore, Dinah**; **Television**; **Vaudeville**.

Herbert M. Druks

Further Reading: Goldman, Herbert G. *Banjo Eyes: Eddie Cantor and the Birth of Modern Stardom*. New York: Oxford University Press, 1997.

CANTORS IN AMERICA

Mickey Mantle, Willie Mays, and Duke Snider were pretty popular names in our Brooklyn neighborhood, but Moshe and David were no less iconoclastic. Mantle, Mays, and Snider each roamed center field for the three New York Baseball teams, but the Kussevitzky brothers, singers of Jewish liturgy and prayer, were champions of the pulpit in their respective local synagogues, or "shuls."

I was born in the Boro Park section of Brooklyn in 1946. Starting around the turn of the century, we had a big immigration of Jews to this country from Europe. Along with the people came their culture. These people, by and large, were poor and did not frequent the opera halls or legitimate theater venues for their entertainment. Music sung by cantors was their escape from hard weekly labor, and they got it for free at their shul.

The first of the "star" cantors, who arrived in New York City in 1912, was **"Yossele" Josef Rosenblatt** (1882–1933). As it turned out, nobody before or since achieved the fame of this little man, small in stature and golden of voice. Yossele's appeal was not exclusive to Jews. When he officiated in Harlem, the jazz artists and opera singers of the day came to shul to hear him. He, in turn, loved American and operatic music and utilized many such motifs in his compositions. Musicians such as Cab Calloway (1907–1994) used cantorial "riffs" in their songs, so you had a kind of "cross pollination" between musical genres which reinforced one another. With the advent of the phonograph, Rosenblatt's popularity soared. He became an American household name, thus benefitting the cause of cantorial music greatly.

Some of the other greats of the time were Mordecai Hershman (1888–1940), a tenor of such sweetness and power that he was compared to the great Benjamino Gigli (1880–1957), successor to Enrico Caruso (1873–1921) at the Met; David Roitman (1884–1943), known as the "Poet of the Pulpit"; Zavel Kwartin (1874–1952), a baritone with a phenomenal top voice, great, rolling, coloratura; and Moshe Oysher (1907–1958), among many others. Moshe Oysher was a crossover artist, who also starred in **Yiddish film** and **theater**. Oysher was a versatile artist who not only starred in Yiddish film and theater, but whose music also resonated with the jazz community.

Growing up in my mostly Jewish shtetl, the sounds of cantorial music were "in the air." My parents owned a kosher **delicatessen** called Sachs and Mendelson's, on 5413 New Utrecht Avenue, under the elevated subway (not a contradiction in terms). It was normal for the waiter to break out into cantorial song while waiting to take an order. The waiter's favorite was a brilliant cantor by the name of Pierre Pinchik (1900–1971), of whom it was said: "He scratched the Jews where they itched." The radio in the deli was tuned to station WEVD, the all-Jewish station, where the sounds of cantors were heard all day long—sometimes in live broadcasts sponsored by Grossinger's Rye Bread or Maxwell House Coffee. A weekly live broadcast was done by the great cantor Moshe Ganchoff (1902–1997), who later became my teacher and mentor.

A friend, Mark Bieler, son of Chaim Bieler, who was host of a WEVD weekly program, tells of a pre-High Holiday live broadcast that he saw in the studio at age 10. Moshe Oysher, and the great former-cantor-turned-opera-star, Richard Tucker (1913–1975), were in the booth, behind the glass, singing their hearts out. It was late August, and the temperature hovered in the high 90s with no air conditioning in the studio. Mark noticed that they were in their shirtsleeves, smoking cigars while singing. As he crept up to the window, he stood on tip toe, and he saw that all they wore below was their underwear!

My personal experience with cantorial music began with singing alto in the Ben Friedman "Double Symphonic" choir. Moshe Kussevitzky (1899–1966) was the cantor, and like all of the greats, he sang with a choir made up of men and boys, as the synagogues were for the most part Orthodox. The great majority of these choirs, while professional, were not very good. Falsetto-singing men were the sopranos, then there were tenors, basses, and boy altos who also sang solos and duets with the cantor. The main function of the choir was to accompany the cantor by humming chords to his improvisations. It was this that the choirs excelled at, as opposed to singing written compositions. As a matter of fact, the entire congregation of 2000 hummed in harmony with Kussevitzky. He had a magnificent voice, with a superhuman upper register. He would sing climactic high Cs and Ds with no apparent effort. The same could be said for his brother David (1912–1985), who served a conservative synagogue around the corner.

From my bird's-eye view in the choir loft, I could see congregants sitting in rapture. Some would actually take out tuning forks to determine just how high a particular note was. People came for the cantorial music, or chazzanut, and nothing else. After the shacharit, or morning service, there was a mass exodus from the building during the reading of the Torah, where serious critical analysis of the cantor took place. They came back for the replacing of the scroll in the ark (after all, there were juicy high notes not to be missed in this liturgy), then there was an exodus for the rabbi's sermon, followed by a final return. All of this was capped off by a debriefing of all the musical highlights on the way home for lunch. This was our theater! This was our entertainment!

The Kussevitzkys were an anomaly. Before they arrived, chazzanut was an art form. Now it was a high note contest. Not that the brothers were not good cantors, for indeed they were, but those that followed only tried to imitate the vocal pyrotechnics and not the art. Had they not come along, chazzanut would have lasted much longer than it did, because art lives longer than fad. In discussing Yossele Rosenblatt, the great jazz saxophonist Ornette Coleman recently said: "I think he's singing pure spiritual. He's making the sound of what he's experiencing as a human being, turning it into the quality of his voice, and what he's singing to is what he's singing about. We hear it as 'how he's singing'. But he's singing about something. I don't know what it is, but it's baaad" (Anjou, 2006). What Coleman discovered in the mid-1980s at the home of a friend was mother's milk to generations of Jews who would talk about being at a particular service, or brag about singing in the choir with such and such cantor, for their entire lifetimes, as if they were present when Babe Ruth hit his 60th home run. I was born at the tail end of this cantorial golden age and witnessed family members not speaking to each other over a perceived slight to a beloved cantor. One can only imagine what the atmosphere was like in the true heyday of these greats.

Today, we are witness to slight rumblings of activity in the mostly dormant cantorial world. There are several orthodox congregations in New York City that have engaged "star quality" cantors, sort of as status symbols. These chazzanim arose out of the phenomenon of the Orthodox cantorial concert circuit, where four or five cantors stand up, and, generally accompanied by piano, sing old chestnut compositions (mostly Kussevitsky) into a microphone so heavily amplified it would put a rock concert to shame. The real Kussevitsky brothers, being classically trained, hardly ever used amplification. Also, sadly, this new breed of cantor knows nothing about music or musical theory, learning their music by heart from recordings. The golden age cantors were, for the most part, master musicians who wrote their own material. Still, we can hope that from these beginnings a revival might ensue. It would only take one or two good ones to ignite the fire. In the liberal branches of Judaism, there is some real hope for a resurgence. The woman's voice in cantorial music is a fascinating subject that would take pages to write about. Suffice it to say that women cantors are most interested in the subject and are working toward the goal of learning the fine art while trying not to imitate the male sound, and they are in many cases succeeding. It is from this corner of the universe that I believe the Jewish people may rediscover the great art of chazzanut.

Jacob Ben-Zion Mendelson

Further Reading: Anjou, Erik. *A Cantor's Tale.* Documentary Film. Teaneck, NJ: Ergo Media Inc., 2006.

CAPP, AL (1909–1979)

Al Capp was the highly successful and controversial creator of the "Li'l Abner" comic strip, which appeared from 1934–1977 and at its peak had a readership of 60,000,000. Born in New Haven, Connecticut as Alfred Gerald Caplin, Capp was the eldest child of Otto Philip and Tillie Caplin, Orthodox Jews whose parents had emigrated from czarist Russia. Ethnic identity played an important role in Capp's family life. A memoir/eulogy by Al Capp's brother, Elliot, recounts how their paternal grandfather, Zayde (Samuel), after arriving in America from Latvia, changed his name from "Cowper" to "Caplin," ostensibly because it sounded less Jewish and would not be a hindrance to his dry goods and notions business.

Similarly, Elliott Caplin recalled how his mother's brother, Uncle Aryeh Labe, changed his name to Archie Lionel, an unusual choice for a rabbi. Indeed, in his mother's family he discerned a desire for assimilation, a wish to become "more American than Sergeant York" (Caplin, 1994). This was not a betrayal of ethnic identity but a survival mechanism for the new environment. Jewish identity was also important in the Caplin family.

Zayde Caplin was devoutly Orthodox and also a very successful businessman. He was able to enroll his firstborn, Otto Philip, at Yale. At some point, perhaps influenced by his Ivy League experience, Otto Philip changed his name to "Caplin." His education did not, however, translate into financial success. Elliott Caplin describes his brother as moody, temperamental, and gifted. Al Capp assumed a special niche in the family when, at the age of nine, he lost a leg in a trolley accident. Elliott Caplin describes his family struggling on the brink of poverty, caught between the improbable economic schemes of his dreamer father and a strict and somewhat emotionally detached mother.

While their mother was devoutly religious, none of her children were. This did not mean that they had no pride in being Jewish. New Haven's immigrant community was like many other enclaves in urban America before World War II. In their ghettos African Americans followed the exploits of Joe Louis, the Brown Bomber, because he was fighting their fight. The Caplin boys admired **Benny Leonard**, Lightweight Champion of the World and also Jewish.

Just as intangible as ethnic pride was the financial support which Otto Philip Caplin gave his oldest son, Al. He enrolled him in Philadelphia's School of Fine Arts but neglected to pay the tuition. According to Caplin's memoir, however, his brother never became angry with his father. Everyone else was a target for his anger, but he and his father were kindred spirits—dreamers. Capp's affinity to his father manifested itself in his interest in literature.

On visits to his paternal grandparents, Capp reportedly enjoyed his grandfather's library, which contained many of the popular authors of the day. As an adolescent his taste changed, and he voraciously read Ford Madox Ford, George Bernard Shaw, James Cabell, and especially William Cowper Brann (1855–1898). Elliott Caplin underscores the importance of Brann, editor of the journal *The Iconoclast,* and Charles Dickens to his brother's perceptions of society in his comics.

Alfred Caplin also changed his name. He became Al Capp and in 1932 launched his career doing a daily comic strip, "Colonel Gilfeather," for the Associated Press. Ham Fisher, the creator of "Joe Palooka," lured Capp to that strip, where he did a great deal of the work until he had a falling out with Fisher. During his time with Fisher, Capp created the figure of "Big Liviticus," and when he struck out on his own that character became the central figure in "Li'l Abner." This comic strip became a piece of Americana. The characters, the fictional locales of Dogpatch and Lower Slobovia, as well as Sadie Hawkins Day, all became elements of America's popular culture vocabulary.

A satirist and iconoclast by conviction, Capp was widely attacked when he began to lampoon the Left instead of establishment institutions. This shift, plus a number of sexual indiscretions on college campuses, led to great disaffection with a man who had been undoubtedly the most popular cartoonist in American history. Illness, family tragedies, and his slipping popularity darkened his final years, and his creative life ended two years before his death. *See also* **Comic Books**.

Leroy T. Hopkins Jr.

Further Reading: Caplin, Eliott. *Al Capp Remembered.* Bowling Green, OH: Bowling Green State University Popular Press, 1994.

CARLEBACH, SHLOMO (1925–1994)

Shlomo Carlebach was a well-known Jewish religious singer and neo-Hasidic rabbi and teacher. Carlebach was born in Germany into a well-known German rabbinic family. His father, grandfather, and various uncles were all Orthodox rabbis in Germany. His uncle, Rabbi Josef Carlebach, was the last chief rabbi of Hamburg, and rather than leave his congregants, he chose to die a martyr's death under the Nazis. After the advent of the Nazi regime, Shlomo's father, Rabbi Dr. Naphtali H. Carlebach, took his family to the United States. Although strictly Orthodox, Rabbi Naphtali Carlebach was an adherent of the school of the German Rabbi Samson Raphael Hirsch, who stressed the integration of Torah study with secular culture. Settling in the Crown Heights section of Brooklyn, the senior Carlebach assumed the pulpit of a large, mainstream Orthodox synagogue on Eastern Parkway. The young Carlebach and his twin brother Eli Chaim were for the first time exposed to Hasidism in an intensive manner. Although Carlebach studied in a so-called Lithuanian yeshiva in Lakewood with the great Talmudist Rabbi Aaron Kotler and at Yeshiva Rabbi Chaim Berlin in Brooklyn under Rabbi Isaac Hutner, his chief spiritual influences were the sixth and seventh Lubavitcher rebbes, Rabbi Joseph I. Schneerson (died 1950) and his son-in-law Rabbi Menachem M. Schneerson (died 1994), both of whom resided in Crown Heights. In addition, Carlebach was influenced by several other Hasidic masters, such as the Bobover rebbe, Rabbi Shlomo Halberstam, and the Modsitzer rebbe, Rabbi Saul Y. Taub (died 1948). Thus, Carlebach identified with both the yeshiva world and the world of Hasidim, particularly Chabad.

Carlebach was known both as a good Talmudic scholar—a scholar of Hasidic thought—and a fine singer of Hasidic melodies. His brother Eli Chaim even married into the Schneerson family and became an official in the court of the sixth Lubavitcher rebbe.

In the early 1950s, Carlebach, with his friend Rabbi Zalman Schachter, traveled to various colleges and universities seeking to spread the message of Orthodox Judaism as unofficial emissaries of the seventh Lubavitcher rebbe. Carlebach and Schachter gained a reputation among many spiritually attuned young Jews as spiritual teachers. Although they remained lifelong friends, Schachter and Carlebach traveled different roads in spreading Jewish spiritual thought. Carlebach also embarked on a singing career. Blessed with a wonderful voice, he started singing songs he had written based on biblical passages, especially from the Psalms. His first fans were students at various yeshivas in greater New York. By the late 1950s, a wider audience was attracted to Carlebach's combination of American folk and Hasidic music, which he accompanied on his own guitar. Carlebach performed at West Village coffee houses, concert halls, homes of his followers, and at synagogues. Carlebach morphed not only into a singer but also into a storyteller and neoHasidic rebbe, offering spiritual teachings to his followers. By the late 1960s Carlebach was recognized by many as a New Age Jewish guru. In the early 1960s both Carlebach and Schachter split from the official Lubavitch movement, mainly because of the Orthodox practice of strict public separation of the sexes. Carlebach was known to hug and caress female fans, a practice frowned upon by the Orthodox and Hasidic communities. This practice hurt Carlebach's reputation among the Orthodox during his lifetime, and the issue of his relations with women was raised in a controversial article in *Lilith* magazine after he died.

With the arrival of the sexual revolution and the hippie period, Carlebach was to be found on the West Coast both singing and preaching Judaism in Berkeley to New Age spiritual followers. To cater to his newfound followers he started the "House of Love and Prayer" in Berkeley. Similar synagogues and drop-in centers were also functioning in Israel and other places in the United States. To Carlebach's chagrin these places were constantly plagued by drug use and sexual promiscuity.

Following his father's death in 1967, he also became co-rabbi of the Carlebach Synagogue on New York's Upper West Side, together with his brother, Rabbi Eli Chaim, who by this time had become a Bobover Hasid. Eventually, this synagogue became the official center for Carlebach's teachings and spiritual work; however, he was always in motion, going around the world and giving both commercial and unofficial concerts, as well as recording numerous record albums, all of which sold very well.

By the 1970s, Carlebach's music had become the most popular musical format in the Orthodox Jewish world, even though Carlebach and his teachings were off limits to most Orthodox Jews. Exceptions to this were the Hasidic rebbes of Amshinov and Modsitz in Israel, who received Carlebach with open arms. Carlebach was also a pioneer in the Soviet Jewry movement, writing the song that became the anthem of this movement—"Am Yisroel Chai."

In 1972, Carlebach was married to a Canadian school teacher, Neilah. They had two daughters together and soon after divorced. Until his death, Carlebach spent his time traveling about giving concerts and speaking at New Age conferences about Jewish spirituality. Although he attracted many people to Judaism, few stayed with him. Most moved on to other forms of Judaism.

Carlebach would not give any official institutional structure to his movement. His followers in Israel lived on several communal settlements and were constantly beset by internal quarrels and by drug use.

At some point prior to his death, Carlebach made overtures to the Orthodox community about returning to the fold, but neither side seems to have been truly engaged in this process. Carlebach died suddenly on a flight to Canada. His followers were shocked at his death, and attempts were made to accord Carlebach the status of a Jewish "saint" on par with the Baba Sali and the Lubavitcher rebbe. It was only after his death that followers attempted to create a framework for his teachings through a series of institutions. But this was plagued by internal squabbles, between Carlebach's wife and daughter Neshama, who sought the mantle of leadership, and other followers of both his teachings and musical style. Many Carlebach-style prayer groups sprung up after his death, marked by intensive congregational singing, mostly of Carlebach's songs, and exhibiting an informal atmosphere. The official center of Carlebach followers seems to be his former synagogue, which is now led by his grand-nephew, Rabbi Naphtali Citron, a young Lubavitch follower. Neshama, his daughter, embarked on a singing career of her own but was hurt by Orthodox community restrictions against females singing in public. Her lack of intensive Jewish religious knowledge also hurt her. Rabbi Shlomo Carlebach made a tremendous contribution to twentieth-century Jewish life by creating a new mode of religious spirituality through song. His influence as a teacher of Jewish spirituality affected many young Jews, but seemingly he failed to leave a lasting impact on the American Jewish religious community. His spiritual role has best been described by **Rabbi Michael Lerner** in an obituary in *Tikkun* magazine following his death. Lerner praised Carlebach's efforts and teachings but described him as a "wounded healer." Carlebach's music continues to be available on CDs.

Zalman Alpert

Further Reading: Blustain, Sarah. "A Paradoxical Legacy: Rabbi Shlomo Carlebach's Shadow Side." *Lilith,* Spring 1998. Dickter, Adam. "Facing A Mixed Legacy." *The Jewish Week,* September 8, 2004. Edelman, Marsha Bryan. "Reinventing Hasidic Music: Shlomo Carlebach." MyJewishLearning.com, 2003. Goldman, Ari L. "Obituary of Rabbi Shlomo Carlebach." *New York Times,* October 22, 1994. Musleah, Rahel. "Shlomo Carlebach: The Music Man." *Hadassah Magazine,* October 2008, 51–56.

CARLISLE HART, KITTY (1910–2007)

An elegant, eternally youthful entertainer and cultural icon, Kitty Carlisle's career in movies, musicals, opera, television, radio, and stage spanned 75 years. Kitty Carlisle Hart (née Catherine Conn, pronounced "Cohen") was born into a German Jewish family in New Orleans on September 3, 1910. Her father, Dr. Joseph Conn, a gynecologist, died when Conn was 10. Her ambitious mother, Hortense Holtzman Conn, was the daughter of the first Jewish mayor of Shreveport, Louisiana. Somewhat of a self-hating Jew, Hortense Conn was a social climber, determined to break into Gentile society. In 1921 she escorted her daughter abroad, intent upon marrying her into European royalty. Failing in this, Catherine Conn remained in Europe and received her education in London, Paris, Switzerland, and Rome. Having decided that she wanted to be an actress, Conn was accepted into London's Royal Academy of Dramatic Art. She also trained at the Theatre de l'Atelier in Paris.

By the time mother and daughter returned to the United States in 1932, Catherine Conn had renamed herself Kitty Carlisle. She got her start as an apprentice at the historic Buck's County Playhouse in New Hope, Pennsylvania. Her appearances in such musicals and operettas as *Rio Rita, White Horse Inn,* and *Champagne Sec* brought her to the attention of Hollywood. Although her film career was brief, she did play a featured role in the classic 1935 **Marx Brothers** movie *A Night at the Opera.* Carlisle appeared in 10 movies; the last was the 1993 film *Ten Degrees of Separation.* Carlisle married Pulitzer Prize-winning playwright Moss Hart, whom she met at a dinner party given by writer Lillian Hellman. She appeared in a number of his works, including the classic *The Man Who Came to Dinner,* which was written about their friend, the noted theater critic Alexander Wollcott. Moss Hart died at age 57, in 1961. Carlisle, who never remarried, spent the rest of her life keeping his memory alive.

Turning to television in the 1950s, Carlisle became a household name as a panelist on the long-running quiz show *To Tell the Truth*. For nearly 45 years, she was known to audiences for her cultured diction, her Prince Valiant hairstyle, and her haute couture gowns.

An important and beloved doyen of the arts, Carlisle served as chair of the New York State Council of the Arts for over 20 years. In 1966, she made her Metropolitan Opera debut as Prinz Orlofsky in Strauss's *Die Fledermaus*. In 1991, she was awarded the American National Medal by the National Endowment for the Arts.

At age 95 she was still performing her one-woman act, which consisted of anecdotes about the great men in American theater she had known, including **George Gershwin** (who at one time proposed marriage), **Irving Berlin**, Kurt Weill, Cole Porter, Jerome Kern, Oscar Hammerstein, and Frederick Loewe.

Kitty Carlisle Hart died of heart failure at the age of 96, on April 17, 2007. She is survived by her son Christopher, daughter Catherine, and three grandchildren. *See also* **Popular Music**.

Kurt F. Stone

Further Reading: Carlisle, Kitty. *Kitty: An Autobiography.* New York: Doubleday, 1988.

THE CATSKILLS

A strong argument can be made to support the concept that domestic tourism began in the Catskill Mountains. The lordly Hudson River provided the first access to the picturesque region, which is, in some places, as rich in history and folklore as it is in scenery. Turnpikes, railroads, and modern highways all provided access and tourist populations. The Catskills were and are beautiful.

As the nineteenth century blended into the twentieth, the region spawned hotels, gated residential parks, several artists' colonies, and thousands of boardinghouses, rooming houses, and bungalow colonies. The Catskills' resort was shaped by two groups: old-line Protestants, who first developed the region, and the Jews, who indelibly marked it. The relationship between these groups has not always been friendly or easy.

Generations of travelers and excursionists sailing up and down the Hudson River saw it in the distance—a hulking, majestic Greek-porticoed white building, high on an escarpment beyond the town of Catskill. Standing until it was destroyed by the New York State Department of Conservation in 1964, the landmark was the Catskill Mountain House, the first great resort hotel in America. It was the flagship of an enterprise that eventually launched at least 1,114 other hotels. New York's Catskill Mountains once housed the greatest concentration of resorts in America. Some were opulent, and others were quite modest. The early resorts catered to a Christian-only population, but beginning in the 1890s, vacation spots in the Fleischmann-Tannersville-Hunter region began to admit Jewish guests. After more than a century of exclusion, the Catskill Mountain House became a Jewish resort, as did its chief rival, the largest hotel ever built in the Catskills, the 1,200-room Hotel Kaaterskill. Other smaller hotels remained exclusionary until the passage of civil rights legislation in the late 1960s—and some even beyond.

By the early twentieth century, for many, the terms "Catskills" and "Jewish" were synonymous. This, in large part, is thanks to the development of the famed Borscht Belt in the southern Catskills, or, technically, the Shawangunks. In the northern Catskills, the "real" Catskills, German Jews broke down the religious barrier. In the Borscht Belt region, it was the Polish and Russian Jews that broke down the barriers, who immigrated to America between 1880 and 1924. They, too, wanted their place in the country—in the mountains, on the lakes, or along the swimmable rivers.

The early hotels of the northern Catskills relied on the steamboats that carried passengers up from New York City to the stagecoaches and wagons that transported travelers to the resorts. Trips were long, and sojourns were longer yet. Before the arrival of the railroad, it took three and a half hours to reach the Catskill Mountain House from the town of Catskill, only 12 miles away. By 1892, the railroad shortened the entire trip time from New York City to the hotel to under three and a half hours.

The initial development of the resort industry of the southern Catskills is completely related to the railroad. The railroad was followed by the automobile and the highway. The area was opened to tourism by the railroad known as the New York, Ontario, and Western (O & W). Beginning in the 1870s, the railroad issued annual editions of *Summer Homes,* which promoted the scenic province. This newer resort area grew rapidly during what local historians consider the "Silver Age." This was the Christian-only phase, and although Sullivan County had grand hotels such as Ye Lancashire Inn in Liberty (built in 1893–1894), it never really competed in grandeur with the region to the north. Rapidly it spawned myriad smaller hotels and boardinghouses, many of which catered to Irish and German immigrants. Because of its high elevation and clean air, in addition to resorts, the Liberty region became home to numerous tuberculosis sanatoria. Vacationers were understandably wary of being near tuberculosis sufferers. Many hotels, accommodating vacationers' fears and prejudices, advertised, "no Hebrews or consumptives accepted."

Gentile farmers took in Gentile boarders, and boardinghouses and hotels grew in importance. Jews first entered this Christian world of farms and summer resorts early in 1892, when Yana "John" Gerson bought an abandoned farm in Glen Wild, near Woodridge. He soon built a successful dairying operation and boardinghouse. Others followed. Jews were not welcomed, but they persisted. By the 1920s, the Borscht Belt was firmly established as a Jewish resort, where Jews could feel at home.

The terms "Sullivan County," "the Catskills," "the Country," the Mountains," and "the Borscht Belt" became synonyms for the famed resort area. Classic Borscht Belt Sullivan County is really only the eastern part of the county, with a bit of southern Ulster County included. The western part of the county, which borders on the Delaware River, never developed an extensive resort industry, although it is now becoming an increasingly expensive center of second homes, often for expatriates from the Borscht Belt.

Most of the soil in the lower Catskills is poor, and few Jewish farmers (like their Christian predecessors) could scratch more than subsistence living from the unyielding ground. Many followed the lead of Yana Gerson and started taking in boarders. Farmers not only rented out sections of their farmhouses, they also fed the boarders the food that they raised and could not market. As inexpensive as boardinghouses were, some New Yorkers could afford only cheaper accommodations, and the *kuchalein,* "cook for yourself," was born. The summer people shared a common kitchen, outhouse, and bathtub that often sat out behind the barn, with separate hours for men and women. Many *kuchaleiners* never used these (often filthy) tubs and preferred to wash in the Neversink River or a nearby lake. They also chose, or sometimes were required, to buy food from their landlord. Because so many early resorts developed from farms, many renters referred to the landlords as farmers, whether they farmed or not.

There were hundreds of *kuchaleins* but, by the 1920s, a demand for more privacy grew. Some "farmers" started to build shacks on their grounds. These structures usually had no cooking or plumbing, and tenants shared the common facilities with the rest of the *kuchalein.* By the mid-1930s, a few of these shacks added a kitchen and a bathroom, and the rental bungalow came into being. By 1956 there were well over 2,000 bungalow colonies in the region of eastern Sullivan

County and southern Ulster County. The typical bungalow had two rooms: a kitchen and a bedroom. A more luxurious unit might have two bedrooms. No bungalow had a separate living room, but there might be a screened porch. During the week, the resort was a matriarchy. The mothers stayed up with the kids, and the fathers came up on the weekends. If they had a vacation, fathers might spend a week or two.

By the 1950s, bungalow colonies had evolved from crude clusters of shacks into comfortable resorts. The average resort might have about 20 units (often a combination of apartments and bungalows), while some larger places, such as Cutler's Cottages in South Fallsburg, counted accommodations in the hundreds. Soon the larger resorts started mimicking the area's famed hotels, offering professional entertainment and even an occasional indoor swimming pool. The question of who went to a bungalow colony and who went to a hotel was based on preference rather than economics. If you wanted three big meals a day and the opportunity to change clothes all day, you went to a hotel. If you wanted a more casual experience, you went to a colony. The 1999 film *A Walk on the Moon* beautifully depicts the vanished world of the Borscht Belt bungalow colony.

At the resort industry's height (1930 to 1970) it seemed as if there was a hotel on every hill. Hotels in the region trace their development to two main sources, conveniently symbolized by the two most famous of the hotels in the Borscht Belt: Grossinger's and the Concord. The Grossinger family, like the Brickmans and Posners (Brickman's Hotel) and the Slutskys (Nevele Hotel), were farmers who, with their children, built great resorts. Others bought existing hotels. Real estate transactions changed the Sha-Wan-Ga Lodge and the White Roe Lodge instantly from "no Hebrews or consumptives accepted" houses to "dietary laws observed" establishments. Most famously, Arthur Winarick set out to build the greatest hotel in Sullivan County. Using money earned from Jerris hair tonic, he built the extraordinary Concord from a modest preexisting facility. Grossinger's prided itself on being *haimish* (homelike), while the Concord was proudly sleek and modern.

The Borscht Belt became a separate-but-better-than-equal resort for New York's Jewish population. During the "Golden Age" of the hotels, immediately following World War II, there were hundreds of hotel choices. These ranged from schlock houses (dumps), little better than boardinghouses, to grand palatial establishments. It can be argued that the Catskill hotels made it possible for the masses to enjoy a luxury vacation. While rich businessmen and their families might spend a summer at Grossinger's or Brown's or the Laurels, their secretaries would save up for a week at the same places. Their accommodations might be more cramped (often two to a bed), but the facilities were the same—open to all. Hotels hired college boys to attract single girls, and the Catskills became one great marriage broker.

The hotels became known for their glitz and abundance; their guests, for their flamboyance. Hotels competed in offering ever more facilities. Guests demanded to know what was new, before making reservations. Swimming pools became filtered pools, followed by indoor pools. Indoor ice rinks also became a must. Entertainment was everywhere. By 1950, some 600 shows were presented on Saturday nights. Entertainers honing their craft in the region are legendary. They included **Danny Kaye**, **Sid Caesar**, and **Sammy Davis Jr.**. "Catskill Comic" entered the language. Performers seen on *The Ed Sullivan Show* on Sunday evening would often play the Concord the next Saturday night. Meals were enormous. People were often proud of how many pounds they gained on vacation. This proved that they got their money's worth. The meals usually offered Jewish favorites, never giving up on lox, herring, and brisket. To the extent that a kosher kitchen would allow, hotels also served variations of Chinese and Italian food. Most hotels were kosher until a few broke and began serving "Jewish American cuisine," which meant that you could have lox and eggs for breakfast and broiled lobster for dinner.

Guests arrived with many suitcases, and women were expected to change clothes at least three times a day and never to wear the same dress twice in the dining room. By the mid-1950s, even before air conditioning became mandatory, every woman needed her mink stole for Saturday night, as well as a mink-trimmed cashmere sweater for less formal occasions. While several movies were set in the Catskill hotels, most famously *Dirty Dancing,* only one, *Sweet Lorraine,* was actually made there and tells the most authentic story.

Today *kuchaleins* are gone, killed off by changing lifestyles and prosperity. Only a handful of traditional hotels remain in Sullivan County. The normative bungalow colonies are mostly gone. Jews who continue to go to the Catskill resorts, and especially the bungalow colonies, are mostly the ultra-Orthodox and the Hasidim. They continue to go because their religion demands a community that provides them with kosher food and Orthodox services. Why did mainstream Jews abandon Sullivan County? The answer is complex. The rise of suburbia, the women's movement, and air conditioning all changed society, as did the civil rights legislation of the 1960s that outlawed discrimination at places of public accommodations. Cheap airfares opened the world to the Americanized Jews. As one hotel owner lamented, "I used to compete with the hotel down the road; now I compete with the world." It was an uneven battle, and the world won. The Catskill tradition of lavish hospitality lives on. It has merely changed venue.

It is no accident that the people who created, or reinvented, our most popular contemporary resort destinations had the Catskills in their past. Ben Novak, the son of the owners of the Laurels Country Club in Monticello, built Miami Beach's incredible Fountainbleu Hotel, which was a high point in the development of Miami Beach's lavish hotel life. Many Catskill hotel owners had hotels in Miami Beach, some as early as the 1920s. The Weiners of the White Roe Inn owned the Plymouth and the Adams hotels. The Levinsons built the Algiers, and the Grossingers bought the Pancoast, a restricted hotel whose clientele changed. Bunny Grossinger tells the story of a longtime Christian guest of the Pancoast calling for his regular winter reservations. When told that the management had changed and dietary laws were now observed, he replied innocently, "Good, I can use a diet." Steve Wynn, who developed several of Las Vegas's most elaborate resorts, including the Bellagio, spent his summers at Grossinger's.

Even at its most Jewish time, the Catskills had hotels catering to other ethnic groups. Peg Leg Bates Hotel, opened by the famed entertainer, catered to African Americans. The Villa Roma Resort in Callicoon still flourishes and attracts an Italian American crowd as it rebuilds from a 2006 fire. While only one large old-style Jewish resort survives in the Catskills today—Kutsher's Country Club—the vital essence of the Catskills lives on. The spirit of over-the-top food and entertainment pioneered in the Catskills has simply changed location. Many of today's most popular cruise ships are nothing more than reconfigured Catskill-style resorts that float. The Catskill Institute, which maintains a list of (mostly past) Catskill hotels, now counts 1,115 hotels. More names are continually being added. More cruise ships are being added, but their numbers will never match those of their inspiration. It is no accident that the principal owners of Carnival Cruise Lines are very familiar with the Catskills of yesterday.

Irwin Richman

Further Reading: Brown, Phil. *Catskill Culture: A Mountain Rat's Memories of the Great Jewish Resort Area.* Philadelphia: Temple University Press, 1999. Catskill Institute Web Site: http://catskills.brown.edu. Kanfer, Stefan. *A Summer World: The Attempt to Build a Jewish Eden in the Catskills*. New York: Farrar, Straus and Giroux, 1989. Richman, Irwin. *Borscht Belt Bungalows: Memories of Catskill Summers*. Philadelphia: Temple University Press: 1998.

CHABON, MICHAEL (1963–)

Chabon, one of America's most celebrated writers, whose most popular work, *The Amazing*

Adventures of Kavalier & Clay, won the Pulitzer Prize in 2001, was born on May 24, 1963 to Robert and Sharon Chabon, an average American couple whose parents were Eastern European Jewish immigrants. A child of the 1960s, living in the suburbs of Columbia, Maryland, Chabon's youth was relatively uneventful, colored mostly by his avid collection of comic books and his parent's divorce around the time he turned 11. These early experiences stayed with the author so that themes of divorce and single-parenthood, along with explorations of genre—fiction and the American Jewish experience—played a central role in his novels later in life.

The first of these novels, *The Mysteries of Pittsburgh,* was written in completion of his 1987 MFA degree in creative writing at the University of California–Irvine. The work was secretly sent off to an agent by Chabon's graduate advisor and ultimately sold to William Morrow Publishers for $155,000. This sum was unheard of for a first-time writer's novel. This financial return said volumes about the author's potential, and the novel's content too was indicative of Chabon's muse. Chabon demonstrated his ability to channel personal experience and explore identity formation with this story about the coming of age of a Jewish mobster's son who deals with his own sexuality and his love of two men.

In the years that followed, Chabon attempted to match his first success with an oversized second work entitled *Fountain City.* Losing the piece's direction, Chabon abandoned the project and turned that creative struggle into his actual second novel, *Wonder Boys* (1995). Drawing again on immediate experience, Chabon told the story of an author fighting creative stagnation and the fear of becoming a one-hit wonder. The novel was well received, yet Chabon and his critics identified a need to move beyond self-inspired first-person narratives.

By the year 2000, *The Amazing Adventures of Kavalier & Clay* marked a new direction in Chabon's writing. The book won a host of awards and accolades, crowned by the Pulitzer Prize. Chabon had demonstrated a new plane of sophistication as well as appreciation for the trials and triumphs of the Jewish experience in America around World War II. Though he had stepped out of himself to produce the work, Chabon was no less present in this saga of two young Jews in America and their rise through the ranks of comic book greats. Acclaimed as his magnum opus, the book was likewise the most central expression yet of his own Jewish background. It demonstrated sensitivities and understandings about the Holocaust, its refugees, and the impact that event would have on future generations. Jewish history and identity had begun to inspire Chabon's work.

His seven-year follow-up, *The Yiddish Policemen's Union,* was one of Chabon's most intricate and potentially alienating works. Jewish themes ran throughout it. A counter-historical narrative set in the style of 1940s film noir, the novel challenged established concepts of Jewish reality by presenting a world in which the State of Israel has been destroyed in a failed war for independence. In its stead, Chabon created a **Yiddish**-speaking Jewish autonomy situated physically in Sitka, Alaska and metaphorically in what he termed the "backwater" of history. The book received mixed reviews. Some heralded its ingenuity; others denounced it as disrespectful of the State of Israel and the cultural legacy of the Holocaust. Chabon claimed that the book was simply an effort to reexamine contemporary Jewish identity, as well as reevaluate historical ideas that developed since the Holocaust.

Reaching the number two slot on the *New York Times* bestseller list and remaining there for the next six weeks, *The Yiddish Policemen's Union* did not jeopardize Chabon's literary standing. Chabon, however, promised a more mainstream topic for his next work. Introducing Jewish issues into his writings may prove the author's greatest contribution: demonstrating just how American it has become to pursue Jewish self-exploration.

Chabon currently lives in Berkeley, California, with his wife and fellow writer, Ayelet Waldman. The couple has four children: Sophie, Isaac, Rosie, and Abraham. *See also* **Literature**.

Alan Amanik

Further Reading: Behlman, Lee. "The Escapist: Fantasy, Folklore, and the Pleasures of the Comic Book in Recent Jewish American Holocaust Fiction," *Shofar* 22, no. 3 (2004): 56–71. Wisse, Ruth. "Slap Shtick: Review of *The Yiddish Policemen's Union,* by Michael Chabon." *Commentary* 124, no. 1 (2007): 73–77.

CHAYEFSKY, PADDY (1923–1981)

Born Sidney Aaron Chayefski to Ukranian Jewish parents, Paddy Chayefsky, as he later called himself, was an acclaimed dramatist, playwright, Hollywood screenwriter, and a pioneer in dramatic writing for television. His best known teledrama, *Marty* (1953), was made into a film in 1955, starring Ernest Borgnine, which won the Academy Award for Best Picture. Born in the Bronx, Chayefsky attended the City College of New York and Fordham University and subsequently served in the U.S. Army during World War II, for which he was awarded a Purple Heart. While recuperating from his wartime wounds, Chayefsky turned to writing for the theater and penned the books and lyrics to a musical called *NO T.O. for Love* (1945), which toured army bases all over Europe. The show was subsequently brought to London, where it opened at the Scala Theater on the West End. Chayefsky was a television pioneer in the writing of teledramas. He wrote nine teleplays one season and during the 1950s and early 1960s wrote for such programs as *The Armstrong Theater, Playhouse 90, The U.S. Steel Hour,* and dozens of other short-lived anthology shows. His greatest fame as a television writer is associated, however, with *Marty* (1953), which featured Rod Steiger. The success of *Marty* led to his writing of screenplays for Hollywood, which included such films as *The Goddess* (1957); *The Bachelor Party* (1957), which, like *Marty,* was first written for television; *Paint Your Wagon* (1969); *The Americanization of Emily* (1964); and he won Oscars for the screenplay for *The Hospital* (1971) and *Network* (1976). Chayefsky also wrote for the Broadway stage. His two most successful plays were *Middle of the Night* (1956) and, the most Jewish of his work, *The Tenth Man* (1959). Within the Jewish community, Chayefsky became somewhat of a hero when, in response to Vanessa Redgrave—who had won Best Supporting Actress for her role in *Julia* (1978) and took the opportunity to denounce the "Zionist hoodlums," who were protesting her support for the Palestinian cause—he, while presenting an Oscar award, responded, "I would like to suggest to Miss Redgrave that her winning an Academy award is not a pivotal moment in history, and does not require a proclamation, and a simple 'thank you,' would have sufficed" (Brady, 1981). Later, Chayefsky stated that he was offended by her "crack about Jews." Chayefsky died of cancer in 1981 at the age of 58. *See also* **Film**; **Television**; **Theater**.

Jack R. Fischel

Further Reading: Brady, John. *The Craft of the Screenwriter.* New York: Simon and Schuster, 1981. Campbell, Colin. "Paddy Chayefsky Dead at 58; Playwright Won Three Oscars." *New York Times,* August 2, 1981.

CHESS

The game of chess has been prominent in Jewish culture since the Middle Ages, and many of the game's greatest players have been of Jewish descent. In the eleventh century Abraham Ibn Ezra produced *Haruzim,* a poem on chess that might be the earliest European account of the game's rules. Both Maimonides and Judah Halevy refer to chess, and there is even an apparent reference to the game in a version of the Babylonian Talmud. Why Jews have had an affinity for chess is unclear. Some experts say that the habit of mind engendered by Talmudic dialectic is similar to chess analysis. Grandmasters Akiba Rubinstein (1882–1961) and Aron Nimzowitsch (1886–1935), for example, emerged from schools of rabbinic training, and it is not hard to imagine the intellectual qualities needed to excel in chess integrated nicely with the traditional Jewish love of learning.

Since the late nineteenth century, American Jews have been vital to the growth and popularity of chess worldwide. Wilhelm Steinitz (1836–

1900), the first official World Chess Champion, was an Austrian Jew who resided in America in his later years. It was in New York, St. Louis, and New Orleans that Steinitz played the first sanctioned world championship match in 1886 against Johannes Zukertort (1842–1888), a Polish Jew. Steinitz won by a score of 10–5 with 5 draws. In his play, writings, and personal appearances Steinitz proposed and developed the theory of positional chess, which is the basis for the modern game. According to this theory, a player should try to accumulate small, subtle advantages that in aggregate can be converted into tangible gains.

Steinitz lost the title in 1894 to Emanuel Lasker (1868–1941), a German Jewish mathematician, by a score of 10–5 with 4 draws. Lasker's toppling of the great Steinitz astounded the chess world. American chess fans, many of whom were recent Jewish immigrants, had a new hero. Lasker had many distinguished colleagues and friends, including **Albert Einstein**, who wrote a charming sketch of Lasker for Hannak's biography of him. Lasker finished his career with the highest winning percentage of any world champion, holding the title for an unprecedented 27 years. His victory at the age of 56 in the great New York 1924 tournament, ahead of younger rivals Jose Capablanca (1888–1942) and Alexander Alekhine (1892–1946), is a high mark of chess history.

American hegemony in international chess during the 1930s, when the United States won four consecutive Olympiads (Prague 1931, Folkestone 1933, Warsaw 1935, and Stockholm 1937), can be traced to the groundwork laid by Steinitz and Lasker. In 1920, Samuel Reshevsky (1911–1992), a Polish Jew, immigrated with his parents to the United States. The nine-year-old "Sammy" gave memorable blindfold exhibitions throughout America, exploits no chess prodigy has ever surpassed. Reshevsky went on to capture six U.S. championship tournaments (1936, 1938, 1940, 1942, 1946, and 1969) and at his zenith was ranked among the world's top three players. If Reshevsky had not taken a five-year hiatus from serious competition to pursue religious studies he might very well have won the world championship.

The first native-born American Jew to distinguish himself in international chess was Isaac Kashdan (1905–1985). During the late 1920s and early 1930s he was America's best player, though he was never able to capture the U.S. title. In 1928, at the Hague Olympiad, he spearheaded the U.S. team to second place behind Germany. Kashdan won the first-board prize with a score of 13–2. For many years he was the chess editor of the *Los Angeles Times*. He also co-founded *Chess Review* in 1933 with Al Horowitz (1907–1973) and Fred Reinfeld (1910–1964).

Despite Kashdan's talents, Reshevsky's true rival in the 1930s and 1940s was Reuben Fine (1914–1993). Although Fine never won the U.S. Chess Championship, his achievements internationally may have outstripped Reshevsky's. In 1937, Fine was second for world champion Max Euwe (1901–1981) in his title defense against Alekhine. Then, in 1938, he was co-winner, along with Estonia's Paul Keres (1916–1975), of the major event sponsored by AVRO (an acronym for a Dutch radio station), generally considered one of the strongest tournaments of all time. It consisted of the world's eight best players in head-to-head match-ups. (In the same tournament Reshevsky finished fourth-sixth, tied with Alekhine and Euwe.)

The world's best speed-chess player in the late 1930s and early 1940s, Fine opted not to compete in the 1948 Hague-Moscow world championship tournament, retiring from competition for a career as a **Freudian** psychoanalyst. Fine was a preeminent writer, and several of his books have remained staples in the game's repertoire, including *Basic Chess Endings* (1941), *The Ideas Behind the Chess Openings* (1943), and the controversial *The Psychology of the Chess Player* (1967).

Other American Jews who competed successfully in the pre-Bobby Fischer years were Arnold Denker (1914–2005), 1944 U.S. Chess Champion; Herman Steiner (1905–1955), 1948 U.S. Chess Champion; Arthur Bisguier (b. 1929), 1954 U.S. Chess Champion; and Larry Evans

(b. 1932), winner of four U.S. Chess Championships (1951, 1961–1962, 1968, and 1980). An accomplished journalist and writer, Evans was Bobby Fischer's official second in the 1972 World Chess Championship.

In addition to Evans, whose best-known work is *New Ideas in Chess* (1967), important literary contributions were made by Horowitz, publisher of *Chess Review* (1933–1969), chess editor of the *New York Times* (1963–1973), and author of more than 20 books; Irving Chernev (1900–1981), an engaging writer and coauthor, with Kenneth Harkness (1898–1972), of the bestseller *Invitation to Chess*; Reinfeld, the most prolific writer in the history of the game, with more than 200 titles to his credit; and Burt Hochberg (1933–2006), who authored a number of excellent books on chess instruction and culture, such as *How to Open a Chess Game.* From 1966, when he took over as editor in chief of *Chess Life,* a position he held for 13 years, until his death in 2006, Hochberg was considered to be America's foremost chess editor and journalist.

Before Garry Kasparov, the highest-rated player of all time was Robert James Fischer. "Bobby" Fischer (1943–2008), the son of a Jewish American mother and reputedly a German father—though in recent years the identity of Fischer's father has come into question—was born in Chicago, Illinois. Fischer moved to Brooklyn, New York with his family in 1949. He was taught how to play chess that same year by his 11-year-old sister, though, according to Fischer, he did not "get good" until he was 12. Once Fischer got going, there was no stopping him.

In 1956, he won the U.S. junior championship. Later that year, in the Rosenwald Tournament, he played the "Game of the Century" against Donald Byrne (1930–1972). Experts consider that chess game the greatest ever played by a prodigy. At 14, Fischer became the youngest player ever to win the U.S. Chess Championship. Indeed, he won it all 8 times in which he competed (1957–1958, 1958–1959, 1959–1960, 1960–1961, 1962–1963, 1963–1964, 1965, and 1966). In 1958, at 15, he became the youngest grandmaster ever, and in the 1963–1964 U.S. Chess Championship Fischer triumphed over the entire field 11–0, the first and only time in the event's history that the victor has won all his games.

But Fischer's greatest achievements arguably occurred in the early 1970s. In 1970, he crushed former world champion Tigran Petrosian (1929–1984) by a score of two wins, two draws, and no losses in the USSR-vs-the Rest of the World Match. He then won the Palma de Mallorca Interzonal with 15 wins, 7 draws, and 1 loss. Fischer's victory made him one of the eight official challengers for the world championship held by Russia's Boris Spassky (b. 1937). To meet Spassky, Fischer had to defeat three of the world's top grandmasters in one-on-one matches. First up was Russia's Mark Taimanov (b. 1926), who Fischer overwhelmed 6–0, the first shutout of a grandmaster in modern times. Next was Denmark's Bent Larsen (b. 1935), and once again Fischer annihilated his opponent 6–0. That left only former champion Petrosian. As in their previous 1970 showdown, Fischer won easily, with 5 wins, 3 draws, and 1 loss, winning the last 4 games straight.

Fischer and Spassky began their historic world championship match in Reykjavik, Iceland, on July 11, 1972. Remarkably, Fischer blundered away the first game and failed to show up for the second, forfeiting it. Spassky had a two-game edge. Then Fischer won the third, fifth, sixth, eighth, and tenth games (the fourth, seventh, and ninth were drawn), building a lead that Spassky found insurmountable. When Spassky resigned the 21st game on September 1, Fischer had become the first American to win the World Chess Championship and the only non-Russian to hold the title since 1937. (In 2007, the championship was won by India's Viswanathan Anand.) Fischer opted not to defend his title in 1975, having withdrawn from public life after his 1972 victory. Thus, Anatoly Karpov (b. 1951) of Russia was awarded the title without having defeated Fischer.

It must be said, regrettably, that though Fischer contributed much to the development of American chess, there is a sad chapter in the story. Perhaps because of the pressure of the limelight, or for reasons remaining unknown, Fischer returned to the public arena in 1992. Facing Spassky in what was nothing more than a ridiculously hyped exhibition match, Fischer won decisively and then humiliated himself by remarks that were blatantly anti-American and anti-Semitic. Friends and associates tried to minimize those pronouncements as the product of a strained existence, but there is little doubt that Fischer's luster was greatly diminished.

Prior to 1992, Fischer's spectacular success had inspired a whole new wave of young talent, with American Jews once again wonderfully represented. Leading the way was Brooklyn native Joel Benjamin (b. 1964). From the age of nine, and throughout his adolescence, Benjamin was the top U.S. junior. He broke Fischer's record at 13, becoming the youngest American master, and eventually was awarded the title of grandmaster in 1986. Among his many achievements was the prominent role he played in the defeat of then-World Champion Kasparov in his Man Vs Machine confrontation with IBM's Deep Blue in 1997. It was Benjamin who served as IBM's chief chess consultant, actively taking part in the development of the super computer's arsenal of tactical and strategic weapons. In 2008, Benjamin chronicled these achievements in his winning memoir, *American Grandmaster.*

Another American Jew inspired by the game was Joshua Waitzkin (b. 1976). During the 1980s and early 1990s Waitzkin became possibly the most successful U.S. scholastic chess player, winning at least eight national events. It was Waitzkin's father, Fred Waitzkin (b. 1945), writing about his son's capturing of the 1986 National Elementary Chess Championship, who penned the acclaimed *Searching for Bobby Fischer* (1988, Simon and Schuster). In 1993, that book was turned into a revealing Paramount film of the same title. The film lured millions around the globe to chess. After becoming an International Master at 15, Waitzkin moved on to a new interest in the martial art of Tai Chi. By 2005, he had captured several prestigious distinctions, including the title of Middleweight World Co-Champion in Moving Step Push Hands. He would write about his personal approach to success in his much-admired 2007 book, *The Art of Learning.*

Other American Jewish standouts in chess during the period include grandmaster, *Chess Life* columnist, and 1989 National Open Champion Michael Rohde (b. 1959); grandmaster Patrick Wolff (b. 1968), author of *The Complete Idiot's Guide to Chess;* grandmaster and 1988 U.S. Chess Champion Michael Wilder (b. 1962); and International Master and bestselling chess author Jeremy Silman (b. 1954).

It must be added that as America has always drawn talents from foreign shores, many renowned chess players, among them numerous Jews, have immigrated to the United States to continue their achievements. Among the most prominent are Russian-born grandmaster and noted chess author Lev Alburt (b. 1945), who won the U.S. Chess Championship three times (1984, 1985, and 1990); Russian-born grandmaster Max Dlugy (b. 1966), who won the World Junior Chess Championship in 1985 and became president of the U.S. Chess Federation in 1990; German-born (though of former Russian citizenry) grandmaster Boris Gulko (b. 1947), who won the U.S. Chess Championship in 1994 and 1999; Russian-born grandmaster and trainer Leonid Yudasin (b. 1959); and Hungarian-born grandmaster Susan Polgar (b. 1969), eldest of the famed Polgar sisters, who was Women's World Chess Champion from 1996 until 1999 and the "American Grandmaster of the Year" in 2003.

In recent years Bobby Fischer has been dethroned as the game's leading exponent. When Garry Kasparov (born in 1963 as Garri Weinstein, an Armenian Jew) retired in 2005, his Elo rating of 2851 made him the highest-rated player in history. While he is a citizen of Russia, where in 2007 he announced his candidacy for the Russian presidency, his writings and charismatic personality continue to impact the game around the world. In the United States the effects of his success can be seen in the many scholastic programs he has inspired and the flourishing study of the game he has encouraged in the use of software and the Internet.

Bruce Pandolfini

Further Reading: Edmonds, David, and John Eidinow. *Bobby Fischer Goes to War.* New York: Harper Collins, 2005. Gaige, Jeremy. *Chess Personalia: A Biobibliography.* Jefferson, NC: McFarland, 1987. Greenberg, Martin. *Jewish Lists.* New York: Schocken, 1979. Pandolfini, Bruce. *The Best of Chess Life and Review,* vols. 1 and 2. New York: Simon and Schuster, 1988. Ribalow, Harold, and Meir Ribalo. *The Great Jewish Chess Champions.* New York: Hippocene, 1987. Salzmann, Jerome. *The Chess Reader.* New York: Greenberg, 1949. Shenk, David. *The Immortal Game.* New York: Doubleday, 2006. Whyld, Ken. *Chess: The Records.* New York: Oxford University Press, 1986.

CHILDREN'S LITERATURE

The first source of literature for Jewish children was naturally the Bible itself. The stories of the Bible provided a rich source of stories and morality tales that were told and retold to children. Often Jewish children learned the Bible stories secondhand, through the midrashic collections. In the United States, one of the earliest collections was *The People of the Book: A Bible History for School and Home,* by Dr. Maurice Harris (1890). Other early collections include *The Jewish Child's Bible Stories: Told in Simple Language* by Addie Richman Altman (1915), *Scripture Stories Retold for Young Israel* by Rabbi Mendel Silber (1916), *Illustrated Bible Stories* by Hyman Goldin (1930), and *Bible Tales for Very Young Children* by Lenore Cohen (1934). The goal of these books was to educate Jewish American children about sacred text and Jewish tradition. Most of these volumes were written by rabbis, or the wives of rabbis, and all were published by Jewish publishing houses.

Children's literature as a whole came into its own only in the twentieth century. The first editor to work exclusively on books for children was appointed by the Macmillan Company in 1919. As this genre established itself and quality literature intended for children was beginning to be widely published, a body of literature for American Jewish children began to emerge as well. Rather than providing accessible and appropriate versions of biblical or rabbinic texts for children, these books were meant to provide Jewish content for American children who were familiar with secular children's literature. One of the classics that appeared during this time was *The Adventures of K'tonton* (1935), by Sadie Rose Weilerstein, featuring a miniature Tom Thumb type of character. The stories taught children about the Jewish holidays and the Hebrew letters as they followed K'tonton on his adventures. Weilerstein was a pioneer in the genre of Jewish children's literature, also publishing holiday-based and value-based story books such as *Danny Bumps into Chanukah* (1937) and *Dick, the Horse That Kept the Sabbath* (1955).

In 1951, Sydney Taylor began to publish her All-of-a-Kind-Family series, about a group of Jewish sisters (and eventually one brother) growing up on the Lower East Side in New York City. Taylor's fondly nostalgic portrayal of Jewish life introduced a generation of Jewish Americans to a gently whitewashed version of their parents or grandparents' lives. The five sisters, Ella, Charlotte, Sarah, Henny, and Gertie, are Jewish and celebrate Jewish holidays against a backdrop of immigration and genteel poverty. Unlike the books that were published to teach American Jews how to seamlessly maintain their Judaism while being authentically and comfortably American, these books focus on learning to become American. Their aspirations are those of first-generation Americans who know what it is to be Jewish, but who strive to succeed as Americans. The books deal with issues like learning how to get a library card, not being embarrassed by a newly arrived relative's accent, and real fears like scarlet fever. Though they are a large, poor family squeezed into a small tenement apartment, the outlook of these books is cheerful and optimistic.

Judaism is presented as a colorful backdrop rather than the primary point of the stories. In their wholesome sunniness and can-do attitude, these books were a Jewish version of Laura Ingalls Wilder's Little House series. What is also significant about Taylor's series is that it was originally published by Follett, a secular trade publisher, rather than a Jewish publisher. Marketed to a wide audience, these books introduced non-Jewish readers to Judaism in a nonthreatening, heartwarming way.

Jewish publishers like the Jewish Publication Society, Union of American Hebrew Congregations, and Behrman House were also involved in helping to establish a body of American Jewish children's literature. These included a series of holiday books by Sophia N. Cedarbaum and illustrated by Clare and John Ross. Published by the Reform Movement's Union of American Hebrew Congregations in the 1960s, this series about a pair of siblings, Debbie and Danny, attempted to portray Jews as modern Americans. There is not one kippah in the books—even the rabbi is bareheaded. While Weilerstein's K'tonton books showed a more Conservative Jewish approach to being a Jew in America, Cedarbaum's books reflected an authentic Judaism in sync with Reform Judaism of that time. Jewish children were able to see their lives reflected in the pages of Cedarbaum's books as they read about Debbie and Danny leading fully American lives in a Jewish context. This series was followed in the early 1970s by a group of books written by Molly Cone and known as the Shema series. These books use Jewish folktales to address ideas about God and Jewish peoplehood. They have remained so popular that they were revised and repackaged into one volume entitled *Hello, Hello, Are You There, God?* (1998).

In the late 1960s and early 1970s the number of Jewish-themed children's books published by commercial trade publishers began to increase substantially. As distinct from the Jewish publishers, these books were aimed at the secular Jewish market and the library market, as well as the multicultural market. Rather than vehicles to inculcate Jewish values or customs, these books were meant to be literature with Jewish themes that were universal enough to be understood and appreciated by Jews and non-Jews alike. One author who made the transition from Jewish children's books meant for a sectarian market to books for a wider readership was Shulamith Ish-Kishor. Largely unknown today, in the 1930s and 1940s she published books intended for Jewish religious school use like the three-volume *Children's History of Israel from Creation to the Present* (1933). Later she wrote Jewish-themed novels, most notably *A Boy of Old Prague* (1963), a National Jewish Book Award winner, and *Our Eddie* (1969), which was a Newbery Medal Honor Book and received a Sydney Taylor Book Award.

In 1968, the Association of Jewish Libraries (AJL) created a children's book award called the Shirley Kravitz Children's Book Award. The first award was given to Esther Hautzig in 1968 for *The Endless Steppe,* a novel about her family's experiences during World War II. After the death of Sydney Taylor, author of the All-of-a-Kind Family series, in 1978, the award was renamed the "Sydney Taylor Book Award." The purpose of the award is to "encourage publication of outstanding books with positive Jewish content for children" (AJL). Two awards are given in different age groups, and Honor Books and Notable Books are selected as well.

The Sydney Taylor awards, along with the National Jewish Book awards, are highly respected and represent significant honor for a book. In addition to these awards, there are two major awards given by the American Library Association for children's books, the Caldecott Medal and Honor awards, for outstanding illustration of a children's book, and the Newbery Medal and Honor awards, for distinguished contributions to the field of children's literature. These awards are often used by librarians and teachers, as well as parents, to determine the quality of books for children. As a body of Jewish literature developed for children, Jewish-themed books began to win Caldecott and Newbery awards, signaling their appeal beyond the Jewish world.

The themes found in Ish-Kishor's novels, of immigration and ethnicity, remain a frequent theme for Jewish Young Adult (YA) literature. *Letters from Rivka* by Karen Hesse (1993), a National Jewish Book Award winner, dealt with the immigration of Jewish girl from Russia to America. Israel is another theme of Jewish YA novels, with examples like *The Garden* by Carol Matas (1996), which tells the story of a teenage Holocaust survivor working on a kibbutz during the founding of Israel in 1947, and *Real Time* by Pnina Moed Kass (2004), a Sydney Taylor Book Award winner, which deals with the painful realities of contemporary Israel. However, the most common theme for Jewish YA novels by trade publishers are **Holocaust**-related novels, like *The Upstairs Room* by Johanna Reiss (1972), a Newbery Honor Book, and *When Hitler Stole Pink Blanket* by Judith Kerr. Noteworthy additions in this category also include *The Devil's Arithmetic* by Jane Yolen (1988) and *Number the Stars* by Lois Lowry (1990), a Newbery Medal book. The Holocaust has also been a topic for children's picture books, with examples like David Adler's *The Number on My Grandfather's Arm* (1987), which received a Sydney Taylor Book Award.

Story collections are an important part of Jewish children's literature. **Isaac Bashevis Singer**, winner of the Nobel Prize for Literature in 1978, published several collections which have a significant place in the canon. These include *Zlateh the Goat and Other Stories* (1967) and *When Shlemiel Went to Warsaw and Other Stories* (1969), both of which were named Newbery Honor Books. Singer's stories introduced American children to life in Eastern Europe and his retellings of the cleverly foolish Chelm stories have enabled those characters to remain alive for subsequent generations. Newer story collections include *My Grandmother's Stories: A Collection of Jewish Folk Tales,* by Adele Geras (1990); *The Adventures of Herschel of Ostropov,* by Eric Kimmel and illustrated by Trina Schart Hyman (1995); and *The Angel's Mistake: Stories of Chelm,* by Francine Prose and illustrated by Mark Podwal (1997).

In the picture book category, many of the Jewish books put out by trade publishers fall into one of five theme areas. A popular theme is retellings of Jewish folk tales, including both Eastern European stories set in the Old Country like *It Could Always Be Worse: A Yiddish Folktale* by Margot Zemach (1990), a Caldecott Honor Book, and *Joseph Had a Little Overcoat* by Simms Taback, a Caldecott Medal book (1999), as well as stories from other parts of the Jewish world like *The Shadow of a Flying Bird: A Legend from the Kurdistani Jews* by Mordicai Gerstein (1994). The many books based on the legend of the Golem figure are also part of this group. Most notable are *The Golem: A Jewish Legend* by Beverly Brodsky McDermott (1977), a Caldecott Honor Book, and *Golem* by David Wisniewski (1997), a Caldecott Medal winner.

Retellings of Bible stories like *David and Goliath* by Leonard Everett Fisher (1993) and *The Moses Basket* by Jenny Koralek (2003), a Sydney Taylor Honor Award winner, remain a central part of Jewish children's literature, with contemporary authors continuing to find inspiration in the biblical text. As in the YA category, a third theme is related to immigration to America, with examples like *Molly's Pilgrim* by Barbara Cohen (1983). A very common theme is Jewish holidays, with Hanukkah and Passover the two most popular.

Eric Kimmel is a highly respected author of Jewish children's books who has written many holiday picture books, including the Caldecott Honor book *Hershel and the Hanukkah Goblins,* illustrated by Trina Schart Hyman (1994). Other examples are Barbara Diamond Goldin and Jane Breskin Zalben who have both written numerous holiday-themed books, many of which have won awards. The last, though probably quickly disappearing group in the picture book category is books that tell stories about Jewish life several generations back in the United States, and in particular on the Lower East Side, most notably *The Carp in the Bathtub* by Barbara Cohen (1983) and *The Castle on Hester Street* by Linda Heller (1982), a Sydney Taylor Award winner. Other examples from Jewish American history include *A Mountain of Blintzes* (2001) by Barbara Diamond Goldin, unusual in that it captures Jewish life at its peak in the **Catskills**, and *Chanukah on the Prairie* by Burt Schuman and illustrated by Rosalind Charney Kaye (2002), a Sydney Taylor Honor book, which tells the story of pioneer Jewish life in Grand Forks, North Dakota.

In addition to the Sydney Taylor Book awards, the Association of Jewish Libraries has been giving Sydney Taylor Body of Work Awards periodically since 1971 to authors who have made significant contributions to Jewish children's literature. The first winner of this award was Isaac Bashevis Singer. Other winners include Molly Cone (1972), Barbara Cohen (1980), Barbara Diamond Goldin (1997), and Eric Kimmel (2004).

Hara Person

Further Reading: Cullinan, Bernice E., and Diane G. Person, eds. *The Continuum Encyclopedia of Children's Literature.* New York: Continuum Publishing, 2001. Krasner, Jonathan. "A Recipe for American Jewish Integration: The Adventures of K'tonton and Hillel's Happy Holidays" from *The Lion and the Unicorn* 27, no. 3 (2003): 344–361.

COBB, LEE J. (1911–1976)

Lee J. Cobb was one of the entertainment industry's most versatile actors who excelled on both the stage and in film. The son of a newspaper editor, Cobb (Leo Jacoby) was born on New York's Lower East Side in 1911. Cobb was a musical prodigy, mastering both violin and harmonica at an early age. When a broken wrist dashed any hope of a career as a violinist, the 16-year old Cobb headed to Hollywood as a member of Borrah Minevitch and His Harmonica Rascals. Unable to find work in Hollywood, Cobb returned to New York, where he attended City College of New York and began appearing on stage. Cobb made his Broadway debut in a short-lived production of Dostoevsky's *Crime and Punishment*. In 1935, Cobb became a part of the Group Theatre, where he received glowing reviews for his performances in **Clifford Odet**'s *Waiting for Lefty* and *Golden Boy.*

Over the next decade, Cobb moved between Broadway and Hollywood. In the 1939 film version of *Golden Boy,* Cobb portrayed the father of violinist-turned-boxer Joe Bonaparte, played by William Holden. Only seven years older than Holden, Cobb played a convincing older man, something he would do for the rest of his career. In 1949, Cobb scored his greatest Broadway triumph as the original Willy Loman in **Arthur Miller**'s *Death of a Salesman.*

A much-celebrated character actor, Cobb appeared in more than 100 films. Among his best-known were *On the Waterfront* (1954), *12 Angry Men*(1957), ***Exodus*** (1960), and *How the West Was Won* (1963). From 1962–1966, Cobb starred in the acclaimed television series *The Virginian.*

In the 1950s, Cobb was subpoenaed before the House Un-American Activities Committee to answer charges of whether he had ever been a communist. Likely, the charges stemmed from having been a member of the left-wing Actor's Theater. When Cobb's wife suffered a nervous breakdown, Cobb decided to testify and "name names." Ironically, he would receive his first Academy Award Nomination for 1954's *On the Waterfront,* whose screenwriter (**Budd Schulberg**) and director (Elia Kazan) had also been friendly witnesses.

Cobb, who was the original choice to play the idiosyncratic detective "Columbo," died of a heart attack in Woodland Hills, California at age 64. *See also* **Film**; **Theater**.

Kurt F. Stone

Further Reading: Navasky, Victor S., *Naming Names.* New York: Viking Press, 1980.

THE COEN BROTHERS

Joel (1954–) and Ethan (1957–) Coen are award-winning and critically acclaimed filmmakers. They were born in St. Park, Minnesota, a suburb of Minneapolis, the sons of Jewish parents, Edward and Rena Coen. Both parents were academics. Their father taught economics at the University of Minnesota and their mother, art history at St. Cloud State University. This privileged background likely played a role in the brothers' intellectual and creative development.

As children they experimented with filmmaking and began a habit that would be the hallmark of their more mature film productions: borrowing and adapting classic film subjects and individuals from recent American history. Reportedly, **Henry Kissinger** was the subject of one of their earliest films. Another was an adaptation of the classic Cornel Wilde film *The Naked Prey* (1966) in which Ethan played a spear-toting native, not in the American West, but in Africa.

Both brothers attended college in Great Barrington, Massachusetts but parted ways academically after graduation. Joel earned a degree at New York University's Film School, while Ethan received a degree in philosophy from Princeton with a thesis on Ludwig Wittgenstein, the Australian British philosopher. The 1980s marked the beginning of the brothers' creative collaborations. Joel had gained valuable experience in film editing working with filmmaker Sam Raimi, and he and Ethan wrote and directed their first film *Blood Simple* (1984).

This noirish drama was warmly received by critics, who were enthused by the brothers' mixture of elements of the classic detective drama with horror. Critical reception of this first effort set high expectations for future work. The film's star, Frances McDormand, appeared in five other Coen brothers productions. She also married Joel. Ethan also married into the film industry: his wife is Tricia Cooke, a film editor. Both couples reside in New York City.

After *Blood Simple* the Coen brothers produced an uneven series of films that were alternately acclaimed and lambasted by critics. These included *Raising Arizona* (1987), *Barton Fink* (1991),*The Hudsucker Proxy* (1994), *Fargo* (1996), *The Big Lebowski*—a film that apparently owes much to their Jewish heritage (1998), *O Brother, Where Art Thou* (2000),*Intolerable Cruelty* (2003), and the recent award-winning *No Country for Old Men* (2007). In these films the Coen brothers were alternately praised and criticized for recycling themes and treatments found in classic film noir and screwball comedies of the 1930s and 1940s. Their originality in adapting Homer's *Odyssey* to the Depression-era South is matched by the creative approach they bring to film production.

Storyboarding, the technique of plotting film sequences, is applied by the brothers to every segment of their productions. In this way they control every aspect of their films. Besides utilizing innovative camera and editing techniques, the brothers have also assumed the disparate roles of screenwriter, editor (under the pseudonym of Roderick Jaynes), director, and producer.

Combining a penchant for recycling film classics, a predilection for graphic violence, and a tendency to capture various aspects of urban and rural America, the Coen brother creations have been nominated for nine academy awards, winning three for screenplays and direction (*Fargo* and *No Country for Old Men*). Frances McDormand received the Oscar for Best Actress for her work in *Fargo*. In addition the brothers have won awards from BAFTA (British Academy of Film and Television Arts) and at the Cannes Film Festival. Much is expected from them in the future. *See also* **Film**.

Leroy T. Hopkins Jr.

Further Reading: Allen, William Rodney, ed. *The Coen Brothers Interviews.* Conversations With Filmmakers Series. Jackson, MS: University of Mississippi Press, 2006. Rowell, Erica. *The Brothers Grim: The Films of Ethan and Joel Coen.* Latham, MD: The Scarecrow Press, 2007.

COLEN, DANIEL (1979–)

Colen is a young American Jewish artist who has received acclaim for his paintings, which have been exhibited at the Whitney Museum in New York and solo shows in Los Angeles, Berlin, and London. Daniel Colen was born on July 13,

A photo of *Do Not Disturb,* a mixed-media sculpture work by artist Dan Colen, who has exhibited at the Whitney and major museums in Berlin and London. [Dan Colen—Private Collection, Courtesy Peres Projects, Los Angeles, Berlin, Athens]

1979 in Leonia, New Jersey, and is a graduate of the Solomon Schechter Day School. Two years after graduating from Rhode Island School of Design, he moved to New York City's East Village, where he became a key player in the downtown cultural scene and had his first solo show. His paintings combine realism and fantasy, seriousness and whimsy, spiritual ambiguities and existential mysteries. In June 2006, Dan Colen had his breakout year as an artist. His work was shown in museums in New York City, London, Oslo, and Passariano and in solo shows in Manhattan, Los Angeles, and Berlin. One sculpture sold on the secondary market for $500,000, a tenfold leap from his previous benchmark price. *Vanity Fair* magazine selected him in the December 2006 issue as a "Rising Star in the Art Universe."

While his originality, edginess, and daring, as well as virtuoso brushwork, composition, and color remain constant, his subjects, styles, and mediums are increasingly diverse: from slick, stylized portraits of friends, Colen turned to hip-hop culture and painted a series of diamond studded pendants worn by rap stars, with hundreds of meticulously rendered jeweled facets. The effect was dazzling.

His tours de force at the Whitney Biennial 2006 were three faux boulders, six feet high, painted as if covered in graffiti, gum, and bird poop. (One was purchased by the museum.) By the show's end, Colen's work was coveted by top collectors on three continents.

For his solo show in Berlin, he produced over 60 paintings, sculptures, drawings, photographs, a collage, and an installation. The work ranged from realistic to abstract. A seven-foot sculpture topped with Jewish prayer shawls was Colen's audacious way of introducing himself as a Jew to the German public.

For inspiration, Colen draws upon personal experiences, feelings, and imagination, as well as the work of artists such as Ed Ruscha. He is deeply affected by the youth culture—its angst, nonconformity, edginess, turbulence, chutzpah, cool, cynicism, and loyalties; its searching, addictions, irreverence, hopes, humor, and vernacular. His art explores terrain from nostalgia to nonsense; from devastation to preservation; from the metaphorical to the shocking; from the inevitability of death to questions of faith, memory, and immortality, and from the Zeitgeist and passage of time to the shaping of experience.

Continuing a family tradition of tzedakah, Colen's most recent gift was a painting in support of an art enrichment program for Ethiopian Israeli youth. *See also* **Artists**.

Sy Colen

Further Reading: Levy, Ariel. "Chasing Dash Snow." *New York Magazine,* January 15, 2007. Wakefield,

Neville. "Share Your Feelings" (interview with Dan Colen). *I.D.,* February 2007.

COMEDY

In twentieth-century America, the roll call of Jewish comics to have made their mark on stage and screen, or in nightclubs, **vaudeville**, **radio**, and **television** spanned the alphabet from A to Z, from Allen to Zero; that is, **Zero Mostel**. American comedy has sometimes appeared to be a Jewish invention. There is no greater sign of modernity or of cultural cachet than the fact that only a generation after Jews were changing their names wholesale to pass as Americans, a African American comedian born Caryn Elaine Johnson gave a rocket boost to her visibility by taking the stage name of Whoopi Goldberg.

Jews been so omnipresent in comedy that in the period between roughly 1920, when they entered the mainstream of American entertainment, until the present, they have revolutionized American comedy. Their earthy wit, irreverent satire, bold idioms, and tart one-liners—uttered as if in preparation for fight or flight, their extravagant routines, and the machine-gun-chatter of their deliveries constituted a new style—a style that replaced the droll and folksy humor associated with the likes of Mark Twain and Will Rogers and, in our time, Garrison Keillor. "Indeed it is difficult," claim William Novak and Moshe Waldoks in *The Big Book of Jewish Humor* (1981), "to imagine what would remain of American humor in the twentieth century without its Jewish component." **Woody Allen** (Alan Stewart Konigsberg), Morey Amsterdam, Roseanne Barr, Belle Barth, **Jack Benny** (Benjamin Kubelsky), **Milton Berle** (Milton Berlinger), Shelly Berman, Joey Bishop, David Brenner, **Mel Brooks** (Melvin Kaminsky), **Lenny Bruce** (Leonard Schneider), **Red Buttons** (Aaron Chwatt), Myron Cohen, Billy Crystal, Rodney Dangerfield (Jacob Cohen), Shecky Green, Buddy Hackett (Leonard Hacker), Goldie Hawn, **Danny Kaye** (David Daniel Kaminsky), Robert Klein, Jack E. Leonard (Leonard Lebitsky), Sam Levenson, **Jerry Lewis** (Jerome Leivitch), the **Marx Brothers**, **Jackie Mason** (Yacov Moshe Maza), Bette Midler, the **Ritz Brothers**, Gilda Radner, Don Rickles, **Joan Rivers**, Mort Sahl, **Soupy Sales** (Milton Supman), **Jerry Seinfeld, Sarah Silverman**, Sophie Tucker, **Gene Wilder** (Jerome Silberman), and **Henny Youngman** are names extracted from a list so long that an encyclopedia entry could be composed out of names alone.

This astonishing Jewish presence in American comedy begs for explanations, and they have been abundant. Those most commonly adduced are variants on the "laughter through tears" thesis that contends that humor arose among the Ashkenazic Jews of Eastern Europe and Russia during times of poverty and persecution as a way of maintaining community morale. American Jewish comedy, in this view, is the flip side of poverty, heartbreak, and the disasters of a long diaspora existence among cruel strangers. Jewish laughter was an import that came wrapped in Jewish tears. A translator of Sholem Aleichem, Hillel Halkin, praises the "therapeutic force" of Sholem Aleichem's humor, which left the Jews of his time "feeling immeasurably better about themselves and their fate as Jews" (1996). Such explanations cannot be denied, for it does seem that humor and comedy flourish among oppressed peoples, who cultivate laughter as a balm for their wounds. The rich strains of comedy in Ireland and Black America appear to give cross-cultural confirmation of this thesis.

While "laughter through tears" says something about the therapeutic purposes of Jewish humor and comedy, it says nothing about their unique forms—the incisive social observation, the nervous physical movements, the tension that detonates in the punch line, the breakneck pace of delivery, the supersonic monologue sometimes called "the shpritz"—or about how it was that Jews should flourish as comics in America, where the tears of the past were stanched by opportunities on a scale unparalleled in the history of the diaspora.

If American Jewish comedy was conceived in grief, it came of age in a land of rising expectations. "Laughter through tears" also leaves us unenlightened about how a Jewish comedy of sorrow gained such eager applause from Yankees, Italians, Irish, Poles, and African Americans. One might surmise from this broad appeal that though Jewish comedy acted out the uniqueness of Jewish culture and history, it also served to ease assimilation for other groups new to, or feeling oppressed by, America. Bringing Jewish voices into the center of American life—by radio, television, and film—made it clear that for all their differences, Jews were like everyone else, only more so. The voice might be Jewish, but the echo chamber was America.

It is one of the ironies of comedy that the language of the Jewish comics in America has been largely English, though an English steeped in the tumult, fret, feistiness, and homely realism of **Yiddish**. Jewish humor and comedy—and the two should be distinguished—rrived in the New World ready to be unpacked and assembled. It was already embodied in a tradition of storytelling, a treasury of folk sayings and anecdotes, and an astringent wit that needed only the opportunity and staging grounds to become as American as the bagel nosh.

Despite the dire and sometimes desperate circumstances of Jewish history or the unremitting sobriety of the Jewish holy books, humor has been a defining feature of Ashkenazic Jewish culture. Doubtless the ultimate sources of this comic spirit are buried in the unrecorded folk life of Ashkenazic Jewry. Humor has little place in the Jewish holy books and played a minor role in rabbinic Judaism, and as for the theater, it was disdained by the rabbis of the Middle Ages as the "seat of the scornful." The one significant point of contact between rabbinic Judaism and the Yiddish comic spirit was in the festival of Purim. Purim, which celebrates the rescue of the Persian Jews from Haman, lieutenant of King Ahasuerus, by Queen Esther and her cousin Mordecai, was traditionally celebrated as a festival of license in which common restraints were abandoned and conventional pieties mocked. Drunkenness was encouraged, vulgarity and profanity were given license, masquerading and cross dressing between men and women promoted, and Torah and Talmud were held up to ridicule.

The centerpiece of the Purim festivity was the Purim *shpil,* the recitation by a "Purim rabbi" of a ludicrous "Purim Torah," which parodied some familiar liturgical text and ridiculed the subtleties of Midrash. The Purim *shpil* was sometimes accompanied by a comic play performed by clowns and fools, and there was even, according to Nahma Sandrow, historian of the **Yiddish theater**, a typology of such clowns: "the *lets, nar, marshelik, badkhen,* and *payets*" (1977). *Lets* and *nar* were simple clowns who did slapstick and pratfalls, while the *marshelik* was a master of ceremonies who specialized in Talmudic wordplay and disputation. The *badkhen,* also a master of wordplay, traditionally performed at weddings, where he recited long rhymed sermons. The *payets* was the narrator and stage director of the Purim play. This normalization of a comic and even insurrectionary spirit under the umbrella of the Purim festivity suggests a strategy by which the religious life accommodated the comic and turned anarchic tendencies to the service of observance itself: binding restless Yiddish folk humor by giving it the limited sanction of its own festival.

If the Purim *shpil* and the Yiddish theater are the proximate ancestors of modern Jewish comedy, then comedy inherited something of the unruliness of those institutions, inherited the tension between rabbinic Judaism and cultural Yiddishism that reached a pitch in the nineteenth century, when Yiddish asserted itself as a language of art and culture. If Jewish humor is continuous with the folk life of the Ashkenazic Jews, touching with affection all things, sacred and secular, that constituted that life, then Jewish comedy (as distinct from humor) may even dispense with that affection and be mutinous and discordant. The humorist acts as a mirror, reflecting back to the community in exaggerated form its particular slant on life. The comedian, however, is a figure apart in the community, but not of it. At his most extreme he is a shaman, who takes upon his shoulders the sins of the community and purges them through his sufferings. Think of Lenny Bruce. The early travails of **Philip Roth** sometimes appeared sacrificial in that way. If we think of Jewish humor as it crystallized in the writing of Sholem Aleichem and would be carried to the stage by the likes of Myron Cohen, Jack Benny, Woody Allen, or Jerry Seinfeld; and if by comedy we mean the aggressive farce and mad antics of the Marx Brothers, **Sid Caesar**, or Mel Brooks; or the insult comedy of Don Rickles, Joan Rivers, and Roseanne Barr, then it is plain that we are dealing with different forms of the comic spirit and different refractions of Jewish life. The humorists are sentimental, gemütlich, and warm; the comics agitated, theatrical, and prickly.

Old-World import, it was not until it hit the New World that anyone saw Jewish comedy but Jews. Imagine the Marx Brothers performing in Odessa or Krakow. "A Night at the Opera" would have quickly become "A Night at the Pogrom." They would have been in "Duck Soup." Only in America was Jewish humor exposed to a larger public—to become show business for all Americans. This transformation took place in New York's **Catskill Mountains** where, early in the twentieth century, vacationers congregated to relax, play, mate, and eat lavishly. The great hotels like the Concord, Grossinger's, and Kutcher's are now names deeply embedded into the lore of American Jewish life. There it was that the*nar* worked up his *narishkeit* and the *badkhen* was transfigured into the *tummler*: a stirrer up of tumult.

Typically, the aspiring entertainer was a jack-of-all-trades for hotel shows: producer, director, writer, actor, song-and-dance man, emcee, comedian, set designer, stagehand, electrician, even waiter. As Joey Adams remembers it, "after the show he had to mingle with the guests, dance with the fat old women and romance the dogs. In addition, he was the *shadchen* or marriage broker" (Brown, 2002). What talent hatched from that incubator: Buddy Hackett, Danny Kaye, Sid Caesar, Milton Berle, Jackie Mason, and others. The Borscht Belt was a sweatshop for the mass production of comedians, specializing in ready-to-laugh, and in the 1950s, when television was live and comedy was king, comedians skilled in the needle trades were at a premium. No other American ethnic culture produced anything remotely comparable.

No word on Jewish comedy is complete without remarking on the place of Yiddish in its formation. Jewish comedy's fundamental repertoire of mannerisms originates in the Yiddish language, whose earthiness and realism made it ideal for deflating pretension. The qualities that suited Yiddish for comedy derive from its subordination as a homely jargon, a *mamaloschen,* to the *loshen ha-kodesh* of the Jews: Hebrew. The Ashkenazim of Eastern Europe inhabited two worlds. One was the world of labor and trade, money, politics, love, marriage, family, hunger, flight, death. Its domain was sundown on Saturday through sundown the following Friday, and its language was Yiddish. The other was the world of the Sabbath, of prayer and study, Torah and Talmud, faith and prophecy. Exalted and transcendent, its language was Hebrew. In daily life the languages tended to fuse, as Yiddish penetrated the language of prayer and Hebrew formed a sacred canopy over common speech.

This jostling of higher and lower within the mental theaters of the Jewish people set the terms for a comedy of deflation, whose basic maneuver was a sudden thrusting downward from the exalted to the workaday. Yiddish was tailor-made for creating punch lines. From Sholem Aleichem to Sid Caesar to Woody Allen, this comedy of internal juxtaposition has been fundamental. In Sholem Aleichem's *The Adventures of Menahem-Mendl,* for example, the ritual openings of all the letters between the wandering Menahem-Mendl and his long-suffering wife, Sheineh-Sheindl, are stylistic melanges, in which the exalted sentiments of the Hebrew salutation are brought low by plain truths uttered in Yiddish.

> To my dear, esteemed, renowned, and honored husband, the wise and learned Menahem-Mendl, may his light shine forever. In the first place, I

> want to let you know that we are all, praise the Lord, perfectly well, and may we hear the same from you, please God, and never anything worse. In the second place, I am writing to say, my dearest husband, my darling, my sweet one—may an epidemic sweep all enemies away! You villain, you monster, you scoundrel, you know very well that your wife is on her deathbed after the reparation which that wonderful doctor made on me—I wish it on all your Yehupetz ladies! The result is I can hardly drag my feet. (Sholem Aleichem, *The Adventures of Menahem-Mendl,* translated from the Yiddish by Tamara Kahana. New York: G.P. Putnam's Sons, 1969.)

Even in translation, it is clear that the comedy of the elevated, formal, and false is being sabotaged by the plain, vernacular, and honest. Jewish comedy is always like this. Consider the hoary joke quoted by **Sigmund Freud** in his *Jokes and their Relation to the Unconscious* (1905). It virtually defines the genre.

> A doctor, having come to deliver the baby of a Baroness, pronounced after examining her that the moment had not come and suggested to the Baron that they in the meantime enjoy a game of cards in the next room. After a while a cry of pain from the Baroness struck the ears of the two men: *"Ah, mon Dieu, mon Dieu, que je souffre!"* The Baron sprang up, but the doctor signaled to him to sit down: "It's nothing. Let's go on with our game!" A little later there were again cries from the pregnant woman: *"Mein Gott, Mein Gott, welche schreckliche Schmerzen!"* "Aren't you going in to her, Doctor?" asked the Baron. "No, no, it's not time yet." At last there came from next door an unmistakable scream of "Oh, Gottenyu! Gottenyu!" The doctor threw down his cards and exclaimed: *"Now* it's time."

"Gottenyu" is Yiddish for "Dear God," and I have heard this joke with the even more earthy punch line of simply "Gevalt, gevalt." This joke strips away the pretensions in the Baroness's self-exposure of—guess who?—a Yid.

So much Jewish humor takes this form. Woody Allen's humor is an almost routine yoking of the elevated and the common, which sometimes produces explosive punch lines. In *God,* a one-act play on the death of God, a modern rendition of a Greek tragedy goes haywire and gets away from both cast and playwright, until Zeus is lowered from on high to put things in order and is accidentally strangled by the machinery. "God is dead," announces an actor. "Is he covered by anything?" responds a physician rushing up from the audience. But unlike the traditional "Gevalt" joke, or the humor of Sholem Aleichem, this is now American comedy: a comedy of deflation, anti-profundity, of Sophocles strangled, of Nietzsche on his knees.

It is this ready availability of formal designs that are also ancient properties of the Jewish mind in exile, more so than the specific details of Jewish history, that have made Jewish humor and comedy possible. Russian poet Osip Mandelstam famously said, "As a little bit of musk fills an entire house, so the least influence of Judaism overflows all of one's life" (1905). We can alter that ever so slightly in accounting for the persistence of Jewish comedy, even in places where the Yiddish language is no longer spoken. "As a little bit of musk fills an entire house, so the least influence of Yiddish overflows all of one's life."

The Yiddish language in passing left behind its musk: earthy, blunt, rebellious, powerfully musical, that promises a continued vitality for Jewish comedy among those who continue living in its afterglow. That musk remains, even as Jewish life and culture is being transformed—in America, in Israel, in Russia—into something quite different from what either Sholem Aleichem or the Catskill comics could have imagined it to be. *See also* **The Catskills**; **Yiddish**; **Yiddish Film**; **Yiddish Theater**.

Mark Shechner

Further Reading: Aleichem, Sholem. *Tevye the Dairyman and the Railroad Stories,* translated by Hillel Halkin. New York: Schocken, 1996. Boskin, Joseph. *Rebellious Laughter.* Syracuse, NY: Syracuse University Press, 1997. Brown, Phil, ed. *In the Catskills: A Century of the Jewish Experience in "The Mountains."* New York: Columbia University Press, 2002. Cohen, Sarah Blacher, ed. *From Hester Street to Hollywood: Jewish-*

American Stage and Screen. Bloomington, IN: Indiana University Press, 1986. ———, ed. *Jewish Wry: Essays on Jewish Humor.* Bloomington, IN: Indiana University Press, 1987. Epstein, Lawrence J. *The Haunted Smile: The Story of Jewish Comedians in America.* New York: Public Affairs, 2001. Novak, William, and Moshe Waldoks, eds. *The Big Book of Jewish Humor.* New York: Harper and Row, 1981. Sandrow, Nahma. *Vagabond Stars: A World History of Yiddish Theater.* New York: Harper and Row, 1977.

COMIC BOOKS

The first American retail comic book was published by Max Ginsberg Gaines and Harry L. Wildensberg in February 1934. It was entitled *Famous Funnies.* It was a collection of backlog comic strips like *Joe Palooka, Mutt and Jeff,* and *Hairbreadth Harry.* Others soon followed, but soon they ran out of the newspaper comic strips that could be reprinted and had to turn to unemployed writers and artists to fill the gap. These writers were unemployed because they were too young, or inexperienced, or perhaps because they were Jewish and employers would not hire Jews. Newspapers and advertising companies of that time rarely hired Jews such as Milt Gross and Rube Goldberg. Comic book companies like Timely Comics or DC Comics, on the other hand, were run by Jewish publishers and did not hesitate to hire Jewish cartoonists.

Lyonel Feininger, 1871–1956, a founder of the Bauhaus, became a celebrated painter who worked as a comic artist from 1906 to 1907 and produced *The Kin-der-Kids* and *Wee Willie Winkie's World* for the *Chicago Tribune.* Although he was not Jewish, his wife was part Jewish, and both were forced to leave Germany when the Nazis came to power in 1933.

William Eisner, 1917–2005, author of *The Spirit, Expose Protocol of Elder of Zion,* and *Expose of Fagan,* used background to portray the psychological state of his characters. *The Spirit,* which was inaugurated in 1940 and continued until 1952, was an important bridge between comics and comic books. He is credited with publishing the first modern graphic novel, entitled *A Contract with God and Other Tenement Stories.* Eisner also pioneered in the comic book industry as a "packager," by creating the assembly line method of production. Working in a loft, he supervised and participated in the creation of thousands of pages of comic stories. Eisner later became an instructor in the animation department of the School of Visual Arts.

Jules Feiffer, also from New York, was born in the Bronx in 1929. As with many other artists, he developed an interest in drawing when he was a youngster, but he wrote novels, plays, and screenplays as well. Many of his drawings dealt with modern life, politics, and folk ways of the American people. His work was followed by people throughout the world. As he grew up in the Bronx his favorite cartoons were *Popeye, Terry and the Pirates,* and *Flash Gordon.* After James Monroe High School Feiffer enrolled in the Art Students' League. He wanted very much to become a cartoonist. From 1947 to 1951 he studied at Pratt Institute and became an assistant to Will Eisner working on *The Spirit.* As Eisner stopped working on *The Spirit,* from 1952 Feiffer became its main writer. By that time he had his own comic feature called *Clifford.* When he was in the army he produced cartoons for the Signal Corps. He continued his career as a cartoonist once his military service ended.

By 1956 Feiffer's political cartoons appeared in the *Village Voice.* His weekly comic strip was called *Feiffer.* He would author various plays and books. In 1967 he authored a musical comedy called *Little Murders* which was made into a film in 1968. Among the list of his plays are: *Crawling Around* (1961), *Only When I Laugh* (1967), *The White House Murder Case* (1969), *Knock Knock* (1976),*Grownups* (1981), and *Carnal Knowledge* (1971). Among his children's books are: *The Man in the Ceiling* (1993), *A Barrel of Laughs* and *A Vale of Tears* (1995), *Meanwhile* (1997), *I Lost My Bear* (1998), *Bark* and *George* (1999). In the area of political cartoons Feiffer attacked Richard Nixon and Lyndon Johnson for the war in Vietnam. He received a Pulitzer Prize for his editorial cartooning.

Jack Kirby (1917–1994) was one of the most productive and influential artists in the world of comic books. He is said to have produced more than 24,000 pages of comic book art and authored with Joe Simon the patriotic story of Captain America—super soldier in 1941, the Fantastic Four, the Hulk, and Thor. Kirby was born Jacob Kurtzberg in New York City, on August 28, 1917. He grew up on the Lower East Side. He liked drawing from the time he was a child. Often one would find him drawing on the walls and floor of the tenement building where he lived. As a teenager, with little or no professional training, he found a job at Max Fischer's animation studio, where he drew "in-between" frames for the *Popeye* cartoons. Shortly thereafter he landed a job drawing for the Lincoln Newspaper Syndicate. By 1938 he entered the comic book field drawing such superheroes as Blue Bolt. He teamed up with Joe Simon, and in 1940, Timely Comics asked them to produce a patriotic superhero. They came up with Captain America, who was dedicated to fighting Hitler and the German Nazis. This was followed in 1942 by *Boy Commandos,* which featured a group of heroic young American soldiers. It sold more than a million copies per issue.

With Stan Lee (1922–), born Stanley Martin Lieber, the son of Romanian Jewish immigrants, Kirby founded Marvel Comics and subsequently penned some of the most popular comic heroes, such as the Fantastic Four in 1961 and the Incredible Hulk in 1962, among others. Both Kirby and Lee were drafted and served during World War II. When they came back they found the comic book industry in a slump, as religious leaders and psychologists claimed that comic books contributed to juvenile delinquency and crime. But in 1956, Kirby was employed by DC Comics, where he drew the adventures of the Green Arrow and worked on various mystery and science fiction comics. From there he was hired by Marvel Comics and teamed up with Stan Lee. In 1961, they created comics which included Nick Fury, Iron Man, X-Men, and the Avengers.

After a dispute over creative rights, Kirby left Marvel Comics (Lee remained to become its president and chairman of the board) and returned to DC Comics, where he worked on Jimmy Olsen, Superman's pal. From there he drew Mister Miracle, the New Gods, and the Forever People. During the 1980s he returned to Marvel to work on animated films and such shows as *The Fantastic Four.* He continued working until 1986 and died in 1994. After his collaboration with Kirby, Lee developed *Spider-Man* and *Daredevil.*

Harvey Kurtzman, 1924–1993, was contributor and editor of *Mad Magazine,* which commenced publication in 1952. He also published *Help!* and the humorous and ribald *Little Annie Fannie,* first developed for *Playboy.* It was one of the works that helped inaugurate the social, political, and sexual rebellion of the 1960s and 1970s. Another cartoon comics author who helped usher in that American counterculture time was R. Crumb and his *Mr. Natural, Fritz the Cat,* and *Keep on Trucking.*

The *Superman* comic book inaugurated the "Golden Age" of comic books. Jerry Siegel and Joseph "Joe" Shuster were the coauthors of *Superman,* and they helped revolutionize comics, transforming them from a relatively unimportant part of the American media into a multi-million-dollar industry. It was the American response to the German Nazi racist Aryan Superman. The American was just the opposite of what the German was. The American Superman stood for justice, law and order, decency, fair play, anti-hoodlumism—the ultimate good-guy hero.

Jerry Siegel from Cleveland Ohio was born in 1914, the son of parents who ran a men's clothing store. Somewhat shy, he found his niche in reading science fiction and fantasy. When he was 15, attending Glenville High School in Cleveland, he began publishing his own science fiction magazine entitled *Cosmic Stories.* He hoped to become a science fiction novelist but changed his mind when he discovered that he could make more money as a script writer for comics. Siegel died in 1996.

Joe Shuster was born in Toronto, Canada in 1914 to parents who had immigrated to North America. His father had come from Rotterdam, Netherlands and his mother, Ida, was from Kiev, Russia. He had talent and a desire to draw on walls, white butcher paper, anything. He found rolls of wallpaper that had been discarded and for years he used it for his drawings. He likewise had a passion for movies. He and his cousin would go to the theater, where his father was the projectionist, and watch the movies. His favorite comic strips included the *Katzenjammer Kids, Barney Goggle,* and*Little Nemo* by Winsor McCay. It was McCay who introduced him to the world of fantasy and science fiction. In 1931, Shuster and Siegel met and became good friends and collaborators in a science fiction publication. In January 1933 their science fiction pulp magazine included a story under the pen name of "Herbert S. Fine." The story was called "The Reign of the Superman," and it was illustrated by Shuster. Inspired by one of the first comic books, entitled *Detective Dan,* it was then that they thought that their Superman could be a hero rather than a villain. They did not have any luck trying to find a publisher. "Creating comics was easy," said Siegel, "selling them wasn't."

Shuster found part-time work as a delivery boy and in selling ice cream on the streets of New York. Siegel continued working on the Superman story. Some of his ideas came from other comic book heroes of the time. *Gladiator* was a 1930 novel by Philip Wylie—both Superman and Spider-Man were influenced by the main character, Hugo Danner.

Danner was bulletproof, leapt great distances, and could bend steel. He may also have been influenced by the writings of Friedrich Nietzsche and George Bernard Shaw. Siegel and Shuster tried hard to sell their *Superman* comic book to the comic book publishers but did not succeed. Finally, in 1938, DC Comics bought the rights to Superman for $130. By 1939, Siegel and Shuster had a Superman radio show and Superman magazine which sold one million copies a month. That same year Superman got his own syndicated comic strip, which was published in over 2,000 newspapers for over 20 million readers. Siegel and Shuster did not benefit from Superman's successes. Ultimately, DC Comics hired them to work on comic books, and they received a combined income of $150 a year—an insignificant amount of money in comparison to the $15 million a year DC earned from Superman movies, radio, television, comic books, and comic strips. When DC produced the adventures of Superman as a youth, Siegel and Shuster sued and won a payment of $94,013.16. When they were dismissed from DC Comics in 1948, Siegel found work with other comic book publishers and created other characters like the Star Spangled Kid, Robotman, G.I. Joe, Kid Cowboy, Joe Yank, and Nature Boy. For a short few years Siegel went back to DC Comics to write scripts for Superman and other characters, but he did not receive royalties for his work. During the 1970s he lived in California near Shuster, who had left the comic book industry to work as a clerk and enjoyed listening to classical music. Shuster died in 1992 and Siegel died four years later.

Superman's equal in comic-book popularity was *Batman,* created by Bob Kane, born Robert Kahn (1915–1998). Kane, like Batman, disguised his identity, which was that he was a Jew, a fact he did not mention in his autobiography. Like Shuster and Siegel in Cleveland, Kane grew up in a Jewish neighborhood in the Bronx, where his father worked as an engraver of printing plates. There is no evidence that his family had any religious inclination, but his Bronx environment suggest that they were exposed to at least some form of cultural Judaism. The creation of *Batman* was DC Comics's response to *Superman,* and its editor hired Kane along with Bill Finger (Kane's friend, a fellow Jew, who was at the time working as a shoe salesman) to devise a character that subsequently became Batman. The DC character was a composite of other comic characters such as the Shadow, the Phantom, and a little of a pulp hero called the Black Bat.

There was no so-called "Jewish character" in these superhero characters, but there was some Jewish reference or significance to some. Joe Simon and Jack Kirby created Captain America, and they had him fighting a Nazi agent named Red Skull. Steve Rogers, who became Captain America after taking a serum, could be seen as representing Jews, who were stereotyped as frail and passive. But as Captain America, Rogers was transformed into a superhero. That serum was concocted by Professor Reinstein, a reference perhaps to **Albert Einstein**, physicist. Superman beat up the German Nazis from 1941 to 1945. Joseph Goebbels, propaganda minister of the Third Reich, rose during one session of the German Reichstag to denounce Superman as a Jew.

Max Gaines, born Maxwell Ginzberg (1894–1947), was the co-publisher of All-American Publications, a precursor to the color-comics format that became the standard for the American comic book industry. Gaines was responsible for introducing comic book heroes (and heroines) such as Wonder Woman, Hawkman, and the Green Lantern. When Gaines died, his son Bill took over and renamed his father's publication as Entertainment Comics. In the process he also changed its direction, to include titles such as *Picture Stories from the Bible, Tales from the Crypt,* and *The Vault of Horror.*

By the 1950s, Jewish comic book artists slowly introduced their Jewishness in their work. Harvey Kurtzman's comic book entitled *MAD* included **Yiddish** expressions like "ganef," "Oy," and "fershlugginer." During the late 1970s comic book writers like Chris Claremont, building on the original Jack Kirby and Stan Lee *X-Men* strip, introduced such Jewish characters as Kitty Pryde, who wore a Star of David necklace, in the updated version of *X-Men,* as well as the enigmatic character Magneto, an Auschwitz survivor, who may or may not be Jewish.

Art Spiegelman's *Maus* series, based on the experiences of his parents as concentration camp survivors, illustrated the **Holocaust** through the media of comics and was awarded a special Pulitzer Prize in 1986. *Maus* was awarded a special Pulitzer Prize in 1986. **Al Capp** (1909–1979) was the highly successful and controversial creator of the Li'l Abner comic strip which appeared from 1934–1977. At its peak the strip had a readership of 60,000,000. Al Capp, born in New Haven, Connecticut as Alfred Gerald Caplin, was the eldest child of Otto Philip and Tillie Caplin, Orthodox Jews whose parents had emigrated from czarist Russia. Caplin changed his name to Al Capp and in 1932 and launched his career doing a daily comic strip, "Colonel Gilfeather" for the Associated Press. Ham Fisher, the creator of *Joe Palooka,* lured Capp to that strip, where he did a great deal of the work until a falling out with Fisher.

During his time with Fisher, Capp created the figure of "Big Liviticus," and when he struck out on his own, that character became the central figure in *Li'l Abner.* This comic strip became a piece of Americana, running daily as a comic strip from 1934 to 1959. A successful Broadway musical version of the strip was staged in 1956, followed by the film version of the play in 1959. The characters, the fictional locales of Dogpatch and Lower Slobovia, as well as Sadie Hawkins Day, all became elements of America's popular culture vocabulary.

The art and writings produced by these animation/cartoon artists provided an avenue for expressing their talents as well as an income. Publishing venues such as the *New York Times* and broadcasting networks such as CNN, CBS, and ABC enabled these cartoonists to reach readers throughout the world. The comics influenced a wide variety of people.

Herbert M. Druks

Further Reading: Fingeroth, Danny. *Disguised as Clark Kent: Jews, Comics, and the Creation of the Superhero.* New York: Continuum, 2007. Kaplan, Arie. *From Krakow to Krypton: Jews and Comic Books.* Philadelphia, PA: The Jewish publication Society, 2006. Weinstein, Simcha. *Up, Up, and Oy Vey! How Jewish History, Culture, and Values Shaped the Comic Book Hero.* Baltimore: Leviathan Press, 2006.

COPLAND, AARON (1900–1990)

Aaron Copland, internationally renowned composer of American music, was born in Brooklyn, New York on November 14, 1900. He was the youngest of five children born to Russian Jewish immigrants Harris Morris Copland, a department store owner, and his wife, Sarah Mittenthal Copland. (The original name "Kaplan" was mistakenly changed by a British immigration officer during passage). In America, Copland's father opened his own department store and became president of Beth Israel Anshei Emes, the oldest synagogue in Brooklyn.

Copland's interest in music began at an early age. Copland's first exposure to music centered on his family's Jewish life. Violin playing, piano playing, and singing were an integral part of the Copland household, as were the weddings Copland attended at the family's Conservative Jewish synagogue. There, he heard the music of Jewish dances (horas) and the melodies sung a capella by the cantor, traditional tunes handed down through the generations.

Despite these impressing experiences (including a Bar Mitzvah), Copland emerged a nonreligious, nonobservant adult without any connection to organized religion. Not surprising therefore, only two works in his entire output, *Vitebst* and *In the Beginning,* show any direct link to Judaism. The conscious effort to be seen as an American composer must certainly have driven Copland to avoid outward signs of his Jewish background.

A brief glance at the aforementioned works, however, provides a window into the subjects that inspired Copland during two different periods in his career. *Vitebst,* an early work, subtitled "Study on a Jewish Theme," was written in 1929. This chamber work, written for piano, violin, and cello, has as its main theme a Hasidic melody from Vitebsk in Russia (hence the title). Copland first heard this tune while attending a performance of Ansky's play *The Dybbuk* and later borrowed it to tell a story of harsh Jewish life in the shtetlach of Eastern Europe. Copland's dissonant chords and quarter-tones on the strings provides a sense of the cruel treatment these people endured under the Russian czar. The shofar is included on the piano to evoke the Days of Awe, and at the end the folk melody resolves all tension. Considering the sequence of events that the music clearly evokes, it seems implausible that Copland's intention was merely to experiment with timbres and dissonant harmonies. That Copland chose to make a purposeful link to his Jewish heritage with this work can only be speculation, but it deserves attention.

The second interesting link to Judaic themes can be found in Copland's dramatic choral work *In the Beginning,* written for the Harvard Symposium on Music Criticism. Unlike the earlier *Vitebst,* there is no direct relationship to Jewish melodies, but Copland does use a recurring main motive that bears a strong resemblance to the beginning of the traditional Ashkenazic "Kol Nidre" tune. The text is taken directly from Genesis 1 (hence the title) and follows the story word for word. After the opening phrase is sung softly to the words in the title, the chorus, in four-part dissonant chords, gradually builds to a climax when the words "light of day" are proclaimed. A remarkable synthesis is made between the ancient text and Copland's music, a feat reminiscent of his earlier *Lincoln Portrait* (1942) for narrator and orchestra. But coming amidst so many secular works at this later stage in his career, who can say what influenced Copland's choice of the religious text for this piece. The question remains unsolved.

As for the evolution of Copland's career, it is noteworthy to mention that he had the full support of his parents from the time he expressed his desire to be a composer. His first piano lessons began in 1914 with Leopold Wolfsohn in Brooklyn, followed by studies in harmony and counterpoint with the esteemed Rubin Goldmark (teacher of **George Gershwin**) and Clarence Adler. During this period, Copland composed numerous short pieces for piano, or piano and another instrument, such as "The Cat and the Mouse" (1920) for solo piano, which has become part of today's standard repertoire.

In 1921, Copland moved from New York to France, where he continued his formal training. Under the formidable influence of his renowned teacher, Nadia Boulanger of the Paris Conservatory (1921–1924), Copland was greatly encouraged to break the chains of European classical tradition and forge a new path with jazz motives within serious music. The result: three of Copland's large jazz-related works—Symphony for Organ and Orchestra (1925), which was later revised without organ and renamed *First Symphony; Music for the Theater* (1925); and the Piano Concerto (1926).

Upon his return to the United States, Copland continued to pursue his artistic aims. Out of this fruitful period (mid-1930s) came several large jazz-related works. A trip to Mexico inspired the *El Salon Mexico* concert piece that includes South American popular songs and jazz rhythms. After a journey across the States, Copland wrote two ballet scores evoking Western settings: *Billy the Kid* and the *Rodeo* suite. In *Appalachian Spring,* Copland again tells the story of a people, this time of an 1800s Quaker community in Pennsylvania. The tone poems "Lincoln Portrait" and "Fanfare for the Common Man" are especially noteworthy for their universal messages, and offer a window into Copland's secular humanism.

Copland's contributions to film are largely western-style motives, as in his "Hoe-down" from the *Rodeo* suite. Most notable was the score for William Wyler's *The Heiress* (1949), which won Copland an Academy Award. Besides composing, Copland played a leading role as teacher, conductor, and writer. He lectured extensively (1927–1937) at the New School for Social Research in New York City, taught young musicians during summer sessions at the Tanglewood Music Center, Lenox, Massachusetts (1940–1965), and published music-appreciation books for the general audience.

As conductor, Copland led great orchestras performing his own music. As a scholar, Copland wrote more than 60 articles and essays on music, and 5 books. He organized, along with Roger Sessions, the Copland-Sessions concerts (1928–1931) in New York City, which featured works by American composers, and he worked with the American Composers' Alliance to especially aid younger American composers in beginning their careers.

The Copland House, the composer's longtime home near New York City, stands as a living tribute to an "uncommon man" who was given the title "Dean of American Music." Inspired by Copland's lifelong advocacy of American music, the restored home provides space for live concerts featuring the music of contemporaries and Copland's own works. Located in the lower Hudson River Valley, the Copland House is a dwelling of historical interest, since it is the only composer's residence in the United States devoted to nurturing American composers.

Quiet, simple, unassuming, devoted, and generous are a few of the traits that have won Copland the esteem of his contemporaries, especially **Leonard Bernstein**, who performed Copland's works with special understanding and warmth. In paying tribute to his lifelong friend, Bernstein likened Copland to the biblical Aaron, describing him as the high priest of American music and a leader adored by his disparate tribes.

Copland was the recipient of numerous awards, including the Pulitzer Prize (1945), New York Music Critic's Circle Award (1954), an Oscar for *The Heiress* (1950), the Presidential Medal of Freedom (1964), and honorary degrees from Princeton, Oberlin, Harvard, and Brandeis universities.

Copland never married. He died on December 2, 1990, in North Tarrytown, New York, at the age of 90. *See also* **Film**; **Theater**.

Ann Leisawitz

Further Reading: Copland, Aaron, and Vivian Perlis. *Copland Since 1943*. New York: St. Martin's Press, 1989. Hansen, Peter S. *Twentieth Century Music*. Upper Saddle River, NJ: Allyn and Bacon, Inc. 1971. Kerman, Joseph. *Listen*. London: Worth Publishing Ltd., Inc. 1976. Lyman Darryl. *Great Jews in Music*. New York:

Jonathan David Publishers, Inc., 1986. Rothmuller, Aron Marko. *The Music of the Jews*. A.S. Barnes Publishing Co., 1975.

COPPERFIELD, DAVID (1956–)

Magician and illusionist David Copperfield is best known for his television specials combining illusions and storytelling. Born David Seth Kotkin in 1956 in Metuchen, New Jersey, he became interested in magic at age 12 after seeing the effect it had on an audience. Subsequently, he became the youngest member to join the Society of American Magicians. Four years later, before his childhood peers graduated from high school, Kotkin taught a course in magic at New York University. In 1974, three weeks after enrolling at Fordham University, he was cast in the lead role of the musical *The Magic Man,*. There, he adopted the stage name David Copperfield, in deference to Charles Dickens's classic.

Headlining in hotels around the country, Copperfield starred in *The Magic of ABC* in 1977. From 1978 until 1994, he enjoyed his own yearly television special, *The Magic of David Copperfield,* usually featuring acts that confounded his audience—such as a trick involving the immovability and impenetrability of a monument, making the Statue of Liberty disappear (1983), levitating over the Grand Canyon (1984), passing through the Great Wall of China (1986), escaping from Alcatraz (1987), and traveling over Niagara Falls (1990). In addition to levitation, Copperfield creates illusions with air, fire, earth, and water.

Copperfield has played himself in the film *Prêt-à-Porter* (1994), starred in his own Broadway show *David Copperfield: Dreams and Nightmares* (1996), and has been the recipient of 21 Emmy Awards. He has also sold more tickets than any other solo artist. Through much of his career, Copperfield played in over 500 shows a year, often touring with his father Hy, until he passed away in 2006.

Copperfield has been awarded a Hollywood star, a knighthood in France, and a wax likeness at London's Madame Tussauds's Wax Museum. Of his many achievements, the most rewarding has been the Magic Project he created in 1982. The project's inspiration came when a wheelchair-bound magician asked David to help arrange a *The Tonight Show* appearance. Since then, over 1,000 hospitals worldwide have adopted the Magic Project, wherein therapists and magicians help disabled patients to regain lost or damaged skills by using sleight-of-hand magic as a form of physical therapy.

Although not an observant Jew, Copperfield was brought up by parents who observed the Jewish holidays and sent him to Hebrew school to study for his Bar Mitzvah. Looking back, Copperfield has said that although he "hated" going to Hebrew school, "I'm happy for the experience now and if I'm lucky enough to have children someday, I'll do the same thing for them—to give them a sense of purpose and place" (Pogrebin, 2005). After six years of marriage, Copperfield divorced model Claudia Schiffer.

Steve Krief

Further Reading: Pogrebin, Abigail. "David Copperfield." *Stars of David*. New York: Broadway Books, 2005.

CURTIS, TONY (1925–)

Film star and television personality Tony Curtis is best known for light comic roles, such as in films like *Some Like It Hot* (1959) with Jack Lemmon and Marilyn Monroe, as well as serious dramatic roles, such as the escaped convict in *The Defiant Ones* (1958), which earned him an Academy Award nomination. Curtis was born Bernard Schwartz on June 3, 1925 in the Bronx, New York. His parents, Emanuel and Helen Schwartz, were Hungarian Jewish immigrants. Young "Bernie" Schwartz and his brothers, Julius and Robert, were raised in rooms adjacent to their father's tailor shop. Raised under difficult circumstances (both his mother and one of his brothers were schizophrenics; another brother died in an accident), "Boinie," as he was called, escaped to the local movie theater. Mesmerized by all the "fencing, horseback riding and kissing the girls," Schwarts thought, "why can't I do that?"

Following a three-year hitch in the U.S. Navy aboard a submarine tender, Schwartz studied acting alongside Elaine Stritch, Walter Matthau, and Rod Steiger. He received good reviews in an off-Broadway production of *Golden Boy* (1948) and was offered a contract with Universal Studios. Studio bosses changed his name to Tony Curtis and gave him a small role in the noir classic *Criss Cross*. His first leading role was in the 1951 action adventure *The Prince Who Was a Thief.*

During the 1950s and 1960s, Curtis was much in demand, starring in such movies as *The Sweet Smell of Success* (1957), *The Defiant Ones* (1958), *Some Like It Hot* (1959), and *Spartacus* (1960). Legend has it that his extraordinary popularity with teenage girls led Elvis Presley to adopt Curtis's "ducktail" hairstyle.

Tony Curtis has appeared on television, costarring with Roger Moore in the series *The Persuaders!* and in *Vega$* with Robert Urich. In all, Curtis has appeared in nearly 140 films and television shows.

Tony Curtis has been married six times. His first and most famous wife was actress Janet Leigh (1927–2004), with whom he had two daughters, the film stars Jamie Leigh Curtis and Kelly Curtis. Since 1998, Curtis has been married to Jill Vandenberg, who is 45 years his junior. Asked to comment on the fact that his wife was young enough to be his granddaughter, Curtis joked that he would "never be caught dead with a woman old enough to be my wife!"

Since the early 1980s, Curtis has had a second career as a painter. His works go for upwards of $50,000. His painting *The Red Table* was put on display at Manhattan's Metropolitan Museum in 2007. *See also* **Film; Film Stars.**

Kurt F. Stone

Further Reading: Curtis, Tony, and Peter Golenbock. *American Prince: A Memoir.* New York: Random House, 2008. Curtis, Tony, and Barry Paris. *Tony Curtis: The Autobiography.* New York: William Morrow and Co., 1993.

CURTIZ, MICHAEL (1886–1962)

Academy Award-winning Hungarian American film director Curtiz directed at least 50 films in Europe and more than 100 in the United States, which included *Casablanca, Yankee Doodle Dandy,* and *White Christmas*. Michael Curtiz was born Manó Kertész Kaminer, in 1886, to a well-to-do Jewish family in Budapest, Hungary. Curtiz's father was an architect, his mother an opera singer. Given to telling tall tales, Curtiz, in later life, claimed that he had run away from home to join the circus and was a member of Hungary's fencing team at the 1912 Olympic Games. At age 26, following studies at both Markoszy University and the Royal Academy of Theater and Art in Budapest, Curtiz, now using the name Mihály Kertész, began his career as an actor and director at the National Hungarian Theater. In 1913, Curtiz spent six months at the Nordisk Studio in Denmark, learning how to direct movies.

When the Hungarian film industry was nationalized in 1919, Curtiz moved to Vienna, where he directed 21 films. When one of his films caught the attention of Jack Warner, Curtiz came to America, where he began a career that included more than 100 Hollywood motion pictures. Known for his temper and lifelong struggle with English, as well as for his cinematic style and efficiency, Curtiz often directed four pictures a year. His body of work ranged from adventure in *The Adventures of Robin Hood* (1938) to westerns such as *The Santa Fe Trail* (1940) and crime drama like *Angels With Dirty Faces* (1938), to costume epics such as *The Private Lives of Elizabeth and Essex* (1939). Nominated four times for a Best Director Oscar, Curtiz won in 1942 for the classic romance *Casablanca*.

Known as a consummate studio director, Curtiz often rode roughshod over the actors in his films. Nonetheless, he guided such stars as Humphrey Bogart, Joan Crawford, Errol Flynn, James Cagney, and Elvis Presley in some of their best work.

His grasp of the English language led to many famous Hollywood anecdotes. Once, when he was chewing out an assistant, he told the underling, "the next time I want an idiot do this, I'll do it myself!" (Marton, 2006).

Curtiz was married three times. His third marriage— to screenwriter Bess Meredyth—lasted from 1929 until his death in 1962. He died one year after completing his final film, *The Comancheros,* with John Wayne. *See also* **Film**.

Kurt F. Stone

Further Reading: Harmetz, Aljean. *Round Up the Usual Suspects: The Making of "Casablanca."* London: Orion Books, 1993. Marton, Kati. *The Great Escape: Nine Jews Who Fled Hitler and Changed the World.* New York: Simon and Schuster, 2006.

D

DANCE

Traditionally, Jews have used dance as a means for expressing religious fervor and celebrating other simchas (festive occasions). This is especially true among Orthodox Jews, where a separation of men and women exists. On Jewish holidays, such as Simchat Torah, Jews congregating in synagogue (especially among the Hasidim) would dance with the Torah and engage in other forms of revelry. Similarly, dancing has always been a part of celebrating Bar and Bat Mitzvahs, where the hora, a dance which originated in Israel, characterized by people holding hands and spinning around in a circle, has become a traditional dance of celebration. Ashkenazic Jews, living in Eastern Europe, created dances corresponding to different forms of **klezmer music**. Though Jewish dances influenced and were influenced by Gentile neighbors, the Jewish roots remained recognizable. Jewish dancers expressed themselves in highly identifiable ways, through hand and arm motions and intricate leg movements.

Jewish dance forms, whether social or folk, connect American Jews to their ancient roots. These same traditional forms have then been added into twentieth-century American dance. By incorporating these dance traditions in American dance, Jewish choreographers have contributed to the growth of a contemporary art form that embraces racial, religious, and ethnic diversity, female expression, and excellence.

Great Jewish choreographers, consciously or not, have explored and wrestled with their Jewish identity through dance. Pearl Lang, **Sophie Maslow**, **Jerome Robbins**, Anna Sokolow, and Helen Tamiris used their creations as a means for demonstrating the uniqueness of the Jewish voice in American dance. Each has explored critical themes faced by Jewish immigrants, including the immigrant experience, the effects of the **Holocaust** on the Jewish psyche and people, feelings of isolation, importance of community, and the problems surrounding assimilation into broader American society.

As the twentieth century dawned, the world of modern dance reflected larger American social conventions. Thus, quotas restricting Jewish participation were found at dance schools such as Ruth St. Denis and Ted Shawn's Denishawn Co. In protest over these discriminatory policies some non-Jewish prominent dancers such as Martha Graham, Doris Humphrey, and Charles Weidman broke with these companies. Martha Graham, eventually, became a favorite teacher at New York's Lower East Side Neighborhood Playhouse. In the 1920s, the Neighborhood

Playhouse provided a training venue for many Jewish choreographers, including Helen Tamiris, Sophie Maslow, and Anna Sokolow. Developed by Irene and Alice Lewisohn, the playhouse dance classes offered immigrant children a pathway into American culture.

In the late 1920s, the modern dancer and choreographer Doris Humphrey noted the grace of movement displayed by the Jewish girls in her company. Modern dance attracted Jewish women because despite expressiveness of body motion, it was different from the comic antics displayed by dancers in vaudeville and Broadway chorus. Jewish women formed the core group within the dance revolution. These modern dancers involved themselves in the social, political, and aesthetic issues of the day through their dancing. Jewish women battled anti-Semitism and along with fellow Americans expressed growing concerns about social justice and building a national culture. Dance became a political tool for Jewish women as they filled modern dance classes, companies, organizations, and picket lines.

Helen Tamiris (b. Helen Becker, 1905–1966) petitioned the federal government for increased attention to dance. Tamiris directed the Federal Dance Project of the WPA with her husband, Daniel Nagrin. Their dances often dealt with themes of brotherhood and emancipation. Tamiris's company included many Jewish dancers such as Mura Dehn, Sue Ramos, and Pauline Bubrick Tish. Edith Segal used dances such as *The Belt Goes Red* and *Black and White* as vehicles for social protest. Other socially aware dancers included Miriam Blecher, Lily Mehlman, and Muriel Mannings, who created the New Dance Group school. Assimilation into American culture pushed some choreographers to glorify American folk ways. Maslow's *Dust Bowl Ballads* provides one example of this trend. Other dancers maintained Jewish concerns for social justice and rights. Dance was even used to mount opposition to fascism. Dance concerts were held to support Spanish democracy during in the Spanish Civil War. Ruthanna Boris from the American Ballet Theater joined forces with modern dancers for this cause.

Martha Graham's modern dance company included the largest number of Jewish dancers. Most notable of her performers were Anna Sokolow, Lillian Shapero, and Sophie Maslow. Other Jewish dancers in her company were Bertram Ross, Robert Cohan, Stuart Hodes, Linda Margolis Hodes, and Pearl Lang.

Another important venue for Jewish involvement in American dance was the 92nd Street "Y" (Young Men's and Women's Hebrew Association). Founded in 1874, the Y provided young Jewish men with a place to gather. In 1930, its administrators decided to add an arts program, which included dance. The first dance director, a performer and choreographer from the Habima theater group in Moscow, named Benjamin Zemach, left after a short time because he was denied an opportunity to present a few dance concerts each year. In 1934, William Kolodney arrived at the Y, and though he concentrated his efforts on his great loves, poetry and music, he recognized that young Jews loved the new art of modern dance.

In 1936, the 92nd Street Y established its Dance Center. Martha Graham, Doris Humphrey, and other leading figures helped to build the center. For years it was the only theater to produce modern dance. The Y elevated the art of American modern dance by providing its best- and least-known practitioners with facilities to produce. It also offered a venue for black American ballet, modern, and ethnic dance performers and choreographers. In 1985 the Dance Center formed an affiliation with the Harkness Foundation for Dance, which supports several Y dance programs. Blossoming into a full partnership, in 1994 the project was renamed the 92nd Street Y Harkness Dance Center. During its 2004–2005 season the Harkness Dance Center offered a year-long program that celebrated the contributions of Jews to American life over the last 350 year. *Gotta Dance: Jews in American Dance* was presented as part of the Y's scheduled performances.

The Nazi regime destroyed all forms of dance in Germany by the mid-1930s. Performers from

Kraus's Viennese Company who escaped and reached America during World War II included Fred Berk, Katya Delakova, and Claudia Vall. Berk established the Jewish Dance Division at the 92nd Street Y. He used Jewish-themed dances on tours and provided an opening for Israeli folk dance. Other choreographers also used Jewish themes. Pearl Lang (1922–), a major choreographer, emerged from the Martha Graham Dance Company. Of her many dances with Hebraic themes, perhaps the best known was *Shirah* (1960), based on a mystical Hasidic tale. Lang also utilized Jewish sources in *Song of Deborah* and in *Legend,* based on Ansky's *Dybbuk.* Two other major figures who had danced with Graham also used some Jewish themes—Anna Sokolow and Sophie Maslow.

Sokolow (1910–2000) created *Kaddish* (1946), based on the prayer for the dead. She also staged and performed in a theater-dance production of S. Ansky's play *The Dybbuk* (1951). This work represented one of Sokolow's early attempts to combine dance with mime and the spoken word. Following *The Dybbuk,* Sokolow's focus switched from public performance to choreography. She showed concern for the individual in contemporary society. Her *Dreams* was an indictment of Nazi Germany. Sokolow continued to experiment with combinations of music, dance, and theater. In such works as *Act Without Words* (1969), *Magritte, Magritte* (1970), and *From the Diaries of Franz Kafka* (1980), she mixed art forms. In 1969, she created a new company. Her Lyric Theatre was devoted specifically to dance compositions of mixed art forms. It is now known as the Sokolow Dance Foundation. Though she left the production of *Hair* before it was staged, she had great influence on the dance and music. She died on June 25, 2006 in Manhattan at age 95.

Sophie Maslow began her dance training with Blanche Talmud at the Neighborhood Playhouse. She became a member of Graham's Dance Company in 1931, performing many solo roles, until 1943. She created her own dance troupe, the Sophie Maslow Dance Company and, with others, established the Dudley-Maslow-Bales Trio in 1942. In 1948, she performed and was a faculty member at the first American Dance Festival held at Connecticut College. Ms. Maslow's choreography includes *The Village I Knew,* depicting the life of Jews in czarist Russia; *Dust Bowl Ballads; Folksay,* based on Carl Sandburg's poem of the same name; and the off-Broadway musical *The Big Winner,* about a poor tailor and his winning lottery ticket. In 1951, she choreographed *The Dybbuk* for the New York City Opera. In 1952, 1955, 1956, and 1960–1962, Maslow choreographed the Chanukah Festivals held at Madison Square Garden.

Later choreographers who delved into their Jewish past include Eliot Feld, Meredith Monk, Amy Sue Rosen, and Anna Halprin (aka Ann), who experimented with dance improvisation. Driven by her roots, her work for her 80th birthday in 2000, *Memories from My Closet, Grandfather Dance,* has Jewish references and klezmer music.

Classical ballet in America also benefited from Jewish patronage and involvement. The New York City Ballet company was founded in 1948 by Lincoln Kirstein andchoreographer George Balanchine, with musical director Leon Barzin. The company grew out of earlier troupes. Lincoln Kirstein was born in Rochester, New York, to a wealthy Jewish family. His interest in ballet and George Balanchine started when he saw a Ballet Russe performance. He was determined to get Balanchine to America. Kirstein brought Ballanchine to America and supported him in his creative endeavors. Other Jews involved in the world of ballet include Nora Kaye, who was perhaps America's greatest dramatic ballerina. She danced in Jerome Robbins's *The Cage* (1951), Anthony Tudor's *Pillar of Fire* (1942), and Herbert Ross's (her husband) version of *The Dybbuk.* She also served as associate director of the Ballet Theatre from 1977–1983. Herbert Ross collaborated with **Leonard Bernstein** and with his wife (Nora Kaye) to choreograph ballets.

Notable contributions to American ballet and the broader world of dance were made by Jerome Robbins and Michael Kidd. Jerome Robbins is generally credited with winning attention for American dance in the wider world. During the 1950s, Robbins continued to create dances for the Ballet Theatre, alternating between musicals and ballet for the better part of two decades. With George Balanchine he choreographed *Jones Beach* in 1950 and directed and choreographed **Irving Berlin**'s *Call Me Madam*.

In 1951, Robbins created the celebrated dance sequences in *The King and I*. That same year, he choreographed *The Cage* for the New York City Ballet. Robbins collaborated on *The Pajama Game* (1954) and worked on the show *Peter Pan* (1955). He also directed and co-choreographed (with Bob Fosse) *Bells Are Ringing* (1956). In 1957, he choreographed and directed what some feel is his crowning achievement: ***West Side Story***.

West Side Story is a 1957 version of *Romeo and Juliet*. The musical marked the first collaboration between Robbins and **Stephen Sondheim**, who wrote the lyrics. Although it opened to good reviews, it was overshadowed by *The Music Man* at that year's Tony Awards. *West Side Story,* an American classic, earned Robbins his second Tony Award for choreography.

Robbins's hits continued with *Gypsy* (1959). When a show was in danger of failing, Robbins was called upon to fix the problem. He took over the direction of two troubled productions and helped turn them into box office hits. In 1962, he saved *A Funny Thing Happened on the Way to the Forum* (1962), a musical farce. Robbins staged an entirely new opening number, which laid out the show for the audience, and the production played beautifully. In 1964, he took on a problematic *Funny Girl* and the show ran for 1,348 performances. The musical helped make **Barbra Streisand** a superstar. That same year, Robbins won Tony Awards for his direction and choreography in ***Fiddler on the Roof*** (1964). That show ran for 3,242 performances. The subject matter allowed Robbins to return to his religious roots.

Robbins always retained connections to ballet. He continued to choreograph productions for the Joffrey Ballet and the New York City Ballet into the 1970s. Robbins became ballet master of the New York City Ballet in 1972 and worked there almost exclusively throughout the next decade. The anthology show *Jerome Robbins' Broadway* (1989) recreated the most successful production numbers from his 50-plus-year career. The show included numbers that had been cut from shows, like Irving Berlin's "Mr. Monotony" and well-known ones like the "Tradition" number from *Fiddler on the Roof.* The anthology show earned Robbins a fifth Tony Award.

Michael Kidd (1915–2007) choreographed for stage and screen. Born Milton Greenwald, he was the son of Abraham Greenwald and his wife, Lillian. Kidd attended New Ultrecht High School. Interested in dance, he studied under Blanche Evan, a dancer and choreographer. In 1937, he was granted a scholarship to the School of American Ballet, and his chemical engineering studies ended.

His work for the 1954 film *Seven Brides for Seven Brothers* was noted for a series of dances depicting ordinary frontier activities. He also choreographed Fred Astaire and Cyd Charisse in the 1953 musical film *Band Wagon.* Kidd won five Tony Awards and an honorary Academy Award in 1996 "in recognition of his services to the art of dance" ("Choreographer," 2008). Some of his other works include Broadway dancing in *Filling Station* (1939), *Pocahontas* (1939), and *Fancy Free* (1946); and serving as choreographer in *Finian's Rainbow* (1947), *Guys and Dolls* (1950), *Can-Can* (1953), *Subways are for Sleeping* (1961), *Skyscraper* (1965), *The Rothschilds* (1970), *The Music Man* (1980 revival), and *The Goodbye Girl* (1993). Kidd died of cancer at the age of 92 years.

Over the last several decades, more Jewish choreographers have been exploring their cultural and religious identities through dance. Some create entire numbers with Jewish themes; others use traditional gestures from Israeli dance. Still others inform their work through the traditional Jewish questioning and interpreting about life's questions and issues. By incorporating different Jewish aspects into their choreography, each helps address questions about life and dance and how they connect to, or concern, American Jews.

Dance historian Rebecca Rossen, in her 2000 solo (later performed by David Dorfman) *Make Me a Jewish Dance,* weaves modern dance with humorous Yiddishisms and Jewish gestures. The piece explores stereotypes and seems to conclude that there is not necessarily "Jewish dance." Judith Brin Ingber, another historian-choreographer, creates dances with biblical themes.

Choreographer Julia Adams draws on Jewish ritual. In 2004, she created a piece for the Houston Ballet called *Ketubah* (a legal Jewish marriage document), which centers on a Jewish wedding. She uses traditional pirouettes rather than the hora, but she does use a piece of sheer fabric to represent the mikvah, the traditional ritual bath Jewish women take before getting married; the dektikhl, the bride's veil; and the huppa, a Jewish wedding canopy.

The Holocaust is another theme used by many Jewish choreographers. Carolyn Dorfman's 2001 piece *Mayne Mentshn* (My People) moves through different aspects of joy and pain in Jewish life. As a child of Holocaust survivors, she claims her work is ultimate belief in the human spirit.

David Dorfman (no relation to Carolyn) also connects with his Jewish background. His 1992 piece called *Dayenu* alludes to the Passover prayer meaning "it would have been enough." The prayer is traditionally used by Jews to thank God for their escape from slavery in Egypt. The prayer maintains that had God helped them with one thing, it would have been enough, but a loving God did more. Dorfman uses a different interpretation. His mother's losing battle with multiple sclerosis, and the death of friends due to AIDS, prompts him to claims it is not enough. Dorfman says his reinterpretation of the prayer is in line with the Jewish faith because it encourages questioning and individual understanding. Nina Haft insists that one can look at something in differing ways and still find meaning. Her dance encourages searching a variety of meanings, for this is part of a Jewish approach.

Jewish influence in American dance can also be seen at a more grassroots as well as the professional level. Arthur Murray (1895–1991) brought ballroom dancing to a vast population. Born in Austria-Hungary in 1895 as Moses Teichman, he was brought to America by his mother, Sarah. They settled in the Lower East Side of Manhattan. In 1912, he began teaching dance at night, while working during the day as a draftsman. Arthur studied under the popular dance team of Irene and Vernon Castle and went to work for them. At the outbreak of World War I, under pressure of anti-German feeling, Teichman changed his name.

In 1919, while attending Georgia Tech, he taught ballroom dancing. His first business, selling dance lessons by mail, failed. His second, a mail-order business, drawing and selling "footprints" which dancers could follow to learn how to dance, succeeded. In 1925, he began his third business, franchising. He trained dance instructors who would give lessons at various hotels; Murray kept a portion of the profits from each franchise. This business expanded in 1938, when an Arthur Murray dance studio franchise was opened in Minnesota. Others followed.

After World War II, Murray's business grew as people's interest in Latin dance increased. During the 1950s Murray taught dance and broadcast in Cuba. Murray and his wife Kathryn hosted a television dance program, *The Arthur Murray Party,* in the early 1960s. The couple retired in 1964 with over 3,560 dance studios in place. In 2007, there were only 220 Arthur Murray studios still in operation. The Murray name and franchise remain part of our popular legacy.

Whether dealing with classical, modern, or more mainstream dance forms, Jews have contributed to much of what we recognize as dance within the nation's popular culture. Though some have incorporated their Jewish roots more openly in their work than others, there is a common thread among them—a commitment to self-exploration, questioning, and highlighting society's ills. *See also* ***Fiddler on the Roof*****; Klezmer**

Music; **Maslow, Sophie**; **Robbins, Jerome**; ***West Side Story***.

Susan M. Ortmann

Further Reading: "Choreographer Michael Kidd Dies." Theater-MSNBC.com. Accessed April 25, 2008. www.msnbc.msn.com/id/22394186. Dunning, Jennifer. "Celebrating Seven Decades of a Modern Dance Crucible." *New York Times,* February 24, 2004. Foulkes, Julia. "Angels 'Rewolt!': Jewish Women in Modern Dance in the 1930s." *American Jewish History* 88 (2000). Graft, Ellen.*Stepping Left: Dance and Politics in New York City, 1928–1942.* Durham, NC: Duke University Press, 1997. Jackson, Naomi. *Converging Movements: Modern Dance and Jewish Culture at the 92nd Street Y.* Macon, GA: Wesleyan University Press, 2000. Jowitt, Deborah. *Jerome Robbins: His Life, His Theater, His Dance.* New York: Simon and Schuster, 2004. Tomko, Linda J. *Dancing Class: Gender, Ethnicity and Social Divides in American Dance, 1890–1920.* Bloomington, IN: Indiana University Press, 1999.

DAVID, LARRY (1947–)

Best known as the writer who propelled *Seinfeld* into comedic orbit, Larry David, writer, producer, and comic has rocketed himself into stardom with HBO's sitcom *Curb Your Enthusiasm.* A native of Brooklyn, David was born and raised in Sheepshead Bay. His father was a clothing salesman, his mother, Shirley, a housewife. After graduating from Sheepshead Bay High School, he attended and graduated from the University of Maryland, earning bachelors' degrees in history and business.

David was a stand-up comedian for 15 years, while he worked as a brassiere salesman and limousine driver. As a comedian, his claim to fame was his decision to walk off the stage if he felt the audience was not responding to his jokes. He also would walk on stage and remain silent as he counted audience members. If the audience didn't seem quite right to David, he would say "never mind" and walk off the stage.

From 1980–1982, David was producer/writer with ABC's *Fridays.* He worked as a writer for *Saturday Night Live* during the 1982–1983 season. David appeared in *Can She Bake a Cherry Pie?* written by Henry Jaglom and in *Second Thoughts,* by Steve Brown, in 1983. In 1987, he appeared in **Woody Allen**'s film *Radio Days,* and in 1989, he appeared in Allen's film *New York Stories,* an anthology also directed by Allen.

David teamed up with his sidekick, **Jerry Seinfeld**, to create *Seinfeld* in 1990. He served as a writer for the show for six years and returned in 1998 to write the show's final season. During his two-year hiatus from *Seinfeld,* David wrote and directed the film *Sour Grapes* (1998), which was not successful.

Since 1999, Larry David has been playing Larry David on *Curb Your Enthusiasm.* The show is unscripted, so viewers watch as life's mundane activities become bigger-than-life events for David. Most episodes portray the star as the victim of life's circumstances. Similar to *Seinfeld, Curb Your Enthusiasm* is usually about nothing, but often the nothing is deeply rooted in Larry's stereotypical Jewishness.

Nominated seven times for an Emmy for *Seinfeld,* David received an Emmy for Outstanding Individual Achievement in Writing in a Comedy Series in 1993. He also shared an Emmy in 1993 for Outstanding Comedy Series, and in 1994 he again shared the PGA Golden Laurel Award with Seinfeld for Most Promising Producer in Television. The United States Comedy Arts Award presented David with the AFI Start Award in 1999. He was nominated for the Golden Globe Award in 2005 for the Best Performance by an Actor in a Television Series–Musical or Comedy and the same year was voted as one of the top 50 greatest comedy acts ever in a poll to select The Comedian's Comedian. David was nominated for a Best Actor Award Emmy in 2006.

Married to Laurie Lennard since 1993, David lives with his wife and two children in Pacific Palisades, California. *See also* **Television**.

Robert Ruder

Further Reading: Dolan, Deirdre. *Curb Your Enthusiasm: The Book.* New York: Gotham Books, 2006. Lapidos, Juliet. "Oh, How We've Missed You!" *Slate.* Accessed September 23, 2007. www.slate.com.

DAVIS, SAMMY, JR. (1925–1990)

Sammy Davis Jr., born December 8, 1925 in Harlem, was a song and dance man, actor, and nightclub entertainer, and he was one of the first African American performers to win widespread acclaim from white audiences. He began his professional career at the age of four with the vaudeville troupe in which his father performed. He eventually became the group's star performer and made a number of recordings and television appearances. His success led to starring roles in the Broadway shows *Mister Wonderful* (1956) and *Golden Boy* (1964). He also became famous for being a member of the "Rat Pack," a group of fast-living, hard-drinking Hollywood performers of the early 1960s which included Frank Sinatra, Dean Martin, and Peter Lawford. He appeared in such films as *Ocean's Eleven* (1960) and *Sergeants 3* (1962), as well as the 1959 film version of *Porgy and Bess*.

In 1954, Davis lost his left eye and almost died in a car accident. While in the hospital, his friend **Eddie Cantor** told him of the similarities between the Jewish and African American cultures, and Davis subsequently converted to Judaism under the tutelage of Rabbi Max Dussbaum at Temple Israel in Hollywood. He later recalled a book he had read on Jewish history, that "I got hung up on one paragraph: The Jews would not die. Three centuries of prophetic teaching had given them an unwavering spirit of resignation and had created in them a will to live which no disaster could crush" (Weiss, 2003). However, the Jewish community never fully embraced Davis, and his conversion also met with considerable controversy within the African American community.

His autobiographies, *Yes I Can* (1965) and *Who Me?* (1989), detailed the racial discrimination that dogged him from his early career, as well as his extravagant private life. He was married three times, once to actress May Britt, who was white (and also converted by Rabbi Dussbaum).

Davis continued performing into the 1980s, despite heavy drinking, drug use, and chain smoking, all of which contributed to his poor health. He died May 16, 1990 of throat cancer, age 64, at his home in Los Angeles. *See also* **Film Stars**.

Leslie Rabkin

Further Reading: Davis, Sammy, and Burt Boyar and Jane Boyar. *Sammy: The Autobiography of Sammy Davis, Jr.* New York: Farrar, Straus and Giroux, 2000. Fishgall, Gary. *Gonna Do Great Things: The Life of Sammy Davis, Jr.* New York: Scribner, 2003. Weiss, Beth. "Sammy Davis, Jr." The Jewish Virtual Library, March 19, 2003. Accessed June 14, 2008.

DERSHOWITZ, ALAN (1938–)

One of the most prominent attorneys in the United States, Alan Dershowitz has had a distinguished career as a constitutional lawyer and legal scholar, criminal appellate attorney, and prolific author. In 1966, at the age of 28, he became the youngest tenured law professor in the history of Harvard University. His prominent clients have often made national headlines: sports stars O. J. Simpson and Mike Tyson, hotel magnate Leona Helmsley, financier Michael Milken, deposed Philippine leader Ferdinand Marcos, *Deep Throat* actor Harry Reems, televangelist Jim Bakker, CIA agent Frank Snepp, and even fellow attorney F. Lee Bailey, to name a few.

Dershowitz has chronicled his law career and philosophy in more than two dozen books and numerous journal and magazine articles. His bestselling book about the Claus von Bulow trial, *Reversal of Fortune* (1990), became a blockbuster film. In an interview, he expressed concern that his pro bono work, probably constituting more than 50 percent of his legal practice, is relatively unknown.

While "Dersh" receives widespread media attention throughout the country for his legal cases and writings on constitutional law, Jews in the United States and around the world know him as an articulate and vocal advocate for Israel and a variety of other Jewish concerns. He was the attorney for Soviet "refusenik" Natan Sharansky and for many years played a very active role in the Soviet Jewry movement. The author of *The Case for Israel* (2003) and *The Case for Peace: How the Arab-Israeli Conflict Can Be Resolved* (2005), Professor Dershowitz, who has no official position with any Jewish organization, is a leading advocate, but not an uncritical supporter, of Israel and Zionism. He frequently speaks on American and also European college campuses to sometimes hostile audiences.

When Professors John Mearsheimer (University of Chicago) and Stephen Walt (Harvard Kennedy School of Government) posted a polemical monograph critical of the so-called "Israel Lobby" on Harvard's Kennedy School of Government web site, Dershowitz promptly demanded and was accorded comparable space to rebut their assertions. During the Israel-Hizbollah war in the summer of 2006, Dershowitz regularly appeared on television and other media outlets to criticize the lack of media coverage of war crimes committed by this Shi'ite Muslim group. When Jimmy Carter published his controversial work *Palestine: Peace not Apartheid,* Dershowitz publicly challenged him to a debate at Brandeis University. While the 39th president claimed his book was written to stimulate a national discussion about the long-festering Arab-Israeli conflict, Dershowitz pointedly noted that Carter refused to engage him in such a debate. Carter later acknowledged that he was not as skilled a debater as the Felix Frankfurter Professor of Law at Harvard University.

Dershowitz's pro-Israel advocacy has often evoked harsh and even malicious comments from some detractors. Former Senator James Abourezk (D-SD), who once registered as a foreign agent of the Islamic Republic of Iran, has called Dershowitz "a snake." Norman Finkelstein, a virulent critic of Israel who was denied tenure at several universities, has blamed Dershowitz for many of his academic woes.

Born in the Williamsburg section of Brooklyn, Dershowitz had an Orthodox Jewish upbringing. His great-grandfather, known as "Reb" Zecharia, although not a rabbi, came to the United States in 1888 and founded a *shtiebl* (small storefront synagogue) in his Brooklyn community. Dershowitz's grandfathers, both of whom were cantors, established the first Orthodox yeshiva in Brooklyn. In the 1930s, his grandfather Louis Dershowitz devised an ingenious plan to save some European Jews: he began hiring several rabbis from Europe for his congregation, thus circumventing the strict immigration laws. Dershowitz's father, a merchant, helped found the local Young Israel synagogue.

Dershowitz attended the Brooklyn Talmudical Academy, commonly called BTA. During the summer, he went to Camp Massad, a Hebrew-speaking camp with a strong Zionist orientation, located in the Pocono Mountains of Pennsylvania. Linguist and vocal critic of Israeli policies towards the Palestinians, Noam Chomsky, who is several years older, was a counselor there, but they did not know each other. More than 50 years later, the MIT and Harvard professors had an acrimonious debate about the Arab-Israeli conflict before a standing room-only crowd at Harvard, which was later broadcast on cable television.

Often contentious in his yeshiva classes, Dershowitz once remarked that his "teachers said I should do something that requires a big mouth and no brain . . . so I became a lawyer" (Stull, 2003). He attended Brooklyn College and then went to Yale Law School, where he graduated at the top of his class and was editor in chief of the *Yale Law Journal.* Despite his academic accomplishments, Dershowitz was rejected for a summer job by 32 out of 32 Wall Street firms. "That certified me as an outsider," he told one interviewer. After receiving his law degree, Dershowitz clerked for Supreme Court Justice Arthur Goldberg and then started his more than four-decade career at the Harvard Law School in 1964.

His popular and widely-discussed book *Chutzpah* (1991) expressed his lifelong philosophy about the obligations and responsibilities of being Jewish: "American Jews need more chutzpah. Notwithstanding the stereotype, we are not pushy or assertive enough for our own good and for the good of our vulnerable brothers and sisters in other parts of the world" (Dershowitz, 1991).

Dershowitz has described himself as a "secular Jew who loves to go to shul," Asserting his religious orientation is "post-denominational," he and his wife hold simultaneous memberships in Orthodox, Conservative, and Reform synagogues.

Despite his deep and abiding commitments to Judaism and Israel, he has not been immune from criticism by his coreligionists. During the O. J. Simpson trial, he received harsh criticism, including hate mail, from some Jews who felt he was defending a murderer. His defense of convicted spy Jonathan Pollard and also Jewish Defense League member Sheldon Seigel, who set a bomb that killed an innocent young woman, also evoked negative community reactions. His book *The Genesis of Justice: Ten Stories of Biblical Injustice That Led to the Ten Commandments and Modern Law* (2000), which resulted from a popular course he taught at the Harvard Law School, drew criticism from some observant Jews who questioned his interpretations of biblical events. Many secular leftist Jews have written scathing attacks on Dershowitz's politics while, on the other end of the spectrum, politically conservative Jews are uncomfortable with many of his liberal views and also his steadfast defense of the right of neo-Nazis to march in Skokie, Illinois, in 1977.

Dershowitz has been awarded honorary doctorates from several institutions including Yeshiva University, Hebrew Union College, Monmouth College, and Haifa University. The Anti-Defamation League presented him with the William O. Douglas First Amendment Award for his "compassionate, eloquent leadership and persistent advocacy in the struggle for civil and human rights" (Israel News Agency).

Married twice, Dershowitz lives with his second wife, Carolyn, a psychologist, and they have one daughter. He has two sons from a previous marriage and two grandchildren.

Donald Altschiller

Further Reading: Dershowitz, Alan M. *Chutzpah.* Boston: Little Brown, 1991. Dershowitz Web Site: http://www.alandershowitz.com. Israel News Agency Staff. "Dershowitz: Israel's Sharon, Jews to Blame for Pollard's Continued Imprisonment." Accessed January 2008. http://www.israelnewsagency.com/jonathanpollarddershowitzisrael480626.html. Stull, Elizabeth. "Son of Brooklyn Brings Home Legacy of High-Profile Trials: Alan Dershowitz Donates Archives to Brooklyn College." *Brooklyn Daily Eagle,* September 25, 2003. Accessed August 12, 2006.

DETECTIVE FICTION

Dorothy L. Sayers began her epic 1929 anthology of detective fiction, *Omnibus of Crime,* with two selections from ancient Israelite texts. The first was the story of "Bel and the Dragon," and the second the story of "Susanna," both taken from apocryphal sections of the book of Daniel. It is only natural that a genre so centered on inquiry and analysis, on the pursuit of truth and justice, should have deep connections with a religion devoted to those very same principals. In a very real sense, detective fiction is a fulfillment of Judaism's desire for a world perfected. As in the story of creation, every mystery begins with chaos—a crime, most often murder. Through an inquiry that is often almost Talmudic, the detective solves the crime, metaphorically restoring God's order.

The first prominent Jewish mystery writer was Israel Zangwill (1864–1926). Zangwill was a friend to Jerome K. Jerome, H. G. Wells, and G. K. Chesterton. As a humorist and Jewish activist, Zangwill was best known for his advocacy of Zionism and his writings about the Jewish community of London, including *Children of the Ghetto* (1892), *Ghetto Comedies* (1907), *Ghetto Tragedies* (1893), and *King of the Schnorrers* (1894). Although less well known as a mystery writer, Zangwill made a huge contribution to the field with his 1892 novel *The Big Bow Mystery,* recognized as the first novel to incorporate the "locked-room" device (first used by Poe in his short story "Murders in the Rue Morgue"), in which a murder occurs in a sealed room with no apparent way for a killer to get in or out.

The person who did the most to advance the mystery genre was actually two people. "Ellery

Queen" was the nom de plume of two Brooklyn-born cousins, Manfred Lee (born Manford Lepofsky, 1905–1971) and Frederick Dannay (born Daniel Nathan, 1905–1982). In the late 1920s, the two boys entered a novel-writing contest sponsored by *McClure's Magazine*. That novel, *The Roman Hat Mystery* (1929), launched a career that would last more than 40 years and a name still synonymous with mystery.

In addition to more than 30 novels featuring amateur sleuth "Ellery Queen," Dannay and Lee wrote for film and radio, edited anthologies and histories of the mystery genre, and spawned **comic books**, board games, and two **television** series. One of their most important contributions to the field was the creation of *Ellery Queen's Mystery Magazine,* in 1941, which launched the careers of many mystery writers and continues publishing short stories today.

The July 1943 issue of *Ellery Queen's Mystery Magazine* included a story written by 15-year-old James Yaffe. Chicago native Yaffe (1927–) wrote six stories featuring super-sleuth Paul Dawn of NYPD's Department of Impossible Crimes. Yaffe abandoned detective fiction when he graduated high school and was drafted into the navy. But in his mid-twenties, Yaffe wrote another story for Ellery Queen, "Mom Knows Best" (1952), featuring the ultimate armchair detective, a Jewish mother whose homicide detective son and Wellesley-educated daughter-in-law come for Shabbos dinner each Friday. During the course of dinner, between tossing malapropisms and jabs at her daughter-in-law, "Mom" manages to solve whatever crime her son happens to be involved in by using Old-World wisdom and Jewish family analogies. Beginning in the late 1980s, Yaffe launched a series of novels featuring "Mom," relocating her and her son (now widowed) to Mesa Grande, Colorado. The series includes *A Nice Murder for Mom* (1988), *Mom Meets Her Maker* (1990), *Mom Doth Murder Sleep* (1991), and *Mom Among the Liars* (1993).

Another discovery made by Dannay in his role as editor of *Ellery Queen's Mystery Magazine* was Harry Kemelman (1908–1996), a Boston native, and like Yaffe, an academic. Kemelman's first published fiction appeared in the April 1947 issue of Ellery Queen. "The Nine Mile Walk," the first of several stories featuring college professor and amateur sleuth Nicky Welt, is considered one of the best examples of a puzzle mystery. Kemelman's 1964 novel *Friday the Rabbi Slept Late* became a bestseller and established one of mystery's most popular series. The series features David Small, a young rabbi at a Conservative synagogue in the fictional New England town of Barnard's Crossing. As the series progresses, Rabbi Small becomes older and wiser, often contending with the tensions of synagogue politics in addition to his crime-solving aptitude. In 1976, the series was adapted as a made-for-television movie starring Stuart Margolin as Rabbi Small and Art Carney as his friend, Police Chief Lanigan. Bruce Solomon played the role of Rabbi Small in the 1977 series *Lanigan's Rabbi,* part of the ongoing *NBC Mystery Movie*.

In the mid-1980s, two mystery series debuted. These were written by two Jewish writers living in Los Angeles, who happened to be husband and wife. Child psychologist Jonathan Kellerman (1949–) and dentist Faye (Marder) Kellerman (1952–) met at UCLA, and were married in 1972. Jonathan's series featured child psychologist Alex Delaware, and began with *When the Bough Breaks* (1985), which won Edgar and Anthony awards for Best First Novel. The series often involves traumatized child-witnesses and gory, disturbing crimes.

While her husband's books tend to remain wedded to the secular world, Faye Kellerman's books are rich in Judaic content. *The Ritual Bath* (1986) introduces Peter Decker, an LAPD detective who was raised by a Southern Baptist family even though his biological parents were Jewish. While investigating a rape that occurred in the mikvah (ritual bath) of a yeshiva community, Decker meets Rina Lazarus, a young Orthodox widow and daughter of Holocaust survivors. The two fall in love, and while solving crimes in the series, they struggle to resolve religious and cultural differences before eventually marrying (prior to the events in *Day of Atonement,* 1991).

The Kellermans have four children, and they are the only married couple to have appeared on the *New York Times* bestseller list simultaneously for two different books. The couple has produced other novels in addition to their series work, including Faye's historical novel *The Quality of Mercy* (1989), Jonathan's Jerusalem thriller *The Butcher's Theater* (1988), and two books that the couple coauthored. The couple's son Jesse (1978–) is also a crime novelist.

Film historian Stuart Kaminsky (1934–) was directing Northwestern University's School of **Radio**, Television, and **Film** while he was establishing himself as one of America's most versatile and prolific mystery writers. *Bullet for a Star* (1977) introduced Toby Peters (born Tobias Pevsner), a private detective frequently employed by Warner Brothers Studios. The series, which has spanned 24 novels set in the 1930s through 1950s, has seen Peters working with the likes of Errol Flynn, Judy Garland, the **Marx Brothers**, John Wayne, and Salvador Dali. Kaminsky has written 14 novels featuring Moscow police detective Porfiry Petrovich Rostnikov, including *Death of a Dissident* (1981) and *A Cold Red Sunrise* (1988); the latter won an Edgar Award for Best Novel. Kaminsky relocated to Florida in 1989, where he taught at Florida State University. It was during this time that he wrote *Lieberman's Folly* (1990), the first of 10 novels to feature sixty-something Chicago police detective Abe Lieberman. Known as "rabbi" to his police colleagues, Lieberman is frequently found at his brother's deli, where he regularly meets with a group of friends known as the "alter cockers." Lieberman is active at his synagogue, where his wife served as its first female president. The Lieberman novels are noted for their honest, poignant, and touching portrayal of its aging protagonist. Kaminsky's other novels include a series about process server Lew Fonesca, two novels based on television's *Rockford Files,* and three *CSI: New York* novels.

Rabbi Joseph Telushkin (1948–), currently the senior rabbi at Los Angeles' Synagogue for the Performing Arts, is the author of numerous books about Judaism including *Jewish Literacy* (1991), *The Book of Jewish Values* (2000), and (with Dennis Prager) *The Nine Questions People Ask about Judaism* (1981). In 1987 Telushkin wrote the first of three novels featuring Daniel Winter, a Los Angeles-based rabbi and talk radio host (modeled in part on himself as well as his long-time friend, Dennis Prager). *The Unorthodox Murder of Rabbi Wahl* (1987), *Final Analysis of Dr. Stark* (1988), and *An Eye for an Eye* (1991) each use the mystery genre as a vehicle for exploring issues of Jewish ethics.

Another Los Angeles Jewish mystery author is Rochelle Krich, daughter of Holocaust survivors, who has explored her own Orthodoxy in her two series featuring LAPD homicide detective Jesse Drake and crime journalist Molly Blume, as well as her five stand-alone thrillers. Before turning to writing full time, Krich was chair of the English department at Yeshiva University of Los Angeles High Schools. Coincidentally, she took over this role from Judith Greber, who had also left the job in order to pursue a successful mystery writing career under the name "Gillian Roberts."

Richard "Kinky" Friedman (1944–) is best known as a politically incorrect humorist, a Texas gubernatorial contender, and the front man for the country western band "Kinky Friedman and the Texas Jewboys." But in 1986 Friedman set down his guitar to write *Greenwich Killing Time,* a mystery featuring himself as an amateur sleuth. He has subsequently written more than 25 books; more than half of these are mysteries.

Other notable Jewish mystery writers include Mystery Writers of America (MWA) Grand Master Lawrence Block, S. J. Rozan, Roger L. Simon, Harlan Coben, Laura Lippman, Sara Paretsky, and Reed Farrel Coleman.

Steve Steinbock

Further Reading: Raphael, Lawrence W. *Mystery Midrash.* Woodstock, VT: Jewish Lights, 1999. Roth,

Lawrence. *Inspecting Jews: American Jewish Detective Stories*. New Brunswick, NJ: Rutgers University Press, 2004. Yaffe, James. *My Mother, the Detective*. Norfolk, VA: Crippen and Landru, 1997.

DIAMOND, NEIL (1941–)

Neil Diamond is one of pop music's most enduring and successful singer-songwriters. Neil Diamond was born on January 24, 1941 to Rose and Akeeba Diamond. He and his brother often lived with their grandparents, and since his parents moved from neighborhood to neighborhood, the boys attended a variety of schools. Music, especially cowboy ballads, appealed to Diamond. He sang in the same choral group as **Barbra Streisand** at Erasmus High School. At age 16 he received his first guitar. He learned to play and wrote his first song, "Hear them Bells."

The family respected Diamond's ability. He did well in fencing and biology in school and was accepted at New York University with a scholarship for premed and fencing. His love of music, however, began to overshadow his interest in biology. Often he wandered the **Tin Pan Alley** area of the city trying to have his music published. He dropped out of college six months before graduation to accept an offer at the Sunbeam Music Company as a staff writer. Earning $50 a week, he sat in a small cubicle and wrote whatever was demanded. Jerry Bock and Sheldon Harnick, who wrote the music for ***Fiddler on the Roof***, sat in cubicles around him. When his contract for Sunbeam ended, he wrote for a few other companies.

In 1965, he began his own company. That year his song "Sunday and Me" was recorded by a popular group, Jay and the Americans. The song hit the charts as one of the year's top 100. In 1966, he recorded "Cherry, Cherry," his first big hit. It rose to number six on the charts.

Diamond began singing at a Greenwich Village club called the Bitter End and started recording songs that were popular there. Among the singles he recorded for Atlantic Records were "Kentucky Woman," and "Girl, You'll Be a Woman Soon." In 1967, *Crashbox Magazine* took a poll of disc jockeys, and Diamond was chosen as one of their favorite composers and singers. Two of his songs, "I'm a Believer" and "A Little Bit Me, A Little Bit You," made the top of the hit parade in 1966–1967.

Diamond moved to California and began recording with MCA Universal Studios. "Sweet Caroline," written for President J. F. Kennedy's daughter Caroline, became a great hit. It was followed by a number of hits. By 1970, Diamond was one of the most popular male vocalists in America. In 1971, he produced an album and autobiographical song "I am, I said." The title came from a line inspired by **Lenny Bruce**, the controversial comedian.

Diamond went through a period of depression, but as he came out of it, he produced such uplifting songs as "Play Me" and "Song Sung Blue." Those songs earned him worldwide sales of over $2 million. By October 1972, Diamond had become one of the first **rock and roll** stars to headline Broadway, as well as the first solo artist since **Al Jolson** to be booked at the Winter Garden Theatre.

Diamond continued working on his professional development and studied classical music. Among his recordings during 1973 were "Rainbow," "Jonathan Livingston Seagull," and "Serenade." In 1974, he won a Grammy, a Golden Globe Award, and an Oscar Nomination for "Jonathan Livingston Seagull." His recording of "You Don't Bring Me Flowers" (1978) with Barbra Streisand became a number one hit record.

Diamond starred in a new film version of ***The Jazz Singer*** in 1980. The songs he composed for the film include, "Hello Again," "America," and "Love on the Rocks." Throughout the 1990s he produced one hit album after another, such as *Up on the Roof—Songs from the Brill Building*. By 2000, Diamond recorded a movie album of his favorite motion picture songs, titled *As Time Goes By*, which sold over 10 million copies. Diamond was inducted into the Songwriters Hall of Fame in 1984, and then in 2000 he was given the Sammy Cahn Lifetime Achievement Award. His 46th album, *Home before Dark* (2008), was the first of his albums to reach number one on the charts.

Diamond married Jaye Posner in 1963, and they had two children, Marjorie and Elyn. They divorced in 1969. His second marriage to Marcia Murphey produced two children, both sons—Jesse Michael Diamond and Micah Joseph Diamond. Diamond's second marriage failed in 1995. He has been involved with Australian native Rachel "Rae" Farley, 31 years his junior, since 1996. *See also* **Popular Music**; **Rock and Roll**.

Herbert M. Druks

Further Reading: Jackson, Laura. *Neil Diamond: His Life, His Music, His Passion.* Toronto, Ontario: ECW Press, 2005.

THE DIARY OF ANNE FRANK

See **The Holocaust in American Culture**

DOCTOROW, E. L. (1931–)

Edgar Lawrence Doctorow authored novels, short stories, screenplays, essays, a play, and is a college professor. He is considered one of the most important American authors today. He was born on January 6, 1931, in New York City, to lower middle-class Jewish parents with artistic interests, David Richard and Rose Levine Doctorow. Doctorow attended the Bronx High School of Science, graduating in 1948, and then enrolled at Kenyon College, where he majored in philosophy, earning his degree with honors in 1952. At Columbia University he pursued graduate work in drama for a year. Doctorow then served in the Army Signal Corps in Germany from 1953 until 1955, during which time he married writer Helen Esther Seltzer, on August 20, 1954.

After the army Doctorow worked in New York for Columbia Pictures, reading seven books a week for three years, writing reports on the potential for movie production. Only one of his recommendations was filmed. Desiring since childhood to write, Doctorow decided he could do better than the authors he read. He wrote *Welcome to Hard Times* (1960), a western novel set in the 1870s Dakota territories. Doctorow had not been west of Ohio, but he preferred emotional truth in his fiction rather than historical accuracy. The novel was a critical success and was made into a 1967 movie starring Henry Fonda. It questions stereotypical westerns in which good guys win over bad, examines the complex reality of the history of the American west and the sometimes less-than-admirable motives of those who settled there. Doctorow next wrote *Big As Life* (1966), a science fiction novel about two slow-moving giant humans from another dimension, who arrive naked in New York Harbor. This too was a critical success, but neither of these early works sold especially well.

Doctorow's third novel, *The Book of Daniel* (1971), his most Jewish work, brought him financial success. Doctorow tried yet another genre, the historical novel, examining the impact the deaths of Julius and Ethel Rosenberg, communists executed in 1953 for treason against the United States, had on their son. The central character is Daniel, son of Rochelle and Paul Isaacson, the fictionalized Rosenbergs. Like *Welcome to Hard Times,* this novel undercuts the simplistic positive image Americans sometimes have of their history.

Doctorow's next novel, *Ragtime* (1975), written while a Guggenheim fellow, is his most successful. It sold 4.5 million copies. Inspired by writer's block, this novel debunks a view of an ideal America in the good old days by means of interactions among a large cast of real and fictional characters. The real include J. P. Morgan, Henry Ford, Emma Goldman, **Harry Houdini**, and Evelyn Nesbit; the fictional include a well-to-do family living in Doctorow's own town of New Rochelle, New York, an immigrant family, and an African American ragtime musician named Coalhouse Walker, whose striking rebellion reveals all is not perfect in early twentieth-century America.

Drinks Before Dinner, a play, was published in 1979, followed by *Loon Lake* in 1980. The latter is another history-oriented novel, this time set during the Great Depression and depicting the amazing rise to wealth and power of a drifter named Joe. Doctorow again questions and satirizes American mythology, in this case related to the American dream. More recent novels are *World's Fair* (1985), *Billy Bathgate* (1989), *The Waterworks* (1994), *City of God* (2000), and *The March* (2005). *World's Fair* is about a Jewish boy growing up in New York City during the Depression and is generally considered autobiographical. As in all of Doctorow's historical novels, *Billy Bathgate* places a higher significance on literary truth than on historical fact. This novel is set again in New York during the Depression, focusing this time on a young boy who rises to wealth and power through his association with the ruthless gangster Dutch Schultz. It is in part an examination of the American fascination with outlaws. *The March* follows the campaign of General William Tecumseh Sherman from Atlanta to Savannah and beyond, in his effort to bring the Civil War to an end. As in earlier novels, fictional and historical figures (including Sherman and Lincoln) cross paths and create an intriguing and iconoclastic picture of America past.

Doctorow has written essays collected in *Jack London, Hemingway, and the Constitution* (1993), *Reporting the Universe* (2003), and *Creationists* (2006); and short stories collected in *Sweet Land Stories* (2004), and *Lives of the Poets: Six Stories and a Novella* (1984); and screenplays (not his favorite genre)—*Three Screenplays* (includes *Ragtime, Daniel, Loon Lake,* 2003). Some of his novels have been made into movies: *Welcome to Hard Times, Daniel, Ragtime* (also produced as a stage musical), and *Billy Bathgate.* He has received numerous awards, including four National Book Critics Circle Awards for *Ragtime* (1976), *Loon Lake* (1982), *Billy Bathgate* (1989), and *The March* (2006); a National Book Award for *World's Fair* (1986); and two PEN/Faulkner Awards for *Billy Bathgate* (1990) and *The March* (2006). He has also served as an editor, both at the New American Library (1959–1964) and at the Dial Press (1964–1969), and as a professor—at several schools, but mostly at New York University, as Glucksman Professor of English and American Letters (he has taught creative writing since 1982). As an author he sets a strenuous schedule, working from early in the morning until 7:30 at night, with a break in the middle of the day. He also believes in careful revision, correcting his work as many as eight times. He and his wife of more than 50 years have lived for many years in New Rochelle, New York, and they have three children: Jenny, Caroline, and Richard. Doctorow is likely to be long remembered as a first-rate storyteller, for his deconstruction of American myth, his moral concern, and his innovative and diverse narrative techniques. *See also* **Literature.**

Alan Kelly

Further Reading: Bloom, Harold, ed. *Modern Critical Views: E. L. Doctorow.* Philadelphia: Chelsea House Publishers, 2001. Doctorow, Edgar L. *Creationist: Selected Essays: 1993–2006.* New York: Random House, 2006.

DOUGLAS, KIRK (1916–)

Kirk Douglas is an American actor, film producer, and novelist. Born Issur Danielovitch Demsky in Amsterdam, New York on December 12, 1916, he was the fourth of eight children of Herschel Danielovitch and Bryna Sanglel, poor and illiterate Russian Jewish immigrants. His father was a "ragman," buying scraps, throwaways, and junk, who barely eked out an existence. Despite his family poverty, Danielovitch had a Bar Mitzvah and worked himself through St. Lawrence University in Canton, New York as an usher, bellhop, waiter, and professional wrestler, becoming the 1939 class president and receiving his BA in 1939. After college Danielovitch received a scholarship at the prestigious American Academy of Dramatic Arts in New York City, and while there, he changed his name to Kirk Douglas. He made a brief Broadway acting debut in 1941, but from then until 1944, when he was diagnosed with amoebic dysentery, he served as an ensign in the navy.

After the war, he returned to New York to continue his career on Broadway. A small part in a 1945 production brought him to the attention of Hal B. Wallis, a Hollywood producer, who tapped him to play opposite Barbara Stanwyck in the *Strange Love of Martha Ivers* (1946). His portrayal in 1949 of a prizefighter in *Champion* confirmed his reputation as a leading dramatic artist. He had memorable roles in *Young Man with a Horn* (1950), *The Bad and the Beautiful* (1953), *Lust for Life* (1956), *Gunfight at the O.K. Corral* (1957), and *Lonely are the Brave* (1962). Douglas eventually formed his own company, Bryna Productions, in memory of his mother, and made the antiwar *Paths of Glory* (1957) and *Spartacus* (1960). He starred in both.

He also played an important role in breaking the Hollywood blacklist when he insisted on giving the blacklisted screenwriter Dalton Trumbo full on-screen credit for his *Spartacus* screenplay.

Douglas has also identified himself with Israeli causes and starred in *The Juggler* (1953), which was filmed in Israel, and in 1966 he played the lead in *Cast a Giant Shadow,* Col. **David "Mickey" Marcus**, the American hero of the War of Independence. In his eighties, Douglas also had a second Bar Mitzvah to reaffirm his faith.

He has also been involved in a wide variety of humanitarian causes, and, in 1981, he received the Presidential Medal of Freedom from President Jimmy Carter, the highest U.S. honor a civilian can receive. *See also* **Film**; **Film Stars**.

Leslie Rabkin

Further Reading: Douglas, Kirk. *Climbing the Mountain: My Search for Meaning*. New York: Simon and Schuster, 2000. ———. *The Ragman's Son*. New York: Simon and Schuster, 1988.

DREYFUSS, RICHARD (1947–)

Richard Dreyfuss, an award-winning actor, was born in Brooklyn, New York on October 29, 1947 to a Jewish family. When he was a child, his parents relocated to Beverly Hills, California. As a child he began acting in school productions at the Beverly Hills Jewish Community Center. By the 1970s Dreyfuss's career seemed to be heading in the right direction with a small role in *The Graduate,* which served as a catalyst to larger roles, including *American Graffiti* (1973), and his first lead role, in *The Apprenticeship of Duddy Kravitz* (1974). The character of Duddy Kravitz is a brash Jewish kid from Montreal who is determined to "make it"—whatever "it" takes. Dreyfuss was horrified at his performance in the film and feared it would end his career. His anxiety caused him to jump at the role of "Matt Hooper," a major character in **Steven Spielberg**'s blockbuster *Jaws* (1975). After *Jaws,* Spielberg cast Dreyfuss as the lead in *Close Encounters of the Third Kind* (1977). In 1978, at the age of 29 he became the youngest actor to win a Best Actor Oscar in *The Goodbye Girl.* By the decade's end, Dreyfuss had established himself as a major film star.

In the early years of the 1980s his films were not so well received, and, hurt by a cocaine problem, he appeared to be in downward spiral. Dreyfuss entered a rehab program and slowly made a comeback with the film *Down and Out in Beverly Hills* (1986). In 1995, he earned another Oscar nomination for his role as a caring music teacher in *Mr. Holland's Opus.*

Dreyfuss remains connected to his Judaism, even if he is not particularly religious. In 1994, he participated in the Papal Concert to Commemorate the Shoah (**Holocaust**) in Rome, Italy. This was a major event of reconciliation arranged by Pope John Paul II at the Vatican, attended by the chief rabbi of Rome, and dedicated to the memory of the Jews of the Holocaust. At this event, Dreyfuss recited the Kaddish, which was part of the performance of **Leonard Bernstein**'s Third Symphony.

He has been married three times—first to Jeramie Raim, in 1983, with whom he had three children. The couple divorced in 1995. In 1999 he married Janelle Lacey, and this marriage also ended in divorce. In 2006, he married Russian-born Svetlana Erokhin.

Dreyfuss is active politically and is supportive of the Israeli peace movement which seeks an equitable solution to the Israeli-Palestinian conflict. *See also* **Film**; **Film Stars**.

Judith Lupatkin

Further Reading: Pogrebin, Abigail. "Richard Dreyfuss." *Stars of David.* New York: Broadway Books, 2005.

DYLAN, BOB (1941–)

An acclaimed rock star, Bob Dylan was born Robert Allen Zimmerman on May 24, 1941 in Duluth, Minnesota, to Abraham and Beatrice Zimmerman, Dylan grew up in Hibbing, surrounded by mines and farms, where cold weather freezes rebellious enthusiasms and hard work keeps the local youth focused. It is a place where some teenagers found refuge wearing James Dean's leather jacket. The wish to accompany great artists such as Little Richard was mentioned in Zimmerman's 1959 high school yearbook. Though Robert enjoyed Hank Williams, Gene Vincent, and Bill Haley, Little Richard brought a fresh, lively approach to the music. These spirited performances motivated Zimmerman to play the living room instrument.

He also learned the guitar and harmonica, playing country and blues songs grabbed from the radio or record albums. Forming his first band, the Shadow Blasters, Zimmerman performed at a Hibbing High show in 1957. By imitating Little Richard's moves and Harpo Marx's sweet destructiveness, he drove the principal to close the curtain. Robert toured high school parties with his second band, the Golden Chords, before joining the Rock Boppers, the Satin Tones, and the Shadows (featuring Bobby Vee).

Schmoozing around Dinkytown's jazz clubs and bars, Robert enrolled in 1959 at nearby University of Minnesota. He adopted poet Dylan Thomas's first name for his last and, while roaming from clubs to libraries, soaked up the musical inspiration of Harry Belafonte. He also took every opportunity to read "Beat" literature. He read authors hitch-hiking their own path—not to redemption or purgatory, but to self-discovery. Among his readings was Woody Guthrie's autobiography, *Bound for Glory,* which draws a map with songs about encounters and interpretations. Woody's Jewish mother-in-law, Yiddish poet Aliza Greenblatt, influenced him to write songs such as "Hanuka Dance." By the mid-1950s, blacklists and sickness drove Guthrie to hospitals, where he was visited by young artists such as Bob Dylan and Joan Baez.

Baez and Dylan met in April 1961 at Gerde's Folk City when he opened for John Lee Hooker —the same place where, five months later, Robert Shelton saw him play such songs as "Talkin' Hava Negeilah Blues," which made him famous with an article in the *New York Times.* Dylan's first album, *Bob Dylan* (1962), is mostly based on traditional and gospel songs heard during his musical education and in Greenwich Village. Two years later, Baez and Dylan appeared at the Monterey Folk Festival. She invited him to be a surprise guest on her summer tour, and both headlined the Newport Folk Festival. They forged an artistic and romantic liaison from 1963 to 1965, singing at rallies such as Martin Luther King's March on Washington.

Also in 1961, Dylan met Suze Rotolo, who appeared on the cover of his second album, *Freewheelin'* (1963), and inspired the songs "Don't Think Twice, It's All Right" and "Boots of Spanish Leather." Both Baez and Rotolo helped raise Dylan's political consciousness. In 1964, his name appeared on a petition written by another mentor, **Allen Ginsberg**, protesting **Lenny Bruce**'s arrest. Gradually, Ginsberg's "Howl" and Dylan's "Hard Rain" made their way onto pages and airwaves, as both share poems in Jack Kerouac's Garden or the cardboard conversations that take place in the back alleys written about in Dylan's 1965 song "Subterranean Homesick Blues."

Dylan hitchhiked from one encounter to another, surprising audiences before they labeled him. He was never anti-American. Dylan was always among the first to anticipate evolution and darkness in the 1960s, and he defended the First Amendment. While French journalists harassed him in 1966 about his supposedly anti-American stance, and French crowds at the Olympia in Paris awaited condemnations of U.S. policy in Vietnam, Dylan opened the curtain with a huge American flag behind him, surfing on the jeers.

In the early 1970s Dylan participated in George Harrison's Concert for Bangladesh, Sam Peckinpah's film *Pat Garrett and Billy the Kid* (which features the song "Knockin' on Heaven's Door"), and a live album, *Before the Flood,* recorded on his tour with The Band. In 1975, Dylan traveled to Rahway Penitentiary to meet Rubin "Hurricane" Carter. For a few weeks, he went to see the framed boxer and learned about his case. A few encounters led to an 8:32 slam, "Hurricane." The song was played every night on the Rolling Thunder Revue tour, and Baez and Ginsberg accompanied him. Dylan recorded songs with the latter in 1971, including William Blake poems. After the Rolling Thunder Revue, Dylan embarked on a spiritual odyssey with Christianity and Orthodox Judaism.

Slow Train Coming (1979) and *Saved* (1980) reveal Dylan's relationship to Christianity and the figure of Jesus, a presence he says he felt in the room with him in late 1978. Some see in this turn no blind devotion, no blatant conversion, but simply the company of another Jewish man in his thirties who lived 2,000 years ago. Was he a rabbi, a prophet, and/or the Son of God? Many fans hear too many certain answers from the man who had previously used his gift of words to ask questions, not answer them. Whatever one's perspective, both ends of the spectrum can agree Dylan preferred non-moralizing virtues over organized institutions, and his explicit rock evangelism was already on the wane by the release of *Shot of Love* (1981). This record includes a song about another charismatic Jewish man, one who was labeled a sick comedian, social commentator, prophet, and devil: Lenny Bruce. Dylan shared a short cab ride with Bruce and was inspired by the man's chutzpah," abstruse feelings, and his expansive comprehension of human nature.

In 1981, for his 40th birthday, Dylan traveled to Jerusalem, visiting the Western Wall. That same year, Israel launched a preventive strike on Saddam Hussein's nuclear facilities. The world forgets Hussein aimed his bombs at Israel and Dylan rushed to defend Israel. Ranting against injustice, just as he did in "Hurricane," Dylan

Bob Dylan, born Robert Zimmerman. Photo of the almost-legendary rock star taken before a sell-out crown at Madison Square Garden in New York City on December 8, 1975, at a benefit to support efforts for former boxer Reuben "Hurricane" Carter to get a new trial after his conviction for murder. Dylan performed the song "Hurricane," which he wrote for this occasion. [AP Photo]

explains in "Neighborhood Bully" (*Infidels,* 1983), how Jews are criticized and condemned just for living. They are expected to take cyclical beatings with a decent placating smile. This is reminiscent of what Serge Gainsbourg did with his 1967 song "Le Sable et le Soldat," which supported Israel during the Six Day War. In 1982, Dylan celebrated his son's Bar Mitzvah in Jerusalem.

In the mid-1980s, Dylan enjoyed various musical experiences, including a Lubavitcher (Chabad) charity event where he sang "Hava Nagila" with his son-in-law, Peter Himmelmann. He and actor Harry Dean Stanton joined the USA for Africa artists (1985) and also toured with Tom Petty

(1986) and the Grateful Dead (1987). The album *Under the Red Sky* (1990) is dedicated to Gabby Goo Goo, which turns out to be his daughter, Desiree Gabrielle Dennis—Dylan's motto, born in 1986 to his new wife, Carolyn Dennis. Grammy Awards, the French Légion d'Honneur, the Kennedy Center Honor presented by Bill Clinton, a role as a chauffeur with Ben Gazzara in *Paradise Cove,* a concert in front of the pope, and musical work with Slash, David Crosby, and Elton John—as well as the continuation of the Neverending Tour, still in train at this writing, round out the 1990s.

The first decade of the twenty-first century requires the artistic definition of Dylan to be plural, not only in experiences but also in persons. His son Jakob sings with *The Wallflowers* while Jesse is a successful director. Bob Dylan continues to sing freely about wars, racism, great deeds, and common, everyday experiences. Never a member of a party or exclusive club, he joins collective movements when the spirit moves.

Dylan's vast awareness and talent has facilitated great encounters with such important and different artists as Joan Baez, Jimi Hendrix, Johnny Cash, George Harrison, Roy Orbison, Tom Petty, Guns N' Roses, David Crosby, Lou Reed, David Bowie, **Gene Simmons**, Martin Scorsese—who directs *No Direction Home* (2005), a brilliant biographical document including interviews of Dylan's early friends—Allen Ginsberg, and Dylan himself. Noting that some of Dylan's detractors decry his tendency to change musical style, Malcolm Jones writes, "The one sure thing about Bob Dylan is that there is no sure thing. In a musical career stretching over more than three decades, he has proven time and again that he owns the most bottomless bag of tricks in the business. With changeling grace, he has embraced folk music, rock and roll, country, and gospel" (Jones, 1995). Art for Dylan has always been about change. Of fans who want him to continue performing his old songs exactly the way he recorded them, he says, "I'd rather live in the moment than some kind of nostalgia trip, which I feel is a drug, a real drug that people are mainlining. It's outrageous. People are mainlining nostalgia like it was morphine. I don't want to be a drug dealer" (ibid.). Traveling the same road twice for an artist such as Dylan offers no real reward unless he is accompanied by new muses and companions.

In 2008, Dylan was awarded the Pulitzer Prize for his "profound impact on popular music and American culture, marked by lyrical compositions of extraordinary poetic power." *See also* **Rock and Roll**.

Steve Krief

Further Reading: Dylan, Bob. *Chronicles: Volume I.* New York: Simon and Schuster, 2004. Gray, Michael. *The Bob Dylan Encyclopedia.* Continuum International, 2006. Jones, Malcolm, Jr. "A Primitive's Portfolio." *Newsweek,* March 20, 1995. Marqusee, Mike. *Wicked Messenger: Bob Dylan and the 1960s.* Seven Stones Press, 2005.

E

EINSTEIN, ALBERT (1879–1955)

Albert Einstein, a Nobel Prize-winning theoretical physicist, is easily recognized by his distinctive appearance, which graced the cover of *Time* when in 1999 it named him the "person of the century." His professional colleagues added to his praises by identifying him as the greatest physicist of all time. Albert Einstein remains an iconic figure in American popular culture. His expressive face and distinctive hairstyle can still be found on billboards, t-shirts, films, and novels, and his name continues to be used as a synonym for "genius." Einstein was born in the German city of Ulm to Hermann and Pauline Einstein. His father was a salesman and engineer. When Einstein was five, his father showed him a pocket compass, and he realized that something in empty space was moving the needle. Later he would recall this experience made "a deep and lasting impression" that inspired him to study science. At his mother's insistence, Einstein at age six took violin lessons, and, although he eventually quit, the experience provided him with a lifelong love of Mozart's violin sonatas. He built models and mechanical devices for fun and began to show a talent for mathematics, as well as for philosophy. By age 12, he learned Euclidean geometry from a school booklet. Soon thereafter he began to investigate calculus, although of the sciences, his favorite was physics. Einstein did not like the authoritarian nature of the German school system, nor was he fond of German society. Throughout his life he believed that schools should have a free atmosphere. He noted that it is a horrible experience to be in a school where teachers worked with the methods of "fear, force, and artificial authority." Throughout his life he believed that "imagination is more important than knowledge. I never came upon my discoveries through the process of rational thinking" (Isaacson, 2007). Like many Jews of his generation, Einstein as a child went through a religious phase and then rebelled against it. His parents were entirely irreligious. His father, in fact, referred to Jewish rituals as "ancient superstitions," and, when Einstein was six, he sent him to a Catholic school where he took the standard religious courses and did so well in his studies that he helped his classmates. Nevertheless, young Einstein could not help being aware of his Jewish roots, perhaps a result of often being taunted about his racial characteristics. Einstein biographer Walter Isaacson states that "physical attacks and insults on the way home from school were frequent . . . and they were sufficient to consolidate, even in a child, a lively sense of being an outsider" (Ibid.).

Despite his parents' rejection of Judaism, young Einstein developed a passion for Judaism, and he was so fervent in his belief that he observed religious strictures in every detail. He did not eat pork, kept the kosher dietary laws, and observed the Sabbath. Einstein's commitment to Jewish ritual and observance, however, was a short one. The reading of scientific books took him away from Judaism, once he reached the conclusion the Bible stories could not be true. Nevertheless, anti-Semitism would continue to plague Einstein into adulthood, even after he discovered the theory of relativity. In 1900, he completed four years of study at the Federal Polytech Academy in Zurich, Switzerland and passed the state examinations, which enabled him to teach. In 1901, he was admitted to the University of Zurich as a lecturer and found he enjoyed teaching, but he failed to attain a permanent academic position, due to his quirky personality and his Jewish heritage. Einstein for some time worked in a Swiss patent office in order to earn a living.

In 1903, he had married Mileva Maric, who had been a fellow student. She was Catholic, and his family did not approve of her. Their first child, Albert, was born a year after their marriage. A second child, Edward, was born, and because at that point in his life his Jewish roots were of no consequence, his children were raised in the faith of their mother. Einstein avoided religious ritual for the rest of his life and especially had "an aversion to the orthodox practice of the Jewish or any traditional religion, as well as to attendance at religious services" (Ibid.). When Maric had their two children baptized, Einstein's response was, "They've turned Catholic. Well, its all the same to me." His rejection of religious creeds also inculcated him against all forms of dogma and authority. He was finally awarded his professorship, in 1909, after acquiring a reputation in the field of physics. In 1905 he published his first essay on relativity, entitled "Towards the Electrodynamics of Moving Bodies, the Theory of Relativity." Some years later he was asked how he had come to the theory, and he responded that he was convinced of the harmony of the universe. Elsewhere, he said of his theory that "if my theory is proven correct Germany will say I am one of the greatest Germans and the French will say that I'm a citizen of the world. But if it should happen the theory is incorrect, I am sure that the French will call me a German and the Germans will call me a Jew" (Ibid.). Einstein separated from his first wife, Mileva, in 1914, but he promised her that should he win the Nobel Prize, he would give her the monetary award, which he did after being awarded the Nobel Prize in Physics in 1921 for his service to theoretical physics. During World War I he declared himself a pacifist, a conviction he held his entire life. Einstein abhorred conflict and stated that in such times one realizes "to what a sad species of animals one belongs . . . How I wish that somewhere there existed an island for those who are wise and of good will" (Clark, 1984). After his divorce from Mileva, Einstein wed his cousin Elsa, a marriage that lasted the rest of their lives. Isaacson's biography of Einstein about the second marriage contends, "So even if it (marriage to Elsa) was not the stuff of poetry, the bond between them was a solid one. It was forged by satisfying each other's desires and needs, it was genuine, and it worked in both directions" (2007). By 1919, he was quite famous because of his theory of relativity. German nationalists and some of his fellow German physicists, however, hated him. In the aftermath of the assassination of the German Foreign Minister Walter Rathenau—a Jew and a friend—by a German nationalist, Einstein realized just how brutal the politics of anti-Semitism were throughout the Weimar Republic. When he learned that he was the next target to be murdered by the German nationalists, Einstein decided to leave his post at the Berlin Academy and the Kaiser William Institute for Physics, stating that "I would never have thought that hatred, blindness and ingratitude could go to such extremes" (Isaacson, 2007). Anti-Semites continued to attack his theories as revolutionary and destructive of physics. He left Germany permanently in 1933 as the Nazis came to power. After traveling around the world, Einstein settled in the United States, where he

Photo of Albert Einstein with Talmudic scholar Chaim Tchernowitz taken in Einstein's study in Princeton, New Jersey in January or February 1945. [Forward Association]

continued his work at the Institute for Advanced Study in Princeton, New Jersey, a position created for him by a Jewish philanthropist, **Louis Bamberger**. At Princeton, Einstein continued his scientific work without teaching or administrative responsibility.

Some of his colleagues criticized his attitude. They were annoyed by his informality, his relaxed manner, his dress—a staple of which was slacks and a sweatshirt, and at times, shoes without socks. One biographer of Einstein noted that his dressing was "an extension of his philosophy, which sought to reduce everything personal to its simplest level. Not wearing socks, for example, eliminated the need for anyone to darn them . . . He wore his hair long because it helped him avoid wasting time at the barber shop" (Ibid.). Despite his critics, Einstein thrived at the institute. One of his favorite pastimes was sailing on board his small boat, yet he did not know how to swim and he did not have life-jackets on board. The idiosyncrasies he was criticized for endeared him to the public-at-large. Einstein was not a conventional agnostic. Not unlike some of America's founding fathers, he believed in a Creator of the universe, but not in a religious sense. He was awed by the wonders of nature, stating that "nature has many puzzles and marvels and there are many things that we do not understand yet about nature. This is why my religion is really the universe" (Einstein, 1954). Around the time Einstein turned 50, he began to articulate more clearly his deepening appreciation of his Jewish heritage, and somewhat separately, his belief in God—albeit a rather impersonal, deistic concept of God, owing more to Spinoza than to Torah. Einstein's turn to a Creator resulted from his empathy for his fellow Jews because of their continued oppression. It seemed that his awareness of anti-Semitism, especially on the eve of Hitler's "seizure of power" in 1933, reawakened some of his lost religious sentiments. Isaacson has noted, "Whether embracing the beauty of his gravitational field equations or rejecting the uncertainty in quantum mechanics, he displayed a profound faith in the orderliness of the universe. This served as a basis for his scientific outlook—also his religious outlook" (2007).

Einstein wrote in 1929 that "the highest satisfaction of a scientific person is the realization that God Himself could not have arranged these connections any other way than that which exists, any more than it would have been His power to make four a prime number" (Isaacson, 385). Einstein's religious feelings of awe and humility also informed his sense of social justice and drove him to eschew excess consumption and materialism and to dedicate his life to efforts on behalf of the oppressed. As a teacher who liked to simplify his subject, Einstein often explained his theory of relativity in laymen's terms. He once explained to a journalist that the theory boiled down to this: "When a man sits with a pretty girl for an hour, it seems like a minute. But let him sit on a hot stove for a minute—and it's longer than any hour. That's relativity" (*Journal of Exothermic Science,* 1938).

After he left Germany in 1933, the Hebrew University offered him a post, but he declined the offer because he felt that the university's president, Judah Magnes, ran the institution in too dictatorial a manner. He stated that he would accept the invitation only if Magnes resigned. Although Einstein never joined the Hebrew University, he had an intense sense of identity with his Jewish heritage, its culture, a deep respect for the Jewish intellectual tradition, and a dedication to the preservation of the Jewish people—which led him to support the creation of a Jewish state in Palestine. Offered the presidency of Israel after the passing of Chaim Weizmann, Einstein rejected the honor but told Israeli Ambassador Abba Eban that he saw the birth of Israel as one of the few political acts in his lifetime that had a moral quality. Nevertheless, he was concerned that the Jewish state was having trouble learning to live with the Arabs and warned that "the attitude we adopt towards the Arab minority will provide the real test of our moral standards as a people" (from a January 1955 letter used in Isaacson, 2007). During his years at the Institute for Advanced Study, in Princeton, Einstein spoke out on political issues. He believed that the economic anarchy brought on by capitalism was the cause of economic hardship. He considered "the crippling of individuals as the worst evil of capitalism. Our whole educational system suffers from this evil. An exaggerated competitive attitude is inculcated into the student who is trained to worship acquisitive success as a preparation for his future career" (Einstein, 1949).

An avowed socialist, Einstein believed that "if a socialist economy would replace the capitalist society then many grave evils would be eliminated" (Ibid.). Einstein found that in America the sense of equality and human dignity was "mainly limited to men of white skins." He believed that slavery had ruthlessly suppressed and exploited Africans brought to America and that contemporary prejudices towards blacks were "the result of the desire to maintain this unworthy condition" (Einstein, 1946). Einstein remained an outspoken critic of racial prejudice throughout his life in the United States.

Although best known for his theory of relativity, Einstein's theories had various practical applications for the American public. A list of products that benefited directly or indirectly from his scientific theories would include fluorescent lights, television, compact disc players, remote controls, microwave ovens, electric stoves, photographic film (from photochemistry), air conditioners and refrigerators (from his work on diffusion), nuclear reactors, laser-guided missiles (from photo-electricity), and his contribution to the production of both the atomic and hydrogen bombs (from his work on mass-energy equivalence). On August 9, 1939, Einstein wrote to President Franklin D. Roosevelt one of the most historically important letters ever received by an American president:

> Some recent work by Enrico Fermi and L. Szilard which has been communicated to me in manuscript, leads me to expect that the element of uranium may be turned into a new and important source of energy in the immediate future. Certain aspects of the situation seem to call for watchfulness and, if necessary, quick action on the part of the administration, I believe, therefore, that it is my duty to bring to your attention the following facts and recommendations. In the course of the last four months it has been made possible probable—through the work of Fermi and Szilard in America—that it may become possible to set up nuclear chain reactions in a large mass of uranium, by which vast quantities of new radium-like elements would be generated. Now it appears almost certain that this could be achieved in the immediate future. This new phenomenon led to the construction of bombs, and it is conceivable—though much less certain—that extremely powerful bombs of a new type may be constructed. A single bomb of this type, carried by boat or exploded in a port, might very well destroy the whole port together with some of the surrounding territory. However, such bombs prove to be too heavy for transportation by air. I understand that Germany has actually stopped the sale of uranium from Czechoslovakian mines which she has taken over. That she should have taken such early action might perhaps be understood on the ground that the son of the German Under-Secretary of State, von Weizsacker, is attached to the Kaiser-Wilhelm Institute in Berlin, where some of the American work on uranium is now being repeated.

The letter, which recommended that President Roosevelt build an atomic bomb, lest the Germans develop it first, led to the Manhattan Project, which ultimately built the bombs that were used on Hiroshima and Nagasaki in 1945, thus ending World War II. Einstein wrote President Truman, in 1945, to tell him that he supported the president's call to open Palestine to 100,000 Jewish survivors of the Holocaust. During the Cold War, Einstein continued to speak out on political issues. He joined in the appeal of many intellectuals appealing to President Truman to void the execution of Julius and Ethel Rosenberg, both of whom were accused for spying for the Soviet Union. Truman passed the matter of the Rosenbergs on to his successor Dwight D. Eisenhower, who subsequently ordered the execution to proceed. Einstein, who regretted the letter he sent to President Roosevelt that led to the building of the atomic bomb, became an advocate to put an end to further nuclear bomb research or development and urged an international force under United Nations auspices to keep the peace. He also urged those brought before the so-called McCarthy Committee investigating un-American activities to refuse to testify with the caveat that "this refusal to testify must be based on the assertion that it is shameful for a blameless citizen to submit to such an inquisition." His activism led followers of the demagogic Senator Joseph McCarthy to label Einstein a security risk and a communist. Adding fuel to the fire, Albert Einstein was also somewhat naïve in his associations. His support for the leftist former Vice President Henry A. Wallace and Paul Robeson Jr., a singer as well as apologist for Josef Stalin, led Edgar Hoover, the director of the FBI to keep a close watch over Einstein's activities and compile a file on the famed scientist. Despite the growing number of enemies that he attracted because of his political activism, Einstein remained a beloved figure among his fellow Americans. His growing fame, his warmth as a human being, and his iconic stature allowed him to continue his outspoken defense of peace, equality, liberty, and support for causes that too often were associated with the Left. In the last 10 years of his life, Einstein dedicated himself to world peace through the establishment of effective international cooperation to prevent war through arms control. For Einstein, there was no alternative to peace, and nuclear war meant the end of life. In the nuclear age, stated Einstein, "what was at stake was the very life or death of our society. . . . Today it is too late to think in terms of military power or technical superiority. What one group of men have discovered, other intelligent and patient workers will surely learn too. There is no secret" (Isaacson, 2007). Albert Einstein was one of the greatest personalities and humanists of the twentieth century. He was a very special human being whose genius was only surpassed by his humanity and humility.

Herbert M. Druks

Further Reading: Clark, Ronald W. *Einstein: The Life and Times*. New York: HarperCollins, 1984. Einstein, Albert. *Ideas and Opinions*. New York: Crown Publishers, 1954. ———. "The Negro Question." Essay. 1946. ———. "Why Socialism?" *Monthly Review*, May 1949. Frank, Philipp. *Einstein: His Life and Times*. Cambridge, MA: Da Capo Press, 2002. Isaacson, Walter. *Einstein: His Life and Universe*. New York: Simon and Schuster, 2007. *Journal of Exothermic Science and Technology* 1, no. 9 (1938).

EISNER, WILLIAM (1917–2005)

William Eisner, a renowned comics writer and artist, was born in Brooklyn, New York, the son of Jewish immigrants. His father, Samuel Eisner, an immigrant from Austria, was a painter and a not-so-successful manufacturer in Manhattan's garment district. Eisner's father had once aspired to act in the **Yiddish theater**, but earning a living for his wife and three children placed that dream beyond his reach. To help make ends meet, young Will Eisner sold newspapers on Wall Street. There he discovered comics. He started drawing for the DeWitt Clinton High School newspaper in 1933, and soon after graduation Eisner, at nineteen, went to work for *Wow; What a Magazine,* where he drew an adventure script called *Captain Scott Dalton*. The magazine, however, only lasted for four more issues. Eisner joined forces with Jerry Iger to co-found the Eisner and Iger Studio, a "packaging house" which contracted artists and writers' works for publishers. Staffers included future comic artists such as Jack Kurtzberg (later known as Jack Kirby, the co-creator of *Spiderman* and *The Fantastic Four*), Bob Kahn (later Bob Kane, the creator of *Batman*), and other future comic artists in the comic book industry.

Eisner's early comic characters included Sheena, the Queen of the Jungle, Dollman, and Blackhawk. Eisner and Iger, to their later regret, turned down a crude submission called *Superman* by equally young comic artists Jerry Siegel and Joe Shuster.

In 1940, after selling out his share of the company to Jerry Iger, Eisner created his most famous character, the Spirit, a masked crime fighter. At the height of the character's popularity, *The Spirit* appeared in 20 major market newspapers with a combined circulation of 5 million readers. From 1942–1945, Eisner served as a warrant officer in the military. During the war, he created motivational posters and pioneered the use of cartoons for instructional purposes with the publication of *Army Motors*. The magazine, which illustrated preventive maintenance, eventually sold 1,500,000 copies.

From 1945 to 1951, Eisner returned to work on *The Spirit* at his new office at 37 Wall Street. From that time to the present, the character of *The Spirit* has rarely been out of print. Since 2000, DC Comics has undertaken an ambitious program to reprint all 645 stories in color hardcovers as *The Spirit Archives* and in 2006 launched a new series of authorized *Spirit* stories.

Cartoonist, playwright, and Eisner's most trusted assistant, **Jules Feiffer** has called Eisner "a rabbi of the comic art form" and "a national treasure."

In the 1970s, Eisner turned to longer storytelling forms. He created the very first graphic novel with the publication of *A Contract with God and Other Tenement Stories* (1978). In his creation of the graphic novel, Eisner married comics and literature in the same way that William Blake blended his drawings and prose. The semi-autobiographical novel revolutionized the art form and became the fastest-growing genre of its kind. Eisner published 20 additional graphic novels, including such classics as *The Building* (1987), *A Life Force* (1988), and *The Name of the Game* (2003). W.W. Norton reissued many of Eisner's graphic novels beginning with *The Contract with God Trilogy* (2005), a hardcover combining three titles, which focuses on a single mythical block in the Bronx. The books include *The Contract with God, Dropsie Avenue,* and *A Life Force.*

In the reissue of *A Contract with God and Other Tenements Stories* in 2001, Eisner revealed that the inspiration for the novel grew out of the 1969 death of his daughter, Alice, who suffered from leukemia. Until then, only his closest friends had been aware that he had a daughter.

In other graphic novels Eisner maps abandoned neighborhoods (*Dropsie Avenue*) and destroyed buildings (*The Building*). He dedicated *Invisible People* (1993) to Carolyn Lamboly, a poor invalid buried anonymously, who died after a computer error discontinued social assistance. Eisner's work is honored in many different venues—at the Angoulême Festival, in a Brazilian documentary, and in Michael Chabon's *The Amazing Adventures of Kavalier & Clay.*

In the graphic novel *To the Heart of the Storm* (1991), Eisner recounts the trauma of walking to school each day while neighborhood bullies referred to Julian Eisner, Will's brother, as "Jewleen." Eisner shares this moment in his semi-autobiographical graphic tale of his early childhood, where he invites us to discover the family background which inspired him to become one of the greatest contributors to comic books ever. Eisner, Stan Lee, Jack Kirby, Harvey Kurtzman, and other Jewish comic book writers helped shape the comic book industry by incorporating the language of the street, films, and the stories they shared in the ethnic neighborhoods that they grew up in. But in the novel Eisner also reveals much about the anti-Semitism of the 1930s. It is not coincidental that in some of his last works, Eisner turned to themes dealing with anti-Semitism and Jewishness.

In *Fagin the Jew* (2003), Eisner attempts to get past the negative stereotype portrait of Fagin in Charles Dickens's *Oliver Twist.* In his last graphic novel, *The Plot: The Secret Story of The Protocols of the Elders of Zion* (2005), Eisner tackled the subject of the infamous anti-Semitic tract that continues to disseminate vicious falsehoods about Israel and Jews in general. Inspiration for writing *The Plot* resulted from Eisner's collision with *The Protocols of the Elders of Zion* text after September 11. Middle Eastern governments re-released the book at that time, in an attempt to whip up anti-Semitic feelings. Angered by the resurgence of this canard, Eisner deconstructs the *Protocols* message of hate, recalling its use against Jews by anti-Semitic states including that of Hitler's Germany. About *The Plot* Eisner wrote: "The people who I want to read this are the people for whom *The Protocols of Zion* is being published" (Eisner, 2006). Ironically, the French editor of *The Plot,* Grasset, published the hoax in the 1920s and Eisner's book 80 years later. The book concludes with Eisner touring the States, tirelessly debating with those exploiting the hoax.

In 1988, the comics community paid tribute to Eisner by creating the Will Eisner Comic Industry Awards, more commonly known as the "Eisners," to recognize achievements each year in the comics medium. Eisner enthusiastically participated in the awards ceremony, congratulating each recipient. In 2002 Eisner received a Lifetime Achievement Award from the National Federation for Jewish Culture. In the same year, *Wizard* magazine named Eisner "the most influential comic artist of all time."

Eisner died in Lauderdale Lakes, Florida of complications from quadruple bypass surgery performed in 2004. He is survived by his wife, Ann Weingarten Eisner, and their son, John. Eisner is buried in the plot next to his daughter Alice. *See also* **Comic Books**.

Steve Krief

Further Reading: Cooke, Andrew, and Jon Cooke. *Will Eisner: The Spirit of an Artistic Pioneer.* Documentary. Montilla Pictures, 2006. Chabon, Michael. *The Amazing Adventures of Kavalier & Clay.* New York: Random House, 2000. (Chabon has said that the novel is based in good part on Eisner.) Eisner, Will. *The Plot: The Secret Story of The Protocols of the Elders of Zion.* W.W. Norton, 2006.

EPHRON, NORA (1941–)

Nora Ephron, American film director, producer, screenwriter, and novelist, was born in Brooklyn, New York on May 19, 1941. At age three, Ephron and her three younger sisters, Delia, Amy, and Hallie, moved to Beverly Hills, California with their parents, screenwriters Henry (1911–1992) and Phoebe (1914–1971) Ephron (*There's No Business Like Show Business, Carousel, Desk Set*). Nominally Jewish, the Ephrons considered themselves atheists and raised their children accordingly. Absent from Ephron's upbringing was any exposure to Judaism or Jewish tradition. They did value "verbal jousting," and one Ephron daughter compared the family meals to the fabled Algonquin Round Table. Ephron graduated from Beverly Hills High School and Wellesley College, where she earned a degree in journalism in 1962. Her parents based their 1963 comedy *Take Her, She's Mine,* on letters Ephron sent them from college.

Upon graduating from Wellesley, Ephron briefly interned in the John F. Kennedy White House and subsequently moved to New York, where she found work as a reporter for the *New York Post.* She quickly became a well-known journalist, her work appearing in *Esquire* and *New York Magazine.* Three of her nonfiction works, *Crazy Salad, Scribble, Scribble,* and the current *I Feel Bad About My Neck,* are bestsellers.

Ephron has been married three times. Her first marriage, to writer Dan Greenberg, ended in divorce. Her second husband was investigative journalist Carl Bernstein. When pregnant with their second child, Max, Ephron learned that her husband was engaged in a torrid affair. The Bernsteins divorced, and Ephron turned the situation into a bestselling novel and film, *Heartburn* (1986), which starred Meryl Streep and Jack Nicholson. Ephron has written and directed such successful films as 1998's *You've Got Mail* (which she co-wrote with her sister Delia) and the 1993 hit *Sleepless in Seattle.* She has also written the screenplay for *Silkwood* and served as producer for *Michael* and *My Blue Heaven.* In her career, Ephron has been nominated for three Academy Awards.

Since 1987, Nora Ephron has been married to crime journalist/screenwriter Nicholas Pileggi, who has penned such films as *Goodfellas* (1990) and *Casino* (1995). Ephron, who has two sons, Jacob and Max, lives with her husband in a palatial apartment on New York's Upper West Side. *See also* **Film**.

Kurt F. Stone

Further Reading: Pogrebin, Abigail. "Nora Ephron." *Stars of David.* New York: Broadway Books, 2005.

EXODUS

"A novel of Israel" that Doubleday published in 1958 became the most wildly popular work of American fiction ever devoted to a Jewish historical subject. For over a year **Leon Uris**'s *Exodus* remained on the *New York Times* bestseller list, including 19 weeks perched at number one, and was a Book-of-the-Month Club alternate selection. The hardcover edition has never gone out of print, after quickly selling over half a million copies in more than 40 printings, and the Bantam paperback was frequently reordered at a rate of 2,000 per month, soon reaching up to almost 7 million copies after 63 printings.

Leon Uris (1924–2003) had dropped out of a Baltimore high school (where he had flunked English) to join the U.S. Marines at the age of 17 and, inspired by his experience in World War II, published *Battle Cry* (1953). Three years later he became a war correspondent to cover the Sinai campaign and claimed to have traveled nearly 50,000 miles for his research in preparation for *Exodus.* It differed from previous propaganda novels that exerted a sensational impact upon mass taste. Unlike *Uncle Tom's Cabin, The Jungle,* or *The Grapes of Wrath,* Uris's book was not designed to stir indignation over a domestic problem. Even more remarkably, *Exodus* was published when interest among American Jewry in the new state of Israel was slight and when levels of both philanthropy and tourism were, by later standards, strikingly low. By 1958, even ethnic consciousness appeared to be vanishing, dismissed as a vestige of the immigrant past. *Exodus* somehow filled a vacuum that few observers had realized even existed—so much so that, in the year that the novel was published, ex-Prime Minister David Ben-Gurion proclaimed: "As a piece of propaganda, it's the greatest thing ever written about Israel" (McDowell, 1987).

How did Uris do it? He outflanked or evaded the customary concerns of the ethnic novel—the tension between old world authority versus new world freedom. Ignoring earlier Jewish literary themes (such as the peril posed to the family or the crises of belief), he drew heavily on the exploits of Yehuda Arazi, a Mossad agent who had operated "illegal" Zionist ships in the Mediterranean under the British Mandate and had drawn press attention to the plight of Jewish refugees. Uris transposed to the Middle East the adventure formulas that middle-brow American readers already expected. In portraying Jewish characters as heroes adept with guns, the ex-Marine knew how to keep the action flowing and thus tapped a subterranean Jewish nationalism and pride when the path toward full assimilation had seemed clear. Probably for that reason rather than stylistic excellence, *Exodus* won the National Jewish Book Award. And even though the romance between a sabra and a Gentile nurse (the only important American character in the novel) is foregrounded, Uris shattered interfaith conventions by having Kitty Fremont join the Jewish independence fighters rather than having the Jewish protagonist (Ari Ben Canaan) yearn to become absorbed into the majority culture of the United States. The dream of the melting pot was thus upended.

Outside of the United States, *Exodus* appeared in over 50 translations. By far the most important language was Russian. Entitled *Ishkod,* it circulated illegally and secretly in the Soviet Union in the form of samizdat; and its impact in awakening Jewish national feelings after the Stalinist era is incalculable. At least two Jews were imprisoned for distributing the book, which Natan Sharansky testified "had an enormous influence on Jews of my generation," stimulating them to apply to emigrate to Israel and elsewhere. Jerry Goodman, the executive director of the National Conference on Soviet Jewry, claimed that "for Soviet Jewish activists *Exodus* was probably more meaningful than even the Bible." This American novel constituted "the only knowledge they had of the Jewish experience" (Medding, 1992).

In 1960 the independent producer Otto Preminger directed the United Artists screen adaptation, starring **Paul Newman** and Eva Marie Saint. The advanced sale on *Exodus* ($1.6 million) was the largest till then in movie history; the film grossed $13 million. Its popularity was apparently unaffected by picket lines that George Lincoln Rockwell of the American Nazi Party formed in Eastern U.S. cities. From the film score by Ernest Gold, crooner Pat Boone quarried a hit song that was notable for its individualistic assertiveness ("This land is mine, / God gave this land to me!"), undoubtedly boosting a successful packaged tour organized in 1960 as well, tracing the route of episodes depicted in Uris's novel. The following year El Al Airlines announced a 16-day tour that promised to cover the very places where Preminger and his crew had shot scenes for *Exodus. See also* **Film**; **Uris, Leon**.

Stephen J. Whitfield

Further Reading: McDowell, Edwin. "'Exodus' in Samizdat: Still Popular and Still Subversive." *New York Times,* April 26, 1987. Medding, Peter Y., ed.

Studies in Contemporary Jewry Volume VIII: A New Jewry? America Since the Second World War. New York: Oxford University Press USA, 1992. Moore, Deborah Dash. "Exodus: Real to Reel to Real," in *Entertaining America: Jews, Movies, and Broadcasting,* ed. J. Hoberman and Jeffrey Shandler. Princeton, NJ: Princeton University Press, 2003. Uris, Leon. *Exodus.* Garden City, NY: Doubleday, 1958.

F

FALK, PETER (1927–)

Peter Falk, a star of stage, screen, and television, has an international reputation and is arguably one of the most popular actors on stage and television. Born in New York City, the son of Madeline and Michael Falk, many of his fans thought Falk was Italian. In truth, his father was of Russian Jewish descent, and his mother was Polish Jewish. In his autobiography he makes no reference to ethnicity other than to refer to his grandmother as "Oma," a German appellation.

Initially, Falk pursued a typical middle-class career path. After graduating as president of his senior class at Westchester County's Ossining High School, he joined the United States Merchant Marine as a cook. Service in another branch of the military was out of the question because his right eye had been removed due to a malignant tumor. He earned a bachelor's degree in political science at the New School for Social Research, in 1951, and then he earned a masters in public administration at Syracuse University, in 1953. This path was not surprising in that his parents were also in the business world. His mother was an accountant and buyer; his father a retail merchant.

After attempting to find employment with the CIA, Falk found employment as a management analyst with the Connecticut State Budget Bureau. Government service apparently did not satisfy him, and he decided to become an actor. Connecticut's White Barn Theatre provided him with the basics, and in 1956, he left the Budget Bureau to appear off Broadway in Molière's *Don Juan*. In the same year he made his debut on Broadway in Shaw's *Saint Joan*. Falk's talent, extreme versatility, and range as an actor soon became apparent.

He has mastered a full range of characters from comedy to serious drama and even avant-garde. Working with his good friend, the late John Cassavetes, he helped produce striking independent films that were critically acclaimed (*Husbands, Woman under the Influence*). The German filmmaker Wim Wenders included him in one of his important productions *Wings of Desire* (1987), where Falk appeared as himself. Nominated for two Best Supporting Actor Oscars for roles in *Murder, Inc.* (1960) and *Pocketful of Miracles* (1961), Falk has gained his most enduring fame working on television. He has won five Emmys and a Golden Globe nomination for his appearances on television. His most enduring characterization is, of course, the lead character in *Columbo.*

Lieutenant Columbo, brilliantly created by Falk, hid a Sherlock-Holmesian intellect under a crumpled exterior and a bumbling manner. The series followed a formula whereby the crime and its perpetrator were always revealed at the outset, and the audience then concentrated on the sometimes brilliant manner in which Columbo solved the crime and apprehended the criminal.

Longevity is one measure of success, and since its debut in 1968, Falk has performed, as of 2003, in 69 *Columbo* episodes. Such exposure normally raises the possibility for type-casting, but it has been of little concern to Falk. To date he has appeared in 45 feature films. *Columbo* does hold a special place in his creative life. His autobiography, whose title reflects a favorite mannerism of his fictional persona, *Just One More Thing,* is replete with details of how Falk was not just an actor but was also involved in writing, producing, directing, and costuming some of the roles he assumed.

Now in his eighties, Falk's popularity and his interest in acting seem undiminished. In 2005 his hometown honored him by renaming a street after him. In typical fashion the new name was covered by an old raincoat, which he removed to unveil the new name. *See also* **Television**.

Leroy T. Hopkins Jr.

Further Reading: Byrne, Bridget. "Peter Falk." *Us Magazine* 3, no. 102 (May 15, 1989): 48–52. Falk, Peter, and Jeff Kaye. "Rumpled and Ready: Columbo Returns! What You Can Expect from Him Now." *TV Guide* 37, no. 5 (February 4, 1989): 10–12. Sherman, Eric. "Peter Falk Reigns in Columbo's Trench Coat." *Ladies' Home Journal* 107 no. 3 (March 1990): 98–100.

FASHION

Jews have played an important role in the world of fashion, and although their contribution to the industry occurred primarily in the twentieth century, no history of the subject would be complete without mention of one of its founding fathers, Levi (Loeb) Strauss (1829–1902). Strauss was a German Jewish immigrant who started the first company to manufacture blue jeans. News of the California Gold Rush reached Strauss, residing in New York City, who proceeded to move West. Strauss, the designer for blue jeans or "Levi's," apparently owed the conception of his pattern, so the story goes, to a gruff old prospector who chided young Strauss for not having brought along a supply of pants, because prospecting for gold was rough on pants. Strauss cut his canvas and stitched it into trousers that were an instant success and were known as "Levis." The success of his durable trousers was so overwhelming that he soon opened his own company, Levi Strauss and Co., on Battery Street in San Francisco. Since that time, nothing essential has changed in this "piece of national heritage," except that the company switched from canvas to serge de Nimes—denim—dyed with indigo. Long after the death of its founder, the company continues to operate as a denim and clothing company, and the word "Levis" has become a synonym for blue jeans.

Fashion has evolved into a significant part of the popular culture. It has become a steady feature in major newspapers, television reports, and, of course, has a line credit in films. The designer is not only responsible for the creative aspect of the garment industry, but also for the selection of the fabric, color, and every aspect that contributes to the final appearance of the outfit. Talent and unique vision afford designers a special role in deciding how people appear in society and how people achieve that special panache that marks personal style. Within the fashion industry there are also tailors or "stitchers," sales personnel, fashion reporters, models, and dressers. Their roles may seem invisible, yet their influence in fashion is undeniable.

Fashion's economic impact is also impressive. In the United States of America the fashion industry represented, in terms of personal consumption in 2005, $180.5 billion dollars in women's and children's fashions (U.S. Department of Commerce, Bureau of Analysis). That influence, in terms of the United States economy, has a spillover effect that can be felt worldwide.

How do Jews figure into the world of fashion? Almost without exception, the Jewish designers who achieved prominence in the field of fashion in twentieth-century America had some early exposure to the garment trade from a close member of their families. Parents or other close relatives who were tailors, shopkeepers, salesmen, or models provided background to both the business and the creative aspect of the industry. Many of these families came from Europe to America to search for a better opportunity or to leave difficult political situations in their native countries. The skills they brought with them enabled them to earn a living in the United States. The following material provides an overview of the major designers who were Jewish and who set the pace in design for men and women's clothes for about eight decades. Their ideas set the styles for their own generation and still influence the "look" of fashion today.

As the twentieth century opened, the film industry was growing, and along with it came a need for creative persons to provide costumes that would enhance the characters in films. An early designer who worked for the Goldwyn Studio (later MGM) was Sophie Wachner (1879-–960). She left her career as a school teacher and went to work as a costume designer in New York City for the theatrical producers Charles Dillingham and Florenz Ziegfeld. In 1919 at age 40 she became director of costumes for the Goldwyn Studios. In 1924 she began to work for Fox Studios, where she worked until 1930.

One of the most prolific designers in Hollywood was Adrian (Gilbert Adrian Greenburgh, 1903–1959). After studying at the Parsons School of Design in New York City, and spending a year in Paris, he began to work as a film and theater designer in New York City, where he remained from 1921 to 1928. Adrian came to Hollywood to work briefly for Cecil B. DeMille before going to work for MGM for 14 years as head designer. His "coat hanger" or "V" silhouette was created to achieve a balanced screen appearance for Joan Crawford, who had wide hips. Adrian's clothes had a timeless quality and have appeared in retrospective exhibitions of garments from the period.

Edith Head (Edith Claire Poesner, c. 1897–1981), the daughter of Max Poesner and Anna Levy, began her work in the film industry after a career change from teaching to designing. Head was detail-oriented, and all aspects of the film, from the script to the actors involved, were reviewed before costumes were developed. She was noted for her ability to camouflage figure flaws and well known for her special way of dealing with difficult personalities in the field. Head received 8 Oscars and over 30 nominations for Best Costume Design. The history of fashion will remember her for her creativity, resolute personality, and longevity.

Helen Rose was offered a contract at MGM in the post-Adrian era. Rose was born in Chicago in 1904 and began designing night club and stage costumes at age 15. Her costumes focused on the silhouette and were described as very elegant and understated. In 1956, Rose received publicity as the designer of the dress Grace Kelly wore when she married Prince Rainier of Monaco. In 1966, she entered the wholesale garment business and created expensive, ready-to-wear dresses sold in department stores. She died in 1985.

Irene Sharaff (1910–1993) had a varied background in art and design. She studied at the New York School of Fine and Applied Arts, the Grande Chaumiere in Paris, and the Art Students League in New York City. Sharaff's early work began in the theater in New York City as a costume designer. In 1942 she came to MGM as a designer for musicals. Sharaff prepared costumes for over 40 films. She received Academy Awards for *An American in Paris,* 1951; *The King and I,* 1956; *West Side Story,* 1961; and *Who's Afraid of Virginia Woolf?* 1966.

On the East Coast the theater attracted the designing talent of Aline Bernstein (1880–1955), born the daughter of Joseph Frankau and Rebecca Goldsmith Frankau. She attended Hunter College and began her work in the theater as a set and costume designer in New York City. On the strength of Bernstein's work she was invited to join what was then an all-male union. In 1926, she was sworn in as "Big Brother," the first woman member of the United Scenic Artists Union of the American Federation of Labor.

New York City has always been a dynamic center for the garment industry, and many creative people were either born there or came there from other parts of the United States. The following are Jewish designers of upscale clothing based mainly in New York City.

Nettie Rosenstein came to the United States with her parents, Joseph and Sara Rosencrans, from Austria circa 1890. She began making her own clothes at age 11. As a young married woman, Rosenstein started designing and making clothes from her home. She said that her "teachers" were the materials she worked with and the mistakes she made. Her eye for quality placed her creations in high demand. Rosenstein died in 1980.

Hattie Carnegie (1889–1956) was born Henrietta Kanengeiser. At some point after the family came to the United States they changed the name to Carnegie. Carnegie was unable to sew or draw, but she told others what she wanted, and they made the garments to her specifications. Her dresses and suits avoided any influences from French fashion but appealed to the American taste in fashion.

Maurice Rentner was born in Poland in 1889 and lived and worked in New York City. His design philosophy was based on a feminine quality expressed in soft suits and graceful dresses. Rentner created clothes that would enhance the women wearing them.

Sally (Knobel) Milgram (1891–1994) was a designer of women's clothes in the early 1920s. One of her best-known dresses was a light blue gown worn by Eleanor Roosevelt at the presidential inaugural ball in 1933. From the 1930s through the 1950s Milgram and her husband operated custom and specialty stores in several U.S. cities.

Omar Kiam (1894–1958) started his fashion career working for a millinery firm in St. Louis. He relocated to New York City to work for a retail fur company, but his talent led to assignments to work with coats, gowns, and ensembles, as well as fur coats. After a five-year stint in Hollywood, where he worked in the film industry, he returned to New York in 1941 and became the chief designer for Ben Reig Corporation, a wholesale dress, suit, and coat company. The September 11, 1950 issue of *Life* magazine described his work as one of "expensive elegance."

Sophie Gimbel, also known as Sophie of Saks, was born Sophie Haas in 1896. Her parents were Felix Haas and Carolyn Kiam Haas. Her father died when she was four years old, and her stepfather was Harry Rossback. She married Adam Gimbel, owner of Saks. Sophie Gimbel was a leading designer at Saks for almost 40 years, and she was given credit for introducing the culotte or divided skirt. In the 1940s, she had a higher retail volume than any other American designer. In 1947 Gimbel was featured on the cover of *Time* magazine. She died in 1981.

Jo Copeland's (1899–1982) parents were Sam and Minna Copeland. She studied at the Parsons School of Design and the Art Students League in New York City. Copeland's chief fashion innovation was the buttoned, two-piece suit to be worn without a blouse. She designed for the American look in women's fashions. Experts in the field described her garments as sophisticated, with simple lines and attention to detail.

Norman Norell (1900–1972) was born in Noblesville, Indiana, the son of Harry and Nettie Levinson. Norell was five years of age when the family moved to Indianapolis, where his father operated a haberdashery. Norell's talent for design was recognized at an early age, and his parents arranged for his study at the Parsons School of Design in New York City, followed by a period of study at the Pratt Institute in Brooklyn. In 1922 he was hired by the New York studio of Paramount Pictures, where he designed costumes for Rudolph Valentino and Gloria Swanson. He also prepared costumes for Broadway productions of Florenz Ziegfeld and the Cotton Club. In 1928, Norell was hired by Hattie Carnegie and under her supervision learned the importance of cut, fit, and fabric quality in garment design. Norell accompanied Carnegie to Paris, where he was exposed to the high quality of couture fashion. The hallmark of his work was simple, well-made dresses that would last and remain in fashion for many years. Norell was the first designer to have his name on a dress label and the first to produce a successful American fragrance. During the war years 1941–1945, America was cut off from the influence of the fashion houses of Paris. Norell came into prominence with his all-American look.

Founder and designer for Iris Lingerie, Sylvia Pedlar was born Sylvia Schlang in 1901. She studied art and fashion illustration at Cooper Union School and the Art Students League, New York City. Her creations were noted for their elegance. Pedlar was especially recognized as the creator of the "bedside toga" for women who slept in the nude. The toga became a bestseller when it was featured on the cover of *Life* magazine in 1962. She died in 1972.

Mollie Parnis (1905–1982) was the daughter of Abraham and Sara Rosen Parnis. She had no specialized training in fashion design but developed an "intuition" for what women wanted to wear. Her philosophy for design was one of understated chic.

Carolyn Schnurer (1908–1998) was born the daughter of Henry and Rebecca Gronner Goldsand. She was a school teacher, and it was at her husband's suggestion that she decided to attend school to study fashion design. At age 32 Schnurer was a relative latecomer to the field. Her approach, although very simple, was fundamental—"the designer must understand the purpose for which the clothes are designed." To gain inspiration for her creations she traveled to foreign countries. In 1944 Schnurer introduced the "Cholo" coat—a loose-fitting, hip-length jacket based on attire worn by South American shepherds.

The daughter of Russian émigrés, Pauline Trigere was born in Paris in 1908. Her father was a tailor, and her mother was a dressmaker; Trigere's early exposure to the trade led her to a job cutting muslins at a couture house in Paris. She was married with two children when the rising tide of Nazism in Europe caused the family to leave France for America. She found work with Hattie Carnegie as an assistant designer but left in 1941 to start her own collection. With the help of her brother, who assisted in sales, her company flourished. Trigere was noted for fit and quality with superb mastery of the bias cut. Rather than working with sketches of patterns, she preferred to drape fabric on a form and cut directly into the material. She said that "fashion is what people tell you to wear, while style is what comes from your own inner things" (Nemy, 2002). Later in her career she traveled to Israel to help with Maskit, a project that used native craftsmanship in helping to build Israel's fashion industry. She died in 2002.

Rudi Gernreich (1922–1985), avant-garde designer of the 1950s and 1960s, was born in Austria, the son of Seigmund and Elizabeth Gernreich, in 1922. He has been labeled as a visionary and innovator with his topless swimsuits, miniskirts, patterned hosiery, see-through blouses, and use of neon colors. A precedent setter, Gernreich changed the interpretation of fashion as it had been known up until that time. He was featured on the cover of *Time* magazine, December 1967 issue.

Anne Klein (Hannah Golofsky, 1923–1974) must be considered one of the designers that ushered in the modern age of fashion design. Her focus was building a wardrobe foundation of basic pieces, including a good blazer, a well-tailored pair of trousers, and shirts that were affordable. Klein also developed a collection for the woman who wore a junior size. With her premature death at age 51, Donna Karan and Louis Dell'Olio were selected to head the design division of Anne Klein Company.

There were many other Jewish designers in the fashion world, and the following roster lists their names and their field of specialization starting from the early 1920s to the present. Florence Eiseman (1899–1988), children's clothes; Mr. John (John Pico Hargerger, 1902–1993), women's hats; Clare Potter (1903–1999), women's clothes; Lily Dache (1904–1989), millinery; Sally (Josephs) Victor (1904–1977), women's hats; Gloria Sachs (1907–), sportswear, separates;

Herbert Kasper (1926–1954), sportswear; Chester Weinberg (1930–1985), classic women's garments; Arnold Scaasi (1931– [reverse spelling of Isaacs]), of the "more is more" design philosophy; Ronald Talsky (1934–1995), costume design for television and film. Stuart Weitzman (1942–), shoe designer; Bill Kaiserman (1942–), men's and women's fashions; Barry Kieselstein-Cord (1943–), jewelry, accessories; Eric Javits (1956–), women's hats; Rebecca Moses (1956–), simple designs, off-beat color combinations; Mark Eisen (1960–), noted for denim suits; Marc Jacobs (1960–), dress designer; Jay Strongwater (Jay Feinberg, 1960–), jewelry; Molly Rebecca Stern (1972–), designer for women's plus sizes; Diane von Fürstenberg (Diane Simone Michelle Halfin, 1946–), best known for her hallmark wrap dress; Richard Blackwell (Richard Sylvan Seltzer, 1922–2008), well-known fashion critic, journalist, television personality, artist, former child actor, and fashion designer, known internationally as Mr. Blackwell—he is the creator of the "Ten Worst-Dressed Women" list; and Zac Posen (1980–), dresses, blouses, and coats.

Within the span of a few years, three designers entered the world of fashion and captured the imagination of the fashion world in the United States. Ralph Lauren (Lifshitz, 1939–), Calvin Klein (1942–), and Donna (Faske) Karan (1948–) were destined to make an unprecedented impact on the fashion scene, not only in the United States but on an international basis as well.

Lauren was in his early twenties, working as a glove salesman by day and attending night school at City College of New York studying courses in business. His first creative effort was in men's fashion—a wide, handmade, very expensive tie. With success in selling the tie he went on to develop a line of menswear he named "Polo." In 1971, he branched out with a line of tailored shirts for women. His subsequent work in the field of design included collections for women with various themes—the "prairie look," the "English gentlewoman," and so on. The Lauren name is also associated with housewares, shoes, furs, and eyewear. Lauren has been successful because of his understanding of the market as well as an instinct for what people want to buy.

Klein decided before he was three that he wanted to enter the field of fashion. After graduating from the Fashion Institute of Technology in 1963, he worked for a women's clothing manufacturer before opening his own business in 1968. A childhood friend, Barry Schwartz, loaned Klein $10,000 to launch the business. Klein's designs were an immediate success, and the company did a million dollars of business the first year. Collections started with women's coats and suits and expanded to sweaters, dresses, shirts, and pants, with a menswear line introduced in 1978. Both lines were simple, nothing extreme. Klein introduced a line of jeans that was marked by notoriety due to provocative advertising. He has reigned over a clothing empire for nearly four decades. He also has licensing in bed linen, cosmetics, and perfumes. In 2003, the company was sold to Phillips-Van Heusen with royalties for Klein to continue until 2018.

It was a summer job with Anne Klein Company that opened the door for Donna Karan. Karan attended the Parsons School of Design in New York City. Her work was so outstanding that when Anne Klein died in 1974, Karan, along with Louis Dell'Olio, was invited to design for the collections of Anne Klein. Karan's underlying premise for women's clothes was to always accentuate the positive. In order to be able to exercise more creative control, she started her own line of garments in 1985. Karan's designs featured body suits, unitards, black cashmere, stretch fabrics, and body wraps. For over 30 years Karan and her staff have shown a consistent market-savvy marketing strategy, as well as season after season of attractive clothes. Donna Karan International also includes men's clothing, teens and children's clothing, accessories, beauty products, and home furnishings. In 2001 DKI was sold to LVMH (Moet Hennessy Louis Vuitton), a French luxury group.

Other Jewish fashion designers have become notable in the fashion industry as well:

Isaac Mizrahi (1961–) was born in Brooklyn and is a graduate of the Yeshiva of Flatbush, as well as the High School of Performing Arts and the Parsons School of Design. He is both a noted fashion designer as well as a popular figure on many television programs, including making appearances on *Sex and the City, Ugly Betty,* and playing himself in *The Apprentice,* season one. A film, *Unzipped,* about his 1994 Fall Fashion Collection, was released in 1995. Many of Mizrahi's designs can be found exclusively in Target stores, but in 2008, the everyman's fashion designer decided to leave behind his popular cheap chic clothing collection for the Target stores to be the creative designer for Liz Claiborne, a more upscale clothing line.

American fashion designer Michael Kors (1959–) was known for bringing a casual chic to his sportswear line. Kors was born Karl Anderson Jr. in Long Island, New York, the son of Joan Krystosek Kors, a former model. Kors's mother is Jewish, and Kors was Bar Mitzvahed in 1972. Designing since he was 19, he launched his first line at Saks Fifth Avenue in 1981 and subsequently launched the Michael Kors women's wear line at Bergdorf Goodman, Lord and Taylor, Neiman Marcus, and Saks Fifth Avenue. Building on his success, Kors was named the first-ever women's ready-to-wear designer and creative director for the French fashion house Celine in 1997. In his tenure at Celine, Kors turned the fashion house around with blockbuster accessories and a critically acclaimed ready-to-wear line. Kors left Celine in October 2003 to concentrate on his own brand runway line. Kors launched his menswear line in 2002. The MICHAEL and KORS lines were launched in 2004. The MICHAEL line includes women's handbags and shoes, as well as women's ready-to-wear apparel. The KORS line contains footwear. Currently, Kors has collection boutiques in New York, Beverly Hills, Las Vegas, Natick, Massachusetts, and South Coast Plaza in Costa Mesa, California.

Michael Kors was awarded the Elle/Cadillac Fashion Award for Excellence in 1995. In addition, he has won two Council of Fashion Designers of America (CFDA) awards, the most prestigious award in the fashion industry. In 1999, he received the CFDA award for womenwear designer of the year, and in 2003, he received the CFDA award for menswear designer of the year.

Kors has became one of the most loved and respected names in American fashion, so much so that for many seasons he has been a judge on Bravo's award-winning popular television fashion reality show *Project Runway.*

Kenneth Cole (1954–) is a clothing designer. He was born in Brooklyn, and his father Charlie Cole owned the El Greco shoe manufacturing company. Cole graduated from Emory University with a BA and in 1982 launched his own company, Kenneth Cole Productions, with the debut of his ladies' footwear. In 1994 Kenneth Cole went public and has been included on the Forbes annual list of 200 Best Small Companies approximately four times. In 2000, he added the Kenneth Cole Women's Collection.

Currently, Kenneth Cole designs men's and women's footwear, men's and women's clothing, and also accessories under the Kenneth Cole Reaction Line. Overall, Kenneth Cole Productions sells clothing and accessories under the following lines: Kenneth Cole New York, Kenneth Cole Reaction, Unlisted, Tribeca, and the licensed name Bongo. The company now operates over 90 retail and outlet stores worldwide and sells in catalogs and web sites.

In addition to being a renowned fashion designer, Cole is also a humanitarian. He was among the first in the fashion industry to take a public stand against HIV. The company's logo maintains that "what you stand for is more important than what you wear."

In 1986, Cole met Maria Cuomo, and they married a year later. Maria Cuomo Cole is the daughter of former New York Governor Mario Cuomo and sister of current New York State Attorney General Andrew Cuomo and ABC News journalist Chris Cuomo. Kenneth and Maria Cole have three daughters.

Marc Ecko (Marc Milecofsky, 1972–) was born in East Brunswick, New Jersey in 1972 and grew up in Lakewood, New Jersey. Ecko is a Jewish fashion designer and entrepreneur. He started selling t-shirts in the mid-1980s and founded his clothing brand, *eckō, in 1993.

Marc Ecko Enterprises has grown to include many separate *eckō unltd. apparel and accessories lines, the contemporary Marc Ecko "Cut & Sew" collection, G-Unit Clothing Company, Zoo York, Avirex Sportswear, Complex magazine, and Marc Ecko Entertainment—a full service production company, with a focus on interactive entertainment. In 2004, Marc Ecko Enterprises reported international sales of approximately $1 billion. The company also recently signed a deal with MTV Films for the film adaptation of Marc Ecko's first video game project, "Getting Up Content Under Pressure."

Over the years, Ecko has also dedicated himself to a number of socially conscious initiatives, including working to set up a children's home for underprivileged Jewish youth in the Ukraine and trying to help reverse the plight of the world's threatened rhino population.

Fashion, however it may be defined within a particular historical context, gives us the opportunity to express ourselves in the clothing we wear. Jewish designers have, over recent decades, expressed "the spirit of the times" in what they have created for us to wear. The garment industry influences culture and society even as it generates economic profits for this nation and nations worldwide.

Marie Zubatsky

Further Reading: Downey, Lynn. *Levi Strauss and Company.* Mt. Pleasant, SC: Arcadia Publishing, 2007. Lee, Sarah Tomerlin, ed. *American Fashion.* New York: Quadrangle/The New York Times Book Company, 1975. Leese, Elizabeth, ed. *Costume Design in the Movies.* New York: Dover Publications, Inc., 1991. Nemy, Enid. "Pauline Trigère, Exemplar of American Style, Dies at 93." *New York Times,* February 14, 2002. Watson, Linda. *20th Century Fashion: 100 Years of Style by Decade and Designer,* in association with *Vogue.* Buffalo, NY: Firefly Books, 2004.

FEIFFER, JULES (1929–)

An author, playwright, and award-winning cartoonist, Jules Feiffer was born in the Bronx on January 26, 1929. He won a gold medal in an art contest at age five and entered the Art Students League during his high school years. While studying drawing at the Pratt Institute (1947–1951), he assisted comic book legend **William Eisner** on his comic strip *The Spirit,* whose title character Feiffer assumed to be Jewish.

Feiffer spent his military service making short cartoon films for the Signal Corps and spending his off-duty hours drawing anti-military cartoons. This led to the creation of his Academy Award-winning animated short *Munro* (1961), about a child mistakenly drafted into the army. Beginning in 1956, he drew editorial cartoons for the *Village Voice,* earning a Pulitzer Prize for his work in 1986. During his 42-year tenure on the paper, he created a weekly strip first called *Sick, Sick, Sick* and later simply *Feiffer.* These strips were drawn sparingly and featured neurotic fictional anti-heroes such as Bernard Mergendeiler, who fretted about personal problems and world affairs.

Feiffer does not often refer directly to Jews and Judaism in his self-titled comic strip. "I seem to belong to that fast vanishing breed of secular Jews who didn't make a big thing of their Jewishness, any more than they made a big thing of their neighborhoods," he noted. But he acknowledged that "the angst, attitude, and atmosphere" of his weekly strip derives from a Jewish sensibility (Surrence, 1996).

Many of the characters in his plays—such as the 1968 Obie-winning *Little Murders* (the film version was released in 1971)—and screenplays —such as *Carnal Knowledge* (1971)—are Jewish. In the latter, the non-Jewish Jack Nicholson was cast as the Jewish character Jonathan, which necessitated a little **Yiddish** coaching. "I had to teach Jack to say 'shmuck,'" Feiffer recalled. "He kept saying 'smuck'" (ibid.).

But it was real-life characters who were the targets of Feiffer's political cartoons, particularly Presidents Johnson and Nixon. His cartoons have appeared in major national publications and been collected in 19 books. In 1997, the *New York Times* commissioned Feiffer to start its first op-ed page comic, which continued until he decided to give up cartooning in 2000. Feiffer has written award-winning children's books, five novels, and plays such as *Hold Me!* (1977) and the Pulitzer-nominated *Grown-Ups* (1981). Both of these were adapted for television, a medium in which Feiffer himself has been the subject, as in the PBS documentary "Feiffer's America." Other plays include Tony-nominated *Knock Knock* (1976) and Obie Award-winning *Little Murders* (1968). Other motion-picture work includes screenplays for *Carnal Knowledge, Popeye,* and *I Want To Go Home,* winner of the Best Screenplay Award at the Venice Film Festival in 1989.

Feiffer was married to Judith Sheftel from 1961–1983. After their divorce, he married Jenny Allen, and the couple worked together on *The Long Chalkboard* (2006) with Feiffer illustrating. That same year he won the Benjamin Franklin Creativity Laureate Award. In 2004 Feiffer received the National Cartoonist Society Milton Caniff Lifetime Achievement Award. Prior to that, he was elected into the American Academy of Arts and Letters (1995). Feiffer's academic affiliations have included Southhampton College, Northwestern University, the Yale School of Drama, and Columbia University, where he served as a senior fellow of its National Arts Journalism Program. He donated his papers and hundreds of cartoons to the Library of Congress. *See also* **Comic Books**; **Eisner, William**.

Barry Kornhauser

Further Reading: Feiffer, Jules. *Feiffer: The Collected Works, Volumes 1, 2, 3.* Seattle, WA: Fantagraphics Books, 1989. Surrence, Matthew. "Jules Feiffer Draws Curtain on Theater, Writes for Kids" *Jewish News Weekly,* March 8, 1996.

FELDSHUH, TOVAH (1952–)

Tovah Feldshuh has played impressive women in her career, including the roles of Sarah Bernhardt, Stella Adler, Sophie Tucker, Tallulah Bankhead, and Katharine Hepburn. But the role that she is best remembered for is Golda Meir, in the Broadway play *Golda's Balcony* (2003). Feldshuh had been studying the role for years, traveling from Golda's birthplace in Milwaukee to her Knesset colleagues in Jerusalem. William Gibson's *Golda's Balcony* set a record for advance sales (above $1.3 million) at the Helen Hayes Theatre and another one for the longest-running one-woman play on Broadway. In 2004, Feldshuh was nominated for a Tony Award for Best Actress in a Play, a year after winning a Drama Desk Award.

Born Terry Sue Feldshuh in New York's Westchester County, after graduating from Sarah Lawrence College, Feldshuh worked with director Michael Langham at Minneapolis's Guthrie Theatre. Unlike most other Jewish artists, Feldshuh used her Hebrew name, Tovah, as her stage name. In 1973, Feldshuh made her Broadway debut in *Cyrano*. Two years later, she won a Drama Desk Award for *Yentl,* which also earned her a Tony nomination. Feldshuh was nominated for an Emmy for her role in the drama series *Holocaust* (1978).

For the last three decades, Feldshuh has played in a number of movies with Jewish themes, such as **Sidney Lumet**'s fictionalized story about the son of Ethel and Julius Rosenberg, Daniel (1983); the short movie *Saying Kaddish* (1991); *Citizen Cohn* (1992), the story of lawyer Roy Cohn as played by James Woods; *A Day in October* (1992), about the rescue of Denmark's Jews during the Holocaust; adding her voice to the animated comedy *The Real Shlemiel* (1995); she played in *A Walk on the Moon* (1998); *Kissing Jessica Stein* (2001); *A House Divided* with F. Murray Abraham (2006), an Israeli-Palestinian love story; and in Israeli author Zeruya Shalev's *Love Life* (2007) with Assi Dayan and in Goyband (2008), the hip-hop version of ***Fiddler on the Roof***. In Elie Chouraqui's *O Jerusalem* (2006), based on the novel, she played Golda Meir. In 2008 Feldshuh starred in the Broadway musical *Salt and Honey*. Feldshuh married New York attorney Andrew Harris Levy in 1977. They have two children, Garson and Amanda. For her charity work, she is the recipient of the Eleanor Roosevelt Humanities Award, Hadassah's Myrtle Wreath, and the Israel Peace Medal. The National Foundation for Jewish Culture honored her with the 2002 Jewish Image Award and the Performing Arts Award in 2006. Her brother David Feldshuh is the Pulitzer Prize-nominated playwright of *Miss Evers' Boys*. *See also* **Film**; **Theater**.

Steve Krief

Further Reading: American Theatre Wing. "Tovah Feldshuh." Biography. Updated 2006. Accessed August 2008. www.americantheatrewing.org/biography/detail/tovah_feldshuh. Bernardo, Melissa Rose. "Tovah Feldshuh 'In a Nutshell.'" *Entertainment Weekly*, March 7, 2008.

FERBER, EDNA (1885–1968)

Edna Ferber, American novelist, short story writer, and playwright, was born in Kalamazoo, Michigan, on August 15, 1885. Her father, Hungarian-born Jacob Charles Ferber, and mother, Julia Neumann Ferber, were both Jewish, and although Edna was not a practicing Jew, she never failed to acknowledge her Jewish background. She was proud of her middle-class, Midwestern, American Jewish roots. Throughout her life, she argued against the evils of anti-Semitism that she often encountered in Kalamazoo where her father owned a general store. When her family moved to Ottumwa, Iowa, Ferber recalled witnessing a lynching and having to put up with numerous anti-Semitic epithets. She described Ottumwa as possessing "all the sordidness and none of the frontier."

The family moved to Chicago, where they spent time with Ferber's maternal grandmother before settling in Appleton, Wisconsin, a city with a small, but active Jewish population. Ferber called Appleton "the American small town at its best." She completed her formal education in Appleton. Jacob Ferber became an invalid and his wife had to take over the family store. Edna could not attend Northwestern University School of Elocution because of limited finances. She began working as a reporter for various publications. When her father died in 1909, the Ferbers moved back to Chicago, where Edna continued her work as a reporter and began to submit short stories to various magazines.

Between 1911 and 1915, Ferber wrote a series of stories, later collected in three books, about a divorced mother and traveling saleswoman named Emma McChesney. Emma became the prototype for all Ferber's heroines in her subsequent novels, a woman forced to fend for herself in a world dominated by men, a "new" type of woman. Ferber once told an interviewer that Emma was a springboard for her own feminist views.

In 1917, Ferber wrote the first of two autobiographical novels, *Funny Herself*, which tells the story of a Jewish girl growing up in Appleton, Wisconsin. Although anti-Semitism is a subtext in almost all of her writings, *Funny Herself* and *A Peculiar Treasure* are the only stories in which Ferber deals directly with Judaism. Literary critics emphasize, however, that many of her major works focus on outsiders and minorities, an emphasis that results from Ferber's Jewish background.

During her half-century writing career, Edna Ferber produced 12 collections of short stories, 12 novels, 2 autobiographies, and collaborated on 9 plays. Twenty of her novels, short stories, and plays were adapted to film, some several times. During most of Ferber's prolific career, she lived in New York, where she became a regular at the Algonquin Hotel. She was one of the famous Round Table group of writers and theater people.

Her most popular novels were *So Big* (1924), for which she won the 1925 Pulitzer Prize; *Show Boat* (1926), which was made into a Broadway musical by Jerome Kern and Oscar Hammerstein II and then into a motion picture; *Cimarron* (1930); *American Beauty* (1931); *Saratoga Trunk* (1941); *Giant* (1952); and *Ice Palace* (1958). She joined forces with noted playwright George S. Kaufman on six plays, most notably *Royal Family* (1927), *Dinner at Eight* (1932), and *Stage Door* (1936).

Ferber's works, especially her novels, have been lauded and criticized. Critics complain that Ferber's novels are too predictable and lack depth; they all contain strong, able female protagonists who are married to weaker husbands. They claim that though her books examine American values, they lack profundity, tend to be too preachy, and are escapist fiction. On the other hand, Ferber has been acclaimed for writing stories that readers want to read—romantic, nostalgic, exciting, enjoyable books set in intriguing American locales. Supporters praise her careful research and commend her for presenting a broad view of how America grew and developed.

During the last decade of her life, Edna Ferber developed trigeminal neuralgia, an extremely painful disease more commonly known as tic douloureux. Her only opportunity for relief was an operation which would sever nerves and cause paralysis of half her face. Ferber opted to live with the pain.

In 1965, Edna Ferber developed cancer, and she died on April 17, 1968. At the time of her death, she was making notes for a novel about the Native American. *See also* **Film.**

Burton Boxerman

Further Reading: Ferber, Edna. *A Kind of Magic.* New York: Doubleday, 1963. ———. *A Peculiar Treasure.* Garden City, NY: Doubleday Doran and Co., 1939. Gilbert, Julie Goldsmith. *Ferber—A Biography.* New York: Doubleday, 1978. Goldstein, Malcolm. *George S Kaufman—His Life, His Theater.* New York: Oxford University Press, 1979.

FIDDLER ON THE ROOF

Almost closing on the road, *Fiddler on the Roof* opened in 1964 on Broadway without high expectations. The show proceeded to win nine Tony Awards, and when it closed eight years later, its 3,242 performances made it the longest-running musical up to that time. *Fiddler on the Roof,* a musical that was written by librettest Joseph Stein, with a score by Jerry Block and lyrics by Sheldon Hanick, even exceeded the run of the longest non-musical ever produced on Broadway, *Life with Father.* Their work was based on the **Yiddish** tales of Sholem Aleichem, the first of which appeared in Warsaw in 1895; the eighth and last was published in 1914. United Artists released a film adaptation of *Fiddler on the Roof* in 1971. Music Theatre International licenses any community or amateur staging of this work and has reported its consistent ranking among the company's five most popular musicals, with over 500 productions staged annually in the United States.

Perhaps even more striking has been the international success of *Fiddler on the Roof.* It has played to packed houses and enthusiastic audiences on every inhabited continent. In London, the show was so sensational that it ran four and a half years.

It was also performed at the Komische Oper in East Berlin, and when the wall crumbled, 23 versions of *Fiddler* were mounted in the former German Democratic Republic. The show was so popular in Tel Aviv that three Tevyes were eventually needed (including Chaim Topol, who starred as Tevye in the movie). Even as the Hebrew-language version was running for a year and a half, a Yiddish version was added, enabling a Russian-born Tevye to belt out "Ven Ich Bin a Rothschild" instead of "If I Were a Rich Man." His counterpart in Tokyo helped *Fiddler on the Roof* to set a record as the longest-running musical in Japanese history.

What accounts for such an impact? On Broadway credit is due primarily to **Jerome Robbins**, whose surname at birth (Rabinowitz) was so close to that of Sholem Aleichem (Solomon Rabinovitsh) as to hint at a special, intimate link. With sharpness Robbins remembered a childhood visit to Poland, and in and in choreographing *Fiddler* (for which he won two Tony Awards, Best Director and Best Choreographer), he was able to convey his feelings about the devastated culture of East European Jewry to future generations. The only member of the original Broadway cast who could speak Yiddish was **Zero Mostel**, who turned in a legendary, Tony-winning performance as Tevye. Because Mostel could sing, dance, and act, the plot blended into the dynamic use of music and choreography. Of the 14 songs in *Fiddler on the Roof,* Tevye sings all but four (in part or whole, solo or with others); this musical achieves a unity of elements which the genre of the musical had long aspired to reach, and it becomes an American Gesamtkunstwerk.

The uniqueness of this show must be acknowledged: no previous musical consecrated to an overtly Jewish subject had ever before triumphed on Broadway. In 1964–1972 Tevye's struggle to overcome adversity surely packed a wallop with predominantly Jewish audiences, whose accounts with their Eastern European past had not been settled. *Fiddler on the Roof* enjoyed the advantage of immediacy. Set in 1905, it was close enough chronologically to the sensibility of American Jews who were only a generation or two removed from villages like Anatevka. But the show also had the benefit of distance. Jews who saw this family and this shtetl on stage were far enough removed to memorialize their heritage without having to honor any particular claims it might make, and they could also do so without submitting to any moral mandates that the Judaism to which Tevye subscribes might demand.

Sholem Aleichem had himself already highlighted the dilemma of romantic love as the challenge that this family must face. Such love is the disruptive force that shatters what this humble and impoverished milk-wagon driver cherishes. Enlightened ideals of liberalism and individualism have penetrated the only cultural universe that Tevye knows. His sense of fitness is tested when he cannot arrange marriages for daughters who want to choose their own husbands. He is bedeviled by the question of whether "tradition" can be loosened or even transcended. The sting of modernization that pains him is hardly restricted to Jewish history and therefore helps account for the worldwide impact of *Fiddler on the Roof. See also* **Theater**.

Stephen J. Whitfield

Further Reading: Altman, Richard, with Mervyn Kaufman. *The Making of a Musical: Fiddler on the Roof.* New York: Crown, 1971. Stein, Joseph, and Sheldon Harnick. *Fiddler on the Roof.* New York: Crown, 1965.

FIERSTEIN, HARVEY (1954–)

A Tony Award-winning actor, Harvey Forbes Fierstein was born the son of a handkerchief manufacturer and a school librarian, in Brooklyn on June 6, 1952 (some sources claim 1954). He began his theater career at age 11 as a founding actor in the Gallery Players Community Theatre in Brooklyn. He earned an MFA from Pratt Institute in 1973 and then embarked on what would prove to be an extraordinary, multifaceted theater career.

Fierstein began performing as a drag queen in Manhattan clubs as early as age 15. He turned these experiences into three one-act plays, which were produced and mounted individually between 1976 and 1979. In 1981, Fierstein began performing his show, now entitled *Torch Song Trilogy,* in an off-off-Broadway theater. Before long, Fierstein's writing and performing talents were recognized, and the show opened on Broadway to ecstatic reviews. For his efforts, Fierstein became the first performer to win simultaneous Tony Awards for both best actor and author (1983). In 1988, *Torch Song Trilogy* was made into a movie, starring Fierstein, Anne Bancroft, and Matthew Broderick.

Fierstein also won Tony Awards in 1984 for his libretto [book] for *La Cage aux Folles* and in 2003 as Best Actor in a Musical for his role as Edna Turnblad in *Hairspray.* His four Tonys in four different categories is a feat matched only once, by Tommy Tune.

Fierstein has appeared in some 40 motion pictures, including *Mrs. Doubtfire* (1993) and **Woody Allen**'s *Bullets Over Broadway* (1994). Fierstein has also starred on Broadway as Tevye in the 2005 revival of ***Fiddler on the Roof.***

The burly, gravel-voiced Fierstein has characterized himself as the first "real-life, out-of-the-closet queer on Broadway." Eminently quotable, he once opined, "Never be bullied into silence. . . . Accept no one's definition of your life; define yourself" (Fierstein, "A 12-step"). In an April 2007 *New York Times* op-ed piece Fierstein wrote, "You cannot harbor malice toward others and then cry foul when someone displays intolerance against you. Prejudice tolerated is intolerance encouraged" (Fierstein, 2007). *See also* **Theater.**

Kurt F. Stone

Further Reading: Fierstein, Harvey. "A 12-Step Program Guaranteed to Change your Life." Transcript of Harvey Fierstein's Commencement Speech to the Bennington College Class of 1992. www.qrd.org/qrd/media/people/1992/harvey.fierstein.speech-12.30.92. ———. "Our Prejudices, Ourselves." *New York Times,* April 13, 2007. ———. *Torch Song Trilogy.* New York: Random House, 1984.

FILM

The history of Jewish representation in American film is a history of gradual assimilation, resulting temporarily in virtual disappearance, followed by a resurgence of activity that is still in full development. Throughout the history of American motion pictures, Jews have dominated film production, serving as producers, writers, composers, directors, and businessmen. In recent years they have also become performers in growing numbers.

The Early Silent Era. Jewish images proliferated during the era of silent cinema, revealing stories of European hardships and the tribulations of American immigrant life, all redeemed by opportunities in the Land of Promise. These stories were contrasted by a large number of comedies featuring ethnically stereotyped Jewish performers. In the United States the first images were also documentaries. In 1903, Thomas Edison released two one-minute films called *Arabian Jewish Dance* and *A Jewish Dance at Jerusalem* featuring Hasidic men doing a hora.

Following these earliest moving pictures were a large number of short comedies and dramas. Typical of these was *Cohen's Fire Sale* (1907), which featured a large-nosed, gesticulating merchant who makes profits on naïve customers. Produced by the Edison Company, it reflected the prevailing anti-Semitism of the day. More sympathetic were films such as *The Romance of a Jewess* (1908), directed by D. W. Griffith, which dramatizes the tragic consequences for young Ruth when she goes against her father's wishes and marries the man of her choice.

In the main, these films fell into three general categories. The first, ghetto films, depict immigrant life on New York's Lower East Side, establishing several character types who persist through the decades—namely, the patriarchal father with Orthodox commitments; the prodigal son, who chooses a different path, usually toward assimilation; and the Rose of the ghetto, the innocent virginal typical of the Victorian era, ever on the verge of being violated. These characters turn up in such films as: *Child of the Ghetto* (1910), *The Ghetto Seamstress* (1910), *Solomon's Son* (1912), *The Jew's Christmas* (1913), and *A Passover Miracle* (1914).

The second genre, the pogrom films, drew inspiration from events in czarist Russia. Here Jewish oppression was graphically portrayed, with rescues provided by the intervention of Christian lovers. Often these works ended as the family set off for the Promised Land. Over a dozen of these films were made. Titles include *In the Czar's Name* (1910), *Russia, the Land of Oppression* (1910), *The Sorrows of Israel* (1913), *Escape From Siberia* (1914), and *Vengeance of the Oppressed* (1916).

Two dramas deserve special mention: *A Passover Miracle* (1914) and *The Jew's Christmas* (1913). The first feature chronicles a prodigal son's philandering and eventual return to the fold. Produced and distributed with the aid of the Bureau of Education of the Jewish Community of New York, the film is an early effort to depict Jewish life and ritual in the hopes of furthering religious tolerance. The second work, produced by Lois Weber and Phillip Smalley, non-Jews, also aimed at interfaith understanding, but through different means. Here intermarriage is not only condoned, but the patriarchal rabbi, who is the first portrayal of a rabbi in American film, ends up celebrating Christmas as emotion triumphs over religious difference. It is this scenario that becomes the dominant message in the years to come.

The third genre, the comedies, display character types including scheming merchants, as in *Levitsky's Insurance Policy* (1908) or *Foxy Izzy* (1911), or Jewish weaklings, as in *The Yiddisher Cowboy* (1909 and 1911) and *How Mosha Came Back* (1914), who use their brains to overcome their physical limitations.

In addition to these three categories, Jews appeared in the various adaptations of classic literature, such as *The Merchant of Venice* (1908, 1912, 1914) and *Oliver Twist* (1909, 1910, 1912, 1916), serving to perpetuate anti-Semitic stereotypes.

The 1920s. During the twenties, there was a plethora of films with Jewish subjects. Most were outgrowths of the earlier period, especially stories from the New York ghetto. Many character types persisted—the patriarchal father, the prodigal son, and the Rose of the ghetto. Added to these was a new figure, the long-suffering mother. The struggle for dominance within the immigrant family and the conflict between traditionalism and assimilation continued to be the central concerns. However, during the twenties the balance of power clearly shifted to the younger generation. Sons rejected their fathers. Families are reconstituted, but seldom do sons "go back home again."

An important feature of this period is the emphasis placed on "making it." Many films deal with sudden financial success and the movement out of the ghetto, reflecting the upward mobility of many Jews. Closely tied to satisfying the great American dream is the ready acceptance of assimilationist ideas. As in the earlier period, this usually manifests itself in a marriage contract between Jew and Gentile, a narrative element that constitutes a happy ending to a large number of works. The "melting-pot" mentality also emerges through the portrayal of relationships with the Gentile community at large. Frequently non-Jews appear as business partners as well as romantic lovers in films with such wonderful titles as *Kosher Kitty Kelly* (1926) and *Clancy's Kosher Wedding* (1927). As in the earlier films, the Irish appear over and over again.

During the twenties, comedies evolved from one- and two-reelers to feature works. Like the melodramas, many center on ghetto life. Jewish shopkeepers continue to conduct business, but the scheming merchant disappears. The comedies tend to be structured around several leading Jewish performers, each of whom developed a unique film persona. The most popular was George Sidney. Beginning with *Busy Izzy* (1915), he portrayed throughout the silent era the small, rotund immigrant, struggling to stay on top of the situation. These appearances culminated in the 1926 film *The Cohens and Kellys,* a blockbuster that spawned six sequels. In addition, Alexander Carr and Sammy Cohen found their niches, creating comic characters such as Morris Perlmutter and Sammy Nosenbloom.

Representative of the twenties are also several prominent motion pictures. Inaugurating the decade is *Humoresque* (1920), a prestige production released by Paramount, based on a work by Fannie Hurst. The story follows the life of Leon Kantor who, spurred on by the encouragement and sacrifice of his mother, rises to great fame as a violinist. As one critic pointed out, "the spectator is not looking at the Jewish family life from the outside in but from the inside out." In large measure, *Humoresque* set the pattern for the films to follow, including *The Good Provider* (1922), *Hungry Hearts* (1922), and *Salome of the Tenements* (1925).

Also influenced by *Humoresque* is the decade's most celebrated feature, ***The Jazz Singer*** (1927). Remembered in history as the first talking film, *The Jazz Singer* featured **Al Jolson** as Jack Robin, a prodigal son, intent upon following a Broadway career rather than becoming a fifth-generation cantor as his father wishes. Supported by a loving mother, Jack not only reaches his ambition but also captures the heart of the lovely Mary, the shiksa. The film's popularity made this pejorative term known to millions of non-Jewish Americans.

In between these two melodramas were several other ghetto films, most importantly *His People* (1925), *We Americans* (1928), and *The Younger Generation* (1929). *His People,* directed by Edward Sloman, and *The Younger Generation,* directed by Frank Capra, feature immigrant families and peddler fathers. Starring eminent actors such as Rudolph Schildkraut and Jean Hersholdt, the films depict sons who achieve the American dream as lawyers, boxers, and successful businessmen. Although these works questioned the price for such upward mobility, in the main they affirm the goal. *We Americans* goes a step further, depicting intermarriage among different national groups and different religions as the natural result of good-hearted men.

The comedies echoed many of the same themes as the dramas. Two series typify the era—the three Potash/Perlmutter comedies (1923–1926), featuring two irascible Jewish partners, and the mishaps of the Cohens and Kellys (1926–1929).

The decade ended with perhaps the most affirmative plea for intermarriage, *Abie's Irish Rose,* released in 1928 with talking sequences. Clearly, Levy and Murphy, the fathers, represent the "old way" as well as the old world, while their children, Abie and Rosemary, have solved the problems of religious difference through marital bliss and the birth of a baby. As with the dramas, this resolution becomes more dominant as we approach the thirties.

The 1930s and the Era of Sound. In the two years following Warner Brothers' *The Jazz Singer,* Hollywood frantically set about converting to sound. As the studios began importing New York talent, many Jews landed in Hollywood. Among the Jewish performers who made their way west were **Jack Benny**, Ben Blue, **Fanny Brice**, **George Burns**, Harry Green, Ted Lewis, the **Marx Brothers**, Sophie Tucker, and Ed Wynn. In addition, directors and writers shifted from theater to film, including men such as George Cukor, Reuben Mamoulian, Sidney Buchman, Norman Krasna, Charles Lederer, Joseph Mankiewicz, S. J. Perelman, Robert Riskin, Morrie Ryskind, and **Ben Hecht**.

In film, the **Hollywood mogul** soon replaced the Jewish businessman as an object of jest and a character of self-parody. He turns up in *Once in a Lifetime* (1932), wherein the producer Julius Saxe demands a scenario of *Genesis* in 300 words, and in *The Cohens and Kellys in Hollywood* (1932).

Upward mobility continued to occupy the minds of screenwriters; however, in the films of the 1930s, there is an increasing ambivalence or, at least, a somber realization that every gain has its concomitant loss. Sometimes this theme is treated nostalgically, as in *Symphony of Six Million* (1932), when Felix Klauber decides to give up his fancy Park Avenue medical practice and return to the ghetto; sometimes comically, as in *The Heart of New York* (1932), where the Mendels do the same thing in an effort to once again be with their old friends; and sometimes dramatically, as when George Simon, the protagonist of **Elmer Rice**'s *Counsellor at Law* (1933), must reexamine the values that made him one of New York's top criminal attorneys.

By the mid-thirties even assimilated Jews were of little interest to studio producers. The degree to which Hollywood eliminated a Jewish presence can be assessed by comparing *The House of Rothschild* (1934) with *The Life of Emile Zola* (1937). The former deals with the famous banking family and forthrightly depicts historic anti-Semitism rampant in the Germany of their day (and by analogy the 1930s as well). In this film, starring George Arliss who had twice depicted Benjamin Disraeli on the screen, there is no question of Rothschild's identity. In contrast, *The Life of Emile Zola* depicts the infamous Dreyfus Affair, yet oddly, throughout the entire film the fact that Dreyfus was a Jew is never mentioned. Instead, he is portrayed as just an innocent French officer unfairly accused.

Despite Hitler's appointment in 1933 as chancellor of Germany, the growing militarization, the suspension of civil liberties, and the subsequent legislated discrimination against Jews, Hollywood remained totally silent on the subject throughout the thirties. The producers reflected the policy of isolationism that emanated from Washington. MGM's *Three Comrades* (1938) and Warner Brothers' *Confessions of a Nazi Spy* (1939) merely intimated the true horror of the Third Reich.

Only one voice dealt directly with the plight of Jews. Charlie Chaplin, a non-Jew, who had worked independently since the 1920s, broke ranks by producing *The Great Dictator* (1940), a film that depicted contemporary conditions in his mythical Tomania. Despite its comic demeanor, the film ends with a passionate plea for hope and triumph over evil.

The 1940s and World War II. With the onset of World War II, Hollywood set about dealing with fascism, although it was less explicit about Jewish persecution. Several titles reached the screen at the beginning of the 1940s: *Escape* (1940), *The Mortal Storm* (1940), and *So Ends Our Night* (1941). It was not until the Japanese bombed Pearl Harbor in December 1941, however, that Hollywood went to war in full force. Increasingly, the victims are identified as Jews rather than non-Aryans, ironically a Nazi classification. These films included *The Pied Piper* (1942), *None Shall Escape* (1944), and *Address Unknown* (1944).

The war also saw the rise of the combat film, usually depicting a fighting unit of ethnically and geographically diverse soldiers. Among the films with Jewish characters who were fighting to keep the world safe for democracy were *Air Force* (1943), *Bataan* (1943), *Guadalcanal Diary* (1943), and *Action in the North Atlantic* (1943). Most typically the Jews' function was to provide the comic relief.

More serious depictions of Jewish participation in World War II can be found in *The Purple Heart* (1944) and *Pride of the Marines* (1945). Consistently, all the characters evidence intelligence, bravery, and patriotism.

Following the war and the full knowledge of the Nazi atrocities, it was natural to ask, "How could this happen?" "Could it happen here?" The response to these questions was two films, both released in 1947—RKO's *Crossfire* and 20th Century Fox's ***Gentleman's Agreement***.

Crossfire treats anti-Semitism as the cause for a seemingly unmotivated murder in a typical 1940s film noir. *Gentleman's Agreement* presents journalist Gregory Peck posing as a Jew to get firsthand experience of what it feels like to suffer discrimination. Both films received critical and popular acclaim and, despite initial concern on the part of the Jewish agencies, both works proved through testing to be effective tools in combating prejudice. Although advanced for its day, the message of *Gentleman's Agreement* (we are all alike except for what we call ourselves) leaves something to be desired.

Another response to the war was the creation of the Motion Picture Project in 1947, an organization funded by the major U.S. Jewish agencies, which sought to encourage Jewish themes in Hollywood films and to create positive images. Headed by a former schoolteacher, John Stone, the project accomplished its task quietly and effectively, working with producers and screenwriters behind the scenes. It accomplished its task so successfully that it was disbanded in 1967.

The 1950s and the Postwar Era. The postwar period also produced an unexpected backlash against Jews, most particularly in Hollywood. Spurred on by anticommunist fears, conservative individuals were able to act out their prejudices through the workings of the House Un-American Activities Committee. Of the original "Hollywood Ten" who faced investigation and later faced charges, seven were Jewish. Also, anti-Semitism emerges from the official records, as evidenced by comments such as Representative John Rankin's description of **Walter Winchell** as "a little slime-mongering kike" (Erens, 1984).

In many ways, the films of the 1950s that deal with Jewish characters and themes can be seen as a direct result of the Motion Picture Project. In no decade are the screen Jews so intelligent, patriotic, and likable. At no other time are religious tolerance and good will so consistently echoed. Beginning in 1951 with the biopic *The Magnificent Yankee,* in which Louis Brandeis, a paragon of wisdom and virtue, fights to become the first Jewish Supreme Court justice, until 1960, when a sensitive, young Jewish cadet, wounded by social discrimination, commits suicide in the screen adaptation of *Dark at the Top of the Stairs,* the films all preach the same message—Jews are deserving of full acceptance; anti-Semitism is no longer acceptable and is un-American. As if to prove the point, most of the Jewish roles were taken by non-Jewish actors, thus playing down differences, but also confusing the issue.

In between these two works, several important films came to the screen. In 1952, **(Isidore) Dore Schary** adapted Sir Walter Scott's novel *Ivanhoe* for the screen, with Elizabeth Taylor in the role of Rebecca. Her father, Isaac of York, a moneylender, is not only distinguished in his white beard but proves his loyalty by ransoming Richard the Lion-Hearted. In 1953, the first remake of *The Jazz Singer* appeared with Danny Thomas in the lead role. The once Orthodox family have now become assimilated Reform Jews. In *Good Morning, Miss Dove* (1955), Jennifer Jones uses the presence of a Polish Jewish immigrant to teach her class a lesson in religious tolerance, first by studying Palestine, the "original home of the Jews," and second by visiting the Jewish student's home.

Three Brave Men (1957) deals with the Abraham Chasanow case, in which a government employee is accused of communist activities. Not only do the charges prove false, but the film's main characters are clearly the exemplary all-American family. Other positive images appear in *Home Before Dark* (1958), which portrays a Jewish college professor, and *The Last Angry Man* (1959), in which Paul Muni plays a kindly doctor who puts the welfare of his patients before material ambition. Two war films, based on best-selling novels, depict anti-Semitism in the United States Army—**Norman Mailer**'s *The Naked and the Dead* (1958) and Irwin Shaw's *The Young Lions* (1958), with much sympathy going out to Montgomery Clift playing the role of the Jewish character Noah Ackerman.

Only *Marjorie Morningstar* (1958), *Me and the Colonel* (1958), and *The Diary of Anne Frank* (1959) deal with other themes. *Marjorie Morningstar,* which was filmed on the strength of its popularity as a novel by **Herman Wouk**, is one of the first films since the 1920s to focus on Jewish domestic life and anticipates the emergence of the ethnic consciousness of the 1960s, especially in its self-critical approach to contemporary Jewish values. Both *Me and the Colonel* (starring **Danny Kaye**) and *The Diary of Anne Frank* were based on successful Broadway plays which treat the plight of Jews both during the war and the **Holocaust**. As initial steps into a difficult terrain, they are to be applauded. In comparison with the more directly engaged material that is to follow, these efforts seem light indeed. Also of note, the major roles of Marjorie Morningstar and Anne Frank, following precedent, went to non-Jewish actresses—Natalie Wood and Milly Perkins.

Lastly, *The Juggler* (1953), starring **Kirk Douglas**, became the first U.S. production shot entirely in Israel, and it sets the tone for a positive image of the land. This film is later eclipsed by the epic ***Exodus*** (1960), which not only creates heroic Jewish men and women but also created a positive image of Israel in American popular culture.

The 1960s and the Reawakening of Jewish Identity. With the arrival of the 1960s, the scene was set for major changes. Not since the silent era had so many Jewish characters appeared, especially in major roles. And once again, Jewish actors and actresses were cast for these parts, with some glaring exceptions. During this decade, there also emerged a growing recognition of the Jew as an identifiable individual who has experienced a unique fate. This is mirrored on screen by several Jewish characters of great suffering, dignity, or courage—Sol Nazerman in *The Pawnbroker* (1965), Colonel **David "Mickey" Marcus** in *Cast a Giant Shadow* (1966), and Yakov Bok in *The Fixer* (1968).

The reawakening of ethnic identity was being felt by almost all national, racial, and religious groups. For the most part, Jews had followed a path of acculturation, assimilating in their public life, while keeping Jewish customs in the privacy of their homes and synagogues. By the 1960s, new attitudes were being voiced by many minorities.

Beginning in 1968, a series of comedies set a new direction and established Jewish humor as a major trend for the next two decades. Most prominent are *Bye, Bye Braverman* (1968), *The Producers* (1968), *Funny Girl* (1968), *Take the Money and Run* (1969), and *Goodbye, Columbus* (1969). In *Goodbye Columbus,* based on **Philip Roth**'s collection of stories, the film introduces Brenda, the personification of the "Jewish American princess," as played by Ali McGraw, a non-Jew, acting in her first starring role. The film also depicts an unflattering picture of her upper-class Jewish family. Together these films highlight the Jewish urban experience, their continued drive to succeed, and the outsider's perspective on American life.

The comedies also introduced to film audiences a group of young Jewish actors and actresses who openly acknowledged their heritage by the parts they chose to play, by their personal publicity, and by the sound of their names. Unlike the Jewish performers in Old Hollywood (**Edward G. Robinson**, Sylvia Sydney, **John Garfield**, **Tony Curtis**, and **Jerry Lewis**, among others not previously mentioned), the new performers were able to assume star roles without having to sacrifice their religious or ethnic identities. **Barbra Streisand** clearly led the way in *Funny Girl.* Other members of this group include **Dustin Hoffman**, Richard Benjamin, **Richard Dreyfuss**, Elliott Gould, Jeannie Berlin, and, of course, the director-actors **Mel Brooks** and **Woody Allen**.

Although comedy dominates the decade in terms of Jewish film, the Holocaust is approached in two works with forceful impact. First, *Judgment at Nuremburg* (1961) soberly approaches the range of Nazi injustices. Although Jews as a group are perplexingly not mentioned, documentary footage of the camps is shown as part of the trial. In 1965, *The Pawnbroker*—based on a novel by Edward Lewis Wallant, independently produced and distributed by Ely Landau, and directed by **Sidney Lumet**—stars Rod Steiger (a non-Jew) in the role of a German Jewish survivor. The film is the first American fictional work to treat the camp experience with such harrowing reality. The virulent anti-Semitism that set the stage for the Holocaust is depicted in *Ship of Fools* (1965). Closely related, *The Fixer* (1968), starring Alan Bates, depicts Jewish victimization under the czarist regime and by implication called attention to the then-prevailing anti-Semitism in the Soviet Union.

The decade closes with one of the most celebrated films about Jewish life ever to reach the screen—***Fiddler on the Roof*** (1969). Based on Sholem Aleichem's story of Tevye and his five daughters, the film exposed millions around the world to the warmth of Jewish family life and the traditions associated with life in the Russian shtetl.

The 1970s, 1980s, and Jewish Self-Parody. Overwhelmingly, the Jewish films of the seventies concentrated on speaking the unspoken. For such purposes, comedy represented an ideal medium, and it is not surprising that a majority of the films in this decade are comedies, seriocomedies, or comic romances.

As in the twenties, the Jewish family once again emerges as central. Although the same character types appear—father, mother, son, and daughter—many shifts have occurred. Whereas the father-son conflict dominated earlier ghetto films, the contemporary works focus on the mother-son relationship. In many cases, the father is totally absent.

In his place appears the mother, totally metamorphized. In the ghetto films, although her position is insignificant, she is the adored long-suffering mother. Beginning in the postwar period, she slowly evolves into the suffocating mother, an object of fear and scorn. By the 1970s, the central conflict is no longer the need to break with traditional Judaism and assimilate, but rather the son's efforts to sever the emotional umbilical cord and to establish his manhood and autonomy.

Two films that portray the suffocating mother are *Where's Poppa* (1970) and *Portnoy's Complaint* (1972), based on the Philip Roth novel. As the memorable Mama Hocheiser, Ruth Gordon is obscene and senile, possessive, and intent upon making her son's life as miserable as possible. Likewise, Lee Grant as Sophie Portnoy appeared dominating and self-serving, holding her son (played by Richard Benjamin) emotionally captive. Quite expectedly, these women produced neurotic sons, the heroes of the above-mentioned works, as did mothers in *Move* (1970), *The Steagle* (1971), and the Woody Allen classic films—*Play It Again, Sam* (1972), *Annie Hall* (1977), and *Manhattan* (1979). These sons were fearful, indecisive, and insecure men, craving boundless sex and affection, most frequently from shiksas as unlike their mothers as possible. Despite their infantile tendencies, these characters were frequently sympathetically presented, a result of their Jewish male authorship.

Compared to the depiction of Italian gangsters in film, Jewish underworld figures have gotten short shrift in the movies. Nevertheless, there have been a number of films made about Jewish underworld figures. The story of the so-called "Murder Incorporated" group, or Brownsville Boys, was turned into a film based on Burton B. Turkus's book *Murder, Inc.* (1951), which was about the mostly Jewish gang. The film version, *Murder, Inc.* (1960), was a commercial film in which **Peter Falk**, who played the Jewish **gangster** Abe "Kid Twist" Reles, was nominated for an Oscar for Best Supporting Actor. In the 1968 film *Funny Girl*, based on the life of Fanny Brice, Omar Sharif played the famous gambler Nicky Arnstein, who was married to Brice and was the friend of the notorious gangster Arnold Rothstein, who fixed the 1919 World Series. Francis Ford Coppola's *The Godfather* (1972) featured Lee Strasberg as Hyman Roth, a Jewish gangster based on Meyer Lansky. The life of the notorious Jewish gangster Louie Lepke was depicted in *Lepke* (1975), in which Tony Curtis played the title role. The success of *The Godfather* films spurred the Italian filmmaker Sergio Leone to produce *Once Upon a Time in America* (1984), which featured Robert De Niro and James Wood, among others. The film tells the story of Jewish ghetto youngsters who rise to prominence in New York City's world of organized crime during the Prohibition era.

Jewish womanhood came off little better during this period. The Jewish heroines of *Such Good Friends* (1971), *Made for Each Other* (1971), *The Heartbreak Kid* (1972), and *Sheila Levine Is Dead and Living in New York* (1975) are as equally insecure and dependent as their brothers, a marked contrast to the Jewish American princess of the previous generation. Only those films with a strong female input—such as *The Way We Were* (1973), starring Barbra Streisand; *Hester Street* (1975), written and directed by Joan Micklin Silver; and *Girlfriends* (1978), written and directed by Claudia Weill—avoid the stereotypes. These works also make other contributions; for example, *The Way We Were* implies that intermarriage does not always work; *Hester Street* focuses on Orthodox Jewish life, a topic untreated since the late 1920s; and *Girlfriends* depicts an autonomous Jewish woman who is not looking for a husband.

The seventies also introduce many new types: the Jewish gambler (*The Gambler*, 1974), the Jewish madam (*For Pete's Sake*, 1974), black-listed artists (*The Front*, 1976), the Jewish gumshoe (*The Big Fix*, 1976), the Jewish lesbian (*A Different Story*, 1978), a Yiddish cowboy (*The Frisco Kid*, 1979), a Jewish union organizer (*Norma Rae*, 1979), a Jewish murderess (*The Last Embrace*, 1979), and an elderly Jew pushed to violence (*Boardwalk*, 1979).

The Frisco Kid deserves special mention. Despite its high comedy, the film is one of the few Hollywood works to treat Jewish values as a serious topic. Briefly stated, the film shows the influence of Talmudic piety, as practiced by a rabbi played by **Gene Wilder**, as it confronts American pragmatism, portrayed in the person of Harrison Ford, and how the two characters influence each other as Jew meets Gentile in the American West.

The Holocaust and Israel continued to provide material for scenarios; however, the tendency was to create thrillers from this material rather than thought-provoking works. Two films, however, stand apart in this genre—*Cabaret* (1972), which deals with the rise of the Nazis in the Germany of the 1920s, was the cinema version of the award-winning Broadway musical, and *The Man in the Glass Booth* (1975), loosely based on the trial of Adolf Eichmann, was also the film version of the Broadway stage play. Other films include *The Odessa File* (1974), *Marathon Man* (1976), and *The Boys From Brazil* (1978), plus *The Jerusalem File* (1975), *Rosebud* (1975), *The Next Man* (1976), and *Black Sunday* (1977).

In the main, the 1980s continued the themes and characters from the 1970s, through a preponderance of comedies and a barrage of minor characters, some familiar, like doctors, lawyers, businessmen, moguls, and performers; others more novel, like werewolves, basketball coaches, and cops.

The major comedies focused once again on domestic life; some with a nostalgic look toward the past, others with a derisive look at the present. Films include *My Favorite Year* (1982), *Down and Out in Beverly Hills* (1986), *Brighton Beach Memoirs* (1987), and *Radio Days* (1987).

Jewish women finally arrive, displaying strength of character as a result of Jewish women's participation in production. Beginning with *Private Benjamin* (1980), co-produced by and starring Goldie Hawn as the Jewish American princess who finally grows into an autonomous woman, Jewish women are admirably depicted in *Tell Me a Riddle* (1980), *Baby, It's You* (1983), *Hannah K* (1983), *Yentl* (1983), *St. Elmo's Fire* (1985), *Sweet Lorraine* (1987), and *Dirty Dancing* (1987). Among the Jewish women active in film as directors, screenwriters, and producers are Barbra Streisand, Susan Seidelman, Claudia Weill, Lee Grant, Joan Micklin Silver, Gail Parent, and Sherry Lansing.

Several of the works of the 1980s feature exclusively Jewish worlds, even the world of Orthodox Jewry, for example, *The Chosen* (1981) and *Yentl.* Other films that deal with Jewish life include *Brighton Beach Memoirs, Sweet Lorraine, Tell Me a Riddle, Dirty Dancing, Crossing Delancey* (1988), *Enemies: A Love Story* (1989), and *The Plot Against Harry* (1989). Here the Gentiles are the outsiders, the marginal group.

In fact, the differences between "us" and "them" continue to fascinate filmmakers who deal with Jewish subject matter. Whereas during the 1940s, films seemed to go to great lengths to prove we were all alike under the skin, contemporary works stress the opposite. Woody Allen, long obsessed with this issue, deals with it again in *Hannah and Her Sisters* (1986), in *Radio Days* (1987), and in *Crimes and Misdemeanors* (1989). Likewise, the issue seems at the heart of such diverse works as *The King of Comedy* (1983), *Desperately Seeking Susan* (1985), *Dirty Dancing,* and *Broadcast News* (1987), or even in *Sophie's Choice* (1982), where the traditional roles of victim and victimizer are reversed.

The 1990s into the Twenty-First Century. The 1990s witnessed a number of Holocaust films produced both in the United States and in Europe. First and foremost among the films that made an impact on American audiences was **Steven Spielberg**'s ***Schindler's List*** (1984). The film, which won seven Academy Awards, including Best Picture, Best Director, and Best Cinematography, chronicled the story of Oscar Schindler, a Nazi businessman who saved the lives of hundreds of Jews during the Holocaust by employing them in his factory. Not without its detractors, the film still remains the definitive representation of the Holocaust in American commercial cinema.

In addition to *Schindler's List,* there were other Holocaust films of note. *Jakob the Liar* (1999) was a remake of a Czech production. Featuring Robin Williams, Lieb Schreiber, and **Alan Arkin**, the film told the story of a concentration camp inmate who attempts to raise the spirits of his fellow prisoners by inventing fictitious radio reports of the advancing Soviet army. *The Grey Zone* (2001) took a painful look at the Sonderkommandos, the special squads of Jews who processed the corpses from the crematoria at the Birkenau death camp. Equally chilling was HBO's dramatization *Conspiracy* (2001), a reenactment of the 1942 Wannsee Conference where top Nazi officials worked out the details for "the Final Solution."

During the 1990s, Hollywood filmmaking, like filmmaking elsewhere in the world, became increasingly global with director, producer, stars, and crew coming from different countries. Thus, the designation of "American" becomes increasingly blurred. This section will therefore include several films that were widely seen in the United States and which have an American component, although technically they are foreign films. For these works, the country of origin will be included.

Roberto Benigni's *Life is Beautiful* (1997) from Italy caused quite a stir because of the comic treatment of the Holocaust. Critics spoke out on both sides of the divide. The film is a dark comedy that depicts a Jewish father trying to shield his son from the horrors of the death camp by convincing him that what is happening is merely a game. The film won three Oscars (Best Foreign Language Film, Best Director, and Best Actor).

Another foreign film on the Holocaust to win a Best Director award was Roman Polanski's *The Pianist* (2002), a co-production from France, Germany, Poland, and Britain. The work gave many Jewish viewers what they did not receive in *Schindler's List,* namely, a Jewish hero. As directed by Polanski, a survivor of the Krakow Ghetto, the film followed the life of the talented Jewish pianist Wladyslaw Szpilman, played by Adrian Brody, as he struggled to remain alive during the dark years of World War II.

In addition, two other foreign films which dealt with aspects of the Holocaust were *Nowhere in Africa* (2003) and *The Counterfeiters* (2007). Both films received Oscars for the Best Foreign Language Film.

A unique treatment of the Holocaust was *Everything is Illuminated* (2005), a goofy comic drama directed by Liev Schreiber. Based on a novel by **Jonathan Safran Foer**, the story follows a young American Jew to the Ukraine as he searches for information about his family history during World War II.

Related to the subject of the Holocaust were those films that focused on anti-Semitism. One unique work, *Homicide* (1991), written and directed by **David Mamet**, revolved around a Jewish detective who unwillingly accepts an assignment investigating the murder of a wealthy Jewish businessman. In order to solve the crime, which has anti-Semitic roots, the detective must first come to understand his own roots.

School Ties (1992), produced by Sherry Lansing, dealt with a teenage Jewish athlete from Scranton, Pennsylvania who attends an exclusive boarding school in New England, who becomes the target of anti-Semitism when his carefully hidden Jewish identity is revealed. *Focus* (2001), based on an **Arthur Miller** novel, told the story of a husband and wife mistakenly identified as Jews by their anti-Semitic Brooklyn neighbors during the waning days of World War II. Also released in 2001, *The Believer,* a powerful and disturbing Canadian production written and directed by Henry Bean, followed the exploits of a young neo-Nazi as he moves from hatred of Jews towards self-hatred and eventual suicide. The character was loosely based on the life of Daniel Burrows, who, before his death, was exposed as having Jewish origins.

The film that stirred the most controversy, however, was Mel Gibson's independently produced *The Passion of The Christ* (2004). The film once again put the blame for the death of Jesus squarely on the shoulders of the ancient Israelites, who are depicted in an ugly, stereotypical manner. Because the film was widely promoted by religious groups in America, many Jewish organizations publicly voiced their opposition to dredging up old anti-Semitic beliefs. Fortunately, the film was not followed by any hostile acts, although professionals were still concerned about the film's ability to create negative feelings towards the Jews. Another film that played upon an old stereotype was Roman Polanski's version of *Oliver Twist* (2005). The film did little to counter the image of Fagin, although he comes across as tragic as well as venal.

Turning anti-Semitism into riotous comedy was a new twist in the early part of the twenty-first century. *Borat: Cultural Learnings of America for Make Benefit Glorious Nation of Kazakhstan*

(2006) was written and directed by and starred the British comedian Sacha Baron Cohen, posing as a country rube from Kazakhstan, who comes to America and discovers, among other things, home-grown anti-Semitism. Building on his television popularity, Cohen found a receptive audience in the United States.

As in the past, Jewish gangsters and criminals continued to hold a fascination for some segment of the population. *Bugsy* (1991) followed the life of Benjamin "Bugsy" Siegel, played by Warren Beatty, as he worked towards realizing his dream with the creation of Las Vegas. *Lansky* (1999), starring **Richard Dreyfuss**, chronicled the life of Meyer Lansky. *Swoon* (1991) recounted the Leopold-Loeb case, and the "crime of the century." This version used the actual court records for details and included references to the boys' homosexual relationship. On the good side of the law, *American Gangster* (2007) featured the real-life, incorruptible Jewish police detective Richie Roberts (Russell Crowe), as he brings to justice the Harlem crime boss, Frank Lucas.

A new theme in the 1990s was the subject of aging. *Used People* (1992) featured a Jewish widow as she faces aging and a new romance. *The Cemetery Club* (1993) was set in the world of an elderly retirement community. This theme is reprised in *Boynton Beach Bereavement Club* (2005). Two variations on the theme are *Driving Miss Daisy* (1989), featuring an elderly Southern, Jewish woman (Jessica Tandy) and her black driver as they forge a relationship over a 25-year period. It won best picture for the year. In *I'm Not Rappaport* (1996), two older men, one Jewish, the other black, meet in New York City's Central Park over a period of years to talk about life and politics.

As always, the largest categories representing Jewish characters and Jewish themes are the comedies and comic-dramas. Many of these feature Jewish family life. One of the first films of the 1990s was Barry Levinson's *Avalon* (1990), which depicted the most universal story in American Jewish life—immigration and assimilation. The story followed a somewhat typical Baltimore family as things change from one generation to the next. In this work, Levinson drew upon his childhood memories, also depicted in *Diner* (1982).

A less typical family story is seen in *The Slums of Beverly Hills* (1998), starring **Alan Arkin** as a single father who moves his kids from one cramped apartment to another so that they can get an education in the prestigious Beverly Hills school district.

Family comedies, which often go hand in hand with comic romances, were in full force beginning with the new millennium. In *Meet the Parents* (2000) a lovely non-Jewish woman brings home her new Jewish boyfriend (**Ben Stiller**), which results in a series of hilarious incidents. The sequel *Meet the Fockers* (2004) reverses the situation when Greg Focker brings home his girlfriend to meet his parents (Dustin Hoffman and Barbra Streisand). Both films did well at the box office, but many viewers felt *Meet the Fockers* played upon old, demeaning stereotypes. *Ira and Abby* (2007) presented another update on the theme of interfaith courtship. The film also featured a large array of Jewish psychoanalysts. The Jewish analyst made another appearance in *The Treatment* (2007), mostly as the nemesis of the Jewish protagonist.

Ethnic humor and dysfunctional families mix in *When Do We Eat?* (2006). The film is a comedy centered on a Passover Seder where everything goes wrong. Another Jewish celebration is featured in *Keeping Up with the Steins* (2006). Here, a large a cast of Jewish actors romp and collide as they prepare for a family Bar Mitzvah. **Adam Sandler**'s *Eight Crazy Nights* (2002), a riff on Hanukkah, offered an animated feature that managed to offend everyone. The film included Sandler's popular "Chanukah Song." The fact that all of the above works include Jewish religious holidays demonstrates how familiar Jewish cultural traditions have become in mainstream American society.

Since 1990, Woody Allen has continued to release approximately one film a year with greater or lesser results. In those works in which he appears, he is, as always, a Jewish character, regardless of whether this is openly acknowledged or not. The major change in his career was his decision, beginning with *Match Point* (2005), to film in London.

Several film dramas, some with comic aspects, took a more serious look at Jewish family life. *It Runs in the Family* (2003), starring **Kirk Douglas** and his son Michael, held a mirror up to father-son relationships, as well as three generations of one family. In Noah Baumbach's semi-autobiographical *The Squid and the Whale* (2005), the narrative featured two young boys as they watch their parents go through the painful experiences of a divorce.

In addition to the already mentioned works, other comedies with Jewish content include *Clueless* (1995); the **Coen Brothers**' *The Big Lebowski* (1997); Joan Micklin Silver's *A Fish in the Bathtub; South Park: Bigger, Longer, Uncut* (1999), based on the successful television animated show; David Mamet's dark comedy, *State and Main* (2000); *Saving Silverman* (2001); *The Hebrew Hammer* (2002), a satire on comic book heroes; and *Dummy* (2003).

Turning to the representation of Jewish women, there was a strong body of work released during the 1990s and after. *The Governess* (1998), written and directed by Sandra Goldbacher, turned its lens on the British Sephardic community of the 1800s. Here a young woman (Minnie Driver) takes a position in Scotland in order to support herself. Posing as Gentile, she becomes a photographic assistant and then lover to the man of the house. Eventually she sets up her own studio in London. The focus on this seldom depicted part of the Jewish community, as well as that of an independent nineteenth-century woman, was a fresh contribution to Jewish cinema.

Also in 1998, *A Price above Rubies* depicted the American Orthodox Jewish community. Here, an unfulfilled mother (Renee Zellweger), hemmed in by the rigid life of the community, finds escape in two love affairs and a part-time job. Eventually she gains the courage to go off on her own. *A Walk on the Moon* (1999) starred Diane Lane as a Jewish wife and mother in the **Catskills** during the summer of 1969. She finds herself drawn into a love affair with a non-Jewish salesman. Eventually everything is sorted out with the help of her wise and sensible mother-in-law (**Tovah Feldshuh**). It is significant that all three films about Jewish women starred non-Jewish actresses and that all three women found temporary satisfaction in the arms of non-Jewish men.

In the realm of comedy, *Amy's O* (aka *Amy's Orgasm*) released in 2001, starring writer/director Julie Davis, chronicled the trials and tribulations of an attractive, successful, nice Jewish girl trying to find a nice Jewish man. In the same vein, *Kissing Jessica Stein* (2002) presented a frustrated heroine who turns to a lesbian relationship when no worthy man seems to present himself. Like Amy, Jessica (Jennifer Westfeldt, also co-scriptwriter), finally finds her match. Reprising her role as the understanding mother figure, Tovah Feldshuh finally puts to rest the old stereotype of the interfering Jewish mother. Also focusing on women's relationships, *In Her Shoes* (2005) took a look at two very different sisters and the influence of their grandmother who lives in Florida.

A film that ran counter to the works mentioned above was *Welcome to the Dollhouse* (1996). Here an awkward seventh grade Jewish girl functions as the center of an often uncomfortable story. Another uncomfortable film was **Sarah Silverman**'s *Jesus is Magic* (2005). Based on her edgy brand of stand-up comedy, Silverman offered her own take on sex, race, and religion.

The Middle East became the subject of two hotly anticipated films. First Steven Spielberg's *Munich* (2005) told the story of a group of underground Israeli agents whose mission it is to murder the terrorists who killed the Israeli Olympic athletes in 1972. The script was cowritten by Tony Kushner. The second work, *A Mighty Wind* (2007), starred Angelina Jolie as Mariane Pearl, the wife of Wall Street journalist Danny Pearl, who was kidnapped and executed by a Muslim militant group in Karachi in 2002.

Finally, there were several works that featured biography, genius, science, and history. Musical prodigy David Helfgott's life story and struggle to recover from mental illness is recounted in the film *Shine* (1996). *Pi* (1998), directed by Darren Aronofsky, focused on a Jewish mathematical genius who is approached by a Hasidic group hoping to further understand the Kabbalah. *Infinity* (1996) centered on the life of Richard Feynman, a 1965 Nobel Prize-winning physicist, and his work on the development of the atomic bomb during World War II. *Enigma* (2001) told the story of the British efforts to break the Nazi Code. *American Splendor* (2002) focused on the life of cartoonist **Harvey Pekar**. And *Bee Season* (2005) presented a Jewish school girl whose spelling triumphs are touched by religion and mysticism.

All told, the last 20 years have seen the continuation of specifically Jewish themes related to the Holocaust and anti-Semitism. Likewise, the areas of comedy and Jewish family life still constitute the largest categories for screen narratives. Within these categories, however, several changes are apparent. The films reflect a greater sense of ease at being Jewish in America, and the old stereotyping that plagued works in previous decades has practically disappeared.

The biggest change, however, was in the representation of Jewish women. The number of female Jewish protagonists, as well as the range of their roles, expanded dramatically. No doubt this trend reflects the new opportunities available for American women in general and for Jewish women in particular. As Jewish women increasingly found their way into writing, directing, and producing, especially in the independent sector, it is not surprising that their input would be reflected in a positive way on the screen.

In sum, the last 20 years have been a productive period for Jewish filmmaking, especially for films produced independently. This is true for Jewish documentary filmmaking as well, although the documentaries are not covered in this entry. The more than 50 Jewish film festivals throughout the United States attest to an active audience willing to support these works. In short, Jewish film is still alive and well.

Patricia Erens

Further Reading: Baron, Lawrence. *Projecting the Holocaust into the Present: The Changing Focus of Holocaust Feature Films Since 1990.* Lanham, MD: Rowman and Littlefield, 2005. Carr, Steven Alan. *Hollywood and Anti-Semitism: A Cultural History up to World War II.* Cambridge, MA: Cambridge University Press, 2001. Doneson, Judith E. *The Holocaust in American Film.* Philadelphia, PA: Jewish Publication Society, 1987. Erens, Patricia. *The Jew in American Cinema.* Bloomington, IN: Indiana University Press, 1984. Friedman, Lester D. *Hollywood's Image of the Jew.* New York: Ungar Publishing Company, 1982. Gabler, Neal. *An Empire of Their Own: How the Jews Invented Hollywood.* New York: Crown Publishing Group, 1988. Hoberman, J., and Jeffrey Shandler. *Bridge of Light: Yiddish Film Between Two Worlds.* Princeton, NJ: Princeton University Press, 2003. Rogin, Michael. *Black Face, White Noise: Jewish Immigrants in the Hollywood Melting Pot.* Berkeley, CA: University of California Press, 1996.

FILM STARS

The Jewish presence in the American film industry has been massive. Most of the famous Hollywood studios were founded by Jews and while all the major studios are now in the hands of large, publicly traded companies, Jewish executives continue to hold many key positions. Likewise, Jews were and continue to be heavily represented in "creative" fields like screenwriting, directing, and movie music composition. In the last century, however, the number of American major film stars who were (or are) Jewish has declined, and several reasons may well account for this drop in representation.

Moviemaking was a relatively low-status and wide-open field when the major Hollywood studios were founded in the first two decades of the twentieth century. Jews got in on the "ground floor" and, as critic Neil Gabler aptly put it, they could and did create "an empire of their own." The Jewish founding fathers of the Hollywood studios were acutely aware that their film product was scrutinized by a large portion of the public through the prism of anti-Semitic and anti-immigrant sentiment. An ongoing criticism of the film industry posits that Hollywood presents images that are counter to "American" or "Christian" values. So, studios largely trimmed their sails and, until the mid-1960s, mostly produced films that portrayed an idealized view of America. The stars of these films were usually very attractive, and the vast majority exemplified what came to be known as "all-American good looks." That look was Northern European.

The studio heads' perception was that a large percentage of the American film-going public was biased and would not spend their money to see films that starred actors without that all-American WASPy look. So, they gave that portion of the public what they wanted, while tamping down the perception of Hollywood as something "alien" and "Jewish." Since persons blessed with "all-American" beauty were told that they "could be" a film actor or actress, an astonishing number of these physically beautiful people, often with no acting training, tried to break into the movies. The lucky ones almost completely filled the ranks of Hollywood stars until 1970. Even so, the all-American look still is somewhat favored today.

By contrast, "character roles" were and are filled by the less beautiful. "Semitic" looks are unimportant when casting a character actor. Most character actors made a conscious decision to enter into the acting field. Knowing that they would almost certainly be denied star status, for their success they depended on genuine acting talent. For cultural reasons, Jews have ignored these drawbacks and have disproportionately filled the pool of character actors. Many, over time, have built successful careers. To date, one can probably count 20 steadily working Jewish character actors for every Jewish film star.

The Silent Era (c. 1903–1927). Just three Jews stand out as genuine screen stars during the silent screen era: Theda Bara (1885–1955), Gilbert "**Broncho Billy**" Anderson (1880–1971), and Ricardo Cortez (1899–1977). Bara, who is often labeled the first "vamp" or "sex star," was born Theodosia Goodman in Cincinnati to a middle-class Jewish family. Her fame is largely based on films made in New York between 1915 and 1919, and her career somewhat predated the Hollywood preference for the "all-American look." In the earliest days of the American film industry, there was a bit more room for an exotic, non-WASPy sexy look like Bara's. By 1925, even very good-looking Jewish actors and actresses had a much harder time becoming stars if they appeared "Semitic." Bara's Jewish background was never disclosed by Fox Studio, and stories depicting her background as, for example, an Arab princess, were created. Although her first films were hits, her career faded, and she retired from the screen in 1926.

Anderson was born Max Aaronson in Arkansas. He acted (as Gilbert Anderson) in the first major American movie, *The Great Train Robbery* (1903). Soon thereafter, Anderson set up his own studio and began turning out hundreds of Western movie shorts. He starred in most of these films under the name "Broncho Billy" Anderson. Broncho Billy is universally described as the first Western cowboy star. Anderson's acting career declined after 1920, and he turned to producing films.

The surprising success of Rudolph Valentino, an Italian immigrant, as a "Latin Lover" led other studios to try and invent their own Valentinos—enter a former Wall Street broker named Jacob Kranz, who was born into a Viennese Jewish family. His studio dubbed him Ricardo Cortez, and he starred in a number of hit silent films as an exotic, sexy Latin lover. When sound came in, his accent did not fit the Latin image, and he successfully switched to character roles, working steadily until he retired in 1959.

The most famous silent star, Charlie Chaplin, was not Jewish in any way. He was a fierce opponent of anti-Semitism. Chaplin's long-term companion, actress **Paulette Goddard**, born Paulette Levy, is sometimes described as Jewish, but she only had one Jewish grandparent.

Hollywood's Golden Age (1927–1965). Very few films made between 1927 and 1947 even mentioned the word "Jew," but through a quirk, the first important talking picture, ***The Jazz Singer*** (1927), had a Jewish theme (a popular singer torn between his Jewish faith and showbiz) and a Jewish star—the **vaudeville** and Broadway superstar **Al Jolson** (1886–1950). The novelty of hearing Jolson sing and talk made *The Jazz Singer* a huge hit. But Jolson didn't really have a big film career, making just a few musical films through 1935. Jolson had a high-energy, "hammy" style that worked well on the stage, but that style was way too broad for the more intimate experience of film.

The two biggest male Jewish stars of the 1930s were Paul Muni and **Edward G. Robinson**. Both were "accidental" stars who broke out of the "character actor ghetto" by virtue of electrifying performances in modest budget films. These performances so captured the public's imagination that their studio took a chance and gave them leading man roles, despite their lack of leading man good looks.

Paul Muni (1895–1959) was born in the Ukraine as Meshilem Meier Weisenfreud. He came to America in 1902. His parents were **Yiddish theater** actors, and Muni first made his name as an actor in the Yiddish theater—where he was known by his Yiddish name, Mooney Weisenfreud—and on the Broadway stage. He was signed by Warner Brothers Studio, which was near bankruptcy in the early 1930s and was willing to risk putting out edgy films about outcasts and **gangsters** that the other studios shied away from. In 1932, Muni gave a great performance as a wrongly imprisoned man in *I Am a Fugitive from a Chain Gang* and followed that up that same year as a scary gangster in the original *Scarface.* Similar pictures did not make Muni a matinee idol, but the public appreciated his talent and turned out for a "Muni movie." Due to his popularity, Warner Brothers decided to cast Paul Muni as the starring actor in many of their pro-democracy bio-pics.

Most of the studio heads in the 1930s (Jews and non-Jews) were political conservatives, totally obsessed with the bottom line. Most were afraid to anger even Nazi Germany with their film product. However, (the Jewish) Jack Warner and his brothers were Democrats who were willing to take a risk. Starting in the mid-1930s, they released films that, at least obliquely, support anti-fascism and anti-Nazism.

In 1937, Muni won a best actor Oscar (the first Jewish actor to win an Oscar) playing the title role in Warner Brothers' *The Story of Louis Pasteur.* The film depicted the famous French biologist as an enemy of ignorance. The same year he made *The Life of Emile Zola,* about the famous French journalist who risked his life to defend the French Jewish army officer Alfred Dreyfus from false charges of treason in the 1890s. Arrayed against Zola were the same forces of reaction that were supporting fascism in the 1930s. While the script barely mentioned that Dreyfus was Jewish—the point was made. In 1939, Muni made his last bio-pic, *Juarez,* about the courageous Mexican president of Indian blood who stood firm and reversed, in the 1860s, the conquest of his country by French forces led by the dictator Napoleon III.

Muni never got along with the studio executives and made just a few more films after *Juarez.* For the most part, he quit film work after 1940 and returned to the stage.

Edward G. Robinson (1893–1973) was born in Romania, and his family came to America in 1903. He acted with Paul Muni in the Yiddish theater. Like Muni, he went from the Broadway stage to breakout film stardom playing a gangster in a Warner Brothers movie. Robinson's role was *Little Caesar* (1933), a gangster part he would forever be associated with. Almost ugly, Robinson teetered between character actor and leading man status during the 1930s and 1940s and then simply became a character actor. While he continued to play tough guys for most of his long career, he did all sorts of roles, including comedies. His favorite role was playing the title character in the Warner Brothers pro-democracy bio-pic *Dr. Ehrlich's Magic Bullet* (1940). It was the story of Dr. Paul Ehrlich, a German Jewish scientist who won a Nobel Prize before World War I for the discovery of the first effective syphilis treatment. While it was Ehrlich's Jewish heritage that was underplayed, audiences still, for the most part, understood the message—Nazis were driving Jews out of Germany, even those as distinguished as Ehrlich.

Robinson was very proud of being Jewish, and his fierce anti-Nazism led him to support what later became labeled as communist front groups. Although never a communist, he was blacklisted around 1950, and he could not get decent roles until director Cecil B. DeMille, a militant anti-communist, cast him (1955) in *The Ten Commandments*. After that film, Robinson continued to work regularly in film and television until his death. He was given an honorary Oscar just before his death. He is still regarded as one of the most memorable actors in film history.

Unlike Robinson, the Hungarian-born Jewish actor Paul Lukas (1891–1971) never became close to being a true American film star. However, unlike Robinson, he did win a best actor Oscar for *Watch on the Rhine* (1943), in which he played an anti-Nazi. Additionally, English Jewish actor Leslie Howard, who also never attained true American stardom, is still remembered for playing the personification of the Southern WASP gentleman, Ashley Wilkes, in *Gone with the Wind*.

The "star" picture for Jewish actresses was extremely bleak in the 1930s. The Austrian-born (1910) Louise Rainer, now the oldest living Oscar winner, won two best actress Oscars back-to-back —in 1936 for *The Great Ziegfeld*, and in 1937 for *The Good Earth* (in which she and Paul Muni played a Chinese peasant couple!). However, she never got along with Louis B. Mayer, the head of MGM studio, and she was released from her contract in 1939.

It is hard to call Rainer a star, despite her two Oscars—her American film career was brief, and she did not achieve stardom in any other country's cinema. It is also hard to decide whether to call Hedy Lamarr (1913–2000) an American film star of the first rank. She began her film career in her native Austria and came to the States in the late 1930s. Incredibly beautiful, she had some starring roles in the late 1930s and early 1940s (*Algiers* and *Ziegfeld Girl*) and then faded until she had a hit with 1949's *Samson and Delilah*. Then, again, her career faded. The Jewish background of Lamarr and Rainer was unknown to the general public, and few of their associates were aware of it. Both came from assimilated backgrounds.

This was not true of Sylvia Sidney (1910–1999), an American Jewish actress who got some good parts in the 1930s, including the costarring role in *Dead End*. She worked steadily until her death at age 88, earning an Oscar nomination for Best Supporting Actress in 1973. Sidney, who was born in Brooklyn as Sylvia Kosnow, was always up-front about her Jewish background and proud of it. While virtually every filmgoer in the 1930s would have known her name, Sidney was never a first-rank star. While certainly pretty, her almost-Eurasian look probably did not help her early career or choice of roles.

The male counterpart to Sylvia Sidney's gritty "urban" persona was found in **John Garfield** (1913–1951), born Julius Garfinkle in New York. Garfield was the first Jewish actor of the talking film era who had leading man looks and, for a time, a real star career. Garfield came out of the leftist, heavily Jewish Group Theatre of New York. (The Group Theatre pioneered the "emotional" Method School of acting). Garfield's talent and good looks got him a Hollywood contract in 1938, and he scored a best supporting actor Oscar nomination for his first film (the otherwise so-so movie *Four Daughters*). In 1939, he played Paul Muni's top Mexican aide in *Juarez*.

Garfield spent most of World War II entertaining the troops (he could not serve due to a heart condition) and starring in "B" pictures. After the war, he had a string of hits that made him a star, albeit not quite a superstar. He stood out from most Hollywood actors of that era because of his naturalistic style of acting and "big city" persona. Virtually every film critic sees him as the direct "ancestor" of Marlon Brando and Montgomery Clift, the Method actors who transformed American film acting in the 1950s.

In 1946, Garfield starred in *The Postman Always Rings Twice,* which is still a classic. Also in 1946, he made the hit *Humoresque* with Joan Crawford. In 1947 was the release of *Body and Soul,* a boxing picture which earned Garfield a best actor nomination, and *Gentleman's Agreement.* The latter film was the first major Hollywood film that tackled the issue of anti-Semitism head on. Garfield had a supporting, but major role in the film as a Jewish army officer whose smooth return to civilian life is complicated by anti-Semitism. Garfield, while never a member of the Communist Party, refused to "name names" and was blacklisted out of Hollywood not long before his death from a heart attack.

Jewish comedians and comic acts were very successful on the stage and on radio, but less so in the movies before the 1950s. **Jack Benny** and **George Burns** (whose wife/partner, Gracie Allen, was Catholic) were big **radio** stars but had only modest film careers. Singer and comic **Eddie Cantor**, big on radio and the stage, had a couple of comic film hits in the early 1930s but did not sustain a major film career. Only the **Marx Brothers**, with long stage experience, had major comedy film hits in the '1930s, but their collective film career faded in the early 1940s.

Lauren Bacall (b. 1924) and **Kirk Douglas** (b. 1916) have had somewhat parallel careers. Bacall was born Betty Perske to a lower middle-class New York Jewish family. She was blessed with what most would define as WASPy good looks, with perhaps a touch of exoticism around her eyes. Bacall studied acting (she met Kirk Douglas, a lifelong friend, at acting school) and was a successful fashion model before she was 18. At 20, she made her first movie, the 1944 classic *To Have and Have Not,* opposite Humphrey Bogart. They married in 1945. In the four years following their marriage, Bogart and Bacall made several classic pictures which made Bacall a movie star (the biggest star of any Jewish actress of "the Golden Age"). For a variety of reasons, Bogart (who died in 1957) was enshrined as a cultural icon in the 1960s. Bacall was enshrined with him as a "screen legend," even though she was still a relatively young woman. But it was legendary status with an asterisk.

Bacall took a lot of time off before she was 40 to have and raise children with Bogart and her second husband, actor Jason Robards. Most of the films she did make in the 1950s were not very memorable, and her stardom declined. She picked up the pace of her career in the late 1960s and still acts in quality projects. Yet, she has never come close to recapturing that moment in the late 1940s when she was the hottest female star in Hollywood.

Douglas was born Issur Danielovitch Demsky, the son of very poor Russian immigrants. He was made for the movies—handsome, with fair features, a strong voice, and a physique that reflected his background as a college wrestler. In 1946, Bacall helped him secure his first film role. From 1949 through 1960, he was certainly one of the top five American film stars, as judged by any criteria from box office to the quality of his work. He earned three Oscar nominations for Best Actor and was active as a producer, bringing to the screen such great movies as *Spartacus* (1960) and *Paths of Glory* (1958).

After 1960, great scripts eluded him, and only a handful of his later films are really worth watching. Douglas embraced his Jewish heritage and Judaism after a near-fatal helicopter crash in 1991 and achieved luster in his later years as an important figure in the Jewish community and as a best-selling author. He was given an honorary Oscar in 1996.

Like Douglas, **Tony Curtis** was made for the movies. In his own words, "I was the best looking Jewish kid, ever." Born (1925) Bernard Schwarz, into a family of poor Hungarian Jewish immigrants in New York, he knew early on he wanted to be an actor. His features were so strikingly handsome (almost pretty) that he could get away with being more swarthy than most aspiring Hollywood leading men. Curtis had little acting experience when he signed a Hollywood contract in 1948. He starred for most of the next decade as a "pretty boy" in unmemorable pictures that did well at the box office.

He was the first Jewish actor to be a "teen idol," and he was a major Hollywood star throughout the 1950s.

In 1957, he showed he had some real acting ability in the dark film *Sweet Smell of Success.* In the next two years, he would make his two other best movies: *The Defiant Ones* (which earned him a best actor Oscar nomination) and *Some Like It Hot,* a great farce. In 1960, Curtis would star opposite Kirk Douglas in *Spartacus,* and, like Douglas, after 1960 his acting career took a slow, but steady downward turn. Curtis married frequently and had many children to support, so he often took roles in mediocre films and television shows just for the paycheck.

While in some sense he remains a star to this day, he really has been in few projects of note since 1960. He has done a lot of charitable work for the Jewish community in Hungary. (Jamie Lee Curtis, Tony's daughter, has had acting success but has not quite become a film star. Even though her late mother was not Jewish, Jamie Curtis more-or-less identifies as Jewish. Her husband of many years is Christopher Guest, the well-known actor/director. He is the child of secular Jewish parents.)

Comedian **Jerry Lewis** (b. 1926) was at least as big a box office star in the 1950s as Douglas or Curtis. Born Joseph Levitch, the son of a small-time comedian, Lewis hit pay dirt right after World War II when he paired up with singer Dean Martin in an incredibly popular nightclub act. The act worked well on the big screen, and Martin and Lewis's silly film comedies were box-office gold until the team broke up in 1956. Lewis then turned himself into an auteur—writing, directing, and starring in a series of Jerry Lewis movies that found a big audience until around 1965. Some were pretty good and still stand up, like *The Nutty Professor.*

Lewis's somewhat juvenile humor tired as he aged, and his own projects since 1965 have been flops. He has worked fairly steadily in other people's movies and on television. He turned in a sterling performance as a talk show host in Martin Scorsese's *King of Comedy* (1983). His famous annual charity telethon has also kept him in the public eye.

Burning brightly for a short time was **Judy Holliday** (1921–1965), a pretty actress who could put on a funny, ditzy personality, although she was really very intelligent. She earned the best actress Oscar for her second film, 1950's *Born Yesterday,* and made a few other hit films in the 1950s, before the cancer which eventually took her life ended her career around 1960.

Worthy of a note is **Paul Newman** (1925–2008), the incredibly handsome actor who became a star in the 1950s, earned many Oscar nominations (and one win), and has led a model professional and personal life. Newman's father was Jewish, but the little religious training he had was in his mother's Christian faith. As an adult he has followed no religion, and he has really never self-identified as Jewish. He did star as the perfect Israeli hero in *Exodus* (1960), and he has done a bit of work for Israel-related causes.

Also noteworthy are Elizabeth Taylor and Marilyn Monroe. Both converted to Judaism in the 1950s after very brief periods of study, but they never practiced after their respective short marriages to Jewish men. There are more serious converts to Judaism in the acting profession (including **Sammy Davis Jr.**, Robert Lansing, Scott Glenn, and Kate Capshaw), but none have achieved film stardom.

The Culture Cracks (1965–1977). By 1965, what was referred to as the Hollywood studio system was collapsing. No longer could the studios afford to keep armies of production workers on salary, sign young actors and make them stars, and bankroll virtually all movies. The moviegoing audience had shrunk since 1950 with the advent of television, and an antitrust action around the same time stripped the studios of their ownership of movie theaters. Gradually, a system emerged where the studios became mostly distributors of movies, with financing from various sources put together on a movie-by-movie basis. The expensive movie musical was an early casualty; however, just before the Hollywood musical soundstages were shuttered, the "most Jewish" star actress in film industry history got a chance to shine—**Barbra Streisand** (b. 1942).

The Brooklyn-born Streisand electrified Broadway, television audiences, and record buyers with her singing voice and "spunk" before her film debut in the hit movie, *Funny Girl* (1969). She won the best actress Oscar for this role, which she had created on Broadway. *Funny Girl* was the story of **Fanny Brice**, a "very Jewish" comedian and singer who was a Broadway star but was relegated to almost-demeaning humorous shorts by the 1930s. Like Brice, Streisand "looked Jewish" (even if she was a lot sexier than Brice). Like Brice, Barbra wasn't demure, was "big city," and could wisecrack back. There were many film character actresses who provided comic relief in years past, but leading ladies were a different breed until Streisand tore down the barrier (at least for herself).

Even Streisand's talent could not get audiences to see her lesser movie musicals, and her roles *Hello, Dolly* and *Funny Lady* flopped. She did much better in romantic dramas and comedies, even if she did not sing (*The Way We Were* and *What's Up Doc?*). Also worthy of note is *Yentl,* a Jewish story that Streisand directed and starred in. While not a big hit, it was only made because Streisand, a big star, insisted.

Hollywood floundered in the late 1960s, while looking for a formula to bring moviegoers back. Through the late 1970s, studios were open to trying new tacks, including giving first time directors a chance and helping to bankroll "small" films starring actors who looked like "regular people." In 1967, Jewish director Mike Nichols cast stage actor **Dustin Hoffman** (b. 1937) as the star of *The Graduate,* because he wanted a Jewish-looking, "urban" actor whose very persona was a contrast to the world of "white-bread" suburban conformity that confronted Hoffman's character. The film was a monster hit and in some ways embodied the rebelliousness of the era. Hoffman went on to a stellar career that included two best actor Oscars. While never a matinee idol, Hoffman's talent was so appreciated by moviegoers that he got many leading man roles.

During this same time, George Segal (b. 1937) and Walter Matthau (1920–2000) emerged as film comedy stars. Segal, a good-looking, if not gorgeous man, started in drama, earning a best supporting actor Oscar nomination for 1964's *Who's Afraid of Virginia Woolf?* He shifted to charming, urbane comedies in the early 1970s. Many of these films were hits, if not blockbusters. His box-office streak ran out in the late 1970s, and he has mostly worked in television since. Matthau's homely looks made him an unlikely leading man, but his everyman personality and his great comedic timing clicked with the public. He labored in character parts, mostly dramatic, until he earned a best supporting actor Oscar in the 1966 comedy *The Fortune Cookie.* Two years later, he cemented his star status by recreating his Broadway role as the costar of the hit comedy *The Odd Couple.* From then on he played leading roles in comedies or dramas in which he was able to give his character a humanizing touch.

Woody Allen (b. 1935) began making comedy films in the mid-1960s. In his early broad comedy films, he played the character he perfected in his former stand-up act—a nebbishy, if very witty urban Jew. His early films were modest box office hits, and with that track record, Allen was able to find enough financing to completely control his own destiny as the writer, director, and usually the star of "Woody Allen" movies. In 1977, he moved out of broad comedy and into much more sophisticated work with *Annie Hall,* one of a very few comedies to win the best picture Oscar. While there have been a few more box office hits for Allen (and even more pictures that critics liked), he has never been a really "bankable" star in Hollywood terms. His pictures rarely make much money and usually do better in Europe than in America. His star-laden casts work for union scale for the opportunity to be in an Allen film.

Nobody has ever accused **Mel Brooks** (b. 1926) of being overly sophisticated, and he really can't be classed as a film star, because the Mel Brooks-directed/-written movies that starred Mel Brooks have not been among his big hits. However, for a brief time, Jewish actor **Gene Wilder**

(b. 1933), who is only marginally better looking than Woody Allen, had a burst of film stardom in Brooks's films. His first costarring film role was in Brooks's 1968 film *The Producers*. It did not make any money, but Wilder went on to star in (and cowrite) Brooks's early 1970s hits, *Young Frankenstein* and *Blazing Saddles*. He had two more hits right after with *Silver Streak* and *Stir Crazy*. Then, for whatever reason, Wilder's stardom ended with a few lackluster movies.

Unlike Wilder, James Caan (b. 1940) had the ruggedly handsome look of a Hollywood star, and he has referred to himself as "the Jewish cowboy." Caan worked in television and film for a decade before becoming a star when he played Sonny Corleone in *The Godfather* (1972). He made some hit films in the 1970s, but his acting career was hampered by a severe drug abuse problem in the 1980s. He remains a well-known name and has a recent hit television show to his credit.

The Blockbuster (1977–2007). Ironically, a "nerdy" Jewish director, **Steven Spielberg**, helped to end the post-1965 era when Hollywood turned out interesting "little films" that featured "ethnic" or less-than-"hunky" actors in starring roles (such as Dustin Hoffman, Al Pacino, Gene Hackman, and others). The incredible box office success of *Jaws* (1975) encouraged film companies to go formulaic and invest in big-budget films. After a time, producers also decided to "retro-cast" and stick classically good-looking actors and actresses into starring roles in these would-be blockbusters. Spielberg, however, did not know he was making a blockbuster with *Jaws* and cast **Richard Dreyfuss** (b. 1947), a simply average-looking Jewish actor as the costar.

Dreyfuss would get another career boost in 1977 as the star of Spielberg's huge hit, *Close Encounters of the Third Kind*. The same year he would win the best actor Oscar as the star of the charming comedy *The Goodbye Girl*. Since then, Dreyfuss has had a few hits and more misses in something of a roller coaster career.

Spielberg's buddy, the non-Jewish director George Lucas, gave a stellar boost to the blockbuster "movement" with his 1977 mega-hit, *Star Wars,* and its sequels. *Star Wars* costarred Harrison Ford (b. 1942) and Carrie Fisher (b. 1956), both of whom have one Jewish parent. Ford, the handsome son of a Jewish mother and an Irish Catholic father, was a virtual unknown before *Star Wars*. In the decade following *Star Wars,* he became a huge box office star in action pictures and dramas including *Raiders of the Lost Ark* and *Witness*. While his star is fading now, he is still an important actor.

Ford was raised without religion, and while he has never hid his Jewish "half," it is hard to discern what would define him as a Jewish actor beyond birth. "Jewishness" is not really evident in his personal life or choice of roles. Carrie Fisher, on the other hand, has referred to herself as Jewish (although she was not raised in a religion), and there is something of the Jewish comedic style in her acting and in the critically acclaimed novels she's written. (Carrie's father is Jewish singer **Eddie Fisher**. Her film career has not been at star-level since *Star Wars*.)

Ford is the forerunner of a trend, the emergence of many well-known actors and actresses of partial Jewish background whose ties, cultural or otherwise, to "Jewishness," are small or not clear. The increase in the number of such actors is not surprising, given the fact that American Jews have been intermarrying with non-Jews at higher and higher rates since the 1960s. Michael Douglas (b. 1944) is the son of a Jewish father (Kirk Douglas) and a non-Jewish mother. Like Ford, he was raised without religion, and while he has done some Jewish cultural "things" (like narrating a documentary on the 1972 massacre of Israeli Olympic athletes), he has consistently avoided being identified as Jewish in a religious sense. He always reminded reporters who labeled him as "Jewish" while interviewing him that his mother is not Jewish.

Douglas's early film career was in the shadow of his famous father, whom he greatly resembles. His first Oscar came as a producer, but in the middle 1980s his own dramatic acting career finally caught fire with hits like *Romancing the Stone, Fatal Attraction,* and *Basic Instinct*. In 1987,

Michael won the best actor Oscar for *Wall Street.* He has cooled off since the mid-1990s but still remains a relatively important film actor.

In the mid-1980s, the average-looking Jewish comic actor **Billy Crystal** (b. 1947) had a brief burst of film stardom with two very well-written hit films, *When Harry Met Sally* (maybe the best romantic comedy ever) and *City Slickers.* But Crystal did not have the "star power" to turn a so-so movie into a hit, and all but one (*Analyze This*) of his subsequent movies did only modest business. He remains popular and is famous as the best host ever of the Oscar awards ceremony, but his time as a film star was brief.

Debra Winger's (b. 1955) star blazed between 1980 and 1985. Pretty, gritty, and vibrant, she had a string of hits including *Urban Cowboy, Terms of Endearment,* and *An Officer and a Gentleman.* While she was nominated twice for the best actress Oscar, her reputation as "difficult" and her unwillingness to take many roles shortened her time as a film star.

Marlee Matlin (b. 1965) has had a remarkable career, but she cannot be called a film star despite the fact she won the best actress Oscar in 1986 for *Children of a Lesser God.* It was her first film role, and she remains the youngest actress (21) to win the best actress Oscar. Matlin, who is very pretty, was born deaf, and her Oscar performance was as a deaf person at a school for the deaf. Matlin defied expectations and has continued to work very steadily, often getting roles that could just as easily be played by a hearing actor.

The equally beautiful Winona Ryder (b. 1971) had a string of hits between 1986 and 2000 and was a darling of critics during this period. She made her first film at 14 and became a "Generation X" icon with starring roles in "X" faves like *Heathers, Reality Bites,* and *Edward Scissorhands.* She got Oscar nominations for performances in two period pieces: *Little Women* and*The Age of Innocence.*

Around 2000, she seemed to care less and took roles in lesser quality movies. Ironically, one of her worst movies, 2002's *Mr. Deeds,* starring **Adam Sandler**, was her biggest box-office hit. In late 2001, she was arrested for shoplifting and inexplicably put herself through a circus-like trial and media frenzy. She has worked relatively little since, admitting in 2007 that she had needed a rest for years. She has quite a few films in the pipeline as of late 2007, but time will tell whether she can reestablish, at 40, a film star career. Ryder's father is Jewish, and her mother is not. While she was not raised in any faith, she has referred to herself as Jewish.

Adam Sandler (b. 1965) often gets "no respect" because most of his comedy films have a lot of juvenile humor and have been much more popular with the masses than with critics. But he is, to my mind, a breakthrough Jewish actor in some respects. Sandler first gained fame as a member of television's *Saturday Night Live* cast. He starred in his first comedy film in 1995 and, with just a couple of exceptions, his comedies have been very high-grossing films. He has shown some acting depth in dramatic films like *Punch Drunk Love* and *Spanglish* but is still awaiting a role in a dramatic film that is really liked by the critics.

There is no doubt that Sandler is Jewish. His three satirical Hanukkah songs, which received a lot of airplay, proclaim his Jewishness while bringing the whole American public into the (hitherto inside-the-Jewish-community) game of guessing which important entertainment figures are Jewish. Sandler is a post-Ghetto Jew, a little crazy, but in a "regular guy way," and not neurotic like a Woody Allen. He is, or was, a "good old boy" who happens to be Jewish. One can imagine him fitting in almost anywhere without denying he is Jewish.

The willowy blonde "goddess" Gwyneth Paltrow (b. 1972) seems far-removed from Adam Sandler's earthiness, but she shows a surprisingly Jewish-type wit in interviews. Paltrow is the daughter of the late Jewish director Bruce Paltrow and non-Jewish actress Blythe Danner. Gwyneth was raised Jewish, and director Steven Spielberg has been her unofficial godfather since birth. She had a string of films that did well at the box office in the early 1990s. In 1996, she won the best actress Oscar for *Shakespeare in Love.* Her career since 2000 has been more low-key. She has taken fewer roles so as to be able to raise her kids, and the films she did make have not made much money. One exception was the broad 2001 comedy *Shallow Hal,* which did pretty well at the box office.

Paltrow's *Shallow Hal* costar was the almost rotund **Jack Black** (b. 1969). Black's mother is Jewish, and his father converted to Judaism. He was raised Jewish. His early career took two tracks—as a comic rock musician and as an actor. Black got small roles through 2000, when he got a meaty supporting role in *High Fidelity,* and his sharp comedic timing attracted notice. *Shallow Hal* was his first starring role. His real breakthrough came in 2002 as the star of the mega-hit *School of Rock.* He played an amiable slacker who turned a bunch of young kids into a great rock band. This film turned Black into a star, albeit not a superstar. Currently, his career is good, but another big hit in the near future would help.

Ben Stiller (b. 1965), is the son of comic Jewish actor Jerry Stiller and comedian Anne Meara, who converted to Judaism. Stiller was raised Jewish. His early film roles were in intelligent small movies like *Reality Bites* and *Flirting with Disaster.* In 1998, he starred in the surprise big comedy hit *There's Something About Mary.* In this film he played what came to be his signature character—a nebbishy guy, often identified as Jewish, who chases after a lovely non-Jewish goddess character and comically humiliates himself along the way. Stiller was explicitly Jewish and the same nebbish in follow-up films that were also hits (*Meet the Parents, Meet the Fockers,* and *Along Comes Polly*). He has also costarred in a number of other film comedies. Stiller has made something of a devil's pact with the public. His earlier work is most admired by critics, but his "loser" character has made him a film star.

The gorgeous Jennifer Connelly (b. 1970) labored in small, intelligent indie films until she scored a great role in 2001's *A Beautiful Mind* and earned a best supporting actress Oscar for her work. She has not had any major hits since, but she has steadily costarred in good mid-budget movies like *Blood Diamond* and *Little Children.* Connelly, whose mother is Jewish, was not raised in any faith.

Scarlett Johansson (b. 1984) began acting as a child and costarred (1998) with Robert Redford in *The Horse Whisperer.* She worked in small movies (*Ghost World*) until a costarring role opposite Bill Murray in 2003's *Lost in Translation* made the world notice that she could act and that she had developed a blonde bombshell figure to go with her pretty face. Scarlett became a beauty icon, appearing on the covers of leading magazines. Most of her films since *Lost in Translation* have had problematic scripts. A minor hit was Woody Allen's 2005 "comeback" film, *Match Point,* and she has been heralded as Allen's new favorite actress. She is a rare "A" list star with almost no major hits on her resume. Johansson is the daughter of an American Jewish mother and a Danish non-Jewish father. She was not raised in any faith but has referred to herself as Jewish.

Natalie Portman (b. 1981) also began acting in films while still a young teen. George Lucas tapped her to play a major role in his three *Star Wars* prequel films that were released between 1999 and 2005. These films made Portman a worldwide name. Portman took time off to study and graduate from Harvard. She is intelligent, well-spoken, and has lived a quiet private life. Portman's father, a doctor, was born and raised in Israel, and while Natalie grew up in the States, she has strong ties to Israel and speaks fluent Hebrew. She is very pretty in a gamine, Audrey Hepburn-type way.

In 2004, she earned a best supporting actress Oscar nomination in Mike Nichols's adult film, *Closer.* The same year, she starred opposite Jewish actor Zach Braff in the surprise indie hit *Garden State.* The movie was made because Portman recognized the script's quality and agreed to star in the movie. Portman's Israeli ties and the model way she has conducted herself have made her a special favorite of the worldwide Jewish community. Portman has noted that every major Jewish film role is offered to her first.

Shia LaBeouf (b. 1986) is a young actor who is building a star career. In 2007, he starred in *Transformers* and *Disturbia,* both of which were major box office hits. He also has been cast opposite Harrison Ford as the adventurous son that Indiana Jones never knew he had in an *Indiana Jones* movie that Steven Spielberg filmed in 2008.

LaBeouf is the son of a non-Jewish father and a Jewish mother. He was raised Jewish. His father's drug addiction led to a family crisis—his mother literally did not know where their next meal would come from. Shia went out, found an agent, and managed to get cast in a hit Disney Channel series before he was 15. As he says, that series saved his family's life. *See also* **Film**.

Nate Bloom

Further Reading: Bial, Henry Carl. *Acting Jewish : Negotiating Ethnicity on the American Stage and Screen.* Ann Arbor, MI: University of Michigan Press, 2005. Hoberman, Jim, Jeffrey Shandler, and Maurice Berger (eds.). *Entertaining America: Jews, Movies, and Broadcasting.* Princeton, NJ: Princeton University Press, 2003.

FINKEL, FYVUSH (1923–)

Fyvush Finkel is an Emmy Award-winning actor who began acting on the Yiddish stage as a child in 1931. Born in Brooklyn in 1923 to a tailor, Harry Finkel and his wife Mary, he played supporting roles in musical comedies after World War II when the **Yiddish theater** was in the midst of a slow decline. Throughout his over 30-year career on the Yiddish stage, Finkel played goofy characters with his pants pulled up too high exposing long white socks, while appearing in such Yiddish shows as *The Old Maid* starring Nellie Casman (1947), *Go Fight City Hall* (1961), and a starring role in *Mama, I'm in Love* (1962).

Finkel was in his forties before he performed on the English language stage, where he had his greatest successes. For 12 years, he was on tour with the company of ***Fiddler on the Roof,*** first playing a small role before taking over the lead part of Tevye. He also appeared as Mushnik in the hit musical *Little Shop of Horrors* off Broadway. In 1988, he won an Obie Award for his portrayal of a waiter in the revival of Hy Kraft's *Cafe Crown,* a play set in a fictionalized version of the Cafe Royal, the legendary after-theater spot for Yiddish actors and their audiences. In a review of Cafe Crown, New York Times theater critic Frank Rich wrote: "Mr. Finkel, a longtime Yiddish theater performer, is priceless, the soul of meticulous clowning whose every contemptuous glare and shambling step reflects decades of comic practice" (1988). In 1990, Finkel toured with his one man show *Finkel's Follies.* He won an Emmy Award in 1994 for his portrayal of lawyer Douglas Wambaugh in David E. Kelly's television series, *Picket Fences.* He also appeared as a history teacher in the television show *Boston Public* and in the remake of *Fantasy Island.*

Finkel has been married to Trudi Lieberman since 1947. They have two sons, Elliot and Ian, who create the backup band for Finkel during his one-man show *Fyvush Finkel: From Second*

Undated photo of Fyvush Finkel when he was a young actor on the Yiddish stage and made his Broadway debut in *Fiddler on the Roof.* He later in life would become well known for his roles in the television production of *Picket Fences* and *Boston Public.* [Forward Association]

Avenue to Broadway. In 1998, as a result of his success in Hollywood, Finkel's name was emblazoned on a star on the Second Avenue sidewalk alongside the names of Yiddish theater luminaries **Maurice Schwartz**, Joseph Buloff, and Aaron Lebedev. *See also* **Television**; **Yiddish Theater**.

Caraid O'Brien

Further Reading: Gates, Anita. "Theater Review: Legends of Yiddish Stage Brought to Life." *New York Times,* December 30, 1997. Lovece, Frank. "Fast Chat: Fyvush Finkel." *Newsday,* Newsday.com, January 6, 2008. Musleah, Rahel. "Fyvush Finkel." *Hadassah Magazine.* October 2008, 68–71. Rich, Frank. "'Cafe Crown,' Bygone World of Yiddish Theater." *New York Times,* October 26, 1988.

FISHER, EDDIE (1928–)

A popular singer and entertainer, Edwin John Fisher, the fourth of seven children born to Joseph and Kate Winokur Fisher, was born in Philadelphia on August 10, 1928. The family's original name, Fisch, was anglicized when his Russian-born family arrived at Ellis Island from Russia. From an early age, it was obvious that Fisher—known as "Sunny Boy" to his family—had a beautiful singing voice. He started singing in and winning numerous amateur contests. By 1946, he was singing with various bands. In 1949, while appearing at Grossinger's resort in the Borscht Belt, he was heard by legendary showman **Eddie Cantor**, who gave him a spot on his network radio show. With the exposure came fame; in 1949, he was signed to a contract with RCA Victor.

Fisher was drafted into the U.S. Army in 1951 and served a year in Korea. From 1952–1953, he was the official soloist in the United States Army Band in Washington D.C. After his discharge, he began singing in nightclubs. He also had a television show, *Coke Time with Eddie Fisher,* from 1953–1957. The show was so successful that Coke offered him an unheard-of $1 million contract to be their national spokesman. A pre-rock and roll singer, Fisher's strong and melodious tenor made him one of the most popular singers of the 1950s. He scored 17 songs in the "Top 10" between 1950 and 1956, and 35 in the "Top 40." His signature song was "Anytime."

In 1955, Fisher married actress Debbie Reynolds, with whom he costarred in the 1956 comedy *Bundle of Joy.* A highly publicized affair with Elizabeth Taylor led to his divorce in May 1959. Later that month, he married Taylor, the widow of his best friend, producer **Mike Todd** (Avrom Hirsch Goldbogen). The publicity severely damaged Fisher's career. Eventually Taylor divorced Fisher and married her *Cleopatra* costar, actor Richard Burton. From that point on, his career consisted mainly of stage shows in Las Vegas and New York.

Fisher has been married five times. He has five children, the oldest of whom is the accomplished actress/author Carrie Fisher. *See also* **Popular Music**.

Kurt F. Stone

Further Reading: Fisher, Eddie. *Been There, Done That.* New York: St. Martin's Press, 1999. ———. *My Life, My Loves.* New York: Harper Collins, 1984.

FOER, JONATHAN SAFRAN (1977–)

An American writer, Jonathan Safran Foer was born in 1977 in Washington D.C. Publishing his first novel at the age of 25, Foer was quickly recognized as a promising young talent in both Jewish and mainstream American cultural circles. Among all of his activities, the author is most noted for the post-Holocaust sensibilities demonstrated at the onset of his career.

Foer's literary debut came in 2002 with the publication of his first novel, *Everything is Illuminated.* Therein, Jonathan Safran Foer—the work's offbeat protagonist, not to be confused with its author—journeys from America to the Ukraine in search of his grandfather's past before and during the Holocaust. In the story that ensues, three acts tell the above-mentioned plot-line, and the fabricated and mystic origins of the grandfather's village, along with the harsh realities surrounding its destruction. Since its publication, many have criticized the novel as an excessively postmodernist manipulation of time, fantasy, and language; still the initial majority opinion was of great praise. Shortly after publication, the work won both the National Jewish Book Award as well as the Guardian's First Book Award, and in 2005 it was successfully adapted to film.

Among scholars, Foer's early work has been understood as an expression of the frustrations and concerns of a new generation of American Jews maturing in the most recent decades of the post-Holocaust period. Anna P. Ronell sees Foer like many other contemporary Jewish writers as having responded to "a perceived urgent need to capture the vanished world of Ashkenazi Jewry" (Ronell, 2007). The resultant multi-layered imagining of Jewish Eastern Europe, its painful destruction, and the eventual confrontation between the young Jewish everyman of Foer's generation with each of these realities demonstrates the desire to comprehend and recover an otherwise fading history.

Though Foer's subsequent work did not deal with the Holocaust in the same way as his first novel, its influence is nonetheless present. In 2005, for instance, the author's second book, *Extremely Loud and Incredibly Close,* followed in suit and in formula telling the story of an equally peculiar hero, nine-year-old Oskar Schell and his own muted quest across New York for any and every connection possible to the memory of his father, who was killed in the World Trade Center attacks of September 11, 2001. According to critic Elaine Safer, despite the very different context and circumstances of that tragedy, the emotional response that Foer projected in his second narrative not only "shared a common concern with memory" as in *Everything is Illuminated,* but was also informed by "the painful need Jews have to grasp, and somehow make palpable, the experiences of loved ones who died in the Holocaust" (Safer, 2007). This novel too met with mixed reviews, finding its harshest critics among those disapproving of Foer's extra-literary devices such as a 12-page flipbook ending the work, animating the reversed leap of a Trade Center victim whom Oskar continually speculates is or is not his father.

Following the success of his first two novels, Foer set his sights on affecting American Jewish life beyond the realm of literature. In 2006, he teamed up with Humane Kosher, an organization seeking to expose alleged animal cruelty within the factories of certain kosher meat providers. Foer's role in the project included narrating an unapologetically graphic documentary titled "If This is Kosher . . ." as well as taking his own tour across America interviewing specialists in biology, farming, ethics, and nutrition for a forthcoming book that promised to "chronicle his road adventure and the ecological crisis he observed."

Less controversial perhaps was Foer's 2007 announcement to the ***Jewish Daily Forward*** of plans to compile a new English language version of the Passover Haggadah. His hope was to reinvigorate the spirit of the holiday in order to "inspire people toward a greater commitment for social change," listing the genocide in Darfur as one cause among many towards which Jews should focus the holiday's spirit of freedom.

Given the projects, literary and not, that have most prominently defined the author, it is no wonder that his first work and the Holocaust explain him to his audience. The lasting contribution of Foer's early career may well be the unique intersection that it speaks to within the American Jewish community of recent years, where one generation has come of age as another of survivors inevitably succumbs to it. In that overlap lies an interesting and increasingly relevant commentary on the legacy of the Holocaust—both experienced and imagined—its place within popular culture, and the most recent manifestation of the event's influence on American Jewry.

Foer currently lives in Brooklyn, New York with his wife and fellow author, Nicole Krauss. The couple has one son named Sasha. *See also* **Literature**.

Alan Amanik

Further Reading: Ronell, Anna P. "American-Jewish Writers Imagine Eastern Europe: Thane Rosenbaum,

Rebecca Goldstein, and Jonathan Safran Foer." *Polin: Studies in Polish Jewry* 19 (2007). Safer, Elaine. "Illuminating the Ineffable: Jonathan Safran Foer's Novels." *Studies in American Jewish Literature* 25 (January 2007): 112–132.

FOOD

Ruth Reichl, editor of *Gourmet Magazine,* once said she has never had a great Jewish meal, because she does not like heavy, brown Eastern European food—it may be because she has never visited one of the many innovative kosher restaurants in New York City or tried the recipes for Jewish holidays printed in her own magazine.

American Jewish food in the twenty-first century, is a far cry from what our parents and grandparents ate. Jewish food follows kosher laws that are set forth in the book of Leviticus, requirements demanding that only four-legged animals that have cloven hooves and chew their cud are allowed to be eaten, whereas birds of prey are prohibited. Furthermore, animals and birds that meet the biblical requirements must be ritually slaughtered. Fish, as long as they have gills and fins, are permitted to be eaten. Kosher laws also require that meat and dairy products are not to be served during the same meal.

Over the centuries, these rules led to a very restrictive diet among Eastern European Jews. These restrictions followed those who immigrated to the United States. Their diet was complicated by using only those foods familiar to them. Eggplants and tomatoes, for example, were alien to them in the old country, so these items were not part of their food intake. Root vegetables—potatoes, onions, parsnips, and turnips—on the other hand, were familiar and a staple of their diet.

The most popular seasoning was chicken fat. Bellin's *Jewish Cook Book* (1958) suggests putting a hamburger on a bun after spreading it with chicken fat. Today, though a recipe may call for fat as an ingredient in making old-fashioned matzah balls for holiday cooking, chicken fat is rarely mentioned in Jewish cookbooks. Some cookbook authors even suggest ways to make fake chicken fat, using onions and olive or canola oil. Today's Jewish food and cooking would astonish the Eastern European immigrants of old. Jewish food has become light and updated. Kosher restaurants in New York City are plentiful, expensive, and have menus that rival any fancy restaurant. Le Marais, named for the Jewish district in Paris, has been open for 10 years. The 2006 Zagat survey rated it as "very good," saying "it won't disappoint." The menu for this restaurant is in French, with English translation. It offers poultry, fish, and many different cuts of beef. None of the items would have been offered on a kosher restaurant menu even as late as the 1960s. Meals are served with "baby vegetables," grilled stone fruits, and only the mushrooms and peas sound familiar. Another New York restaurant serves meals that are just as "New American" as those found in "regular" non-kosher restaurants. Selections from their menu that appear in the *Great Kosher Restaurants Magazine* include Macadamia Crusted Chicken, Cashew Crusted Sea Bass, and a Green Tea Sashimi Special.

Whatever contemporary restaurants feature can be ordered in kosher restaurants (there are also kosher Chinese restaurants). One can find kosher wraps, panini, pizzas, and sushi. At the same time, even though many of the delis have disappeared, one can still find Israeli restaurants serving shawarma, hummus, and falafel, as well as old staples of kosher cuisine such as pastrami and corned beef sandwiches.

Substitutes for fat and dairy have made it much easier for cooks to stick to kosher requirements. Crisco, a vegetable shortening, has provided an alternative to using chicken fat or butter for cooking. Today's kosher cooks can also use chemically made margarine that imitates butter to make cookies and cakes as well as other dishes. Cooks also have soy milk, soy cream cheese, and soy sour cream. In addition to soy milk, there are milks made from rice, almonds, grains, and oats, according to Levana Kirschenbaum, the author of a recently published cookbook called *Levana Cooks Dairy-Free* (2007). In the introduction to her cookbook Kirschenbaum advocates the use of only natural products such as nut butters and alternative sweeteners. She calls her products and her recipes "politically correct . . . from a nutritional as well as a kosher standpoint."

Buying kosher food in the United States has become easier as more large food corporations have made their plants kosher. There were headlines in the Jewish press when Oreo cookies and many other Nabisco products became kosher, in 1998. Many food products today have one of the many kosher hechshers (rabbinically approved, usually listed with a "K" or marked with an "OU"). Even on Passover, a time of restrictive eating, there are more and more foods in the "kosher for Passover" category. Items such as cereals, bagel mixes, roll mixes, cake mixes, and spaghetti sauces, and even a form of baking powder are made for the Passover market. Many manufacturers are rushing to get their foods certified, since this market brings a larger percentage of the food dollar.

During the November 2007 Kosherfest, a trade show for kosher food products, exhibits showed that new manufacturers as well as older ones are rushing into this market and follow the trends with natural and organic products as well as gluten-free foods. In addition to bakery products, chocolates, chips, dips, juices, and pretzels, there were also shelf-stable prepared foods and frozen meals. More exciting was a whole range of products from other cultures and countries to help the home cook, restaurant chef, and caterer.

Examples of the foods shown at this year's Kosherfest demonstrate the huge difference in American Jewish foods of today. Olive oils, pasta sauces, or seemingly authentic Chinese sauces would never have been used by earlier generations of Eastern Europeans. What can be termed "Jewish food" has become less distinct as it has begun to embrace the cooking of many lands outside Eastern Europe. *See also* **Jewish Delicatessens**.

Renee Hartman

Further Reading: Bellin, Mildred Grosberg. *The Jewish Cook Book*. Garden City, NY: Doubleday and Company, Inc., 1958. Kirschenbaum, Levana. *Levana Cooks Dairy-Free*. New York: Skyhorse Publishing, 2007. Kornblum, Elan, ed. *Great Kosher Restaurants Magazine*. Brooklyn, NY: Elan Kornblum, 2007.

FOOD INDUSTRY

In the late nineteenth and early twentieth centuries, Jewish immigrants came to the United States in great numbers. Given the problems they had in their native countries, a land of economic opportunity like America attracted them. Yet America challenged them. One obstacle was the problem of maintaining their religious rules concerning food. In the American Jewish diaspora, Jews needed to trade with non-Jews to achieve economic success. The more they exchanged goods, the harder they found it was to keep kosher or find Eastern European-style food. Of course, as more Jews immigrated to America and the demand for kosher food increased, Jewish-owned food businesses soon filled the niche. For example, wine suitable for a Friday night kiddush or a special holiday had to meet specific requirements. It was kosher only if Jewish workers made it and a mashgiach, a rabbi who supervised the wine making, certified it as kosher. The Mogen David Wine Corporation and the B. Manischewitz Corporation arose from humble beginnings to become two well-known kosher wine producers.

Since there isn't space in this article to review the history of every American Jewish food corporation, presented below are two case studies—a longer one for the B. Manischewitz Company and a shorter one for the Acme Smoked Fish Corporation. The Manischewitz case exemplifies a business originally started to supply matzah, unleavened bread, for Passover (that is, to meet kosher laws). The case is special because the company's early use of economies of scale in its production process differentiated it from competing companies. The Acme case concerns the supply of certain fish products (that is, foods popular with American Jews craving tastes left behind in Eastern Europe).

A leading marketer of kosher foods in America for many years, the B. Manischewitz Company,

LLC, originated in Cincinnati, Ohio. The company began in the spring of 1888 when Rabbi Dov Ber Manischewitz opened a small matzah bakery. Largely for religious reasons, he began to make matzah for Passover, first for his family and a few friends, but soon for many of the city's observant Jews. His bakery evolved into a successful, innovative, and prosperous company that paid close attention to its customers' religious needs. By the end of the nineteenth century, demand for his matzah became so great that the rabbi turned to the use of gas-fired ovens, replacing the older coal stoves that other Jewish bakers used. The newer ovens allowed for much more careful control of the baking speed, ensuring consistent and standard quality matzah.

He also introduced portable traveling tunnel ovens and was the first to package his matzah for shipment to places beyond his bakery's immediate neighborhood. He began shipping his matzah overseas to such diverse places as England, Japan, France, Hungary, Egypt, and New Zealand. His bright, clean bakery would become a model for future kosher bakeries, both in America and abroad.

In 1940, the company produced its first "Tam Tam" cracker. The product signaled the initial departure from its line of matzah products. About the same time, in a licensing arrangement, many firms throughout the country began to sell Manischewitz wines. In 1954, as the company continued to expand into products other than matzah, it purchased a processing plant located in Vineland, New Jersey. This facility manufactured all the company's canned and jarred products, including favorites like gefilte fish, chicken soup, and borscht. Workers there pack about 2,000,000 pounds of fish and 1,000,000 pounds of beets each year. There the company developed other products including other soups, chicken broth, olive oil, and egg noodles.

The Manischewitz Company routinely bought out competitors until 1998, when it became part of the R.A.B. Food Group, a private company in Secaucus, New Jersey. Today R.A.B. Holdings owns and operates the company as a subsidiary. In August 2004, The B. Manischewitz Company, LLC, changed its name to R.A.B. Food Group, LLC, although it still markets food under the Manischewitz name.

The Acme Smoked Fish Corporation began in the early 1900s when Harry Brownstein arrived in New York from Russia. He found a job in the smoked fish business as a "wagon jobber," picking up fresh, hot fish from smokehouses with his horse-drawn wagon and hand-delivering them to small grocery stores. Eventually, through his hard work and dedication, he achieved the dream of owning his own Brooklyn smokehouse.

Harry Brownstein passed his skills, passion, and pride for quality to his son and son-in-law. Then, he passed them on to his grandsons, Eric and Robert Caslow and Mark and Gary Brownstein. Now, a fourth generation, Eric's son David Caslow, manages the company and continues the tradition started by his great-grandfather nearly a century ago.

Today, the family is responding to the growing popularity of smoked fish. It is modernizing its Brooklyn factory, dramatically increasing production capabilities, while keeping an emphasis on quality and safety. Additionally, to meet the varied demand for smoked fish products, the company launched the Blue Hill Bay Smoked Seafood product line in July 2000, adding such products as Alaskan Black Cod, Brook Trout Fillets, Peppered Mackerel Fillets, Cold Smoked Yellowfin Tuna, Whitefish Fillets, Baked Salmon Spread, and Chunky Whitefish Spread. Still family owned and operated, Acme Smoked Fish Corporation, located in Brooklyn's Greenpoint section, is now one of America's largest processors of smoked fish and herring.

In recent years, there has been much consolidation among traditional American Jewish food corporations, although the future is bright given the rapidly growing American kosher food market. American shoppers spend more than $50 billion a year on kosher foods. With sales growing by double digit percentages each year, industry insiders estimate that traditional Jewish customers now only account for one of five buyers of kosher foods. American food-producing corporations, including many neither Jewish-owned nor Jewish-managed are having many of their food products certified as kosher. *See also* **Manischewitz Family**.

Marvin Margolis

Further Reading: Blech, Zushe Yosef. *Kosher Food Production.* Oxford, United Kingdom: Blackwell Publishing, 2008. Diner, Hasia R. *Hungering for America: Italian, Irish, and Jewish Foodways in the Age of Migration.* Cambridge, MA: Harvard University Press, 2001.

FREUD, SIGMUND (1856–1939)

Though, in current times, Sigmund Freud may not be seriously regarded as a scientist, his cultural legacy remains. Contemporary America's therapeutic culture and popular humor would be unimaginable without his notions of the subconscious psyche (Id, Ego, Superego), repression, neurosis and hysteric symptoms, the symbolism of dreams, emotional transference, passive-aggressive behavior, Oedipal and Electra complexes, libido and death instincts, revealing slips of the tongue, memories of childhood trauma, and penis envy. Freud's core concept of the individual's subconscious struggle of the self between irrational instinct, painful memories, and repressive reason remains a touchstone of popular culture.

Freud had his conflicted qualities. Though he was clearly a man of his warring and annihilating age, Freud's generalizations about human society and culture remained ahistorical—outside of time and with no attention to events or change. A secular Jew, he was conflicted about his own Jewishness (see his essay "My Subconscious Jewishness" in *The Current Jewish Record* of November 1931). Yet Freud's genius was his ability to synthesize and popularize his theoretical concepts—he was successful at reaching the wider society.

A European import, Freudian theory became a mass phenomenon in the United States only after his death and the end of World War II. Replacing the Enlightenment's idea of a rational human nature with the conflicted subconscious offered a compelling explanation for the irrational horrors of modern warfare and collective racial savagery. Ironically, it also encouraged the idea of life led as an individual distinct from family or society, which fit well with the intensified individualism of an early twentieth-century America. Psychoanalysis became chic in America by the 1950s. The professional, upper middle classes sought out therapists for personal, social, and even corporate executive problems.

Freudian theory was custom-made for Jews in America, struggling with their own identity concerns amid efforts to use education as a way to assimilate into the professional classes.

Sigmund Freud, the father of psychoanalysis, was born in Austria and is best known for his theories of the unconscious mind. In 1933 the Nazis took control of Germany and burned his books along with those of other prominent Jews. When the Nazis annexed Austria in 1938, Freud and his family went into exile "to die in freedom" and left for England, where he died of cancer in 1939. [Photofest, Inc.]

Therapeutic talk about emotions, anxiety, and guilt over an admixture of self-love and self-loathing, combined with the pursuit of personal betterment, were prescriptions for negotiating how to remain Jewish while becoming American. It is not surprising that a disproportionate number of therapists and patients were Jewish. Popular Jewish interpreters of the human psyche emerged (for example, see Rabbi **Joshua Loth Liebman**'s *Peace of Mind* in 1946). But for many Catholics and conservative Protestants, Freud represented a heretical exodus from traditional Christian values.

Examples of Freudian theory in postwar popular culture are myriad. The child-rearing manuals of Benjamin Spock (1946) and Erik Erikson (1950) to novels like *Catcher in the Rye* (1951) and *Portnoy's Complaint* (1967) and classic movies like *Rebel Without a Cause* (1955), explored the angst-ridden experiences of childhood and youth in Freudian terms. Stream of consciousness novels like James Joyce's *Ulysses* (1922), *Finnegans Wake* (1939), and Virginia Woolf's *The Lighthouse* (1927) and *The Waves* (1939) created a new genre of popular literature. Plays like Eugene O'Neill's trilogy *Mourning Becomes Electra* (1931) reframed classical themes with psychoanalytical meaning, while films like *Spellbound* (1945), *The Three Faces of Eve* (1957), and *Marnie* (1964) popularized psychiatrists and their patients' subconscious compulsions.

Bestselling social science books like *Modern Woman: The Lost Sex* (1947) and popularizers such as Dr. **Joyce Brothers** and Ann Landers applied Freudian concepts to the everyday world of suburban middle-class women. Even conceptual high art made its Freudian imprint on popular culture through works like Salvador Dali's surreal ticking clocks. On a humorous note, who has not seen the ubiquitous image of the *Peanuts* character Lucy Van Pelt offering her services as a shrink to Charlie Brown for a nickel, or of **Woody Allen** as the lifelong poster child for Freudian anxiety and humor? Freud still makes comic appearances on the cartoon television show *The Simpsons,* and even the violent mafioso Tony Soprano is humanized through frequent sessions with his therapist. Freud's concepts and language continue to shape popular culture.

Freud's generation-long postwar psychoanalytic popularity was eventually eclipsed by the highly publicized repressed memory wars of the early 1990s. But his abiding legacy has never been so much about the science of individual diagnosis through psychotherapy as it has been about the cultural condition of the individual in modern mass society. If not in the realm of critical psychology and psychiatry then surely in the realm of popular culture, Freud lives on in our subconscious. *See also* **Popular Psychology**.

Joseph P. Huffman

Further Reading: Adler, Jerry. "Freud in Our Midst." *Newsweek* 147, no. 13 (March 27, 2006): 42–49. Caplan, Eric. *Mind Games: American Culture and the Birth of Psychotherapy.* Berkeley and Los Angeles: University of California Press, 2001. Erwin, Edward, ed. *Freud Encyclopedia: Theory, Therapy, and Culture.* London: Routledge Press, 2002. Kramer, Peter D. *Freud: Inventor of the Modern Mind.* New York: Harper Collins, 2006. Roth, Michael S., ed. *Freud: Conflict and Culture. Essays on His Life, Work, and Legacy.* New York: Knopf, 1998.

FRIEDAN, BETTY (1921–2006)

Considered founder of second-wave feminism, since the 1963 publication of her first book, Friedan defined "the problem that has no name" as a mind-numbing sense of failure suffered by educated women with goals limited to marriage and child rearing.

Friedan was born Bettye Goldstein in Peoria, Illinois, daughter of Harry Goldstein, a Russian immigrant, and 18-year-younger Miriam Horwitz, only child of an Illinois physician who immigrated from Hungary and went on to become state health commissioner. Freidan was oldest of three children; her sister, Amy, was considered the pretty one, and her brother, Harry Jr., was so named despite Jewish traditional practice.

Friedan grew up sensitive to her mother's discontented idea that she had married below her class. Although Harry Goldstein was successful, having moved from selling buttons to owning Goldstein Jewelry, he spoke with an accent and was not educated. His demeanor embarrassed his college graduate wife. Miriam further resented being forced to give up her position as editor of the local society pages at the time she married.

The Goldsteins attended the Reform rather than Orthodox synagogue, and Friedan informed her rabbi that she did not believe in God shortly before her confirmation. She was unaware of anti-Semitism in Peoria until high school, when she was refused admission to a sorority because she was Jewish. From that point she understood exclusion and, although bitter about her status as outsider, sought success through achievement rather than social connection. She read voraciously, wrote, worked on the school newspaper, co-founded the literary magazine, and graduated valedictorian. Those years were influenced by world events, which included the rise of Hitler and Mussolini, and the popularity of anti-Semite priest/radio host Charles Coughlin. Friedan's early writings indicate the beginnings of feminist ideas: ambivalence about sex appeal, domesticity, prettiness, and intellectual assertiveness. Friedan applied to, was admitted to, and chose Smith. She was editor of the weekly paper when America was attacked at Pearl Harbor. Since even the intellectually distinguished women at Smith were more interested in marriage than careers, Friedan found no role models for the professional woman. When she graduated in 1942 she dropped the "e" from her first name.

Friedan did a year's graduate work in psychology at Berkeley but declined a fellowship for her PhD partly out of fear of academically outdoing the men in her department. She moved to New York and worked in journalism for five years, notably at Federated Press and United Electrical, Radio and Machine Workers of America. Her articles focused on progressive, sometimes radical, political activism especially regarding women's issues.

In 1947, Friedan married Carl Friedan (divorced in 1969). She took maternity leave when her first son was born but was fired when she got pregnant with her second son. Her last pregnancy, with a daughter, forced the family to move from their small Queens apartment. She attempted to settle into suburban domesticity and freelance writing. In preparing and analyzing a questionnaire for Smith graduates 15 years after graduation, Friedan discovered she was not alone in frustration with the role of housewife. She expanded the questionnaire into an article and, for the first time in her career, had an article turned down. Realizing the editors of the women's magazines she freelanced for found her article threatening, she devoted five years to writing *The Feminine Mystique*. An immediate bestseller that defined and raised consciousness about the problem, the book did not suggest vehicles for change. Friedan went on to co-found the National Organization of Women (1966) and to help organize the National Abortion Rights Action League (1969) and the National Women's Political Caucus (1971).

In 1971, Friedan organized the Women's Strike for Equality. Fifty thousand women marching to demand equality closed down Fifth Avenue. When she addressed the crowd she altered the Orthodox Jewish prayer to declare, "From this day forward women all over the world will be able to say, 'I thank Thee, Lord, I was created a woman'" (Antler, 1998).

Friedan came to object to the sexual politics that invaded the movement when young leaders took over NOW. In 1981 she wrote *The Second Stage* to reassess feminism and urge it remain mainstream; many radical feminists reacted with hostility.

Friedan claimed to have moved past feminism and in 1993 published *The Fountain of Age*, which addressed the psychology of aging. Her last book, a memoir, *Life So Far*, was published in 2000. Friedan died at 85 of congestive heart failure. *See also* **Jewish Women and Popular Culture**.

Marion Schotz

Further Reading: Antler, Joyce. *The Journey Home: How Jewish Women Shaped Modern America*. New York:

Shocken, 1998. Hennesee, Judith. *Betty Friedan: Her Life*. Harmondsworth, Middlesex, UK: Penguin, 1999. Horowitz, Daniel. *Betty Friedan and the Making of The Feminine Mystique: The American Left, the Cold War and Modern Feminism.* Amherst, MA: University of Masschusetts Press, 1998.

FRIEDMAN, DEBBIE (1952–)

Debbie Friedman is one of the most influential contributors to American Jewish sacred music. Many of her melodies have entered the canon of American Jewish prayer, and on any given Saturday morning, countless congregations are singing her settings of traditional liturgy. Friedman, working parallel to composers like **Shlomo Carlebach**, helped reinvigorate Jewish sacred music by pairing folk and popular sensibilities and traditional liturgy.

Ms. Friedman was born in upstate New York in 1952, but at age five, her family relocated to St. Paul, Minnesota, where her family joined a Reform congregation and she attended a Conservative day school. Inspired by one of her peers, Friedman picked up the guitar at age 16 and taught herself to play by playing along with recordings of Peter, Paul and Mary.

Beginning with songleading for her temple youth group, Friedman soon attended a songleader workshop at UAHC Kamp Kutz, the national leadership camp of the Reform Movement. Friedman's first song—a version of the ve'ahavta—followed shortly thereafter. She wrote it for a creative service that the campers had put together, and she quickly realized the potential power of setting traditional liturgy to contemporary musical styles.

In 1972, she recorded her first album "as a fluke," with sales that far exceeded her expectations. The following year, with her reputation spreading, she moved to Chicago, where she worked while still performing in concerts around the country. From the beginning, she composed new settings of traditional prayers as well as English translations of popular passages. Songs from her earliest records, such as "Im Tirtzu" and "Not By Might, Not By Power" were sung by a whole generation of Jewish children in schools and summer camps across North America. Similarly, countless school children have learned their "Aleph Bet" by singing along with Friedman's melody.

For 20 years, Friedman continued writing music, recording, and releasing albums of original material, which she sold at her concerts. Her approach to liturgy and composition matured, and she began penning other songs that reflect her political and cultural sensibilities. Songs like "L'chi Lach" and "Miriam's Song" reflect a more egalitarian view of contemporary Jewish life, and her setting of "Mishebeirach" has become as widely popular as any other contemporary worship song.

To celebrate her 25th anniversary in the world of Jewish music, Friedman played three sold-out programs at Carnegie Hall. Since she began writing and recording in the early 1970s, Friedman has recorded over 19 albums and sold more than 250,000 units. Her melodies are practically ubiquitous in Conservative, Reform, and Community educational and worship settings. Friedman's popularity and longevity evidence her ability to capture the sentiment of worship in music and to write in a style that resonates deeply and powerfully with American Jews. By introducing a more popular or contemporary sound to Jewish prayer, Friedman irreversibly changed the tone and texture of American Jewish prayer, and her impact, along with her music, is still deeply felt. *See also* **Carlebach, Shlomo**.

Ari Y. Kelman

Further Reading: Friedman, Debbie. *Best Of Debbie Friedman.* Milwaukee, WI: Hal Leonard Corporation, 1997. ———. *Miracles & Wonders: Musicals for Chanukah and Purim.* Clifton, NJ: Sounds Write Productions, 1992.

FRIEDMAN, KINKY (1944–)

Texas's most famous singing Jewish cowboy was born in Chicago on October 31, 1944 to Dr. S. Thomas Friedman, a psychology professor and supporter of Texas Hillel at the University of Texas at Austin, and his wife, Min, a speech therapist. The couple had two other children, Roger and Marcie. The family moved to Kerrville, Texas in 1953, where they established Echo Hill Ranch, a summer camp for children and Kinky Friedman's current residence.

Friedman attended Hebrew school and celebrated his Bar Mitzvah in Houston. He graduated from the University of Texas–Austin (1966), where he was an honors student and a psychology major. It was as a freshman that he earned the nickname "Kinky" because of his hairstyle.

Inspired by John F. Kennedy, Friedman joined the Peace Corps, working in Borneo for two years. Upon his return to the United States, Friedman enjoyed modest success as a singer, with Kinky Friedman and the Texas Jewboys. Their repertoire included "They Ain't Makin' Jews Like Jesus Anymore," "Get Your Biscuits in the Oven and Your Buns in the Bed," and "Ride 'Em, Jewboy," described as a tribute to the victims of the Holocaust, as well as less-familiar country songs with Jewish themes.

When the band folded in the early 1970s, he began a new career writing humorous detective novels with himself as the protagonist.

Friedman, who has never married, has described himself in interviews as "of the Jewish persuasion, but not religious." He established the Utopia Animal Rescue Ranch, which cares for stray, abused, and aging animals. Like **Paul Newman**, Friedman established a merchandising business—including such products as Kinky's Private Stock Salsa and Kona Kosher Blend Coffee, as well as a line of cigars—to finance his philanthropic work.

In 2006, Friedman threw his cowboy hat in the ring as an Independent candidate for Texas governor. His campaign slogan: "How Hard Can It Be?" He finished in 4th place with less than 13 percent of the vote. Columnist Molly Ivins wrote that Friedman was "exactly who he says he is. He is a Texas Jew Boy. And he's just as Jewish as he is Texan, and there's no contradiction" (*CBS,* 2005).

Ron Kaplan

Further Reading: "Kinky Friedman Turns to Politics: Humorist, Musician, Writer, Is Now Gubernatorial Hopeful In Texas." *CBS Sunday Morning,* August 21, 2005. Kinky Friedman Web Site: http://www.kinkyfriedman.com. "Still Kinky After All These Years," *Moment Magazine,* August 2004.

FRIEDMAN, THOMAS (1953–)

Thomas Friedman, noted author and columnist, was born in St. Louis Park, Minnesota on July 20, 1953, to Jewish parents who exposed him at an early age to matters pertaining to Jewish culture and politics. In 1975, he received a BA in Mediterranean studies from Brandeis University and then, after receiving a Marshall scholarship, attended Oxford University in England, where his received his MA in Middle East studies.

Friedman's unofficial career in journalism started when he sent an op-ed piece to his local paper in Minnesota. He received his first professional reporting position at the London Bureau of United Press International after graduating from Oxford. In 1982, he was hired by the *New York Times* and was dispatched to Beirut to cover the 1982 Israeli invasion of Lebanon. His coverage of the Lebanon war, and in particular the Sabra and Shatila massacre, earned him his first Pulitzer Prize for International Reporting. From 1984 to 1988, he was assigned to Jerusalem to cover the first Palestinian Intifada, for which he received his second Pulitzer Prize and about which he wrote his first book, the bestselling *From Beirut to Jerusalem* (1989). Following the presidential election in 1992, Friedman was assigned by the *New York Times* to cover the Clinton White House. In 1995, the *Times* moved Friedman to the paper's op-ed page to write on foreign policy and economics, where he presently remains.

His op-ed pieces cover many topics: American politics, globalization, the Arab-Israeli conflict, global warming, and international terrorism. Since the publication of *From Beirut to Jerusalem,* Friedman has written three additional books, all bestsellers as well as commercial successes; all deal with aspects of globalization—*The Lexus and the Olive Tree* (1999), *Longitudes and Attitudes: Exploring the World after September 11* (2002), *The World is Flat: A Brief History of the Twenty-First Century* (2005), and his most recent book, *Hot, Flat, and Crowded* (2008). The widespread popularity of Friedman's books, together with his frequent appearances on television shows, such as *Meet the Press,* has made him a popular and much sought-after speaker at corporate conferences, college campuses, and other events. Friedman was the recipient of the 2004 Overseas Press Club award for Lifetime Achievement.

As someone who writes about subjects that affect the world and America's role in it, he is not without detractors. He has been criticized for his support of the Iraq war in his op-ed columns, although he has increasingly become critical of Bush administration policies in Iraq and the Middle East. Friedman believed that the establishment of a democratic state in Iraq would force the other states in the region to liberalize and modernize. He became disillusioned, however, with the manner in which the Bush White House has mismanaged the occupation and reconstruction of Iraq.

Thomas and Ann Friedman, a graduate of Stanford University, live in Bethesda, Maryland, and have two daughters—Orly, who attends Yale University, and Natalie, who is a student at Williams College. Both Friedman daughters were born in Israel during the period that he served the *Times* as its correspondent. See also **Journalism**.

Jesse Ulrich

Further Reading: Friedman, Thomas. *From Beirut to Jerusalem*. New York: Doubleday Publishing, 1989. ———. *Longitude and Attitudes: Exploring the World after September 11*. New York: Farrar, Straus and Giroux, 2002. ———. *The World is Flat: A Brief History of the Twenty-First Century.* New York: Farrar, Straus and Giroux, 2005.

FUCHS, LEO (1911–1994)

Leo Fuchs was the last great comedian of the Yiddish musical stage. He was born Abraham Leon Springer Fuchs in Lemberg (Lwow), Austria-Hungary (now Lviv, Ukraine) in 1911, the son of Yiddish actors, Yakov and Rosa Fuchs. Fuchs started acting in the **Yiddish theater** with his parents at the age of five. His father, a character actor, died when Fuchs was 10, and his mother, a leading musical theater actress, was killed in the Holocaust. After securing a reputation as a promising young actor in Europe, Fuchs immigrated to America when he was in his twenties. A comic actor with matinee idol looks, Fuchs was also an accomplished violinist. He became a star in New York in the Alexander Olshanetsky musical *Lucky Boy* at the Second Avenue Public Theater in 1935.

Admiring his versatility as an actor, singer, dancer, and musician, the *New York Times* wrote of his performance in *Lucky Boy* that he was "every inch a one man show." Fuchs was the inheritor of a style of Yiddish comedy developed by such stars as Sigmund Mogulescu, Ludwig Satz, and **Menasha Skulnik**—nebbishy, surprisingly charming anti-heroes who always get the girl. In fact, Fuchs reprised several roles originated by Skulnik, including parts in the plays *Yona Searches for a Bride* (the first ever musical adaptation of George Bernard Shaw's *Pygmalion*), *Wish Me Luck,* and **Clifford Odets**'s *The Flowering Peach*.

Fuchs married the Yiddish actress Mirele Gruber in 1936. They toured Poland together performing in musical comedies before divorcing in 1941. Fuchs performed dramatic roles with **Maurice Schwartz**'s Yiddish Art Theatre in 1939, appearing in Sholem Asch's*Salvation* and Sholem Aleichem's *If I Were a Rothschild*. In 1940, he had a starring role in the **Yiddish film** *American Matchmaker,* directed by Edgar G. Ulmer. Considered a precursor to the films of **Woody Allen**, Fuchs played a wealthy, neurotic commitment phobe in search of a wife. Fuchs also appeared in the Yiddish films *I Want to Be a Mother* (1937) and *Mazl Tov Yidn* (1941). In 1947, he toured London with his second wife, actress Rebecca Richman, in *The Galician Cowboy,* selling out the Alexander Theater like no other visiting Yiddish star. Other Yiddish musicals starring Fuchs include *Cigarettes with Herman Yablokoff* (1936), *I Want a Wife* (1946), *The Rabbi's Son* (1949), *Laugh and Be Happy* (1950), *Hired Groom* (1952), *Private Mendel* (1953), *Bei Mir Bistu Schoen* (1961), *Poor Millionaire* (1965), *Cowboy in Israel* (1962), *Here Comes the Groom* (1973), and *One of a Kind* (1980).

Fuchs had his English language debut in a touring production of *Girl Crazy* in 1951. From that point on, he moved continuously between the Yiddish stage and Hollywood. He appeared on television in *Wagon Train, Mister Ed, The Ed Sullivan Show, Sanford and Son,* and *Valentine's Day.* He was Herr Schulz in the original touring production of *Cabaret* and performed supporting roles in the films *The Frisco Kid* and *Avalon*. He also portrayed the grandfather in the televised version of Clifford Odets's *Awake and Sing!* starring Walter Matthau. Decades earlier, Matthau had appeared as an extra in the Yiddish theater in plays starring Fuchs. The Yiddish theater documentary *Almonds and Raisins* includes an interview with Fuchs in English. Fuchs died on December 31, 1994 in Los Angeles, California. He and Richman, who died in 1990, had one son. *See also* **Yiddish Film**; **Yiddish Theater**.

Caraid O'Brien

Further Reading: Karel, Russ, director. *Almonds and Raisins: A History of the Yiddish Cinema.* Film. New York: Brooks Productions, 1983. Ulmer, Edgar G., director. *American Matchmaker.* Film. Waltham, MA: National Center for Jewish Films, Brandeis University, restored from 1940 version.

G

GANGSTERS

Like other immigrant groups who came to America in the late nineteenth and early twentieth century for a chance at a better life, Jews had a difficult time adjusting. Many opportunities in business and education were closed to them. To escape poverty and degradation, some turned to crime. Youngsters would start off small, perhaps by swiping merchandise from pushcarts on crowded city streets. Those with an aptitude might be recruited by older criminals to do errands, "graduating" to higher levels of more daring and often more violent acts. In some circles, Jewish gangsterism took on a romantic aura, disproving the notion that Jews were weak and timid and creating a subculture of "tough Jews."

One of the earliest criminal organizations was the Yiddish Black Hand, a trio of thugs on the Lower East Side of New York City who extorted merchants by threatening to kill or injure their horses. But such groups were not limited to the East Coast. There was also a presence of organized crime in Los Angeles, Detroit, and Minneapolis. (As suited their needs, and despite their notoriety, municipal officials actually sought out Jewish gangs to help quell pro-Nazi rallies in the years leading up to World War II. Short of murder, these gangs were given free reign to disrupt these meetings, a job they did with a good deal of pride.)

The most ruthless of these gangsters—including Louis "Lepke" Buchalter, Benjamin "Bugsy" Siegel, Meyer Lansky, and Arthur "Dutch Schultz" Flegenheimer—extended their "evil empires," building large enterprises during Prohibition that revolved around liquor, drugs, prostitution, numbers running, and other nefarious concerns. These crime rings fought amongst themselves as well as with rival ethnic organizations.

While most first-generation Jewish criminals came from Orthodox families, they generally shunned ritual, although some of the more successful among them supported synagogues and other Jewish institutions (including Israel). These men led violent lives and for the most part followed their own code. Several of the leading criminals, including those working for Siegel, Lansky, and Buchalter, were responsible for the establishment of a "company" of assassins dubbed Murder Incorporated. Killings, voted on by committee, were designed to take care of internal housecleaning by eliminating troublemakers, informants, and others who failed to follow ersatz rules. Ironically, Schultz was himself rubbed out by Murder, Inc. in 1935 for seeking to put a hit on his own personal Javert, U.S. Attorney Thomas E. Dewey. When his cohorts refused to go along with the request as being too dangerous, Schultz persisted, insisting he would do the deed himself. Fearful of such a loose cannon, Murder, Inc. put a contract on Schultz.

There were several more notorious Jewish gangsters:

Arnold Rothstein (1882–1928) was one of the premier bootleggers during Prohibition and the mastermind behind the 1919 Black Sox gambling scandals, in which members of the Chicago White Sox conspired to throw the World Series. Rothstein was murdered in 1928.

Louis "Lepke" Buchalter (1897–1944) was first arrested for burglary at the age of 18. He served as the leader of Murder, Inc. for six years and was responsible for hundreds of killings. Sentenced to 30 years in Sing Sing in 1940 on charges of racketeering, he was executed in 1944 for the murder of a candy store clerk in Brooklyn. "Lepke" is Yiddish for "Little Louis."

Arthur "Dutch Schultz" Flegenheimer (1902–1935) dropped out of school and started his life of crime at the age of 14, when his father abandoned the family in New York City. He was arrested for burglary and served his only jail sentence when he was 17. He received his nom de guerre as tribute to his toughness. He began work in a speakeasy and soon became partners in the enterprise. Schultz realized there was money to be made in the distribution of beer and was powerful enough to extort his competitors into buying his stock. Although he was said to be responsible for scores of murders, U.S. Attorney Thomas Dewey brought Schultz to trial on charges of tax evasion. Schultz beat the rap thanks to a change of venue for the trial, but he was so angered at Dewey's prosecution (and persecution) that he politicked Murder, Inc. to have him killed. Instead he was mortally wounded at a restaurant in Newark, New Jersey when the group decided to eliminate him. As he lay dying in the hospital, he asked for a priest to administer the last rites so he could die as a Catholic.

Meyer Lansky (1902–1983) emigrated with his family from Russia to the Lower East Side when he was nine years old. He met Lucky Luciano in grade school and Bugsy Siegel as a teenager, and they later formed the Bugs and Meyer Mob. Lanksy's mob was unofficially engaged to disrupt Nazi sympathizer gatherings in New York in the 1930s; during the war he aided the Office of Naval Intelligence by having members of his organization watch out for German infiltrators and saboteurs. In his later years, Lanksy, fearful of indictment on tax evasion charges, tried to move to Israel. He was returned to the United States, where he was eventually acquitted of the charges. He died of lung cancer at the age of 80.

Abraham "Kid Twist" Reles (1906–1941) is another example of a Jewish gangster who began his career as a youngster in an attempt to escape poverty in Brooklyn. A violent felon with a short temper, Reles used an ice pick as his murder weapon of choice. During Prohibition, he and his associates specialized in illegal slot machines, encroaching into the territory of the Shapiro Brothers and instigating a tit-for-tat conflict. Finally arrested for his crimes and facing the death penalty, Reles chose to turn informant, "dropping the dime" on Louis "Lepke" Buchalter. He died under mysterious circumstances while in custody; FBI files claim he committed suicide by jumping from a sixth floor window at the Half Moon Hotel in Coney Island, New York, where he was being held before the trial of crime boss Albert Anastasia; other sources say he may have been pushed by policemen working for Frank Costello.

Benjamin "Bugsy" Siegel (1906–1947) was born in Brooklyn, New York, where he started his life of crime in small gangs, befriending Meyer Lansky as a teenager. He made his reputation as a bootlegger, smuggling liquor during Prohibition. He later moved to the West Coast, where he became infatuated with the entertainment industry. His attempt to open one of Las Vegas's first casinos failed so miserably that it resulted in his assassination by order of Murder, Inc., which suspected him of absconding with mob funds. In fact, he had been betrayed by his paramour, Virginia Hill, who had stolen the money over a period of time and had fled to Europe. Siegel is memorialized by a plaque in the Bialystoker Synagogue on Manhattan's Lower East Side.

Abner "Longy" Zwillman (1899–1959—though some sources put his year of birth as 1904) is another case of a young man dropping out of school and turning to crime as a way to escape poverty. Born in Newark, Zwillman mixed bootlegging, gambling, prostitution, and labor racketeering with legitimate business interests, including influence peddling. Following the death of Dutch Schultz, Zwillman became known as "the Al Capone of New Jersey." He managed to stay relatively clear of the hands-on violent dirty work that was the hallmark of Schultz and Kid Twist. Shortly after receiving a subpoena to appear before the McClellan State Committee Hearings on Organized Crime in 1959, Zwillman was discovered hanging in his home in West Orange, New Jersey. Rabbi Joachim Prinz, president the American Jewish Congress, officiated at the funeral.

Ron Kaplan

Further Reading: Cohen, Rich. *Tough Jews: Fathers, Sons, and Gangster Dreams.* New York: Simon and Schuster, 1998. Fried, Albert. *The Rise and Fall of the Jewish Gangster in America.* New York: Columbia University Press, 1993. Rockaway, Robert. *But He Was Good to His Mother: The Lives and Crimes of Jewish Gangsters.* New York: Geffen Publishing House, 2000. *Once Upon a Time in America.* DVD. Warner Brothers Home Video, 2008.

GARFIELD, JOHN (1913–1952)

John Garfield was an actor who achieved stardom playing defiant, working class characters. As a Jew, he is probably best known for playing one in the groundbreaking film that examined "polite" anti-Semitism in mid-twentieth-century America, ***Gentleman's Agreement*** (1947). He has been characterized as the first of the "Method" actors—predating Marlon Brando, Montgomery Clift, and James Dean—who revolutionized acting in America. Jacob Julius Garfinkle was born on March 4, 1913, on New York City's Lower East Side to Russian Jewish immigrants—David, a clothes presser and part-time cantor, and Hannah Garfinkle. The family later moved to Brooklyn, where Hannah gave birth to another son in 1918. After a difficult pregnancy, she died two years later when "Julie"—as Garfield was known all his life—was seven. A tough street kid and gang member, Garfield was sent to live with relatives in the Bronx. He entered P.S. 45, a school for difficult children, and came under the influence of Principal Angelo Patri. The innovative educator encouraged Garfield to take up boxing and enroll in acting classes to correct a stammer. With a new focus, Garfield's academic performance and social behavior improved. The teenage Garfield also possessed a talent for debate and won a statewide contest sponsored by the *New York Times*. Patri helped Garfield win a scholarship at the Heckscher Foundation Drama Workshop. Garfield also studied at the American Laboratory Theatre and served as an apprentice at the Civic Repertory Theatre. In 1931, he journeyed across the country, hitching rides, jumping freight trains, and working odd jobs. After returning to New York, he contracted rheumatic fever, which permanently damaged his heart. In his late teens, Garfield began landing bit parts on the New York stage. He made his Broadway debut in 1932 under the name "Jules Garfield." By 1934, he had joined the avant-garde Group Theatre, starting lifelong personal and professional associations with such luminaries as **Clifford Odets**, Stella and Luther Adler, Morris Carnovsky, and Elia Kazan. In 1935 Garfield married his childhood sweetheart, actress Roberta "Robbie" Seidman. Garfield's stage career was ushered in by his portrayals in two Group Theatre productions by Odets, *Waiting for Lefty* and *Awake and Sing!* When he was passed over for the lead in the Group's staging of *Golden Boy*—which Odets wrote for him—he accepted an offer from Warner Brothers and went to Hollywood in 1938. Jack Warner thought "Jules" sounded "too Jewish" and changed the actor's first name to

John. Garfield's first film performance in 1938 as a bitter, cynical, out-of-work musician in *Four Daughters* was critically acclaimed and earned him an Oscar nomination for Best Supporting Actor. The film made him a star. For the remainder of his career, Garfield fought typecasting in similar outsider roles.

Although Garfield's heart condition excluded him from military service in World War II, he became a tireless supporter of the American war effort, joining entertainment troupes and selling war bonds. He and Bette Davis founded the Hollywood Canteen for servicemen in Los Angeles. Among his 35 films, Garfield is remembered in particular for standout performances in *Juarez* and *They Made Me a Criminal* (1939), *Sea Wolf* (1941), *Destination Tokyo* (1943), and *The Postman Always Rings Twice* (1946). In *Humoresque* (1946), Garfield played a Jewish violinist who leaves behind his friends and family in the old neighborhood as he rises to fame. Garfield was one of the first Hollywood stars to establish his own independent production company when his Warner Brothers contract expired in 1946. His portrayal of a Jewish boxer who fights his way out of the slums, in the company's first project, *Body and Soul* (1947), earned Garfield his second Oscar nomination for Best Actor. His insistence that the black actor Canada Lee appear in the film demonstrated his commitment to civil rights. One of Garfield's most memorable roles was in *Gentleman's Agreement,* 1947's Oscar winner for Best Picture, where Garfield played Dave Goldman, the Jewish friend of journalist Phil Green (played by Gregory Peck), who is posing as a Jew to write an exposé of anti-Semitism. An ardent liberal, Garfield was ensnared in the Red Scare of the late 1940s and early 1950s. His wife had been a member of the Communist Party, but there was no evidence that he had ever been a communist. Nevertheless, he was called before the House Un-American Activities Committee in April 1951 and, after refusing to "name names," became a victim of the notorious Hollywood black list. When few film roles came his way, Garfield returned to Broadway, at long last playing the lead role in a 1952 revival of *Golden Boy.* Subsequently, Garfield achieved critical recognition in *The Big Knife* (1949) and *Peer Gynt* (1951), both directed by Group Theatre founder Lee Strasberg. Despite these stage successes, Garfield sought to redeem his name and claimed that he had been tricked by the Communist Party. Confused and desperate, he became estranged from his family, and it was believed that the stress of being blacklisted exacerbated his health problems, which led to his fatal heart attack at the age of 39 on May 21, 1952. His funeral at Riverside Memorial Chapel was mobbed by more than 10,000 fans. He was buried at Westchester Hills Cemetery in Hastings on Hudson, New York. Roberta and John Garfield had three children: Katherine (b. 1938), who died after an allergic attack in 1945; David (b. 1943), who became an actor and film editor and died of heart failure in 1994; and daughter Julie (b. 1946), an actress and acting teacher. Roberta, who remarried in 1954, died in 2004. *See also* **Film**; ***Gentleman's Agreement***; **Odets, Clifford**; **Theater**.

Abby Meth Kanter

Further Reading: Beaver, Jim. *John Garfield: His Life and Films.* Cranbury, NJ: A.S. Barnes and Co., 1978. Nott, Robert. *He Ran All the Way: The Life of John Garfield.* New York: Limelight Editions, 2003.

GEHRY, FRANK (1929–)

A Pritzker Prize-winning architect based in Los Angeles, Frank Gehry has won every architectural award and is a household name in the world of architecture. He was born Ephraim Owen Goldberg in Toronto, Ontario on February 28, 1929. A creative child, he and his grandmother Caplan would create tiny cities out of scraps of wood. At age 17, Goldberg moved to southern California, where he drove a truck and began studies at Los Angeles City College. He graduated from the University of Southern California School of Architecture in 1954 and studied city planning at the Harvard Graduate School of Design for one year. In the 1950s, Goldberg married Anita Snyder, whom he claims convinced him to change his name to Frank Gehry. They divorced in the mid-1960s. Several years later, he married his second wife, Berta. Gehry has two sons and two daughters.

Gehry's creations are generally classified as part of the Deconstructionist, or "DeCon" school of postmodernist architecture. Gehry disavows this, insisting that he is affiliated with no school of design. Most of his structures have a "warped" form—undulating lines that easily capture the imagination. Gehry's best-known works are the titanium-covered Guggenheim Museum in Bilbao, Spain, the Walt Disney Concert Hall in Los Angeles, and his personal residence in Santa Monica, California, which essentially jump-started his career. Unlike most architects, who spend years working "on paper" before ever seeing their designs realized, Gehry found success in near record time.

Frank Gehry's creations extend beyond the world of concrete and glass. He has designed a wristwatch, a bottle for Wyborowa Vodka, and jewelry for Tiffany. His most recent project is the Barclays Center, the new home of the basketball New Jersey Nets.

In addition to being known for his undulating designs, Gehry is renowned for bringing his buildings in on time and rarely for more than the projected cost—a rarity in the world of upper-end architecture. He is the recipient of most of the major prizes the architectural world has to offer, along with honorary doctorates from Harvard, Yale, and the Rhode Island School of Design.

Kurt F. Stone

Further Reading: Pollack, Sydney, director. *Sketches of Frank Gehry.* Documentary. Sony Pictures, 2005.

GENTLEMAN'S AGREEMENT (1947)

Gentleman's Agreement, a novel by Laura Z. Hobson about the scourge of anti-Semitism in American society in the wake of World War II, was quickly transformed into a successful feature film by 20th Century Fox and released the same year in order to qualify for that year's Academy Awards. The author was born Laura Kean Zametkin (1900–1986), the daughter of Jewish socialist immigrants. Her father, Michael Zametkin, was at one time the editor of the ***Jewish Daily Forward***.

Before becoming a film, *Gentlemen's Agreement* was number one on the *New York Times* best-sellers list. The story is about Philip Schuyler Green (played by Gregory Peck), a widower who has a young son. Green moves to New York to work for a news magazine. As his first assignment, Green, an award-winning journalist, decides he wants to "blow the cover" off anti-Semitism by pretending to be Jewish so he can observe the subtle and not-so-subtle faces of bigotry.

Green is faced with a number of situations that demonstrate anti-Semitism. His young son, Tommy (Dean Stockwell), must also pretend to be Jewish and is taunted with anti-Semitic slurs and beaten by schoolmates. Green's mother (Anne Revere) is Tommy's caregiver. When she falls ill, a Gentile doctor chafes at Green's request for the name of a Jewish physician. Green's best friend, Dave Goldman (**John Garfield**), following his release from military service arrives in town for a job interview, only to find it difficult to find a place to live, which he believes is due to his ethnicity. Another major event involves Green's attempt to make reservations at an exclusive (that is, "restricted") hotel. His confrontation with the manager pushes him to the edge of violence.

Even Green's personal secretary—a Jew trying to conceal her religion—displays disdain towards "the kikey ones" who cause trouble for the rest of the community.

Green's project makes his courtship of Kathy, his boss's niece (Dorothy McGuire), problematic. Although she is in on the subterfuge, she wants him to be more forthcoming about his true identity, lest her family and friends—part of that genteel society he seeks to expose—think he actually is Jewish.

It is worth noting that at no time in the film is there any evidence of Judaism as a religion: no religious services, no traditional items in the household. Yet, according to film critic Bosley Crowther in the *New York Times,* "The shabby cruelties of anti-Semitism which were sharply and effectively revealed within the restricted observation of Laura Z. Hobson's 'Gentleman's Agreement' have now been exposed with equal candor and even greater dramatic forcefulness in the motion-picture version of the novel."

The film received numerous awards, including three Oscars (Celeste Holm, Best Supporting Actress; Elia Kazan, Best Director; and Best Picture) and an additional five Oscar nominations, including best actor, actress, and screenplay (by Hart Moss).

Gentleman's Agreement was not the first feature film to deal with anti-Semitism in America. After a long reluctance to deal with the issue, Hollywood, in addition to *Gentleman's Agreement,* also produced *Crossfire* (which was nominated for five Oscars), which was released by RKO in July 1947, preceding 20th Century Fox's film by less than four months. *See also* **Film**; **Garfield, John**.

Ron Kaplan

Further Reading: Crowther, Bosley. "Review of Gentleman's Agreement," *The New York Times,* November 12, 1947. Hobson, Laura Z. *Gentleman's Agreement.* New York: Simon and Schuster, 1947. ———. *Laura Z.: A Life*. Westminster, MD: Arbor House, 1983.

GERSHWIN, GEORGE (1898–1937)

"True music must repeat the thought and aspirations of the people and the time. My people are Americans. My time is today ... What I have done is what was in me; the combination of New York where I was born ... with the centuries of hereditary feeling back of me" (Jablonski, 1987). So wrote George Gershwin, arguably America's most beloved and versatile composer of popular music. In partnership with his brother Ira (1896–1983), he wrote 10 Broadway musicals and numerous popular songs that place him in the elite circle of America's greatest music composers. His talent and accomplishments were not limited to popular music, however. He achieved great success in the world of classical music, opera, and dance as well. Gershwin's worldwide fame was as much for *Rhapsody in Blue* (1924) and *An American in Paris* (1928) as it was for " I Got Rhythm" (1930), "Swanee" (1920), and "S'Wonderful" (1927).

Gershwin was the great-grandson of a rabbi, the grandson of a mechanic, and the son of a tailor and baker. George's father Morris (Moshe) Gershovitz left the family home in St. Petersburg, Russia, to escape military service and married Rose Bruskin. By that time he had changed the family name to Gershvin, ultimately changed by his son, Jacob (who later changed his name to George), to Gershwin after he began his musical career. George Gershwin's earliest passion was baseball, not music, but when his brother Ira showed little interest in the recently purchased family piano, it was George who sat down and played. His musical education training flourished with classical piano training under the strict tutelage of Charles Hambitzer (1878–1918), who refused to allow the teenager to play popular music, focusing exclusively on the musical skills necessary for the "masters."

Receiving limited formal education, in May 1914, Gershwin left school at 16 to become the youngest staff "song plugger" (pianist-salesman) for the Jerome H. Remick Company at a salary of $15 per week. With the intervention of "the last of the Red Hot Mammas," Sophie Tucker (1884–1966), Gershwin wrote and published his first song, "When You Want 'Em, You Can't Get 'Em; When you Got 'Em, You Don't Want 'Em" in 1916. While the song only earned him five dollars, it introduced him to new lyricists and composers, ultimately leading him to interview for master **Tin Pan Alley** songwriter **Irving Berlin** (1888–1989). Gershwin played Berlin an arrangement of one of Berlin's own songs, but, while offered the job, he was urged by Berlin to write his own songs. Instead he went to Max Dreyfus (1874–1964), the head of the T.B. Harms publishing house, who hired Gershwin as staff composer—$35 a week just to write songs. It was a brilliant investment, for Gershwin stayed

Jewish music composer George Gershwin, who composed such classics of American popular culture as *Porgy and Bess, Rhapsody in Blue, Strike Up the Band, Funny Face, Of Thee I Sing,* and *Crazy for You.* [Photofest, Inc.]

with Dreyfus for most of his creative life. His first major hit song, "Swanee," came in 1920, beginning 18 years of unprecedented creativity.

Four years later, in 1924, Gershwin produced his jazz classic, *Rhapsody in Blue,* commissioned by bandleader Paul Whiteman (1890–1967). Gershwin was able to bridge the popular, Broadway, and classical musical worlds for the remainder of his career. George and Ira's Broadway show hits included *Lady, Be Good* starring Fred (1899–1987) and Adele (1896–1981) Astaire, *Strike Up The Band* (1927), *Girl Crazy* (1930) starring Ethel Merman (1908–1984) and Ginger Rogers (1911–1995), and *Of Thee I Sing* (1932). In addition to the classical compositions mentioned previously, Gershwin produced such classical works as Concerto in F for Piano (1925), *Preludes for Piano* (1926), *Cuban Overture* (1932), and his masterwork, his opera, *Porgy and Bess* in 1935.

Surprisingly, *Porgy and Bess* was rejected by opera critics as being too much like Broadway, and by many Broadway critics as being too operatic. In the passage of time, it has been accepted as a landmark of American music, enjoying numerous revivals and recordings, becoming a staple of opera companies and theatrical stages around the world.

The decidedly mixed response to *Porgy and Bess* and the economic collapse of Broadway following the onset of the Depression encouraged the Gershwins to migrate to California to write for Hollywood. Their outstanding films *Damsel in Distress* (1935), *Shall We Dance* (1937), and *The Goldwyn Follies* (1938) included song standards "A Foggy Day," "They Can't Take That Away from Me," "Let's Call the Whole Thing Off," "Love Walked Right In," and "Our Love Is Here to Stay."

During the spring of 1937, Gershwin suffered deep depression and terrible headaches. He died on July 11, 1937 from an undiagnosed brain tumor. Gershwin was memorialized at Temple Emanu-El in New York in a eulogy written by Oscar Hammerstein II (1895–1960) and delivered by film star **Edward G. Robinson** (1893–1973). Gershwin's legacy was recognized in a very profound way in 2007 with the creation of the Gershwin Prize, presented by the Library of Congress. The citation reads: "The Gershwin Prize is a milestone in the Library's mission to recognize and celebrate creativity in order to spark imagination in this and future generations." The first recipient was singer-songwriter-activist **Paul Simon** (b. 1941). To paraphrase Ira Gershwin's lyrics, George Gershwin's contributions to the world's stages, concert halls, and silverscreens "are here to stay." *See also* **Jazz and Blues**; **Popular Music**.

Kenneth Kanter

Further Reading: Jablonski, Edward. *Gershwin.* New York: Doubleday, 1987. Jablonski, Edward, and Lawrence Stewart. *The Gershwin Years.* Garden City, NY: Doubleday, 1973. Kanter, Kenneth A. *The Jews on Tin Pan Alley.* New York: Ktav, 1982. Kimball, Robert, and Alfred Simon. *The Gershwins.* New York: Atheneum, 1973.

GINOTT, HAIM G. (1922–1973)

Known as Haim Ginsberg in Israel, Haim G. Ginott was a clinical psychologist, child therapist, parent educator, and author whose work has had an outstanding educational impact on the way adults relate to children. Ginott began his career in Israel as an elementary school teacher in 1947 before immigrating to the United States. He attended Columbia University in New York City and earned a doctoral degree in clinical psychology in 1952.

Ginott was the first psychologist to teach parents and teachers the importance of setting clear boundaries when working with children, while using compassion and empathy. Dr. Ginott claimed it was not an "either/or" proposition. He showed respect for children's feelings while setting limits on their behavior. Ginott used this approach when he worked with children at the Guidance Clinic in Jacksonville, Florida and it proved to be effective. He said he was strict with unacceptable behavior, but permissive with feelings. He has been praised by other professionals for teaching parents how to socialize with their children while cultivating their emotional well-being. He married Dr. Alice Ginott, and they had no children.

Ginott published three books during his lifetime. The first one, *Between Parent and Child,* was published in 1965. It sold to over five million people and was translated into 30 languages. In 2003, Alice Ginott, a psychologist, revised the book with the assistance of Dr. H. Wallace Goddard. It has made her husband's work even easier to read and understand. She said it was her labor of love. *Between Parent and Teenager* was published in 1967 and followed by *Teacher and Child in* 1972. But it was his first book that made him a national hero. His good sense of humor also helped make him a success when he appeared on television with Barbara Walters, Steve Allen, Phil Donahue, and Hugh Downs.

Other respected authors such as Dr. John M. Gottman believed Ginott was a genius. He urged parents to buy Ginott's book, saying their children would always be grateful if they did. There is no doubt that Ginott's greatest contribution and continuing legacy comes from teaching the communication skills that help parents relate to their children in a caring and understanding way without diminishing parental authority. Jane Brody, who writes for the *New York Times,* said it was Ginott's book that helped her become a more effective parent.

Dr. Haim Ginott's work rings truer today than ever before because its foundation adheres to universal principles that have not changed. It is clear in his work that adults must be good models for children, not judges. He believed that respectful communication between adults and children works because it is mutual. Millions of parents and teachers worldwide continue to be grateful to Ginott for sharing his philosophy of parenting. *See also* **Popular Psychology**.

Ann Moliver Ruben

Further Reading: Ginott, Haim. *Between Parent and Teenager.* New York: Macmillan, 1967. ———. *Teacher and Child.* New York: Macmillan, 1972. Ginott, Haim G., Alice Ginott, and H. Wallace Goddard. *Between Parent and Child.* New York: Three Rivers Press, 2003.

GINSBERG, ALLEN (1926–1997)

No history of the "Beat Generation," which first emerged in the 1950s, would be complete without calling attention to the prominent role that Allen Ginsberg played in the movement. His participation was central to the movement's critique of what was perceived as the degenerative force of materialism and conformity in American society during the years of the Eisenhower presidency.

Allen Ginsberg was born in Newark, New Jersey but grew up in Patterson, the son of poet Louis Ginsberg and communist activist Naomi Levy. His family and the poets he was exposed to in high school, Walt Whitman and William Blake, became important influences in his emergence as a major American poet and political activist. At age 11, Ginsberg began keeping a journal that included, among its entries, a description of an anti-Nazi rally (1938) in which he participated. He graduated from Eastside High School in 1943. A scholarship from the Young Men's Hebrew Association of Patterson made it possible for him to attend Columbia University. During his freshman year, Ginsberg contributed to the *Columbia Review Literary Journal* and the *Jester,* and he subsequently won the university's prestigious Woodberry Poetry Prize. Before Ginsberg received his BA from Columbia University in 1949, however, he was suspended from the institution for a year because of his involvement in a robbery investigation involving one of his friends, a heroin addict by the name of Herbert Huncke. Ginsberg was arrested as an accessory to crimes carried out by Huncke and his friends, who had stored stolen goods in Ginsberg's apartment. As an alternative to a jail sentence, Ginsberg's professors Carl Van Doren and Lionel Trilling arranged with the Columbia dean for a plea of psychological disability, on condition that Ginsberg be admitted to the Columbia Presbyterian Psychiatric Institute, where he spent eight months.

It was at Columbia that Ginsberg met Jack Kerouac, author of *On the Road* (1951), which is generally considered the "Bible" of the Beat movement. They first met at a party and, after a few insults were exchanged, got into a fight. A few parties later they became the best of friends. The two radically changed poetry and literature for the second part of the twentieth century.

Kerouac and Ginsberg are the pillars of what is defined as the 1950s Beat Generation. The movement was influenced by jazz's rhythm and soul beat, especially Charlie Parker's stream of consciousness. Beat also referred to the beatitude and the downer felt by drug users. The art produced by this generation of nonconformists was manifested in their poetry, writing, film, photography, art, and homosexual lifestyle. They produced a counter to mainstream American culture.

In New York, Ginsberg was part of a group which included Lucien Carr, Edie Parker (Kerouac's girlfriend), and subsequently Neil Cassidy. It was in 1945 that both Ginsberg and Kerouac were expelled from Columbia and, as was the case with **Lenny Bruce** and Kerouac, Ginsberg joined the Merchant Marine and discovered marijuana.

Ginsberg's subsequent life and work brought him into contact with many in the counterculture. The list includes William Burroughs, junkie Herbert Huncke, poet Gregory Corso and his long time lover and fellow traveler, Peter Orlovsky. In 1961 they toured Israel, where Ginsberg met his cousin, who revealed that they were related to one of the founders of Zionism, Ahad Ha'am. Subsequently, Ginsberg also became friends with Buddhist ecologist Gary Snyder and jam session companion **Bob Dylan**.

On October 7, 1955, Allen Ginsberg read the beginning of *Howl,* his most famous poem and one of the landmark works of the Beat movement, at San Francisco's Six Gallery: "I saw the best minds of my generation destroyed by madness, starving hysterical naked, dragging themselves through the negro streets at dawn looking for an angry fix, angel headed hipsters burning for the ancient heavenly connection to the starry dynamo in the machinery of night . . . " In 1956, City Lights published *Howl and Other Poems,* for which Lawrence Ferlinghetti was served with a warrant for publishing obscenity. In 1957, Judge Horn declared that *Howl* was "not obscene." The same judge gave a similar ruling regarding Lenny Bruce's trial a few years later.

The death of Ginsberg's mother in 1956 and his difficulty in dealing with her mental illness was the inspiration for *Kaddish* (the Jewish prayer for the dead), one of Ginsberg's most important poems. During the Vietnam era, Ginsberg became involved in peace demonstrations against the war. In 1973, Ginsberg founded the Jack Kerouac School of Disembodied Poetics in Boulder, Colorado. Interviewed by a French magazine that lauded his world contribution to poetry and peace, Ginsberg humbly responded, "I'm just a student of Jack Kerouac's poetry."

Ginsberg's embrace of both Buddhism and Hinduism began after traveling to India, where he became friends with Buddhist teachers and with A. C. Bhaktivedanta Swami Prabhupada, the founder of Hare Krishna. Ginsberg backed the Swami with money and his reputation and helped him establish the first Hare Krishna temple. He also toured with him to promote the movement. Ginsberg claimed that he was the first person on the North American continent to chant the Hare Krishna mantra. Subsequently, music and chanting became an integral of Ginsberg's poetry readings.

Despite his relationship to Hare Krishna, the body of Ginsberg's poetry is Jewish. The poet and critic Gerald Stern has noted that Ginsberg's Jewishness can be found "in his fierce prophetic utterances, in his humor, in his sense of humor, in his irreverence, in his sense of social justice, in his uncanny location of 'persecution,' in his passion for knowledge." Stern notes that "Howl," "America," "Sunflower Sutra," and "Kaddish" are Jewish poems, even as they are partially derived from Whitman, Blake, and the French Surrealists (Stern, 1992).

Ginsberg won the National Book Award for his book *The Fall of America* in 1993. He is buried in a Jewish cemetery in Elizabeth, New Jersey. *See also* **Dylan, Bob**.

Steve Krief

Further Reading: Podhoretz, Norman. "At War with Allen Ginsberg," in *Ex-Friends*. New York: Free Press, 1999. Raskin, Jonah. *American Scream: Allen Ginsberg's Howl and the Making of the Beat Generation*. Berkeley, CA: University of California Press, 2004. Schumacher, Michael. *Dharma Lion: A Biography of Allen Ginsberg*. New York: St. Martin's Press, 1994. Stern, Gerald. "Poetry." *Jewish-American History and Culture: An Encyclopedia,* edited by Jack Fischel and Sanford Pinsker. New York: Garland Press, 1992.

GITTLESOHN, RABBI ROLAND B. (1910–1995)

Rabbi Roland B. Gittlesohn's eulogy of March 26, 1945 during the dedication of the Fifth Marine Division cemetery on Iwo Jima is one of the most famous and important eulogies delivered by an American rabbi. Gittlesohn was born in Cleveland, Ohio, received a BA from Western Research University in 1931 and a BH from Hebrew Union College in Cincinnati 1934, and he was ordained by the Hebrew Union College in 1936. He also did graduate work at Teachers College of Columbia University and the New School in New York. He was a rabbi at the Central Synagogue of Nassau County on Long Island from 1936 to 1953 before being appointed as rabbi at Temple Israel in Boston, New England's most prestigious Reform congregation.

During his tenure at Temple Israel, Gittlesohn continued his predecessor's tradition of social activism. Particularly noteworthy was his involvement in the civil rights movement, prison reform, and opposition to the Vietnam War. He wrote several books, including *The Meaning of Modern Judaism* and *Lower than Angels*. He was married twice. His first wife was Ruth Frayer, with whom he had a son, David B. Gittlesohn, and a daughter, Judith Fales. His second wife was Hulda Tishler.

Gittlesohn was a committed pacifist and yet volunteered to be a chaplain in World War II. He reconciled this seeming contradiction by arguing that the conflict was a "just war" and thus sanctioned by Jewish tradition. Gittlesohn served in the navy and was assigned to the U.S. Marine Corps. He was the first Marine Corps Jewish chaplain in history and was with the Fifth Marine Corps Division when it went ashore at Iwo Jima on February 19, 1945. The battle for Iwo Jima was the bloodiest in Marine Corps history and the only battle in the Pacific in which the United States incurred more casualties than the Japanese. Three of the six men from the Fifth Division who raised the flag on Mount Suribachi were killed in the battle, along with 600–800 other Marines. These comprised one-third of all Marine Corps deaths in World War II.

Reverend Warren Cuthriell, the head chaplain of the Fifth Division and a Protestant minister, asked Gittlesohn to deliver the eulogy during the dedication of the cemetery. Cuthriell believed this to be appropriate in light of the ecumenical and democratic nature of the American war effort. Two Protestant and six Catholic Marine Corps chaplains on Iwo Jima protested and threatened to boycott the ceremony. The Catholic chaplains were particularly adamant. They were theologically opposed to all ecumenical religious services and argued that it was inappropriate for a Jew to deliver a eulogy at a cemetery in which over 90 percent of those interred were Christians. Although Cuthriell was not intimidated, Gittlesohn did not want to create controversy and decided instead to give his eulogy at a service solely for the Jewish fallen. Seventy persons attended this ceremony, including three Protestant chaplains who were appalled by the treatment of Gittlesohn.

Unexpectedly, Gittlesohn's four-minute eulogy was widely publicized. It was picked up by the armed forces radio network, reprinted in the *Congressional Record,* and reported on in *Time* magazine. Gittlesohn later modestly claimed that no one would have heard of his sermon had it not been for the protests. In fact, the eulogy was one of the most eloquent wartime statements on what the war should mean for Americans. Echoing themes and terminology found in Lincoln's Gettysburg Address, Gittlesohn emphasized that out of the sacrifices of those who perished on Iwo Jima a better America should emerge, one in which Christians and Jews, whites and blacks, and rich and poor would live together in democratic fellowship and social equality. "The war has been fought by the common man; its fruits of peace must be enjoyed by the common man!"

While there was nothing distinctively Jewish about Gittlesohn's eulogy and it could just as easily have been delivered by a Christian chaplain, it anticipated major themes of the civil religion of American Jews in the immediate postwar decades. Especially important among these themes were the elimination of racial and religious prejudice, the abolition of war, and the expansion of the welfare state. So prescient was his eulogy that after the war it became unthinkable in Jewish circles for anyone to claim to be a good Jew without also being a liberal and equating democracy with liberalism.

Edward S. Shapiro

Further Reading: Gittlesohn, Roland B. "Brothers All?" *The Reconstructionist,* February 7, 1947. Moore, Deborah D. *GI Jews: How World War II Changed a Generation.* Cambridge, MA: Harvard University Press, 2004.

GLASS, PHILIP (1937–)

A three-time Academy Award-nominated classical music composer, Philip Glass is considered one of the most influential composers of the late twentieth century. Glass was born in Baltimore, Maryland on January 31, 1937. His parents, Lithuanian Jewish immigrants, owned a record store with a highly refined collection of music. From his many hours of listening to these mostly unsold records, Glass developed a keen interest in all genres of music. Glass entered an accelerated program at the University of Chicago at age 15, where he studied both mathematics and philosophy. Moving on to Juilliard, Glass studied composition with Vincent Persichetti (1915–1987) and William Bergsma (1921–1994). Glass also studied with Darius Milhaud (1892–1974] and, at age 23, went to Paris, where he studied with the eminent French composer Nadia Boulanger (1887–1979). While in Paris, Glass discovered Indian classical music while transcribing the works of sitar master Ravi Shankar. It was a turning point for the young composer.

In 1966, Glass traveled to North India, where he came in contact with Tibetan refugees. Ever since, he has been a strong supporter of the Tibetan cause. In 1987, he co-founded the Tibet House with, among others, actor Richard Gere. This institution houses a permanent Cultural Center and Library, whose purpose is to share Tibet's unique spiritual and artistic heritage.

Many consider Glass's composition style to be austere; he prefers calling it "minimalist," or even better, "theatre music." His works are based on additive rhythms, along with a sense of timing influenced by the Irish littérateur Samuel Beckett. Additive rhythms consist of large periods of time constructed from smaller sequences of smaller rhythmic units.

Glass has worked with a diverse group of musical artists ranging from **Paul Simon**, David Bowie, and Brian Eno to Coldplay, Talking Heads, and Phish. He has scored music for nearly 80 films and been nominated for 3 Academy Awards. Glass, who has been married twice, has two children, Zachary and Juliet (a writer); he lives in New York and Nova Scotia.

Kurt F. Stone

Further Reading: Glass, Philip. *Music By Philip Glass.* New York: Harper and Row, 1987.

GODDARD, PAULETTE (1910–1990)

Paulette Goddard was an Oscar-nominated American film and theater actress who was a major star of the Paramount Studio in the 1940s. She was born Pauline Marion Levy in Whitestone Landing, New York, in 1910. Reference books list her as Jewish, and her father, Joseph Russell Levy, was a Jew, but her mother, Alta Mae Goddard, was an Episcopalian. There is no evidence that she identified with her father's religion. Her father had little influence on her life and career, because he disappeared soon after her parents divorced. Her maternal uncle, Charles Goddard, became the male figure in her childhood.

"Uncle Charlie" Goddard found the teenage Pauline jobs as a fashion model. By 1924, 14-year-old Pauline was a "Ziegfeld Girl." In 1926, Pauline, now renamed Paulette Goddard, made her stage acting debut in *The Unconquerable Male.* Following a brief marriage to wealthy businessman, Edgar Morris (they were divorced in 1930), Paulette headed for California, where she began making films for Hal Roach. She played uncredited bit parts in many Laurel and Hardy films.

The turning point in her career came in 1932, when she signed with Samuel Goldwyn and met Charles Chaplin. Goddard became a "Goldwyn Girl," along with future stars Lucille Ball, Jane Wyman, and Betty Grable. By 1936, she was living with Chaplin, who had purchased her contract from Goldwyn. She co-starred with Chaplin in *Modern Times,* a film that made her a star. Goddard came close to being cast as Scarlett O'Hara in *Gone with the Wind* but was supposedly denied the role because of her "immoral" relationship with the much-older Chaplin. In 1940, she once again co-starred with Chaplin, this time in *The Great Dictator.*

Goddard's relationship to Chaplin remains a source of controversy. At the premier of *The Great Dictator,* Chaplin introduced her as his wife, but there is little evidence they were legally married. Nevertheless, in 1942, Goddard "divorced" Chaplin and soon after married actor Burgess Meredith. Divorced from Meredith in 1950, in 1958, she married German novelist (*All Quiet on the Western Front*) Erich Maria Remarque. This marriage lasted until his death in 1970.

Goddard's career flourished throughout the 1940s. In 1944, she received a best supporting actress nomination for *So Proudly We Hail.* Independent, intelligent, and unconventional, Paulette Goddard appeared in nearly 60 films. Goddard died in Ronco, Switzerland in April 1990. In her will, she left $20 million to New York University. Paulette Goddard Hall is located at 79 Washington Square East in New York City. *See also* **Film**; **Film Stars**.

Kurt F. Stone

Further Reading: Gilbert, Julie. *Opposite Attraction: The Lives of Erich Marie Remarque and Paulette Goddard.* New York: Pantheon Books, 1995. Morella, Joe. *Paulette: The Adventurous Life of Paulette Goddard.* New York: Random House, 1991.

THE GOLDBERGS

See **Radio**; **Sitcoms**; **Television**

GOLDEN, HARRY (1902–1982)

A journalist, a bestselling raconteur and humorist, and the most prominent Jew of his era residing in the South, Harry Golden achieved fame mostly as the editor of a monthly tabloid, *The Carolina Israelite.*

Born in Mikulintsy in the Galician corner of the Austro-Hungarian Empire, Herschel Goldhirsch was not yet three when his parents, Leib (a Hebrew teacher) and Anna Klein Goldhirsch, brought him and their four other children to the United States. At Ellis Island the family surname became Goldhurst, and on the Lower East Side, the family lived in poverty. After graduating from high school, Harry Goldhurst took on a number of jobs, becoming a stock broker during the speculative craze of the 1920s. In 1926, he married Genevieve Alice Marie "Tiny" Gallagher, an Irish Catholic. They had four sons, three of whom (Richard Goldhurst, William Goldhurst, and Harry Golden Jr.) became writers or teachers. The fourth was mentally handicapped and was institutionalized before dying at age 19.

In 1929, Goldhurst was caught committing mail fraud and was sentenced to four years in an Atlanta federal prison. After his release, he attempted to hide his past by changing his name to Golden, and he returned to the Northeast. During the Great Depression, he became increasingly aware of the peril that Nazism posed, and he later acknowledged that the Third Reich made him intensely conscious of his ethnic identity.

An opportunity to work for a labor newspaper in North Carolina brought him to Charlotte, where he founded *The Carolina Israelite* in 1942. It was a remarkable solo act; the 16-page newspaper had no other contributors. Drawing upon the wide reading of an autodidact, as well as his fond memories of New York, Golden pounded out essays on his typewriter while consuming bourbon and branch water. Brandishing no photographs or attention-grabbing headlines, *The Carolina Israelite* could barely be called a newspaper, since it contained observations and opinions but no actual news. What started as a monthly eventually became a bi-monthly, and it sold for three dollars a year by subscription. Within five years, *The Carolina Israelite* became self-sustaining, and by 1958 it attracted 16,000 subscribers. The following year circulation fell just short of 45,000 and was evenly divided between Gentiles and Jews.

Golden's topics were ambitious but concentrated. He professed to harbor only "three passionate loves in this life; the Jewish people, America and the South" (Golden, 1969). He foresaw the possibility of linking his Jewish identity to the advocacy of equal rights for black Americans, an association that might be realized in the region. Golden's vocation was to try to liberate Southern white readers from the inertia of their tradition. So successful was he that, only two decades after he moved to Charlotte, the executive director of the Southern Regional Council praised Golden as "the man who has done more than any other to teach Southerners and Americans generally to see the irony of their racial foolishness." In his "Letter from the Birmingham Jail" (1963), Martin Luther King Jr. also hailed Golden for "having written about our struggle in eloquent and prophetic terms."

In 1958, the first collection of his essays, mostly drawn from *The Carolina Israelite,* leaped to the top of the bestseller list. About a quarter of a million copies of *Only in America* sold in hardcover, and at least five times that number sold in paperback. The author's amiable charm became familiar to viewers of the television programs of Dave Garroway, Arthur Godfrey, and Jack Paar. Golden also wrote a syndicated newspaper column (unsurprisingly entitled *Only in America*), even though his time as a convict was exposed. But his reputation was unharmed. Indeed, Golden's fame was enhanced with the publication of a second collection of essays, *For 2 Cents Plain,* in 1959. It was perched in third place among the year's bestsellers, competing with *Only in America* (ranked number nine in 1959), even as the playwriting team of Jerome Lawrence and Robert E. Lee was adapting the earlier volume for a brief run on Broadway. Audiences could not seem to get enough of the editor of *The Carolina Israelite.* Eventually he published close to a dozen and a half other books.

"I got away with my ideas in the South," the author once explained, "because no southerner takes me—a Jew, a Yankee, and a radical (sic)—seriously." That was untrue (or at least exaggerated). A liberal who exuded the stereotypical attributes of a Yiddish-speaking New Yorker, he was graciously adopted by the Bible Belt. Golden tried hard, he said, "to be an American and a Jew in full measure, each to the enrichment of the other" (Golden, 1969). He died in Charlotte. *See also* **Journalism**.

Stephen J. Whitfield

Further Reading: Golden, Harry. *Only in America.* Cleveland, OH: World, 1958. ———. *The Right Time: An Autobiography.* New York: G.P. Putnam's Sons, 1969.

GOODMAN, BENNY (1909–1986)

Goodman was a bandleader and clarinetist known for some five decades as "The King of Swing." He was born Benjamin David Goodman on May 30, 1909 in Chicago, the 9th of 12 children of Jewish immigrants, David and Dora (Reginski) Goodman. His father came from Warsaw, his mother from Kovno in Lithuania, and the parents met and married in Baltimore in the 1890s. They moved to Chicago in 1903, where David Goodman, a tailor by trade, worked in the garment industry and in the stockyards.

Although the family was impoverished, David believed that music could be a ticket out of poverty for his children. When Goodman was 10 years old, he and two of his brothers were enrolled for music lessons at the Kehelah Jacob Synagogue. The older brothers were given a tuba and trombone, while Goodman received a clarinet. The next year he joined the boy's club band at Jane Addams' Hull House, where he received lessons from the director, James Sylvester. During this period he also received instruction from the classically trained clarinetist Franz Schoepp.

By the age of 16 Goodman was a full-fledged member of one of Chicago's best jazz groups. He formed his first band in New York City in 1934, and the concert by his band at the Palomar Ballroom in Los Angeles in August 1935 was credited with ushering in the Swing Era. In 1936 Goodman hired African American pianist Teddy Wilson, thereby becoming the first major bandleader to front a racially integrated group.

On January 16, 1938, the Goodman band became the first jazz ensemble to perform in New York City's Carnegie Hall. This concert, billed as *From Spiritual to Swing,* was the band's greatest moment. It brought down the house with the unforgettable 22-minute version of "Sing, Sing, Sing."

Goodman continued to lead a band until 1950. He tried briefly but failed to adapt to the jazz style known as bebop that supplanted swing after World War II. Sporadically through the 1950s, 1960s, and 1970s, he formed small groups and big bands for concert tours. Of these, the most important was a trip to the Soviet Union in 1962 under the auspices of the U.S. State Department.

Goodman was also the first major musician to have dual careers in jazz and classical music. He commissioned and performed two of the best-known modern classic works featuring the clarinet, Béla Bartók's *Contrasts for Clarinet, Violin and Piano,* and **Aaron Copland**'s Clarinet Concerto. Goodman died on June 13, 1986, age 77, of cardiac arrest in New York City. *See also* **Jazz**; **Popular Music**.

Leslie Rabkin

Further Reading: Collier, James Lincoln. *Benny Goodman and the Swing Era.* New York: Oxford University Press, 1989. Goodman, Benny, and Irving Kolodin. *The Kingdom of Swing.* New York: Stockpale, 1939.

GOODMAN, PAUL (1911–1972)

An archetypal, secular Jewish intellectual, Paul Goodman was born in New York City, the son of Barnett and Augusta Goodman. After a business failure Barnett Goodman deserted his family, and Goodman and his three siblings grew up in poverty. Goodman attended Hebrew school and later graduated from Townsend Harris High School, in 1927, at the top of his class. Entering the City College of New York, he became an anarchist and fell under the spell of the legendary philosopher Morris Raphael Cohen. Graduating with honors in 1931, Goodman struggled during the Great Depression to complete doctoral requirements at the University of Chicago by 1940. He did not receive his degree until 14 years later, when the University of Chicago Press published his thesis on *The Structure of Literature*. By then Goodman had a minor reputation for short stories, poems, and essays that were published in mostly avant-garde periodicals.

A pacifist who avoided military service during World War II, he held firm throughout his adult life to nonviolent, independent, communitarian anarchism. The fervor of his repudiation of social and political conventions consigned him, until the 1960s, to the margins of intellectual life. Goodman mostly earned a living as a lay therapist, practicing for about 25 hours a week at the New York Institute for Gestalt Therapy. An acolyte of Wilhelm Reich, who asserted that physical satisfaction grounds mental and emotional health, Goodman coauthored, with Frederick Perls and Ralph Hefferline, a textbook on *Gestalt Therapy* (1951).

Sexual liberation, the urgency of desire, as well as the frustration of homosexual yearnings, are themes that haunt his fiction. His bisexuality and the openness of his predominant homosexuality caused him social difficulties. His candor also resulted in dismissal from at least two teaching positions, at the Manumit School of Progressive Education in New York (1942) and at the experimental Black Mountain College in North Carolina (1950). Goodman's two marriages were common—law because, as he explained, "I don't believe that people's sexual lives are any business of the state; to license sex is absurd" (Widmer, 1980). He was married to Virginia Miller from 1938 until 1943; they had one daughter. Sally Duchsten was his second wife, from 1945 until his death; they had one son and another daughter.

In 1960 Random House published Goodman's loosely connected set of essays, *Growing Up Absurd*. The 49-year-old author moved quickly from being an itinerant teacher and bohemian to being famous. His book reactivated the radical tradition with salvos against a society that "thwarts aptitude and creates stupidity" and that lacks "honest public speech." Initially serialized in *Commentary* (the monthly sponsored by the American Jewish Committee), Goodman's criticism helped stimulate the political and social transformations of the 1960s and made them intelligible. *Growing Up Absurd* stemmed from Goodman's anarchist conviction that human nature is intrinsically creative and loving but that what he called "the Organized System" blunted generous impulses.

The acclaim bestowed upon *Growing Up Absurd* enabled its author to publish some of his older rejected manuscripts. Five books appeared in 1962 with so remarkable a range that soon 21 separate categories were needed by cataloguers of the New York Public Library. He insisted, however, that "everything I do has exactly the same subject—the organism and the environment," especially its urban version. His older brother, Percival Goodman, the most prolific synagogue architect in the United States, collaborated with him on a classic of urban planning and communitarian theory, *Communitas* (1947, rev. ed. 1960).

Goodman devoted much of the 1960s to denouncing militarism and became conspicuous in protesting against the Vietnam War. By the end of the decade, he had split from his "crazy young allies" for their apparent eagerness to jettison scientific inquiry and professional standards.

Goodman frequently taught at New York University, the University of Wisconsin, Sarah Lawrence College, and elsewhere. He found time to write four volumes of short stories and five volumes of plays, which found admirers and critics. He lived on the West Side of Manhattan and also on a farm in North Stratford, New Hampshire—which is where, five years after his son's death in a mountaineering accident, Goodman died of a heart attack.

Stephen J. Whitfield

Further Reading: Parisi, Peter, ed. *Artist of the Actual: Essays on Paul Goodman*. Metuchen, NJ: Scarecrow,

1986. Widmer, Kingsley. *Paul Goodman*. Boston: Twayne, 1980.

GRADE, CHAIM (1910–1982)

The Yiddish poet and novelist Chaim Grade (pronounced GRA-deh) was a brilliant yeshiva student who left religious life to become one of the most admired Jewish writers of the twentieth century. He was born in Vilna, Lithuania in 1910, the son of Hebrew teacher Shlomo Mordecai Grade and his second wife, Vela Blumenthal. The family lived in extreme poverty. After Grade's sister Ettele died of starvation when she was six, Grade lived in the back of a blacksmith shop with his mother, who supported them as an itinerant fruit seller. At 13, Grade was sent to the rigorous Novaradok Musar Yeshiva where he was a star student, studying with its most revered scholar, Rabbi Avrohom Yeshaya Karelitz, the "Chazon Ish." Expected to become the Talmudic mind of his generation, Grade began writing Yiddish poetry in secret during his last year at the yeshiva. His first published poem, "My Mother," appeared in 1932 in *Der Vilner Tog*. Grade's loving depiction of his mother in particular and of women in general became a hallmark of his writing style.

As a young poet, Grade joined a group of talented Yiddish artists called Yung Vilne (Young Vilna). He published his first book of poems, *Yau* (*Yes*), in 1936. Described as "the newest genius in Yiddish poetry," he had a second edition that appeared the next year. Three years later, Grade published *Musernikes,* a collection of poems based on his experiences in the Musar yeshivas.

In the late 1930s, he married a nurse from Warsaw, Frumme-Liebe, the daughter of a Zionist rabbi. In 1941, he fled Vilna, carrying with him a Hebrew Bible and a German translation of Dante's *Divine Comedy*. His mother and wife stayed behind, believing the Nazis would only imprison able-bodied men. Grade spent the war years digging trenches in Russia. His prescient poem from 1936 *Geveyn fun Doros* (*Cry of the Generations*) was read by the Jews in Auschwitz who believed he had written it expressly for them. In 1945, Grade returned to Vilna to discover that his wife, his mother, his city, and almost everyone he had ever known had been destroyed. He wandered the ruins of the Jewish quarter alone for almost half a year.

Grade had more books published in the five years after the war than at any other time in his life, including several books of poetry: *Doros* (*Generations*), *Farvoksene Vegn* (*Overgrown Paths*), *Plitim* (*Refugees*), *Der Mames Tsavoe* (*My Mother's Will*), and *Shayn fun Farloshene Shtern* (*The Glow from Extinguished Stars*). Grade married his second wife, Inna Hecker, in 1945 before spending two years in France as president of the Yiddish Literary Union of Paris. Moving to New York in 1948, he wrote novels in serial form for the newspapers *Der Morgan Journal* and the ***Jewish Daily Forward***. His memoirs, *Der Mames Shabosim* (*My Mother's Sabbath Days*) were published in 1955 and dramatized by the Folksbiene **Yiddish Theatre** in New York in 1960.

While his poetry addressed the atrocities of the Holocaust, his novels vividly recreated Jewish life in pre-war Eastern Europe. Although he would never set foot in his home city again, Grade always returned to Vilna in his work, writing about his neighbors as they lived, reawakening a Jewish way of life that no longer existed. Influenced by Dante, Spinoza, and Doestoevsky, questions of Jewish law feature prominently in his work. His novel *The Agunah* chronicles a debate between two rabbis over whether a young deserted wife is allowed to remarry. The protagonist of his epic two-volume novel *The Yeshiva* wants to start his own yeshiva but doubts the existence of God. Grade's philosophical dialogue about the Holocaust, "My Quarrel with Hersh Rasseyner," first appeared in English translation in 1954. It was made into a film, *The Quarrel,* in 1992.

Grade's novels translated into English include*The Well, The Agunah, The Yeshiva, The Sacred and the Profane* (also called *Rabbis and Wives*) and *My Mother's Sabbath Days,* his tender depiction of his mother's courtyard in Vilna before the war as well as his return to its ruins in 1945. Grade made his living primarily as a lecturer and in 1978 delivered the first lecture ever given in Yiddish at Harvard University. *Rabbis and Wives* was a finalist for the Pulitzer Prize in 1983. The Jewish Theological Seminary, Yeshiva University, and Hebrew Union College all awarded Grade honorary degrees. He died in the Bronx on July 26, 1982. See also **Literature**.

Caraid O'Brien

Further Reading: Grade, Chaim. *My Mother's Sabbath Days: A Memoir, Chana Kleinerman Goldstein and Inna Hecker Grade.* New York: Jason Aronson, 1997. ———. *The Yeshiva.* Trans. Curt Leviant. New York: Bobbs Merril Co., 1976. Howe, Irving, and Eliezer Greenburg. "My Quarrel with Hersh Rasseyner," *A Treasury of Yiddish Stories.* New York: Viking Press, 1954.

GREEN, GERALD (1922–2006)

Gerald Green, a novelist, is best known for writing the screenplay for *The Holocaust,* the critically acclaimed 1978 television miniseries that won eight Emmy Awards and was credited with persuading the West German government to repeal the statute of limitations on Nazi war crimes. Green also turned *Holocaust* into a novel, which became a bestseller. Green was born in Brooklyn, New York on April 8, 1922, where his father, Sam Greenberg, was a doctor. Green earned a BA from Columbia University (1942), where he was elected to Phi Beta Kappa and edited the school's humor magazine, *Jester.* During World War II, Green served as editor of the army's *Stars and Stripes* newspaper. Following the war, he returned to the Columbia School of Journalism, where he earned a master's degree.

Following a brief stint as editor for the International News Service, Green joined NBC television where, from 1950 through the early 1960s, he worked as writer, director, and producer of the *Today* show, which he and Dave Garroway had created in 1952.

In 1950, Green published his first novel, *His Majesty O'Keefe.* The film version (1954) starred Burt Lancaster. In 1956, Green published his best-known work, *The Last Angry Man,* which tells the story of Samuel Abelman, MD, a crotchety 68-year-old Brooklyn general practitioner who achieves tabloid celebrity for saving the life of a black woman who has been gang-raped. Columbia Pictures purchased rights to the novel and made it into a successful movie starring Paul Muni and Luther Adler.

Gerald Green published 20 novels, several works of nonfiction, and wrote/produced numerous motion pictures and television dramas, including 1986's *Wallenberg: A Hero's Tale.* Green was known for writing gritty works on social issues and historical events.

Gerald Green died in Norwalk, Connecticut on August 29, 2006. He was survived by his wife, Marlene, 3 children, 3 stepchildren, and 20 grandchildren. See also **The Holocaust in American Culture**.

Kurt F. Stone

Further Reading: Green Gerald. *Holocaust.* New York: Rosetta Books, 1978. ———. *The Last Angry Man.* New York: Rosetta Books, 1957.

GREEN, SHAWN DAVID (1972–)

Shawn David Green was a two-time major league all-star who drove in 100 runs four times, hit 40 or more home runs three times, won both a Gold Glove Award and a Silver Slugger Award, and set the Dodgers single-season record in home runs. Considered by many to be the greatest Jewish slugger since **Hank Greenberg**, Green, the son of Ira and Judy, was born on November 10, 1972 in Des Plains, Iowa. He was the top draft pick of the Toronto Blue Jays in 1991, making his major league debut two years later. Green spent seven seasons with the Blue Jays before being traded to the Los Angeles Dodgers. In 2001, he broke a 415 consecutive game streak to sit out in honor of Yom Kippur. Green said at the time he felt he owed it to his young Jewish fans to serve as a role model. Comparisons to **Sandy Koufax**, the Hall of Fame pitcher for the Brooklyn/Los Angeles Dodgers who passed up pitching the first game of the 1965 World Series to observe the day, were inevitable. In subsequent years when the holiday fell during the playing schedule, Green made similar accommodations, either sitting out a game on the eve of Yom Kippur and playing the following day, or vice versa.

Green was traded to the Arizona Diamondbacks in 2005, where he played until being dealt to the New York Mets in August 2006. Green is the highest-profile Jewish ballplayer since Koufax. His 328 home runs and 1,070 runs batted in (as of the end of the 2007 season) rank behind only Hank Greenberg for Jewish major leaguers; his 2,003 career hits puts him in second place behind Buddy Myer (2,131).

Green set the Major League mark for total bases in a single game (19) when he hit four home runs, a double, and a single against the Milwaukee Brewers in 2002.

Although he reportedly never attended Hebrew school or had a Bar Mitzvah ceremony, Green has been involved in Jewish communal work. In 2007, he donated $180 to United Jewish Appeal for each run he batted in, a sum matched by the Mets and sports memorabilia entrepreneur Brandon Steiner.

Green married Lindsay Bear in 2001. They are the parents of two daughters, Presley Taylor (born December 22, 2002) and Chandler Rose (August 26, 2005). *See also* **Sports**.

Ron Kaplan

Further Reading: Singer, Tom. "Hammerin' Hebrew: Shawn Green carries the torch as baseball's latest Jewish All-Star." *Atlanta Jewish News,* August 4, 2000 (http://atlanta.jewish.com/archives/2000/080400cs.htm).

GREENBERG, HANK (1911–1986)

Considered along with **Sandy Koufax** as one of the two greatest Jewish baseball players of all time, Henry Benjamin "Hank" Greenberg grew up in an observant Jewish household in New York City. His parents, David and Sarah, were Romanian immigrants who settled in the Lower East Side but moved to the Bronx when their son was six. His siblings included Ben, Joe, and Lillian. He attended Hebrew school and celebrated his Bar Mitzvah.

Greenberg, a first baseman, was recruited by the New York Yankees while attending James Monroe High School in the Bronx, but since the team already had Lou Gehrig firmly fixed at his position, he decided to attend New York University. He signed with the Detroit Tigers after his freshman year for $9,000 and made his debut with the team on September 14, 1930.

The photo of the Hall of Fame plaque of Henry "Hank" Greenberg, who was elected in 1956. The pride of "Jewish" America, Greenberg was also one of the first Jewish superstars in American professional sports. He garnered national attention in 1934 when he refused to play baseball on Yom Kippur, the Jewish Day of Atonement, even though the Tigers were in the middle of a pennant race. [AP Photo]

"Hammerin Hank" was the first superstar Jewish athlete, breaking the stereotype of the un-athletic Jew. He faced a good deal of anti-Semitism during his career, often challenging opponents who baited him with slurs. With Adolf Hitler and his Nazi regime ascendent in Europe, Greenberg realized his importance as a role model to American Jewry.

Facing the decision of playing on the High Holidays in 1934 with his team in the thick of a pennant race, Greenberg consulted with rabbis and reached a compromise. He played on Rosh Hashanah, clubbing two home runs to give the Tigers a victory, but he declined to play during Yom Kippur. In *Speaking of Greenberg,* Edgar Guest wrote about this decision that was hailed by rabbis across the country for setting an example for Jewish youth. Greenberg has become the standard against which modern-day Jewish players are measured when it comes to "the Yom Kippur dilemma."

Greenberg was the first baseball player to earn a salary of $100,000. He was traded to the Pittsburgh Pirates in 1947 and received the admiration of many groups for his kindness to Jackie Robinson, who broke baseball's color line that year.

Conceivably Greenberg's baseball statistics might have been greater than those achievements that earned him a place in the Hall of Fame, but he missed three full seasons and parts of two others to military service during World War II. He was drafted in 1940 and received an honorable discharge on December 5, 1941, but immediately reenlisted after the attack on Pearl Harbor. He graduated from Officer Candidate School and was commissioned as a first lieutenant, eventually serving in the Burma Theater. Greenberg also missed part of the 1936 season because of injury. In 13 seasons, he amassed 331 home runs, 1,276 runs batted in, and achieved a .313 batting average. Serious baseball fans project "what might have been," had he and his contemporaries not lost significant periods of time to World War II.

Greenberg married Caral Gimbel (daughter of the New York department store family) in 1946. They had a daughter, Alva, and two sons, Glenn and Stephen; the latter played for five seasons in the Washington Senators/Texas Rangers minor league system. Greenberg subsequently divorced his wife and married Mary Jo DeCicco in 1966.

After his retirement as a player, Greenberg served as general manager for the Cleveland Indians and Chicago White Sox. In 1956, he became the first Jewish player enshrined in the Baseball Hall of Fame; he was also inducted into the National Jewish Sports Hall of Fame, the International Jewish Sports Hall of Fame, and the Jewish American Hall of Fame. *See also* **Sports**.

Ron Kaplan

Further Reading: Greenberg, Hank, and Ira Berkow. *The Story of My Life*. Crown, 1989. Kempner, Aviva, director. *The Life and Times of Hank Greenberg* Documentary. Also written and produced by Aviva Kempner. Ciesla Foundation, 2003.

H

HECHT, BEN (1894–1964)

Ben Hecht was a Hollywood screenwriter, playwright, reporter, short story writer, and novelist. He was also a Jewish activist. Hecht fought for a Jewish homeland in Palestine and was a critic of President Franklin Roosevelt's failure to do more to prevent the destruction of European Jewry during the Holocaust.

Hecht's parents were Jewish immigrants from Russia who settled in Racine, Wisconsin. Hecht became a reporter for the *Chicago Daily News,* often covering the crime beat. His first book, *101 Afternoons in Chicago,* was based on his crime reporting, which brought him prominence, as did his role in solving a sensational murder case in Chicago. Hecht was invited to Hollywood, where he became a scriptwriter, often collaborating with writer Charles MacArthur. He was involved with 70 films, many of which were Academy Award winners. Such greats as *A Farewell to Arms, Gunga Din, Front Page,* and *Mutiny on the Bounty* were shaped by Hecht. Often he was a ghost writer and editor, receiving no credits.

In 1933, with the advent of Hitler, his Jewish identity was awakened. Some of his films, such as *Foreign Correspondent* (1940)—Hecht wrote the final scene, which was not credited—attacked Nazism. He also became a supporter of Peter Bergson, a Palestinian Jew who represented the Revisionist wing of the Zionist movement. Bergson arrived in the United States during World War II, with the mission of arousing public support for a Jewish state in Palestine. Towards this end, the Revisionists and their military arm, the Irgun, engaged in military confrontation against the British in Palestine. In contrast, the Labor Zionists, led by the future prime minister of Israel, David Ben-Gurion, and their supporters in America, believed in achieving a Jewish state through diplomacy with Great Britain.

In addition to his active support for the "Bergson Group," during the 1940s, Hecht used his pen to awaken Americans to the Holocaust and the plight of Jewish refugees, as well as to work on behalf of a Jewish state in Palestine. He wrote and placed ads in major newspapers to publicize the Nazi death decree against European Jews. One ad read, "For Sale To Humanity 70,000 Jews Guaranteed Human Beings at $50 A Piece" (*New York Times,* 1)—the ad explained that three and a half million dollars would rescue the then-trapped Romanian Jews. Hecht subsequently produced, along with Kurt Weil, *We Will Never Die* (1943), a major stage pageant that revealed the Nazi plan to annihilate European Jewry. The dramatic presentation attracted thousands of concerned

Ben Hecht—screenwriter, playwright, and literary figure, who was active in his efforts to awaken the United States to the ongoing Nazi Holocaust and subsequently worked tirelessly in behalf of a Jewish state in Palestine. [Photofest, Inc.]

Americans as the pageant, which opened in Madison Square Garden, toured the country. After the war ended, Ben Hecht produced another major pageant, this time about establishment of the State of Israel, called *A Flag is Born,* which glamorized Jewish resistance to British and Arab rule.

Following the establishment of Israel in 1948, Hecht opposed Ben-Gurion's Labor Party government and sponsored the Irgun munitions ship the *Altalena,* which the Israeli government blew up. His book *Perfidy* (1961) was an attack on the Jewish Agency in Palestine for failing to alert the Hungarian Jewish community to their doom at the hands of Nazis. Much of Hecht's role in working for a Jewish state can be found in his 1954 autobiography, *A Child of the Century.*

Hecht has been credited with writing more than 70 films and authoring 35 books. He received the best original story Academy Award in the first-ever Oscar ceremony, for *Underworld* (1927) and another for *The Scoundrel* (1935). He was nominated for four additional screenplay Academy Awards for *Viva Villa* (1934), *Wuthering Heights* (1939), *Angels Over Broadway* (1940), and *Notorious* (1946). Hecht died of a heart attack on April 19, 1964, while working on the script of *Casino Royale* (1967). Despite his achievements as a Hollywood scriptwriter and prolific author, he will be best remembered as a man who sacrificed a lucrative career to devote himself to rescue Jews trapped in the Holocaust, and as a man who worked for the creation of Israel. *See also* **Film.**

Philip Rosen

Further Reading: Hecht, Ben. *A Child of the Century.* New York: Simon and Schuster, 1954. Kovan, Florine Whyte., *Rediscovering Ben Hecht: Selling the Celluloid Serpent.* Washington, DC: Snickersnee Press, 1999. MacAdams, William. *Ben Hecht: The Man Behind the Legend.* New York: Scribners, 1990. *New York Times,* February 16, 1943, p. 1.

HEEB MAGAZINE (2002–)

Heeb Magazine, a quarterly publication, was launched in 2002 with a $60,000 grant from the Joshua Venture: A Fellowship for Jewish Social Entrepreneurs, funded by **Steven Spielberg** and Charles Bronfman, among others.

Heeb was founded by Jennifer Bleyer, a graduate of Columbia University, who had worked on the *Webzine Mazel-Tov Cocktail* (she now writes for the *New York Times*) and Joshua Neuman, a graduate of Harvard University Divinity School, who serves as editor in chief. Neuman described his project's philosophy as "trying to poeticize this fluidity of Jews between their religious and secular self" (*New York Times,* 2007). The founders chose their title, normally considered a Jewish slur, as an act of defiance against their staid ancestors and the outside world. These "young Turks" were not afraid to tackle any subject, no matter how taboo. Subtitled "The New Jew Review," *Heeb* covers arts, culture, and politics and is known for its parody advertisements of familiar Jewish products, such as Gold's Horseradish and **Manischewitz** wines.

Aimed at young hip Jews, most issues center around loose themes including guilt, money, sex, food, and kids, and since *Heeb*'s inception, the editors have mostly eschewed "A-list" profiles in favor of up-and-comers in various fields. The "*Heeb* 100" includes representatives from art, fashion, entertainment, comedy, television, and film, among others, most of whom are under 35 years of age, further evidence of the editors' target audience and philosophy.

This offbeat publication, which has a reported subscription of 30,000, has enjoyed mixed success. In 2004, both the Anti-Defamation League and the Catholic League criticized the publication for its parody of Mel Gibson's *The Passion of the Christ*. *See also* **Journalism**.

Ron Kaplan

Further Reading: "Marketers, Gingerly, Bite at Parody Bait." *New York Times,* March 28, 2007.

HELLER, JOSEPH (1923–1999)

Iconoclastic novelist, dramatist, and Fulbright Scholar, Joseph Heller was born into a poor Jewish family in Brooklyn, New York, on May 1, 1923. His father, Isaac Donald Heller, who was a bakery truck driver, died in 1927. Heller was subsequently raised by his mother, Lena Heller. He graduated from Abraham Lincoln High School in June 1941. By that time he had already written several short stories and planned to pursue a literary career. He took a job as a blacksmith's helper in Norfolk, Virginia. With the declaration of war in December 1941, Heller and several Brooklyn friends volunteered for military duty. He flew 60 bombing missions while assigned to the 12th Air Corps.

After the war, Heller earned a BA in English from NYU and an MA in literature from Columbia University. He spent two years at Oxford as a Fulbright Scholar. Returning to the United States in 1950, he became a professor of English at Pennsylvania State University. Later he worked as an advertising copywriter for *Time, Look,* and *McCall's* magazines.

In 1961, Heller published his first novel, *Catch-22*. Based in part on his military experience, the book was a scathingly satirical antiwar novel filled with logical absurdities and dark humor. After slow initial sales, *Catch-22* became an immense success and is generally recognized as a classic of American literature. Its protagonist, Yossarian, became a cult hero, and the title phrase entered the common lexicon—a no-win situation created by law, bureaucracy, or circumstances.

After writing several screen and Broadway plays, Heller published his second novel, *Something Happened,* in 1974. Subsequent literary efforts included novels *Good as Gold* (1979), *Picture This* (1988), and *God Knows* (1984). *No Laughing Matter* (1986) is the story of his recovery from Guillain-Barre Syndrome and *Closing Time* (1998) is a touching memoir of his boyhood days. Despite critical acclaim, Heller never again achieved the success he gained with his first novel. When an interviewer observed that Heller had never written anything as good as *Catch-22,* Heller simply replied, "Who has?" He suffered a heart attack and died on December 13, 1999. His final novel, *Portrait of an Artist as an Old Man,* was published in 2000, after his death.

Good as Gold was Heller's first fictional use of his Jewish heritage. Bruce Gold, a college professor, is writing a book about "the Jewish experience," but secretly he yearns for a career in politics. Offered a high government position after writing a positive review of a book written by the president, Gold is offered an appointment in government. Gold accepts, leaves his wife and children, and finds himself immersed in Washington's farcical bureaucracy where public officials speak in a confusing version of double-talk. The novel harshly satirizes former Secretary of State **Henry Kissinger**, a Jew who has essentially forsaken his Jewishness. As a result, the author draws an analogy between the pursuit of political power and the corruption of Jewish identity. When his older brother dies, Gold realizes the importance of his Jewish heritage and family and decides to leave Washington.

R. Z. Sheppard, writing in *Time* magazine, called the book "a savage, intemperately funny satire on the assimilation of the Jewish tradition of liberalism" into the American mainstream. "It is a delicate subject," Mr. Sheppard wrote, "off limits to non-Jews fearful of being thought anti-Semitic and unsettling to successful Jewish intellectuals whose views may have drifted to the right in middle age" (1979).

In Heller's next novel, *God Knows,* he retells the biblical story of King David, in the form of a monologue in which Heller uses anachronistic speech, combining the Bible's lyricism with a Jewish American dialect reminiscent of the comic routines of such humorists as **Lenny Bruce**, **Mel Brooks**, and **Woody Allen**.

Heller wed Shirley Held in 1945, and the marriage dissolved in 1986, the same year that Heller contracted Guillain-Barre Syndrome, a life-threatening neurological disease. At Mt. Sinai Hospital he met Valerie Humphries, a nurse, who cared for him during his illness. They married in 1987. Heller died of heart failure in 1999 and was survived by a daughter, Erica, and a son, Theodore. *See also* **Literature**.

John M. McLarnon

Further Reading: Pinsker, Sanford. *Understanding Joseph Heller.* Columbia, SC: University of South Carolina Press, 1991. Sheppard, R. Z. "Speaking About the Unspeakable." *Time,* March 12, 1979. Vogel, Speed. *No Laughing Matter.* New York: G.P. Putnam's Sons, 1986.

HESCHEL, ABRAHAM JOSHUA (1907–1972)

Rabbi Heschel was the leading Jewish theologian and religious thinker in the United States following World War II. He was also a well-known social and political activist, a leading figure in the civil rights movement of the 1960s and the anti-Vietnam War movement in the same era. Heschel was born in Warsaw into a prominent family of Hasidic rebbes. He was part of the Apter and Novomisker dynasties and also related to the dynasties of Rizhin and Chernobel, among others. He was also a descendant of the founder of the Hasidic movement, Rabbi Israel ben Eliezer, the Baal Shem Tov (died 1760). As a child he was taught in the spirit of joy of his ancestors and also the more strict and elitist manner of the Kotzker Hasidim, the chief force in the nineteenth-century Polish Hasidic movement. Heschel excelled in his religious studies and was ordained as a rabbi at a young age. He did not, as expected, assume the family mantle of Hasidic leadership as a rebbe. Rather, he chose to go to Vilna in Lithuania and study the secular world and develop his literary flair; he became a Yiddish poet of some note.

Heschel moved to Germany and studied Judaism at the Liberal Rabbinical Seminary in Berlin known as the Hochschule fur die Wissenschaft des Judentums. He also worked toward his doctoral studies at the University of Berlin. He received his doctorate and was ordained as a Liberal rabbi. Following a number of teaching positions in Nazi Germany he was expelled as a Polish citizen and assumed a position in Warsaw teaching Judaism.

Eventually Heschel arrived in the United States and served as a faculty member at the Hebrew Union College in Cincinnati, Ohio, where he taught various areas of Judaism between 1940–1946. Strong disagreements with the Jewish religious outlook expressed at HUC led to his joining the faculty of the Jewish Theological Seminary in New York, the rabbinical school of the Conservative movement. Here Heschel, ever the traditionalist, felt more at home.

Heschel was a multi-faceted academic whose interests included Polish Jewry, mysticism, Medieval Jewish religious thought, Maimonides, Hasidic thought, and Jewish ethics. Heschel, a prolific author, published numerous book and articles before his death in 1971. But Heschel was not a dry academic aiming at cold scholarship. Rather, through his writings Heschel hoped to renew and revive the relationship between God, Israel, and heritage. His interest in mysticism and Jewish theology brought him to the attention of the Christian religious community, to whom he became the chief proponent of Jewish religious thought and interpreter of Jewish religious tradition. He became close friends with theologians such as Reinhold Niebuhr.

Heschel was not only a scholar, he was a mystic —and this strand of his personality was reflected in the poetical style of many of his works. *Sabbath* and *Man Is Not Alone* were not typical dry academic studies; these works carried a deep mystical and poetical nature, revealing the God of the book's author. Heschel taught that every Jew and every person had the opportunity to come in contact with God the Creator, and that prayer was the manner in which this communication could be achieved. Heschel was also very interested in the post-biblical nature of prophecy, essentially arguing that a true saint can gain access to the true spirit of God.

A frequent speaker at both Jewish and non-Jewish religious conferences, Heschel had many lectures that were published as books or essays. He was also very active in the interfaith dialogue movement, especially in regards to the Second Vatican Council. Heschel traveled to Rome a number of times and not only met the pope several of them, but he also became friendly with important Catholic theologians such as Cardinal Bea of Germany. Heschel's participation at the Council remains controversial because some, like Rabbi Joseph Baer Soloveitchik of Yeshiva University, believed that Heschel exaggerated his role in the deliberations.

Heschel gained respect for his personal involvement in the civil rights movement. He strongly supported the African American community's struggle to attain equal rights. He not only participated, but he took a leadership role, becoming a close friend and confidant of the Reverend Martin Luther King Jr. He joined King in many of the movements' historic marches and demonstrations, thus emerging as the Jewish face in this struggle. During these marches he likened marching to "praying with your feet." A stalwart leader in the anti-Vietnam War movement, Heschel was one of the best-known religious voices against the war. He joined the Berrigan brothers and the Reverend William Sloane Coffin of Yale as the religious leaders of this struggle.

By the time of his death, Heschel was regarded by the Christian community as a modern incarnation of an Old Testament prophet and as a man of supreme moral principles. He was also held in very high regard in the Jewish community. Though he was not regarded as a great classroom teacher, individual students like Rabbis Wolfe Kelman, Seymour Siegel, Art Green, and Samuel Dresner, among others, were his true disciples. Since the seminary was chiefly interested in cold intellectual scholarship, Heschel was looked upon with suspicion, because of his mystical nature and his philosophy of depth theology.

Heschel was a strictly observant Jew in his private life and remained under the influence of his Hasidic ancestors throughout his life. Except for some close relatives (the Kopishnitzer rebbe and Boyaner rebbe) and some personal friends (Rabbi Leib Cywiack), he had almost no connection with the Orthodox institutional world. Although he spent time in Berlin in the 1930s with such Orthodox luminaries as Rabbi Joseph B. Soloveitchik and the Lubavitcher rebbe, Rabbi Menachem M. Schneerson, there is no evidence that they were close or in contact while he was in the United States. Heschel was also active in other areas of interest such as the Soviet Jewry movement and Jewish education. Today Heschel is chiefly remembered in the popular sense by his Old Testament image of a flowing white beard and by his criticism of the social ills of the United States in the 1960s, as evidenced by the mistreatment of American blacks and the reckless American adventure in Southeast Asia. Heschel not only preached against these injustices, but he took a personal role in the crusade.

Heschel died of a heart attack in December 1972. He embodied the phrase he coined, "Life without commitment is not worth living." He lived a very committed life. Heschel's daughter, Dr. Susannah Heschel, holds the Eli Black Chair in Jewish Studies in the Department of Religion at Dartmouth College.

Zalman Alpert

Further Reading: Kaplan, Edward K. *Abraham Joshua Heschel in America, 1940–1972.* Yale University Press, 2007.

HOFFMAN, DUSTIN (1937–)

Dustin Hoffman is a two-time Academy Award and six-time Golden Globe recipient whose role starring in *The Graduate* made him one of the most famous actors in film history. Hoffman was born in Los Angeles on August 8, 1937, to a Polish Jewish family. His mother, Lillian Gold, was a jazz pianist, and his father, Harry Hoffman, worked as a prop supervisor/set decorator at Columbia Pictures before becoming a furniture salesman.

While he was not raised in a Jewish-oriented family (he did not know he was Jewish until age 10), his connection to his Jewish heritage was always present. He credits his second wife, Lisa Gottsegen, for his embrace of Judaism. As he reveals in Abigail Pogrebin's book *Stars of David,* "My wife changed everything," he said, "two sons bar mitzvahed, two daughters bat mitzvahed." He continued, about his connection, "I have very strong feelings that I am a Jew," punctuating the declaration with his fist, stating, "and particularly, I am a Russian, Romanian Jew. I love herring and vodka; I feel it comes from something in my DNA. I do love these things. And I know I have a strong reaction to any anti-Semitism."

As a young man, Hoffman had hopes of making it big in the movies, but it took him quite a while to do so. He worked as a waiter, as a typist for the yellow pages, and as a fragrance tester for Maxwell House. It wasn't until Mike Nichols cast him opposite Anne Bancroft in *The Graduate* that he gained some success. Initially, he was not sure he would be right for the role of Benjamin Braddock, once saying, "I had read the book, and I said, 'Mr. Nichols, I'm not right for this part. Benjamin Braddock is tall, he's blond, he's Anglo-Saxon. I'm too Jewish. And when I don't feel connected, I get in trouble, I get tied up in knots and I argue with everyone.' 'Read it again,' Mike said, 'but this time, think of Ben as Jewish' " (Pogrebin, 2005). The rest is, as they say, history.

After his turn as a disaffected college student in *The Graduate,* he was offered a number of similar roles. Wanting to avoid being typecast, he accepted the role of Ratzo Rizzo in *Midnight Cowboy.* This part, such a direct departure from his role of Benjamin, earned him recognition for his acting versatility. He has won two Academy Awards, one in 1979 for *Kramer vs. Kramer* and the other in 1989 for *Rain Man.* In 1999, he was honored by the American Film Institute with a lifetime achievement award. *See also* **Film.**

Judith Lupatkin

Further Reading: Pogrebin, Abigail. "Dustin Hoffman." *Stars of David.* New York: Broadway Books, 2005.

HOLIDAYS AND RITUALS

The Sabbath. The holiest day on the Jewish calendar, the Sabbath, which begins on Friday at sundown and concludes on Saturday evening, is a day when observant Jews, mostly among the Orthodox, refrain from, among other activities, work, transportation, and lighting fire. It is also a day devoted to prayer and the study of Torah. The laws in regard to the Sabbath emanate from the Torah and the Talmud, but in practice many Jews ignore these prohibitions. This may be because most Jews generally do not follow the Halacha (or Jewish law) pertaining to the Sabbath or most other Jewish holidays. This lack of observance, added to the general assimilation of most Jews to the secularism of American life, has resulted in treating the Sabbath as a day of relaxation and play, not unlike their non-Jewish neighbors.

The High Holy Days. The Jewish High Holy Days—Rosh Hashanah, the Jewish New Year, and Yom Kippur or Day of Atonement, a day of fasting, are considered, next to the Sabbath, the holiest days of the Jewish calendar. During both Rosh Hashanah and Yom Kippur, the emphasis is on synagogue attendance, where the focus of the service is on prayer and contemplating the "sins" committed during the past year, as well as asking forgiveness from those who may have been maligned. Unlike Rosh Hashanah, where traditional holiday meals are prepared after services, Yom Kippur is a day wherein Jews fast for 25 hours. During the Yom Kippur service we plead to God for forgiveness for our transgressions and to place our name in the "Book of Life" for the coming year.

In Hollywood, the solemnity of Yom Kippur was displayed in *The Jazz Singer,* the first movie with sound (1927), starring Al Jolson, and its remake with Neil Diamond (1980), which tells the quintessential story of the conflict between maintaining tradition and assimilating into secular society that many first- and second-generation Jews faced and still face in America.

Specifically, on Rosh Hashanah, the solemnity of the day is offset by the special meals that are served after the synagogue services, which include dipping apples in honey with the meal, signifying the hope for a "sweet" year. There is the also the popular ceremony of Tashlich (casting), whereby Jews will go to a nearby stream and empty their pockets, a symbol of casting away one's sins. Like the Sabbath, there is a prohibition on work and travel, although as more Jews have moved to the suburbs, they have been forced to travel to synagogue. Even in Orthodox synagogues, many rabbis have "looked the other way" when it comes to their congregants using automobiles to come to services, lest none show up at all. On Yom Kippur, the requirement is to fast for 25 hours. Inasmuch as all Jewish holidays, including the Sabbath, begin at sundown, commencing with the lighting of candles, the fast does not conclude until sundown the next day.

The Three Pilgrimage Festivals. The ancient Hebrews were commanded to celebrate the "Shalosh Regalim—Three Festivals" "in the place the Lord your God will choose" (Deuteronomy 16:16). All of the major Jewish holidays originate in the Torah or the Five Books of Moses. These holidays are not only religious in the sense of observance but also reflect the history and agricultural year of the ancient Israelites. These are:

1. "Pesach—Passover—The Festival of the Spring" (Nisan 15, normally in the beginning of April).
2. "Shavuot—Feast of Weeks—Harvest Festival" (observed two days in America, one day in Israel Sivan 6, around May or June).
3. "Sukkot—Tabernacles" (eight days including "Shemini Atzeret—Eighth Day of Solemn Assembly," beginning on Tishre 15, soon after Passover).

Pesach—Passover. Passover, the first of the three Pilgrimage Festivals, celebrated for eight days in the Diaspora and for seven days in the land of Israel, has both a historical and an agricultural significance.

According to the Torah, Pesach commemorates the exodus of the children of Israel from Egyptian slavery. The agricultural significance is as a spring festival celebrated at the beginning of the barley harvest.

Passover is referred to by various names as well.

1. Chag ha-Matzot—The Festival of Unleavened Bread (Exodus 12:15).
2. Pesach-Passover—Referred to in the Bible as the angel of death who "passed over" the houses of the children of Israel when he slew all the firstborn of the Egyptians (Exodus 12:27). This also applied to the paschal lamb (korban pesach).
3. Z'-man Che-ru-tenu—The Season of Our Freedom. Passover celebrates the liberation of our ancestors from Egyptian bondage and the Jewish peoples' emergence as a free nation.
4. Chag ha-Aviv—The Spring Festival, which marks the beginning of the barley harvest.

The first two days of Passover are celebrated with a Seder each evening (in Israel, only one day). At the Seder, the Haggadah or book (the word means "telling") is read, which recounts the story of the Israelites' liberation from slavery as told in the book of Exodus. At the Seder, special foods are eaten. In addition, a Seder plate, which consists of a boiled egg, greens, a shankbone, and bitter herbs are prominently displayed for the purpose of symbolizing the bitterness of slavery. Matzah or unleavened bread is also included to commemorate the Hebrews' sudden departure from Egypt and the makeshift bread that they ate in the desert. Observant Jews do not eat bread for the entire length of the holiday and substitute matzah instead as well as non-grain or wheat derivatives. During the Seder, the tradition is to drink four cups of wine to represent the joy of freedom; another cup of wine, the Elijah cup, considered to be the "Cup Of Salvation," is also placed on the Seder table to symbolize the coming of the Messianic age.

More than any other Jewish holiday, Passover is the one most familiar to non-Jews. Some historians believe that the Last Supper was actually a Seder, attended by Jesus and his disciples in observance of Passover. In recent years the Passover Seder has been symbolically reproduced in many Christian churches. Because the Passover Seder is observed in the home as opposed to the synagogue, the ecumenical nature of the holiday has involved non-Jews. Christians are often invited to participate in the Seder ceremony by their Jewish neighbors, especially in those families where the Seder is conducted in English. Although the movie does not deal directly with Passover, Hollywood indirectly told the story first in the silent film version of *The Ten Commandments* (1923) and then again in the blockbuster remake in 1956 starring Charlton Heston as Moses. More recently, Broadway utilized the Passover Seder in the play *Beau Jest,* a hilarious comedy in which the father, portrayed by Bernie Landis, specializes in leading a shortcut Seder, emphasizing wine and food at the expense of religious ritual ("We were slaves, and then we were free, let's eat"). Hollywood turned to Passover with its release of *When Do We Eat?* (2005). The comedy involves a dysfunctional family gathered around the Seder table, when the family patriarch is slipped a hallucinogenic drug during the meal, which turns the overly critical head of the family to embrace the spirit of the holiday, vowing to guide his contentious clan toward forgiveness and harmony.

Shavuot—Feast of Weeks—Harvest Festival. Shavuot is the second of the major festival holidays. The name "Weeks" derives from the biblical instruction according to Exodus 34:22, Leviticus 23:15, and Deuteronomy 16:9–10 to count seven weeks from the time of the Passover harvest festival, at the end of which a second harvest festival was to be observed. Shavuot is also called, according to Exodus 23:16, "Chag ha-Katsir" (the Harvest Festival) and according to Numbers 28:26 "Yom ha-Bikkurim" (the Day of the First Ripe Fruits)—when the Israelites were to bring a special thanks-offering to the Temple. After the Temple's destruction, the main emphasis has shifted to the festival's identification as the anniversary of the giving of the Torah at Mount Sinai, when the "Asseret ha-Dibrot" (the Ten Commandments) were proclaimed to the assembled children of Israel.

Observant Jews attend synagogue where, in addition to the regular holiday service, the book of Ruth is read. Over the years, the custom has arisen to eat dairy meals on this holiday. The meaning and requirements of these major Jewish holidays are observed in synagogues but also are taught in Jewish day schools, yeshivas, and Talmud Torahs in all branches of Judaism—Orthodox, Conservative, Reform, and Reconstruction, albeit with different interpretations as well as forms of observance.

In many communities (particularly in America), the festival also marks the graduation of teenagers from the formal synagogue educational framework, or Confirmation.

Sukkot. Sukkot, or Booths, which in the Jewish calendar follows Rosh Hashanah and Yom Kippur, recalls the wandering of the Hebrews in the desert following the exodus from Egypt; Jewish law requires that following the Day of Atonement, a sukkah be constructed where meals are eaten, replicating how the Israelites of old survived for 40 years before reaching the promised land. Simchat Torah concludes the eight-day holiday that commenced with Sukkot. The Torah is read in the synagogue every Monday, Thursday, and Saturday, as well as on the major Jewish holidays, and Simchat Torah celebrates the conclusion of the reading of the last book of the Torah. The Torah is not only believed by observant Jews to be a work of divine creation, but it was also seen by such secular Jews as David Ben-Gurion, Israel's first prime minister, as the history of the ancient Jewish people.

The various names given to this festival provide a comprehensive explanation of its purpose:

1. Chag ha-Asif—The Festival of the Ingathering [of crops] (Exodus 23:16, 34:22), pointing to its agricultural importance.
2. Chag ha-Sukkot—The Festival of Tabernacles (Leviticus 23:34, Deuteronomy 13, 16), commemorating Israel's experience in the wilderness under God's protection.
3. Chag—The Festival (Leviticus 23: 39–41, Numbers 29:12), a name popular with the rabbis, as if to suggest that Sukkot was the holiday par excellence, and
4. Zeman Simchatenu—The Season of our Rejoicing (Deuteronomy 15:14–15), a liturgical designation reflecting the Bible's commandment to "be altogether joyful!"

Hanukkah. When we turn to Hanukkah, we deal with a minor Jewish festival which has become Judaism's most popular holiday. Celebrated for eight days with specials prayers, songs, and the lighting of the "Chanukiah" or "Menorah" (Hanukkah Candelabra, which utilizes either olive oil or candles) every night of Hanukkah, followed in many households by the giving of presents, the holiday normally occurs on or around the time Christians celebrate Christmas. Most unfortunately, there are Jews who feel more excluded on the Christmas holiday than during any other holiday on the calendar. Although some Jews view it as an American holiday (Irving Berlin thought as much and composing "White Christmas" was his testimony to this belief) and have Christmas trees in their homes, without truly realizing what they are doing by celebrating Christmas/Hanukkah they are desecrating the true meaning of either holiday, and many Christians feel insulted by this practice. Then, there are other Jews who understand and respect that it is a Christian holiday.

Envying the glitz and overwhelming presence of Christmas in American culture, Jews have attempted to make Hanukkah its equivalent in terms of appeal to its own community. Hanukkah in America, therefore, has become a holiday characterized by the giving of presents, Hanukkah pageants, and dinners in synagogues.

Hanukkah celebrates the victory of the ancient Hebrews over the Assyrian Greeks, who sought to desecrate the Temple and destroy Judaism. Led by Mattit-ya-hu, the high priest, and later succeeded by his son, Judah Maccabee, and his followers, the ancient Hebrews triumphed and proceeded to reclaim and cleanse the Holy Temple. The lighting of the Hanukkah candles is associated with the miracle of Hanukkah, whereby in purifying the Temple in Jerusalem, the Hebrews found a container of pure olive oil, bearing the unbroken seal of the Kohen Gadol (the "high priest"), which contained enough oil to last one night—but it lasted miraculously for eight days. Hence the miracle of Hanukkah is a holiday which resonates with the American public because the Hebrews fought for the principle of religious freedom.

Hanukkah, unlike the Sabbath or the major Jewish holidays, has no special restrictions, but there are special foods, such as Potato Latkes (potato pancakes) fried in olive oil (for Jews of Eastern European descent) and Sufganiyot, (doughnuts) fried in oil (for German Jews and Israeli Jews). For the young, there is the game of dreidel (Sevivon) and Hanukkah Gelt (chocolate that is shaped like a coin and wrapped in golden foil).

Adam Sandler's popular "Chanukah Song" is most certainly an inaccurate representation of the real meaning of Hanukkah. It is rather a funny, comedic presentation which actually demeans and cheapens the holiday. In the same category is the treatment of the holiday in several episodes of *The Simpsons,* among other examples, which has made its way into popular culture. On the other hand, there is "Light One Candle" by

Peter Yarrow, performed by Peter, Paul and Mary on their album "A Holiday Celebration," which exemplifies the real heart and spirit of Hanukkah.

But there is also another side to the Christmas-Hanukkah holiday season. Exacerbating the Christmas-Hanukkah divide is the manner in which the holiday season is observed. Many Jews (but also Hindus, Buddhists, atheists, and other non-Christians) object to Christmas trees, representations of nativity scenes, and Christmas celebrations in government spaces, as well as in public schools, as a violation of the separation of church and state. Some Orthodox Jews, especially among the Lubavitcher Hasidim, do not seem to object to the crèche in public places; they actually encourage it as long as there is also a Menorah to counterbalance it. The Orthodox Jews who feel this way also believe, along with their Evangelical counterparts, that there should be no separation of church and state. This way they could benefit from federal funding for their private parochial schools. Thus, along with the joy of the season, there also exists an ongoing culture war between Christians and some Orthodox Jews, on one side, and those who oppose the holiday displaying any religious symbols, on the other side. This is especially a problem in schools where not only is there conflict over the placement of Christmas trees and over the type of songs that are used in Christmas concerts or holiday concerts, but also there is conflict in the way the celebration is defined. Is it a "holiday" or "winter" concert? Or a "Christmas" concert? Christian groups have charged that "Christ is being taken out of Christmas" (rightly so), and they resent that holidays like Hanukkah gain parity with the true meaning of the holiday season. Thus, as we have become a more multicultural society, the schools have become a primary battleground for this culture war with no easy resolution in sight.

Purim. Purim, like Hanukkah, is a minor holiday on the Jewish calendar. The holiday celebrates the deliverance of the Jews of Persia from annihilation because of the intervention of Queen Esther who, along with her Uncle Mordecai, thwarted the plans of Haman to murder the Jews. The story is told in synagogues from the biblical scroll of Esther (Megillat Esther), which relates how the king's chief minister, Haman, cast lots to determine the day upon which to exterminate the Jews. During the reading of the Megillat, a gragger (ra-ashon) or a noisy rattle is used to drown out the name of Haman whenever his name is mentioned in the reading. Purim is characterized by gift-giving, special food—such as the triangular-shaped cookies called "Hamantashen," the giving of charity to the poor, and taking part in other customs including drinking wine; this is the only Jewish holiday where Jews are permitted to become inebriated, to the point where they do not know the difference between the names of "Haman" or "Mordecai." Some synagogues include a Queen Esther contest as part of the celebration.

A politician running for office recently was criticized for comparing Purim to Halloween, but their only similarity is in the dressing up in costumes that is characteristic of both celebrations. Hollywood has made two films about the Purim story, *Queen Esther* (1948), and *One Night with the King* (2005). Neither films were commercial successes.

Tisha B'Av—The Ninth of Av. During the Hebrew month of Av (normally around August), Tisha B'Av, the "Ninth of Av," is the saddest day in the Jewish calendar—a day of fasting and mourning. This day commemorates the destruction of the First Temple by the Babylonians under Nebuchadnezzar in 586 BCE and the destruction of the Second Temple by the Roman legions of Titus in 70 CE. The destruction of Jerusalem and the loss of the Jewish state are not the only sad events that have occurred on the ninth of Av. The Mishnah enumerates the following: "On the ninth of Av it was decreed against our fathers that they should not enter the Land of Israel" (Numbers 14:29); in 135 CE, Bar Kochba's last surviving fortress, Betar, fell to Hadrian's legions; traditionally this occurred on Tisha B'Av, and Jerusalem was ploughed up.

On July 18, 1290 (coinciding with the Fast of Av), the Jews were expelled from England, and the expulsion of the Jews from Spain occurred on the same day in 1492. Tisha B'Av also marked the outbreak of World War I, beginning a long period of suffering for the Jewish people. Not only did this period witness the pogroms and massacres perpetrated against the Jews of Russia, Poland, and other countries of Eastern Europe, but it was also a prelude to World War II and the savage destruction of six million Jews. Tisha B'Av has became synonymous with oppression and exile.

The special scroll reading for Tisha B'Av is the book of Lamentations (Megillat Echah), which describes the destruction of Jerusalem and the Temple in poetic and moving terms.

Despite the tragedy associated with the Ninth of Av, it is held that Tisha B'Av will eventually become an occasion for rejoicing (Zechariah 8:19), and the rabbis identified it with the birthday of the Messiah.

In the State of Israel, thousands attend services at the Western Wall below the Temple Mount, and Tisha B'Av is observed as a day of public mourning. All restaurants and places of entertainment are closed, while radio and television programs emphasize various aspects of the occasion.

Rites of Passage. Every religion has rites of passage, and Judaism is no exception. The most enduring rites are the Brit Milah and the Bar and Bat Mitzvah.

Brit Milah. Brit Milah or ritual circumcision owes its origins to the Torah, where it is written, "This is my covenant that you shall observe between Me and you and your children after you, to circumcise your every male. You shall circumcise the flesh of your foreskin, and it shall become the sign of the covenant between Me and you" (Genesis 17:1). For thousands of years the Jewish people have followed this commandment, which is carried out eight days after the birth of a male child. The Brit is performed by a mohel, a Torah-observant Jew (often the mohel is also a rabbi or cantor), trained not only in Jewish law but also in medical laws pertaining to the Brit Milah, with a special expertise in Jewish ritual circumcision.

Although in a growing number of Jewish families the decision to have "the circumcision" is being made to have the ritual performed by a pediatric surgeon at the hospital, it does not fulfill the biblical requirement of a Jewish ritual circumcision.

The mohel and circumcision in general are often portrayed as objects of ridicule in popular culture, in the form of bad jokes. In 1970, a *Saturday Night Live* parody car commercial for a Royal Deluxe II showed the smoothness of the car's ride by having a mohel perform a circumcision in the backseat while the chauffeur is driving 40 miles per hour on a bumpy road.

Thirty-three years later, in September 1993, this was further exemplified in a notorious episode of *Seinfeld* where the circumcision is performed by a mohel who is portrayed as a borderline lunatic. It portrays Brit Milah as a humorous and barbaric act. What makes it worse is that many of the writers for these shows are Jewish, and all they accomplish is to denigrate their own religion for a laugh.

Bar—Bat Mitzvah. "Bar" and "Mitzvah" are popularly translated as "son [or daughter] of the commandment." The Mishnah (Avot 5.21) states that 13 is the age for observing the commandments (Mitzvot). There is no evidence, however, of a Bar Mitzvah ceremony prior to 1400, and major codifiers of the Oral Law, such as Isaac Alfasi (11th century) and Maimonides (12th century) do not mention it.

When a boy reaches age 13 and a girl age 12, they automatically assume the responsibility of being a young adult member of the Jewish community, counted as a part of the minyan, the quorum of 10 required for a formal prayer service and to read the Torah and recite the mourner's Kaddish. Nowhere mentioned in the Torah, the Bar and Bat Mitzvah ceremony is not required, but it has become a common practice for both boys and girls to study in Hebrew school their portion of the Torah (the section that corresponds with their Hebrew birthday) and be called up to chant it in a synagogue service to mark this milestone event, which is generally followed by a celebration to commemorate this rite of passage. The celebration, however, has been the subject of much criticism as many parents attempt to outdo one another in the lavish affair that follows the synagogue service.

CBS in 1981 aired a failed 100-minute television pilot called "Rivkin: Bounty Hunter," based on the real-life episodes of "Stan Rivkin," a father, widower, and Jewish bounty hunter. The film starred Ron Leibman as Rivkin, Abraham Barzak as the rabbi, and Harry Morgan as a kindly old retired priest neighbor who lived next door to Rivkin and his physically disabled, wheelchair-bound 12-year-old son—who is, oddly, being tutored by the retired priest for his becoming a Bar Mitzvah.

On the Sabbath of his son's Bar Mitzvah, Rivkin had an emergency call to track down a bail jumper. The suspense builds as the service continues with everyone watching the door. Just as the boy, with tears in his eyes, is about to recite the Torah Blessings, his father comes bursting into the synagogue in the nick of time. This was a tender, somewhat meaningful portrayal of a modern-day Bar Mitzvah.

The recent comedy film *Keeping Up with the Steins* (2006), however, satirizes this religious ceremony when it depicts how too many Jewish families see a Bar Mitzvah or Bat Mitzvah not as a coming of age for their son or daughter, but rather as an excuse to throw an outrageously expensive party. Unfortunately there has been too much emphasis placed on the "Bar" and not enough on the "Mitzvah"; hopefully our modern-day clergy are remedying this situation.

Israel J. Barzak

Further Reading: Bloch, Abraham P. *The Biblical and Historical Background of the Jewish Holy Days.* Ktav, 1978. Raphael, Chaim. *The Festival Days: A History of Jewish Celebrations.* Weidenfeld and Nicholson, 1990). Schauss, Hayyim. *The Jewish Festivals: History and Observance.* Schocken Books, 1962. Strassfeld, Michael. *The Jewish Holidays: A Guide and Commentary.* Harper and Row, 1985. Zevin, Rabbi Shlomo Yosef. *The Festivals in Halachah: An Analysis of the Development of the Festival Laws.* Two volumes. Mesorah Publications, 1999.

HOLLIDAY, JUDY (1921–1965)

Born Judith Tuvim (Hebrew for "holidays") in New York on June 21, 1921, Judy Holliday was a precocious child who became a movie star playing "dumb blondes." Hiding her intelligence became her trademark in movies such as *Adam's Rib* (1949) and *Born Yesterday* (1950). In both of these films she displayed a wide-eyed innocence, but in her alleged simplicity, she often expressed profound truths. Holliday began performing on the night club circuit in the 1940s, joining Betty Comden and Adolph Green as *The Revuers.* They sang and performed skits.

Judy Holliday went to Hollywood in the late 1940s. *Adam's Rib* was her first major role, in which she starred with Katharine Hepburn and Spencer Tracy. Holliday played the part of a wronged wife who, after shooting her husband, is defended in court by Katharine Hepburn. Hepburn uses the courtroom as a forum for feminism. The movie, a comedy, gave all of the principals an opportunity to show off.

Holliday was raised as an only child by her **Yiddish**-speaking, socialist parents, Abe and Helen Tuvim. They divorced when she was two, and her mother encouraged her artistic talents by enrolling her in ballet school when she was a child. She graduated at the top of her class from Julia Richman High School in 1938 and immediately went into show business. In 1948, she married David Oppenheim and had a son, Jonathan, in 1952. The couple divorced in 1957.

Holliday won an Oscar in 1950 for *Born Yesterday,* and though she had two further hits, *The Solid Gold Cadillac* (1956) and *Bells Are Ringing* (1960), Hollywood had a hard time casting her. During the early 1950s, when Congress and the Senate were investigating Hollywood communist-front organizations, Judy Holliday was called before the Senate Internal Security Subcommittee in 1952, and she was advised to "play dumb." She did and was not indicted or blackballed by Hollywood producers. Nevertheless, her movie career declined. Judy Holliday died of breast cancer on June 7, 1965. *See also* **Film; Film Stars**.

June Sochen

Further Reading: Jewish Women's Archives. "Jewish Women in Comedy." www.joo.com.pl/jewish-woman.php.

HOLLYWOOD MOGULS

The American film industry was created by a handful of first- or second-generation Jewish American immigrants, who, as film historian Neal Gabler has explained, virtually invented Hollywood. Each of the six major film studios can trace its origins to the vision of these entrepreneurs—Metro-Goldwyn-Mayer (Louis B. Mayer), Warner Brothers (Jack and Harry Warner), Paramount (Adolph Zukor), and 20th Century Fox (William Fox), Universal-International (Carl Laemmle), and Columbia (Harry Cohn). They came from Jewish immigrant families that had strong ties to their faith. Yet, as they moved into adulthood, they retained tenuous connection to Judaism and the Jewish community. They were assimilationists in their personal life and conservative in political views. Their films, made under the rigid Motion Picture Production Code, were patriotic and moralistic and painted a vision of America that was decent, optimistic, and strong. Unlike movies of the later era, evil was never found in the upper reaches of the American government.

These moguls were defensive and fearful of anti-Semitic attacks. In the years prior to Pearl Harbor, they were pressured by isolationists such Ambassador Joseph P. Kennedy, Senator Gerald Nye, Senator Burton Wheeler, and Charles Lindbergh for their pro-British, pro-intervention political support and for their anti-Nazi films. Joseph Kennedy warned the major Jewish studio heads in a private meeting held in 1940 that they should stop making anti-Nazi pictures and using films to influence public opinion. He warned of growing anti-Semitism and that the Jews would be blamed for any American involvement in the war. In a famous speech in Des Moines, Charles Lindbergh made a very similar point. Those attacks ended with Pearl Harbor, and Hollywood films once again were tuned into American patriotic spirit.

During the Cold War the studio heads, in a climate of public anticommunist sentiment, reassured critics of their unqualified opposition to communist influence. In November 1947, meeting at the Waldorf-Astoria in New York, film executives representing all major studios issued a statement promising that the five members of the Hollywood Ten still in their employ would be fired as would anyone else who refused to answer questions about their communist affiliations.

Who were these creators of Hollywood? Harry Cohn (1891–1958), the son of a German Jewish tailor and a Russian Jewess, left school at an early age and pursued a variety of dead-end jobs. He began a film career in 1918 as the personal secretary to Carl Laemmle. Two years later he, along with his brother Jack and others, founded the C.B.C. Film Sales Company. Harry soon left for Hollywood to begin film production under the aegis of the company. The company became Columbia Pictures (1924), with Harry as the studio chief. In the ensuing decades, Cohn elevated Columbia from a "poverty row" operation to the rank of major studio. In the 1930s Columbia produced many of the legendary Frank Capra films, and in the 1940s the company profits skyrocketed through the production of slick "B" pictures and occasional major productions such as *Gilda*.

Like many of the other moguls, Harry Cohn rejected Judaism and avoided any association with a synagogue or formal Jewish organization. He had a reputation as a bully and vulgar despot; he regularly spied on his employees, hiring and firing them at will. Some considered him the most hated man in Hollywood. Nonetheless, he had an uncanny understanding of the film business. Under Cohn's leadership Columbia became a major studio.

Louis B. Mayer (1885–1957) was born in Minsk, Russia. His family immigrated to New Brunswick, Canada when he was three. The son of a junk dealer, he moved to Boston as young man. There he met his first wife, Margaret Shenberg, and briefly established a scrap metal business. When the business failed in 1907, Mayer leased a burlesque house in Haverhill, Massachusetts and converted it into a motion picture house. Soon he had the largest chain of movie theaters in New England. He became a film distributor, making a considerable profit from the distribution of the legendary film *Birth of a Nation.* He took those profits and invested in his own production company, Louis B. Mayer Pictures. With the success of his first picture, *Virtuous Wives,* Mayer moved his family and his company to Hollywood. In 1924 the company merged with the Metro-Goldwyn company, controlled by Marcus Loew, the owner of the largest theater chain in America. The company was called Metro-Goldwyn-Mayer (MGM). Louis Mayer became the vice president and general manager, a position he held until 1951.

Under Mayer's guidance, MGM became the gold standard of the industry. Mayer, as did other Hollywood Moguls, ruled the company as his own family. He dictated the public behavior of his stars and punished insubordination. He had a capacity to select talent and he understood popular taste. Mayer hired brilliant production chiefs such as Irving Thalberg and **(Isidore) Dore Schary**, and he built legendary stars such as Greta Garbo, Norma Scharer, Joan Crawford, Lana Turner, Judy Garland, Clark Gable, Spencer Tracy, Robert Taylor, and William Powell. His films, mostly wholesome and patriotic, extolled and idealized American life.

An active Republican and political conservative, Mayer had a marginal association with Judaism and the Jewish community. He was personally closer to made leading Catholic prelates. In 1951, he struggled with Dore Schary and was ousted from the studio. Schary became his successor. Mayer's ouster marked the beginning of the end of a Hollywood era in which big studios controlled the business and films conformed to a rigid production code.

Adolph Zukor (1873–1976) was born in Risce, Hungary and came to the United States at the age of 15. Raised by an uncle, Kalman Lieberman, a devout and scholarly Jew, Adolph was expected to enter the rabbinate. His brother, Arthur, became a rabbi in Berlin; Adolph, once in America, had no such interest in the profession or in Judaism. By the time he was 30, Zukor made a substantial fortune in the fur business. He invested in penny arcades and Marcus Loew's motion picture theater chain. In 1912, he purchased the rights to distribute a French-made feature film, *Queen Elizabeth,* starring the great Sarah Bernhardt. The success of the film proved to Zukor that there was a market for feature-length films. He opened his own production company, Famous Players. Though movies were considered cheap entertainment for the lower classes, Zukor attempted to raise the sophistication level to reach a broad middle-class audience. His first productions were film versions of such classic novels as *The Count of Monte Cristo, The Prisoner of Zenda,* and *Tess of the D'Urbervilles.* He soon signed Mary Pickford, perhaps the most popular of the silent film stars, whose films became a gold mine. Famous Players soon acquired a small film company, Paramount, and adopted its name. By 1920 Zukor had achieved his goal. Motion pictures had become the most popular entertainment in America, and Paramount had become a major studio, whereby Zukor, as president of the company, became one of the most powerful men in the business. Zukor, as president of the company, became one of the most powerful men in the business.

In 1936, he was replaced as president, but he remained the figurehead chairman of the board. He continued his association with the company until his death at the age of 103.

Carl Laemmle (1867–1939) was born to a middle-class German Jewish family in Laupheim in southwestern Germany. He arrived in America in 1884. During his early years in America he moved from one dead-end job to another. When he moved to Oshkosh, Wisconsin, he found stability (a wife and family) and a decent job as clothing store manager. In 1906, Carl moved his family to Chicago and invested his savings in a storefront movie theater. Unlike the other movie theaters of that day, which were dirty and at the low end of the social scale, Laemmle's theater was clean and bright and designed to appeal to a middle-class audience. Soon he was also in the film distribution business, renting films to other theater owners. By 1909, the Laemmle Film Service was one of the largest film distributors in America. He defied pressure from Thomas Edison's Motion Picture Patents Company, which attempted to control film production and distribution. Laemmle started a production company known the Independent Motion Picture Company of America (IMP) and competed directly with Edison. He launched the company with a 16-minute film version of the famous Longfellow poem *Hiawatha.*

Laemmle was one of the first filmmakers to understand the value of glamour in the industry. He hired many stars of the day and provided them with plenty of publicity. As IMP flourished, Laemmle merged his company with a number of small companies to form Universal Pictures. By 1915, after a series of corporate battles, Laemmle was in control of Universal and opened the largest studio in the business. He a had strong sense of family loyalty, hiring numerous family members, including the young William Wyler. He also recognized talent, therefore hired Harry Cohn and Irving Thalberg as assistants.

Universal fell on hard time during the Depression, and Laemmle, battling health problems, turned the studio over to his son, Carl Laemmle Jr., who badly mismanaged it. As a consequence the Laemmles had to sell the studio in 1935 for a paltry sum of $5 million. The company made a comeback and remains one of the giants of the industry.

Jack Warner (1892–1978), the youngest and most famous of the brothers, was born in London, Ontario. He was one of 12 children of Jewish immigrants from Poland. In 1903, Jack, along with his older brothers Harry (1881–1958), Albert (1884–1967), and Sam (1888–1927) opened a nickelodeon in New Castle, Pennsylvania, and within a few years the brothers were in the film distribution business. Discouraged by the competition from Edison's Patents Company, they also went into the film production business. With the proceeds from their first success, *My Four Years in Germany,* an anti-German film that struck a popular chord during World War I, and with support from First National Bank, they purchased a studio in Los Angeles, calling it Warner Brothers. In 1925, with financial backing from the major Jewish investment house Goldman Sachs and Company, the Warners acquired the Vitagraph studio and its distribution network and were able add sound to movies. They began to purchase a network of movie theaters.

The Warners were on the cutting edge of a film revolution, producing the first major talking film, ***The Jazz Singer,*** with **Al Jolson**. *The Jazz Singer* tells the story a of a rabbi's son torn between carrying on his tradition and lure of show business. It was one of the few films the Jewish studio heads dared to produce that dealt explicitly with Jewish themes and the question of assimilation. The film brought tremendous success to the studio. The money they acquired was invested in over 500 movie theaters, record companies, and foreign film patents. They even financed Broadway shows.

Harry handled the company's finances, and Jack ran the studio. Jack Warner used a heavy hand to run the studio, which featured such legendary stars as Bette Davis, Humphrey Bogart, Jimmy Cagney, Joan Crawford, **Edward G. Robinson**, and Errol Flynn. Jack was tight fisted. His films were often social dramas, gangster movies, and black and white musicals. Warner Bros. did not produce the lavish spectacles characteristic of MGM. Harry and Jack feuded bitterly over the years, and eventually Harry sold his shares in the company. Jack stayed on as studio head until 1967. Today the company is part of the Time Warner communications empire.

The modern film industry was largely created by these self-educated American Jews, who embraced their new country with little regard for or interest in their own. Their films helped to create common culture to which many immigrants, Jews and others, gravitated. The industry became as essential an element in the story of American assimilation.

Robert Bresler

Further Reading: Gabler, Neal. *An Empire of Their Own: How the Jews Invented Hollywood.* New York: Doubleday, 1988. Schatz, Thomas. *The Genius of the System: Hollywood Filmmaking in the Studio Era.* New York: Pantheon Books, 1988.

THE HOLOCAUST IN AMERICAN CULTURE

American popular culture has engaged the Holocaust through literature, art, music, television, film, and cultural institutions since the end of World War II. Some of the best-known examples include the book *Anne Frank: The Diary of a Young Girl,* the television miniseries *Holocaust,* the **United States Holocaust Memorial Museum**, and the film ***Schindler's List***. The impact and significance of these efforts to understand the tragedy, and the questions of whether and how the Holocaust has been "Americanized," have been addressed, discussed, and debated by scholars and laypeople alike.

Perhaps the most popular book in the United States about the Holocaust is *Anne Frank: The Diary of a Young Girl,* first published in 1947 in Dutch. Having received a diary as a 13th-birthday present, Anne Frank began to write just three weeks before going into hiding in Amsterdam. In August 1944, the family's secret apartment was raided, and they were deported. Anne died in Bergen-Belsen in March 1945, just prior to liberation. After the war, her Dutch neighbors, who had found and saved Anne's writings, returned them to her father. Anne's work was published in English translation in 1952. It sold more than five million copies in the first two decades and was turned into a Pulitzer Prize- and Tony Award-winning play in 1955 and into a movie watched by millions when it premiered in 1959. The book has been translated into 67 languages and sold more than 31 million copies. It is often required reading for students, and many people who have not read the book still know Anne Frank's name and connect her with the Holocaust. While many first-person testimonies of the Holocaust have been published, the volume's popularity has been attributed to the ease with which young people are able to identify with the author, who writes not only about events outside of the hiding place, but also about her problems and thoughts as an adolescent. Anne Frank's story has come to be seen as representative of the scale of the atrocities and suffering that victims endured under the Nazis.

Such stories of unrelieved misery were traditionally shunned by television networks, but NBC decided to air the miniseries *Holocaust* in April 1978. In nine-and-a-half hours over four nights, the series recounted the Holocaust and its history from the perspective of a German Jewish family and a German family. Although the characters in the program were fictional, the docudrama referenced many Holocaust events, including Kristallnacht, the creation of ghettos, the deportations to camps, and the use of gas chambers. Approximately 120 million viewers watched at least some of the program, which earned a 49 percent market share and won 8 Emmy Awards, including Best Limited Series. Although *Holocaust* generated generally positive responses, they were not unanimous. Reviewers praised the cast (which included Meryl Streep, James Woods, and Michael Moriarty) and the script (written by **Gerald Green**), but critics argued that this historical atrocity had been turned into a soap opera. Many viewers also found the commercials too cheerful for the subject matter. The way for the broadcast was paved, however, by the previous year's miniseries about American slavery, *Roots,* which scored the largest Nielsen ratings in broadcast history (66 percent market share). For viewers, *Holocaust* was straightforward and accessible, and made millions—who might not otherwise have been—aware of the Holocaust.

President Jimmy Carter announced, just two weeks after the miniseries aired, the establishment of a commission to recommend a national Holocaust memorial, and the United States Holocaust Memorial Museum opened on April 22, 1993, as America's official memorial to the millions of European Jews and others killed and persecuted during the Holocaust by the Nazis and their allies. One of the most visited museums in Washington D.C., its goal is to advance and disseminate knowledge about the Holocaust, to preserve the memory of those who suffered, and to encourage visitors to reflect upon the questions raised by this unprecedented tragedy. The institution currently receives 1.6 million visitors a year, and it reaches millions more through its website (www.ushmm.org) and through outreach programs to students and educators; law enforcement officials and the military; and college students, graduate researchers, and professors in the United States and abroad via its Center for Advanced Holocaust Studies. The United States Holocaust Memorial Museum is the largest of the many institutions devoted to remembrance and teaching about the Holocaust that have been established throughout the United States since the late 1970s.

The opening of the United States Holocaust Memorial Museum was not the only major Holocaust-related cultural event in 1993. **Steven Spielberg** also released the motion picture *Schindler's List,* about a Sudeten-German Catholic businessman, Oskar Schindler, who saved more than a thousand Polish Jews during the Holocaust. Spielberg's film was based on Thomas Keneally's 1982 book of the same title (published initially in the United Kingdom as *Schindler's Ark*), inspired by Holocaust survivor Poldek Pfefferberg, a former laborer in Schindler's factory. Spielberg's film starred Liam Neeson as Schindler, Ralph Fiennes as SS officer Amon Göth, and Ben Kingsley as Schindler's secretary, Itzhak Stern. A box office success that grossed $96 million in three years, *Schindler's List* won seven Academy Awards, including Best Picture and Best Director. As with NBC's 1978 *Holocaust,* the film was accompanied by educational materials, was watched by more than 120 million Americans, and was the catalyst for a new institution for memorialization (that is, the Survivors of the Shoah Visual History Foundation). The educational impact of *Schindler's List* was even broader than *Holocaust,* however, because of the medium of motion pictures and the involvement of hugely successful director Steven Spielberg.

These four examples illustrate that the Holocaust as a topic has become increasingly mainstream within American culture, but scholars, religious leaders, and laypeople continue to debate the value of this greater awareness. Some are concerned that a focus on the tragedy of the Holocaust may come to outweigh other elements of Jewish identity, while others argue that initial interest in the Holocaust may lead students and adults to develop broader knowledge of Jewish history, culture, and religion. The Holocaust may also serve as a moral agent reminding people of the need to be tolerant of religious, cultural, and ethnic differences. If the last 60 years are any indication, discussion of the impact and role of the Holocaust in American culture is sure to continue far into the future.

Aleisa Fishman

Further Reading: Flanzbaum, Hilene, ed. *The Americanization of the Holocaust.* Baltimore: The Johns Hopkins University Press, 1999. Mintz, Alan. *Popular Culture and the Shaping of Holocaust Memory in America.* Seattle: University of Washington Press, 2001. Novick, Peter. *The Holocaust in American Life.* Boston: Houghton Mifflin, 1999.

HOLOCAUST REMEMBRANCE DAY

Responding to the near-successful state-authorized murder of European Jewry during World War II, but not limiting his response to this alone, professor and lawyer Raphael Lemkin coined and defined the term "genocide" as actions of deconstruction and elimination directed against individuals who are members of a national entity: "Generally speaking, genocide does not necessarily mean the immediate destruction of a nation, except when accomplished by mass killings of all members of a nation. It is intended rather to signify a coordinated plan of different actions aiming at the destruction of essential foundations of the life of national groups, with the aim of annihilating the groups themselves. The objectives of such a plan would be disintegration of the political and social institutions, of culture, language, national feelings, religion, and the economic existence of national groups, and the destruction of the personal security, liberty, health, dignity, and even the lives of the individuals belonging to such groups" (Lemkin, 1944). Lemkin's study influenced the original draft of the United Nations 1948 Convention on the Prevention and Punishment of the Crime of Genocide. Contextually and intellectually, the nuances and complexities related to the draft's definitions of physical genocide, biological genocide, and cultural genocide are implicit in Holocaust Remembrance Day.

Holocaust Remembrance Day is a day that has been set aside to remember the victims of the Holocaust and to educate Americans about what can happen to civilized people when anti-Semitism, racism, hatred, and indifference are not checked. To teach effectively against "dislike of the unlike," a unanimous act of the U.S. Congress in 1980 chartered the U.S. Holocaust Memorial Council, which was charged to build the United States Holocaust Memorial Museum, "America's national institution for the documentation, study, and interpretation of Holocaust history." The museum, adjacent to the National Mall in Washington D.C., was opened to the public in April 1993 after a somber dedication ceremony in the museum's Hall of Remembrance, which featured the lighting of the eternal flame by noted Holocaust survivor Elie Wiesel and President Bill Clinton. Among its activities, the museum sponsors annual Holocaust commemorations known as Days of Remembrance, highlighted by Holocaust Remembrance Day. Holocaust Remembrance Day is observed according to the Hebrew calendar date set by the Knesset of Israel to commemorate Yom ha-Shoah u-Mered ha-Getaot (Shoah and Ghetto Revolt Day), the national day of remembrance in Israel.

On April 12, 1951, the Knesset proposed Nisan 27 to be the date of remembrance. This was officially established by Israeli law in 1959. Viewpoints reflecting Jewish thought about the Shoah, such as, was the Great Catastrophe part of providential design, history, or a combination of both, generated debate over the date. Some argued that the Shoah is commensurable to the destruction of the Jerusalem Temple and thus the day should be observed on Asarah b'Tevet or Tishah b'Av. Others proposed April 19 to memorialize the Warsaw Ghetto uprising. However, the Knesset's 1951 reading of "The Decision Regarding the Establishment of a National Holiday Commemorating the Holocaust and Ghetto Revolt Remembrance" followed the reading for Yom ha-Atsmaut (Israel Independence Day), suggesting a conscientious redemptive link between the birth of the modern State of Israel and the destruction of European Jewry, a connection poignantly reflected in the cited prophetic verse delivered from God to Jerusalem: "And when I passed by thee, and saw thee wallowing in thy blood, I said unto thee: In thy blood, live; yea, I said unto thee: In thy blood, live" (Ezekiel 16:6).

Annual Holocaust Memorial Day is encouraged and supported by the United Nations, which acknowledges a shared responsibility to fight the evils of anti-Semitism, racism, genocide, xenophobia, and discrimination. Aside from the Jews, all victims of National Socialism are recognized. Thus the commemorative date of remembrance is January 27, the anniversary of the liberation of Auschwitz death camp by the Soviet Army in 1945. *See also* **The Holocaust in American Culture**; **United States Holocaust Memorial Museum**.

Zev Garber

Further Reading: Garber, Zev. "Dating the Shoah: In Your Blood Shall You Live," in Z. Garber, *Shoah:*

The Paradigmatic Genocide. Lanham, MD: University Press of America, 1994. Lemkin, Raphael. *Axis Rule in Occupied Europe: Laws of Occupation—Analysis of Government—Proposals for Redress.* Washington, DC: Carnegie Endowment for International Peace, 1944.

HOUDINI, HARRY (1874–1926)

Shrouded in mystery and known for sensational acts of escapism, the magician Houdini continues to capture the imagination and interest of fans almost 100 years after his death. Born Ehrich Weiss in Budapest, Hungary to Cecilia and Mayer Samuel Weiss (Weisz), Houdini, his sister, and two brothers settled in Appleton, Wisconsin where his father served as rabbi of the Zion Reform Jewish Congregation synagogue. In Appleton, a third brother was born to the Weiss family. After a string of failed rabbinic positions, Ehrich Weiss and his father moved to New York City and lived in a boarding house. Weiss began working at an early age, finding work where he could. At the age of nine Weiss was a trapeze artist in a neighborhood circus and soon became known as "Ehrich, The Prince of the Air." In 1891, after rediscovering his childhood interest in magic, 17-year-old Weiss partnered with Jacob Hyman and became the "Brothers Houdini." In 1893, when Weiss became a professional magician, he began calling himself "Harry Houdini" because he was heavily influenced by French magician Jean Eugène Robert-Houdin.

After the death of Weiss's father in 1892, the Brothers Houdini began performing an array of magic and card tricks at venues in upstate New York. By 1893 they expanded their tour to include the Midwest and performed at the World's Columbian Exposition of 1893. Dash Weiss, Ehrich's brother, replaced Hyman in 1894. The "Brothers Houdini" became the "Houdinis" that same year, and Weiss married Wilhelmina Beatrice (Bess) Rahner, a fellow performer, who became his assistant.

A fellow performer, Martin Beck, suggested Houdini move from card tricks to handcuffs and other escape acts. Houdini followed Beck's advice and became an expert at escaping from handcuffs, chains secured with padlocks, knotted ropes, and straitjackets. Impressed with Houdini's magical skills, Beck booked Houdini on the Orpheum vaudeville circuit. Houdini was soon performing at vaudeville houses across the United States. In 1913, Houdini introduced the Chinese Water Torture Cell. Mystifying audiences, Houdini escaped from a locked steel and glass enclosure while suspended upside down.

In 1913 Erich Weiss legally changed his name to Harry Houdini. He became president of the oldest magic company in the United States, Martinka and Co., in 1919. After his mother's death in 1920, Houdini devoted his energies to revealing fraud among those who claimed to be psychics and mediums. Believing that most spiritualists were trained as magicians, he revealed their deceptive practices. Houdini's boldness alienated him from long-time friend Sir Arthur Conan Doyle. Doyle rejected Houdini's opinions about mystics and psychics.

Harry Houdini's final performance took place on October 24, 1926 at the Garrick Hotel in Detroit, Michigan. He died on Halloween in 1926 from a ruptured appendix at the age of 52. For 10 years after his death, his wife participated in séances, awaiting Houdini's return from the other side. The Harry Houdini Museum in Scranton, Pennsylvania, operated by magicians Dorothy Dietrich and Dick Brooks, continues to hold séances on the anniversary of Houdini's death. Sidney H. Radner, a protégé of Houdini, also holds a séance each year in a location that holds a significant connection to Houdini's life. *See also* **David Copperfield**.

Robert Ruder

Further Reading: Christopher, Milbourne. *Mediums, Mystics and the Occult.* New York: Thomas Y. Crowell, 1969. Fleischman, Sid. *The Story of the Great Houdini.* New York: Greenwillow Books, 2006. Henning, Doug, with Charles Reynolds. *Houdini: His Legend and His Magic.* New York: Time Books, 1978. Houdini, Harry. *Miracle Mongers and Their Methods.* Charlottesville, VA: University of Virginia Library; Boulder, CO: NetLibrary, 1996. ———. *The Right Way to Do Wrong.*

Boston, MA: Harry Houdini, 1906. ———. *Secrets of Handcuffs*. London: George Routledge and Sons, 1910. Kalush, William, and Larry Sloman. *The Secret Life of Houdini: The Making of America's First Superhero*. New York: Simon and Schuster, 2006.

HUROK, SOL (1888–1974)

Solomon Isaievich Hurok (Gurkov), a producer and impresario, was born in Pogar, Russia on April 9, 1888. His father, Israel Gurkov, was a retail trader. In 1906, the 18-year-old Hurok was sent to study at the Karkhov Trade School, but he instead used his tuition money to immigrate to the United States.

Hurok was a master of self-aggrandizement; he also had an almost infallible sense of what would "project" and sell to an audience. In the early 1920s, he convinced Russian ballerina Anna Pavlova (1881–1931) that he should be her manager. Under his guidance, Pavlova became a major success in America. Hurok was on the map. Many believe that Hurok's "in" with Russian artists was his ability to speak Russian; Isaac Stern once observed, "Hurok knows six languages—and all of them are **Yiddish**!" (Robinson, 1994).

Hurok eventually represented such talents as pianist Efrem Zimbalist Sr., cellist Mstislav Rostropovich, singer Feodor Challiapin, pianists Van Cliburn and Artur Rubinstein, and dancers Dame Margot Fonteyn and Isadora Duncan. In 1935, Artur Rubinstein introduced Hurok to African American singer Marion Anderson. Hurok immediately decided to organize her concerts in the United States. Because of the prevailing prejudice towards "Negroes," Anderson was barred from most "elite" halls in America, whereupon Hurok presented Anderson at an open-air performance at the Lincoln Memorial. The concert, staged on April 9, 1939, was attended by some 75,000 people; it made Marion Anderson an international celebrity.

During the height of the Cold War, Hurok continued bringing Russian ballet companies to the United States under the "S. Hurok Presents" banner. This drew the fire of those opposed to American-Soviet rapprochement. In 1972, his offices were bombed. He died two years later, on March 5, 1974. More than 2,500 people filed into Carnegie Hall for his memorial service.

Hurok was married twice: to Tamara Shapiro and Emma Borisovna Runich.

Always quotable, Hurok was best known for saying "Get pleasure out of life . . . as much as you can. Nobody ever died from pleasure."

Kurt F. Stone

Further Reading: Robinson, Harlow. *The Last Impresario*. Penguin Press, 1995. ———. "Sol Hurok: America's Dance Impresario." *Dance Magazine,* November 1994.

I

IWO JIMA EULOGY

See **Gittlesohn, Rabbi Roland B.**

J

JAZZ AND BLUES

Jews and Blues. Popular belief holds that American Jews are demographically an urban and northern people, yet they had a considerable presence in the Deep South. The Dixie Diaspora, during the antebellum period, witnessed a large Jewish population in such cities as Charleston and New Orleans. Jews fought on both sides in the Civil War and, at its end, they replaced many local southerners as purveyors of goods to African Americans throughout much of the Mississippi Delta and Tennessee regions. These two areas spawned the early blues. Much has been made over the parallels in Jewish music, with its krechts, which is a catch in the voice, its preference for minor keys, and its readiness to syncopate, to the blues. Although similarities are evident and mutual influences possible, any suggestion of co-dependency, at this point, is extra-historical. The two traditions remain parallels that enjoy *occasional* intersection.

The roots of the blues have actually been traced to West African and partly Islamic musical structures. West African musicians, despite centuries of distance, could have sat in on blues sessions in the Mississippi Delta and recognized a common musical language. The cry-from-the-soul element paralleling the krechts sound in Jewish music was a legacy of West African proprietary tradition, suffering, and perhaps from distant memories of calls to prayer.

The blues sprang, more immediately, from a fusion of spirituals sung in African American churches with secular country forms. The call and response preaching tool used in churches dictated much of the structure of blues. Church provides a cultural line that does intersect through subject matter and story origins. A large portion of the lyrical material in spirituals came from Tanach sources. The stories of the Bible, particularly those concerning Moses's leading the Israelites from slavery, were prominent in this music. In its reborn form, contemporary "gospel" music, this biblical feature of spirituals is somewhat de-emphasized, but in the pivotal days of its formation, the blues remade Tanach and New Testament stories into the moral and mythological vision of their world. The moral vision came into play effectively when the blues/folk style became a rallying point for social protest. Leadbelly's compositions and his "Hitler Song," in particular, were early examples of this. Leadbelly called for the destruction of Hitler because he "dragged the Jews from their homes" (Jones, 1963). Looking out over the Mississippi River tied the blues to the river Jordan.

The blues is relatively simple music covering a wide palette of subject matter. A crucial moral point might appear close to a raunchy lyrical line as the secular and the religious often intertwine in a thematic counterpoint. The sermon element was kept alive through itinerate preachers who wandered the landscape, like many Hasidim, saving souls and spreading the blues gospel. The Reverend Gary Davis and Blind Willie Johnson made religious blues their fare and adapted ancient Jewish stories as teaching tools. Gary Davis's songs "If I Had My Way" and "Samson and Delilah" provided a heartfelt cry against the evils of the earth. Even the most earthy blues men, like Son House, Skip James, and the musing and philosophical Mississippi John Hurt, kept a number of religious blues songs in their repertoire.

As the blues moved north, the Jewish world's natural affinity for African American music made it easy to spot its value, even if many tended to treat it as a quaint musical curiosity. The Jewish community through pioneering blues recordings, through promoting and employing blues artists, and by producing a few blues artists of their own, became enablers of this essentially African American creation. **Tin Pan Alley** and theater composers like **George Gershwin** and Harold Arlen gave blues a presence in the mainstream.

George Wein and his partner, Albert Grossman, teamed with **Theodore Bikel**, Oscar Brand, and Pete Seeger to form the Newport Blues Festival. By the early sixties, blues had formed an important, but somewhat neglected underground following. The festival drew in blues artists like John Hurt, Brownie McGhee and Sonny Terry, John Lee Hooker and Reverend Gary Davis. Sharing the stage with these giants was a young **Bob Dylan**, the lead voice in the folk-blues protest scene. Methodical archivists and ballad hunters, such as blues guitarist Stefan Grossman, transcribed and published much of the great blues music.

The excitement around the blues-folk movement led to a resurgence of the blues recording industry. Jewish producers included Leonard and Phil Chess, whose Chess label included performances by Bo Diddley, Etta James, and Muddy Waters. Bruce Iglauer formed Delmark and Alligator Records; the Solomon brothers started Vanguard Records. Jewish record producers Moses "Moe" Asch, Lester Melrose, Art Rupe, the Bihari Brothers, and Ralph Bass helped blues greats achieve a bit of immortality through recording and promotion efforts. Talent promoters such as Jerry Wexler and **radio** personalities such as Alan Freed furthered the offshoots of soul and black **rock and roll**, respectively.

In recent years, new generations of Jewish musicians have come onto the blues scene. Mike Bloomfield, who got his first guitar as a Bar Mitzvah gift, became a blues star. Peter Green and Dave Specter became bluesmen in their own right, often learning on the job. Bob Margolin, Steve Freund, Rick Estrin, Ronnie Earl, and Tad Robinson are now ably filling the vacant shoes of their blues predecessors. Blues artists Israeli bassist Avishai Cohen, Lazer Lloyd, and Chicago vocalist Bob Bell have also been an important part of the thriving blues circuit.

The contribution of blues to Tin Pan Alley and to American song will, no doubt, prove inestimable. The works of George Gershwin and the opportunities of writing songs such as "Strange Fruit"—the heartrending showstopper made famous by Billie Holiday and written by Jewish school teacher Abe Meeropol—would not have emerged without blues. An entire spectrum of feeling and thought would never have found its voice. Blues provided the world of popular music a momentum that carries it along to this day.

Jazz through World War II. New Orleans has been dubbed the cradle of jazz. As early as the mid-1800s, the city broke with its oppressive traditions for a few hours on Sundays and allowed slaves to express themselves musically in the part of town known as Congo Square. The musical fest became a weekly ritual, and slaves, Creoles, and freed blacks used this circumscribed opportunity to dance and play music that was widely regarded by white southerners as a cultural and physical threat. This pastime operated as a safety valve for bitterly suppressed cultural feelings and provided the city with a tourist attraction.

The prime catalyst for the evolution of jazz, ironically, was the city's adoption of segregation laws in the late 1890s. This pushed local Creoles (a mixed-race population) into quarters that had traditionally separated them from more purely African Americans. Creoles leaned strongly on their European roots and were often trained in some of Europe's finest conservatories. The blending of Creole and African American skills provided the needed mix for jazz to emerge.

The first acknowledged combination of African music and European orchestral instrumentation may be traced to the inventiveness of a Jewish Creole named Louis Moreau Gottschalk (1829–1869). The son of a Jewish businessman from London and a white Creole Haitian, Gottschalk was a piano prodigy, hailed by Chopin. He was one of the first American musicians to achieve international fame. His "Bamboula-Danse des Negres" combined classical music and African and Latin drums and syncopation. His work begins as a subtly disorienting evocation of the dances Gottschalk heard in Congo Square and then flirts with musical strains that almost break into ragtime. This proto-jazz was premiered successfully nearly a half century before the recorded birth of ragtime. Gottschalk traveled to Latin America, where he introduced musical ideas that later influenced the formation of samba and chorino—a song typified by a near-cantorial lament.

A half-century later, the known Jewish contribution to the evolution of jazz centered on an atypical addition to a Jewish family living near the ghettoized New Orleans section called Storyville. Here, amid brothels, bars, and dance halls, Jewish merchants supplied goods to local concerns. One family, the Karnovskys, took in a small African American child to help with their coal wagon. They cared for him, fed him, gave him a coronet, and included him in family singing. A particular favorite of his was a Russian lullaby they sang to him at night. The child, the young Louis Armstrong, later acknowledged that they gave him a gift of music that spurred on his own God-given genius. He wore a Star of David the rest of his life in memory of the kindness and support he had received.

As jazz and "Louie" Armstrong moved north during the great migration of African Americans, they encountered a network of Jewish entrepreneurial and artistic talent that was hungry for ideas. The network found its creative impetus with this new musical form and used it to transform the American musical scene. Jazz evolved from a cultural niche phenomenon into an industry.

In the North, jazz encountered American popular song. Although this often resulted in only slightly syncopated renditions of European music, there were a number of Jewish jazz concerns that more closely emulated their African American counterparts. As early as 1915, Stein's Original Jazz Band spread ragtime and incubated future jazz musicians. At the same time, Willie "the Lion" Smith (born William Bertholoff) emerged onto the jazz scene. Born of a Jewish father and an African American mother, Smith was one of the greatest jazz pianists of all time and was, perhaps, the most feared stride master of his day. The stride was a night-long musical duel that became regular feature in early jazz clubs.

The enclave of publishers, composers, and performers of Tin Pan Alley acquired a predominantly Jewish character. This creative hothouse included George Gershwin, **Irving Berlin**, Jerome Kern, Harold Arlen, and a host of musical greats. It was well placed and able to inject jazz into the market mainstream. The venues that enabled this new musical form, such as the Orpheum Circuit, as well as Broadway Theater, had a strong Jewish contingent. Jazz definitions have been and remain elusive, bewildering, and often erroneously restrictive; thus, much of this early effort presented jazz as heard with an Eastern European ear.

The jazz of **Al Jolson**'s ***The Jazz Singer*** was primarily an up-tempo Tin Pan Alley-jazz mélange that would have been as uneasily received in Harlem as in contemporary jazz venues. The film did, however, expand public awareness about jazz and Jews. This first American talkie featured the Kol Nidre, a number of jazz-influenced tunes, and a young Jew putting on black face to help him return to his Jewish identity while wanting to sing music he perceived to be jazz. Despite its echoes of the degrading world of minstrelsy, the film became an honest, if schmaltzy exploration of basic human themes.

Blackface, an ingrained custom in American entertainment, was one of the more drastic means of assimilation. In the stratified world in which it began, putting on a gloss of African American identity gave Jews societal permission to engage in popular song. The practice was often necessary for blacks as well as whites. The African American star of the Ziegfeld Follies, a "corked up" Bert Williams, used a cartoon version of black people for the stage. In Williams's act, his wise-cracking nephew was played by the similarly compromised **Eddie Cantor**. The two managed to use their enforced guise to strategic satirical effect. Eventually, and to his enduring credit, Eddie Cantor became one of the first to refuse using blackface.

As social barriers relaxed and jazz itself entered the mainstream, Caucasian (often Jewish) orchestra leaders like Paul Whiteman began to move from improvisation to using set, publishable orchestrations. The newly created ASCAP (American Society of Composers, Authors and Publishers), which featured the talents of Irving Berlin and Jerome Kern, began to turn musical composition into a legally protected product.

The great publishing houses, which sported Jewish names like Stern, Remick, Bornstein, Feist, and Witmark, infuriated the nation's ethnically vigilant. Henry Ford in large part helped Jews and African Americans form a new ghettoization in the American mind.

Ford's opening salvo was the essay "The International Jew" (1920), published by his newspaper, the *Dearborn Independent*. Inspired by Ford's reading of *The Protocols of the Elders of Zion,* the essay enjoyed wide distribution. This essay was followed by his rant "Jewish Jazz - Moron Music - Becomes our National Music—the Story of Popular Song Control in the United States" (August 6, 1921). Ford railed against Jewish success in all aspects of music and claimed jazz was a Jewish creation meant to destroy the American character. Although Ford was forced to retract many of his anti-Semitic statements because of lawsuits, the essays entered American and European consciousness.

Various reports argue Paul Whiteman's Jewish origins, but he commissioned Gershwin's *Rhapsody in Blue,* which premiered with Whiteman's orchestra and featured Gershwin as the piano soloist. Whiteman was a proclaimed "King of Jazz," although it has been pointed out that the coronation did not take place in Harlem. As a popular bandleader and a major innovator in jazz orchestration, Whiteman considered it his mission to take jazz from the speakeasy and brothel and make it "respectable." Respectability can be a minus, but jazz was given a boost toward acceptance with passage of the Volstead Act (1920). In major cities, the anti-liquor laws usually received a pass in black areas. Noted jazz strongholds such as the Savoy, the Lafayette, and the Apollo were Jewish owned and managed, and they featured the refreshment and jazz the public craved. Harold Arlen, demonstrating an ability to compose for African American entertainers, was a creative force at the Cotton Club. Producer Irving Mills introduced Cab Calloway to the Cotton Club. Calloway often used mock cantorial runs in his music. This is recognizable in his hit "Hi Di Ho."

The Broadway stage, via the Rodgers and Hart creation of *Showboat,* introduced blues, jazz, and more boldly racial themes. The musical generated acclaim and controversy. Theater giants such as George Gershwin, Jerome Kern, Irving Berlin, Harold Arlen, and others began increasingly to employ jazz, albeit modified, to striking effect. As many theater and concert composers were lured to Hollywood, they fueled a golden age of film musicals.

The cross-fertilization of sources and styles during the period is demonstrated by events leading to the production of a musical hit. In 1938, Sammy Cahn and his pianist were invited to watch the performers Johnnie and George at the Apollo Theater. To Cahn's surprise, the team sang "Bei Mir Bis du Schoen" in a beautiful Harlem-inflected **Yiddish**. They brought down the house.

Cahn purchased the song from its Jewish composer, commissioned English lyrics, and turned it over to Jewish band leader Vic Schoen. Schoen arranged it for a trio of Lutheran siblings, the Andrews Sisters. It was an instant hit on their first Decca recording.

The world of classical music was beginning to take note of jazz. Igor Stravinsky became intrigued with jazz during a visit to Harlem and then while listening to New Orleans and Chicago bands. He composed *Ebony Concerto,* which was less a jazz composition than an effort to understand the new concept. The first full-length composition incorporating jazz elements was Darius Milhaud's ballet *Creation of the World.* Milhaud, an Americanized French Jew, pioneered the inclusion of jazz in the conservatory curriculum. His most noted student was jazz great Dave Brubeck.

During the Great Depression much of the class structure that had kept jazz "a music apart," broke down. The country was singing the blues, and poverty encompassed the entire color spectrum. Poverty, by necessity, became somewhat respectable. The public recognized its Job-like kinship to much of the lyrical poetics of jazz. In a gesture that would have been unheard of earlier, **Benny Goodman** formed an integrated jazz quartet that performed in Carnegie Hall (1938). Irving Mills also employed integrated bands for his recording sessions. Jazz increasingly told the nation's story, while giving vent to America's irrepressible optimism. Swing bands like those of Goodman and Leo Reisman vaulted Jewish musical personalities to popularity and became a training ground for future talent.

Jazz became the voice of the American soul. With the advent of World War II, jazz reaffirmed the hard-won American experience and offered a unique way for the country to redefine itself. Material rationing put the recording industry on hold, but jazz spread via the radio. Shortwave, the Internet of its day, brought the musical language of America to every continent.

Jazz was used as a weapon of war. Numerous musical acts were transported across the globe to serve as military morale boosters. The hit tunes of World War II had been, mostly, reminiscent of the British Music Hall, but the music of World War II was mainly jazz, and Jewish musicians and composers were abundantly represented. The Goodman, Artie Shaw, and Glenn Miller orchestras carried American musical identity across theaters of the war.

These bands were joined with all-woman bands featuring musicians such as Rosalind Cron and Betty "Roz" Rosner. In 1926, Sophie Tucker became the first woman to lead a popular jazz band. She hired African American composers and sought the great African American singer Ethel Waters as a coach. Jewish jazz musicians of both sexes reminded American fighting men of home and their reason for fighting. Initially seen as an oddity, woman groups were given a well-deserved chance to shine by the depletion of manpower. The most famous of these was Ada Leonard's "All Girl Band," booked by the impresario **Billy Rose**. Ada Leonard had been a stripper, but she reinvented herself as a first-rate jazz conductor. She delivered first-rate jazz performances.

All Americans, as well as Jews around the world, faced the same enemy. The ancient theme of return that had long resonated with Jews now captured the minds of Americans who longed for the safe return of the troops. The nation began redefining itself, with both Jews and jazz closely included.

Jazz During the Nazi Era. Thousands of African American troops served in World War I and returned from a comparatively color-blind Europe to a segregated America. They shared their experiences with family and musicians back home. Others chose to remain in Europe, and alongside expatriate white artists were many of the brightest jazz minds. African American entertainers such as Josephine Baker became the toast of Europe. Sydney Bechet and Coleman Hawkins earned a respectful audience with their first musical reviews. Ernest Ansermet who, as a conductor, had premiered much of Stravinsky's work in recording, wrote the classical world's first jazz review, a critical rave for Sydney Bechet.

Following this trend, the Delaunays, a family of Jewish jazz aficionados, teamed with critic Hugues Panassie to form *Le Jazz Hot,* the first magazine devoted to criticizing and promoting jazz. This boosted the influence of their Le Jazz Hot Club of Paris, the prime hub of European jazz. Jewish promoters and journalists became dominant in the Monmarte jazz scene.

Europe loved jazz, and Jewish musicians figured prominently. Ady Rozner, the "Russian Satchmo," recognized as the best trumpet player in Europe, fled the continent at the right time. The popular Russian jazz scene featured two other Jewish jazz artists, Leonid Utesov and Alexander Tsfasman. They survived the war because Stalin and some of his henchmen were fans of Utesov. In Germany, Harry Frommerman started the close-harmony singing group the Comedian Harmonists, whose wild popularity eventually extended to the elite of the Third Reich.

Nazi ascendancy interrupted this brief golden age. Taking their cue from Wagner, who attacked Jewish presence in the musical world, and more immediately from the essays of Henry Ford, the Nazis viewed jazz as a cultural and ethnic threat. Various attacks on the art form appeared in print and broadcast. The phrase "nigger-jew jazz" became the Nazi label of choice. In 1937, Goebbels issued a proscription of jazz in broadcasting. Jews were forbidden radios. Accompanying the infamous Düsseldorf Degenerate Art exhibition of 1938 was its companion piece "Degenerate Music. The poster for the exhibition featured a monkey-featured black man playing jazz on a saxophone. On his lapel was a Star of David.

The Nazis further tightened the net with the assembly of the "Lexikon Der Juden in Der Musik." This listed all known Jews in the musical world. First a tool of exclusion, it soon became a death list. Musicians who did not flee the continent were rounded up and sent to concentration camps.

Many Jewish musicians were sent to Theresienstadt to take part in the sham that the Nazis prepared for Red Cross inspectors. The lovely city of Jews that the Nazis wanted the world to see was laced with musical groups playing with stars on their chest and forced smiles on their starving faces. Jazz, the happy Jewish music the Nazis held it to be, was featured by the Ghetto Swingers, a group of Jewish musicians arrested months before. Among them was the young Heinz Jakob "Coco Schumann." They serenaded citizens of the ersatz city during the Red Cross inspection. Once the inspection was over, the film-set city was struck.

What the Red Cross considered a safe haven of humane treatment was, in reality, a processing plant for death camps. Many musicians were sent to Auschwitz. Jazz musicians who survived incarceration and transport were formed into a group whose task was to greet trains full of newcomers with up-tempo music—music that could also be heard in the cold Polish air by those being sent to their deaths. The Nazis exercised their penchant for euphemism by naming the group the Happy Five. In a macabre pep talk to ensure top-notch playing, one guard reputedly pointed at smoke rising from the stacks and quipped that those were previous unsatisfactory musicians.

The prisoners also entertained prison guards while they dined or when desired. This role provided the inmates a slightly protected status. Access to different parts of the camp gave them the opportunity to scavenge from a wider array of food sources. Despite these slim advantages, only Coco Schumann and 3 of the original 16 Jazz musicians survived Auschwitz. Schumann, the last survivor, gave an enthusiastically received jazz concert at the Berlin Jewish Museum in 2005.

Before the war, Europe celebrated the career of Jewish jazz trumpeter Louis Bannet, head of the Louis Bannet Rhythm Five. He was hailed as the "Dutch Louis Armstrong." Bannet, sipping tea in his favorite bakery, was spotted by one of his fans, a Gestapo agent. He was transported to Auschwitz. There, a gaunt Louis Bannet played his beloved Louis Armstrong jazz on the trumpet of another murdered inmate for carousing Nazi officers at a party honoring Josef Mengele. This was, apparently, all within earshot of his fellow prisoners. Bannet survived the war, having literally played for his life.

For some, another alternative was to play jazz for Goebbels's pet project, Propaganda Ministerium. Jazz was popular with the German officer corps. British and American jazz was broadcast to the continent from England, and even the Luftwaffe tuned in for a bit of entertainment during bombing runs. Hitler and Goebbels hit upon the idea to fire jazz back over the airwaves, but a jazz reworked with propagandistic and viciously anti-Semitic lyrics. This brainstorm launched "Charlie and his Orchestra." Their broadcasts continued throughout the war. The project gave musicians like Jewish-blooded drummer Freddie Brocksieper a safe pass until V.E. Day.

World War II to the Present. The end of the war brought energy and exuberance to the American scene. A new Jazz Age began. The long struggle to lay the foundations for jazz began to pay off. Every aspect of the American artistic and entertainment world found itself influenced by this once marginalized form.

The movement of musical ideas overseas had not been a one-way street. Jazz artists in Europe and jazz's recent acceptance as an art form opened the way for new compositional ideas. Stravinsky, who had tinkered with jazz earlier, started to influence jazz musicians. Miles Davis, Dizzy Gillespie, John Coltrane, and Charlie Parker attuned themselves to the works of Koussevitzky, Stravinsky, and Schoenberg. Jazz was entertainment and intellectual "high-brow" music. Classical artists such as Jascha Heifetz recorded and performed jazz.

New Jewish producers, along with older ones, combined to give jazz artists long overdue prominence and respect. Sandra and Allan Jaffe took over an ailing art gallery and opened Preservation Hall to revitalize jazz in New Orleans. The Jaffe family, also in the vanguard of the civil rights movement, bravely bore the brunt of entrenched segregation. The indomitable George Wein broke new ground with his Newport Rhode Island Jazz Festival (1959). The festival showcased the finest known artists and promoted relative unknowns. It served as the model for all future festivals.

Norman Granz, concert promoter, talent rep, and record producer made numerous contributions to jazz. In 1944, he produced the short film *Jammin' the Blues* and went on to create the *Jazz at the Philharmonic* series. Granz was also among the first to pay his black artists the same salary as whites. He was known for once insisting that white cab drivers take his black artists as customers, even as he was threatened by a policeman's gun. He guided the careers of many jazz greats of his day and was, perhaps, most proud of his long-term collaboration with Ella Fitzgerald.

The recording industry, all but crushed by material shortages during the war, began its resurgence. Jewish-owned and -managed record labels like A&R, Blue Note, and Fantasy records, as well as Granz's own Verve and Pablo Labels, drove new markets. The industry was vaulted forward by technological breakthroughs that permitted an enhanced experience for jazz listeners. The phonograph, invented by Emile Berliner mere decades before, was improved by the efforts of another Jewish inventor. Peter Carl Goldmark (1906–1977) rolled out the first long-playing record and turned the previously fragmented listening experience into an evening-long concert. This new product brought a fidelity to the sound and worked well with the packaging of jazz concept albums. Extended themes of great jazz recordings like Miles Davis's "Bitches Brew" were not possible on the older technology.

The symphonic film scores of such greats as Dimitri Tiomkin, John Steiner Alfred Newman, and others were joined by an increasing number of jazz-inspired works. The first full-blown jazz film score came from Alex North for *A Streetcar Named Desire*. This groundbreaking choice opened the door for a tradition of jazz-influenced film scores. Elmer Bernstein and Jerry Goldsmith lead a list of Jewish film composers who worked extensively with jazz. Marvin Hamlisch's light reworking of Scott Joplin's ragtime composition "The Entertainer" became the hit score for *The Sting*.

Classical composers such as **Aaron Copland**, Louis Gruenberg, and Morton Gould have touched jazz. Their momentum was carried forward by classical composers working in Broadway Theater. German Jewish theater composer Kurt Weill came to America to create new works. The legacy of jazz on the Broadway stage reached its zenith with **Leonard Bernstein**'s score for symphonic-jazz ***West Side Story***. This powerful score cowritten, in part, by Stephen Sondheim, also translated brilliantly to film and won Academy scoring awards.

The fifties produced the Beat Generation, and jazz became an enclave for the socially rebellious. Norman Mailer's landmark essay "The White Negro" pointed out a new blip on the social scene. The leader of this movement was the legendary Mezz Mezzrow, who had stared down Al Capone, opted to obliterate his Jewish identity, and became his version of an African American. The phenomenon still exists, most noticeably in **rap and hip hop**. It is satirized by British comedian Sascha Baron Cohen through his "Ali G" black "wannabe" character.

Bugsy Siegel's move to bring the entertainment industry west to Las Vegas ushered in a new era of live shows featuring jazz artists. African American Jews like **Sammy Davis**, Jackie Wilson, the Velvet Fog of Mel Tormé, **Dinah Shore**, and an entire circuit of jazz musicians found venues. The list of Jewish jazz greats grew exponentially during this period. In the sixties, composer-singers like **Bob Dylan** and Laura Nyro created bridges between jazz and other musical styles.

One hundred years after Gottschalk brought his new musical ideas to Latin America, Jewish jazz composers like Herb Alpert responded with innovative work in Latin jazz. Stan Getz's Bossa Nova recordings created a new market for that musical style. Vocalist Flora Purim carries the jazz legacy adroitly in her native Brazil. Ms. Purim also has performed with Dizzy Gillespie's Grammy-winning United Nations Orchestra.

British Jews like Ronnie Scott, Ray Noble, Andre Previn, Monte Norman, and Victor Feldman were pivotal influences on the British jazz scene. French director Bertrand Tavernier directed the film *Round Midnight* (1986), which some have claimed is a tribute to Dexter Gordon. Gordon was considered a great jazz tenor saxophonist. Gordon starred in the movie *Round Midnight* as Dale Turner, an expatriate jazz musician much like himself.

Earlier scattered efforts at jazz journalism paved the way for jazz historians such as Leonard Feather, Floyd Levin, Nat Hentoff, and George T. Simon. Magazines like *Downbeat* and *The Village Voice* (created by Al Lipschultz) devoted much of their energies to jazz criticism. Darius Milhaud's introduction of jazz to the university curriculum found its fulfillment in Dan Morgenstern's work as head of the Jazz Conservatory at Rutgers.

The world is now awash in jazz festivals featuring many Jewish artists. The festival phenomenon is especially strong in Israel, with the Red Sea Jazz Festival becoming a world-reviewed concern.

Through technological advances jazz recordings can fit in a person's pocket or be blasted across the Internet. People can get as much jazz as they want. **Klezmer**, the Jewish music that had much to do with the Jewish affinity for jazz, is itself being described as both a parallel musical tradition and a genre of jazz. The new generation of jazz artists such as Harry Connick Jr., Michael Feinstein, Steven Bernstein, John Zorn, Lew Tabacken, Dave Koz, and Dan Levinson are determined to see the further popularization of jazz. Whether they and the wide-ranging roster of new jazz talents are proverbial dwarfs standing on the shoulders of their titanic predecessors or giants themselves has yet to be determined.

At present, jazz, an ever-resilient art form whose acceptance and destiny in this country have so closely mirrored that of the Jewish world, lives in hope. A century after the Karnovskys provided Louis Armstrong with his first musical instrument, despite the recent devastation of Katrina, old traditions are resuming in New Orleans, albeit with some promising changes in place. Social aid and pleasure clubs dating back to late nineteenth-century benevolent societies have resumed their jazz parades. One of the oldest and finest of these benevolent associations, the

African American Prince of Wales Social Aid and Pleasure Club, was recently led by its newest member. Joe "White Boy" Stern, a 65-year-old Jewish trumpeter, played jazz at the head of the band, triumphantly blasting away at whatever walls lay ahead. It was the first time in anyone's memory that a white person was presiding over a brass-band-led "second line" parade for one of New Orleans's traditional African American social, aid, and pleasure clubs. Jazz and the people who love it continue to blast away at the obstacles separating people. *See also* **Goodman, Benny**; ***The Jazz Singer*; Tin Pan Alley**.

Richard Gould

Further Reading: Burns, Ken, and Geoffrey Ward. *Jazz, a History of American Music*. Knopf, 2000. Jones, Leroi. *Blues People: Negro Music in White America*. New York: William Morrow, 1963. Merwin, Ted. *In Their Own Image: New York Jews in Jazz Age Popular Culture*. New Brunswick, NJ: Rutgers University Press, 2006. Scaruffi, Piero. *A History of Jazz Music: 1900–2000*. Omniware, 2007.

A poster for *The Jazz Singer*. [Photofest, Inc.]

THE JAZZ SINGER (1927)

Although the movie musical is generally referred to as the first feature talkie film, the reality is it was only in part a talkie, consisting of dialogue and musical selections with the use of captions. The film featured **Al Jolson**, who sang five songs, including "Mamie." Produced by Warner Brothers, the path-breaking film had its premier on October 6, 1927. The plot has a strong Jewish theme and was close to another film story, "Day of Atonement." Jolson plays the protagonist Jackie, the son of a cantor in a family boasting many generations of cantors. Jackie, however, would rather sing jazz than cantorial melodies, and he is caught by his father singing in a nearby bar. When his Orthodox father beats him, Jackie runs away. His mother is more understanding of the boy and is willing to accept her son's desire to be a jazz singer.

Jackie returns years later as Jack Robin, a jazz singer. He returns for an opening night performance of his show which falls on the evening of Yom Kippur, the holiest day of the Jewish calendar. His girlfriend, Mary, a Gentile, has used her influence to get Jackie a major singing part. He discovers, however, that his father is very sick, and this circumstance presents Jackie with a dilemma. It is traditional for the cantor to sing Kol Nidre, the opening prayer on the eve of Yom Kippur. The movie plot hinges on whether Jackie will return to the synagogue in his father's place or sing in the secular play on Yom Kippur. In the film's denouement, the son sings the Kol Nidre prayer, while the father hears him from his bed at home, which is close to the synagogue. The old cantor expires believing his son has returned to the Orthodox fold. However, this is untrue since the son has decided to devote his life to jazz singing. The film's message is that assimilation triumphs over tradition and religion. The generational religious conflict ends in a victory for the assimilated, Americanized, younger generation. This is very similar to what really happened to many second-generation American Jews, especially in Hollywood. The film concludes with Al Jolson singing "Mamie" to his adoring mother, who seems resolved to accept her son's Americanization. The film certainly mirrored Hollywood's Jewish film community as its members assimilated into the American "melting pot." *See also* **Film**; **Jolson, Al**.

Philip Rosen

Further Reading: Dines, Tim. *The Jazz Singer* (1927), www.filmsite.org. Hoberman, J., and Jeffrey Shandler. "The Jazz Singer," in *Entertaining America: Jews, Movies, and Broadcasting*. Princeton University Press, 2003.

JESSEL, GEORGE (1898–1981)

George Jessel was a screen, stage, radio, and television actor and comedian. He was born in New York City on April 3, 1898, the son of Joseph Jessel, a playwright and traveling salesman, and Charlotte Schwartz. Jessel began entertaining when he was nine years old, serenading customers in his maternal grandfather's tailor shop. He launched his professional career that same year, singing baritone with the Imperial Trio at the Harlem Theater where his mother worked as a ticket-taker. Jessel had only six months of formal education when his father died in 1908. Jessel quit school to join Gus Edwards's Boys and Girls, a popular vaudeville touring show, staying with Edwards until 1914. He then toured England as a singer and comedian for three years.

Jessel returned to the United States in 1917. For the next eight years he played in vaudeville houses, appeared in several two-reel silent movies, wrote and produced a few vaudeville and Broadway productions, and tried his hand at theatrical management.

In 1925, Jessel was cast in the lead role of Jack Robin in the original Broadway stage version of *The Jazz Singer.* Robin was not a comic role, but it became Jessel's most popular character, one he performed more than 1,000 times. The play tells the tale of a rabbi's son who yearns for the stage but gives up his career to return home to his family. Two years later the film adaptation of *The Jazz Singer* became the signature role for **Al Jolson**. Jessel had been offered the part, but he refused to star in the movie version because Hollywood changed the ending.

In 1927, Jessel had a second hit on the Broadway stage, *The War Song,* the story of a Jewish songwriter who ends up on the front lines in World War I. Like his previous hit, *The Jazz Singer, The War Song* focused on the theme of Jewish assimilation into American culture through show business. This theme would remain at the core of Jessel's concerns throughout his career.

During the 1930s, Jessel continued to appear in motion pictures and in vaudeville. He also ventured briefly into a new medium—radio, where he was not as successful. In late 1943, Jessel signed a contract as a director for 20th Century Fox and went to Hollywood, where he remained for 10 years. In 1953, he abandoned the movie industry and began raising money for charitable causes. One of his first efforts was a cross-country tour selling bonds for Israel. He then began raising money for other organizations, most notably the City of Hope Medical Center. Because of the many after-dinner speeches he gave in support of political, social, and humanitarian causes, Jessel became known as the "Toastmaster General of the United States." He also toured extensively for the United Service Organizations, putting on shows for American service personnel overseas. For these efforts, Jessel was made an honorary member of the United States Air Force. Other honors included the Jean Hersholt Humanitarian Award in 1969, presented to Jessel by the Academy of Motion Picture Arts and Sciences,and B'nai B'rith's Man of the Year Award, in recognition of his service to many Jewish and Israeli causes.

Jessel died of a heart attack on May 23, 1981, shortly after he appeared in the award-winning movie *Reds.*

He had married four times and had one daughter from his third marriage. In assessing his career, some critics maintain Jessel was more successful as a writer and producer of Broadway shows and Hollywood motion pictures than as an entertainer. Most agree that Jessel's major contribution came in his role of banquet toastmaster and charitable fundraiser. *See also* **Comedy**; **Vaudeville**.

Burton Boxerman

Further Reading: Franklin, Joe. *Joe Franklin's Encyclopedia of Comedians*. Citadel Press, 1979. Jessel, George. *Elegy in Manhattan*. Holt, Rinehart and Winston, 1961. ———. *Hello, Momma*. World Publishing Company, 1946. ———. *This Way Miss*. Henry Holt, 1955. ———, and John Austin. *The World I Lived In*. Regenery, 1975. Smith, Bill. *The Vaudevillians*. Macmillan, 1981.

JEWISH DAILY FORWARD

The *Forward* or *Forvats*, in **Yiddish**, was first published in 1897 as a Yiddish language daily under the editorship and inspiration of **Abraham Cahan**. Its audience was the Jewish working class that had flocked to America from Eastern Europe. Following the assassination of Czar Nicholas II in 1882, czarist Russia began persecuting Jews more rigorously. One third of Eastern Europe's Jews migrated to America between 1881 and 1924. In 1924 the United States Congress, guided by a racist pro-Nordic bias, enacted into law the National Origins Act, which severely restricted immigration from Southern and Eastern European countries. The law, in part, was aimed at the number of immigrants who arrived in the United States with radical ideas. Many of the new Jewish immigrants, for example, came with attitudes which not only reflected hatred of old world despotism, but, for a sizable number, a belief in the promises of socialism.

Regardless of their political preferences, the Jewish immigrants could unite around their lingua franca, Yiddish. Cahan's Yiddish-printed newspaper attempted to meet their needs. The paper provided them with world and local news, human interest stories, fiction, short stories, and even serialized novels. Such Jewish personalities as the revolutionary Leon Trotsky, the socialist-anarchist Morris Winchevsky, and the novelist

The *Forward* Building, located at 175 E. Broadway in Manhattan, was the home of the *Jewish Daily Forward*, the most popular newspaper in the immigrant Jewish community of the Lower East Side, which was founded in 1897 as a daily newspaper in Yiddish by Abraham Cahan. Presently the *Forward* is published weekly in separate Yiddish and English editions. [Forward Association]

Isaac Bashevis Singer found space in the paper. Its editorial policies and articles advocated democratic socialism, and its pro-labor union policy favored the American Federation of Labor, particularly the Jewish-led International Ladies Garment Workers Union. The *Forward* was also non-Zionist and favored the politics of the European Jewish Socialist *Bund*. Like the *Bund*, Cahan embraced a socialist agenda.

The 1920s saw the apogee of the newspaper. It had 11 daily editions as far west as Chicago, with a readership of 275,000. Its readers turned quickly to a "Dear Abby"-style column called the "Bintel Brief," which consisted of letters where contributors appealed to the editor to solve personal problems, many of which were a result of coming to a new world that was alien to the newly arrived immigrants. The paper sought to Americanize and acclimate its readers. However, the process of "Americanization," the decline of new immigrants, and the rapid movement of Jews from the working class into the middle class decimated the *Forward*'s circulation. By 1939, it was down to a readership of 170,000. Cahan had visited the Jewish settlement in Palestine and became an admirer of its efforts, thus softening his non-Zionist views. Subsequently, the paper embraced President Franklin Roosevelt and his New Deal and abandoned its attachment to the Socialist Party.

Seth Lipsky, a *Wall Street Journal* editor, persuaded the *Forward* in 1995 to start an English-language edition. Financial wizard and philanthropist Michael Steinhardt joined and became its vice president, as well as purchasing 50 percent of the English edition, with the Forward Association holding the rest. In the same year, a Russian edition started. Each version is a completely independent edition with its own editors and staff. Each became a weekly rather than daily. The paper long ago cut its ties to socialism, but, while staffing a number of conservative writers, it generally leans toward a liberal point of view in its content. All editions are published at 49 East 33rd Street in New York. *See also* **Cahan, Abraham**; **Journalism**; **Yiddish**.

Philip Rosen

Further Reading: Howe, Irving. *World of Our Fathers.* New York: Harcourt Brace, 1978. Metzker, Isaac, and Harry Golden. *A Bintel Brief; Sixty Years of Letters from the Lower East Side to the Jewish Daily Forward.* Doubleday, 1971.

JEWISH DELICATESSENS

If anything could be said to have united the diverse, fractious membership of the American Jewish community during the twentieth century, it was a shared fondness for the Jewish delicatessen. "Eating deli" became, in the words of Joan Nathan, "the Jewish eating experience in this country," one shared by Jews of every practice and persuasion (1994). The word "delicatessen" comes from a German word that means "delicacies." The first delis in this country were started in the late nineteenth century by Germans and Alsatians; they catered to fellow immigrants who craved a taste of the old country. Jewish "delicatessen stores" followed this model; they initially sold cured meats, canned beans, pickles, and other products that were the "fast food" of their time. They soon added tables and became full-fledged restaurants. Not all were kosher; Katz's Deli, founded in 1888 and still in business on New York's Lower East Side, never served kosher meat.

By the interwar era, two distinct types of Jewish delis had emerged in New York, where more than 1,500 such establishments were located. Reuben's, Lindy's, the Gaiety, and the Stage were among the renowned theater district delis that served overstuffed, non-kosher pastrami and corned beef sandwiches named after the celebrities of the day. In stark contrast were the ubiquitous kosher delis in Brooklyn and the Bronx, which were on par with the synagogue as gathering places for the local community. While they sidestepped Jewish law by remaining open on the Sabbath and other Jewish holidays, these delis served no dairy products with their sandwiches, which were made from Hebrew National, Zion Kosher, and other popular brands of kosher meat.

Both types of delis were known for their sarcastic waiters, who were always ready with a wisecrack or a putdown. And as Jews became increasingly involved in all branches of the entertainment industry, a plethora of plays, films, songs, television shows, and advertising campaigns revolved around the consumption of deli food. Perhaps the most famous is **Rob Reiner**'s 1989 film *When Harry Met Sally,* in which Sally, played by Meg Ryan, pretends to have a sexual climax in Katz's.

In the years following World War II, delis became integral to Jewish life in many North American cities, including Chicago, Miami, Los Angeles, and Montreal. When Jews moved to the suburbs, delis sprang up on main streets and in shopping malls. But their clientele, which included many non-Jews, soon gravitated toward other kinds of ethnic food, especially Chinese and Italian. The rise of health consciousness in the 1970s led many to demonize deli meat as excessively fatty, salty, and cholesterol-laden. Even Orthodox Jews embraced gourmet kosher cuisine rather than plebeian deli fare.

Jewish deli foods, as bagels had done before them, gradually became part of the overall American cuisine. When chains like Subway and Quiznos, along with warehouse stores like Costco, started selling pastrami sandwiches, they preempted the deli's claim to fame. Some famous delis—the Carnegie and the Stage in New York, Manny's in Chicago, Canter's and Nate 'n Al's in Los Angeles—live on. But, except perhaps in nostalgia, the deli no longer serves a vital function in the lives of most American Jews. *See also* **Food**.

Ted Merwin

Further Reading: Nathan, Joan. *Jewish Cooking in America,* New York: Knopf, 1994. "Old Style Jewish Delicatessens for Goyim (non-Jews)." October 24, 2001. Accessed August 20, 2008. Epinions.com.

JEWISH MUSEUMS IN THE UNITED STATES

Jewish museums are the product of the modern age and developed almost simultaneously beginning in the late nineteenth century in Europe, the United States, and the land of Israel. The history of these museums is integrally linked with Jewish experience in the twentieth century and has been indelibly marked by the changing circumstances and events which have altered the very course of Jewish life during the past hundred years. Today there are nearly 300 Jewish museums across the globe.

In 1904, Judge Mayer Sulzberger (1843–1923) presented the Jewish Theological Seminary Library (JTS) in New York with 26 ceremonial objects that served as the nucleus for creating the Jewish Museum. This historic gift was preceded by the formation of the earliest Judaica collection in the United States in 1889 at the Smithsonian Institution. The curator, Cyrus Adler (1863–1940), a cousin of Sulzberger's, became president of the JTS Board in 1902. Like many of his coreligionists in Europe, Adler's goal was to use modern critical scholarship to counteract age-old stereotypes. Beyond that, his aim was to gain acceptance for Jews as truly equal partners in American society. Adler and Sulzberger had family ties to the closely knit leadership group of largely German Jews who were responsible for the establishment of many institutions that were to shape American Jewish life. Adler was also a key figure in the founding of the American Jewish Historical Society (AJHS) in 1892. The AJHS, distinguished as the first ethnic historical organization in the United States, pioneered the collection of archives, books, and artifacts of American Jewry.

In 1925, JTS acquired the Sephardic Judaica of Hadji Ephraim Benguiat (d. 1918), which Adler previously arranged to borrow for the Smithsonian's installation at the 1893 World's Fair and subsequently in Washington until 1924. Though Adler's museum experience at the Smithsonian emphasized education through exhibitions, at JTS, there was only a small museum display in the library beginning in 1931.

The impending crisis in Europe brought additional collections to the Jewish Museum. In 1939, through a plan to help Danzig's Jews emigrate, the American Jewish Joint Distribution Committee sent funds to Danzig, and ceremonial objects were sent for safekeeping to the Jewish

Museum. Also in 1939, Benjamin Mintz brought his Judaica collection from Poland, ostensibly to be shown at the World's Fair. The Mintz Collection was purchased by the museum in 1947.

While the JTS Library continued to maintain a large and important collection of illustrated manuscripts, illuminated ceremonial texts, and prints, a new era was inaugurated with the museum's move to its current location on Fifth Avenue in 1947. The museum embarked on an ambitious program of exhibitions and collections development that set a high standard for the field. A unique contribution was made by Harry G. Friedman (d. 1965), a collector who acquired Jewish art and ceremonial objects during the war years and gifted some 6,000 items to the museum. In 1956 the museum pioneered the movement to create contemporary Jewish ceremonial objects with the establishment of the Tobe Pascher Workshop. Ludwig Wolpert (1900–1981) trained as a silversmith at the Bauhaus, a crafts and fine arts school in Germany. He became a professor at Jerusalem's New Bezalel Academy for Arts and Crafts in 1935. Wolpert was invited, in 1956, to the Jewish Museum in New York by Drs. Abraham Kanof and Stephen Kaiser. There he established and was designated director of the Tobe Pascher Workshop. Another trendsetting initiative was to commission prominent American artists to create an original graphic for the Jewish New Year.

In 1962, the Jewish Museum briefly altered direction, exhibiting avant-garde secular art. This course was reversed in 1971 to focus on the Jewish cultural heritage and its interpretation in the context of social history and art. Attuned to the importance of media, in 1984, the Jewish Museum established the National Jewish Archive of Broadcasting. Recent collections development and exhibitions have highlighted the museum's particular niche as an art museum that presents Jewish culture. In a series of landmark exhibitions, the Jewish Museum has been at the forefront of presenting the work of contemporary artists.

America's second Jewish museum was founded in 1913 at the Hebrew Union College in Cincinnati by the National Foundation of Temple Sisterhoods, whose members recognized the importance of saving family heirlooms at a time when liberal Jews were no longer observing traditional Jewish rituals. The Union Museum also focused on collecting with limited educational outreach. Adolph Oko (1883–1944), HUC's librarian, purchased four important European collections, including that of Salli Kirschstein of Berlin of over 6,000 items. While material cultural of the American Jewish experience was only incidentally added to the collection, in 1947, the American Jewish Archives was founded at HUC by Jacob Rader Marcus (1923–2004). For many years, the collection lay dormant in storage. The museum was reestablished in 1948 by HUC president Dr. Nelson Glueck (1900–1971), and a series of exhibitions and publications was launched. Glueck, an archaeologist, added artifacts from his excavations in Israel to the collection.

The collection was moved to the HUC Los Angeles campus in 1972 and renamed the Skirball Museum. In the 1980s HUC began plans for a new cultural center to focus on the American Jewish experience. The Skirball initiated Project Americana, to collect material culture of the American Jewish experience, which increased the museum's holdings by some 6,000 objects. In 1996, the museum opened in greatly expanded quarters in the new Skirball Cultural Center, now an independent affiliate of HUC which presents a broad array of exhibitions, performing arts, film, literary, and children's and family programs. A branch of the Skirball Museum remains in Cincinnati and the HUC Klau Library maintains an important collection of visual arts. The Hebrew Union College-Jewish Institute of Religion Museum in New York, established in 1983, showcases contemporary Jewish art and ceremonial objects.

In the postwar period, there was a heightened sense of the importance for Jews in the United

States and in the new state of Israel to preserve Jewish culture. In the aftermath of World War II, the Jewish Cultural Reconstruction (JCR) was given the authority by the U.S. State Department to identify and redistribute Nazi-looted Judaica that was located in Germany's American Zone of Occupation when no heirs could be found. The JCR was based at the Jewish Museum through 1952. Hannah Arendt (1906–1979) was the executive secretary.

YIVO, Institute for Jewish Research, formerly headquartered in Vilna (now Vilnius, Lithuania) established a new home in New York. Today, YIVO is the preeminent center for the study of East European Jewry and Yiddish language, literature, and folklore and the influence of that culture in the Americas. The Leo Baeck Institute (LBI), dedicated to the history of German-speaking Jewry, was founded in New York in 1955. Sister institutions were established in Jerusalem and London and LBI, New York, opened a research branch at the Jewish Museum, Berlin.

There was also a growing interest among private individuals in collecting Judaica, and some of these formed the core of new Jewish museums. The B'nai B'rith Klutznick National Museum in Washington, D.C. was founded in 1957 with the collection of Joseph B. and Olyn Horwitz of Cleveland. The Spertus Museum in Chicago was formed in 1968, at the then-College of Jewish Studies, with the collection of Maurice Spertus. Opening a major new facility in 2007, the museum of the renamed Spertus Institute of Jewish Studies has articulated its mission as being to "re-examine Jewish culture in order to celebrate, challenge, and advance modern Jewish identity." The Judah L. Magnes Museum was established in Berkeley, California in 1962 as a community-based endeavor by Seymour Fromer, who served as its director for more than 30 years. Interest in local history led to the creation of the Western States Jewish History Center at the Magnes in 1967.

The Yeshiva University Museum in New York opened in 1973, incorporating collections of Jewish art previously acquired by the university's library, including items from the JCR. Sylvia Herskowitz, founding director, has guided the museum's multidisciplinary perspective and an exhibitions program featuring both social history exhibitions and contemporary artists working on Jewish themes. The National Museum of American Jewish History (NMAJH) in Philadelphia opened in 1976 in honor of the United States Bicentennial, adjacent to Independence Mall and the Liberty Bell, where it has shared its site with Congregation Mikveh Israel, founded in 1740. The NMAJH is dedicated to exploring the American Jewish experience as well as issues of American ethnic identity, history, art, and culture. In 2005, the museum was gifted the Peter H. Schweitzer Collection of Jewish Americana, with 10,000 items, the largest and most significant private collection of its type. The NMAJH will open a new facility in 2010.

In 1977, at a meeting of the Association of Jewish Studies, Dov Noy of the Hebrew University proposed the formation by American Jewish museums of an organization to further their efforts to "collect, preserve, and interpret Jewish art and artifacts." The Council of American Jewish Museums (CAJM) has grown from 7 to 80 institutional and associate members. CAJM membership ranges from major institutions to small organizations. Some are independent, and the largest percentage, about one-third, are synagogue museums. Others are affiliated with institutions of higher learning, some with Jewish federations and Jewish community centers. The collections, exhibitions, and programs of a number of the museums are broad in scope, encompassing the 4,000 years of Jewish cultural heritage. Others are more focused in their subject area, including local/regional history, the Holocaust, and contemporary art and ceremonial objects. Three are children's museums. The Jewish Women's Archive is unique in that all of its programs and exhibitions are online.

Beginning in the 1980s, there was a tremendous growth in the number of Jewish museums. The interest in preserving Jewish cultural heritage has reached communities large and small throughout the United States, paralleling a general preoccupation with ethnicity which emerged at the time and which encompasses a major component of contemporary identity.

Founded as the Jewish Historical Society of Maryland in 1960, the Jewish Museum of Maryland (JMM), considered the first regional American Jewish museum, is one of the largest in the United States related to regional and American Jewish history.

Situated in a historic Jewish neighborhood, the JMM saved and restored two synagogues, the Lloyd Street Synagogue (1845) and B'nai Israel Synagogue (1876), and incorporated them into a museum complex.

The Museum of the Southern Jewish Experience, now incorporated as part of the Goldring/Woldenberg Institute of the Southern Jewish Experience, was founded in 1986, through the initiative of Macy Hart to represent Jewish culture in the states of Mississippi, Louisiana, Alabama, Arkansas, and Tennessee, with plans to cover all 12 states of the south. The museum collects artifacts and archives, provides planning assistance for congregations, and works to save historic properties and to care for untended cemeteries.

The Jewish Museum of Florida in Miami Beach restored Congregation Beth Jacob, an art deco building dating from 1936. The museum originated as MOSAIC, a project organized by Marcia Kerstein Zerivitz, as a statewide grassroots preservation effort on the history of Jewish life in Florida. From 1984–1992, the MOSAIC team identified some 6,000 relevant items, many of which were donated to the museum. MOSAIC traveled for four years, and a version of the exhibition is on view at the museum. The museum's collection now numbers some 100,000 items.

The Oregon Jewish Museum, located in Old Town Portland, was founded in 1986 and in 1996 merged with the Jewish Historical Society of Oregon, acquiring its archives of 150 years of Jewish experience in Oregon and the Pacific Northwest. Other historical societies and museums of local Jewish history include: Alaska Jewish Historical Museum in Anchorage, Jewish Historical Society of MetroWest, New Jersey; Jewish Heritage Foundation of North Carolina (JHFNC), which maintains the Rosenzweig Museum at Judea Reform Congregation in Durham; the Milwaukee Jewish Historical Society opened a new Jewish Heritage Museum in 2007; the Sherwin Miller Museum of Jewish Art in Tulsa also serves as the Jewish Historical Society of Oklahoma; the Bremen Museum of Jewish Heritage in Atlanta includes a focus on the experience of the Jews in Georgia; and though without a permanent home, the Jewish Historical Society of the Upper Midwest organizes temporary exhibitions.

The National Yiddish Book Center grew out of a project established by Aaron Lansky in 1980 to rescue and preserve Yiddish books. In 1997, the Center's headquarters, described as a lively "cultural shtetl," opened in Amherst, Massachusetts, with a collection of over 1.5 million books, archives, and artifacts.

The Contemporary Jewish Museum was established in 1984 as the Jewish Museum, San Francisco. Included in the roster of innovative presentations has been a series of invitationals to encourage contemporary design for the celebration of Jewish life. This initiative reflects the virtual renaissance in the field of Jewish art, with artists working in a wide variety of materials and styles to explore their personal Jewish identity by creating contemporary artifacts. In 2008, the Contemporary Museum moved to its new home designed by Daniel Libeskind. The building is an adaptive reuse of the 1907 Jessie Street Power Substation.

The National Museum of American Jewish Military History, in Washington, D.C., under the auspices of the Jewish War Veterans of the United States, documents and educates about the contributions of American Jews who heroically served in the armed forces.

Numerous synagogue museums have been established in the past 30 years. Rabbi Abba Hillel Silver (1893–1963) pioneered the plan to establish a museum at the Temple Tifereth Israel in Cleveland in 1950, the centennial of the congregation. In 2005, the Temple's Judaica collection was incorporated as a gallery of the new Maltz Museum of Jewish Heritage in Beachwood, a Cleveland suburb. The Maltz Museum also features a core exhibition on the experience of the Jewish community in Cleveland as "An American Story." Also established in the 1950s is the Elizabeth S. and Alvin I. Fine Museum of Congregation Emanu-El, San Francisco, which has actively presented exhibitions since that time.

Some major synagogues saved commemorative artifacts and ceremonial objects that later formed the basis of museum collections in those congregations. In Boston, Temple Israel's Wyner Museum traces its origins to a 1910 exhibition. Congregation Emanu-El of the City of New York established a collection in 1928 with the collection of Henry Toch, a trustee, and it dedicated the Herbert and Eileen Bernard Museum decades later in 1997.

A number of museums have been formed in historically important synagogues. The Touro Synagogue in Newport, Rhode Island, built in 1763, was the first prominent synagogue to be built in America, and it is the only one to survive from the colonial era. The beginnings of Kahal Kadosh Beth Elohim in Charleston, South Carolina can be traced to 1775. The Temple and a museum are housed in an 1841 Greek Revival building that is the second-oldest synagogue in the United States and the oldest in continuous use. The Jewish Historical Society of Greater Washington is housed in the Adas Israel Synagogue dedicated in 1876. The Beth Ahabah Museum and Archives in Richmond, Virginia maintains materials dating back to the eighteenth century. The Eldridge Street Synagogue on New York's Lower East Side, completed in 1887, was the first designed and built in America by immigrants from Eastern Europe. Temple Emanu-El, (the Historic Stone Avenue Temple) in Tucson, Arizona, built in 1910, is home to the Jewish Heritage Center of the Southwest. The Vilna Shul, built in 1919, is now the Boston Center for Jewish Heritage.

Since the late 1970s the most profound aspect of the emphasis on history as memory has been the establishment of Holocaust museums and memorials in nearly every state. The Association of Holocaust Organizations was founded in 1985. The museums and memorials are historical resources, serve as places of remembrance, and provide a context for developing awareness of the contemporary implications of the Holocaust and related issues of human rights.

In 1978, President Jimmy Carter created the Presidential Commission on the Holocaust, which led to the formation of the **United States Holocaust Memorial Museum** in Washington dedicated in 1993. The USHMM, a federal institution, serves as America's national institution for the documentation, study, and interpretation of Holocaust history, and as the memorial of the United States to the millions of victims. The Simon Wiesenthal Center, Museum of Tolerance in Los Angeles, which opened in 1993, is named in honor of Simon Wiesenthal (1908–2005) who survived the Holocaust and dedicated his life to bringing the perpetrators to justice. The Wiesenthal Center is dedicated to the furthering the cause of human rights. The Museum of Jewish Heritage in New York opened in 1997. It is sited in view of the Statue of Liberty and Ellis Island and just five blocks form the former site of the World Trade Center. The museum was "created as a living memorial to the Holocaust" to honor the lives and legacy of the victims of the Holocaust even as it recounts the tragedy of their deaths.

An innovative model for maximizing cultural and fiscal resources led to the establishment of the Center for Jewish History, located in New York City in 2000. The self-described purpose is to "present a unique opportunity to preserve the Jewish heritage, advance Jewish scholarship, art and culture, and build on the richness of the Jewish past." The Center houses the combined holdings of the American Jewish Historical Society, American Sephardi Federation, Leo Baeck Institute, Yeshiva University Museum, and YIVO Institute for Jewish Research. The largest repository of Jewish artifacts, archives, and historical materials in this country, the CJH houses over one hundred million archival documents, a half million library volumes, and tens of thousands of artifacts and art works.

Undoubtedly the brightest note in the Jewish museum world in the United States today is the focus on special installations for children and their families and the creation of independent Jewish children's museums. Independent museums include the Zimmer Children's Museum in Los Angeles and the Jewish Children's Learning Lab and the Jewish Children's Museum in New York.

In a time of rapid change and many challenges for the Jewish community in America, Jewish museums seek to explore and advance contemporary Jewish identity. Through innovative exhibitions, public programs, and special projects they have positioned themselves to play a role in guaranteeing a strong and vital future for American Jewry as well as to reach a broader and more diverse audience. *See also* **United States Holocaust Memorial Museum**.

Grace Cohen Grossman

Further Reading: Frazier, Nancy. *Jewish Museums of North America*. John Wiley and Sons Inc., 1992. Grossman, Grace Cohen. *Jewish Museums of the World*. Hough Lauter Levin Associates, Inc.; Beaux Arts Editions, 2003.

JEWISH WOMEN AND POPULAR CULTURE

It is in twentieth-century America that Jewish women actors, singers, dancers, and comics got their greatest opportunity to display their talents. In Europe, during earlier periods, women's chances of performing on a public stage were much more limited. Prejudice against Jews and against women denied them an active role in public performances. In sharp contrast, many factors combined to make the American scene inviting to women entertainers: a growing population in urban areas (particularly a Jewish one); the commercialization of entertainment; the presence of Jewish entrepreneurs in vaudeville, burlesque, the theater and movies; and the seemingly insatiable need for enjoyment, even among the immigrant poor. Combine these ingredients with the agnostic and secular capitalistic view of "whatever sells is okay," and you have conditions enabling talented and ambitious women to appear in public. This was a major departure from the norms regarding women's behavior in both Jewish and Christian society. The religious imperatives of both traditions demanded that women remain in the home, behave modestly, and be obedient to their fathers and husbands. Appearing on the stage, often in skimpy costumes, was a radical break with the past. But it happened in twentieth-century America.

Impresarios and entrepreneurs in the new but growing industry of show business looked for talent to attract audiences, particularly male audiences (before the family market was targeted). Attractive young women offered sure-fire appeal. Religious issues were not the only challenges immigrant Jewish women (and immigrant women of all ethnicities) faced. They had to rid themselves of any accent, speak English well, shed their modesty, and learn ways to amuse and engage an audience. Once they accomplished this, they faced the normal difficulties of getting a break in the business. Many Jewish women who aspired to a career in entertainment shed their Jewish identity willingly. Fewer of them retained their Jewish persona and built their image on that very identity. This essay focuses upon Jewish women entertainers who integrated their Jewish identity, however tenuous, to their performance. Those who rejected their Jewish heritage are not included in this survey.

The first step toward popular success for some Jewish women was the **Yiddish theater**, which flourished in big cities with large Jewish populations. Few women stars of that stage, however, made the transition to the American theater. Their facility in English was limited, and their acting style was too exaggerated for the American stage. There were exceptions such as Bertha Kalisch and **Molly Picon**, who had a limited career in the American theater, but most of their fans were housed in Yiddish theaters. It was the daughters of immigrants, already a step closer to assimilation, who became the famous vaudevillians, burlesque queens, and singers on Broadway. These women were already accustomed to American ways, and they had the necessary ambition, along with no reluctance to give up their religious traditions. They traveled with vaudeville troupes on the Jewish Sabbath and Holy Days and fit in with Christian Americans. And yet in the cases to be described, they retained a connection to their Jewish heritage and proudly proclaimed it before their audiences. For Jewish women entertainers, the tie to Judaism was cultural, not religious. Indeed, many were not quite sure what it means to be Jewish, but they publicly acknowledged that identity nonetheless.

Fanny Brice (1891–1951) is the best example of this soon-to-be assimilated generation of stars. New York-born, but not Yiddish-speaking, Brice won an amateur singing contest while a teenager and went on to appear in small parts on Broadway. Eventually, she became a headliner in the Ziegfeld Follies and remained a Ziegfeld star for most of the 1920s. She combined a great voice with a comedic manner to enthrall her audiences. Brice learned an **Irving Berlin** song that satirized Salome of the seven veils and, to add to the humor, she sang it with a Yiddish accent (taught to her by Berlin). Brice often made fun of her own people, which, she once said, she did to show that she both identified with Jews and recognized their vulnerabilities. Her skit-songs became legendary and audiences insisted upon repeat performances.

"Mrs. Cohen at the Beach," for example, made gentle fun of a possessive and overly proud mother who thought her children were superior to all others. Brice's very expressive face and great timing conveyed the message effectively. "I'm an Indian," another Brice classic, describes a maiden who had been captured by the Indians; only later does everyone discover that she is Rosie Rosenstein, a nice Jewish girl. Because New York was the home to multiple immigrant cultures in the 1910s and 1920s, audiences, Jewish and Christian alike, enjoyed the gentle mocking that Brice offered. Everyone could identify with her characters, their ambitions, and their anxieties.

Sophie Tucker (1884–1966) is another example of a successful Jewish woman entertainer whose career began in the early decades of the twentieth century. Tucker's main success came in the new nightclubs, an intimate venue that allowed performers to do off-color jokes and sing songs with double entendres. Sexual content was possible in night clubs but not in the larger settings of vaudeville, or later radio and the movies. Many Jewish women flourished in this medium; being naughty, displaying an independent streak, and showing a shocking willingness to say the forbidden, made bawdy stars like Tucker and her contemporary Belle Barth very popular. In nightclubs like Reisenweber's in New York City, Tucker sang "A Good Man Is Hard to Find," and "I'm the Last of the Red Hot Mammas." A physically large woman with a gravelly voice, she expressed her desire for sexual satisfaction in many songs. Her audiences laughed when she declared her interest in sex as they were both titillated by a lady singing about such a subject and amused that a heavy woman shared the same yearnings as a skinny lady. In 1925, Jack Yellen wrote "My Yiddishe Mamma" for her, and this song became a regular number in all of her performances. Combining sentimental with the sexual became her trademark.

When silent movies became the rage in the 1910s and 1920s, Jewish women entertainers found that the movie studio heads, though predominantly Jewish, were not particularly interested in hiring Jewish actresses. The Jewish entrepreneurs wanted to demonstrate their American credentials and advised Jewish performers to change their names and hide their Jewish identity. Theodosia Goodman, a nice Jewish girl from Philadelphia, became Theda Bara. She was presented as an exotic, as a symbol of an Oriental beauty. While **Al Jolson** in ***The Jazz Singer*** portrayed the conflict between traditional Jewish life and the lure of America, there is no equivalent female treatment of the subject. Jewish women actresses distinguished themselves in the movies as actresses, but their identity no longer included their Judaic heritage.

It is not until the 1950s, in early television, that we see an openly Jewish woman live comfortably in her identity. Born in New York City to a family that ran a resort hotel in the **Catskill Mountains**, Berg spent every summer there and began to write and produce skits at an early age. Gertrude Berg, known as Molly Goldberg in a weekly television show, became a very popular star portraying a nurturing and humorous Jewish mother. In 1929, Berg starred in *The Rise of the Goldbergs* on the NBC Blue Network. The show was on the air for five years and in another incarnation was broadcast on CBS from 1938 to 1945. In 1949, it went to television and endured for five years reaping good ratings and good reviews. Berg's character, Molly Goldberg, had a husband Jake, children Rosalie and Sammy, and a boarder Uncle David. Molly listened patiently to peoples' troubles and offered commonsensical words of advice. Yiddishisms were sprinkled throughout the conversations, with a lot of "oy veys" and "nus." In Cold War America, Molly Goldberg provided soothing assurance to American audiences that families remained strong in the heart of American life. Her popularity also confirmed that ethnic differences were still recognized in multicultural America.

Perhaps the most spectacularly successful Jewish woman entertainer of the twentieth century is **Barbra Streisand**. A singer, actress, and film director, she has won awards for her stage performances, for her recordings, and for her films. Beginning on Broadway in 1961 as Miss Marmelstein in *I Can Get It For You Wholesale,* Streisand's fabulous voice, her fine articulation, and her comic talents distinguished her from other aspiring performers. Her portrayal of Fanny Brice in the stage version of *Funny Girl* two years later made her a star. The film version in 1968 won her an Oscar. Streisand as Brice seemed to be a natural fit: a Jewish woman singer-comic who was not conventionally beautiful and who becomes a big hit on Broadway and, in Streisand's case, Hollywood.

Funny Girl was the first of many roles in which she played a Jewish character. In four of her most memorable movies, a Jewish woman is the main character—in *The Way We Were* (1973) Streisand plays a radical student activist in the 1930s who marries the quintessential goy, Robert Redford, and follows him to Hollywood during the heyday of the Red Scare after World War II. In *Yentl* (1983) she is a Jewish girl in shtetl Europe who masquerades as a boy so that she could study Torah. In *The Prince of Tides* (1991) she plays a psychiatrist who wonders aloud why she falls for Gentile men. And in the 1996 *The Mirror Has Two Faces,* she is a college professor with a nagging mother played by **Lauren Bacall**. Streisand openly acknowledges that Jewishness is a factor in all of these movies.

While Fanny Brice had her nose fixed in the 1920s, Streisand never changed her stereotypically Jewish nose. She seemed comfortable with her Jewish identity and in her role as a liberal Democrat in Hollywood. Her music did not include explicitly Jewish themes, but her prominence as a singer, actress, and film director made her religious identity common knowledge. In the early twenty-first century, reports indicated that she was studying Kabbalah, the mystical tradition of Judaism, with a Los Angeles rabbi.

Bette Midler, a contemporary of Streisand's, is the last example of a very popular concert singer and film star of the 1970s and 1980s who identified as a Jew. In her public pronouncements as well as her fondness for Sophie Tucker songs and shtick, she referred to herself as Jewish. Born in Honolulu to a Jewish father and Christian mother, she wrote a comic autobiography called *A View from a Broad* (1980) and recounted how being white and Jewish in Hawaii was unusual, and, she quipped, she was not sure what it meant to be a Jew either. Midler began her career in 1965 by playing a small part and then Tsaytl, Tevye's oldest daughter, in *Fiddler on the Roof.* She developed a night club act which included the persona called the *Divine Miss M*. In the

1980s, she made a few very successful comedies including *Ruthless People* (1986), *Outrageous Fortune* (1987), and *Beaches* (1988). In the 1990s, she returned to concertizing and toured the country in her updated 1970s show. Her movie versions of *Stella Dallas* and *Gypsy* did not match her earlier cinematic successes and, in the early twenty-first century, she returned to the concert stage.

While there have been occasional Jewish actresses on television dramas (Kyra Sedgwick in *The Closer*) and situation comedies (Debra Messing in *Will and Grace,* and Sarah Jessica Parker in *Sex in the City,* for example), their number has been few and far between. Jewish women comics, by contrast, have flourished in recent years in venues reminiscent of the early twentieth century: instead of the intimate nightclubs, they perform in comedy clubs and on cable television. **Sarah Silverman** is a recent example; few, however, can be seen on mainstream television or big screen movies. While the golden moment when a large urban Jewish migration merged with the rise of entertainment has passed, Jewish women entertainers will continue to reinterpret themselves and their careers to accommodate the ever-changing entertainment industry.

June Sochen

Further Reading: Berg, Gertrude, and Charney Berg. *Molly and Me*. New York: McGraw Hill, 1961. Grossman, Barbara W. *Funny Woman: The Life and Times of Fanny Brice*. Bloomington, IN: Indiana University Press, 1991. Hyman, Paula E., and Deborah Dash Moore, eds. *Jewish Women in America: An Historical Encyclopedia*. New York: Routledge, 1997. Sochen, June. *Consecrate Every Day: The Public Lives of Jewish American Women, 1880–1980*. Albany, NY: SUNY Press, 1981. ———. *From Mae to Madonna: Women Entertainers in 20th Century America*. Lexington, KY: University Press of Kentucky, 1999.

JOEL, BILLY (1949–)

Piano-playing rock star Billy Joel was born in New York on May 9, 1949 and grew up in Hicksville, New York. His father, Howard Joel, was a Jewish Holocaust survivor from Germany, whose father, Karl Amson Joel, owned the fourth-largest mail order company in Germany before being dispossessed by the Nazis. His mother, Rosalind Nyman, was born in England, to an agnostic Jewish family. Howard Joel barely escaped from Germany in 1939 before the Nazis implemented their plan to exterminate the Jews of Europe. The blows of losing their business and possessions, being forced to flee, and spending three years as refugees in Cuba may have caused the Joels to keep their Jewish roots under wraps when the family arrived in the United States in 1942. Upon their arrival in the United States in 1943, Howard Joel was drafted and was among the American troops who liberated Dachau, the infamous concentration camp in southern Germany. "I had relatives that were in concentration camps—although not Dachau—and some of them were put to death. But at Dachau . . . it was terrible. We were too late to help," Howard Joel said in a 1994 Billboard interview. Given the family history, it's no coincidence that so many of Billy Joel's songs champion the underdog.

Billy Joel's parents divorced in 1960, and his father returned to Europe, resettling in Vienna, Austria. Billy Joel has two siblings—a sister, Judith Joel, and a half-brother, Alexander Joel, who is an acclaimed classical pianist and conductor in Europe, now living in New York.

As Billy Joel was raised by his mother, he developed an intense interest in music. He was especially fond of classical music. Some of the neighborhood bullies thought that he was studying to become a ballet dancer, and he became the victim of beatings and teasing, which led Joel to take up boxing in order to defend himself. He was good at boxing and entered the Golden Gloves circuit, where he won some matches, but he chose to give it up after his nose had been broken. Rock and roll was the music of his time, but he fell in love with the melodies of Paul McCartney and the Beatles. They inspired him to write songs of his own. Between jobs to help support his mother, his sister, and his music, he did not have much time to devote to school work. He was supposed to graduate from Hicksville High School in 1967, but he lacked one English credit, and in order to get that diploma he would have to attend summer school, but he chose to pursue his musical career instead. (Twenty-five years later the Hicksville school board waived the English requirement for Joel and granted him his diploma.) He joined a local band and attempted some recordings, but they did not turn out so well. In 1971 he tried to record a solo album entitled *Cold Spring Harbor,* but it likewise did not turn out so well. He moved to Los Angeles and performed at a piano bar, which would give him the experience for later recordings such as the *Piano Man* album, which was released in 1973 and became a bestseller. Over the years he would sell some four million copies of that album, which also included such titles as "Captain Jack," "The Ballad of Billy the Kid," and "You're My Home."

As he contracted with Columbia Records he was on his way to becoming one of the most successful musicians in America. His recordings included such songs as "Just the Way You Are," "Only the Good Die Young," "She's Always a Woman."

In 1980–1981 he had success with such songs as "Honesty," "Don't Ask Me Why," and "It's Still Rock and Roll to Me." That year he won a Grammy for the Best Rock Vocal Performance.

In June 1987 he performed in such Soviet cities as Moscow and Leningrad. The trip was a financial disaster, but he felt that his rock and roll concerts had helped better relations between the United States and Russia and that brought some good will.

His songs would be among the top 10 hits for three decades from the 1970s, 1980s, to 1990s, and he was to be a six-time Grammy Award winner. Some have seen in his song "We Didn't Start the Fire" Joel's defense of the Jewish community against anti-Semitism. The single, from the album *Storm Front,* was released in September 1989, and it became Joel's third number one hit, spending two weeks at the top of the charts. His early 1990s album entitled *River of Dreams* won four Grammy Awards for Record, Album, Song of the Year, and Best Male Pop Vocal Performance.

Billy Joel sold some 150 million records worldwide and was inducted into the Songwriter's Hall of Fame in 1992, the Rock and Roll Hall of Fame in 1999, and the Long Island Music Hall of Fame in 1996. He did some work on Walt Disney's *Oliver Twist* (1997), where he composed and acted. Among the songs he sang in the film was "Why Should I Worry?"

In 1997 he received a Lifetime Achievement Award from the American Society of Composers and Authors and in 1999 the Award of Merit from American Music Awards. Soon thereafter he returned to recording singles, starting with "All My Life." In 2000 he recorded his 17th album, called *The Millennium Concert,* for which the Smithsonian Institute awarded him the James Smithson Bicentennial Medal; a few months later Southampton College awarded him an honorary Doctor of Music degree. In 2001 he released *Fantasies and Delusions,* a recording of classical compositions for the piano.

Joel married his business manager Elizabeth Weber in 1973, and they divorced in 1982. He married Christie Brinkley in 1985. Their daughter, Alexa Ray Joel, was born in 1986. Joel and Brinkley's marriage ended in divorce in 1994. In 2004, Joel married 23-year-old culinary artist Katie Lee. Joel's second wife, Christie Brinkley, attended the union and gave the couple her blessing. *See also* **Popular Music**; **Rock and Roll**.

Herbert M. Druks

Further Reading: Benarde, Scott. *Stars of David: Rock 'n' Roll's Jewish Stories.* Brandeis University Press, 2003.

JOHANSSON, SCARLETT (1984–)

Award-winning actress Scarlett Johansson was born in Manhattan, New York on November 22, 1984 to Melanie Sloan and Karsten Johansson. Her mother's family is Jewish of Danish and Polish descent. Johansson attended the Professional Children's School in Manhattan, where she graduated in 2002. By the time she was 17, she had appeared in 11 movies; by 2007, Johansson had appeared in almost 30 feature films.

Johansson made her stage debut off-Broadway at the age of eight. She first appeared on television the following year during *Late Night with Conan O'Brien*. In 1994, she appeared in her first feature film, *North* (1994), directed by **Rob Reiner**. In 1998, she appeared in the breakthrough film *The Horse Whisperer,* which led to critically acclaimed appearances in *Ghostworld* (2001) and *Lost in Translation* (2003), among many others.

The actress has received critical acclaim and maintained popular appeal. Johannsson has received recognition from prestigious organizations such as the British Academy of Film and Television Arts, as well as organizations more closely linked to pop culture (that is, the MTV Movie Awards, Teen Choice Awards, and People's Choice Awards). In 1998, Johansson received a Hollywood Reporter Young Star award for her appearance in *The Horse Whisperer.* In 2003 she received Golden Globe nominations for her appearances in *Girl with a Pearl Earring* (2003) and *Lost in Translation*. In 2005, she received a Golden Globe nomination for her appearance in the **Woody Allen** film *Match Point*. In 2007, she was named Harvard University's Hasty Pudding Theatricals "Woman of the Year." Johansson made several films in 2008, including *The Other Boleyn Girl* and *Vicky Cristina Barcelona*.

In September 2008, Johansson married actor Ryan Reynolds. As of this writing, Johansson has several films in production, including Woody Allen's *Spanish Project,* and she is developing a singing career. *See also* **Film**.

Danny Rigby

Further Reading: Roberts, Chris. *Scarlett Johansson: Portrait of a Rising Star*. Carlton Publishing Group, 2007.

JOLSON, AL (1886–1950)

The great Al Jolson (given name was Asa Joelson) who entertained millions of people from 1920s to 1950 with his unique baritone voice was born on March 26,1886 in a Lithuanian village in Imperial Russia. He was the fourth surviving child of Moshe and Naomi Yoelson. The family was Orthodox, and their father made a living as a cantor and rabbi. Moshe Yoelson left his family for America in order to earn enough passage money so that they could all leave Russia and establish themselves in America. In 1894 Yoelson was hired to become the head of a Washington, D.C. congregation. He then sent his family money to come to America. A year after they arrived in New York, Naomi died. It was a shattering time for the Yoelsons, and Al Jolson would never be the same, always haunted by the death of his mother.

Jolson and his brother Hirsh were attracted to show business, and subsequently both brothers were booked with a comedy act called "The Hebrew and the Cadet." In 1904 Jolson started performing blackface at Kennedy's Theater in Brooklyn. Soon thereafter he was hired to perform for vaudeville's Orpheum circuit. The blackface act had been used in vaudeville since the early 1900s and was part of American comedy that used racial and ethnic groups as objects of humor. Jolson was no racist; he used blackface because it was normative for many showmen of the time as a vehicle to entertain rather than to consciously ridicule African Americans.

Harry quit the team when he realized that he was holding his brother back from becoming a star. In 1906 he was a solo act as a "singing comedian." He performed in San Francisco and then toured the West. Within a year he married Henrietta Keller, then joined a minstrel troupe that headed for New York, where he was an outstanding success. It was about this time that he incorporated whistling as part of his act. He performed in the Winter Garden Theater in 1911 and was a great success. As was the experience of many Jewish composers and show business personalities, such as George Gershwin, Al Jolson was influenced by the rhythms of African American music, such as jazz, blues, and ragtime. Many of his popular songs, such as "Swanee," "My Mammy," and "Rock-A-Bye Your Baby with A Dixie Melody," were derivative of this musical genre.

A photo of Al Jolson performing in blackface as Jack Robin in the 1927 feature-length motion picture *The Jazz Singer.* The film, which dealt with the issue of assimilation, heralded the commercial ascendance of the "talkies" and the decline of the silent film era. [AP Photo]

Jolson was also among the first popular entertainers to make a spectacular "event" out of singing a song. Prior to Jolson, popular singers would stand still, with only minimal gesturing as they performed. In contrast, Jolson displayed enormous energy, and it was common for him to sit on the end of the stage and have personal interaction with the audience.

Jolson's success in vaudeville was mirrored by his Broadway stage career. His first starring role on Broadway was in *Robinson Crusoe, Jr.* (1916), followed by the hit play *Sinbad,* which was the most successful play of the 1918–1919 season. The show included two songs that would later be identified with Jolson: "Swanee," composed by George Gershwin, and "My Mammy." By 1920, Jolson was one of the biggest stars on Broadway, and his prominence on stage continued throughout the decade.

In 1927 Warner Brothers cast Jolson in the "first" talking film, *The Jazz Singer.* Jolson sang five songs in the film, including "Mamie." In 1928, Jolson made his first "all-talking" picture, *The Singing Fool,* and subsequently went on to make more than 16 films between 1928 and 1949. Towards the end of his film career, he lent his voice to such movies as *The Jolson Story* (1946), which featured Larry Parks as Jolson, as well as the sequel, *Jolson Sings Again* (1949), and in *Oh, You Beautiful Doll* (1949).

Al Jolson was one of the greatest entertainers of his time. Four years after his death the United States Postal Service issued a postage stamp in his honor. In 2006, Al Jolson had a street in New York named after him. He died of a massive heart attack on October 23, 1950. *See also* **Film; *The Jazz Singer*; Popular Music; Vaudeville.**

Herbert M. Druks

Further Reading: Dunning, John. *On the Air: The Encyclopedia of Old-Time Radio.* Oxford University Press, 1998. Oberfirst. *Al Jolson: You Ain't Heard Nothin Yet.* Barnes, 1980.

JONG, ERICA (1942–)

Erica Jong is the author of 8 novels and 19 books of poetry. Her best-known novel is *Fear of Flying* (1973), a work of fiction with autobiographical overtones. Like many of her other works, the novel includes explicit sexuality. Other themes of concern to women include issues of independence, self-esteem, wisdom, power, and courage.

Jong was born in Manhattan's Upper West Side to Russian Jewish Seymour Mann and Eda Mirsk. Her parents were Barnard graduates who were artistic, musically inclined, and poets, and her Jewish consciousness manifested itself in a bohemian lifestyle at university, where she majored in English literature. She married four times, first to her college sweetheart, Michael Werthman; her second husband was Chinese American psychiatrist Allan Jong, with whom she had a daughter, Molly Jong-Fast (who is the author of three books); her third husband was novelist and social work educator Jonathan Fast. Her present spouse is Ken Burrow, a New York divorce lawyer.

Erica's strong Jewish awareness is reflected in her novels. They are peppered with **Yiddish** phrases, quotations from the Talmud, Yiddish proverbs, and references to Jewish history. In *Fear of Flying* there are echoes of the Holocaust. The novel *Parachutes and Kisses* tells of a pilgrimage to the Nazi World War II killing center at Baba Yar. In *Inventing Memory, a Novel of Mothers and Daughters* (1997) her main character Sarah Solomon experiences a Russian pogrom, and, in America a Jewish neighborhood of radicals and bohemians. The novel traces four generations of Jewish women. In *Shylock's Daughter* (1987), the main character is transported back through time to Shakespeare's Venice and the home of the controversial moneylender.

This "red diaper" baby (a reference to the children of communists, anarchists, and anyone considered radical) expressed her idea about what Jewishness means to very secular Jews as their being people who remain Jewish because they love memory, love words, and revere the written word. Jong attributed this to the Jewish religion which worships a scroll (the Sefer Torah). Even though she was slow to recognize it, Erica Jong's writing has been deeply influenced by her Jewish roots. As she ages she says she feels more comfortable among her own people with whom she has so much in common. *See also* **Literature**.

Philip Rosen

Further Reading: Jong, Erica. *Seducing the Demon: Writing for My Life.* Tarcher, 2006.

JOURNALISM

Jewish young men gravitated to journalism in the early part of the twentieth century. Encouraged by their parents to avoid factory work or petty storekeeping and enter professions upon graduation, they found many careers restricted, even closed. Journalism provided an opening for intellectual, highly articulate, urbane, verbally gifted, and well educated people. Politically, they were liberal. They knew and understood a generation that suffered a 70-hour week, a 7-day week, child labor, union busting, and a cruel free market society unfettered by regulation. They were not, however, unsympathetic to government intervention to correct the abuses of capitalism and social welfare measures to help the poor and working classes.

There was a small settlement of Jews in Palestine (Yishuv), but Zionism, the movement to create a Jewish state in Palestine, was unpopular. Most Orthodox Jews rejected the movement for theological reasons, while Reform Jews disdained Jewish nationalism, considering the Jewish people to be a religious group. Many Jews felt it was unpatriotic to say that there was a homeland outside the United States; their Zion was America.

Even this new Zion in America presented problems. During the 1930s, American Jews were timid, fearful of anti-Semitism, and frightened as events in Europe threatened the lives of their brethren. The German American Bund and the Ku Klux Klan marched in the streets. Radio priest Father Charles Coughlin (1891–1979) ranted to 15 million people against "the international Jewish conspiracy." Economic and social discrimination was blatant throughout the country. Jews, including Jewish journalists, did not want to bring up Jewish identity. This essay will discuss Jewish journalists in reference to liberalism, conservatism, Zionism, and Jewish identity.

One could make a division between the Jewish journalists from the early part of the century to the 1960s. Few Jewish journalists in publishing, radio, television, or newspapers revealed their Jewish identity or political views. Walter Lippmann (1889–1974), editorial columnist, author, and political pundit was considered the dean of journalism and a major foreign policy expert. He helped President Woodrow Wilson (1856–1924) write his "Fourteen Points" (1918). Lippmann shed his youthful socialist inclinations and his Jewish identity early. In his career not a word did he write about Jewish concerns, even as the terrible **Holocaust** raged and the new State of Israel was born and came under attack. Adolph Ochs (1855–1935) bought the *New York Times* in 1896 and kept it in the family. The family did not want the paper to appear as a Jewish publication. The paper relegated Jewish concerns, even the horrors of the Holocaust, to small articles on inside pages.

There were some exceptions. Some Jewish journalists revealed interest in Jewish-related subjects and politics. Liberalism prior to our own time did not include such issues as abortion, stem cell research, religion in the public square, or gay marriage. It was concerned with social justice for working people, anti-fascism and anti-militarism. I. F. Stone (1907–1989) wrote for the left wing *P.M.* newspaper and had his own *I. F. Stone Weekly,* where he challenged the foreign policies of the administration and the premises of the Cold War. He favored the Jewish pioneers of the Yishuv, and when Israel was born, he featured it but soon became a friendly critic. The **Yiddish** papers reported the German atrocities, while the Anglo-Jewish press was generally reluctant to feature the evolving Holocaust. The ***Jewish Daily Forward*** espoused social democracy, while the small circulation *Freiheit* was communist and pro-Soviet. Howard Fast (1914–2003) was a communist who wrote glowingly about the Soviet Union until the revelations about Stalin in 1956. Gilbert Seldes (1898–1970) was fiercely anti-Nazi and pro-New Deal in his weekly *In Fact,* as was radio and feature gossip and political columnist **Walter Winchell** (1897–1972). Winchell later became an obsessive red-baiter. Nathan Fleischer, Yiddish radio commentator, favored left-wing presidential candidate Henry Wallace and the Progressive Party in 1947–1948.

Ben Hecht (1894–1964), like so many Jewish journalists, ignored Jewish and Zionist issues until he met Peter Bergson (1915–2001), representative of the right-wing Zionist Revisionist Party in 1941. In an epiphany, Hecht took a strong stand for Jewish identity, Zionism, and he publicized the Yishuv, the Holocaust, and American apathy. Postwar, Hecht wrote about Nazi war criminals, at a time when very few in the Yiddish and Anglo-Jewish press did. (Nor did the general press, which, like the American government, was trying to appease the U.S. ally West Germany.) Writer **Meyer Levin** (1905–1981) wrote about the Holocaust, the postwar difficulties of European Jews, and the problems of the Yishuv. His play about Anne Frank was repressed by playwright Lillian Hellman (1905–1984). She promoted a version absent of Jewishness, such was the timidity of the Jewish literary intelligentsia.

With the cultural revolution of 1960s a new group of journalists came forth. They rejected social and economic liberalism and New Left counterculture. Its origin was Barry Goldwater's failed presidential attempt in 1964. The movement came together in 1970. Many Jewish journalists defected to this anti-liberal rejectionist position. The term "neoconservative" was coined by the democratic socialist writer Michael Harrington (1928–1989). He said neoconservative journalists believed that liberals did not know what they are talking about, and furthermore their ideas were counterproductive; foremost thinkers were Irving Kristol (b. 1920), long time editor of *Commentary,* founder of magazines *Encounter, Public Interest,* and *National Interest*—

as well as Norman Podhoretz (b. 1930) *Commentary's* chief editor. They attacked government planning and its unintended consequences, high taxes, and they favored a vigorous and well funded military. The neoconservatives criticized the black equality movement (including affirmative action) and the antipoverty movement. Poverty, they claimed, was mainly due to poor character traits rather than socioeconomic factors. They opposed the women's rights movement and restrictions on the free market. They supported a militant, proactive, anticommunist foreign policy and were favorable to the Vietnam War. The vanguard included such Jewish policy intellectuals as Paul Wolfowiz (b. 1943), Douglas Feith (b. 1953), Richard Perle (b. 1948), and Felix Rohatyn (b. 1928). They rallied around Senator Henry "Scoop" Jackson's (1912–1983) presidential campaigns (1972, 1976). Then they moved to support Ronald Reagan (1911–2004) in his presidential campaigns of the 1980s. Their major plank was that American power should intercede around the world promoting U.S. interests. They favored aiding and supporting the State of Israel.

President George W. Bush's policies after September 11 catapulted the neoconservatives into the limelight. A Bush speechwriter and commentator for the neoconservative flagship journal, the *Weekly Standard,* David Frum (b. 1960) coined the term "axis of evil," which was used by the president to characterize the states Iraq, Iran, and North Korea. It suggested preemptive war. Max Boot (b. 1969) then-editor of the pro-administration newspaper *Wall Street Journal,* opined that the United States "must stop terrorists overseas and play the role of global policeman" ("The Bush Doctrine," 2002).

Barry Rubin (b. 1966), author and research scholar in terrorist affairs, claims that the neoconservative label is a pejorative, code word for Jew. Anti-Semites and anti-Israel writers assert that support for Israel is to the detriment of true American interests. David Horowitz (b. 1939), ex-Trotskyite, now a stout right-wing Israel supporter, has his own media organizations, the David Horowitz Freedom Center and the cyberspace/online *Frontpage Magazine.* He claims the term "neoconservative" is used exclusively by those who oppose the Iraq war and are appeasers in the war against what he calls "Islamofascism." This term conflates some modern Islamic groups and movements with the twentieth-century European fascist movement. Islamofascists are to be distinguished from devout Muslims who reject terrorist means.

Another major Jewish columnist who writes on "Islamofascism" (better known as radical jihadists) is Daniel Pipes (b. 1949). He heads his own creation, a think tank in Philadelphia called the Middle East Forum, which hosts a staff of writers who monitor and comment on what they believe is false and hostile anti-Israel materials in the media.

There are other organizations that act as watchdogs over the media and try to correct anti-Israel, pro-Palestinian material. They are private subscriber online and print organizations—*Flame, Honest Reporting,* and *Camera.* They reproduce articles by Harvard Professor **Alan Dershowitz** (b. 1938), Caroline Glick (b. 1978)—editor of the *Jerusalem Post,* and historian Michael G. Bard (b. 1959).

Jews are well represented in the top tiers of publishing, ownership, and chairmanships. Gerald Levin (b. 1947) heads Time Warner, a huge conglomerate which includes *Time* and the television all-news station CNN. Michael Eisner (b. 1942) heads the Walt Disney Company, a conglomerate that includes ABC, ESPN, and A&E. Mortimer Zuckerman (b. 1937) owns *U.S. News & World Report, Atlantic Magazine,* and the *New York Daily News.* Howard Stringer (b. 1942) heads Sony of America. Samuel (b. 1927) and Donald Newhouse (b. 1930) took over from their father, Samuel Sr. (1895–1976), a publishing empire. It consisted of 31 daily newspapers, 7 radio stations, 6 television stations, and 15 cable stations. It included the *Cleveland Plain Dealer,* the *New Orleans Times Picayune,* and the Sunday supplement *Parade.* It later expanded to the magazines *The New Yorker, Vanity Fair, Vogue, Glamour, Bride,* and *Gourmet.*

Ralph J. Roberts (b. 1920) founded Comcast, the huge cable network. (It is now headed by his son, Brian Roberts.) Sumner Redstone (b. 1923) controls Viacom, which holds CBS. Leslie Moonves (b. 1949) is the president of CBS Television. David Westin (b. 1950) is president of ABC News. Peter Chernin (b. 1951) is the CEO of Israel-friendly Fox News, where he manages the news section.

The most influential American newspapers are published by Jewish owners and have a number of Jewish writers. The *New York Times,* as was mentioned, was in the hands of the Ochs family. The current editor Arthur Ochs Sultzberger (b. 1926) is the product of marriage with the Sultzberger family. This is a media empire that includes 32 other papers. The *Boston Globe* and magazines *McCall's* and *Family Circle* belong to it. The *Times* employs both conservative and liberal columnists. William Safire (b. 1929) is conservative with a pro-Israel slant. David Brooks (b. 1961) is a neoconservative who also serves as senior editor of the *Weekly Standard.* He is pro-Israel. **Thomas Friedman** (b. 1953) is the *Times* Middle East specialist. He mentions his Jewish identity, takes a position recognizing Israel's terrorist problems, sees a two-state solution, and yet is often critical. Frank Rich (b. 1949) and economist Paul Krugman (b. 1953) are the most left and are critical of the conservatives and the Bush administration. Both rarely mention Israel. Editorially, the *Times* takes a centrist position regarding Palestinian-Israeli issues. Editorially, the paper does criticize the administration, but it is not the flaming left-wing journal its critics make it out to be.

The *Wall Street Journal* has the largest circulation of the newspaper dailies. Peter R. Kann (b. 1942) is the chairman and publisher. Both its paper and online edition take a pro-Bush administration position and are very sympathetic to Israel's interests. Kann also heads Dow Jones Co., the parent company of the *Journal.* Dow publishes 24 other newspapers, including the financially oriented *Barrons,* edited by Max Boot.

The *Washington Post* was bought by Eugene Meyer, a financier, in 1933 and was run by his daughter Katherine Meyer Graham (1917–2001) —who, incidentally, converted to Christianity. Her son Donald (b. 1945) now is the CEO and publisher. Editorially, it is mildly liberal and pro-Palestinian. Richard Cohen (b. 1952), a major columnist, stated that the creation of Israel was a mistake. David Broder (b. 1928) and Carl Bernstein (b. 1944), both centrists politically, ignore Jewish-related issues. However, reflexive pro-Israel Charles Krauthammer (b. 1950) is godfather of the neoconservative movement. His essay in *Foreign Affairs,* advocating the use of American power to impose its interests upon the world, is the core of neoconservatist foreign policy.

The *New York Post* was purchased by Dorothy Schiff (1903–1989, daughter of the financier Jacob Schiff), and under her tenure it was liberal, supporting unions, the New Deal, and social welfare measures. Max Lerner (1902–1992) a pro-Israel progressive was a featured columnist. Financier Rupert Murdoch (b. 1931) purchased the paper and turned it conservative, often featuring Daniel Pipes.

The *New York Sun* is recent, publishing its first edition in 2002. Its investors include Michael Steinhardt (b. 1940), Thomas Tisch (b. 1955) and Roger Hertog. The editor in chief is Seth Lipsky (b. 1946), former editor of the English version of the *Forward.* Its editorial policy claims it is a "proponent of Israel's right to defend itself" and greater Israel. It is strongly neoconservative, considering the paper to be a foil to the *New York Times.*

The *Los Angeles Times* is generally conservative. It is owned by the Tribune Company, headed by Sam Zell (b. 1941). It boasts columnists Jonah Goldberg and Max Boot (mentioned already). Columnist Joel Stein (b. 1971), a liberal, identifies with Jewish issues. However, editorially, the paper is hostile to Israel. It ignores Israel's suffering, emphasizes Palestinian suffering, humanizes suicide bombers, makes immoral equations between murderous attacks and Israeli defensive measures, and views defensive measures negatively.

The two main national Jewish papers differ. The English version *Forward* is liberal, but it is no longer an outlet for the garment unions and Workmen's Circle. It is pro-Israel, it favors a compromise, a two-state solution, but it entertains some anti-Israel criticism. The *Jewish Press* is an Orthodox outlet—Republican, conservative, and hard-line hawkish regarding Israel, desiring retention of the West Bank.

The far left magazines are hostile to Israel, often comparing Israeli counteractions to terror as Nazi-like. They are convinced that the Bush administration and Congress take orders from the American Israel Political Action Committee (AIPAC). The *Nation, Progressive, Mother Jones, New Yorker,* and online *Counterpunch* and *ZNet* are reflexively Israel-hostile. They feature Noam Chomsky (b. 1928), Matthew Rothschild (b. 1946) and Howard Zinn (b. 1920); all of them are Jews who characterize Israel as a tool of American imperialism. Seymour Hersh (b. 1937) of the *New Yorker* detects an Israeli cabal pulling U.S. political strings in the Middle East. **Rabbi Michael Lerner** (b. 1943), publisher and editor of the monthly progressive magazine *Tikkun,* favors a two-state solution, and he often takes a critical view of Israel's policies. He appears with hard-left Israel-bashers but claims he is uncomfortable with them.

Conservative magazines tend to be pro-Israel. *Commentary,* an intellectual pace setter and strongly neoconservative, features Norman Podhoretz (b. 1930), who turned over editorial duties to his son, John Podhoretz (b. 1961). The *Weekly Standard* is the flagship for neoconservatives and pro-Israel supporters. The *Standard*'s neoconservatives include Irving Kristol (b. 1920), a founder of neoconservatism; his son, the editor in chief, William Kristol (b. 1952); David Brooks (b. 1961), Fred Barnes (b. 1952), and David Gelender.

The *National Review* was founded in 1955 by a traditional Christian conservative, William Buckley (1925–2008). The *Review* transformed into a strong neoconservative bastion and about 1970 dropped the early conservatism demonstrated by Robert Taft and Russell Kirk. The advocacy opinion journal has Jewish editors—Michael Ledeen (b. 1941) and Richard Lowry (b. 1968). The *National Review Online,* as well as the print form, is the megaphone for well-known neoconservatives. Writers Mona Charen and Anne Bayefsky (who specializes in the UN anti-Israel bias) have a voice. The writers and columnists are affiliated with the American Enterprise Institute, the Heritage Foundation, the Manhattan Institute, and the Hudson Institute—think tanks who supply the media with opinion pundits.

Time tends to be centrist politically and is mildly pro-Israel. Michael Kinsley and Joe Klein (b. 1971), columnists, are liberal. Charles Krauthammer, mentioned before, appears often. *Newsweek* also is moderate. Its chief political correspondent and commentator is Howard Fineman, who is rather centrist, mildly liberal, and pro-Israel.

Radio and television hosts are well represented by Jewish journalists. Dennis Prager (b. 1948) and Michael Medved (b. 1948), strongly neoconservative, openly announce their Jewish observance on the air and their unqualified support for the well being of the Jewish state. Michael Savage (b. 1942), born Jewish, follows the neoconservative agenda pugnaciously. There is a liberal radio analyst, Daniel Schorr (b. 1916), now in his nineties, who is friendly toward Israel. That is not common on National Public Radio. It is also not common on television's *Democracy Now,* hosted by Amy Goodman (b. 1957). She is reflexibly anti-Israel, giving much time to Palestinian suffering without any mention of Arab provocation. Matt Drudge (b. 1966), in the tradition of Walter Winchell, mixes celebrity gossip with news on political figures in his online report. He is moderately conservative and mum on Jewish issues.

The all-news cable station CNN employs a number of Jewish journalists: Aaron Brown (b. 1948), who is no longer an anchor with the station, **Larry King** (b. 1933), Paula Zahn (b. 1956), and Jeff Greenfield. Wolf Blitzer (b. 1948) is a former *Jerusalem Post* writer. They try to present an objective picture of Israeli-Palestinian events. Blitzer appears on panels defending Israel. They do not deny Jewish identity, nor do they bring it up. Lesley Stahl (b. 1941) and Morley Safer (b. 1931) of *60 Minutes* do the same. **Mike Wallace** (b. 1918) often has been critical of Israeli policies. Fox News entertains many of the neoconservatives and commentators mentioned in this article, who are strongly pro-Israel.

Though it is difficult to ascertain just how religiously and culturally Jewish these reporters are, their ethnicity seems to have little or no influence on their journalistic writings. Among opinion columnists the very pro-Israel neoconservatism stands out; they have had a great deal of influence on the presidency of George W. Bush. Since polls taken within the Jewish community show that most vote overwhelmingly Democratic and are liberal, the idea that they influence a conservative administration seems contradictory.

Philip Rosen

Further Reading: "The Bush Doctrine." *Think Tank,* PBS. July 11, 2002. Friedman, Murray. "Opening the Discussion of American Jewish Political Conservatism." *American Jewish History* 87, no 2 and 3 (June and September 1999). Goldberg, J. J. *Jewish Power: Inside the American Jewish Establishment.* New York: Perseus Book Group, 1996. Medved, Michael. "Jews Run Hollywood, So What?" *Momemt,* August 1996. Rothman, Cliff. "Jewish Media Stranglehold." *The Nation* 275 (July 8, 2002).

JUNGREIS, ESTHER (1935–)

Although Orthodoxy has yet to ordain a female rabbi, it does have a female superstar religious leader. Esther Jungreis, also known as "Rebbetzin" (the honorific title of a rabbi's spouse), has served as a revivalist, outreach worker, and preacher for almost 40 years. Rebbetzin Jungreis was born in Hungary before World War II to a prominent Ashkenazic rabbinical family. Her ancestor was the famed Rabbi Asher Anschel Jungreis, who was not only a prominent Talmudist but was also well known as a miracle worker. He authored a volume of rabbinic novellas called *Menuchoth Asher.*

As a child, Rebbetzin Jungreis was held in the Bergen-Belsen concentration camp, but she, her father, and some other siblings managed to survive until the liberation by British forces. She arrived in the United States in 1947 and attended Stern College (the female undergraduate division of Yeshiva University). She even appeared on the *College Bowl Television Program* representing Stern in the weekly scholastic duels between schools. She married another member of the Jungreis rabbinic clan, Rabbi Theodore Jungreis, and served as rebbetzin in her husband's synagogue in Long Island.

Her first public exposure came as a weekly columnist in the Brooklyn-based Orthodox English weekly, the *Jewish Press.* In her column she offered advice on all manner of personal, religious, and social problems faced by the new baby boomer generation of Orthodox Jews in New York.

In 1973, she founded the Hineni movement, which was dedicated to combat assimilation and intermarriage in the United States. As such she embarked on an ambitious speaking tour across the United States, commencing with a mass rally at Madison Square Garden in November of 1973. Her message was fairly simple—that after the Holocaust and the murder of six million Jews, it was incumbent upon all Jews to remain Jewish and raise Jewish families. Her message was chiefly a message based on ethnic and nationalistic ideals. Religion played a secondary role at that point. Her rallies were well attended, and her column in the *Jewish Press,* together with the column of the late Rabbi Meir Kahane (the founder of the Jewish Defense League) helped define the identity of the *Jewish Press* and of many of its readers. The Rebbetzin expanded the scope of her work to include activities for single Jews, via prayer services directed by male family members of the Jungreis clan in Upper Manhattan, along with weekly classes held in Congregation Kehillath Jeschurun on Manhattan's Upper East Side. These lectures proved to be very successful and were an important event in the weekly schedule of New

York Jewish singles. Although based in New York, Hineni also had branches in other parts of the world such as Israel and South Africa. Besides her column in the *Jewish Press,* she also appeared regularly on cable television and authored several books. The best known was her first, *Jewish Soul on Fire* (1981). It sold well among the Orthodox population in the United States. Her most recent book is *Life Is a Test,* published in 2006. Although Jungreis is clearly an Orthodox Jew, her message is tailored to appeal to all Jews. She emphasizes the lessons of the Holocaust and support for the State of Israel. It has often been difficult to decide if she belongs to the modern Orthodox camp or the Charedi branch of Orthodoxy.

Part of Jungreis's fame rests on her media and public image; she would dress in a blonde sheitel (wig) as befitting an Orthodox rebbetzin and used make up very liberally. She spoke English softly with a thick Hungarian accent and was sort of an Orthodox Jewish version of the Gabor sisters. Although very vocal in her message against assimilation, she could hardly be termed an activist and was rarely seen in demonstrations or rallies other than peaceful ones. As such, she was different from other Jewish revivalists, such as Rabbi Avi Weiss or the late Rabbi Meir Kahane. Although she was one of the few women in Orthodox Judaism with a public following, she was not identified with the Orthodox Jewish feminist movement led by people such as Blu Greenberg.

Since the death of her husband, Hineni seems to have diminished its public role, and the Rebbetzin's schedule has been sharply curtailed.

Rebbetzin Esther Jungreis has provided Orthodox Judaism with a unique figure, a sort of Jewish Amy MacPherson, a Jewish female evangelist, whose message is the importance of Jews marrying Jews and preserving Jewish identity, especially given the disasters of the Holocaust. *See also* **Carlebach, Shlomo**.

Zalman Alpert

Further Reading: Jungreis, Esther. *The Jewish Soul on Fire.* New York: William Morrow & Company, 1982.

K

KATZ, MICKEY (1909–1985)

Mickey Katz, a sharp clarinetist, a brilliant comic, a rebel parodist, and a clever linguist, was a musical alchemist who turned the goyishe wonderland of fifties U.S.A., from its vanilla suburbs to its vanilla pop charts, into Shvitzville, U.S.A. He scored a hybrid mix of **klezmer**, mambo, swing, **rock and roll**, and easy-listening pop. The son of Latvian and Lithuanian immigrants, Katz was born and raised on Cleveland's east side. He grew up playing jazz clarinet, including a gig at the Golden Pheasant Chinese Restaurant, where his fellow Clevelandite Artie Shaw also paid his dues. Katz toured with the Maurice Spiltany Orchestra, did a United Service Organizations (USO) run backing Betty Hutton, and finally landed a noisy sound effects spot with the Spike Jones band. It wasn't until he struck out on his own, however, with a Yiddish-English goof on "Home on the Range" (1947) that Katz began to reach his professional peak in the 1950s through series of full-length albums for Capitol.

He made an acclaimed album of traditional Eastern European klezmer recordings, *Music for Weddings, Bar Mitzvahs, and Brisses,* and a deferential and nostalgic salute to ***Fiddler on the Roof.*** Katz is perhaps best remembered for what the sleeve notes to *Mickey Katz and His Orchestra* describe as his "humorous treatment of the nation's favorite songs," a polite way of characterizing the 90-plus anarchistic, irreverent, and wildly ethnic klezmer parodies of mid-century popular songs. For the bulk of Katz's work, the formula was as simple as it was radical: take any song that was popular with mainstream American audiences, bludgeon it with explosive blows of reeling Eastern European klezmer, and re-write the lyrics into unpredictable stories of Jewish American feats and foibles delivered in a nasal rapid-fire mix of English and Yiddish, or "Yinglish."

Katz turned Tennesse Ernie Ford's 1955 coal-mining tale of manual labor and piling debt, "Sixteen Tons," into a kosher deli work-song ("You load sixteen tons of hot salami / Corned beef, rolled beef, and hot pastrami") and Patti Page's "Doggie in the Window" into "Pickle in the Window" ("I read in the papers, there are burglars / A ganef who robs you in bed / A pickle will come in so handy / With a pickle I'll break him his head"). The combined result was nothing short of a cultural hijack, a relentless Judaizing of American culture. Being the fifties, of course, that tactic was not always welcomed by Katz's fellow Jews, who feared anti-Semitic stereotypes were still too fresh in the postwar world. Katz was often beloved in private but reviled in public, his performance of American Jewishness "too Jewish" for many Jews of the 1950s who preferred the more assimilated byways of social mobility.

Katz's revival in the 1990s by African American clarinetist Don Byron rescued Katz's work from the obscurity of novelty bins and helped earn him a new legacy, one of twentieth-century Jewish music's most important pop cultural thinkers. *See also* **Klezmer Music**; **Rock and Roll**.

Josh Kun

Further Reading: Kun, Josh. "The Yiddish Are Coming: Mickey Katz, Antic-Semitism, and the Sound of Jewish Difference." *American Jewish History* 87, no. 4 (December 1999): 343–374.

KAYE, DANNY (1913–1987)

Danny Kaye was a phenomenally successfully Jewish American actor, singer, and comedian. Born in Brooklyn as David Daniel Kaminsky, Kaye was the son of Jewish immigrants from the Ukraine. He never completed a formal education but instead left high school to pursue a career in entertainment. As a teenager he entered the world of Jewish American entertainment by becoming a "tummler," a **Yiddish** term for an entertainment director, in the **Catskills**' Borscht Belt.

Kaye's film career began in 1935 when he appeared in the comedy *Short Moon over Manhattan*. Two years later he began a series of short comedies in which he drew on his Slavic heritage to play a fast-talking Russian. Playing opposite him were newcomers such as June Allyson and Imogene Coca. The series was abruptly terminated in 1938 when the production company was closed. Kaye soon found success in the 1941 hit Broadway production of *Lady in the Dark*. His performance of "Tchaikovsky," a Kurt Weill and Ira Gershwin song featuring a string of Russian composers' names sung at breakneck speed, established him as comedian of some stature.

Kaye had to overcome ethnic stereotypes. Reportedly, he resisted an attempt by Samuel Goldwyn to change his nose because Goldwyn felt that Kaye looked too Jewish. When Kaye refused, a compromise was reached and he dyed his hair red. This was done so that he could play in *Up in Arms* (1944), Goldwyn's remake of his own 1930 production *Whoopee!* starring **Eddie Cantor**. Kaye's successful film career lasted three decades.

He appeared in such notable films as *The Secret Life of Walter Mitty* (1947), *The Inspector General* (1949), *Hans Christian Anderson* (1952), *White Christmas* (1954), *The Court Jester* (1956), and the *Five Pennies* (1959). Kaye's reputation as an artist was largely based on his comedic talents and linguistic virtuosity, as demonstrated in tongue-twisting songs frequently composed by his wife, Sylvia Fine. Besides his film career Kaye had a brief stint in radio (1945–1946) and on television in his own show (1963–1967).

Kaye was able to translate his phenomenal success as an entertainer into other pursuits. An avid baseball fan, he was an original owner of the Seattle Mariners' franchise and also composed a theme song for his hometown favorite Brooklyn Dodgers, "The D-O-D-G-E-R-S (Oh really? No, O'Malley)," which still enjoys some popularity as a classic baseball tune. Outside of the commercial arena, Kaye was honored for his devotion to charitable enterprises. Notably he served as the first international ambassador for UNICEF.

Kaye's interests were far-reaching and included medicine, cooking, and music. The library of the Culinary Institute of America in Hyde Park, New York, is named for him, possibly in recognition of his skill as a cook. Music was an essential element in Kaye's success, and he was a celebrity conductor for UNICEF's fundraisers; during his career he reportedly helped raise over $5,000,000 for musicians' pension funds. For all of these activities Kaye received an honorary Academy Award in 1955 and the Jean Hersholt Humanitarian Award in 1982.

During the last phase of his creative life, Kaye received critical acclaim for two dramatic roles in the 1980s. In 1981 he assumed the role of Max Feldman, a survivor in the television-movie *Skokie,* a cinematic depiction of an attempt by neo-Nazis to march in Skokie, Illinois, a community in which a large number of Jewish immigrants and survivors of the Holocaust lived. Also notable was his depiction of Gaspar, a character in an episode of *The New Twilight Zone* titled "Paladin of the Lost Hour" that aired on November 8, 1985. The script was written by science-fiction writer Harlan Ellison and was also the title of his award-winning novelette. The television production has a science fiction premise in which race and ethnicity are underlying if not explicitly stated themes.

In his last performance, an appearance on the *Cosby Show,* Kaye returned to his métier, comedy, in 1986. He died as the result of an heart attack on March 3, 1987. *See also* **Film**; **Television**.

Leroy T. Hopkins Jr.

Further Reading: Gottfried, Martin. *Nobody's Fool: The Lives of Danny Kaye.* Simon and Schuster, 1994.

KAZIN, ALFRED (1915–1998)

From World War II to the end of the twentieth century, Alfred Kazin was among America's most notable literary critics and intellectuals, as well as one of a select group of Jewish writers and critics known as the "New York Intellectuals." He received a BA from City College in 1935, and an MA from Columbia in 1938. In 1942 he published his first book of criticism, *On Native Ground,* a review of late nineteenth-century and early twentieth-century literature, which brought Kazin recognition as an authority on American literature and culture. He also taught at several universities and wrote numerous book reviews and essays for leading U.S. newspapers and literary magazines.

Kazin was born in the Brownsville section of Brooklyn, New York, the son of immigrant Jewish parents who came from czarist Russia. His father, Charles Kazin, was a house-painter and sympathizer of Eugene Debs's Socialist Party. His mother, Gita Kazin, was a garment worker. The language spoken at home was **Yiddish**.

His trilogy of memoirs, *A Walker in the City* (1951), *Starting Out in the Thirties* (1965), and *New York Jew* (1978), evoke the Jewish immigrant's experience in twentieth-century America. They also address the political and cultural odyssey of the generation which grew up in proletarian Jewish neighborhoods during the depression years and matured under the impact of the Spanish Civil War and Nazism.

Walker in the Street is suffused with bittersweet recollections of his childhood difficulties. At the core of these remembrances is an evocation of his family, his neighborhood, and his Jewish identity. It is written in sensuous prose, portraying the thoughts of the boy Alfred Kazin, growing up amidst the varied sights, smells, and the voices of the ghetto.

These books also portray what have become stereotypic images of Jewish immigrant life—the dominance of the kitchen, the claustrophobic intensity of family relationships, the tension between impoverished, fearful parents and the urgent movement out and beyond of their sons and daughters. Kazin describes his sometime-embarrassment of parental ways, as when his father "kept slurping the soup and reaching out for the meat with his own fork," as well as the parental self-denial of pleasure and fidelity to the past.

Kazin's work describes the growth of his lifelong passion for reading, focusing on the development of literature in the United States he was later to chronicle. He wrote: "I read as if books would fill my every flaw, let me in at last into the great world that was anything just out of Brownsville" (Kazin, 1997).

In *A Walker in the City,* Kazin offered his own take on being a Jew, who as a child in synagogue felt "I was being pulled into some mysterious and ancient clan" and "whether I agreed with its beliefs or not, I belonged . . . I was a Jew . . ." and was expected "to take my place in the great tradition."

Kazin died at his home in New York City June 5, 1998, after suffering from prostate and bone cancer. *See also* **Literature**.

Leslie Rabkin

Further Reading: Cook, Richard M. *Alfred Kazin: A Biography.* New Haven: Yale University Press, 2007. Kazin, Alfred. *A Walker in the City.* Bel Air, CA: MJF Books, 1997. ———. *On Native Grounds: An Interpretation of Modern American: Prose Literature.* New York: Harcourt, 1995.

KELLERMAN, FAYE

See **Detective Fiction**

KELLERMAN, JONATHAN

See **Detective Fiction**

KING, ALAN (1927–2004)

"We few, we happy few, we band of brothers"—it's with this William Shakespeare quote that comedian Alan King starts a chapter of his autobiography *Name Dropping: The Life and Lies of Alan King* (1996). A member of the Friars, the New York City club known for its celebrity roasts, King discloses in his book that in 1945, at the age of 17, he was sponsored as a "Friarling" by **Milton Berle**. He first met Berle after King performed his stand-up act at a New York City night club. Berle greeted the youngster with a cigar in his mouth, which King knew was Berle's trademark. King subsequently adopted it as his own. Since imitating a fellow and well-known comedian was a common practice among novice entertainers, King became Berle's protégé. He was influenced by Berle's humor, as well as that of another member of the Friars, **Jack Benny**. A Friar for over 50 years, Alan King served as the club's abbot and was roasted in 1961.

Alan King was born Irwin Alan Kniberg to Minnie and Bernard Kniberg, a handbag cutter. He grew up in Manhattan's Lower East Side, and later the family moved to Brooklyn. His entry into show business was at the age of 14, when he performed "Brother, Can You Spare A Dime" on the *Major Bowes' Original Amateur Hour* radio program. At 15, King dropped out of high school to perform comedy at the Gradus Hotel in the **Catskill Mountains**. Subsequently he became a professional prize fighter and won 20 straight bouts before losing. He took the name "King" from the fighter who beat him. King decided to give up boxing and pursue a career in comedy after his nose was broken.

In addition to the influence of fellow Friars, King's type of comedy benefitted from two encounters. After his marriage to Jeanette Sprung in 1947, King agreed to move to the suburbs of Queens. This experience became grist for his humor, as he incorporated the absurdities of suburban life into his comedy act. The other important influence was Danny Thomas. When King saw him perform in the early 1950s, he noted that Thomas developed a rapport with his audience that comedians who confronted their audiences failed to master. He proceeded to adopt Thomas's technique.

King's odyssey as a comedian commenced with performances in the Catskills, the Paramount Theater in New York, and major night clubs. He was often the opening act for singers such as Frank Sinatra, Judy Garland, and Nat King Cole. Subsequently, King performed on major television variety shows, performing 93 times on *The Ed Sullivan Show,* as well as being a frequent guest on *The Tonight Show Starring Johnny Carson.*

In Martin Scorsese's film *Casino* (1995), Alan King convinces Robert De Niro to manage the mob's casino in Las Vegas. King actually knew the city well, having performed during the Sands' golden age in the sixties, when the "Rat Pack" was in its glory. In addition to his career as a comedian, King was also an actor in films (often playing gangsters and rabbis), a theater and movie producer, a comedy writer, the master of ceremony for President John F. Kennedy's inaugural party in 1961, and the emcee for the 1972 Academy Awards, as well as the long-standing host of the Friars' roasts. The prolific King even created a tennis tournament in Las Vegas. But he always found time for causes that he cared for, such as civil rights. On stage he poked fun at racism, and he accompanied Martin Luther King on several of his protest marches. His keen observation of contemporary life motivated Jerry Stiller to call him "the Jewish Will Rogers."

He also participated in various charities, including the Nassau Center for Emotionally Disturbed Children in Long Island, the creation of a chair in dramatic arts at Brandeis University, the Laugh Well program (organizing comedy shows in hospitals), and the Alan King Diagnostic Medical Center in Jerusalem. In 1988, King received the first American Jewish humor award from the National Foundation for Jewish Culture—an award renamed for him since.

King died of lung cancer in 2004. *See also* **The Catskills**; **Comedy**; **Film**.

Steve Krief

Further Reading: King, Alan. *Matzo Balls for Breakfast and Other Memories of Growing Up Jewish*. Simon and Schuster, 2000. ———. *Name Dropping: The Life and Lies of Alan King*. Simon and Schuster, 1996.

KING, LARRY (1933–)

Larry King, host of CNN's *Larry King Live,* was born Lawrence Harvey Zeiger in Brownsville, Brooklyn, New York on November 19, 1933. He was the second child of Jennie and Eddie Zeiger, Russian Jewish immigrants who ran a successful bar and grill, but they sold it so that King's father could work at a defense plant in Kearny, New Jersey. When King's father died of a heart attack while working at the plant, Jennie Zeiger was forced to find work in New York's garment district so that she could support herself and her two sons.

Ten-year-old Larry Zeiger suffered greatly because of his father's death; at first he regarded his father's death as a desertion, and he worried about who would leave him next. He lost interest in school and graduated from Brooklyn's Lafayette High School in 1951 with a grade point average of 66 percent. Larry spent a great deal of his time listening to Brooklyn Dodgers baseball games and other radio broadcasts. He was fascinated by Arthur Godfrey's show, newsman **Walter Winchell**, and the comedy team of Bob Elliot and Ray Goulding. At times he would travel to Manhattan to see live broadcasts of his favorite shows.

After high school he went to work as a United Parcel Service delivery man, and in the course of his delivery route he visited the various broadcasting studios. One CBS announcer suggested that he find a job as a small town broadcaster.

Eventually, Larry found a broadcasting job. At the age of 23 he was hired as a morning disc jockey in Miami, Florida. It was there that he changed his name from Zieger to King. By 1960 he tried television broadcasting and began writing columns for the *Miami Herald* and the *Miami News*. The *Larry King Talk Show,* the outcome of his endeavors as a broadcaster and columnist, was heard nightly by more than three and a half million people throughout North America, Canada, and Mexico. His success earned him the title of the "King of Talk."

King, unfortunately, spent beyond his means, gambled, and failed to pay his taxes. He was befriended by a Florida financier named Lou Wolfson, who financed New Orleans District Attorney Jim Garrison's investigation of the JFK assassination. Wolfson supposedly asked King to deliver money to Garrison, and allegedly Larry kept some of the money to pay his debts.

In 1971, King moved to the West Coast, where he continued his broadcasting career. By the early 1970s the *Larry King Show,* a national call-in show, had millions of listeners. According to the talk show host, his most memorable program was the night John Lennon was assassinated at the Dakota in Central Park West. After receiving news of the shooting at 11:45 P.M., King devoted the rest of the night to John Lennon. People from all walks of life throughout the United States, Canada, and Mexico called in to share their memories of John Lennon. Many cried as they talked and shared their recollections of Lennon.

King was hired by CNN to do a television interview show called *Larry King Live*. On February 20, 1992, Texas billionaire Ross Perot came on King's show to announce that he would run for president. Thereafter King's show became the place to which presidential candidates often came to announce their candidacy and talk about the issues of the campaign. On *Larry King Live* national and international figures have come to be interviewed and present their point of view to the man wearing the shirt with suspenders. Over the many years King has received many broadcasting awards, including the George Peabody Award for Excellence in Broadcasting, Broadcaster of the Year from the International Radio and Television Society, and the Jack Anderson Investigative Reporting Award. King has been married several times, twice to the same woman, and has several children. *See also* **Radio**; **Television**.

Herbert M. Druks

Further Reading: King, Larry. *The Best of Larry King Live: The Greatest Interviews.* Turner Publishers, 1995. ———, and David Gilbert. *How to Talk to Anyone, Anytime, Anywhere: The Secret of Good Communication.* Random House, 2004. The Museum of Broadcast Communications. www.museum.tv/archives/etv/K/htmlK/kinglarry/kinglarry.htm.

KIRBY, JACK

See **Comic Books**

KISSINGER, HENRY (1923–)

Diplomat and former Secretary of State Henry Kissinger was born in Fuerth, Germany in 1923. His family left Germany because of the Nazi persecution of Jews and moved to the United States in 1938. On June 19, 1943, Kissinger became a naturalized American citizen. His mother, Paula Stern, and father, Louis Kissinger, a schoolteacher, were middle-class German Jews. In Manhattan, Kissinger attended high school and City College of New York. In 1943, the army drafted him and sent Kissinger to Clemson College in South Carolina. At Clemson he was taught to be a German interpreter for the 970 U.S. Counter Intelligence. Following the war, Kissinger's ability to speak German helped him to ferret out and arrest former Gestapo agents in postwar Germany.

Using his GI Bill, Kissinger earned his BA degree Summa Cum Laude from Harvard in 1950, and he earned MA and PhD degrees from Harvard University in 1952 and 1954 respectively. A brilliant student, he was retained by Harvard as a member of the faculty in the Department of Government and Center for International Affairs (1962), where he was appointed the director of the Harvard Defense Studies Program. A liberal Republican, Kissinger was consultant to a number of government agencies, as well as an advisor to Nelson Rockefeller, who sought to win the Republican presidential nomination in 1960, 1964, and 1968.

After Richard Nixon won the presidency (1968), Kissinger became the national security advisor and then secretary of state, a position he also held under President Gerald Ford. During the 1973 Yom Kippur War, he was instrumental in the crucial U.S. airlift of arms to Israel. Kissinger subsequently negotiated the peace between Israel and Egypt that ended the war. He also negotiated an end to U.S. involvement in Vietnam, for which he was awarded the 1973 Nobel Peace Prize. His achievements as the 56th secretary of state, with the Nixon and Ford administrations (1973–1977), helped implement détente with the Soviet Union and communist China.

Kissinger has come under heavy criticism for his role in U.S. policy toward Chile, Cyprus, East Timor, India, and Bangladesh. Recently, Kissinger has met regularly with President George W. Bush to discuss the war in Iraq.

Married twice, Kissinger has two children by his first wife, Ann Fleischer; Elizabeth and Davis. He was divorced in 1964. He currently resides in Kent, Connecticut with his second wife, Nancy Maginnes, whom he married in 1974. In private business, he runs a foreign policy consulting organization called Kissinger Associates. He is a registered Republican, a world figure, and is widely sought for interviews by television networks and the media on foreign policy issues. During his tenure as secretary of state, he became something of a celebrity, often photographed by the press with Hollywood stars such as

Jill St. John. During those years the press dubbed him with the sobriquet "Super K." His books and articles on foreign policy have won him many awards as contributing to international understanding.

Philip Rosen

Further Reading: Isaacson, Walter. *Kissinger: A Biography.* London: Faber and Faber Ltd., 1992.

KLEZMER MUSIC

Klezmer music refers to a type of Jewish instrumental music that originated in the Middle Ages in Central and Eastern Europe. "Klezmer," the **Yiddish** word for a musician who plays this music, means "vessel of song," from "kley" (vessel) and "zemer" (song). "Klezmorim" (plural of klezmer) formed bands (kapelye) which played primarily at Jewish weddings and other joyous occasions in Eastern Europe from around 1500 into the twentieth century.

Klezmer music initially developed as an instrumental imitation of the vocal ritual music of Judaism—the chants of the cantors who assisted rabbis in the officiating of Jewish rituals and services, as well as the niggunim, the wordless melodies sung by the Hasidim, a Jewish mystical sect that developed in the late 1700s in Eastern Europe. Since the destruction of the second Temple in 70 CE, the rabbis (in mourning) discouraged instrumental music except at weddings and a few other joyous occasions, but the Hasidic love of dancing and music allowed the klezmorim an outlet for their playing.

Klezmorim in Europe were usually underemployed, very poor, and considered to be among the least prestigious classes in society. In order to make a living as musicians, klezmorim often played for non-Jews as well. Their exposure to non-Jewish music sometimes led the klezmorim to develop music that was a mixture of Jewish and non-Jewish music. In particular, klezmer dance music was highly influenced by Gypsy, Romanian, and Bulgarian elements. This fusion of Jewish religious and dance music with the dance music of other European ethnic groups helped klezmer music to continue developing over the centuries.

Klezmer music was an integral part of the Jewish culture in Europe before the twentieth century. As millions of Eastern European Jews moved from small rural villages into larger European cities, or immigrated to the United States in the late nineteenth and early twentieth centuries, Jews shed klezmer music (along with other aspects of their old culture) as they assimilated rapidly into their new environments.

In the 1970s a variety of forces, particularly the search by African Americans for their cultural roots, influenced young Jews to search for and embrace their own ethnic and spiritual roots. Young Jewish musicians such as Lev Lieberman, Andy Statman, Henry Sapoznik, and Hankus Netsky, rediscovered klezmer music and began to form groups such as the Klezmorim, Kapelye, and the Klezmer Conservatory Band. This revival of klezmer music attracted other Jewish musicians who began to combine klezmer with other musical genres, just as their ancestors had. The result was a fusion of the European klezmer music that the Jewish immigrant musicians had brought with them two generations before combined with a wide variety of contemporary musical styles, including **jazz and blues**, folk, African Cuban, **pop**, and more.

The revival and renaissance of klezmer music in the United States began to spread around the world during the last decades of the twentieth century. When the great violinist **Itzhak Perlman** began performing and recording klezmer music in the mid-1990s, an increasingly large and diverse audience for klezmer emerged. *See also* **Katz, Mickey; Yiddish**.

David Stameshkin

Further Reading: Sapoznik, Henry. *Klezmer! Jewish Music from Old World to Our World.* New York: Schirmer Books, 1999. Slobin, Mark, ed. *American Klezmer: Its Roots and Offshoots.* Berkeley, CA: University of California Press, 2002.

KLUGMAN, JACK (1922–)

Film and television actor Jack Klugman (Jacob Joachim Klugman) was born to a poor Jewish family in South Philadelphia on April 22, 1922. Klugman was one of six children; his father was a house-painter and heavy drinker, who died when Klugman was 12. The family was not religious, although his grandfather was devout (his devotion embarrassed Jack's father). Klugman and his brothers were never Bar Mitzvahed. To support the family, Klugman's mother turned her parlor into a millinery shop and made hats. Despite the family's poverty, there was a respect for education and culture. After serving in the army, Klugman attended Carnegie Mellon under the GI bill, where he enrolled in the drama program. Despite being discouraged by a member of the faculty who advised him that he was "a lousy performer," he continued to pursue a career in acting.

Klugman studied at the American Theater Wing and made his stage debut at the Equity Liberty Theater production of *Saint Joan*. While a struggling actor in New York City, he shared an apartment with a fellow budding actor, Charles Bronson. During the 1950s, Klugman's acting career began to blossom as both a television and film actor. Klugman appeared on *The US Steel Hour, Alfred Hitchcock Presents,* and *The Twilight Zone*. In 1954, he appeared with Humphrey Bogart and Henry Fonda in a live television production of *The Petrified Forest,* a role he regarded as his greatest thrill.

In 1957, he costarred in the film classic *12 Angry Men,* which was his favorite role. In 1959, Klugman got his break on Broadway when he was cast opposite Ethel Merman in *Gypsy* and received an Emmy nomination for Best Actor in a Musical.

Klugman received the first of several Emmys for an appearance in a television episode of *The Defenders*. But it was his role as Oscar Madison in the *Odd Couple* (1970–1975), where he costarred with Tony Randall, that made him a star. *The Odd Couple* earned him two more Emmy Awards (1971, 1973), as well as a Golden Globe award in 1974 for Best TV Actor—Musical/Comedy, before he moved on as the lead for seven successful seasons in *Quincy, M.E.* (1976–1983).

In 1989, Klugman was diagnosed with lung cancer and lost half of his larynx, which limited his acting career. In 2005, Klugman published *Tony And Me: A Story of Friendship,* a tribute to his *Odd Couple* costar, the late Tony Randall.

Klugman married Brett Somers in 1956 and had they two children, Adam and David. The couple separated in 1974. In February 2008, Klugman married his partner of 20 years, Peggy Crosby.

Klugman has appeared in 18 films in addition to *12 Angry Men,* including *Cry Terror* (1958), *Days of Wine and Roses* (1962), *Act One* (1963), *The Detective* (1963), *Goodbye, Columbus* (1969), *The Odd Couple: Together Again* (1993), *Dear God* (1996), *The Twilight of the Golds* (1997), and *When Do We Eat* (2005). *See also* **Film**; **Television**.

Jack R. Fischel

Further Reading: Klugman, Jack. *Tony and Me: A Story of Friendship*. Good Hill Press, 2005.

KOCH, EDWARD (1924–)

Congressman, mayor, and radio/television personality, as well as an often-brash and forthright public figure, Ed Koch is a true New Yorker, born in the Bronx. His father, a furrier, moved the family to Newark during the Great Depression. His mother, Joyce, died when he was young. Koch served in the army during World War II as a rifle infantryman. Discharged in 1946, he attended New York University Law School and was admitted to the bar in 1949.

Working for the Democratic Party in Greenwich Village, he was tapped for the New York City Council in 1968. On the Democratic-Liberal ticket he was elected to the U.S. Congress in 1969, where he served until 1977. In 1978, he became the 105th mayor of New York City. A witty bachelor and colorful figure, he held office for three terms until 1989, although in 1982, he ran unsuccessfully in the Democratic Party primary for governor against Mario Cuomo.

Known for mixing with "the people," he frequently asked his constituency how he was doing. As mayor, he helped the city achieve financial stability and established a merit system for the selection of judges. Noted for his pro-gay rights position, he issued executive orders prohibiting discrimination against gays, while insisting he was not a homosexual himself.

In 1989, he was defeated for a fourth term in the mayoralty primary by David Dinkins. Koch returned to law and became a partner in a Manhattan law firm, Robinson, Silverman, et al. He did not fade into obscurity. He became a film critic, an adjunct professor, and a mock television judge. A practicing Jew, he wrote, lectured and commented on television and in newspapers, much of which included his defense of the State of Israel.

In recent years, Koch's politics has veered to the political right. Once a liberal Democrat, he has campaigned for Republican candidates and considers the Democrats "too leftist" for his taste. Koch is an ardent supporter of President George W. Bush, particularly his policies on the "war on terror" and the invasion of Iraq.

In his eighties, Koch is vigorous even though he has suffered a minor stroke, and he continues to comment on the New York and national scene on television and in his newspaper column.

Philip Rosen

Further Reading: Koch, Ed, and Pat Thaler Koch. *Eddie, Harold's Little Brother.* Grosset and Dunlap, 2004. Koch, Edward I., and Daniel Paisner. *Citizen Koch: An Autobiography.* St. Martin's Press, 1992. Newfield, Jack, and Wayne Barrett. *City for Sale: Ed Koch and the Betrayal of New York.* Harper Row, 1988.

KOPPEL, TED (1940–)

Ted Koppel (birth name Edward James), best known as the original anchor of ABC's award-winning news broadcast *Nightline,* was born February 8, 1940 in Lancashire, England, after his Jewish parents fled Nazi Germany. Koppel's family moved to the United States when he was 13 years old, and he acquired American citizenship in 1963. After receiving his BA degree in speech from Syracuse University in 1960, Koppel completed his MA degree in mass communication research and political science at Stanford University in 1963. He began a journalism career that has spanned more than four decades.

One of Koppel's first assignments as an ABC radio news correspondent was covering John F. Kennedy's assassination for the daily *Flair Reports Program.* By the 1970s Koppel hosted several television specials for ABC News, including *The People of People's China* in 1973 and *Kissinger: Action Biography* in 1974. He was ABC News's chief diplomatic correspondent from 1971–1980 and anchored *ABC's Saturday Night News* from 1975–1977. Koppel also coauthored his first book, *In the National Interest,* in 1977. By March 1980, Koppel's reputation earned him the position of senior news analyst and anchor for ABC's prime time news show, *Nightline,* a position he held for over two decades. After leaving *Nightline* in 2005, Koppel joined the Discovery Channel in 2006 as a managing editor focusing on major global issues.

Koppel is internationally acclaimed and has earned every major award in journalism including 41 Emmy Awards and 6 George Foster Peabody Awards. In 1985, he was awarded the first Golden Baton in the history of the DuPont-Columbia Awards for his weeklong news coverage aired from apartheid-era South Africa. In 1987, he was voted best radio and television interviewer by the *Washington Journalism Review* and broadcaster of the year by the International Television and Radio Society. In 1994, Koppel was named a Chevalier de l'Ordre by the Republic of France. Koppel has also received numerous honorary degrees and is a member of the Broadcasting Hall of Fame.

Koppel has been married since May 17, 1963 to Grace Anne Dorney. They have three daughters, Deirdre, Tara, and Andrea; one son, Andrew; and three grandchildren. *See also* **Journalism**; **Television**.

Maury I. Wiseman

Further Reading: Koppel, Ted. *Off Camera: Private Thoughts Made Public.* Knopf, 2000. ———, and Kyle Gibson. *Nightline: History in the Making and the Making of Television.* Times Books, 1996.

KOUFAX, SANDY (1935–)

Sandy Koufax, the Hall of Fame pitcher, was born Sanford Braun on December 30, 1935 to Evelyn and Jack Braun in the Borough Park section of Brooklyn. Three years after his parents divorced his mother remarried. Braun, age nine at the time, took the name of his stepfather, Irving Koufax. The family, which included his sister, Edie, moved to Rockville Centre, Long Island but returned to Brooklyn after Koufax completed middle school.

Although heralded as one of the two most significant Jewish baseball players (with **Hank Greenberg**), Koufax never received religious education or had a Bar Mitzvah ceremony.

As a teenager, he preferred basketball over baseball, honing his skills at the Jewish Community House in Bensonhurst. He was named captain of the Lafayette High School team and ranked second in the school's division in scoring, with 165 points in 10 games. He also played on the school's baseball team, primarily as a first baseman but later as a pitcher as well.

Koufax attended the University of Cincinnati on a basketball scholarship; he also pitched for the school's baseball team. He found the demands of pursuing a degree in engineering boring and soon left school to pursue a career in baseball. Koufax had tryouts with the New York Giants and Pittsburgh Pirates before eventually signing with the Brooklyn Dodgers, who were obliged to keep him on the big league roster because of the rules governing "bonus babies" (Koufax signed for a $6,000 contract, with a bonus of $14,000). His wildness kept him on the bench, and he was used haphazardly during his first several years. Later biographies refer to Koufax's belief that anti-Semitism on the part of the team's front office and manager Walter Alston also played a role in his lack of use, thereby hindering his improvement.

For the first several years Koufax—who made his debut on June 24, 1955 in a relief appearance against the Milwaukee Braves—was a mediocre pitcher. His win-loss record from 1955–1961 was 54–53 with 501 walks, 952 strikeouts, and a 3.94 earned run average in 947.3 innings. From 1962–1966, Koufax was baseball's most dominant pitcher, posting 111 wins against 34 losses, striking out 1,444 batters in 1,377 innings, allowing just 1.94 earned runs per game. He led the National League in ERA (Earned Run Average) for five consecutive years and established the modern-day record for most strikeouts by a left-hander, with 382 in 1965. Koufax pitched four no-hitters, including a perfect game against the Chicago Cubs in 1965.

He was named to the National League All-Star team seven times and won the National League Most Valuable Player Award (1963) and three Cy Young Awards, emblematic of the game's best pitcher (1963, 1965, 1966).

Like Greenberg, from a generation before, Koufax made headlines by refusing to play on Yom Kippur, most notably skipping his opening game assignment in the 1965 World Series against the Minnesota Twins. He won two decisions, including a courageous 2–0 complete game victory in the deciding contest, and was named the Series MVP.

Following the 1966 season, Koufax, who had long pitched in pain and was battling circulatory problems as well as arthritis, retired at the age of 31. He was voted into the Baseball Hall of Fame in 1972, his first year of eligibility. In 1999, Koufax was named by *The Sporting News* as one of the 100 Greatest Baseball Players of All Time, as well as selected as a member of the Major League Baseball All-Century Team.

A notoriously private person, Koufax had a brief but uncomfortable stint as a commentator for NBC's *Game of the Week* following his retirement. He was married—and divorced—twice and has no children. In recent years, Koufax has attended the spring training camp for several teams, including the Dodgers, New York Mets, and Texas Rangers, serving as an unofficial coach and living legend. In 2006, he was "drafted" by the Modi'in Miracle of the newly-formed Israel Baseball League as tribute to his significance to the Jewish community. *See also* **Sports**.

Ron Kaplan

Further Reading: Leavy, Jane. *Sandy Koufax: A Lefty's Legacy.* Harper Collins, 2002.

KRAMER, STANLEY (1913–2001)

The career of Stanley Kramer exemplifies the belief that films, as a vehicle of popular culture, can educate the public about issues of great importance. As the director of many of the most important "message" films of the 1950s through the 1970s, Kramer reflected a liberal point of view at a time when the nation was confronting issues such as civil rights, nuclear warfare, and the genocidal criminality of Nazi Germany.

Kramer was born in Brooklyn, New York but was raised by his maternal grandmother in the Hell's Kitchen section of Manhattan. His father abandoned him at an early age; his mother, Mildred Kramer, and his grandmother lived in near poverty in a cramped, cold-water flat. There is little evidence that young Kramer ever received any Jewish education, but we know that education was important to his family, and consequently he split his time between odd jobs and school. At age 15, he entered New York University with the expectation that he would eventually become a lawyer. This career move was sidetracked when his mother, who did clerical work for Paramount Studios in New York, exposed him to the world of filmmaking. At NYU, he won a writing contest which led to an internship at 20th Century Fox. He subsequently left New York for Hollywood, where he hoped to become a screenwriter.

After a series of experiences as a production assistant and working for an army film unit in New York, Kramer organized an independent production company in 1948. His first success as a film producer was *Champion,* starring **Kirk Douglas** (1948), which received six Academy Award nominations. During the next three years Kramer produced *Home of the Brave* (1949), which tackled the subject of race; *The Men* (1950), a film which dealt with the issue of trauma suffered by World War II veterans, which also marked Marlon Brando's screen debut; and a screen adaptation of **Arthur Miller**'s *Death of a Salesman* (1951).

Subsequently, he co-produced *High Noon* (1952), which some critics interpreted as a response to McCarthyism. *The Juggler,* starring **Kirk Douglas**, was one of Hollywood's first films dealing with the Holocaust and was filmed in Israel (1953). In 1954, he produced the cult film *The Wild One* and *The Caine Mutiny,* based on **Herman Wouk**'s bestselling novel about World War II.

As a director, Stanley Kramer's résumé includes 13 films. Among the most controversial, given the time period, were *The Defiant One* (1958, which dealt with race), *On the Beach* (1959, dealing with the aftermath of nuclear war), *Inherit the Wind* (1960, a fictionalized version of the Scopes Trial and the controversy over evolution), *Judgment at Nuremberg* (1961, which dealt with Nazi war crimes), and a film that anticipated the later films about the Holocaust, *Ship of Fools* (1965), a film whose theme was Nazi anti-Semitism. *Guess Who's Coming to Dinner* (1967) was perhaps Kramer's most controversial film. It concerned issues of race relations and showed that racial prejudices was not confined to the South. Kramer died in Los Angeles in 2001 after suffering from pneumonia. He was survived by his wife, Karen Sharpe, and his three daughters and a son. *See also* **Film**.

Jack R. Fischel

Further Reading: Kramer, Stanley. *A Mad, Mad, Mad, Mad World: A Life in Hollywood.* New York: Harcourt Trade Publishers, 1997.

KUBRICK, STANLEY (1928–1999)

Film director Stanley Kubrick was born in New York City, the first son of Jacob and Gertrude (Perveler); a sister, Barbara, was born in 1934.

The Kubrick and Perveler families emigrated from the Austro-Hungarian Empire at the turn of the century. Kubrick's father was a West Bronx physician who introduced his son to reading, chess, and photography. His mother closely followed his film career, and an uncle, Martin Perveler, financed Kubrick's first feature film, *Fear and Desire* (1953).

Kubrick's family was not religious, and he did not have a Bar Mitzvah, although the Kaddish was read at his funeral. His first two wives were Jewish—Toba Metz was the daughter of a jeweler born in Latvia; Ruth Sobotka emigrated with her family from Vienna in 1938. Kubrick's third wife, Christiane Harlan, was a non-Jewish German he met while filming *Paths of Glory* (1957) in Munich. Harlan, niece of Nazi film director Veit Harlan and daughter of a musician who worked at the German Theater in Nazi-occupied Holland, had one daughter, Katharina Hobbs, from a previous marriage and two daughters, Anya and Vivian, with Kubrick.

Kubrick's 13 feature films display a dark view of humanity, exploring the inextricable mix of good and evil he saw in people and the world. This reflected the era of fascism and war in which he grew up. Kubrick admitted to a lifelong fascination with the history of Nazi Germany. Kubrick's cinema was inspired by the brooding concerns of German Expressionism, while the perpetrators of evil who dominate Kubrick's films often have German names, pasts, and associations: Dr. Zempf in *Lolita* (1962), *Dr. Strangelove* (1964), Gunnery Sergeant Hartman in *Full Metal Jacket* (1987), and Victor Ziegler in *Eyes Wide Shut* (1999).

Kubrick drew his dark satirical style from German Jewish directors Marcel Ophuls, Fritz Lang, and Erich von Stroheim. His favorite writer was the German Jewish Franz Kafka, and he was captivated by **Sigmund Freud**'s psychoanalysis. His last film, *Eyes Wide Shut,* was based on Jewish physician Arthur Schnitzler's novella about the psychological and social discontents of turn-of-the-century Vienna. Though Kubrick avoided Jewish characters in his films for box office reasons, characteristically changing the characters in *Schnitzler's Dream Story* (1926) from Jews to Gentiles, he always wanted to make a film about the **Holocaust**. That he never made such a film —writing only a screenplay, *Aryan Papers,* based on Louis Begley's autobiographical novel *Wartime Lies* (1991), reflected deep personal and artistic reservations. References to the Holocaust in Kubrick's cinema are indirect, in line with his "open narrative" presentation of ideas through props, music, colors, and sounds. Kubrick's horror film *The Shining* (1980) contains a deeply laid visual and aural subtext on the Holocaust informed by Raul Hilberg's *The Destruction the European Jews* (1961), Kafka's *The Castle* (1922), and Thomas Mann's *The Magic Mountain* (1924), along with music by Béla Bartók and Krzysztof Penderecki composed in response to the Nazi regime and its murderous policies. *See also* **Film**.

Geoffrey Cocks

Further Reading: Cocks, Geoffrey. *The Wolf at the Door: Stanley Kubrick, History, and the Holocaust*. New York: Peter Lang, 2004. ———, et al., eds. *Depth of Field: Stanley Kubrick, Film, and the Uses of History.* Madison, WI: University of Wisconsin Press, 2006. Raphael, Frederic. *Eyes Wide Open: A Memoir of Stanley Kubrick*. New York: Ballantine, 1999.

KUNITZ, STANLEY JASSPON (1905–2006)

Stanley Kunitz, poet laureate of the United States (2000), was born in Worcester, Massachusetts on July 29, 1905. His father, Solomon, who was a dressmaker, committed suicide just six weeks before his son's birth. Kunitz's mother, Lithuanian-born Yetta Jasspon, refused to speak of her late husband and "locked his name in her deepest cabinet." Yetta Jasspon then married Mark Dine, who died when the future poet was 14. Kunitz's sisters also died young; much of his future poetry would be filled with complex themes such as time, the chaos of inner life, and loss: "My mother never forgave my father for killing himself" ("The Portrait," *Passing Through,* 1995).

Kunitz won a scholarship to Harvard. As a student, he was enthralled with the poetry of Keats, Blake, Tennyson, and especially, Robert Herrick (1591–1674). Kunitz graduated from Harvard summa cum laude in 1926. Unable to secure a teaching post there because of his religion, Kunitz went to Europe, where he edited the *Wilson Library Bulletin.* He also began publishing poetry in *The Nation, The New Republic,* and *Commonweal.*

Kunitz published his first volume of poetry, *Intellectual Things,* in 1930. He would not publish another volume for over 14 years. During World War II, Kunitz, a conscientious objector, served in the army as an editor, stationed in North Carolina. In 1944, he published *Passport to War,* which, despite containing one of his most celebrated poems, *Fathers and Sons,* was largely unnoticed and soon out of print. It would be another 14 years before Kunitz found favor with critics; his 1958 volume, *Selected Poems,* won the Pulitzer Prize.

Kunitz taught at Bennington, Yale, Princeton, Columbia, and the New School. With fame came awards: the Robert Frost Medal and the National Medal of Arts. He served two terms as consultant on poetry for the Library of Congress—the precursor title to poet laureate.

Stanley Kunitz died at the age of 100. Of morality, he once wrote, "The deepest thing I know is that I am living and dying at once, and my conviction is to report that dialogue" (Lehmann-Haupt, 2006).

Kurt F. Stone

Further Reading: Kunitz, Stanley. *Passing Through: The Later Poems and Selected.* New York: W.W. Norton, 1995. Lehmann-Haupt, Christopher. "Stanley Kunitz, Poet Laureate, Dies at 100." *New York Times,* May 16, 2006. Orr, Gregory. *Stanley Kunitz: An Introduction to the Poetry.* Columbia University Press, 1984.

KURTZMAN, HARVEY

See **Comic Books**

KUSHNER, HAROLD S. (1936–)

This well-known author and rabbi laureate of Temple Israel in Natick, Massachusetts, Rabbi Kushner, is affiliated with the Conservative movement and has served as the spiritual leader of Temple Israel for 24 years. Kushner has gained international recognition for his inspirational and motivational writings.

Kushner was born in Brooklyn, graduated from Columbia University, and received his rabbinical ordination from the Jewish Theological Seminary in 1960. He received his doctorate in Bible from JTS in 1972. A prolific writer, Kushner has authored best-selling books that include *When Bad Things Happen to Good People* (1981), *When All You've Ever Wanted Isn't Enough* (1985), *How Good Do We Have to Be?* (1996), *Living A Life That Matters* (2001), and *Overcoming Life's Disappointments,* published in 2006.

Rabbi Kushner has received six honorary doctorates and has taught at the Jewish Theological Seminary and Clark University. In addition, Kushner has received the Christopher Award for *When All You've Ever Wanted Isn't Enough* and was recognized by the Christophers for being one of 50 people who have made the world a better place in the last 50 years.

Kushner's first book, *When Bad Things Happen to Good People*, was written after the loss of his son at an early age. Kushner's subsequent writings speak to the importance of family and friendship in leading a successful and gratifying life. He stresses the importance of self-sacrifice and charity and claims a person's positive deeds may make a difference in the world even if only one person is the benefactor.

Using his years of rabbinical experience, Kushner encourages readers to make the best of who they are, despite the obstacles they encounter. He tells readers to be resilient and forgiving, and to continue pursuing their dreams and life goals. Known for his ability to provide an uplifting message to his readers, Rabbi Kushner's writings transcend Judaic theology.

Kushner is an energetic and enthusiastic speaker who delivers messages that are practical and apply to daily life, family relationships, friendships and self-improvement.

Rabbi Kushner lives in Natick with his wife of 43 years, Suzette, and is the father of a daughter. *See also* **Popular Psychology**.

Robert Ruder

Further Reading: Kushner, Harold. *How Good Do We Have to Be? A New Understanding of Guilt and Forgiveness.* Back Bay Books, 1996. ———. *Overcoming Life's Disappointments.* Anchor, 2006. ———. *To Life! A Celebration of Jewish Being and Thinking.* Grand Central Publishing, 1994. ———. *When Bad Things Happen to Good People.* Avon, 1981. ———. *When Children Ask about God: A Guide for Parents Who Don't Always Have All the Answers.* Schocken Books, 1971.

L

LANDAU, MARTIN (1931–)

Oscar-winning film and television actor, Landau was born in Brooklyn, New York to a Jewish family on June 20, 1931. During World War II, his Austrian-born father rescued relatives from the Nazis. In late 1939, he helped smuggle eight ancient Torahs out of Hitler's Europe and delivered them to his Orthodox shul in Brooklyn. Landau remembers "a joyful procession down the street." Landau began his artistic career at age 17 as a cartoonist for the *New York Daily News*. In 1955, after several off-Broadway and regional stage roles, and television appearances in programs such as *Playhouse 90* and *Studio One,* Landau auditioned for the Actors Studio. Of 2,000 applicants, only he and Steve McQueen were accepted. A year later, moving into a landmark off-Broadway revival of *Uncle Vanya,* the actor began to draw notice. He debuted on Broadway in *Middle of the Night* (1957) and received broad acclaim. Touring that show, Landau found his way to the West Coast, where he found his first film work. *Pork Chop Hill* (1959) was his first film, but he is better remembered for the *heavy* he played that same year in Alfred Hitchcock's *North by Northwest.*

It was his television work that first brought Landau true celebrity. After performing in several episodes of *The Outer Limits,* he was offered the role of Mr. Spock on Star Trek, but he turned it down to play *Mission Impossible*'s master-of-disguise, Rollin Hand. The program also featured Barbara Bain, whom Landau had married in 1957. Although originally intended only as a recurring role, Hand was so well received that Landau was made a series regular. For each of his three seasons on the show, he was nominated for an Emmy as Outstanding Lead Actor in a Drama, and he won the Golden Globe in 1968 as Best Male TV Star. But after a salary dispute, he and his wife chose to leave the series in 1969. (Ironically, Leonard Nimoy, who had taken the role of Mr. Spock in his stead, replaced him.)

Artistic setbacks for the couple followed during the next years, as little successful work came their way. In 1975, the two moved to England to take the lead roles in series *Space: 1999.* Critics panned it, and Landau himself was critical of the scripts. The show was canceled after two seasons, although it had gained cult status. Careers of both husband and wife reached a low point over the next few years, as exemplified by roles in *The Harlem Globetrotters on Gilligan's Island* (1981).

Reviving his career might have seemed a "mission impossible" for the actor, but a remarkable resurgence began in 1988 when Francis Ford

Coppola cast him in *Tucker: The Man And His Dream,* a role that earned Landau an Academy Award nomination as Best Supporting Actor and his second Golden Globe win. **Woody Allen**'s *Crimes And Misdemeanors* followed the next year, as did a second consecutive supporting actor Oscar nod. Landau finally won that award in 1994 for his portrayal of Bela Lugosi in Tim Burton's bio-pic *Ed Wood.* This role also earned the actor yet another Golden Globe, as well as many other top honors. A year earlier, he and Barbara Bain divorced, but not before raising two daughters—Susan and Juliet. Martin Landau continues to work today as one of the nation's leading character actors. *See also* **Film**; **Television**.

Barry Kornhauser

Further Reading: Pfefferman, Naomi. "The 'Majestic' Martin Landau." *Jewish Journal.com.* December 21, 2001. Lindsey, Robert. "Martin Landau Rolls Up in a New Vehicle." *New York Times.* August 7, 1988.

LATIN MUSIC

In 1959, the legendary Puerto Rican bandleader and timbale master Tito Puente headlined the grand ballroom at Grossinger's Hotel, the flagship Jewish getaway destination in the **Catskill Mountains**. It was not the first time the beloved boricua and his "World Famous Orchestra" had played for the vacationing Jewish masses at Grossinger's, but it was the first time that one of his Sullivan County Catskills sessions was recorded and soon after released, by his label RCA, as a full-length album—*Cha Cha Cha: Live at Grossinger's.*

Puente might have been the star of the album's front cover, but the back cover was pure Catskills promo, peppered with idyllic photos of the mountains' most well-known and iconic resort. Come enjoy the tennis courts and Olympic-size pool. Come ice skating or paddle the lake in a row boat. Come hear Puente turn "Baubles, Bangles, and Beads" into a sweltering pachanga. It was, to be sure, a public relations tag-team: hype for Puente's music and hype for the mountain getaway in Liberty, New York that had helped make Puente a favorite with, at leisure, Jews who were eager to try out the mambo steps they learned in dance class earlier that day.

For all the promotional buzz, *Cha Cha Cha: Live at Grossinger's* documents a cross-cultural, mid-century relationship between Latinos and American Jews that speaks as much to the financial dealings of commercial entertainment as it does to the pleasures of black-tie dance contests, living room listening sessions, and late-night mambo parties. Yes, Puente was Jewish entertainment that night, but the Grossinger's Jews were Puente people too—he was their beloved headliner; they were his beloved audience. "Would the band and the crowd really 'dig' each other?" the liner notes asked, but there was really never any question if the Puerto Rican band and the Jewish crowd would "dig" each other. This was, after all, New York in the fifties, and the whole city was caught up in the golden age of the Jewish Latin Craze. But it was bigger than that. It spoke to a larger history of Latino-Jewish musical exchange. Or as the humorist **Harry Golden** remarked just a year earlier, "The history of Jews in America: from Sha sha to Cha cha" (Golden, 1958).

Golden's statement came at the tail end of the mambo craze of the 1950s and the previous rumba craze of the 1930s. Each was marked by the heavy participation of American Jews. Indeed, as early as 1932, **George Gershwin**—who is typically cited as a pioneering architect of black-Jewish musical exchange but not of Jewish-Latino musical exchange—spent three weeks in Havana and came back with his rumba-riffing *Cuban Overture.* From the 1930s on, numerous Jewish musicians recorded tributes to the Jewish love of Latin American music (from Ruth Wallis's "It's A Scream How Levine Does the Mambo" on her *Rumba Party* album to the Barton Brothers' "Mambo Moish" and the Irving Fields Trio's *Bagels and Bongos*), many radio DJs who were actively involved in the dissemination of mambo and the promotion of Latino musicians to Latino and non-Latino audiences alike were Jewish (Symphony Sid, Dick "Ricardo" Sugar, Art "Pancho" Raymond), and more than a few Jewish musicians managed to become mainstays of the scene (Alfredo "Mendez" Mendelsohn in the thirties, Al "Alfredito" Levy in the fifties, Larry "El Judio Maravilloso" Harlow in the sixties). When Jewish entrepreneur Maxwell Hyman's famed ballroom and "Home of the Mambo," the Palladium, adopted its "all-Latin" policy in 1949, Jewish fans of Latino music—soon renamed in Yiddish as "mamboniks"—had a place to go to listen and dance (especially on Wednesday nights, when "Killer Joe" Piro gave dance lessons to Jews and Italians).

Due to the close proximity of Jews and Latinos in places like East Harlem, local Jewish businessmen, for whom Latin music was a daily soundtrack, became some of the first to capitalize on its growing popularity and some of the key players in promoting and supporting the careers of Latin musicians. One of the earliest to get involved was Sidney Siegel, whose Casa Siegel general store in East Harlem was soon parlayed into Seeco Records, a label he dedicated to "the finest in Latin-American recordings." Seeco built consumer bases in New York, Cuba, and Puerto Rico (at times even boasting 75 percent of their sales on the islands), and in 1954, Seeco released the first Latin recording ever on a 12-inch LP.

The 1940s and 1950s saw the birth of two other crucial early Latin labels, Alegre Records and Tico Records. Al Santiago, owner of Manhattan's Casalegre record store, founded Alegre Records in 1955 with the financial support of Jewish businessman Ben Perlman (the owner of the store next to Santiago's, Grossman's Clothes). Tico was the joint venture of Art Raymond, the Latin radio star, and George Goldner, the ragman-turned-music-man with a Puerto Rican wife. Their first major hit, Tito Puente's "Albaniquito," featured the legendary likes of Mario Bauza, Mongo Santamaria, and Vicentico Valdes.

The Jewish-Latin craze's most sacred laboratories, however, were in the hotels of the Catskill Mountains. The Catskills were, as one guest typically recalls, a "Mecca for Latin music." Leading Latino musicians like Alberto Socarras and Jose Curbelo played Grossinger's as early as 1944. Cuban Latin **jazz** pioneers Mario Bauza and Machito had both played the Concord, another popular Catskills hotel, by 1947. Machito released his own testament to Latino-Jewish vacation intermingling on Kiamesha Lake, *Vacation at the Concord,* which came complete with Machito's own resort-specific mambo, "Mambo la Concorde" (written with Bauza and Rene Hernandez).

As some of these examples suggest, exchanges between Jews and Latinos were not unidirectional. Jews may have been fans of Latin music, played in Latin bands, and helped promote and sell Latin music, but Latinos were quick to answer back. Pupi Campo covered the Barton Brothers' Yiddish radio goof "Joe and Paul" in 1948 and then recorded "Mambonik," a tribute to mambo-identified Jews everywhere. Joe Quijano, the Puerto Rican percussionist who once boasted, "Yo soy el son cubano" ("I am the Cuban son"), did ***Fiddler on the Roof*** *Goes Latin.* Eddie Cano recorded "Hava Nagilah Pachanga," Machito chimed in with "Israeli Sha Sha," Perez Prado made the twist go mambo and Jewish with "The Twist of Hava Nageelah," and Al Gomez and his orchestra did a straight-up Yiddish rumba "Shen Vi Di L'Vone." As late as 1973, Sabu Martinez paid tribute to Martin Cohen, the founder of the country's leading Latino musical instrument company, Latin Percussion, with "Martin Cohen Loves Latin Percussion," an instrumental that opened his *Afro Temple* album.

One of the more interesting contributions to this intercultural musical conversation came in the mid-1950s when Ray Barretto, Willie Rodriguez, and Charlie Palmieri teamed up with John Cali, Doc Cheatham, and Clark Terry to form Juan Calle and His Latin Lantzmen, an alleged Latin-Jewish supergroup; they recorded an album called *Mazel Tov Mis Amigos,* wherein they turned such classic Yiddish songs as "Hava Nagila" into a cha cha cha and "Die Greene Koseene" into a merengue.

The questions "Why Jews?" and "Why Latin music?" are answered by examining forces that are historically musicological and immediately sociological. Many have attributed it to the ghost of genetic memory, as twentieth-century Jews heard some of Latin music's roots in the Arabic cultures of North Africa, which shared stylistic connections to the music of fifteenth-century Sephardic Jews (and their eventual dispersal into a global diaspora of Catholic conversos).

Jazz trumpet player Steve Bernstein, whose 1999 album *Diaspora Soul* bridged rhythm and blues, New Orleans jazz, Yiddish music, **klezmer**, and Latin rhythms, has offered an alternative geography of influence and recognition that ends with the Jewish hora as a distant cousin of the Afro-Cuban clave. This leads to thinking about a Gulf Coast sound, rather than a New Orleans sound. This Gulf Coast sound encompasses Texas, Cuba, and part of the Gulf Coast around to Miami. The most popular Cuban export of the 1950s was the "cha cha cha." Who loves a cha-cha more than the Jews? And the final piece of the grail, the hora bass pattern—one, two-and, and-four-and—is the first half of the clave, the heart of Afro-Cuban music.

Latin music typically served as an alternate mode of Jewish performance, a space where Jewish tradition was engaged by being changed, and Jewish memory activated while refusing monolithic attachment to a stable, too-easily shared notion of Jewishness. By playing and listening to Latin music—especially in the many cases of listening to Latin versions of Yiddish songs—Jews were simultaneously tied to collective memory and freed from the rules and constraints of a preordained identity.

One of the 1950s' more Latinized Jewish songs was "Channa From Havana," composed by Eli Basse and sung by the Barry Sisters. This 1952 klezmer-mambo hit tells of the story of Channa's 10-day cruise to Havana with her husband and her return to Miami as a "Cubaphile." The song describes Channa as only wanting to dance mambo and cha cha cha, and she even begins calling her bubele husband "Bubalu." Her newfound love of Cuban music convinced Channa she did not need her husband, and she fell for a Latino man, a Mexican (Meksikaner) rather than a Cuban. Just when Channa thought she had left her life as Channa Cohen of Miami behind, Basse and the Barry Sisters, who sang in both English and Yiddish, with only bits of Spanish, pulled a typical Jewish-Latin craze trick. It turned out the Meksikaner was named Sam Shapiro. Shapiro was another Jew who went Latin to find himself. All the while, the song's Latin shuffle is continually interrupted by a blaring old-school Eastern European klezmer freilach that fades in and out but never goes away. Just like her Mexican man, Channa's new Cuban identity was partly a Jewish one. *See also* **The Catskills**; **Popular Music**.

Josh Kun

Further Reading: Golden, Harry. *Only in America*, New York: World Publishing Co., 1958 (republished in 1972). Schorsch, Jonathan. "Making Judaism Cool," *Best Contemporary Jewish Writing*. Michael Lerner, ed. Hoboken, NJ: Jossey-Bass, 2001.

LAZARUS, EMMA (1849–1887)

Lazarus was an American-born Jewish writer whose poetry and prose contributed to the fabric of American Jewish life on three fronts: democracy, Zionism, and feminism. Her sonnet "The New Colossus" was placed on a plaque in 1903 and affixed to the Statute of Liberty. Her essays in *The Century* and *The American Hebrew* established her as a herald of Zionism on the American shore. Her extensive writing oeuvre helped inaugurate the voice of femininity in American Jewish writing.

Emma Lazarus was born on July 22, 1849, in New York. She was the fourth of seven children (Sarah, Mary, Josephine, Emma, Eliezer Frank, Agnes, and Annie) born to Moses and Esther Nathan Lazarus. The close-knit Sephardic family was mildly observant and belonged to the Shearith Israel Congregation. Moses made his fortune refining sugar and was a founder of the Knickerbocker Club. The prominent family had roots that reached back to the time of the American Revolution. Reserved and studious, Lazarus was taught by private tutors, who taught her European languages (French, German, Italian) and culture. Her persona and early education are reflected in *Poems and Translations* (1866), a collection of melancholic poems and translations from Hugo, Dumas, Schiller, and Heine. Her youthful talent attracted the attention of Ralph Waldo Emerson, who, in letters written from 1868–1869, suggested that she read Thoreau, Whitman, and Shakespeare, among others, to sharpen her rhetoric. *Admetus and Other Poems* (1871) was dedicated to Emerson in appreciation and gratitude.

She wrote a romance novel, *Alide* (1874), based on a love incident in the life of the great German poet and dramatist Johann Wolfgang von Goethe, and a historical tragedy, *The Spagnoletto* (1876), set in seventeenth century Italy. Her translation of the poems and biography of the German Jewish poet and critic Heinrich Heine were published in 1881.

Lazarus's interest in Jewish memory and identity is evident from the start. Her "In the Jewish Synagogue at Newport" was published in her maiden volume, *Admetus and Other Poems*. She published translations of outstanding Jewish poets such as Judah Halevi and Solomon Gabirol (1879) and especially Heine. The dire effects from the heightened Russian pogroms of 1881–1882 changed her focus from idyllic Jewish subjects in memory past to a more activist commentary on present-day Jewish persecution. Her advocacy and concern for victimized Jews of Russia and East Central Europe was meant to reject anti-Semitism and urge assimilated American Jews to receive nearly arrived ghetto Jewish refugees. In essays in non-Jewish publications, *The Century* (1882) and *The Critic,* she spoke out against the causes and effects of virulent hatred of Jews. She met with Jewish refugees on Ward's Island, and, driven by a socialist-humanitarian ethos, she believed that these downtrodden ghetto Jews would contribute to American democracy. Her regular contributions to *The American Hebrew* demonstrated her passion for Jewish culture and history.

In drama, poetry, and prose, Lazarus identified with the plight and right of Jews in history. Her reference to the bittersweet spirit of the Jews is apparent in *Songs of a Semite* (1882), which features *The Dance of Death,* a historical tragedy in five acts that speaks about the burning of Jews of Nordhausen and Eisenach in Thuringia during the Black Plague (May 1349), along with poems in praise of rediscovered Jewish nationalism, for example, "The New Ezekiel" and the "Banner of the Jews." Her *An Epistle to the Hebrews* (1882–1883) set forth in prose what she sang in verse: her ideas and views for the revitalization of Jewish life by a cultural and national revival in America and in Eretz Israel. Emma Lazarus believed and breathed the particularity and the universality of the Jewish idea: choose life.

Noteworthy are two poems she composed in 1883: "Gifts" and "The New Colossus." In the former, the Jews forswear wealth, beauty, and power, for wisdom and truth. In the latter, quoting from the Mother of Exiles: "Give me your tired your poor, your huddled masses yearning to breathe free, the wretched refuse of your teeming shore. Send these, the homeless, tempest-tossed to me, I lift my lamp beside the golden door." In the spirit of the Torah and the American way, Lazarus envisioned that the handmaiden of life is freedom grounded in truth and justice for one and all. *See also* **Literature.**

Zev Garber

Further Reading: Merriam, Eve. *Emma Lazarus Rediscovered.* New York: Biblio Press, 1998. Schappes, Morris U. *Emma Lazarus: Selections from Her Poetry and Prose.* New York: Emma Lazarus Federation of Jewish Women's Clubs, 1978.

LEIBER, JERRY AND STOLLER, MIKE

See **The Brill Building Songwriters**

LEIBOVITZ, ANNIE (1949–)

With more than 25 years of high-profile magazine and commercial photography to her credit, Annie Leibovitz is especially known for her unique portraits of celebrities. Whether it is Pete Townsend —with bloody fingers, Demi Moore—nude and pregnant, or Whoopi Goldberg—immersed in a bathtub of milk, Leibovitz's unconventional images of celebrities always reveal something personal about the subject. One of six children, Anna-Lou Leibovitz was born in Westport, Connecticut on October 2, 1949. Her father Samuel served as an officer in the air force, and her mother Marilyn taught modern dance. In 1967 Leibovitz began studying painting at the San Francisco Art Institute, and she graduated four years later with a bachelor's degree in fine arts. In 1968, Leibovitz received her first camera and traveled to Japan. In 1969, Leibovitz lived in an Israeli kibbutz, where she completed her first serious photography series.

The newly formed magazine *Rolling Stone* hired Leibovitz in 1970 and assigned her to photograph John Lennon for an early cover image. Within three years, she had become the magazine's chief photographer. Several high-profile assignments followed, including the role of official photographer for the Rolling Stones' 1975 world tour.

In 1980 she photographed Lennon again for *Rolling Stone,* this time with Yoko Ono. One particular photo from this session—a nude Lennon curled around a fully clothed Ono—has become an iconic image in popular culture. This session was the last time Lennon was photographed before he was murdered. In 2005, the American Society of Magazine Editors named Leibovitz's portrait of Lennon and Ono the best magazine cover in 40 years. Leibovitz became the first contributing photographer for *Vanity Fair* magazine; her first book, *Annie Leibovitz Photographs,* was published in 1983.

In 1989, Leibovitz met **Susan Sontag** and began a long-term relationship that lasted until Sontag's death in late 2004. The scholarly influence of Sontag had a profound effect on Leibovitz's work.

More than eight books of Leibovitz's photographs have been published. Her most recent book, *A Photographer's Life: 1990–2005,* provides the most intimate look at the artist's own life. Leibovitz has three daughters: Sarah, Susan, and Samuelle.

Shauna Frischkorn

Further Reading: Leibovitz, Annie. *Photographs—Annie Leibovitz, 1970–1990.* New York: Harper Collins, 1991. ———. *Women.* New York: Random House, 1999. *Life Through a Lens.* DVD. Custom Flix, 2007.

LEONARD, BENNY (1896–1947)

Known as the "Ghetto Wizard," the nickname given to him by sports columnists, Benny Leonard was born Benjamin Leiner on Manhattan's East Side. He was a tough kid who had to guard his back, as gangs often fought each other with pipes and clubs in the densely populated, multiethnic, poor neighborhood. Leonard used his head, fighting with great skill—he was a boxer noted to be wily, speedy, and a stylized puncher. He entered the ring at age 15 as a means of earning money to avoid the crushing low pay and conditions in factories and sweatshops. He had his greatest success as a lightweight—5 feet, 5 inches and 139 pounds, achieving 180 wins, 69 knock outs, and 21 losses. Sporting News rated him in 1997 as "the best boxer in 75 years."

Leonard was a proud Jew. He wore a six-pointed star (Mogen David) on his trunks and did not fight on Jewish holidays. He supported the Jewish sports competitions known as the Maccabiah Games. His Orthodox mother hated the sport, considering boxing "goyish." His Russian-born father thought it was better than working in the sweatshop as he did. Responding to the pleas of his mother, Leonard finally gave up boxing in 1924, and he retired as the undefeated lightweight champion of the world, holding the title from May 1917 to May 1925.

Retiring as a millionaire, he lost it all in the great stock market crash of 1929. Without funds, he returned to the ring in 1931. A year later, weakened by the time off, he lost by a technical knock out to Jimmy McLarnin in the sixth round and left the ring permanently. Trying a number of occupations, including a brief career in the movies, he joined the Merchant Marine, earning the rank of lieutenant commander during World War II. In 1943, Leonard became a boxing referee. He died in the ring on April 18, 1947 of a massive heart attack.

This ring craftsman left a legacy. Benny Leonard helped bring about acceptance of Jews by fair-minded people. *Ring Magazine* dubbed him as the greatest lightweight who ever lived. Lightweights following him adopted his crafty, smart-punching boxing style, including the head weave and the damaging left jab. Other individuals in the ethnic minority found boxing a way to gain social acceptance and mobility. *See also* **Sports**.

Philip Rosen

Further Reading: Bodner, Allen. *When Boxing Was a Jewish Sport.* Praeger Trade, 1997.

LERNER, RABBI MICHAEL (1943–)

Rabbi Lerner, the rabbi of progressive (religiously and politically) congregation Beyt Tikkun in Berkeley, California, also founded *Tikkun* (1986), a liberal alternative to *Commentary,* the neoconservative Jewish magazine. *Tikkun,* the Hebrew word for restoration, is derived from the Jewish mystical belief in Tikkun Olam, or "repair of the world," an objective which characterizes Lerner's approach to politics. The magazine publishes Jewish-oriented critiques of politics and culture, with a circulation of around 100,000 readers. Its position on the Israeli-Palestinian conflict represents an alternative approach to the American Israel Public Affairs Committee (AIPAC), the mainstream pro-Israel lobby.

In regard to Israel, Lerner would end settlements, withdraw from the military occupation of the West Bank, return to Israel's pre-1967 borders, assume some responsibility for Arab refugees, and create an independent Palestinian state. He is also an ardent supporter of the Israel peace movement, Peace Now. Although Lerner has marched with antiwar leftist groups, as a Zionist he has denounced their passionate anti-Israel rhetoric. In regard to other issues, Lerner favors an immediate end to America's occupation of Iraq, opposes the religious right's promotion of the integration of church and state, advocates religious pluralism, supports political programs which favor minorities, immigrants, and the less fortunate in American society, and in general, he promotes a "politics of meaning," translated as a kinder, highly ethical, and more loving society.

Michael Lerner received his BA from Columbia University and also took courses at the Jewish Theological Seminary (JTS). It was at JTS that Lerner came under the influence of the noted Jewish theologian **Abraham Joshua Heschel**, whose "prophetic" Jewish activism emphasized the need to heal the world. Lerner went on to earn two PhD degrees, one in philosophy (1972) and another in psychology (1977) at the University of California at Berkeley. While attending the University of California–Berkeley, he was a leader in the anti-Vietnam War movement. While acting as a psychotherapist for working-class people (1979), he became convinced that the left had to address spiritual needs and be friendly to religion.

He received his rabbinical ordination, in 1995, from the Jewish Renewal Beth Din (religious court), headed by Rabbi Zalman Schachter-Shalomi, an ordination questioned by some mainstream Orthodox, Conservative, and Reform rabbis. In 2005, Lerner co-founded the Network of Spiritual Progressives along with Cornel West and Benedictine Sister Joan Chittister. Lerner married Nan Fink in 1986. They had one child, Akiva. Divorced in 1991, he married Deborah Kohn in 1998. Lerner has authored a number of books, including *The Politics of Meaning* (Addison Wesley, 1997), which caught the attention of then-First Lady Hillary Clinton. Subsequently, he became for a short time an advisor to Mrs. Clinton.

Considered by some the most controversial Jew in America, he now lives with his wife, Rabbi Deborah Kohn, in Berkeley, and he serves as rabbi of Beyt Tikkun and editor of *Tikkun* magazine.

Philip Rosen

Further Reading: Handler, Judd. "Michael Lerner: The Most Controversial Jew in America." *San Diego Jewish Journal,* March 26, 2007.

LEVIN, IRA (1929–2007)

Levin, the son of successful toymaker Charles Levin and Beatrice Schlansky, was born in New York in 1929. Levin attended Horace Mann High School and earned degrees in English and philosophy from NYU. Levin's father wanted him to go into the family toy business; the son wanted to be a writer. So, they compromised: his father would support him for two years. If at the end of that time he had no success as a writer, he was to work for his father. In 1949, CBS ran a contest for original teleplays. Levin's entry, *The Old Woman,* a murder mystery, won second place and was eventually filmed as an episode on the mystery-thriller *Lights Out.* Levin never went into the toy business.

No Time for Sergeants (1956), Levin's first play, was adapted from a novel by Mac Hyman. The play was a comedy about a hillbilly inducted into the U.S. Army. It was staged on Broadway, launching the career of the then-unknown Andy Griffith. Turned into a film, it led to the television series *Gomer Pyle, USMC.* Levin's first novel, *A Kiss Before Dying* (1953) won the prestigious Edgar Award and was purchased by Hollywood, where it was filmed twice. His next novel, the eerie *Rosemary's Baby* (1967), a story about a couple's involvement with friends who turn out to be devil worshipers, was made into a film in 1968, and it moved Roman Polanski into the front rank of Hollywood directors.

The Tony-nominated *Deathtrap* (1978) was made into a film starring Michael Caine and Christopher Reeve (1982). A remake of the film was released in 2007 with Michael Caine and Jude Law. *Deathtrap* holds the record for the longest-running mystery on Broadway. Writer Stephen King, an acknowledged master of the mystery genre, once described Levin as "the Swiss watchmaker of suspense novels . . . he makes the rest of us look like cheap watchmakers in drugstores" (Guttridge, 2007).

Levin's oeuvre includes such well-known works as *The Stepford Wives* (1972), produced as a film in 1975, and *The Boys from Brazil* (1976); the film version was made in 1978. He was married twice, to Gabrielle Aronsohn and Phyllis Finkel; both marriages ended in divorce. Levin had three sons from his marriage to Ms. Aronsohn: Adam, Jared, and Nicholas; he also has three grandchildren. *See also* **Film**.

Kurt F. Stone

Further Reading: Guttridge, Peter. "Ira Levin." Obituary. *Independent,* November 15, 2007.

LEVIN, MEYER (1905–1981)

Possibly the twentieth century's foremost writer on Jewish subjects, Meyer Levin was born in 1905 in Chicago. His parents, Joseph Levin and Golda, were Jewish Lithuanian immigrants. Meyer started his career on the *Chicago Daily News* as a reporter. He also wrote essays for the Jewish-oriented periodical *The Menorah Journal,* which chronicled news of interest to its Jewish reading audience. While traveling as a reporter for the Jewish Telegraphic Agency and the U.S. Office of War Information, Levin was present at the liberation of the concentration camps.

His autobiographical book *In Search* (1949), as well as *Eva* (1959) and *The Stronghold* (1965), tells about Jewish survivors of the Holocaust. Levin was a strong Zionist and supporter of the Jewish community in Palestine. As early as 1931, he wrote about life in a kibbutz (collective farm) in Jewish Palestine in his novel *Yehuda.* His later novels, *The Settlers* (1972) and *The Harvest* (1978), deal with the same theme.

After World War II he joined the Jewish underground Haganah which engaged in "smuggling" European Jewish survivors into Palestine. He related this experience in his documentary *The Illegals* (1947). His *My Father's House* was the first Palestinian feature film.

Meyer Levin is probably best known for his novel about the Leopold-Loeb case, which later was filmed as *Compulsion* (1959). The docudrama told the story of the two Jewish college students who cold-bloodily murdered a little neighborhood boy. Levin had gone to the University of Chicago with the defendants.

Levin's greatest disappointment in life was his failure to have his play based on Anne Frank's diary produced. The first to recognize the diary's great literary potential, Levin befriended Anne's father, Otto, and believed he had an agreement for the subsequent Broadway production. Lillian Hellman, however, believed the Levin version was "too Jewish," and she pushed for the Hackett version to reach Broadway. Levin's side of this controversy can be read in the book *Obsession* (1974), which details how the play was altered to emphasize the universal aspect of Anne Frank's diary at the expense of its Jewish content.

Levin married twice, first to Tereska Torres, then to Mabel Schamp. He fathered Jonathan, Dominique, Gabriel, and Mikael. Meyer died in Jerusalem of unspecified causes in 1981. *See also* **Film**; **Theater**.

Philip Rosen

Further Reading: Graver, Lawrence. *An Obsession with Anne Frank*. University of California Press, 1985.

LEWIS, JERRY (1926–)

Jerry Lewis is a comedian, award-winning actor, producer, writer, and director, best known for his slapstick humor and charity-fundraising telethons for the Muscular Dystrophy Association. Jerry Lewis was born Jerome Levitch into a show business family in Newark, New Jersey on March 17, 1926. His parents, Danny and Rae Lewis, trod the boards of the Borscht Belt. A 2001 article in the *New York Times* noted that his Bar Mitzvah was attended only by his grandmother Sarah, who raised the boy while his parents were on the road; they did not make it to the synagogue in time for the celebration.

Lewis made his professional debut at the age of five, singing "Brother Can You Spare a Dime." By the time he began Irvington High School he had lost whatever taste he had for formal education and dropped out at the age of 15 to begin a solo career with middling success. Then he met a singer named Dean Martin.

During their heyday, Martin and Lewis were the highest-paid act in show business. Martin would croon and Lewis would *fonfer*, cracking up both the audiences and his partner.

An "appreciation" in the *Forward* in 2006, marking the comedian's birthday, noted "how 'ethnic' (Martin and Lewis's) improvised antic routines were, and how utterly at ease each appears in his Italian American or Jewish American funny bones," particularly "Lewis's surreal screechy 'up-talk,' with its Yiddish lilt and reversals of syntax ("So giant malted, I should drink?")" (Weber, 2006). Prominently displayed on Lewis's desk in his Las Vegas office is a placard with the phrase "Super Jew."

Lewis, a self-described workaholic, tried his hand in every aspect of the entertainment world: actor, writer, producer, director, even musical composer. After his breakup with Martin, Lewis played the title role in a 1959 television production of ***The Jazz Singer***, in which he sought reconciliation with his ailing cantor father by chanting Kol Nidre in greasepaint. He also directed and starred in the ill-fated feature film *The Day the Clown Cried*, a 1972 project that was never completed, in which he played a German clown interred in a concentration camp who was compelled to march children to their deaths.

His career suffered a lull during the 1960s and 1970s, but his performance in *The King of Comedy* marked something of a comeback. In all, Lewis has appeared in more than 40 feature films and hosted three television series.

Although health problems complicated by his physical humor have plagued Lewis in recent years, he has been the guiding force behind the Jerry Lewis Muscular Dystrophy Association Labor Day Telethon since its debut broadcast in 1966. A favorite in France, Lewis was awarded the French Legion of Honor in 1984. He was inducted into the International Humor Hall of Fame in 1992 and received a Lifetime Achievement Award from the Comedy Hall of Fame in 1998. A *Newsweek* poll in 2001 had Lewis in a fifth-place tie with Pope John Paul as the most recognized person on the planet.

Lewis married Patti Palmer in 1945. The couple had four children, Scott, Christopher, Anthony, and Gary—who enjoyed some fame of his own as leader of Gary Lewis and the Playboys. They also adopted another son, Ronald, and divorced in 1980. Lewis married SanDee Pitman in 1992; the couple had one daughter, Danielle, born in 1992. *See also* **Comedy**.

Ron Kaplan

Further Reading: Lewis, Jerry, with James Kaplan. *Dean and Me (A Love Story)*. Doubleday, 2005. Neibhur, James L., and Ted Okuda. *The Jerry Lewis Films*. McFarland, 1994. Weber, Donald. *Forward,* March 10, 2006.

LEWIS, SHARI (1933–1998)

Host of the popular 1960s *Shari Lewis Show* and creator of Hush Puppy, Charlie Horse, and Lamb Chop, Lewis was born Sonia Hurwitz in New York City. Influenced by her parents, Ann Ritz Hurwitz (coordinator of music for the New York City public school system) and Abe Hurwitz (professor at Yeshiva University), Lewis became an accomplished ventriloquist, puppeteer, songwriter, actor, and dancer. Lewis's first husband was Stan Lewis.

Lewis studied music theory, orchestration, piano, and violin at New York City's High School of Music and Art. She studied acting at the Neighborhood Playhouse and danced at the School of American Ballet. While she was interested in pursuing a career in song and dance, Lewis's father encouraged her to develop her ventriloquism skills. At 19 she won first place in the Arthur Godfrey Talent Scouts. Lewis's television debut was in the form of a 15-minute show entitled *Facts and Fun with Shari,* an educational program that aired on Saturday mornings in New York. Her television career was launched in 1957 when she and Lamb Chop appeared on the *Captain Kangaroo Show.*

The Shari Lewis Show followed a few months later, showcasing Lamp Chop and other characters. Capturing and sustaining the interest and imagination of children, the show ran from 1960 to 1963. As her cast of puppets encountered life's dilemmas, Lewis helped them resolve their conflicts by encouraging them to make appropriate choices. Using songs or conversations to solve problems, the lessons learned by Lamp Chop, Hush Puppy, and Charlie Horse were designed to assist children in addressing obstacles encountered in life's journey. Always integrating humor into her show, Lewis believed that learning should be musical, magical, and fun.

Lewis was the recipient of the Action for Children's Television Award, the Peabody Award, the John F. Kennedy Center Award for Excellence and Creativity, 7 Parents' Choice Awards, and 12 Emmy Awards. Hofstra University awarded Lewis an honorary doctorate in education in 1993. She was the author of 60 books for children and collaborated with her husband in writing "The Lights of Zetar," a *Star Trek* episode.

After an almost 20-year hiatus from children's television, Lewis launched *Lamb Chop's Play Along* on PBS in 1992. The show aired for five years. In 1998 Lewis began work on a PBS television series called *The Charlie Horse Music Pizza*. The show was a collaborative venture of Lewis's husband of 40 years, Jeremy Tarcher, and daughter, Mallory Tarcher. During her work on *The Charlie Horse Music Pizza,* Lewis was diagnosed with uterine cancer, and she died the same year. *See also* **Television**.

Robert Ruder

Further Reading: Dickenson, Amy. "Dishing Up Lamb Chop; On PBS, Shari Lewis's Second Generation." *Washington Post,* April 4, 1994.

LEWISOHN, LUDWIG (1882–1955)

During the 1920s and for several decades following, Ludwig Lewisohn was one of the most popular, often-seen-as-infamous novelists in the country. On the heels of *The Case of Mr. Crump* (1926) and *The Island Within* (1928), and several other works seen in the minds of many as quite autobiographical, he was portrayed by some as a dissolute writer who had left his wife and embarked upon a series of failed relationships with women.

Ludwig Lewisohn, born in Germany in 1882, was brought to this country in 1890 by his German Jewish assimilated parents; he was brought up in Charleston, South Carolina, where his parents converted to Christianity, and where he was an honors student in high school. Lewisohn graduated with a simultaneous BA and MA from the College of Charleston. In New York City, he entered Columbia University in 1902 for his doctorate in English. Along the way he met and married Mary Child, an English woman 20 years his senior; she was divorced with children.

While writing his dissertation Lewisohn was told by a member of his committee that Jews would not be hired by any English department. Stung by the words, he dropped out and got a job in first one and then another mid-western university in the German department. During World War I, due to anti-German prejudice he moved to New York City, where he became the drama critic for *The Nation*.

As he came to realize that his marriage was a mistake, his wife hired a detective to follow him. Lewisohn ran off to Paris with a young woman 20 years his junior. The two had a son but never married. Though his books were praised by such luminaries as Thomas Mann and **Sigmund Freud**, his wife refused to give him a divorce, sued him, and prevented him from collecting royalties.

Some readers of *The Case of Mr. Crump* (later titled "The Tyranny of Sex") believed the novel was about Lewisohn and his wife. For the discerning reader it was a story of an artist, a genius, trying desperately to survive in a new world, as Ralph Melnick put it, shaped by bourgeois tastes and moral and cultural decay, and, as others have noted, by sexual hypocrisy and double standards. Known widely as a translator who had published books on German drama and literature, and having published several well-received novels that freed literature from sexual repression and American puritanism, Lewisohn gained an international reputation in the 1920s that lasted several decades

In *The Island Within*, Jewishness reigned as the dominant world system. Marginalized as a Germanophile during World War I, Lewisohn's interest in Judaism, once awakened, never declined. He became a Zionist and in his last years helped found and was part of Brandeis University. A man of great talent and emotion, he was a brilliant and prolific novelist, translator, and essayist. Though very popular and well known for decades, his work is now lamentably neglected. *See also* **Literature**.

Daniel Walden

Further Reading: Lewisohn, Ludwig. *The Island Within*. Syracuse University Press, 1928.

LIEBERMAN, JOSEPH (1942–)

Joseph Isadore Lieberman, known popularly as Joe Lieberman, earned a place in American history as the first Jew to stand for national election on a major party ticket when presidential candidate Al Gore selected him as his vice-presidential running mate in 2000. He also landed a place in popular culture during the campaign for his advocacy for faith-based politics and monitoring of the entertainment industry for sexual and violent content. He remained in the public eye after the election as a presidential primary candidate in the 2004 election when his reference to "Joementum" became part of popular discourse and in the 2006 senatorial election when a kiss placed on his cheek by president George W. Bush after the state of the union speech was captured for visual and material culture.

Lieberman was one of three children (sisters Rietta and Ellen) born to Henry Lieberman (1915–1986), a liquor store owner, and Marcia Manger (1914–2005), Jews of Polish and Austrian backgrounds, respectively. In Lieberman's memoir *In Praise of Public Life* (2000), he recalled the influence of his maternal grandmother, Minnie, who had immigrated to the United States after she was married and had children. He credited her with setting a standard for service in his family, as a founder of the Hebrew Ladies

Educational League in his hometown of Stamford, Connecticut. It was in his view a classic immigrant, self-help, pre-welfare organization, one which raised money and gave it to the needy in the Jewish community. Later in life, he encouraged as a matter of public policy the involvement of faith-based organizations in welfare and community development programs.

As a summer intern in the office of Democrat Senator Abraham Ribicoff, a fellow Jew, Lieberman gained political experience. There he met his first wife, Betty Haas, but they divorced in 1981 after what Lieberman described as religious differences (she was a Reform Jew, and he was moving toward modern Orthodoxy) and his intensive public life. After graduating from Yale Law School in 1967, he entered politics as a Connecticut state senator in 1970, campaigning as a Reform Democrat on an anti-Vietnam War platform. He gained statewide notice in 1974 when he rose to the position of majority leader.

From 1982 to 1988 Lieberman served as attorney general, which was followed by his election to the United States Senate in 1988. In 1983, he married Hadassah Freilich (born 1948 in Prague, Czechoslovakia), a daughter of Rabbi Samuel Freilich, a Holocaust survivor. Lieberman politically supported advocacy for a strong national defense (support for war in Iraq), support for Israel, environmental protection (for example, the Clean Air Act of 1990), and regulation of the entertainment industry.

Lieberman drew national attention for including cultural values in his campaign in order to curb sales of video games with sexual and violent content. In 1995, he pushed for requiring the "V-chip" in televisions to block undesired shows and channels. He wrote in his book *In Praise of Public Life* that this movement was motivated by concerns for his youngest daughter as television became more sexual and violent. He targeted the video game *Postal,* developed by Running with Scissors, which he claimed indulged homicidal behavior. In retaliation, developers of the sequel included a banner that read "Lieberman, God sees your lies" and featured a newspaper announcing the apocalypse with, "Lieberman blames Doom." Lieberman became further associated with promoting morals when he parted with Democratic Party colleagues by publicly blasting President Bill Clinton in 1998 for having an affair with White House intern Monica Lewinsky.

During the 2000 vice presidential campaign, questions arose about possible conflicts between his Sabbath observance and his public duties. Instead of sparking anti-Semitism, his espousal of the role of his faith in public life drew praise from Christian conservatives who supported promotion of "traditional values" in public policy. Lieberman's public avowal of Jewishness revived an old debate about whether the goal of assimilation as a success strategy in America sacrifices Jewish ethnic display and continuity. Jewish cultural studies scholar Simon Bronner conceptualized this "balancing act" by Jews between a public and private persona in America as the "Lieberman Syndrome." The dilemma is epitomized by Lieberman's labored explanation of himself as a participant-citizen in the American polity, despite his Orthodox Jewish belief and practice. The relative paucity of Jewish politicians in American life was traced to this Jewish concern about having a public ethnic profile.

Jokes circulated during the 2000 election campaign regarding Jewish politicians who hide their Jewishness, only to demonstrate their ethnicity in a dialect expression, relation to the Jewish mother figure, or ethnic food craving. After the election, Lieberman became a celebrity face for Jewish social causes and the encouragement for more Jewish participation in American politics. He wrote the introduction to *Jews in American Politics* (2001). Lieberman's role became pronounced because of the pivotal role played by Florida in the election and the expectation that Lieberman would be effective in garnering the state's Jewish vote. In a close vote, the state went for Bush.

Making a run for president before the New Hampshire primary in 2004, Lieberman told CNN's Wolf Blitzer that despite disappointing poll results, he was picking up "Joementum," linguistically a portmanteau word or a new word formed by joining two others and combining their meanings. He ended up placing a disappointing fifth among the candidates, and he dropped out of the race. In the years that followed, the term showed up in blogs, news reports, and humor to refer to any candidacy that is slipping in popularity and bound to fail despite the candidate's hope or optimism. It also was a term used in anti-Lieberman blogs during his 2006 senatorial reelection campaign against fellow Democrat Ned Lamont.

Lieberman lost his primary bid against Lamont, but he ran as an independent and won the general election. Any discontent Democrats had with Lieberman was due mainly to his support for the war in Iraq. Lieberman's agreement with the administration's policies in Iraq was on open display when the president planted a kiss on his cheek following the 2005 state of the union address. Pictures of the kiss were emblazoned on signs, buttons, and parade floats. The message of the kiss had, according to critics, the connotation of the mafia godfather kiss that accords vassal status to the person being kissed.

Many commentators have observed Lieberman's popularity as a sign of change in Jewish political culture. Once characterized as staunchly liberal in social, diplomatic, and economic policies, the Jewish voter has been harder to pigeonhole since the late twentieth century. Lieberman has often been cited as an example of the independent-minded Jew in national politics—combining conservative positions on affirmative action, censorship, and the war in Iraq with strict environmental protection, public utility regulation, and liberal immigration policy. Senator Lieberman supported Republican John McCain in the 2008 presidential election and angered many of his former Democratic Party colleagues when he spoke at the Republican convention in behalf of the Arizona senator.

Simon J. Bronner

Further Reading: Bronner, Simon J. "The Lieberman Syndrome: Public and Private Jewishness in American Political Culture." *Journal of Modern Jewish Studies* 2 (2003): 35–58. Lieberman, Joe, and Hadassah Lieberman. *An Amazing Adventure: Joe and Hadassah's Personal Notes on the 2000 Campaign.* New York: Simon and Schuster, 2003. Lieberman, Joseph I., with Michael D'Orso. *In Praise of Public Life.* New York: Simon and Schuster, 2000.

LIEBMAN, JOSHUA LOTH (1907–1948)

Although during the 1940s Joshua Liebman was a radio personality with a large audience, he is best known for his million-plus bestseller, *Peace of Mind* (1946). His was one of the earliest books which emphasized self-help and self-acceptance as a guide for self-fulfillment. A Freudian, he believed that religion and depth psychiatry could bring greater happiness to people.

In 1945, veterans who had lived through the most devastating war of the century were returning home anxious about their ability to reintegrate themselves in a peacetime setting. Liebman urged his readers to accept themselves, recognize that everyone has imperfections and limitations, and accept what life brings to gain inner peace. *Peace of Mind* was the first bestseller by a religious Jew. It also marked the first time a serious publication introduced both Judaism and Jewish theology to a mass non-Jewish audience. On the radio, Liebman was a charismatic speaker and by 1940 gained a huge audience of two million listeners that was thought to be about 70 percent Gentile.

Joshua Liebman was the son of Simon and Sabina Liebman (née Loth). After their divorce they sent him from Hamilton, Ohio to his paternal grandparents in Cincinnati. His grandfather was a Reform rabbi. He encouraged Joshua's interest in religion. Joshua entered the University of Cincinnati at age 15 and won highest honors. He went on to earn a PhD in Hebrew letters at the Hebrew Union College, and he subsequently married his cousin Fran Loth. The couple adopted a daughter, Leila, a Holocaust survivor. (She became a child psychiatrist.)

After several pulpits, he accepted a position at Temple Israel in Boston in 1939. This assignment brought with it the radio program that beamed him to an ecumenical audience. He remained there until his unexpected death in 1948 of a massive heart attack.

Liebman was an outspoken Zionist at a time when Reform Judaism was anti-Zionist. He also advocated racial equality and full citizenship for blacks. His view of God was similar to the founder of the Reconstructionist movement, Rabbi Mordechai Kaplan, who rejected the revelation at Sinai in favor of God as a power in nature that made for salvation. Likewise, he rejected Christian views of sin based on the "fall" as described in Genesis. *See also* **Popular Psychology**.

Philip Rosen

Further Reading: Heinze, Andrew R. *Jews and the American Soul.* Princeton University Press, 2004.

LINDEN, HAL (1931–)

The genial star of Broadway musicals best known for playing the good-natured precinct captain on the long-running television comedy *Barney Miller,* Linden was born Harold Lipschitz, the son of Charles and Francis Rosen Lipschitz, in the Bronx, New York on March 20, 1931. He was educated at the High School for the Performing Arts, Queens College, and City College of New York. As a teen, Linden studied classical clarinet and played regularly with symphony orchestras. During his time in the army, he sang and provided entertainment for the troops, thus sparking an interest in becoming an actor. Upon his discharge, he trained in voice and drama at the American Theatre Wing.

While on his way to one of his first acting jobs, Lipschitz saw the looming water tower in Linden, New Jersey; from that day on, he was Hal Linden. After a stint in summer stock, Linden made his Broadway debut as understudy for Sidney Chaplin in the musical *Bells Are Ringing.* During the run of the show, Linden met dancer Francis Martin; they married in 1958. The Lindens have four children: Amelia, Jennifer, Nora, and Ian.

Hal Linden built an impressive résumé of roles throughout the 1960s in such musicals as *Anything Goes, The Apple Tree,* and *The Pajama Game.* In 1971, he won the Tony Award for his role in *The Rothschilds.* This success led directly to a career in television. In 1975, Linden began a long stint on the television comedy *Barney Miller.* The show, staged on a single set, had Linden starring as the eponymous New York City police captain, leading a precinct of loveable zanies. *Barney Miller* garnered dozens of Emmy nominations. It concluded its successful run in 1982.

Linden continues to guest star on television shows, tour with orchestras, and take an occasional film role. For several years, he served as chair of the March of Dimes, and he is currently a spokesperson for the Jewish National Fund.

As of 2007, Linden was touring with costar Barbara Eden (*I Dream of Jeannie*) in the romantic two-person play *Love Letters. See also* **Television**.

Kurt F. Stone

Further Reading: Brumburgh, Gary. "Hal Linden Biography." Internet Movie Database, 2008.

LITERATURE

The first Jews who came to American in 1654 were descendants of those who had been expelled from Spain and Portugal in the 1490s. At the time of the American Revolution, these Sephardic Jews, who numbered less than 2,500, had made extraordinary contributions to their new homeland. Beginning with the 1830s, thousands of German Jews arrived in the United States. There were now about 50,000 in America, mostly on the East Coast. Since they came from a country where the Enlightenment had spread its doctrine of rationalism, these Jews embraced and extended Reform Judaism. With the news of the assassination of Czar Alexander II in 1881 and the subsequent massacres of Jews in Russia, **Emma Lazarus** extended her heart to the "huddled masses yearning to breathe free." Between 1881 and 1914, more than two million Jews from

Russia-Poland arrived in America. It was the "promised land" to Mary Antin, fresh from Polotzk. It was also the land of opportunity, where Abraham Cahan's David Levinsky was told, "It isn't Russia. . . . Judaism has not much of a chance here . . . A man must make a living here" (1917). Coming from Russia-Poland, most from shtetlach (little Jewish towns), the Jews of the New Immigration and their descendants have dominated American Jewish life numerically, economically, and culturally almost since they arrived. But they have lived with a paradox: at the same time that they wanted more than anything else to be American, they wanted to remain Jews. The attempts to define what it meant to be a Jew in the old country, what it meant to be a Jew here, and how a Jew was acculturated (and perhaps assimilated in an ever-changing culture) while still holding to an ethnic identity, are grist for its writers, who have described the unique experience of being Jewish. The new immigrants, numbering perhaps 500,000 by 1900 and close to 3 million in 1914, came to the New World with little or no money and few skills. Arriving too late to duplicate or even carry on the experience of the German Jews, they were received with hostility by most Christians and viewed with contempt by the German Jews. Speaking **Yiddish**, looked down on by the German Jews, they were called coarse peasants and were seen as a threat to the comfortable assimilation and economic stability of their predecessors. The threat proved to be real; as we know from historians Moses Rischin and Ronald Sanders and from **Abraham Cahan**'s classic, *The Rise of David Levinsky,* the Russian Jews succeeded the German Jews as entrepreneurs, owners, and workers in the clothing industry in New York City. As Russian Jews became more visible, anti-Semitism surfaced and grew. Fortunately, the plans to cut off immigration did not become effective until after World War I. By that time, three and a half million Jews had landed. Ironically, though it is often forgotten, Catholic immigrants from Russia, Poland, Italy, and Greece were far more numerous and visible. Most Jews who arrived here between 1881 and 1914 were nominally Orthodox. Those willing to venture to the New World were those least committed to the practice of their religion. From the Enlightenment, Jews learned how to enter European civilization: literature from outside the Jewish community (like Dostoevsky, Tolstoy, and Marx), science, and the impact of urbanism combined to dissolve the medieval isolation of the ghettos. As a synthesis developed, it became clear that the ideas of the Enlightenment had been diluted even as they penetrated the ghetto, while the orthodoxy of extreme piety and ritual crumbled even as the essence of the Jewish heritage held on. That there would be two Zions in their lifetime, one in the United States and the other in Israel, was not foreseen. That Yiddish culture, Eastern European culture, would endure, though the Yiddish language would diminish, was also not seen. Driven by pogroms at home and lured by the American Dream, they chanced the journey to what was literally a New World. By the 1920s, America's Jews, now American Jews, with one foot in the old country and one in the new, were struggling with problems no longer tied to the ghetto. As Jews, their adherence to traditional values and ethics was honored. As American Jews, shown in Samuel Ornitz's anonymously published novel *Haunch, Paunch and Jowl* (1923), the compulsion to succeed and to wield power, no matter how corruptly, surfaced for the first time. Though it was an isolated case, surrounded by pathos and humor, it went beyond David Levinsky's acceptable entrepreneurship in its earthiness—so much in the Yiddish tradition—and grotesqueness. Myron Brinig's Singermann family saw some of the same forces and emotions. In a country in which an allegedly "lost generation" flourished, emulation was common. As the drama of the generations was played out, Jews as Jews and as American Jews rebelled against their parents, struggled for their own identities, succeeded and failed, cried and laughed, as did others. Jews were in the forefront in creative areas. The success of Ira and **George Gershwin**, **Irving Berlin**, **Eddie Cantor**, and **Al Jolson** in the world of entertainment matched the success of **Albert Einstein,**

Marc Chagall, and Ben Shahn and many others in science and in the creative arts. In the 1930s, in the grip of the Great Depression, Jews moved into prominence in movies, in the theater, and in literature. Luther and Stella Adler, **John Garfield**, and the playwright **Clifford Odets** made their marks in legitimate theater; Paul Muni, **Edward G. Robinson**, Irving Thalberg, and many actors and producers in Hollywood enriched the screen. In literature, whether through proletarian novels or novels with social impact, writers fought the system that bound and fought their families as well. Nathanael West, Tillie Lerner, Albert Halper, Daniel Fuchs, Anzia Yezierska, Michael Gold, Henry Roth, **Meyer Levin**, and Edward Dahlberg were some of those in whose works social and economic and generational and religious problems appeared. Writing about intellectuals and workers, hoboes and farmers, they concentrated on the attempts of people to identify with the poor and the oppressed. Some glorified the new energy of the Soviet Union or the Communist Party at home, as alternatives to what appeared a sick society. Most reflected the external pressures of a depression-ridden society in which Jews struggled to be Americanized and survive. Many also joined in the decade's widely supported protests, spearheaded by President Roosevelt's New Deal for some, and the Communists' program for others. Exchanging religious attachments for secularism, they sought new answers, perhaps new messiahs, in the social order. Caught up in the conflict of generations, young Jewish writers sometimes moved beyond acculturation. Although their motives were good their arguments, that ranged from a belief in assimilation to a belief in class over religion, meant very little. To a people recently arrived from Eastern European persecution, sensitive to overt anti-Semitism in American, excuses or rationales were hard to accept. It was almost unique that **Henry Roth**'s *Call It Sleep* (1934) shifted focus in so many ways. Unlike any other novel of the era, this superb psychological work, written as seen through the eyes of a child, summed up the truths and the traumas of the immigrants' experience. Confronted by a father who was maddened by ghosts of the past and present poverty and despair, little David Schearl's existence balanced precariously between the traditional values of his mother and the cheder (religious school) and those of the outside world. Even before 1930, American Jewish novelists used the themes of sex and love. They are persistent needs in the work of Anzia Yezierska and in Cahan's *David Levinsky,* a kind of Jewish Horatio Alger, as they continually tried to find love. That Levinsky ended with loneliness, a millionaire, only highlighted the paradox: his success was a measure of his estrangement from the community of old.

Until the 1960s, American Jewish writers did not easily use these themes. In any case, the image of the Jew was more meaningful than it had been. An inarticulate sense of inherited identity, later to be articulated, reflected a growing interest. Secular and cultural Judaism, generational problems, intermarriage, all vied with traditional forms. Apparently there were millions of Americans who wondered about the God of their fathers, the American Dream, man's manipulation of man, and the necessary persistence of the natural and compulsory Jewish communities of earlier days. American Jewish writers have had to fashion their product out of the life they knew, and they worked usually in an uncaring or hostile framework. For too long, as in the case of black literature, stereotypes persisted, drawn mainly by the host culture but aided and abetted by the minority. Even as "Sambo" and Amos and Andy perpetuated the Negro stereotype, so Potash and Perlmutter, Cohen on the telephone, **Mickey Katz**, and chocolate matzahs continued the travesty of Jews by Jews. Overcoming these images was one aspect of the writers' problem. Learning the language and the symbols was another. Most important, the writers had to deal with a Jewish image brought into existence by Gentiles and Jews and then create what had never existed before—an American Jewish literature and later a Jewish American literature. America's major writers, from the early nineteenth century on, have been preoccupied with man's condition and his attempts to find meaning in it. They were conscious of the disparity between what Americans said they believed in and what they did. Sensitive to this gap, to the fraudulent, self-righteous, commercial aspects of American culture that overshadowed the ethical-human, they used their insights to hold mirrors up to us all. In the twentieth century this socio-literary examination and analysis continued in the works of Dreiser, James, Hemingway, Dos Passos, Faulkner, Fitzgerald, and Wolfe, to name a few. In this tradition the American Jewish writers came of age. They are American Jewish writers because they were born Jewish, and, regardless of the intensity of their religious or cultural commitment, they have written about some essential aspect of the Jewish experience in America. Unlike the Lost Generation writers—Gentiles who seldom wrote about urban or ethnic conditions—the Jewish writers had to wait until they had become American Jews and the Jewish community was defined enough to support their work. In the cultural vacuum that existed in the early 1940s, American Jewish writers, now Jewish American writers, responded as no other group to the country's urgent cultural need. The biblical past, the rise of Hitler, the **Holocaust**, the new State of Israel, and the need of Americans to again believe in humanity helped. As **Saul Bellow** put it, affirming his belief in the humanity of the patriarch Abraham, he knew his debt—it had to do with the presence and continuation of life, it had to do with creating a significant pattern, it had to do, as he put it in *Mr. Sammler's Planet,* with honoring the contract that we all knew. For the American Jewish writers, from the cities, towns, and shtetlach of Russia-Poland, arriving at a time of national reform and psychic crisis, of primary importance were the problems of adjustment to the new culture and reconciliation of their old country culture with that of the New World. Scrambling for a dollar, everyone working, they endured so that their children might become Americans. "Who has ever seen such optimism?" asked **Harry Golden**. For the American Jewish writer, under the pressures of the Americanizing process, new problems were added. With disdain for his parents' ways, dress, and accent, he often opted for the New at the expense of the Old. Traditions, values, religion—all were subordinated to the need to emulate the Americans or the Jews who were no longer greenhorns.

The joys and the tragedies of the generational experience were not unique, of course, but the works of those writers from Cahan on, in the first generation, and from Ornitz through Henry Roth in the next, show that the context, the insights, and the style of the generational experience are novel, a breakthrough. For the first time, Jews who bridged the two cultures in a host country wrote of the ongoing bridging experience. Their literary talents explored the sociological dimensions of a minority. And as the up-from-the-ghetto literature gave way to fiction as a living form, as Jewish self-consciousness benefited from the national and international processes, so the Jewish American writer wrote of himself, his people, anti-Semitism, the War, middlebrow America, and the attempt to understand himself and the society he inhabited.

The fact of their quest for identity, the effort to create a literature in a non-WASP context, the excellent and near-excellent quality of the work seem to me significant because they created a new genre in literature and demonstrated that the American Jew was beginning to feel at home. Because of their writings, fertile, talented minds, conversant with the subject, created the images of the American Jew; the gross, distorted portraits of the past, as a result, have been dissolved in the subtler and more artful, and thus truer, images of the Jewish American moderns.

Many of America's Jews have succeeded materially. Their children, fortunate to have middle-class parents, are Americans, who are Jewish. Their dress, their likes and dislikes, their speech, their music, their foods, are urban- and exurban-oriented, with few memories of Europe's death camps and little active acquaintance with anti-Judaism at home. A generation brought up on the "Jewish" experiences of **Allen Ginsberg**, Abbie Hoffman, **Bob Dylan**, and Don Rickles is not likely to look to Dachau or the cheder for its reference points. Yet, uncertain as they are of their precise Jewish identity, for many there is no struggle with being identified as Jewish. Influenced by the **rock and roll** and the Youth Cult, they are also possessed by the desire to understand the human condition, themselves, and the country they live in. Rejecting that part of America where the bland lead the bland, they seek roots and truth.

In the same way, the contemporary American Jewish writers were influenced by the same forces, as well as those of the Depression, the Spanish Civil War, Hitler and World War II, Franklin D. Roosevelt, and the Korean War and McCarthyism. In their common quest, compelled by an indefinable feel of one's heritage, it is the writers who have asked the questions about other Jews, because that is whom they know and love, and hate, and because they care deeply and want to find out what it means to be a Jew, or an American Jew, or a Jewish American, or an American who is a Jew. Jews in the United States have responded in many ways to the pressure of the New World. Some from the beginning and into the present desired to be and were quickly or eventually assimilated. Some attempted to find a middle way by which they could become Americans and still retain their sense of being Jews. Some were so alienated or estranged as to drop out and pass into the great other, the Gentile world. Still others were doubly alienated, no longer at home, either in the Jewish or non-Jewish context. And some didn't care one way or the other. Meyer Levin, accepting biculturalism, wrote, "Godless though I profess myself, I have responded with more than warmth to the mystical elements of Chasidism. As a writer, I have considered that I accept the material as folklore. But in my soul I know that I take more than this from these legends" (Levin, 1950). Albert Halper spoke of Yiddish as a "bastardized language," while Edward Dahlberg, a Jew who was in a Catholic, and then a Jewish, orphan asylum, sought a faith he could not find. And **Ben Hecht** vacillated from self-hating and nearly anti-Semitic prose to some essays and stories in the 1940s calling on Jews to defend Jewish rights. For Saul Bellow, who had no struggle in identifying himself as Jewish, there was unconcern for the definition of what that means. The Jewish people's experience was a universal metaphor. Inasmuch as the modern writer specializes in what are called grotesque facts and cannot compete with the news itself, as Bellow and Roth and others pointed out, he must go beyond reality. He must turn away from current events, but without losing focus. For what seems lacking, concluded Bellow, was a firm sense of a common world, a coherent community, a genuine purpose in life. Man had to strive for a life of significant pattern. With the same goals in mind, **Bernard Malamud** quested for moral salvation and self-realization. As one of the Hasidic rabbis said, I would rather be devout than clever, but rather than both devout and clever, I should like to be good. Achieving the essential Jew, therefore, by his own actions, is what was sought. But that goal, shared by **Philip Roth**, is at least distantly related to what Bellow refers to as the consummation of a heart's need. That there are similarities in the work of some Jewish American writers can be demonstrated. The differences are more striking; Roth, for instance, has written most often about extreme behavior in ordinary situations. In short, we lean from Philip Roth that the fantastic situation must be accepted as reality as we accept the reality of the fantastic and the horrible. The world of fiction, Roth argues, frees us of circumscriptions that society places on feeling and allows both writer and reader to respond to experiences in ways not always available in day-to-day conduct. Through writing and reading a people passes on its collective experience. From Yiddish literature the old country can be remembered; even some of that whole wonderful body of literature, in English translation, can bring back the hard, dirty, primitive life of the old world, of the shtetlach. It will also bring back the warmth and earthiness of life in a Jewish family in a Jewish community in a world that no longer exists. So it is with the sensitively written recollections of Harry Golden and **Alfred Kazin** and the creative memories of the American Jewish writers from Abraham Cahan into the present. Thus, Bellow, as he recreates the joys and sadnesses of growing up in Montreal and Chicago, or describes an Augie March or a Herzog, also demonstrates an ambivalent faith in man's ability to realize himself in an ambiguous world. The resonance of two-ness is always present. For Malamud, redemptive suffering is what comes through from a New York City past; for Roth, who grew up outside of Elizabeth, New Jersey, insanity or estrangement are not what he sees as the good life, yet an examination of what appears insane in a framework of normality is compelling. For others, the flight from impotence into machismo in Bruce Jay Friedman and the significance of the existential in Edward Lewis Wallant are important. And no wonder, if one recalls the shtetl (in spite of the romanticized ***Fiddler on the Roof***) or the Holocaust, as in Wallant's *The Pawnbroker* (1961), then pain is an everyday experience that coexists with love and comfort. What Jew can ever forget the death camps in Germany and Poland? How many can forget how their grandparents hid in the forests from the Cossacks or townspeople, or fled Russia to avoid the draft, persecution, humiliation, and often forced conversion? But, the question must be asked, what has all this to do with today? During the latter part of the twentieth century, and now in the twenty-first century, a new wave of Jewish American writers has emerged. Delving with fiction into their Jewish roots, into the traditional ways, into feminism in various manifestations, into the state of Israel and its past and future, into the Holocaust by way of the second and even third generation, using narrative, fantasy, modernism and post-modernism, its writers are carving out a broadening of interests beyond questions of identity, assimilation, and acculturation. **Cynthia Ozick** and **Chaim Potok**, two very great writers who have bridged the space and time from those in the first generation, from Cahan and Henry Roth and Yezierska to Bellow, Malamud, and Philip Roth, have led the way. Starting with her first published novel *Trust* (1966), Cynthia Ozick tried to avoid writing a "woman's novel," by avoiding what female authors wrote about and by making her narrator neutral. Not an adherent of the new feminism, adhering to her own "classical feminism" and resisting the locution "Jewish writer," she has carved out a niche as a rationalist and a sceptic, hostile to mystery and magic, in her imaginative constructions. "The Pagan Rabbi" and her subsequent works attest to her reach, her stature. Yet at the same time she has tried to keep faith with her own culture, as she wrote in 1983 in *Art and Ardor,* by composing "midrashim," that is, by trying to transform English into the language of a culture that is centrally Jewish in its concerns and thereby liturgical in nature.

Chaim Potok, on the other hand, is trying to present core-to-core cultural confrontations—that is, a subculture, Judaism, versus the surrounding American secular majoritarian culture; or Orthodox Judaism versus Hasidic Judaism. He has imaginatively done what no one else has succeeded in doing. In *The Chosen* and in *My Name is Asher Lev,* for example, he pointed out, himself an Orthodox Jew, the problems that a traditional, believing Jew faces dealing with the ultra-religious or the outside world. Among the newer and younger writers, Allegra Goodman, Rebecca Goldstein, Thane Rosenbaum, Jonathan Rosen, Melvin Bukiet, Dara Horn, Myla Goldberg, Aryeh Lev Stollman, Nomi Eve, **Jonathan Safran Foer**, and **Michael Chabon** stand out. Goodman, in *Kaaterskill Falls,* her first novel, showed the "small desolations" and "the mystery of private being" in the Kaaterskill Orthodox, the simple village life in a religious community, even the little everyday disturbances that distract most of her peers. In Rebecca Goldstein's *Mazel,* three generations of women insiders, who have left Judaism, try to make the requirements of the faith consistent with their feminism, as they try to maintain their relationships with their daughters and granddaughters. As Goldstein explains in "Against Logic," here we all are, "having sufficiently assimilated the culture" and the "inner worlds of characters to whom Jewishness is nothingness; here we all are, against logic, dreaming Jewish dreams" (2005).

For Thane Rosenbaum, son of survivors, there is a genetic component involved in the transmission of the parents' experience as well as a barely concealed rage, so powerfully and imaginatively shown in *Elijah Visible, Second Hand Smoke* and *The Golems of Gotham*. For Bukiet, also the son of survivors, his *Stories of an Imaginary Childhood* challenges the old pieties as he traces the imaginative reconstruction of "before" with foreshadowing of the Shoah itself. *Everything is Illuminated,* by Jonathan Safran Foer, on the other hand, as Janet Burstein has written, recalls "home" in the image of the East European shtetl, yet when memory comes, its effect is deadly, not life-giving. Michael Chabon's *The Amazing Adventures of Kavalier and Clay,* which won the Pulitzer Prize, portrayed a few Jewish cousins, through a golem-like **comic book**, as they fight Nazi Germans. *The Yiddish Policemen's Union* (2007) explores how 3.2 million Israeli Jews in Sitka, Alaska, showing the absurdity of shtetl life in Alaska, displace the indigenous Tlingit Indians. As Courtney Hodell, Chabon's editor, put it: " [It's] a meditation on home and identity and sense of place and dislocation 'illustrating' in some ways that connection to a particular plot of land is illusory" (see Jewel, 2007).

Certainly Irving Howe and Leslie Fiedler never anticipated the emergence of the new Jewish American writer. They saw the Jewish American novel as immigrant fiction dependent on the immigrant's memory. Now we are seeing a new, post-immigrant Jewish American sensibility. As Andrew Furman put it, in the *Chronicle of Higher Education,* July 6, 2001, we are seeing "a renaissance in Jewish American culture that is not a resurgence of traditional Judaism, per se, but a transformation of it, as contemporary Jews in America, now thoroughly integrated into mainstream society, explore through their works ways of establishing a meaningful Jewish ethos in a secular country, apparently devoid of redemptive possibilities."

What can be seen is a growing body of Jewish American novels that are seeking new ground, new space. No one writer has yet achieved the stature of Saul Bellow, but rather than lament the passing of the twentieth-century giants, we can rejoice in the richness and inventiveness and the reach of these, the literary grandchildren of Bellow and Malamud.

To young Americans who are Jews, the memories and suffering of the past are subordinated to the middle-class comforts and security of post-World War II America, as they should be. Like Descartes, they ask: "I am certain that I am, but what am I?" The case of Franz Kafka, an acculturated Jew, might be a help. Conscious of being an outsider, he somehow felt his way into Jewishness. *The Metamorphosis* was "no dream," he wrote. What was at stake, according to young Jewish Americans, was that many struggles were going on, the outcomes of which were dreadfully important to them. They had to find a way to bring peace to the contending forces; to find some harmonic middle way between the material-hedonistic and the ethical-moral was necessary. No longer capable of determining their destinies, while being taught individualism as a supreme virtue, they alternately pursued the chimera of achievement and escape from the frustration of despair. It was clear to them that the love of suffering, of what they saw as the dead past, was a waste of time. It was not clear that playing the doomsday theme, or playing at crises, alienation, apocalypse, and desperation, with tools like mind expanders and religious cults, were also suffering. They didn't see that individualism cut two ways: a triumph on the one hand for justice and self-realization, it was also a bearer of possible trouble with its dreams of unlimited leisure and liberty, nothing remains the same. Jews have always disappeared, but the Jew has lived on. Just as the Jews of antiquity differed from those of the Middle Ages, the Jews of Eastern Europe differed from the American Jews and from the Jewish Americans. But as the Jewish American writers have made plain, they were all Jews, and they are still ethically and morally committed, still concerned with right behavior, and, as the Bible commands, in spite of the secular and assimilative tendencies of American life, they still choose life.

For a long time many people have accepted the premise that a work of art is important in itself: that it is a social action in itself. So it is with the Jewish American writer. Asking, "What do people think?" and exposing the sensitive issues others avoid, he is not held back by criticism. He is concerned with the honesty and depth of his work. It is the human predicament and the human condition that engage him. In defense of values, he rejects pessimism, and quests for values. The possibility of meaningful individual life is what he seeks, in whatever way he can. For if it is man, a little lower than the angels, in whom we are interested, then it is man's questionable or diminished state in the real world that is at stake. *See also* **Bellow, Saul**; **Chabon, Michael**; **Kazin, Alfred**; **Levin, Meyer**; **Potok, Chaim**; **Roth, Philip**.

Daniel Walden

Further Reading: Burstein, Janet. *Telling the Little Secrets: American Jewish Writing Since the 1980s*. University of Wisconsin, 2006. Jewel, Carolyn. "What's It Like to Be a Fiction Writer? Read On." *Writers Diary* by Carolyn's Blog. April 27, 2007. Levin, Meyer. *In Search*. New York: Horizon, 1950. Rubin, Lois, ed. *Connections and Collisions: Identities in Contemporary Jewish American Women's Writing*. University of Delaware, 2005. Walden, Daniel, ed. *On Being Jewish: American Jewish Literature From Abraham Cahan to Saul Bellow*. Fawcett, 1974.

LORRE, PETER (1904–1964)

Peter Lorre became an international sensation in 1931 with his portrayal of a serial killer who preys on little girls in the German film *M*. Later he became a popular featured player in Hollywood crime films and mysteries, notably alongside Humphrey Bogart and Sydney Greenstreet, and as the star of the successful Mr. Moto detective series. The son of Alois and Elvira Löwenstein, he was born Láslów Löwenstein in Rószahegy/Rosenberg, Austria-Hungary in 1904. By 1912, the family had moved to Moedling, Austria, where Löwenstein received his education. After high school, Löwenstein landed a job as a bank teller in Vienna. Working by day at the bank, he spent his nights studying acting at the Theater of Spontaneity. Before completing his apprenticeship, the theater's director, Jacob Moreno, renamed the actor "Peter Lorre," due to his resemblance to Struwwelpeter, a character in classic German children's literature.

Lorre's stage work brought him to the attention of Bertolt Brecht, who cast him in his play *Pioniere in Ingolstadt* (*Engineers in Ingolstadt*). Lorre quickly became "the hottest thing on the Berlin stage." In 1931, director Fritz Lang starred Lorre as a psychopathic child murderer in the film *M*. This role cemented Lorre's filmic image. The Nazis used his image from *M* on publicity posters for the film *The Eternal Jew* (1933), as an example of the "typical Jew."

In 1934, Lorre fled to Paris, days before the burning of the German Reichstag. Later that year, he made his first English-language film, Alfred Hitchcock's *The Man Who Knew Too Much*. Lorre arrived in America in 1934, where, over the next half-dozen years, he played everything from Raskolnikov in *Crime and Punishment* to "Mr. Moto." In 1941 and 1942, Lorre played two of his signature roles: Joel Cairo in *The Maltese Falcon* and Ugarte in *Casablanca*. In 1951, Lorre returned to Berlin to direct and star in *Der Verlorne* (*The Lost One*), a noir film about a doctor who murders his fiancée during World War II. Although praised, the film failed at the box office.

Returning to Hollywood, Lorre continued portraying mad doctors, scientists, and con artists. Lorre was married three times and had one child, Catherine, born in 1953. He died in Los Angeles on March 23, 1964. Since his death the Lorre voice and demeanor has provided the inspiration for dozens of characters, including Ren in the cartoon series *Ren and Stimpy*. See also **Film**; **Film Stars**.

Kurt F. Stone

Further Reading: Youngkin, Stephen D. *The Lost One, A Life of Peter Lorre*. University of Kentucky Press, 2005.

LUBAVITCHER MOVEMENT

See **Boteach, Shmuley**

LUMET, SIDNEY (1924–)

Actor, director, producer, and writer Sidney Lumet began his career in show business as an actor at the age of 4, made it to Broadway by age 11, and appeared in film at age 15. After World War II, Lumet transitioned from acting to directing, first working in theater, then in live television, and finally in feature films. Over the next 5 decades Lumet directed 45 feature films, most set in New York City. During his career, Lumet earned recognition as a socially progressive filmmaker, a gifted director of actors, and an effective stylist. Despite critical acclaim for many of his films—*12 Angry Men, The Pawnbroker, The Appointment, Serpico, Murder on the Orient Express, Dog Day Afternoon, Network, Prince of the City, The Verdict*—Lumet never received the recognition accorded major Hollywood-based filmmakers.

Committed to art that has purpose, Lumet makes films that often explore the human condition. As of 2008, 44 of Lumet's 45 feature-length films are fictional narratives, including many adaptations of theater works. While he has directed films in a variety of genres, Lumet's most successful films portray inner struggles of everyday men who confront larger systems or institutions. Even his lone documentary, *King: A Filmed Record . . . Montgomery to Memphis*, follows this pattern by chronicling Dr. Martin Luther King's civil rights initiatives. As a Depression-era baby, Lumet attributes his lifelong focus on social issues to his "Lower East Side poor Jewish upbringing" (Margolick, 1989).

Born in Philadelphia in 1924 to actor Baruch Lumet and dancer Eugenia Wermus Lumet, Lumet started his career in show business as a child actor in New York's Yiddish Art Theatre at the age of four. Growing up Jewish in the city, Lumet asserts that his daily efforts to avoid beatings developed significant professional skills; he believes "that immigrant experience not only gives you a tremendous sense of time, place and limits, it also gives you a tremendous energy, because you have to pay attention, all the time." In 1935, Lumet performed in his first show on Broadway, *Dead End*, and in 1939 he acted in his first film, *One Third of a Nation*. After serving in the army in World War II, Lumet returned to New York, founded an off-Broadway school for actors, and began to direct theater. In 1950, CBS recruited him to direct live television.

Along with other talented television directors, Lumet transitioned from television to film in the late 1950s. In 1957 his debut film, a thoughtful jury-room drama entitled *12 Angry Men*, garnered wide critical acclaim. Noted for its strong performances, its intelligent dialogue, its moral undertones, and its effective filming techniques, *12 Angry Men* set the stage for similar achievements in Lumet's later films.

As his career developed, Lumet continued to direct for the stage and television as well as for the screen. In the 1960s Lumet's love of theater resulted in a number of adaptations of works by master playwrights such as Williams (*The Fugitive Kind*, 1960), Miller (*A View from the Bridge*, 1962), O'Neill (*Long Day's Journey Into Night*, 1962), and Chekhov (*The Sea Gull*, 1968). Lumet's career peaked in the 1970s, when he directed some of American cinema's most innovative films, including *Serpico* (1973), *Dog Day Afternoon* (1975), and *Network* (1976). These three films reflect several of Lumet's central concerns, including social justice, moral challenge, and the human conscience. Lumet's impressive run in the early 1970s was followed by some notable flops, often with lighter, entertainment-oriented pictures like *The Wiz* (1978).

In assessing his own career, Lumet notes that his focus has always been on "the process," on "how everybody gets functioning on their best" (Rapf, 2006). Renowned for his abilities to work with actors to achieve exceptional performances,

Lumet has directed some of the industry's best, including Marlon Brando (*The Fugitive Kind*), Richard Burton (*Equus*), Henry Fonda (*12 Angry Men* and four other films), Katharine Hepburn (*Long Day's Journey into Night*), **Dustin Hoffman** (*Family Business*), Al Pacino (*Serpico, Dog Day Afternoon*), and **Paul Newman** (*The Verdict*). As of February 2007, 18 of his actors had been nominated for Academy Awards for their work in his films.

To complement these great performances, Lumet keeps his cinematic style simple and unobtrusive. Whatever his subject, Lumet's style serves the narrative; it remains unseen but felt. Good examples of this purposeful style include *The Pawnbroker*'s (1965) use of subliminal editing to represent the emerging memories of a Holocaust survivor and *Dog Day Afternoon*'s energetic, documentary-style camerawork to capture the developing intensity of a bank robbery/media event. Even though Lumet changes his stylistic approach to complement his narratives, critics associate him with the "New York School" of film directors; these unrelated New York directors created films that featured a grittier, more realistic cinematography reflecting the varied realities of the City.

In addition to Lumet's contributions to popular culture as an actor's director and stylist, Lumet created memorable characters who put into circulation some of cinema's most quoted lines. Viewers sympathized with Sonny, *Dog Day Afternoon*'s ill-fated, bisexual, Vietnam veteran as he taunted authority with screams of "Attica! Attica!" They echoed *Network*'s aging newsman Howard Beale's rousing cry of "I'm mad as hell, and I'm not going to take this anymore!" To this day, Lumet's rebels and their catch phrases remain significant presences in American cultural consciousness.

Now in his eighties, Lumet continues to direct major films. After three marriages that ended in divorce (to Rita Gam, Gloria Vanderbilt, and Gail Lumet Buckley), he is currently married to Mary Gimbel. His two children with Gail Lumet Buckley, Amy and Jenny Lumet, both work in the movie industry. In 1995 Lumet authored *Making Movies* to pass on his knowledge of the craft. In 1993 the Director's Guild honored Lumet with its prestigious D.W. Griffith Award. The American Academy of Arts and Sciences recognized Lumet's achievements in direction by nominating him for Best Director for four of his films, *12 Angry Men* (1957), *Dog Day Afternoon* (1975), *Network* (1976), and *The Verdict* (1982). Although Lumet did not win for these films, in 2005 the Academy recognized his important contributions to American cinema with an honorary Academy Award for his "brilliant services to screenwriters, performers and the art of the motion picture." *See also* **Film**.

Roberta Jill Craven

Further Reading: Cunningham, Frank R. *Sidney Lumet: Film and Literary Vision*. University Press of Kentucky, 1991. Lumet, Sidney. *Making Movies*. New York: Alfred A. Knopf, 1995. Margolick, David. "Again, Sidney Lumet Ponders Justice." *New York Times,* December 31, 1989. Rapf, Joanna, ed. *Sidney Lumet: Interviews*. University Press of Mississippi, 2006.

M

MAILER, NORMAN (1923–2007)

From the start of his career, Norman Mailer was a literary celebrity with outsized ambition, determined to make an impact on America. Many said he had chutzpah; others called it courage. Mailer had an extremely long and prolific career, including novels, plays, poetry, journalism, essays, and biographies. An innovator in New Journalism or the "non-fiction novel," he wrote some of the finest political reportage of his time.

A renaissance man, Mailer also wrote and directed movies—including one Hollywood feature called *Tough Guys Don't Dance* (1987, based on his 1984 novel), acted, helped found *The Village Voice,* and twice ran for mayor of New York City. In the opening manifesto of *Advertisements for Myself* (1959) he announced, "The sour truth is that I am imprisoned with a perception which will settle for nothing less than making a revolution in the consciousness of our time." If he did not make a revolution, he boldly and sometimes recklessly stormed the battlements of the culture.

Mailer's heroes tend to be either WASPs or only part Jewish, perhaps because he thought of himself more as an American than a Jewish American writer. His persistent themes were sex, violence, and power in American life, but behind his radicalism is a moral, proselytizing (one might even say rabbinical) streak. His work can be considered one long quest for a hero fit for our times: a man able to resist the drift of history and help to shape the future.

Mailer came from a middle-class Jewish family and grew up in the Eastern Parkway section of Brooklyn—which he called "the most secure Jewish environment in America," graduated from Harvard in 1943, and served in the Philippines in World War II. He gained fame at the tender age of 25 with the big bestseller *The Naked and the Dead* (1948), one of the classic American war novels. In the 1950s, he flirted with Hollywood but became a fixture in the New York bohemian scene and fashioned himself into the official bad boy of contemporary letters, staking out as his subject the extremes of experience, including murder, rape, orgy, and psychosis.

For years, Mailer was more notorious for his public misbehavior—drunken brawls, arrests, marrying six times, stabbing one wife, than for his work. In the 1970s, he became controversial for his denunciations of homosexuality and feminism. But as he aged, he mellowed, serving as president of PEN (Poets, Essayists and Novelists) and becoming a respected elder statesman of American letters. He won the National Book Award for Arts and Letters in 1969, the Pulitzer

Prize in 1969 and 1980, and in 2005 was awarded the National Book Medal for Distinguished Contribution to American Letters.

Highlights of his career include *Advertisements for Myself* (1959), a selection of his short fiction and essays, the most candid confession of the pressures of the literary marketplace on the serious American writer since F. Scott Fitzgerald's *The Crack Up* (1936). *An American Dream* (1965) is a novel about a man who gets away with murdering his wife that critics denounced as self-indulgent and morally repugnant, or praised as a powerful dream vision of American life. *Why Are We in Vietnam?* (1967), a savage comedy with a teenage hero, indicts American civilization for the violence of the Vietnam War. *The Armies of the Night* (1968), one of the most influential works of the New Journalism of the 1960s, recounts the events surrounding his arrest and imprisonment stemming from his participation in an anti-Vietnam War march on the Pentagon in 1967. *The Executioner's Song* (1979), a "true life novel," deals with the last year in the life of Gary Gilmore, the Utah murderer. The work won the Pulitzer Prize. Mailer returned to epic form with *Harlot's Ghost* (1992), a 1,300-page-long chronicle of the CIA from the Berlin Airlift to the assassination of John F. Kennedy.

Toward the end of his career, he continued to deal with big questions—good and evil, God versus the devil—in novels such as *The Gospel According to the Son* (1997), in which Jesus narrates his life, and *The Castle in the Forest* (2007), in which the devil narrates the life of Hitler. Mailer's work, for all its unevenness, showed a wide scope and flexibility, an epic ambition, and a willingness to experiment and to tackle controversial, major themes which place him in the top rank of American writers. *See also* **Literature**.

Andrew M. Gordon

Further Reading: Gordon, Andrew M. *An American Dreamer: A Psychoanalytic Study of the Fiction of Norman Mailer.* Cranbury, NJ: Associated University Presses/Fairleigh Dickinson University Press, 1980. Manso, Peter. *Mailer: His Life and Times.* New York: Simon and Schuster, 1985.

MALAMUD, BERNARD (1914–1986)

The renowned and prolific writer of fiction Bernard Malamud was born in Brooklyn, New York to Max Malamud and Bertha Fidelman, Jewish immigrants from Russia who struggled to survive on the meager income from their tiny grocery store. Malamud's early desire to write full time was frustrated by the Great Depression. He graduated from Erasmus Hall High School, attended City College (BA, 1936), and Columbia University (MA, 1942) but afterward earned barely enough at odd jobs to pay for food and rent. In 1940 he was employed as a clerk in the U.S. Census Bureau. As Herman Melville and Walt Whitman before him, Malamud tried to finish his required government work in the morning, so that he could free up afternoons for writing. In 1945, he married Ann de Chiara, an Italian American Roman Catholic and had two children, Paul (1947) and Janna (1952). Malamud taught high school in Brooklyn and Harlem before being employed on the staff of Oregon State College from 1949–1961. There he wrote his first novel *The Natural* (1952) and then taught at Bennington College (1961–1986) and Harvard University (1966–1968).

Malamud produced seven memorable novels, as well as allegorical short stories. A master of the short story, Malamud frequently set his stories in the grim context of urban Jewish immigrant life and drew from Jewish folklore and Yiddish literature. Indeed, in stories like "Angel Levine," "The Jewbird," "Talking Horse," and in novels and in collections of short stories such as *The Magic Barrel* (1958), *Idiots First* (1963), and *Rembrandt's Hat* (1974), the humor—involving luftmenschen, schnorrers, ubiquitous lost souls, and the irony of **Yiddish** immigrant speech—hovers just above Malamud's "high art" and the gravity of his serious moralism.

His first novel, *The Natural,* an unorthodox fantasy about baseball and its mythological place in American life, resonates with the legend of the Holy Grail. This novel, which has no significant Jewish character, offered little reason to suspect that Malamud would be categorized among the important "Jewish writers" of the postwar period (**Saul Bellow**, **Philip Roth**, **Cynthia Ozick**, and the like).

During his years in Oregon Malamud wrote more than a dozen stories filled with "Yiddishkayt," reflective of the old-world work of Sholem Aleichem, Moyshe Kulbak, and Irena Klepfisz. He finished *The Assistant* (1957), a dark novel set in Brooklyn which drew heavily on his own childhood ("autobiographical essence" Malamud later said, as distinct from "autobiographical history"). *The Assistant* is widely judged as Malamud's magnum opus. The novel wrestles with the perennial question of what it means to be a Jew. Critics have argued that the novel infers a Jew is defined as someone who suffers, and that through suffering moral wisdom is gained. But the "answer" Malamud gives in *The Assistant* is cryptic or, at best, ambiguous. It is not clear in this novel, or in the bulk of Malamud's oeuvre, whether a person (Jewish or not) is doomed to suffer (and therefore to be a Jew!); nor is it clear that suffering, rather than love, empathy, and wholehearted responsibility to other people is what imparts the deepest human understanding.

Over the years, Malamud was asked directly about suffering: "Suffering? I'm not for it," Malamud said. "The less we have, the better. . . . I'm against it, but when it occurs why waste the experience?" (Davis, 2007). He told an audience of Holocaust survivors, when accepting the Jewish Heritage Award in 1977, that he did not live the Jewish experience of day-to-day humiliation or terror. In his imagination, however, he was affected by it deeply. Early in life Malamud had married a non-Jew and eschewed his Jewish identity. Near the end of World War II, when he learned about the Holocaust and that Jews were killed for being Jews, and that a vast number of Jewish refugees were "wandering from nowhere to nowhere," he reevaluated his Jewish identity.

Although Malamud knew a great deal about Jewish history and literature, he came to his knowledge of Jewish life, he said, "mostly through people." In his fiction, Malamud has several characters argue that "there are many ways to be a Jew." For Malamud the most meaningful way was to recognize the responsibility of peoplehood. The responsibility of Jew for Jew (and Malamud took the Jew as his starting point for what was most human in humankind) is dramatized in many of his stories, particularly "Idiots First," wherein the protagonist pleads climactically, "Don't you understand what it means—human!?" In "The Last Mohican" (*Pictures of Fidelman,* 1969) Bronx-born Arthur Fidelman, an art student in Italy, pestered maddeningly by Susskind, a classic schnorrer, comes to see through an epiphany that to be truly open to another person means to get "mixed up" with him and even hurt by him. This, Malamud seems to imply, can mean being a blunderer and a victim—a schlemiel—but unlike other Jewish writers, who make the schlemiel a pathetic figure to be pitied or ridiculed, Malamud's schlemiel is interchangeable with the idea of being a Jew, a *mentsh,* a humane figure—one who assumes a moral stance and recognizes the responsibility of peoplehood.

Nowhere is the responsibility of peoplehood more starkly or darkly demonstrated than in *The Fixer* (winner of the National Book Award and the Pulitzer Prize for Fiction in 1966). Yakov Bok, the fictional version of Mendel Beilis, the Russian Jew wrongly accused of murdering a Christian in the infamous czarist "blood-libel" case in 1913, tries to evade the responsibility of his Jewish identity (the life of a Russian Jew was a dangerous one!) by changing his name, dumping his tefillin (phylactery) into the Dnieper River and rejecting the God of his people.

But *The Fixer,* like Malamud's other novels, *A New Life* (1961), *The Tenants* (1971), *Dubin's Lives* (1979), and *God's Grace* (1982), are not susceptible to simplistic interpretation, and, as Malamud said, he was not "out to prove anything." Malamud's art was complex and elusive, but what is accessible and lives on in his work is his celebration of morality and love, and his recognition that life without compassion and without *mentshlikhkayt* is no life at all. *See also* **Literature**.

Gerald Sorin

Further Reading: Avery, Evelyn, ed. *The Magic Worlds of Bernard Malamud.* State University of New York, 2002. Bloom, Harold, ed. *Bernard Malamud: Modern Critical Views.* Chelsea House, 1986. Davis, Philip. *Bernard Malamud.* Oxford University Press, 2007. Smith, Janna. *My Father is a Book.* Houghton Mifflin, 2006.

MAMET, DAVID (1947–)

Author, essayist, playwright, screenwriter, and film director David Mamet is known for his works' clever, terse, sometimes vulgar dialogue and arcane stylized phrasing, as well as for his exploration of masculinity. Mamet was born on November 30, 1947 to assimilated Jewish parents in Flossmoor, Illinois. He was educated at Goddard College in Vermont, a progressive liberal arts school, as well as at the Neighborhood Playhouse School of Theater in New York. From 1977 to 1990 he was married to actress Lindsay Crouse. The couple had two children, Willa and Zosia. Divorced, he married Rebecca Pidgeon, also an actress, who converted to Judaism and bore two children, Clara and Noah.

Author, playwright, director, screenwriter, producer, Mamet was awarded the Pulitzer Prize in 1984 for his play *Glengarry Glen Ross,* as well as having received a Tony nomination, for *Speed-the-Plow* in 1988. In addition, Mamet has earned kudos and awards for his many screenplays, including *The Postman Always Rings Twice* (1980), an Academy Award nomination for his script for *The Verdict* (1982), and an Oscar nomination for *Wag the Dog* (1997). He made his film-directing debut in *House of Games* (1987), the film version of *Glengarry Glen Ross* (1992), *American Buffalo* (1996), and the political satire *Wag the Dog* (1997).

Mamet identifies strongly with Jews and Judaism. A number of his works deal with Jewish identity, assimilation, the claims of memory and tradition, the ache of displacement, the disablement of self-hatred, and the loneliness of lapsed Jews. His film *Homicide* (1991) dealt with the conflict of a Jewish detective who denies his Jewish heritage when confronted by Jewish zealots who seek his aid against neo-Nazis. *Lansky* (1999) dealt with the life of the Jewish gangster and included scenes from the American Jewish

David Mamet, author, playwright, screenwriter, and film director. Mamet, who received a Tony nomination for *Glengarry Glen Ross* (1984) and an Oscar nomination as screenwriter for *Wag the Dog* (1997), has authored *The Old Religion* (1997), about the lynching of Leo Frank; *The Wicked Son* (2006), a study of Jewish self-hatred and anti-Semitism; and *Five Cities of Refuge: Weekly Reflections on Genesis, Exodus, Leviticus, Numbers and Deuteronomy.* [Photofest, Inc.]

ghetto. His book *The Old Religion* (1997) explores the mind of Leo Frank, the Jewish Atlanta factory owner lynched by anti-Semites in 1913's Georgia. His book *The Wicked Son* (2006) lambasts Jews who attack Israel, exhibit self-hatred, and leave the Jewish community.

He continues to write and direct the television series *The Unit* and blogs political cartoons for the *Huffington Post* online newsletter. Mamet's most recent book, published in 2007, *Bambi vs. Godzilla: On the Nature, Purpose and Practice of the Movie Business,* is a critical assessment of the film industry. *See also* **Film.**

Philip Rosen

Further Reading: Heilpern, John. "How Good Is David Mamet, Anyway?" Salon.com, December 3, 1999.

MANILOW, BARRY (1943–)

Singer-songwriter, musician, arranger, producer, and conductor Barry Manilow is best known for such recordings as *I Write the Songs Mandy, Weekend in New England,* and *Copacabana.* Manilow's achievements include sales of more than 76 million records worldwide. In 1978, five of his albums were on the bestselling charts simultaneously—a feat equaled only by Frank Sinatra and Johnny Mathis. Barry Manilow was born Alan Pincus in Brooklyn, New York, to a Jewish mother, Edna Manilow, and an Irish father, Harold Kelliher, who were divorced when Barry was two. Manilow was raised in Brooklyn by his mother and grandparents, Esther and Joseph Manilow, immigrants from Russia. Manilow started his singing career while preparing for his Bar Mitzvah, and he shortly after changed his name to Manilow to carry on the surname of his grandfather. His first musical instrument was the accordion, which he hated. He refined his music on the piano.

Manilow attended the Juilliard School of Music upon graduation from high school. He paid his way through school by working at CBS as a mail clerk and later as the musical director of a show called *Callback.*

Manilow worked at a variety of jobs. He wrote and performed in advertisements for such companies as Dr. Pepper soft drinks, McDonald's, and Kentucky Fried Chicken. He found work as a composer and music accompanist for Bette Midler and others. By the 1970s he had written several successful songs, including "Mandy" (1974) and "I Write the Songs" (1975).

Early in 1984, he produced a jazz album with Sarah Vaughan, Mel Torme, and Gerry Mulligan. During the next few years, he produced international albums and sang duets in French, Italian, Portuguese, and Japanese. In the 1990s he produced albums with popular Broadway show tunes and also recorded an album in tribute to Frank Sinatra. He is probably most famous for his hit songs "Mandy," "I Write the Songs," "Looks Like We Made It," "Copacabana," and "Can't Smile Without You."

During the course of his career, Manilow has sold over 75 million records. Manilow also wrote the music for animated films such as *The Pebble and the Penguin* and *Thumbelina.*

Manilow has also composed for the stage. Together with Bruce Sussman, Manilow wrote the music for *Harmony,* a play based on the true story of the Comedian Harmonists, a musical group of German Jews and Gentiles who gained fame in Europe and returned to Germany at the moment of the Nazi seizure of power in 1933. The Jewish members of the group became victims of the Nazi purge of Jews from German life. Manilow composed 18 songs for the two-act play.

In an interview with the *Jewish Advocate* (December 2007), Manilow stated that "the tragic part of their story moves me more because I'm Jewish and because my relatives went through the Holocaust . . . There are moments in the script that we refer to traditional Jewish rituals, such as the wedding scene when the groom breaks the wine glass, that I was moved to tears." As of this writing, Manilow hopes to bring the play to Broadway.

In recent years Manilow has seen a resurgence in popularity. His album *The Greatest Songs of the Fifties* debuted at number one on the Billboard charts in 2006 and sold more than 3 million copies. In the same year, *The Greatest Songs of the Sixties* debuted at number two, and his album *The Greatest Songs of the Seventies* was in the top 10 in 2007.

Manilow has been active in television and earned an Emmy in 2006 for his PBS special *Manilow: Music and Passion*. He has appeared on such television shows as *The View* and *The Oprah Winfrey Show*. In December 2007 Rhino released *Barry Manilow: The First Five Television Specials,* a boxed DVD set of his televised shows between 1977 and 1988. *See also* **Popular Music**.

Herbert M. Druks

Further Reading: Butler, Patricia. *Barry Manilow: The Biography.* Music Sales, 2007. Manilow, Barry. *Sweet Life: On the Way to Paradise.* McGraw-Hill 1987.

MANISCHEWITZ FAMILY

The Manischewitz family was among the pioneer families in the production of kosher food in the United States, and their name was synonymous with kosher food products. The firm was first started by Rabbi Dov Ber Manischewitz in Cincinnati, Ohio in 1888. Manischewitz was born in Lithuania and was a disciple of Rabbi Israel Lipkin, better known as Rabbi Israel Salanter. After first serving as a shochet, or ritual slaughterer, Manischewitz dedicated his skills to the production of matzah for the American Jewish community. While most matzah was still baked by hand in Europe, there had been many attempts at baking matzah by machine in central Europe in the mid-nineteenth century. In the United States following the great emigration of 1881, most matzah was either baked by hand or by primitive machines. In Europe most rabbinic authorities opposed the innovation of machine-baked matzah. Using his Lithuanian Orthodox background, Manischewitz was able to obtain rabbinical approval from American rabbinic authorities (who were all from Lithuania) for his new innovative manner of baking matzah via mass production. In this sense, Manischewitz was to matzah what Henry Ford was to automobiles. His bakery in Cincinnati was extremely successful and matzah was not only supplied for the Passover holiday but became a year round staple for American Jewry. The matzah was known as Manischewitz Matzah and Cincinnati Matzah. The company also started exporting matzah to Europe and Palestine, and Manischewitz became the "gold standard" of matzah. It is well known that such a great rabbinic personality as Chief Rabbi Abraham Isaac Kuk of Palestine asked for Manischewitz Matzah by name during his sojourn in England in World War II. The company also began production of other kosher food products, such as wine and Jewish specialty items. Ber Manischewitz died in 1914 and was succeeded by his five sons. The best known of these was Rabbi Hirsch Manischewitz, who was not only an able merchant but was also a leading activist in American Orthodox Jewish life He started a yeshiva in Palestine in memory of his late father. Under his leadership the company moved a good portion of its operations to Jersey City, New Jersey, in 1932. By that time the company controlled over 75 percent of the matzah market in the United States. Yet it faced competition from other family-owned brands such as Goodman's, Streits, and Horowitz-Margareteen.

Ownership of the company eventually passed into the hands of a third generation of the Manischewitz family, but in 1990 it was sold to Kohlberg and Co., thus ending family ownership. Although no longer under family control, the Manischewitz Company still is the leading producer of matzah in the United States as well as other kosher specialty food items. *See also* **Food Industry**.

Zalman Alpert

Further Reading: Goldberg, Howard G. "Manischewitz Only Sweet? Not Anymore," *New York Times,* March 23, 1994.

MARCUS, DAVID "MICKEY" (1901–1948)

David "Mickey" Marcus was a United States Army colonel who assisted Israel during the

1948 Arab-Israeli War and who became Israel's first general. His life and death was the subject of a major motion picture, *Cast a Giant Shadow* (1966), starring **Kirk Douglas**. David Daniel Marcus, an assimilated Jew who served in the U.S. Army during World War II, volunteered to serve as a strategic military advisor to the Jewish army, the Haganah in 1947. The United States War Department granted him leave, and he arrived in Jewish Palestine (Yishuv) in January 1948, where he designed a command and control structure for the soon-to-be-declared State of Israel. Using his experiences as commander at the U.S. Ranger School, he identified the Yishuv's weakest points. When war came, as a result of the invasion by six Arab states following the declaration that created Israel in 1948, Marcus was granted the rank of major general. He commanded operations to lift the Arab siege of Jerusalem by designing a makeshift military road, which effected a breakthrough for the fledgling Jewish army.

Marcus was born in Brooklyn to Mordecai and Leah Marcus, immigrants from Romania. He attended Boys High School in Brooklyn, New York and graduated from West Point in 1924. Marcus attended Brooklyn Law School, where he received law degrees in 1927 and 1928. In 1927, he married Emma Hertzenberg, and during the 1930s, he was a United States Attorney in New York, gaining notoriety as the prosecutor of Lucky Luciano. His court skills led to Mayor Fiorello LaGuardia appointing him commissioner of corrections for Manhattan.

With the coming of war with Japan, he became executive officer to the military governor of Hawaii. In 1942, he was commandant of the U.S. Army's Ranger School. The Rangers are an elite force who develop unconventional and innovative warfare tactics. In 1944, against orders to remain in the States, he managed to serve with the 101st Airborne in the battle of Normandy.

At war's end, he helped to draw up surrender terms for Germany and then served in the occupation government. He found ways to feed the starving millions who were recently freed by the Allies and helped clean up the infamous Nazi concentration camps. Named chief of the War Crimes Division, he planned legal procedure for the Nuremberg trials. His experience with Nazi crimes and the suffering of Jewish survivors of the concentration camps convinced Marcus that Palestine was the place for Jewish refugees.

In 1947, David Ben-Gurion asked Marcus to recruit "an American officer" to serve as key strategic military advisor to the nascent Jewish army, the Haganah. Marcus decided to "volunteer" himself and in 1948, the United States War Department granted him leave to advise the fledgling Jewish army. Marcus disguised his name and rank to avoid problems with the British government, which was the mandatory authority in Palestine.

He identified Israel's weakest points in the Negev south and Jerusalem. Following Ben-Gurion's reading of the declaration that created Israel, the Arab armies invaded the Jewish state, and Marcus was appointed as commander of the Jerusalem front and given the rank of aluf, major general.

Just before the ceasefire on June 9, 1948 that created the armistice between Israel and the Arab states, Marcus was accidentally shot by a Jewish sentry. His body was taken to West Point, where he was buried. His tombstone reads: "A soldier for all humanity." His efforts in behalf of Israel were the subject of a major Hollywood film, *Cast a Giant Shadow* (1966), which featured Kirk Douglas as Marcus. *See also* **Film.**

Philip Rosen

Further Reading: Berkman, Ted. *Cast A Giant Shadow: The Story of Mickey Marcus Who Died to Save Jerusalem.* Manifest Publications, 1999.

THE MARX BROTHERS

During the first half of the twentieth century the Marx Brothers unleashed their unique brand of zany, anarchic comedy in vaudeville, theater, and film. While the family Marx boasted five biological brothers who participated over the years in acts labeled as variations of "The Marx Brothers," the three eldest brothers developed the central characters that constituted the heart of the comic team. Leo (later Leonard), whose stage name was Chico (1887–1961); Adolph (later Arthur), whose stage name was Harpo (1888–1964); and Julius, whose stage name was Groucho (1890–1977), perfected fast-faced comedy routines that often took aim at the establishment and poked fun at high society. As supporting characters in the brothers' comedy acts, the two younger Marxes typically played the straight men, and both left show business to pursue other careers. Milton, whose stage name was Gummo (1892–1977), left the brothers' vaudeville act during World War I to join the army. He was replaced by Herbert, whose stage name was Zeppo (1901–1979). Zeppo worked in both vaudeville and film and then retired from acting in 1934 after completing the Marx Brothers' last Paramount film, *Duck Soup*. After capturing Broadway by storm with their popular revues in the 1920s, the Marx Brothers starred in 13 films together, making them household names from 1929 on. Their memorable stage personalities and their invaluable contributions to comedic form elevated their name to a unique signifier within popular culture: the concept of "The Marx Brothers" grew beyond referring to their biological selves, beyond even naming the comic team in films, to designating an iconic construct symbolizing an unbridled zaniness, a refreshing anarchism that challenges both pretension and privilege (Groch 1990, 35).

The legendary status of the Marx Brothers was promoted largely by their film antics but also fueled by their rumored off-screen exploits as well as their larger-than-real-life personas. They got their start in New York City as the sons of two Jewish European immigrants, Simon Marx (nicknamed "Frenchie," from Alsace Lorraine) and Miene Schönberg/Schoenberg (from Germany). Both parents changed their names to assimilate: Simon became Sam and worked as a tailor, while Miene became Minna and then Minnie and followed her parents in the world of show business. In Germany, Minnie's parents had had a wagon show; her father had been a magician and her mother a harpist. In the States her brother, Abraham Elieser Schoenberg, had become the Shean half of Gallagher and Shean, a respected vaudeville comedy act. Given the show business in her blood, Minnie decided to bring some of her boys into the family business. As a result of their poverty, their dispositions, and the opportunities to make money around them, the older Marx boys had all left school early, and so Minnie began to chart their futures by moving the middle sons, Julius (later Groucho) and Milton (later Gummo), into vaudeville.

The boys began their early vaudeville period in 1907, with Groucho and Gummo performing as singers first with Mabel O'Donnell and then with Lou Levy in the Three Nightingales; the group changed to the Four Nightingales when mother Minnie added Harpo, who couldn't sing, to the act. They continued to perform on the vaudeville circuits until 1909, adding occasional comic bits to their act. At this point, the family moved to the vaudeville hub of Chicago, and Minnie began to use the name Minnie Palmer as she built her career as a producer on the circuits. After a brief stint in 1910 as the Six Mascots (when Minnie and Aunt Hannah joined the act), the three Marx brothers transitioned into comic routines, dropped their singing name, and traveled the country doing madcap antics as the Three Marx Brothers and Company. Their initial vaudeville show, *Fun in Hi Skool/Skule* (1911–1912), metamorphosed into *Mr. Greene's Reception* (1912–1914) with the addition of Chico in 1912 and finally into the long-running *Home Again* (1914–1919). During *Home Again* Gummo left to serve in the army during World War I; Minnie Marx filled his vacant straight-man role with his younger brother Zeppo.

It was in front of these live vaudeville audiences that Marx brothers Leo, Adolph, and Julius began to develop and mature the personas they would later play in the films. Even at this early stage, the characters who would crystallize as the Marx Brothers were forming: for example, in the production of *Home Again*, brother Arthur donned

The Marx Brothers, 1930s. Shown clockwise from upper left: Zeppo, Groucho, Harpo, and Chico. The team of Jewish brothers was perhaps the greatest troupe of comedy performers in the history of show business. [Photofest, Inc.]

an old raincoat and performed his role without speaking. It was also during these years that their stage names emerged, reputedly during a poker game with Art Fisher, who was joking about a comic strip character called Knocko the Monk and his name's impact on vaudeville names. The Marxes then were named for their characteristic hobbies (for his chasing "chicks," Leo became "Chicko," which became "Chico" due to a typing error), their unique talents (for his playing harp, Arthur became "Harpo"), their unusual temperaments (for his variable moods, Julius became "Groucho"), and their distinctive clothing selections (for his gumshoes, Milton became "Gummo"). Even though the names began as a gag, the brothers decided to keep them, and even family members called the brothers by their stage names later in life, after their stage and screen careers had long faded.

The stage personalities that emerged during these early vaudeville years would come to be some of the most famous in comedy history. Significantly, they started out as specifically ethnic characters. As the eldest son of a Jewish family growing up in an ethnically mixed Upper East Side of New York, Leo (Chico) had learned to mimic foreign accents to avoid potential hostilities in the city. In his vaudeville days, Leo would use this talent for creating personas to develop "Chico," a likeable, extroverted, not-so-bright Italian character who characteristically donned a pointed hat and old jacket. Adept at making up schemes and twisting the English language, the character of Chico also graced the stage with accomplished piano solos—he'd even "shoot" the keys with comic flair. The Marxes' second son, Adolph, called "Ahdie" and later Arthur, would develop the consummate comic mime character, Harpo. He began his career creating an Irish, Patsy-Brannigan-type character. With a curly red (and later, for the screen, blonde) wig, a bulb horn stuck in his pants, and a big raincoat that produced just about any object, Harpo easily magnified the mayhem even without a voice. And yet, amidst all the frenetic high jinks, this clownish character would stop a scene to play an ethereal harp solo (much to his brother Julius's real-life discontent). The middle child, Julius, known as Groucho, who had been more bookish than his older brothers, crafted a persona that embodied strong comic visual aspects topped off by a sharp verbal wit. In the early revues, his character started off as a Dutch schoolteacher with a German accent, but with the advent of World War I Groucho moved away from the German traits. Wearing a wide greasepaint moustache complemented by large greasepaint eyebrows, glasses, and a big cigar, Groucho was amusing even before he opened his mouth, especially as he crouch-loped across the stage. But once he began with his quick one-liners, amusing non-sequiturs, and outrageous insults, his verbal ingenuity often dominated the act. Since the fourth brother, Milton (Gummo) was active only during the vaudeville years, he never developed a well-known persona. The youngest Marx brother, Herbert (Zeppo), routinely played the straight romantic lead as a necessary part of the act. Overshadowed by his older siblings, Zeppo acted an assigned part with neither a comic persona nor substantial lines. Thus, the character triad of Chico, Harpo, and Groucho became the commercially significant core of the stage and screen entity known as "The Marx Brothers."

In making the transition from vaudeville to the real stage, the brothers experienced about four years of trials before they hit it big. In 1918 or 1919, the brothers, with newcomer Zeppo, made their first real musical, *The Cinderella Girl,* which flopped. They reverted to their revue show, which eventually was titled *N'Everything.* By 1921, they were doing another New York show entitled *On the Mezzanine,* which they took to England in 1922 as *On the Balcony.* This fast-paced show was so poorly received that they switched to performing *Home Again.* Late in 1922 they got involved in a production called the *Twentieth Century Review,* which went bankrupt. Also during this early vaudeville period, the brothers made reels of a silent film called variously *Humor Risk, Humorisk,* or *Humoresque,* which is lost. Despite their mixtures of successes and failures, brother Chico confidently pushed the brothers toward the big time of Broadway.

The turning point in the Marx Brothers' career was a musical comedy revue called *I'll Say She Is,* which ran for over a year before reaching Broadway in May of 1924. This Broadway revue would launch the brothers to fame when, on May 20, 1924, major New York critics like Alexander Woollcott (who would later become a close friend of Harpo's) lauded their comic accomplishments in the press. By their next revue show, *The Cocoanuts* (1925–1928), the Marxes were recognized stars, and this prestige garnered them such talent as producer Sam Harris, writer George S. Kaufman, and composer **Irving Berlin**. Harris and Kaufman would also work with the brothers on *Animal Crackers* (1928–1930), another revue which became a hit even in spite of the stock market crash.

In 1929 the Marx Brothers began their film careers, which would comprise 13 films over 2 decades. From 1929–1933, they made five films with Paramount: *The Cocoanuts* (1929),*Animal Crackers* (1930),*Monkey Business* (1931),*Horse Feathers* (1932), and *Duck Soup* (1933). The first two films were adaptations of their work in the theater that were filmed in New York. Their debut film, *Cocoanuts,* was one of Paramount's first sound features; as a recording of the 1920s revue format, it holds special significance in its own right. Notably, this first successful film established a pattern for future Marx Brothers' films: in *Cocoanuts* Chico, Harpo, and Groucho played their established vaudeville characters, Zeppo played the romantic lead, and actress Margaret Dumont presented the first of several performances as Groucho's wealthy, high-class female foil. *Animal Crackers,* their second film based on a Broadway stage hit, would feature Groucho posing as an African explorer who is the special guest of Mrs. Rittenhouse (played by Margaret Dumont), a wealthy socialite whose prized painting unexpectedly goes missing. It would feature what would become Groucho's trademark song, "Hooray for Captain Spaulding." Their third film, *Monkey Business,* marked the Marx Brothers' transition to the Hollywood studios. It also was the first film written specifically for them for the screen; notable writers as S. J. Perelman and Nat Perrin, among others, were hired to script the insanity of stowaways on a cruiseline. Their two final Paramount films—*Horse Feathers,* a satire on college, and *Duck Soup,* a satire on war—are considered some of their career's best. *Duck Soup*'s ingenious scene of Harpo playing Groucho's mirror image would be hailed as comic genius and later referenced in other works, including Harpo's recreation of the scene with Lucille Ball in a 1955 episode of *I Love Lucy.*

In 1935 Metro-Goldwyn-Mayer (MGM) producer Irving Thalberg convinced the Marx Brothers, now minus Zeppo, to work for MGM; he also persuaded them to add more credible story and romance to their films. For both *A Night at the Opera* (1935) and *A Day at the Races* (1937) the brothers used preproduction roadshows to improve the timing and lines of their skits so that their on-screen delivery would be optimal. *A Night at the Opera,* with its famous stateroom scene, would become one of the Marx Brothers' most acclaimed films. *A Day at the Races,* unfortunately, would be their last film with Thalberg, whose death during the film's preproduction in 1936 marked a turning point in the Brothers' careers.

The last six films of the Marx Brothers are generally considered lesser works with limited energy and ingenuity. *Room Service* (1938) was a play moved to film for RKO rather than a film written for the Marx Brothers, as all the films since *Monkey Business* had been. MGM then brought the Marx Brothers back for three films: *At the Circus* (1939), *Go West* (1940), and *The Big Store* (1941). After the Marx Brothers finished their work together with *A Night in Casablanca* (1946) and *Love Happy* (1950), they went their individual ways.

The personal lives behind the screen personas were as divergent as the personas themselves. Chico, indulging his real-life passions for women and an addiction to gambling, reportedly spent much of his life broke. He married his first wife, Betty Karp, in 1917; they raised one daughter, Maxine. Their marriage ended in divorce, and in 1958 Chico married Mary Dee (aka Mary DiVithas), who had been his steadfast companion for years. He died in 1961 of a heart attack. Harpo, a gentle and well-liked man offscreen, waited the longest to marry; he settled down with Paramount actress Susan Fleming in 1936, and together they adopted four children (Bill, Alexander Woollcott, James Arthur/Jim, and Minnie). After his screen career faded, he lived a happy life painting, playing the harp, and enjoying family life in his Palm Springs home until his death after vascular surgery in 1964. His story is recounted in his 1961 autobiography, *Harpo Speaks!*

In contrast to Harpo's happy married life, Groucho was married and divorced three times, to Ruth Johnson in 1920 (son Arthur, daughter Miriam), to Catherine (Kay) Marvis Gorcey in 1945 (daughter Melinda), and to Eden Hartford in 1954. He also authored a number of books, including his autobiography *Groucho and Me* (1959) and *Memoirs of a Mangy Lover* (1963). Groucho died in 1977 of pneumonia. After leaving the brothers' vaudeville act to serve in the army during World War I, Gummo worked in the garment industry as his brothers earned their fame; once they were famous, he became their manager. In 1929 he married a young widow named Helen von Tilzer, who had a daughter (Kay) from a previous marriage, and they had a son, Robert, together. Gummo died of natural causes a few months before Groucho in 1977.

Zeppo married actress Marion Benda (born Bimberg) in 1927, and they raised two sons, Timothy and Thomas. After leaving the act in 1934, Zeppo formed his own theatrical agency, Marx, Miller, and Marx, and retired from show business in 1949. He also patented a few inventions. After his divorce from Marion, he married and divorced Barbara Blakely, who already had a son (Robert) from a previous marriage. The last Marx brother standing, Zeppo, died of lung cancer in 1979.

Over the years, the Marx Brothers established a reputation for irreverent shenanigans both on and off the screen, and ultimately it is hard to decipher where reality leaves off and legend begins. Did the brothers really roast potatoes nude in Irving Thalberg's office because he was late? While it's hard to tell which of the many memorable anecdotes are true, the sheer number of anecdotes points to showmen who pushed boundaries and defied authority and convention off the screen as well as on it. Lieberfeld and Sanders attribute the Marxes' penchant for the continual disruption of the powerful status quo to their Jewish heritage: "Under the protective guise of humor, (the Marx Brothers) . . . enacted immigrants' collective resentment toward elites whose prejudices they found threatening. By parodying anti-immigrant stereotypes, the Marx Brothers drain them of their potency. . . . Their humor elevates low-brow immigrant culture in response to the snobbish refinement and elitism of those insiders and sophisticates who define their social position by exclusion" (1995, 108). However, Groucho appears to acknowledge a different strategy for their ethnic portrayals: "We Marx Brothers never denied our Jewishness. We simply didn't use it. We could have safely fallen back on the **Yiddish theatre,** making secure careers for ourselves. But our act was designed from the start to have a broad appeal" (Louvish, 2000). Whatever its source, the Marx Brothers' continual challenges to authority, decorum, and high society added a potent social dimension to their film productions.

Coming to the cinema at the very beginning of sound film, the Marx Brothers captured their anarchic **vaudeville** routines on film and then developed for film some of cinema's most beloved comedies and comic personalities. Working with some of the industry's most talented writers, including Bert Kalmar, Harry Ruby, George S. Kaufman, Morrie Ryskind, S. J. Perelman, Will B. Johnstone, Nat Perrin, Arthur Sheekman, Buster Keaton, and Herman Mankiewicz, the Marx Brothers developed a unique blend of visual comedy and verbal wit that masterfully played off of and developed the three individual comic personas of Chico, Harpo, and Groucho. Although the team's real-world antics created a reputation for them as "undirectable" and unpredictable, interviews reveal that the brothers did work solidly from a script, with Groucho occasionally ad libbing and Harpo authoring some of his visual material. Their films' combination of antiestablishment plots, freewheeling visual humor, and creative, fast-paced dialogue has yet to be equaled. While no one can match them, the Marx Brothers' inimitable style opened up the possibilities for future comedians on film.

Even though the brothers filmed their last film together in 1949, their influence continued well into the next century. Individually, Chico, Harpo, and Groucho went on to participate in their own projects, the most significant of which was Groucho's hosting of the game show *You Bet Your Life* (on radio from 1947–1950 and on television from 1950–1961), the success of which brought new fans to the older films. During and after their careers, the Marx Brothers influenced a number of artists in varied fields—people like Eugene Ionesco and Woody Allen—and counted many important artists as admirers, including Salvador Dali (who wrote an unproduced screenplay, *The Marx Brothers on Horseback Salad,* for them) and Antonin Artaud.

In April of 1974 the film industry recognized their profound influence by offering an honorary Academy Award to Groucho "in recognition of his brilliant creativity and for the unequalled achievements of the Marx Brothers in the art of motion picture comedy"; Groucho accepted the award, saying, "I only wish Harpo and Chico could have been here—and Margaret Dumont, who never understood any of our jokes." Some of the brothers' long-term pop cultural influences include their roles as "comedy/antiestablishment icons"; as significant developers of the "lunatic" comedy movement and antiheroic comedy; and as pioneers of "saturation" comedy, the fast-paced antics setting the stage for acts like Ernie Kovacs, Rowan and Martin's *Laugh-In,* and Monty Python (Gehring 1989, 27–31). From rock groups like Queen naming albums after Marx Brothers' films (*A Day at the Races, A Night at the Opera*), to director Woody Allen naming films after their lyrics (*Everyone Says I Love You*), to director Rob Zombie naming film characters after the Marxes' own characters, to little kids' donning fake glasses, noses, and moustaches that resemble Groucho, the Marx Brothers' influence, thankfully, continues. Perhaps their longevity is a result of the liberatory aspects of their acts. Something about their freedom to flout society's restrictive conventions and constraints remains enduringly attractive; their audacious antics and creative wordplay kindle the fires of imagination, hopefully for new generations of Marxists to come. *See also* **Film**.

Roberta Jill Craven

Further Reading: Adamson, Joe. *Groucho, Harpo, Chico and Sometimes Zeppo: A History of the Marx Brothers and a Satire on the Rest of the World.* New York: Simon and Schuster, 1973. Gehring, W. D. "The Marx of Time" *Thalia: Studies in Literary Humor* 11, no. 1 (1989): 25–33. Groch, John R. "What is a Marx Brother." *The Velvet Light Trap* 26 (1990): 28–41. University of Texas Press. Lieberfeld, D., and J. Sanders. "Here Under False Pretenses: The Marx Brothers Crash the Gates." *American Scholar* 64 no. 1 (1995): 103–108. Louvish, Simon. *Monkey Business: The Lives and Legends of the Marx Brothers.* New York: St. Martin's Press, 2000.

MASLOW, SOPHIE (1911–2006)

The dynamic, innovative choreographer, modern dancer, and teacher and founding member of the New Dance Group, Sophie Maslow was born in New York City on March 22, 1911. Creativity ran in her family; her first cousin, Leonard Baskin (1922–2000), was an accomplished sculptor and graphic artist. As a young girl, Sophie Maslow began studying dance with Martha Graham at the Neighborhood Playhouse School. From 1931–1943, she performed many solo roles with the Graham Company, including "Death and Entrances," based on the lives of the Brontë sisters.

In 1943, she joined Jane Dudley and William Bales in a dance trio that performed together for nearly a decade. When they disbanded in 1952, she formed her own troupe, the Sophie Maslow Dance Company. Maslow was also a founding member of the New Dance Group, a company dedicated to using dance to make social and political statements.

Among Maslow's best known works are 1941's "Dust Bowl Ballads," with music by Woody Guthrie; 1942's "Folksay," based on the Carl Sandberg poem of the same name; and 1963's "Poem," with music by Duke Ellington and based on a work by poet Lawrence Ferlinghetti.

"Dust Bowl Ballads" depicted the endurance of people in the rural Southwest during the Depression. The cheerful "Folksay" blended dancing with dialogue and songs sung by troubadour Pete Seeger. "Poem," set in a San Francisco beatnik hangout, was proclaimed an "instant hit." Maslow also choreographed *The Snow Queen* (1953), a retelling of Hans Christian Andersen's fairy tale; "Decathlon Etude" (1976), which turned sports movement into dance; and "Voices" (1980), a lyrical piece set to the Romantic music of Schumann.

Maslow also choreographed several Jewish pieces, including "The Village I Knew," based on the stories of Yiddish writer Sholem Aleichem, and "Israel through the Ages." She also choreographed many of the annual Hannukah festivals staged at Madison Square Garden.

Sophie Maslow was married for many years to the artist Max Blatt. They had one daughter, Abigail. Sophie Maslow died in Manhattan on June 25, 2006. She was 95 years old. *See also* **Dance**.

Kurt F. Stone

Further Reading: Chujoy, Anatole. *The Dance Encyclopedia.* New York: Simon and Schuster, 1967. McDonagh, Don. *The Complete Guide to Modern Dance.* New York: Doubleday and Company, 1976.

MASON, JACKIE (1934–)

Stand-up comedian and actor on stage, screen, radio, and television, Mason is best known for his controversial appearance on *The Ed Sullivan Show* in 1964. In recent years he has acted in a series of one-man shows on Broadway. Jackie Mason was born Yacov Moshe Maza in Sheboygan, Wisconsin, where his father, a rabbi, had a pulpit. To encourage his four sons to enter the rabbinate, the family moved to New York's Lower East Side. After graduating at age 25 with a BA from City College of New York, Mason followed in his father's footsteps and was ordained as a rabbi in Latrobe, Pennsylvania. Three years later he left the rabbinate to become a comedian. Mason followed the classic comedy route of the 1960s, which led him to New York City comedy clubs, to the **Catskills**, and on cross-country tours. He gained prominence as a comedian, appearing regularly on television until he made television history on *The Ed Sullivan Show.*

On October 18, 1964, Mason appeared on *The Ed Sullivan Show.* Shortly after Mason began his routine, President Johnson's live television broadcast interrupted the program. Sullivan gestured with his finger to Mason that he was to be interrupted. When the show returned, Mason mocked Sullivan by pointing his index finger to the audience, the producers, himself, and finally to Sullivan. Ed Sullivan interpreted Mason's use of his finger as a lewd gesture and responded by threatening the comedian with the words, "I will destroy you in show-business." Mason graduated to *The Ed Sullivan Show* black list, never to be invited back. Mason insists that he never raised the "obscene finger." After a hiatus from show-business, he returned to the stage in the mid-1980s. Not the least rancorous, Mason included the controversial finger-pointing episode as part of his comedy routine along with a hilarious imitation of the famed television host. Mason's take on Sullivan also adorns the cover of his book, *How to Talk Jewish* (1991).

In 1973, Mason traveled to Israel during the Yom Kippur War, along with artists such as Isaac Stern and Mike Brant, to entertain the troops and the wounded. Israelis were not accustomed to Mason's **Yiddish** dialect and classic punch lines. His quick wit, however, endeared him to the audience when Mason reacted to a seemingly indifferent soldier with the "threat," "I will punch you in the face!" Everyone laughed.

Mason's movie career includes *The Stoolie* (1972), *The Jerk* (1979), a role in **Mel Brooks**'s *History of the World: Part 1* (1981), *Caddyshack II* (1988), and *The Hitchhiker's Guide to the Galaxy* (2005). Mason has also appeared in a television series, the short-lived *Chicken Soup* (1989). But most prominently, Mason lent his voice to the character of Rabbi Hyman Krustofski, on the *Simpsons* episode "Like Father, Like Clown," for which he won an Emmy in 1992. In 2005, Mason started a daily talk show, *The Jackie Mason Show,* which appeared on the CN 8 television network. Mason currently hosts a nationally syndicated radio program which originated in 2006.

Mason's greatest successes have been achieved on Broadway and in other live stage performances. His one man show *The World According to Me,* which originated in Los Angeles, moved to Broadway for a two-and-a-half-year run. Mason's one-man performances also include such shows as: *Brand New* (1990), *Politically Incorrect* (1994), *Love Thy Neighbor* (1996), *Much Ado about Everything* (1999), *Prune Danish* (2002), and *Freshly Squeezed* (2005). Mason has performed before Queen of England and Nelson Mandela.

Together with attorney Raoul Felder, Mason has written a regular column on the Internet and in the *Washington Times*. In 2007, they teamed up to write a controversial book titled *Schmucks.* In recent years, his humor has become increasingly political. In 2006, Mason, an avowed Republican, posted two rants a week on *Youtube* and provoked controversy when he defended Mel Gibson by claiming that the actor's anti-Semitic diatribe against a Los Angeles cop was the act of a drunk rather than that of a bigot.

Jackie Mason recently opened a new show called *Jackie Mason: The Ultimate Jew* (2008), at the Off Broadway New World Stages.

In 1991, Mason married Jyll Rosenfeld. *See also* **Comedy**.

Steve Krief

Further Reading: Mason, Jackie. *How to Talk Jewish.* St. Martin's Press, 1991.

MATISYAHU, HASIDIC MC (1979–)

Matisyahu is a Hasidic MC and beatboxer who amazes Jewish and non-Jewish audiences alike with his unique fusion of hip hop, reggae, and jamband music. In the early 1970s, the term

"MC" became associated with what would change to become known as the "rapper" in hip hop/rap music and culture. Originally, the term was simply used as "master of ceremonies." As hip hop progressed, the title MC has been thought to mean a number of acronyms such as "microphone controller," "microphone commander," "mic checka," "music commentator," and one who "moves the crowd." The use of the term MC when referring to a rhymer originates from the dance halls of Jamaica. At each event, there would be an announcer or master of ceremonies who would introduce the different musical acts and would say a toast in the style of a rhyme, directed at the audience and to the performers. Since his debut, Matisyahu has received positive reviews from both rock and reggae outlets. Most recently, he was named "Top Reggae Artist of 2006" by Billboard.

Matisyahu is taking his mission of redemption to the masses as a khozer b'teshuva (or "born again Jew"). And while he may not be winning —or even necessarily seeking—converts to "the faith," he is winning converts who were first skeptical of the appeal of a Hasidic reggae singer.

Matisyahu was born in West Chester, Pennsylvania as Matthew Paul Miller on June 20 1979, which corresponds on the Jewish calendar to Tammuz 5, 5740. His family moved to Berkeley, California and eventually settled in White Plains, New York. He was brought up as a Reconstructionist Jew. As a child Miller was sent by his parents to Hebrew school several times a week—he was no different from many other children his age; he was not too happy about the extra hours of school. He was often threatened with expulsion from school for disrupting his class.

At the age of 14, Matthew Miller lived the lifestyle of a typical teenage rebel. He fell in with the "Dead Head" group, grew dreadlocks, and wore Birkenstocks all year round. He learned how to beat box in the back of his classroom and played bongos in the lunchroom

As an 11th grader he almost burned down his chemistry class. It was then he began to realize that something was missing in his life. He set off on a spiritual quest by going on a camping trip to Colorado, far from his typical suburban lifestyle in White Plains, New York. It was amidst the beauty and splendor of the Rocky Mountains where Miller's metamorphosis began to take shape. In this peaceful, serene, and majestic environment he started to realize there was some greater power and awesome spirit in the universe.

His spiritual journey continued when he took his first trip to Israel; it was there that his Jewish identity and his Jewish heart came to life and merged as one. He began to feel a personal relationship and spiritual connection with that same greater power and awesome spirit he had encountered in Colorado. He came to the realization that this higher being was God. He prayed and danced everywhere he went in Israel.

Upon returning to White Plains, Miller didn't quite know how to maintain his new connection with Judaism. He sometimes performed under the alias "MC Truth" for MC Mystic's Soulfari band. As a young man Miller was often depressed, which led him to drop out of high school He subsequently decided to follow the rock band Phish on a national tour.

On the road, Miller thought seriously about his life, his music, and his strong feelings for Judaism. He returned home burnt out and broke. His parents insisted that he "straighten" himself out at a wilderness program, and he completed high school in Bend, Oregon. The high school encouraged artistic pursuits, and Miller took advantage of this time to delve further into his music. He studied reggae and hip hop. He attended a weekly open-mic timewhere he rapped, sang, beat boxed, and did almost anything he could to stay creatively charged. It was there that he started to develop the unique reggae-hip hop sound for which he would one day become known. After two years in the "sticks," the 19-year-old Matthew returned to New York a changed man. He moved to the city to attend the New School, where he continued honing his musical craft and also dabbled in theater. During this time, he happened on the Carlebach Shul, a synagogue on the Upper

West Side, well known for its hippie-friendly vibe and exuberant singing. This encounter further fueled his soul-fire, turning him on to the mystical power of song in Hasidic Judaism. Now, instead of beat boxing in the back of the classroom, he was leaving the classroom to pray on the school's roof.

Around 2001 he seriously turned to Orthodox Judaism, becoming a baal teshuva (a Jew who decides to return to Judaism and strictly observe the laws of the Torah) and performing with the Jewish band Pey Dalid.

While studying at the New School, Matthew wrote a play entitled *Echad* (*One*). The play was about a boy who meets a Hasidic rabbi in Washington Square Park and through him becomes religious. Shortly after the play's performance, Matthew's life strangely imitated his art; years after the initial sparks were lit, Matthew met a Lubavitch rabbi in the park, spurring his transformation from Matthew to Matisyahu.

No one remembered what Hebrew name Matthew Miller received at his Brit Milah (ritual circumcision ceremony at eight days of age). In Hebrew school it was assumed to be "Matisyahu" because of the connection between "Matthew" and "Matisyahu." Many years later, he came across the original certificate from his brit, and he discovered that his real Hebrew name was actually "Feivish Hershel," not "Matisyahu." (His friends call him "Mates.") He was advised by his rabbis to continue using the Hebrew name he had grown up with, "Matisyahu," which means "gift of God." From 2001 through July 2007, Matisyahu has been a member of the Chabad-Lubavitch Hasidic community in Crown Heights, Brooklyn, New York. However, on July 17 2007, Matisyahu told the*Miami New Times* in an interview that he no longer "necessarily" identifies with the Lubavitch movement. In the interview, he stated that "the more I'm learning about other types of Jews, I don't want to exclude myself. I felt boxed in." In the autumn of 2007, while on a family vacation spent primarily in Jerusalem, he expressed interest in another Hasidic sect, that of Karolin.

Matisyahu studied Torah in Hadar Hatorah, a yeshiva for returnees to Orthodox Judaism; he wrote and recorded his first album while still a student there. He counts Bob Marley, Phish, God Street, Wine, and Rabbi **Shlomo Carlebach** among his musical inspirations, while giving credit to Rabbi Simon Jacobson's book *Toward a Meaningful Life* for the lyrical inspiration to the title song of his album, *Youth*.

In an interview with Chabad.org, a popular Jewish web site, Matisyahu states: "All of my songs are influenced and inspired by the teachings that inspire me. I want my music to have meaning, to be able to touch people and make them think. Chasidism teaches that music is 'the quill of the soul.' Music taps into a very deep place and speaks to us in a way that regular words can't" (Chabad.org, 2006).

Matisyahu's towering presence and traditional Hasidic garb (black suit, white shirt, black hat, and long beard) present a striking image. Whether blending eighteenth-century Hasidic melodies (known as "niggunim") with Uptown beat box technique, or singing ancient Hebrew psalms in a Caribbean lilt over dancehall rhythms, Matisyahu manages to take the cultural outgrowth of three disparate ghettos—Poland, the Bronx, and Trenchtown—and merge them into one musical form, while retaining the distinct ambience and energy of each.

His albums include *Shake Off the Dust . . . Arise,* released November 1, 2004 under the JDub Records Label; *Live at Stubb's,* released April 19, 2005 under the JDub/Or/Epic Records Label, US RIAA Certification—Gold; *Youth,* released March 7, 2006 under the JDub/Or/Epic Records Label, US RIAA Certification—Gold; and *No Place to Be* (CD/DVD), released December 26, 2006 under the Sony Music Records Label. Matisyahu's second album, *Live At Stubb's* (Or Music), took the third spot atop the Billboard reggae charts.

He has performed with such musical greats as Dave Matthews, the Allman Brothers, Modest Mouse, De La Soul, and former members of the Grateful Dead. He also headlined Carifest, New

York City's biggest Caribbean Island music festival, where he joined a pantheon of dancehall dons, including Buju Banton, Bounty Killer, Luciano, and Capleton.

In spring of 2006, right before the release of *Youth,* Matisyahu cut ties with his managers at JDub Records, which resulted in some controversy due to Matisyahu's role in the founding of the label. Contrary to popular belief, JDub managed Matisyahu's act, but was not his record label. In July 2007, Matisyahu began writing new songs for his third studio album, which is due for release sometime in late 2008 or early 2009. Despite the obvious bravado necessary to any MC, Matisyahu remains incredibly humble and grounded. This is because he attributes his success solely to God.

"No doubt the Hasidic thing has helped, in two senses," offers Matisyahu. "In one sense it's the gimmick thing—it helps with publicity. But the truth behind the Hasidic thing, I believe, is that I gave myself to God. I told God, if you want, I won't do music. I'll do whatever you want me to do. And then the music thing happened. I don't think I'd be successful without God" (Chabad.org, 2006).

The "final redemption," Matisyahu believes, is incumbent on more than the arrival of any one person. "Moshiach" will be both a person and a consciousness. It's not just that a person's going to come and "it's gonna happen." It's gonna happen when people already start changing their reality. It's going to happen as a result of the people. Matisyahu is working to bring that message to the people. The people are still "feelin' "him, whether they're heeding the call or not.

In recent years, Matisyahu has appeared on television and radio. A list of the better-known shows that he has been a guest on would include *The Tonight Show* (2005), MTV (2005), *Late Night with Conan O'Brien* (2005), *Jimmy Kimmel Live* (2006), and *CBS Sunday Morning* (2006). In 2006 Matisyahu was awarded *Esquires*' "Esky Music Award" as the "Most Lovable Oddball." The magazine went on to name him "the most intriguing reggae artist in the world."

Matisyahu married a former NYU student named Thalia in August 2004; the couple has two sons. *See also* **Rap and Hip Hop Music**.

Israel J. Barzak

Further Reading: Blum, Brian. "Who?" *Shabbat Shalom,* June 15, 2006. Chabad.org. Interview with Matisyahu, April 15, 2006. "Matisyahu Tonight at the Sound Advice Amphitheatre." *Miami New Times* Blog, July 17, 2007. Relic, Peter. New CDs: "Matisyahu, Juvenile." *Rolling Stone,* March 6, 2006. Sisaro, Ben. "Hasidic Reggae Singer Surprises His Managers." *New York Times,* March 14, 2006.

MATTHAU, WALTER

See **Film Stars**

MERRILL, ROBERT (1917–2004)

Robert Merrill was a famous operatic baritone who wrote two memoirs and acted in a film, but relatively late in his singing career, he became known for singing "The Star-Spangled Banner" at Yankee Stadium. He first sang the national anthem to open the 1969 baseball season, and it became a tradition for the Yankees to bring him back each year on opening day and special occasions. Robert Merrill was born Morris (Moishe) Miller in the Williamsburg section of Brooklyn to an Orthodox Jewish family. His father, Abe Miller (originally Milstein), was a sewing machine operator, and his mother Lillian, née Balaban, had been an amateur singer. Both had immigrated from Warsaw. Early on, Merrill had two great passions—his love of baseball and his desire to become a crooner like his then-idol, Bing Crosby. Merrill was cursed with a horrible stutter that was a constant source of ridicule and embarrassment. His mother, who back in Poland had been denied a potential singing career by social constraints, vigorously guided Merrill towards a career in music A turning point in his life came when he was delivering dresses on a clothes rack near the Metropolitan Opera. Claiming that they were costumes, he sneaked into the Met and heard the great Lawrence Tibbett performing the role of

Germont in *La Traviata*. The boy was awestruck. Little did he know that he was staring into his own destiny. He would one day succeed Tibbett at the Met and debut in that very role. Merrill's road seemed clear—he wanted to sing opera. Money was tight for the Merrill family, and so the young singer partially paid for lessons by working as a semi-pro pitcher. The acquired athletic prowess served him well in the rigorous world of classical opera. He also sang whenever possible on radio, at Bar Mitzvahs, and he even did extensive entertainment work in the **Catskill** resorts, playing the so-called Borscht circuit with such talents as Phil Silvers, and he even schilled in burlesque for the likes of Pinky Lee. A second turning point came with his audition for the great singing teacher Samuel Margolis, a Jewish immigrant from Latvia, who saw in the shy young man the potential for an operatic voice. Under Margolis's tutelage, Merrill made his opera debut in *Aida* in New Jersey (1944) and his debut at the Met as Germont in *La Traviata* in 1945. During the same year, Merrill cut a 78 rpm record set with Jeanette MacDonald, in which they sang duets from such musicals as *Up in Central Park.*

Merrill's performance was followed by offers to sing as one of the resident artists at the Met. After several seasons, Merrill jeopardized this opportunity by asking for a leave of absence to do a Hollywood musical film. The request was denied by then-head of the Met Rudolph Bing, but Merrill took the time off anyway, and he was fired from the company. The resulting film, *Aaron Slick from Punkin' Crick* (1952), was beneath the talents of Merrill. Despite some wonderful but poorly staged singing, the film was a flop. It took several years of wooing and a personal and public apology, but Bing eventually relented, and the Metropolitan Opera became Merrill's home and primary artistic focus. Though he went on to sing all over the world and performed several times in Las Vegas with the likes of **Danny Kaye** and Louis Armstrong, Merrill always worked around his commitments to the Met. He would remain at the world-famous opera house for 31 years and sing nearly every major baritone role in over 500 performances. His hard-won technique and golden timbre remained with him throughout his life Merrill was also noted for his work with Arturo Toscanini who, at the urging of the great baritone Giuseppe de Luca, had heard a broadcast of Merrill singing *Verdi.* Toscanini knew that he wanted him for an upcoming performance of the newly formed NBC Orchestra. Over the course of his career, Merrill was a consummate and ever-improving performer who combined high art with the common touch. For 30 years he suited up in a New York Yankees shirt and tie and proudly sang "The Star-Spangled Banner" at each Yankees season opener. His autobiography reveals a deeply modest man of engaging humor who was a loyal friend and colleague. Merrill was married twice: the first time was to fellow Met star Roberta Peters. The marriage ended after a tumultuous 10 weeks, and the two remained friends and colleagues throughout their careers. The second time was to pianist Marian Marchno, who had been introduced to him by an old-world style matchmaker. The marriage was a successful and happy one, and she often accompanied Merrill in recitals. The couple bore two children. Merrill died in his New Rochelle home on October 23, 2004. Robert Merrill's voice is preserved in numerous recordings, some of which have been in print for about 50 years. Videos of his work with *The Bell Telephone Hour* and *Voice of Firestone* are a welcome release.

Richard Gould

Further Reading: Merrill, Robert. *Between Acts.* McGraw Hill, 1976. ———. *Once More from the Beginning*. Macmillan, 1965.

MILLER, ARTHUR (1915–2005)

Arthur Miller was one of the major dramatists of the twentieth century. Before his death he often was called the "greatest living American playwright." He earned this reputation during his 70-year-plus career, in which he wrote his first plays as an undergraduate at the University of Michigan in the 1930s. He achieved critical success in the 1940s with *All My Sons* and *Death of a Salesman.* In the 1950s he wrote *The Crucible* and *A View From the Bridge,* refused to "name names" at his appearance before the House Un-American Activities Committee, and married actress Marilyn Monroe. In the 1960s and 1970s, he served as president of the literary organization International P.E.N. (Poets, Essayists, Novelists) and delegate to two Democratic Conventions. In 1987 he produced a critically acclaimed autobiography, *Timebends,* and premiered new plays on Broadway and in London in the 1990s. In the new millennium, Miller remained as active as at the beginning of his career, publishing a collection of essays, *Echoes Down the Corridor,* and completing two new plays, *Resurrection Blues* and *Finishing the Picture.* Recipient of the New York Drama Critics Circle Award for *All My Sons, Death of a Salesman,* and *A View From the Bridge;* the Pulitzer Prize for *Death of a Salesman;* a Tony Award for *All My Sons, Death of a Salesman,* and *The Crucible;* and a Lifetime Achievement Award and the Olivier Award for *Broken Glass,* Miller ranks with other great figures of American drama like Eugene O'Neill, Tennessee Williams, and Edward Albee —and the pantheon of great world dramatists such as Anton Chekov, August Strindberg, George Bernard Shaw, and Samuel Beckett.

Arthur Miller was a literary giant and one of the more significant political, cultural, and social figures of his time. He was well known as a man of conviction with rock-solid integrity, who frequently took unpopular stands on many issues. At his death, the front page headline of the *New York Times* called him the "moral voice of the American stage."

A native New Yorker, Miller was born in Manhattan, the second son of Isadore and Augusta Barnett Miller. His older brother, Kermit, was a businessman, and a younger sister is the actress Joan Copeland. The Millers (his father was a Jewish immigrant from Poland, and his mother was born on the lower East side of Manhattan to Polish Jewish émigrés) were wealthy from their coat and suit factory, a family business his father had built up. The Millers lived in upper middle-class splendor on West 110th Street in a large apartment overlooking Central Park. Hard times, however, came early for the Millers. Isadore Miller's business collapsed before the stock market crash of 1929. He relocated his family to Brooklyn in 1928, when Miller was 13. The move was a step down, and the family settled into a little six-room house where Miller shared a bedroom with his maternal grandfather.

The move to Brooklyn and the onset of the Depression were the most defining events of Miller's youth. Miller was so influenced by his upbringing during the Depression that the borough became the prime setting for many of his plays and fiction. He attended James Madison and Abraham Lincoln high schools in Brooklyn, where he was an average student and played on the second squad of the Lincoln football team. In 1932, Miller graduated during the depths of the Depression. His poor grades and his family's finances kept him out of college. For two years he worked in a succession of odd jobs. During this time, Miller first encountered anti-Semitism, and it became a major theme in his work.

In 1934 Miller entered the University of Michigan at Ann Arbor. He immersed himself in university life, which then had the reputation of being a hotbed of 1930s leftist political radicalism. Miller's years at Michigan are most notable as the start of his playwriting career. He entered and twice won the college's annual $250 Avery Hopwood Writing Award. After graduation, Miller joined the Federal Theater Project. An old football injury made him ineligible for the draft, so to assist the war effort and earn some money, he wrote half-hour radio plays and worked in the Brooklyn Navy Yard while continuing to work on his plays. In 1940, he married Mary Slattery, a fellow student and a Catholic. They settled in Brooklyn Heights and had two children, Jane and Robert. In early 1943, Miller left the navy yard to write a screenplay of *Here is Your War,* a collection of columns by America's beloved war reporter, Ernie Pyle. Miller toured army camps gathering background material and used his research for a book of reportage called *Situation Normal* (1944), his first published book.

In 1944, Miller had his first play produced on Broadway, *The Man Who Had All the Luck,* which opened to almost universally negative reviews. It closed after four performances. In 1945, Miller published his only novel, *Focus,* one of the first important American works about anti-Semitism. The novel was successful, selling 90,000 copies. *Focus* tackles a theme that is a major part of Miller's dramatic canon: all humanity shares a responsibility for the suffering of the Jews. In 1947, Miller's next play, *All My Sons,* was his first Broadway hit. The play focuses on Joe Keller, a small factory owner who confronts his legal and moral crime of knowingly selling defective airplane parts during World War II. With the production of *All My Sons,* Miller began his professional and personal association with the film and stage director Elia Kazan.

In late 1948, Miller wrote his masterpiece, *Death of a Salesman.* The play depicts the last 24 hours in the life of Willy Loman, a 63-year-old traveling salesman. When the play, directed by Kazan, opened on February 10, 1949 at the Morosco Theater, the critical reaction was overwhelming. It ran for 742 performances, won the Antoinette Perry Award (Tony), the Drama Critics' Circle Award, and the Pulitzer Prize. Within a year of its premiere, *Salesman* was playing in every major city in the United States and within a few years began its incredible run of international productions. The enduring universal appeal of *Death of Salesman* to audiences, theater critics, and scholars lies in its focus on the American Dream as a central theme.

In 1950, Miller wrote an adaptation of Henrik Ibsen's *An Enemy of the People.* During this time, the United States was entering a period of political and social upheaval that had a lasting effect on Miller's career and personal life. Miller witnessed the rise of the Army/McCarthy hearings and the establishment of the House Un-American Activities Committee (HUAC) in response to the "Red Scare" threat from the Soviet Union and communist China. People were called before these committees in order to admit to alleged radical pasts, and the targets were often high-profile celebrities whose appearances would guarantee publicity. Miller saw his friends and colleagues, including the playwright Clifford Odets, **Lee J. Cobb** (the original Willy Loman), and Elia Kazan, "name names" during their testimony. Kazan's decision to inform caused a breach in his personal and professional relationship with Miller that lasted a decade. In 1953, Miller wrote *The Crucible* about the Salem Witch Trials. He likened these so-called communist witch hunts to the earlier Salem madness.

In *A View From the Bridge* in 1955, Miller explored the Sicilian immigrant society of the Brooklyn docks. At this time, Miller had begun his affair with Marilyn Monroe, was about to divorce his wife, and was becoming a target of the HUAC. He entered a period of personal and political turmoil that kept him from the Broadway stage for nine years. In 1956, Miller encountered troubles with the government over alleged leftist activities. He suspected that the publicity over his marriage to Monroe would draw the attention of the HUAC. Miller was subpoenaed, and the hypocrisy of the committee was evident to him when his lawyer told him that Pennsylvania Representative Francis E. Walter, chairman of the committee, proposed that the hearing might be canceled if Monroe agreed to be photographed shaking hands with him. Miller cordially answered the committee's questions about his association with political groups, and gave his opinions on freedom of speech and Communist conspiracies. Miller was asked about his attendance at a meeting of communist writers a decade earlier. He freely admitted his presence but refused to give the names of others in attendance. Miller was warned that he would be in contempt of Congress for refusing to answer. Miller still refused and was cited. He was tried for contempt of Congress and was found guilty on two counts. His sentencing was deferred for an appeal, and in 1958 the U.S. Court of Appeals overturned his conviction. Miller's personal, professional, and political reputation is often judged by this well-known period.

In 1960, he revised a short story he had written, "The Misfits," into a screenplay for Monroe. Monroe and Miller's marriage was failing during the making of the film, and they divorced within the year. *The Misfits* was the last vehicle for Monroe and her costar Clark Gable. Gable died of a heart attack a few days after the film's final shooting. Monroe was found dead, apparently from an overdose of barbiturates, in August 1962.

In 1962, Miller married Ingeborg Morath, a renowned photographer, whom he had met on the set of *The Misfits*. He and Morath had two children, Rebecca and Daniel. Rebecca Miller is married to the stage and film star Daniel Day-Lewis. In 1964, Miller's first play in nine years, *After the Fall*, premiered for the Lincoln Center Repertory Theater. The play was the result of a trip Miller and Morath took to Germany and Austria, where Miller had the opportunity to attend the Nazi war trials, which he covered for the *New York Herald Tribune*. The play is partly autobiographical. There was criticism of the character, Maggie, who seemed too Monroe-like.

After the Fall, a significant play in Miller's canon, marks the first time he devoted a play to the Holocaust. No other American playwright has been as prolific in writing about the Holocaust. Miller produced three other plays which directly dramatize the topic: *Incident at Vichy* (1964), *Playing for Time* (teleplay 1980, stage script 1985), and *Broken Glass* (1994). Discussion of Miller's Holocaust plays often centers on his classification as a Jewish American playwright. Despite the fact that he was raised in a household of observant immigrant Jews, Miller as an adult was neither a practitioner nor a believer in its faith. Although he became a self-described "Jewish atheist," the noted scholar Christopher Bigsby has judged, "To a greater extent than critics have supposed, to greater extent than perhaps he would himself once have acknowledged, the story of Arthur Miller is that of a Jewish writer. It is his default setting" (*Critical Study*, 477). As a playwright who described one of the functions of a writer to be a "rememberer," Miller did not deny his Jewishness in his life or art. Miller said in his acceptance speech after being awarded the Jerusalem Prize in 2003: "It may be that as a Jew of a certain generation, I was unable to forget the silence of the Thirties and Forties when fascism began its destruction of our people, which for so long met with the indifference of the world." Miller's Holocaust plays dramatize the horror as confrontations between the public and the private. He shows how the Holocaust forces his characters to confront their personal struggles as they become embroiled in world affairs.

Miller continued to create plays and boldly express his interest in morality and politics. He actively protested against the Vietnam War. *The Price* in 1968 was Miller's biggest Broadway hit since *Death of a Salesman*. In 1977, Miller wrote *The Archbishop's Ceiling*. This followed his experiences visiting Eastern European countries behind the iron curtain, where he found himself in living rooms he was certain had been "bugged" by the regimes. In the 1980s, he supported the Polish Solidarity movement, protested Israel's West Bank settlements, and continued to defend the rights of artists and writers living under repressive governments.

Miller's railing against the Tiananmen Square massacres was particularly relevant since he had directed an acclaimed version of *Death of Salesman* in Beijing in 1984. Miller also began to more increasingly criticize the commercialization of the American theater. In the 1990s Miller wrote the plays *The Last Yankee, Broken Glass, The Ride Down Mt. Morgan,* and *Mr. Peter's Connections,* as well as a screenplay for *The Crucible,* for which he received an Academy Award nomination. He also published a novella, *Homely Girl,* and oversaw revivals of his work around the world. He continued to write essays and political tracts, many of which appeared as op-ed pieces in the *New York Times.* One op-ed concerned the controversy over Elia Kazan's honorary Oscar, which Miller insisted Kazan deserved.

In 2001, Miller gave the annual Jefferson Lecture in Washington, D.C. and caused a stir with his controversial opinion on the disputed election between Al Gore and George W. Bush, a speech which he called "Politics and the Art of Acting."

Miller's third wife, Inge Morath, died in 2002. Miller's final play, *Finishing the Picture,* premiered a few months before his death on February 10, 2005. *See also* **Film**; **Theater**.

Steve Marino

Further Reading: Arthur Miller Society Web Site: http://www.ibiblio.org/miller/ Bigsby, Christopher. *Arthur Miller, A Critical Study.* United Kingdom: Cambridge University Press, 2005. Centola, Steven R., and Michelle Cirulli, eds. *The Critical Response to Arthur Miller.* Connecticut: Greenwood Press, 2006. Miller, Arthur. *Timebends: A Life*. New York: Grove Press, 1987.

THE MINSKY BROTHERS

Minsky! The name is synonymous with burlesque . . . globally. In 1917, the four Minsky brothers, Abraham, Billy, Herbert, and Morton, originated burlesque on the top three floors of a **Yiddish theater** in New York which they called the Winter Garden. Meanwhile Louis Minsky, the brothers' father, spent his spare time studying the Talmud.

Burlesque was the outgrowth of **vaudeville**, with roots firmly planted in old minstrel shows. The rowdy, risqué, baggy-pants comics performed pieces of theater based on venerated bits of culture . . . novels, opera, and ballet, making fun of them, thumbing their noses at highbrow theater. No one took themselves seriously. Their bawdy slapstick "send-ups" created the word "shtick," which had its origins in burlesque. burlesque comedy perfected the pun and double entendre. Their humor was deliciously incorrect. Interestingly, they *never* used a four-letter word.

During the 1930s, the four Minsky brothers had 15 shows running on Broadway. This is startling, considering that now it takes a village of producers to produce one Broadway show. They were personally responsible for making burlesque a classic American art form. They were a sensation, albeit at times not far from financial ruin. Billy Minsky was a juggernaut of promotion. Crowds flocked to see the time-honored Minsky formula —shows consisting of long-stemmed American beauties in lavish costumes, novelty acts, and outrageous comics. The Minsky shows of the 1920s and 1930s created a scandal. Religious groups consisting of Christians and Jews picketed the burlesque theaters, resulting in police raids. The Minsky brothers were constantly embroiled in legal battles to maintain their licenses.

Minsky shows launched the careers of **Red Buttons**, Phil Silvers, Robert Alda, Dan Dailey, Bert Lahr, and Gypsy Rose Lee. Burlesque has never really gone away. Everywhere you look, you see the products of burlesque. Its gaudy, brassy jokes and physical comedy are all over television, the movies, and music. It's as modern as MTV.

The Minsky dynasty continued with Harold Minsky, son of Abraham. Abraham put Harold, the last of the producing clan, in charge of his own theater, the Gotham in New York. Mayor Fiorello La Guardia shut Minsky down in New York in 1942, criticizing the shows' racy content. After months of litigation, La Guardia's ban was upheld by the Supreme Court. Minsky had no alternative but to declare bankruptcy.

Minsky dusted himself off and hit the road, producing touring shows in Chicago, Miami, Cincinnati, and Hollywood. He introduced his first burlesque show to Las Vegas in 1954. Minsky's shows played the Dunes, Aladdin, Silver Slipper, Thunderbird, Frontier, and Fremont hotels. The 1967 film *The Night They Raided Minsky's* immortalized the family's contributions.

Harold Minsky, the inveterate showman, was a mild-mannered impresario much beloved by show folk. He died on December 25, 1977, shortly after his last show closed at the Fremont Hotel in Las Vegas. *See also* **Vaudeville.**

Marilyn Mayblum

Further Reading: Minsky, Morton, and Milt Machlin. *Minsky's Burlesque : A Fast and Funny Look at America's Bawdiest Era.* Arbor House, 1986.

MOSTEL, ZERO (1915–1977)

Zero Mostel was a stage and film actor best known for his portrayals in Eugene Ionesco's

The original Tevye, Zero Mostel, poses with the cast of the hit musical *Fiddler on the Roof,* following its opening performance at the Imperial Theatre in New York City on September 22, 1964. From left to right: Maria Karnilova, who played Tevye's wife Golde, Tanya Everett as Chava, Julia Migenes as Hodell, and Joanna Merlin as Tzeitel. [AP Photo]

absurdist drama *Rhinoceros* (1961); as the freedom-loving Roman slave Pseudolus, in Stephen Sondheim's *A Funny Thing Happened on the Way to the Forum* (1962); in the role of Tevye, the poor Russian Jewish dairyman determined to marry off his daughters in *Fiddler on the Roof* (1964); and as the unscrupulous Max Bialystock in **Mel Brooks**'s hilarious film *The Producers* (1967). The role of Tevye was recognized as the high point of his career, and he returned to it in several revivals. *Newsweek* noted, "When he sings 'If I were a rich man . . .' he follows the words with a sighing, dream-tasting spiral of **Yiddish** scat-syllables, which become the anthem of yearning for poor men everywhere" (Kroll, 1964).

Mostel was born Samuel Joel Mostel in the Brownsville section of Brooklyn on February 28, 1915, the seventh of eight children of Israel Mostel and Cina (Celia) Druchs. Both parents were Eastern European Jews who had immigrated separately to the United States. A failed attempt to make a living on a Connecticut farm caused the family to return to New York and settle on the Lower East Side of Manhattan. There Mostel attended public school and developed a talent for painting and drawing in the art classes of Ben Shahn at the Educational Alliance, a Jewish institution for immigrants.

Mostel graduated from the City College of New York in 1935, and, with no job prospects in view, he joined the Federal Art Project (part of the Works Projects Administration), teaching art at the 92nd Street Young Men and Young Women's Hebrew Association. He also gave gallery talks in New York museums and found that people were amused by his sense of humor. He soon became a stand-up comedian in Greenwich Village, recognized for his nutty, exaggerated, improvisational style. It was during this period that a club press agent nicknamed him "Zero," because he was a guy "who started from nothing."

After his World War II military service, Mostel played character roles in several films, but his career crashed when the House Un-American Activities Committee blacklisted him as a communist. Although he did hold leftist political views, Mostel denied he was a member of the Communist Party and refused to provide information about his friends.

His career in shambles, Mostel painted to support his family. In 1958, his career resumed when a friend got him the part of Leopold Bloom in the off-Broadway production of *Ulysses in Nighttown,* for which he won an Obie. Mostel's experiences during these difficult years are depicted in Martin Ritt's film *The Front* (1976), about an actor victimized by the Hollywood blacklist. This proved to be Zero's last film role before his death of cardiac arrest in Philadelphia on September 8, 1977. *See also* **Film**; **Theater**.

Leslie Rabkin

Further Reading: Kroll, Jack. Review of *Fiddler on the Roof. Newsweek,* September 29, 1964. Sainer, Arthur. *Zero Dances: A Biography of Zero Mostel.* New York: Limelight Editions, 2004.

MUNI, PAUL

See **Film**; **Film Stars**.

MYERSON, BESS (1924–)

On September 8, 1945, Bess Myerson was chosen as the first, and to-date only, Jewish Miss America. Myerson was born in the Bronx into a working-class **Yiddish**-speaking family and graduated from Hunter College in 1945. She entered the Miss America competition partially to further her musical ambitions. She hoped to use any winnings to buy a good piano, which her father, a house painter, could not afford. The year after becoming Miss America, Myerson married Allan Wayne. In 1949, she gave birth to her daughter, Barra, the couple's only child. They divorced in 1958. Myerson married Arnold Grant in 1962 and divorced him in 1967.

Myerson's fame as Miss America resulted in a career in television during the 1950s and 1960s, when she co-hosted *Candid Camera,* was a panelist on *I've Got a Secret* and *The Name's the Same,* and worked as an actress on other shows. She became active in New York City politics in the 1960s, serving as the city's first commissioner of consumer affairs during the John Lindsay administration and as commissioner of cultural affairs under Mayor **Edward Koch** in the 1970s. Myerson often campaigned with Koch during his first race for mayor, and cynics hinted this was done to refute suspicions that Koch was homosexual. Certainly Koch benefitted from the support of Myerson, the city's best known and most recognizable Jewish woman.

Myerson was unsuccessful in her 1980 effort to win the Democratic nomination for the United States Senate seat held by Jacob Javits. It was said that she seemed "too tall and beautiful" to be a senator. Any political ambitions she had ended in 1987 when Myerson was indicted for bribery, conspiracy, and mail fraud. She was acquitted of all charges, but in 1988 she pled guilty to a shoplifting charge in Williamsport, Pennsylvania.

The circumstances surrounding her selection as Miss America were both dramatic and symbolic for American Jews. The war in Europe had ended four months earlier, and all were in shock because of the continuing revelations of the Holocaust. For a Jew to be selected Miss America exemplified the differences between the United States and Europe and the opportunities open to America's Jews. Her victory was not merely an individual success but was a collective triumph over bigotry. If a Jew could be selected Miss America, then anything was possible. Myerson's victory was also prophetic, anticipating the postwar ascent of American Jews in social, cultural, and economic fields.

It was not only that she won, but who she was and how she won that endeared Myerson to American Jews. Myerson was raised in the Sholom Aleichem Cooperative Houses, an apartment complex inhabited by left-wing Jews in a solidly Jewish neighborhood. As a child, she participated in pro-radical political demonstrations and attended the Sholom Aleichem Folkschule, an afternoon socialist Yiddish school. Many other American Jews had grown up in immigrant, Yiddish-speaking, working-class, left-wing milieus, and they identified closely with Myerson. She was one of them.

Jews also admired Myerson's refusal to hide her background. She would compete as a New York Jew or not at all. She rejected suggestions to change her name. American Jews perceived Myerson to be their personal champion. "Bess

Myerson was the most important female image in your life," one Jewish woman, then a teenager, recalled. "We didn't just know about her. We felt her" (Dworkin, 1987). Strangers came up to her during the week of competition at Atlantic City to tell her how important her winning would be to them and to Jews throughout the world. A Jewish New York clothing manufacturer provided her evening gowns at no cost so that she could represent Jews in style. The residents of the Sholom Aleichem Houses and other left-wing Jews, for whom beauty contests embodied the sexism, decadence, and competitiveness of capitalism, rooted as hard for Myerson as did other American Jews. And when word reached the displaced persons camps in Europe of Myerson's victory, it made Jewish refugees even more determined to settle in the golden land of America. Myerson became an iconic figure for American Jews in 1945, and she was frequently described as the most famous Jewish woman since Queen Esther. *See also* **Koch, Edward**.

Edward S. Shapiro

Further Reading: Alexander, Shana. *When She Was Bad*. Dell, 1991. Dworkin, Susan. *Miss America, 1945: Bess Myerson's Own Story.* Newmarket Press, 1987. Shapiro, Edward S. *A Time for Healing: American Jewry Since World War II.* Johns Hopkins University Press, 1992.

N

NEWMAN, PAUL (1925–2008)

Actor, race car driver, and philanthropist, even as he entered his eighties, Paul Newman had an ever-growing group of admirers. Handsome and blue-eyed, Newman was a legend as a screen actor appearing in over 65 motion pictures. His career spanned more than 50 years.

Newman was born in Shaker Heights, Ohio. His father, Arthur S. Newman, was the son of Jewish immigrants from Europe. His mother, Theresa Fetzser, who immigrated to the United States from Hungary, was Catholic but converted to Christian Science. Newman's parents operated a successful retail business while raising him and his brother, Arthur. At the age of seven, Newman appeared in his school's production of *Robin Hood,* where he portrayed the court jester.

After graduating from Shaker Heights High School, Newman began his college career at Ohio State University in Athens. He left Ohio State and enlisted in the navy. His hopes of becoming a pilot were dashed because he was color-blind. Newman served in the South Pacific as a radio operator on board torpedo bombers. At the conclusion of the war, Newman received an athletic scholarship to Kenyon College, where he became involved with the drama program. He performed in college productions as well as summer stock with the Wisconsin-based Williams Bay Repertory Company. He graduated in 1949 with a bachelor of arts degree in English. Newman performed with the Woodstock Players in Chicago before moving to Connecticut, where he studied acting as a graduate student at Yale and at New York's Actors Studio.

Newman first appeared on Broadway in William Inge's original production of *Picnic. The Silver Chalice* (1954) was Newman's first motion picture. In 1960, he starred in ***Exodus*** as Ari Ben Canaan, a member of a socialist Zionist military organization. His role resulted in his friendship with Israeli veterans, and he became a contributor to Jewish causes. Newman once said he considered himself Jewish "because it is more challenging" (Bernstein, 2008).

He was nominated nine times for Academy Awards for acting and once as a producer. He won the award in 1986 for his role in *The Color of Money.* He was awarded the Golden Globe in 1969 for directing *Rachel, Rachel.* In 1984 he captured the Golden Globe Cecil B. DeMille Lifetime Achievement Award. The Academy presented the Jean Hersholt Humanitarian Award to Newman in 1994. He was also awarded a Golden Globe Award, a Screen Actors Guild Award, and an Emmy in 2005.

In 1949, Newman married actress Jackie Witte, with whom he had three children, Scott, Stephanie, and Susan. The marriage ended in 1958. He married actress Joanne Woodward in 1958. They had three children, Melissa Steward, Elinor Teresa, and Claire Olivia. When asked why he chose not to wander during his almost 50 years of marriage, Newman responded, "Why fool around with hamburger, when you have steak at home?"

The creation of Newman's Own food products in 1982 began with a line of salad dressings and has expanded to include spaghetti sauces, lemonade, popcorn, cereal, salsa, and other fine foods. By 2006, the proceeds after taxes from Newman's Own products exceeded $200 million, all of which go to charity. The best-known benefactors of Newman's generosity are the Hole in the Wall Camps, located in Ashford, Connecticut, as well as sites in Israel, France, and Ireland. The camps are for children suffering from serious illnesses. In addition, Newman was a cosponsor of the $25,000 PENN/Newman's Own First Amendment Award, the purpose of which is to recognize those who protect the written word.

Paul Newman died of lung cancer on September 26, 2008, at his home in Westport, Connecticut. *See also* **Film**.

Robert Ruder

Further Reading: Bernstein, Adam. "The Blue-Eyed Antihero." Obituary, *Washington Post,* September 28, 2008. Berson, Misha. "Cool and Dashing, Paul Newman Was a New Kind of Jewish Star." *Forward,* October 10, 2008, 1, 9. Lax, Eric. *Paul Newman: A Biography.* Turner, 1999. Oumano, Elena. *Paul Newman.* St. Martin's Press, 1989.

NIMOY, LEONARD (1931–)

Leonard Nimoy was born March 26, 1931 to Max (a barber) and Dora (a housewife) Nimoy, Ukrainian Jewish immigrants to the United States. Early in life, Nimoy knew that acting would be his vocation. He first appeared onstage at age 8 in a production of *Hansel and Gretel* and continued with his amateur theater work until, at age 18, he left Boston and Boston College for Hollywood.

Nimoy's first role was in the 1951 movie *Queen for a Day.* His big break came in 1952, when he got the lead in the movie *Kid Monk Baroni.* Three years later he joined the army for 18 months. It was during his time in the military that Nimoy directed his first play, *A Street Car Named Desire,* while performing the part of Stanley with the Atlanta Theater Guild. Nimoy also wrote, directed, and emceed GI shows.

Upon his return to Hollywood, Nimoy continued to act, while he supported his family by driving taxicabs and working as a soda jerk. When acting in an episode of the television drama *The Lieutenant,* Nimoy caught the attention of Gene Rodenberry, who was working on the show. Rodenberry was also working on a new science fiction series, *Star Trek.* He invited Nimoy to join the cast. Nimoy accepted because he could relate to the character of Spock. The role made Nimoy an icon of popular culture. For Leonard, having grown up a Jew in the Catholic city of Boston, playing an alien was not alien. *Star Trek* embodied many Jewish values for Nimoy, because the crew of the Enterprise was educated, committed to social justice, and tolerant of differences.

After three years the series ended, and Nimoy joined the popular adventure series *Mission Impossible,* where he played the part of Paris for two years (1969–1971). After Nimoy left the series, he did guest appearances on various television shows. Nimoy also returned to the stage, performing in ***Fiddler on the Roof*** in 1971. Nimoy also toured in *Vincent,* a play he wrote, directed, and starred in for over 150 performances.

Leonard has pursued other interests, in addition to acting. In 1967, Nimoy released his first album, *Leonard Nimoy Presents Mr. Spock's Music from Outer Space,* which produced a hit single, "Visit to a Sad Planet," and proved so popular that Nimoy released *The Two Sides of Leonard Nimoy* in 1968. He recorded music on records and CDs, and his narrations of stories and televisions shows are also available on CD.

Nimoy has directed both television and movies, such as an episode of *TJ Hooker* which starred **William Shatner**, his costar on *Star Trek* and his best friend. He also wrote the film versions of the "cult" series *Star Trek III: The Search for Spock, Star Trek IV: The Voyage Home,* and *Star Trek VI: The Undiscovered Country.* Over the years he has published three books of poetry, two autobiographies, and a novel.

In 1973 Nimoy had his first photographic exhibition, and by the 1990s he became a groundbreaking photographer with his exhibition of nude women titled *Shekhina*. Museums such as the Los Angeles County Museum of Art, the New Orleans Museum of Art, the Jewish Museum in New York, and the Museum of Fine Art in Houston have purchased his photos. In addition, the Elise Monte Dance Company performed a dance piece based on Nimoy's *Shekhina* photographs (2004).

Education is an important part of Leonard Nimoy's life. Truly a renaissance man, in 1977, Nimoy completed his master's in education at Antioch College and, in 2000, Antioch University awarded Nimoy an honorary doctorate of humane letters.

In 1954, Nimoy married Sandy Zober, with whom he had two children: Julie and Adam. In 1986, the Nimoys divorced, and three years later Nimoy married Susan Bay. In 2003, Leonard and Susan Bay Nimoy founded the Nimoy Foundation, whose goal is to encourage contemporary artists. It funds artists and foundations, connecting artists with organizations that can help with their careers, and it encourages artists to teach and mentor upcoming artists. *See also* **Television**.

Mara W. Cohen Ioannides

Further Reading: Nimoy, Leonard. *I Am Not Spock.* New York: Ballantine/Del Rey, 1977. ———. *I Am Spock.* New York: Hyperion Books, 1995. ———, and Donald Burton Kuspit. *Shekhina.* Photographs by Leonard Nimoy. Brooklyn, NY: Umbrage Editions, 2002.

O

ODETS, CLIFFORD (1906–1963)

Clifford Odets was a Depression-era playwright, Hollywood screenwriter, actor, and socialist, whose plays *Waiting for Lefty* and *Awake and Sing* are often considered masterpieces of the Broadway stage. Odets was born to Jewish immigrants Louis J. Odets and Pearl (Geisinger) Odets on July 18, 1906. The Odets family lived in Philadelphia, where Louis Odets worked at selling newspapers and peddling salt. Pearl worked in a factory. At the age of six, Clifford Odets and his two younger sisters moved with their parents to the Bronx. There his father rose from a position as feeder in a printing plant to become plant owner. Although Odets always insisted that until the age of 12 he was the son of a worker, the family was far from financially strapped. They lived in a Bronx apartment building that had an elevator, and they owned an automobile. Later the family returned to Philadelphia, where Louis Odets owned an advertising agency.

Despite a financially secure childhood, Odets described himself as having experienced a melancholy childhood. His mother was not happy in her marriage, and Odets's relationship with his father was strained, at best. Louis Odets had plans for his son to enter his advertising business. Young Odets had other ideas; he wanted to become an actor. Odets's father remained highly critical of him and continued to berate him, even when he later in life helped support his family. In an interview, Odets recalled his father smashing a typewriter to stop his son from wasting his life pursuing a career in the arts.

Because he considered schooling unnecessary, Clifford Odets dropped out of Morris High School in 1923 and tried his hand at writing poetry. Odets spent the next seven years occupied with a variety of minor theatrical jobs. He acted with the Drawing-Room Players, a neighborhood company that presented one-act plays, and with Harry Kemp's Poet's Theatre. He wrote plays for radio ads and worked as an announcer for a small station in the Bronx. He also gave performances reciting poetry. At the age of 20, he was hired as a juvenile in Mae Desmond's Stock Company, but his acting talent proved limited.

In 1929, Odets finally had an opportunity on Broadway. He was hired as understudy to Spencer Tracy in Warren F. Lawrence's *Conflict*. A member of the cast introduced Odets to the Theatre Guild, which led him to join the Group Theatre in 1930. This event truly marked the beginning of Odets's career. The Group Theatre was mostly made up of first- and second-generation Jewish Americans. Founded by three idealists, the group intended to restore dignity to acting. Their theatrical ideology of working as a collective provided a perfect vehicle for Odets's plays, which stressed the psychological interactions between persons with one another and their world.

Odets's melancholy continued to haunt him. Before the age of 25 he had attempted suicide three times. Living in New York City, Odets grew increasingly aware of the suffering of the working and middle classes as he witnessed the impact of the Great Depression. Drawing on his sympathy, Odets wrote his first play, *9–10 Eden Street.* He could not have been happy with the result, since *9-10 Eden Street* was never produced. *Awake and Sing,* his next play, was also rejected, despite Odets's association with the Group Theatre.

Odets wrote his next play, *Waiting for Lefty* (1935), for a contest. It won, and it was performed. This introduction into the New York theater world brought Odets much acclaim, and within a year he had three plays running on Broadway. *Waiting for Lefty* was a play filled with anger. It was based on the incidents of the 1934 New York City cab strike. The staging was simple and stark, and the play's impact was devastating as the first audiences saw their own hurt and broken hope depicted by the characters. Not everyone was thrilled with *Waiting for Lefty.* It was banned in seven cities for its communist message.

Odets had busy years in 1935 through 1936. *Awake and Sing* provided the Broadway stage with one of its first portrayals of a Jewish American family. Then *Till the Day I Die* (1935), one of the first successful anti-Nazi plays to appear in New York, described the Nazis' torture and breakdown of a German underground worker. Audiences and critics now eagerly awaited Odets's next play, *Paradise Lost* (1936). It marked an unexpected turning point in his career; it failed miserably. But his earlier works provided Odets with an escape. Hollywood courted him for a screenwriting job. Odets was torn; he saw the promise of Hollywood and financial success, yet he worried about leaving the Group Theatre and the artistic freedom it offered. Ultimately, he decided that by leaving he could help finance the Theatre with his earnings. When he left New York, many accused him of betraying his ideals for monetary security.

Affiliations with the Communist Party increased the controversy surrounding Odets. Although Odets had joined the Communist Party for eight months, he later quit, claiming it interfered with his freedom to write. He also joined a delegation traveling to Cuba in 1935 to investigate conditions there. On their arrival in Havana, the members of the commission were arrested and forced to return to the United States. After lodging a protest with the Cuban Consul General, the commission published a pamphlet, *Rifle Rule in Cuba,* and Odets began a play (which he never finished) that was intended to bring the incident to the attention of the public.

Though Odets moved to Hollywood, he continued to focus his work on man's desire to maintain his identity and dignity in a hostile world. In *Golden Boy* (1937) he muted his political and economic ideology quite a bit and earned critical acclaim. Some critics declared his next play, *Rocket to the Moon* (1938), his finest work. From the late 1930s until the 1960s, whether writing alone or in collaboration with others, Odets produced an impressive body of work that included *None But the Lonely Heart* (1944), *Deadline at Dawn* (1946), *Humoresque* (1946), *The Country Girl* (first produced on Broadway in 1950), *The Sweet Smell of Success* (1957), *The Story on Page One* (1960), and *Wild in the Country* (1961).

Odets's personal life was no less complicated than his career path. He married actress Louise Rainer on January 8, 1937 and divorced her in May 1940. His next trip to the altar was with actress Bette Grayson, with whom he had two children. He later divorced Grayson. When in 1954 she died unexpectedly, Odets was left to raise their two children, Nora and Walter, as a single parent. Thus, in the spring of 1952, when Odets's brief affiliation with the Communist Party brought him to the attention of the subcommittee of the House Un-American Activities Committee (HUAC), he could hardly afford to lose his Hollywood paycheck. During his testimony, Odets "named names" of individuals he believed to have been members of the Communist Party. Odets's testimony cost him friends and haunted him throughout his remaining years.

His last play, *The Flowering Peach* (1954), seems to focus upon Odets's loss of political faith and his attempt find a way to accept the change. After *The Flowering Peach* closed in 1955, Odets returned to California, where he lived the rest of his life. Though he professed his determination to write more plays, he did not. Odets was hospitalized in 1963 while working on scripts for *The Richard Boone Show.* He died of cancer three weeks later.

Despite success, Odets continually questioned the depth of his talent. In 1940, he began keeping a journal, *The Time Is Ripe.* This diary was intended for publication as an instructive piece for young writers. In it he documents his surprise at the success he was enjoying, writes of socializing with elite artists and literary figures, and comments about the difficulties of writing and about his worries that his best work was already behind him. His fears were not completely unfounded. The events of the 1930s had spurred Odets to write plays that influenced the way people felt about their everyday lives and work. During the Depression, America thirsted for someone to give voice to their anger, fears, and hopes, and Clifford Odets's plays offered that release. As the despair of the thirties faded, however, so did the feelings that provided a connection to Odets's plays. His work seemed to lose its relevance. Some critics and scholars over the years have dismissed his talent and claimed he failed to live up to his promise. Yet, Odets's accomplishments cannot be ignored. The character types Odets created have inspired generations of writers and actors, and theater groups continue to stage his plays. *See also* **Theater**.

Susan M. Ortmann

Further Reading: Breneman-Gibson, Margaret. *Clifford Odets—American Playwright—The Years from 1906–1940.* Atheneum, 1981. Lahr, John. "Stage Left." *New Yorker,* April 17, 2006. Mendelsohn, Michael J. *Clifford Odets: Humane Dramatist.* New York: Everett/Edwards, 1969. Weales, Gerald. *Odets the Playwright.* London and New York: Methuen, 1985.

OZICK, CYNTHIA (1928–)

Cynthia Ozick is counted within the front ranks of the great living American writers in contemporary fiction. Cynthia Ozick was born in New York City in 1928, the second child of Celia and William Ozick, who ran a pharmacy in the Pelham Bay section of the Bronx. Coming from the Lithuanian region of Russia, her parents favored the skeptical, rational, anti-mystical attitudes of the region. Cynthia grew up working in the drugstore, learned Yiddish at the same time as she learned English, entered cheder when she was five, and began to embrace feminism when the rabbi at the school told her grandmother that girls didn't have to be educated. Fortunately her "bobbe" took her back the next day and insisted on her being accepted. At P.S. 71, she was an excellent student but was attacked as a "Christ-killer" and humiliated when she, on principle, would not sing Christmas carols.

The saving grace in her childhood was the traveling library, the fairy tales especially, which transported her to another world and set in motion the desire to be a writer. As she told an interviewer, "I think one of the reasons from earliest childhood I felt free to be a writer is that if I had been a boy, I would have had to go be something else" (*Paris Review,* 1987).

After college, Cynthia pursued a master's degree in English at Ohio State University, writing on "The Later Novels of Henry James." She worked at various jobs while writing *Mercy, Pity, Peace and Love,* a long, Jamesian unpublished novel. With the publication of *Trust* and "The Pagan Rabbi" in 1966, as well as *Envy; or, Yiddish in America,* in 1969, her reputation began to grow. In 1971 *The Pagan Rabbi and Other Stories* appeared; *Bloodshed and Three Novellas* came out in 1976 and *Levitation: Five Fictions* in 1982. In 1984 the editor of *The Best American Short Stories* named her one of the three greatest American writers of stories alive.

In the 1950s and 1960s Ozick underwent a transformation culturally and intellectually. She became "Judaized" as she read voraciously in the Jewish Textual tradition, separated herself from the influence of James, and became a "Jewish writer"—a term she has struggled with as she had with "woman writer" for many years. Meanwhile as she published *The Cannibal Galaxy* (1983), *The Messiah of Stockholm* (1987), *The Puttermesser Papers* (1997), and *Heir to the Glimmering World* (2006), she wrote the superb "The Shawl" and "Rosa" and several collections of essays—*Art and Ardor* (1983), *Metaphor and Memory* (1989), *Fame and Folly* (1996), *Quarrel and Quandary* (2001), and *The Din in the Head* (2006).

One of the most important themes in Ozick's work is the Greek/Hebrew dichotomy. Setting up oppositions of fate and free will, aestheticism and moral seriousness, the gods of nature and the God of history, Ozick presents a protagonist in *Trust* whose Hebraic analytic voice opposes the appeal of the Hellenic influence. Similarly in "The Pagan Rabbi," Rabbi Kornfeld, forced to choose between Jewish and pagan values, chooses Nature as god. Inveighing against idol worship and adoration of magical events in her novels and stories, she argues against art for art's sake in her essays while advocating a Judaic literature, "advancing the theme of freedom to change one's life," as Lillian Kremer puts it, "the energy of creative renewal, the sense that we are morally responsible." Implicit in this Hebraic literature, Kremer continues, "is the fluid, changing possibilities of humankind in opposition to the Hellenic fated or static view of life" (Kremer, 1989).

In 1971, Cynthia Ozick published an essay called "The Demise of the Dancing Dog," on the exclusion (and self-exclusion) of women, then an anomalous and isolating act. It was her way of proposing the Ovarian Theory of Literature. Ten years later in "Literature and the Politics of Sex: A Dissent," she argued that the term "woman writer" was a new political term, signaling that there are male and female states of intellect, an absurdity. To her "a writer is a writer." "When I write," Ozick stated, "I am free. I am, as a writer, whatever I wish to become . . . In life, I am not free" (Ozick, 1984). In short, classical feminism was concerned with the end of false barriers and boundaries, while not denying the body, self-image, and self-knowledge.

Cynthia Ozick is a literary powerhouse among America's most important and influential novelists and critics. She was a finalist for the National Book Award for *The Puttermesser Papers,* widely named as one of the top 10 books of the year; she won the National Book Critics Award in 2001 for *Quarrel and Quandary,* and *Heir to the Glimmering World* was selected as a best book of the year by the *New York Times,* the *Washington Post,* and the *San Francisco Chronicle. See also* **Literature.**

Daniel Walden

Further Reading: Kremer, S. Lillien. *Witness Through the Imagination: Jewish-American Holocaust Literature.* Detroit, MI: Wayne State University Press, 1989. Ozick, Cynthia. *Art and Ardor: Essays.* New York: E.P. Dutton, 1984. ———, and Elaine M. Kauvar. *A Cynthia Ozick Reader.* Bloomington, IN: Indiana University Press, 1996. "An Interview with Cynthia Ozick." *Paris Review* 102 (Spring 1987).

P

PALEY, WILLIAM (1901–1990)

A pioneer of television and radio, William Paley built CBS into one of the world's leading networks, serving as president and then chairman of the board from 1928 until 1990.

Paley was a son of Russian Jews who had immigrated to Chicago, where he was born and where his family established a prosperous cigar business. In 1928, with money provided by his father, Paley purchased a moribund radio network with only 16 affiliate stations, renamed it the Columbia Broadcasting System, and made himself president. He built the network into a world-class communications empire on the strength of one big idea: it was national advertisers, and not the affiliates, who were the network's primary clients. Paley's approach, novel for the time, was to provide network programming to affiliate stations at low cost and thereby create the widest possible audience for advertisers. Affiliates, required to carry network shows, shared in the national advertising revenue.

A key to CBS's success was Paley's sense of the public's taste in programming. CBS radio launched shows such as *Mercury Theatre on the Air,* founded by Orson Welles and John Houseman, and was famous for the *War of the Worlds* broadcast of 1938. CBS radio gave exposure to writers including **Arthur Miller** and Norman Corwin and performers including Katharine Hepburn, Burgess Meredith, Helen Hayes, and Laurence Olivier. In the 1940s CBS's programming department created shows such as *Our Miss Brooks* and *Gunsmoke.* Paley was able to bring diverse talents to the radio network, including **Jack Benny**, Frank Sinatra, Bing Crosby, Bob Hope, **George Burns** and Gracie Allen, Amos and Andy, and Will Rogers, many of them lured away from rival networks. When television began to supplant radio, Paley already had most of the popular stars in his stable, easing the network's transition to the new medium.

CBS was equally successful in its television programming throughout Paley's stewardship, with such well-known hits as *The Ed Sullivan Show, Playhouse 90, I Love Lucy, All in the Family,* and *M*A*S*H.* Paley was responsible for both quality programming and escapist fare, such as *The Beverly Hillbillies.*

Perhaps Paley's most singular achievement was developing CBS News into a first-rate organization with its own full-time newsgathering service and a group of news stars including Edward R. Murrow, H. V. Kaltenborn, Eric Sevareid, **Mike Wallace**, Morley Safer, Dan Rather, and Walter Cronkite. In 1968, the news division created *60 Minutes,* one of the longest-running, highest-rated, and most highly regarded television shows of all time.

Not all of Paley's business ventures were successful. Enormous sums were lost on CBS's investments in a television manufacturing company, the publishing firm of Holt, Rinehart, and Winston, and the New York Yankees baseball team. CBS bought the Yankees for $11.2 million in 1964 and sold the team for $8.7 million in 1973. Today the Yankees are worth an estimated $1.2 billion. Paley offset these occasional missteps with successful ventures such as CBS Records, sold to Sony in 1987 for $2 billion, and investments in Broadway shows such as *My Fair Lady.*

Paley was married twice—to Dorothy Hearst, former wife of William Randolph Hearst Jr., and to socialite Barbara "Babe" Cushing Mortimer, with whom he had two children. Despite their social standing and great wealth the family found themselves barred from Long Island country clubs because of Paley's Jewish heritage.

During World War II, Paley served as deputy chief of the army's Psychological Warfare Division. He was an avid art collector, bequeathing his collection, including works by Picasso, Matisse, Pollock, Cézanne, Gauguin, and Toulouse-Lautrec, and valued in the hundreds of millions of dollars, to New York's Museum of Modern Art. Paley served the museum as president and chairman for 23 years. In 1975 Paley founded the Museum of Television and Radio, which in 2007 was renamed The Paley Center for Media. The Center houses 145,000 hours of radio and television shows. *See also* **Radio**; **Television**.

Howard C. Ellis

Further Reading: Paley, William S. *As It Happened: A Memoir.* Garden City, NY: Doubleday, 1979. Slater, Robert. *This . . . Is CBS: A Chronicle Of 60 Years*. Englewood Cliffs, NJ: Prentice-Hall, 1988. Smith, Sally Bedell. *In All His Glory: The Life of William S. Paley, the Legendary Tycoon and His Brilliant Circle.* New York: Simon and Schuster, 1990.

PATINKIN, MANDY (1952–)

Mandy Patinkin is an actor of stage, film, and television, as well as a tenor vocalist. He is known for his roles in television series such as *Chicago Hope, Dead Like Me,* and the first two seasons of *Criminal Minds*. His most notable film roles film include *The Princess Bride, Yentl, Men With Guns,* and *Dick Tracy,* and Patinkin won a Tony for his stage role as Che in *Evita*. Mandel Bruce Patinkin was born in Chicago, Illinois in 1952, to Doris "Doralee" (Sinton) Patinkin, a homemaker and the author of *Grandma Doralee Patinkin's Jewish Family Cookbook*. His father, Lester Patinkin, was head executive of an iron, stee,l and scrap corporation. Growing up in a middle-class Jewish family, Mandy took an early interest in music and acting. He attended the University of Kansas and later the Juilliard School of Drama.

As a child Mandy sang in his Temple's choir, which may have sparked the flame that has characterized his nearly 30-year career in show business. Patinkin's initial success came in musical theater, commencing with the role of Che in Broadway's *Evita* (1979), which earned him a Tony Award for the Best Actor in a Featured Role—Musical. Patinkin moved on to movies, and among the more than 20 films he has acted in are *Ragtime* (1981), *Yentl* (1983, for which he was nominated for a Golden Globe and for Best Performance by an Actor in a Motion Picture—Comedy/Musical), *Daniel* (1983), and the *Princess Bride* (1987). In 1995, he won an Emmy for Outstanding Lead Actor in a Drama Series, for *Chicago Hope*. Patinkin played the lead role in CBS's *Criminal Minds* before he departed the hit show after its second season.

Throughout his career Patinkin's commitment to his Jewish roots has remained strong. In 1998 he recorded *Mamaloshen,* an album of classic Yiddish songs. He has been quoted as saying, "I say prayers everyday; every Shabbos, we have a wonderful dinner in our house. Being Jewish, singing the songs, saying the prayers—it gives me a wonderful feeling. If there's a message I want to convey it's 'investigate your heritage' " (Levitt, 2000).

In 1980, he married fellow actress Kathryn Grody; they have two sons, Isaac and Gideon. In 2004, he was diagnosed with prostate cancer, and when he was given a clean bill of health, he celebrated his recovery with his son Isaac by completing the 280-mile charity bike ride for the Arava Institute Israel Ride: Cycling for Peace, Partnership and Environmental Protection. He is also on the board of Hazon, a nonprofit Jewish organization that seeks to expand the Jewish community through outdoor and environmental education. *See also* **Television**; **Yiddish**.

Judith Lupatkin

Further Reading: Levitt, Beverly. "A Lifetime of Seders: Mandy Patinkin's Jewish Connections Go Well Beyond Mamaloshen." *Jewish Journal*, April 13, 2000. Rubin, Doralee Patinkin, and Mandy Patinkin. *Grandma Doralee Patinkin's Holiday Cookbook: A Jewish Family Celebration.* New York: St. Martin's Press, 2001. ———. *Grandma Doralee Patinkin's Jewish Family Cookbook: More than 150 Treasured Recipes from My Kitchen to Yours.* New York: St. Martin's Press, 1999.

PEKAR, HARVEY (1939–)

Harvey Pekar is an underground comic book writer best known for his autobiographical *American Splendor* series. In 2003, the series inspired a critically acclaimed film adaptation of the same name. Harvey Pekar, who has been variously described as a "working-class everyman" and a "world-class curmudgeon," was born to Jewish immigrants from Poland in Cleveland, Ohio on October 8, 1939. Pekar grew up in a mostly African American neighborhood, where he was known as "white cracker" and suffered daily beatings. Pekar responded to his less-than-joyous existence by retreating from most of the things he enjoyed, like sports. He found solace in reading. As a young man, he joined the navy but was "asked to leave" when it was found that he lacked "the flexibility for the navy life." According to Pekar, part of the problem was he did not know how to wash his own clothes. In 1966, Pekar started working as a file clerk for a local Veteran's Administration Hospital in Cleveland, a job he held for 35 years.

Pekar began his writing career as a jazz music and book critic. His reviews were published in *Downbeat*, the *Boston Herald*, and *Jazz Times*, among other journals. His friendship with legendary underground comic guru R. Crumb led to the creation of Pekar's autobiographical comic series, *American Splendor.* The series, written by Pekar and drawn by leading underground cartoonists, documents Pekar's humdrum "everyman" life in his Cleveland neighborhood. The success of *American Splendor* led to eight appearances on the *Late Show with David Letterman.* In 1994, Pekar and his wife, Joyce Brabner, published the autobiographic comic *Our Cancer Year,* detailing his year-long struggle fighting the disease.

A film adaptation of *American Splendor,* starring Paul Giamatti as Pekar, hit the screen in 2003; it was nominated for an Academy Award. Pekar turned his experience with the movie (in which both he and his wife Brabner had cameos) into *American Splendor: Our Movie Year.*

Pekar's other comic works include *The Quitter* (2005), *Ego & Hubris: The Michael Malice Story* (2006), and *Macedonia* (2007). Now retired, Pekar continues to live in Cleveland with his wife and their foster daughter. *See also* **Comic Books**.

Kurt F. Stone

Further Reading: Pekar, Harvey. *American Splendor: The Life and Times of Harvey Pekar.* Ballantine Books, 2004. ———, Joyce Brabner, and Frank Stack. *Our Cancer Year.* Running Press Books, 1994.

PERLMAN, ITZHAK (1945–)

Itzhak Perlman, world-famous violinist, was born in Tel Aviv, Israel, on August 31, 1945. His parents, Chaim and Shoshana, met and married when they independently migrated to Palestine from Poland in the mid-1930s.

Perlman's career began at the age of three, when he heard the sound of a violin over the radio and immediately expressed a desire to play the instrument. His parents bought him a toy violin (he refused to play it because of its horrible sound) and soon afterward Perlman received a real instrument. When he was four years old, Perlman was stricken with polio, leaving him permanently paralyzed in both legs. Despite his disability, Perlman continued to practice his violin and received a scholarship from the America-Israel Cultural Foundation to be enrolled at the Tel Aviv Academy of Music. He received his initial training from Rivka Goldgart and gave his first solo recital at the age of 10.

In 1958, 13-year-old Perlman won a talent contest which resulted in his coming to the United States for two successful appearances on *Ed Sullivan's Caravan of Stars,* a televised showcase for promising young artists. After an amazing rendition of the technically demanding "Flight of the Bumble Bee" and first movement of the Mendelssohn Violin Concerto, Perlman won international acclaim. This event led to an American concert tour under the sponsorship of the Zionist Organization of America. A scholarship to the Juilliard School in New York next led to Perlman's studies with the legendary Ivan Galamian and Dorothy DeLay.

Perlman's professional debut took place at Carnegie Hall in 1963, with a stirring performance of the Wienawski F-sharp Violin Concerto. A year later, he was awarded the prestigious Leventritt prize in international competition, which opened the door to world-wide concert tours. Perlman appeared extensively throughout the United States, Canada, South America, Europe, Israel, the Far East, and Australia.

Today, Perlman is recognized as the most beloved reigning violin virtuoso in the world. With his extraordinary talent and boundless generosity, he brings joy and inspiration to audiences of all ages and cultures. Perlman's repertory is wide and varied, extending from baroque, classical, romantic, and jazz music to the nostalgic old world melodies of **klezmer**, drawn from his own East-European background.

Perlman makes his Stradivarius violin "speak" with an instinctive directness of musical expression. Each sound is carefully refined with his brilliant technique and aristocratic tone. Moreover, Perlman has the innate ability to immediately engage his audience through his sheer love of music. His stage manner is immediately infectious, often humorous and casual, yet, tinged with emotion and dedication to every note.

Perlman's Jewish connection is an essential core of his whole being. This link can be heard in various collaborative projects he has accomplished in recent years. Some of his proudest achievements are the heartrending violin solos he contributed to the John Williams soundtrack score in **Steven Spielberg**'s 1993 Oscar-winning movie *Schindler's List.* Perhaps the best example of Perlman's close link to his Jewish heritage is his close affinity for klezmer music. Growing up in a **Yiddish**-speaking household in Israel made this connection quite natural. Klezmer derives from the Jewish folk music of Eastern Europe, which was home to Perlman's parents and grandparents. In playing klezmer music, Perlman sees himself as a direct line from the past to the present. In his 1995 PBS documentary film *In the Fiddler's House,* Perlman states he grew up with klezmer music and performs it as if he has been playing it all his life. The music is infectious, and Perlman has an instinctive feeling for its syncopated rhythms, minor-key melodies, and quick-changing moods. Just as klezmer is designed for dancing, so does Perlman's "fiddle" dance to the music.

In the Fiddler's House won an Academy award in 1997. The filming takes place in several locations: first Poland, where Perlman takes the viewer to his ancestral neighborhood in Krakow; then on to New York City for a visit with two Yiddish-speaking comedians from the old Borscht Belt circuit, **Red Buttons** and **Fyvush Finkel**, at a Romanian restaurant on the Lower East Side. The final destination is Lincoln Center, where Perlman performs freylekhs (East European circle dances) and produces the characteristic "wails" with several well-known klezmer bands.

In July 1997, a concert at the Tanglewood Music Festival in Massachusetts brought Perlman together with a group of classically trained klezmer musicians. The performance ended with a rousing tribute to Perlman to the tune called "Itzhak Mach a Groise Simcha" ("Itzhak Made a Great Celebration").

Perlman maintains a close affiliation with the Israel Philharmonic and has made many international tours with the orchestra, beginning with the Warsaw/Budapest tour in 1987. In the spring of 1990, Perlman took the orchestra to the Soviet Union for the first time, a historic event of immense proportions, recorded on PBS with the title *Perlman in Russia*. In 1994, Perlman continued touring, with a visit to China and India.

African American music provides Perlman with another love. In a collaborative set of recorded transcriptions featuring Scott Joplin's ragtime music, Perlman, along with pianist Andre Previn, adds yet another dimension to Joplin's classical piano rags with their own unique interpretations. Another jazz-related Telarc recording entitled *Side by Side* came as a result of Perlman's collaboration with Oscar Peterson's trio. For this venture, Perlman injected jazzy improvisations into a variety of popular tunes by **George Gershwin** and **Irving Berlin**, among others.

Teaching is an important aspect of Perlman's persona. He speaks passionately about educating promising musicians. Never forgetting the early training and encouragement from his own master teachers, Perlman offers master classes throughout the world. In conjunction with his wife, Toby, herself a violinist and graduate of Juilliard (they married in 1967), Itzhak established the Perlman Music Program for Young People in 1998, in Shelter Island, New York. Perlman also joined the teaching staff at the Juilliard School of Music in 1999 and was appointed to the Dorothy Richard Starling Chair of Violin Studies. He continues to teach full time every summer at the Perlman Music Program, and he advises his students to actively listen and soul-search to arrive at the essence of music. He enjoys working with young people and likes the challenge of trying to figure out how his students will sound in a few years. When Perlman teaches, he says he makes new discoveries about his own playing, a humble admission for an artist of his caliber.

Perlman's busy concert schedule includes appearances on the conductor's podium. The list of orchestras he has conducted includes the New York Philharmonic, the Chicago Symphony, the Philadelphia Orchestra, the Boston Symphony, the National Symphony, the Los Angeles Philharmonic, and the Saint Paul Chamber Orchestra, among others. In 2000, Perlman was appointed principal guest conductor of the Detroit Symphony, and in the 2004–2005 season, he conducted both the Detroit and St. Louis symphony orchestras. Internationally, Perlman has conducted the Berlin Philharmonic, the Concertgebouw Orchestra, the London Philharmonic, the English Chamber Orchestra, and the Israel Philharmonic.

Perlman has also appeared on several television programs such as *Sesame Street* and *Live from Lincoln Center* and has received four Emmy Awards. A PBS documentary, *Perlman in Shanghai*, highlights the Perlmans' music program. The finale of this film takes place at the Shanghai Grand Theater with a performance by 1,000 young American and Chinese violinists, prodigies of the Perlman program.

Perlman's EMI recordings regularly appear on the bestsellers' charts and have garnered 15 Grammy Awards. The list of releases over the past decades include orchestral performances, solo recitals, chamber music, and klezmer music, to popular hits from movies such as *Schindler's List* and live performance with jazz combos.

Perlman continues to expand his career, and the world continues to fall in love with his music. Numerous publications and institutions have paid tribute to Perlman for the unique place he occupies in the music world. Prestigious universities such as Harvard, Yale, Brandeis, Yeshiva and the Hebrew University in Jerusalem have awarded him honorary degrees. He was one of 12 first-generation Americans to be honored with the Medal of Liberty in recognition and appreciation of his contributions to the United States. More recently, President Clinton awarded Perlman the National Medal of Arts at the Kennedy Center for Performing Arts.

When Perlman turned 50, 19,000 people celebrated with him at the Tanglewood Music Festival in Lenox, Massachusetts. This tremendous outpouring speaks for all those who have heard or seen Perlman in concerts or recorded performances. His musicality represents the highest level of artistry and humanism, and we, the audience, remain in awe of his many accomplishments. *See also* **Jazz**; **Klezmer Music**.

Ann Leisawitz

Further Reading: Lyman, Darryl. *Great Jews in Music.* Jonathan David Publishers, Inc., 1986. Rogovoy, Seth. *The Essential Klezmer.* Algonquin Books, 2000. Strom, Yale. *The Book of Klezmer.* A Capella Books, 2002.

PICON, MOLLY (1898–1992)

The Golden Globe-nominated actress Molly Picon was a star of the **Yiddish musical theater** and Broadway whose impish charm and boundless energy transcended language, age, nationality, and gender. At a time when the leading actresses of the Yiddish stage were sturdy matriarchs and voluptuous sirens, the elfish Picon made her mark playing acrobatic short-haired ingénues and wide-eyed yeshiva boys. She simultaneously fulfilled dual careers in both English and Yiddish, often portraying the American girl on the Yiddish stage, while singing Jewish songs in English for vaudeville shows at the Palace Theatre. As a 14-year-old teenager, she played Jacob P. Adler's elderly mother in the Yiddish theater. In her sixties, she somersaulted across the Broadway stage to a Tony nomination in Jerry Herman's *Milk and Honey.* Picon was born on New York City's Lower East Side in 1898 to Russian Jewish immigrants, Clara Ostrick and Louis Pyekoon. The family soon moved to Philadelphia, where her mother worked as a seamstress in the Yiddish theater. Picon's career in show business began when she won a talent competition at the age of five. In 1918, when her tour with an English-language vaudeville troupe was derailed in Boston because of the flu epidemic, Picon auditioned for Jacob Kalich's Yiddish company at the Grand Opera House. Kalich, a former rabbinical student from Austria, cast Picon as a scene-stealing school boy in *The Polish Jew.* After they married in 1919, Kalich brought his new wife on a tour of Europe to perfect her **Yiddish** and to introduce her as a star to the Jewish communities. Inspired by her early success playing a boy, Kalich wrote the play *Yankele Goes to the Synagogue* for her, which became a signature role. In 1923, Picon debuted *Yankele* at the Second Avenue Theater in New York. It was an instant success followed by other starring vehicles, including *Tsipke, Shmendrik, Mamele, Circus Girl,* and *Molly Dolly.* When not appearing in Yiddish, Picon performed in English-language **vaudeville** with the prestigious RKO circuit. In the twenties and thirties, Kalich and Picon made several concert tours of the Yiddish-speaking world, performing in Eastern Europe, Russia, South America, Palestine, South Africa, and throughout Canada and the United States. In Palestine, Picon performed in Yiddish at a time when the country's attitude toward the language was hostile. Picon wrote almost all the lyrics to the songs she sang in Yiddish including, most famously, "Abi Gezunt." She also wrote a column for the Yiddish newspaper *Der Tog.* At the forefront of both the film and radio industries, Picon appeared in the oldest-surviving Yiddish film, *East and West,* in 1923. In 1930, she began performing on the radio, headlining variety shows for Jell-O, Colgate, and Maxwell House Coffee. In 1937 and 1938, Picon filmed two movies in Poland with director Joseph Green—*Yiddle with a Fiddle* and *Mamale.* In addition to being among the best Yiddish films, these works capture Eastern European Jewish life on the eve of its destruction. In 1940, Picon made her Broadway debut as the matriarch in *Morning Star,* Sylvia Regan's play about the Triangle Shirtwaist Factory fire. No longer playing the impish school girl or boy, she was finally cast as a full grown woman. In 1942, she returned to Broadway in an autobiographical play written by Kalich in a mixture of Yiddish and English, entitled *O, What a Life.* After World War II, Picon and her husband toured the displaced persons (DP) camps in Germany, performing Yiddish theater for the Jewish refugees. In 1954, she performed in Yiddish for the Knesset in Israel. In the 1960s, Picon starred in *A Majority of One* in London and in *Milk and Honey* on Broadway. She continued to star in Yiddish musicals, including *The Kosher Widow* and *The Mixed up Honeymoon*.

Although her career thrived on playing young boys and girls well into her forties, most of America came to know Picon as the eccentric old lady—from "Yente the Matchmaker" in ***Fiddler on the Roof*** to "Mrs. Goldfarb" in both *Cannonball Run I* and *Cannonball Run II*. In 1963, she was nominated for a Golden Globe for playing Frank Sinatra's mother in *Come Blow Your Horn*. Picon guest-starred on many television shows, including *Car 54 Where Are You?, Trapper John MD,* and *The Johnny Carson Show.* After her husband's death in 1975, Picon toured with her one-woman show, *Hello Molly,* at the age of 81. She died on April 6, 1992. *See also* **Yiddish**; **Yiddish Film**; **Yiddish Theater**.

Caraid O'Brien

Further Reading: Picon, Molly. *So Laugh a Little*. New York: Paperback Library, 1966. ———, with Jean Grillo., *Molly! An Autobiography.* New York: Simon and Schuster, 1980.

PINSKY, ROBERT (1940–)

Three-time poet laureate of the United States (1997–2000), Robert Pinsky was born in Long Branch, New Jersey to optician Milford Simon Pinsky and Sylvia Eisenberg. He was raised in a kosher home and attended Hebrew school. Pinsky stated, however, that the family was highly secularized and saw the inside of a synagogue only three times a year for the Jewish High Holy Days. In college he struggled with his faith. Although his father's fortunes fell, placing the family in poverty in 1947, Pinsky did attend Rutgers, earning his BA, and later, Stanford University, where he received his PhD. Before taking a position at Boston University, he taught at Wellesley and the University of California. Although his work deals primarily with creative writing, Pinsky never took a writing course. In 1961 he married Ellen Jane Bailey, a clinical psychologist. They have three daughters.

Pinsky's poetry deals with a variety of subjects, including themes that incorporate the ordinary and the mundane. He won awards for *The Inferno of Dante* (1994). Pinsky is the author of 19 books, many of which are collections of poetry, including *The Figured Wheel: New and Collected Poems 1966–1996*. His poem *The Unseen* deals with a dream about the horrors of Auschwitz. His recent book of prose, *Life of David,* about the great Jewish king and poet-warrior, earned him the National Foundation for Jewish Culture's 2006 Jewish Cultural Achievement Award in the Literary Arts. Pinsky likes to think that he is a "people's poet," writing works they can relate to and encouraging reading, writing, and reciting poems in their daily lives. His mastery of poetic meter has earned him praise by fellow poets for following a tradition shared by poet-critics such as Samuel Taylor Coleridge and W. H. Auden. He has also won kudos for taking everyday images and imbuing them with order and profound meaning. Pinsky's poems and literary criticism appear online in the cyber magazine *Slate,* where he serves as poetry editor.

Pinsky recently became more a part of popular culture as a result of his guest-starring role in a 2002 episode of *The Simpsons,* entitled " Little Girl in the Big Ten," and as a guest on the *Colbert Report* (April 2007). Pinsky, a true public advocate of poetry, lives with his wife in Newton's Corner, Massachusetts and teaches a poetry workshop to Boston University graduate students.

Philip Rosen

Further Reading: "The Art of Poetry." *Paris Review* 166, 1997.

PLAIN, BELVA (1919–)

Belva Plain is a bestselling author of mainstream women's fiction. Plain is a third-generation American. She was born in 1919 in New York City to Oscar (a contractor) and Eleanor Offenberg and subsequently moved to New Jersey, where she now resides. Plain graduated from Barnard College with a degree in history and published her first short story at age 25. She was married for 40 years to the late Irving Plain, an ophthalmologist, who died in 1989. They raised their three children in New Jersey, where she has made her home for more than a half-century. While raising her family, she continued writing and publishing short stories in national magazines such as *McCall's, Good Housekeeping, Redbook,* and *Cosmopolitan.*

In 1978 Plain, at the age of 59, published her first novel, *Evergreen.* It quickly topped the *New York Times* bestseller list and remained there for nearly 10 months. *Evergreen* tells the story of Jewish immigrants Iris and Joseph Friedman, following their lives and the lives of their progeny through four tumultuous generations. *Evergreen* was to become the first of four novels in the Werner Family Saga. Other novels in the multigenerational chronicle include *Golden Cup* (1986), *Tapestry* (1988), and *Harvest* (1990). *Evergreen* was turned into a television miniseries in 1985.

Plains's novels are largely multigenerational page-turning epics that feature beautiful, talented, accomplished (and largely Jewish) women whose happiness is endangered by crisis and a long-held, deep, dark secret. In Plain's fiction, the women usually make the decisions about love, marriage, and children that shape the lives of their families.

Plain has written that much of her public fiction is vaguely autobiographical, drawing from her own experiences as well as from stories of her own family, Jewish immigrants who came to the United States in the mid-nineteenth century. Her writing treats Jewish issues as historical social artifacts, used by Plain to enhance or threaten the family life of her characters. Nevertheless, it has been pointed out that the philosophy that characterizes her novels grows from the fundamental Jewish tenet mentioned in the *Golden Cup,* "Choose life that thy children may live."

Belva Plain has written 27 novels which have reached an estimated 30 million readers in more than 20 languages. Her readers purchase them in supermarkets, drugstores, bookstores, and from book clubs such as the Literary Guild and Doubleday. It may not be an exaggeration to call her, as the cover of paperback editions of her works state, "America's most beloved best-selling author."

Kurt F. Stone

Further Reading: Belva Plain Web Site. "A Conversation with Belva Plain." www.randomhouse.com/features/belvaplain. Vespa, Mary. "Philip Roth Beware: Novelist Belva Plain's the New One-Woman Jewish Mother's Defense League." *People,* August 7, 1978.

POMUS, DOC

See **The Brill Building Songwriters**

POPULAR MUSIC

Without the contribution made by American Jews, popular music, as we know it today, would not exist. Popular music mirrors the history, religious beliefs, mores, lifestyles, and interests of those about whom and for whom it were written and performed. These songs have been central in the educative and political processes, emphasizing major social and political issues such as abolition and slavery, women's suffrage, prohibition, and even jingoistic patriotism. Popular songs allowed lower, economically challenged classes to fantasize about places they could never visit. Songs portrayed and exported the "American Dream" to countries around the world.

Jewish contribution to popular music began soon after their immigration to America commenced. The first major composers, John Howard Payne (1791–1852) and Henry Russell (1812–1900) wrote during the 1840s when Jewish presence in America was small, numbering no more than 15,000 in a population of 17 million. With transportation and communication links expanding, the popular song served as more than entertainment; it became educational. With the beginning of burlesque and **vaudeville**, Jewish influence on music increased. David Braham (1838–1905) provided songs for the Gentile vaudeville team Edward "Ned" Harrigan (1845–1911) and Tony Hart (1855–1891) that made fun of new immigrants. Polish-born Jews Joe Weber (1867–1942) and Lew Fields

(1867–1941) continued this comedic tradition with slapstick ridicule of "greenhorns," the new Jewish immigrants, like themselves, coming to America. Vaudeville fostered many of the great American popular music composers including **Irving Berlin** (1888–1989), Jerome Kern (1885–1945), Irving Caesar (1895–1996), and Charles K. Harris (1867–1930).

Publishers made these songs available to large audiences. Immigrant Jews largely dominated the music publishing business and songwriting. Among the more prominent publishers of sheet music was the firm of Marcus Witmark & Sons, established in New York City in 1886. Although Marcus Witmark was the head of the company, from the beginning the company was run by his sons, Isidore (1869–1941), Jay (1873–1950), and Julius (1870–1929). Immigrant Jews who were also prominent in music publishing and songwriting included Charles K. Harris (1867–1930), Joseph Stern (1870–1934), Harry Von Tilzer (1872–1946) and his brother Albert (1878–1956), Leo Feist (1869–1930), and Irving Berlin (1888–1989).This cohort of musical entrepreneurs were among the vanguard of the entertainment enterprise known as **Tin Pan Alley**, a name coined by Jewish journalist-lyricist Monroe Rosenfeld (1861–1918) when interviewing Harry Von Tilzer in New York's Flat Iron Building. To Rosenfeld, the sounds of so many song pluggers playing pianos in small cubicles reminded him of coins dropped on a tin collection plate—hence, the name "Tin Pan Alley."

Charles K. Harris, a Milwaukee Jew, was the first composer of a "million seller." His masterpiece, "After the Ball" (1892) sold over five million copies of sheet music in seven years, two million alone in the first. The most prolific composer of Tin Pan Alley (he claimed to have written 8,000 songs), Harry Gumm (1872–1946) changed his name to honor his mother's hometown of Tilzer, Germany, adopting the pen name of Harry Von Tilzer. Their songs became part of American cultural fabric. Summers are incomplete without "Take Me Out to the Ball Game," (1908) written by Harry's brother Albert, and September requires at least one rendition of "School Days" by Gus Edwards (1878–1945).

Jerome Kern's insistence on the unity of script and song paved the way for those who succeeded him in the Broadway theater, including Irving Berlin and George and Ira Gershwin. Berlin, a Russian-born immigrant born Israel Baline in Temun, Siberia, revolutionized the popular music profession. His songs called men and women to war in World War I and II and popularized two secularized Christian holidays, Christmas and Easter. Berlin also wrote what many consider to be our second national anthem, "God Bless America" (1939), originally written as a song to be performed by soldiers in his World War I musical, *Yip Yip Yaphank* (1918), written to raise money for an enlisted men's social center for Camp Upton on Long Island, New York. Berlin decided that the song was redundant and shelved it until 1939, when radio personality Kate Smith requested a patriotic ballad. Jerome Kern said of him, "Irving Berlin has no place in American music, he IS American music" (Bergreen, 1996).

George Gershwin (1898–1937), born Jacob Gershovitz, and brother Ira Gershwin (1896–1983), born Israel Gershovitz, enlarged the scope of popular music by proving that theatrical and popular music composers could also compose the more serious music of the orchestra hall and that of **jazz**. The quintessential American music idiom, jazz, was enriched by Gershwin when on February 12, 1924 the Aeolioan Hall audience was electrified by *Rhapsody in Blue;* even if most of the critics were not. After a string of successful Broadway musicals, Gershwin wrote his masterwork, *Porgy and Bess,* in 1935.

American popular music benefited enormously from the work of German immigrant and lyricist Gus Kahn, who wrote such songs as "Memories" (1915), "Pretty Baby" (1916), "Yes Sir, That's My Baby" (1922), and "Carolina in the Morning" (1925). Harry Ruby (1895–1974) composed many song hits, including "Who's Sorry Now" (1923), "I Want to be Loved By You" (1928), and "Three Little Words" (1930), but he may be best remembered for the scores to the **Marx**

Brothers' classic films, *Animal Crackers* (1930), *Horse Feathers* (1932), and *Duck Soup* (1933). Sammy Fain, born Samuel Feinberg (1902–1989), wrote many classics including "Let a Smile Be Your Umbrella" (1927), "I'll Be Seeing You" (1938), "Secret Love" (1954), and "Love is a Many-Splendored Thing" (1955); Joseph Meyer (1894–1987) will always be remembered for such songs as the **Eddie Cantor** (1892–1964) signature song "If You Knew Susie" (1925) and "California, Here I Come" (1921), written with the greatest entertainment star of his day, **Al Jolson** (1884–1950).

Many others who went on to great success in Broadway and film careers began in Tin Pan Alley. The son and grandson of two great New York musical entrepreneurs, Oscar Hammerstein II (1885–1960) wrote the lyrics for many of our most treasured musicals including *Showboat* (1925), *Oklahoma* (1943), *Carousel* (1945), and *South Pacific* (1949). The grandson of opera impresario and developer Oscar Hammerstein I (1847–1919), an early competitor of the Metropolitan Opera and builder of Harlem's Apollo Theatre, and son of Willie Hammerstein (1870–1914), theater producer and manager, Hammerstein worked with numerous composers, but his two most meaningful collaborators were Jerome Kern and Richard Rodgers (1902–1988).

When the phrase "Broadway musical" is mentioned, most people immediately think of *The Sound of Music* (1959) or *The King and I* (1951). Both are among the hugely popular productions of Rodgers and Hammerstein. It is less known that Rodgers wrote with many lyricists, including Alan Jay Lerner (1918–1986), Sheldon Harnick (b. 1924), Martin Charnin (b. 1934), and **Stephen Sondheim** (b. 1930). His most prolific partner was Lorenz Hart (1895–1943), lyricist for such classic songs as "With a Song in My Heart" (1929), "The Lady is a Tramp" (1937), "My Funny Valentine" (1937), and "This Can't Be Love" (1938). Their long relationship deteriorated because of Hart's bouts with alcoholism and depression, which prematurely ended his brilliant career.

Almost 70 years after the Depression, E. Y. "Yip" Harburg (1898–1981) is remembered as the writer of the classic political anthem "Brother, Can You Spare a Dime" (1932), but he will always be remembered for his classic film score to the world-beloved *Wizard of Oz,* containing one of the most famous songs ever written, "Somewhere over the Rainbow," a thinly veiled commentary on contemporary events in Europe and the Far East during that troubled time. With Russian-born composer Vernon Duke (1903–1969), born Vladimir Dukelsky, Harburg wrote "April in Paris" (1932).

The World War II years introduced a new generation of composers and lyricists to the American popular music scene. Frank Loesser (1910–1969) built on the accomplishments of World War I songwriters like George M. Cohan (1878–1942) and Irving Berlin in writing patriotic songs for the Second World War, such as "Praise the Lord and Pass the Ammunition" (1942). Loesser also wrote the music for the Broadway classic *Guys and Dolls* (1950) and *The Most Happy Fella* (1956). Jule Styne (1905–1994) composed several classic Broadway shows which included such songs as "Diamonds are a Girl's Best Friend" from *Gentlemen Prefer Blonds* in 1949, the show that catapulted Carol Channing (b. 1921) to stardom, and "People" from the fictionalized biography of **Fanny Brice**, *Funny Girl* (1964), which did the same for **Barbra Streisand** (b. 1942). Styne's most acclaimed score, *Gypsy* (1959), was written with lyricist Stephen Sondheim and included such songs as "Everything's Coming Up Roses" and "You Gotta Have a Gimmick"—the secret to success for a stripper! While the original production was a tour de force for Broadway legend Ethel Merman (1908–1984), it has been revived on Broadway several times, starring English-born Angela Lansbury (b. 1925), television actress Tyne Daly (b. 1946), and Bernadette Peters (b. 1948).

Gypsy's lyricist Stephen Sondheim had previously written the lyrics for ***West Side Story*** (1957) and later for *Do I Hear a Waltz* (1965) with music by Richard Rodgers. Sondheim was the composer/lyricist for many milestone Broadway musicals, including *A Funny Thing Happened on the Way to the Forum* (1962), derived from comedies by the classic Roman playwright Plautus; *Company* (1970), about relationships in contemporary New York; *Follies* (1972), the history of a Broadway theater soon to be razed and the reunion of its former dancers and performers; and *A Little Night Music* (1973), based on Ingmar Bergman's film *Smiles of a Summer Night* (1955), set in turn-of-the-century Sweden. The score, written in waltz time, contained Sondheim's most popular song, "Send in the Clowns."

West Side Story, which Sondheim wrote with **Leonard Bernstein** (1918–1990)—whose previous musicals had included *On the Town* (1944) with its outstanding song "New York, New York" and *Wonderful Town* (1953)—included a number of outstanding songs, including "Tonight," "Maria," and "I Feel Pretty." Parts of *West Side Story* were reproduced in the self-created musical retrospective by the choreographer **Jerome Robbins** in *Broadway* (1989).

Sammy Cahn (1913–1993), the lyricist for *Funny Girl,* also wrote the lyrics for such popular hits as "Bei Mir Bist Du Schoen" (1937). It set new English words to the **Yiddish** song by Sholom Secunda, "Papa, Won't You Dance with Me?" (1947) from Cahn's first musical *High Button Shoes,*, which starred vaudevillian and comedian Phil Silvers (1911–1985), who was soon nationally recognized for his work in comedy on **television**. Cahn wrote songs for films and television as well, most notably "Three Coins in the Fountain" (1954), for which he and Jule Styne received the Academy Award for best song, and "Love and Marriage" with Jimmy Van Heusen (1913–1990) for singer Frank Sinatra (1915–1998), from a television version of *Our Town.*

The 1940s and early 1950s introduced several composers and lyricists who went on to great success. Alan Jay Lerner (1918–1986), son of the Lerner Stores family, and Frederick Loewe (1904–1989), the son of a prominent Viennese opera singer and cantor, wrote such Broadway musicals as *Brigadoon* (1947), with songs "Almost Like Being in Love" and "Heather on the Hill," and their masterful musicalization of the George Bernard Shaw (1852–1950) play *Pygmalion* (1913). *My Fair Lady* (1956), which starred Rex Harrison (1908–1990) and Julie Andrews (b. 1935), contained numerous standards, including "Get Me to the Church On Time," "I Could Have Danced All Night," and "On the Street Where You Live." Other Lerner and Loewe musical successes include *Camelot* (1960), the story of King Arthur and the Knights of the Round Table, which starred Julie Andrews, Richard Burton (1925–1984), and Robert Goulet (b. 1933), as well as both the film and musical of *Gigi* (1958), taken from the Collette novel.

Richard Adler (b.1921) and Jerry Ross (1926–1955) began writing popular music with their hit "Rags to Riches" (1953), but completed their careers together writing the hit Broadway shows *Pajama Game* (1954) and *Damn Yankees* (1955) including hit songs "Hey There" (1954) and "You Gotta Have Heart" (1955). Adler was to continue his career with several Broadway shows including most successfully *Fosse* (1999), a retrospective of director-choreographer Bob Fosse (1927–1987).

Jerry Herman (b. 1932) is responsible for many hugely successful musicals, as well as several that broke new ground in sensitive issues. Among these was *Milk and Honey* (1961), a tribute to the then 13-year-old state of Israel that starred Yiddish theater performer **Molly Picon** (1898–1992) and opera star Robert Weede (1903–1972); *Hello Dolly* (1964), which starred the irrepressible Carol Channing (b. 1921) portraying matchmaker Dolly Levi; and *La Cage Aux Folles* (1983), based on the French movie of the same title that made musical comedy history by featuring a partnered male couple as the show's protagonists, writing the so-called "gay anthem" "I Am What I Am."

Charles Strouse (b. 1928) worked with several partners to write such popular Broadway shows as *Bye, Bye Birdie* (1960), a tongue-in-cheek tribute to an Elvis Presley-like singer whose popularity invades a stereotypical Midwest town, and *Applause* (1970), a musicalization of the Bette Davis film *All About Eve* (1950) that starred Lauren Bacall (b. 1924). Strouse's greatest hit was the musical *Annie* (1977), based on the comic-strip character Little Orphan Annie. While Strouse has written many songs, none reached the success of Annie's "uber-optimistic" anthem "The Sun Will Come Out 'Tomorrow.' "

John Kander (b. 1927) and lyricist Fred Ebb (1932–2007) were responsible for such dramatic/musical theatrical productions as *Cabaret* (1966), which used pre-Nazi Berlin as its setting for themes of anti-Semitism, homophobia, drugs, and xenophobia; *Zorba* (1968) was taken from the Kazantzakis novel *Zorba the Greek; Chicago* (1975) satirized the gangster 1920s in the Windy City; and *Kiss of the Spider Woman* (1992) was a musical retelling of the story of political repression in South America. Several of Kander and Ebb's musicals have been revived, achieving even greater success than when first produced, and their musical *Chicago* received the Oscar for best film at the Academy Awards in 2003. Kander and Ebb have contributed prominently to the specialty music field, writing, producing, and directing one-person shows, especially for Liza Minnelli (b. 1946).

Jerry Bock (b. 1928) and Sheldon Harnick (b. 1924) are Tony Award- and Pulitzer Prize-winning songwriters. Their first successful Broadway musical, *Fiorello!* (1959), about New York City's diminutive mayor Fiorello La Guardia (1882–1947), earned both the Tony Award for best musical and the Pulitzer Prize. Their huge joint success came in 1964 when they wrote the score for ***Fiddler on the Roof***, at the time the longest-running musical in Broadway history. Their Jewish-themed musicals continued with *The Apple Tree* (1966), retelling **Jules Feiffer**'s (b. 1929) view of the Creation story, and *The Rothschilds* (1970), about the international Jewish banking family.

Marvin Hamlisch (b. 1944), Broadway composer and film music arranger, received great acclaim for his Academy Award-winning score, which he adapted from the music of Scott Joplin, for the film *The Sting* (1973). His first Broadway musical, *A Chorus Line* (1975), became the longest-running musical in Broadway history, only to be revived thirty years later for another successful run. Hamlisch's songs include *A Chorus Line*'s "What I Did for Love" and the Academy Award-winning "The Way We Were" (1973).

While not popularly known as a songwriter, the highly successful comedian, writer, director, and actor **Mel Brooks** (b. 1926), born Melvin Kaminsky, must be included in this article of popular music writers. The composer, lyricist, and producer for the most Tony Award-honored Broadway musical in history, *The Producers* (2001), Brooks has written music for several of his films, including *The Producers* (1968), *Blazing Saddles* (1974), *History of the World: Part 1* (1981), and *Spaceballs* (1987). His most recent Broadway musical, *Young Frankenstein,* opened in 2007. He is one of the very few who has received Emmy Awards, Grammy Awards, Oscars, and Tony Awards for his creative efforts.

Cy Coleman, born Seymour Kaufman (1929–2004), a well-known jazz musician, wrote many highly regarded Broadway musicals, including *Wild Cat* (1960), which starred comedienne-television performer Lucille Ball (1911–1989). The musical included the hit song "Hey Look Me Over"; *Sweet Charity* (1966) with Gwen Verdon included "Big Spender"; *Seesaw* (1973), *City of Angels* (1990), and *The Will Rogers Follies* (1991). Coleman was a Tony- and Oscar-winning composer. His several-time partner, lyricist Dorothy Fields (1905–1974)—the daughter of vaudevillian Lew Fields (1867–1941) of Weber and Fields fame—was a respected songwriter before collaborating with Coleman. Among her most famous songs are "I Can't Give You Anything But Love, Baby" (1928) and "On the Sunny Side of the Street" (1930). With Coleman she wrote one of her standards, "If My Friends Could See Me Now" (1966) from *Sweet Charity.*

The music scene of the 1950s and 1960s experienced an enormous growth in songwriters representing varied musical genres. Hal David

(b. 1921) and Burt Bacharach (b. 1928) wrote popular songs such as "One Less Bell to Answer" (1967), "I'll Never Fall in Love Again" (1968), "Raindrops Keep Falling on My Head" (1969), and "Close to You" (1970), as well as their successful Broadway show *Promises, Promises* (1968). Another big song-writing team was Max C. Freedman (1893–1962) and James Myers (1919–2001), whose 1953 classic "Rock Around the Clock" contributed to the rock and roll music of that decade. Far and away, however, the most successful and widely known Jewish songwriting team of the 1950s were Jerry Leiber (b. 1933) and Mike Stoller (b. 1933), who wrote such classics for Elvis Presley (1935–1977) as "Hound Dog" (1956), "Lovin' You" (1957), "Treat Me Nice" (1957), and "Jail House Rock" (1957). Songs for other performers included "Yakkety Yak" (1958), "Is That All There Is" (1969) for Peggy Lee (1920–2002), and "Love Potion #9" (1959). Their influence was widespread, from the Motown composers to the Beatles. They were inducted into the Songwriters Hall of Fame (1985) and Rock and Roll Hall of Fame (1987).

The 1960s saw a return to the musical themes of political, social, and cultural upheavals as found in the post-World War I-Depression period. With the growth of political protest songs came meaningful works by Jewish songwriters and performers. Among the most important was **Bob Dylan** (b. 1941), born Robert Zimmerman, with such songs as "Blowin' in the Wind" (1962), "Mr. Tambourine Man" (1964), "The Times, They Are a Changin' " (1964), and "Like a Rollin' Stone" (1965). Dylan wrote his musical commentaries on the issues of his day—racial bigotry, the arms race and the Cold War, Vietnam and war in general. Dylan contributed to the politicization of popular music that would continue for the next half-century, to the present time. **Neil Diamond** (b. 1941) contributed such songs as "I Got the Feelin' " (1966), "I'm A Believer" (1966), "Song Sung Blue" (1972), and a widely successful updating of the early **Al Jolson** film ***The Jazz Singer*** (1980), with Diamond as composer-lyricist and onscreen star. Neil Sedaka (b. 1939), who began writing in the 1950s, had numerous song hits, but he had huge impact in the early 1960s with such ballads as "Happy Birthday, Sweet Sixteen" (1961), "Breakin' Up is Hard to Do" (1962), "Calendar Girl" (1962), "Laughter in the Rain" (1975), and "Love Will Keep Us Together" (1975) with Howard Greenfield (b. 1942). Sedaka's career has stretched over five decades with his ability to update his hits of the 1950s and 1960s into the different styles of 50 years later. Sedaka was one of the several great New York-born Jewish songwriters who wrote at the **Brill Building**.

Rock and Roll's Tin Pan Alley! Spouse songwriting teams included Gerry Goffin (b. 1939) and Carole King (b. 1942), whose songs include "Go Away Little Girl" (1962), "One Fine Day" (1963), and "Natural Woman" (1967). King has been hugely successful with her own songs, including "You've Got a Friend" (1971) and "You Light Up My Life" (1974). Barry Mann (b. 1939) and Cynthia Weill (b. 1942) wrote such classics as "You've Lost That Lovin' Feelin' " (1965), and "On Broadway" (1963); Jeff Barry (b. 1938) and Ellie Greenwich (b. 1940) wrote "Leader of the Pack" (1963), and "I'm a Believer" for the Monkees in 1966. Barry and Greenwich discovered Neil Diamond and wrote several huge hits for him, including "Kentucky Woman" in 1966. Another woman who looms large in the songwriters of the 1960s and following is Carly Simon (b. 1945), of the Simon and Schuster publishing family. Her hits have included "You're So Vain" (1971) and "Anticipation" (1973), the appeal of which fostered a very popular television advertising campaign. The theater world was shocked on January 25, 1996 to learn of the death of Jonathan Larson (1960–1996) who had written the score, lyrics, and libretto for the groundbreaking musical *Rent,* a modern downtown New York treatment of *La Boheme*. While Larson only wrote two musicals that were actually produced, *Rent* is so important that his biography is included in this article. Born in Westchester in a committed Jewish family, Larson later studied theater at Adelphi University and began to compose for student productions. The recipient of both a Richard Rodgers Award and the Stephen Sondheim Award, Larson's promise would never be reached. Tragically, he died the night before *Rent* was to open off-Broadway. After a hugely successful run, the show was moved to the Nederlander Theatre on Broadway. Larson received posthumously the Pulitzer Prize for Drama, Tony Awards for Best Musical, Best Score and Book, and similar awards from the NY Drama Circle and Outer Critics. The show has run for almost 5000 performances, making it one of the top 10 musicals in Broadway history. It seems appropriate that the last biography included in this article of Popular Music should be a third-generation American Jewish songwriter. Adam Guettel (b. 1965) has an extraordinary theatrical pedigree. He is the son of Broadway composer Mary Rodgers (b. 1931), composer of, among others, *Once Upon A Mattress* (1959), *Working* (1978), and the *Madwoman of Central Park West* (1979), a one-woman show written for Phyllis Newman (b. 1933). Guettel is the grandson of Broadway scion Richard Rodgers, half of the Rodgers and Hart and the Rodgers and Hammerstein partnerships. Guettel has written several Broadway shows, with two most memorable—*Floyd Collins, Love's Fire* (1996) and *The Light in the Piazza* (2005). In spite of mixed reviews, this dazzling show received the Tony Award for Best Original Score and for Best Orchestrations.

The enormity of the contribution by Jews to American popular music can only be understood when realizing that the names and songs included are only the peak of a creative mountain that contains hundreds more individuals and thousands of songs. Over the past 175 years this music contributed profoundly to American culture and the image of America around the world. Though Jerome Kern wrote, "Irving Berlin has no place in American music; he IS American music" for a specific person, that statement might be accurately paraphrased: "American Jews have no place in American music; they ARE American music." *See also* **Berlin, Irving**; **Bernstein, Leonard**; **Brooks, Mel**; **Dylan, Bob**; **Rock and Roll**; **Sondheim, Stephen**; **Theater**; **Tin Pan Alley**; ***West Side Story.***

Kenneth Kanter

Further Reading: Bergreen, Laurence. *As Thousands Cheer: The Life of Irving Berlin.* Cambridge, MA: Da Capo Press, 1996. Ewen, David. *All the Years of American Popular Music.* Englewood Cliffs, NJ: Prentice-Hall, 1977. Green, Stanley. *The World of Musical Comedy.* South Brunswick, NJ: Barnes, 1976. Kanter, Kenneth A. *The Jews on Tin Pan Alley,* New York: Ktav, 1982. Norton, Richard. *A Chronology of American Musical Theatre.* New York: Oxford University Press, 2002. Starr, Larry, and Christopher Waterman. *American Popular Music.* New York: Oxford University Press, 2003.

POPULAR PSYCHOLOGY

On May 3, 1908, **Sigmund Freud** wrote to his faithful colleague, Karl Abraham, defending the anointing of Carl Jung as his "successor and crown prince." Marshaling all of his considerable rhetorical charms, Freud explained to Abraham that psychoanalysis desperately needed the Gentile Jung to be its front man to ensure that his creation, psychoanalysis, would not become "a Jewish national affair."

Had the professor lived to witness the heady days of the mid-twentieth-century American psychotherapy profession, he would have *plotzed.* For the surveys of the 1960s were all quite uniform in their findings: some 50 percent of clinical psychologists, psychoanalysts, psychiatrists, and social workers were Jewish. Nobody was kvetching, of course. After all, the famous 1962 Midtown Manhattan Study plainly showed that Jews outnumbered Gentiles by more than three to one as seekers of one form or another of the talking cure.

The reasons for this interesting turn of events can be attributed to a wide variety of historical, cultural, sociological, and psychological causes. For one thing, these figures were likely due to the fact that the New York Jewish population tapped by the Manhattan study were predominately Eastern European immigrants and their offspring. Their high prevalence rates for emotional distress would reflect matters of Jewish socialization and the sociological strains to which these generations had been subject.

Even earlier, in 1924, the Jewish American psychiatrist Isadore Wechsler attributed the psychological stresses of Jews to social pressures, an overemphasis on educational success, overly close family ties, with their intimate links to guilt feelings and stern religious values, which provided few of the escapist avenues found in the more mystical promises and rituals of Christianity. Jews were viewed as locked in a struggle between their overdeveloped conscience and the reality of their situation, which called for a tenacious will to survive against tough environmental odds. Conflicts about assimilation hung heavy over this early cohort of Jewish Americans.

Later in the century, the American (Gentile) psychiatrist Karl Menninger wrote an article entitled *The Genius of the Jew in Psychiatry* (1959), in which he proposed a list of values that Jews have imbued and which make them exemplary healers and eloquent spokespersons concerning the human condition. The attributes Menninger set forth included identification with the suffering of others; separateness that has invoked curiosity about how people behave; a sensitivity to insecurity, producing dubiousness about human motives; an intense pleasure from the verbal expression of emotions; and an analytic stance towards all phenomena.

If we add to this line-up factors such as Jewish marginality and a press for upward mobility; an abhorrence of discrimination; the intellectual rigor of Talmudic pilpul (intellectual hair-splitting); the Enlightenment tradition of self-examination; the *mame-loshen*'s (Yiddish language) clinical and social uses of irony character delineation; and insight into the follies of human behavior, we can better understand what led Jews to become so important in shaping America's "therapeutic culture."

Freud and the American Unconscious. In American popular culture, Freud has been viewed as the promoter of new and daring theories of sexuality. The popularization of his concepts has been abetted by the striking and novel subject matter of psychoanalysis, its dreams, complex parent-child relationship, and "suppressed desires," which must be confronted, understood, and managed to achieve mental health. For more than 100 years, the analyst's role has been that of a guide during periods of changing mores—a guide that helps assuage, rather than exacerbate guilt.

When Freud made his visit to America, in 1909, the nation's most important psychologist, William James, greeted him with the prophetic words, "Yours is the psychology of the future!" Despite this fulsome praise, Freud himself remained distressed by his growing popularity in America. The spread of psychoanalysis in the New World, he rightly came to believe, produced knowledge that was not profound, critical, or accurate. As he wrote to his acolyte and biographer, Ernest Jones, "America is a mistake; a gigantic mistake, it is true, but none-the-less a mistake" (circa 1919; Jones, 1955).

Nevertheless, American culture quickly began to develop an interpretation of psychoanalysis to suit its own needs. This paved the way for the encouragement of personal improvement and productivity, as well as the development of an approach-avoidance attitude concerning the mysterious unconscious. The American unconscious was at once perceived to be a private realm and an unlimited, fathomless territory for psychological exploration and manipulation.

This hybrid American conception of the unconscious made therapeutic transformation become at once *more* straightforward and *more* mysterious, thus necessitating that it be under the control of a trained cadre of medical experts using a new, complex scientific technology. The mental health professions began their hegemony over the inner world.

The Cult of Self-Improvement. By the turn of the twentieth century, Americans were already ardent readers of self-help and improvement literature. For example, self-control and "nervousness" were notable concerns, and among the popular books of 1920 was *The Nervous Housewife,* penned by the Jewish psychiatrist Abraham Myerson. The various mental health experts of the time focused their attention on such cultural bugbears as feelings of anxiety, depression, exhaustion, and boredom.

Since the end of World War II, the pursuit of self-improvement has become a central feature of American life, and personal "growth" and the search for pleasure and fulfillment have been anointed as among the most valued aspects of life. In turn, these desires have brought forth the expansion of enterprises ministering to these needs, such as the cosmetic, diet, and plastic surgery industries, as well as the self-improvement industry that includes professional psychotherapy, pop psychology, and pop religion.

Jewish Eytses-Gebers *(Advisers).* From the 1960s to the present, the sure sign that we inhabit a "psychological society" has been the proliferation of self-help manuals that crowd bookstore shelves and present themselves by the hundreds on Amazon.com. These tomes assure us that our marriages can be bettered; our sex lives raised to new levels of hedonistic exaltation; our shyness, procrastination, fear of flying, or "complexes" overcome; our ability to "get along with others" improved; our children brought to love, honor, and obey us; our aging transcended; and even our deaths made "meaningful."

Another extremely popular helpmeet for the insatiable psychological needs of Americans has been the newspaper advice column, and both of these self-help productions have been very much a Jewish affair.

Some of the most famous *eytses-gebers* of the past 100 years are **Abraham Cahan**, the editor of the ***Jewish Daily Forward,*** who introduced the "Bintel Brief" ("Bundle of Letters") in 1906, providing a venue for aiding the immigrant Jewish masses to adjust to life in the New World; psychologist Dr. Joseph Jastrow, who hosted a syndicated column in the *Philadelphia Public Ledger* from 1927 to 1932 entitled "Keeping Mentally Fit"; Israel Lutsky, the "Jewish Philosopher," who from 1931 to the mid-1960s had a fervent following, despite the fact that the "letters" to which he responded were actually written by his copywriter!; Dr. Rose Fransblau, a psychologist with a 1935 PhD from Columbia, whose *New York Post* column "Human Relations" (1949–1976) offered Freudian-style advice for her readers' problems; "**Abigail Van Buren**" (Pauline Esther Friedman)—Friedman wrote for decades as "Dear Abby," gathering a faithful following of millions of readers of her widely syndicated newspaper column; and "Ann Landers" (Esther Pauline Friedman), the twin sister of Pauline Esther, who spent 40 years providing witty and sarcastic advice. Ann was more outspoken than her sister in opposing racism and anti-Semitism. She passed away in 2000. There is Dr. **Joyce Brothers** (Joyce Diane Bauer), who became an overnight celebrity in 1955 when she won the prize on *The $65,000 Question* game show as an expert on boxing. She wrote a monthly column in *Good Housekeeping* for four decades, as well as appearing on radio and television and in the movies. She holds a PhD in psychology from Columbia; **Dr. Ruth Westheimer** was born in Germany and sent by her parents to Switzerland at age 12. The parents perished at the hands of the Nazis. Westheimer went to Israel and joined the Haganah during the War of Independence, then went to Paris and on to New York. She began her radio career in 1980 with the program *Sexually Speaking* and has since appeared in various movies and television roles. In 2007 she resuscitated the "Bintel Brief" in the English language *Forward;* Dr. Laura (Laura Catherine Schlessinger) was born in 1947 and hosts a cultural conservative radio call-in program. She is a "born again Jew" (on her father's side; her mother was Italian), and, with much fanfare began practicing as an Orthodox Jew in 1999. She abandoned her practice in 2003, explaining that she felt no connection with God!

Three Khakhomim *(Jewish Wise Men) Who Enriched the American Therapeutic Culture.* Psychologist Abraham Maslow (1908–1970 was one of the founders of humanistic psychology. During the 1960s and 1970s he espoused the concepts of "self-actualization," "peak experiences," "creativity," "self-expression," and "human potential" as part of a counterculture crusade against all the institutions that thwarted the individual and blocked what he called "the highest reaches of human nature."

Psychoanalyst Erich Fromm (1900–1980) came to the United States as a refugee from the Nazis in 1934. Unlike Freud, his interests were in social, political, and cultural issues and their impact on individual personality. He also did something few psychoanalysts have done—he wrote openly and knowledgeably about his Jewishness and his upbringing in an Orthodox family and how it significantly informed and shaped his psychological theories. He wrote a series of highly successful books in an Old Testament prophetic voice and was a leading social critic who decried the wickedness of the times and pointed to an urgent need for redemption through a return to justice and love.

Fromm had a significant impact on American culture of the 1940s and 1950s, enjoying a large audience among lay persons, especially in his highlighting postwar America as a society in which style was valued over substance, opportunism over loyalty, salesmanship over integrity, and mobility over stability. For Fromm, freedom was an aspect of human nature that we either embrace or escape.

Psychoanalyst Erik Homburger Erikson (1902–1994) arrived in America as a refugee in 1933. He was most famous for his book *Childhood and Society,* which lauded the American character and introduced the concept of an "identity crisis," involving young people's "inability to settle on an occupational identity." His description of this state of being had a great impact on the development of decades of American students, while certain other of the terms he introduced, such as "ego identity" and "moratorium," have passed from the technical literature into the vernacular.

Erikson believed that individuals needed to protect themselves from the seductive power of mass conformity, and he saw the ideal of "ego integrity" as the highest stage of character development. Erikson personally demonstrated his ego integrity when on the faculty of the University of California at Berkeley, during the McCarthy era, he refused to sign a loyalty oath. His statement on why he could not do so in good conscience is one of the most moving defenses of academic freedom ever penned.

Coda. Dr. Freud would not have approved of American's love affair with popular psychology. His admonition to his American front man, A. A. Brill, suggests that the lofty goal of public enlightenment may not be the primary aim of the producers of such literature: "You have submitted far too much to the big vices of America," the professor lamented, "the greed and the respect of public opinion."

Leslie Rabkin

Further Reading: Hale, Nathan G., Jr. *Freud and the Americans.* New York: Oxford University Press, 1971. Heinze, Andrew R. *Jews and the American Soul.* Princeton University Press, 2004. Jones, E. *Sigmund Freud: Life and Work. Vol 2: The Years of Maturity 1901–1919.* London: Hogarth Press, 1955. Zaretsky, Eli. *Secrets of the Soul: A Social and Cultural History of Psychoanalysis.* New York: Vintage, 2005.

PORTMAN, NATALIE (1981–)

In the third version of his "Chanukah Song," **Adam Sandler** sings: "Chanukah is the Festival of Lights . . . Hey, Natalie Portmanica it's time to celebrate Chanukah." If there's a Jewish symbol that relates to Natalie Portman, it might as well be the Menorah, an extendable chandelier around which symmetrical branches bring a sense of balance, reciprocity, and the infinite. From Luc Besson to Milos Forman, via Michael Mann, George Lucas, and Mike Nichols, actress Natalie Portman continues to enjoy an extraordinary career. In a little more than a decade, Portman has grown with every experience, relying on strong roots and wide branches.

Natalie Portman has said that although she "really love(s) the States . . . my heart's in Jerusalem. That's where I feel at home" (Heath, 2002). She is an only child and very close to her parents, who are often seen with her at her film premieres. Natalie Portman was born Natalie Hershlag in

A 2008 photo brings together two of the most popular actresses in film today, who also happen to be Jewish, Natalie Portman and Scarlett Johansson. The picture was taken in Berlin at the screening of *The Other Boleyn Girl.* [AP Photo]

Jerusalem to Avner and Shelley Stevens Hershlag. Her father is an Israeli medical doctor, and her mother was born in the United States; she is a homemaker who serves as Natalie's agent. Natalie later took the last name of her maternal grandmother. Her father's parents made aliya (immigrated) to Israel from Poland, and her paternal grandfather's parents died in Auschwitz. A surgeon at Hadassah Hospital, Avner Hershlag moved to the United States in 1984 in order to pursue his medical training. The family lived in Washington D.C., where they enrolled their daughter in the Charles E. Smith Jewish Day School. They then moved to Connecticut, before settling in Syosset, New York in 1990.

Natalie's mother enrolled her in dance classes as well as encouraging her interest in theater, while Natalie's father exposed her to his work in the delivery room and by taking her to medical conferences. Portman's Jewish education continued in New York as she attended the Solomon Schechter High School of Glen Cove, then attending Syosset High School, graduating in June of 1999. Portman reportedly had to miss the premiere of *Star Wars: Episode I* so she could study for her high school final exams. An excellent student, education has always been important to Natalie Portman, who has stated that "I'd rather be smart than be a movie star," indicating that her goal was to graduate from college even if it ruined her acting career.

After high school, Portman enrolled at Harvard University, where she graduated with a bachelor's degree in psychology in 2003. As a Harvard undergraduate, she did research for Harvard Professor **Alan Dershowitz**'s book *The Case for Israel* (2003). In 2005, Portman pursued graduate studies at Hebrew University in Jerusalem and then returned to Harvard, where she was also a research assistant in Dr. Stephen M. Kosslyn's psychology lab and made a guest-lecturer appearance in the terrorism and counterterrorism course at Columbia University in early March of 2006, discussing themes from her film *V for Vendetta* (2006). In addition to Hebrew and English, Portman has studied or can speak French, Japanese, and German. She has recently been learning to speak Arabic. She also understands Spanish.

Portman's professional career was inspired by the work of Bob Fosse, and she initially wanted to become a dancer. Her mother encouraged her to model and study acting. In 1991, a Revlon representative noticed Natalie in a pizza parlor and signed her for an advertising campaign. At that time that she adopted her maternal grandmother's name, Portman.

Natalie Portman's film career began in 1994 with her lead role in *The Professional.* This was followed by a succession of films, including *Heat* (1995), *Beautiful Girls* (1996), *Mars Attack* (1996), and *Everyone Says I Love You* (1996). The George Lucas *Star Wars* trilogy made Portman an instant Hollywood star and included *Star Wars: Episode I—The Phantom Menace* (1999), *Star Wars: Episode II—Attack of the Clones* (2002), *Star Wars: Episode III—Revenge of the Sith* (2005). Portman has also acted in *Anywhere But Here* (1999); *Cold Mountain* (2003); *Garden State* (2004); *Closer* (2004), for which Portman was nominated for an Oscar for Best Supporting Actress in a Drama but won the Golden Globe Award—Best Supporting Actress—Motion Picture; *V for Vendetta* (2006), for which she won a Saturn Award for Best Actress; *Everyone Says I Love You* (2006); *The Darjeeling Express* (2007); and *The Other Boleyn Girl* and *Brothers* (2008).

Portman's stage career includes *The Seagull* (2001). She made her mark on Broadway in *The Diary of Anne Frank* in 1997. The play has special meaning to Portman because of the loss of relatives in the Holocaust. Though her parents were not religious or involved in their local synagogue, Portman has remarked that the first time she "felt comfortable in a religious institution was in college, because campus Hillel was inclusive. And it's nice having a Shabbat dinner every week" (Pogrebin, 2005). Portman says that she's always fasted on Yom Kippur and continued to do so in college. As for marriage, she says that "a priority for me is definitely that I'd raise my kids Jewish," but she doesn't think it necessarily takes two Jews to maintain the continuity of a Jewish family. For Portman, "the most important concept in Judaism is that you can break any law of Judaism to save a life . . . Which means to me that humans are more important than Jews are to me . . . or than being Jewish is to me" (ibid.). *See also* **Film.**

Steve Krief

Further Reading: Heath, Chris. "The Private Life of Natalie Portman." *Rolling Stone,* June 2002. Pogrebin, Abigail. "Natalie Portman." *Stars of David.* Broadway Books, 2005.

POTOK, CHAIM (1929–2002)

With a repertoire of fiction and nonfiction, Chaim Potok is considered one of the greatest American writers. Potok spent his writing career resisting the title "American Jewish writer" because he never saw critics using a similar title for Protestant or Catholic writers.

On February 17, 1929 in New York City, Benjamin and Molly (née Friedman) Potok had their first of four children. This child was named Herman Harold Potok, though Benjamin and Molly called him Chaim Hersch, and he later took the name Chaim. Mrs. Potok was a descendant of the Reizener Hasidic dynasty and Benjamin a descendant of a Hasidic family, so they raised their children in a deeply Orthodox, bordering on the Hasidic, home in the Bronx. Potok attended a yeshiva and completed a degree in English literature, summa cum laude, in 1950 at Yeshiva University, New York. In 1954 he completed his master's in Hebrew Letters (MHL) at the Jewish Theological Seminary of America, New York. This latter degree was a method for improving his writing by gaining a more holistic understanding of Judaism.

Upon completion of the MHL, Potok was ordained as a Conservative rabbi and joined the army as a chaplain, serving in Korea. Potok also received a doctorate in secular philosophy at the University of Pennsylvania in 1965. La Sierra University granted Potok an honorary Ddoctorate in humane letters in 1997.

In 1943, Potok read Evelyn Waugh's *Brideshead Revisited,* which changed his life. For Potok, writing was as much a part of life as breathing. He wrote for self-satisfaction, rather than for an audience. As a teenager without money to buy paper, Potok composed on the bedroom walls. When he was about 17, the editor of the *Atlantic Monthly* requested he write a novel to publish because they were so impressed by a story of Potok's.

The Chosen (1967), Potok's first published novel, received the Edward Lewis Wallant Award. He wrote it while writing a doctoral dissertation about Salomon Maimon, an eighteenth-century philosopher. Publishing 13 more books, 5 plays, and a screenplay, Potok won other awards, including the Athenaeum Prize for *The Promise,* the National Book Award for Fiction for *The Gift of Asher Levi,* the Barrymore Award for Outstanding New Play for *The Chosen,* the O'Henry Award for his short story "Moon," as well as the Jewish Cultural Achievement Award and the Delaware Valley Mensa award for "Creative Use of Intelligence to Benefit Others" in 1988.

The first novel Potok wrote was not published until 1992. It was given the title of *I Am Clay* and is based on Potok's experiences in Korea. In addition, Potok wrote about theology. Potok edited two different volumes of Torah commentary, one for the Jewish Publication Society (JPS) and the other for the Conservative Judaism movement.

In 1966, Potok became editor in chief of JPS and then special projects editor. Until then, JPS's publication philosophy had been one of publishing exclusively scholarly material. Potok reworked that vision to include fiction. Under his direction, JPS published a Torah commentary, considered one of the best.

Potok was the scholar-in-residence at Har Zion, Philadelphia and taught at the University of Pennsylvania, Philadelphia, as well as at Bryn Mawr College, Philadelphia, and Johns Hopkins University, Baltimore. *See also* **Literature**.

Mara W. Cohen Ioannides

Further Reading: Abrahamson, Edward A. *Chaim Potok.* Boston: Twayne, 1986. Potok, Chaim. *Wanderings: Chaim Potok's History of the Jews.* New York: Knopf, 1978. Walden, Dan, ed. "The World of Chaim Potok." *Studies in American Jewish Literature* 4 (special issue), 1985.

R

RADIO

As with any American mass medium, the relationship between the medium and American minorities is often fraught with troubling histories, grotesque stereotypes, and other problematic encounters. The relationship between Jews and the American mass media, in general, has been troubled from the very beginning, as Jews have long made important contributions to American popular cultures and have often been intimately involved with the media that transmits culture.

In film, the Hollywood moguls profoundly influenced the growth and development of Hollywood. In American musical theater, Jews represented a majority of composers and songwriters. American popular music, as well, had a disproportionate percentage of American Jews in its rosters. The same prominence of Jewish influence is found with radio.

Exploring this relationship in any depth or sophistication requires us to establish distinctions between three groups of Jews involved with radio. First were the Jews who worked in radio, but rarely appeared on radio. This group includes people like **David Sarnoff** and **William Paley**, who established NBC and CBS, respectively. The second group includes Jewish performers on radio—people like **Jack Benny**, **Al Jolson**, **Eddie Cantor**, or Arthur Tracey, all of whom appeared on radio, although they were not necessarily explicitly identified as Jewish performers. And, finally, the third group features primarily Jewish characters, played by any number of Jewish and non-Jewish performers. A handful of performers could be included in two of these categories, and others, like Gertrude Berg, transcended all three.

Another helpful distinction to make at this point is that between English language radio and **Yiddish** radio; although both types of entertainment played over the same radio, and both attracted Jewish audiences, they operated in relative independence of one another. Mainstream, English-language, largely network-based radio generally operated without consideration for Yiddish (or Italian, German, Polish, or any other immigrant tongue), while Yiddish radio played to an immigrant audience with the safe assumption that nobody other than Jewish immigrants would understand, let alone care to listen.

So, with these distinctions in place, let us proceed to discuss each group in turn.

Jews Behind the Scenes. The three most influential Jews in radio who rarely appeared on radio were William Paley, David Sarnoff, and Gertrude Berg. Born in Russia, Sarnoff immigrated with his family at age nine and showed entrepreneurial spirit practically from the start. He began selling newspapers and soon bought his own newsstand. As a teenager, he worked for the American Marconi Company and shortly after landed a job managing the radio station at Wanamaker's department store, one of the most popular early radio stations. When the American Marconi Company split from its parent company in 1919, Sarnoff helped transition the new company and develop it as the Radio Corporation of America (RCA). Under Sarnoff's leadership, RCA bought up a handful of independent broadcast stations and in 1926, RCA launched the first national network. Sarnoff assumed the presidency of RCA in 1930 and oversaw its growth and development over the next few decades.

Sarnoff's counterpart at CBS, William Paley, was born in Philadelphia to a relatively successful family. Through fortuitous circumstances, Paley entered the radio business in the late 1920s, as the sponsor of a radio program. In 1928, he assumed control of the Columbia Phonograph Broadcasting System, which soon shortened its name to CBS, and hardly one month later, Paley oversaw the debut of CBS's national network. Paley was known for his hands-on style, which many of his employees found difficult to tolerate. But Paley also prided himself on the quality of his networks' offerings, earning CBS the monicker the "Tiffany Network" to indicate the network's high standards.

Gertude Berg, whose program *The Goldbergs* debuted on NBC in 1929, was a one-woman radio production team, and she oversaw every step of the production process from scriptwriting to sponsorship agreements to performing. Berg, who wrote many of the program's scripts herself, also played "Molly Goldberg," the matron of the program's fictional family. *The Goldbergs* aired five nights a week and, in Jewish dialect, told the story of a Jewish family living in the Bronx (though they eventually moved to the suburbs). More important, however, was the program's popularity and subsequently, Berg's power at the network.

Jews on the Air. Berg's performance as Molly Goldberg established the stereotype of the Jewish mother in the American popular imagination. Loud, wise, and malaprop-prone, Molly Goldberg set the tone for English-language American Jewish popular drama. Although not the only Jewish woman on the air—**Fanny Brice**, Sophie Tucker, and Belle Baker were among others who had careers on the radio—Berg's on-air persona proved larger than life. So large, in fact, that throughout the remainder of her career, she became so closely associated with Molly that countless fans did not bother to tell the fictional Molly from the real-life Gertrude.

Because of radio's debt to **vaudeville** and live theater, many of the popular performers from those live venues made the transition to radio, with great success. Arthur Tracey (née Abba Tracousky) became one of radio's early sensations when he performed as the "Street Singer" and used the mystery of radio to attract audiences. Although a popular vaudeville performer, Tracey really found fame on the radio. Similarly, Mel Blanc, the famous voice-over artist, began his career contributing to more than 20 programs per week on stations all over Los Angeles. For other performers, like Al Jolson, Eddie Cantor, and **Groucho Marx**, radio became another venue for their already substantial success. Jolson made his radio debut the year after he starred in ***The Jazz Singer*** (1927), and Marx, although he appeared as a youngster on the radio, really did not find his place on radio until 1947, as the host of *You Bet Your Life*. Likewise, Eddie Cantor was already well known for his work in the Ziegfeld Follies before he joined the ranks of radio performers and hosted one of radio's most popular programs during the early 1930s. Jack Benny and **George Burns** achieved modest fame, but their roles on radio catapulted them into the entertainment elite. Benny's performances as the host of his eponymous show, and Burns's witty repartee with wife and straightwoman Gracie Allen set the standard for radio comedy. By 1937, *The Jack Benny Show* had become the most popular program on radio.

As radio began to change during the 1940s and move away from the kinds of programming that typified radio during its golden age, announcers known soon as "disc jockeys" became even better recognized than earlier stars. Perhaps no radio announcer is as significant as Alan Freed, the Cleveland DJ who is credited with coining the term "rock and roll." Though Freed was eventually fired in 1959, his radio program introduced the music of black America to white audiences and helped usher in the popular musical styles that would come to dominate American music in the latter half of the twentieth century.

Jewish Characters. Some performers, like Gertrude Berg, played Jewish characters, while other Jewish characters were played by "character actors" who had mastered the dialect comedy once so popular on the vaudeville stage. Berg's Molly stands out as one of a handful of Jewish characters that became part of the popular culture pantheon. Jack Benny's Mr. Kitzel (played by Artie Auerbach) is another, but beyond those two, few radio characters were widely memorable. That does not mean that there were not Jewish characters. The local New York station WBNX hosted a program during the early 1930s called the *Bronx Marriage Bureau,* which featured a roster of Jewish characters in comic situations. CBS aired a program called *Meyer the Buyer* in 1932. It was a radio adaptation of Harry Hershfeld's popular cartoon strip *Abie the Agent.* Hershfeld, along with fellow Jewish cartoonist Milt Gross, performed together in a short-lived series called *The Jewish Poker Game,* which basically consisted of the men trading one-liners in Jewish dialect. Potash and Perlmutter, the title characters of a series of popular short stories, also earned their own program, while *Mama Bloom's Brood* appeared during the 1930s, as a tale of a Jewish family with all the hallmarks of golden age melodrama intact. Following the success of *The Goldbergs* and Eddie Cantor, NBC surveyed its audiences and found that people responded positively to characters "of a Jewish type." Thus, it is likely that there were other shows as well that featured Jewish characters that debuted and disappeared during the 1930s.

Still other characters, like Mrs. Nussbaum on *The Fred Allen Show,* the Jack Benny program's Shlepperman, and Henry Burbig, a dialect actor who appeared as a performer on his own program on CBS and then NBC in the years around 1930, capitalized on the popularity of Jewish dialect performance. While other programs featured a polyglot cast of dialect performers in programs like *Houseboat Hannah,* which told the story of Hannah O'Leary and included a character named Abe Finkelstein, or Mr. Horowitz, who offered a Jewish counterpoint to *Life with Luigi*'s Italian title character.

Yiddish Radio. From 1923 until the late 1970s, Yiddish language broadcasting was a regular fixture on American airwaves. Typically operating out of small, shoestring operations in large American cities like New York, Chicago, Detroit, Baltimore, Philadelphia, and Los Angeles, Yiddish language programs also appeared on stations in smaller markets like Rochester, New York; Tuscaloosa, Alabama; and, in 1960, Honolulu, Hawaii. Despite this geographic diversity, New York housed the majority of radio stations that carried Yiddish programs and produced more Yiddish-speaking performers than any other city. Therefore, this survey will have a slight New York bias, trying to account for Yiddish programming in other cities.

The stations that housed Yiddish language programs were typically owned by Jewish immigrants or members of other immigrant groups. These multiethnic and multilingual stations did not have the financial resources necessary for a full-time program director, so they hired programmers and advertisers in each of the languages in which they broadcast. Jews handled the Jewish accounts, Italians handled the Italian accounts, and so on.

Because they operated within their own ethnic communities, Yiddish-speakers in the radio industry often played more than one role. Rabbi Aaron Kronenberg owned station WARD, gave radio sermons, and hosted a variety of programs like *Matchmaker Rubin's Yiddish Hour.* Similarly, Michl Levitzky worked for a number of stations as their advertising agent and also read the news and made announcements. In Baltimore, Nathaniel Yongelson became the voice of Yiddish radio beginning in 1933, while in Philadelphia William Zigenloib seemed virtually omnipresent on Yiddish programs. Miami's Yiddish radio programming did not take root until much later, but it, too, followed a similar model as Jacob Shachter took responsibility for almost every aspect of programming.

Popular **cantors** like Moshe Oysher, Moshe Genshoff, Pinchas Levanda, and **"Yossele" Josef Rosenblatt** regularly performed on the air. Similarly, countless local rabbis also took advantage of the new medium to appeal to their congregants, the most popular of which was Rabbi Shmuel Rubin, who hosted a Yiddish version of the *People's Court,* on which he convened a rabbinical court for hearing complaints by members of the community broadcast as entertainment. Yet, radio also provided a platform for performers who would not otherwise have been able to find an outlet for their skills. Women like Freydele Oysher and Jean Gornish performed cantorial music on the radio, because Jewish law prohibited them from performing in synagogues.

Theater performers also used radio to promote their upcoming performances and to supplement incomes. Composers Alexander Oleshanetzky, Sholom Secunda, Maurice Rauch, and Abraham Ellstein all wrote music and played on the radio. Herman Yablokoff developed a successful career performing as "Der Payatz" ("The Clown"), while **Maurice Schwartz** tried his hand at a variety of performance styles, including one that invited members of the listening audience to sing along with him on the radio. Female stars of the Yiddish stage like **Molly Picon** and Jennie Goldstein also established long careers on the radio. Editor of the *Leksikon fun Yiddishen Teater* Zalman Zilberczweig also took advantage of radio and hosted a program from his home in Los Angeles.

The entire world of Yiddish radio was by and for Jews, so to document each of the players would require creating a roster of anyone ever involved in the effort. Such a task is virtually impossible, but it is possible here to highlight some of the industry's most prominent and influential players, as well as some of the ways in which Yiddish radio departed from its English-speaking counterpart. Because of the scarcity of resources, Yiddish radio programs were frequently irregular, and many came and went without notice.

The first star of Yiddish radio, Rubin Goldberg, recorded a novelty record for Columbia called *Shloime afn radio* (*Shloime on the Radio*) in 1923, some three years before the first Yiddish-language radio program even aired. Goldberg went on to host a variety of programs and fancied himself the "Jewish Rudy Vallee." He even went so far as to broadcast his own wedding on radio. Goldberg did not ultimately have the impact he desired. That role fell to a trio of other men: Nukhem Stutchkoff, Victor Packer, and Zvee Scooler.

Stutchkoff single-handedly wrote and starred in more than 10 Yiddish radio dramas between 1932 and 1958. No other writer came close to Stutchkoff's level or variety of productions. Others, like Mendel Osherovitch, Chaim Tauber, or Mark Schweid, specialized in a particular type of Yiddish program (dramatic adaptations of literature for Osherovitch, and dramatizations of historical events for Schweid). Stutchkoff, however, specialized in the creation of original family dramas that sounded so realistic that he often introduced his programs with a disclaimer stating that the story was fictional and that his performers were, in fact, actors.

Victor Packer was one of the most creative and ambitious Yiddish radio performers and spent the majority of his career at WLTH. Packer played advertiser, host, copywriter, poet, agent, and interviewer for the station, owned by Norman Warembud. Like Michl Levitzky, his counterpart at WEVD, Packer hosted quiz shows, amateur hours, man-in-the-street interview programs and, where regular programming fell short, read his own poetry along with translations of other famous works. He read serialized versions of popular novels and would do almost anything to keep his audience interested and his sponsors satisfied. Yet, whereas Levitzky could barely speak Yiddish (which did not stop him from becoming an announcer and successful host), Packer was extraordinarily literate and his fluency in Jewish culture is clearly audible in nearly everything he performed.

Zvee Scooler, the only one of these radio men with a stage career of note, began his radio career during the mid-1930s, appearing with his partner, Yehuda Bleich, as part of a comedy duo. Bleich and Scooler contributed weekly rhyming monologues on every topic under the sun, including an entire year's worth of commentaries on the Torah portion of the week. Bleich soon left radio, and Scooler ensconced himself as "Der Grammeister" ("The Rhyme-Master") on WEVD's Yiddish-language *Forward Hour*. Each week, Scooler would write and perform a 10-minute rhyming monologue on contemporary issues, on Jewish life, or on the news. Scooler, who eventually starred as the rabbi in the movie version of ***Fiddler on the Roof***, continued to appear on radio as he also developed a successful career in Hollywood films and television.

The Yiddish airwaves were also open to women such as Chana Spector, who wrote and performed the *Women's Matinee Hour*, and Esther Feld, who performed as the "Jewish-Gentile Lady" throughout the 1930s and 1940s. Lesser-known performers like Celia Budkin, Jennie Moskowitz, Lilian Lux, and others sang and appeared on serials throughout this period.

By the early 1950s, changes were underway, and while Stutchkoff, Packer, and Scooler continued to broadcast, new performers joined them. The two people who would contribute much to Yiddish radio in America were the husband and wife team of Miriam Kressyn and Seymour Rexite. The pair specialized in contemporary Yiddish versions of popular English songs and newly arranged versions of classic Yiddish numbers. Both had modestly successful careers on the Yiddish stage, and both found their greatest successes on the radio.

Although the number of Yiddish radio outlets declined over the remainder of the twentieth century, Yiddish radio in New York remained strong through the late 1970s, thanks to WEVD, which became known as "the station that speaks your language." In terms of total hours, Yiddish radio hardly declined at all, as WEVD attributed more of its broadcast hours to programming in Yiddish. Yiddish programming in cities with significant Yiddish-speaking audiences like New York and Miami adapted to changes in radio more broadly, playing more records and reading more news, as their English counterparts underwent similar changes. The broad industrial changes that spelled the end of radio's "golden age" did not immediately spell the end of Yiddish radio, as the audience that grew up listening in the 1930s, still tuned in through the 1970s. *See also* **Paley, William**; **Sarnoff, David**; **Television.**

Ari Y. Kelman

Further Reading: Siegel, David S., and Susan Siegel. *Radio and the Jews: The Untold Story of How Radio Influenced America's Image of Jews 1920s–1950s*. Book Hunter Press, 2007.

RAMONE, JOEY (1951–2001)

Joey Ramone was born Jeffrey Hyman on May 19, 1951. He was the lead singer for the prototypical punk rock band the Ramones. Hyman was raised in the middle-class, predominantly Jewish neighborhood of Forest Hill Queens. His father, Noel Hyman, headed Hyman Trucking Corporation in Manhattan. His mother, Charlotte Hesher, ran an art gallery in Queens.

In 2001, *Spin Magazine* marked the onset of the punk movement with the 1976 release of the first Ramones album. The band's July 1976 appearances in London set off United Kingdom punk, profoundly influencing bands such as the Clash and the Sexpistols. The Ramones played 2,200 shows and placed 15 albums on the Billboard charts during their 22-year run. In 2002 the Ramones were inducted into the Rock and Roll Hall of Fame.

Hyman played his first show with the Ramones in 1974. He originally played drums but switched to vocals shortly after they formed. Hyman's musical influences included 1960s girl groups such as the Ronettes, surf groups such as the Trashmen, and Detroit hard rock acts like the MC5 and the Stooges. The singer's influences were reflected in the band's sound, which was an amalgam of bubblegum-pop and up-tempo hard rock. Hyman's vocal abilities eventually caught the attention of legendary record producer Phil Spector, who recorded the Ramones' *End of the Century* in 1980.

After the Ramones disbanded in 1996, Hyman remained involved with music. Hyman DJ'd in various clubs and supported upcoming as well as more established musicians. In 1999 Hyman produced an EP (extended play 45rpm) for former Ronettes lead singer Ronnie Spector. Hyman spent three years recording a solo album entitled *Don't Worry About Me,* which was released posthumously in 2002.

Hyman developed lymphatic cancer in 1995. On April 15, 2001, he succumbed to the disease at New York Presbyterian Hospital. Hyman was 49 at the time of his death. *See also* **Rock and Roll**.

Danny Rigby

Further Reading: Beeber, Steven Lee. *The Heebie-Jeebies at CBGB's: A Secret History of Jewish Punk*. Chicago: Chicago Review Press, Inc, 2006.

RAND, AYN (1905–1982)

Author and philosopher Ayn Rand was born Alissa Rosenbaum, to Fronz and Anna Rosenbaum in St. Petersburg, Russia on October 15, 1905. The oldest of three daughters born into an assimilated Russian Jewish family, Rand received almost no formal religious training and declared herself an atheist as a young child, a belief she held her entire life. Her father was a successful chemist and pharmacist, which allowed the Rosenbaums to live outside the Pale, something rare for a Jewish family of this time.

As a teenager, Rand witnessed both the Kerensky revolution, which she supported, and the Bolshevik revolution, which she opposed. In order to avoid the fighting, the Rosenbaums escaped to the Crimea, where Rand finished her high school education. After the communists consolidated power, they confiscated the Rosenbaums' pharmacy as part of their collectivist policies, an event of significant importance in Rand's early life. In *Atlas Shrugged* (1957), one of Rand's best-known novels, the character John Galt announces to the American people that each person should take responsibility for their lives and be a rationalist, individualist, and producer. Conversely, the great enemies to the realization of one's potential are irrationalism, collective morality, and altruism. While Galt's speech represents the core of what became Rand's philosophical commitments (known as Objectivism), it is also indicative of the impact that her family's financial loss had on Rand's subsequent intellectual development.

When her family returned from the Crimea, she enrolled at the University of St. Petersburg, where she studied history and philosophy. Years later, she would recall her university days in *We the Living* (1936). After her graduation, Rand decided to pursue her interest in Western film by enrolling at the State Institute for Cinema Arts in 1924 to study screenwriting. In 1925, Rand received permission to go to the United States to visit relatives. After six months living with relatives in Chicago in 1926, she was determined never to go back to Russia, and after receiving an extension on her visa, Rand moved to Hollywood to pursue a career in screenwriting.

A fluke encounter with Cecil B. DeMille on her second day in California led to a job, first as an extra and then as a script reader on the set of the movie *King of Kings*. On the set, Rand met actor Frank O'Connor, whom she married in 1929 and remained with until his death 50 years later. In the immediate years following her marriage, Rand struggled to find an audience interested in her stage and movie writing, but in 1932 Universal Studios bought her screenplay *Red Pawn* and saw her first play, *Night of January 16th,* produced in Hollywood and later on Broadway in 1935. The modest royalties made from this play afforded Rand the time to concentrate on her first love, going back to her childhood, of becoming a writer. It is on her role as a writer that much of Rand's fame rests. In particular, her novels *Anthem* (1938), *The Fountainhead* (1943), and *Atlas Shrugged,* established her as a bestselling author. Her popularity as an author led to the making of a movie version of *The Fountainhead* starring Gary Cooper and Patricia Neal, in which Rand wrote the screenplay.

By the 1950s, there emerged a devoted following of college students who wanted to emulate characters in Rand's novels. The success of her novels also led Rand to become more visible in American popular culture, appearing in 1967 on *The Tonight Show Starring Johnny Carson* and years later on *The Phil Donahue Show.* The Canadian progressive rock band Rush thanked Rand in the liner notes of their celebrated science-fiction album based on *Anthem* entitled *2112* (1976). Other admirers of importance include former Federal Reserve Chairman Alan Greenspan, who earlier in his career wrote for Rand's newsletter, the *Objectivist.* While few professional philosophers take Rand's work seriously, her novels continue to sell yearly close to a quarter million copies.

Other works by Rand include *For the Intellectual* (1961), *Capitalism: The Unknown Ideal* (1966), and *Introduction to Objectivist Epistemology* (1967).

Joshua Fischel

Further Reading: Baker, James T. *Ayn Rand.* Boston: Twayne, 1987. Branden, Barbara. *The Passion of Ayn Rand.* New York: Doubleday, 1986. Branden Nathaniel, and Barbara Branden. *Who Is Ayn Rand?* New York: Random House, 1962. Mayhew, Robert. *Essays on Ayn Rand's The Fountainhead.* Lexington Books, 2006. O'Neill, William. *With Charity Toward None: An Analysis of Ayn Rand's Philosophy.* New York: Philadelphia Library, 1971.

RANDALL, TONY (1920–2004)

Best known for his television portrayal of Felix Unger in the *Odd Couple,* Tony Randall was an actor of great range. His roles included that of a teacher in *Mr. Peepers,* a host of the *Texaco Opera Quiz,* a Jewish gay man (he was heterosexual) in *Love Sidney,* and a skeptical reporter in the Broadway production of *Inherit the Wind.* Randall was a television personality, although he had roles in radio, on stage, and in movies. He founded the National Actors Theater (1991), a repertoire theater which attracted many well-known entertainers. His debonair, witty, and educated patter earned him 90 appearances on the *David Letterman Show* and many host appearances on the *Steve Allen Show* and *Arthur Godfrey and His Friends.*

Tony Randall was born Leonard Rosenberg in Tulsa, Oklahoma to a Jewish family. His father was an art dealer and his mother a housewife. He majored in theater at Northwestern University and the Neighborhood Players School. He had a short career in radio and a hitch as a second lieutenant in the U.S. Army Signal Corps during World War II (1942–1946). His career took off with his role in *Mr. Peepers.* His wife of 54 years, Florence Gibb, died childless. Randall married Heather Harlan, a woman 3 times younger than him, and at age 77, fathered his first child, Julia, in 1997. Another child, Jefferson, came in 1998.

The fussy half of the *Odd Couple* died at age 84 in 2004 of complications due to heart surgery. The funeral service, a traditional Jewish one, was held at New York's Riverside Chapel. **Jack Klugman**, the other half of the *Odd Couple,* delivered the eulogy. Burial took place in Hastings-on-the-Hudson at Westchester Hills Cemetery, a non-denominational resting place for entertainers. *See also* **Film**.

Philip Rosen

Further Reading: Randall, Tony. *Biography: Tony Randall.* A&E Home Video, 2000.

RAP AND HIP HOP MUSIC

One of the main assumptions about hip hop music, or rap music, is that it is an entirely African American enterprise—that it was created, owned, controlled, and consumed by African

Americans, and only African Americans. This is a false assumption. As in the case of jazz music, over 40 years earlier, and more recently the role that Jewish composers played in writing rock and roll music, Jews had a hand the rise of rap, which is meant to express the despair and joys of living in America's inner cities.

The study of Jews in American popular culture usually ignores rap music, but rap and hip hop benefited from Jewish influences. Many Jews were involved in rap music's infancy, but the most important was **Rick Rubin**, co-founder of Def Jam Records. Lyor Cohen, another co-founder of Def Jam Records, was also Jewish (the non-Jewish co-founder of the trio was Russell Simmons). Def Jam Records was one the first hip hop labels, and with artists such as Run-DMC, LL Cool J, and the **Beastie Boys**, Def Jam Records was among the most successful rap recording companies.

Rick Rubin (Frederick Jay Rubin) was born on Long Island in 1963 and is now the co-head of Columbia Records. Rubin's influence on rap was extensive in the 1980s. He helped to bridge the gap between rock and roll and rap music when he asked Aerosmith to collaborate with Run-DMC on a cover of Aerosmith's hit "Walk This Way."

Lyor Cohen, who is presently the chairman and CEO of the Warner Music Group, was also born in New York City, the child of Israeli immigrants, making the early influence on rap not only an American Jewish experience, but an Israeli one as well. Lyor Cohen has not always been a positive influence on rap, because he had many run-ins with the law and disputes with artists.

Another earlier Jewish producer of rap music was James Iovine, born March 11, 1953, in Brooklyn. As chairman of Interscope Records he helped launch the solo careers of Dr. Dre and Eminem. These three men, all Jewish, are still involved in the rap and hip hop industry

One of the rap movement's earliest successes was a group called the Beastie Boys, who recorded the bestselling rap album of the 1980s, *License to Ill. License to Ill* sold over five million copies and was the first rap album to go number one on the Billboard album chart. All four members of the Beastie Boys are Jewish and from New York City. Michael Diamond, Adam Yauch, Adam Horovitz, and Michael Schwartz have one of the longest continuously running hip hop acts and were inducted into the Rock and Roll Hall of Fame in 2007. While the Beastie Boy's Judaism has not been important in their lives, their presence at the birth of rap music represents the nexus between the Jewish and African American cultures that have contributed so greatly to popular music.

The proximity between Jewish and African American settlements in the inner city created a connection between the two peoples. Jews who helped produce and distribute the rap albums in the early years had an affinity for the emotional core of rap music. Both Jews and African Americans viewed themselves as "outsiders" and were determined to keep their culture intact rather than adopt that of bland Protestant, white America. Many books have been written on the shared experiences of African Americans and American Jews. The manner in which Jewish entertainers, composers, and producers, from **George Gershwin** to Leiber and Stoller, to Rick Rubin, have been influenced by the music of African Americans sheds light on the history of popular music in the twentieth century.

While the majority of rap's performers have not been Jewish, there are a number of rap groups that featured Jewish performers. They include the Whooliganz, a 1990s hip hop music group led by Scott Caan (the son of actor James Caan; Scott eventually went into acting) and Alan Maman. The duo went by the names "Mad Skillz" and "Mudfoot." Chutzpah is a Los Angeles-based Jewish rap group who call themselves the "first ever Jewish hip hop super group." The group includes Master Tav, an ex-cantorial student turned rapper; MC Meshugenah; Jewdah, the Rastafarian philosopher rapper; and their leader, Dr. Dreck. The group's film, *Chutzpah, This Is?* was an official selection at the Newport Beach, Cedar Rapids, and Washington D.C.

Jewish Film Festivals. Blood of Abraham is a hip-hop duo featuring Benyard (Benjamin Mohr) and Mazik (David Saevitz). A key characteristic of the group is their unapologetic Jewish identity. Their best-known track is "Niggaz and Jewz (Some Say Kikes)," an irreverent call for Jewish-black unity. There were also a few novelty Jewish rap acts like Two Live Jews and Members of the Tribe (M.O.T.), but both of these groups satirized what was currently going on in rap music at that time. Neither group brought anything new to the genre.

The most recent Jewish performer in the world of rap/hip hop is **Matisyahu**. While Matisyahu technically sings reggae music, his musical inspiration is drawn from a wide spectrum. Unlike the Beastie Boys or novelty acts such as Two Live Jews or M.O.T., Matisyahu is a Hasidic Jew who is attempting through music to bring Jews back to Judaism. This is a stark contrast to the majority of rap albums, which explore beliefs about the essence of African American culture.

Although for many American Jews there is a failure to appreciate rap, the reality is, whether rap is demonstrated through the fallout from mid-1990s East Coast/West Coast violence, the misogynist lyrical nature of rap songs, or the negative and violent nature of many rappers, there is a strong connection between rap music and American Jews. In fact, the largest consumers of rap and hip hop are middle class, white children, the socioeconomic class that incorporates most American Jews. This audience continues to validate the musical form with their wallets. Rap and hip hop may well remain popular among young people for the foreseeable future.

Jesse Ulrich

Further Reading: Khazzoom, Loolwa. "Hip Hop's Jew Crew Takes Center Stage." *Jewish Journal,* December 9, 2004. Merino, Noel. *Rap Music (Introducing Issues With Opposing Viewpoints).* Farmington, MI: Greenhaven Press, 2008. Quinn, Christopher. "Faith Sets the Beat for Jewish Rapper."*Modesto Bee,* http://www.modbee.com/, 2008.

REICH, STEVEN (1936–)

Described by the British *Guardian* as one of the few composers who have "altered the direction of musical history," Reich is a seminal twentieth-century composer. His minimalist compositional style is known as phase shifting. It is characterized by gradual, slow changes.

Reich was born in New York City on October 3, 1936. His mother was the songwriter June Carroll ("Love is a Simple Thing"). His parents divorced when he was one; consequently, Reich was raised in both New York and California. At age 14, he began studying music. He began first by studying drums in order to play jazz. Reich graduated with a BA in philosophy from Cornell in 1957; his senior thesis was on Ludwig Wittgenstein. In 1995 he set texts by the philosopher to music in *Proverb* (1995), a composition for three sopranos, two tenors, two vibraphones, and two electric organs.

Following study at Juilliard and Reed College (where his teacher was Darius Mihaud), Reich embarked on a musical journey that saw him studying everything from African music in Ghana to cantillation in Jerusalem. The latter influence appeared in his 1981 work *Tehillim,* the first of his works to draw explicitly on his Jewish heritage. *Tehillim* is a work in four parts, scored for an ensemble of four women's voices and a host of brass, woodwind, and percussion instruments.

In 1993, Reich collaborated with his wife, video artist Beryl Korot, on an opera called *The Cave,* which explores the roots of Judaism, Christianity, and Islam. Reich's compositional style has had a profound influence on composers like Philip Glass and visual artists such as Bruce Nauman. Reich has won two Grammy awards: for *Music for Eighteen Musicians* and for *Different Trains,* a piece for string quartet and tape. Reich's compositional innovations include the use of tape loops, repetitive figures, and phrasing effects. His compositions frequently take on social, political, and historical issues.

In 2006, performing organizations around the world celebrated Reich's 70th birthday. In 2007, he received both the prestigious Polar Music Prize and a Chubb Fellowship at Yale.

Kurt F. Stone

Further Reading: Reich, Steve. *Writings on Music, 1965–2000.* Oxford University Press, 2002.

REINER, ROB (1945–)

Rob Reiner is an actor, director, producer, writer, and political activist who first came to national prominence as Archie and Edith Bunker's son-in-law, Michael "Meathead" Stivic, on the television comedy *All in the Family.* Rob Reiner was born in the Bronx on March 6, 1945 and moved with his family to New Rochelle, New York. New Rochelle was the setting for the television comedy *The Dick Van Dyke Show,* which was directed by his father, Carl Reiner. When Reiner turned 13, the family moved again, this time to the Los Angeles area. There Reiner graduated from Beverly Hills High and then studied at the UCLA film school.

He first gained national prominence as an actor in the role of Michael "Meathead" Stivic on the landmark sitcom *All In the Family* (1971–1977), a role that earned him two Emmy Awards. Reiner has, since that time, become better recognized as a director, producer, and political activist. The range of films he has overseen demonstrates his versatility as a filmmaker. Among them are such critically acclaimed box-office hits as the "Rockumentary" *This Is Spinal Tap* (1984), *The Princess Bride* (1987), *Misery* (1990),*Sleepless In Seattle* (1993),*The American President* (1995), and *Ghosts of Mississippi* (1996). The Directors Guild of America honored him with three Best Director nominations for his work on *Stand by Me* (1986), *When Harry Met Sally* (1989), and *A Few Good Men* (1992).

From 1971–1979, Reiner was married to actress/director Penny Marshall. After their divorce, he wed photographer Michele Singer in 1989. With his second wife, he founded the Parents' Action for Children, a foundation that promotes early child development initiatives. In 1998, he served as chairman of California's Proposition 10 campaign. Its success resulted in the formation of First 5 California, a program providing early childhood services, which Reiner chaired from 1999–2006. He also campaigned for California's Proposition 82, a state-funded preschool program, which failed to win popular support. Reiner is a member of the Social Responsibility Task Force, which advocates moderation in the depiction of violence, substance abuse, and the like in the entertainment industry, remaining active in environmental issues and liberal politics.

He was touted as a possible Democratic candidate for the California governorship in 2006 but chose not to run. Reiner has also worked as a movie and television writer and even composed music for his film *This Is Spinal Tap.* *See also* **Film**; **Television**.

Barry Kornhauser

Further Reading: *The Hollywood.com Guide to Film Directors.* New York: Carroll and Graf Publishers, 2004.

REUBENS, PAUL (1952–)

Paul Reubens, best known as Pee-Wee Herman, was born Paul Rubenfeld to Milton and Judy Rubenfeld on August 27, 1952 in Peekskill, New York. Raised in Sarasota, Florida, Rubenfeld attended Boston University for a year before moving to California, where he changed his last name to Reubens and pursued a career in Hollywood.

Reubens landed several minor acting roles by the late 1970s, including appearances on *The Gong Show* and in the movie *The Blues Brothers.* But his breakthrough came with the creation of the character Pee-Wee Herman in 1977, while a member of the Groundlings, a Los Angeles-based improvisational group that included Reubens's close friend, Phil Hartman. Pee-Wee Herman was conceptualized as a talentless comedian, yet the overgrown juvenile in the tight gray suit and red bowtie was immensely successful. Pee-Wee made bad jokes and showed the audience his toys, invariably following his comments with his famous staccato laugh or his childish response to ridicule, "I know you are, but what am I?" Pee-Wee's success led HBO to film his performances, resulting in *The Pee-Wee Herman Show* in 1981. Despite Pee-Wee Herman's success, Reubens failed to make the cast of *Saturday Night Live* in 1984.

Capitalizing on Pee-Wee's popularity, Reubens refined his act and made a movie. *Pee-Wee's Big Adventure* cost $7 million to produce in 1985, but grossed over $45 million. The film's success spurred CBS to offer Reubens a contract for a sanitized version of Pee-Wee Herman to air Saturday mornings beginning in 1986. Fueled by a $325,000 budget per episode, few creative restrictions, and a cast that included Phil Hartman as Captain Carl and Laurence Fishburne as Cowboy Curtis, *Pee-Wee's Playhouse* received 22 Emmy Awards over the course of its 5 years and 45 episodes on CBS, nearly 1 award for every 2 episodes.

After a decade as Pee-Wee Herman, Reubens diversified his acting career following his infamous 1991 arrest for indecent exposure in Sarasota, Florida. Appearing at the 1992 MTV Awards, Reubens memorably mocked his recent arrest, asking the crowd, "Heard any good jokes lately?" Since then he has performed in several movies, including *Batman Returns, Mystery Men,* and the 2001 box-office smash, *Blow.* Reubens continues acting and plans a return of Pee-Wee Herman. *See also* **Television**.

Maury I. Wiseman

Further Reading: Smith, Ronald L. *Who's Who in Comedy: Comedians, Comics, and Clowns from Vaudeville to Today's Stand-Ups.* New York: Facts on File, 1992, 214–216.

RICE, ELMER (1912–1967)

Elmer Rice was an American playwright, novelist, author, stage director, and civil libertarian who had a remarkably productive career during the first half of the twentieth century. His more than 50 plays ranged in genre from farce and comedy through melodrama, fantasy, naturalism, and expressionism.

Rice was born Elmer Leopold Reizenstein in Manhattan's Upper West Side on September 28, 1912, the grandson of German Jewish immigrants; he was raised by his parents, Jacob and Fanny. His family maintained a tenuous connection with their Jewishness, and Rice refused to become a Bar Mitzvah. The family was poor, and at age 14, Rice dropped out of school and began working. He earned a high school equivalency diploma and in 1908 entered New York Law School, from which he graduated cum laude in 1912. Although he passed the bar exam, he put law aside to begin a career as a playwright. His first play, *On Trial* (1914), a courtroom drama, became a Broadway hit, ran for a year, and earned him $100,000. At the end of the play's run, Reizenstein changed what he called his "foreign-sounding name" to Rice.

As a playwright, Rice was known for his use of experimental technique, his realism, and his portrayal of the problems of his time, especially the issue of social injustice. He is best remembered for the expressionistic *The Adding Machine* (1923) and for the realistic drama *Street Scene* (1929) that presents life in a slum tenement and reaches its climax in a double murder. It was one of the first stage productions to include realistic sound effects throughout the performance, and it won a Pulitzer Prize. In 1947 it was made into an opera by American poet Langston Hughes and the German-born American composer Kurt Weill.

A number of Jewish characters appear in Rice's plays. For example, in *Street Scene* he presents Abraham Kaplan, an old radical writer for the Yiddish press; in *Counselor-at-Law* (1931) the lead part of George Simon (played by Paul Muni) offers a plea for the liberation of human potential and freeing oneself from dehumanizing illusions; and in *Flight to the West* (1940), a young Jewish pacifist (like Rice himself) tries to persuade his Gentile wife that personal participation in the fight against Nazi barbarity is necessary and proper.

Rice died May 1, 1967 in Southampton, England of pneumonia, after having been evacuated off the liner *France* a week earlier when suffering a heart attack. *See also* **Theater**.

Leslie Rabkin

Further Reading: Palmieri, Anthony F. R. *Elmer Rice: A Playwright's Vision of America*. New Jersey: Fairleigh Dickinson University Press, 1980. Rice, Elmer. *Minority Report: An Autobiography*. New York: Simon and Schuster, 1963.

THE RITZ BROTHERS

The Ritz Brothers were a comedy team who appeared in 1930s films and as live performers from 1925 to the late 1960s. The three Joachim brothers—Al (1901–1965), Jimmy (1904–1985), and Harry (1907–1986), were the sons of Austrian-born haberdasher Max Joachim. The brothers grew up in New Jersey and Brooklyn, independently deciding to go into show business. Al, the oldest, became a dancer; brothers Jimmy and Harry followed suit, securing solo bookings as both dancers and comedians. In 1925, the brothers became a song-and-dance comedy act. Legend has it that they went from "Joachim" to "Ritz" after seeing the name on a laundry truck. With their brother George acting as agent, they soon broke into vaudeville, where their zany antics won them a loyal following.

Over their nearly six decades on the stage and in films, the brothers' act remained remarkably constant: precision dancing, tongue-twisting satires of popular song hits, and slapstick comedy. The Ritz Brothers first appeared in film in the 1934 two-reel comedy *Hotel Anchovy*. This led to a contract with 20th Century Fox, which saw them as possible rivals to MGM's wildly popular Marx Brothers. Fox—and then Samuel Goldwyn—used them primarily as comic relief in such big-budget musicals as *Sing Baby Sing* (1936), and *The Goldwyn Follies* (1938). In 1939, the boys played comic foils in Fox's production of *The Three Musketeers*. After this film, the Ritz Brothers' Hollywood fortunes begin to fade; in total, the brothers appeared in over a dozen pictures. After the demise of their film career, they spent the next quarter-century performing on stage and in nightclubs, also making guest appearances on television. Following Al Ritz's death in 1965, Harry and Jimmy struggled to keep the act together. When, in a 1975 interview, writer/producer **Mel Brooks** proclaimed "this [Harry Ritz] is the funniest man in the world," the two surviving brothers made a brief comeback, replacing the **Three Stooges** in *Blazing Stewardesses* (1975) and having brief cameos in *Won Ton Ton: The Dog Who Saved Hollywood* (1976). Jimmy Ritz passed away in 1985, his brother Harry in 1986. *See also* **Film**.

Kurt F. Stone

Further Reading: Stein, Harry. "Mel Brooks Says This Is the Funniest Man On Earth." *Esquire Magazine*, June 1976.

RIVERA, GERALDO (1943–)

Geraldo Rivera is an attorney, television reporter, war correspondent, and former talk show host. He is known to have an affinity for dramatic, high-profile stories. Rivera hosts the news magazine program *Geraldo at Large*, and he appears regularly on Fox News Channel. Gerald Michael Rivera was born in New York City July 4, 1943. His father, Cruz "Allen" Rivera, was an immigrant from Puerto Rico; his mother, Lillian Friedman, the daughter of Jewish immigrants. "Jerry" Rivera grew up in Brooklyn and West Babylon, New York. Rivera is an alumnus of the University of Arizona and earned a JD from Brooklyn Law School in 1969. While working as attorney for the Young Lords, a Puerto Rican activist group, he attracted the attention of a news producer, who offered Rivera a job with ABC News. He also suggested that he use the name "Geraldo."

Rivera was hired as a reporter for Eyewitness News. In 1972, he garnered national attention and an Emmy for reporting on conditions for mentally retarded patients at Staten Island's Willowbrook State School. Soon after, Rivera began hosting *ABC's Goodnight America*, reaching a national audience. In 1987, Rivera began producing and hosting the daytime talk show *Geraldo,* which ran for 11 years. Derided by *Newsweek* as "trash TV," *Geraldo* featured provocative stories and one infamous melee, in which Rivera had his nose broken by angry skinheads.

In 1997, Rivera signed a 5-year, $30 million contract with NBC, for whom he covered the Clinton impeachment. After September 11, he took a cut in pay and joined Fox News, which sent him to Afghanistan. While embedded with American troops in Iraq, Rivera disclosed an upcoming military operation. Brought to task, Rivera soon began reporting the war from Kuwait. Rivera has also hosted *Geraldo at Large* and appeared as himself in dozens of movies and television shows.

One lasting urban legend claims he was born "Jerry Rivers" and changed his name in order to attract a Hispanic audience. This is untrue. Rivera has been married five times and has five children; his second wife, Edie, was the daughter of novelist Kurt Vonnegut. Rivera has won 10 Emmys and the Peabody Award. Rivera on many occasions has identified himself as a Jew and takes pride in his ethnic heritage. *See also* **Journalism**; **Television**.

Kurt F. Stone

Further Reading: Rivera, Geraldo. *Exposing Myself.* Bantam, 1991.

RIVERS, JOAN (1933–)

Joan Rivers is a comedian, actress, and television talk show host. She is known for her brash manner and loud, raspy voice with a heavy metropolitan New York accent. Rivers grew up in Larchmont, New York, far removed from her immigrant parents'—Meyer and Beatrice Molinsky—first home in America—Brooklyn. Her father became a doctor, and her ambitious mother doted on her two daughters, Rivers and her older sister, Barbara. While her sister went to law school, Joan Molinsky insisted upon a career in show business, after satisfying her parents' wish that she graduate from college (Barnard, 1954). Rivers displayed a sharp wit and entered the perilous field of stand-up comedy, a field that, in the 1950s, had few women practitioners. She developed a self-deprecatory style that grew in audacity as she gained success. Not a conventionally beautiful woman, Rivers used her physical attributes (which included small breasts) to her comic advantage. She began in the **Catskill Mountains** resorts like so many other Jewish comics and quipped that at the beginning, a Yiddish translator stood alongside her and after every line, repeated the joke in **Yiddish**. The result, she noted, was that her material bombed twice.

Her appearance on Johnny Carson's *The Tonight Show* in 1965 launched her career on national television. Rivers wrote her own material and branched out to write film scripts in the 1970s. Her greatest successes came on late night television talk shows and in appearances in Las Vegas. She made fun of her skinny body, her less-than-glamorous looks, told off-color jokes, and made fun of famous people. Her salacious humor made her a kin to the early twentieth-century bawdy Jewish comics, who could never have been broadcast in prime time television. Rivers has written and discussed her philosophy of comedy frequently, arguing that the sharper and more vulgar remarks were always chosen over the tamer and more staid because that is the essence of humor. Rivers believes that comedy should be subversive, explosive, and offensive, or it is meaningless.

She made fun of herself and anyone else who struck her fancy in her comedy routines. In recent years, she appeared on television promoting sales of her line of jewelry. With her daughter Melissa, she is seen on a variety of cable shows. In 2005, BBC Channel 4 conducted a poll to find "The Comedian's Comedian," and Rivers was voted among the top 50 comedy acts by her peers. In the spring of 2007, she was touring with Jewish comic Don Rickles, still active as a stand-up comedian. *See also* **Television**.

June Sochen

Further Reading: Joan Rivers Web Site: http://www.joanrivers.com/. Rivers, Joan. *Still Talking.* New York: Random House, 1991.

ROBBINS, HAROLD (1916–1997)

Harold Robbins is among the world's bestselling authors, publishing over 20 books which were translated into 32 languages and sold over 750 million copies. There are two stories about Harold Robbins's early life. One has him born Francis Kane in New York City on May 21, 1916, spending his early childhood in a succession of orphanages. According to this tale, he was given the adoptive name "Harold Rubin," which he eventually changed to "Robbins." The second story would have it that he was the son of well-educated Russian and Polish immigrants named Rubin, his father being a successful pharmacist.

Robbins graduated from George Washington High School and soon began working at menial jobs, including working as a numbers runner. By 20, after buying options on farmers' produce, Robbins became a millionaire. A move into sugar options lost him his fortune. He then found work as a shipping clerk at Universal Studios. Robbins slowly began making his way up the corporate ladder.

In 1948, supposedly on a dare from a studio executive, Robbins wrote his first novel, *Never Love a Stranger.* The novel followed the life of an orphan from the streets of New York. Its graphic sexuality created a major stir and gave rise to the story that Robbins had been an orphan from the streets. Made into a film in 1958, *Never Love a Stranger* would be the first of 11 Robbins novels to find their way onto the silver screen.

From 1948 to shortly before his death in 1997, Robbins wrote more than two dozen novels, most thinly-veiled stories of people like Howard Hughes and Lana Turner. Among his best-known works are *A Stone for Danny Fisher* (1952), *The Carpetbaggers,* (1961), and *Where Love Has Gone* (1962).

Harold Robbins lived life fast and furiously. He indulged in drugs and drink, and he married at least five times.

Robbins died in Palm Springs, California on October 14, 1997. Since his death, several of his story ideas have been turned into posthumously ghosted novels.

Kurt F. Stone

Further Reading: Carson, Tom. "Harold Robbins: The Man Who Invented Sex." Book review. *New York Times,* October 21, 2007. Severo, Richard. "Harold Robbins, 81, Dies; Wrote Best Sellers Brimming with Sex, Money and Power." Obituary. *New York Times,* October 15, 1997.

ROBBINS, JEROME (1918–1998)

Jerome Robbins was an award-winning film director and choreographer whose work has included everything from classical ballet to contemporary musical theater. Jerome Wilson Rabinowitz was born at the Jewish Maternity Hospital on New York's Lower East Side on October 11, 1918. His parents, Lena and Harry Rabinowitz, were Russian Jews who emigrated to America to escape czarist pogroms. His parents gave their son his middle name, Wilson, to honor then-President Woodrow Wilson. When Robbins was 10, the Rabinowitz family moved to Weehawken, New Jersey, where his father and uncle opened a successful business. As a child, Robbins studied both piano and violin before turning his interest to ballet After briefly studying chemistry at New York University, the soon-to-be-named Robbins (the name Rabinowitz resonated as too ethnic for him) began studying virtually every aspect of dance: ballet, Spanish, folk, modern, and dance composition. By 1939, Robbins was dancing in the chorus of many Broadway shows choreographed by George Balanchine.

Robbins first gained public notice as a soloist with the American Ballet Theatre, where he scored triumphs in *Petrouchka, Helen of Troy,* and *Romeo and Juliet.* In 1944, Robbins choreographed and performed the world premiere of *Fancy Free,* a ballet about three sailors on shore leave. *Fancy Free* was a success; it also provided critical attention to the ballet's composer, **Leonard Bernstein**, with whom Robbins collaborated throughout his career. Later that year, Robbins, together with Bernstein, choreographed the world premiere of *On the Town,* which launched his Broadway career. Two years later, he choreographed another hit, the Keystone Kops ballet in *High Button Shoes* (1947), for which he won his first Tony Award. In the 1950s, Robbins choreographed and/or directed 15 other musicals, including such hits as *The King and I* (1951), *The Pajama Game* (1954), *Peter Pan* (1954), *Bells Are Ringing* (1956), *West Side Story* (1957—for which he earned his second Tony Award for choreography), *Gypsy* (1959), and ***Fiddler on the Roof*** (1964). Robbins also co-directed (along with Robert Wise) the film version of *West Side Story* (1961), for which they shared the Oscar for Best Director.

It was also in 1953 that Robbins appeared before the House Un-American Activities Committee, where he "named names" of former colleagues as members of the Communist Party. In years to come, he received the opprobrium of some artists and colleagues in the entertainment industry.

The 1960s were an especially good decade for Robbins. In 1964, he won Tony Awards for his direction and choreography of *Fiddler on the Roof,* which ran an incredible 3,242 performances. In all, Robbins won five Tony Awards.

In 1981, Robbins was honored by the Kennedy Center for his artistic achievement. In 1983, following the death of George Balanchine, Robbins accepted the post of artistic director of the New York City Ballet with Peter Martins, a position he held until 1990. In 1988, he received the National Medal of the Arts. In 1989, he briefly returned to Broadway with an anthology of past hits entitled *Jerome Robbins' Broadway.* Robbins, who was characterized by one obituary writer as "likely the richest choreographer of all time," died of a stroke on July 29, 1998. *See also* **Dance**; **Theater**; ***West Side Story.***

Kurt F. Stone

Further Reading: Jowitt, Deborah. *Jerome Robbins: His Life, His Theatre, His Dance.* Simon and Schuster, 2005. Lawrence, Greg. *Dances With Demons: The Life of Jerome Robbins.* Berkeley Trade, 2002. Vaill, Amanda. *Somewhere: The Life Of Jerome Robbins.* Broadway Books, 2006.

ROBINSON, EDWARD G. (1893–1973)

Born Emmanuel Goldenberg in Bucharest, Romania on December 12, 1893, Edward G. Robinson was a skilled and forceful actor, appearing on stage and screen for 60 years. He was best known for his tough-talking gangster role in the film *Little Caesar* (1930), a performance that became a prototype for movie portrayals of gangsters.

Robinson, one of six sons of Morris and Sarah (Gutman) Goldenberg,, came with his mother to join his father in New York when he was nine years old. The family first lived in a Lower East Side tenement and then moved to the Bronx, where his father ran a candy store and bought and sold antiques. Robinson celebrated his Bar Mitzvah at the Romanian synagogue on Rivington Street in Manhattan.

After graduating from Townsend Harris High School and a brief stay at City College, Robinson won a scholarship in 1911 to the American Academy of Dramatic Arts, changed his name, and began his career as an actor in 1913 with a Binghamton, New York stock company. In 1915, he made his Broadway debut, and he came to prominence in the 1920s with the Theater Guild, appearing in a wide variety of plays, including *The Kibitzer* (1929), a comedy of which he was part author.

The success of *Little Caesar* launched his movie career. Although he was long typecast as a gangster, he broadened his range and became a skilled actor in a variety of parts. These included *Dr. Erlich's Magic Bullet* (1940), *All My Sons* (1948), *The Ten Commandments* (1956), and *The Prize* (1963). He also returned to the stage on occasion, notably in Arthur Koestler's *Darkness at Noon* (1951) and in **Paddy Chayefsky**'s *Middle of the Night* (1956).

During World War II, Robinson devoted himself to various patriotic and specifically Jewish causes. In 1943, he and the actors Paul Muni and Jacob Ben-Ami participated in a mass memorial for Jewish victims of the Nazis written by **Ben Hecht** and entitled "We Shall Never Die."

In the 1950s, a notorious anticommunist magazine, *Red Channels,* claimed that Robinson had been connected with communist organizations. Robinson insisted on appearing before the House Un-American Activities Committee to clear his name. He testified three times, offering his record of contributions and wartime activities. On April 30, 1952, he was cleared. The committee concluded that, "according to the evidence to this committee, you are a good, loyal and intensely patriotic American citizen." In 1956, he was forced to sell his world-renowned French Impressionist art collection as part of a divorce settlement with actress Gladys Lloyd, his wife of 29 years.

Robinson celebrated his 75th birthday at a Madison Square Garden salute connected with the 1968 Hanukkah Festival of Lights, which included the world premier of a ballet dedicated to him. Never nominated for an Academy Award, in 1973 Robinson was posthumously awarded an honorary Oscar. He died from cancer on January 26, 1973 at the age of 79, two months before the award ceremony. He was interred in the family mausoleum at Beth-El Cemetery in Ridgewood, Queens, New York. *See also* **Film**.

Leslie Rabkin

Further Reading: Beck, Robert. *The Edward G. Robinson Encyclopedia*. Jefferson, NC: McFarland and Co., 2002. Gansberg, Alan L. *Little Caesar: A Biography of Edward G. Robinson.* Blue Ridge Summit, PA: Scarecrow Press, 2004.

ROCK AND ROLL

Understanding the influence of American Jews on rock and roll is to understand American Jews' influence on music in America. Whether it was big band, swing, or **Tin Pan Alley**, Jews were involved from the beginning of what would become American popular music. When it comes to rock and roll there are two kinds of influence. There is the "behind the scenes" and the "on stage."

Early in the history of rock and roll, from the late 1940s to the early 1960s, American Jews were behind the scenes as songwriters. Artists like Elvis Presley and Jerry Lee Lewis did not write their own material. Most of their songs were written by Jews. Men like Jerry Leiber, Mike Stoller, Doc Pomus, Jerry Wexler, Jerry Ragovoy, and Phil Spector were the writers, even though only Phil Spector's name would be recognizable to people familiar with music. Phil Spector continued in the music business as a producer and invented the "wall of sound," which revolutionized how albums were produced.

There were many reasons for the lack of Jewish performers in the early days of rock and roll. For Jewish performers, even to this day, their names created problems. Many of them changed their name in order to fit into what the record companies believed had box-office appeal. Some changed their names because they wanted to sound "cooler." **Bob Dylan** provides the best example of that reasoning for a name change. The annals of rock history are full of studio musicians and band members who changed their names and then regretted their action.

During the 1960s, Jewish artists moved from the writing room to the stage; four in particular would help to shape rock and roll for the rest of the century: Bob Dylan, **Paul Simon**, Lou Reed, and Leonard Cohen.

Bob Dylan, born Robert Allen Zimmerman, started his career as an antiwar and civil rights activist. Playing his acoustic guitar, he became the reluctant leader of the antiwar folk movement. His leadership in this movement ended when he switched to the electric guitar, which changed the sonic landscape of popular music ever since. His influence on music also expands across the Atlantic, if one believes the story that it was Dylan who introduced the Beatles to marijuana, which has been attributed to the sonic changes in the later and more popular Beatles albums.

Paul Simon, the singer and songwriter behind the duo Simon and Garfunkel, helped shape the continuation of folk music in the 1960s and would continue changing the musical landscape as a solo artist. Introducing American music listeners to world music in his albums *Graceland* and *Rhythm of the Saint,* his influence on American music is still being felt today. He is one of the few rock and rollers to be inducted into the Rock and Roll Hall of Fame twice—as a solo artist and as a member of Simon and Garfunkel. He is also the first recipient of the Library of Congress's Gershwin Award for Popular Song.

Lou Reed—born Lewis Allen Reed—performed as lead guitarist and songwriter for the band Velvet Underground as well as performing as a solo artist. He pioneered the use of different effects on the sound of the guitar. By using distortion, feedback, and nonstandard tuning, Reed changed how the guitar sounded and helped promote newer forms of rock and roll. While not as successful as a solo artist as he was as a member of Velvet Underground, he now plays the role of an elder statesman of rock and roll.

Leonard Cohen, born Leonard Norman Cohen, as a songwriter holds the distinction of being one of the most-covered artists in rock and roll. As a poet and singer-songwriter, he wrote songs that explored the themes of religion, isolation, and sexuality. Another distinction that Leonard Cohen holds is that he might be the only Jewish rock and roller who is now an ordained Rinzai Buddhist monk.

More recent Jewish rock and rollers include Lenny Kravitz, Paula Abdul, **Matisyahu**, all three members of Guster, and three of the four members of the uber-jamband Phish. Bands like Phish and Guster, who constantly tour and improvise on stage, have had a very strong influence on Americans in their twenties and thirties. On Phish's album *Hoist,* if listeners have the patience to listen past the last track, they will hear the first verse and refrain of the Hebrew song "Yerushalayin shel Zahav" ("Jerusalem of Gold"). One of the members of Guster, Adam Gardner, created a side project called the LeeVees and released an album called *Hanukkah Rocks* (2005) which consists of humorous and original Jewish holiday songs. With this album Adam Gardner attempts to recapture the popularity of **Adam Sandler**'s "Chanukah Song," which first appeared on *Saturday Night Live* in 1994 and reprised in 1999.

Jewish rock and roll performers whose parents were Holocaust survivors include Keith Reid, the non-performing member of the British classical rock band Procol Harem; co-founder of Kiss **Gene Simmons**, whose mother was sent to a concentration camp at the age of 14; rock artist **Billy Joel**; War's harmonica player, Lee Oscar; Ten Wheel Drive lead singer Genya Ravan; Bob Glaub, the bass player for Jackson Browne; singer Linda Ronstadt; songwriter Dan Bern; Dan Draiman, the lead vocalist of Disturbed, is a grandchild of Holocaust survivors.

The influence on rock and roll by American Jews is pronounced and influential. Jewish artists such as the band Phish expanded the sonic landscape, while the Ramones reel it in. Moreover, Jewish influence has been felt from the beginnings of the genre just as it has in Broadway, television, and the movies.

Jesse Ulrich

Further Reading: Benarde, Scott. *Stars of David: Rock 'n' Roll's Jewish Stories.* Brandeis University Press, 2003. Billig, Michael. *Rock 'n' Roll Jews.* Syracuse University Press, 2000.

ROSE, BILLY (1899–1966)

The legendary showman Billy Rose had many successful careers—secretary, songwriter, producer, nightclub owner, impresario, financier, art collector, and patron. A self-made multimillionaire, he was born William Samuel Rosenberg on September 6, 1899 in New York City, the oldest surviving child of Russian Jewish immigrants Fanny and David Rosenberg.

Rose grew up on Cherry Street in a tenement on the Lower East Side. His father, a pharmacist back in Russia, became an unsuccessful salesman in America. As a teenager, Rose was a champion at shorthand, winning national competitions, which eventually led to a job as secretary to the head of the War Industry Board, Bernard Baruch, during World War I. After the war, noticing how much money songwriters made, Rose decided to try his hand at the profession. He spent months in the library deconstructing the qualities of a hit song.

Rose went on to pen over 400 songs, many of which were hits. His first score was with the song "Barney Google" in 1922. His other hits included "Without a Song," "Me and My Shadow," "That Old Gang of Mine," "More Than You Know," "It's Only a Paper Moon," "I Found a Million Dollar Baby in a Five and Ten Cents Store," and "Does the Spearmint Lose Its Flavor on the Bedpost Overnight?"

He ran several after-theater supper clubs, some financed by the Mafia, including the Casino de Paree (which became Studio 54), Billy Rose's Music Hall, the Diamond Horseshoe, the Backstage Club, and the Fifth Avenue Club. His acts featured showgirls such as Gypsy Rose Lee, alongside some of the top entertainers of the day—dancers Buck and Bubbles and Eleanor Powell, band leader **Benny Goodman**, and crooner Seymour Rexite. He sold the title of his club—Billy Rose's Diamond Horseshoe—to 20th Century Fox for $100,000.

Billy met his first wife, Broadway star **Fanny Brice**, while writing vaudeville sketches for her after she admired his popular tune "In the Middle of the Night." He then decided to become a theatrical producer, and his first show was the musical revue *Sweet and Low* starring his new wife. It was a flop, so he changed its name to *Crazy Quilt* and put it on the touring circuit. He made his money back.

Rose became known as a showman of the highest order with his circus musical—*Jumbo*—starring Jimmy Durante opposite Big Rosie the elephant. **Ben Hecht** and Charlie MacArthur wrote the script; George Abbott directed. Rodgers and Hart wrote the score, featuring the hit songs "The Circus is on Parade," and "The Most Beautiful Girl in the World." It rehearsed for six months and was sold out, but it lost money because of its high overhead. After *Jumbo,* he was paid $1,000 a day in 1936 to create a show for the Fort Worth Centennial.

Rose put together the dinner theater cabaret *Casa Manana,* starring the fan dancer Sally Rand, on the world's largest revolving stage in an amphitheater that seated 7,500 for the Fort Worth Frontier Days. He met his second wife, olympic swimmer Eleanor Holm, while directing the water spectacle *The Aquacade* (a word he coined) at the 1937 World's Fair in Cleveland, in which she starred. He brought *The Aquacade* to New York in 1939. In 1943, Rose scored both a critical and a popular success as producer of *Carmen Jones,* Oscar Hammerstein's retelling of Bizet's opera *Carmen* with an all-black cast. In 1944, he bought the Ziegfeld Theater, running it as a legit theater for 11 years before leasing it to NBC as a television studio. In 1959, he bought and refurbished his second Broadway theater, a 1200-seat house on 41st Street, renaming it the Billy Rose Theater. It was home to many long-running productions, including Edward Albee's *Who's Afraid of Virginia Woolf?* in 1962.

Rose was also a syndicated columnist, art collector, and investor, and when he died he was the largest shareholder of AT&T. He donated over a million dollars' worth of art to Israel, creating the Billy Rose Sculpture Garden at the Israel Museum in Jerusalem. He had no children but was married and divorced five times, twice to the same woman, actress Joyce Matthews. In addition to Eleanor Holm and Fanny Brice, he was also married to Doris Warner Vidor, the daughter of film producer Harry Warner. He died at his home in Montego Bay, Jamaica at the age of 66 on February 11, 1966. He bequeathed his fortune to a charitable foundation that bears his name and continues to fund the arts in New York City today. *See also* **Brice, Fanny**; **Popular Music**.

Caraid O'Brien

Further Reading: Gottlieb, Polly Rose. *The Nine Lives of Billy Rose.* New York: Crown Publishers, Inc., 1968. Nelson, Stephen. *Only a Paper Moon: The Theatre of Billy Rose.* Ann Arbor: UMI Research Press, 1987.

ROSENBLATT, "YOSSELE" JOSEF (1882–1933)

Yossele Rosenblatt was the leading American cantor in his lifetime. He was born in the Ukraine to Hasidic parents loyal to the Sadigorer Hasidic community (part of the Ruzhiner dynasty) and received a traditional Orthodox upbringing directed by his father, also a cantor. At an early age, it was apparent to all that he was blessed with an exceptional voice and singing talent. Soon he was traveling with his father as a soloist and assisting in leading Jewish prayer services. As a teenager he became the cantor in the city of Munkatch, a stronghold of Hungarian Hasidism. However, his reputation spread, and he was soon lured to the city of Bratislava as chief cantor of the central Orthodox synagogue. Following his tenure there he accepted a position as chief cantor of the Orthodox synagogue in Hamburg, Germany.

Rosenblatt toured Europe giving concerts and was enthusiastically received by audiences. He also recorded a number of record albums, which sold well. At the start of World War I, he was regarded as the world's "king of cantors." He was also respected for his loving and kind personality.

In 1912 Rosenblatt accepted a generous offer to become cantor of the First Hungarian Congregation in New York City, located in Harlem. This was a westernized Orthodox synagogue headed by Rabbis Hillel Klein and Bernard Drachman. Rosenblatt was enthusiastically received and highly regarded, not only by his congregants, but by American Jewry in general. In America he continued to give concerts, and he recorded on the RCA Victor label. His salary at his synagogue was astronomical for that time.

Though he had an excellent tenor voice, Rosenblatt became famous for his falsetto. Unlike other cantors, he not only sang but also composed musical melody. His music was borrowed by many fellow cantors, and his liturgical compositions have become classics in the cantorial world.

As a strict Orthodox and Hasidic Jew, Rosenblatt would not compromise his religious principles by trimming his beard or appearing with female vocalists. He also refused to perform in non-Orthodox synagogues. Rosenblatt, however, did agree to participate in ***The Jazz Singer*** (1927), playing himself. Because of his prominence as a cantor, he caught the attention of the non-Jewish public and was a much sought-after musical personality. He was probably the only Orthodox Jew to become well known in American popular culture and gain respect for his religious devotion. He resisted the temptations of Hollywood and show business.

Rosenblatt was not only a great vocalist but was a generous philanthropist as well, and as such he was always donating his time and energy to various charitable causes. His chief cause, however, was the continuity of Orthodox Judaism. In the 1920s, a number of acquaintances persuaded him to invest in a new, ultra-Orthodox **Yiddish** newspaper called *Di Yiddishe Licht.* Unfortunately, it was run by people who were less than honest. Rosenblatt lost all his money in this venture and was forced to declare bankruptcy.

Even though it was clear that the publishers of this paper used and tricked Rosenblatt, he decided to honor his debts. He embarked on a rigorous schedule of **vaudeville** tours. He was unhappy with the need to make appearances, but they were necessary to pay his creditors. In 1933, he decided to visit Palestine and produce a movie to pay off his debts. He was enthusiastically received by all sectors of the Jewish population. While there, he suffered a stroke and died. Rosenblatt was buried in Jerusalem.

Rosenblatt left a large family, and several of his children were active in Jewish music. His eldest son, Dr. Samuel Rosenblatt, was a well-known Modern Orthodox rabbi and scholar in Baltimore as well as a professor at Johns Hopkins University.

Rosenblatt remains the unchallenged king of cantors to this very day. His records are still popular and in print, and his compositions are sung by a new generation of American and Israeli cantors. *See also* **Cantors in America**.

Zalman Alpert

Further Reading: Halberstadt, Alex. "The Man With the $50,000 Beard." Nextbook.org, June 11, 2007. Olivestone, David. "Standing Room Only: The Remarkable Career of Cantor Yossele Rosenblatt." *Jewish Action,* 1964.

ROSS, BARNEY (1909–1967)

Boxing historian Allen Bodner ranked Barney Ross as the fifth-greatest Jewish boxer of all time. During the 1930s, Ross was lightweight, junior welterweight, and welterweight world champion. He won 74 out of 81 professional fights and was the only Jew to be world champion in three different weight divisions. He was later inducted into the International Boxing Hall of Fame, the World Boxing Hall of Fame, and the International Jewish Sports Hall of Fame. The classic 1949 boxing film *Body and Soul* starring **John Garfield** as the Jewish boxer Charley Davis was loosely modeled on Ross's life.

Ross (Dov-Ber Rasofsky) was born in December, 1909 on New York City's Lower East Side to Isadore (Yitchak) and Sarah Epstein Rasofsky. His parents were immigrants from Brest-Litovsk in White Russia. His father was a rabbi and a student of the Talmud, and the Rasofsky home was strictly Orthodox. In 1911, the Rasofskys moved to Chicago's tough and teeming Maxwell Street Jewish ghetto, where the elder Rasofsky operated a grocery store. Ross's parents hoped their son would become a Talmudic scholar. "If Pa had lived," Ross recalled, "I think he would have killed me before he ever would have permitted me to put on a pair of gloves and climb into a ring" (Kolatch, 1966).

In 1923, Isidore Rasofsky was murdered in a holdup in his store. Out from under control of his strong-willed father, Ross turned to petty crime and boxing in a desperate and successful effort to keep his family of four brothers, a sister, and mother together. Ross was employed briefly as a messenger by Al Capone and during his hoodlum days formed a lifelong friendship with Jacob "Sparky" Rubenstein, alias Jack Ruby.

Ross rejected the Orthodox ways while a teenager, but he never turned his back on the Jewish people or Judaism. At a time when boxers emphasized their ethnicity, he and his handlers capitalized on his Jewish background. He would enter the ring to the tune of "My Yiddish Mama," while wearing a white and blue robe. Ross contributed generously to Jewish charities and was an ardent Zionist. Prior to the establishment of the State of Israel, he was involved in arms running for Jewish forces in Palestine and volunteered to fight for a Jewish state in a Jewish American army. The army was never established, but Ross did tour Canada and the United States selling Israel bonds and speaking in support of a Jewish state.

Ross's autobiography *No Man Stands Alone: The Story of Barney Ross* (1959) recounted how anti-Semitism motivated him as a boxer. "The news from Germany made me feel I was . . . fighting for all of my people." During the 1930s, Ross was one of the great folk heroes of American and Canadian Jews. His prowess in the ring refuted the anti-Semitic calumny that Jews were weak, cowardly, and disdained physicality. Ross showed that Jews could fight back, a personification of the "muscular" Judaism advocated by Max Nordau and other early Zionists.

Jewishness was an ever-present aspect of Ross's public persona. In 1934, he insisted that the date of his defense of the welterweight championship be changed because it fell on the Jewish New Year. This preceded **Hank Greenberg**'s more celebrated refusal in 1934 to play a game for the Detroit Tigers because it conflicted with Yom Kippur. Ross's demand resulted in the rescheduling of the fight, whereas Greenberg's gesture had only symbolic importance since the Tigers had already clinched the American League pennant.

Ross's stature as a Jewish (and American) hero grew during World War II. He enlisted in the U.S. Marine Corps soon after Pearl Harbor at the relatively advanced age of 32 after receiving an age waiver, and he was severely wounded on Guadalcanal on November 19, 1942. He received a Distinguished Service Cross and a Silver Star, America's third-highest military honor, for conspicuous gallantry and intrepidity in action.

During his convalescence at a military hospital, Ross was administered morphine to relieve pains from his wounds and malaria, and he became a drug addict. His addiction grew stronger during 1943 and 1944 while he toured the country, speaking at war rallies at factories and Red Cross centers. His autobiography and the melodramatic 1957 film *Monkey on My Back* discusses his long and painful struggle to kick his drug habit. After his recovery, Ross lectured frequently at high schools on the dangers of drug addiction. He died in January 1967 from cancer of the jaw. *See also* **Sports**.

Edward S. Shapiro

Further Reading: Bodner, Allen. *When Boxing Was a Jewish Sport*. Praeger Trade, 1997. Kolatch, Alfred J. *Great Jewish Quotations*. New York: Jonathan David Co., 1966. Levine, Peter. *Ellis Island to Ebbets Field: Sports and the American Jewish Experience*. New York: Oxford, 1992. Ross, Barney. *No Man Stands Alone: The Story of Barney Ross*. London: Stanley Paul, 1959.

ROSTEN, LEO (1908–1997)

Leo Rosten was a novelist, essayist, screenwriter, and editor who carved a place in popular culture before World War II by creating a comedic literary character named Hyman Kaplan. Kaplan represented the efforts of early twentieth-century Jewish immigrants challenged to assimilate to America through the use of the English language and its cultural contexts. If Hyman Kaplan takes joy in learning English, as much as he maligns it, Rosten paid homage to the *mame loshn* (mother tongue) of many East European Jewish immigrants by writing *The Joys of* ***Yiddish*** (1968). He followed that work with *Hooray for Yiddish!* (1982) and *The Joys of Yinglish* (1989), to show that Yiddish lived on in the hybridized forms used in American English. He was often quoted as a witty speaker and writer, and he took interest in compiling quotations of Jews that left a mark in popular culture with *Leo Rosten's Treasury of Jewish Quotations* (1988). Known primarily as a humorous writer, he had a serious, sociological side expressed in nonfiction that dealt with the social dynamics of the film industry, comparative American religions, public policy, and journalistic practice.

Rosten was born in Lodz, Poland, to Yiddish-speaking parents Samuel and Ida Rosten. His parents brought him to the United States when he was three. They followed the great wave of immigration that was prompted by the push of national intolerance of Jews in Eastern Europe and the pull of industrial opportunities in America. He studied at the University of Chicago as an undergraduate and earned a doctorate in political science in 1937. He worked his way through school by teaching English in night school. There, he encountered a student who provided the inspiration for the ebullient, confident Hyman Kaplan in a collection of humorous stories published as *The Education of H*Y*M*A*N K*A*P*L*A*N* (1937) under the pen name of Leonard Q. Ross. Trying to establish his credentials as an intellectual, he published his dissertation under his own name with the title *The Washington Correspondents* (1937).

The Hyman Kaplan stories were received well, and he published two sequels: *The Return of H*Y*M*A*N K*A*P*L*A*N* (1959) and *O K*A*P*L*A*N, My K*A*P*L*A*N* (1976) under his own name. Many of the stories were literary adaptations of orally circulating dialect jokes in which Jewish Kaplan, speaking with Yiddish intonations, flummoxes the proper English teacher named Mr. Parkhill. The asterisks in the book titles referred to Kaplan's habit of inserting them between each letter of his name on papers he wrote. Critics have debated whether readers found the stories appealing because Kaplan was marginalized due to his immigrant status, which was apparent because of his difficulty with English and understanding cultural contexts, or if the appeal lies in Kaplan's getting the better of Parkhill, who represents normative Anglo-Protestant-dominated society. For some critics, Kaplan was another ethnic dolt, for others he was a sage hero who showed Jewish and immigrant enthusiasm for the American dream.

Kaplan was a vintage first-generation figure; however, Rosten created another comic male character representing the second generation in the form of Jackson Leibowitz. Leibowitz was a newly arrived, neurotic orderly in a psychiatric unit of a military hospital during World War II for the book *Captain Newman, M.D.* (1961). The book was quickly adapted for the Hollywood screen (1963) starring **Tony Curtis** in the role of Leibowitz, Gregory Peck playing Newman, and Angie Dickinson as Lt. Francie Corum. Leibowitz's character continued Rosten's commentary on Jewish assimilation. As a new arrival Jackson is cast as different and misunderstood. Although he has talent, he displays nerdy "Jewish angst" for comic effect. This type of comedy was used by **Woody Allen** and **Jerry Lewis** to express the struggle of being successful in society without being accepted.

By the 1960s, use of Yiddish as a workaday language among the second- and third-generation immigrants declined, and a nostalgia for the "old country" of the Eastern European immigrants swept the Jewish community. National interest also rose with the success of ***Fiddler on the Roof*** and *Funny Girl* on Broadway. Academic linguistic work went into dictionaries such as Uriel Weinreich's *Modern English-Yiddish/Yiddish-English Dictionary* (1968), but what distinguished Rosten's *Joys of Yiddish* (1968) as a reference work was its narrative form. Meanings of Yiddish words such as "chutzpah" and "shlemiel" were explained in anecdotes, reminiscent of the didactic method of the Jewish parable tradition. Although some critics hailed Rosten for creating popular compassion for the language as a symbol of American ethnic roots, others found in the humor a socially sanctioned outlet for conflicts between an emerging assimilated, suburbanized Jewish identity and the need for ethnic display and authenticity to establish a public Jewish presence.

As an immigrant who liked to play with language, Rosten identified with Hyman Kaplan, indicated by the title *The Many Worlds of L*E*O R*O*S*T*E*N* (1964). Rosten was also compared to other wits and wordsmiths such as Sholem Aleichem, using old world Jewish storytelling, and Mark Twain, whose quips are enshrined in oral tradition. Rosten holds a place in popular culture for memorable quotations that dispense wisdom in short declarations or answers to questions such as "Why did God give me two ears and one mouth? So that I will hear more and talk less." *See also* **Yiddish**.

Simon J. Bronner

Further Reading: Bronner, Simon J. "Structural and Stylistic Relations of Oral and Literary Humor: An Analysis of Leo Rosten's H*Y*M*A*N K*A*P*L*A*N Stories." *Journal of the Folklore Institute* 19 (1982): 31–45. Shiffman, Dan. "The Comedy of Assimilation in Leo Rosten's Hyman Kaplan Stories." *Studies in American Humor* 3 (2000): 49–63.

ROTH, DAVID LEE (1955–)

Rock vocalist, songwriter, actor, author, and radio personality David Lee Roth is best known as the lead singer for Van Halen. David Lee Roth was born on October 10, 1955, in Bloomington, Indiana. Though Roth achieved commercial success as a solo recording artist and, briefly, as a radio disc jockey, he is best known as the former lead singer for the legendary rock group Van Halen. Van Halen was inducted into the Rock and Roll Hall of Fame in 2007.

As a youth, Roth migrated with his family from Indiana to southern California. Roth eventually sang lead in a band called the Red Ball Jets, which often played shows with another unknown band from Pasadena, Mammoth. Roth soon became friends with Mammoth's guitar player and drummer—Edward and Alex Van Halen. In 1972 Roth joined the Van Halen brothers (and bass player Michael Anthony) and reportedly suggested the quartet call itself "Van Halen."

As the lead singer for Van Halen, Roth set the mold for the quintessential hard-rock front man. His stage style and antics were copped by countless spandex-wearing imitators. Roth claimed his stage persona and energy arose from his rejection of Jewish stereotypes and anti-Semitism. Thus, Roth's conception of his own Jewish identity ultimately became a major influence on the glam-metal scene which emerged in Van Halen's wake in the mid-1980s.

Van Halen enjoyed immense commercial success with Roth as its front man. The band's 1978 self-titled debut album and *1984* each sold over 10 million copies. All of the other discs recorded with Roth went platinum. In 1983 Van Halen received a record-breaking fee for headlining the 1983 US Festival in San Bernadino, California. Van Halen remained successful after Roth's departure in 1985, but many Van Halen fans lost interest in the band after Roth left. *See also* **Rock and Roll**.

Danny Rigby

Further Reading: Roth, David. *Crazy From the Heat.* Ebury Press, 2000.

ROTH, HENRY (1906–1995)

Author Henry Roth is best known for his first novel, *Call it Sleep*. It was later acclaimed a classic of American Jewish literature but virtually disappeared from view for 30 years because Roth suffered a massive writer's block. The block prevented further major works for twice that length of time. Herschel Roth was born February 8, 1906, in Tysmenitz in the Galicia region of Austria-Hungary. In 1907, he and his mother, Leah, came to New York, where his father, Chaim or Herman, was already living. The family lived in Brooklyn from 1908 to 1910, when they moved to the Jewish Lower East Side. Four years later they moved to Harlem, which was home chiefly to Irish and Italian immigrants. Roth's failure to find acceptance in the neighborhood in part led to his increasing abandonment of Jewish observance. It was at his parents' insistence that he became Bar Mitzvahed in 1919.

Roth graduated from DeWitt Clinton High School in 1924 and began to write while a student at City College of New York (from which he graduated in 1928). He was encouraged by poet and English literature professor Eda Lou Walton, who became his mistress. While living with Walton, who was 12 years his senior, Roth met such notable writers as Hart Crane and Margaret Mead. Roth published the novel *Call It Sleep*—dedicated to Walton—in 1934. Influenced by the works of James Joyce and T. S. Eliot, he was among the first to introduce interior monologue and stream of consciousness into American literature. The life of eight-year-old David Schearl is presented from the hypersensitive Jewish immigrant boy's perspective. Through his eyes, the reader views David's confrontation with the mysteries—religious, sexual, societal—of the world around him, chief among them the domineering and persistent rage of his father and the all-enveloping love of his mother. In the pre-World War I Lower East Side's teeming population of immigrants, David must also face his fears of anti-Semitism and the threats of brutal street gangs.

Roth, who had joined the Communist Party in 1934, was devastated when leftist critics dismissed the novel. They complained that its focus on the psychological landscape of its characters, its linguistic innovations, and its literary flourishes prevented it from accomplishing what they viewed as the only true role of the novel: a means of dramatizing the class struggle and a tool to instigate social change. *Call It Sleep* went out of print and effectively disappeared after the publisher went bankrupt. Roth began a second novel designed to appease his communist critics and completed a number of stories, but he abandoned writing in the early 1940s. He destroyed all his manuscripts and notebooks and entered into a decades-long fallow period, a writer's block ascribed variously to the pressures of the political critics, his self-loathing and depression, his negative self-image as a Jew, his guilt at having misrepresented what was actually an easy early childhood in the Jewish precincts of the Lower East Side, and his then-secret shame over his incestuous relationship with his sister. In 1938, Roth met pianist and composer Muriel Parker at the Yaddo artists' colony in Sarasota Springs, New York. They married the next year and had two sons, Hugh and Jeremy. In 1946, the family moved to Maine.

There and later in New Mexico, Roth found work as, among other occupations, a firefighter, laborer, psychiatric aide, teacher, and waterfowl farmer. His job as a precision tool grinder was his contribution to the war effort. Over the years, there was sporadic interest in *Call It Sleep*. In 1956, it was included on the American Scholar's list of "The Most Neglected Books of the Past 25 Years" and was republished in 1960 as a result of prompting by writer and editor Harold Ribalow. But the work was truly given a second life in 1964 when Irving Howe praised it on the cover of the *Times Book Review*—the first time a paperback had been reviewed in the publication. One million copies of the book were sold, and *Call It Sleep* was widely recognized as a masterpiece of Depression-era American literature. In 1965 Roth received a $2,500 grant from the National Institute of Arts and Letters. Roth's self-abnegation as a Jew, born in part from his view of the Jew as history's perennial victim, was reversed with Israel's victory in the 1967 Six Day War. The Soviet Union's backing of the Arab states whose aim was Israel's destruction effectively broke his embrace of communism. He began to study Hebrew and Jewish history in his return to Judaism, and he began to write again. A small portion of a novel he had begun about Jews during the time of the Spanish Inquisition, a subject inspired by a visit to Seville, was published in the *New Yorker* in 1966. After a summer living near Taos as a D. H. Lawrence Fellow at the University of New Mexico, he and Muriel moved to Albuquerque in 1968. In January 1987, Roth was awarded the Nonino International Prize, one of Italy's most important literary awards. That same year, Roth's *Shifting Landscape: A Composite, 1925–1987,* a collection of short stories, was issued. The first two volumes of his second novel—*A Star Shines Over Mt. Morris Park* and *A Diving Rock on the Hudson* were published shortly before his death in 1995. An autobiographical work, *Mercy of a Rude Stream,* was intended as a six-part novel. However, Roth was able to complete only the first four before his death and left behind two final manuscripts that remain unpublished. *Mercy of a Rude Stream* consists of *A Star Shines Over Mt. Morris Park* (1994), *A Diving Rock on the Hudson* (1995), and the last two volumes, *From Bondage* (1996) and *Requiem for Harlem* (1998), were published posthumously. Among the tributes Roth received were honorary doctorates from the University of New Mexico and Hebrew Union College in Cincinnati. He posthumously received *Hadassah Magazine*'s Harold U. Ribalow Prize, and February 7, 2006, was proclaimed "Henry Roth Day" in New York City. Muriel died in 1990. Roth died at 89 on October 13, 1995, in Albuquerque. *See also* **Literature**.

Abby Meth Kanter

Further Reading: Fiedler, Leslie. "Henry Roth's Neglected Masterpiece." *Commentary Magazine,* 1960. Kellman, Steven G.*Redemption: The Life of Henry Roth.* W.W. Norton, 2005. Michaels, Leonard. "The Long Comeback of Henry Roth: Call it Miraculous." *New York Times Book Review,* August 15, 1993. Rosen, Jonathan. "Writer, Interrupted: The Resurrection of Henry Roth." *New Yorker,* August 1, 2005.

ROTH, PHILIP (1933–)

Philip Roth, one of America's most celebrated writers, was born in Newark, New Jersey, on March 13, 1933, the year Adolf Hitler rose to power in Germany. That year marked the beginning of one of the darkest times in world history in general and Jewish history in particular: the period that culminated in worldwide warfare and the **Holocaust**, (also known as the Shoah). Roth, who was raised in the solidly Jewish household of his parents, Herman and Bess Roth, grew up aware of the dangers that German fascists posed to European Jewry. He also perceived the potential consequences their genocidal drive could have for American Jews who, at the time, were making real progress in fighting pervasive anti-Semitism and were entering the mainstream of American life to a much great extent than ever before.

Under the tutelage of his parents and the close-knit Jewish community in Newark, which later became the setting for many of his novels, Roth came to recognize that "history is everything that happens everywhere." This concept of history, quoted here from *Plot Against America* (2004), binds together not only Jews, but all people. Moreover, it informs Roth's treatment of major historical events, ranging from Eastern European totalitarianism to the American involvement in Vietnam. Arguably, this notion of empathic experience applies to Roth's view of cultural and even personal history as well.

Following the fall of Nazi Germany, Roth, then a teenager attending Weequahic High School, observed a number of Holocaust survivors who settled in Newark, which was then predominantly Jewish. Their accounts of Nazi atrocities kindled a keen spiritual kinship with the now-destroyed civilization that had given birth to Franz Kafka and Anne Frank, two major literary figures who inspired and influenced Roth's artistic development. The pull of the old country from where his own family hailed and the tragic fate of European Jewry permeates much of his work, and these serve as touchstones, indeed, as moral points of reference throughout his fiction. As his writings attest, during his years at Rutgers University (1950–1951), at Bucknell University (AB, 1954), at the University of Chicago (MA, 1955), in the military (1955–1956), and throughout his whole literary career, he could not face his Jewishness or his Americanness without sensing the shadows of the Shoah.

Roth's first book, *Goodbye, Columbus* (1959), which consists of the title novella and five short stories, won the National Book Award. The collection explores many themes that have preoccupied the author throughout his career. It also marks the beginning of an often uneasy relationship between Roth and the Jewish community. *Goodbye, Columbus* examines the quandaries and moral conflicts faced by second- and third-generation American Jews. Struggling with issues of self-definition as both Americans and Jews, they leave behind their inner-city, ethnic enclaves and move into suburban communities that are populated mostly by Gentiles. Their aspirations for upward mobility and full acceptance by the mainstream Gentile community require them to become conspicuously affluent, a circumstance that often causes them to distort their values. In turn, their misplaced values bring about a moral decline. And those characters who become obsessed with wealth and willfully estrange themselves from their Jewish roots invariably suffer an identity crisis. Their disconnection from the moral teachings of Judaism typically results in a sterile assimilation that leaves them spiritually unfulfilled.

As evidenced in most of Roth's writing, fidelity to one's Jewish identification becomes especially important in America. For instance, "Eli, the Fanatic," another story in *Goodbye, Columbus,* shows that in the aftermath of the Holocaust, assimilation and estrangement from Jewish roots are not viable solutions to the long history of Jewish suffering and persecution. The story shames and condemns the deracinated Jews of Woodenton, Long Island, who think that by leaving their neighborhoods and moving into a predominantly Protestant environment they can melt into a new American landscape and thereby absolve themselves from their responsibilities as Jews. In particular, they try to avoid being labeled Jews, identifying themselves as Americans instead. Moreover, they repudiate their responsibilities to a group of Holocaust survivors, 18 children among them, who, in 1948, come to Woodenton to establish a yeshiva within the security of American democracy. Upon meeting the survivors, Eli, the emissary appointed by the Woodenton Jews to rid the town of the yeshiva, undergoes a "conversion" and aligns himself with the Hasidic Jews. He even contemplates raising his newly-born son in a tradition that secured Jewish survival throughout millennia. Finally, the timing of the story, set in 1948, is significant, because the State of Israel was founded that year. In this respect, "Eli, the Fanatic" initiates Roth's career-long representation of Israel as a monument to Jewish resiliency and revival, as well as a safe haven for Jews in the post-Holocaust era. Indeed, Israel goes on to serve as a frequent destination both for Philip Roth the writer and for several of his fictional characters, who endure the controversies and conflicts generated by the establishment of the Jewish homeland and who cope with the complexities of Jewish lives and counter lives.

Goodbye, Columbus thus treats many real-life issues and acrimonies that the American Jewish community faced in the second part of the twentieth century. Whatever they may be: intergenerational tensions, the relationship of individuals to their communities, the role of writers in the formation of a social and cultural consciousness, ethnic relations in America, competing national allegiances, and/or materialism and spiritual depravity, Roth examines these issues not only as a Jew but also as an American. Indeed, Roth stands primarily as an American artist whose Jewishness reinforces his sense of Americanness. From his earliest stories in *Goodbye, Columbus,* through such mid-career publications as *The Ghost Writer* (1979), to his 21st novel, *The Plot Against America,* being an American remains synonymous with being a Jew, because both enjoy the freedom to shape their own destinies, guaranteed respectively by secular and sacred law, and both are thus charged with using their freedom wisely and responsibly.

It is not hard to understand the reasons for Jewish sensitivities and insecurities in the aftermath of the Shoah and America's reluctance to join the fight against Nazi Germany before December 1941. But in spite of accusations by some critics and community leaders that he ignored these sensitivities and depicted Jews in disparaging ways, Roth felt he needed to engage the social and cultural milieu he knew so intimately and cared for so deeply, one that has remained a source of his artistic inspiration throughout his prolific career. Therefore, while acknowledging the historical vulnerability of the Jewish people, Roth nevertheless insisted that America provides Jews with a rare opportunity to assert their equality, to live in dignity, and to laugh at themselves, if they choose to do so.

With this in mind, in his second novel, *Letting Go* (1962), he continues to explore the complicated familial relationships between Jewish parents and their sons, examine the vicissitudes of male and female friendships, and scrutinize the increasingly tighter interaction between the Jewish and non-Jewish worlds. In his next novel, *When She Was Good* (1967), Roth gives his readers a glimpse into the world of several generations of Gentile Midwestern families. Although some critics maintain he wrote it to distance himself from his Jewish subjects, in order to avoid criticism of self-hatred and anti-Semitism, the novel reaffirms Roth's implicit identification of Jews and Americans by demonstrating how the turbulence and intimate concerns experienced by members of Jewish families mirror those experienced by non-Jews.

Roth's foray into the non-Jewish world did not placate some of his Jewish detractors, and when he published *Portnoy's Complaint* in 1969, the earlier charges of self-hatred were supplemented by new accusations that Roth was ridiculing the mother-child and father-son relationships in Jewish families. Fueling these charges was outrage among some members of the Jewish community over protagonist Alex Portnoy's sexual exploits, which introduced elements of amorality and pornography into the fiction. Others viewed Roth's comic portrayal of a possessive Jewish mother and a constipated father as an assault on the Jewish middle-class, which often regarded sexual pleasure and traditional morality as incompatible. Even Irving Howe, a seasoned critic and early supporter of Roth, turned his back on the young writer and predicted his rapid artistic decline.

Overall, Roth's serious exploration of Portnoy's effort to balance the restrictive, moral Jewish traditions with the seductive forces of contemporary American culture was often overlooked. Nonetheless, in spite of the novel's being misread and despite the many mistaken efforts to identify him with his lascivious protagonist, Roth maintains that *Portnoy's Complaint* and some of his other writings perceived critical of Jews have blessed him by enabling him to engage a Jewish audience whose "expectations, disdain, delight, criticism, their wounded self-love, their healthy curiosity" fuel his imagination and provide him

American Jewish novelist Philip Roth receiving the 2002 National Book Foundation's Medal for Distinguished Contribution to American Letters in New York City, November 20, 2002. The author best known for *Portnoy's Complaint* (1969) has written more than 25 novels. [AP Photo]

with subjects that turn into artistic obsessions worthy of serious inquiry.

America has been and remains one of those subjects. As a prelude to a close examination of his native country in his later novels, in the 1970s Roth began to focus upon various aspects of American public life, including the country's political leadership; America's role in world affairs; and the damaging affects of McCarthyism, the Cold War, the Vietnam War, and the Watergate affair. In *On the Air* (1970), *Our Gang* (1971), and *The Great American Novel* (1973) Roth employs satire and parody, rather than the realism of his earlier works, to explore how these developments in American history have become imprinted upon the once "pastoral" fabric of American existence.

His often acrimonious encounters with Jewish critics, however, and the controversies generated by his earlier writings weighed heavily on Roth's mind and raised several issues about life and art that he felt he needed to address. *My Life As a Man* (1974) introduces Nathan Zuckerman, Roth's celebrated protagonist and alter ego who reappears in many subsequent novels. *My Life As a Man* examines the relationship between Zuckerman's life and his art, and the ways he translates personal experiences into artistic achievements. This investigation continues in the *Professor of Desire* (1977), where Roth again dwells on the uneasy relationship between one man's longing for erotic and sensual pleasure and the social pressures on him to lead a dignified and orderly life. The issue leads David Kepesh, the book's protagonist, to take a closer look at the uses of literature and its functions. His visit to Kafka's grave in Prague and his deeper appreciation of how artists and intellectuals struggled to survive meaningfully under totalitarianism affect him profoundly. Finally, Kepesh realizes that literature offers tools for measuring the success and failure of existence and for enabling him to escape the self-absorption and self-centeredness that had afflicted him and other American intellectuals.

From his earliest publications to the present, Roth has focused primarily on the interplay between the artist's inner self and the artist's vocation. His frequent visits to Eastern Europe and his decision to move to London in 1976 with Claire Bloom, the famous British actress, mark the "globalization" of Roth's fiction. Although the ever-present "tension between license and restraint" that gave rise to and informed Roth's art continued to permeate his novels, in the 1980s and 1990s that tension was mostly refracted through narratives about European and American history and the birth of the State of Israel. These pit Roth's various versions of the Portnoy/Kepesh/Zuckerman selves against broad historical events, including World War II and the Holocaust, Stalinist repressions and European xenophobia, the Red Scare and civil turbulence of the 1960s, and, of course, the Middle East conflicts. These novels reflect a "struggle between personal liberty and the forces of inhibition" set against historical calamities that pose a constant threat to the autonomy of the individual self and the autonomy of art.

The Zuckerman Bound trilogy charts a long journey of a Jewish American artist from Newark to Prague. Consisting of *The Ghost Writer* (1979), *Zuckerman Unbound* (1981), and *The Anatomy Lesson* (1983), and followed by an epilogue, the *The Prague Orgy* (1985), the Zuckerman series commences with the young artist/narrator of *The Ghost Writer* seeking to find his own voice, so he may "say something new and wrenching to Gentiles about the Jews, and Jews about themselves." It ends with his realization that a Jewish writer needs to be bound by the Jewish collective past and with a dictate to commemorate the victims of the Holocaust, so that the Shoah can be removed from its enormous inhuman dimension and brought closer to human beings. In *The Ghost Writer* young Nathan Zuckerman imagines Amy Bellette, an aspiring writer and Holocaust survivor he meets in the Berkshires, to be Anne Frank and the woman he wants to marry. Retelling the story of Anne Frank as if she were still alive not only underscores the tragedy of the teenage writer's murder, it also binds the connection between eradicated European Jewry and its American decedents.

Zuckerman Unbound and *The Anatomy Lesson* demonstrate that this connection often will be challenged by fame, money, and the seductive allure of assimilation. *The Prague Orgy,* however, makes it abundantly clear that a Jewish writer's artistic imagination is nourished by his continuous efforts to sanctify the connection between the Jewish past and the Jewish present and to safeguard the integrity of that connection. Nathan Zuckerman undertakes a pilgrimage to Prague to retrieve the manuscripts of a Jewish writer who perished in the Holocaust and whose story is being distorted by anti-Semitic communists. This is a pilgrimage against oblivion and historical revisionism. But, although successful in reclaiming the manuscripts, Zuckerman fails to smuggle them out of the country. Labeled a Zionist agent and a thief, he is compelled to surrender the writings and is expelled from the country. Ultimately, Roth intimates that the ongoing effort to victimize the Jews, even dead Jews, must be countered by the continued survival of a Jewish homeland and by holding America responsible for living up to the promise of its own dreams. These conclusions are elaborated in more detail in *The Counterlife* (1986), in which Zuckerman travels to Israel, where he encounters alternate paths of life that he might have followed had he been born there. And although Zuckerman, after a short sojourn in England, chooses to return to America, he acknowledges the importance of Israel to world Jewry and its collective destiny.

In 1988, Roth took stock of his career in *The Facts: A Novelist's Biography,* in which he questions the very nature of autobiographical writing. About the same time the author's long sojourn in England was coming to a close. But before turning a page in the book of his own life, he paused briefly to write *Deception* (1990), Zuckerman/Roth's romantic farewell to extramarital felicity in London, the heart of Christendom. *Deception* introduces metaphysical musings and thematic obsessions that Roth further develops in his subsequent work. Although a welcome turn of events, Roth's taking leave of Europe coincided with his very painful separation from his father, who died in 1990. *Patrimony: A True Story* (1991) pays tribute to Herman Roth, a father whose resiliency, zest for life, and an enviable knowledge of self and the world stand in stark opposition to the uncertainties that Philip Roth's fictional characters experience on the "darkling plains" of their own existence.

Orphaned, Roth again set his sight on Israel, a country his father loved passionately. Based on his visit there to witness the trial of John Demjanjuk (1987–1988), the notorious concentration camp guard, Roth's next novel, *Operation Shylock: A Confession* (1993), fuses fact and fiction in its depiction of Israel as a place of often incomprehensible political and ideological controversies and competing national agendas. Nonetheless, one thing remains constant: the importance of safeguarding the Jewish homeland in the aftermath of the Shoah. The book also investigates post-Holocaust Jewish consciousness and destiny, as well as the pleasures and agonies of exile.

As it turns out, the source of these pleasures and agonies is America, the land of promise and artistic imagination whose binding and beckoning forces Roth could fully understand only by temporarily distancing himself and his protagonists from their native country. *The Sabbath Theatre* (1995) is, according to Roth, the "real turning back to American stuff," and Mickey Sabbath, its Dionysian, larger-than-life protagonist, is an authentic American voice struggling to be heard and understood through the cacophony of voices from competing American backgrounds and circumstances. Religious, racial, ethnic, political, generational, and gender disparities inform much of twentieth-century American history, and Roth renders the interplay among them in *American Pastoral* (1997), *I Married A Communist* (1998), and *The Human Stain* (2000). Designed to depict the "ideological ethos of postwar America," the trilogy is narrated by a wiser and older Nathan Zuckerman. In these novels Roth issues a fictional report card for America. Assigned a barely passing grade, America the Beautiful nevertheless promises to remain one of Roth's primary sources of pleasure and pain. More importantly, it remains a rich spring well of artistic creativity and inspiration.

"To shake loose of the dark Zuckerman take on American life," Roth wrote *The Dying Animal* (2001), a playfully serious novel that yet again has its protagonist, David Kepesh, test his manhood against societal restrictions and norms. Nothing is playful, however, about 2001, the year *The Dying Animal* was published. The shadow of horrific September 11 attacks on the Pentagon and New York's World Trade Center casts a dark spell on the four novels Roth published following September 11: *The Plot Against America, Everyman* (2006), *Exit Ghost* (2007), and *Indignation* (2008).

According to *Everyman*'s protagonist, "the catastrophe had subverted everyone's sense of security and introduced an eradicable precariousness into their daily lives." When the very ideas of freedom and democracy come under attack the sense of vulnerability citizens experience becomes a "fear of the unforseen" and a tragic state of existence that prevents a parent from making a child's fate seem predictable.

The Plot Against America explores these fears and vulnerabilities when it recreates the lives of Herman and Bess Roth and their two children, Sandy and Philip, during the early 1940s. An alternative history, or uchronia, as Roth calls it, the novel's premise is that Charles Lindbergh, the aeronautical hero, is elected president and makes good on the promise the real Lindbergh actually made in a speech on September 11, 1941 that America will stay out of the war in Europe while the Jews were dying in the Holocaust. Under Lindbergh's presidency, the Roth family is exiled within their own country. They are on the verge of experiencing the horrific fate of their Jewish counterparts in Europe. Lindbergh's timely demise and America's love for freedom saves them, and potential genocide is averted. But it could have happened, had democracy given way to totalitarianism, or had Herman Roth failed to act as a dignified Jew and a patriotic American when defending his family and his country.

Roth continues his investigation of the consequences of the September 11 tragedy in *Everyman,* where his main character engages in a process of self-reflection and introspection in order to examine the validity of his values as he faces illness, old age, and death in a world torn apart by war and terror. Nathan Zuckerman, the protagonist of *Exit Ghost,* undergoes a similar journey of self-reflection as an artist whose time has come to contemplate issues of mortality and literary legacy. Roth's recent works make it clear that Zuckerman would have never become the writer he is had Franz Kafka and Anne

Frank not been part of his artistic pilgrimage, and if Philip Roth, his creator, had not been born in a country where "growing up Jewish . . . and growing up American seemed to [him] indistinguishable."

Philip Roth's artistic achievements have been richly rewarded by numerous literary awards. The Library of America has committed to publishing eight volumes of Roth's writings, a rare distinction for a living author. *See also* **Literature**.

Asher Z. Milbauer

Further Reading: Cooper, Alan. *Philip Roth and the Jews* (SUNY Series in Modern Jewish Literature and Culture), 1996. Podhoretz, Norman. "The Adventures of Philip Roth." *Commentary,* October 1998. Safer, Elaine B. *Mocking the Age: The Later Novels of Philip Roth* (SUNY Series in Modern Jewish Literature and Culture), 2006.

RUBIN, RICK (1963–)

Frederick Jay (Rick) Rubin is one of the most influential music producers of the last three decades. Rubin was born on March 10, 1963 in Lido Beach, Long Island, New York. His grandparents, Birdie and Jack Rubin, kept a kosher home. Rubin's parents, Martin (Mickey) and Linda Rubin, are Conservative Jews who observe many of the Jewish holidays. Rubin went to Temple Israel in Long Beach, New York and had his Bar Mitzvah at Singer's Hotel in Spring Valley, New York in June 1976.

Rubin was among the first generation of suburban youth to embrace the emerging urban hip hop scene in the late 1970s and early 1980s. His major contribution to popular music was coupling the hip hop sound with heavy metal, leading to the commercial success of both of these underground genres and innovating the music industry. Rubin began producing music while a film student at New York University, but his notoriety in the music industry grew after he joined Russell Simmons to form Def Jam Records in 1984. Under the Def Jam label, Rubin produced early hip hop legends including Public Enemy, LL Cool J, and Run-DMC, as well as metal bands like Slayer and Danzig. But it was Rubin's unique contribution of mixing metal and hip hop genres, most evident in Run-DMC and Aerosmith's chart-topping coverage of Aerosmith's classic "Walk This Way" in 1985 and in the production of the **Beastie Boys**' top-selling 1986 album *Licensed to Ill,* that profoundly influenced popular music.

By 1988 Rubin split with Simmons and moved to Los Angeles, where he formed the Def American label. He continued working with both hip hop and metal artists, producing several highly successful albums, including the Red Hot Chili Peppers' *Blood, Sugar, Sex, Magik* in 1991, before dropping "Def" from the label title in 1993. Under the new title American Records, Rubin produced the late Johnny Cash's Grammy Award-winning compilation, *The American Recordings.* Rubin's knack for juxtaposing music styles and artists impacted Cash and is exhibited in Cash's renditions of the Nine Inch Nails' "Hurt" and Soundgarden's "Rusty Cage." Rubin helped rejuvenate **Neil Diamond**'s, Tom Petty's, and Donovan's careers as well. Despite his widespread influence and market success, Rubin only won his first Producer of the Year Grammy Award in 2007 after three previous nominations in 1994, 1995, and 1999.

In 2007 Rubin was also named one of *Time* magazine's 100 most influential people. Rubin continues producing music and working with diverse artists ranging from Justin Timberlake, the Dixie Chicks, and System of a Down to U2, Jay-Z, and Lil Jon. *See also* **Rock and Roll**.

Maury I. Wiseman

Further Reading: Hirschberg, Lynn. "The Music Man: Can Rick Rubin Save the Music Business?" *New York Times Magazine,* September 2, 2007, 26–33, 46, 49–50.

S

SAGAN, CARL (1934–1996)

Carl Sagan entered popular culture via television and in film. He appeared frequently on *The Tonight Show.* The movie *Contact* (1997) is based on his book, while the television documentary *Cosmos* (again based on his book) is still popular. Sagan is noted for his search for extra terrestrial intelligence (SETI). He warned America about the dangers of nuclear war by explaining nuclear winter in over 100 scientific articles. As advisor to NASA, he helped with space missions both manned and unmanned. His predictions of what the missions would discover were remarkably accurate.

Born in 1934, in a working-class Jewish section of Brooklyn, his parents, Sam Sagan and Rachel Molly (née Gruber), were poor. His father was a garment worker and his mother an amateur writer. Sagan received all his degrees, including his PhD in physics and astronomy, from the University of Chicago. He was married three times: Lynn Marguiles (1957), Linda Salzman (1968), and Ann Druyan (1981–1996). He fathered five children.

Sagan was a freethinker, an atheist, and a skeptic and severe critic of religion. His book *The Demon-Haunted World* (1995) attacks religious beliefs. His writings about religion mock conventional views about God. His son, Dorion, wrote *Atheist Universe* (2006). The scientist who popularized the cosmos died of bone cancer in Seattle in 1996. He is buried with a plastic stone in a non-denominational cemetery.

Philip Rosen

Further Reading: Davidson, Keay. *Carl Sagan: A Life.* John Wily and Sons, 2000.

SALES, SOUPY (1926–)

Soupy Sales is best known for his long-running daily children's television show, *Lunch with Soupy Sales.* The show was originally called *12 O' Clock Comics* and was later known as *The Soupy Sales Show.* Improvised and slapstick in nature, *Lunch with Soupy Sales* was a rapid-fire stream of sketches, gags, and puns, almost all of which resulted in Sales's receiving a pie in the face, which became his trademark. Born Milton Supman, Sales was the youngest of Irving and Sadie Supman's three sons. The Supmans moved from Baltimore to Franklinton, North Carolina, where they operated a dry goods store. In time, the Supman family relocated to Huntington, West Virginia. Milton Supman graduated from Huntington High School and Madison University.

Using his nickname "Soupman" and the last name of Charles (Chic) Sale, a comedian popular in the 1920s, Supman invented his show business persona, Soupy Sales. Sales began his career as a disc jockey and host of *Soupy's Soda Shop,* a television dance show for teenagers that aired in Cincinnati in 1950. Sales attained national recognition when *The Soupy Sales Show* replaced ABC's *Kukla, Fran and Ollie* during the summer of 1955. The show was broadcast live and ran for 15 minutes.

The Soupy Sales Show aired from 1964 to 1966. The show was a nonstop barrage of one-liners, pies-in-the-face, and celebrity guest spots, including Frank Sinatra, **Sammy Davis Jr.**, and Dean Martin, as well as imaginary guests whose arrival was signaled by a loud knock on the door. Sales's conversations with his costars White Fang and Black Tooth and their unintelligible grunts, groans, and wild waving of their huge paws were present in many episodes, often causing Sales to roar with laughter because of the unexpected and unusual nature of the dialogue. Complementing the show was Sales's every present sidekick, Pookie the Lion, who offered an abundance of advice, as well as Bubbles, who was Sales's female alter ego. *The New Soupy Sales Show* aired in 1979 but was short lived. Sales also appeared on many television shows. He was a regular panelist on the syndicated revival of *What's My Line.*

Sales's edgy humor has been a subject of controversy. Adult humor and double entendre were always woven into the fabric of the show, and viewers always looked forward to his next performance. References to his Jewish heritage were occasionally included in Sales's "shtick" and usually followed by his deadpan facial expression. Philo Kvetch, one of his characters, provided his viewers with a subtle **Yiddish** connection. Cast and crew members who understood Yiddish could be heard laughing as Sales moved through his performance. A story describing Mrs. Supman sharing Hamantaschen (Purim cookies) with the neighbors in Huntington and Sales's mother's recipe for Milchig (Dairy) Fish Soup are included in a collection of kosher recipes at lynnescountrykitchen.net.

In 2003, Sales's autobiography, *Soupy Sez!: My Zany Life and Times,* was published. Soupy received a star on the Hollywood Walk of Fame in 2005. Sales's first wife was Barbara Fox, whom he married in 1950. After divorcing her Sales married his second wife, Trudy Carson, in 1980, who was a professional dancer and Rockette at Radio City Music Hall. Soupy is the father of two sons, Hunt Sales and Tony Fox Sales, who are musicians and formed the band Tony and the Tigers. *See also* **Television**.

Robert Ruder

Further Reading: Sales, Soupy. *Did You Hear the One About: The Greatest Jokes Ever Told.* M. Evans, 1987. ———. *Soupy Sez!: My Zany Life and Times.* M. Evans, 2003. ———. *Stop Me If You've Heard It!: Soupy Sales' Favorite Jokes.* M. Evans, 2003.

SALINGER, JEROME (1919–)

J. D. Salinger was born in New York on New Year's Day, 1919. His father, Saul, was a prosperous importer of kosher cheese; his mother, Marie Jillich, was half Scottish, half Irish. Marie changed her name to Miriam and passed herself off as Jewish; her son did not learn this until after his Bar Mitzvah. Salinger began writing while a student at Valley Forge Military Academy.

Drafted in 1942, Salinger saw action at Normandy and the Battle of the Bulge. He used much of his wartime experience in his writing. While in Europe, he met Ernest Hemingway who, upon reading a few Salinger's stories, remarked, "Jesus, he has a helluva talent."

Salinger's first published story, "The Young Folks," appeared in 1940. In 1942, Salinger's "Slight Rebellion off Madison" was accepted by the *New Yorker* but did not run until 1946. The story featured a semi-autobiographical character named Holden Caulfield. Salinger's 1948 story "A Perfect Day for Bananafish" so impressed the magazine's editors that they signed him to a contract in which they received "first right of refusal."

Salinger gained literary immortality with *The Catcher in the Rye,* a novel driven by the nuanced, intricate character of Holden Caulfield. It received glowing reviews. It was also banned in many places for its bold, and to some, offensive language. Nonetheless, it is still a "required read" in most American high schools.

In 1953, Salinger moved to Cornish, New Hampshire, where he has since lived a hermetic life. In addition to *The Catcher in the Rye,* Salinger has published three collections of short stories. A major theme of Salinger's work is the strong, yet delicate mind of "disturbed" adolescents and the redemptive capacity of children in the lives of such young men. Many believe that his works are largely autobiographical, including his novel *Franny and Zooey* (1961).

Salinger has been married three times and has two adult children, Margaret, who later published a memoir of her family life entitled *Dream Catcher* (2000), and Matt, who became an actor. Although raised as a Jew, Salinger moved away from Judaism and for a time was attracted to Hinduism, where he was initiated into the practice of Kriya Yoga. Subsequently, he gravitated to Scientology and later was attracted to a number of spiritual and medical belief systems including Christian Science, the teachings of Edgar Cayce, and sitting in a Reichian "orgone box" to accumulate orgone energy. In 1999, he was the subject of the documentary *JD Salinger Doesn't Want to Talk.* *See also* **Literature**.

Kurt F. Stone

Further Reading: Alexander, Paul. *Salinger: A Biography.* Los Angeles: Renaissance, 1999. Crawford, Catherine, ed. *If You Really Want to Hear About It: Writers on J. D. Salinger and His Work.* New York: Thunder's Mouth, 2006. Salinger, Margaret. *Dream Catcher: A Memoir.* New York: Washington Square Press, 2000.

SANDLER, ADAM (1966–)

Anger Management (2003) is set in Brooklyn in 1978 and opens as fifth grader Sarah Plowman invites Dave Buznik to give her his first kiss in front of everyone. A second before the big moment, neighborhood bully Arnie Shankman pulls down Dave's shorts. Everyone laughs, including Sarah. This episode traumatizes Dave for 25 years, making him shy away from his emotional and financial ambitions. In the 1970s, overrated movies about personal traumas were perceived as portrayals of New York Jewish humor. But Adam Sandler, comedian, singer, actor, screenwriter, and producer, brought back to these portrayals the raw energy that **Woody Allen** hid under a couch through endless therapies of nostalgic remembrances of **Groucho Marx**.

Sandler was born in Brooklyn to Judy and Stanley Sandler, respectively a nursery school teacher and an electrical engineer. They provided Adam with a Jewish upbringing. When he was five, Adam's family moved to Manchester, New Hampshire, where he graduated from Central High School, the school to which he dedicated his song "Lunchlady Land." Adam began his career in stand-up humor at a Boston comedy club at age 17. While studying Fine Arts at New York University, Adam continued performing in comedy clubs and played Theo's friend "Smitty" on *The Cosby Show,* which landed him a job hosting the game show *Remote Control* on MTV.

Dennis Miller, a *Saturday Night Live* (*SNL*) performer, discovered Sandler and recommended him to the show's producer, Lorne Michaels. Sandler was hired as a writer but quickly became a featured player. From 1991 to 1995, Sandler played many characters, such as scout "Canteen Boy" and "Iraqi Pete." He also wrote songs, many of which have become classics, such as "The Hanukkah Song." *SNL* works because of camaraderie of the cast, and Adam made his mark in sketches with fellow comedy performers such as Rob Schneider, Kevin Nealon, John Lovitz, Chris Rock, David Spade, and Chris Farley. Some of the show's greatest moments were performed by the duo of Sandler and Farley.

Sandler left *SNL* in 1995 to work full-time in films. His earlier films, *Going Overboard* (1989), *Shakes the Clown* (1992), *Coneheads* (1993), and *Airheads* (1994), were moderate commercial successes. Beginning with *Billy Madison* (1995), Sandler's "star" power rose, and he became a bankable comedy actor in such commercial hits as *Happy Gilmore* (1996), *The Wedding Singer* (1998), *The Waterboy* (1998), and *Little Nicky* (2000). Sandler's films showcased his comedic talents, and film critics were less than enthused.

His serious side as an actor became apparent in the critically well-received film *Punch-Drunk Love* (2002), for which he received a Golden Globe nomination. Other films that have contributed to Sandler's status as a film star include *Anger Management* (2003), *50 First Dates* (2004), *Spanglish* (2004), *Click* (2006), and *Reign Over Me* (2007). Sandler has been involved in 35 movies as of 2007.

Sandler has maintained a strong identification with the Jewish community through his three "Hanukkah Song" recordings. Impersonating Bin Laden in the third "Hanukkah Song," Sandler parodies Osama when he reveals that the terrorist leader began to hate Jews when he lost a figure-skating match to Jewish champion skater Sarah Hughes. The three Hanukkah songs also confront anti-Semitic stereotypes with lyrics such as "People think Ebenezer Scrooge is Jewish, well he's not, but guess who is, all three Stooges." He even produced a cartoon, *8 Crazy Nights* (2002), which includes his Hanukkah song in the credit.

Above all, Sandler is appreciated for being a mensch. His motto could be "help your friends discreetly and despise those who are indiscreet with friends' misadventures and departures." When journalists became more interested in Drew Barrymore's private life than her acting ability, Sandler offered her the leading role in *The Wedding Singer* (and received the MTV Award for Best Movie Kiss). Sandler's web site features three personal videos on his home page: an updated newsreel, a special message for the troops fighting in Iraq, and one for his father and mentor, Stanley Sandler. In *50 First Dates* (2004), Barrymore and Sandler again teamed up to tell the story of Dr. Henry Roth, who falls in love with Lucy, a woman who suffers from short-term memory loss. Henry must get Lucy to fall in love with him each time they meet, as she has no memory of ever having met him before. *Reign Over Me* (2007) provided Sandler the opportunity to take on a more serious role as a man who lost his family in the September 11 attack on New York City. He runs into his old college roommate, and rekindling the friendship is the one thing that appears able to help the man recover from his grief.

On June 22, 2003, Sandler married actress Jacqueline Samantha Titone, and they are the parents of Sadie Madison Sandler, born May 6, 2006 at Cedars-Sinai in Los Angeles. (Sandler lives with his family in Los Angeles, though he also has a home in New York.) *See also* **Comedy**; **Film**.

Steve Krief

Further Reading: Pfefferman, Naomi. "Crazy for Chanukah: An Animated Adam Sandler Brings the Festival of Lights to Pop Culture." *Jewish Journal,* November 28, 2002.

SARNOFF, DAVID (1891–1971)

Sarnoff was a businessman and pioneer of American commercial **radio** and **television**. He founded the National Broadcasting Company (NBC), and throughout most of his career he led the Radio Corporation of America (RCA) in various capacities from shortly after its founding in 1919 until his retirement in 1970. David Sarnoff was the eldest of five children. He was born on February 27, 1891, in a small Jewish community called Uzlian not far from the Russian city of Minsk. Abraham Sarnoff, his father, hoped that his eldest would also become a tradesman, but his mother wanted him to become a scholar. When his father left for America, his mother sent young Sarnoff to study Talmud with her uncle, who was a rabbi. By the time Abraham Sarnoff sent for his family to come to America in the summer of 1900, David Sarnoff was able to memorize some 2,000 words of Talmud a day, but two days after arriving in America, he was selling newspapers in the streets to help support his family. Sometimes he also ran errands for the local butcher. Soon he had his own newsstand, which he opened in the early mornings and late afternoons. He also earned money as a boy soprano for the choir of his synagogue.

His father died when Sarnoff was 15. The boy left school to become a messenger boy for the Commercial Cable Company. He bought himself a telegraph, learned Morse code, and within a few months applied for a job as an operator at the Marconi Wireless Telegraph Company of America. They hired him to be an office boy rather than a telegraph operator. In his spare time he read and studied technical books. By 1908 the company sent him to the Marconi station at Nantucket Island. There he continued his studies using books from the technical library. Within a year he was transferred to Sea Gate, Coney Island. After work he took courses in electrical engineering at Pratt Institute in Brooklyn. In 1911, he worked as a marine radio operator on board the S.S. *Beothic* on an Arctic sealing expedition and then on the S.S. *Harvard* sailing between Newark and Boston and on cross-Atlantic trips.

When John Wanamaker of Philadelphia installed the most powerful radio station of the time atop his New York store, Sarnoff applied for the job as a radio operator. It was Sarnoff who picked up the message from the S.S. *Titantic* on April 14, 1912: "ran into an iceberg sinking fast." For the next 72 hours he received various messages from the *Titanic* and relayed the details of the disaster and the names of survivors to the news media. As a reward for his work the Marconi Company appointed him radio inspector and instructor at the Marconi Institute. By 1913 he became chief radio inspector and assistant chief engineer, and in 1914 he was promoted to be contract manager. Sarnoff was on his way as a radio pioneer.

In 1915, Sarnoff presented the Marconi Company with an idea that he called a "radio music box." He suggested that music could be sent over the air and that it could be picked up by a simple radio receiver arranged for different wave lengths. It would be changeable by the throwing of a switch or the pressure of a single button. On April 29,1921, he submitted the proposal once again to the newly formed Radio Corporation of America, which had taken over American Marconi. They were impressed by his idea. He further demonstrated the idea by transmitting a blow-by-blow broadcast of the 1921 Dempsey-Carpentier championship fight. That first broadcast had more than 200,000 amateur wireless operators listening in to Sarnoff's broadcast.

When RCA began the manufacture of receiving sets in 1923, it chose David Sarnoff to be one of their vice presidents. Three years later RCA launched the National Broadcasting Company under the leadership of Sarnoff, who came up with the concept of combining radio and phonograph in one cabinet. When in 1923 Dr. Vladimir Zworkin invented the iconoscope, Sarnoff set up a special NBC station (B2XBS) to work on what came to be known as "television."

In 1929, Sarnoff traveled to Europe to help set up the "Young Plan" to help Germany pay World War I reparations. When Sarnoff returned on January 3, 1930, he was named president of RCA. Among his achievements during his tenure as president of RCA was inaugurating the Music Appreciation Hour conducted by Walter Damrosch, introducing broadcasts of grand opera from the stage of the Metropolitan Opera house in New York, and establishing the NBC Symphony Orchestra under the great Italian conductor Arturo Toscanini.

The inaugural demonstration of television was conducted by NBC at the opening of the New York World's Fair on April 30, 1939. Sarnoff apparently said, "Now at last we add sight to sound." In 1941 NBC started commercial television broadcasting from Station WNBT, New York. When he was called to active duty on March 20, 1944, Sarnoff was sent overseas to serve as General Eisenhower's communications consultant. After the war he was an ardent supporter of the United Nations and suggested that it establish an independent international broadcasting system to promote peace and understanding. In July 1947 he was elected chairman of the board of RCA. In addition to his leadership at

RCA, he was very much involved in the Metropolitan Opera Association and was a trustee of both NYU and Pratt Institute. He was one of the leading pioneers in world broadcasting, but he never returned to his study of the Talmud.

In 1917 he married Lizette Hermant, and they had three sons. He died December 12, 1971. *See also* **Radio**; **Television**.

Herbert M. Druks

Further Reading: Lyons, Eugene. *David Sarnoff.* New York: Harper & Row, 1966.

SCHARY, (ISIDORE) DORE (1905–1980)

Dore Schary was a motion picture director, writer, producer, playwright, and liberal political activist, and he served as national chairman of the B'nai B'rith's Anti-Defamation League. Schary was born in Newark, New Jersey, to parents who were of Central European background. They ran a hotel and catering business. Schary attended Newark Central High School but dropped out at the age of 14 to work as a salesman and a printer for the *Newark Sunday Call.* It was there that he began his writing career.

Schary turned his focus to playwriting, and by age 33, a few of his works, such as *Too Many Heroes,* had been produced by New York's legitimate theater. By 1934, he was freelancing for Paramount, Warner Brothers, and MGM. Over the next 6 years he authored some 35 screenplays. *Boy's Town,* written during this period, won an Oscar. Among the other screenplays to his credit were *Young Tom Edison, Edison the Man, Married Bachelor,* and *Broadway Melody.*

During World War II, Schary produced films such as MGM's *Journey for Margaret, Lassie Come Home, Bataan,* and *Joe Smith, American.* In 1944, he joined David O. Selznick's Vanguard Productions and made hit films such as *I'll Be Seeing You.* From 1945 through 1946 he worked for RKO Radio Pictures. At RKO he produced four pictures: *The Spiral Staircase, Till the End of Time, The Bachelor and the Bobby-Soxer,* and *The Farmer's Daughter.*

Schary was selected to be vice president in charge of production at RKO in 1947. That year he made *Crossfire,* a film about anti-Semitism in America. A few years later he developed a film that advocated tolerance called *The Boy with Green Hair.* These films were significant in that they were produced while the House Un-American Activities Committee was investigating communist influence in the country. Schary's deep interest in social problems stemmed from his upbringing in New Jersey, where daily fights took place among boys from different ethnic backgrounds. His fight against bigotry earned him the position of National Chairperson for B'nai B'rith Anti-Defamation League.

Not all of his films had a serious message; in 1948, he released the lighthearted *Mr. Blandings Builds His Dream House* starring Cary Grant and Myrna Loy. After completing *Berlin Express,* in 1948, Schary left RKO. Howard Hughes had gained control of the company, and Schary disagreed with Hughes when it came to making pictures. After signing with MGM, Schary purchased the rights for several World War II films. He continued to work at MGM Studios for the next 14 years.

Following his departure from MGM, he wrote the Broadway play *Sunrise at Campobello,* which was a story about Franklin Delano Roosevelt. The play won five Tony Awards. He wrote and produced the motion picture of the same name in 1960 and had a brief role in the film, playing the delegate from Connecticut.

Schary died in 1980 and was interred in the Hebrew Cemetery, West Long Branch, New Jersey. To honor his memory, the Anti-Defamation League established the Dore Schary Awards in 1982. *See also* **Film**; **Theater**.

Herbert M. Druks

Further Reading: Schary, Dore. *Heyday: An Autobiography.* Boston: Little, Brown, 1979.

SCHINDLER'S LIST (1993)

In the language of anthropologists, Oskar Schindler (1908–1974) is "thrice born." His first birth is biological, born in Svitavy in the Sudetenland and nurtured by Catholic German upbringing. His second birth is as a Nazi confident, profiteer businessman, *Direktor* of a prison camp, and a protector of Jews during the German occupation of Krakow and Zablocie (outside of Krakow), 1939–1944, and Zwittau-Brunnlitz (Brnenc, Sudetenland, now part of the Czech Republic), 1944–1945. His third birth is a book (Australian writer Thomas Keneally's *Schindler's Ark* (1982), published in the United States as *Schindler's List*) and a film (**Steven Spielberg**'s *Schindler's List,* released December 15, 1993) about his ventures as a self-described "profiteer of slave labor." The ambiance of ghettos (Krakow and Zablocie), labor camps (Plazów, noted for the brutality of its commandant, Amon Leopold Göth), and extermination camps (Gross-Rosen, Auschwitz) provide the backdrop of the true story of a man who saved about 1,200 Jews, whose descendants number more than the Jews alive today in Poland, the land of Plazów and Auschwitz.

Spielberg's quest for inner healing ("I wanted to tell people who had told me to be ashamed of my Jewishness that I was proud to be a Jew") was the stimulant for his adaptation of Keneally's international bestseller. His powerful Academy Award-winning film (1993) bears cinematic wizardry in relating the horrors of the Shoah by juxtaposing one more day in the life of the *Schindlerjuden* with the evolving scenes leading to the Final Solution, such as the pitiful sight of children hiding in outhouse cesspools and the smokestacks bellowing human ashes from the death factories of Auschwitz-Birkenau.

The screenplay by Steven Zaillen (writer-director of *Searching for Bobby Fischer*) and the haunting black and white cinematography of Janus Kaminski brilliantly weave into a seamless garment the fate of Oskar Schindler and the faith of Krakow Jews. *Time* magazine film critic Richard Schickel wrote that Spielberg told the cast, "we're not making a film, we're making a document" (*Time,* 1993). The testimony of Itzhak Stern, Leopold Pfeferberg (aka Poldek Page), Justice Moshe Bejski of the Israeli Supreme Court, and other *Schindlerjuden* graphically describe Jewish life in Nazi-occupied Poland in life and death hues. The life of the Jew in the street, ghetto, factory, camps; the elderly, women, children, qualified and unfit workers for German labor; and the Jew haters are vivid reminders to "think people" as the essential starting point in the Shoah universe.

Some images are anguished testimony to the difficult privilege of Jewishness, such as the scenes in which Jews are forced into the ghetto or endure the depravity of camp life. Others are diary in vignette—journey of beginnings, interruptions, and endings. A number are fashioned with black irony, white heat, and jarring historical reality. The ultimate effect is gothic documentation that conveys transformation and commitment. For example, Itzhak Stern (played by Ben Kingsly), the Jewish accountant with contacts with the underground Jewish business community, stubbornly insisted and then composed the list of names which in turn served as a guide to Schindler's conscience. Also, the wandering girl in the red coat who is last seen dead upon a cartful of bodies parallels changes in Schindler's persona, from a coldhearted business entrepreneur to profiteer to an altruistic individual who saves the lives of his workers.

The stereotype of Evil perennially dramatized in the media is an SS officer swaggering, sneering, and barking out his murderous commands. What is lost, however, are the essential lessons from the Shoah, including survival with morality. Arguably, the Shoah is absolute evil. The Nazi atrocity is an atrocity forever, and its consequences become part of the living fabric of the Jewish present and future. Therefore, validated testimony and historical research are essential for all to learn in an era when many are indifferent (in 1994, the Roper Organization public-opinion poll reported that a third of the American adult population was not sure about the Nazi murder of European Jews), when pseudo-scholars have denied or reviled the Holocaust, and when anti-Zionists invert the lessons into anti-Jewish propaganda (for example, saying that Israel is a Nazi offshoot engaged in a policy of extermination against the Palestinian people, and the like).

Tragically, in the current decade of global terrorism, despite the efforts of some, the message of the Shoah for America and the world community is threatened. This is due in part to the fact that we cannot existentially understand a past others have suffered. Additionally, we relate the Shoah to all other horrors of the past and present, which leads to Shoahcide (revision and distortion of Holocaust facts). Therein lies the value of *Schindler's List,* which cinematically testifies to the deadly weight of the Shoah on the living and the stubborn persistence of one man's determination (materialistic, humanitarian, spiritual) to confront the unbearable by discharging the Talmudic wisdom that "whoever saves one life, saves the entire world" (film tagline).

Spielberg's film begins in darkness, the last flicker of Shabbes candles (flame in color, symbol of the Dual Torah that has governed Jewish life ever since Sinai) in a Krakow apartment—and the movie ends in the light of Zion, with a procession of today's Schindler Jews around Schindler's tombstone in the Catholic Latin cemetery in Jerusalem. This is a memorable scene of gratitude to the memory of Oskar Schindler, who gave hope and life to a despised people in the face of extraordinary evil.

Steven Spielberg's share of profits for making *Schindler's List* established the Righteous Persons Foundation. A separate gift funded the Shoah Foundation (1994), which became the USC Shoah Foundation Institute for Visual History and Education (2006). The Shoah Foundation develops educational resources for teachers, students, and universities worldwide. *See also* **Film**; **The Holocaust in American Culture**; **Spielberg, Steven**.

Zev Garber

Further Reading: Keneally, Thomas. *Schindler's List.* New York: Penguin Books, 1983. Schickel, Richard. "Heart of Darkness," *Time,* December 13, 1993. USC Shoah Foundation Institute for Visual History and Education Web Site: www.usc.edu/schools/college/vhi.

SCHULBERG, BUDD (1914–)

The son of movie pioneer Benjamin Percival ("B. P.") and Adeline Jaffe Schulberg, Budd Wilson Schulberg was born in New York City on March 27, 1914. He was educated at the Deerfield Academy and Dartmouth, where he wrote for the school newspaper and studied sociology. It was at Deerfield that Schulberg first encountered anti-Semitism, despite the fact that his family was marginally religious and Budd didn't consider himself Jewish. While attending Dartmouth, Schulberg's father was ousted as head of production for Paramount Studios, an event for which the younger Schulberg never forgave Hollywood.

After graduation, Schulberg moved to Hollywood, where he began screenwriting for producer David O. Selznick and collecting anecdotes about the film community. Among his earliest uncredited works were *A Star is Born* (1937) and *Nothing Sacred* (1937). In the late 1930s, Schulberg published a series of short stories in *Liberty Magazine* starring a fictional character named Sammy Glick. Random House head Bennett Cerf urged Schulberg to turn the stories into the novel that became *What Makes Sammy Run?* Published in 1941, it became an instant bestseller and won the National Critics' Choice Award for Best First Novel of the Year. It also got Schulberg blacklisted from Hollywood.

In Sammy Glick (loosely based on screenwriter/producer Jerry Wald), Schulberg created the ultimate Hollywood anti-hero: venal, amoral, and maniacally driven. Although made into a successful, though long-forgotten musical, *What Makes Sammy Run?* has yet to be made into a motion picture. As of 2006, its rights are owned by actor **Ben Stiller**.

From 1937 to 1940, Schulberg belonged to the Communist Party. During hearings on communist involvement in the film industry, Schulberg named names as a "friendly witness." In 1954, Schulberg won an Academy Award for *On The Waterfront,* a film directed by another "friendly," director Elia Kazan. Among Schulberg's other successful works are the novels *The Harder They Fall* (1947), *The Disenchanted* (1950), and the film *A Face in the Crowd* (1957).

Married four times, Schulberg has five children. He resides in Westhampton, New York. *See also* **Film.**

Kurt F. Stone

Further Reading: Schulberg, Budd. *Moving Pictures: Memories of a Hollywood Prince.* New York. Stein and Day, 1981.

SCHWARTZ, MAURICE (1890–1960)

Impresario Maurice Schwartz founded the longest running repertory company in New York City's history—the Yiddish Art Theatre, which ran continuously from 1918 until 1950. Born in 1890 in Sedikov, Ukraine, at 12 Schwartz was separated from his family during their journey from Russia to America. Surviving alone in London, Schwartz's only respite from his life as a street urchin was to sneak into the Yiddish theaters. After two years, Schwartz was found and sent to America to rejoin his parents, Isaac and Rose. His religious father resented Schwartz's passion for theater, and the young man left home at 16.

As a teenager, Schwartz created an amateur company where he was discovered playing the part of an elderly man. He went on to perform professionally in Baltimore, Chicago, Cincinnati, and Philadelphia. After passing his third audition into the notoriously selective Hebrew Actors Union, Schwartz worked under the esteemed Yiddish tragedian David Kessler on Second Avenue, taking over the direction of that company for a season in 1917.

In 1918, Schwartz published a manifesto in the New York Yiddish papers detailing his plans for creating a better Yiddish theater, devoted to presenting sophisticated productions of literary plays. Yiddish art theaters like the one Schwartz envisioned were emerging throughout Europe at this time, among them the Vilna Troupe and the Moscow Yiddish Art Theater. Unlike his European counterparts who performed in small halls, Schwartz was determined to present literary theater on a grand scale. His first season opened at the 900-seat Irving Place Theater in 1918. Peretz Herschbein's poetic depiction of Jewish peasant life—*The Secluded Nook* was their first success.

Schwartz staged plays by Yiddish writers such as Osip Dymov, H. Leivick, and David Pinsky, as well as translations into Yiddish of works by George Bernard Shaw, Oscar Wilde, Anton Chekhov, and Henrik Ibsen. Schwartz also successfully adapted an epic Yiddish novel by I. J. Singer and Sholem Asch. Schwartz's most famous production was his dramatization of Singer's *Yoshe Kalb* in 1932, which ran for over 300 performances before touring the world. Schwartz brought his shows to Broadway in English translation including Leonid Andreyev's *Anathema* in 1923 and *Yoshe Kalb* in 1933. Schwartz was the first to present plays in Yiddish on Broadway, producing several seasons of the Yiddish Art Theatre at the Nora Bayes Theater on 44th Street. In 1926, the company moved to its permanent home, the 1,265-seat Yiddish Art Theatre on Second Avenue and 12th Street.

Schwartz loved spectacle and excelled in staging mass scenes—Sholem Asch's *Kiddush ha Shem* had 42 speaking roles plus 50 extras. As a director, Schwartz experimented with different styles of performance, moving from realism and farce to the stylized avant-garde. Schwartz knew every aspect of theater intimately, developing his own special effects, writing the scripts, staging the production, starring in the show, and infuriating his cast by giving them line readings. Actors who began their careers working with Schwartz include Academy Award winner Paul Muni, Vilna Troupe actors Joseph Buloff and Luba Kadison, Jacob Ben-Ami, acting guru Stella Adler, radio personality Isaiah Sheffer, and television star

Leonard Nimoy. Schwartz hired legendary set designers Boris Aaronson and Sam Leve.

As an actor Schwartz shone in Jewish patriarchal roles like Sholem Aleichem's Tevye and as Shylock in *Shylock's Daughter*. Schwartz starred in and directed the Yiddish films *Tevye* and *Uncle Moses*. Based on the same work that inspired the Tony Award-winning musical *Fiddler on the Roof*, Schwartz's *Tevye* became the first non-English film to be included in the National Film Registry by the Library of Congress in 1991.

Schwartz's wife Anna Bordofsky was also his business manager. They adopted two child refugees from World War II: Risa and Marvin. After his theater closed in 1950, Schwartz played small parts in Hollywood films, acted on Broadway in a one-man show, and attempted to rebuild the Art Theater, opening it for one more season in 1955. In 1960, Schwartz went to Israel to build a permanent Yiddish theater there. Schwartz died in Israel that year during rehearsals for Sholem Asch's *Kiddush ha Shem*.

From 1918 until 1960, Schwartz was the dominant figure in the New York Yiddish theater. His influence went far beyond the Yiddish world, however. The most famous New York repertory theater, the short lived Group Theatre, included actors such as Stella and Luther Adler who began their careers with Schwartz. Schwartz produced *Chekhov* in Yiddish translation a year before the Moscow Art Theater came to America and was credited with introducing *Chekhov* to the American stage. As *New York Times* critic Brooks Atkinson wrote in 1946, "the Yiddish art theater has always been one of the most interesting stage organizations in this city."

Caraid O'Brien

Further Reading: Lifson, David S. *The Yiddish Theatre in America.* Thomas Yoseloff, 1965.

SCIENCE FICTION

Defining the science fiction genre (also referred to as sci-fi) is, at best, a difficult task. In simplest terms it may be seen as the attempt to combine the rational (science) and the irrational (fiction). Science fiction provides a means of understanding the world through storytelling. The sci-fi medium has encompassed a broad and ever-expanding variety of fictional forms. "Hard" science fiction is characterized by rigorous attention to accurate detail in quantitative sciences, especially physics, astrophysics, and chemistry, while "soft" science fiction is the antithesis of hard science fiction. It may describe works based on social sciences. In some of the literature the boundaries between the hard and soft genres tend to blur. The soft science fiction has spawned related branches such as speculative fiction that portray a utopian or dystopian world. *Brave New World* and *1984* provide examples of this.

In the early 1980s, the "cyberpunk" genre emerged. Common themes in cyberpunk include advances in information technology and artificial intelligence. Alternate history stories are based on the premise that historical events might have turned out differently, while military science fiction is set in the context of conflict between national, interplanetary, or interstellar systems, such as the stories written for the Battlestar Gallactica series. Other related science fiction branches include "new wave" science fiction, apocalyptic and post-apocalyptic fiction, fantasy, and horror. Though some contend these last two elements should be considered separately from science fiction, others commonly describe them as science fiction with fantasy or horror elements. Isaac Asimov and other writers sometimes incorporate horror and/or mystery elements in their science fiction.

What are the roots of this broad fictional genre? According to historian-librarian Eli Eshed, the first works of science fiction can be traced back to mythology. Eshed contends the earliest stories developed in what is now Israel, in the third century BCE in the Apocryphal Books of Enoch, featuring a biblical hero traveling in space and time searching for secrets of creation (*Locus,* Oct. 1996, p. 43). From that point forward, Jewish science fiction and fantasy writers took inspiration from religion, the Diaspora, humor, Kabbalah, and a host of other traditions.

The Diaspora and the sense of "otherness" imposed on Jews, over centuries, has produced tension between the Jew's attempting remain faithful to his or her culture and trying to assimilate into the culture of the country in which he or she settled. Jews located in a variety of locales, from east to west, have felt the need to live double identities as they become more enmeshed in popular culture. Despite their efforts, they have often been regarded as different, separate. Science fiction gives voice to tensions inherent in living a dual identity. It enables those rejected due to language, religion, and culture to express their dilemma. Through science fiction, American Jewish artists can explore their hopes and fears. For example, *Wandering Stars: An Anthology of Jewish Fantasy and Science Fiction,* edited by Jack Dann (1974), along with the two volumes that have succeeded the 1974 text, provides short stories addressing some subjects long troubling many Jews. In these tales the disturbing realities of assimilation and dispersion take center stage as characters struggle to retain a connection with their past while dealing with the modern world and the difficult question of "who is a Jew?"

In science fiction one can be a person and a mutant, a person and a telepath. This ability to live a dual identity helps spur discussion concerning questions about Jewish identity. Questions about Jewish problems take center stage in the medieval legend of Rabbi Moreynu Ha-Rav Low of Prague and his "Golem." The word "golem," originally meaning "shapeless matter," dates back to the Hebrew Bible, where it appears in Psalm 139:16. Adam praises the Creator for forming his "imperfect substance" ("golem") from the earth. The earliest reference to a golem as a creation of man is found in a text in the Talmud. The rabbi in the legend created his Golem to protect the Jewish people. Although several different endings have been used for this tale, the most popular version claims the rabbi loses control of his monster and must destroy it. This story inspired such well-known science fiction tales as *Frankenstein.* For many authors the golem fable provides a rich tradition to draw upon. Two winners of the Nobel Prize for Literature recounted the various golem tales in published form: **Elie Wiesel** in 1983 and **Isaac Bashevis Singer** in 1984.

Ideas from Jewish law and tradition also find their way into science fiction. Kabbalah contains the keys to the secrets of the universe, as well as to the mysteries of the human heart and soul. Great sages have taught that every human being is born with the potential for greatness. Kabbalah is the means for activating that potential. Kabbalah tells of the intervention of angels and demons. These demons and angels become material for American Jewish science fiction writers. Kabbalah also explores Hebrew numbers and Hebrew letters. Numbers, or numerology, afford a connection between the world of humans and the structure of the universe. This mystical connection often finds its way into science fiction. Writers attempt to link the world above with the world below. Humans may be relegated to the earth, but they often fix their eyes upon the heavens.

Jewish humor has also influenced science fiction. Jack Dann contends insecurity, discomfort, frustration, hypocrisy, nostalgia, satire, ironic self-mockery, and exaggeration as the foundations for Jewish comedy. As Dann has written, "Humor provides an effective armor against a hostile society" (Dann, 1974). Thus, comedic writers such as **Woody Allen** have chosen to utilize science fiction. Allen's film *Sleeper* is the slapstick saga of a health freak that enters the hospital for an operation in 1973 and wakes up 200 years later into a world where everything is automated. The only things he recognizes are a Volkswagen Beetle and a copy of the *New York Times.* The film employs classic Jewish humor as it follows the antics of the Allen character, who outwits a group of police thugs and devious scientists while he resists joining the New Order.

For decades, American Jewish science fiction writers have inspired other writers and the general public with their stories. From Isaac Asimov to

Steven Spielberg, some of our most celebrated artists had career breaks in the science fiction industry: Steven Spielberg made his filmmaking debut as a young man overseeing production on the pilot episode for the Rod Serling series *Night Gallery,* which was the successor of the classic *The Twilight Zone.* **Leonard Nimoy**, who played Mr. Spock on "Star Trek," used the centuries-old secretive hand signals of the Jewish priests for his famous Vulcan hand signal. Paul Levinson, author and past president of the Science Fiction and Fantasy Writers of America, claims a distinction exists between explicitly Jewish themes and themes that are Jewish but not identified as such, yet there is a Jewish aspect to most science fiction today. For example, Gregory Benford and David Brin in *Heart of the Comet* explore humanity's relation to the universe as man struggles to improve his condition and the condition of the world he inhabits. This struggle is a Jewish concept.

The **Holocaust**, a tragedy that belied any belief in human improvement, inspired a new group of Jewish writers to utilize modern science fiction as the vehicle for their ideas. Robert Silverberg, Alfred Bester, Robert Sheckley, Harlan Ellison, and Avram Davidson (an Orthodox Jew whose second published work was titled *The Golem*) began to write for science fiction magazines. Though most of these individuals, born and raised in America, did not personally experience the horrors of Nazism, science fiction literature provided an outlet for expressing their revulsion and remembrance. From the late 1940s forward, the Holocaust played a symbolic role in a myriad science fiction tales. Jack Dann insists the Holocaust was a defining moment and that those who come generations after the Holocaust must testify, or forget. That sense of "otherness" portrayed in many sci-fi stories, whether it be through Vulcans, androids, or a wide variety of other characters, is a vital ingredient in American Jewish postwar science fiction.

The number of American Jewish authors who have made significant contributions to the genre is too long to list here, but some of the major contributors to the genre include Isaac Asimov, Avram Davidson, and Harlan Ellison. Isaac Asimov is widely considered a master of the science fiction genre and one of the "Big Three" science fiction writers during his lifetime. Asimov's most famous work is the Foundation series; Avram Davidson is primarily recognized for short fiction. His stories deal with the fantasy element of science fiction. Davidson won a Hugo Award, which is given every year for the best science fiction or fantasy works and achievements of the previous year. He also won three World Fantasy Awards in the science fiction and fantasy genre, as well as a Queen's Award and an Edgar Award in the mystery genre. Harlan Ellison's most famous stories were published within the genre of speculative fiction, and he has won multiple Hugo and Nebula awards. He was also very active in the science fiction community He served as the Science Fiction and Fantasy Writers of America's first vice president, in the 1960s.

There are others, such as Robert Albert Bloch, who wrote hundreds of short stories and over 20 novels, usually crime fiction, science fiction, and, perhaps most influentially, horror fiction (*Psycho*). He was the recipient of the Hugo Award for his story "That Hell-Bound Train." Bloch was also a major contributor to science fiction fanzines and fandom in general. David Brin's body of science fiction is normally categorized as hard science fiction. Although his Uplift stories make up a minority of Brin's works, they have won a large following in the sci-fi community, twice winning the Hugo Award in the Best Novel category. Paul Levinson writes science fiction, fantasy, and sci-fi mystery hybrids. He has received multiple nominations for the Hugo, Nebula, Sturgeon, Prometheus, Edgar, and Audie awards. His novel *The Silk Code* won the Locus Award for Best First Novel of 1999. Joseph Haldeman served as a combat engineer in Vietnam, and his wartime experience was the inspiration for *War Year,* his first novel. Haldeman's most famous novel is *The Forever War,* which won both the Hugo and Nebula awards. Robert Silverberg is a multiple-time winner of both the Hugo and Nebula

Awards. His first published novel, a children's book called *Revolt on Alpha C,* appeared in 1955, and in the following year, he won his first Hugo as Best New Writer. Joel Rosenberg has published a number of science fiction novels, including *Ties of Blood and Silver* (1984) and *Emile and the utchman* (1986), which are both set in the same universe.

William Tenn, whose real name is Philip Klass, began writing sci-fi while serving in World War II. From 1946 until the mid-1960s, he was a moderately prolific author, mostly of short stories and novelettes. He was a central figure in the dominant magazines of the time, *Galaxy* and *The Magazine of Fantasy and Science Fiction.* His essay and interview collection, *Dancing Naked,* was nominated for a Hugo Award for Best Related Book in 2004. He was given the Author Emeritus honor by the Science Fiction and Fantasy Writers of America in 1999. There is another series of books, written by Harry Turtledove, which presents an alternative history, one in which the earth is invaded by lizard-like extraterrestrials at the beginning of World War II, leading to strange earth alliances of, for example, Nazis and Jews. A sense of Jewish influence runs through many of Mike Resnick's stories. For instance, many of his main characters, much like the early prophets, wish to avoid taking up their roles in society, yet they cannot escape their need to find some meaning in life in order to save humanity. Resnick's book with an overt Jewish theme, *The Branch,* describes a future in which the Hebrew biblical Messiah, instead of the Christian Messiah of love and peace, comes back to earth.

American Jewish women writers of science fiction tend to include materials found in places where Jews were oppressed in their stories. For example, fabrics help remind of us of the sweat shops in the garment industry. Documentation of the reality of the Holocaust and pilgrimages by the artists to Israel are also included. Judith Merril's most significant contributions to the sci-fi genre were: *Daughters of Earth, That Only a Mother,* and *Shadow on the Hearth.* The last two were written during the McCarthy era of the 1950s. They explore the terror of nuclear holocaust, and they reflect the oppression that American citizens felt under McCarthyism. The "alien" in her work often represents those who don't fit into the mainstream American culture. Growing up Jewish in America helped Judith, when writing her stories, to connect with the alien. Lisa Goldstein is a Nebula, Hugo, and World Fantasy Award-nominated fantasy and science fiction writer. Her 1982 novel *The Red Magician* won the American Book Award for best paperback novel. Esther Friesner writes science fiction and fantasy and is best known for her humorous pieces. She has been nominated a number of times for the Hugo and Nebula awards, winning the Nebula Award for Best Short Story in 1995 and 1996. Jane Yolen is an author of children's books, fantasy, and science fiction, including *Owl Moon,Devil's Arithmetic,* and *How Do Dinosaurs Say Goodnight?* Some of Jane Yolen's awards include the Caldecott Medal, two Nebula Awards, two Christopher Medals, the World Fantasy Award, the Golden Kite Award, the Jewish Book Award, and the Association of Jewish Libraries Award.

In recent decades science fiction ideas have become increasingly mainstream, and though some of the feeling of otherness may have diminished, Jewish culture and thought has made science fiction writing a richer genre. Despite oppression and prejudice, Jews and their culture have remained intact and influenced those societies in which they struggled to live. Time may change all things, but the next millennium and beyond seems to bode well for science fiction writers. Our ever-expanding knowledge of the world around us will provide a vast amount of material for authors as they incorporate new ideas into their work. *See also* **Nimoy, Leonard**; **Shatner, William**; **Television**.

Susan M. Ortmann

Further Reading: Berkwits, Jeff. "Stars of David." *San Diego Jewish Journal,* October 2004. Dann, Jack, ed. *Wandering Stars: An Anthology of Jewish Fantasy and Science Fiction.* New York: Harper and Row, 1974.

Metzger, Rebecca. "Jewish Visions of the Fantastical Future." *Culture Currents,* January 2000.

SEDAKA, NEIL

See **The Brill Building Songwriters**.

SEINFELD, JERRY (1954–)

Jerry Seinfeld is the main protagonist on the television sitcom *Seinfeld* (1989–1998), one of television's most successful and critically acclaimed comedy shows. This semi-fictionalized version of comedian Jerry Seinfeld was named after, based on, and played by Seinfeld himself. Jerome Seinfeld was born in Brooklyn on April 29, 1954. His father, Kálmán Seinfeld, who owned a sign company, was of Hungarian descent; his mother, Betty, a home-based tailor, came from a Syrian Jewish family. Seinfeld grew up in Massapequa, New York and graduated from Queen's College. Having decided by an early age that one could make a living from comedy, Seinfeld began performing at New York's Catch a Rising Star comedy club. His hard work and dedication to his craft led to a spot on a Rodney Dangerfield HBO special, a brief role on the sitcom *Benson,* and successful appearances with Johnny Carson, Merv Griffin, and David Letterman.

In 1989, Seinfeld teamed up with writer/director Larry David to create a television sitcom originally called *The Seinfeld Chronicles,* later shortened to *Seinfeld.* At first plagued by low ratings, *Seinfeld* evolved into a "funny, literate, cynical sitcom about an anal-retentive, Superman-obsessed comic and his small circle of friends" (Haberman and Shandler, 2003). The show didn't reach the top 30 until its 4th season; by its 6th season, it was television's highest-rated program. Played on a single set, *Seinfeld* mined comedy from the ordinariness of everyday life. Indeed, critics nicknamed it the "Show About Nothing."

Seinfeld ran in primetime until 1998. The show's producers reportedly offered Seinfeld $5 million per episode—for 22 episodes—to continue for one additional season. Seinfeld said no, and the show went into syndication. According

The cast of one of television's most successful comedies, *Seinfeld.* Shown from left: Michael Richards (as Cosmo Kramer), Jason Alexander (as George Costanza), Julia Louis-Dreyfus (as Elaine Benes), Jerry Seinfeld (as Jerry Seinfeld). [NBC/Columbia TriStar Television/Photofest]

to *Forbes* magazine, Jerry Seinfeld made $267 million during the show's final season.

After his sitcom went off the air, Jerry Seinfeld returned to stand-up comedy and recorded a much-praised comedy special entitled *I'm Telling You For the Last Time.* In 2002, director Charles Christian made the documentary *Comedian,* which chronicled Seinfeld's process of developing and performing new material at clubs around the world. Seinfeld is also a bestselling author, most notably for his 1993 book *Seinlanguage.*

Known for his many public romances, Jerry Seinfeld married Jessica Sklar in December 1999. They have three children and live in Manhattan. *See also* **Sitcoms**; **Television**.

Kurt F. Stone

Further Reading: Haberman, J., and Jeffrey Shandler. *Entertaining America: Jews, Movies, and Broadcasting.* Princeton University Press, 2003.

SENDAK, MAURICE (1928–)

Sendak is an award-winning writer and illustrator of children's literature who is best known for his book *Where the Wild Things Are,* published in 1963. Sendak was born on June 10, 1928, in Brooklyn, New York, to Jewish immigrant parents. Early influences were comic books, Mickey Mouse, and European illustrators. As a young artist he was nurtured by the influential children's book editor Ursula Nordstrom. After Sendak was first published as an illustrator for an adult book, *Atomics for the Millions* (1947), Nordstrom hired him to illustrate *The Wonderful Farm* by Marcel Ayme (1951).

Sendak's work was strikingly different from other children's book illustrations in the 1940s and 1950s. His working-class Brooklyn childhood helped him create memorable characters like Rosie, who has a big mouth and even bigger dreams. Rosie first appeared in *The Sign on Rosie's Door* (1960) and later became the star of *Really Rosie,* an animated musical collaboration with Carole King. In an era of blond, well-mannered, neat-looking children, Sendak created a fantastical universe of dark, disheveled, and frequently disobedient children. Sendak believed that fantasy enabled children to deal with the pain, anxiety, and struggle of growing up.

In Sendak's work, fear, humor, and fantasy intermingle. Sendak is most well known for *Where the Wild Things Are,* which won a ALA Caldecott Medal in 1964. In this book, Max misbehaves and is sent to his room without supper, whereupon he embarks on a journey to the land of the Wild Things. He enjoys adventures with scary but humorous beasts until he is ready to go home, where his mother has left dinner waiting for him after all. Hailed as a classic of children's literature for reassuring children that no matter how badly they behave, their parents will still love them, *Where the Wild Things Are* was also met with criticism. Some parents, teachers, and librarians thought it was too frightening and denounced the book for allowing Max to express his anger at his mother.

Sendak is no stranger to controversy. *In the Night Kitchen* (1970), a Caldecott Honor book, is a joyous, nocturnal dreamscape that features Mickey, a little boy who wakes up, falling through the dark past his sleeping parents, out of his clothes, and landing in a bowl of dough being mixed by nighttime bakers who resemble Hardy of Laurel and Hardy fame. Many teachers and librarians objected to the nudity in the illustrations, and it was criticized for being an allegory about masturbation.

Sendak's father's family lost many relatives in the Holocaust, and this influence is seen in his work. *Brundibar* (2003), retold by playwright Tony Kushner, is the story of a Czech opera performed by children in the Theresienstadt concentration camp. The main characters are an evil hurdy-gurdy player, who resembles Hitler in Sendak's illustrations, and a penniless brother and sister trying to find milk for their sick mother; the children come up against the evils of society and manage to triumph. Sendak and Kushner collaborated on an opera production of *Brundibar* in 2006.

Children's author and illustrator Maurice Sendak, best known for his book *Where the Wild Things Are* (1963), is the author of more than 20 children's books and the illustrator of approximately 60 additional books. [Photofest, Inc.]

Sendak received seven Caldecott Medal Honor Awards, as well as the 1964 ALA Caldecott Medal for *Where the Wild Things Are*. In addition, he was awarded the Hans Christian Andersen Medal for Illustration (1970), the National Medal of the Arts (1996), the Jewish Cultural Achievement Award (1998), and the Astrid Lindgren Memorial Award for Literature (2003). In 1983, he was awarded the Laura Ingalls Wilder Award by ALA in recognition of his body of work. Sendak's work includes both books he has written and those he has illustrated. The following are examples of the books he has written—*Kenny's Window* (1956), *Higglety Pigglety Pop!, Or, There Must Be More to Life* (1967), and *Outside Over There* (which won the Caldecott Medal Honor Award, 1982). Sendak's illustrated books include *A Very Special House* by Ruth Krauss (1953), *Dear Mili* by Wilhelm Grimm (1988), and *Brundibar* by Tony Kushner (2003). *See also* **Children's Literature**.

Hara Person

Further Reading: Marcus, Leonard S. *Ways of Telling: Conversations on the Art of the Picture Book.* New York: Dutton Children's Books, 2002.

SHATNER, WILLIAM (1931–)

William Shatner, born in Montreal, Canada, is most notably known as the actor who played the character Captain James Tiberius Kirk of the United Star Ship Enterprise, from the three-year television series and seven Star Trek movies. However, Shatner has more than one role to his credit.

Born March 22, 1931 to Ann and Joseph Shatner, William Shatner was raised in a Conservative Jewish home in a city plagued with anti-Semitism. On numerous occasions Shatner fought with schoolmates over the issue of religion. One of Shatner's greatest teenage disappointments was being replaced on the high school football team since he missed a practice because the Jewish laws governing the holy day of Yom Kippur forbade activities other than prayer and rest.

After completing high school, Shatner attended McGill University, completing a degree in commerce. During his time at McGill, Shatner participated in university theater productions, and in the summers he performed with the Royal Mount Theater Company. Upon graduation in 1952, Shatner worked with the National Repertory Theater of Ottawa. From there, Shatner moved to New York City in hopes of furthering this career.

Trained as a classical Shakespearean actor, Shatner performed at the Shakespearean Stratford Festival of Canada in Stratford, Ontario, where he played a range of roles that included Henry V and Marlowe's Tamburlaine the Great. Shatner made his Broadway debut in the latter. In 1954, he was cast as "Ranger Bill" on the Canadian version of *The Howdy Doody Show.*

Shatner's first feature role in film was in the screen version of *The Brothers Karamazov* (1958) opposite Yule Brenner. He became a household name in his famous role as Captain James T. Kirk in the television series *Star Trek*. The science-fiction drama ran for three years, 1966–1969, and has become a cult classic spawning seven films and four other television series (*Star Trek the Animated Series, Star Trek: The Next Generation, Star Trek Voyager,* and *Enterprise*). Shatner acted in several other series (for example, *T.J. Hooker* and *Boston Legal*) and movies (including *The Andersonville Trial,* 1970, and six *Star Trek* films).

Shatner's acting ability has not gone unrecognized. He has won two Emmys—the first in 2004 for Outstanding Guest Actor for a guest role on *The Practice* and another in 2005 for Best Supporting Actor on *Boston Legal.* In 1983, Shatner was honored with a star on the Hollywood Walk of Fame, and in 2007 Shatner was inducted into the Hall of Fame of the Academy of Television Arts and Sciences.

In addition to his acting, Shatner is a respected author, having written the science fiction *TekWar* series with science fiction writer Ron Goulart, along with *Star Trek V: The Final Frontier.* He has also directed and produced in television and film. He directed numerous episodes of the television series *TekWar* and *T. J. Hooker,* as well as the film *Star Trek V: The Final Frontier;* he also produced, among other shows, *TekWars.*

His sense of humor is legendary. Shatner has appeared in numerous skits parodying the character of James Kirk. It is not uncommon for Shatner to convince fans to help with practical jokes planned against friends. Married four times—to Gloria Rand, Marcy Lafferty, Nerine Kidd, and Elizabeth Anderson Martin—Shatner has three daughters with his first wife, Gloria Rand: Leslie, Lisabeth, and Melanie Shatner. A lover of horses, Shatner owns a horse farm in Kentucky where American Saddlebred and Quarter horses are bred and trained. These horses are shown by Shatner and his fourth wife, Elizabeth Anderson Martin. Shatner promotes equine therapy for disabled children and produces the annual Hollywood Charity Horse Show, which raises money for children's charities. *See also* **Film**; **Television**.

Mara W. Cohen Ioannides

Further Reading: Shatner, William, with David Fisher. *Up Till Now: The Autobiography.* New York: Thomas Dunne Books, 2008.

SHELDON, SIDNEY (1917–2007)

Sidney Sheldon was as an Academy Award-winning writer who won awards in three careers —as a Broadway playwright, a Hollywood television and movie screenwriter, and a bestselling novelist. Sheldon, the son of Jewish parents, Otto and Natalie Schechtel, was born in Chicago on February 11, 1917. Sheldon sold his first written work—a poem—for $10 at age 10. He attended Northwestern University, but financial problems forced him to drop out before he received his degree. In 1936, Sheldon moved to New York, intent upon becoming a songwriter. Crushing mood swings (bipolar disorder) cut short his career. Moving to Hollywood in 1937, Sheldon found work as a $22-a-week script reader. By the early 1940s, he was writing screenplays. In 1947, his screenplay for *The Bachelor and the Bobby-Soxer* won an Oscar. His other notable screenplays included *Easter Parade* (1948), *The Barkleys of Broadway* (1949), and *Annie Get Your Gun* (1950). Sheldon also triumphed on Broadway. At one time, he had three successful musicals running at the same time.

In 1959, Sheldon won a Tony Award for *Red Head,* starring Gwen Verdon. In the early 1960s, Sheldon moved into television, creating, writing, and producing three successful sitcoms: *The Patty Duke Show, I Dream of Jeannie,* and *Hart to Hart.* While writing and producing *I Dream of Jeannie,* Sheldon began writing novels. His first effort, *The Naked Face* (1970), sold 3.1 million copies and won an Edgar Allen Poe Award from the Mystery Writers of America. His next novel, *The Other Side of Midnight* (1973), was number one on the *New York Times* bestseller list.

Sheldon would go on to write nearly 20 novels, which were translated into 51 languages and sold in excess of 250,000,000 copies worldwide. Many of his works made their way onto the screen. Sheldon's page-turning novels, which critics lambasted but readers loved, were peopled by shockingly beautiful women, square-jawed heroes, and fiendish villains. His novels also had an undeniable aura of authenticity: "If I write about a meal, I've been there. If I write about a meal in Indonesia, I've eaten there in that restaurant" (as quoted in "Sidney Sheldon," *Deathwatch Central,* 2007).

Sidney Sheldon was married in 1951 to Jorja Curtright, an actress, who died in 1985; in 1989 he married Alexandra Kostoff. At the time of his death in Palm Springs of complications from pneumonia, his estimated net worth was in excess of $3 billion. It is estimated that close to 300 million copies of his 18 novels remain in print in a total of 51 languages.

Kurt F. Stone

Further Reading: Sheldon, Sidney. *The Other Side of Me.* Warner Books, 2005.

SHORE, DINAH (1919–1994)

Singer, actress, and television personality Dinah Shore was the most popular female singer during the Big Band era of the 1940s and 1950s, as well as the first female singer of her era to achieve huge solo success. Dinah Shore was born in Winchester, Tennessee to Anna and Solomon Shore. She kept her surname, but after singing on the radio she changed her first name from Frances to Dinah. Shore's mother died in 1934, and she and her sister, Bessie, eight years her senior, visited New York with her sorority where she was given an opportunity to sing. The experience convinced her to enter show business. Shore's career began on radio, after having visited the Grand Ole Opry. She auditioned for radio station WSM (AM) in Nashville, where she made her debut in 1938. She decided, however, to return to New York City to pursue a career as a vocalist, and she auditioned for orchestras and radio stations. In many of her auditions, she sang the popular song "Dinah," and subsequently she changed her name from Frances to Dinah. In 1939 she was hired as a vocalist with the Leo Reisman Orchestra. This led to a spot on the *Eddie Cantor Radio Show.* Her 1940 recording of "Yes, My Darling Daughter" was a huge success. In 1944, "I'll Walk Alone" was the year's biggest hit. Shore married George Montgomery, Gentile star of western movies, in 1944. They raised two children, Melissa Ann and an adopted son, John David.

Shore tried her luck in six movies, but only Danny Kaye's *Up in Arms* (1944) was notable. Shore's success was on television, starring in the *Dinah Shore Show* (1951–1956) then the *Dinah Shore Chevrolet Show,* which lasted seven seasons. She hosted talk variety shows, *Dinah* and *Dinah's Place,* to 1979. After that she toured many cities in concert. Her image was one of a feminine, self-confident, non-confrontational, talented woman, aging gracefully. Dinah died of ovarian cancer close to her 77th birthday in February 1994. She was buried in Culver City's Jewish cemetery for Hollywood stars. *See also* **Popular Music.**

Philip Rosen

Further Reading: Hyman, Paula E., and Deborah Dash Moore, eds. *Jewish Women in America,* vol. II. Routledge, 1997.

SIEGEL, JERRY, AND JOE SHUSTER

See **Comic Books**

SILLS, BEVERLY (1929–2007)

World-famous opera star Beverly Sills was born Belle Miriam Silverman on May 25, 1929 in Brooklyn, New York. Her mother Shirley (Bahn) was a Russian Jew born in Odessa, and her father, Morris, of Romanian descent, immigrated to the United States when he was a baby and became an insurance broker. Sills is the youngest of three children, having two brothers, Sidney and Samuel. The close-knit Silverman family lived a typically middle-class American Jewish life in Brooklyn, and Sills always considered herself to be an American Jew.

Few twentieth-century singers have enjoyed as much popularity and public affection as Sills. Her personality was as "bubbly" as her nickname. (The name "Bubbles" was adopted at the age of seven for publicity purposes, but originally it was given to Sills by her doctor at birth because she was born with a huge bubble of saliva in her mouth.) Sills's dream of eventually becoming an opera star was hers alone. However, her mother, an avid opera lover, was largely responsible for providing the nurturing environment that set her daughter on the path to stardom. Before any formal lessons were provided in voice, piano,

Beverly Sills was a link between highbrow and popular culture. In this photo she is taking her bows in her last performance as an opera diva in the role of Rosalind in *Die Fledermaus,* on October 27, 1980, the role she made her debut in 25 years earlier. [AP Photo]

elocution, and tap dancing, seven-year-old Sills had already listened to recordings of coloratura arias on 78-rpm phonograph recordings and memorized the Italian words to 22 concert arias.

The direction Sills's career was to take was mainly shaped by her supportive, loving mother and her one and only singing teacher, Estelle Leibling. It was under Leibling's constant supervision that Sills developed her beautiful coloratura voice and charming personality. Leibling's teaching methods, derived from her own experience as a disciple of the Mathilde Marchesi School, emphasized the bel canto style of singing, a style which eventually became Sills's trademark.

Leibling was also instrumental in arranging appearances for Sills, beginning with an audition for CBS radio show, *Major Bowes' Amateur Hour* in 1936, and for many years after making contacts with large opera companies and impresarios both at home and abroad. Early on, 12-year-old Sills was forced into retirement by her parents, who wanted their daughter to live a more normal childhood, but these plans never materialized. By 1944, Sills was back on stage, starring in a tour of Gilbert and Sullivan operettas.

The decision to leave light opera behind and focus on serious opera represents a major turning point in Sills's career. Under Leibling's supervision, Sills became groomed for such leading roles as her debut performance as the Spanish gypsy Frasquita in Bizet's *Carmen* with the Philadelphia Civic Opera (1947), and later as Manon in Massenet's *Manon* with the Baltimore Opera (1953). A major breakthrough occurred when Sills became a permanent member of the New York City Opera in 1955, debuting as Rosalinda in Strauss's *Die Fledermaus.* At last, Sills reached the highest level by becoming that company's premier diva. After the long association with Leibling ended with her teacher's death in 1970, Sills continued to pay homage to the woman she regarded as her "second mother."

Sills's renewed connection to her Jewish roots came about in 1970, when she was invited to sing with the Israel Philharmonic. With her husband Peter Buckley Greenough (they were married in a civil ceremony at Leibling's New York apartment in 1956), Sills toured Jerusalem and Tel Aviv for the first time. Seeing her name on Hebrew posters, visiting the Western Wall in Jerusalem, and meeting her father's relatives from Romania had an enormous impact on Sills. "I made up my mind then that I would do everything I could to help Israel survive," Sills stated, and she continued these ties the rest of her life (Sills, 1981).

Another important dimension to Sills's persona was her role as devoted wife and mother. When tragedy struck in 1959 with the discovery that her daughter, Meredith ("Muffy"), suffered from a profound loss of hearing, coupled with the fact that her son Bucky, born in 1961, was mentally retarded, Sills took a leave of absence from her work and devoted her time to her children, seeing that they received the best therapy and excellent educations. Because of her personal experiences, Sills was long active on behalf of the Mother's March on Birth Defects, supporting this cause with generous commitment. Serving as national chairperson of the March of Dimes Foundation, Sills helped to raise upward of $80,000,000.

After numerous stage appearances and major roles with top opera companies, including an acclaimed debut at London's Covent Garden in Donizetti's *Lucia di Lammermoor,* Sills reached the pinnacle of her career with her long-awaited debut in 1975 at New York City's Metropolitan Opera in Rossini's *The Siege of Corinth.* After additional triumphs, she started experiencing vocal unevenness and announced that she would retire in 1980. In 1979 she was appointed the co-director general of the New York City Opera, where she turned a debt-ridden organization into a financially self-sustaining company. Sills also became chairwoman of the Lincoln Center and the Metropolitan Opera organizations, where she remained until she announced her retirement from arts administration in 2002.

In retirement, Sills devoted her time and energy to fundraising, public speaking, and appearing in numerous televised broadcasts and documentaries, such the PBS broadcast *Beverly*

Sills: Made in America, now available on DVD. With characteristic warmth and wit, she continued to charm her audiences with personal stories and humorous vignettes, told from the perspective of an artist/humanitarian.

In her honor, the Beverly Sills Artist Award was established, offering a $50,000 prize to be awarded annually to singers between the ages of 25 and 40. Other accolades are honorary degrees from Temple, New York University, the New England Conservatory of Music, California Institute of the Arts, and Harvard, not to mention the Presidential Medal of Freedom which she received in 1980.

Among Sills's many achievements are televised recordings of 18 full-length operas, for which she received national and international recognition, along with a televised special with Carol Burnett titled *Sills and Burnett at the Met* and more recently *A Conversation with Beverly Sills.*

Sills died on July 2, 2007 at her home in Manhattan. The cause was lung cancer, although she was never a smoker.

Ann Leisawitz

Further Reading: Sills, Beverly. *Beverly, An Autobiography.* Bantam, 1981. ———. *Bubbles: An Encore.* Grosset and Dunlap, 1981. ———. *Bubbles: A Self Portrait.* MacMillan, 1976.

SILVERMAN, SARAH (1970–)

Sarah Silverman is an Emmy Award-nominated comedian, writer, singer, and actress. Her satirical comedy addresses social taboos and controversial topics such as racism, sexism, and religion. Silverman was born in Bedford, New Hampshire on December 1, 1970 to Donald (author of the novel *The Enemy is Me*) and Beth Ann Silverman. Sarah has three sisters: Rabbi Susan Silverman-Abramowitz; Laura, cast as the comedian's younger sister on *The Sarah Silverman Program* (2007–), which premiered on Comedy Central in 2007; and Jodyne Speyer, a screenwriter. Sarah has said that she considers herself "Jewish technically but . . . not religious at all" (Paul, 2006). Known for her colorful language, she also incorporates Jewish themes into her material.

Silverman attended New York University for one year, but she left school to concentrate on her career. She made her stand-up debut in 1988 at Stitches, a comedy club in Boston. She was a writer and cast member on *Saturday Night Live* (1993–1994) and made her first important on-camera appearance in *Seinfeld* in 1997. Her résumé includes appearances on more than 30 television programs and movies, including guest appearances on *Frasier* (2003) and *Entourage* (2004), where she played herself.

Silverman has frequently found herself at the center of controversies because of her style of humor, as evidenced by concert movie *Jesus is Magic* and *The Aristocrats* (both released in 2005), which highlight her uncensored, stream-of-consciousness manner. Known by her nickname as "Big S" or Sarah "Big S" Silverman, her humor is known for satire, societal taboos, and controversial topics such as racism, sexism, and religion.

Silverman has been open about her lifelong battle with clinical depression, crediting her current freedom from attacks of despair to her use of prescription Zoloft. *See also* **Comedy**; **Film**; **Television**.

Ron Kaplan

Further Reading: Paul, Pamela. "Sarah Silverman-Interview." *Slate,* November 10, 2006. Solomon, Deborah. "Funny Girl, Interview with Sarah Silverman." *New York Times,* January 21, 2007.

SIMMONS, GENE (1949–)

Following the 2006 war between Israel and Hizbollah guerillas, Ron Weinrich, an Israeli tank crewman paralyzed from the waist down, rested in a Haifa hospital. He was unable to attend his brother's wedding, so his brother organized it in his brother's hospital room, by way of a video of the wedding. It had the following message: "Hi Ron, this is Gene Simmons. I'm talking to you from my home. I can't tell you how proud I am of you, and how much the world and Israel owes you a debt of gratitude. From the bottom of my heart, you are a real hero, you are everybody's hero, you are my hero and I wish I could be there with you." And then in Hebrew: "My name is Chaim, I was born in Haifa."

Chaim Witz, better known as "the Demon" in the hard rock band Kiss, was born in Haifa, Israel in 1949 to Feri and Flora (born Florence Klein, a Hungarian Jewish immigrant to Israel, who was the only member of her family to survive the Holocaust) Witz. One of his earliest memories is the machine gun left by his father, which symbolized for him Israel's continued fight for survival. Feri Witz abandoned his family, and in 1953 Flora took her son and immigrated to the United States. Flora Witz struggled to feed and protect her only child. She taught him the importance of education.

In the United States Chaim Witz changed his name to Gene Klein. In the 1960s he again changed his name, this time to Gene Simmons. Simmons first saw America through movies, and he was enamored with the entertainment world, especially television. During his teens, he loved variety television shows, which featured musical performers. His mania for music was enhanced by the appearance of the Beatles on *The Ed Sullivan Show.* The teenaged Simmons learned to play musical instruments and joined his first band, the Lynx, later renamed the Missing Links.

In 1970, Simmons met musician Paul Stanley. Stanley included Simmons in his band, Wicked Lester. Stanley and Simmons soon left the group and formed a Beatles-on-steroids band that fit their image and ambition. During a rite de passage trip to Sullivan County, a fraternal knot was tied when they recruited Peter Criss and Ace Frehley. The band, named Kiss by Paul Stanley, dressed in black with a character for each member; Simmons, the fire-throwing blood-spitting devil, was known as the Demon. From 1972 to 1974, assisted by manager Bill Aucoin, record executive Neil Bogart, and Dj Nightbird, they rose to the top of glam rock. They recorded three albums and a band anthem, "Rock and Roll All Night." The band, in great demand, soon played in stadiums and performed in Madison Square Garden (1976), as well as in Europe and Japan. All had succumbed to Kiss mania.

In 1977, Simmons met cartoonist Stan Lee, who provided Kiss with its own Marvel comic, which broke sale records. After the band made one movie, *Kiss Meets the Phantom of the Park* (1978), a series of live recordings and solo albums, the Kiss army invaded Australia. They were fueled by the huge success of "I Was Made for Loving You."

The band began to have problems when a depressed Peter Criss was voted out of the band and replaced by Eric Carr. Ace Frehley and Bill Aucoin then left the group, and Neil Bogart died. Following their setbacks, Kiss became self-managed and made changes in their act. In 1983 they decided to take their masks off on MTV. The band enjoyed a resurgence that continued into the 1990s. At the 1996 Grammy Award show, hosted by Tupac Shakur, the four original members reconciled. In 1998, the band released *Psycho Circus,* its first album in almost 20 years; since then the original group has again dissolved. Charismatic performer and astute manager Gene Simmons participates in various projects such as reality shows and other Kiss concerts and ventures, remaining part of the third most-successful band in history.

Gene Simmons lives with former Playboy Playmate and "B" movie star Shannon Tweed. They have two children, Nick and Sophie. The four of them act together on the reality television show *Gene Simmons Family Jewels,* on A&E. *See also* **Rock and Roll**; **Television**.

Steve Krief

Further Reading: Gebert, Gordon G. G., and Bob McAdams. *Kiss & Tell.* Pitbull Publishing, 1997. Gill, Julian. *The Kiss Album Focus* (3rd edition), Volume 2. Philadelphia, PA: Xlibris Corporation, 2005. ———. *The Kiss & Related Recordings Focus: Music! the Songs, the Demo, the Lyrics and Stories!* Philadelphia, PA: Xlibris Corporation, 2005.

SIMON, NEIL (1927–)

America's most prolific and popular playwright was born Marvin Neil Simon to a Jewish family in the Bronx on the Fourth of July, 1927. Simon grew up in the Washington Heights section of Manhattan, the son of Irving, a garment salesman, who would periodically desert the family. During these times, mother Mamie worked at Gimbel's department store and relied on friends and relatives to support her sons Neil and Danny. Simon acquired the nickname "Doc" early in life as he enjoyed playing with a toy stethoscope. After his parents' divorce, Simon moved in with relatives in Forest Hills.

He briefly attended NYU (1944–1945) and the University of Denver (1945–1946) before joining the army, where he began writing for his camp newspaper. Upon his discharge, Simon found employment in the mailroom of Warner Brothers' East Coast offices back in New York City. He and Danny Simon began writing material for resort comics and radio. Comedian **Sid Caesar** invited the two to join other young Jewish humorists such as **Woody Allen** and **Mel Brooks** in writing his television program *Your Show of Shows*. After working on *The Phil Silvers Show* and other early television programs and winning several Emmy nominations along the way, the Simon brothers began to write gags and sketches for Broadway musicals in the late 1950s.

Neil Simon soon broke out on his own as a playwright, creating what became an unprecedented string of Broadway hits, beginning with *Come Blow Your Horn* in 1961. His works ultimately earned 17 Tony nominations and won 3 Tonys as Best Play. In the 1966–1967 season, Simon had four shows running concurrently—*Barefoot In the Park, Sweet Charity, The Star Spangled Girl,* and*The Odd Couple,* the first of his "Best Play" winners. Three years later, three more of his works graced the Great White Way simultaneously—*Last of the Red Hot Lovers, Plaza Suite,* and*Promises, Promises*. Then in 1973, his wife, dancer Joan Baim, died. This was followed by several stage failures in the mid-seventies, marking a nadir in Simon's life. A move to California and the success of *California Suite* (1976) proved revitalizing.

Simon married his second wife, actress Marsha Mason, and wrote *Chapter Two* in 1977 based on his own renewal. He has since been married three more times—twice to Diane Lander, and now to Elaine Joyce. He is the father of three—Nancy and Ellen by first wife Baim, and Bryn, a child he and fifth wife Joyce adopted. Despite his unparalleled commercial success, universal critical acclaim eluded Simon until the 1980s, when he penned an autobiographical trilogy of plays featuring alter ego Eugene Jerome. *Brighton Beach Memoirs* (1983) explored his turbulent youth and family life; *Biloxi Blues* (1985), another Tony Award-winning "Best Play," revisited his brief army life; and *Broadway Bound* (1986) chronicled the start of his showbiz career.

In 1991, yet another autobiographical work, *Lost In Yonkers,* earned Simon his third "Best Play" Tony Award and also the Pulitzer Prize for Drama. More of Simon's plays have been adapted for the screen than those of any other American playwright, three of which earned him Academy Award nominations for Best Adapted Screenplay—*The Odd Couple* (1968), *The Sunshine Boys* (1975), and *California Suite* (1978). He also wrote nearly a dozen original screen comedies. Other honors garnered by Simon include the Screen Writers Guild Award, the Evening Standard Award, the New York Drama Critics Circle Award, the Shubert Award, the Outer Circle Award, a Golden Globe for his screenplay of *The Goodbye Girl,* an American Comedy Lifetime Achievement Award, a Kennedy Center Honor, and the 2006 Mark Twain Prize for American Humor. Simon was awarded an honorary LHD degree from Hofstra University and a DHC from Williams College. He is also the only living playwright to have a Broadway theater named after him. *See also* **Comedy**; **Theater**.

Barry Kornhauser

Further Reading: Simon, Neil. *The Play Goes On: A Memoir*. New York: Simon and Schuster, 1999. ———. *Rewrites: A Memoir.* New York: Simon and Schuster, 1996.

SIMON, PAUL (1941–)

Simon is a songwriter, musician, and member of the Rock and Roll Hall of Fame. In 2006, *Time* magazine called him one of the 100 "people who shape our world." Paul Simon, born Paul Frederic Simon, was born to Jewish parents, Belle and Louis Simon, on October 13, 1941. His mother, Belle, was an English teacher and his father, Louis, was a professional bass player, playing in jazz bands and teaching. Simon released his first single, "Hey, Schoolgirl," with his friend Art Garfunkel in 1957, under the name Tom and Jerry. Their first song reached 49th on the pop charts, but the LP *Wednesday Morning, 3am* did not sell well at first. It was not until 1964 that they released their first album as Simon and Garfunkel. The two parted ways and Simon moved to England, where he attempted to start a solo career, writing and recording what would become the *Paul Simon Song Book*. The songs in this book helped fill later albums.

Back in the United States, Simon and Garfunkel's first album sold because of the track "The Sound of Silence," and Columbia asked the duo to record a follow-up album, *Wednesday Morning, 3 A.M.* Over the next four years Simon and Garfunkel produced a highly successful catalog of albums: *Sound of Silence* (1966), *Parsley, Sage, Rosemary and Thyme* (1968), *Bookends* (1968), and *Bridge Over Troubled Waters* (1969). Simon was also heavily involved in the soundtrack for the movie *The Graduate* (1968), which featured the song "Mrs. Robinson." Following the recording of the soundtrack for *The Graduate,* Simon and Garfunkel again went their separate ways. They reunited occasionally—once in 1975, releasing the top 10 single "My Little Town," which was featured on Art Garfunkel's first solo album. In 1981, they reunited again for a free concert in New York City's Central Park, which was released as an album and sold well. In 1990, they were inducted into the Rock and Roll Hall of Fame, and in 2003 they both received the Grammy Lifetime Achievement Award. The meeting in 2003 led to the idea of another tour together, named the "Old Friends" Tour, which was popular and produced another live collaboration. Their most recent reunion took place in 2007 when Paul Simon was the first recipient of the Library of Congress Gershwin Prize for Popular Song.

Simon's solo career spans 1971 to the present day. His first album released in 1972, entitled *Paul Simon,* features the hit "Me and Julio Down by the School Yard"; his next album, *There Goes Rhymin' Simon,* released in 1973, features the hit "Kodachrome," which gained later fame in the hit movie *Coneheads.* In 1975 he released *Still Crazy after All These Years,* with hits that included the title track and "50 Ways to Leave Your Lover." His next two albums were not as successful, *One Trick Pony* (1980) and *Hearts and Bones* (1983).

With *Graceland* (1986) and *Rhythm of the Saints* (1990), Paul Simon helped to popularize the genre of world music, and he won his first Grammy as a solo artist for the album *Graceland.* The popularity of these albums gave Simon the chance to have a concert in Central Park, with a band consisting of both South African and Brazilian artists. His next album, *You're the One,* was followed by *Surprise* (2006). While both of his recent albums were not as financially successful, they helped reestablish Paul Simon as one of the best singer-songwriters in the history of music. While his Judaism never came out through his songs, his embrace of world music and the fact that he won the first Library of Congress Gershwin award, named after another Jew, **George Gershwin**, attests to the Jewish influence on popular music in the twentieth century. *See also* **Rock and Roll**.

Jesse Ulrich

Further Reading: Billig, Michael. *Rock 'n' Roll Jews.* Syracuse University Press, 2000.

SINGER, ISAAC BASHEVIS (1904–1991)

Isaac Bashevis Singer was a Nobel Prize-winning Polish Jewish American author and one of the leading figures in the Yiddish literary movement. I. B. Singer was born Icek Hersz Zynger in a small town near Warsaw. Singer's father was a Hasidic rabbi and judge of the local Jewish court. His mother was descended from a long line of rabbis. Singer decided to place "Bashevis," meaning "son of Bethsheva" (his mother) as his middle name. To avoid the ravages of World War I, his family moved to the maternal grandmother's shtetl home, a venue that gave Singer firsthand exposure to the cultural life of the Jewish people of Poland (then czarist Russia). Israel Joshua Singer, his brother eight years his senior and an established writer, introduced Isaac Singer to the world of letters. Singer proofread for his brother's Warsaw magazine, the *Literarische Bleter,* of which he was an editor—but subsequently he started his own magazine, *Globus,* with his friend, **Yiddish** poet Aaron Zeitlin. He published his first novel, *Satan in Goray,* in the periodical (the novel was his second novel translated into English, which was published in the United States in 1955)—it was a fictional account of the effects of the murderous Cossack pogroms in 1648 on a Jewish town.

In 1935, fearing an attack on Poland by Nazi Germany, Singer emigrated to the United States, leaving behind a wife and child who ultimately found their way to Palestine. Both his wife and child vanished from Singer's life. In New York City, he went to work as reviewer of Jewish literature for the New York Yiddish paper, the ***Jewish Daily Forward***. In 1940 he married a German Jewish refugee, Alma Wasserman, a union that lasted his lifetime. In 1943 he became an American citizen and began a series of stories, always written in Yiddish, in the *Forward*. His first novel published in English was *The Family Moskat* (1950); it dealt with the destruction of the Jewish communities in Poland during the World War I and II. But it was his short story "Gimpel the Fool," included in the first collection of Singer's short stories in English (1957), about a cuckold, that brought him wide recognition. Discovered by Irving Howe, and translated by **Saul Bellow**, who used his influence to have it published in the *Partisan Review,* the story caused Singer to emerge as a major figure in the literary world.

Singer went on to write 18 novels, 14 children's books, and hundreds of short stories. The body of his work described Eastern European folk beliefs: blessings, curses, demons, ghosts, spirits, charms, making no sharp distinction between the natural and the supernatural. Singer himself believed in the supernatural. His description of the activities of the common folk (including rabbis) included adultery, prostitution, womanizing, philandering, rape, and sexual aberrations. Like Hamlet, Singer believed he was holding a mirror up to life. Some critics accused him of writing pornography, while others charged him with airing Jewish dirty linen in public. Singer's response to his critics was to argue that a writer was a good storyteller, not a reformer.

In his novels and hundreds of short stories, Singer makes fun of tradition and authority and depicts the world as malicious. His characters are playthings of supernatural forces or at the mercy of bad luck. His short stories for children recount the trials and tribulations of the not-so-fictitious town of Chelm, whose inhabitants are among the most foolish and hilarious Jews in all of his fiction. Two of his novels became movies: *Yentl* (1983), about a young woman disguised as a yeshiva boy, and *Enemies, A Love Story* (1989), which deals with a post-Holocaust love triangle.

Singer called his personal religion private mysticism. He was a skeptic, a loner, a nonconformist, a believer in the occult, yet respectful of Orthodoxy and Jewish tradition. His writings reflect the tensions of free thinking versus traditional Judaism, the old ways versus the new. In 1978, he won a Nobel Prize for literature. His address to the Swedish assembly was in Yiddish. It bemoaned the loss of tradition in the world and extolled the Yiddish language. The medal he received had this inscription in English and Yiddish: "Free will is life's essence."

In the autumn of his life, Singer maintained an apartment in Miami and taught creative writing at the University of Miami. Despite fame and fortune he lived as he always did—modestly, mingling almost daily with ordinary folk. After

Polish-born Yiddish storyteller and prolific author Isaac Bashevis Singer is applauded by Sweden's King Carl Gustaf after receiving his Nobel Prize in Literature on December 10, 1978. [AP Photo]

several heart attacks, he died on July 24, 1991. *See also* **Literature**.

Philip Rosen

Further Reading: Norville, Florence, and Catherine Temerson. *Isaac B. Singer, A Life*. Farrar, Straus and Giroux, 2006.

SITCOMS

Jewish representation has been a major part of television history. Since the early days of television, Jewish humor has been a fixture in variety shows, stand-up performances, and sitcoms. Although comedy programs have changed in style and content through the decades, one aspect of sitcoms has evidenced little, if any, alteration—the self-deprecating humor and stereotypes of Jews. When television became popular in U.S. households, during the late 1940s and early 1950s, the first "Jewish" sitcom, *The Goldbergs* (1949–1956), appeared on NBC. The ways in which Jews were presented in that program bear a remarkable similarity to the representation of Jews in currently popular sitcoms. A "Jewish" sitcom may be defined in numerous ways, but for this essay, it is a television show that encompasses Jewish humor, characters, and themes. Examples include *Rhoda* (1974–1979), *Welcome Back,*

Kotter (1975–1979), *Barney Miller* (1975–1983), *Seinfeld* (1989–1998), and *Will and Grace* (1998–2006). Dry humor and the "comedy of pain" are inherent in these sitcoms. Another regular feature is the focus on cultural Jewishness rather than religious Judaism. Televisual history shows that many "Jewish" comedians often utilized Jewishness, not Judaism, in their sitcoms in order to appeal to mass audiences, who would have likely rejected the religious aspects of the Jewish faith.

Jewishness is distinctly different from Judaism because it focuses on cultural values rather than on religious ideals. Jewishness entails compassion, connection, and endurance. Jews are the paradigmatic diaspora people, having been exiled from their homes. From *galut* (exile), prejudice, and diaspora, a Jewish identity developed. Jewishness embodies chutzpah and tzedakah (charity), from which certain characteristics—gesticulations, intonations, and expressions sustain. While the exact meaning of "Jewishness" adapts and changes over the years, it remains a vital element in Jewish sustenance and community relations. By making various races, religions, and ethnicities laugh, Jews could relate to "others" in an unthreatening environment.

Hundreds of famous comedians, from the early variety shows to present stand-up comedy and sitcoms, were Jewish, including the 1940s and 1950s legends **Milton Berle**, **Sid Caesar**, **Jack Benny**, **Groucho Marx**, **George Burns**, and **Eddie Cantor**. Today, Jewish comedy persists through the work of comics such as **Mel Brooks**, **Woody Allen**, Paul Reiser, **Adam Sandler**, **Jon Stewart**, and **Jerry Seinfeld** dominating much of show business. Lawrence J. Epstein writes, "...the ability of Jews to laugh at themselves even in times of adversity is an essential aspect of 'Jewishness,' and may be a reason that Jewish comedy persists and connects to secular sensibility" (Epstein, 2001).

The Goldbergs (1949–1956). The "Jewish" sitcom emerged in 1949 with *The Goldbergs*. In 1929, this show began as an NBC radio series and, because of its popularity, became a television sitcom two decades later. The family-based sitcom revolved around Molly Goldberg (Gertrude Berg), her husband Jake (originally Philip Loeb), their teenage son and daughter, Sammy (Larry Robinson) and Rosalie (Arlene McQuade), and Uncle David (Eli Mintz). As a pioneering ethnic sitcom, *The Goldbergs* addressed immigrant problems of the time, such as assimilation anxiety. The program dealt most particularly with "old world" parents and their Americanized children. Molly, Jake, and David spoke with heavy **Yiddish** accents and followed traditional Jewish customs, while their children, Sammy and Rosalie, conducted a more secular life, which included typical American schooling and social events.

In every episode, a new dilemma arose, and Molly, clever and resourceful, solved it. Molly Goldberg epitomized the lovable "Yiddishe Mama" of the pre-World War II era. Vincent Brook notes that as "Matriarch-extraordinaire," she was a "yenta" (busybody), a matchmaker, head of the household and the voice of reason. Because of its resonance with immigrant culture, this "Jewish" sitcom charmed the American audience, and "the show rated seventh overall for the 1949–1950 television season" (Brook, 2003).

The Goldbergs began to lose its audience in the mid-1950s. Critics marked the sitcom "too Jewish." Molly Goldberg's "Yiddishisms," neighborly chats, and gefilte fish were seen as overly identifiably Jewish. In an effort to save the show, producers tried to "Americanize" the Goldberg family and emphasize their "whiteness" by moving them to the suburbs. A complete transformation occurred. The sitcom now featured an all-American family that displayed aspects of Jewishness.

From *The Goldbergs,* producers learned that audiences could accept shows about Jewishness, as long as culture, not religion, remained the primary focus. Two decades passed before the next Jewish sitcom aired, although Gertrude Berg tried unsuccessfully to revive her character in the 1960 *Molly Goes to College*. When Jewish sitcoms made a comeback, they still encompassed Jewish sensibility and humor and still sidelined Judaism and spiritual ideologies.

The 1950s and 1960s: Where Are the Jews? For two decades Jewish sitcoms declined. Vincent Brook suggests that, during these years, Jews successfully pursued other cultural avenues, such as film, literature, music, and painting. Instead of television careers, Jews were enjoying their acceptance in more established vocations that had traditionally been closed to them. He also suggests that movies provided an outlet for Jewish actors such as George Segal, Elliott Gould, **Barbra Streisand**, Woody Allen, Richard Benjamin, and **Dustin Hoffman**. These stars were now "in" as they appeared in movies, with "big noses, kinky hair, and nasal New York accents." These Jewish thespians remained staples of the movie industry. The Jewish sitcom did reemerge in the 1970s, but as a less ethnic genre than was viewed in *The Goldbergs*.

Rhoda, a spin-off of the popular *Mary Tyler Moore Show* (1970–1977), aired from 1974–1979. Not as popular as its predecessor, *Rhoda* still appealed to diverse audiences and enjoyed a five-year run. Although in *The Mary Tyler Moore Show,* the character of Rhoda Morgenstern (Valerie Harper, a non-Jew) played the nasal-inflected Jewish Woman in Search of Marriage . . . New York Jewish 'rye' to Mary Richard's white-bread, Minnesota WASP, she was transformed in the sitcom as "less Jewish." Because it attracted a segment of an older viewing audience, Rhoda's Jewishness and Jewish humor was sustained throughout the series, but her character shed many of the physical and behavioral characteristics of being Jewish.

Rhoda's likeable characteristics, including chutzpah, are often associated with Jews. But Rhoda's toned-down character demonstrated that only a soft-pedaled version of Jewish sensibility was acceptable to television audiences. As long as *Rhoda* adhered to the newfound formula for sitcoms, which included cultural Jewishness and excluded Judaism, the show appealed to diverse viewers.

Through the 1970s and 1980s, Jewish sitcoms were sparse, but they did not disappear altogether. *Barney Miller* (1975–1983) and *Taxi* (1979–1983) had Jewish protagonists and discourse, but television executives placed little or no emphasis on Jews in their shows. This marginalization continued until the 1990s, when a collection of Jewish sitcoms altered television's landscape.

Surge of the "Jewish Sitcom" in the 1990s. The introduction of *Seinfeld* in 1989 changed television sitcoms. The role of Jews and "Jewishness" on television shifted, and in the 1990s a number of new shows incorporating Jewish humor and Jewishness premiered. America loved Jerry Seinfeld, George Costanza (Jason Alexander), Elaine Benes (Julia Louis-Dreyfus), and Cosmo Kramer (Michael Richards). *Seinfeld* garnered huge audiences, as the series' cast of neurotic and self-deprecating television characters became weekly guests in living rooms. At the peak of the show's popularity, Thursday night became the most profitable night on television for NBC.

Seinfeld's Jewish humor came through, either directly or indirectly, in each episode. Mainstream audiences were attracted to *Seinfeld,* since it focused on Jewishness rather than Judaism. The show highlighted Jewishness in secular, cultural terms, and while Jewishness was central to *Seinfeld*'s success, the sitcom often mocked Jewish religious practices For example, in a fifth-season *Seinfeld* episode titled "The *Bris,*" Judaism is portrayed as negative and foolish. The story line has Jerry and Elaine asked to be godparents for a Jewish friend's new baby. This responsibility requires Elaine to find a mohel (professional circumciser) and for Jerry to hold the baby during the circumcision. They complain about these duties and, during the ceremony, disaster ensues. The mohel Elaine finds is a neurotic, unstable *meshugganah* (crazy person), who yells at the guests and cuts Jerry's finger off. He inappropriately rants, "I could've been a Kosher butcher like my brother . . . money's good!" and has no remorse for his foul behavior. This representation of a Jewish figure may be humorous for some, but it is inaccurate and offensive for many Jews. The portrayal of the *Bris* belittles Jewish religious practices.

Generational gaps are also portrayed on *Seinfeld* and other Jewish sitcoms. The main characters' parents and relatives are often portrayed as stereotypical old world Jews, while the main characters, the "Jerrys" and others, are depicted as "Baby Boomer Jews." In the episode "The Pony Remark," Jerry, his parents, and Elaine attend a celebration dinner for his great-Aunt Manya's 50th anniversary. Jerry exclaims at the dinner table, "I hate anyone who ever had a pony when they were growing up!" His great-Aunt Manya, with her heavy Eastern European accent replies, "I had a pony," and continues in her broken English, "When I was a little girl in Poland, we all had ponies . . . what's wrong with that?" Jerry tries to backpedal as Manya stomps out of the room. While the other relatives at the table give him disapproving looks, Jerry digs himself deeper. Later in the episode, Manya passes away suddenly and everyone blames Jerry and his pony remark.

This episode encompasses Jewishness, with Manya's *zaftigkeit* (fleshiness) and Polish accent and Jerry's mocking of the Jewish peasants from the old country. The pony symbolizes the difference between Jewish culture, past and present. When Manya was young, a pony represented working-class identity, while, for Jerry, the animal is a symbol of affluence and vanity. The dissonance between the younger and older generations shows little hope of reconciliation. Jerry then considers not attending the funeral because it overlaps with a baseball game. This demonstrates even more strongly his disrespect for his elders and his indoctrination into American culture.

Ridiculing old world Judaism seems to be a trend in Jewish sitcoms. One is left to consider whether television is reflecting reality or reality is reflecting television.

Jerry epitomizes the "new nineties Jew." Journalist J. J. Goldberg elaborates on this developing type, "It's a Baby Boomer Jewishness: at home in America, taken for granted, more than a little ambivalent. 'Jewishness' is as much a part of them as family, sex and work, and just as ripe for satire. There's nothing worshipful there" (Goldberg, 1998). This aptly describes Jerry's connection to his Jewish identity. Jerry dates Gentile women, eats pork, and enjoys Friday nights out. Similar to many Jewish Americans, Jerry does not practice Judaism as a religion, but he does identify ethnically as a Jew. Seemingly, negotiating one's Jewish and American identity is the key to acceptance and success in America. Jerry's carefully constructed identity appeals to audiences because it is not "too Jewish." Throughout its nine-year run, *Seinfeld* was a television triumph. The Jewishness of *Seinfeld* connected with people of differing ethnicities and religions, as well as a changing Jewish population.

The Nanny ran from 1993–1999. Fran Drescher played the openly Jewish nanny employed by the elite, conservative Sheffield family. Drescher's character, with her flashy style, high-pitched nasal voice, heavy New York accent, and obsession with shopping, was representative of the "Jewish American Princess." Hired by a British Broadway producer, Maxwell Sheffield (Charles Shaughnessy), as a nanny for his three children, Fran Fine (Drescher) moves into the mansion and changes the family's lives with her "ethnic flavor" and fun-loving persona.

The lower-class, heavily-Jewish Fran is depicted as crass, gauche, whining, materialistic, manipulative, and addicted to food and shopping. Her "Jewishness" runs through the show, with Yiddishisms, frequent visits from her pushy mother, Sylvia Fine (Renee Taylor), constant noshing and kibitzing (gossiping).

Similar to *Seinfeld, The Nanny* mocks Judaism, Jewish rituals, and traditions. Fran and her mother are secular Jews. In one episode, "The Cantor Show," Fran suggests the cantor at her mother's synagogue try out for Mr. Sheffield's musical (*The Nanny,* third season). When he gets the lead role, the cantor leaves the synagogue. The congregation is furious at Fran and Sylvia. They are banished to the back row of the temple. When attending sevices, Sylvia pulls out a BLT sandwich to protest her banishment. The scene portrays Fran and Sylvia as disrepectful and treats Judaism insensitively.

Jews have been and remain a staple of the American television sitcom. Producers, writers, and actors in "Jewish" sitcoms unconsciously use cultural Jewishness to make religious Judaism non-threatening for multicultural audiences. While Jewishness as a stereotype is prominent on these sitcoms, Judaism, as a religion, is mocked and marginalized. The main characters are never "too Jewish." Jewish humor appeals to audiences as does the more secularized behavior of the characters.

Caroline Forman Litwack

Further Reading: Altman, Sig. *The Comic Image of the Jew: Explorations of a Pop Culture Phenomenon.* Rutherford, NJ: Fairleigh Dickinson University Press, 1971. Antler, Joyce. "Not 'Too Jewish' for Prime Time," in *Television's Changing Image of American Jews.* Neal Gabler, Frank Rich, and Joyce Antler, eds. New York: The American Jewish Committee and The Norman Lear Center, 2000. Brook, Vincent. *Something Ain't Kosher Here: The Rise of the 'Jewish' Sitcom.* New Brunswick, NJ: Rutgers University Press, 2003. Epstein, Lawrence J. *The Haunted Smile.* New York: Public Affairs, 2001. Freedman, Samuel G. *Jew vs. Jew: The Struggle for the Soul of American Jewry.* New York: Touchstone, 2000. Goldberg, J. J. "Seining Off." *The Jewish Journal of Greater Los Angeles,* May 15, 1998. Zurawik, David. *The Jews of Primetime.* Hanover, NH: University Press of New England, 2005.

SKULNIK, MENASHA (1890–1970)

One of the most popular comedians in **Yiddish theater** history, Menasha Skulnik became a Broadway star in his sixties. The seventh of eight children born to Morris Skulnik and Sarah Weinberg in Poland in 1890, Skulnik sang in a children's chorus. As a teenager, the budding actor played female roles in amateur productions. Immigrating to America in 1913, Skulnik worked as a stage manager playing small parts in the Philadelphia Yiddish theaters. Early in his career, Skulnik performed with Yiddish theater stars **Molly Picon**, **Maurice Schwartz**, and Jacob Ben-Ami. In 1927, The Hebrew Actors Union accepted Skulnik as a character comedian, and the actor joined a venerable line of Yiddish theater actors including Sigmund Mogelescu and Ludwig Satz in perfecting the part of the hapless nebbish who nevertheless gets the girl. This Yiddish theater archetype was a precursor to the comedic styles of such comedians as **Jerry Lewis** and **Woody Allen**. As Irving Howe writes in his book ***World of Our Fathers***: "Woody Allen was a reincarnated Menasha Skulnik, quintessential schlemiel of the Yiddish theater" (Howe, 1978).

Standing just five feet, four inches in an undersized pork pie hat and an absurdly checked jacket, Skulnik was a comedian who loved to make his audience cry. *New York Times* critic Brooks Atkinson wrote about Skulnik's Broadway debut: "There are not many things in life more enjoyable than a melancholy Jewish comedian" (Atkinson, 1953). A serial improviser, Skulnik preferred scripts that had, instead of his dialogue, just the words "Menasha enters." When the audience applauded his entrance, Skulnik would often shuffle downstage, shrug his shoulders, and stutter in **Yiddish**—"You know me?"

From 1927–1933, Skulnik performed Yiddish theater in the provinces headlining Brooklyn, Buenos Aires, and the Bronx, playing the earnest fool in musical comedies such as *Gezl becomes a Groom* and*Shmendrick's Wedding.* In 1933, Skulnik had a hit show in Brooklyn, *Yoina Searches for a Bride* by Yitshak Freedman, the first ever musical adaptation of George Bernard Shaw's *Pygmalion.* Skulnik then conquered Manhattan, becoming one of the biggest names on Second Avenue, the Yiddish Broadway. Like the majority of Yiddish theater stars, Skulnik also acted as producer of his own shows including *The Jolly Village, The Little Tailor, The Wise Fool,* and *Yossel and His Wives.*

In addition to his career on the Yiddish stage, Skulnik appeared in English language radio, television, and theater. Often, he would hop in a cab after a show on Second Avenue and race uptown to record a part on the radio. He played the role of Uncle David in Gertrude Berg's radio serial *The Rise of the Goldbergs* from 1929–1946, later appearing in the televised version. In 1950, Skulnik's short-lived television show *Menasha the Magnificent* was canceled after three months. Skulnik made his celebrated Broadway debut in 1953 as dress manufacturer Max Pincus in Sylvia

Regan's *The Fifth Season,* which ran for almost two years. Also on Broadway, Skulnik originated the role of Noah in **Clifford Odets**'s *The Flowering Peach* and title roles in *The Zulu and the Zayde* and *Uncle Willie.*

Skulnik married Sarah Kutner in 1913, with whom he had a daughter, Hanna. After the death of his first wife, Skulnik married actress Anna Tietelbaum, and they also had a daughter, Maya. In 1970, the almost 80-year-old Skulnik became ill while rehearsing a show out of town. Skulnik returned to New York, where he died in June of that year. *See also* **Television**; **Yiddish Film**; **Yiddish Theater**.

Caraid O'Brien

Further Reading: Lifson, David S. *The Yiddish Theatre in America.* Cranbury, NJ: Yoseloff, 1965. Rosenfeld, Lulla. *Bright Star of Exile: Jacob Adler and the Yiddish Theatre.* New York: Crowell, 1977. Sandrow, Nahma. *Vagabond Stars: A World History of Yiddish Theatre.* New York: Harper and Row, 1977.

SONDHEIM, STEPHEN (1930–)

Fifty years ago, a Broadway musical premiered combining current events with a familiar drama of 400 years earlier. *West Side Story*'s score was written by composer-conductor-television personality **Leonard Bernstein** (1918–1990). His lyricist was the relatively unknown Stephen Sondheim, who soon became the most creative and honored personality on Broadway. The recipient of a Pulitzer Prize, seven Tony Awards—the most of any composer, an Academy Award, numerous Grammy awards, and the Kennedy Center Lifetime Achievement Award, Sondheim dominated the American musical theater for the last 30 years of the twentieth century. Stephen Joshua Sondheim was born in New York City on March 22, 1930. His childhood, even in the lap of luxury, was difficult, with belligerent parents who ultimately divorced. His father, Herbert, a successful dress manufacturer, abandoned his wife and child. Sondheim's mother, Janet, known by the nickname "Foxy," had grown up in a traditional Jewish home, but she did not pass this education to her son and only child. A dress designer, her relationship with her son was very distant.

At the time of his parents' divorce, Sondheim became close friends with Jimmy Hammerstein, the son of Oscar Hammerstein II. This relationship proved pivotal, for the distinguished playwright and lyricist became a teacher, mentor, friend, sounding board, and surrogate father for Sondheim. Sondheim took advantage of this relationship when, after writing a musical for his school, he brought the text to Hammerstein to critique. The lyricist of *Show Boat* (1927), *Oklahoma* (1943), and *Carousel* (1945) took this opportunity seriously and deconstructed the young man's efforts, point by point. He then explained how it could be improved, giving the young man a master class in musical writing. An extraordinary mentoring relationship developed, with Hammerstein creating musical assignments for Sondheim, followed by his critique.

Sondheim attended Williams College, where he studied composition with Milton Babbitt, who provided a formal classical foundation to the practical skills learned from Hammerstein. Sondheim graduated in 1950 and began four difficult years of songwriting and writing for the popular television show *Topper.* He enjoyed his first big break, writing the lyrics for ***West Side Story*** with music by Bernstein, book by Arthur Laurents, and direction from **Jerome Robbins**. Even though *West Side Story* ran over 700 performances, Sondheim has often spoken of his disappointment with the level of his own work on this show.

Two years later, he was invited to write the lyrics for Jule Styne's (1905–1994) musical *Gypsy,* starring Ethel Merman. *Gypsy*'s librettist was *West Side Story* colleague Arthur Laurents. This show was a great success, running for over 700 performances. Some of Sondheim's most successful songs came from this score, including "Everything's Coming Up Roses" and "Let Me Entertain You," yet Sondheim was not happy writing lyrics alone.

This changed in 1962 when Sondheim wrote both music and lyrics for *A Funny Thing*

Happened on the Way to the Forum, which was based on the bawdy farces of the Roman playwright Plautus, with the libretto by comedy writers Burt Shevelove and Larry Gelbart. The show ran more than 960 performances and won several Tony Awards including Best Musical, but Sondheim's efforts were not critically recognized. His frustration continued with the flop musical *Anyone Can Whistle* (1964), starring British-born film actress Angela Lansbury, which ran for nine performances. It was followed by *Do I Hear A Waltz,* with legendary composer and producer Richard Rodgers.

The 1970s provided Sondheim success and praise. His innovative and creative concept musicals began with *Company* in 1970, set in contemporary New York. In 1972, Sondheim honored the golden age of Broadway with his show *Follies.* The show a tribute to the Broadway revues of the past, Sondheim echoed their styles in his songs. 1973 saw the hugely successful show *A Little Night Music,* which contained Sondheim's only "hit parade" song, "Send in the Clowns." Based on the Ingmar Bergman film *Smiles of a Summer Night, A Little Night Music* was written in waltz time.

Sondheim followed these groundbreaking musicals with his most unusual, *Pacific Overtures,* the story of Japan's opening to Western commerce. Sondheim's only operatic score followed, with *Sweeney Todd* (1979), the story of a wronged man killing those who had convicted him, providing their corpses for meat pies!

Most recently, Sondheim has written several unique shows. *Merrily We Roll Along* (1981), another brief run, was followed by *Sunday in the Park with George* (1984) based on the neo-Impressionist painter Georges Seurat (1859--1891), starring **Mandy Patinkin** and Bernadette Peters—for which Sondheim received the Pulitzer Prize. This was followed by the fairy tale *Into The Woods* (1987), the political/historical *Assassins* (1990), *Passion* (1994), and a revised *Frogs* (2004) taken from Aristophanes.

Sondheim was honored with several revues based on his own songs, most prominently *Side by Side by Sondheim* in 1976 and *Putting it Together* in 1993. As Martin Gottfried wrote, "Stephen Sondheim is the giant of the modern musical stage. He is to today's Broadway what Kern and Gershwin, Hammerstein and Hart were to yesterday's" (Gottfried, 1993). *See also* **Popular Music**; ***West Side Story.***

Kenneth Kanter

Further Reading: Gordon, Joanne. *Art Isn't Easy.* Carbondale: Southern Illinois University, 1992. Gottfried, Martin. *Sondheim.* New York: Harry Abrams, Inc., 1993. Horowitz, Mark. *Sondheim on Music: Minor Details and Major Decisions.* Lanham, MD: Scarecrow Press, 2003. Secrest, Meryle. *Stephen Sondheim: A Life.* New York: Alfred Knopf, 1998. Zadan, Craig. *Sondheim & Co.* New York: Harper and Row, 1986.

SONTAG, SUSAN (1935–2004)

Susan Sontag, the sole woman among the so-called "New York intellectuals," was the daughter of Jack and Mildred Rosenblatt. Her father died in 1940 of tuberculosis, and her mother married Nathan Sontag in 1947. Susan Sontag and her sister Judith took their stepfather's name. Brought up in a highly secularized Jewish family, Sontag did not receive a formal Jewish education. She attended the University of California at Berkeley and the University of Chicago, then Harvard, receiving master's degrees in literature and philosophy. In 1950, at age 17, she married Philip Reif, a social psychologist (divorced 1958). The union produced one son, David.

Susan spent 12 years in the academic world, teaching at colleges, and she for a time wrote for *Commentary,* the Jewish-oriented current affairs magazine. Between 1962 and 1965, she published 26 essays, the genre in which she established her reputation. In the 1960s and 1970s she wrote her first novel, *The Benefactor,* then a second novel, *Death Kit* (1967); she completed six novels and some short stories. Susan wrote scripts and directed three experimental films, including *Promised Lands,* which dealt with the Yom Kippur War. In 2001 she was awarded the Jerusalem Prize, which is given every two years to a writer whose work explores the freedom of the individual in society. While sympathetic to the Jewish state, she criticized the settlement movement and collective punishment against Arabs because of terrorist attacks. She shocked the left by equating Soviet bloc countries with fascism and the right by charging the white race with genocide and being a cancer on the world. Her most critically acclaimed novel, written in 1992, *The Volcano Lover,* retold the story of the romance between Admiral Lord Nelson and Lady Hamilton. Altogether, she authored 17 books, 3 plays, and 6 films. Sontag won numerous awards and recognition. She was a founding member of the New York Institute for the Humanities and became president of the writers' prestigious PEN American Center from 1987 to 1989.

Sontag's nine major essays have won her fame and criticism. Declaring she should not be categorized by gender, political inclination, or faction of religion, she claimed she was an universalist, demanding cultural autonomy and refusing to be bound by one critical perspective.

Her short essay "On Camp" (1964) defined the boundaries of that term, denoting "art which is so bad, it is good." Her essays "Illness as a Metaphor" (1978) and "AIDS and Its Metaphors" (1989) dismantled cultural metaphors which placed the blame for the disease on its victims.

Ms. Sontag was diagnosed with breast cancer in 1975. After intense chemotherapy treatment, she lived until 2004, when at age 71, she was diagnosed with leukemia (believed to be a result of cancer treatments). At her request, she is buried in Montparnesse cemetery in Paris. The cemetery, neutral religiously, is the resting place of intellectual and artistic elites.

Philip Rosen

Further Reading: Rollyson, Carl, and Lisa Paddock. *Susan Sontag: The Making of an Icon.* W.W. Norton, 2000.

SPECTOR, PHIL

See **The Brill Building Songwriters**

SPELLING, AARON (1923–2006)

Aaron Spelling was born on April 22, 1923, in Dallas, Texas to Jewish parents who emigrated from Poland. Spelling had three brothers and two sisters. His mother, Pearl, worked as a homemaker, while his father, David, was employed by Sears-Roebuck. As a boy, Spelling was the only Jewish student at his school, and his classmates constantly harassed him. The bullying eventually took its toll, and at the age of eight, Spelling lost the use of his legs due to trauma. He was confined to bed for a year.

Spelling served in the United States Army Air Force during World War II and was awarded the Bronze Star and Purple Heart with Oak Leaf Cluster. After his military service Spelling attended Southern Methodist University as a journalism student, graduating in 1949 with a BA. While attending Southern Methodist University, Spelling won the prestigious Harvard Award for the best original one-act play.

In 1953 Spelling married actress Carolyn Jones, and the couple left Dallas for Hollywood, where Spelling earned his living as a bit actor. He played small roles in classics such as *Dragnet, Gunsmoke,* and *I Love Lucy,* and he wrote for the *Zane Grey Theatre, Playhouse 90, Wagon Train,* and *The Jane Wyman Theater.* Spelling's career as an actor faltered, but his profession as a scriptwriter began to show promise.

While Spelling's acting roles gradually diminished, his wife Carolyn's star was on the rise. Though the two stayed together for a time, their marriage ended in divorce in 1965. Spelling remarried in 1968. He and his new wife Carol Jean (Marer) Spelling had two children, Tori and Randy.

Spelling wrote and helped produce 14 television productions between 1957 and 1974. *Burke's Law* and *Daniel Boone* were two of the programs he was involved in, but his breakthrough in television occurred with the 1968 hit *The Mod Squad.* The show gained attention from viewers because it featured counterculture characters. The series garnered six Emmy Award nominations.

In 1972, he oversaw the creation of Aaron Spelling Productions, which went public in 1986 as Spelling Entertainment. The company produced some of America's best-known programs, including *Starsky and Hutch, Dynasty, Beverly Hills 90210, Charmed, 7th Heaven, The Love Boat, Charlie's Angels,* and *Fantasy Island*. As a master of escapist television, Spelling brought many of his more than 200 projects to the small screen as television series.

Throughout his career, admirers and critics often attributed Spelling's success to his ability to know what audiences wanted to watch. Though most of his television series were noted for their escapist genre, Spelling managed to produce some critically acclaimed television. For example, *Family,* the highly praised drama about American life that aired from 1976–1980, tackled the previously taboo subjects of divorce, homosexuality, and domestic violence. In film, Spelling's work ranges from *Soapdish* and the horror flick *Satan's School for Girls* (the 1973 original and the 2000 remake) to the acclaimed HBO film *And the Band Played On,* which earned the critics' praise for its handling of the subject of AIDS. Spelling has received numerous industry awards, and he has been given the NAACP's Image Award six times.

Aaron Spelling was a lifelong smoker and was diagnosed with oral cancer in 2001. On June 18, 2006, Spelling suffered a stroke, and he died five days later on June 23. He was 83 years old. *See also* **Film**; **Television**.

Susan M. Ortmann

Further Reading: Spelling, Aaron, and Jefferson Graham. *Aaron Spelling: A Prime-Time Life*. New York: St. Martin's Press, 1996. "Spelling's Final Print Interview." *Sydney Morning Herald,* September 2004.

SPIEGELMAN, ART (1948–)

Best known for his Pulitzer Prize-winning, graphic **Holocaust** novel-memoir *Maus,* which he based on the experiences of his parents as concentration camp survivors, Art Spiegelman was born on February 15, 1948 in Stockholm, Sweden. He immigrated to the United States at an early age with his parents, Vladek and Anja Spiegelman (his mother's maiden name was Zylberberg), Polish Jewish refugees. The family settled in Queens, New York, and subsequently Spiegelman graduated from the High School of Art and Design in Manhattan, where he studied cartooning.

At age 16, he started to draw professionally, and he later attended Harpur College in Binghamton, New York, where he majored in art and philosophy. After leaving college in 1968, he joined the underground comix movement and first published "Maus" in *Funny Animals* in 1972. Spiegelman expanded the story line into a full-blown graphic novel, which he drew from 1980 to 1986, with the Jews presented as mice and the Nazis as cats (the Katzies). The book *Maus: A Survivor's Tale* earned Spiegelman celebrity status. He completed the story in 1991 with *Maus II: From Mauschwitz to the* ***Catskills***. For his work, Art Spiegelman received the Pulitzer Prize in 1992. Together with *The Diary of Anne Frank,* the television adaptation of **Gerald Green**'s novel *Holocaust,* and **Steven Spielberg**'s film ***Schindler's List***, *Maus* entered the mainstream of popular culture as a creative work that exposed the American public to the Nazi extermination of European Jewry. The inspiration for the graphic novel can be found in Spiegelman's family history. He had one brother, named Richieu, who died before Spiegelman was born. During the German occupation of Poland, which commenced in 1939, Richieu was sent to live with an aunt, Tosha, since the ghetto where she resided seemed safer than the Sosnowiec-S'rodula ghetto, where he had been confined. When the Nazis started to deport people from the Zawiercie ghetto, Tosha poisoned herself, Richieu, her own daughter (Bibi), and her niece (Lonia). This is all recorded by Spiegelman in *Maus* (volume 1). Spiegelman mentions in *Maus* that he felt like he had a sibling rivalry with a photograph, since his parents never overcame the death of their firstborn son. The second volume of *Maus* was dedicated to Richieu Spiegelman and to Art's daughter, Nadja. Although the success of *Maus* gained Spiegelman national recognition, especially on college campuses, he had already established himself as an artist in the comix industry. Spiegelman was a regular contributor to various underground publications, including *Real Pulp, Young Lust,* and *Bizarre Sex,* and, using different pen names, such as "Skeeter Grant" and "Al Flooglebuckle," he drew comic characters such as "Ace Hole, Midget Detective," "Nervous Rex," "Douglas Comics," and "Cracking Jokes." In 1975, he co-founded *Arcade,* an influential comix revue. Besides his cartooning career, Art Spiegelman edited several comix magazines. In 1980 he started the magazine *Raw* with his wife, Francoise Mouly, where he helped identify important new talents like Mark Beyer, Chris Ware, Charles Burns, J. Otto Seibold, and Kaz and Jerry Moriarty, as well as artists from foreign shores, such as Ever Meulen, Pascal Doury, Jacques Tardi, and Joost Swarte, among others. Hired by Tina Brown in 1992, Spiegelman worked for *The New Yorker* for 10 years but resigned a few months after the September 11 terrorist attacks. The cover created by Spiegelman and Mouly for the September 11 issue of *The New Yorker* received wide acclaim. In the 1990s, besides illustrating for books and for *The New Yorker,* Spiegelman put together the children's magazine *Little Lit,* containing comics for children and adults, which included the work of artists outside the comics field such as William Joyce, **Maurice Sendak**, Ian Falconer, David Macaulay, Barbara McClintock, and Harry Bliss. In the wake of the disaster of September 11, 2001, which happened around the corner from where he lives (Green Street/Canal Street), Spiegelman subsequently wrote a graphic novel about the terrorist assault on the World Trade Center in New York, called *In the Shadow of No Towers* (Pantheon, 2004). In 2005, *Time* magazine named Spiegelman one of their "Top 100 Most Influential People." Spiegelman is a prominent advocate for the medium of comics. He has taught courses in the history and aesthetics of comics at schools including the University of California–Santa Cruz and the School of Visual Arts in New York. He is a very sought-after speaker on college campuses, where he presents a lecture he calls "Comix 101." An anthology of interviews with Spiegelman, spanning 25 years and a wide variety of printed venues, was published by University Press of Mississippi in 2007 as *Art Spiegelman: Conversations.* He lives in downtown Manhattan with Mouly and their two children, Nadja and Dashiell. *See also* **Comic Books**.

Jack R. Fischel

Further Reading: Gordon, Andrew. "Jewish Fathers and Sons in Spiegelman's *Maus* and Roth's *Patrimony.*" *Image Text,* no. 1, 2004. Spiegelman, Art. *Maus: A Survivor's Tale.* Pantheon, 1973–1991.

SPIELBERG, STEVEN (1946–)

Steven Spielberg is a film director and producer. In 2006, the magazine *Premiere* listed him as the most powerful and influential figure in the motion picture industry; *Time* listed him as one of the 100 "greatest people of the century." At the end of the twentieth century, *Life* named him the most influential person of his generation. Born in Cincinnati, Ohio on December 18, 1946, Spielberg grew up in Camden, New Jersey; Haddon Township, New Jersey; Phoenix, Arizona; and Saratoga, California. He traces his ancestors to an Austrian city called Spielberg. Film was always his great interest, and he started making films as a teenager with an eight-millimeter camera. He attended Saratoga High School in Saratoga, California and graduated in 1965. High school was the "worst experience" of his life and was "hell on earth." By the time he was 21 he did a short film for theatrical release called *Amblin* (1968). Years later he would name his production company Amblin Entertainment. Spielberg was an Eagle Scout and established the merit badge for cinematography. He enrolled in California State University where he majored in English, but he dropped out in 1968. Some 30 years later he completed his degree requirements via independent projects.

Spielberg entered the world of television production. His early résumé includes a number of episodes of *Marcus Welby M.D., Name of the*

Game, and *Columbo.* He then moved on to complete television movies such as *Duel* (1971), and *Something Evil,* which was similar to *The Exorcist* (1972). The first of his projects for the big screen was *The Sugarland Express,* a chase movie about a couple seeking to regain custody of their baby. Next came *Jaws,* a box-office hit that told of a series of shark attacks along the New England coast. *Jaws* earned Spielberg three Academy Awards and grossed some $100 million. He considered it to be the hardest film he had ever made, and he refused to do any of the sequels. His next endeavor was *Close Encounters of the Third Kind,* in 1977. It was one of the few films that he wrote and directed, and for his efforts he was nominated for an Oscar for Best Director.

In 1981 he joined *Star Wars* author George Lucas to make *Raiders of the Lost Ark,* with Harrison Ford as Indiana Jones. It won numerous Oscar nominations. Spielberg once again was nominated for Best Director. The following year he returned to space fantasy with *E.T.: The Extra-Terrestrial.* It was a touching story of a boy who became best friends with an adorably short and big-eyed alien. It was Spielberg's big hit and his own personal favorite.

Spielberg again teamed with Lucas to make another Indiana Jones film, entitled *Indiana Jones and the Temple of Doom.* In 1985, he made the film *The Color Purple* with Whoopi Goldberg and Oprah Winfrey, which was based upon Alice Walker's Pulitzer Prize-winning novel. It was another hit for Spielberg. The film received 11 Academy Award nominations, but Spielberg did not receive a Best Director nomination.

The prolific director turned his attention to making a "Peter Pan" film entitled *Hook.* Peter Pan was played by Robin Williams and Captain Hook by **Dustin Hoffman**. It was a financial success but failed to earn the acclaim most had expected.

In 1993 Spielberg had better success when he turned *Jurassic Park,* Michael Crichton's novel about dinosaurs propagating and roaming through a tropical island, into another popular movie. As with *E.T.* it became one of the top 10 money-producing films.

During 1993, he also produced ***Schindler's List***. It was based on the life of Oskar Schindler, a German industrialist who helped save some 1,100 people from Nazi destruction. Spielberg thought it was his most important film, even though he still considered *E.T.* his masterwork. Some observed that it was one of the most accurate and poignant portrayals of the **Holocaust**. Spielberg won his first Academy Award for Best Director, and the film also took top honors as the year's best picture.

Spielberg used the money made from that film to establish the Shoah Foundation, whose goal it is to provide an archive for the filmed testimony of as many survivors of the Holocaust as possible. Thousands of survivors gave testimony of what happened to them, but some scholars found the tapings to be poorly done. In 1999, the American Film Institute named *Schindler's List* to the ranks of the 10 greatest films ever made.

Four years later Spielberg did *Lost World* and *Amistad,* which was a story about enslaved Africans who rebelled against their captors. It was his second film about the plight of blacks in America; his first had been *The Color Purple.*

Among his other enterprises Spielberg has produced a number of successful cartoons, including *Tiny Toon Adventures, Animaniacs, Pinky and the Brain* and *Freakazoid!*

In 1998, he directed *Saving Private Ryan,* a drama about the Allied landing at Omaha Beach in Normandy, World War II. *Private Ryan* won the artist his second Academy Award for directing. Some of his other films include *Munich,* which details how Israeli intelligence agents sought revenge for the Arab terrorist killing of Israeli athletes during the Munich Olympics in 1972. Many of his films have been creative, innovative, courageous, and some, like *Schindler's List* and *E.T.,* are unforgettable. *See also* **Film**; ***Schindler's List***.

Herbert M. Druks

Further Reading: Baxter, John. *Steven Spielberg: The Unauthorized Biography.* Harper Collins, 1997. McBride, Joseph. *Steven Spielberg.* Faber and Faber, 1997.

SPITZ, MARK (1950–)

Mark Spitz is a retired swimmer, best known for winning seven gold medals at the 1972 Munich Olympic Games, an achievement surpassed only when Michael Phelps won his eighth gold medal at the 2008 Beijing Olympics in China. Spitz, born February 10, 1950, was the oldest of Lenore and Arnold Spitz's three children. When Spitz was two years old, Arnold Spitz, a steel company executive, was transferred to Honolulu, Hawaii, where young Spitz began to swim daily at Waikiki Beach. His family soon recognized his athletic ability and encouraged him to swim competitively.

The Spitz family returned to California and he began training at the Sacramento YMCA. Three years later, he trained at the Arden Hills Swim Club and by age 10 had won 17 age-group events. When Spitz faced a scheduling problem with his after-school swim workout and Hebrew school, his father intervened with the rabbi and the conflict disappeared. Eventually, the family relocated so that Spitz could train with the celebrated George Haines at the Santa Clara Swim Club.

The 1965 Maccabiah Games in Tel Aviv provided Spitz with his first international competition. The 15-year-old Spitz won four gold medals and was named outstanding athlete of the games. He returned to Israel in 1969 to compete in the Maccabiah Games, and this time he won six gold medals and again was named the competition's outstanding athlete.

A pre-dental student, Spitz accumulated swimming awards, medals, and world records in college. He won eight individual NCAA titles and the 1971 Sullivan Award as the country's top amateur athlete, and he was named World Swimmer of the Year in 1969, 1971, and 1972. After graduating from Indiana University, he prepared to compete in the Olympics.

At the 1972 Olympic Games in Munich, Germany, Mark Spitz won seven gold medals. He won the 200-meter butterfly, the 200-meter freestyle, the 100-meter butterfly, and won medals as a member of the 400-meter freestyle relay team, the 800-meter freestyle team, and the 400-meter medley relay team. The world was awed by Spitz's achievements in swimming.

World attention, however, soon turned to the horrendous terrorist situation unfolding at the games. Just hours after Spitz won his final gold medal, Palestinian terrorists broke into the athletes' compound. They killed two members of the Israeli delegation and took nine others hostage. Because he was Jewish and had earned international fame at the games, Spitz was surrounded by nervous German police, intent on ensuring his safety when he talked to the press. Spitz called the murders tragic and refused to comment further, departing for London before the closing ceremonies. Spitz was criticized for his seemingly cold reaction to the tragedy (all the hostages died during a rescue attempt).

Nevertheless, Spitz was hailed as a hero upon returning home. At age 22, he retired from competitive swimming, put aside plans for dental school, and looked over endorsement offers. Spitz was signed as a spokesperson for the Schick Company, the California Milk Advisory Board, Adidas, Speedo, and numerous other companies. The years 1973–1974 were busy for Spitz. He married Suzy (née Weiner) in 1973, who was also Jewish. The couple had two sons, Matthew (b. 1981) and Justin (b. 1991).

During that same 1973–1974 period, Spitz worked to establish a show business career. Spitz appeared on *The Tonight Show Starring Johnny Carson, The Sonny and Cher Comedy Hour,* and *Emergency!* But critics called Spitz's performances on *Bob Hope's Special* and other shows bland. Offers from Hollywood and commercial clients declined. Although Spitz continued in broadcasting for a while, within a few years his Hollywood career faded. He eventually began a successful real estate company in Beverly Hills.

In 1985, Spitz opened the Maccabiah Games, lighting a torch along with three children of the Israeli Olympians murdered at the Munich Olympics. At the age of 41 he attempted to stage a comeback for the 1992 Barcelona Olympics. Spitz failed to qualify, but his accomplishments are still memorable. In 2005, he was chosen to be the flag bearer for the United States delegation to Israel's 17th Maccabiah Games, and when Amanda Beard made her first appearance in a television commercial in 2007 with her own seven medals, the production featured a cameo appearance by another winner of seven gold medals, Mark Spitz.

Spitz, his wife, and their sons still live in Los Angeles. Spitz enjoys sailing and traveling. Having given up his real estate business, he continues to do promotional work.

See also **Sports**.

Susan M. Ortmann

Further Reading: "Bionic Man." *Sports Illustrated,* October 23, 1989, 80–82. Pogrebin, Abigail. "Mark Spitz," in *Stars of David.* Broadway Books, 2005. "Super Swimmer Mark Spitz." *People,* January 15, 1990, 86–88.

SPORTS

The Suffolk (Long Island) Y Jewish Community Center is home to the National Jewish Sports Hall of Fame and Museum. It is the largest of 18 comparable institutions situated in Jewish communities throughout the United States. Its mission is to put the lie to perhaps the most famous popular cultural reference to Jewish involvement in sports. The line comes from the 1980 movie *Airplane,* where a flight attendant's response to a passenger's request for some "light" reading while on board was: "How about this leaflet, Famous Jewish Sports Legends?" In less tolerant times, the suggestion that Jews have not participated or succeeded in great American pastimes has taken on downright anti-Semitic dimensions when, for example, supposed "cowardly" Jewish inactivity on the athletic field of honor was linked to their alleged absence from the military battle field during the Second World War—or during the national debate of a century ago over whether to restrict East European immigrants, when opponents presumed Jews to be non-athletic, weakling newcomers who could not make the necessary cultural adjustments to become true Americans. To answer the cinematic comment and to counter these cruel canards, organizations like the Suffolk Y have set out to dispel such myths and to chronicle and celebrate Jewish athletic participation. With a bow towards the cultural pluralistic values that inform our times, they aver that what they are doing for Jews—shattering stereotypes —may sensitize all people to false notions harbored about all groups.

Earlier efforts to identify Jewish champions were explicit in outright apologetics. One writer in the 1950s believed, for example, that the sight of a Jewish "fighter wearing a Jewish star" was proof enough of that group's "admirable war record." Several years later, a massive *Encyclopedia of Jews in Sports* appeared. So anxious were its editors to produce a large tome that they occasionally presumed Gentiles with Jewish-sounding names were Jewish and blithely added these stars. The contemporary effort to recount Jewish participation in sports includes an American Jewish Historical Society, supported online archives, several other "Jews in sports" web sites, a collection of Jewish baseball cards (which offers its thousands of fans background and statistics on the more than 150 Jewish players who made it to the Major Leagues from 1870 to the present), not to mention a bi-monthly *Jewish Sports Review* which digs up the names of Jewish young men and women who play professional, scholastic, and collegiate sports.

There is a full pantheon of American Jewish sports achievers, some of whom have been instrumental in the development of their respective sports in this country. For example, basketball was once considered a "Jewish game" by virtue of the exploits of men such as Barney Sedrin and Nat Holman. Sons of immigrants, both grew up on New York's Lower East Side and were stars in the early amateur and professional leagues that grew up in the early twentieth century. Holman coached at CCNY and produced some eight Jewish All-Americans. Sedrin and Holman helped "roundball" emerge from its Springfield YMCA roots as a mid-winter programming substitute into a game that is popular in this country and, when it comes to fan enthusiasm, is second only to soccer around the world. In the 1930s, an acerbic New York sports writer named Paul Galico actually alleged that Jews had a natural affinity for basketball based on their supposed deceptiveness and "smart aleckness."

Three great Jewish "Reds" raised American and Jewish consciousness about basketball. Arnold "Red" Auerbach coached his Boston Celtics to professional basketball supremacy in the 1950s–1960s. William "Red" Holzman who played for Holman at CCNY brought that city-style of game to the New York Knicks in the late 1960s to early 1970s. Winning their two league championships, that team captured the imagination of New Yorkers at "America's greatest arena," Madison Square Garden. In tribute to Holzman's achievement, the Garden hung a banner carrying his name and the number 613 from its rafters. For observant Jews who might attend Garden games, that popular icon has additional significance. That number signifying the total of games Red Holzman won as a coach also corresponds to the number of commandments in the Torah. Meanwhile, operating in a more modest setting, Holzman's earliest athletic mentor at the Jewish Workmen's Circle, Bernard "Red" Sarachek, coached Yeshiva University and was renowned as a "coaches' coach" who developed creative plays and patterns that other coaches studied and implemented.

One of the Reds' contemporaries, Oscar "Ozzie" Schechtman, was credited in 1946 with scoring the first basket in the history of the Basketball Association of America, a forerunner of the contemporary National Basketball Association. In 2007, Schechtman became the eponym of a documentary film appropriately called *The First Basket,* which chronicled Jews involvement with that sport. In the 1950s, Dolph Schayes was the league's all-time leading scorer. Danny Schayes, Dolph's son, was the last Jew to play major league basketball in this country, concluding his 18-year career in 1999–2000. In 1996, the Women's National Basketball Association was founded, and Nancy Lieberman was one of its earliest stars. Today, she often appears as an announcer on that league's telecasts and continues to promote the distaff version of that game.

Generations ago, immigrant Jews aspired to be the "Pride of the Ghetto" as prize fighting was, in fact, a tough but rewarding economic way out of the downtown's regions. In the 1920s, some 17 Jews held world championship belts in different weight classifications. Among the best known pugilists were Abe Attell, **Benny Leonard**, and **Barney Ross**. Out of the ring, Attell, in particular, suffered some acute notoriety for his involvement in 1919 that led to the fixing of that year's World Series, the so-called Black Sox scandal. In the 1930s, heavyweight champion Max Baer, a Christian, became what has been characterized as a "situational Jew." He wore a Jewish star on his trunks to attract Jewish fight fans to his corner. Jews were then recognized among the most devoted followers of the "sweet science"; they were especially ready to plunk down their money when the man in the ring ostensibly carried with him the honor of his people. Today, in 2007, Ukrainian Jewish welterweight Dimitryi Salita has attracted a loyal Jewish following for his fighting skills and his advocacy of Orthodox religious practice, through his involvement with the Lubavitch Hasidic movement.

Legendary baseball manager John McGraw of the New York Giants was well aware that Jewish fans bought tickets to cheer on stars from their religious group. That box-office consideration contributed to promoting second baseman Andy Cohen to the "Big Show" in the late 1920s. His saga inspired the parody poem "Cohen at the Bat," a take-off on the celebrated "Casey at the Bat." Cohen was only one of some 150 Jews to play major league baseball. In the 1930s–1940s, slugger **Hank Greenberg** was the most prominent Jewish player of his time. He is remembered in American Jewish history for the anti-Semitism that he faced when he challenged Babe Ruth's one-season home run record and for the pressure that he was subjected to when, in 1934, the end of the baseball season coincided with the Jewish High Holidays and his Detroit Tigers were in contention for the pennant. Greenberg decided to play on Rosh Hashanah but absented himself on Yom Kippur (by then the American League race was basically decided and he was free to stand down). His absence on this Jewish holiday garnered him much respect in synagogues in the Motor City and throughout the United States. His life as an American Jew was the subject of a 1998 prize-winning documentary, *The Life and Times of Hank Greenberg*.

Los Angeles Dodgers pitcher **Sandy Koufax** filled the roles of greatest Jewish baseball player and religious standard bearer in the 1960s. Selected by *Sports Illustrated* as its favorite athlete of the twentieth century, this man, who hurled four no-hitters, is best remembered for his own refusal in 1965 to pitch in the World Series on Yom Kippur and for the positive response his prideful stand evoked throughout a more culturally-pluralistic United States.

Jews have produced relatively few gridiron stars as demographics played a significant role in limiting their participation. In many of the areas where football is king, like Western Pennsylvania, Texas, and the rural South, Jews did not settle in large numbers. And while big-city Jewish boys may have played "Association," a street-game version of football, they generally did not acquire the formalized training necessary to succeed in that regimented sport. Still, a good half-dozen Jews, including quarterbacks Benny Friedman and Sid Luckman, running-back Marshall Goldman, and legendary coaches Sid Gilman and Marv Levy earned recognition in the college and professional football halls of fame.

For more than a century, ever since Sam Berger struck gold in St. Louis as a boxer and Daniel Frank earned a silver medal in the long-jump, American Jewish men and women have been winners in the Olympic Games. Charlotte Epstein captained the first American women's swim team in the 1920 Antwerp Olympiad, and 12 years later Lillian Copeland broke world and Olympic records at the Los Angeles games as she captured gold in the discus. These women are among the featured athletes in the 2005 documentary film *Jewish Women in Sports: Settlement House to the Olympics*. Perhaps, the two most important American Jewish Olympians were two runners who never received a chance to participate in the 1936 Games. U.S. Olympic officials and coaches dropped Marty Glickman and Sam Stoller from the 4-man by 100-meter relay squad so as not to embarrass the Nazis with the possibility of triumphant Jews standing on the Berlin Stadium victory stand. This politicization of the games constitutes an ugly preamble to the world's disinterest in the fate of the Jews during the Holocaust. Similarly, Palestinian terrorists' murdering of 11 Israeli athletes at the 1972 Munich Olympics overshadows historically the achievement of **Mark Spitz** in garnering 7 swimming gold medals in the Munich pool.

When "on their game," the more sophisticated Jewish sports halls of fame have taken note of Jewish involvement in every aspect of sports, which has become an American popular cultural phenomenon. American Jewish entrepreneurial history intersects with this country's sports saga when, for example, the business activities of Pittsburgh Pirates owner Barney Dreyfuss (1902–1932) are counted in. During this same time period, Jewish fighters made their way economically out of the ghetto through the prize ring, and their owners and managers demonstrated profound economic acumen as they promoted their manly art successfully. In an ironic twist of fates and political cultures, Joe Jacobs, aka "Yussel the Muscle," the most famous Jewish manager of his time, was in Max Schmeling's corner for the German's renowned battle in 1938 against Joe Louis—a fight with international significance and repercussions. Concomitantly, long-time owner of the Harlem Globetrotters, Abe Saperstein, beginning in 1926 integrated the athletic and entertainment values of sports. In more recent times, the dedicated and altruistic Fred Lebow, a devotee of the 1970s running boom, turned the New York City Marathon into a major sporting attraction and an annual moment in time where that city's multiple and disparate ethnic and racial groups all turn out to cheer on tens of thousands of runners who traverse the metropolis's streets and before an international television audience.

Jewish involvement in American labor history has been played out in the sports venue as Jewish union organizers and agents have massively protected and enhanced the rights and salaries of competitors. As a result of their victories for their clients, they have transformed the economics of these popular attractions, starting with their impact on the rising cost of tickets. Consumers have largely borne the high costs of what present-day athletes earn. In this realm, Marvin Miller, former executive director of the major leagues baseball players union (1966–1982) stands out. In 2000, *The Sporting News* rated him 5th among the 100 most powerful people in twentieth-century sports. A similar encomium was tendered to him in 1994 when *Sports Illustrated* designated him as the seventh most influential personality in sports.

Sitting on the other side of the negotiating table are the three Jewish commissioners of major American sports. David Stern is head of the National Basketball Association. Gary Betteman leads the National Hockey League, and Bud Selig is the chief executive officer of Major League Baseball. Among Selig's own clients is Fred Wilpon, owner of the New York Mets and high school teammate of Sandy Koufax.

As members of the media, Jews have played a major role in the promotion of public interest in sports. Well-known sports scribes included, in prior generations, Shirley Povich, Milton Gross, and Roger Kahn. In contemporary times, Jerry Izenberg, Gerald Ezkenazi, Maury Allen, Murray Chass, Ira Berkow, George and Peter Vecsey, John Feinstein, L. John Wertheim, and the recently-deceased David Halberstam have been the most outstanding Jewish newspaper and magazine writers. Absent an unofficial czar for the under-regulated sport of boxing, editor Nat Fleisher, from his founding of *Ring Magazine* in 1922 and for close to half a century thereafter, often served as the voice and conscience of American pugilism. On May 25, 1965, he actually determined a famous fight that was still in progress. At a bizarre scene in Lewiston, Maine, with former champion Sonny Liston prone on the canvas and the histrionic Muhammad Ali dancing around the ring, Fleisher authoritatively, notwithstanding his undesignated role, counted Liston out. Fleisher's call stood.

In the years that followed, radio and television commentator Howard Cosell played a far more decisive role in Ali's career. Respected and reviled for his "tell it like it is" persona, Cosell departed from the boosterism that often characterized "home-team" sports writing, adding a controversial new dimension to sports journalism. Drawing upon his training as an attorney, Cosell often prosecuted unpopular causes. None was as controversial as his advocacy of Ali's claim for designation as a "conscientious objector," absolving him from service in the U.S. Army during the Vietnam War. The fighter demanded exemption as a Black Muslim minister. His refusal to accept induction led to his being stripped of his heavyweight title and to three and half years of enforced idleness while appeal of his legal offense dragged on. Through it all, Cosell stood by the erstwhile champion as together they came to be viewed as one of the symbols of both African American and Jewish youth opposition to this unpopular war. Cosell, a noteworthy Jew, evidenced through his stance that sports were intrinsically intertwined with the most significant contemporary issues of the day. During Munich, 1972, Cosell had his own consciousness raised when as a result of seeing fellow Jews (Israelis) slaughtered, he started to exhibit a stronger sense of ethnic identity.

While Cosell was renowned and ridiculed both for his points of view and his idiosyncratic commentator's voice, he was once lampooned on the *Odd Couple,* a popular 1960s–1970s television series, as possessed of "an inane nasal drone"; other more stentorian Jewish voices have long been associated with the broadcasting of American sports. Bill Stern, the same Marty Glickman of 1936 Olympic fame, Mel Allen, and Bill Mazer, among others, earned their stripes first in radio booths, before adding television to their résumés. The Albert family, Marv and his brothers, Steve and Al, and his son, Kenny, have become a broadcast dynasty. But it remained for Al Michaels to provide the most memorable American sports sound bite of the late twentieth century. As telecaster of the improbable United States hockey team triumph over the Soviet Union in the 1980 Lake Placid Winter Olympics, Michaels gave triumphant voice to an entire nation's exaltation when he shouted as time expired on the Russians: "Do you believe in miracles? Yes!" At that moment, Michaels helped lift the spirits of his countrymen, who, it has been said, were suffering from a spiritual malaise during the period of the Iranian hostage crisis.

In the final decades of the twentieth century, viewers and listeners have become increasingly attuned to female Jewish voices on the air. The aforementioned Nancy Lieberman has done "color commentary" on her favorite sport. Linda Cohn has the anchor's chair on ESPN's national *Sports Center*. Suzyn Waldman has been both a beat reporter and analyst describing the activities and games of the New York Yankees. Her trained voice—she once considered the cantorate as a career—can also be heard occasionally belting out the national anthem at major league ball games.

The Jewish high profile in off-the-field activities—as managers, owners, agents, reporters, and chroniclers of the games Americans play—has provided occasional grist for anti-Semites, who chafed at alleged Jewish control of the country's sports culture. Canards range from the old stand-by assertions that Jews do not play sports, rather they own them, to even more invidious characterizations of Jews as corruptors of national pastimes. Henry Ford articulated the most outrageous group censure when he identified a Jewish conspiracy behind the aforementioned infamous 1919 "Black Sox" scandal. Drawing upon his belief in the message of the arch-forgery of the twentieth century, *The Protocols of the Elders of Zion,* which he published in 1921 in his *Dearborn* (Michigan)*Independent*—with his own contemporary updates—Ford argued Jews corrupted the sport most dear to Americans and alleged this was part of the Jews' well-thought-out agenda to break the American spirit and takeover the United States. Factually, though Abe Attell and gambler Arnold Rothstein were deeply involved in the Sox scandal, so were Gentile coconspirators. And although the American Jewish community did not strongly dissociate itself from Rothstein's actions, there was no group plan to do violence to America.

In recent times, unfocused anger has often been directed at Jewish sports agents who, again, do not play the game but seemingly control athletic labor unrest. Emulating Ford's view of the world, contemporary anti-Semitic bloggers point out the number of Jews in sports management and control positions, from New England Patriots owner Robert Kraft to Atlanta Braves, Thrashers, and Hawks president Stan Kasten to Randy Levine of the New York Yankees, as proof that Jews are in possession of national games and sports.

In a tolerant twenty-first-century America, most sports fans are oblivious to the religious backgrounds of athletic corporate types, even of those like Robert Kraft, who frequently and pridefully acknowledge their Jewish heritage. On occasion, the public has been fascinated with the decisions high-profile Jewish athletes have made when balancing sports with residual Judaic values. In 2004, Los Angeles Dodgers fans watched a replay of the Greenberg-Koufax-High Holiday saga when the team's outfielder, **Shawn David Green** dealt openly with his personal conflict over suiting up for a pennant-race game on the holiest day in the Jewish calendar. With supporters—both within and without the team's clubhouse—leaving the choice up to him, Green dealt with the pressure. He decided to play Kol Nidre night and absent himself the day of Yom Kippur. For the record, no divine punishment was visited on the slugger who hit out a game-winning home run on the evening of his transgression.

Two years earlier, in August 2002, a 12-year-old Jewish athlete was accorded a few days of international renown when he decided not to play on the Jewish Sabbath. Micah Golshirazian was then a member of the Worcester, Massachusetts squad competing in the Little League World Series in Williamsport, Pennsylvania. With the crucial semi-finals scheduled for late Saturday afternoon, and committed to being part of a national championship-caliber team without violating Sabbath strictures, Golshirazian and his family stayed at a hotel close to the field. He walked to the field and waited patiently in the dugout until the holy day ended. ESPN was duly fascinated with this unusual act of faith. The cable network counted down until 8:43 P.M. with a clock in the corner of the screen. Usually, such television timing is reserved for the moments before presidential campaign debates. Extending the electoral-media analogy, for that moment, the young man became a "**Joseph Lieberman** in a baseball uniform," a high-profile Jew who garnered public attention and approbation in a tolerant and accepting contemporary environment.

Golshirazian's Sabbath of celebrity, his brief shining moment, was essentially a one-shot deal. The four-year saga of Tamir Goodman (1999–2003) remains the most publicized contemporary example of the American media's continuing fascination with Jewish athletes. The talented ones are still projected as exceptions, and in this case an additional feature was in play. The young man was deeply committed to his Orthodox faith. Dubbed uncritically as the "Jewish Jordan," the "Lubavitch Laker," or the "Chassidic Celtic," Goodman burst onto the national sports scene when as a high school junior at the Baltimore Talmudic Academy, serious discussions were held with the University of Maryland about granting him an athletic scholarship to play basketball for their Terrapins with the understanding that he would not have to compete on the Sabbath. Over 1,500 web sites and countless newspapers, magazines, and radio and television programs reported on the twists and turns in this story which included talk that the Atlantic Coast Conference, where Maryland is a member, might adjust the game times of its multimillion-dollar postseason tournament to enable Goodman to remain true to his observant religious values. These outlets also followed his peregrinations from his yeshiva to a Seventh-Day Adventist high school for his senior year, where he sought to hone his skills further while not violating the Sabbath. This idiosyncratic Christian school does not schedule games on Saturday. At one point he was even the subject of a Jewish rap song, "The Kid with the Lid," that made much of his wearing a yarmulke when he played. The cameras and writers followed him through his problematic denouements with the Terrapins. His scholarship never came to fruition. The Maryland coaching staff ultimately judged his talents unsuitable for their Division I squad.

And the media was there to report on the major accommodations that a smaller-time program, Towson State University in Maryland, was willing to make to allow Goodman to compete at their level. Towson, and its Colonial Athletic Conference, in fact, revised its basketball calendar to allow him to balance, on a weekly basis, his sports and Jewish identities. Goodman left Towson in his second year of competition because of nasty disagreements with his coach. The conflicts had nothing to do with his Jewish values and everything to do with his on-court performances. Some of the same sports experts who had unconditionally lauded his talents backed off, red-faced, and declared as *Sports Illustrated* did that "in retrospect, maybe we went a little too far with the whole 'Jewish Jordan' thing" ("Terps," 1999). Goodman eventually migrated to Israel where for a few years he played minor league professional basketball, while remaining true to his religious beliefs and assisting the Lubavitch movement in promoting Jewish practice among his people.

When American Jewish sports history moves beyond apologetics and the chronicling and crowning of champions, that group's and faith's encounter with a basic aspect of contemporary popular culture serves as an uncommonly useful lens through which Jewish acceptance, adjustment, and accommodation in this country may be related and evaluated.

Jeffrey S. Gurock

Further Reading: Gurock, Jeffrey S. *Judaism's Encounter with American Sports*. Bloomington, IN: Indiana University Press, 2005. Levine, Peter. *Ellis Island to Ebbets Field: Sport and the American Jewish Experience*. New York: Oxford University Press, 1992. Riess, Steven A., ed. *Sports and the American Jew*. Syracuse, NY: Syracuse University Press, 1998.

STEINEM, GLORIA (1934–)

A writer, editor, and political activist, Steinem is a founder of both *Ms.,* the first national woman's magazine run by a woman, and the National Women's Political Caucus, an organization to motivate women to run for political office. She became deeply involved in the Women's Liberation Movement of the 1960s and remains one of the strongest feminist voices today.

Born Gloria Marie in Toledo, Ohio on March 25, Steinem is the daughter of Leo, a Jewish American antique salesman, and Ruth Nuneviller, a newspaper reporter. Steinem's paternal grandmother, Pauline Steinem, was a suffragist and the first woman to serve on a school board in Ohio.

Steinem's family was dysfunctional, her childhood difficult. The Steinems spent summers in Clark Lake, Michigan, trying to develop a resort Leo had purchased with the intent of turning it into a venue for big bands. The rest of the year the family traveled in a trailer, collecting antiques for Leo to sell. They were never in one place long enough for Steinem to enroll in school, so her mother tutored her. When Steinem was 11, her parents divorced and her father moved to California. By that time Steinem's mother had suffered a nervous breakdown and was severely disabled by depression and anxiety. For the next four years, Steinem lived in poverty, caring for a totally debilitated mother as best she could. She analyzes this period of life in a memoir, *Ruth's Song (Because She Could Not Sing It)*. Steinem's father agreed to care for Ruth in California for one year in order to allow Steinem to spend her senior year in high school living with her 10-year-older sister. When Steinem gained admission and some financial aid to Smith College, her sister arranged for their mother to be hospitalized at a mental institution outside Baltimore.

Steinem graduated magna cum laude and as a member of Phi Beta Kappa in 1956. She won a fellowship to study at the Universities of Delhi and Calcutta, and her exposure to life in India made her aware of suffering in the human condition. She became committed to social justice and determined to become a journalist.

In 1960 Steinem moved to Manhattan to begin her freelance career. She became assistant editor of *Help!* magazine and wrote occasional scripts for the television show *That Was the Week That Was.* Her breakthrough article, an assignment for *Show Magazine,* was the exposé "I Was a Playboy Bunny." To prepare for the article, Steinem was hired and worked as a "bunny" for about three weeks. She exposed the low pay, poor working conditions, and demeaning values of Hugh Hefner's *Playboy* philosophy. Still it was difficult for Steinem to get jobs on serious topics, because magazine editors preferred men reporters. Finally, in 1968, she became a contributing editor for *New York Magazine* and did regular political analysis in her column, "The City Politic." At about that time she began working for Democratic political causes and candidates including the United Farm Workers, **Norman Mailer**, Eugene McCarthy, and Robert Kennedy.

Steinem's involvement with the antiwar and civil rights movements during the 1960s probably led to her feminist career. She credits her initial involvement with the movement to her attendance, as a reporter, to a meeting of the Redstockings, a women's liberation group, on the dangers of illegal abortion. She became deeply committed to women's rights to control their own bodies and embarked on an intense, nationwide speaking tour. Concerned that the movement might be construed as a white, middle-class cause, she made certain she was always accompanied by Dorothy Hughes Pittman, Florynce Rae Kennedy, or Margaret Sloan, all accomplished black feminist speakers.

In 1971 Steinem, **Bella Abzug**, Shirley Chisholm, and **Betty Friedan** formed the National Women's Political Caucus. In 1972 Steinem became one of six founding editors of *Ms.*, the first national feminist magazine; the title changed the way American women were addressed. She wrote articles for *Ms.* until it was sold in 1987. The magazine enhanced her popularity, and she spent the next 20 years speaking on feminist causes, including the sex caste system, reproductive freedom, abortion rights, rape, equal opportunity, gender roles, child abuse, violence, and the extension of the date for ratification of the Equal Rights Amendment.

Her books include *Outrageous Acts and Everyday Rebellions* (1983), *Marilyn* (1986), *Revolution from Within* (1992), and *Moving Beyond Words* (1994).

In 2000, when she was 66, Steinem married David Bale; he died of lymphoma of the brain only 3 years later.

Steinem has said that the values of Judaism greatly influenced her life. She gave her name in support of the New Israel Fund and the Jewish Alliance for Justice and Peace. She was among the group of feminists who held the first women's Seder and has participated in it for more than 30 years. *See also* **Friedan, Betty**.

Marion Schotz

Further Reading: Daffron, Carolyn. *Gloria Steinem*. New York : Chelsea House Publishers, 1988. Heilbrun, Carolyn G. *The Education of a Woman: The Life of Gloria Steinem*. New York: Dial, 1995.

STERN, HOWARD (1954–)

Radio's most famous "Shock Jock," was born in Roosevelt, Long Island to Ben and Ray Stern. Howard Stern's father owned a record studio and encouraged his son's interest in radio. His mother was a homemaker, and the self-proclaimed "King of All Media" had one sister, Ellen. Stern was an excellent student at Boston University, where he received a BA in communications in 1976. In 1978, he married Alison Berns, his college girlfriend at Temple Ohabei Shalom in Brookline, Massachusetts and subsequently had three children—Emily Beth (b. 1983), Deborah Jennifer (b. 1986), and Ashley Jade (b. 1993). In 2001, the couple divorced.

Stern received his first radio program at Boston University in 1973, but after the first "King Schmaltz Bagel Hour" he was fired on air. He subsequently turned down an offer to work at Westchester, New York's WRNW, but Alison convinced him to call back, and the station hired him as a disc jockey and program director. He moved on to Hartford, Connecticut's radio station WCCC, where he organized a "cadaverathon" for the local university. At Detroit's W-4, he assembled the Wack Pack and won the Billboard Award. In 1981, while working at radio station DC 101 in the nation's capital, Stern met and began his long professional relationship with Robin Quivers. Stern liked her consumer reports and, specifically, enjoyed her nonjudgmental interview with a prostitute on Washington's DC 101.

Quivers and Stern formed a team that improvised and sought to catch their guest with their "pants down," so to surprise and expose them. In his autobiography *Private Parts* (1993), Stern describes his role as an interviewer: "What we try to do with humor is show the absurdity of the differences between people, as **Lenny Bruce** did when he used words like nigger and kike and wop in an attempt to demystify them and rob them of any power they may have. Underneath all the differences, we're all in this together." Hired at WNBC in 1982, he shared the air waves with Don Imus. Fired in 1985, Stern signed with K-Rock and topped Imus in the ratings with his morning show. On the show, Stern introduced the character of "Fartman," the "hero" Stern impersonates, who took on diplomats, politicians, and celebrities, and when his questions went unanswered, his guests were met with the loosening of a sphincter.

Stern's shtick is sometimes serious, such as his denunciation of the "fatwa" placed by Iran's mullahs on Salman Rushdie and his condemnation of China over the massacre at Tiananmen Square. One of his finer on-air moments was his handling of September 11, giving an extensive and grave account of the terrorist attack. Most of the time, he is simply outrageous. He used his "Fartman" character to steal the show at the 1991 MTV awards. On one of his shows, Stern recruited a stutterer to ask Gennifer Flowers if Bill Clinton used a condom.

Stern and his entourage have feuded with many media personalities. His fans have been known to disrupt live shows. Showbiz friends and enemies interviewed are frequently embarrassed with revelations of sexual inhibitions or urged to engage in erotic exhibitions. Stern, nevertheless, manages to debunk hypocrisies regarding attitudes toward sex, racism, and freedom of speech. One of Stern's segments involved a televised game, "Guess Who's the Jew?" where he has an official KKK member rating his hatred on a billboard held by a "Hassidic Shaft Stern."

Not everyone enjoys Stern's antics. The FCC investigated Stern's show when a Mississippi minister organized a national campaign against him in 1988 because a caller complained about Stern's on-air satire of a Christmas party. Eventually, Stern was found guilty of "indecent" broadcasting. This drove him to become more political. For example, in 2004, he "campaigned" for the presidency against President Bush. Embroiled in legal battles, heavy censorship, and excessive editing by management, Stern left his radio and television programs for Sirius satellite radio in 2006. *See also* **Radio**.

Steve Krief

Further Reading: Stern, Howard. *Miss America.* Regan Books, 1996. ———. *Private Parts.* Simon and Schuster, 1993.

STEWART, JON (1962–)

Jon Stewart, host of *The Daily Show,* Comedy Central's popular faux news program, was born Jonathan Stuart Leibowitz on November 28, 1962 to Donald, a physicist, and Marian, an educational consultant; he has one brother, Larry Leibowitz. His parents divorced in 1971. Growing up in Lawrenceville, New Jersey, Stewart played trumpet in a kids' swing combo called the Lawrence Stage Band, which once appeared on *The Captain Noah Children's Hour,* a children's television show produced in Philadelphia. As the only Jewish student in Lawrence High School, Stewart has said he was subjected to considerable harassment from some of his classmates. His first comedy "award" came when he was voted Best Sense of Humor in his high school yearbook. Stewart attended the College of William and Mary in Virginia, where he majored in psychology and played on the soccer team, which ultimately led to hernia and knee surgery due to injuries sustained on the field. The "Leibo Award" is now given annually in his honor to the member of the team who experiences the most personal growth and provides the most laughs for his teammates. Stewart spoke at the commencement ceremonies at his alma mater in 2004 and was presented with an honorary doctor of arts degree. Among the list of jobs he had before he got his big break were "puppet master" in southern New Jersey grade schools to sensitize children to people with disabilities, and "live mosquito sorter" for the New Jersey Department of Health. Stewart's first appearance on the stand-up circuit took place in 1986 at The Bitter End. His first joke: What do they call lunch hour in the diamond district when all the Hasidim are causing a traffic jam in the streets? Yidlock.

In addition to his career as a stand-up comedian, Stewart has appeared in movies and on several television programs and is the author of *Naked Pictures of Famous People,* a collection of "what-if" essays, as well as the bestselling *America (The Book): A Citizen's Guide to Democracy Inaction.* Stewart married Tracey Lynn McShane, a veterinary technician, in 2000. The couple has two children, Nathan Thomas (named after Stewart's grandfather) born in 2004, and Maggie Rose, born in 2006. Stewart hosted his own show (*The Jon Stewart Show*) on MTV from 1993–1995; *The Daily Show* premiered in 1999. He received the Peabody Award for excellence in radio and television broadcasting in 2000 and 2004 for coverage of the presidential elections on *The Daily Show*. He has also received several Emmy Awards and was nominated for others.

Stewart is a frequent guest of talk shows, both those in favor of the faux-news style and those who oppose the concept as "too confusing." In an appearance on *Crossfire* he engaged in a notable on-air confrontation with host Tucker Carlson on the responsibility of the news media. *See also* **Television**.

Ron Kaplan

Further Reading: Stewart, Jon. *America (The Book): A Citizen's Guide to Democracy Inaction.* Grand Central Publishing, 2004. ———. *Naked Pictures of Famous People.* Harper Paperbacks, 1999.

STILLER, BEN (1965–)

The hit film *Meet the Fockers* (2004) united an impressive cast around Ben Stiller, which included Robert De Niro, **Dustin Hoffman**, and **Barbra Streisand**. The film also included Jewish comedian Shelley Berman, who in his early years was part of a improvisational Chicago-based troupe known as the Compass Players. Included in the troupe were comedy team Jerry Stiller and Anne Meara, who met at the Compass Players and later married. Ben Stiller was born to Jerry Stiller and Anne Meara in 1965. While playing in the revival of John Guare's off-Broadway comedy hit *The House of Blue Leaves* (1986) with John Mahoney, Stiller started to create "mockumentaries." Mahoney and Stiller produced a 10-minute short, *The Hustler of Money,* which spoofed Martin Scorsese's *The Color of Money,* where both actors reenact billiard sharks **Paul Newman** and Tom Cruise as bowling hustlers. *Saturday Night Live* (*SNL*) aired it in 1987, the same year Stiller starred in **Steven Spielberg**'s *Empire of the Sun*. After a short stint for *SNL,* in 1989, Stiller wrote, directed, and acted in *Elvis Stories,* a 30-minute spoof of a fictitious tabloid interviewing people who claimed to have had an Elvis sighting. After directing *Going Back to Brooklyn,* where Jerry Stiller plays Danny Aiello's character in a *Do the Right Thing* spoof, MTV aired *The Ben Stiller Show* (1990). The show failed in the ratings but was picked up by the Fox network, where it ran for 12 episodes, and Stiller won an Emmy for comedy writing after the show was cancelled.

A 19-year-old freshman at the University of Southern California, Helen Childress, wrote the screenplay for *Reality Bites* (1994). Stiller acted in and directed the movie, which starred Winona Ryder. In 1996, Stiller fulfilled the two jobs again in *The Cable Guy,* featuring Jim Carrey and **Jack Black**. He also played a nurse terrorizing Adam Sandler's grandmother in *Happy Gilmore* (1996). After appearances on *Friends* and in his short *Derek Zoolander,* made for the 1997 VH-1 Fashion Awards, Stiller gained worldwide fame starring in *There's Something About Mary* (1998), a comedy about abortive love, a subject studied a little differently in *Your Friends and Neighbors* (1998). That same year, he played a dramatic role as a multiple addict in *Permanent Midnight*. A few roles later, he was Anne Bancroft's son Jake Schram in *Keeping the Faith* (2000), a film about a rabbi (Stiller) and a priest, played by Edward Norton, two childhood friends who share a crush on Jenna Elfman.

The beginning of the twenty-first century witnessed Stiller as one of the top names in comedy with such films as *Meet the Parents* (2000), *Orange County* (2002), *Starsky & Hutch* (2004), *Envy* (2004), *Anchorman: The Legend of Ron Burgundy* (2003), *Meet the Fockers* (2004), *Night at the Museum* (2006), and *Night at the Museum 2* (2007). In 2007, Jerry and Ben Stiller played father and son in the *Heartbreak Kid,* a remake of Elaine May's 1972 comedy, but minus the satiric element which depicted Jewish men and their lust for blonde, blue-eyed Gentile females. *See also* **Film**.

Steve Krief

Further Reading: Bankston, John. *Ben Stiller (Real-Life Reader Biography).* Hockessin, DE: Mitchell Lane

Publishers, 2002. Dougherty, Terri. *Ben Stiller (People in the News).* San Diego, CA: Lucent Books, 2006.

STONE, IRVING (1903–1989)

Born Irving Tannenbaum in San Francisco (1903), Stone, who took his family name from him mother's second husband, was the son of Charles and Pauline Rosenberg Tannenbaum. As a child, the bookish Stone decided he wanted to write after poring through novels by Jack London, George Norris, and Sherwood Anderson. Stone worked his way through the University of California–Berkeley, where he majored in political science and graduated with honors in 1923. The following year he received a MA in economics from the University of Southern California. Following brief stints as an economics lecturer at USC and a none-too-successful playwright in New York, he went to Europe, where he chanced upon an exhibit of works by painter Vincent van Gogh. This event changed his life.

Mesmerized by van Gogh's art and life story, Stone decided to write a biographical novel about the artist. Stone supported himself by penning pulp mysteries for magazines and directing plays while conducting extensive research on the life of nineteenth-century Impressionist. Rejected by nearly a dozen publishers, Stone's work *Lust For Life* was finally published in 1934 and became a bestseller. From then on, Stone wrote almost nothing but biographical novels, aided by his wife and editor, and occasional coauthor, Jean Factor, whom he had met while directing a play.

Over the next half-century, Stone wrote best-selling biographic novels on, among others, **Sigmund Freud** (*Passions of the Mind*), Charles Darwin (*The Origin*), Michelangelo (*The Agony and the Ecstasy*), Eugene Debs (*Adversary in the House*), John and Abigail Adams (*For Those Who Love*), and Mary Todd Lincoln (*Love Is Eternal*). Four of his novels were turned into successful motion pictures, with two, *Lust for Life* (1956) and *The Agony and the Ecstasy* (1965) becoming major successes.

Known as much for his intense research as for the quality of his writing, Stone's books sold more than 30 million copies worldwide and were translated into more than 60 languages and dialects.

Stone died in Los Angeles in on August 26, 1989. He was 86 years old.

Kurt F. Stone

Further Reading: Brandt, Randal. "Irving Stone's Lust for Life." *Bancroftiana, Newsletter of the Friends of the Bancroft Library,* no. 123, Fall 2003, bancroft.berkeley.edu/events/bancroftiana/123/stone.html. "Irving Stone, Bestselling Author, Dies." *Washington Post,* August 28, 1989.

STREISAND, BARBRA (1942–)

Barbra Streisand, one of the most accomplished and popular woman singers of the twentieth century, was born in Brooklyn on April 24, 1942. Streisand's father, Emmanuel Streisand, died of a cerebral hemorrhage less than a year and a half after she was born. Diana (Rosen) Streisand and her children, Barbra Joan and Sheldon, found themselves in most difficult economic circumstances. In order to support her family Streisand's mother found a job as a bookkeeper; in 1949, she married Louis Kind, who was anything but kind to Streisand and her brother. They had a daughter they named Rosalin and then divorced. Despite these difficult times Streisand graduated from Erasmus High School in 1959 with an A average and a love for the theater.

After graduation, Streisand left home to pursue a career in show business. While she studied acting and voice, she performed at the Lion Club in New York. Her style and her beautiful voice made her a hit at the cabaret. Eventually, she began performing outside New York, and wherever she sang people became avid fans. She made her television debut in 1961 on *The Jack Paar Show* and appeared on many other popular talk and revue shows such as *The Joe Franklin Show.*

At the age of 19 Streisand appeared as Miss Marmelstein in the Broadway play *I Can Get It for You Wholesale.* Once again she was a success.

In 1963, she met and married Elliot Gould. They had a son and named him Jason Emmanuel, but the couple divorced by 1971.

Columbia Records signed Streisand to a contract, and her first major album came out in 1964. It was a terrific hit and remained at the top of the charts for some 18 months. This helped establish Miss Streisand as one of America's most popular singers. In 1968, she had great success playing **Fanny Brice** in *Funny Girl,* and from there she was cast as Dolly Levy in *Hello Dolly!* Her next role was *On a Clear Day You Can See Forever.* In 1970, her film *The Owl and the Pussycat* was followed by the comedy *What's Up Doc?* The 1973 romantic drama *The Way We Were* was another great success, and it brought her more fans and more money. Towards the end of 1976 she starred in *A Star Is Born.*

In 1981, she recorded the album *Memories,* which was one of her greatest successes. Streisand decided to take up another challenge by directing and playing the lead role in the film version of *Yentl,* **Isaac Bashevis Singer**'s Hasidic story by the same name. The play was based upon a Sholem Aleichem story about a young woman who wants to devote her life to rabbinical studies and falls in love with a rabbinical student. To play this role well she took lessons in the Jewish faith and tradition. She may not have won an Oscar for that role, but it was one of the most meaningful roles she had ever played.

Her movie roles and recordings have earned her success, fame, and wealth. She is devoted to various charitable causes in America and Israel. Often she has given handsomely to these charities to honor her mother and father. She is actively involved with various environmental causes, gay rights, and the Democratic Party. She has publicly lent her support to Democratic candidates such as George McGovern and Bill Clinton. When President Clinton was accused of obstructing justice and was about to be removed from office, Streisand remained one of his most loyal supporters.

Streisand has made a name for herself as a popular singer and a movie star. Of the 50 albums that she recorded, some 30 went gold, and some have even gone platinum. She is one of the most popular singers in America. While she chooses to remain a very private person, she did star in over 15 very successful films. Streisand is one of a small group who has won an Emmy, a Grammy, an Oscar, and a Tony award. Her second and current husband is actor James Brolin, whom she married on July 1, 1998. They have no children together, but Brolin has three children from earlier marriages. *See also* **Film**; **Popular Music**.

Herbert M. Druks

Further Reading: Anderson, Christopher. *Barbra: The Way She Is.* Harper Collins, 2006. Spada, James. *Streisand: Her Life.* Crown Publishers, 1995.

SUSANN, JACQUELINE (1918–1974)

Jacqueline Susann was born in Philadelphia on August 20, 1918, where her father, Robert Susann, a portrait painter, was considered "Philadelphia's answer to John Singer Sargent," and her mother was a schoolteacher. Susann early on decided she wanted to be an actress. Following her high school graduation, she moved to New York. Filled with determination, self-confidence, and startlingly good looks, Susann was hired to understudy Arlene Francis in the original 1936 production of Clare Boothe's *The Women.* Susann found acting jobs scarce; after a year's search, she landed a theatrical job playing a lingerie model.

With her 1939 marriage to press agent Irving Mansfield (1908–1988), Susann began getting better jobs. Theirs was a stormy marriage; the bisexual Susann had affairs with, among others, comics **George Jessel** and Joe E. Lewis and actresses Ethel Merman and Carole Landis. In the late 1940s Susann landed a role as "Lola the Cigarette Girl" on *The Morey Amsterdam Show;* the television program failed after two seasons. Following a stint hawking Schiffli lace on late-night television, Susann decided to write. At first, she thought of writing a show business/drug exposé tentatively titled *The Pink Dolls*—her name for pills. Instead, she wrote a book based on her experiences with her poodle, *Every Night, Josephine!* The book's relative success gave her the cachet to publish her next work, *The Valley of the Dolls* (1966). *Dolls,* a loud, bombastic soap opera of a novel, told the story of a model, a singer, and a bombshell actress. It sold more than 19 million copies, was filmed twice, and at one time was the world's bestselling novel.

Susann followed up *Dolls* with two more bestsellers: *The Love Machine* (1969) and *Once Is Not Enough* (1973). Although roundly lambasted by critics, she became a bestselling author. Afflicted with breast cancer in the early 1960s, Susann died in 1974. She was survived by her husband, son Guy, and her mother. In 1976, her final novel, *Delores,* was published posthumously.

Kurt F. Stone

Further Reading: Seaman, Barbara. *Lovely Me: The Life of Jacqueline Susann.* Seven Stories Press, 1986.

T

TELEVISION

Depending how strictly one defines ethnicity, hundreds of Jewish actors have enjoyed visibility on network television since the medium's beginning in 1947. Although many early television shows were unremarkable, many became popular, and a handful became legitimate classics. Jews were prominent in every genre: situation comedies; soap operas; courtroom, police, and medical dramas; westerns; science fiction; and others. Infrequently, Jewish performers played Jewish characters, but more often they transcended ethnicity.

In the days of live variety and sketch programs, for example, **Milton Berle**, **Jack Benny**, **George Burns**, and **Sid Caesar** were perennial favorites, carry-overs from the shtick of the Borscht Belt/**vaudeville/radio** days when they mixed skits with musical guest appearances. Berle and Caesar received Emmy awards for their work.

Westerns were a popular genre from the late 1950s through the 1960s. Among them was *Bonanza,* the epic tale of the Cartwright family, which ran from 1959–1973, making it the second-longest running western in television history next to *Gunsmoke*. Lorne Greene (Lyon Chaim Green, a Canadian, born to Russian Jewish immigrants) starred as Ben, father of the clan, while Michael Landon (Eugene Michael Orowitz, born to a Jewish father and Irish Roman Catholic mother) played his youngest son, Little Joe. Both actors enjoyed later success on other series. Landon was cast as Jonathan Ingalls, the father on *Little House on the Prairie* (1974–1983), and as an angel on *Highway to Heaven* (1984–1989). One of his daughters on *Little House* was played by the Jewish actress Melissa Gilbert, who went on to serve as president of the Screen Actors Guild from 2001–2005. Greene, meanwhile, portrayed another father figure in the original version of the science-fiction series *Battlestar Gallactica* (1978–1979) and *Gallactica* (1980), portraying Commander Adama. Ross Martin and Robert Conrad—both stars of *The Wild Wild West* (1965–1970), were born to Jewish mothers. Conrad, who specialized in tough-guy roles, also saw duty on *Hawaiian Eye* (1959–1963), and *Baa Baa Black Sheep* (1976-–1978). Gene Barry (b. Eugene Klass) starred in the hit Western *Bat Masterson* (1958–1961) and then went on to star on *Burkes's Law* (1963–1965) which he won a Golden Globe Award for in 1965. Barry had a notable career in television, including his starring role in *The Name of the Game* (1968–1971). The original *Star Trek* (1966–1969), the most famous sci-fi television show in history, featured three

Jewish actors in key roles: **William Shatner** as Captain James Tiberius Kirk, **Leonard Nimoy** as Science Officer Spock, and Walter Koenig as ship's navigator Pavel Andreievich Chekhov.

Shatner went on to campy success in other series, including the short-lived *Barbary Coast* (1975–1976), an espionage/western, and *T.J. Hooker* (1982–1986), a police drama. He has enjoyed a renaissance with his role as lawyer Denny Crane on *Boston Legal*. Nimoy, who maintained a close connection with the Jewish community in private life, traded pointed ears for the life of a spy when he joined the cast of *Mission Impossible* from 1969–1971. He was also the host for *In Search of*...—a nonfiction science/anthropology program. In subsequent revisions of the Star Trek franchise, other Jewish actors have played leading roles, which include Bret Spiner (Data on *Star Trek: The Next Generation,* 1987–1994), and Armin Shimmerman (Quark) and Wallace Shawn (Grand Nagus Zek) on *Star Trek: Deep Space Nine* (1993–1999). *Babylon 5* (1992–97) was a syndicated sci-fi staple with an abundance of Jewish actors, including Koenig, Mira Furlan, Stephen Furst, Melissa Gilbert, Stephan Macht, and Robin Sachs.

Several actors on the popular teen fantasy *Buffy the Vampire Slayer* (1997–2003) are Jewish, including Buffy herself, Sarah Michelle Gellar, as well as Seth Green, Alyson Hannigan (*How I Met Your Mother*), Juliet Landau, Amber Benson, and Michelle Trachtenberg.

Other programs aimed at a teenaged audience featured Jewish performers. The Canadian-produced *Degrassi: The Next Generation* features young stars Aubrey Graham, Sarah Barrable-Tishauer, Jake Goldsbie, Shane Kippel, Lauren Collins, Jake Epstein, and Stacey Farber. *Beverly Hills 90210* (1990–2000), perhaps the first of the teen dramas, starred Ian Ziering, Gabrielle Carteris, and Tori Spelling, whose father, Aaron, was one of the industry's most prolific producers. Soap operas featuring Jewish performers include *General Hospital* (Rena Sofer, who also appeared on *24, Just Shoot Me,* and, currently, *Heroes*; Steve Bond; and Stuart Damon); *Santa Barbara* (Bond and Nancy Lee Grahn); *The Bold and the Beautiful* (Sean Kanan); and *Days of Our Lives* (Sean Kanan and Jason Brooks). Claudia Lonow and Michelle Lee starred in the nighttime soap *Knots Landing* (1979–1993). In the legal/police/espionage genres, which often "cross over," shows and actors include three-time Emmy winner **Peter Falk** for his role in *Columbo* (several incarnations); *Alias* (2001–2006, Victor Garber, Ron Rifkin, Joey Slotnick, Michael Vartan, Kevin Weisman, and Greg Grunberg [also on *Heroes*]); *Homicide: Life on the Street* (1993–1999, Yaphet Koto and Richard Belzer, now with the Law and Order franchise); *L.A. Law* (1986–1994, Michael Tucker and Alan Rachins); *The Practice* (1997–2004, Camryn Manheim and Marla Sokoloff); and *24* (2001– , Jonathan Ahdout, Sara Gilbert, and Mia Kirshner). The *Law and Order* "family" has featured such actors as Steven Hill (an Orthodox Jew who was known for leaving work early on Fridays to observe Shabbat), Judith Light (who also starred in *Who's the Boss* and now as a regular on *Ugly Betty*), Scoot Cohen, Lynn Cohen, and Bebe Neuwirth; and David Krumholtz, Judd Hirsch and Rob Morrow, who currently appear on the show *Numb3rs*.

Film and Broadway actor Ron Leibman, who won a Tony for acting in Tony Kushner's *Angels in America,* starred in the television series *Kaz* (1978–1979), which he won an Emmy for in 1979. He also had a recurring role in *The Sopranos* as Dr. Pepler. Medical shows counting Jews among their casts include *St. Elsewhere* (1982–1988, Howie Mandel, Stephen Furst), *ER* (1994– , Noah Wyle and Julianna Margulies), *Chicago Hope* (1994–2000, **Mandy Patinkin** [who won an Emmy in 1995], **Alan Arkin**, Peter Berg, Barbara Hershey), and *Ben Casey* (1961–1966, Sam Jaffe). CBS's *NCIS* features actress Cote de Pablo (who is not Jewish) as Ziva David, an Israeli Mossad agent assigned to the navy intelligence unit.

One of the rare dramas that dealt with Judaism was *Thirtysomething* (1987–1991), which starred Ken Olin as Michael Steadman, an ambivalent Jew in an interfaith marriage who occasionally questioned his religious philosophy. Melanie Mayron, who played his cousin Melissa, is also Jewish. She won the Emmy for best supporting actress in a dramatic series from 1989–1991. Olin also appeared as a regular on *Hill Street Blues* (1981–1987) and *Bay City Blues* (four episodes, 1983), as well as in guest shots on several other series. Sitcoms claim the lion's share of Jewish stars. One of the most unusual—and a point of contention among Jews in the 1960s—was *Hogan's Heroes* (1965–1971), which was set in a German POW camp during World War II. Many thought it was disrespectful to portray Nazis in a humorous and human light. Ironically three of the main German characters were played by European-born Jews: Colonel Klink (Werner Klemperer), Sergeant Schultz (John Banner), and General Burkhalter (Leon Askin). All managed to escape from the real Nazis, although Askin (née Leo Aschkenasy), was incarcerated in a French internment camp and his parents were killed at Treblinka. Robert Cleary, a French actor who was cast as Corporal Louis Lebeau, spent three years in a concentration camp. Banner spent a short time in a camp, during the early stages of the war, before being released and immigrating to the United States. Jewish organizations protested the series, claiming it trivialized the evils of the Nazi regime.

On shows with less political import, *Car 54, Where Are You?* (1961–1963) was the most Yiddish-inflected sitcom of all time and the one with the most Jewish characters until *Barney Miller* (1975–1982), which featured **Hal Linden** in the title role, Barbara Barrie as his wife, Steve Landesberg as Sergeant Dietrich, and Abe Vigoda as Detective Fish. *Fish* (1977–1978) became a Miller spin-off.

With the exception of Ron Howard and Marion Ross, the major roles on *Happy Days* (1974–1984) were played by Jews, including **Henry Winkler** as "The Fonz," Tom Bosley as Howard's father, and Anson Williams and Don Most as his two best friends. *Rosanne* (1988–1997), another staple of the sitcom world, featured Roseanne Barr, Sandra Bernhard, Sara Gilbert, Tom Arnold (a converted Jew), Michael Fishman, Estelle Parsons, **Shelley Winters**, and John Randolph.

Mad About You (1992–1999) featured Paul Reiser and Helen Hunt (who had a Jewish father) as the interfaith couple, along with Richard Kind and Hank Azaria, better known for his roles on *The Simpsons* (1988–), which also stars Harry Shearer and Julie Kavner. Kavner also appeared as Valerie Harper's younger sister, Brenda, on *Rhoda* (1974–1978), which featured David Groh and Harold Gould. Interestingly, neither Harper (who received critical acclaim when she replaced **Tovah Feldshuh** in the Broadway play *Golda's Balcony*) nor Nancy Walker, who expertly played the Jewish mother, was in fact Jewish.

Linda Lavin starred in *Alice* (1976–1985), the television version of *Alice Doesn't Live Here Anymore,* and headlined *Room For Two* (1992–1993), as well as appearing in secondary roles on *Barney Miller* and *Conrad Bloom* (as a "Jewish mother"). Ed Asner reprised his role on *The Mary Tyler Moore Show* (1970–1977) in the dramatic spin-off *Lou Grant* (1977–1982). *Friends* (1994–2004) included mainstays Lisa Kudrow and David Schwimmer, as well as frequent guest stars Ron Leibman, Elliot Gould, Paul Rudd, and Maggie Wheeler. *Seinfeld* (1990–1998) also featured Jewish actors in key roles, including **Jerry Seinfeld** (who few probably remember for his recurring role on *Benson* from 1980–1981, Julia Louis-Dreyfus (who had a Jewish paternal grandfather), Jason Alexander, Jerry Stiller, and Estelle Harris. Award-winning *Everybody Loves Raymond,* whose initial run on CBS was from 1996—2005 and is now in syndication, included two Jewish leads—three-time Emmy actor Brad Garret (Brad Gerstenfeld) and five-time Emmy actress Doris Roberts (Doris May Metzler).

Born to an American Jewish family in 1949, Gary Shandling was the star of two hit comedies on premium cable television. *The Gary Shandling Show* premiered on Showtime in 1986 and ran for 72 episodes, ending its run in 1990. The sitcom starred Shandling as a self-obsessed stand-up comedian. The show paved the way for his more successful run as late-night talk show host Larry Sanders on HBO's *The Larry Sanders Show.* The sitcom ran from 1992 to 1996 and during its run won both Emmy and Peabody awards. *The Larry Sanders Show* was listed as number 38 on TV Guide's 50 Greatest TV Shows of All Time, and *Time* magazine listed the sitcom as one of the 100 Best TV Shows of All Time. Modeled after *The Johnny Carson Show,* where Shandling often appeared as a guest, Jewish actor Jeffrey Tambor played Larry's sidekick. Both shows included Jewish content, but the most memorable episode occurred on *The Larry Sanders Show* when Tambor decided to become a born-again Jew and insisted on wearing a kippah (skullcap) on the show. Jeffrey Tambor moved on to star in *Arrested Development* (2003–2006), Fox's low-rated but critically acclaimed comedy series about a dysfunctional family. The ensemble cast featured Tambor as George Bluth, a jailed Jewish white-collar criminal. The plot line followed the efforts of his levelheaded son Michael Bluth (Jason Bateman) to take over family affairs after his father's imprisonment. But the rest of his spoiled, zany family make his job unbearable. The show included veteran Jewish actress Jessica Walter as Tambor's wife. Jews and Jewish references are ongoing themes of the Emmy Award-winning *Curb Your Enthusiasm,* which made its debut on HBO in 2000 and stars *Seinfeld* co-creator **Larry David**, who plays himself on the comedy series. As is the case with a number of situation comedies involving Jewish characters, David is married to a shiksa (non-Jewish woman) played by Cheryl Hines. The irreverent comedy has spoofed many aspects of Jewish life, such as the Holocaust, conversion, Jewish holidays, Jews and Christmas, circumcision, and so on. Some Jewish actors have appeared in numerous starring roles over the years, including Bea Arthur (*Maude,* for which she won an Emmy in 1977; *Golden Girls,* another Emmy in 1988; and *Amanda's*), Don Rickles (*The Don Rickles Show, C.P.O. Sharkey*), Judd Hirsh was in *Delvechio* and *Taxi* (for which he won Emmys in 1981 and 1983), Jeffrey Tambor and Jessica Walters (*Arrested Development*), and Jeremy Piven (*Entourage*). Others are perennial guests (Elliot Gould, Harold Stone, Carol Kane, Jeff Goldblum, Steve Guttenberg, Jon Lovitz, Stephen Tobolowsky, Eugene Levy, Charles Grodin, Robert Klein, **Harvey Fierstein**, Carrie Fisher, Madeline Kahn, and Ben Stein, among others. In addition to their iconic roles on *The Odd Couple* (1970–1975), **Jack Klugman** also starred in *Quincy, M.E.* (1976–1983), while **Tony Randall** appeared on *Mr. Peepers* (1952–1955), *The Tony Randall Show* (1976–1978), and *Love, Sidney* (1981–1983). Behind the television cameras, Jews have played important roles as writers, directors, and producers. Some of television's most notable shows have been produced by Jewish producers, including Sheldon Leonard (*Bershad,* 1907–1997), who was a producer, director, writer, and actor. His television credits include *The Andy Griffith Show* (1960–1968), *The Danny Thomas Show* (1953–1964), *The Dick Van Dyke Show* (1961–1966), and *I Spy* (1965–1968). **Paddy Chayefsky** (1923–1981) was an acclaimed dramatist, playwright, and screenwriter for Hollywood. His first major television success was a live production of *Marty* (1954), which was made into a film in 1955, starring Ernest Borgnine. The film won the Academy Award for Best Picture. He wrote scripts for *The Armstrong Theater, Playhouse 90, U.S. Steel Hour,* and dozens of other short-lived television anthologies in the 1950s and early 1960s. Norman Lear (1922–) produced *All in the Family* (1971–1979), *Sanford and Son* (1972–1977), *One Day at a Time* (1975–1984), *The Jeffersons* (1975–1985), *Good Times* (1974–1979), *Maude* (1972–1978), *Archie Bunker's Place* (1979–1983), *Mary Hartman, Mary Hartman* (1976–1978), and *Different Strokes* (1978–1986). David Susskind (1920–1987) was both a producer and a pioneer talk-show host. His talk show, *Open End,* ran from 1958–1967, which became *The David Susskind Show* in 1967 and was televised until 1986. During his almost 30 years as a talk show host, Susskind covered many controversial subjects, ranging from race relations to the Vietnam War. His interview with

Soviet Premier Nikita Khrushchev, which aired in October 1960, drew a large audience and generated national attention. Susskind also brought controversial programming to television when he and Herbert Brodkin produced *The Defenders* (1958–1965), which dealt with police and civil liberties issues, and *East Side/West Side,* a program that dealt with the ills of American society. The show only lasted the 1963–1964 season. Susskind also brought serious drama to television when he produced **Arthur Miller**'s *Death of a Salesman* in 1967 and brought *The World of Sholem Aleichem* to public television as part of its "The Play of the Week" series (1959). Larry Gelbart (1928–), who wrote the Broadway hit *A Funny Thing Happened on the Way to the Forum* (1962), was the force behind the creation of one of television's most iconic series, *M*A*S*H* (1972–1983). He wrote and produced many of its episodes and left after its fourth season. *See also* **Television Stars**; **Sitcoms**.

Ron Kaplan

Further Reading: Brooks, Tim, and Earle Marsh. *The Complete Directory to Prime Time Network and Cable TV Shows, 1946–Present.* Random House, 2007.

TELEVISION STARS

Considering that many television executives, like movie studio heads, were Jews by birth, there was a considerable lack of Jewish content in the early years of the medium. Several reasons played into these decisions. Jewish executives wanted to downplay their ethnicity, since they were embarrassed by, and wished to distance themselves from, their immigrant origins. They married Gentiles and disassociated themselves from their roots, assimilating into American society as did many other first- and second-generation Jews. It is all the more ironic then that they found such success in the entertainment industry, which had been considered an unfit vocation for respectable people. Still, it was one of the few opportunities available for late nineteenth/early twentieth-century Jews, who were unofficially barred from many more-traditional occupations. These men were also concerned that presenting characters or programs that appeared "too Jewish" would alienate a majority of viewers and sponsors. Nevertheless, many of the performers of early television were Jewish, albeit, rarely calling attention to their ethnicity. Among the first Jewish stars who headlined variety or comedy programs were **Milton Berle** (*The Milton Berle Show,* originally *The Texaco Star Theater,* 1948–1956), **Sid Caesar** (*Your Show of Shows,* 1950–1954)—both Berle and Caesar received Emmy Awards for their work—and **Groucho Marx**, who starred in *You Bet Your Life,* which made its debut on radio in 1947 and made the transition to television in 1950. The show, which was a combination quiz show as well a showcase for Marx's humor, remained on television until 1961 (the show was renamed *The Groucho Show* in 1960). There were exceptions. The first important show to exhibit Jewish life was *The Goldbergs,* starring Gertrude Berg as the matriarch of an extended family on the Lower East Side of Manhattan. A carry-over from the popular radio series, the television version of *The Goldbergs* told the story of a Jewish family trying to "learn to be more American." The program was something of an anomaly in that Berg did not play the stereotypical Jewish mother but was rather a strong on-screen presence (as well as behind the scenes). She received the Emmy for best actress in a comedy in 1950. Television continues, for the most part (except for seasonal Christmas episodes), to forego religion as a programming subject, regardless of the faith of the main characters. From the "birth" of network television until the late 1980s, Jewish characters were rare in non-comedy programming and were not cast in lead roles. They basically served as a novelty. When westerns became a staple of prime time viewing, Jews were depicted as "the other," a stranger in a strange land. They were inclined, much to the curiosity and bigotry of others, to hold on to their old country ways while adjusting to their new home; *Bonanza* and *Gunsmoke,* two of television's most popular westerns, featured such plot lines. (*Little House on the Prairie,* a family drama set in the late 1800s—and starring Michael Landon, who had starred on *Bonanza* as "Little Joe"—featured an intermarriage story line. When the couple had twins, they solved the religion question by deciding to raise one child as a Jew and the other as a Christian.) Jewish actors on television were often relegated to professions that have become Jewish stereotypes, such as doctors (Howie Mandel and Stephen Furst, among others on *St. Elsewhere;* **Alan Arkin** and **Mandy Patinkin** in *Chicago Hope*); lawyers (Alan Rankin, Michael Rucker on *L.A. Law*); accountants (Marvin Kaplan on *The Chicago Teddy Bears*); and teachers (Gabe Kaplan in *Welcome Back, Kotter;* **Fyvush Finkel**, *Boston Public;* **Richard Dreyfuss**, *The Education of Max Bickford*). In recent decades, television shows have portrayed Jewish characters as leads, albeit almost always in "mixed" relationships, suggesting the ambivalence of being Jewish in modern society. Michael Steadman (played by Ken Olin) grappled with religious issues on *Thirtysomething,* which won an Emmy Award for best dramatic series in 1988. Likewise, *Northern Exposure*'s main character, Dr. Joel Fleischman (Rob Morrow), found the concept of getting in touch with his Judaism a bit difficult in the isolated community of Cicely, Alaska, when he decided he wanted to say the mourner's Kaddish for a beloved relative (*Exposure* won the Emmy drama award in 1992).

A more recent series that featured a Jewish character—again as part of a mixed marriage—was *The O.C.*, a "teen drama" which introduced "Chrismukkah"—a hybrid of two winter holidays—into popular culture. The cult classic *Everwood* (2002–2006) featured Treat Williams, whose Jewish wife has died, leaving him to raise their two children. During the last year of the series, his daughter has her Bat Mitzvah, an episode that is treated in a dignified and respectful manner.

Jews, when they were identified as such, were often portrayed as caricatures (or, less politely, stereotypes). The loud, sometimes obnoxious family of Bernie Steinberg in the controversial *Bridget Loves Bernie* is an example. Conservative and Reform Jewish groups protested the program, angry at the casual depiction of intermarriage (not to mention the rendering of the Jewish family).

Other characters, while not readily identified by their surnames (few Goldbergs, Horowitzes, or Teitelbaums, but possible Millers, Fishers, and Gordons) were identified by their behavior.

Bridget Loves Bernie was dropped from the CBS line-up after just 24 episodes, the highest-rated program ever canceled. But it wasn't a total loss for the stars: in an example of life imitating art, David Birney and Meredith Baxter became real-life husband and wife. Fran Drescher's portrayal of *The Nanny* was another example. Gaudily dressed, whiny, looking to land a rich husband, she was the poster girl for the Jewish American Princess. *Seinfeld* was an undoubtedly Jewish character, but the sitcom (1993 comedy Emmy) never examined this in depth. In the tradition of **Woody Allen** films, a number of *Seinfeld* episodes came close to mocking Jewish tradition and culture. One such episode featured a bipolar mohel at a *bris,* and another dealt with tricking an observant Jew into eating treif shellfish. In still another episode, Seinfeld complained that his Christian dentist had converted to Judaism "for the jokes." (An additional episode centered on the consequences of Jerry and his date "making out" during a screening of ***Schindler's List*** to the shock and embarrassment of his parents, a doting "Jewish mother" and a know-it-all father.) The three other main Seinfeld characters—Elaine Benes, Cosmo Kramer, and especially George Costanza (and by extension his over-the-top parents), also display what could be considered Jewish "traits." *Brooklyn Bridge* was a latter-day homage to *The Goldbergs.* It featured a close-knit Jewish family in that New York borough in the 1950s. The grandparents, Russian immigrants (one can almost assume that any family with an Eastern European/Russian accent was of Jewish origin), lived in the same apartment building. The ostensible star of *Bridge* was an adolescent boy who had a crush on a neighbor who attended Catholic parochial school, perhaps setting the stage for yet another interfaith relationship had the program lasted longer. Several post-1980s sitcoms continue the theme of a Jewish man and the "shiksa goddess," that is, the worldly, sexy (often blond) female and the nebbishy, neurotic, mother-dominated Jewish male. Examples of this include *Anything But Love,* which starred that perennial loony comedian Richard Lewis and Jamie Lee Curtis; *Chicken Soup,* in which a 52-year-old **Jackie Mason** was still living with his mother while courting Lynn Redgrave; *Love and War* (Jay Thomas/Susan Dey); and *Flying Blind* (Corey Park/Tea Leoni) among others. Many of these were dropped from the prime time schedule before a season had passed. A handful of programs reversed the gender balance, with a Jewish female character still relatively under the thumb of parents who saw her as their "princess." Examples of this included *Rhoda, Dharma & Greg, Friends,* and *Will and Grace*. Compared with sitcoms of the period, dramatic shows with Jews were relatively rare and usually unsuccessful. *Lanigan's Rabbi,* a 1970s detective show based loosely on Harry Kellerman's series of novels about a sleuthing spiritual leader, was canceled after only four episodes. *The Education of Max Bickford* (Richard Dreyfuss as a middle-aged college professor) lasted for 22. The show *100 Centre Street,* directed by **Sidney Lumet** and starring Alan Arkin as Judge Joe Rifkind, aired 30 episodes, while *State of Grace,* which relocated the *Brooklyn Bridge* theme to North Carolina (another fish-out-of-water concept), produced 39 shows over two seasons during roughly the same period. *See also* **Sitcoms**; **Television**.

Ron Kaplan

Further Reading: Brook, Vincent. *Something Ain't Kosher Here: The Rise of the "Jewish" Sitcom*. Rutgers University Press, 2003. Zurawik, David. *The Jews of Prime Time*. University Press of New England, 2003.

THEATER

Eminent British director Tyrone Guthrie noted the necessity of the Jewish contribution to the survival of the American theater. The observation is closer to fact than to hyperbole. Over the last hundred years, Jews have been actively engaged in every dimension of the art, business, and patronage of the theater. One estimate has it that by 1905, as many as 50 percent of those working in American entertainment were Jewish.

The phenomenon is all the more remarkable because it reverses a long tradition. Despite the fact that few people have a more dramatic history and that Jewish rituals abound in performance, Jews customarily made theater only to celebrate Purim. Then came the Haskalah (Enlightenment) and with it, **Yiddish theater**. Introduced in Romania in 1876, it swept through Eastern Europe and six years later crossed the Atlantic. Perhaps the seeds of theatrical creativity germinated in the heritage for centuries waiting for the requisite conditions to blossom. The catalyst was the convergence of history and opportunity in the years of mass migration westward.

Even before the emergence of an indigenous repertoire in the 1910s, Jews had made their entrance in American theater history. As historian Louis Harap has noted, the first Jews to distinguish themselves in American literature—Isaac Harby, Mordechai Manuel Noah and Jonas Phillips—did so in drama, although they rarely wrote plays about Jews. The earliest arrivals on stage were conventional stock types, sometimes villainous, often ludicrous. The "Hebrew comic" who emerged on the post-Civil War vaudeville stage quickly became a popular figure. He dressed funny, talked funny, and *was* funny. However, early Jewish vaudevillians gave the role wide berth, preferring to channel their humor through other ethnic personae. For instance, Joe Weber and Lew Fields (Shanfield) delighted fin-de-siecle audiences as a team of "Dutch" immigrants with preposterous German accents ("Dot vas no lady; dot vas my wife"). Actor David Warfield (Wollfeld), whose Jewishness is uncertain, began as a Hebrew comic but won notable success in a new, more substantial Jewish role. In *The Auctioneer* (1901), Warfield starred as a devoted family man who recovers from near ruin and forgives the brother who defrauded him.

Warfield had been recruited for *The Auctioneer* by theatrical overachiever David Belasco. Actor, playwright, producer, Belasco became a Broadway legend. Except for *The Auctioneer,* however, he confined his Jewish presence behind the scenes. That is where Jewish business aptitude has prospered ever since (Broadway today is still very much a Jewish business). By the beginning of the twentieth century, the major American playhouses were controlled by syndicates and agencies headed by entrepreneurs like Marc Klaw, Abe Erlanger, and the Frohman and Shubert brothers. Many believe that is why the stage door was open to Jews when so many other doors were shut.

As Jews became more conspicuous in America, more Jewish-created Jews appeared behind the footlights. In 1913, transplanted Englishmen, Montague (Marsden) Glass and Charles Klein, scored a hit with the comic adventures of *Potash and Perlmutter.* The Yiddish-inflected pair, partners in the garment industry, quarreled their way into audiences' hearts, inspiring still other plays based on Glass's stories in the *Saturday Evening Post.* From the wildly inventive Aaron Hoffman came dozens of vaudeville skits and full-length plays, many explicitly Jewish. Hoffman's ironically titled comedy, *Welcome Stranger* (1920), makes an emphatic affirmation of the Constitutional rights of American Jews. In a ringing assertion whose candor the stage has yet to surpass, Hoffman's sunny but determined hero reminds his anti-Semitic adversaries that "for some particular reason, God wants us to live and prosper and—what the Hell are you going to do about it?"

"Live and prosper" are apt words for audiences in the years when the nation was molding its cultural profile. It is not always sufficiently recognized that the lifeblood of theater is theatergoers. Newcomers swelled the ranks of working-class spectators who flocked to variety shows, revues, and vaudeville. For newly arrived Jews, the irresistible magnet was the Yiddish theater. It is here that the flood of Eastern European Jews, which peaked between 1881 and 1924, exercised an influence that cannot be overestimated.

In America, theater in Yiddish—perhaps a more accurate concept than "Yiddish theater"—included all manner of performance. The bills ranged from operettas, melodrama, variety shows, and *shund* (trash) to the Yiddish classics, translations of world masterpieces, and new works of high literary quality, like those **Maurice Schwartz** produced at the Yiddish Art Theatre (1918–1950). Artistic quality and aspirations aside, theater in Yiddish mattered because the stage validated the audiences' culture in a language that was uniquely their own and a space where they felt at home—so much so, they sometimes traded food and opinion and talked back to the actors. Shop girls and sweatshop laborers used their lunch money for tickets. Going to the theater became an integral part of Jewish life in America.

Performance houses were quick to exploit the immigrants' devotion. Competitive blood ran hot on Second Avenue. Fans made matinee idols of talented actors like Celia, Jacob, and Sara Adler; Jacob Ben-Ami; Bertha Kalisch; and David Kessler. Gifted performers did not escape notice in the larger theater world. Influential uptown critics—Brooks Atkinson, George Jean Nathan, and Stark Young among them—wrote admiringly of the superior acting on the Yiddish stage.

Soon wider audiences were able to judge for themselves as Yiddish performers made their way to the English-speaking stage: Ben-Ami, Kalisch, Paul Muni (Meshilem Meier Weisenfrend), **Molly Picon**, and **Menasha Skulnik**. Some performers, among them Stella Adler, Luther Adler, Sanford Meisner, and Lee Strasberg (Israel Strassberg), became influential acting teachers. They taught subsequent stars like Marlon Brando, **Dustin Hoffman**, **Paul Newman**, Al Pacino, and Marion Seldes. Brando, trained by Stella Adler, remarked, "If there wasn't a Yiddish theater, there wouldn't have been a Stella. And if there hadn't been Stella, there wouldn't have been all those actors who studied with her and changed the face of theater—and not only acting, but directing and writing" (Kanfer, 2006).

However impossible it is to quantify the extent to which the Yiddish theater promoted the presence of Jews in every dimension of American theater, its impact is everywhere manifest. The appeal of the classic Yiddish plays remains undiminished. They include **Paddy Chayefsky**'s hugely successful *The Tenth Man* (1959), a reworking of Anski's *The Dybbuk* in psychological terms; Tony Kushner's *A Dybbuk* (1997), a demonstration of the enduring power of mysticism; and Sholom Asch's scandalous *God of Vengeance,* adapted by Donald Margulies, who relocates the play to the Lower East Side, setting it in 1923, the year a production of the original play in English was closed down for indecency.

The Yiddish theater shaped the tastes, the leisure time habits, and, frequently, the careers of subsequent generations. In the 1920s when Jewish writers began to dramatize American Jewish life, their plays in English often bore traces of Yiddish antecedents. For instance, family interaction troubled by children's defiance of tradition and culture is a dominant subject in the repertoire of both languages. A famous example is Samson Raphaelson's ***The Jazz Singer*** (1925), in which a talented performer, a second-generation American, is torn between making his debut on Broadway or obeying the deathbed wish of his cantor father that he take his place to chant the Kol Nidre. That *The Jazz Singer,* starring **George Jessel**, became the very first talking film, with **Al Jolson** (Asa Yoelson), illustrates how representative the Jewish experience in America had become by 1928.

Yiddish-inflected mommas and poppas and their rebellious sons and daughters found steady employment in American works. One of the most popular was Gertrude Berg's *The Goldbergs,* which came to the stage in 1946, having aired on radio and, ultimately, television. Less well known are the sentimental scripts Sam and Bella Spewack fashioned with dramatis personae common to the Yiddish repertoire—the stubbornly opinionated father (*Poppa,* 1928), the perennially resourceful Jewish mother (*Spring Song,* 1934. In 1948, the Spewacks wrote the book for his memorable musical *Kiss Me Kate.*

By the 1930s, assimilation, prosperity, and the move to the suburbs, along with the passing of the giants, had taken their toll on the Yiddish stage (a notable exception is the Folksbiene [1915], which is thought to be New York's oldest continuously producing English or Yiddish theater), but Jews were firmly established in the American theater arts (Shepard, 2000). The ethnic composition of two landmark producing companies, the Playwrights Company (1938–1960) and the Group Theatre (1931–1941), illustrates the heterogeneity that characterizes theater creativity in America.

The Playwrights Company was founded by five dramatists devoted to high standards of theatrical writing and production: Maxwell Anderson, S. N. Behrman, Sidney Howard, **Elmer Rice**, and Robert E. Sherwood. Among dozens of outstanding plays, it produced Pulitzer Prize winners *Abe Lincoln in Illinois* (1938) and *There Shall Be No Night* (1940), both by Sherwood, and Tennessee Williams's *Cat on a Hot Tin Roof* (1955).

Elmer Rice (Reizenstein), the company's longest-serving member, a dramatist, director, and producer, was one of the most versatile and innovative pioneers of the American theater. Rice introduced the filmic technique of flashback to the stage in *On Trial* (1914). Fifteen years later, he became the first Jew to win the Pulitzer Prize for drama, for *Street Scene*(1929). During the era of the Federal Theatre Project (1935–1939), he championed uncensored government support for regional theaters across the country. In 1947, Rice collaborated with African American poet Langston Hughes and German refugee Kurt Weill, who had joined Playwrights, to turn *Street Scene* into a critically heralded musical.

One of Weill's earliest works in America, the antiwar *Johnny Johnson* (1936), was produced by a second archetypal company, the Group Theatre. The Group's founders, Harold Clurman, Cheryl Crawford, and Lee Strasberg, were not dramatists, and their mission differed from Playwrights'. They were dedicated to leftwing politics, egalitarianism, and Stanislavsky-influenced dramatic art. The Group's achievements belie its brief history. In 10 years, it launched the careers on the English language stage of some of America's finest actors

—Luther and Stella Adler, J. E. Bromberg, Morris Carnovsky, and **John Garfield**—and influential acting teachers. **Clifford Odets**, a bit player in the Group, discovered that his future lay not in acting, but in playwriting.

The Group had resisted producing Odets's plays until the unanticipated phenomenal success of his one-act agitprop about a taxi drivers' strike, *Waiting for Lefty* (1935). The play swiftly found audiences across the country. The Group quickly mounted Odets's *Awake and Sing!* (1935), thereby giving the American Jewish repertoire its first master work. Set in a Bronx apartment, the play depicts with stunning accuracy the struggles of three generations of the Berger family coping with conflicting goals, the challenges of Depression America, and one another. In *Paradise Lost* (1935), Odets portrayed the downfall of a more prosperous Jewish family, and in *The Flowering Peach* (1954), he styled Noah and his family as Jews. Although Odets used Jewish characters in other plays (*Golden Boy*, 1937; *Rocket to the Moon,* 1939), many of his stage and film scripts plays have no Jewish interest at all. The point is noteworthy because Odets's alternating between Jewish and non-Jewish subjects typifies the practice of almost all American Jewish dramatists.

The winds of political and social unrest that filled the sails of the Group Theatre and launched Odets's career blew strong throughout the Depression-wracked 1930s. Jews, characteristically responsive to injustice and eager for social action, supported theater that used the stage as a weapon. Liberal politics, along with the rigors of pursuing the American dream and the conflicting values of intergenerational family life in a society challenged from many directions, became dominant and broadly representative subjects of American Jewish drama.

These concerns are central for the nation's most famous American Jewish playwright, **Arthur Miller** (1915–2005). His early, unpublished "No Villain" (1936) depicts a strike in the garment industry that sets a threatened manufacturer at odds with his idealistic, labor-allied son. The irreconcilability of social responsibility, personal integrity, and individual fulfillment prevails in *All My Sons* (1947), *The Price* (1968), and Miller's most famous work, *Death of a Salesman* (1949). In *The Crucible* (1953), inspired by the playwright's own experience with the House Committee on Un-American Activities, the topic opens out into a reactionary community (read: country) at war with its own sons and daughters.

While Willy Loman's ethnicity is ambiguous, Miller is explicit when he means to write about Jews. His most powerful Jewish character may be Gregory Solomon, who mediates between warring Gentile brothers when he is summoned to buy their late father's furniture in *The Price* (1968). *Incident at Vichy* (1964) portrays a roundup of Jews for deportation from wartime France. In *Playing for Time* (1980), a television play, a French cabaret singer's music keeps her alive in Auschwitz. *Broken Glass* (1994) concerns an American woman paralyzed by news reports of Kristallnacht and her self-hating Jewish husband.

Arthur Miller was not the only Jewish dramatist who drew audiences' attention to international politics and its perils for world Jewry. Some of the earliest American plays about the growing threat of fascism came from Jewish playwrights: S. N. Behrman's *Rain From Heaven* (1934), Lillian Hellman's *Watch On the Rhine* (1941), Elmer Rice's *Flight to the West* (1940) and his *Judgment Day* (1934), about the Reichstag Fire trial, an arson the Nazis imputed to the communists. Rice's foresight is thrown into relief by *New York Daily News*' naïve review of *Judgment Day*, which charged that the play "overstated the case of Hitler . . . The audience does not believe it humanly possible for so vicious and brazen a travesty of justice to have taken place in any civilized state."

Even after Americans came to a fuller understanding of the magnitude of Nazism, they were still unwilling to confront its horrors in the theater. The stage tended to portray the terrifying subject on the oblique, with minimal references to Judaism, few to the ghettos, and none to the camps. The well-known *Diary of Anne Frank*

(1954) is an early and perennially popular example of what works. Hollywood scriptwriters Alfred Hackett and Frances Goodrich downplayed the work's Jewishness, while the production of **Meyer Levin**'s original, more faithful dramatization of the *Diary* was halted by bitter Jewish infighting. It is fair to say that depictions of the Holocaust do not come from or appeal to the American psyche.

By contrast, the Shoah has become an obsessive constant in plays that draw on what *is* genuinely part of the American Jewish psyche: understanding what it means *not* to have been personally involved, trying to respond to those who were (Barbara Lebow's *A Shayna Maidel,* 1984; Donald Margulies's *The Model Apartment,* 1990; Jeffrey Sweet's *The Action Against Sol Schumann,* 2001) or growing up as the child of survivors (Leeny Sack's *The Survivor and the Translator,* 1980; Adam Melnick and John Tarjan's *Camp Holocaust,* 2000; Deb Filler's *Punch Me in the Stomach,* 1992). The horrifying shadow of the Holocaust pervades plays focused on entirely other subjects. It darkens the end of **Neil Simon**'s *Brighton Beach Memoirs* (1983) and imposes troubling dimensions on Jon Robin Baitz's *The Substance of Fire* (1991) and Margulies's *Sight Unseen* (1992).

Still, the regularity with which American Jews dramatize and view the consequences of the Holocaust is fed by the confidence with which they have come to assert their Jewish identity. The Shoah itself is a reason, but also the emergence of Israel as a state and, with the Six Day War, as a military presence. Another major contributing factor is the rise of ethnic pride in the postwar years. The cultural revolution of the 1960s challenged traditions of every sort and made room for the vigorous affirmation of what had been minority identities. The passionate Zeitgeist animated all the arts, fostering unprecedented governmental, foundation, and university support.

The Jewish theater was among the beneficiaries. One of its most significant patrons is the National Foundation for Jewish Culture, established in 1960. The Foundation supports translations and productions of Hebrew and Yiddish plays and the creation of new works in English. It has subsidized performers, the publication of Jewish plays, and an online international catalog, *Plays of Jewish Interest,* launched in 2007 on the All About Jewish Theatre web site (www. jewish-theatre.com). When in 1980 the Foundation announced the first Annual Jewish Theatre Conference, it was astonished at the breadth of responses that included producing groups in Kansas and rural Vermont. From that event there emerged a network of North American producing companies which, along with playwrights, theater personnel, and scholars, today thrives as the Association for Jewish Theatre. The theaters of the AJT preserve the repertoire, expand it by supporting new work, and mount current plays of Jewish interest that also appear regularly on commercial and regional stages.

It is received wisdom in the industry that the surest way to sell out any auditorium in America is to put on a play by Wendy Wasserstein or Neil Simon. In the last three decades, plays about, and usually by, Jews and the audiences for them have burgeoned. One reason may be that Jewish theater has long engaged social questions that have become increasingly common and compelling. Women who reject traditional life choices, early staged by Rose Franken in *Doctors Disagree* (1943) and *Soldier's Wife* (1944) are central to Wendy Wasserstein's oeuvre, notably *Isn't It Romantic* (1985), the Pulitzer winning *The Heidi Chronicles* (1986), and *An American Daughter* (1997). Franken's 1943 *Outrageous Fortune* was the vanguard of plays that squarely address homosexuality, like **Harvey Fierstein**'s *Torch Song Trilogy* (1982), William Finn and James Lapine's *Falsettoland* (1989), and Tony Kushner's *Angels in America* (1993). **Jules Feiffer** (in *Grown Ups,* 1981), **Woody Allen** (in *The Floating Light Bulb,* 1981), and Neil Simon (from *Come Blow Your Horn,*1961 to his Pulitzer-winning *Lost in Yonkers* 1991) have serious fun with dysfunctional families—a combat zone earlier patrolled by Clifford Odets and the Spewacks.

Yet another determinant of the broad popular appeal of Jewish plays is their frequent examination of what defines identity, an often pressing question in a multicultural society of interracial, intermarried, and multi-hyphenated people. Some scripts question the enduring imperatives and relevance of Jewish identity and even its limits. Daniel Goldfarb's plays, for instance, depict a gamut of challenges. At one end are the competing values of the movie mogul in *Adam Baum and the Jew Movie* (1999). In the midst of celebrating his son's Bar Mitzvah, he upbraids the Gentile writer he hired to outdo MGM's *Gentlemen's Agreement* for "writing too Jewish." At the other extreme, there is the dogged commitment to Judaism of the observant salesman in Goldfarb's *Modern Orthodox* (2005), who is thoroughly disoriented when he has to take off his yarmulke to close a business deal. The first act of Richard Greenberg's *Everett Beekin* (2001) takes place in that most conventionally Jewish of places, a crowded Lower East Side kitchen. The second act, set on a subsequent generation's bare California patio, betrays no indications whatever of identity. One of the characters declares, "I have lost myself." In Mamet's ominously entitled *The Disappearance of the Jews* (1982), two middle-aged friends lament the distance between their unaffiliated adult lives and their Jewish boyhood, belatedly reevaluating the heritage they once took for granted.

Other plays ask how porous or "contagious" is identity, and exactly what determines it. The young commodities trader in **Ira Levin**'s *Cantorial* (1988), responding to Jewish heritage to which he can lay no legitimate claim, neglects his job to restore the former synagogue where he and his Jewish girlfriend have moved. The central question of Margulies's *Collected Stories* (1996) is whether a Gentile woman can write authentically about her Jewish mentor's love affair with a famous Jewish poet.

The Jewish theater likes to laugh. The comic spirit often leavens even the most daunting subjects. Consider a visit from Death in Woody Allen's 1975 play of that name. In *The Sunshine Boys* (1977), Neil Simon found humor in the painful subject of the elderly who have outlived their purpose, the subject as well of Herb Gardner's bittersweet *I'm Not Rappaport* (1986). Not even as formidable a topic as Hitler has escaped the traditional Jewish response to disaster; witness **Mel Brooks**'s deliciously outrageous *The Producers* (1991). It is in plays like these that the American Jewish theater delights audiences with the traditional wisdom that laughter not only diverts us from life's hazards but confers a sense of empowerment over them.

Ellen Schiff

Further Reading: Erdman, Harley. *Staging the Jew: The Performance of an American Ethnicity, 1860–1920.* New Brunswick, London: Rutgers U.P., 1997. Harap, Louis. "The Drama." *The Image of the Jew in American Literature: From Early Republic to Mass Immigration.* 2nd ed. Syracuse: Syracuse U.P., 2003. Kanfer, Stefan. *Stardust Lost: The Triumph, Tragedy, and Mishugas of the Yiddish Theater in America.* New York: Alfred A Knopf, 2006. Schiff, Ellen. *From Stereotype to Metaphor: The Jew in Contemporary Drama.* Albany: State U. of New York, 1982. Shepard, Richard F., and Vicki Gold Levi. *Live & Be Well: A Celebration of Yiddish Culture in America.* Rutgers University Press, 2000, 56.

THE THREE STOOGES

The Three Stooges were a popular, raucous comedy trio known for their antic, fast-paced films and physical slapstick comedy. The actors who played the Stooges were Jews who were born in Brooklyn. The Stooges got their start as a madcap vaudeville act in 1925. Originally called "Ted Healy and His Stooges," the act consisted of Healy singing or telling jokes, while his "assistants" would interrupt him with lowbrow physical humor.

The Three Stooges went through various incarnations. The original members of the group were the Horwitz (Howard) brothers, "Moe" (Harry Moses, 1897–1975), "Shemp" (Samuel, 1895–1955), and long-time friend Larry Fine (Louis Feinberg, 1902–1975). In 1932, Shemp was replaced in the act by the third Horwitz brother, "Curly Joe" (Jerome Lester, 1903–1952). When Joe suffered a stroke in 1946,

Shemp rejoined the act and remained with the group until his death.

In 1930, Ted Healy and His Stooges appeared in their first Hollywood feature film, *Soup to Nuts.* After parting company with Healy, the Stooges signed a contract with Columbia Motion Pictures, for whom they were to make 190 one- and two-reel films over a 23-year period. Each "short" contained a simple plot line in which the threesome, with Moe as the putative "brains," would engage in rough physical humor, generally including eye-gouging, face-slapping, and assorted acts of comedic mayhem. The Stooges also made a handful of full-length films in the 1950s.

In 1959, Columbia syndicated the entire Stooge library to television, thus introducing them to the new generation of Baby Boomers. Through their syndicated television shorts, the Stooges' success continued well on into the 1970s. Throughout their long career, Moe acted as the group's main creative force and business manager. In later Stooge incarnations, vaudeville veterans Joe Besser and "Curly Joe" DeRita would join the group.

In 2000, long-time fan Mel Gibson produced a television movie about the Stooges, starring Paul Ben-Victor as Moe, Evan Handler as Larry, John Kassir as Shemp, and Michael Chiklis as Curly.

Generations of fans will long remember the Stooge routines and catch phrases, including: "Nyuk Nyuk Nyuk!" (Curly laughing); "I'll murderize ya!" and "Soitenly!" (Curly); and "I'm sorry Moe, it was an accident!" (Larry).

Kurt F. Stone

Further Reading: Cox, Steve, and Jim Perry. *One Fine Stooge: A Frizzy Life in Pictures*. Cumberland House Publishing, 2006. Howard, Moe. *Moe Howard and the Three Stooges*. Citadel Press, 1977.

TIN PAN ALLEY

Tin Pan Alley was the name of a center of music publishers and songwriters located in Manhattan between Broadway and Sixth Avenue in West 27th–28th Streets. The name came to that group of musicians possibly because they made a racket that sounded like the banging of tin pans. Early in the nineteenth century, songwriters were seldom rewarded for their efforts, since copyright was poorly regulated in the United States. Publishers printed their own versions of popular songs without compensating the composer. As copyright laws were enforced toward the end of the nineteenth century, composers, lyricists, and publishers worked together for their mutual protection.

Songwriters came to Tin Pan Alley to sell their songs. At times, the more successful songwriters like **Irving Berlin** were put on staff of the music publishing firms. The "Song pluggers" were the musicians and singers who demonstrated the songs in order to stimulate the sale of the sheet music.

ASCAP, the American Society of Composers, Authors and Publishers, was established in 1914 to assist and protect composers and publishers. By 1919 more than 90 percent of the sheet music and phonograph records sold in America paid royalties to ASCAP. The leading Tin Pan Alley composers included Irving Berlin, Irving Caesar, Hogy Carmichael, George M. Cohan, Buddy deSylva, Dorothy Fields, Ira and **George Gershwin**, Gus Kahn, Jerome Kern, Harry von Tilzer, Fats Waller, and Vincent Youmans. Among the hits published through Tin Pan Alley firms were "After the Ball," "The Man Who Broke the Bank at Monte Carlo," "The Sidewalks of New York," "The Band Played On," "A Hot Time in the Old Town Tonight," "Only a Bird in a Gilded Cage," "Bill Bailey, Won't You Please Come Home," "In the Good Old Summertime," "Give My Regards to Broadway," "Shine on Harvest Moon," "Take Me Out to the Ball Game," "By the Light of the Silvery Moon," "Down by the Old Mill Stream," "Let Me Call You Sweetheart," "Alexander's Ragtime Band," "Peg o' My Heart," "God Bless America," "Swanee," "All Alone," and "Baby Face."*See also* **Popular Music**.

Herbert M. Druks

Further Reading: Forte, Allen. *Listening to Classic American Popular Songs.* New Haven, CT: Yale

University Press, 2001. Tawa, Nicholas E. *The Way to Tin Pan Alley: American Popular Song, 1866–1910.* New York: Schirmer Books, 1990.

TODD, MIKE (1909–1958)

Mike Todd, a film and theater producer, was born Avrom Hirsch Goldbogen in Minneapolis, Minnesota on June 22, 1909. Todd was one of Rabbi Chaim and Sophia Hellman Goldbogen's nine children. The family moved to Chicago, where Todd was expelled from sixth grade, allegedly for running a crap game inside the school. In high school he had his first taste of theatrical success, when his production of *The Mikado* proved to be a hit. Todd left school before graduation and went into the construction business, where he made—and then lost—a fortune.

In the 1930s and 1940s, Todd turned his attention to Broadway, where he produced some 30 shows, including a musical version of *Around the World in Eighty Days,* featuring a Cole Porter score and a cast headed by the young Orson Welles. In 1950, Todd, along with broadcaster Lowell Thomas and inventor Fred Wallis, formed the Cinerama Company. "Cinerama," a process invented by Wallis, used three film projectors to create a giant image on a curved screen. Todd's company scored an immediate hit with the 1952 film *This Is Cinerama.* Trying to correct some of Cinerama's minor technical flaws, Todd, in conjunction with the American Optical Company, created and patented a new system called "Todd-AO." The process was first used in the 1955 film *Oklahoma!* In 1958, Todd produced *Around the World in Eighty Days.* The film earned Todd both an Academy Award and a fortune.

Mike Todd was married three times. At age 17, he married Bertha Freshman. The couple had a son, Mike Todd Jr. Freshman died under mysterious circumstances in 1946. The next year Todd married movie actress Joan Blondell. They divorced in 1950. Seven years later, Todd married actress Elizabeth Taylor. The couple had a daughter, Liza, in August of 1957.

On March 22, 1958, Todd's private plane, *Lucky Liz,* crashed in New Mexico, killing everyone on board. Todd, 49, was survived by his wife, his son, Mike Jr., and his daughter, Liza Todd Burton. *See also* **Film**.

Kurt F. Stone

Further Reading: Cohen, Art. *The Nine Lives of Mike Todd.* London: Hutchinson, 1958.

TOKLAS, ALICE B. (1877–1977)

Alice Babette Toklas, Gertrude Stein's life partner, was born into a middle-class Jewish family in San Francisco. Toklas was educated in both San Francisco and Seattle and briefly studied music at the University of Washington. In 1907, Toklas's life changed forever when, at the suggestion of art critic Leo Stein (1872–1947), she moved to Paris, where she met Stein's sister, Gertrude Stein (1874–1946). Shortly thereafter, Toklas and Stein (Toklas referred to Stein as "Lovey" and Stein referred to Alice as "Pussy") moved into an apartment in the Rue de Fleurus. They continued living together until Stein's death in 1946. The two turned their apartment into one of the era's best-known literary salons, hosting writers such as Hemingway and Wilder and avant-garde painters like Picasso and Matisse. Friends from this "Lost Generation" described Toklas as "a chain smoker with a slight moustache, Gypsy earrings and manicured nails" (The *Time* 100, 2003).

In her memoirs, Toklas described the young Stein: "She was a golden brown presence, burned by the Tuscan sun and with a golden glint in her warm brown hair" (Mellow, 1974). Not only a lover and confidante, Toklas acted as cook, secretary, muse, and editor for Stein. In 1933, Stein published her autobiography—the ironically titled *I Love You Alice B. Toklas.* In it, Stein records Toklas's first-person observations of Stein's life and all the people who flocked to their Paris salon.

A gourmet cook, Toklas published *The Alice B. Toklas Cookbook* in 1954. Despite its containing more than 300 recipes, only one is remembered:

"Haschich [*sic*] Fudge." Toklas was immortalized in the 1968 Peter Sellers's movie *I Love You Alice B. Toklas,* in which her cannabis brownies played a significant role.

Toklas and Stein remained in Paris during World War II, where, living under the protection of Marshall Philippe Pétain, they managed to escape persecution. Stein died in 1946. Toklas, who lived another 31 years, died in poverty and obscurity. Shortly before her death, Toklas converted to Catholicism, in the hopes of "meeting Gertrude in heaven." The two are buried side-by-side in Père Lachaise Cemetery in Paris.

Kurt F. Stone

Further Reading: "The *Time* 100: Heroes and Icons." *Time* 2003. Accessed September 8, 2008. www.time.com/time/time100/heroes/romances/romances2.html. Mellow, J. R. *Charmed Circle: Gertrude Stein & Company.* New York: Avon, 1974, reprint 1991. Toklas, Alice B. *Staying on Alone; Letters of Alice B. Toklas.* New York: Liveright, 1973. ———. *What is Remembered.* New York: Holt, Rinehart, and Winston, 1963.

TOYS AND GAMES

According to Pamela B. Nelson, "Toys, like other artifacts of material culture, can tell us a great deal about changing cultural attitudes and values, and about the exercise of power in society." Nelson uses this hypothesis as a point of departure for her essay "Toys as History: Ethnic Images and Cultural Change," an examination of how toys reflected popular attitudes in this country towards ethnic and racial groups since the Civil War. In analyzing the toy production during those decades Nelson found a paucity of "Jewish and Italian-American images."

This absence she found surprising given stereotypes of those groups found in other segments of popular culture. Nelson rationalizes this discrepancy by citing folklorist Henry Glassie's insistence that cultural historians need to embrace "confusion, contradiction, and complexity" when analyzing the past. A fact which Nelson does not consider is the prominent role which Jewish Americans have and continue to play in the toy industry since the Civil War.

One measure of the preeminence and extraordinary contributions of Jewish Americans to the toy industry is their presence among the inductees of the Toy Industry Hall of Fame. Since 1985 the toy industry has honored 55 entrepreneurs for their contributions to the field. Among the Jewish honorees are:

Louis Marx (1896–1982)
Merrill L. Hassenfeld (1918–1979)
Joshua Lionel Cowen (1877–1965)
Benjamin F. Michtom (1901–1980)
Ruth Handler (1916–2002)
Elliot Handler (1938–2002)
Stephen D. Hassenfeld (1942–1989)
Alan G. Hassenfeld (1948–)
Beatrice Alexander Behrman (1895–1990)
Albert Steiner (1895–1977)

The above named represent an incomplete list of the Jewish Americans recognized for their contributions to the toy industry but are representative of a significant development in that industry. The era of scientific innovation and industrial expansion that followed the Civil War had a tremendous impact on the manufacturing of toys. Mass production and the growth of industrial complexes facilitated the growth of a toy industry and signaled the end of the era of the individual craftsman and cottage industry.

In age that prided itself on the seemingly endless march of progress due to scientific innovation, it is interesting that William Fuld (1870–1927), the third child of Jacob and Mary Abell Fuld, should achieve success and wealth capitalizing on the irrationality that coexisted as a substratum in an age of science and reason. Jacob Fuld had emigrated to the United States from Germany in 1854 and married Mary Abell, a resident of York, Pennsylvania. William, their 3rd of 10 children, was born and reared in Baltimore, Maryland.

His parents had apparently abandoned Judaism in the 1880s when they joined Baltimore's Franklin Street Presbyterian Church. William joined the same church in 1894. After attending public school and the Maryland Institute for the Promotion of the Mechanic Arts/Schools of Art and Design, Fuld found employment as painter/varnisher in 1887. He later joined the Kennard Novelty Company (est. 1890), the company usually credited with manufacturing the first Ouija boards, a favored device of the spiritualism movement in the United States at the end of the nineteenth century. Fuld moved up the ranks in the company quite rapidly. In 1892 he received a patent for improvements on the board and soon became the principal manufacturer of the "talking boards."

In November 1897 Fuld and his brother Isaac created Isaac Fuld & Brother. By 1901 the brothers separated and began a feud that was not settled until their grandchildren reached a settlement in 1997. While running his company, William Fuld not only got his own Ouija board trademark, Oracle, in 1902 but also manufactured pool tables, sandboxes, pails, dart boards, doll furniture, and many parlor games. Not just a successful businessman, William Fuld also led a full life of civic engagement.

He became a Freemason, a democratic representative to the Maryland House of Delegates, and a member of the groups representing toy manufacturers and retailers on the local and national levels. A measure of his success was the continual expansion of his business, necessitating the construction of a three-story, 36,000 square foot factory in 1918 at the cost of $125,000. After his death in a tragic accident, his son William managed the business until it was sold in 1966 to Parker Brothers.

William Fuld's career is paradigmatic for the development of toy manufacturing in the twentieth century, which brought the creation of dynastic family enterprises and multinational corporate giants built on toy and game invention, manufacture, and marketing. Louis Marx (1896–1982) followed the same path as Fuld before him. Born in Brooklyn to German Jewish immigrants, Marx joined the company of Ferdinand Strauss, a manufacturer of mechanical toys. By the age of 20 Marx was managing one of Strauss's plants in East Rutherford, New Jersey but was soon fired because of management differences. After serving in the army during World War I he returned to civilian life to find employment with a manufacturer of wooden toys and began a successful career in manufacturing.

In 1919 Marx and his brother created Louis Marx and Company, and through shrewd business tactics they made themselves millionaires by 1922. The Marx Company utilized mass production techniques and recycled old toy designs. In this way they made a fortune redesigning existing toys and games such as the yo-yo. The company was really successful manufacturing and retailing tinplate buildings, toy soldiers, play sets, toy dinosaurs, mechanical toys, toy guns, action figures, dolls, dollhouses, and toy cars and trains. Their hallmark was the creation of quality at a reasonable price. This formula helped the company stay profitable even during the Great Depression, and at its peak in the 1950s, annual sales exceeded $50 million, making it allegedly the largest toy company in the world. Because of his stature as a "toycoon" and the "Henry Ford of the toy industry" Louis Marx was the initial inductee into the Toy Industry Hall of Fame in 1955.

Failure to invest in research on new toy development or marketing led to the Marx Company's decline, and in 1972 it was sold to Quaker Oats Company for $54 million. These strategic errors were avoided by a family-owned business that is one of today's largest toy manufacturers, Hasbro. Founded in 1923 by Henry and Helal Hassenfeld, Jewish immigrants from Poland, the company grew from modest beginnings as a retailer of textile remnants and manufacturer of pencil boxes and supplies to become an industry giant with annual net revenue in 1990 of $1.3 billion. The significance of the company is visible in the honoring of a son and two grandsons of Henry Hassenfeld in the Toy Industry Hall of Fame. Stephen, the most successful of this triumvirate, not only increased the company's profitability 85 percent annually from 1980 to 1986, he was also a noted philanthropist who created a charitable trust and two foundations concerned with the health issues of children, higher education, volunteerism, and special community projects.

The chief competitor of Hasbro is also represented in the hall of fame in the personages of Ruth and Elliot Handler. In 1945 Elliot Handler and his partner, Harold "Matt" Matson created a company to manufacture picture frames, which they named by joining parts of their names: "Matt-El" = "Mattel." From that simple beginning the company evolved into a manufacturer and retailer of dollhouse furniture, until Handler's wife Ruth discovered the German Bild Lilli doll during a trip to Europe. Although intended for adults, the doll was transformed by Ruth Handler, renamed, and debuted at the New York Toy Fair in 1959 as "Barbie." The road to fame beckoned. Television advertising helped smooth that path: the Handlers advertised on the *Mickey Mouse Show* and helped define children's taste in toys for an entire generation. Even though the Handlers resigned from the company under a cloud in 1975, Mattel continued to grow and in 2005 was the largest toy manufacturer in the world in terms of revenue ($5.179 billion), derived from a production line that included over 80 dolls, 18 games, and several video game consoles and handheld electronic games. The company has not been immune to controversy and is currently embroiled in the problems surrounding the importation of toys from China.

Three other honorees in the Toy Industry Hall of Fame that are noteworthy are Joshua Lionel Cowen, Benjamin Michtom, and Beatrice Alexander Behrman. Cowen was born in 1877 as Joshua Lionel Cohen, the son of Jewish immigrants. The spelling change of his name may have been an attempt to ease his acculturation into American society. Although a college dropout, he was a gifted inventor, receiving his first patent in 1899. He is also credited with inventing the flashlight as a device to illuminate flowerpots. But when he had no success marketing it, Cowen sold the patent to Conrad Hubert, who sold it minus the flowerpot and became a multimillionaire. Also in 1899 Cowen became a defense contractor charged with manufacturing mine fuses. In 1900 he founded the Lionel Corporation with a friend and began manufacturing toy trains. He had made his first train as a child and, after trying to use the train as an advertising mechanism for other products, discovered that it was a success all by itself. After 1902 the company concentrated on the manufacture of the toy trains which became synonymous with little boys and Christmas. Cowen retired in 1959 and sold his shares in the company to his great-nephew Roy Cohn, the flamboyant lawyer associated with Senator Joseph McCarthy.

Benjamin Michtom was inducted into the Toy Industry Hall of Fame in 1989 because of his success as a toy promoter; his licensing deals propelled the Ideal Toy Company to the forefront of the industry. His parents, Rose and Morris Michtom, founded the Ideal Toy Company. Inspired by a cartoon drawn by Clifford Berryman depicting Teddy Roosevelt's hunting trip to Louisiana, Morris created the teddy bear in 1903. The success of the toy encouraged the Michtoms to create the Ideal Novelty and Toy Company in 1907. The name was changed in 1938 to Ideal Toy Company. Morris Michtom, a refugee from the pogroms in Russia, apparently never forgot his roots. He and his wife supported the Hebrew Immigrant Aid Society, the Jewish National Fund, and the National Labor Campaign for Palestine as well as other Jewish enterprises. The teddy bear is, of course, an international icon and enjoys a spot in the Smithsonian among other American cultural artifacts.

Beatrice Alexander Behrman (1895–1990) was inducted into the Toy Hall of Fame in 2000 because of her extraordinary achievements in the manufacturing of dolls. Her mother was also a refugee from the Russian pogroms and arrived in New York in 1895 already bearing Beatrice, whose biological father had been killed in Europe. Her mother married Maurice Alexander, who operated a doll hospital. Alexander relied heavily on German sources for the dolls that he repaired and apparently resold. The Allied embargo of

Germany during World War I threatened his business, so Beatrice and her sisters launched a doll-making enterprise that substituted cloth for the porcelain her stepfather had used. During the 1920s Beatrice Alexander (she had married Phillip Behrman ca. 1914) not only expanded her doll manufacturing business, she also became involved in politics, joining the Women's League for Palestine in 1920.

In 1923 the Alexander Doll Company was founded in Harlem (New York City) and began to create a series of dolls that included Alice in Wonderland, Little Women, 3 Little Pigs, Scarlett O'Hara, and Snow White. These were composition dolls with painted-on features. In the 1940s the company switched materials and started manufacturing dolls from plastic. Among "Madame" Alexander's achievements were four Fashion Academy Gold Medal Awards for doll design (1951–1954). In 1955, four years before the appearance of Barbie, the Alexander Doll Company produced "Cissy," described as the "first full-figured, high-heeled fashion doll." In 1981 Beatrice Alexander Behrman received the Distinguished Public Service Award form the Anti-Defamation League. Her highest accolade came perhaps from the industry in which she worked. The Toy Hall of Fame cited her as "the premier American doll maker of the 20th Century."

An individual not recognized (as yet) by the Toy Hall of Fame is Ralph H. Baer (1922–). A refugee from Nazi Germany just before Kristallnacht, Baer was largely self-taught. He graduated from the National Radio Institute as a radio service technician in 1940 and was drafted in World War II, when he served in military intelligence. After the war he received one of the early bachelor of science degrees in television engineering (1949) from the American Television Institute of Technology in Chicago. He worked for several electronic firms, started his own company, and then ultimately joined Sanders Associates, a defense-electronics company, in 1958, where he remained until his retirement in 1987. During his fruitful career as an inventor he is credited with being the creator of the first video game.

For Sanders Associates he developed the "Brown Box" console video system, which was licensed to Magnavox in 1971 and renamed Magnavox Odyssey. The console went public in 1972 and was quite successful. Baer also created the first light gun and game for home use, known as "Shooting Gallery," and also developed "Simon," an electronic game that was quite popular in the 1970s. For his achievements Baer received a Legend Award at the 2005 video game show G-Phoria, and in 2006 President Bush gave him a National Medal of Technology for his "groundbreaking and pioneering creation, development and commercialization of interactive video games." He also received two other prestigious international awards in 2008. In 2006 Baer donated all his prototypes and documents to the Smithsonian.

Additional contributions to the toy industry made by Jews would include the G.I. Joe action toys, which were invented by Hasbro's Stan Weston and Larry Reiner in 1964. There was also independent toy inventor Marvin Glass (1914–1974), whose design studio introduced more than 50 plastic toys and games to the marketplace between 1962 and 1972. Toy inventor Richard C. Levy developed original concepts for 25 years. His 125-plus licensed products include one of the most successful toys of all time, the Furby. His games include Men Are from Mars, Women Are from Venus; Route 66; and Family Reunion. He has created premiums for Procter and Gamble (Crest) and General Foods (Pebbles and Puddin' Pops). Ronald O. Wingartner is a former vice president for inventor relations at Hasbro Games. His product development and marketing involvement have spanned preschool items to computer software. Together, Levy and Weingartner authored *The Toy and Game Inventor's Handbook,* where they estimate that more than half of the 80 leading contemporary American toy inventors are Jewish.

Clearly Jewish Americans have made far-reaching contributions in the field of toy and game manufacturing. It would be difficult to imagine the industry existing as it does today without the contributions of the individuals described above. A common thread in their stories is the successful transfer from one culture and the successful adaptation to American culture. Many Jewish American toy and game manufacturers came either directly or indirectly to this country to flee oppression in Europe and eventually helped shaped the popular culture of the new homeland. One interesting story is that of Mah-jong. According to tradition the game dates back to Confucius, but it did not become popular in this country until the 1920s when American popular culture was in the midst of a phase of "Orientalism" that featured the halt of Chinese immigration, anti-miscegenation laws applied to the Chinese residing in the United States, and the denial of citizenship to Chinese living here (the notable exception to this anti-Chinese sentiment was the popularity of fictional Chinese American detective Charlie Chan).

It is a clear manifestation of the complexity and contradiction which Henry Glassie posits in cultural history that this quintessential Asian game should be considered a "Jewish" game in its American incarnation. The National Mah Jongg League was reported founded by Jewish players in 1937, and many current players and members of the organization are also Jewish. Also to further complicate the image of this cultural artifact there is the **Eddie Cantor** song from the 1920s "Since Ma is Playing Mah Jong" which is extensively quoted on the web site of the German Mah-Jongg Liga (DMJL) e.V. The text combines racist and humorous touches to reflect as toy and games often do, popular attitudes and antipathies to racial and ethnic groups.

Leroy T. Hopkins Jr.

Further Reading: Ralph H. Baer, http://en.wikipedia.org/wiki/Ralph_H._Baer. Deutsche mah-jongg Liga. Mah Jongg Museum, http://www.mah-jongg-museum.de/musik_001.html. William Fuld, www.williamfuld.com/biography.html. Handler, Ruth. *Dream Girl: The Ruth Handler Story.* Longmeadow Press, 1994. Jewish Heroes and Heroines in America from 1900 to WW II: A Judaica Collection Exhibit at Florida Atlantic University: Seymour Brody, "'Madame' Beatrice Alexander: The First Lady of Dolls," http://www.fau.edu/library/bro62a.htm. Jewish Virtual Library, http://www.jewishvirtuallibrary.org/jsource/biography/Michtoms.html. Levy, Richard, and Ronald O. Weingartner. *The Toy and Game Inventor's Handbook.* Alpha Books, 2003. Nelson, Pamela B. "Toys as History: Ethnic Images and Cultural Change." Balch Institute for Ethnic Studies of the Historical Society of Pennsylvania, http://www.ferris.edu/news/jimcrow/link/toys. O'Brien, Richard. *The Story of American Toys.* New York: Abbeville Press, 1990. Toy Industry Hall of Fame. http://www.toyassociation.org/AM/Template.cfm?Section=Hall_of_Fame.

TRILLING, LIONEL (1905–1975)

Lionel Trilling was a renowned teacher, a writer of international stature, and one of the foremost literary critics of the twentieth century. Trilling focused on the influence that culture and history had upon authors and the literature they produced and, in turn, how these earlier writers and works affected the next generation of authors and their writings. By concentrating their efforts on these influences, Trilling and other members of the famed group known as the New York Intellectuals, most of whose members were Jews, emphasized the social and political effects of literature. A liberal humanist, Trilling explored the psychology, sociology, and philosophy of authors and their works' ability to affect the dimensions of the morality and conventions of the culture. Trilling was born July 4, 1905, in Queens, New York, to Jewish immigrants David, a tailor and furrier, and Fannie (Cohen) Trilling. A 1921 graduate of DeWitt Clinton High School, he enrolled in Columbia University at 16, graduated in 1925, and received his master's degree the following year. In 1929, Trilling married writer and cultural critic Diana Rubin (1905–1996); their son, James, was born in 1947. While still an undergraduate at Columbia, Trilling had contributed material to the *Menorah Journal,* a magazine of Jewish thought, and worked as an assistant editor at the publication in 1930. After teaching at the University of Wisconsin–Madison and at Hunter College, he returned to Columbia as an instructor in the English department in 1932, continuing what became a lifelong association with the university. In 1936, Trilling received the news that his appointment at the university was to be terminated; a spokesman for the English department attributed the reason to the supposition that as "as a Freudian, a Marxist, and a Jew," Trilling would be "more comfortable" at another institution. It was only by the intervention of Columbia president Nicholas Murray Butler that Trilling's position was secured.

In 1939, at a president's dinner held to honor publication of Trilling's book on the English poet and critic Matthew Arnold, which was the outgrowth of his PhD dissertation, Butler made it clear that Trilling would be appointed a permanent member of the staff, thus making him the first Jew to receive tenure in the Department of English at Columbia and, indeed, at any Ivy League university. Diana Trilling wrote about these incidents against the background of her husband's family origins in "Lionel Trilling, a Jew at Columbia" in the March 1979 issue of *Commentary* magazine.

Trilling was made an associate professor in 1945 and a full professor in 1948, was named the George Edward Woodberry Professor of Literature and Criticism in 1965, and achieved the institution's highest honor by becoming a university professor in 1970. Trilling was regarded as an iconoclastic, gifted, and devoted teacher; he was particularly popular as the teacher, in partnership for 30-plus years with Jacques Barzun, of the Colloquium on Important Books. Among his students were **Allen Ginsberg** and Norman Podhoretz.

In 1937, Trilling had joined the staff of the Marxist, anti-Stalinist journal *Partisan Review.* The New York Intellectuals, including, among others, Diana Trilling, **Alfred Kazin**, Delmore Schwartz, William Phillips, Clement Greenberg, Harold Rosenberg, Dwight Macdonald, and Mary McCarthy, were closely associated with the magazine.

Trilling wrote one critically successful novel, *The Middle of the Journey* (1947), as well as short stories but was best known for his critical essays on literary works and figures. He published his first collection of essays, *The Liberal Imagination* (1950). Among his other notable works are *The Opposing Self* (1955), *Freud and the Crisis of Our Culture* (1955), *A Gathering of Fugitives* (1956), *Beyond Culture* (1965), and *Sincerity and Authenticity* (1972). *Of This Time, Of That Place and Other Stories,* a collection published four years after his death, included five of his most highly regarded stories, among them "Impediments" and "Notes on a Departure," which were originally published in the *Menorah Journal* in the 1920s. In 1951, Trilling became a member of the National Institute of Arts and Letters and a fellow of the Academy of Arts and Letters. He was the first recipient, in 1972, of the Thomas Jefferson Award in the Humanities. In his studies, covering figures ranging from Jane Austen to E. M. Forster, Tolstoy to **Freud**, he outlined his view that "the primary function of art and thought is to liberate the individual from the tyranny of his culture in the environmental sense and to permit him to stand beyond it in an autonomy of perception and judgment" (Trilling, 1979).

Trilling said, "Being a Jew is like walking in the wind or swimming: you are touched at all points and conscious everywhere" (ibid.) Trilling died on November 5, 1975, in New York City. *See also* **Kazin, Alfred**; **Literature**.

Abby Meth Kanter

Further Reading: Bloom, Alexander. *Prodigal Sons: The New York Intellectuals & Their World.* Oxford University Press, 1986. Krupnick, Mark. *Lionel Trilling and the Fate of Cultural Criticism.* Northwestern University Press, 1986. Trilling, Diana. *Beginning of the Journey.* Harcourt Brace, 1993. Trilling, Lionel. *Beyond Culture: Essays on Literature and Learning.* New York: Viking Press, 1979.

TUCHMAN, BARBARA (1912–1989)

Although she was not trained as a professional historian and did not earn a PhD, Ms. Tuchman won two Pulitzer Prizes for works on military history and served as president of the Society of

American Historians (1970–1973). Her 11 eleven books were praised for their readable style, lucidness, and scholarly research. For her epic account of World War I in *The Guns of August* (1962), Tuchman retraced the battlefields of the Western Front as she followed the advance of the German armies making their way to Paris through Belgium and northern France in a war she considered senseless. In *The Proud Tower: A Portrait of the World Before the War, 1890–1914* (1966), Tuchman covered the rise of U.S. imperialism, socialism, and communism and the passing of the nineteenth-century old order in Europe and North America. In another highly praised work, Tuchman traced the history of warfare in *The March of Folly: From Troy to Vietnam* (1968). For her biography, *Stillwell and the American Experience in China* (1970), she spent two years in China researching her project.

Tuchman was the daughter of a distinguished German Jewish family; her grandfather on her mother's side was Henry Morganthau Sr., Woodrow Wilson's ambassador to Turkey, whose son, Henry Morganthau Jr., was Franklin Delano Roosevelt's secretary of the treasury. Her father, Maurice Wertheim, was a banker, publisher of *The Nation* magazine, a philanthropist, founder of the Theatre Guild, and president of the American Jewish Committee. Tuchman's historical narratives evidenced her Jewish interests. *The Proud Tower* included accounts of the anti-Semitism leading up to the Dreyfus Trial in France. *The Distant Mirror* (1978) is a history of Europe in the fourteenth century, which includes sections dealing with the persecution of Jews and the false accusations of well-poisoning that led to mob violence against Jews during the Bubonic Plague.

Ms. Tuchman had an interest in Great Britain. Receiving a degree from Radcliffe (Harvard's school for women) in history, her honors thesis was *The Moral Justification for the British Empire.* Her book, *Bible and Sword, Relations between Britain and Palestine* (1956) revealed her sympathy for Zionism. Her first job as a reporter for her father's journal *The Nation* gave her access in the 1930s to the diplomacy of Europe, which led to her works on diplomatic and military subjects.

Tuchman told her audience that "the writer's object should be to hold the reader's attention. To obtain this, the narrative should not bog down with an overload of detail but encourage the reader to keep turning until the end" (Brody, 2006).

Philip Rosen

Further Reading: Brody, Seymour. "Jewish Heroes and Heroines in America 1900 to World War II." Florida Atlantic University Libraries, October 19, 2006. Accessed September 8, 2006. www.fau.edu/library/bro94.htm. Hyman, Paula E., and Deborah Dash Moore. "Barbara Tuchman. "*Jewish Women in America,* vol. II. Routledge, 1997.

TUCKER, SOPHIE

See **Jewish Women and Popular Culture**; **Popular Music**

TUROW, SCOTT (1949–)

Author and lawyer Scott Turow was born in Chicago on April 12, 1949. His father, an obstetrician, served as a field doctor during World War II. His father's accounts of his role in that war served as the basis for Turow's 2005 historical novel, *Ordinary Heroes.* Turow reveals his feelings about being Jewish in this novel and notes that among his wartime characters, the Jewish protagonist realizes the extent to which life is about race, religion, and history.

Turow attended New Trier High School and graduated from Amherst College in 1970. From 1971 to 1972, Turow was a fellow at the Stanford University Creative Writing Center, from which he received an MFA. From 1972 to 1975, he taught creative writing at Stanford. In 1975, he entered the Harvard Law School. Turow's first published work of nonfiction, *One-L,* was based on his first year in law school.

Upon receiving his Juris Doctor in 1978, Turow returned to Chicago, where he became an Assistant U.S. Attorney. Serving as prosecutor in several high-profile federal trials, Turow was lead counsel in Operation Greylord, a widely publicized FBI "sting" operation, in which 17 judges, 48 lawyers, 8 court officials, and 1 state legislator were indicted. Turow's work on the case provided background for his 1999 bestseller, *Personal Injuries. Time* magazine named the work "Best Fiction Novel of 1999." Turow was appointed to a panel by then-Illinois Governor George Ryan to study flaws in that state's capital punishment program. He turned that experience into his 2002 thriller *Reversible Errors,* which in turn became a 2004 made-for-television movie starring William H. Macy and Tom Selleck.

Despite his tremendous success as an author, Turow continues to practice law. He is a partner in the Chicago firm Sonnenschein, Nath & Rosenthal, where he takes most of his cases on a pro bono basis. In 1995, Turow won reversal in the murder conviction of a man who spent 11 years on death row for a crime another man confessed. Turow's books, translated into over 25 languages, have sold more than 25 million copies worldwide.

Scott and his former wife, artist Annette Turow, have three grown children.

Kurt F. Stone

Further Reading: Macdonald, Andrew F., and Gina Macdonald. *Scott Turow: A Critical Companion.* Greenwood Press, 2005.

U

UNITED STATES HOLOCAUST MEMORIAL MUSEUM

The United States Holocaust Memorial Museum is dedicated to advancing and disseminating knowledge about the Holocaust, preserving the memory of those who suffered, and encouraging visitors to reflect upon the questions raised by this tragedy. The museum serves as the United States' official memorial to the millions of European Jews and others killed during the Holocaust. Since its opening on April 22, 1993, the museum has welcomed more than 25 million visitors and reached millions more through numerous outreach programs.

Created by a unanimous act of Congress in 1980, the museum was built on federal land adjacent to the National Mall in Washington, D.C. Funding for its construction came from private donations. The museum is located on Raoul Wallenberg Place (formerly 15th Street), named for the Swedish diplomat believed to have saved tens of thousands of Jews in Hungary during World War II. The building was designed by James Ingo Freed (1930–2005) of the architectural firm Pei Cobb Freed & Partners. Freed fled Nazi Germany as a child in 1939.

The museum works to expand public understanding of the Holocaust and its history and serves as a venue for learning, remembrance, and reflection. Using text, photos, maps, film, and artifacts, the museum's permanent exhibition, the Holocaust, tells the history of the systematic murder of millions of Jews and other victims by the Nazis and their allies during World War II. At the exit of the permanent exhibition, the Hall of Remembrance provides a space for quiet reflection. A second permanent exhibit, Remember the Children: Daniel's Story, is a presentation geared for children. Several temporary exhibition spaces allow the museum to mount short-term in-depth exhibits relevant to the Holocaust. The Wexner Learning Center offers resources that encourage contemplation of connections of this history to today's world. Also included in the museum is a library of more than 72,000 items in 55 languages, as well as an archive with more than 42 million pages of documents, 77,000 photographs, 9,000 oral histories, and 985 hours of historical footage.

Education is a key element of the mission, and the museum runs extensive programs both on-site and through outreach for students and educators, law enforcement officials and the military, and college students, graduate researchers, and professors in the United States and abroad. The museum's Center for Advanced Holocaust Studies is a primary venue for Holocaust scholarship, promoting research and support for scholars of the Holocaust in all disciplines and at all career stages. As a memorial to the Holocaust, the museum's Committee on Conscience also strives to prevent genocide in the future. Through its web site (www.ushmm.org) the Museum reaches both national and international audiences, providing information about the Holocaust in several languages. *See also* **The Holocaust in American Culture**.

Aleisa Fishman

Further Reading: Berenbaum, Michael. *The World Must Know: The History of the Holocaust As Told in the United States Holocaust Memorial Museum.* New York: Little, Brown and Company, 1993. Ochsner, Jeffrey Karl. "Understanding the Holocaust through the U.S. Holocaust Memorial Museum." *JAE: Journal of Architectural Education* 48 (May 1995): 240–249.

URIS, LEON (1924–2003)

Bestselling novelist Leon Uris was born in Baltimore, Maryland, to Wolf William Uris, a shopkeeper, and Anna Blumberg. Both parents were Jews of Russian Polish origin. His father, an immigrant from Poland, had spent a year in Palestine after World War I and derived his surname from Yerushalmi, meaning "man of Jerusalem."

Uris grew up in Norfolk, Virginia. He was undersized as well as an asthmatic and once said that "I used to think of myself as a sad little Jewish boy." He was not a particularly good student, having failed English three times in high school, but he was determined to become a writer. Uris never completed high school because following the Japanese attack on Pearl Harbor he enlisted in the U.S. Marine Corps. He left school halfway during his senior year and served as a radio operator in the campaigns on Guadalcanal and Tarawa. His wartime service provided him with the material for his first successful novel, *Battle Cry,* which he based on his Marine experience. Warner Brothers bought the rights to the bestselling novel, and Uris moved to Hollywood to write the screenplay for the movie, which was released in 1955.

Alternating between writing novels and writing for Hollywood, Uris wrote his second novel, *The Angry Hills* (1955), which was about a member of the British Army's Palestine Brigade during World War II, and wrote the screenplay for the film *Gunfight at the O.K. Corral* (1957). His second novel, ***Exodus*** (1958), an epic 600-page story of the Jewish struggle to establish the State of Israel, became a bestseller and was made into a blockbuster film in 1960. Initially, Uris worked on the screenplay but clashed with Otto Preminger, the film's producer, who proceeded to engage the blacklisted writer Dalton Trumbo to write the screenplay for the movie.

Exodus, which was published by Doubleday, was subsequently translated into several dozen languages, and more than any other literary work it engaged the sympathy of the American public for the State of Israel. As the critic Sanford Pinsker has written of Uris, "The mythic Israel he presented is still the mythic Israel in the heads of American Jews" (Ephross, 2003). Continuing to write about themes dealing with contemporary Jewish history, Uris's third novel, *Mila 18* (1961), chronicled the Warsaw Ghetto uprising. The novel was so successful that **Joseph Heller** reportedly changed the name of his novel from "Catch-18" to *Catch-22.* Other novels dealing with the contemporary Jewish experience include *The Haj* (1984), which tells about the birth of Israel from the view of a Palestinian; *The Mitla Pass* (1988), which deals with the Suez Canal Crisis that led to the Suez War of 1956, which saw Israel allied with France and Great Britain against Egypt; and *QBVII* (1970), a fictionalized account of a lawsuit filed against Uris by a Polish doctor, Wladislaw Dering, who was named in *Exodus* as someone who committed atrocities against inmates in Auschwitz. The novel's title refers to the Queen's Bench Courtroom No. 7, where the fictional trial takes place. The novel was later made into a movie for television (1974). The rest of Uris's work includes *Armageddon* (1964); *Topaz* (1967); *Trinity,* about Ireland's struggle for independence (1976); *Redemption,* a sequel to *Trinity* (1995); and *A God in Ruins* (1999), the story of an Irish Catholic presidential candidate who turns out to be Jewish. His last book, *O'Hara's Choice,* is a love story involving the history of the Marines (2003). A popular writer, he was never recognized by the literary critics as being in the same class as **Saul Bellow**, **Bernard Malamud**, or **Philip Roth**. But with regard to his contribution to American Jewish fiction, Uris, along with **Chaim Potok** and **Herman Wouk**, made important contributions to the popular culture in his representation of the Jewish experience to the overall American public. Uris was married three times and had five children. *See also* ***Exodus***; **Film**.

Jack R. Fischel

Further Reading: Ephross, Peter. "Leon Uris Dies—Created 'Mythic Israel' for Generations." *Jewish Telegraphic Agency,* June 27, 2003. Accessed September 4, 2008. www.jewishsf.com/content/2-0-/module/displaystory/story_id/20596/edition_id/421/format/html/displaystory.html. "Leon Uris Biography," at nytimes.com.

V

VAN BUREN, ABIGAIL (1918–)

Abigail Van Buren (Pauline Esther Friedman), the notable advice columnist, was born in Sioux City, Iowa, 17 minutes after her twin, Esther Pauline, the future advice columnist Ann Landers. Their parents, Abraham and Rebecca Rushall Friedman, were Russian immigrants. Abraham was co-owner of a burlesque house. Pauline and Esther, nicknamed respectively "Popo" and "Effie," were so close that they even had a joint wedding in 1939. "Abby" married Morton Phillips, heir to a Midwestern liquor fortune; sister "Ann" married Julius Lederer, founder of Budget Rent-a-Car. Both of the twins attended Morningside College in Sioux City.

Pauline Friedman had never written professionally until 1956, when, at age 38, she contacted the editor of the *San Francisco Chronicle,* informing him that she could write a better advice column than the one he was employing. Granted an interview and asked to prepare several trial columns, Friedman got the job. She soon took to using the name "Abigail Van Buren," taking the name "Abigail" from the Hebrew Bible and "Van Buren" from America's eighth president. Friedman claimed that she took the latter name because of its "aristocratic old-family ring."

Her "Dear Abby" column was an immediate success. Doling out advice on subjects ranging from raising teenagers, to sex, and to how to respond to social slights, "Dear Abby" eventually became the most widely-read syndicated column in the world. One mark of her popularity came the day after the 1964 presidential election, when cartoonist Bill Mauldin ran a sketch of Senator Barry Goldwater on the phone. The caption read: "Dear Abby . . ."

Competition between the twins led to years of estrangement. The two reconciled shortly before Esther's death in 2002.

With the onset of Alzheimer's Disease in the 1990s, Van Buren ceased writing her column. It was taken over by her only child, daughter Jeanne Phillips, who lives in Beverly Hills, California. *See also* **Popular Psychology**.

Kurt F. Stone

Further Reading: Heinze, Andrew R. *Jews and the American Soul.* Princeton: Princeton University Press, 2004.

VAUDEVILLE

The Yiddish word "shtick" literally means a piece or bit of something; it comes from the Old High German word "stukki," the word for a crust or fragment. But when we think of "shtick," we usually think of a comedian's gimmick, his or her unique way of stealing the limelight. If nowadays we are each said to have our own "shtick," our own particular brand of craziness or originality, then we have the Jewish vaudeville entertainers of the early twentieth century to thank for making shtick a style of performance and a way in which we look at the world.

Vaudeville, "from the Old French words Val-de-Vire, the valley in Normandy after which the fifteenth century poet Olivier Basselin named his lively drinking tunes" (Slide, 1994), became a catchall term for a mix of entertainment that embraced everything from "racial" comedy (including, most notably, the blackface minstrel show) to variety shows, animal acts, and burlesque. It was the primary form of theatrical entertainment in late nineteenth- and early twentieth-century America, and it often mined humor from widespread anxieties about immigration and cultural mixing. African Americans and non-British immigrants were believed to be unraveling the nation's social fabric; these fears led to deprecating and denigrating them in popular culture.

Jewish immigrants in particular were the butt of humor from so-called "Hebrew" comics (since Jews were often referred to as "Hebrews" or "Hebes"), who dressed in long black coats, with black derby hats pulled over the ears, crepe beards, and putty ("Jew clay") noses. By speaking in a pseudo-**Yiddish** dialect, gesticulating wildly, and raving about money, these comics helped to stereotype Jews as ridiculously dressed, uncouth, ill-mannered, dishonest, and greedy. Despite nationwide campaigns by Jewish groups to suppress these performances, they flourished well into the interwar era and had a significant effect on the way that Jewish characters were portrayed in such Broadway comedies as Anne Nichols' long-running *Abie's Irish Rose* and in Hollywood films like the series *The Cohens and the Kellys*.

Scholars debate the origin of these early Jewish routines. While theater historian Harley Erdman describes them as typically written and performed by non-Jewish comics for non-Jewish audiences, Jody Rosen has recently collected many recordings by Jewish performers, such as **Irving Berlin**'s "Cohen Owes Me 97 Dollars," sung by the Jewish comic Rhoda Bernard. By far the most financially successful of these Jewish performers was Monroe Silver, best remembered for his Yiddish-accented recording "Cohen on the Telephone," in which an immigrant calls his landlord to complain about a broken window. The routine sold almost a million copies.

A vast number of vaudeville routines were also produced by Jews; Erdman has estimated that close to half the entertainment business in New York was in Jewish hands at the turn of the twentieth century—and not just in New York; in 1886 the Jewish businessmen Marc Klaw and A. E. "Abe" Erlanger created the first theatrical syndicate, which booked the majority of vaudeville productions into theaters around the country. In the late 1910s, the three Shubert Brothers (Lee, Sam S., and Jacob J.), the son of Polish immigrant Duvvid Schubart, wrested control of the industry; they eventually came to own, manage, or book almost a thousand theaters nationwide.

As Jews moved out of the immigrant ghetto on the Lower East Side and into the outer boroughs of New York, they began attending Broadway shows rather than the Yiddish-language plays that had been so important to their parents. This "subway public," a large percentage of which was Jewish, demanded Jewish-themed material in English, a market that was partly satisfied by the routines of **Eddie Cantor**, **Fanny Brice**, **George Jessel**, Sophie Tucker, Belle Baker, and many other second-generation Jewish performers who benefited hugely from the post-World War I wave of economic prosperity and the concomitant growth of Broadway. In the work of this new breed of comics, the complexities of Jewish identity were explored. These performers, many performing in blackface, produced a broad range of material, much of it without any direct Jewish reference. But they also became "known and lionized by their fellow Jews" for skits and songs that were imbued with Jewish content. Even performers like the **Marx Brothers**, who over time pruned overt Jewish references from their stage and film work, remained animated by what most people recognized as a Jewish style and sensibility.

By the middle of the twentieth century, vaudeville-style comedy became the stock in trade of entertainers in the **Catskills**, the mountain range in upstate New York where Jews vacationed during the summer. Known as "tummlers" (from the Yiddish word "tummlen," to make a racket or commotion), **Henny Youngman**, **Alan King**, Jan Murray, **Red Buttons**, Buddy Hackett, and many other Jewish comics were required to produce one-liners all day long, whether serving in the dining room, dancing with unattached women, or just generally making sure guests were enjoying themselves. By the time they had to put on a show, they had enough material for a week.

Early television comedy was also heavily influenced by vaudeville. **Sid Caesar**'s *Your Show of Shows,* modeled on vaudeville-style variety shows, was supplied by a dream team of Jewish writers that included **Mel Brooks**, **Neil Simon**, **Woody Allen**, and Larry Gelbart. Aspects of Jewish vaudeville "including its tendency to make light of the pain and grief that Jews have suffered throughout the ages" later found a home in the pages of *Mad Magazine* (founded by Harvey Kurtzman), the sketch comedy of *Saturday Night Live,* and the work of stand-up comedians Mort Sahl, **Lenny Bruce**, and **Jackie Mason**.

Contemporary Jewish comedians like **Jerry Seinfeld**, **Larry David**, **Sarah Silverman**, and Sacha Baron Cohen have deep roots in Jewish vaudeville, with its mix of verbal and physical comedy, its puncturing of pretension, and its exploiting of the prickly tensions implicit in a dual Jewish American identity.

Ted Merwin

Further Reading: Merwin, Ted. *In Their Own Image: New York Jews in Jazz Age Popular Culture*. Rutgers University Press, 2006. Slide, Anthony. *The Encyclopedia of Vaudeville.* Westport, CT: Greenwood Press, 1994.

WALLACE, IRVING (1916–1990)

Acclaimed author and screenwriter Irving Wallace was born in Chicago on March 19, 1916. His parents, Alexander and Bessie Liss Wallace, were both Russian immigrants. Raised in Kenosha, Wisconsin, where his father was clerk in a general store, Wallace published his first article, "The Horse Laugh," when he was 15. After studying creative writing at the Williams Institute in Berkeley in the 1930s, Wallace began work as a freelance correspondent. In 1941, he married Sylvia Kahn, with whom he had two children: writers David Wallechinsky and Amy Wallace.

During World War II, Wallace served as a writer in the First Motion Picture Unit—the unit in which Ronald Reagan also served. From 1948 to 1958, Wallace wrote more than 20 screenplays for films starring the likes of Alan Ladd, Charleton Heston, and James Cagney. Despite his relative success, Wallace saw Hollywood as a place of "indignity, disrespect and disdain."

After publishing the lackluster *The Sins of Phillip Fleming* in 1959, Wallace struck gold with his 1961 novel, *The Chapman Report,* a work influenced by the "Kinsey Report." The novel dealt with a doctor conducting a study of female sexuality in an American suburb; it was made into a film starring **Shelley Winters** and Jane Fonda.

The lion's share of Wallace's novels—many of which were made into major motion pictures—deal with social issues like pornography and free speech, religious fanaticism and racism. Wallace, along with his son, David Wallechinsky (the original family name), also coauthored the highly successful *The Book of Lists* and *The People's Almanac* series.

Despite (or perhaps due to) his enormous popularity, most critics found Wallace's fiction to be lacking in literary merit. Wallace managed to shrug off their barbs—he believed a bestselling novel stirred up the critics' doubts.

Irving Wallace died of pancreatic cancer in Los Angeles on June 29, 1990. His works, many of which are still in print, have sold upwards of 250 million copies worldwide.

Kurt F. Stone

Further Reading: Leverence, John. *Irving Wallace: A Writer's Profile.* Popular Press, 1974.

WALLACE, MIKE (1918–)

Journalist Myron Leon ("Mike") Wallace was born in Brookline, Massachusetts, the fourth child of Friedl (Frank) and Zina Wolek, who emigrated to America from a small town in czarist Russia in the late nineteenth century; the family's original name was changed to Wallace in the process of immigration to the United States. Wallace's father was a somewhat successful wholesale grocer and insurance broker in Brookline, which was a haven for upwardly mobile Jews and Catholics who were still not welcomed in the Brahmin sections of Boston. Joseph P. Kennedy and family had moved to Brookline in 1914, and Mike attended the same grammar school as Jack Kennedy, but apparently their paths seldom crossed during the years that the Kennedys lived in Brookline.

At Brookline High School Wallace maintained a steady "B-" average, and after graduating from high school in 1935, he attended the University of Michigan in Ann Arbor. He worked as a waiter and dish washer to help pay for his education and planned to become an English teacher, but that ambition changed when he became an announcer at the university **radio** station. He graduated in 1939 with a BA degree and went to Grand Rapids, where he was employed as a radio announcer for station WOOD Wash. (Apparently the station was jointly owned by a furniture store and a laundry thereby the term "WOOD Wash.") At times he was an actor on such radio programs as *The Lone Ranger, The Green Hornet,* and *The Road to Life.* As he reminisced years later, he was "trapped" into broadcasting.

When he moved to Chicago he wrote for the *Chicago Sun,* did some acting, and announced for such daytime serials as *Ma Perkins* and *The Guiding Light.* In 1943 he helped narrate a series that was part of a navy recruiting program which subsequently recruited Wallace into the U.S. Navy. He served as a communications officer in Hawaii, Australia, and at the Great Lakes Naval Training station north of Chicago. Once he returned to civilian life he continued his career as a radio broadcaster in Chicago. He divorced his first wife, Norma Kaphan; the couple had two children, Peter, who died at 19 in a tragic accident, and the future Fox news anchor, Chris Wallace. Wallace proceeded to wed actress Buff Cobb, and they moved to New York where they together broadcast a talk show. The talk/interview show came to an end in 1954 as did their marriage. Their show was characterized by constant arguments and disagreements, which carried over into their marriage.

Wallace made his acting debut in 1954 in a comedy on Broadway, playing the part of a young art dealer, and he subsequently appeared as a panelist on CBS's panel show called *To Tell the Truth* and was the emcee for NBC's quiz show called *The Big Surprise.*

In 1955, Wallace and Ted Yates Jr. organized a news department for WABD-TV, and Wallace began broadcasting the nightly news. They subsequently worked together on an evening interview show called *Night Beat,* which began on October 9, 1956. Some of his guests included Ethel Waters, Steve Allen, Will Rogers Jr., Fannie Hurst, Mary Margaret McBride, and the still relatively unknown Malcolm X.

From April 1957 Wallace's now controversial interview show was known as *The Mike Wallace Interview.* When interviewing his guests, Wallace asked probing questions that resulted in revealing interviews. His guests included Senator Wayne Morse, gangster Mickey Cohen, U.S. Communist Party leader Earl Browder, and the grand wizard of the KKK. One reviewer found him "humorless and witless," and his manner of interview more like an inquisition than an interview. In his own defense, Wallace quoted Supreme Court Justice William O. Douglas as stating that "the function of free speech under our system of government is to invoke dispute. It may indeed best serve its high purpose when it induces a condition of unrest, creates dissatisfaction with conditions as they are, or even stirs people to anger" (*Mike Wallace Interview,* May 11, 1958). Wallace insisted that he did not seek to inquire "for the sake of prying," but that he only tried to encourage "a reasonable exchange of ideas." Despite good ratings the show only lasted some 18 months, and then it was discontinued.

CBS hired Wallace as special correspondent in February 1963. Soon thereafter he did various programs including *Morning News,* the CBS *Midday News,* and a daily *Personal Close-Up.* Don Hewitt persuaded CBS to introduce *60 Minutes,* "a *Life* magazine on the air." Hewitt asked Mike Wallace and Harry Reasoner to be his coeditors and reporters. Wallace's first *60 Minutes* interview was with U.S. Attorney General Ramsey Clark. Later, Dan Rather was added to the team and Morley Safer replaced Reasoner.

Wallace continued to interview controversial people in the news, including Texas millionaire H. L. Hunt; black activist Eldridge Cleaver; Daniel Cohn-Bendit, a radical who led the student riots of Paris in 1968; and Private Paul Meadio and Captain Ernest Medina, two American soldiers who participated in mass killings of Vietnamese civilians (1968) in the My Lai massacres. Wallace also dealt with such investigatory items as heroin addiction, biological warfare, draft evasion, and other "hot topics."

Among the many newsworthy personalities Wallace interviewed during his career were presidents Richard Nixon, Lyndon B. Johnson, and Ronald Reagan, as well as such international personalities as Egypt's president Anwar Sadat, Yasser Arafat, Menachem Begin, Ehud Barak, Ezer Weizman, Shimon Peres, the Shah of Iran, and Ayatollah Khomeini. He often was direct, daring, and inquisitive. At age 90, Wallace still remains a powerful advocate of the rights guaranteed by the United States Constitution and the Bill of Rights. Through his eagerness to seek out the truth and get to the bottom of news stories, Wallace helped protect American democracy from charlatans, gangsters, and frauds.

Although Wallace was raised in a traditional Jewish home, having gone to Hebrew school and being confirmed at age 16, he has distanced himself from the organized Jewish community. He apparently lost any identification with the religious aspect of Judaism when he attended the University of Michigan, and in his professional career, he works on *Yom Kippur,* the holiest day on the Jewish calendar, and celebrates Christmas, something he yearned to do since childhood.

Furthermore, Wallace has fostered the reputation among some in the Jewish community as being a "self-hating Jew." This image derived from his report on Syrian Jewry in 1975 on *60 Minutes,* where he noted that the country's Jews were not as oppressed as Jewish organizations had led Americans to believe. Wallace raised a fire storm among many American Jews, and in an interview in Abigail Pogrebin's book *Stars of David,* he charged that his future boss at CBS, Laurence Tisch, had spread the word that he was a "self-hating Jew." Yet, Wallace has admitted that to the present, when he goes to bed, he says the *Shema,* Judaism's most fundamental affirmation of belief in God. Wallace admitted to Pogrebin that, "I can't go to sleep at night unless I say it." Wallace has described himself as feeling Jewish, but in an ethnic sense. Son Chris Wallace, who is the moderator of the *Fox News Sunday* show, is married to a Catholic woman, considers himself Catholic, and raises his children accordingly. Nevertheless, Wallace told Pogrebin, "Chris is under the impression that he is not really Jewish . . . I mean his mother and father are Jewish, and so is his grandmother, grandfather, and so forth. . . . I've said, Chris, you're Jewish! You may not like it, or may not want to . . ."

His present wife is Mary Yates, whom he married in 1986 following the death of her husband, Ted Yates, who was killed in the Middle East.

Although Wallace has attempted to be evenhanded in the Israeli-Palestinian conflict, Wallace does identify with the Jewish state and has established a fund at the Hebrew University in Jerusalem. *See also* **Journalism**; **Television.**

Herbert M. Druks

Further Reading: Pogrebin, Abigail. "Mike Wallace." *Stars of David.* Broadway Books, 2005, 280–285. *The Mike Wallace Interview,* Transcript. Guest: William O. Douglas talking about his book, *The Right of the People.* Interview from May 11, 1958. Wallace, Mike, with Paul Gates.*Between You and Me: A Memoir.* Hyperion Books, 2005.

WALLACH, ELI (1915–)

Eli Herschel Wallach, an award-winning actor, was born on December 7, 1915 in Brooklyn, New York to a Jewish family. He grew up enjoying **Yiddish theater** and being immersed in Jewish culture, though his childhood neighborhood was also known as "Little Italy." For the past 50 years Wallach has been known as one of America's finest method and character actors. His film and television credits list more than 150 acting roles, including in *Baby Doll* (1956), *The Magnificent Seven* (1960), *The Misfits* (1961), *How the West Was Won* (1962), *Lord Jim* (1965), *The Tiger Makes Out* (1967), two episodes of the *Batman* series on television in which he played "Mr. Freeze" (1967), *The Angel Levine* (1970), the television production of *Skokie* (1981), *The Executioner's Song* (1982), *The Godfather, Part III* (1990), and *Mystic River* (2003).

Wallach won the BAFTA Film Award for Most Promising Newcomer (1957) for his role in *Baby Doll*. In 1966, he won an Emmy for the Outstanding Performance by an Actor in a Supporting Role for his role in *Poppies Are Also Flowers*.

Wallach graduated with a BA from the University of Texas–Austin and an MA from the City College of New York. In 1938, he joined the Neighborhood Playhouse, where he was trained in the art of method acting. During World War II he served in the army's Medical Administrative Corps, eventually attaining the rank of captain.

On March 5, 1948 he married actress Anne Jackson. They have three children, Peter, Katherine, and Roberta.

Now in his nineties, Wallach continues to perform both on the silver screen and on television. In 2006, he made a guest appearance on NBC's short-lived series *Studio 60 on the Sunset Strip* as a 1950s blacklisted television writer, for which he was nominated for an Emmy Award. He also had a supporting role in *The Holiday* (2006), playing opposite Kate Winslet. *See also* **Film**.

Judith Lupatkin

Further Reading: Wallach, Eli. *The Good, the Bad and Me: In My Anecdotage.* Fort Washington, PA: Harvest Books, 2006.

WALTERS, BARBARA (1929–)

Barbara Walters broke through a male-dominated broadcasting system and demonstrated that when given the chance women can achieve stardom in the medium. She was the youngest producer on NBC-TV. As a writer and producer on CBS-TV, Ms. Walters has an ability to put her interviewees at ease and draw out the unexpected, such as in interviews with such notables as Anwar Sadat, Menachem Begin, Fidel Castro, Colin Powell, Hillary Clinton, and the Dalai Lama.

Walters was born in Boston; later her parents, Dena and Lou Walters, moved to New York. Her father owned the Latin Quarter, a nightclub which featured many show business celebrities. Walters felt comfortable in a show business environment, an asset that served her well when she became an interviewer. Her parents did not provide her with a Jewish education (her father was an atheist). To this day Walters states that she practices no religion. Walters graduated from Sarah Lawrence College with a BA in English in 1953. She married three times, to Jewish men. Her first husband was Robert Katz. The marriage was annulled after one year. The second marriage, to Lee Gruber, ended in divorce in 1976; the third, to Mervin Adelson, ended in divorce in 1997. She has an adopted daughter, Jacqueline.

Walters's career in television has earned a remarkable number of awards, and she has amassed a list of "firsts" for a woman in the male-oriented business. She was awarded Emmys for her work as a writer-producer and interviewer in 1975, 1980, 1982, 1986, and 1993. Her career took off when Dave Garaway brought her on to *The Today Show* as a writer and researcher in 1961. In 1974, she became the first female co-host of the program and remained with the show for 10 years. In 1979, ABC hired Walters for their news magazine *20/20,* where she reported for 20 years. She was the first woman news anchor on The ABC *Evening News*. In 2001 the *Ladies' Home Journal* named Walters the fourth most powerful woman in America. Presently she is active as producer and participant on *The View,* the highly-rated, controversial late-morning talk show television program.

Women working as on-air reporters, commentators, news co-hosts, and anchors owe much to

Ms. Walters, who pioneered women's acceptance within the television industry. *See also* **Television**.

Philip Rosen

Further Reading: Hyman, Paula E., and Deborah Dash Moore, eds. "Barbara Walters." *Jewish Women in America,* vol. II. New York: Routledge, 1997. Walters, Barbara. *Audition: A Memoir.* Knopf Publishing Group, 2008.

WESTHEIMER, DR. RUTH (1928–)

Dr. Ruth Westheimer is both a media personality and a cultural icon closely associated with America's sexual revolution of the 1960s and 1970s. Born Karola Ruth Siegel in Frankfurt/Main (Germany) she is the only child of Julius and Irma Hanauer Siegel, a devoutly Orthodox couple who perished in the Holocaust. In 1939 her parents were able to rescue their daughter by sending her on a Kinderstransport to Switzerland. The Nazi governments in Germany and Austria permitted selected Jewish children 10–17 years to depart for exile. Funding was to be provided by Jewish groups to support the children for their "temporary" stays abroad. Karola Siegel traveled to a Swiss-Jewish orphanage in Heiden, where she spent the war years.

Her years in the Swiss home as well as the time prior to her settlement in the United States in 1956 are vividly and memorably depicted in her 1987 memoir *All in a Lifetime.* More than just an autobiography, this entertaining narrative provides a snapshot of the Jewish experience during and after the Holocaust. Westheimer unabashedly professes her Jewishness—not just in word but also in deed. Despite her phenomenal success in show business and academia she continues to live in New York City's Washington Heights, which she considers the home of German Jews in America.

Her narrative, like her life, is multi-layered. On the surface it is an interesting account of her adventures—growing up a war orphan in a neutral but decidedly unfriendly Switzerland; as an ardent Zionist in Palestine, where she was a sharpshooter and courier in the Haganah, the secret Jewish army; and then finally as an emerging scholar struggling on the edge of poverty in France and the United States. On another level one finds very personal statements about her relationship to Judaism and the Diaspora. Her early idealism and her experience of the Holocaust led her to Zionism.

This idealism was apparently tempered by her experiences in Palestine during the early years of the Israeli state. Reading between the lines it is clear that fanaticism of any kind is foreign to Westheimer's nature. While remaining an Orthodox Jew, she admits that she did not rear either her daughter Miriam or son Joel to be Orthodox but was delighted when they chose that path themselves without coercion. Self-realization and personal freedom are clearly very important to her.

In her autobiography she vividly describes her state of denial after World War II and the inability to admit that her parents had been murdered. It is significant that as she was establishing her credentials as a sociologist, psychologist, and sex therapist, she did not forget her roots. She devoted a study to the experiences of the children who had lived with her in the Swiss orphanage. Thus she was able to tell her story without losing the perspective that the Holocaust was not just the fate of an individual but of an entire group. This self-deprecating humility is an essential ingredient in Dr. Ruth's Weltanschauung, a humanism that informs her work as a sex therapist. According to Sigmund Freud's last lecture, Weltanschauung is an intellectual construction which gives a unified solution of all the problems of our existence, a construction in which no question is left open and in which everything in which we are interested finds a place.

The evolution of her career as a sex therapist is a third layer of significance in her autobiography. In 1950 she moved to France, where she studied and taught psychology at the University of Paris. In 1956, she immigrated to New York City, where she earned her master's degree in sociology and a EdD from the New School for Social Research. Subsequently, Westheimer completed postdoctoral work in human sexuality at New York-Presbyterian Hospital. She attracted the attention of a local New York radio station, where she began her evolution from radio personality to cable and television star, and then ultimately to a cultural icon of the sexual revolution known universally as "Dr. Ruth." Her public persona, however, is just one aspect of her life. Westheimer's autobiography places her firmly in the tradition of modern giants such as Piaget and Masters and Johnson. Her special gift is that in her profession as well as her private life Westheimer is genuinely interested in empowering individuals to deal with their problems and achieve their full potential. *See also* **Popular Psychology**.

Leroy T. Hopkins Jr.

Further Reading: Heinze, Andrew. *Jews and the American Soul: Human Nature in the 20th Century.* Princeton University Press, 2004. Melody, Edward Michael. *Teaching America about Sex: Marriage Guides and Sex Manuals from the Late Victorians to Dr. Ruth.* New York U. Press, 1999. Westheimer, Dr. Ruth K. *All in a Lifetime.* New York: Warner Books, 1987, 2001. German American Corner. www.germanheritage.com.

WEST SIDE STORY

Though *The Music Man* won the Tony for the Best Musical of 1957, no musical has proved in retrospect more influential than *West Side Story.* Its prime mover, the choreographer and director **Jerome Robbins**, achieved the ideal of a fully integrated musical, in which the same performers were expected to sing, dance, and act. The play was propelled forward by the "urban jazz" that composer **Leonard Bernstein** considered the most distinctive feature of American popular music. No previous musical had ever been conceived, choreographed, and directed by one person, and Robbins inspired the performers to communicate and advance *West Side Story* most audaciously through dance.

The sheer bleakness of the story was quite unusual for a Broadway musical, with corpses dropped on the stage at the end of both acts. Arthur Laurents's libretto and **Stephen Sondheim**'s lyrics, however, should be credited for ensuring that *West Side Story* would help smash the traditions that Broadway tended to honor when entertaining its audiences.

The theme of *West Side Story* was hardly unfamiliar to the creative team that was responsible for its production. Jews had long hoped that romance might transcend the chasms that artificial and ancestral differences opened. Robbins, Bernstein, Sondheim, and Laurents all belonged to an ethnically homogeneous creative team that was bound to be attracted a musical adaptation and updating of *Romeo and Juliet,* in which the union of lovers is undermined by tribal conflict. To be sure, the romance of Tony and Maria is doomed in *West Side Story,* and it is a tragedy. But the belief that no American in the thrall of love ought to be parochial—subjected to the rigid norms of a sub-community—was bound to draw in the secular Jews who were responsible for this musical. On these shores, Jews—at least as fervently as anyone else—dreamed of a society in which historic demands of group cohesiveness might be abandoned, to satisfy individual desire.

The initial ideas about *West Side Story* occurred late in 1948; Bernstein's diary noted the following telephone conversation: "Jerry R. called today with a noble idea: a modern version of *Romeo and Juliet* set in slums at the coincidence of Easter-Passover celebrations. Feelings run high between Jews and Catholics. Former: Capulets, latter: Montagues. Juliet is Jewish. Friar Lawrence is the neighborhood druggist. Street brawls, double death—it all fits." But the setting was switched from Poland to America, and Tony (née Anton) became merely a "Polack," according to the Puerto Ricans arriving in a city seething with conflicts among ethnic insiders and outsiders. *West Side Story* might be interpreted by some as disguising the Jews as Puerto Ricans—the Sharks are swarthy newcomers; they are strangers who speak accented English. Sondheim disclaimed direct knowledge of either poverty or Puerto Ricans and *West Side Story* isn't supposed to be ethnography. But, the play was not to be realistic, and Jewishness, for the sake of box-office draw, could not be made explicit.

The shared ethnicity that constituted the creative auspices of *West Side Story* was only briefly heard, as when one of the Jets informs, "Dear kindly social worker, / They tell me: earn a buck, / Like be a soda jerker, / Which means like be a shmuck." And a song like "America," which decried the prejudice and violence that could not be officially acknowledged, echoed a more radical dissidence that could be found in the Jewish past and defied an atmosphere of complacency in national politics.

It took Robbins and his collaborators more than eight wrenching years to get from conception to opening night. But the finished product was well worth the work and the wait. By addressing a gnawing urban problem, *West Side Story* provided audiences with something more than entertainment. This musical eschewed escapism with a raw energy that enabled the genre itself to grow up. *See also* **Popular Music**.

Stephen J. Whitfield

Further Reading: Garebian, Keith. *The Making of West Side Story*. New York: Mosaic Press, 1998. Vaill, Amanda. *Somewhere: The Life Of Jerome Robbins*. New York: Broadway Books, 2006.

WIESEL, ELIE (1928–)

Eliezer Wiesel, often referred to as the poet laureate of the Shoah, is obsessed by memory of the Event. *Night* (1960), his memoir, is a canonical text of the Shoah which has been republished in several languages. His concern for memory reveals the author's commitment to the future no less than the past. Firmly rooted in the Jewish tradition, his message is for humans everywhere. In 1986 Wiesel won the Nobel Peace Prize. Egil Aarvik, chairman of the Norwegian Nobel Committee, observed that Wiesel's "aim is not to gain the world's sympathy for the victims or the survivors. His aim is to awaken our conscience because our indifference to evil makes us partners in the crime. The words he uses are simple and the voice that speaks them is gentle. It is a voice of peace. Its power is intense." Wiesel's devotion to the cause of human rights has taken him throughout the world.

The author of over 40 books, Wiesel is professor and Andrew W. Mellon Professor in the humanities at Boston University, where he has won a distinguished teaching award. His public lectures always draw an overflow audience. Wiesel's annual lectures at the 92nd Street Y in New York City have become a highly anticipated event. Wiesel writes on a variety of topics—the Hebrew Bible, Talmud, and Hasidism. Further, he writes in several genres—novels, plays, cantatas, poetry, and essays. All of these works reveal the tension between the God-intoxicated boy that he was and the Buchenwald survivor that he is.

Wiesel was recently brought to the attention of a mass audience when his most important memoir, *Night*, was chosen by Oprah Winfrey for her book club. A new edition of *Night* quickly rose to the top of the bestseller charts.

Born in Sighet, Wiesel was a deeply religious youth. A fervent student of mysticism, he sought to hasten the coming of Messiah. He and his family were deported to Auschwitz in 1944. The author's parents—Shlomo, a leader of the Jewish community, and Sarah—as well as his youngest sister Tzippora, perished in the Holocaust. Wiesel's world view is profoundly shaped by two diametrically opposed forces. On the one hand, he was deeply influenced by the Hasidic tales he heard from Dodye Feig, his maternal grandfather. The youth was fascinated by their affirmation of life, their insight into the human condition, and the vital relationship they display between humanity and God. On the other hand, there was the anti-world of the death camps, which replaced redemption with destruction, freedom with bondage, and human dignity with torture and degradation.

Night is the key to all of his subsequent writings. It is both the end—of his traditional faith, and the beginning—of his search for a viable post-Holocaust image of God. This text, composed after a 10-year period of self-imposed silence, is Wiesel's eloquent and heartfelt cry

Elie Wiesel, Holocaust survivor, Nobel Prize winner, and author of *Night,* as well other books about the Jewish condition, receiving an honorary doctorate from Millersville University, Millersville, Pennsylvania. [Millersville University Archives]

against divine injustice and human cruelty. Wiesel's trial of God (din Torah) paints a stark portrait of the reversal of biblical norms. Instead of the Akedah, in which Abraham was to sacrifice his son Isaac, some sons in Auschwitz, driven mad by hunger and thirst, turned on their fathers. The Exodus of redemption became the death of his traditional faith. Yet it is his questioning of the deity, while refusing to abandon faith, that makes of his memoir a timeless and eternally valid question.

Wiesel went to France after the war. He learned French, the language in which he continues to write, and studied at the Sorbonne. He held a variety of jobs, including choir director, in order to survive and was eventually reunited with his two older sisters, Bea and Hilda, who had also survived. Wiesel also traveled to India and became a newspaper correspondent. He had an important interview with the great Catholic writer Francois Mauriac, who urged Wiesel to write about his experience. Mauriac helped get Wiesel's memoir published and wrote the introduction. Weisel views literature as an element of theology in which prayers become stories. His 1964 novel *The Town Beyond the Wall* is divided into four prayers rather than chapters.

Wiesel's writings influence people in a variety of faith traditions. That his revolt against the traditional image of God occurs from within the tradition gives voice to many whose own faith was called radically into question by the Holocaust. In *Night* he writes that he sympathized with Job. Like the prophet, he believed in God, but not in divine justice. Consequently, the author describes his post-Auschwitz faith as wounded. Additionally, his emphasis on questions—which word contains the word "quest"—means that questions, which unite people, are more important than answers, which are divisive. In a memorable encounter with the late Lubavitcher rebbe, later incorporated in his novel *The Gates of the Forest,* Wiesel asked: "Rebbe, how can you believe in Hashem [God] after the Khourban [Holocaust]?

He looked at me and said, And how can you not believe in Hashem after the Khourban?" The author terms this dialogue a "turning point" in his writing.

His many honors, in addition to the Nobel Prize, include the Presidential Medal of Freedom, the United States Congressional Gold Medal, and the French Legion of Honor with the rank of Grand Cross. Among Wiesel's literary awards are the Prix Medicis for *A Beggar in Jerusalem,* the Prix Bordin de l'Academie Francaise for *Souls on Fire,* and the Prix Rivarol for *The Town Beyond the Wall.* One of the reasons that Wiesel's message has such great universal resonance is that he teaches through stories. A story reveals what is profoundly important to the human condition—its hopes and fears, its longings and questions. His retelling of Hasidic tales emphasizes that the path to God leads through man. *See also* **The Holocaust in American Culture**.

Alan L. Berger

Further Reading: Fine, Ellen. *Legacy of Night: The Literary Universe of Elie Wiesel.* Albany: State University of New York Press, 1982. Wiesel, Elie, and Richard Heffner. *Conversations with Elie Wiesel.* New York: Schocken Books, 2001.

WILDER, GENE (1933–)

Jerome Silberman, more commonly known as comedic actor Gene Wilder, was born in 1933 in Milwaukee, Wisconsin to William and Jeanne (née Baer) Silberman. His father, a Russian Jewish immigrant, manufactured whiskey and beer bottles; his mother was born in Chicago. Neither of his parents were particularly observant Jews, although they attended an Orthodox synagogue, where Wilder's grandfather was president and where Wilder was Bar Mitzvahed. Later the family joined a Conservative Temple. Despite his Jewish upbringing, Wilder has stated that "I have no other religion. I feel very Jewish and I feel grateful to be Jewish. But I don't believe in God or anything to do with the Jewish religion."

Wilder attended the University of Iowa, England's Old Vic Theatre School, and New York's Actors Studio. The United States Army was his home from 1956 to 1958, where he served as a psychiatric medic outside Philadelphia. In Hollywood, he was noticed by Anne Bancroft. Wilder's appearance as an undertaker in*Bonnie and Clyde* (1967), though small, marked his first important film role. This was followed by the classic spoof of Adolf Hitler in *The Producers* (1968), a film which earned him an Oscar nomination and marked his first collaboration with **Mel Brooks**. His portrayal of Wonka in *Willy Wonka and the Chocolate Factory* (1971) catapulted him to stardom.

In addition to*The Producers,* Wilder has acted in a number of productions with Jewish content. Wilder appeared in the Jewish Theological Seminary's television docudrama *Eternal Light* series, on NBC, based on a Sholem Aleichem story (1973). He costarred with Mel Brooks in *Blazing Saddles* (1974), a movie which included **Yiddish**-speaking Indians, and as a Polish rabbi in *The Frisco Kid* (1979). Other notable Wilder performances include *Young Frankenstein* (1974), *Silver Streak* (1976), and *Stir Crazy* (1980).

Wilder has been married four times: Mary Mercier, Mary Joan Schultz, Gilda Radner, and Karen Boyer, his current wife. The death of Gilda Radner devastated him emotionally. Wilder organized Gilda's Club, an institution devoted to cancer research.

The man with the Harpo Marx hair has made millions of people laugh with his classic comedies. *See also* **Film**.

Philip Rosen

Further Reading: Pogrebin, Abigail. "Gene Wilder."-*Stars of David: Prominent Jews Talk About Being Jewish.* Broadway Books, 2005. Wilder, Gene. *Kiss Me Like a Stranger: My Search for Love and Art.* St. Martin's Press, 2005.

WINCHELL, WALTER (1897–1972)

At the height of his popularity in the 1930s and 1940s, Walter Winchell reached 50 million Americans with his newspaper column and radio broadcasts. He is credited with the invention of the gossip column and opinion-laced reporting. While he wrote about financial and current events as well as night life in New York, he pioneered in tabloid journalism—the foibles, marital problems, and gaffes of the rich and famous. With the presidency of Franklin Roosevelt and the New Deal, he became an exponent of liberalism, as well as a foe of anti-Semites and bigotry. Winchell was also a supporter of African American rights, insisting that minorities receive equal treatment. He was, for example, instrumental in integrating New York's famous Lindy's restaurant and the Copacabana night club, a frequent hangout of his. During the Hitler years, his staccato, telegraphic rattle-style voice could be heard over radio hammering both foreign and domestic Nazis. John Rankin, the racist congressman from Mississippi, referred to Winchell as "a little slimy kike."

After World War II his influence began to fade, in part because television was replacing radio as the primary source of news and entertainment. Winchell also lost much of his audience and liberal following because of his red-baiting broadcasts and "cheerleading" for Senator Joseph McCarthy's witch hunts.

Winchell maintained a friendship with J. Edgar Hoover, the director of the Federal Bureau of Investigation, who often became an unnamed "source" for the intrepid reporter; this relationship endured despite Winchell's contacts with gangsters and the underworld. From 1959–1962, Winchell attained a semblance of renewed popularity as narrator of the hit television series *The Untouchables*. After the show ran its course, Winchell fell into obscurity.

Philip Roth, for one, thought Winchell an important enough historical personality of his time that he made him a central character in his 2004 alternative historical novel, *The Plot Against America,* wherein a fictionalized Winchell runs against Charles Lindbergh for the presidency.

Walter Winchell was born into an impoverished Jewish immigrant family in Harlem. He left school at age 13 and worked in vaudeville, where he was a hoofer, along with **George Jessel**, **Eddie Cantor**, and Jack Weiner. He started writing about show business for the magazines *Vaudeville* and *Billboard*. He became an entertainment editor for the *Evening Graphic* and worked as a columnist on the *New York Daily Mirror* from 1929–1963.

Winchell married Rita Greene in 1919, but the marriage did not last. He lived with June Magee without benefit of marriage. The couple had two children, Walter Junior and Walda. Walter Junior committed suicide in 1968.

Winchell's paper, *The Mirror,* folded in 1963, and he was left without a column. Winchell announced his retirement in 1969, using as an excuse the death of his son, but his celebrity status was gone. He spent the last three years of his life suffering from cancer and living as a recluse. Winchell had been active in raising funds for charity and was the driving force behind the creation of the Damon Runyon Cancer Research Fund.

At his burial in a nondenominational cemetery, the only mourner attending his graveside was his daughter Walda.

Philip Rosen

Further Reading: Gabler, Neal. *Winchell: Gossip, Power and Culture of Celebrity.* New York: Knopf, 1994.

WINKLER, HENRY (1945–)

Between 1974 and 1984, no television character so captured the imagination of the American public than did "the Fonz" on ABC's top-rated show *Happy Days*. Played by Henry Winkler, the character of Arthur "Fonzie" Fonzarelli, as well as the actor, became a national icon, along with his famous motorcycle jacket, a prop that was initially censured by ABC because the network feared that the "menacing" outfit would have a negative influence on young viewers. The jacket now hangs at the Smithsonian.

Henry Franklin Winkler was born October 30, 1945 in New York City, several years after his Jewish parents, Harry Irving and Ilse Anna Maria, left Germany shortly before the outbreak of World War II in 1939, because of the Nazi persecution of the Jews. After getting his BA at Emerson College in 1967, Winkler earned his MFA from the Yale School of Drama in 1970. In addition, Winkler received a PhD in Hebrew Literature at Emerson College in 1978. That same year, he married Stacey Weitzman, with whom he has three children, Zoe, Max, and a stepson, Jed, from Stacey's previous marriage to Howard Weitzman.

Winkler earned a Golden Globe for Best Actor in a Television Comedy or Musical twice, in 1977 and 1978, for his role in *Happy Days*. He won a day time Emmy for Outstanding Children's Special for *CBS School-Break Special: All the Kids Do It* (1984) and an additional day time Emmy for Outstanding Performance in an Animated Program for *Cliffords Puppy Days* (2003). Winkler also received a Genesis Award for Best TV Drama for *MacGyver* (1991).

Winkler's film career includes *Lords of Flatbush* (1974), *Heroes* (1977), and *Night Shift* (1982). In *Lords of Flatbush,* which starred Sylvester Stallone, Winkler made his film debut. He played a leather-clad "hood." He used the speech and attitude characteristics developed for the film to create his persona as "the Fonz" in *Happy Days.*

Although his identification as "the Fonz" almost typecast him, his film roles in *Heroes* and in Ron Howard's *Night Shift* enabled Winkler to demonstrate his wide acting repertoire. He acted in three **Adam Sandler** movies—*The Waterboy* (1998), *Little Nicky* (2000), and *Click* (2006). He has also guest-starred on numerous television shows, such as *South Park*. Winkler has been active as both a film and television director as well as a producer. His credits include directing Billy Crystal's *Memories of Me* (1988) and producing television programs such as *MacGyver* and *Sightings.*

Winkler's iconic fame as Fonzie has not prevented him from spoofing himself. For example, in a 1977 *Happy Days* episode, Fonzie jumps over a shark using water skis. Almost 30 years later, Winkler hops over a dead shark on a pier, in a scene from the television series *Arrested Development*. In that same sitcom, while facing the bathroom mirror, Winkler repeats the famous comb move that was so identified with "the Fonz."

Winkler has used his celebrity to promote educational and social projects. When a *Happy Days* episode has Fonzie check out a book from the library, proclaiming, "Everybody is allowed to read," "it provoked a 500% rise in library card registration" ("The Fonz," 2008). Influenced by the values of his Jewish upbringing, Winkler has devoted much of his free time to causes involving youngsters, such as the Children's Action Network, which helps to immunize and feed L.A. kids, the Annual Cerebral Palsy Telethon, and the Special Olympics. Concern for children is paramount for Winkler, who overcame dyslexia in his youth. In 2003, he cowrote with Lin Oliver a series of children's books centering around Hank Zipzer, a dyslexic fourth grade boy. His high sense of tzedakah (charity) has been recognized by various organizations from B'nai B'rith to the UN. *See also* **Television.**

Steve Krief

Further Reading: "The Fonz, Henry Winkler, joins Ed Balls for reading launch." *Telegraph Media Group,* July 2, 2008. Accessed September 7, 2008. telegraph.co.uk.

WINTERS, SHELLEY (1922–2006)

Academy Award-winning actress Shelley Winters was born Shirley Schrift in St. Louis, Missouri to Jewish parents—Jonas Schrift, a designer, and Rose, a singer. The family moved to Brooklyn, New York when Shirley was three years old. Her father was sent to Sing-Sing prison for arson (later exonerated) when Shirley was nine years of age, a traumatic event the memory of which, she later wrote, was a useful tool in her acting career. A high school dropout, Ms. Winters modeled in Manhattan's garment center by day and attended the New Theater School at night. The actress subsequently began her acting career as a nightclub chorus girl and then moved on to the theater scene in New York, where she landed a part in the national company of Meet the People in 1941.

From the stage she went on to a career in film. Her first film was *There's Something About a Soldier* in 1943, and after a number of small parts in some other 17 films, she made her film breakthrough in *A Double Life* (1947). In her autobiography, Winters would later write that "to this day I feel that getting 'A Double Life' was a miracle." Ms. Winters subsequently signed a seven-year contract with Universal Studios and went on to a successful film career of more than 80 movies, including such classics as *A Place in the Sun* (1951), for which she was nominated for an Oscar for Best Actress; *Night of the Hunter* (1955); *The Big Knife* (1955); *The Diary of Anne Frank* (1959), for which she was awarded an Oscar for Best Supporting Actress; as well as one for Best Actress in a Supporting Role in 1965 for *A Patch of Blue.* Other notable films include *Lolita* (1962), the role of Ma Barker in the cult classic *Bloody Mama* (1970), and an Oscar nomination for Best Actress in a Supporting Role for her role as Belle Rosen in *The Poseidon Adventure* (1972).

Shelley Winters was Jewish by ethnicity but not apparently religiously observant. Nevertheless she was always conscious of her Jewish heritage, as when she donated her Oscar for *The Diary of Anne Frank* to the Anne Frank House in Amsterdam. Her career took her from being a blonde sex symbol (she at one time roomed with Marilyn Monroe) to someone who had lost her lifelong struggle to control her weight (she once remarked that obesity was a marketing tool, since there were plenty of prominent normal-weight older actresses but fewer overweight ones, and her obesity would enable her to find work more easily). During the seventies she played more matronly roles, often cast as the stereotypical Jewish mother in such films as *Next Stop Greenwich Village* (1976) and *Over the Brooklyn Bridge* (1984).

An acclaimed dramatic actress, she not only made her mark in film but also on the stage and on television. On Broadway she acted in such plays as *The Night Before Christmas* (1941), *Rosalinda* (1942), *Oklahoma!* (as a replacement for Celeste Holm, 1947), and *A Hatful of Rain* (1955). Winters also made numerous appearances on television. She is probably best remembered for her recurring role in the 1980s and early 1990s as the grandmother in the ABC hit sitcom *Roseanne,* where she played a parody of herself.

Married four times, at the time of her death of heart failure, Shelley Winters was survived by her companion, Jerry DeFord; her daughter, Dr. Vittoria Gassman; and two grandchildren. *See also* **Film**.

Jack R. Fischel

Further Reading: Winters, Shelley. *Shelley: Also Known as Shirley.* Ballantine Books, 1980. ———. *Shelley II : The Middle of My Century.* Ballantine Books, 1989.

WORLD OF OUR FATHERS

World of Our Fathers, Irving Howe's monumental exploration of the journey that East European Jews made to America and the life they found and refashioned, was almost always characterized by reviewers, and even by Howe himself, as an elegy. This beautifully written work was described time and again as a farewell with love and gratitude to **Yiddish** and Yiddishkeit, to Jewish socialism, to Jewish secularism generally. But *World of Our Fathers* is also something much larger and more complex than a mere obituary. It is a search for authentic and enduring Jewish meaning in the collective experience of ordinary Jewish men and women.

Published in 1976 when Howe was 56, *World* represents the culmination of Howe's personal journey from youthful cosmopolitanism and revolutionary internationalism in the late 1930s and 1940s to a "reconquest of Jewishness" by the 1970s, a journey he took without ever abandoning his commitment to democratic radicalism. Indeed, *World,* Howe's first and only bestseller, is an embrace of that distinctive moral impulse in Jewish life and values which continues to see the need for repairing and improving a far from perfect world.

Howe allots a small number of pages to Judaism in the old countries of Eastern Europe, to "Israel and the American Jews," and several paragraphs to "The Holocaust and After," but there is no sustained analysis of religion or attention to the influence of the Shoah and post-World War II Zionism on the life of Jewish America. Howe's limited attention to Judaism is mainly a result of the author's commitment to secular Jewishness as the animating, sustaining force in Jewish culture.

In 1979, Howe recalled a "clever" review of *World,* in which he was attacked for knowing the names of all the Yiddish poets, but not the rabbis. And in 1990 as part of the preface to the Schocken edition of *World,* Howe defended his emphasis on socialism and Yiddish culture and the lack of significant attention to traditional religion as distinct from secular Jewishness. He stood by his original claim that the book was a work of authentic social and cultural history, but he also recognized the cogency of the critical observation that it was an intensely personal book. His father, Howe said, had become for him a representative figure of the old country, and *World of Our Fathers* was a literary extension of what he knew about him: a hard-working but hopeful man who was not particularly observant in faith or behavior, but whose whole life was colored and defined by Jewishness. *World* was also Howe's own story of the secular socialist part of the Jewish immigrant community as he and other sons and daughters moved into the intellectual world.

But *World* was no exercise in nostalgia. Howe knew that Jewish slums in the 1880s and 1890s and into the early decades of the twentieth century bred Jewish crime, wife desertion, juvenile delinquency, gangsterism, and prostitution. In *World* Howe not only described appalling scenes of hunger and destitution, he explicitly cautioned against nostalgia as a proper response to poverty, fatigue, and occasional despair. Nonetheless, for Howe, the immigrant neighborhood, with all its dimensions of gemeinschaft was a "paradise" of a kind, but, he insisted, "a paradise we have left behind because we had to leave it, a paradise lost forever" (Sorin, 2002).

Howe had neither hope nor desire for the re-creation or duplication of the world of our fathers, but in writing *World,* he was paying tribute to the Jewish labor and socialist movements and to the self-educated workers who filled the ranks; he was also pointing to the positive qualities of community and fraternity in Jewish immigrant culture that might be tailored, and thereby salvaged, for his own and future time.

Over a 25-year period, in many printings and various editions, *World* found its way into nearly every Jewish home in America. Jews hurried out to buy the book, Howe guessed, the way African Americans rushed out to purchase Alex Haley's *Roots,* published in the same year.

On the very last page of *World,* while Howe tells us that "the story of the immigrant Jews is all but done," he also intimates that the powerful moral impulse of secular Jewishness continues to show signs of vitality and the potential for renewed commitment to social justice. *See also* **Yiddish**; **Yiddish Film**; **Yiddish Theater**.

Gerald Sorin

Further Reading: Howe, Irving. *A Margin of Hope: An Intellectual Autobiography.* New York: Harcourt, 1982. Michels, Tony. "Socialism and the Writing of American Jewish History: World of Our Fathers Revisited." *American Jewish History* 88, no. 4 (December, 2000): 521–546. Sorin, Gerald. *Irving Howe: A Life of Passionate Dissent.* New York University Press, 2002.

WOUK, HERMAN (1915–)

Bestselling author Herman Wouk is perhaps the only well-known American-born literary figure who is also a practicing Orthodox Jew. Wouk was born in New York and was raised in the Bronx. His father worked as a laundry laborer, and the family did their best to overcome their poverty. His grandfather, Mendel Leib Levine, was a ritual slaughterer and a Lubavitcher Hasid, hailing from Minsk. Wouk seems to have received a basic Jewish education, but as was the trend at the time he chose to reject his Jewish religious tradition and assimilate in the general American culture. By 1931, Wouk's father

American Jewish writer Herman Wouk, the author of such bestsellers as *The Caine Mutiny* (1951), *Marjorie Morningstar* (1955), *This Is My God: The Jewish Way of Life* (1959), *The Winds of War* (1971), and *War and Remembrance* (1978), is shown in his Palm Springs, California home in May 2000. [AP Photo]

became successful in the power laundry business, and the family moved to the more fashionable Manhattan West Side.

Leading a secular lifestyle, Wouk attended Columbia University, graduated in 1934, and began his literary career as a gag man for a radio comedian. Subsequently, he worked as a scriptwriter for *The Fred Allen Show,* from 1936–1941. At some point in his late twenties Wouk decided to return to the religion of his ancestors. Particularly attracted to the Lubavitcher Hasidism of his grandfather, he became an Orthodox Jew. Wouk served in the navy during World War II, an experience that inspired the book that brought him popular name recognition, *The Caine Mutiny* (1951). The novel was a bestseller, a successful film, and earned him the Pulitzer Prize for that year. After *Caine,* Wouk proceeded to publish one bestseller after another, including *Marjorie Morningstar* (1955), which focused on the Jewish Upper West Side of the 1930s and the struggle for assimilation and success in the literary and theatrical world, and *Youngblood Hawk* (1962). Both novels became films. Later bestselling novels (and major made-for-television films) by Wouk included his World War II and Holocaust books, *The Winds of War* (1971) and *War and Remembrance* (1978). Although much more proud of his Jewish identity than many fellow Jewish authors, he never achieved the critical acclaim of his literary peers such as the late **Norman Mailer**, **Philip Roth**, **Bernard Malamud**, and **Saul Bellow**. In the 1950s, Wouk took a much more active and public role as an Orthodox Jew. Together with the newly formed Synagogue Council of Yeshiva University, organized by Dr. Samuel Belkin, the second president of Yeshiva, he was the catalyst in the formation of an Orthodox synagogue in Great Neck, New York. This synagogue split from the local Conservative synagogue and fought an uphill battle for survival. This marked the coming of age of Orthodoxy in America with the formation of a strictly Orthodox congregation in an area of suburbia.

At the same time Wouk took an active role in the lay leadership of Yeshiva University and authored his first nonfiction work, *This Is My God* (1959), which outlined and explained Orthodox Judaism and how Wouk related to it. This short book was printed numerous times and to this day serves as a fine introductory text to the complex and detailed world of Orthodox Judaism. The short book brought the message of Orthodoxy via the medium of the mass-market paperback.

Wouk also was active in other synagogues. As a resident of New York's exclusive Upper East Side, he took the leadership in establishing the Fifth Avenue Synagogue, a strictly Orthodox synagogue that has had a number of prominent rabbinical leaders in the congregation, including Emmanuel Rackman and the late chief rabbi of the United Kingdom, Dr. Immanuel Jakobovitts. Another famous literary figure, **Elie Wiesel**, also is an active member of this synagogue. Wouk was also active in the local synagogue in the Virgin Islands, which served as his vacation home for a number of years.

In September 2008, Herman Wouk was presented with the first Library of Congress Award for lifetime achievement in the writing of fiction. While Orthodox Jews have become well known in many fields since the 1970s such as medicine, science, politics, the law, and the world of commerce, few have achieved fame as writers. As a Jewish American writer, Wouk, as Pearl K. Bell points out, is unembarrassed by his Jewishness and a believer in such discredited forms of commitment as valor, gallantry, and patriotism. *See also* **Film**.

Zalman Alpert

Further Reading: Guttman, Allan. *The Jewish Writers in America.* Oxford University Press, 1971.

Y

YIDDISH

American Jewish popular culture is largely defined by the approximately two million Jews who arrived at these shores from Eastern Europe during the period of mass immigration lasting from the early 1880s to the start of World War I in 1914. These immigrants, the great majority of whom were native speakers of Yiddish, expanded the number of Jews in the United States exponentially and transformed the public presence of Jews in major American cities, especially New York. The arrival of this large number of Yiddish-speaking Jews in the United States coincided with the advent of new technologies (especially sound recordings and silent film) and new social practices (including Yiddish press, theater, and popular song) that engendered an American Jewish popular culture unprecedented in its scope and significance. From the turn of the twentieth century to the present, American Jews' use of Yiddish has undergone a series of threshold changes, as has the language's symbolic value both for the immigrant generations and for their descendants. Indeed, the dynamics of American Jewish popular culture are, to a considerable extent, articulated by the changing role of Yiddish in American Jewish life. Much of this popular culture is indebted to Yiddish and its speech community even when the language's presence is not evident.

As the traditional language of daily life spoken by the great majority of Jews who had come to America from the Russian and Austro-Hungarian empires, Yiddish was at the center of an extensive immigrant popular culture. These practices flourished immediately upon the immigrants' arrival in America in the late nineteenth century, responding to their urgent need to negotiate the great disparities between their Old World past and New World present. In many respects, American Yiddish popular culture paralleled other concomitant cultures created by new arrivals to the United States in Italian, German, Russian, Finnish, and other languages. All these immigrants confronted an unknown political, economic, and social order, as well as an unfamiliar national language. They also encountered an array of new forms of popular culture, especially those immigrants who settled in major cities: cabarets, cafes, dance halls, nickelodeons, amusement parks, photographs, and public libraries. America also presented many of these immigrants with unprecedented freedoms of speech and association, while the burgeoning economy of the United States introduced these new arrivals to a consumer culture that they themselves were helping to transform.

For these reasons, some forms of Yiddish popular culture, notably theater (itself a novelty among Jews in late nineteenth-century Eastern Europe), thrived in America more readily than on the other side of the Atlantic Ocean, where censorship and other restrictions in czarist Russia restricted the development of **Yiddish theater** considerably. In addition to presenting new works by Jewish playwrights—which ranged from sentimental or sensational crowdpleasers to historical dramas and realist social-problem plays—the Yiddish stage introduced its audiences to European drama. Immigrant Jews attended Yiddish-language performances of pioneering works of modern drama and classic playwrights, including popularized and Judaized versions of Shakespeare. As a phenomenon embracing both "high" and "low" art, Yiddish theater soon became the focus of intense public debates about the moral, political, and aesthetic implications of popular culture. Even as it provided entertainment, the Yiddish stage was a powerful modernizing force in immigrant Jewish life and an important public venue for enacting a new immigrant cultural sensibility. Theatrical entertainments also engaged their audiences through the media of sound recordings and sheet music, which enabled the theatergoing public to savor performances by their favorite singers and comedians in the privacy of home and to perform songs made popular in theaters, accompanying themselves on the piano.

The American Yiddish press was the most widely visible venue for this immigrant popular culture. American Yiddish-speakers supported a sizeable number of newspapers and periodicals; by 1914 New York City boasted five Yiddish daily newspapers as well as other weekly and monthly periodicals. These publications provided readers with an array of engagements with Yiddish popular culture. Besides reporting on other practices—ranging from purchasing greeting cards for Rosh Hashanah to vacationing in the **Catskill Mountains**—newspapers were themselves facilitators of popular culture. They published works of popular literature, introduced new amusements such as Yiddish crossword puzzles and cartoons, and invited readers to contribute their voices to the newspaper by writing letters to the editor (exemplified by the ***Jewish Daily Forward***'s renowned advice column, "Bintel Brief") and entering contests for the best recipes or humorous anecdotes. Yiddish newspapers regularly printed poems by leading immigrant writers and also serialized works of fiction, including translations from world literature as well as original works written in Yiddish, many of them *shund-romanen* (sensational "potboiler" novels), which typically dealt with the challenges that readers faced in their daily lives as immigrants in urban America.

Following World War I and the restrictive immigration quotas enacted by the U.S. Congress in the early 1920s, the scope of Jewish immigration from Eastern Europe was severely limited. Increasingly, the American-born children of these immigrants defined the public profile of the nation's Jews. While many of them spoke or at least understood Yiddish, English was, as a rule, their primary language of daily life. Nevertheless, novel forms of Yiddish popular culture flourished in the decades following World War I, especially in the new media of radio and "talking" motion pictures. At the same time that network radiocasts and Hollywood films established a national, Anglophone mainstream culture of unprecedented scope, Yiddish radio and film emerged as alternative popular media for Jewish immigrants and their children.

The several dozen **Yiddish films** made in the United States during the 1930s brought to the screen both literary classics set in the old world —including Peretz Hirschbein's *Grine felder* (*Green Fields,* 1937) and Sholem Aleichem's *Tevye der milkhiker* (*Tevye the Milkman,* 1939)—and contemporary melodramas of intergenerational conflict set in urban America, such as *Vu iz mayn kind?* (*Where Is My Child?,* 1937) and *Hayntike mames* (*Modern Mothers,* 1939). These films both emulated the aesthetics of Hollywood feature and offered its audiences distinctive stories and sensibilities All of these films presented a cinematic world in which Yiddish was the prevailing language, spoken not only by Jews but also by an array of non-Jewish characters, from Ukrainian peasants to German anti-Semites. In its heyday, Yiddish radio programs were heard in New York, Chicago, Los Angeles, and other American cities with large Jewish populations. Beginning in the late 1920s, these broadcasts—which included soap operas, news reports, musical variety programs, interview programs—were, in fact, often bilingual; their programming freely mixed English and Yiddish, sometimes within the same sentence. This language play epitomized the intergenerational negotiation of immigrant parents' sensibilities with those of their American-born children. Yiddish-English bilingualism also informed much Jewish comedy of the 1920s, 1930s, and 1940s, including popular books of Jewish dialect humor by Milt Gross and **Leo Rosten** as well as sound recordings by **Mickey Katz** and **Menasha Skulnik**.

After World War II—which witnessed the murder of half of the world's Yiddish speakers and the destruction of their centuries-old cultural heartland in Eastern Europe—the significance of Yiddish in American Jewish culture changed rapidly. On one hand, growing numbers of American Jews abandoned Yiddish as a language of daily life; on the other hand, Yiddish gained new importance as a symbolic language for memorializing the victims of Nazism and recalling the East European heritage of immigrant generations. During the early postwar years, Yiddish informed numerous efforts to memorialize this vanished world, including popular works of philosophy, anthropology, photography, as well as anthologies of Yiddish literature in English translation. The most renowned and elaborate of these efforts was the hit Broadway musical of 1964, ***Fiddler on the Roof***, based on the fiction of Yiddish writer Sholem Aleichem.

During the postwar years Yiddish also became a fragmented code of Jewish ethnicity, stubbornly defying assimilationist tendencies and challenging established cultural boundaries. Even as many American Jews ceased speaking Yiddish, the nation's non-Jewish population avidly adopted a handful of Yiddishisms. A series of mock dictionaries, with titles such as *Yiddish for Yankees* and *Every Goy's Guide to Common Jewish Expressions,* offered comic explanations of selected Yiddish terms, especially those concerning food, sex, elimination, and states of emotional extreme. An extensive material culture of mass-produced items—refrigerator magnets, coffee mugs, lapel pins, board games, t-shirts, and the like—imprinted with one or more Yiddish words—has also appeared at the same time. These books and objects typically present Yiddish as the language of a raucous, appetitive, subversive Jewishness, contrasting sharply with the prevailing postwar image of Jewish religious life promoted by the major denominations as rational, respectable, and well integrated into the American mainstream.

The resurgent interest in **klezmer**, as the traditional instrumental music of East European Jewry has come to be known, beginning in the 1970s, has fostered a new interest in Yiddish as a heritage language engaged through music. This phenomenon has prompted performers both to learn the repertoires of Yiddish folksong, political song, and theater music and to create new works of Yiddish music. Much of this activity has involved performers who are not native speakers of the language, including a noteworthy number of non-Jews. The American-led klezmer "revival" also inspired similar interest in this music and its attendant Yiddish culture abroad, including in its erstwhile "homeland." Consequently, American musicians and scholars now play leading roles in teaching this "old world" vernacular culture in Eastern Europe.

At the same time, some American Jews maintain a commitment to Yiddish as a language of daily life. This commitment is most extensive among Hasidim, the majority of whom came to the United States after World War II. In contrast to their prewar engagement with the language in Eastern Europe, Hasidim typically use the language today to articulate the difference between their way of life and that of other, less stringently observant Jews, as well as the non-Jewish world. In recent decades, American Hasidim have developed a rich popular culture in Yiddish that combines mainstream cultural forms with content approved for these ultra-Orthodox communities. Examples include songs that set pious Yiddish lyrics to rock and other popular music idioms; Yiddish books, board games, puzzles, and similar items for Hasidic children; historical fiction, spy novels, and other works of "leisure" fiction written in Hasidic Yiddish, prefaced by letters of approval from rabbinic authorities.

For both Jews and non-Jews, American Yiddish popular culture serves as a revealing indicator of changes in the meaning of ethnic difference in the United States and how "ordinary" people (as opposed to religious, political, or intellectual elites) might engage this distinction in the practices of daily life. Whether as an old world heritage language, a language of separatist ultra-Orthodox piety, or a fragmentary language embedded in American mainstream culture, Yiddish has become a language charged with symbolic value, and its use in popular culture is emblematic of the tenacity as well as mutability of Jewishness in America.

Jeffrey Shandler

Further Reading: Hoberman, J. *Bridge of Light: Yiddish Film Between Two Worlds*. New York: Schocken, 1991. Shandler, Jeffrey. *Adventures in Yiddishland: Postvernacular Language and Culture*. Berkeley: University of California Press, 2005. Slobin, Mark, ed. *American Klezmer: Its Roots and Offshoots*. Berkeley: University of California Press, 2002.

YIDDISH FILM

As an effort to retain identity and heritage in the face of the "melting pot" myth, Yiddish cinema transcended territorial, political, and aesthetic boundaries in celebrating the richness of Jewish life. It was a cultural expression that began before World War I as a tool for combating czarist anti-Semitism and as a vehicle for presenting Jewish theater to the masses. Later, with the arrival of sound, Yiddish movies became a medium for entertaining non-English-speaking Jewish immigrants. At its zenith, between 1936 and 1940, Yiddish cinema provided an effective tool for strengthening Jewish identity. To be sure, Yiddish pictures were made to entertain, not to indoctrinate, but their stories and themes continually reinforced a belief in Jewish peoplehood and survival.

In 1911, Yiddish cinema production began simultaneously in Poland, Russia, and the United States. A. Y. Kaminsky arranged to have plays, produced by his Warsaw-based Yiddish theater troupe, filmed directly from the stage. Film prints were then sent to Jewish communities all across the Austro-Hungarian Empire, where they were seen by enthusiastic audiences. Most of Kaminsky's films starred his actress wife Esther Rokhl Kaminska (known as the mother of Yiddish theater), with daughter Ida (much later of *The Shop on Main Street* and *The Angel Levine* fame) appearing in some. At the same time in Moscow, Alexander Arkatov took a different tack by successfully adapting an original story about Jewish life in Russia for the screen; Arkatov used nonactors for his films. Kaminsky continued his film recordings until 1914 when the war made film stock rare and distribution impossible, while Arkatov's last film, an adaptation of a Sholem Aleichem story, was completed in 1917 on the eve of the Russian Revolution.

In the United States, the first Yiddish pictures were made by Sidney Goldin. To protest harsh anti-Semitism in czarist Russia, Goldin identified a new film genre. After World War I, Goldin made films in Austria using noted artists from Yiddish stage, such as **Maurice Schwartz** and **Molly Picon**. The 1920s brought us fine Yiddish films produced in Poland and the Soviet Union. In Poland, with Yiddish theater again thriving, actors from the Warsaw Yiddish Art Theatre helped create these pictures. Artists such as Zygmund Turkow, his brother Jonas Turkow, and Henry Szaro used Yiddish cinema to deal with difficult issues of the day. In the Soviet Union, where cultural development was initially encouraged by the Communist Party, Yiddish filmmaking was seen as an integral part of Soviet cinema production. Several films were produced during the period; they were directed by, written by, and featured some of the most talented Soviet artists, including Alexander Granovsky, Isaac Babel, Solomon Mikhoels, Benjamin Zuskin, Grigori Roshal, and G. Gricher-Cherikover. By the end of the decade though, with changing Soviet ideology, almost all Yiddish film production in Russia ceased. A sound motion picture, Peretz Markish's *The Return of Nathan Becker,* largely a showcase for the virtues of a communist way of life, was made in 1932.

Despite a dominance of Jews in the American film industry of the 1920s, producers were not interested in making pictures aimed at any one ethnic group, especially their own. Still, Jewish subject films with Jewish characters were produced, more often than not, featuring stories of Jews who sought intermarriage and assimilation. Upon achieving "the American dream" their Jewishness was almost always left behind. These films, with their "melting pot" ideology, seemed to appeal to the broad American audience. Yet, for many Jews these films proved objectionable, especially when intermarriage of Jew and Gentile was suggested. As sound in film became the norm by 1927–1928, the immigrant population not fluent in English, which had difficulty following the spoken dialogue, stopped frequenting the movies. Not only did they find the new "talkie" technology problematic, but they grew weary of the "assimilationist" themes of Hollywood movies. For them, Yiddish was not only their *mameloshn*—their mother-tongue; it represented a tradition that encouraged education, upward mobility, and acceptance into society. With that went a strong commitment to remaining a Jew and seeing that one's children would also maintain their Jewishness. Hollywood's film product was just not acceptable.

In response to Hollywood's portrayal of Jews and as a means of providing the 10-million-strong Yiddish-speaking audience with talking pictures they could understand, a Yiddish film industry began to evolve in the 1930s. At first, pictures were cheaply made, churned out in someone's kitchen or filmed off the theater stage. But by the mid-1930s, independent producers realized that better, well-crafted pictures could bring in greater box office returns. Some of the great actors of Yiddish theater, such as Boris Thomashefsky, Ludwig Satz, and Celia Adler, participated in these films. Since many Yiddish-speaking Jews still considered Eastern Europe as "home," many of the films dealt nostalgically with Jewish life back there. For many, Jewish values and culture seemed more clearly defined when living in the shtetl, while life in the West, with the push toward assimilation and acculturation, changed the mores of Jewish existence. The shtetl represented a pure Jewish spirit, lost in Americanization.

In 1936, Joseph Green, a Polish-born American, went back to Warsaw to try and authentically recreate Jewish life, an action that would revolutionize the new Yiddish film industry. Bringing Molly Picon, now a household name on the Yiddish stage, to Poland and coupling her with actors from the Warsaw theater, he made the Yiddish musical *Yidl Mitn Fidl* (Yidl with a Fiddle), the story of a girl who masquerades as a boy in order to join a troupe of klezmorim (traveling musicians). The film did exceptionally well in Poland, and when Green brought the movie to New York the following year, the lines of those waiting to see the picture stretched for blocks.

Green had proved that quality Yiddish films could be made and yield a profit. *Yidl Mitn Fidl* ushered in a "golden age of Yiddish cinema" that lasted from 1936 until 1940. During this five-year period, productions of the highest level were made. Green returned to Poland in 1937 and 1938, with Europe in the throes of Nazi expansion, to produce and direct three more Yiddish pictures. Many issues were tackled in his films, and all revolved around family and holiday celebration.

Sidney Goldin, "grandfather" of the Yiddish cinema, wanted to bring the "golden age" to America. Pointing to the success of Green's *Yidl Mitn Fidl,* he was able to raise sufficient funds for a large budget film, at least by Yiddish film standards. He engaged Moshe Oysher, one of the great vocalists in Yiddish theater, to star in what was actually an adaptation on the singer's story. Unfortunately, in September 1937, Goldin died in the middle of production of *Dem Khazns Zundl* (The Cantor's Son). Like Moses, who only saw the promised land from a distance, Goldin did not live to witness the presentation of high-quality, well-produced Yiddish pictures in America.

In Poland, 11 pictures (including Green's films) were produced during the golden age. These films, all of which exist today, provide a living testament to a vanished world. Performances by Avrom Marevsky, Dzigan and Schumacher, and Dina Halpern add vitality to movies written by some of the finest Yiddish writers of the twentieth century. Some of the films, such as *The Dybbuk* and*Yidl Mitn Fidl,* won international recognition and attracted large non-Jewish audiences. Yiddish cinema in Poland was a phenomenon. As Nazi activity in Europe increased, so did creative Yiddish cinema, as if an expression of resistance.

In America, Edgar G. Ulmer brought his European and Hollywood training to New York and helped usher in the golden age for Yiddish cinema. With his technical know-how and the support of Yiddish theater talents such as Jacob Ben-Ami, he successfully adapted theater classics for the screen. His first film was Peretz Hirschbein's *Green Fields.* Others, such as the noted Yiddish actor Maurice Schwartz and producers Roman Rebush and Abraham Leff, followed his lead. Ten classics were made between 1937 and 1940, including *Tevye, Mirele Efros,* and *The Light Ahead.* There were also numerous low-budget films produced during this period.

With the outbreak of World War II in Europe, worldwide Yiddish film production ground to a halt. One last elaborate production, *Der Vilner Balabesl* (The Vilna Petit-Bourgeois), was begun in America in 1939 and released the following year. Independent producers Ira Greene and Ludwig Landy lavished the Yiddish screen with opulence. They wanted faithful reproduction quality and emulated Hollywood movies by using expensive costumes and a wide variety of elegant sets unprecedented in Yiddish movies. It was to be the last "high-budget" Yiddish picture and an end to the golden age of Yiddish filmmaking.

With the end of World War II came a last effort to bring Yiddish cinema back to life. Several films were made in Poland, West Germany, and the United States. In 1950, however, the same year that the Yiddish Art Theatre closed in New York, Yiddish film production ceased. In Europe, there was barely a Yiddish-speaking audience. In America, Jews were beginning to view themselves differently—how they lived, where they lived, what professions they chose, and how they entertained themselves. Having largely recovered from the trauma of war, American Jews, both native and foreign-born, were finding it easy and comfortable to be just as "American" as their Gentile neighbors. A Yiddish picture, with its language and plot tied to an Eastern Europe of a bygone era, was of little interest. The Holocaust had shattered the illusion of comfort and peace in the "old country." American Jews, more than ever, wanted American culture.

In the 1970s, efforts were begun to restore and rehabilitate Yiddish pictures, and interest in such films grew significantly, drawing a new audience. As world Jewry had begun to rediscover its Jewish heritage, more and more young Jews were drawn to the Yiddish film form. Cinema historians and enthusiasts turned their attention to these creations of an ethnic minority as being among the more interesting examples of independent cinema. By the 1990s, Yiddish films had been released on video and shown on European television. Yiddish film festivals took place across North and South America, Europe, and Israel, and Yiddish pictures became mainstays of Jewish film festivals. Today, many Yiddish movies are available on DVD.

At one point, in the early 1960s, there seemed little future for the Yiddish cinema. As the Yiddish-speaking audience dwindled in size, it seemed less practical to produce Yiddish pictures. Yet, since 1980, Yiddish movies have been produced in Belgium, Israel, Poland, and the United States; others are being developed. A revival, at least a reappraisal, seems very much to be in the making.

Eric A. Goldman

Further Reading: Goldberg, Judith N. *Laughter through Tears*. Rutherford, NJ: Fairleigh Dickinson University Press, 1983. Goldman, Eric A. *Visions, Images, and Dreams: Yiddish Film Past and Present*. Ann Arbor, MI: UMI Research Press, 1983 (reissued in late 2008 by Holmes and Meier Publishers). Hoberman, J. *Bridge of Light: Yiddish Film between Two Worlds*. New York: Schocken, 1991. Kafanova, Ludmila. "Remembering Solomon Mikhoels." *New Leader* 61 (March 13, 1978): 16–17. Paskin, Sylvia. *When Joseph Met Molly*. London: Five Leaves, 1999.

YIDDISH THEATER

Yiddish theater in America was a vast, socially progressive and artistically diverse theatrical movement that dominated New York's Lower East Side from the 1880s until World War II. Taking over the former **vaudeville** houses and German language theaters on the Bowery, Yiddish companies first offered operettas based on biblical themes as well as melodramas dealing with immigrant life. The poet and former rabbinical student Avrom Goldfadn created the first Yiddish theater company in the world in Yasi, Romania in 1876, establishing a theater in Odessa by 1878. His company quickly inspired imitators throughout Europe and Russia, and by the early 1880s a teenage factory worker, Boris Thomashefsky, with the help of newly arrived Yiddish actors from Europe organized the first production of a Goldfadn operetta in America at Turn Hall, in New York City.

Thomashefsky became the first actor-impresario of the Yiddish stage in New York, a matinee idol beloved in plays such as *The Yeshiva Student* and *Alexander Crown Prince of Jerusalem*. By the time Thomashefsky took over the 3,500-seat Bowery theater, he staged *Hamlet* and *King Lear* in Yiddish translation as well as English melodramas such as *The Wages of Sin*. By 1883, the czar outlawed performances in Yiddish in Russia, which compelled many Yiddish performers to immigrate to the Lower East Side, creating what quickly became the largest nexus for Yiddish theater in the world. Soon the Bowery had several competing Yiddish theaters, and the waves of Yiddish-speaking immigrants ensured they had the audiences to fill them all.

America's Yiddish theater was less than a decade old in 1891 when the Russian Yiddish socialist Jacob Gordin arrived in New York. He and the Ukrainian-born actor Jacob P. Adler, who made a name for himself performing in London before settling in New York, strove to guide the Yiddish theater away from melodrama and toward a literary socialist theater of artistic quality. Adler starred in many of Gordin's dozens of plays, including *Siberia,* about the horrors of unjust imprisonment; *God, Man and Devil,* a Yiddish Faust story; and *The Wild Man,* a drama about an abused mentally handicapped man who falls in love with his stepmother and rapes her. The *New York Times* described Gordin in 1909 as: "the man who gave his life to bring the young Jewish mind up on thought, who forced them to make thinking their amusement." Gordin's hard-hitting subject matter was too explicit for the Broadway stage in English translation. When his hit play *The Kreutzer Sonata,* about a Jewish girl who becomes pregnant with her Gentile lover's child and whose father pays a Jewish man to marry her, was produced in English, reviewers were appalled. Similarly, in 1923, a production of Sholem Asch's drama *God of Vengeance,* a play about a Jewish brothel owner, led to the arrest of its entire Broadway cast for lewd behavior.

By the early twentieth century at least a dozen Broadway-sized houses of 2,000 seats or more presented plays in Yiddish on the Lower East Side and in Brooklyn, Harlem, and the Bronx. The first theater built especially for Yiddish theater was the Grand Street Theater in 1903; several others soon followed, many on Second Avenue. At the dawn of the twentieth century as Broadway was creating a home for itself in Times Square, Second Avenue became the center for Yiddish entertainment. New York wasn't the only place for Yiddish theater, however—Philadelphia, Chicago, Detroit, Boston, and Montreal, among other cities, played host to touring stars as well as resident companies.

Beginning with Jacob Gordin, Yiddish theater was divided into two camps—those who preferred melodramas and musicals and those who were interested in serious literary drama. Both types of theater addressed the myriad of challenging social issues facing their audiences. The glory days of the Yiddish musical were in the 1910s, 1920s, and 1930s, when conservatory-trained composers Joseph Rumshinsky, Alexander Olshanetsky, Abraham Ellstein, and Sholem Secunda were writing scores. Rumshinsky, who wrote show tunes imbued with the sound of Hasidic melodies, was instrumental in bringing a full pit orchestra into the Yiddish theaters. He created starring vehicles for the actress **Molly Picon**. The Russian-born Alexander Olshanetsky, a master of the romantic ballad, had a major hit with the song "I Love You Much Too Much," which he originally wrote for the actress Luba Kadison in the Second Avenue show *The Organgrinder.* Sholem Secunda is best known for "Bei Mir Bistu Sheyn," from the Yiddish musical *I Would If I Could,* popularized by the Andrew Sisters in 1938. While the Juilliard-trained Ellstein had many hit musicals on Second Avenue including the **Menasha Skulnik** vehicle—*The Scotsman of Orchard Street*—he also wrote songs for Broadway and an opera, *The Golem,* which debuted at Lincoln Center.

The first great performer of the Yiddish stage was Sigmund Mogulescu. Goldfadn created the roles of Shmendrik and Kuni Leml for him, and together they developed the comedic archetype of the luckless, socially awkward nebbish that was further popularized by the Yiddish actors Ludwig Satz and Menasha Skulnik, which we see in the work of many comedians today, including **Jerry Lewis**, **Woody Allen**, and **Larry David**. The actor David Kessler was known as the greatest tragedian of the Yiddish stage and for many years ran his own company comprised of the best actors in the city—among them a young **Maurice Schwartz**, perhaps the most significant figure in the latter days of the Yiddish stage. After publishing a manifesto in the *Forward* and the *Day* newspapers detailing his plans for creating a better Yiddish theater, Schwartz opened his Yiddish Art Theatre in 1918, which ran in repertory for over 30 consecutive seasons. In 1926, a 1,265-seat theater was built for Schwartz on Second Avenue and 12th Street which is now a Loews movie multiplex. His much-admired company presented new plays by the best Yiddish playwrights, such as Sholem Asch, Dovid Pinski, and Leon Kobrin, as well as translations of work by Ibsen, Chekov, Wilde, and Shaw. Across the street from Schwartz's theater, theater artists and their admirers packed the Cafe Royale, the Sardi's of the Lower East Side.

Ticket prices were higher in the Yiddish theaters, and the performers often made better salaries than their English-language counterparts. Devotees of the Yiddish stage were passionate about their favorite actors and created rival fan clubs that occasionally came to blows. Yiddish daily newspapers had a weekly theater section, and several Yiddish magazines were devoted completely to theater. When a major actor like Adler or Mogulescu died, tens of thousands of mourners followed the coffin down Second Avenue, resulting in some of the largest funerals in New York City history.

The Yiddish actors were almost always their own producers. Actors often married each other, creating profitable producing partnerships like those of Bessie and Boris Thomashefsky and Jacob and Sara Adler. As there was no shortage of starring roles for female performers, women were powerful creative and managerial forces. Goldfadn discovered the teenage soprano Sara Segal, who became the first Yiddish actress ever before moving on to have a successful career in America as Sophia Karp. Anna Held, one of the early stars of Broadway musicals and muse of producer Flo Ziegfeld, began her career with Jacob Adler on the Yiddish stage in London. Jacob Adler's wife Sara starred in Gordin's *Kreutzer*

Sonata, and Bessie Thomashefsky was a coquettish comedienne whose most famous role was as Minka, an impish housemaid. Bertha Kalisch was an actress equally as admired on the Yiddish and Broadway stages. Keni Liptsin was known for her matriarchal roles, originating the title role in Jacob Gordin's *Mirele Efros,* the story of a widow who turns her husband's failing business into an empire but alienates herself from her son. Most of the actors and writers of the American Yiddish stage were born in Russia and Europe, but two of its most beloved stars were born on the Lower East Side: Jennie Goldstein and Molly Picon. Goldstein, the queen of melodrama, began her career as a child star and together with her husband, Max Gabel, presented musicals where she played the jilted lover, abused wife, or bereaved mother. Molly Picon, directed by her husband and collaborator Jacob Kalich, starred as the irrepressible gamine in shows like *Molly Dolly!* and *O What a Girl!*

The Broadway and Yiddish theaters looked to each other for inspiration, both technical and creative. Many of the great writers of the American songbook came from the same background as their counterparts on the Jewish stage—Yiddish-speaking, Lower East Side, theater-going families —**Irving Berlin**, **Billy Rose**, and George and Ira Gershwin, to name a few. The actors Miriam Kressyn and Seymour Rexite, who did a radio show for Maxwell House coffee for over 50 years, performed the hit songs of the 1930s, 1940s, and 1950s in Kressyn's Yiddish translations. Yiddish actor Herman Yablokoff was the first to "mike" actors on stage, an innovation quickly adapted by Broadway producers.

The first actors' union in America was the Hebrew Actors Union, founded in 1899, which was instrumental in the creation of Actors Equity in 1913. Innovative Broadway set designers Boris Aaronson and Sam Leve both got their start on the Yiddish stage. The lighting designer Abe Feder, who lit up the Empire State Building, began his career with Joseph Buloff in the Yiddish theater in Chicago. Buloff, who traveled the world performing in Yiddish, played several roles on the Broadway stage, originating the part of Ali Hakim in *Oklahoma*. The actor-singer Aaron Lebedev, who wrote the classic Yiddish song "Romania, Romania," developed a style of skat singing that was popularized in American films by **Danny Kaye**. Academy Award winner Paul Muni began his career in the Yiddish theater working with his parents in vaudeville. He was later noticed by Broadway producers. In 1903, Jacob Adler performed the role of Shylock in Yiddish on Broadway with the rest of the cast performing in English. Many of Jacob Adler's children had successful careers in the theater, including Celia, Luther, Frances, and of course Stella Adler, who became the famed method acting teacher to Marlon Brando and Warren Beatty.

After World War II, the Yiddish theater began a slow decline. Completing a run of 32 consecutive seasons, Maurice Schwartz's Yiddish Art Theatre closed in 1950. Throughout the next decade, producer and lyricist Jacob Jacobs presented translations of hit Broadway shows on Second Avenue, including *The Student Prince, Anna Lucasta,* and Joseph Buloff's production of **Arthur Miller**'s *Death of Salesman* that "returned Miller's script to its Yiddish original," according to *Commentary* magazine. In the sixties and seventies, variety shows began to dominate. Molly Picon continued to star in light musical comedies such as *The Kosher Widow* and *A Cowboy in Israel,* composed for her by the last living Yiddish composer, Sholem Secunda, who died in 1973. That same year, the last hit show in Yiddish on Second Avenue was Sholem Aleichem's *Hard to Be a Jew,* with music by Secunda and starring Joseph Buloff and Miriam Kressyn, former stars of the Yiddish art and musical theaters, respectively, who would never have appeared together at the height of their careers. By 1977, there were no longer Yiddish theaters on the Lower East Side. There are still companies around the world performing in Yiddish today, however, including the National Yiddish Theater Folksbiene in New York, the Yiddish Spiel Theater in Tel Aviv, the State Jewish Theater in Warsaw, and the Dora Wasserman Theater in Montreal.

Caraid O'Brien

Further Reading: Kadison, Luba, Joseph Buloff, and Irving Genn. *Onstage, Offstage: A Lifetime in the Yiddish Theater.* Harvard University Press, 1992. Lifson, David S. *The Yiddish Theatre in America.* Cranbury, NJ: Yoseloff, 1965. Sandrow, Nahma. *Vagabond Stars: A World History of Yiddish Theater.* New York: Harper and Row, 1977.

YOUNGMAN, HENNY (1906–1998)

Stand-up comedian Henny Youngman was born Yonkel Yungman in Liverpool, England on January 12, 1906. His parents had immigrated from Russia to the United States, where his father was a hat maker and a sign painter. Youngman's father loved opera and arranged for Youngman to take violin lessons in the hope that someday he might play with the Metropolitan Opera orchestra. Youngman never achieved that, but he would use the violin as a prop for his comedy act. He grew up in Bay Ridge, Brooklyn, where he attended Public School 2 and Manual Training High School. After his suspension for classroom clowning and giving facetious answers to his teachers' questions, he spent his time going to New York City to see vaudeville comedians perform. After they expelled him from Manual Training High School, his father managed to have him enrolled in Brooklyn Vocational School so that he could learn the printing profession.

Eventually Youngman formed a band called the Syncopators. In the 1920s he took his band to the Catskill Mountain hotels, where he mixed comedy with music. From the Catskills and Brooklyn he found opportunities with such clubs as the Yacht Club of New York City, but the work was not very steady. From 1936 to 1938 he was on *The Kate Smith Show* for CBS. During those radio broadcasts he made his famous one-liner jokes like "Take my wife, please, get rid of her." Later he streamlined that remark to "Take my wife, please." Although his wife, Sadie Cohen, was often the butt of many of his jokes—such as "On our anniversary my wife said to me, 'For our anniversary I want to go somewhere I've never been before.' I said, 'Try the kitchen!' "—they were a happy couple and remained married for over 60 years until her death in 1987.

Hoping to get film contracts, Youngman arranged for Bud Abbott and Lou Costello to replace him on *The Kate Smith Show,* but film opportunities did not materialize until later in his career. Subsequently he traveled throughout the country doing his comedic performances. For more than 40 years he would average about 200 engagements a year, and some fellow comics would joke: "Everyone's trying to get on TV. Youngman is still trying to get on radio."

Finally, Youngman got lucky when he was hired to do cameo bits on 10 segments of television's *Hee-Haw,* a country version of *Laugh-In.* He also participated in the *Hollywood Squares* and as a guest on the *The Tonight Show Starring Johnny Carson.* In 1974, he recorded for the telephone company, and some three million people called to hear Youngman tell his jokes.

Youngman was known as the "King of the One Liners," a title bestowed upon him by columnist **Walter Winchell**. A typical stage performance by Youngman lasted only 15 to 20 minutes but contained dozens of jokes, spouted in rapid-fire fashion.

His prescription for peace of mind was "Good health for you and your family, and money in your pocket. That's all." *See also* **Comedy**.

Herbert M. Druks

Further Reading: Youngman, Henny, and Neal Karlen. *Take My Life! Please.* Putnam, 1973.

Bibliography

Abrahamson, Edward A. *Chaim Potok.* Boston: Twayne, 1986.

Adamson, Joe. *Groucho, Harpo, Chico and Sometimes Zeppo: A History of the Marx Brothers and a Satire on the Rest of the World.* New York: Simon and Schuster, 1973.

Adler, Jerry. "Freud in Our Midst." *Newsweek* 147, no. 13 (March 27, 2006): 42–49.

Adler, Mortimer. *A Second Look in the Rearview Mirror: Further Autobiographical Reflections of a Philosopher at Large.* New York: St. Martin's Press, 1992.

———.*How to Read a Book: A Guide to Reading the Great Book.* New York: Touchstone Publishing, 1966.

———. *Six Great Ideas: Truth-Goodness-Beauty-Liberty-Equality- Justice.* New York: Simon and Schuster, 1997.

Albom, Mitch. *The Five People You Meet in Heaven,* New York: Hyperion Books, 2003.

———. *For One More Day,* New York: Hyperion, 2006.

———. *Tuesdays with Morrie,* New York: Doubleday, 1997.

Aleichem, Sholem. *Tevye the Dairyman and the Railroad Stories,* translated by Hillel Halkin. New York: Schocken, 1996.

Alexander, Paul. *Salinger: A Biography.* Los Angeles: Renaissance, 1999.

Alexander, Shana. *When She Was Bad.* Dell, 1991.

Allen, William Rodney, ed. *The Coen Brothers Interviews.* Conversations With Filmmakers Series. Jackson, MS: University of Mississippi Press, 2006.

Allen, Woody. *Side Effects.* New York: Random House, 1980.

———. *Without Feathers.* New York: Ballantine Books, 1983.

Altman, Richard, with Mervyn Kaufman. *The Making of a Musical: Fiddler on the Roof.* New York: Crown, 1971.

Altman, Sig. *The Comic Image of the Jew: Explorations of a Pop Culture Phenomenon.* Rutherford, NJ: Fairleigh Dickinson University Press, 1971.

Altschuler, Glenn C., and David I. Grossvogel. *Changing Channels: America in TV Guide.* Urbana, IL: University of Illinois Press, 1992.

American Theatre Wing. "Tovah Feldshuh." Biography. Updated 2006. Accessed August 2008. www.americantheatrewing.org/biography/detail/tovah_feldshuh.

Anderson, Christopher. *Barbra: The Way She Is.* Harper Collins, 2006.

"An Interview with Cynthia Ozick." *Paris Review* 102 (Spring 1987).

Anjou, Erik. *A Cantor's Tale.* Documentary Film. Teaneck, NJ: Ergo Media Inc., 2006.

Antler, Joyce. *The Journey Home: How Jewish Women Shaped Modern America.* New York: Shocken, 1998.

———. "Not 'Too Jewish' for Prime Time." In *Television's Changing Image of American Jews.* Edited by Neal Gabler, Frank Rich, and Joyce Antler. New York: The American Jewish Committee and The Norman Lear Center, 2000.

Apple, Max. *I Love Gootie: My Grandmother's Story.* New York: Grand Central Publishing, 1998.

———. *Roommates: My Grandfather's Story.* New York> Grand Central Publishing, 1994.

Arkin, Alan. *Halfway through the Door: First Steps on a Path of Enlightenment.* Harper San Francisco, 1984.

———. *The Lemming Condition*. Harper One, 1989.

Arthur Miller Society Web Site: http://www.ibiblio.org/miller/

"The Art of Poetry." *Paris Review* 166, 1997.

Atkinson, Brooks. Review of *The Fifth Season,* January 24, 1953.

Atlas, James. *Bellow: A Biography.* New York: Random House, 2000.

Avery, Evelyn, ed. *The Magic Worlds of Bernard Malamud*. State University of New York, 2002.

Bacall, Lauren. *By Myself and Then Some.* New York: Harper-Collins Books, 2005.

Baker, James T. *Ayn Rand.* Boston: Twayne, 1987.

Bankston, John. *Ben Stiller (Real-Life Reader Biography).* Hockessin, DE: Mitchell Lane Publishers, 2002.

Baron, Lawrence. *Projecting the Holocaust into the Present: The Changing Focus of Holocaust Feature Films Since 1990.* Lanham, MD: Rowman and Littlefield, 2005.

Barry, Julian. *Lenny: A Play Based on His Life and Words of Lenny Bruce.* New York: Grove Press, 1971.

Baxter, John. *Steven Spielberg: The Unauthorized Biography.* Harper Collins, 1997.

Beaver, Jim. *John Garfield: His Life and Films.* Cranbury, NJ: A.S. Barnes and Co., 1978.

Beck, Robert. *The Edward G. Robinson Encyclopedia.* Jefferson, NC: McFarland and Co., 2002.

Beeber, Steven Lee. *The Heebie-Jeebies at CBGB's: A Secret History of Jewish Punk.* Chicago: Chicago Review Press, Inc, 2006.

Behlman, Lee. "The Escapist: Fantasy, Folklore, and the Pleasures of the Comic Book in Recent Jewish American Holocaust Fiction," *Shofar* 22, no. 3 (2004): 56–71.

Bellin, Mildred Grosberg. *The Jewish Cook Book.* Garden City, NY: Doubleday and Company, Inc., 1958.

Belva Plain Web Site. "A Conversation with Belva Plain." www.randomhouse.com/features/belvaplain.

Benarde, Scott. *Stars of David: Rock 'n' Roll's Jewish Stories.* Hanover, NH: Brandeis University Press, 2003.

Benny, Jack, and Joan Benny, *Sunday Nights at Seven: The Jack Benny Story.* New York: Warner Books, 1990.

Berenbaum, Michael. *The World Must Know: The History of the Holocaust As Told in the United States Holocaust Memorial Museum.* New York: Little, Brown and Company, 1993.

Berg, Gertrude, and Charney Berg. *Molly and Me.* New York: McGraw Hill, 1961.

Bergreen, Laurence. *As Thousands Cheer: The Life of Irving Berlin.* Cambridge, MA: Da Capo Press, 1996.

Berkman, Ted. *Cast A Giant Shadow: The Story of Mickey Marcus Who Died to Save Jerusalem.* Manifest Publications, 1999.

Berkwits, Jeff. "Stars of David." *San Diego Jewish Journal,* October 2004.

Berle, Milton, and Haskel Frankel. *Milton Berle: An Autobiography with Haskel Frankel.* New York: Dell, 1994.

Bernardo, Melissa Rose. "Tovah Feldshuh 'In a Nutshell.'" *Entertainment Weekly,* March 7, 2008.

Bernstein, Adam. "The Blue-Eyed Antihero." Obituary, *Washington Post,* September 28, 2008.

Berson, Misha. "Cool and Dashing, Paul Newman Was a New Kind of Jewish Star." *Forward,* October 10, 2008, 1, 9.

Bial, Henry Carl. *Acting Jewish: Negotiating Ethnicity on the American Stage and Screen.* Ann Arbor, MI: University of Michigan Press, 2005.

Bigsby, Christopher. *Arthur Miller, A Critical Study.* United Kingdom: Cambridge University Press, 2005.

Bikel, Theodore. *Autobiography of Theodore Bikel.* New York: Harper Collins, 1994.

Billig, Michael. *Rock 'n' Roll Jews.* Syracuse, NY: Syracuse University Press, 2000.

"Bionic Man." *Sports Illustrated,* October 23, 1989, 80–82.

Blech, Zushe Yosef. *Kosher Food Production.* Oxford, United Kingdom: Blackwell Publishing, 2008.

Bloch, Abraham P. *The Biblical and Historical Background of the Jewish Holy Days.* Ktav, 1978.

Bloom, Alexander. *Prodigal Sons: The New York Intellectuals & Their World.* Oxford University Press, 1986.

Bloom, Harold, ed. *Bernard Malamud: Modern Critical Views.* Chelsea House, 1986.

———. *Modern Critical Views: E. L. Doctorow.* Philadelphia: Chelsea House Publishers, 2001.

Blum, Brian. "Who?" *Shabbat Shalom,* June 15, 2006.

Blustain, Sarah. "A Paradoxical Legacy: Rabbi Shlomo Carlebach's Shadow Side." *Lilith,* Spring 1998.

Bodner, Allen. *When Boxing Was a Jewish Sport.* Praeger Trade, 1997.

Boskin, Joseph. *Rebellious Laughter.* Syracuse, NY: Syracuse University Press, 1997.

Bosworth, Patricia. *Diane Arbus: A Biography.* New York: W.W. Norton and Company, 1976.

Boteach, Shmuley, and Uri Geller. *Confessions of a Psychic and a Rabbi.* New York: Element Books, 2000.

Brady, John. *The Craft of the Screenwriter.* New York: Simon and Schuster, 1981.

Branden, Barbara. *The Passion of Ayn Rand.* New York: Doubleday, 1986.

Branden Nathaniel, and Barbara Branden. *Who Is Ayn Rand?* New York: Random House, 1962.

Brandt, Randal. "Irving Stone's Lust for Life." *Bancroftiana, Newsletter of the Friends of the Bancroft Library,* no. 123, Fall 2003, bancroft.berkeley.edu/events/bancroftiana/123/stone.html.

Breneman-Gibson, Margaret. *Clifford Odets—American Playwright—The Years from 1906–1940.* Atheneum, 1981.

Brody, Seymour. "Jewish Heroes and Heroines in America 1900 to World War II." Florida Atlantic University Libraries, October 19, 2006. Accessed September 8, 2006. www.fau.edu/library/bro94.htm.

Bronner, Simon J. "The Lieberman Syndrome: Public and Private Jewishness in American Political Culture." *Journal of Modern Jewish Studies* 2 (2003): 35–58.

———. "Structural and Stylistic Relations of Oral and Literary Humor: An Analysis of Leo Rosten's H*Y*M*A*N K*A*P*L*A*N Stories." *Journal of the Folklore Institute* 19 (1982): 31–45.

Brook, Vincent. *Something Ain't Kosher Here: The Rise of the "Jewish" Sitcom.* New Brunswick, NJ: Rutgers University Press, 2003.

Brooks, Tim, and Earle Marsh. *The Complete Directory to Prime Time Network and Cable TV Shows, 1946–Present.* New York: Random House, 2007.

Brothers, Joyce. *Widowed.* New York: Ballantine Books, 1990.

Brown, M. *Tearing Down the Wall of Sound: The Rise and Fall of Phil Spector,* London: Bloomsbury, 2007.

Brown, Phil. *Catskill Culture: A Mountain Rat's Memories of the Great Jewish Resort Area* Philadelphia: Temple University Press, 1999.

———, ed. *In the Catskills: A Century of the Jewish Experience in "The Mountains."* New York: Columbia University Press, 2002.

Brumburgh, Gary. "Hal Linden Biography." Internet Movie Database, 2008.

Buchwald, Art. *I'll Always Have Paris.* New York: G.P. Putnam, 1995.

———. *Leaving Home: A Memoir.* New York: G.P. Putnam's, 1994.

———. *Too Soon to Say Goodbye.* New York: Random House, 2007.

Buhle, Paul. *From the Lower East Side to Hollywood.* London: Verso, 2004.

———, ed. *Jews and American Popular Culture.* 3 vols. Westport, CT: Praeger, 2007.

Burns, George. *Gracie: A Love Story.* New York: Signer, 1991.

Burns, Ken, and Geoffrey Ward. *Jazz, a History of American Music.* New York: Knopf, 2000.

Burstein, Janet. *Telling the Little Secrets: American Jewish Writing Since the 1980s.* Madison: University of Wisconsin, 2006.

Burton, Humphrey. *Leonard Bernstein.* New York: Doubleday, 1994.

"The Bush Doctrine." *Think Tank,* PBS. July 11, 2002.

Butler, Patricia. *Barry Manilow: The Biography.* Music Sales, 2007.

Byrne, Bridget. "Peter Falk." *Us Magazine* 3, no. 102 (May 15, 1989): 48–52.

Caesar, Sid, with Bill Davidson. *Where Have I Been: An Autobiography.* New York: Crown Publishers, 1982

Caesar, Sid, and Eddy Friedfeld. *Caesar's Hours: My Life in Comedy, with Love and Laughter.* New York: Public Affairs, 2003.

Campbell, Colin. "Paddy Chayefsky Dead at 58; Playwright Won Three Oscars." *New York Times,* August 2, 1981.

Caplan, Eric. *Mind Games: American Culture and the Birth of Psychotherapy.* Berkeley and Los Angeles: University of California Press, 2001.

Caplin, Eliott. *Al Capp Remembered.* Bowling Green, OH: Bowling Green State University Popular Press, 1994.

Carlisle, Kitty. *Kitty: An Autobiography.* New York: Doubleday, 1988.

Carr, Steven Alan. *Hollywood and Anti-Semitism: A Cultural History up to World War II.* Cambridge: Cambridge University Press, 2001.

Carson, Tom. "Harold Robbins: The Man Who Invented Sex." Book review. *New York Times,* October 21, 2007.

Catskill Institute Web Site: http://catskills.brown.edu.

Centola, Steven R., and Michelle Cirulli, eds. *The Critical Response to Arthur Miller.* Connecticut: Greenwood Press, 2006.

Chabad.org. Interview with Matisyahu, April 15, 2006.

Chabon, Michael. *The Amazing Adventures of Kavalier & Clay.* New York: Random House, 2000.

———. *The Yiddish Policeman's Union.* New York: Harper Collins, 2007.

"Choreographer Michael Kidd Dies." Theater-MSNBC.com. Accessed April 25, 2008. www.msnbc.msn.com/id/22394186.

Christopher, Milbourne. *Mediums, Mystics and the Occult.* New York: Thomas Y. Crowell, 1969.

Chujoy, Anatole. *The Dance Encyclopedia.* New York: Simon and Schuster, 1967.

Clark, Ronald W. *Einstein: The Life and Times.* New York: HarperCollins, 1984.

Cocks, Geoffrey. *The Wolf at the Door: Stanley Kubrick, History, and the Holocaust.* New York: Peter Lang, 2004.

———, et al., eds. *Depth of Field: Stanley Kubrick, Film, and the Uses of History.* Madison, WI: University of Wisconsin Press, 2006.

Cohen, Art. *The Nine Lives of Mike Todd.* London: Hutchinson, 1958.

Cohen, Rich. *Tough Jews: Fathers, Sons, and Gangster Dreams.* New York: Simon and Schuster, 1998.

Cohen, Sarah Blacher, ed. *From Hester Street to Hollywood: Jewish-American Stage and Screen.* Bloomington, IN: Indiana University Press, 1986.

———, ed. *Jewish Wry: Essays on Jewish Humor.* Bloomington, IN: Indiana University Press, 1987.

Collier, James Lincoln. *Benny Goodman and the Swing Era.* New York: Oxford University Press, 1989.

Cook, Richard M. *Alfred Kazin: A Biography.* New Haven: Yale University Press, 2007.

Cooke, Andrew, and Jon Cooke. *Will Eisner: The Spirit of an Artistic Pioneer.* Documentary. Montilla Pictures, 2006.

Cooney, John. *The Annenbergs: The Salvaging of a Tainted Dynasty.* New York: Simon and Schuster, 1982.

Cooper, Alan. *Philip Roth and the Jews* (SUNY Series in Modern Jewish Literature and Culture), 1996.

Copland, Aaron, and Vivian Perlis. *Copland Since 1943.* New York: St. Martin's Press, 1989.

Cox, Steve, and Jim Perry. *One Fine Stooge: A Frizzy Life in Pictures.* Cumberland House Publishing, 2006.

Crawford, Catherine, ed. *If You Really Want to Hear About It: Writers on J. D. Salinger and His Work.* New York: Thunder's Mouth, 2006.

Crowther, Bosley. "Review of Gentleman's Agreement," *The New York Times,* November 12, 1947.

Cullinan, Bernice E., and Diane G. Person, eds. *The Continuum Encyclopedia of Children's Literature.* New York: Continuum Publishing, 2001.

Cunningham, Frank R. *Sidney Lumet: Film and Literary Vision.* University Press of Kentucky, 1991.

Cunningham, Steve. "License to Chill." *New Times* (Broward Palm Beach, FL), March 6 2008.

Curtis, Tony, and Peter Golenbock.*American Prince: A Memoir.* New York: Random House, 2008.

Curtis, Tony, and Barry Paris. *Tony Curtis: The Autobiography.* New York: William Morrow and Co., 1993.

Daffron, Carolyn. *Gloria Steinem.* New York : Chelsea House Publishers, 1988.

Dann, Jack, ed. *Wandering Stars: An Anthology of Jewish Fantasy and Science Fiction* New York: Harper and Row, 1974.

Davidson, Keay. *Carl Sagan: A Life.* John Wily and Sons, 2000.

Davis, Philip. *Bernard Malamud.* Oxford University Press, 2007.

Davis, Sammy, and Burt Boyar and Jane Boyar. *Sammy: The Autobiography of Sammy Davis, Jr.* New York: Farrar, Straus and Giroux, 2000.

Dershowitz, Alan M. *Chutzpah.* Boston: Little Brown, 1991.

Dershowitz Web Site: http://www.alandershowitz.com.

Deutsche mah-jongg Liga. Mah Jongg Museum, http://www.mah-jongg-museum.de/musik_001.html.

Dickenson, Amy. "Dishing Up Lamb Chop; On PBS, Shari Lewis's Second Generation." *Washington Post,* April 4, 1994.

Dickter, Adam. "Facing A Mixed Legacy." *The Jewish Week,* September 8, 2004.

Diner, Hasia R. *Hungering for America: Italian, Irish, and Jewish Foodways in the Age of Migration.* Cambridge, MA: Harvard University Press, 2001.

Dines, Tim. *The Jazz Singer* (1927), www.filmsite.org.

Doctorow, Edgar L. *Creationist: Selected Essays: 1993–2006.* New York: Random House, 2006.

Dolan, Deirdre. *Curb Your Enthusiasm: The Book.* New York: Gotham Books, 2006.

Doneson, Judith E. *The Holocaust in American Film.* Philadelphia: Jewish Publication Society, 1987.

Dougherty, Terri. *Ben Stiller (People in the News).* San Diego, CA: Lucent Books, 2006.

Douglas, Kirk. *Climbing the Mountain: My Search for Meaning.* New York: Simon and Schuster, 2000.

———. *The Ragman's Son.* New York: Simon and Schuster, 1988.

Downey, Lynn. *Levi Strauss and Company.* Mt. Pleasant, SC: Arcadia Publishing, 2007.

Dunning, Jennifer. "Celebrating Seven Decades of a Modern Dance Crucible." *New York Times,* February 24, 2004.

Dunning, John. *On the Air: The Encyclopedia of Old-Time Radio.* Oxford University Press, 1998.

Dworkin, Susan. *Miss America, 1945: Bess Myerson's Own Story.* Newmarket Press, 1987.

Dylan, Bob. *Chronicles: Volume I.* New York: Simon and Schuster, 2004.

Edelman, Marsha Bryan. "Reinventing Hasidic Music: Shlomo Carlebach." MyJewishLearning.com, 2003.

Edmonds, David, and John Eidinow. *Bobby Fischer Goes to War.* New York: Harper Collins, 2005.

Einstein, Albert. *Ideas and Opinions.* New York: Crown Publishers, 1954.

———. "The Negro Question." Essay. 1946.

———. "Why Socialism?" *Monthly Review,* May 1949.

Eisner, Will. *The Plot: The Secret Story of The Protocols of the Elders of Zion.* W.W. Norton, 2006.

Emerson, K. *Always Magic in the Air: The Bomp and Brilliance of the Brill Building Era.* New York: Viking, 2005.

Ephross, Peter. "Leon Uris Dies—Created 'Mythic Israel' for Generations." *Jewish Telegraphic Agency,* June 27, 2003. Accessed September 4, 2008. www.jewishsf.com/content/2-0-/module/displaystory/story_id/20596/edition_id/421/format/html/displaystory.html.

Epstein, Lawrence J. *The Haunted Smile: The Story of Jewish Comedians in America.* New York: Public Affairs, 2001.

Erdman, Harley. *Staging the Jew: The Performance of an American Ethnicity, 1860–1920.* New Brunwick, London: Rutgers University Press, 1997.

Erens, Patricia. *The Jew in American Cinema.* Bloomington, IN: Indiana University Press, 1984.

Erwin, Edward, ed. *Freud Encyclopedia: Theory, Therapy, and Culture.* London: Routledge Press, 2002.

Ewen, David. *All the Years of American Popular Music.* Englewood Cliffs, NJ: Prentice-Hall, 1977.

Fagen, Herb, and George Burns. *George Burns: In His Own Words.* New York: Carroll and Graf, 1996.

Falk, Peter, and Jeff Kaye. "Rumpled and Ready: Columbo Returns! What You Can Expect from Him Now." *TV Guide* 37, no. 5 (February 4, 1989): 10–12.

Feiffer, Jules. *Feiffer: The Collected Works, Volumes 1, 2, 3.* Seattle, WA: Fantagraphics Books, 1989.

Fein, Irving. *Jack Benny: An Intimate Biography.* New York: Putnam, 1976.

Feldman, Jan. *Lubavitchers as Citizens.* Ithaca: Cornell University Press, 2003.

Ferber, Edna. *A Kind of Magic.* New York: Doubleday, 1963.

———. *A Peculiar Treasure.* Garden City, NY: Doubleday Doran and Co., 1939.

Fiedler, Leslie. "Henry Roth's Neglected Masterpiece." *Commentary Magazine,* 1960.

Fierstein, Harvey. "A 12-Step Program Guaranteed to Change your Life." Transcript of Harvey Fierstein's Commencement Speech to the Bennington College Class of 1992. www.qrd.org/qrd/media/people/1992/harvey.fierstein.speech-12.30.92.

———. "Our Prejudices, Ourselves." *New York Times,* April 13, 2007.

———. *Torch Song Trilogy.* New York: Random House, 1984.

Fine, Ellen. *Legacy of Night: The Literary Universe of Elie Wiesel.* Albany: State University of New York Press, 1982.

Fineberg, Jonathan. *Art Since 1940.* New York: Harry N. Abrams, Inc., 1995.

Fingeroth, Danny. *Disguised as Clark Kent: Jews, Comics, and the Creation of the Superhero.* New York: Continuum, 2007.

Fisher, Eddie. *Been There, Done That.* New York: St. Martin's Press, 1999.

———. *My Life, My Loves.* New York: Harper Collins, 1984.

Fishgall, Gary. *Gonna Do Great Things: The Life of Sammy Davis, Jr.* New York: Scribner, 2003.

Fishkoff, Sue. *The Rebbe's Army: The World of Chabad-Lubavitch.* New York: Schocken, 2003.

Flanzbaum, Hilene, ed. *The Americanization of the Holocaust.* Baltimore: The Johns Hopkins University Press, 1999.

Fleischman, Sid. *The Story of the Great Houdini.* New York: Greenwillow Books, 2006.

"The Fonz, Henry Winkler, joins Ed Balls for reading launch." *Telegraph Media Group,* July 2, 2008. Accessed September 7, 2008. telegraph.co.uk.

Forte, Allen. *Listening to Classic American Popular Songs.* New Haven, CT: Yale University Press, 2001.

Foulkes, Julia. "Angels 'Rewolt!': Jewish Women in Modern Dance in the 1930s." *American Jewish History* 88 (2000).

Frank, Philipp. *Einstein: His Life and Times.* Cambridge, MA: Da Capo Press, 2002.

Franklin, Joe. *Joe Franklin's Encyclopedia of Comedians.* Citadel Press, 1979.

Frazier, Nancy. *Jewish Museums of North America.* New York: John Wiley and Sons Inc., 1992.

Freedman, Samuel G. *Jew vs. Jew: The Struggle for the Soul of American Jewry.* New York: Touchstone, 2000.

Freud, Sigmund. *Jokes and Their Relation to the Unconscious.* London: Pelican Freud Library, 1905.

Fried, Albert. *The Rise and Fall of the Jewish Gangster in America.* New York: Columbia University Press, 1993.

Friedman, Debbie. *Best Of Debbie Friedman.* Milwaukee, WI: Hal Leonard Corporation, 1997.

———. *Miracles & Wonders: Musicals for Chanukah and Purim.* Clifton, NJ: Sounds Write Productions, 1992.

Friedman, Lester D. *Hollywood's Image of the Jew.* New York: Ungar Publishing Company, 1982.

Friedman, Murray. "Opening the Discussion of American Jewish Political Conservatism." *American Jewish History* 87, no 2 and 3 (June and September 1999).

Friedman, Thomas. *From Beirut to Jerusalem.* New York: Doubleday Publishing, 1989.

———. *Longitude and Attitudes: Exploring the World after September 11.* New York: Farrar, Straus and Giroux, 2002.

———. *The World is Flat: A Brief History of the Twenty-First Century.* New York: Farrar, Straus and Giroux, 2005.

Gabler, Neal. *An Empire of Their Own: How the Jews Invented Hollywood.* New York: Doubleday, 1988.

———. *Winchell: Gossip, Power and Culture of Celebrity.* New York: Knopf, 1994.

Gaige, Jeremy. *Chess Personalia: A Biobibliography.* Jefferson, NC: McFarland, 1987.

Gansberg, Alan L. *Little Caesar: A Biography of Edward G. Robinson.* Blue Ridge Summit, PA: Scarecrow Press, 2004.

Garber, Zev. "Dating the Shoah: In Your Blood Shall You Live," in Z. Garber, *Shoah: The Paradigmatic Genocide.* Lanham, MD: University Press of America, 1994.

Garebian, Keith. *The Making of West Side Story.* New York: Mosaic Press, 1998.

Gates, Anita. "Theater Review: Legends of Yiddish Stage Brought to Life." *New York Times,* December 30, 1997.

Gebert, Gordon G. G., and Bob McAdams. *Kiss & Tell.* Pitbull Publishing, 1997.

Gehring, W. D. "The Marx of Time" *Thalia: Studies in Literary Humor* 11, no. 1 (1989): 25–33.

German American Corner. www.germanheritage.com.

Gilbert, Julie. *Opposite Attraction: The Lives of Erich Marie Remarque and Paulette Goddard.* New York: Pantheon Books, 1995.

Gilbert, Julie Goldsmith. *Ferber—A Biography.* New York: Doubleday, 1978.

Gill, Julian. *The Kiss Album Focus* (3rd edition), Volume 2. Philadelphia, PA: Xlibris Corporation, 2005.

———. *The Kiss & Related Recordings Focus: Music! the Songs, the Demo, the Lyrics and Stories!* Philadelphia, PA: Xlibris Corporation, 2005.

Ginott, Haim. *Between Parent and Teenager.* New York: Macmillan, 1967.

———. *Teacher and Child.* New York: Macmillan, 1972.

Ginott, Haim G., Alice Ginott, and H. Wallace Goddard. *Between Parent and Child.* New York: Three Rivers Press, 2003.

Gittlesohn, Roland B. "Brothers All?" *The Reconstructionist,* February 7, 1947.

Glass, Philip. *Music By Philip Glass.* New York: Harper and Row, 1987.

Going Where I've Never Been Before: The Photographs of Diane Arbus. Videocassette. Camera Three Productions, 1989.

Goldberg, Howard G. "Manischewitz Only Sweet? Not Anymore," *New York Times,* March 23, 1994.

Goldberg, J. J. *Jewish Power: Inside the American Jewish Establishment.* New York: Perseus Book Group, 1996.

———. "Seining Off." *The Jewish Journal of Greater Los Angeles.* May 15, 1998.

Goldberg, Judith N. *Laughter through Tears.* Rutherford, NJ: Fairleigh Dickinson University Press, 1983.

Golden, Harry. *Only in America,* New York: World Publishing Co., 1958 (republished in 1972).

———. *The Right Time: An Autobiography.* New York: G.P. Putnam's Sons, 1969.

Goldman, Albert. *Ladies and Gentlemen: LENNY BRUCE!!* New York: Random House, 1974.

Goldman, Ari L. "Obituary of Rabbi Shlomo Carlebach." *New York Times,* October 22, 1994.

Goldman, Eric A. *Visions, Images, and Dreams: Yiddish Film Past and Present.* Ann Arbor, MI: UMI Research Press, 1983 (reissued in late 2008 by Holmes and Meier Publishers).

Goldman, Herbert. *Fanny Brice: The Original Funny Girl.* Cambridge: Oxford University Press, 1993.

Goldman, Herbert G. *Banjo Eyes: Eddie Cantor and the Birth of Modern Stardom.* New York: Oxford University Press, 1997.

Goldstein, Malcolm. *George S Kaufman—His Life, His Theater.* New York: Oxford University Press, 1979.

Goodman, Benny, and Irving Kolodin. *The Kingdom of Swing.* New York: Stockpale, 1939.

Goodwin, George M. "A New Jewish Elite: Curators, Directors, and Benefactors of American Art Museums." *Modern Judaism,* 18, no. 1 (February 1998).

Gordon, Andrew. "Jewish Fathers and Sons in Spiegelman's *Maus* and Roth's *Patrimony.*" *Image Text,* no. 1, 2004.

Gordon, Andrew M. *An American Dreamer: A Psychoanalytic Study of the Fiction of Norman Mailer.* Cranbury, NJ: Associated University Presses/Fairleigh Dickinson University Press, 1980.

Gordon, Joanne. *Art Isn't Easy.* Carbondale: Southern Illinois University, 1992.

Gottfried, Martin. *Nobody's Fool: The Lives of Danny Kaye.* Simon and Schuster, 1994.

———. *Sondheim.* New York: Harry Abrams, Inc., 1993.

Gottlieb, Polly Rose. *The Nine Lives of Billy Rose.* New York: Crown Publishers, Inc., 1968.

Grade, Chaim. *My Mother's Sabbath Days: A Memoir, Chana Kleinerman Goldstein and Inna Hecker Grade.* New York: Jason Aronson, 1997.

———. *The Yeshiva.* Trans. Curt Leviant. New York: Bobbs Merril Co., 1976.

Graft, Ellen. *Stepping Left: Dance and Politics in New York City, 1928–1942.* Durham, NC: Duke University Press, 1997.

Graver, Lawrence. *An Obsession with Anne Frank.* University of California Press, 1985.

Gray, Michael. *The Bob Dylan Encyclopedia.* Continuum International, 2006.

Green, Gerald. *Holocaust.* New York: Rosetta Books, 1978.

———. *The Last Angry Man.* New York: Rosetta Books, 1957.

Green, Stanley. *The World of Musical Comedy.* South Brunswick, NJ: Barnes, 1976.

Greenberg, Hank, and Ira Berkow. *The Story of My Life.* Crown, 1989.

Greenberg, Martin. *Jewish Lists.* New York: Schocken, 1979.

Groch, John R. "What is a Marx Brother." *The Velvet Light Trap* 26 (1990): 28–41. University of Texas Press.

Grossman, Barbara W. *Funny Woman: The Life and Times of Fanny Brice.* Bloomington: Indiana University Press, 1991.

Grossman, Grace Cohen. *Jewish Museums of the World.* Westport, CT: Hough Lauter Levin Associates, Inc.: Beaux Arts Editions, 2003.

Gurock, Jeffrey S. *Judaism's Encounter with American Sports.* Bloomington: Indiana University Press, 2005.

Guttman, Allan. *The Jewish Writers in America.* Oxford University Press, 1971.

Guttridge, Peter. "Ira Levin." Obituary. *Independent,* November 15, 2007.

Haberman, J., and Jeffrey Shandler. *Entertaining America: Jews, Movies, and Broadcasting.* Princeton: Princeton University Press, 2003.

Haist, Paul. "G. M. Anderson, nee Max Aronson: Reel Cowboy." *Jewish Review* 45 (April 2003): 20, 27.

Hajdu, David. *The Ten Cent Plague: The Great Comic Book Scare and How it Changed America.* New York: Farrar, Straus and Giroux, 2008.

Halberstadt, Alex. "The Man With the $50,000 Beard." Nextbook.org, June 11, 2007.

Hale, Nathan G., Jr. *Freud and the Americans.* New York: Oxford University Press, 1971.

Handler, Daniel. "Interview with Jack Black." *Believer,* July/August 2008.

Handler, Judd. "Michael Lerner: The Most Controversial Jew in America." *San Diego Jewish Journal,* March 26, 2007.

Handler, Ruth. *Dream Girl: The Ruth Handler Story.* Stamford, CT: Longmeadow Press, 1994.

Hansen, Peter S. *Twentieth Century Music.* Upper Saddle River, NJ: Allyn and Bacon, Inc. 1971.

Harap, Louis. "The Drama." *The Image of the Jew in American Literature: From Early Republic to Mass Immigration.* 2nd ed. Syracuse: Syracuse University Press, 2003.

Harmetz, Aljean. *Round Up the Usual Suspects: The Making of "Casablanca".* London: Orion Books, 1993.

Heath, Chris. "The Private Life of Natalie Portman." *Rolling Stone,* June 2002.

Hecht, Ben. *A Child of the Century.* New York: Simon and Schuster, 1954.

Heilbrun, Carolyn G. *The Education of a Woman: The Life of Gloria Steinem.* New York: Dial, 1995.

Heilpern, John. "How Good Is David Mamet, Anyway?" Salon.com, December 3, 1999.

Heinze, Andrew R. *Jews and the American Soul.* Princeton: Princeton University Press, 2004.

Hennesee, Judith. *Betty Friedan: Her Life.* Harmondsworth, Middlesex, UK: Penguin, 1999.

Henning, Doug, with Charles Reynolds. *Houdini: His Legend and His Magic.* New York: Time Books, 1978.

Hirschberg, Lynn. "The Music Man: Can Rick Rubin Save the Music Business?" *New York Times Magazine,* September 2, 2007, 26–33, 46, 49–50.

Hoberman, J. *Bridge of Light: Yiddish Film between Two Worlds.* New York: Schocken, 1991.

———, and Jeffrey Shandler. "The Jazz Singer," in *Entertaining America: Jews, Movies, and Broadcasting.* Princeton, NJ: Princeton University Press, 2003.

Hoberman, Jim, Jeffrey Shandler, and Maurice Berger (eds.). *Entertaining America: Jews, Movies, and Broadcasting.* Princeton, NJ: Princeton University Press, 2003.

Hobson, Laura Z. *Gentleman's Agreement.* New York: Simon and Schuster, 1947.

———. *Laura Z.: A Life.* Westminster, MD: Arbor House, 1983.

Hoffman, Edward. *Despite All Odds: The Story of Lubavitch.* New York: Simon and Schuster, 1991.

The Hollywood.com Guide to Film Directors. New York: Carroll and Graf Publishers, 2004.

Horowitz, Daniel. *Betty Friedan and the Making of The Feminine Mystique: The American Left, the Cold War and Modern Feminism.* Amherst: University of Maschusetts Press, 1998.

Horowitz, Mark. *Sondheim on Music: Minor Details and Major Decisions.* Lanham, MD: Scarecrow Press, 2003.

Houdini, Harry. *Miracle Mongers and Their Methods.* Charlottesville, VA: University of Virginia Library; Boulder, CO: NetLibrary, 1996.

———. *The Right Way to Do Wrong.* Boston, MA: Harry Houdini, 1906.

———. *Secrets of Handcuffs.* London: George Routledge and Sons, 1910.

Howard, Moe.*Moe Howard and the Three Stooges.* Citadel Press, 1977.

Howe, Irving. *A Margin of Hope: An Intellectual Autobiography.* New York: Harcourt, 1982.

———. *World of Our Fathers.* New York: Harcourt Brace, 1978.

———, and Eliezer Greenburg. "My Quarrel with Hersh Rasseyner," *A Treasury of Yiddish Stories.* New York: Viking Press, 1954.

Hughes, Robert. *American Visions.* New York: Alfred A. Knopf, 1997.

Hyman, Paula E., and Deborah Dash Moore, eds. *Jewish Women in America: An Historical Encyclopedia.* New York: Routledge, 1997.

Inglis, I. " 'Some Kind of Wonderful': The Creative Legacy of the Brill Building," *American Music* 21, no. 2 (2003): 214–35.

"Irving Stone, Bestselling Author, Dies." *Washington Post,* August 28, 1989.

Isaacson, Walter. *Einstein: His Life and Universe.* New York: Simon and Schuster, 2007.

———. *Kissinger: A Biography.* London: Faber and Faber Ltd., 1992.

Israel News Agency Staff. "Dershowitz: Israel's Sharon, Jews to Blame for Pollard's Continued Imprisonment." Accessed January 2008. http://www.israelnewsagency.com/jonathanpollarddershowitzisrael480626.html.

Jablonski, Edward. *Gershwin.* New York: Doubleday, 1987.

———, and Lawrence Stewart. *The Gershwin Years.* Garden City, NY: Doubleday, 1973.

Jackson, Laura. *Neil Diamond: His Life, His Music, His Passion.* Toronto, Ontario: ECW Press, 2005.

Jackson, Naomi. *Converging Movements: Modern Dance and Jewish Culture at the 92nd Street Y.* Macon, GA: Wesleyan University Press, 2000.

Jessel, George. *Elegy in Manhattan.* Holt, Rinehart and Winston, 1961.

———. *Hello, Momma.* World Publishing Company, 1946.

———. *This Way Miss.* Henry Holt, 1955.

———, and John Austin. *The World I Lived In.* Regenery, 1975.

Jewel, Carolyn. "What's It Like to Be a Fiction Writer? Read On." *Writers Diary* by Carolyn's Blog. April 27, 2007.

Jewish Heroes and Heroines in America from 1900 to WW II: A Judaica Collection Exhibit at Florida Atlantic University: Seymour Brody, " 'Madame' Beatrice Alexander: The First Lady of Dolls," http://www.fau.edu/library/bro62a.htm.

Jewish Virtual Library, http://www.jewishvirtuallibrary.org/jsource/biography/Michtoms.html.

Jewish Women's Archives. "Jewish Women in Comedy." www.joo.com.pl/jewish-woman.php.

Jones, E. *Sigmund Freud: Life and Work. Vol 2: The Years of Maturity 1901–1919.* London: Hogarth Press, 1955.

Jones, Leroi. *Blues People: Negro Music in White America.* New York: William Morrow, 1963.

Jones, Malcolm, Jr. "A Primitive's Portfolio." *Newsweek,* March 20, 1995.

Jong, Erica. *Seducing the Demon: Writing for My Life.* Tarcher, 2006.

Josefsberg, Milt. *The Jack Benny Show.* New Rochelle, NY: Arlington House, 1977.

Journal of Exothermic Science and Technology 1, no. 9 (1938).

Jowitt, Deborah. *Jerome Robbins: His Life, His Theater, His Dance.* New York: Simon and Schuster, 2005.

Jungreis, Esther. *The Jewish Soul on Fire.* New York: William Morrow & Company, 1982.

Kadison, Luba and Joseph Buloff, Irving Genn. *Onstage, Offstage: A Lifetime in the Yiddish Theater.* Cambridge, MA: Harvard University Press, 1992.

Kafanova, Ludmila. "Remembering Solomon Mikhoels." *New Leader* 61 (March 13, 1978): 16–17.

Kalush, William, and Larry Sloman. *The Secret Life of Houdini: The Making of America's First Superhero.* New York: Simon and Schuster, 2006.

Kanfer, Stefan. *A Summer World: The Attempt to Build a Jewish Eden in the Catskills.* New York: Farrar, Straus and Giroux, 1989.

———. *Stardust Lost: The Triumph, Tragedy, and Mishugas of the Yiddish Theater in America.* New York: Alfred A Knopf, 2006.

Kanter, Kenneth A. *The Jews on Tin Pan Alley,* New York: Ktav, 1982.

Kaplan, Arie. *From Krakow to Krypton: Jews and Comic Books.* Philadelphia, PA: The Jewish publication Society, 2006.

Kaplan, Edward K. *Abraham Joshua Heschel in America, 1940–1972.* Yale University Press, 2007.

Karel, Russ, director. *Almonds and Raisins: A History of the Yiddish Cinema.* Film. New York: Brooks Productions, 1983.

Kaufman, Peter. "The Background on Albert Brooks." *The Buffalo News,* January 22, 2006.

Kazin, Alfred. *A Walker in the City.* Bel Air, CA: MJF Books, 1997.

———. *On Native Grounds: An Interpretation of Modern American: Prose Literature.* New York: Harcourt, 1995.

Kellman, Steven G.*Redemption: The Life of Henry Roth.* W.W. Norton, 2005.

Kempner, Aviva, director. *The Life and Times of Hank Greenberg* Documentary. Also written and produced by Aviva Kempner. Ciesla Foundation, 2003.

Keneally, Thomas. *Schindler's List*. New York: Penguin Books, 1983.

Kennedy, Eugene. "Saul Bellow Teaches an 'Object' Lesson." *Chicago Tribune,* May 31, 1987, sec. 14: 3, 5.

Kerman, Joseph. *Listen*. London: Worth Publishing Ltd., Inc. 1976.

Khazzoom, Loolwa. "Hip Hop's Jew Crew Takes Center Stage." *Jewish Journal.com,* December 9, 2004.

Kiehn, David. *Broncho Billy and the Essanay Film Company.* Berkeley, CA: Farwell Books, 2003.

Kimball, Robert, and Alfred Simon. *The Gershwins.* New York: Atheneum, 1973.

King, Alan. *Matzo Balls for Breakfast and Other Memories of Growing Up Jewish*. Simon and Schuster, 2000.

———. *Name Dropping: The Life and Lies of Alan King*. Simon and Schuster, 1996.

King, Larry. *The Best of Larry King Live: The Greatest Interviews*. Turner Publishers, 1995.

———, and David Gilbert. *How to Talk to Anyone, Anytime, Anywhere: The Secret of Good Communication.* Random House, 2004.

"Kinky Friedman Turns to Politics: Humorist, Musician, Writer, Is Now Gubernatorial Hopeful In Texas." *CBS Sunday Morning,* August 21, 2005.

Kinky Friedman Web Site: http://www.kinkyfriedman.com.

Kirschenbaum, Levana. *Levana Cooks Dairy-Free.* New York: Skyhorse Publishing, 2007.

Klugman, Jack. *Tony and Me: A Story of Friendship*. Good Hill Press, 2005.

Koch, Ed, and Pat Thaler Koch. *Eddie, Harold's Little Brother.* Grosset and Dunlap, 2004.

Koch, Edward I., and Daniel Paisner. *Citizen Koch: An Autobiography.* St. Martin's Press, 1992.

Kolatch, Alfred J. *Great Jewish Quotations.* New York: Jonathan David Co., 1966.

Koppel, Ted. *Off Camera: Private Thoughts Made Public.* Knopf, 2000.

———, and Kyle Gibson. *Nightline: History in the Making and the Making of Television.* Times Books, 1996.

Kornblum, Elan, ed. *The Great Kosher Restaurants Magazine.* Brooklyn, NY: Elan Kornblum, 2007.

Kovan, Florine Whyte., *Rediscovering Ben Hecht: Selling the Celluloid Serpent*. Washington, DC: Snickersnee Press, 1999.

Kramer, Peter D. *Freud: Inventor of the Modern Mind.* New York: Harper Collins, 2006.

Kramer, Stanley. *A Mad, Mad, Mad, Mad World: A Life in Hollywood.* New York: Harcourt Trade Publishers, 1997.

Krasner, Jonathan. "A Recipe for American Jewish Integration: The Adventures of K'tonton and Hillel's Happy Holidays" from *The Lion and the Unicorn* 27, no. 3 (2003): 344–61.

Kremer, S. Lillien. *Witness Through the Imagination: Jewish-American Holocaust Literature.* Detroit, MI: Wayne State University Press, 1989.

Kroll, Jack. Review of *Fiddler on the Roof. Newsweek,* September 29, 1964.

Krupnick, Mark. *Lionel Trilling and the Fate of Cultural Criticism.* Northwestern University Press, 1986.

Kulshrestha, Chirantan. "A Conversation with Saul Bellow." *Chicago Review* 23.4–24.1 (1972): 7–15.

Kun, Josh. "The Yiddish Are Coming: Mickey Katz, Antic-Semitism, and the Sound of Jewish Difference." *American Jewish History* 87, no. 4 (December 1999): 343–374.

Kunitz, Stanley. *Passing Through: The Later Poems and Selected.* New York: W.W. Norton, 1995.

Kushner, Harold. *How Good Do We Have to Be? A New Understanding of Guilt and Forgiveness.* Back Bay Books, 1996.

———. *Overcoming Life's Disappointments.* Anchor, 2006.

———. *To Life! A Celebration of Jewish Being and Thinking.* Grand Central Publishing, 1994.

———. *When Bad Things Happen to Good People.* Avon, 1981.

———. *When Children Ask about God: A Guide for Parents Who Don't Always Have All the Answers.* Schocken Books, 1971.

Lahr, John. "Stage Left." *New Yorker,* April 17, 2006.

Lapidos, Juliet. "Oh, How We've Missed You!" *Slate.* Accessed September 23, 2007. www.slate.com.

Lawrence, Greg. *Dances With Demons: The Life of Jerome Robbins.* Berkeley Trade, 2002.

Lax, Eric. *Paul Newman: A Biography.* Turner, 1999.

———. *Woody Allen: A Biography.* New York: Vintage, 1992.

Leavy, Jane. *Sandy Koufax: A Lefty's Legacy.* Harper Collins, 2002.

Lee, Sarah Tomerlin, ed. *American Fashion.* New York: Quadrangle/The New York Times Book Company, 1975

Leese, Elizabeth, ed. *Costume Design in the Movies.* New York: Dover Publications, Inc., 1991.

Lehmann-Haupt, Christopher. "Stanley Kunitz, Poet Laureate, Dies at 100." *New York Times,* May 16, 2006.

Leibovitz, Annie. *Photographs—Annie Leibovitz, 1970–1990.* New York: Harper Collins, 1991.

———. *Women.* New York: Random House, 1999.

Lemkin, Raphael. *Axis Rule in Occupied Europe: Laws of Occupation—Analysis of Government—Proposals for Redress.* Washington, DC: Carnegie Endowment for International Peace, 1944.

"Leon Uris Biography," at nytimes.com.

Leverence, John. *Irving Wallace: A Writer's Profile.* Popular Press, 1974.

Levin, Meyer. *In Search.* New York: Horizon, 1950.

Levine, Peter. *Ellis Island to Ebbets Field: Sports and the American Jewish Experience.* New York: Oxford, 1992.

Levine, Suzanne Marin and Mary Thon. *Bella Abzug: One Tough Broad from the Bronx.* New York: Farrar, Straus and Giroux, 2007.

Levitt, Beverly. "A Lifetime of Seders: Mandy Patinkin's Jewish Connections Go Well Beyond Mamaloshen." *Jewish Journal,* April 13, 2000.

Levy, Ariel. "Chasing Dash Snow." *New York Magazine,* January 15, 2007.

Levy, Richard, and Ronald O. Weingartner. *The Toy and Game Inventor's Handbook.* New York: Alpha Books, 2003.

Lewis, Jerry, with James Kaplan. *Dean and Me (A Love Story).* Doubleday, 2005.

Lewisohn, Ludwig. *The Island Within.* Syracuse University Press, 1928.

Lieberfeld, D., and J. Sanders. "Here Under False Pretenses: The Marx Brothers Crash the Gates." *American Scholar* 64 no. 1 (1995): 103–108.

Lieberman, Joe, and Hadassah Lieberman. *An Amazing Adventure: Joe and Hadassah's Personal Notes on the 2000 Campaign.* New York: Simon and Schuster, 2003.

Lieberman, Joseph I., with Michael D'Orso. *In Praise of Public Life.* New York: Simon and Schuster, 2000.

Life Through a Lens. DVD. Custom Flix, 2007.

Lifson, David S. *The Yiddish Theatre in America.* Cranbury, NJ: Yoseloff, 1965.

Lindsey, Robert. "Martin Landau Rolls Up in a New Vehicle." *New York Times.* August 7, 1988.

Louvish, Simon. *Monkey Business: The Lives and Legends of the Marx Brothers.* New York: St. Martin's Press, 2000.

Lovece, Frank. "Fast Chat: Fyvush Finkel." *Newsday,* Newsday.com, January 6, 2008.

Lumet, Sidney. *Making Movies.* New York: Alfred A. Knopf, 1995.

Lyman, Darryl. *Great Jews in Music.* New York: Jonathan David Publishers, Inc., 1986.

Lyons, Eugene. *David Sarnoff.* New York: Harper & Row, 1966.

MacAdams, William. *Ben Hecht: The Man Behind the Legend.* New York: Scribners, 1990.

Macdonald, Andrew F., and Gina Macdonald. *Scott Turow: A Critical Companion.* Greenwood Press, 2005.

Manilow, Barry. *Sweet Life: On the Way to Paradise.* McGraw-Hill 1987.

Manso, Peter. *Mailer: His Life and Times.* New York: Simon and Schuster, 1985.

Marcus, Leonard S. *Ways of Telling: Conversations on the Art of the Picture Book.* New York: Dutton Children's Books, 2002.

Margolick, David. "Again, Sidney Lumet Ponders Justice." *New York Times,* December 31, 1989.

"Marketers, Gingerly, Bite at Parody Bait." *New York Times,* March 28, 2007.

Marovitz, Sanford E. *Abraham Cahan.* New York: Twayne, 1996.

Marqusee, Mike. *Wicked Messenger: Bob Dylan and the 1960s.* Seven Stones Press, 2005.

Marton, Kati. *The Great Escape: Nine Jews Who Fled Hitler and Changed the World.* New York: Simon and Schuster, 2006.

Mason, Jackie. *How to Talk Jewish.* St. Martin's Press, 1991.

"Matisyahu Tonight at the Sound Advice Amphitheatre." *Miami New Times* Blog, July 17, 2007.

Mayhew, Robert. *Essays on Ayn Rand's The Fountainhead.* Lexington Books, 2006.

McBride, Joseph. *Steven Spielberg.* Faber and Faber, 1997.

McDonagh, Don. *The Complete Guide to Modern Dance.* New York: Doubleday and Company, 1976.

McDowell, Edwin. " 'Exodus' in Samizdat: Still Popular and Still Subversive." *New York Times,* April 26, 1987.

Medding, Peter Y., ed. *Studies in Contemporary Jewry Volume VIII: A New Jewry? America Since the Second World War.* New York: Oxford University Press USA, 1992.

Medved, Michael. "Jews Run Hollywood, So What?" *Moment,* August 1996.

Mellow, J. R. *Charmed Circle: Gertrude Stein & Company.* New York: Avon, 1974, reprint 1991.

Melody, Edward Michael. *Teaching America about Sex: Marriage Guides and Sex Manuals from the Late Victorians to Dr. Ruth.* New York U. Press, 1999.

Mendelsohn, Michael J. *Clifford Odets: Humane Dramatist.* New York: Everett/Edwards, 1969.

Merino, Noel. *Rap Music (Introducing Issues With Opposing Viewpoints).* Farmington, MI: Greenhaven Press, 2008.

Merriam, Eve. *Emma Lazarus Rediscovered.* New York: Biblio Press, 1998.

Merrill, Robert. *Between Acts*. McGraw Hill, 1976.

———. *Once More from the Beginning*. Macmillan, 1965.

Merwin, Ted. *In Their Own Image: New York Jews in Jazz Age Popular Culture*. New Brunswick, NJ: Rutgers University Press, 2006.

Metzger, Rebecca. "Jewish Visions of the Fantastical Future." *Culture Currents,* January 2000.

Metzker, Isaac, and Harry Golden. *A Bintel Brief; Sixty Years of Letters from the Lower East Side to the Jewish Daily Forward*. Doubleday, 1971.

Michaels, Leonard. "The Long Comeback of Henry Roth: Call it Miraculous." *New York Times Book Review,* August 15, 1993.

Michels, Tony. "Socialism and the Writing of American Jewish History: World of Our Fathers Revisited." *American Jewish History* 88, no. 4 (December, 2000): 521–546.

The Mike Wallace Interview, Transcript. Guest: William O. Douglas talking about his book, *The Right of the People*. Interview from May 11, 1958.

Miller, Arthur. *Timebends: A Life*. New York: Grove Press, 1987.

Minsky, Morton, and Milt Machlin. *Minsky's Burlesque : A Fast and Funny Look at America's Bawdiest Era*. Arbor House, 1986.

Mintz, Alan. *Popular Culture and the Shaping of Holocaust Memory in America*. Seattle: University of Washington Press, 2001.

Moore, Deborah D. *GI Jews: How World War II Changed a Generation*. Cambridge, MA: Harvard University Press, 2004.

Moore, Deborah Dash. "Exodus: Real to Reel to Real," in *Entertaining America: Jews, Movies, and Broadcasting,* Edited by J. Hoberman and Jeffrey Shandler. Princeton, NJ: Princeton University Press, 2003.

Morella, Joe. *Paulette: The Adventurous Life of Paulette Goddard*. New York: Random House, 1991.

The Museum of Broadcast Communications. www.museum.tv/archives/etv/K/htmlK/kinglarry/kinglarry.htm.

Musleah, Rahel. "Fyvush Finkel." *Hadassah Magazine.* October 2008, 68–71.

———. "Shlomo Carlebach: The Music Man." *Hadassah Magazine,* October 2008, 51–56.

Nathan, Joan. *Jewish Cooking in America,* New York: Knopf, 1994.

Navasky, Victor S., *Naming Names.* New York: Viking Press, 1980.

Neibhur, James L., and Ted Okuda. *The Jerry Lewis Films*. McFarland, 1994.

Nelson, Pamela B. "Toys as History: Ethnic Images and Cultural Change." Balch Institute for Ethnic Studies of the Historical Society of Pennsylvania, http://www.ferris.edu/news/jimcrow/link/toys.

Nelson, Stephen. *Only a Paper Moon: The Theatre of Billy Rose.* Ann Arbor: UMI Research Press, 1987.

Nemy, Enid. "Pauline Trigère, Exemplar of American Style, Dies at 93." *New York Times,* February 14, 2002.

Newfield, Jack, and Wayne Barrett. *City for Sale: Ed Koch and the Betrayal of New York.* Harper Row, 1988.

New York Times, February 16, 1943, p. 1.

The New York Times Book Review, September 20, 1953.

Nimoy, Leonard. *I Am Not Spock.* New York: Ballantine/Del Rey, 1977.

———. *I Am Spock.* New York: Hyperion Books, 1995.

———, and Donald Burton Kuspit. *Shekhina.* Photographs by Leonard Nimoy. Brooklyn, NY: Umbrage Editions, 2002.

Norton, Richard. *A Chronology of American Musical Theatre.* New York: Oxford University Press, 2002.

Norville, Florence, and Catherine Temerson. *Isaac B. Singer, A Life.* Farrar, Straus and Giroux, 2006.

Nott, Robert. *He Ran All the Way: The Life of John Garfield.* New York: Limelight Editions, 2003.

Novak, William, and Moshe Waldoks, eds. *The Big Book of Jewish Humor.* New York: Harper and Row, 1981.

Novick, Peter. *The Holocaust in American Life.* Boston: Houghton Mifflin, 1999.

Oberfirst. *Al Jolson: You Ain't Heard Nothin Yet.* Barnes, 1980.

O'Brien, Richard. *The Story of American Toys.* New York: Abbeville Press, 1990.

Ochsner, Jeffrey Karl. "Understanding the Holocaust through the U.S. Holocaust Memorial Museum." *JAE: Journal of Architectural Education* 48 (May 1995): 240–249.

Ogden, Christopher. *Legacy: A Biography of Moses and Walter Annenberg.* New York: Little, Brown and Company, 1999.

"Old Style Jewish Delicatessens for Goyim (non-Jews)." October 24, 2001. Accessed August 20, 2008. Epinions.com.

Olivestone, David. "Standing Room Only: The Remarkable Career of Cantor Yossele Rosenblatt." *Jewish Action,* 1964.

Once Upon a Time in America. DVD. Warner Brothers Home Video, 2008.

O'Neill, William. *With Charity Toward None: An Analysis of Ayn Rand's Philosophy.* New York: Philadelphia Library, 1971.

Orr, Gregory. *Stanley Kunitz: An Introduction to the Poetry.* Columbia University Press, 1984.

Oumano, Elena. *Paul Newman.* St. Martin's Press, 1989.

Ozick, Cynthia. *Art and Ardor: Essays.* New York: E.P. Dutton, 1984.

———, and Elaine M. Kauvar. *A Cynthia Ozick Reader.* Bloomington, IN: Indiana University Press, 1996.

Paley, William S. *As It Happened: A Memoir.* Garden City, NY: Doubleday, 1979.

Palmieri, Anthony F. R. *Elmer Rice: A Playwright's Vision of America.* New Jersey: Fairleigh Dickinson University Press, 1980.

Pandolfini, Bruce. *The Best of Chess Life and Review,* vols. 1 and 2. New York: Simon and Schuster, 1988.

Parish, James Robert.*It's Good to Be the King: The Seriously Funny Life of Mel Brooks.* Hoboken, NJ: Wiley, 2007.

Parisi, Peter, ed. *Artist of the Actual: Essays on Paul Goodman.* Metuchen, NJ: Scarecrow, 1986.

Paskin, Sylvia. *When Joseph Met Molly.* London: Five Leaves, 1999.

Paul, Pamela. "Sarah Silverman-Interview." *Slate,* November 10, 2006.

Pekar, Harvey. *American Splendor: The Life and Times of Harvey Pekar.* Ballantine Books, 2004.

———, Joyce Brabner, and Frank Stack. *Our Cancer Year.* Running Press Books, 1994.

Peyser, Joan. *Bernstein: A Biography.* New York: Beach Tree Books, 1987.

Pfefferman, Naomi. "Crazy for Chanukah: An Animated Adam Sandler Brings the Festival of Lights to Pop Culture." *Jewish Journal,* November 28, 2002.

———. "The 'Majestic' Martin Landau." *Jewish Journal.com.* December 21, 2001.

Picon, Molly. *So Laugh a Little.* New York: Paperback Library, 1966.

———, with Jean Grillo., *Molly! An Autobiography.* New York: Simon and Schuster, 1980.

Pinsker, Sanford. *Understanding Joseph Heller.* Columbia, SC: University of South Carolina Press, 1991.

Podhoretz, Norman. "The Adventures of Philip Roth." *Commentary,* October 1998.

———. "At War with Allen Ginsberg," in *Ex-Friends.* New York: Free Press, 1999.

Pogrebin, Abigail. *Stars of David: Prominent Jews Talk About Being Jewish.* New York: Broadway Books, 2005.

Pollack, Sydney, director. *Sketches of Frank Gehry.* Documentary. Sony Pictures, 2005.

Potok, Chaim. *Wanderings: Chaim Potok's History of the Jews.* NewYork: Knopf, 1978.

Quinn, Christopher. "Faith Sets the Beat for Jewish Rapper."*Modesto Bee,* http://www.modbee.com/, 2008.

Ralph H. Baer, http://en.wikipedia.org/wiki/Ralph_H._Baer.

Randall, Tony. *Biography: Tony Randall.* A&E Home Video, 2000.

Rapf, Joanna, ed. *Sidney Lumet: Interviews.* University Press of Mississippi, 2006.

Raphael, Chaim. *The Festival Days: A History of Jewish Celebrations.* Weidenfeld and Nicholson, 1990).

Raphael, Frederic. *Eyes Wide Open: A Memoir of Stanley Kubrick.* New York: Ballantine, 1999.

Raphael, Lawrence W. *Mystery Midrash.* Woodstock, VT: Jewish Lights, 1999.

Raskin, Jonah. *American Scream: Allen Ginsberg's Howl and the Making of the Beat Generation.* Berkeley, CA: University of California Press, 2004.

Reich, Steve. *Writings on Music, 1965–2000.* Oxford University Press, 2002.

Relic, Peter. New CDs: "Matisyahu, Juvenile." *Rolling Stone,* March 6, 2006.

Ribalow, Harold, and Meir Ribalo. *The Great Jewish Chess Champions.* New York: Hippocene, 1987.

Rice, Elmer. *Minority Report: An Autobiography.* New York: Simon and Schuster, 1963.

Rich, Frank. " 'Cafe Crown,' Bygone World of Yiddish Theater." *New York Times,* October 26, 1988.

Richman, Irwin. *Borscht Belt Bungalows: Memories of Catskill Summers.* Philadelphia: Temple University Press, 1998.

Riess, Steven A., ed. *Sports and the American Jew.* Syracuse, NY: Syracuse University Press, 1998.

Rischin, Moses, ed. *Grandma Never Lived in America: The New Journalism of Abraham Cahan.* Bloomington, IN: Indiana University Press, 1985.

Rivera, Geraldo. *Exposing Myself.* Bantam, 1991.

Rivers, Joan. *Still Talking.* New York: Random House, 1991.

Rivers Web Site: http://www.joanrivers.com/.

Roberts, Chris. *Scarlett Johansson: Portrait of a Rising Star.* Carlton Publishing Group, 2007.

Robinson, Harlow. *The Last Impresario.* Penguin Press, 1995.

———. "Sol Hurok: America's Dance Impresario." *Dance Magazine,* November 1994.

Rockaway, Robert. *But He Was Good to His Mother: The Lives and Crimes of Jewish Gangsters,* New York: Geffen Publishing House, 2000.

Rogin, Michael. *Black Face, White Noise: Jewish Immigrants in the Hollywood Melting Pot.* Berkeley, CA: University of California Press, 1996.

Rogovoy, Seth. *The Essential Klezmer*. Algonquin Books, 2000.

Rollyson, Carl, and Lisa Paddock. *Susan Sontag: The Making of an Icon*. W.W. Norton, 2000.

Ronell, Anna P. "American-Jewish Writers Imagine Eastern Europe: Thane Rosenbaum, Rebecca Goldstein, and Jonathan Safran Foer." *Polin: Studies in Polish Jewry* 19 (2007).

Rosen, Jonathan. "Writer, Interrupted: The Resurrection of Henry Roth." *New Yorker*, August 1, 2005.

Rosenfeld, Lulla. *Bright Star of Exile: Jacob Adler and the Yiddish Theatre*. New York: Crowell, 1977.

Ross, Barney. *No Man Stands Alone: The Story of Barney Ross*. London: Stanley Paul, 1959.

Roth, David. *Crazy From the Heat*. Ebury Press, 2000.

Roth, Lawrence. *Inspecting Jews: American Jewish Detective Stories*. New Brunswick, NJ: Rutgers University Press, 2004.

Roth, Michael S., ed. *Freud: Conflict and Culture. Essays on His Life, Work, and Legacy*. New York: Knopf, 1998.

Rothman, Cliff. "Jewish Media Stranglehold." *The Nation*. 275 (July 8, 2002).

Rothmuller, Aron Marko. *The Music of the Jews*. A.S. Barnes Publishing Co., 1975.

Rothstein, Mervyn. "Comedian Red Buttons Dies at 87." *New York Times*, July 14, 2006.

Roudane, Matthew C. "An Interview with Saul Bellow." *Contemporary Literature* 25.3 (1984): 265–80.

Rowell, Erica. *The Brothers Grim: The Films of Ethan and Joel Coen*. Latham, MD: The Scarecrow Press, 2007.

Rubin, Doralee Patinkin, and Mandy Patinkin. *Grandma Doralee Patinkin's Holiday Cookbook: A Jewish Family Celebration*. New York: St. Martin's Press, 2001.

———. *Grandma Doralee Patinkin's Jewish Family Cookbook: More than 150 Treasured Recipes from My Kitchen to Yours*. New York: St. Martin's Press, 1999.

Rubin, Lois, ed. *Connections and Collisions: Identities in Contemporary Jewish American Women's Writing*. Newark, DE: University of Delaware Press, 2005.

Safer, Elaine. "Illuminating the Ineffable: Jonathan Safran Foer's Novels." *Studies in American Jewish Literature* 25 (January 2007): 112–132.

Safer, Elaine B. *Mocking the Age: The Later Novels of Philip Roth* (SUNY Series in Modern Jewish Literature and Culture), 2006.

Sainer, Arthur. *Zero Dances: A Biography of Zero Mostel*. New York: Limelight Editions, 2004.

Sales, Soupy. *Did You Hear the One About: The Greatest Jokes Ever Told*. M. Evans, 1987.

———. *Soupy Sez!: My Zany Life and Times*. M. Evans, 2003.

———. *Stop Me If You've Heard It!: Soupy Sales' Favorite Jokes*. M. Evans, 2003.

Salinger, Margaret. *Dream Catcher: A Memoir*. New York: Washington Square Press, 2000.

Salzmann, Jerome. *The Chess Reader*. New York: Greenberg. 1949.

Sandrow, Nahma. *Vagabond Stars: A World History of Yiddish Theater*. New York: Harper and Row, 1977.

Sapoznik, Henry. *Klezmer! Jewish Music from Old World to Our World*. New York: Schirmer Books, 1999.

"Saul Bellow." *Playboy Review* (May 1995): 59–68, 166–70.

Scaruffi, Piero. *A History of Jazz Music: 1900–2000*. Houston, TX: Omniware, 2007.

Schappes, Morris U. *Emma Lazarus: Selections from Her Poetry and Prose*. New York: Emma Lazarus Federation of Jewish Women's Clubs, 1978.

Schary, Dore. *Heyday: An Autobiography*. Boston: Little, Brown, 1979.

Schatz, Thomas. *The Genius of the System: Hollywood Filmmaking in the Studio Era*. New York: Pantheon Books, 1988.

Schauss, Hayyim. *The Jewish Festivals: History and Observance*. Schocken Books, 1962.

Schickel, Richard. "Heart of Darkness," *Time*, December 13, 1993.

Schiff, Ellen. *From Stereotype to Metaphor: The Jew in Contemporary Drama*. Albany: State University of New York, 1982.

Schorsch, Jonathan. "Making Judaism Cool." In *Best Contemporary Jewish Writing*. Edited by Michael Lerner. Hoboken, NJ: Jossey-Bass, 2001.

Schulberg, Budd. *Moving Pictures: Memories of a Hollywood Prince*. New York. Stein and Day, 1981.

Schumacher, Michael. *Dharma Lion: A Biography of Allen Ginsberg*. New York: St. Martin's Press, 1994.

Seaman, Barbara. *Lovely Me: The Life of Jacqueline Susann*. Seven Stories Press, 1986.

Secrest, Meryle. *Stephen Sondheim: A Life*. New York: Alfred Knopf, 1998.

Severo, Richard. "Harold Robbins, 81, Dies; Wrote Best Sellers Brimming with Sex, Money and Power." Obituary. *New York Times*, October 15, 1997.

Shandler, Jeffrey. *Adventures in Yiddishland: Postvernacular Language and Culture*. Berkeley: University of California Press, 2005.

Shapiro, Edward S. *A Time for Healing: American Jewry Since World War II*. Johns Hopkins University Press, 1992.

Shatner, William, with David Fisher. *Up Till Now: The Autobiography*. New York: Thomas Dunne Books, 2008.

Sheldon, Sidney. *The Other Side of Me.* Warner Books, 2005.

Shenk, David. *The Immortal Game.* New York: Doubleday. 2006.

Shepard, Richard F., and Vicki Gold Levi. *Live & Be Well: A Celebration of Yiddish Culture in America.* Rutgers University Press, 2000, 56.

Sheppard, R. Z. "Speaking About the Unspeakable." *Time,* March 12, 1979.

Sherman, Eric. "Peter Falk Reigns in Columbo's Trench Coat." *Ladies' Home Journal* 107 no. 3 (March 1990): 98–100.

Shiffman, Dan. "The Comedy of Assimilation in Leo Rosten's Hyman Kaplan Stories." *Studies in American Humor* 3 (2000): 49–63.

The Sid Caesar Collection—The Fan Favorites—50th Anniversary Edition. Starring Sid Caesar, Carl Reiner, Imogene Coca, et al. 3-CDs. New Video Group, 2004.

"Sidney Sheldon, best-selling author, 89." *Deathwatch Central,* cdw@slick.org.January 31, 2007.

Siegel, David S., and Susan Siegel. *Radio and the Jews: The Untold Story of How Radio Influenced America's Image of Jews 1920s–1950s.* Yorktown Heights, NY: Book Hunter Press, 2007.

Sills, Beverly. *Beverly, An Autobiography.* Bantam, 1981.

———. *Bubbles: An Encore.* Grosset and Dunlap, 1981.

———. *Bubbles: A Self Portrait.* MacMillan, 1976.

Simon, Neil. *The Play Goes On: A Memoir.* New York: Simon and Schuster, 1999.

———. *Rewrites: A Memoir.* New York: Simon and Schuster, 1996.

Singer, Tom. "Hammerin' Hebrew: Shawn Green Carries the Torch as Baseball's Latest Jewish All-Star." *Atlanta Jewish News,* August 4, 2000 (http://atlanta.jewish.com/archives/2000/080400cs.htm).

Sisaro, Ben. "Hasidic Reggae Singer Surprises His Managers." *New York Times,* March 14, 2006.

Slater, Robert. *This . . . Is CBS: A Chronicle Of 60 Years.* Englewood Cliffs, NJ: Prentice-Hall, 1988.

Slide, Anthony. *The Encyclopedia of Vaudeville.* Westport, CT: Greenwood Press, 1994.

Slobin, Mark, ed. *American Klezmer: Its Roots and Offshoots.* Berkeley: University of California Press, 2002.

Smith, Bill. *The Vaudevillians.* Macmillan, 1981.

Smith, Janna. *My Father is a Book.* Houghton Mifflin, 2006.

Smith, Ronald L. *Who's Who in Comedy: Comedians, Comics, and Clowns from Vaudeville to Today's Stand-Ups.* New York: Facts on File, 1992, 214–216.

Smith, Sally Bedell. *In All His Glory: The Life of William S. Paley, the Legendary Tycoon and His Brilliant Circle.* New York: Simon and Schuster, 1990.

Sochen, June. *Consecrate Every Day: The Public Lives of Jewish American Women, 1880–1980* Albany, NY: SUNY Press, 1981.

———. *From Mae to Madonna: Women Entertainers in 20th Century America.* Lexington, KY: University Press of Kentucky, 1999.

Solomon, Deborah. "Funny Girl, Interview with Sarah Silverman." *New York Times,* January 21, 2007.

Sorin, Gerald. *Irving Howe: A Life of Passionate Dissent.* New York University Press, 2002.

Spada, James. *Streisand: Her Life.* Crown Publishers, 1995.

Spelling, Aaron, and Jefferson Graham.*Aaron Spelling: A Prime-Time Life.* New York: St. Martin's Press, 1996.

"Spelling's Final Print Interview." *Sydney Morning Herald,* September 2004.

Spiegelman, Art. *Maus: A Survivor's Tale.* Pantheon, 1973–1991.

Starr, Larry, and Christopher Waterman, *American Popular Music.* New York: Oxford University Press, 2003.

Stein, Harry. "Mel Brooks Says This Is the Funniest Man On Earth." *Esquire Magazine,* June 1976.

Stein, Joseph, and Sheldon Harnick. *Fiddler on the Roof.* New York: Crown, 1965.

Stern, Gerald. "Poetry." *Jewish-American History and Culture: An Encyclopedia.* Edited by Jack Fischel and Sanford Pinsker. New York: Garland Press, 1992.

Stern, Howard. *Miss America.* Regan Books, 1996.

———. *Private Parts.* Simon and Schuster, 1993.

Stewart, Jon. *America (The Book): A Citizen's Guide to Democracy Inaction.* Grand Central Publishing, 2004.

———. *Naked Pictures of Famous People.* Harper Paperbacks, 1999.

"Still Kinky After All These Years," *Moment Magazine,* August 2004.

Strassfeld, Michael. *The Jewish Holidays: A Guide and Commentary.* Harper and Row, 1985.

Strom, Yale. *The Book of Klezmer.* A Capella Books, 2002.

Stull, Elizabeth. "Son of Brooklyn Brings Home Legacy of High-Profile Trials: Alan Dershowitz Donates Archives to Brooklyn College." *Brooklyn Daily Eagle,* September 25, 2003. Accessed August 12, 2006.

"Super Swimmer Mark Spitz." *People,* January 15, 1990, 86–88.

Surrence, Matthew. "Jules Feiffer Draws Curtain on Theater, Writes for Kids" *Jewish News Weekly*, March 8, 1996.

Tawa, Nicholas E. *The Way to Tin Pan Alley: American Popular Song, 1866–1910*. New York: Schirmer Books, 1990.

Taylor, Paul. *Jews and the Olympic Games*. Sussex, UK: Sussex Academic Press, 2004.

"Terps Preparing for 'Jewish Jordan.'" Associated Press. February 7, 1999.

Theodore Bikel Web Site: www.bikel.com.

"The *Time* 100: Heroes and Icons." *Time* 2003. Accessed September 8, 2008. www.time.com/time/time100/heroes/romances/romances2.html.Toklas, Alice B. *Staying on Alone; Letters of Alice B. Toklas*. New York: Liveright, 1973.

———. *What Is Remembered*. New York: Holt, Rinehart, and Winston, 1963.

Tomko, Linda. *Dancing Class: Gender, Ethnicity and Social Divides in American Dance, 1890–1920*. Bloomington, IN: Indiana University Press, 1999.

Toy Industry Hall of Fame. http://www.toyassociation.org/AM/Template.cfm?Section=Hall_of_Fame.

Trilling, Diana. *Beginning of the Journey*. Harcourt Brace, 1993.

Trilling, Lionel. *Beyond Culture: Essays on Literature and Learning*. New York: Viking Press, 1979.

Ulmer, Edgar G., director. *American Matchmaker*. Film. Waltham, MA: National Center for Jewish Films, Brandeis University, restored from 1940 version.

Uris, Leon. *Exodus*. Garden City, NY: Doubleday, 1958.

USC Shoah Foundation Institute for Visual History and Education Web Site: www.usc.edu/schools/college/vhi.

Vaill, Amanda. *Somewhere: The Life Of Jerome Robbins*. Broadway Books, 2006.

Van Voolen, Edward. *Jewish Art and Culture*. Munich: Prestel, 2006.

Vespa, Mary. "Philip Roth Beware: Novelist Belva Plain's the New One-Woman Jewish Mother's Defense League." *People*, August 7, 1978.

Vogel, Speed. *No Laughing Matter*. New York: G.P. Putnam's Sons, 1986.

Von Gunden, Kenneth. "Bruce, Lenny." *Jewish American History and Culture*. New York: Garland Publishing, 1992.

Wakefield, Neville. "Share Your Feelings" (interview with Dan Colen). *I.D.*, February 2007.

Walden, Dan, ed. "The World of Chaim Potok." *Studies in American Jewish Literature* 4 (special issue), 1985.

Walden, Daniel, ed. *On Being Jewish: American Jewish Literature From Abraham Cahan to Saul Bellow*. Greenwich, CT: Fawcett, 1974.

Wallace, Mike, with Paul Gates.*Between You and Me: A Memoir*. Hyperion Books, 2005.

Wallach, Eli. *The Good, the Bad and Me: In My Anecdotage*. Fort Washington, PA: Harvest Books, 2006.

Walters, Barbara. *Audition: A Memoir*. Knopf Publishing Group, 2008.

Watson, Linda. *20th Century Fashion: 100 Years of Style by Decade and Designer*, in association with *Vogue*. Buffalo, NY: Firefly Books, 2004.

Weales, Gerald. *Odets the Playwright*. London and New York: Methuen, 1985.

Weber, Donald. *Forward*, March 10, 2006.

Weinstein, Simcha. *Up, Up, and Oy Vey! How Jewish History, Culture, and Values Shaped the Comic Book Hero*. Baltimore: Leviathan Press, 2006.

Weiss, Beth. "Sammy Davis, Jr." The Jewish Virtual Library, March 19, 2003. Accessed June 14, 2008.

Westheimer, Dr. Ruth K. *All in a Lifetime*. New York: Warner Books, 1987, 2001.

Whitaker, Jan. *Service and Style*. New York: St. Martin's Press, 2006.

Whyld, Ken. *Chess: The Records*. New York: Oxford University Press, 1986.

Widmer, Kingsley. *Paul Goodman*. Boston: Twayne, 1980.

Wiesel, Elie, and Richard Heffner. *Conversations with Elie Wiesel*. New York: Schocken Books, 2001.

Wilder, Gene. *Kiss Me Like a Stranger: My Search for Love and Art*. St. Martin's Press, 2005.

William Fuld, www.williamfuld.com/biography.html.

Wilson, Martin, ed. *The Hydrogen Jukebox: The Selected Writings of Peter Schjeldahl, 1978–90*. Berkeley, CA: University of California Press, 1991, 227.

Wilson, Nance. "Judy Blume." In *The Continuum Encyclopedia of Children's Literature*, edited by Bernice E. Cullinan and Diane G. Person. New York: Continuum Publishing, 2001.

Winters, Shelley. *Shelley: Also Known as Shirley*. Ballantine Books, 1980.

———. *Shelley II : The Middle of My Century*. Ballantine Books, 1989.

Wisse, Ruth. "Slap Shtick: Review of *The Yiddish Policemen's Union*, by Michael Chabon." *Commentary* 124, no. 1 (2007): 73–77.

Yaffe, James. *My Mother, the Detective*. Norfolk, VA: Crippen and Landru, 1997.

Youngkin, Stephen D. *The Lost One, A Life of Peter Lorre*. University of Kentucky Press, 2005.

Youngman, Henny, and Neal Karlen. *Take My Life! Please*. Putnam, 1973.

Zadan, Craig. *Sondheim & Co.* New York: Harper and Row, 1986.

Zaretsky, Eli. *Secrets of the Soul: A Social and Cultural History of Psychoanalysis.* New York: Vintage, 2005.

Zevin, Rabbi Shlomo Yosef. *The Festivals in Halachah: An Analysis of the Development of the Festival Laws.* Two volumes. Mesorah Publications, 1999.

Zurawik, David. *The Jews of Prime Time.* Hanover, NH: University Press of New England, 2005.

Index

Abdul, Paula, 339
Abzug, Bella, **1–2**, 397
Adler, Celia, 453
Adler, Mortimer, **2–3**
Adler, Richard, 313
Adrian. *See* Fashion
Albom, Mitch, **3**
Alburt, Lev, 63
Allen, Gracie, 42, 303. *See also* Burns, George
Allen, Woody, **3–5**, 6, 24, 38, 88, 150, 154, 180, 246, 363, 375; Sid Caesar, 46; Comedy, 70, 72; Film, 121, 127, 128, 131; Film Stars, 139; Al Jolson, 221; David Lee Roth, 344; Adam Sandler, 355; Sitcoms, 379; Steven Spielberg, 380, 382; Theater, 408, 413, 431; Yiddish, 4, 456. *See also* Comedy; Film
Alpert, Herb, 206
Amsterdam, Morey, 71
Annenberg, Walter, **5–6**. *See also* Journalism
Anti-Semitism, 101, 107, 119, 231, 342, 346, 348; Film, 124, 125, 126, 127, 128, 131; Film Stars, 134; John Garfield, 160; *Gentleman's Agreement,* 161–62; Abraham Joshua Heschel, 180; Scarlett Johansson, 220; Journalism, 228; Popular Music, 314; Adam Sandler, 356
Apple, Max, **6–7**
Arbus, Diane, **7**
Arkin, Alan, **8**, 129, 404, 408, 409
Arlen, Harold, 201, 202
Artists, **8–14**, 7; Marc Chagall, 260; Mark di Suvero, 11–12; Adolph Gottlieb, 10; Philip Guston, 10; Eva Hesse, 12; Holocaust, 11; Man Ray, 9; Amadeo Modigliani, 8; Louise Nevelson, 11; Barnett Newman, 10; Jules Pascin, 8; Emmanuel Radnitzky, 9; Mark Rothko, 9; George Segal, 12; Richard Serra, 13; Chaim Soutine, 8
Asch, "Moe," 200
Asimov, Isaac, 364
Auerbach, Arnold "Red," 391

Bacall, Lauren, **15–16**, 137, 147, 218
Bacharach, Burt, 33, 315
Baer, Ralph, 420. *See also* Toys and Games
Baez, Joan, 98
Bamberger, Louis, **16–17**, 103
Bara, Theda, 134, 217
Bar Mitzvah, 97, 174, 182, 187–88, 240, 286, 345, 441; Film, 132; Holidays and Rituals, 187–88; Soupy Sales, 352, 354; Television Stars, 408; Theater, 414
Barr, Rosanne, 71
Barry, Gene, 403
Barry, Jeff, 34
Barth, Bell, 71
Batman, 76. *See also* Comic Books
Beastie Boys, **17–18**, 330, 352
Behrman, Beatrice Alexander, 419. *See also* Toys and Games
Beins, Bert, 35
Bellow, Saul, **18–21**; Literature, 261; The Marx Brothers, 271; Isaac Bashevis Singer, 377; Leon Uris, 427; Herman Wouk, 446
Belzer, Richard, 404
Ben-Ami, Jacob, 338, 410, 454
Benjamin, Joel, 63
Benny, Jack, **21–22**; Eddie Cantor, 49; Comedy, 70, 72; Film, 124; Film Stars, 137, 234, 303; Radio, 323, 324; Sitcoms, 379; Television, 403
Berg, Gertrude, 22, 218; Radio, 323, 324; Sitcoms, 379, 407, 411. *See also* Radio; Sitcoms; Television
Berger, Isaac (Ike), **22–23**
Berle, Milton, **23–24**; Alan King, 234; Sitcoms, 379; Television Stars, 407; Theater, 411
Berlin, Irving, **24–26**, 55, 86, 162, 201, 217, 259, 278, 307, 415; The Brill Building Songwriters, 32; Popular Music, 311, 316; Vaudeville, 430; *West Side Story,* 439, 457. *See also* The Brill

Building Songwriters; Popular Music
Berman, Shelly, 71
Bernstein, Aline, 112
Bernstein, Carl, 108, 226
Bernstein, Leonard, **26–27**, 97, 337; Aaron Copland, 79; Jazz and Blues, 206; Popular Music, 313; Menasha Skulnik, 383. *See also* Popular Music; *West Side Story*
Betteman, Gary, 393
Bikel, Theodore, **27–29**, 200
"Bintel Brief," 47, 210, 450. *See also Jewish Daily Forward*
Bishop, Joey, 71
Bisquier, Arthur, 61
Black, Jack, **29**, 142, 399
Blitzer, Wolf, 227, 256
Block, Jerry, 120
Blume, Judy, **29–30**. *See also* Children's Literature
Bock, Jerry, 314
Borscht Belt. *See* The Catskills
Boteach, Shmuley, **30–31**
Brice, Fanny, **31–32**, 312, 323; Film, 124, 128; Film Stars, 139; Jewish Women and Popular Culture, 217, 218; Billy Rose, 340; Barbra Streisand, 401; Vaudeville, 430
The Brill Building Songwriters, **32–36**, 26; Neil Diamond, 94–95; Jerry Leiber, 249; Doc Pomus, 35, 310, 338; Neil Sedaka, 315; Phil Spector, 338, 385; Mike Stoller, 249, 315, 338; Tin Pan Alley, 94, 162, 200, 311, 315, 338, 415–16, 338
Brit Milah, 187, 284, 333. *See also* Holidays and Rituals
Broadway. *See* Theater
Broncho Billy, **36**, 134
Brooks, Albert, **37**
Brooks, Mel, **37–38**, 180, 282, 334, 414; Sid Caesar, 46, 70; Film, 127; Film Stars, 139; Zero Mostel, 291; Popular Music, 314; Neil Simon, 375; Sitcoms, 379; Vaudeville, 431; Yiddish, 441
Brothers, Joyce, **38–39**, 150, 318. *See also* Popular Psychology
Bruce, Lenny, **39–41**, 18, 165, 397, 431; Louis "Lepke" Buchalter, 157; Comedy, 70, 72, 94; Bob Dylan, 98, 99
Buchwald, Art, **41–42**
Burns, George, **42–43**, 303; Film, 123; Film Stars, 137; Radio, 323; Sitcoms, 379; Television, 403. *See also* Vaudeville
Buttons, Red, **43–44**, 70, 305, 431

Caan, James, 140
Caesar, Sid, **45–46**, 4, 403, 431; Mel Brooks, 37, 38; The Catskills, 57; Comedy, 70, 72, 375; Sitcoms, 379
Cahan, Abraham, **46–48**, 209, 318
Cahn, Sammy, 202, 313
Cantor, Eddie, **48–49**, 89, 144, 421; Film Stars, 137; Jazz and Blues, 202; Danny Kaye, 232; Molly Picon, 312; Radio, 323; Dinah Shore, 370; Sitcoms, 379; Vaudeville, 430; Henry Winkler, 442
Cantors in America, **49–51**, 326; Moshe Ganchoff, 50; Mordecai Hershman, 49; Jewish Delicatessens, 50; Moshe Kussevitzky, 50; Moshe Oysher, 50; Pierre Pinchik, 50; David Roitman, 50; "Yossele" Josef Rosenblatt, 49, 50, 341
Capablanca, Jose, 61
Capp, Al, **51–52**, 77
Carlebach, Shlomo, **52–54**, 152, 229, 284
Carlisle Hart, Kitty, **54–55**
Carnegie, Hattie. *See* Fashion
The Catskills, **55–58**, 37, 43, 67, 286, 386; Film, 132; Jewish Women and Popular Culture, 218; Danny Kaye, 232; Alan King, 234; Jerry Lewis, 253; Jackie Mason, 282; Itzhak Perlman, 30; Joan Rivers, 335; Vaudeville, 431; Yiddish, 450
Cedarbaum, Sophia, 65
Chabad, 53
Chabon, Michael, **58–60**, 263. *See also* Literature
Chagall, Marc, 260
Chaplin, Charlie, 125
Chayefsky, Paddy, **60**, 337, 406, 411. *See also* Literature
Chernin, Peter, 226
Chess, **60–64**; Lev Alburt, 63; Alexander Alekhine, 61; Joel Benjamin, 63; Jose Capablanca, 61; Albert Einstein, 101–6; Reuben Fine, 61; Bobby Fischer, 61, 62; Gary Kasparov, 63–64; Emmanuel Lasker, 61; Susan Polgar, 63; Samuel Reshevsky, 61; Michael Rohde, 63; Herman Steiner, 61; William Steinitz, 60–61; Josh Waitzkin, 63; Johannes Zukertort, 61
Chess, Leonard and Phil, 200. *See also* Jazz and Blues
Children's Literature, **64–67**, 29, 30, 368; Sophia Cedarbaum, 65; Holocaust, 66; Eric Kimmel, 66; Shirley Kravitz Children's Book Award, 65; Isaac Bashevis Singer, 66; Sydney Taylor Award, 65; Sydney Taylor, 64
Chomsky, Noam, 90
Cobb, Lee J., **67**, 288
Coben, Harlan, 93
Coca, Imogene, 45, 232
The Coen Brothers, **67–68**, 132
Cohen, Leonard, 339
Cohen, Myron, 71, 73
Cohen, Sasha Baron, 131, 206, 431
Cohn, Harry, 189, 191
Cole, Kenneth. *See* Fashion
Coleman, Cy, 314
Colen, Daniel, **68–70**
Comedy, **70–74**, 5, 24; Woody Allen, 3–5; Jack Benny, 21–22; Milton Berle, 23–24; Mel Brooks, 37–38; Lenny Bruce, 39–41; Red Buttons, 42–43; Sid Caesar, 45–46; Charlie Chaplin, 125; Billy Crystal, 70, 141; Danny Kaye, 232–33; Jerry Lewis, 253–54; The Marx Brothers, 275–281; Jackie Mason, 281–282; The Ritz Brothers, 70, 334; Joan Rivers, 335–36; Soupy Sales, 353–54; Adam Sandler, 355–56; Jerry Seinfeld, 366–67; Phil Silvers, 373; Gene Wilder, 38, 70, 441; Henny Youngman, 458. *See also* The Catskills; Sitcoms; Vaudeville
Comic Books, **74–77**, 52, 264, 305, 371; Albert Einstein, 101–6; William Eisner, 106–7; Jules Feiffer, 118–19; Harvey

Kurtzman, 106, 243, 431; Stan Lee, 107, 374; Joe Shuster, 106; Jerry Siegel, 106; Art Spiegelman, 386–87; *Superman,* 106
Conrad, Robert, 403
Copeland, Jo, 113
Copland, Aaron, **78–80**, 26, 205
Copperfield, David, **80**
Cortez, Ricardo, 134
Cosell, Howard, 393. *See also* Sports
Cowen, Joshua Lionel, 419. *See also* Toys and Games
Crystal, Billy, 70, 141
Curtis, Tony, **80–81**, 127, 137
Curtiz, Michael, **81–82**

Dance, **83–88**, 281, 337; Irving Berlin, 86, 24–25; *Fiddler on the Roof,* 120–21; Holocaust, 87; The Holocaust in American Culture, 192–93; Michael Kidd, 85, 86; Klezmer Music, 206, 237, 248, 305, 451; Pearl Lang, 84; Sophie Maslow, 28; Arthur Murray, 87; Jerome Robbins, 336–37; Anna Sokolow, 83, 84, 85; Stephen Sondheim, 383–84; Barbra Streisand, 400–401; Helen Tamiris, 83, 84; *West Side Story,* 438–39
Dannay, Frederick, 92
David, Hal, 33
David, Larry, **88**, 406, 431, 456
Davidson, Avram, 364
Davis, Sammy, Jr., **89**, 57, 138, 206, 354
Dershowitz, Alan, **89–91**, 47, 225, 319
Detective Fiction, **91–94**; Harlan Coben, 93; Comic Books, 74–77; Frederick Dannay, 92; Film, 122–23; Kinky Friedman, 152–53; Faye Kellerman, 92; Jonathan Kellerman, 92; Harry Kemelman, 92; Manfred Lee, 92; Sara Paretsky, 93, 275–81; Radio, 323–27; Television, 403–7; Joseph Telushkin, 93; Israel Zangwill, 91
Diamond, Neil, **94–95**, 35
The Diary of Anne Frank, 28, 95, 350, 351; Journalism, 224; Meyer Levin, 253; Chaim Potok, 321; Philip Roth, 347; Art Spiegelman, 386; Theater, 412; Shelley Winters, 444
Doctorow, E. L., **95–96**
Douglas, Kirk, **96–97**, 126, 132, 137, 241, 275
Drescher, Fran, 381, 408
Dreyfuss, Richard, **97–98**, 37, 127, 131, 140, 407, 409
Drudge, Matt, 227
Dylan, Bob, **98–100**, 41; Allen Ginsberg, 165; Jazz and Blues, 200, 206; Literature, 261; Popular Music, 315; Rock and Roll, 338

Ebb, Fred, 314
Ecko, Mark. *See* Fashion
The Ed Sullivan Show, 4; The Catskills, 57; Alan King, 234; Jackie Mason, 282; William Paley, 304; Gene Simmons, 374
Einstein, Albert, **101–6**, 17; Chess, 61; Comic Books, 77; Literature, 259
Eisner, William, **106–8**, 74. *See also* Comic Books
Ellison Harlan, 364
Ephron, Nora, **108**
Erikson, Eric Homburger, 319
Exodus, **108–110**, 67; Film, 126; Israel, 108; Paul Newman, 295; United States Holocaust Memorial Museum, 426. *See also* The Holocaust in American Culture; Jewish Museums

Falk, Peter, **111–12**, 7, 128, 404
Fashion, **112–18**; Adrian, 113; Hattie Carnegie, 114; Kenneth Cole, 117; Mark Ecko, 118; Sophie Gimbel, 114; Edith Head, 113; Donna Karan, 116; Ann Klein, 115; Calvin Klein, 116; Michael Kors, 117; Ralph Lauren, 116; Isaac Mizrahi, 117; Mollie Parnis, 115; Maurice Rentner, 114; Helen Rose, 113; Nettie Rosenstein, 114; Carolyn Schnurer, 115; Irene Sharraf, 113; Levi Strauss, 112; Pauline Trigere, 115
Fast, Howard, 224
Feiffer, Jules, **118–19**, 74, 106; Popular Music, 314; Theater, 413
Feldshuh, Tovah, **119–20**, 132, 405
Ferber, Edna, **120–21**
Fiddler on the Roof, **121–22**, 27, 86, 94, 118, 296, 309, 337; Film, 127; Fyvush Finkel, 143; Mickey Katz, 231; Latin Music, 247; Literature, 263; Popular Music, 314; Radio, 327; David Lee Roth, 344; Yiddish, 451. *See also* Theater
Fiedler, Leslie, 264
Fierstein, Harvey, **122–23**, 406, 413
Film, **123–34**, 60, 275, 321, 334, 361, 369, 401, 436; Woody Allen, 4; Alan Arkin, 8; Lauren Bacall, 15; Mel Brooks, 37; The Coen Brothers, 67, 68; Aaron Copland, 79; Tony Curtis, 81; Kirk Douglas, 97; *Exodus,* 108–110; *Fiddler on the Roof,* 120–21; *Gentleman's Agreement,* 161–62; Harry Golden, 168; Hollywood Moguls, 189–92; Al Jolson, 221; Jack Klugman, 238; Stanley Kubrick, 241; Meyer Levin, 252; Peter Lorre, 265; Sidney Lumet, 266–67; Walter Matthau, 285; Paul Muni, 292; Tony Randall, 329; Rob Reiner, 332; Edward G. Robinson, 337; Adam Sandler, 356; (Isidore) Dore Schary, 358; Sarah Silverman, 373; Aaron Spelling, 386; Steven Spielberg, 388; Ben Stiller, 399; Barbra Streisand, 401; United States Holocaust Memorial Museum, 427; Walter Winchell, 441; Herman Wouk, 444, 446
Film Stars, **134–44**; Woody Allen, 4; Alan Arkin, 8; Lauren Bacall, 15; Jack Black, 29; Mel Brooks, 37, 43; The Coen Brothers, 67; Tony Curtis, 80–81; Kirk Douglas, 97; Paulette Goddard, 168; Al Jolson, 221; Danny Kaye, 232; Jack Klugman, 238; Peter Lorre, 265, 285; The

Marx Brothers, 275; Robert Merrill, 285; Paul Muni, 292; Paul Newman, 295; Tony Randall, 329; Rob Reiner, 332; Edward G. Robinson, 337; Ben Stiller, 399; Barbra Streisand, 401
Fine, Reuben, 61
Finkel, Fyvush, **144–45**
Fischer, Bobby, 61, 62. *See also* Chess
Fisher, Carrie, 140, 406
Fisher, Eddie, **145**
Flegenheimer, Arthur. *See* Gangsters
Foer, Jonathan Safran, **145–47**, 130, 263. *See also* Literature
Food, **147–48**, 210
Food Industry, **148–50**; Manischewitz Family, 274
Freed, Alan, 200, 325
Freud, Sigmund, **150–51**, 73, 400, 422; Stanley Jasspon Kunitz, 242; Ludwig Lewisohn, 255; Popular Music, 316. *See also* Popular Psychology
Friedan, Betty, **151–53**, 397
Friedman, Debbie, **153**
Friedman, Kinky, **153–54**, 93
Friedman, Thomas, **154–55**, 226
Fromm, Erich, 319
Fuchs, Leo, **155–56**
Fuld, William, 418. *See also* Toys and Games

Gaines, Max, 77. *See also* Comic Books
Ganchoff, Moshe, 50
Gangsters, **157–59**, 128, 135; Louis "Lepke" Buchalter, 129, 157; Arthur "Dutch Schultz" Flegenheimer, 157; Meyer Lansky, 128, 132, 157; Abraham "Kid Twist" Reles, 158; Arnold Rothstein, 158, 394; Benjamin "Bugsy" Siegel, 157, 158, 159, 206; Abner "Longy" Zwillman, 159
Garber, Vic, 404
Garfield, John, **159–60**, 127, 136; *Gentleman's Agreement,* 161; Literature, 260; Barney Ross, 342; Theater, 412
Garfunkel, Art, 376
Garrett, Brad, 405
Gehry, Frank, **160–61**
Gelbart, Larry, 384, 431
Gellar, Sarah Michelle, 404
Genshoff, Moshe, 326
Gentleman's Agreement, **161–62**, 125, 160. *See also* Film
Gershwin, George, **162–64**, 25, 32, 55, 78; Jazz and Blues, 200; Al Jolson, 222; Latin Music, 246; Literature, 259; Itzhak Perlman, 307; Popular Music, 311; Rap and Hip Hop Music, 330; Paul Simon, 376; Theater, 415; Yiddish Theater, 457. *See also* Jazz and Blues; Popular Music
Getz, Stan, 206. *See also* Jazz and Blues
Gilbert, Melissa, 403, 404
Gilman, Sid, 392
Gimbel, Sophie. *See* Fashion
Ginott, Haim G., **164**
Ginsberg, Allen, **164–66**, 98, 261, 422. *See also* Literature
Gittlesohn, Rabbi Roland B., **166–67**
Glass, Philip, **167–68**
Glickman, Marty, 392
Goddard, Paulette, **168**, 134
Goffin, Gerry, 34, 315. *See also* Popular Music
The Goldbergs, 168; Radio, 324; Sitcoms, 378; Television, 407; Theater, 411
Golden, Harry, **168–70**, 246, 261, 262
Goldin, Sidney, 452, 453–54
Goldmark, Peter Carl, 205
Goldstein, Lisa, 365
Goldwyn, Samuel, 232, 334. *See also* Hollywood Moguls
Golem, 87, 363, 364. *See also* Science Fiction
Goodman, Benny, **170**, 203, 340. *See also* Jazz and Blues
Goodman, Paul, **170–72**
Gottlieb, Adolph, 10. *See also* Artists
Gottschalk, Louis Moreau, 201, 205. *See also* Jazz and Blues
Gould, Elliot, 380, 405
Grade, Chaim, **172–73**
Green, Gerald, **173**, 386
Green, Joseph, 308, 453, 454
Green, Loren, 403
Green, Shawn David, **173–74**, 394
Greenberg, Florence, 33
Greenberg, Hank, **174–75**, 173, 240, 342
Greene, Ira, 454
Greenwich, Ellie, 34
Guettel, Adam, 316
Guston, Philip, 10–11. *See also* Artists

Hackett, Buddy, 72
Hamlisch, Marvin, 205, 314. *See also* Popular Music
Hammerstein, Oscar, 312, 316, 340. *See also* Popular Music
Handler, Elliot, 419. *See also* Toys and Games
Handler, Ruth, 419. *See also* Toys and Games
Hanukkah, 185, 186. *See also* Holidays and Rituals
Harburg, E. Y. "Yip," 312. *See also* Popular Music
Harnick, Sheldon, 312, 314
Hawn, Goldie, 129
Head, Edith. *See* Fashion
Hecht, Ben, **177–78**, 124, 224, 262, 338, 340
Heeb Magazine, **178–79**
Heller, Joseph, **179–80**
Herman, Jerry, 313
Hershman, Mordecai, 49
Heschel, Abraham Joshua, **180–82**, 251
Hesse, Eva, 12, 13
Hip Hop, 206, 285, 329–31. *See also* Rap and Hip Hop Music
Hirsch, Judd, 406
Hobson, Laura, 161
Hoffman, Avi, 48
Hoffman, Dustin, **182**, 41, 399; Film, 131; Film Stars, 139; Sidney Lumet, 267; Sitcoms, 380; Steven Spielberg, 388; Theater, 410
Holidays and Rituals, **182–88**; Bar Mitzvah, 97, 174, 182, 187–88, 240, 286, 345, 441; Brit Milah, 187, 284, 333; Hanukkah, 185, 186; Lubavitcher, 31, 53, 99, 181, 186, 445, 446; Passover, 183, 184; Purim, 186; Rosh Hashanah, 175, 182, 392, 450; Adam Sandler, 131, 141, 185, 319, 339, 355–56, 379, 443; Sukkot, 184–85; Tisha B'Av, 186–87, 194; Yom Kippur, 174, 175, 182, 207, 240, 342, 369, 392, 435

Holliday, Judy, **188–89**, 138
Hollywood Moguls, **189–92**, 124; Harry Cohn, 189, 191; William Fox, 189; Al Jolson, 94, 217, 221–22; Carl Laemmle, 189, 190–91; Louis B. Mayer, 136, 189, 190; (Isidore) Dore Schary, 126, 190, 358; Irving Thalberg, 190, 260, 279; Harry Warner, 189, 191; Jack Warner, 159, 189, 191; Adolph Zukor, 189, 190
Holocaust. *See* The Holocaust in American Culture; United States Holocaust Memorial Museum
The Holocaust in American Culture, **192–93**, 11, 66, 77, 87, 95, 97, 118; *The Diary of Ann Frank,* 28, 95, 350, 351; Film, 126, 128, 130; Jonathan Safran Foer, 145; Chaim Grade, 172; Gerald Green, 173; Ben Hecht, 177; Jewish Museums, 215; Journalism, 223, 224; Klezmer Music, 241; Literature, 261; Bernard Malamud, 271; David Mamet, 273, 289; Chaim Potok, 321; Philip Roth, 346, 351; *Schindler's List,* 359, 360; Science Fiction, 362–67; Isaac Bashevis Singer, 377; Steven Spielberg, 386; Theater, 413; United States Holocaust Memorial Museum, 426; Elie Wiesel, 439, 440, 441; Herman Wouk, 445
Holocaust Remembrance Day, **193–95**. *See also* The Holocaust in American Culture; United States Holocaust Memorial Museum
Holtzman, William "Red," 391
Horowitz, David, 225
Houdini, Harry, **195–96**, 95
House Un-American Activities Committee (HUAC), 105, 125, 288, 300, 412
Howard, Leslie, 136
Howe, Irving, 264, 444
Hurok, Sol, **196**

Israel, 282, 350; Albert Einstein, 104; *Exodus,* 108, 109; Fashion, 114; Film, 126, 128, 132; Holidays and Rituals, 187; Holocaust Remembrance Day, 194; Journalism, 224; Literature, 261; David "Mickey" Marcus, 275; Billy Rose, 340; Philip Roth, 346, 347; Sarah Silverman, 373; Mark Spitz, 389; United States Holocaust Memorial Museum, 426
Iwo Jima Eulogy. *See* Gittlesohn, Rabbi Roland B.

Jazz and Blues, **199–207**; Herb Alpert, 206; Harold Arlen, 201, 202; Moses "Moe" Asch, 200; Irving Berlin, 24–25, 201, 202; Leonard Bernstein, 26–27, 206; Theodore Bikel, 27–28, 200; Sammy Cahn, 202; Eddie Cantor, 48–49, 202; Aaron Copland, 78–80, 205; Sammy Davis Jr., 89, 206; Bob Dylan, 98–100, 200; Alan Freed, 200; George Gershwin, 162–63, 200; Stan Getz, 206; Benny Goodman, 203; Louis Moreau Gottschalk, 201, 205; Marvin Hamlisch, 205, 314; *The Jazz Singer,* 201, 207–8; Al Jolson, 201, 221–22; Jerome Kern, 201, 202, 311; Klezmer Music, 206, 237, 248; Abe Meeropol, 200; Mez Mezzrow, 206; Radio, 200, 323–27; Rock and Roll, 200, 338–39; Billy Rose, 203, 339–40; Dinah Shore, 206, 370–71; Tin Pan Alley, 200, 338; Sophie Tucker, 124, 203, 217; *West Side Story,* 206, 438–39
The Jazz Singer, **207–8**, 217; Neil Diamond, 94; Film, 123; Film Stars, 135; The Holocaust in American Culture, 191; Jazz and Blues, 201; Al Jolson, 207, 208, 221; Meyer Levin, 253; Popular Music, 315; Paul Reubens, 324; "Yossele" Josef Rosenblatt, 341; Theater, 411
Jessel, George, **208–9**, 401; Theater, 411; Vaudeville, 430; Walter Winchell, 442
Jewish Daily Forward, **209–210**, 46, 47, 145, 161, 172, 224; Popular Psychology, 318; Isaac Bashevis Singer, 377; Yiddish, 450; Yiddish Theater, 456
Jewish Delicatessens, **210–11**, 50, 147
Jewish Museums, **211–16**. *See also* United States Holocaust Memorial Museum
Jewish Women and Popular Culture, **216–19**, 151; Lauren Bacall, 218; Theda Bara, 217; Gertrude Berg, 218; Irving Berlin, 217; Fannie Brice, 217; The Catskills, 218; *The Jazz Singer,* 217; Al Jolson, 217; Debra Messing, 219; Bette Midler, 218; Sarah Jessica Parker, 219; Molly Picon, 216–17; Kyra Sedgwick, 219; Barbra Streisand, 218; Sophie Tucker, 217
Joel, Billy, **219–20**, 339
Johansson, Scarlett, **220–21**, 142
Jolson, Al, **221–22**, 94, 217; Film, 123; Film Stars, 135; Hollywood Moguls, 191; Jazz and Blues, 201, 207; Literature, 259; Popular Music, 312, 315; Radio, 323; Theater, 411. *See also* Film; *The Jazz Singer;* Vaudeville
Jong, Erica, **223**
Journalism, **223–28**; Mitch Albom, 3; Walter Annenberg, 5–6; Carl Bernstein, 108, 226; Wolf Blitzer, 227, 256; Art Buchwald, 41–42; Abraham Cahan, 46–47; Peter Chernin, 226; Alan Dershowitz, 89–90, 225; Matt Drudge, 227; Howard Fast, 124, 224; Thomas Freidman, 226; Leo Fuchs, 154; Paul Goodman, 170; Ben Hecht, 124, 224; Holocaust, 192–93, 224; David Horowitz, 225; *Jewish Daily Forward,* 210, 224; Larry King, 235–36, 227; Charles Krauthammer, 226, 239; Rabbi Michael Lerner, 54, 227; Meyer Levin, 224, 252–53; Leslie Moonves, 226; Adolph Ochs,

224; Frank Rich, 226; Geraldo Rivera, 335; Arthur Ochs Sultzberger, 226; Mike Wallace, 228, 435; David Westin, 226; Walter Winchell, 224, 441–42
Jungreis, Esther, **228–29**

Kahn, Gus, 311, 415. *See also* Popular Music
Kahn, Madeline, 406
Kaminska, Esther Rokhl, 452
Kaminsky, A. Y., 452
Kander, John, 314
Kane, Bob, 76, 106. *See also* Comic Books
Kane, Carol, 406
Karan, Donna. *See* Fashion
Kashdan, Isaac, 61
Kasparov, Gary, 61, 62. *See also* Chess
Katz, Mickey, **231–32**, 237, 260, 451. *See also* Literature
Kaye, Danny, **232–33**, 55, 126, 286, 370, 457
Kazin, Alfred, **233–34**, 263, 422
Kellerman, Faye, 92, 234. *See also* Detective Fiction
Kellerman, Jonathan, 92, 234. *See also* Detective Fiction
Kemelman, Harry, 92
Kern, Jerome, 201, 202, 311, 316, 415
Kerouac, Jack, 98
Kiam, Omar, 114
Kidd, Michael, 85, 86. *See also* Dance
Kimmel, Eric, 66
King, Alan, **234–35**, 431
King, Carole, 34, 315, 367
King, Larry, **235–36**, 227
Kirby, Jack, 75, 106, 236. *See also* Comic Books
Kirshner, Don, 34
Kissinger, Henry, **236–37**, 28, 68, 179
Klein, Ann. *See* Fashion
Klein, Calvin. *See* Fashion
Klezmer Music, **237**, 83, 206, 248, 305, 451
Klugman, Jack, **238**, 329, 406
Koch, Edward, **238–39**, 292
Kol Nidre, 201, 207, 253. *See The Jazz Singer*
Koppel, Ted, **239–40**
Kors, Michael. *See* Fashion
Koufax, Sandy, **240–41**
Kramer, Stanley, **241**
Krauthammer, Charles, 226, 227
Kravitz, Lenny, 339
Kressyn, Miriam, 327, 457
Krugman, Paul, 226
Krumholtz, David, 404
Kubrick, Stanley, **241–42**
Kunitz, Stanley Jasspon, **242–43**
Kurtzman, Harvey, 75, 106, 243, 431. *See also* Comic Books
Kushner, Harold S., **243–44**
Kushner, Tony, 132, 367, 404, 411, 413
Kussevitzky, Moshe, 50

Laemmle, Carl, 189, 190–91. *See also* Hollywood Moguls
Lamarr, Hedy, 136
Landau, Martin, **245–46**
Landers, Ann, 429
Landy, Ludwig, 454
Lang, Pearl, 84
Lansky, Meyer, 128, 132, 157
Lasker, Emmanuel, 61
Latin Music, **246–48**; The Catskills, 55–56, 426; George Gershwin, 162–63, 246; Harry Golden, 168–69, 246; Grossinger's Hotel, 246; Popular Music, 310–16
Lauren, Ralph. *See* Fashion
Lavin, Linda. *See* Television
Lazarus, Emma, **248–49**, 258. *See also* Literature
Lear, Norman. *See* Television
Lebedev, Aaron, 457
Lee, Manfred, 92
Lee, Stan, 75, 107, 374. *See also* Comic Books
Leiber, Jerry, 35, 249, 312, 338
Leibovitz, Annie, **249–50**
Lemkin, Raphael, 193, 194
Leonard, Benny, **250–51**, 52, 391
Lepke, Louie, 129
Lerner, Alan Jay, 312, 313. *See also* Popular Music
Lerner, Rabbi Michael, **251**, 54, 227. *See also* Journalism
Levin, Ira, **252**, 414
Levin, Meyer, **252–53**, 224, 260
Levitsky, Michl, 325, 326
Levy, Marv, 392
Levy, Richard, C., 420. *See also* Toys and Games
Lewis, Jerry, **253–54**; Eddie Cantor, 49; Comedy, 70; Film, 127; Film Stars, 138; Leo Rosten, 344; Sitcoms, 382; Yiddish Theater, 456
Lewis, Shari, **254**
Lewisohn, Ludwig, **254–55**
Lieberman, Joseph, **255–57**
Liebman, Joshua Loth, **257–58**, 150
Linden, Hal, **258**, 405
Literature, **258–65**; Saul Bellow, 18–21, 261; Michael Chabon, 59, 263; E. L. Doctorow, 96; Bob Dylan, 98–100, 261; Albert Einstein, 101–6, 259; Edna Ferber, 120; Jonathan Safran Foer, 145, 263; Allen Ginsberg, 164–65, 261; Harry Golden, 168–69, 261; Ben Hecht, 224, 262; Abraham Joshua Heschel, 180; Holocaust, 192–93, 261; Israel, 261; Al Jolson, 221–22, 259; Erica Jong, 223; Mickey Katz, 231–32, 260; Alfred Kazin, 233, 263; Emma Lazarus, 248–49, 258; Meyer Levin, 252–53, 260; Ludwig Lewisohn, 255; Sidney Lumet, 266–67; Norman Mailer, 269–70; Bernard Malamud, 262, 270; Clifford Odets, 260, 299; Cynthia Ozick, 263, 302; Chaim Potok, 263, 322; Philip Roth, 262, 346; Rick Rubin, 352; Isaac Bashevis Singer, 377; Barbara Tuchman, 422
Loesser, Frank, 312. *See also* Popular Music
Loewe, Frederick, 313. *See also* Popular Music
Lorre, Peter, **265–66**
Lubavitcher Movement, 31, 53, 99, 181, 186, 445, 446
Luckman, Sid, 392
Lumet, Sidney, **266–67**, 118, 127, 409

Mah Jongg, 421. *See also* Toys and Games
Mailer, Norman, **269–70**, 7, 126, 130, 446
Malamud, Bernard, **270–72**, 262, 427, 446. *See also* Literature
Mamet, David, **272–73**, 130
Manilow, Barry, **273–74**

Manischewitz Family, **274**, 148–49
Mann, Barry, 34
Man Ray, 9
Marcus, David "Mickey," **274–75**, 97, 126
Martin, Ross, 403
Marx, Louis, 418. *See also* Toys and Games
The Marx Brothers, **275–81**, 18, 22; The Catskills, 55; Comedy, 70; Film, 124; Film Stars, 137; Groucho Marx, 334, 355, 379, 407; Popular Music, 312; Radio, 324; Vaudeville, 430
Maslow, Abraham, 318. *See also* Popular Psychology
Maslow, Sophie, **281**
Mason, Jackie, **281–82**, 70, 409, 431
Matisyahu, Hasidic MC, **282–85**, 331, 339
Matlin, Marlee, 141
Matthau, Walter, 81, 155, 285
Maus, 387. *See also* Comic BooksSpiegelman, Art
Mayer, Louis B., 136, 189, 190. *See also* Hollywood Moguls
Mazer, Bill, 394
Medved, Michael, 227
Meeropol, Abe, 200
Merrill, Robert, **285–86**
Messing, Debra, 219
Mezzron, Mezz, 206
Michaels, Al, 394. *See also* Sports
Michton, Benjamin F., 419. *See also* Toys and Games
Midler, Bette, 218
Miller, Arthur, **286–90**, 7, 67, 241; William Paley, 303; Television, 407; Theater, 412; Yiddish Theater, 457
Miller, Glen, 203. *See also* Jazz and Blues
The Minsky Brothers, **290**
Mizrahi, Isaac. *See* Fashion
Modigliana, Amodeo, 8
Moonves, Leslie, 226
Morrow, Rob, 404
Mostel, Zero, **290–92**, 38, 70, 120
Movies. *See* Film
Muni, Paul, 135, 136, 292, 338, 361, 410, 457
Murray, Arthur, 87
Murray, Jan, 431
Myerson, Bess, **292–93**

Nevelson, Louise, 11. *See also* Artists
Nevins, Al, 34
Newman, Barnett, 10
Newman, Paul, **295–96**, 109, 138, 153, 267, 399, 410
Nimoy, Leonard, **296–97**, 362, 364, 404
Nimzowitsch, Aaron, 60
Norell, Norman, 113

Ochs, Adolph, 224
Odets, Clifford, **299–301**, 288; Lee J. Cobb, 67; Leo Fuchs, 154, 155; John Garfield, 159; Literature, 260; Menasha Skulnik, 382; Theater, 412
Oyster, Moshe, 50
Ozick, Cynthia, **301–2**, 263, 271. *See also* Literature

Paley, William, **303–4**, 323. *See also* Radio; Television
Paltrow, Gwyneth, 141
Paretsky, Sara, 93
Parker, Sarah Jessica, 219
Parnis, Mollie. *See* Fashion
Pascin, Jules, 8. *See also* Artists
Passover, 183, 184. *See also* Holidays and Rituals
Patinkin, Mandy, **304–5**, 384, 404, 408
Pekar, Harvey, **305**, 133
Perlman, Itzhak, **305–8**
Picon, Molly, **308–9**; Jewish Women and Popular Culture, 216; Popular Music, 313; Radio, 326; Sitcoms, 382; Theater, 410; Yiddish Film, 452, 453; Yiddish Theater, 456, 457
Pinchik, Pierre, 50
Pinsky, Robert, **309**
Plain, Belva, **309–310**
Polansky, Roman, 130, 252
Polgar, Susan, 62
Politics: Bella Abzug, 1; Kinky Friedman, 153; Henry Kissinger, 236; Edward Koch, 238; Joseph Lieberman, 255
Pomus, Doc, 35, 310, 378. *See also* The Brill Building Songwriters
Popular Music, **310–16**; Richard Adler, 313; Leonard Bernstein, 26–27, 313; Jerry Bock, 314; Fanny Brice, 31–32, 312; Mel Brooks, 37–38, 314; Sammy Cahn, 202, 313; Cy Coleman, 314; Neil Diamond, 94–95, 315; Bob Dylan, 98–100, 315; Fred Ebb, 314; Jules Feiffer, 117–18, 314; *Fiddler on the Roof,* 120–21, 314; George Gershwin, 162–63; Gerry Goffin, 315; Adam Guetell, 316; Oscar Hammerstein II, 312, 316, 340; E. Y. "Yip" Harburg, 313; Sheldon Harnick, 312, 314; Jerry Herman, 313; *The Jazz Singer,* 207–8, 315; Al Jolson, 221–22, 315; Gus Kahn, 311, 312; Jerome Kern, 201, 202, 311, 316, 415; Alan Jay Lerner, 312, 313; Molly Picon, 308–9, 313; Richard Rodgers, 312, 384; Jerry Ross, 313; Neil Sedaka, 34, 315, 366; Phil Silvers, 286, 290, 313, 375; Carly Simon, 315; Stephen Sondheim, 27, 86, 312, 383–84; Barbra Streisand, 312, 400–401; Charles Strouse, 313; Tin Pan Alley, 315, 415; Vaudeville, 310, 429–31; Harry Von Tilzer, 311; *West Side Story,* 313, 438–39
Popular Psychology, **316–19**; Joyce Brothers, 39; Sigmund Freud, 149–50; Haim G. Ginott, 164–65; Harold S. Kushner, 244; Joshua Loth Liebman, 257–58; Abigail Van Buren, 429; Dr. Ruth Westheimer, 437
Portman, Natalie, **319–21**, 142
Potok, Chaim, **321–22**, 263, 427. *See also* Literature
Purim, 186. *See also* Holidays and Rituals

Queen, Ellery, 92. *See also* Detective Fiction

Radinsky, Emmanuel (Man Ray), 9. *See also* Artists

Radio, **323–27**; Jack Benny, 21, 22; Gertrude Berg, 22, 218, 323, 324, 379, 407, 411; Fanny Brice, 31–32, 124, 128, 139, 323, 340, 401, 430; George Burns, 42–43, 114, 137, 303, 323, 379, 403; Eddie Cantor, 48–49, 137, 144, 202, 232, 312, 323, 370, 379, 421; Film Stars, 137; *The Goldbergs,* 168, 324, 378, 407, 411; Al Jolson, 94, 123, 135, 191, 201, 207, 217, 221–22, 323, 303; The Marx Brothers, 18, 22, 55, 70, 124, 275–81, 324; David Sarnoff, 356–58; Howard Stern, 397–98
Rainer, Louise, 136
Ramone, Joey, **327–28**
Rand, Ayn, **328–29**
Randall, Tony, **329**, 406
Rap and Hip Hop Music, **329–31**; Beastie Boys, 17–18, 330; George Gershwin, 162–63, 330; Matisyahu, Hasidic MC, 282–83, 331; Rick Rubin, 17, 330, 352
Reich, Steven, **331–32**
Reiner, Carl, 37, 38, 46, 332
Reiner, Rob, **332**, 37, 211, 221. *See also* Film; Television
Reiser, Paul, 405. *See also* Television
Reles, Abraham "Kid Twist," 158
Rentner, Maurice. *See* Fashion
Reubens, Paul, **332–33**
Rexite, Seymour, 327, 340, 457
Rice, Elmer, **333–34**, 124, 411, 412
Rich, Frank, 226
Rickles, Don, 335, 406
The Ritz Brothers, **334**, 70
Rivera, Geraldo, **334–35**
Rivers, Joan, **335–36**, 70
Robbins, Harold, **336**
Robbins, Jerome, **336–37**, 27, 83, 85–86, 120, 83, 438. *See also* Popular Music
Robinson, Edward G., **337–38**, 127, 135, 163, 191, 260
Rock and Roll, **338–39**; Beastie Boys, 17–18, 330, 352; The Coen Brothers, 339; Bob Dylan, 98–100, 165, 200, 338; Ben Hecht, 338; Billy Joel, 219–20, 339; Jerry Leiber, 35, 249, 312, 338; Matisyahu, Hasidic MC, 282–83, 331, 339; Joey Ramone, 327–28; Adam Sandler, 319, 339, 355–56; Paul Simon, 339, 376
Rodgers, Richard, 312, 384. *See also* Popular Music
Rohde, Michael, 50, 63
Roitman, David, 50
Rose, Billy, **339–40**, 32, 203, 457
Rose, Helen. *See* Fashion
Rosenberg, Julius and Ethel, 95, 105
Rosenblatt, "Yossele" Josef, **341–42**, 49, 50, 326
Rosenstein, Nettie. *See* Fashion
Rosh Hashanah, 175, 182, 392, 450. *See also* Holidays and Rituals
Ross, Barney, **342–43**, 391
Ross, Jerry, 313
Rosten, Leo, **343–44**, 51
Roth, David Lee, **344–45**
Roth, Henry, **345–46**, 260
Roth, Philip, **346–52**, 16, 72, 127, 262, 271, 427, 442
Rothko, Mark, 9–10. *See also* Artists
Rothstein, Arnold, 158, 394
Rubenfield, Paul. *See* Reubens, Paul
Rubenstein, Akiba, 60
Rubin, Rick, **352**, 17, 330
Ryder, Winona, 141

Sagan, Carl, **353**
Sales, Soupy, **353–54**, 70
Salinger, Jerome, **354–55**
Sandler, Adam, **355–56**; Film, 131; Film Stars, 141; Holidays and Rituals, 185; Natalie Portman, 319; Rock and Roll, 339; Sitcoms, 379; Henry Winkler, 443
Saperstein, Abe, 392
Sarnoff, David, **356–58**, 323
Satz, Ludwig, 453
Schacter, Zalman, 53, 251
Schary, (Isidore) Dore, **358**, 126, 190
Schayes, Dolph, 391
Schindler's List, **359–60**, 305; Film, 129; The Holocaust in American Culture, 192, 193; Art Spiegelman, 386; Steven Spielberg, 388; Television Stars, 408
Schneerson, Rabbi Menachem, 181
Schnurer, Carolyn. *See* Fashion
Schreiber, Lieb, 129
Schulberg, Budd, **360–61**, 67
Schuman, Mort, 35
Schwartz, Maurice, **361–62**, 144, 154, 326, 452, 454
Science Fiction, **362–66**; Woody Allen, 3–5, 363; Isaac Asimov, 364; Robert Albert Bloch, 364; Jack Dann, 363; Avram Davidson, 364; Harold Ellison, 364; Lisa Goldstein, 365; Golem, 363, 364; Holocaust, 192–93, 364; Leonard Nimoy, 296–97, 364; Robert Silverberg, 364; Steven Spielberg, 364, 387–89
Secunda, Sholom, 326, 456
Sedaka, Neil, 34, 315, 366
Sedgwick, Kyra, 219
Segal, George, 12. *See also* Artists
Seinfeld, 88, 366, 380, 405
Seinfeld, Jerry, **366–67**; Comedy, 70, 72; David Copperfield, 80; Sitcoms, 379; Television, 405; Vaudeville, 431
Selig, Bud, 393
Sendak, Maurice, **367–68**, 387
Serra, Richard, 14. *See also* Artists
Shahn, Ben, 291
Shandling, Gary, 405
Sharraf, Irene. *See* Fashion
Shatner, William, **368–69**, 297, 365, 404
Shaw, Artie, 203. *See also* Jazz and Blues
Sheldon, Sidney, **369–70**
Shirley Kravitz Children's Book Award, 65
Shoah. *See* The Holocaust in American Culture
Shore, Dinah, **370–71**, 49, 206
Shuster, Joe, 76, 106. *See also* Comic Books
Sidney, Sylvia, 136
Siegel, Benjamin "Bugsy," 157, 158, 206
Siegel, Jerry, 75, 106. *See also* Comic Books
Sills, Beverly, **371–73**
Silverberg, Robert, 364
Silverman, Sarah, **373**, 70, 132, 219
Silvers, Phil, 286, 290, 313, 375
Simmons, Gene, **373–74**, 100, 339
Simon, Carly, 315
Simon, Neil, **374–75**, 38, 46, 413, 431
Simon, Paul, **376**, 163, 339

Singer, Isaac Bashevis, **376–78**, 66, 209, 363
Sitcoms, **378–82**, 367; Woody Allen, 379; *Barney Miller,* 380; Jack Benny, 379; Gertrude Berg, 380; Milton Berle, 379; Mel Brooks, 379; George Burns, 379; Sid Caesar, 379; Eddie Cantor, 379; Fran Drescher, 381; *The Goldbergs,* 379; Elliott Gould, 380; Dustin Hoffman, 380; Groucho Marx, 379; *The Nanny,* 381; Paul Reiser, 379; *Rhoda,* 380; Adam Sandler, 379; George Segal, 380; Jerry Seinfeld, 379; Jon Stewart, 379, 407, 409; *Welcome Back Kotter,* 379
Skulnik, Menasha, **382–83**, 141, 154, 451, 456
Sokolow, Anna, 83, 84, 85
Solomon Brothers, 200
Sondheim, Stephen, **383–84**, 27, 86, 312, 438. *See also* Popular Music
Sontag, Susan, **384–85**, 250
Soutere, Chaim, 8
Spector, Phil, 34, 338, 385
Spelling, Aaron, **385–86**
Spiegelman, Art, **386–87**, 77. *See also* Comic Books
Spielberg, Steven, **387–89**, 97, 386; Film, 129; Film Stars, 140; The Holocaust in American Culture, 193; Mandy Patinkin, 305; *Schindler's List,* 359; Science Fiction, 364; Ben Stiller, 399
Spitz, Mark, **389–90**, 392
Sports, 22–23, **390–96**; Mel Allen, 394; Arnold "Red" Aurerbach, 391; Gary Betteman, 393; Howard Cosell, 393; Sid Gilman, 392; Marty Glickman, 392; Shawn David Green, 394, 173–74; Hank Greenberg, 174–75; William "Red" Holtzman, 391; Benny Leonard, 250–51; Marv Levy, 392; Sid Luckman, 392; Bill Mazer, 394; Al Michaels, 394; Rosh Hashanah, 175, 182, 392, 450; Barney Ross, 342–43, 391; Arnold Rothstein, 158, 394; Abe Saperstein, 392; Dolph Schayes, 391; Bud Selig, 393; Mark Spitz, 389–90, 392; David Stern, 393; Sam Stoller, 392; Suzyn Waldman, 394; Yom Kippur, 174, 175, 182, 207, 240, 342, 369, 392, 435
Stein, Ben, 406
Stein, Gertrude, 416–17
Steinem, Gloria, **396–97**
Steiner, Herman, 61
Steinitz, Wilhelm, 60
Stern, Bill, 394
Stern, David, 393
Stern, Howard, **397–98**
Stewart, Jon, **398–99**, 379
Stiller, Ben, **399–400**, 131, 142
Stoller, Mike, 35, 249, 315, 338
Stoller, Sam, 392
Stone, Irving, **400**
Strasberg, Lee, 410, 411
Strauss, Levi. *See* Fashion
Streisand, Barbra, **400–401**, 32; Dance, 86; Neil Diamond, 94; Film, 127, 128; Film Stars, 139; Jewish Women and Popular Culture, 218; Popular Music, 312; Sitcoms, 380
Strouse, Charles, 313
Styne, Jule, 383
Sukkot, 184–85. *See also* Holidays and Rituals
Sultzberger, Arthur Ochs, 226
Superman, 75, 76, 106. *See also* Comic Books
Susann, Jacqueline, **401–2**
Susskind, David, 406
Sydney Taylor Awards, 65

Tambor, Jeffrey, 406
Tamiris, Helen, 83, 84, 85
Taylor, Sydney, 64
Television, **403–7**; Woody Allen, 3–5; Alan Arkin, 8, 404; Gene Barry, 403; Richard Belzer, 404; Jack Benny, 21–22, 403; Milton Berle, 23–24, 403; George Burns, 42–43, 403; Sid Caesar, 45–46, 403; Paddy Chayefsky, 60, 406; Robert Conrad, 403; Larry David, 88, 406; Peter Falk, 97–98, 404; Tovah Feldshuh, 118–19, 406; Victor Garber, 404; Sarah Michelle Gellar, 404; Melissa Gilbert, 403; Lorne Greene, 403; Judd Hirsch, 404; Jack Klugman, 238, 406; Tony Kushner, 132, 367, 404; Norman Lear, 406; Hal Linden, 405; Ross Martin, 403; Arthur Miller, 286–87, 407; Rob Morrow, 404; Leonard Nimoy, 296–97, 404; Mandy Patinkin, 305–6, 404; Tony Randall, 329, 406; Paul Reiser, 405; Don Rickles, 335, 406; Jerry Seinfeld, 366–67, 405; Gary Shandling, 405; William Shatner, 368–69, 404; David Susskind, 406; Jeffrey Tambor, 406; Henry Winkler, 405, 442–43
Television Stars, **407–9**; Woody Allen, 3–5, 408; Alan Arkin, 8, 408; Jack Benny, 407; Milton Berle, 23–24, 407; George Burns, 42–43, 403; Sid Caesar, 45–46; Paddy Chayefsky, 406; Robert Conrad, 403; Larry David, 88, 406; Fran Drescher, 381, 408; Richard Dreyfuss, 97–98, 408; Peter Falk, 111–112, 404; Fyvush Finkel, 143–44, 408; Judd Hirsch, 404; Jack Klugman, 238, 406; Tony Kushner, 133, 367, 404; Hal Linden, 405; Ross Martin, 403; Groucho Marx, 407; Rob Morrow, 408; Leonard Nimoy, 296–97, 404; Mandy Patinkin, 305–6, 408; Tony Randall, 329, 406; Paul Reiser, 405; Jerry Seinfeld, 366–67, 408; William Shatner, 368–69, 404; Henry Winkler, 405, 442–43
Telushkin, Joseph, 93
Texaco Star Theater, 24, 407
Thalberg, Irving, 190, 260, 279. *See also* Hollywood Moguls
Theater, **409–14**; Woody Allen, 4, 413; Lauren Bacall, 15–16; Gertrude Berg, 411; Paddy Chayefsky, 60, 337, 406, 412; *The Diary of Anne Frank,* 412; Jules Feiffer, 117–18, 413; *Fiddler on the Roof,* 120, 121; Harvey Fierstein, 121–22, 413; John Garfield, 159–60, 412;

The Goldbergs, 411; Dustin Hoffman, 41, 131, 139, 267; Holocaust, 413; *The Jazz Singer,* 411; Tony Kushner, 411; Ira Levin, 414; Meyer Levin, 413; Arthur Miller, 286–87, 412; Paul Muni, 410; Paul Newman, 295–96, 410; Clifford Odets, 154, 155, 299, 412; Molly Picon, 308–9, 410; Elmer Rice, 411; Neil Simon, 374–75, 413; Menasha Skulnik, 382–83, 410; Lee Strasberg, 411; Kurt Weill, 411; *West Side Story,* 438–39; Yiddish Theater, 410
Thomashefsky, Boris, 453, 455
The Three Stooges, **414–15**, 18, 334
Tin Pan Alley, **415–16**, 32, 36, 94, 162, 200, 311, 315, 338
Tisha B'Av, 186–87, 194. *See also* Holocaust Remembrance Day
Todd, Mike, **416**, 144
Toklas, Alice B., **416–17**
The Tonight Show, 4, 335
Topol, Chaim, 120. *See also Fiddler on the Roof*
Toys and Games, **417–21**; Ralph H. Baer, 420; Beatrice Alexander Behrman, 419–20; Joshua Lionel Cowen, 419; William Fuld, 427–28; Elliot and Ruth Handler, 419; Henry and Hella Hassenfed, 418; Mah Jongg, 421; Louis Marx, 418; Benjamin Michtom, 419; Stan Weston, 420; Ronald Wiengartner, 420
Trigere, Pauline. *See* Fashion
Trilling, Lionel, **421–22**
Tuchman, Barbara, **422–23**
Tucker, Sophie, 124, 162, 203, 217. *See also* Jazz and Blues
Turow, Scott, **423–24**

Ulmer, Edgar G., 454
United States Holocaust Memorial Museum, **425–26**, 192, 215. *See also* The Holocaust in American Culture; Jewish Museums
Uris, Leon, **426–27**, 108–9

Van Buren, Abigail, **429**, 39, 318
Vaudeville, **429–31**, 21, 341; Irving Berlin, 24; Fanny Brice, 31; George Burns, 42, 43; Eddie Cantor, 48; Comedy, 70; Film Stars, 135; *Jewish Daily Forward,* 209; Al Jolson, 221; The Marx Brothers, 280; The Minsky Brothers, 290; Popular Music, 310; Radio, 324; Television, 403; Yiddish Theater, 455
Von Tilzer, Harry, 24

Wachner, Sophie, 112
Waitzkin, Joshua, 62. *See also* Chess
Waldman, Suzyn, 394
Wallace, Chris, 435
Wallace, Irving, **433**
Wallace, Mike, **433–35**, 3, 228, 303
Wallach, Eli, **435–36**
Walters, Barbara, **436–37**
Warner, Harry, 189, 191
Warner, Jack, 159, 189, 191
Warner Brothers, 221, 426. *See also* Hollywood Moguls
Weber, Max, 8. *See also* Artists
Weil, Cynthia, 34
Weill, Kurt, 411
Weingartner, Ralph O., 420. *See also* Toys and Games
Westheimer, Dr. Ruth, **437–38**, 318
Westin, David, 226
West Side Story, **438–39**, 26, 86, 206, 313, 337, 383
Wiesel, Elie, **439–41**, 31, 363, 446
Wilder, Gene, **441**, 38, 70
Winchell, Walter, **441–42**, 40, 125, 224, 235
Winger, Debra, 141
Winkler, Henry, **442–43**, 405
Winters, Shelley, **443–44**, 405, 433
World of Our Fathers, **444–45**, 382
Wouk, Herman, **445–47**, 126, 241, 427

Yiddish, **449–52**, 270, 282, 292, 343, 441; Woody Allen, 4, 5; Judy Blume, 29; Sid Caesar, 45; Abraham Cahan, 47; Michael Chabon, 59; Comedy, 71, 72, 73; Comic Books, 77; *Fiddler on the Roof,* 120; Judy Holliday, 188; Sol Hurok, 196; Jazz and Blues, 202; *Jewish Daily Forward,* 209; Journalism, 224; Danny Kaye, 232, 233; Klezmer Music, 237; Joshua Loth Liebman, 257; Bernard Malamud, 270; Zero Mostel, 291; William Paley, 305; Molly Picon, 309; Popular Music, 313; Radio, 323; Joan Rivers, 335; "Yossele" Josef Rosenblatt, 341; Soupy Sales, 354; Sitcoms, 377, 379, 382; Vaudeville, 430; *World of Our Fathers,* 444
Yiddish Film, **452–55**; Celia Adler, 453; Jacob Ben-Ami, 454; Sidney Goldin, 452, 453–54; Joseph Green, 453, 454; Ira Greene, 454; Esther Rokhl Kaminska, 452; A.Y. Kaminsky, 452; Ludwig Landy, 454; Molly Picon, 308–9, 452, 453; Ludwig Satz, 453; Maurice Schwartz, 361–62, 452, 454; Boris Thomashefsky, 453; Edgar G. Ulmer, 454
Yiddish Theater, **455–58**, 216; Woody Allen, 4, 456; Irving Berlin, 24–25, 457; Comedy, 71; Larry David, 88, 406, 431, 456; Fyvush Finkel, 143, 144; Leo Fuchs, 154, 155; Chaim Grade, 172; Miriam Kressyn, 457; Aaron Lebedev, 457; Jerry Lewis, 106, 456; The Marx Brothers, 280; Arthur Miller, 286–87, 457; Zero Mostel, 290; Paul Muni, 135, 136, 457; Molly Picon, 309, 456, 457; Seymour Rexite, 457; Billy Rose, 339–40, 457; Menasha Skulnik, 382, 456; Boris Thomashefsky, 455; Vaudeville, 436; Herman Wouk, 445;
Yom Kippur, 174, 175, 182, 207, 240, 342, 369, 392, 435
Youngman, Henny, **458**, 70, 431

Zangwill, Israel, 91
Ziegfeld, Florenz, 48
Zukertort, Johannes, 61
Zukor, Adolph, 189, 190
Zwillman, Abner "Longy," 159

About the Editors and Contributors

THE EDITORS

Jack R. Fischel is professor emeritus of history at Millersville University and visiting professor of the humanities at Messiah College. He is the author of hundreds of reviews and articles in such publications as the *Virginia Quarterly,* the *Forward, Midstream, Hadassah Magazine, Holocaust and Genocide Studies, Congress Monthly,* the *Philadelphia Inquirer,* the *Jewish Exponent,* the *Weekly Standard,* and *New Jersey Jewish News,* among other publications. He also coedited *American Jewish History and Culture: An Encyclopedia* (Garland), *The Holocaust* (Greenwood), *The A to Z of the Holocaust* (Scarecrow Press), and he coedited six volumes of *The Holocaust Studies Annual.* Dr. Fischel is also the former editor of *Congress Monthly,* the publication of the American Jewish Congress.

Susan M. Ortmann is currently an adjunct professor of history at Millersville University. She is assistant editor of *John Winthrop's Religious Writing, 1560–1637* (Massachusetts Historical Society, 2005), a contributor to the two-volume *Encyclopedia of Puritanism* (2005), coeditor of *The Religious Implications of the Holocaust* (Greenwood Press, 2002), and coeditor of *Richard Rogers' Seven Treatises on How to Live a Godly Life* (work in progress).

THE CONTRIBUTORS

Zalman Alpert
Yeshiva University

Donald Altschiller
Boston University

Alan Amanik
New York University

Israel J. Barzak
River Garden Hebrew Home, Campus Chaplain

Alan L. Berger
Florida Atlantic University

Nate Bloom
Journalist

Burton Boxerman
Researcher, Author

Robert Bresler
Pennsylvania State University

Simon J. Bronner
Pennsylvania State University

Geoffrey Cocks
Albion College

Sy Colen
Sculptor, Writer

Roberta Jill Craven
Millersville University

Gloria Cronin
Brigham Young University

Herbert M. Druks
Brooklyn College

Howard C. Ellis
Millersville University

Patricia Erens
The School of the Art Institute of Chicago

Joshua Fischel
Millersville University

Aleisa Fishman
United States Holocaust Memorial Museum

Linda Forgosh
Jewish Historical Society of MetroWest

Shauna Frischkorn
Millersville University

Zev Garber
Los Angeles Valley College

Eric A. Goldman
Ergo Media, President

Andrew M. Gordon
University of Florida

Richard Gould
Independent Scholar

Grace Cohen Grossman
Skirball Cultural Center

Jeffrey S. Gurock
Yeshiva University

Renee Hartman
Food Consultant

Leroy T. Hopkins Jr.
Millersville University

Joseph P. Huffman
Messiah College

Mara W. Cohen Ioannides
Missouri State University

Abby Meth Kanter
New Jersey Jewish News

Kenneth Kanter
Hebrew Union College-Jewish Institute of Religion

Ron Kaplan
New Jersey Jewish News

Alan Kelly
Millersville University

Ari Y. Kelman
University of California–Davis

Barry Kornhauser
Fulton Opera House, Lancaster, Pennsylvania

Steve Krief
Independent Scholar

Josh Kun
University of Southern California-Annenberg School for Communication

Ann Leisawitz
Harrisburg Area Community College

Caroline Forman Litwack
Brandeis University

Gabriela Lupatkin
Brandeis University

Judith Lupatkin
NBC Universal, New York University Cinema Studies

Marvin Margolis
Millersville University

Steve Marino
St. Francis College

Marilyn Mayblum
Performing Producer

John M. McLarnon
Millersville University

Jacob Ben-Zion Mendelson
Temple Israel Center, Hebrew Union College-School of Sacred Music

Ted Merwin
Dickinson College

Asher Z. Milbauer
Florida International University

Caraid O'Brien
Playwright

Bruce Pandolfini
New York Chess Club

Hara Person
URJ Press

Leslie Rabkin
Independent Scholar

Irwin Richman
Pennsylvania State University

Danny Rigby
University of Florida

Philip Rosen
Community College of Philadelphia

Ann Moliver Ruben
Palm Beach Community College

Robert Ruder
Educational Consultant

Ellen Schiff
Massachusetts College of Liberal Arts

Marion Schotz
Writer

Jeffrey Shandler
Rutgers University

Edward S. Shapiro
Seton Hall University

Mark Shechner
State University of New York–Buffalo

June Sochen
Northeastern Illinois University

Gerald Sorin
State University of New York–New Paltz

David Stameshkin
Franklin & Marshall College

Steve Steinbock
Hebrew Union College

Kurt F. Stone
Florida Atlantic University

Jon Stratton
Curtin University of Technology–Perth, Western Australia

Jesse Ulrich
Independent Scholar

Daniel Walden
Pennsylvania State University

Stephen J. Whitfield
Brandeis University

Maury I. Wiseman
University of Florida

Marie Zubatsky
Writer